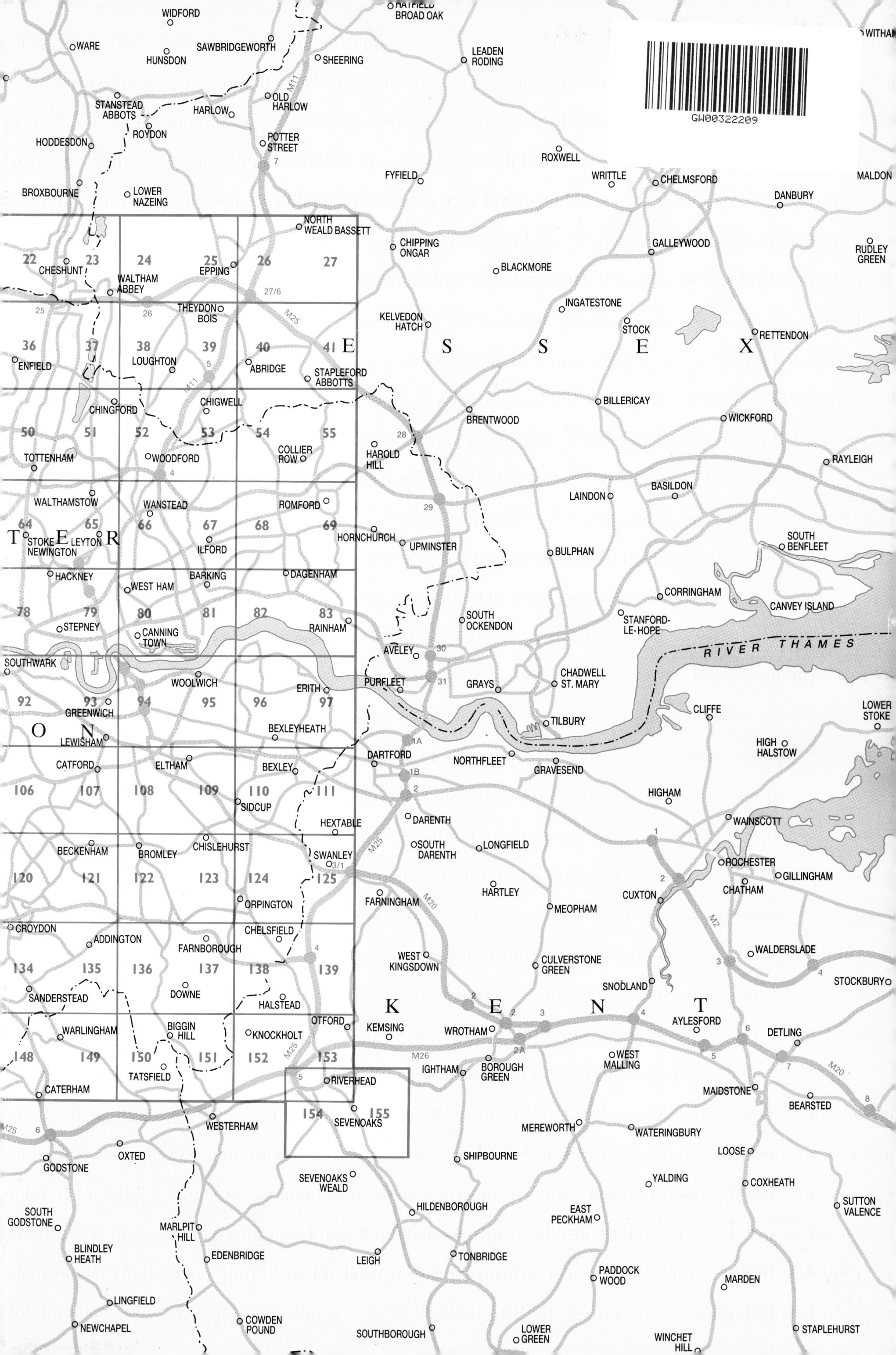

HATFIELD BROAD OAK
WIDFORD
WARE
HUNSDON
SAWBRIDGEWORTH
SHEERING
LEADEN RODING
WITHAM
GW00322209
STANSTEAD ABBOTTS
HARLOW
OLD HARLOW
M11
ROYDON
HODDESDON
POTTER STREET
7
ROXWELL
BROXBOURNE
LOWER NAZEING
FYFIELD
WRITTLE
CHELMSFORD
MALDON
DANBURY
NORTH WEALD BASSETT
CHIPPING ONGAR
GALLEYWOOD
RUDLEY GREEN
22
23
24
25
26
27
CHESHUNT
EPPING
BLACKMORE
WALTHAM ABBEY
27/6
25
26
THEYDON BOIS
M25
INGATESTONE
KELVEDON HATCH
STOCK
RETTENDON
36
37
38
39
40
41
E
S
S
E
X
ENFIELD
LOUGHTON
5
ABRIDGE
STAPLEFORD ABBOTTS
M11
CHIGWELL
BILLERICAY
CHINGFORD
BRENTWOOD
WICKFORD
50
51
52
53
54
55
28
COLLIER ROW
HAROLD HILL
TOTTENHAM
WOODFORD
4
RAYLEIGH
LAINDON
BASILDON
WALTHAMSTOW
WANSTEAD
ROMFORD
29
64
65
66
67
68
69
T
E
R
STOKE NEWINGTON
LEYTON
ILFORD
HORNCHURCH
UPMINSTER
BULPHAN
SOUTH BENFLEET
HACKNEY
WEST HAM
BARKING
DAGENHAM
CORRINGHAM
CANVEY ISLAND
78
79
80
81
82
83
STEPNEY
RAINHAM
SOUTH OCKENDON
STANFORD-LE-HOPE
CANNING TOWN
RIVER THAMES
AVELEY
30
SOUTHWARK
PURFLEET
31
GRAYS
CHADWELL ST. MARY
WOOLWICH
ERITH
92
93
94
95
96
97
GREENWICH
TILBURY
CLIFFE
LOWER STOKE
O
N
LEWISHAM
BEXLEYHEATH
1A
HIGH HALSTOW
DARTFORD
NORTHFLEET
GRAVESEND
CATFORD
ELTHAM
BEXLEY
1B
106
107
108
109
110
111
2
HIGHAM
SIDCUP
DARENTH
HEXTABLE
1
WAINSCOTT
SOUTH DARENTH
LONGFIELD
BECKENHAM
BROMLEY
CHISLEHURST
SWANLEY
M25
ROCHESTER
GILLINGHAM
3/1
2
120
121
122
123
124
125
CHATHAM
HARTLEY
CUXTON
ORPINGTON
FARNINGHAM
M20
MEOPHAM
M2
CROYDON
CHELSFIELD
ADDINGTON
FARNBOROUGH
4
WEST KINGSDOWN
CULVERSTONE GREEN
WALDERSLADE
134
135
136
137
138
139
3
4
STOCKBURY
SANDERSTEAD
DOWNE
SNODLAND
HALSTEAD
K
E
N
T
2
2
3
4
OTFORD
AYLESFORD
WARLINGHAM
BIGGIN HILL
KNOCKHOLT
KEMSING
WROTHAM
6
DETLING
M25
148
149
150
151
152
153
M26
2A
WEST MALLING
5
7
TATSFIELD
IGHTHAM
BOROUGH GREEN
M20
CATERHAM
5
RIVERHEAD
MAIDSTONE
BEARSTED
8
154
155
SEVENOAKS
M25
6
WESTERHAM
MEREWORTH
WATERINGBURY
OXTED
GODSTONE
SHIPBOURNE
LOOSE
SEVENOAKS WEALD
YALDING
COXHEATH
SUTTON VALENCE
HILDENBOROUGH
EAST PECKHAM
SOUTH GODSTONE
MARLPIT HILL
BLINDLEY HEATH
EDENBRIDGE
LEIGH
TONBRIDGE
PADDOCK WOOD
MARDEN
LINGFIELD
NEWCHAPEL
COWDEN POUND
SOUTHBOROUGH
LOWER GREEN
WINCHET HILL
STAPLEHURST

Making moving simple

With the strength of a nationwide network of offices, combined with local knowledge and expertise, Bradford & Bingley Gascoigne-Pees and Bradford & Bingley Alan de Maid are committed to offering the highest level of service on any aspect of home ownership, from the initial moment a customer walks through the door to the day they move into their home.

Services offered

Residential Estate Agency

Financial Services*

Land & New Homes

Residential Lettings & Management

Telephone

Sales 01932 252720 or 01737 766548

Lettings 01737 766548

Land & New Homes 01932 868316

* Bradford & Bingley Estate Agents is a trading name for Bradford & Bingley Estate Agencies Limited. Registered Office 36 Salisbury Square, Hatfield, Hertfordshire AL9 5DD.

Bradford & Bingley Estate Agencies Limited is an appointed representative of Bradford & Bingley Building Society, which is regulated by the Personal Investment Authority for investment business.

Bradford & Bingley
Estate Agents

Trading as Bradford & Bingley Gascoigne-Pees and Bradford & Bingley Alan de Maid in the Greater London area

COLLINS

MASTER STREET ATLAS LONDON

CONTENTS

HarperCollins*Publishers*

Published by Collins
An imprint of HarperCollins*Publishers*
77-85 Fulham Palace Road, Hammersmith, London W6 8JB

Copyright © HarperCollins*Publishers* Ltd 1999
Mapping © Bartholomew Ltd 1995,1997,1998,1999

Mapping generated from Bartholomew digital databases

London Underground Map by permission of London Regional Transport
LRT Registered User No. 99/2818

The contents of this publication are believed correct at the time of printing. Nevertheless, the
publisher can accept no responsibility for errors or omissions, changes in the detail given, or
for any expense or loss thereby caused.

The representation of a road, track or footpath is no evidence of a right of way.

Printed in Italy

ISBN 0 00 448837 7 Paperback
     0 00 448838 5 Hardback   MM10142/MM10140   ANA

e-mail: roadcheck@harpercollins.co.uk   web site: www.bartholomewmaps.com

KEY TO CENTRAL LONDON MAPS

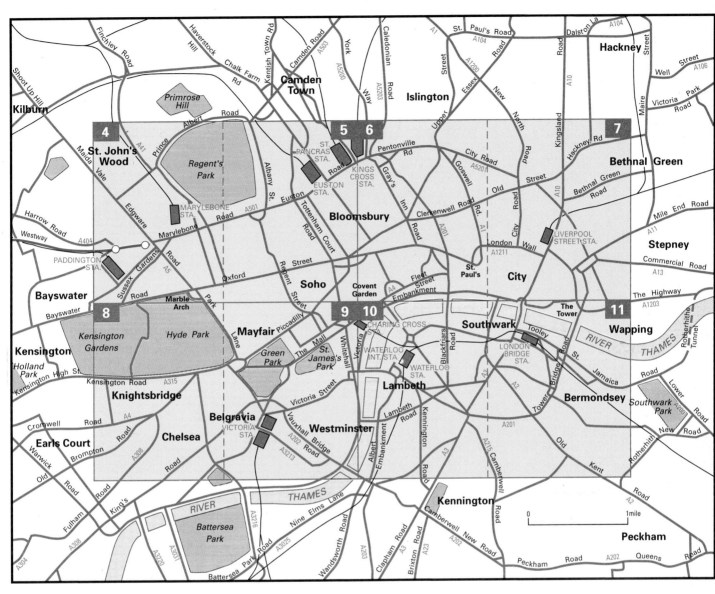

KEY TO MAP SYMBOLS

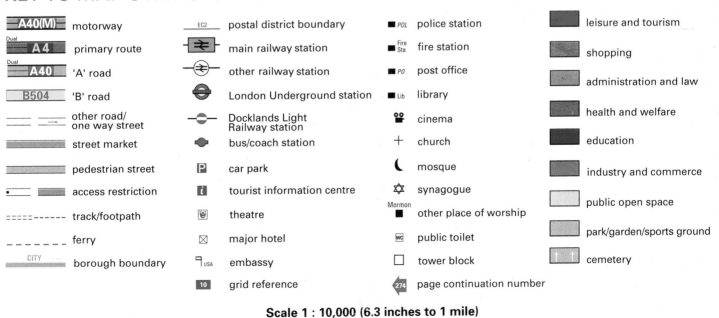

A40(M)	motorway
Dual A4	primary route
Dual A40	'A' road
B504	'B' road
	other road/ one way street
	street market
	pedestrian street
	access restriction
	track/footpath
	ferry
CITY	borough boundary

EC2	postal district boundary
	main railway station
	other railway station
	London Underground station
	Docklands Light Railway station
	bus/coach station
P	car park
i	tourist information centre
	theatre
	major hotel
USA	embassy
10	grid reference

POL	police station
Fire Sta	fire station
PO	post office
Lib	library
	cinema
+	church
	mosque
	synagogue
Mormon	other place of worship
WC	public toilet
	tower block
274	page continuation number

	leisure and tourism
	shopping
	administration and law
	health and welfare
	education
	industry and commerce
	public open space
	park/garden/sports ground
	cemetery

Scale 1 : 10,000 (6.3 inches to 1 mile)

0	0.25	0.50	0.75	1 kilometre
0	1/4		1/2 mile	

A
B
C
D
E
F
G
1
2
3
4
5
6
7
8
9
10
76
8
REGENT'S PARK
ST. JOHN'S WOOD
LISSON GROVE
MARYLEBONE
PADDINGTON
W1
RUNNING TRACK
LONDON ZOO
TOWNSHEND ESTATE
Carlton TV
Prim Sch
ST. JOHN'S WOOD BARRACKS
ST. JOHN'S WOOD
HOSPITAL OF ST. JOHN & ST. ELIZABETH
Arnold House Sch
CONVENT OF MERCY
WELLINGTON HOSP
St. John's Wood Church
LORD'S CRICKET GROUND
MUSEUM
Lord's Tavern PH
Hilton
London Central Mosque
HANOVER GATE
WINFIELD HOUSE
Tennis Cts
BOATING LAKE
OPEN AIR THEA
QUEEN MARY'S GARDENS
THE HOLME
DEPT OF ENVIRONMENT
Parks Dept
Bandstand
LONDON BUSINESS SCH
REGENT'S COLLEGE
Clarence Gate
ROYAL COLL OF OBSTETRICIANS & GYNAECOLOGISTS
Electricity Sta
Our Lady (RC)
LISSON GREEN
TRESHAM EST
NORTH BANK
CANAL WAY
PRINCE ALBERT ROAD
ST. JOHN'S WOOD RD
WELLINGTON ROAD
PARK ROAD
OUTER CIRCLE
INNER CIRCLE
GROVE END RD
LISSON GROVE
EDGWARE ROAD
ROSSMORE ROAD
GLOUCESTER PLACE
BAKER STREET
MARYLEBONE ROAD
MARYLEBONE
MADAME TUSSAUD'S
PLANETARIUM
ROYAL ACADEMY OF MUSIC
PRINCESS GRACE HOSP
UNI OF WESTMINSTER
SHERLOCK HOLMES MUS
Sylvia Young Theatre Sch
ST. EDWARDS CONV.
UNI OF WEST PODIATRIC DEPT
CHURCH STREET ESTATE
PADDINGTON GREEN
CITY OF WESTMINSTER COLLEGE
North Westminster Comm Sch
The Landmark
WESTMINSTER TOWN HALL
EDGWARE ROAD
CHAPEL ST
OLD MARYLEBONE RD
HARBET ROAD
London Metropole
ADULT ED. CEN
NORTH WHARF RD
PADDINGTON BASIN
ST. MARY'S HOSP
MEDICAL SCHOOL
PRAED ST
SUSSEX GARDENS
SEYMOUR STREET
Seymour Leisure Cen
BRYANSTON SQUARE
MONTAGU SQUARE
PORTMAN SQUARE
WALLACE COLLECTION
HEINZ GALL
WIGMORE ST
OXFORD STREET
SELFRIDGES
Selfridge
MARBLE ARCH
CUMBERLAND GATE
Speaker's Corner
PARK LANE
BAYSWATER ROAD
HYDE PARK GARDENS
HYDE PARK SQUARE
HYDE PARK CRES
CONNAUGHT SQUARE
Connaught Ho. Sch
SRI LANKA
Great Western Royal
Royal Lancaster
LANCASTER GATE
Victoria Gate
Marlborough Gate
The Fountain
Lancaster Gate
THE RING
NORTH CARRIAGE DRIVE
GROSVENOR SQUARE
Roosevelt Memorial
UNITED STATES
Marriott
Thistle Marble Arch
Mostyn
Annual Cumberland
BRYANSTON
Bryanston Court
Portman
Churchill
CRAVEN RD
WESTBOURNE TER
GLOUCESTER SQUARE
SUSSEX GDNS
St. James
Mornington
A5
A41
A40
A5205
A4205
A4209
A5204
B507
OXFORD ST where marked is closed to through traffic (except buses & taxis) from 7a.m. - 7p.m. Monday - Saturday

5
H
J
K
L
M
N
P
REGENT'S PARK
CUMBERLAND MKT EST
MORNINGTON CRES
CROWNDALE RD
PANCRAS ROAD
A5202
KING'S CROSS
KING'S CROSS ST. PANCRAS
A5200
1
WHARFDALE RD
CALEDONIA ST
THAMESLINK
ST. PANCRAS
SOMERS TOWN
British Library
AMPTHILL SQ EST
HAMPSTEAD ROAD
A400
EUSTON
EUSTON ROAD
A501
A4200
2
3
ST PANCRAS
GRAY'S INN ROAD
ARGYLE ST
CROMER STREET
EUSTON SQUARE
WARREN ST
GT. PORTLAND ST
REGENT'S PARK
PARK SQUARE GDNS
PARK CRES
A4201
UNIVERSITY COLLEGE LONDON
4
UCL HOSP
TOTTENHAM COURT RD
GOWER ST
WOBURN PLACE
RUSSELL SQUARE
BLOOMSBURY
UNIVERSITY OF LONDON
5
6
B502
THE HOSP FOR SICK CHILDREN
THE BRITISH MUSEUM
BEDFORD SQUARE
GOODGE ST
MIDDLESEX HOSP
7
PORTLAND PLACE
GREAT PORTLAND STREET
B506
BBC Radio
CAVENDISH SQ
OXFORD ST
A40
OXFORD CIRCUS
TOTTENHAM COURT ROAD
NEW OXFORD ST
HIGH HOLBORN
HOLBORN
8
SHAFTESBURY AVE
ST GILES HIGH ST
9
SOHO
REGENT STREET
NEW BOND ST
B406
CONDUIT ST
CHARING CROSS ROAD
A401
COVENT GARDEN
LEICESTER SQ
STRAND
10
WC2
PICCADILLY CIRCUS
A4201
MAYFAIR
NATIONAL GALLERY

6
A
B
C
D
E
F
G
1
2
3
4
5
6
7
8
9
10
141
KING'S CROSS
ST. PANCRAS
PENTONVILLE RD
PENTONVILLE
A501
A5200
CALEDONIA
WHARFDALE RD
THAMESLINK
KINGSWAY COLLEGE
ANGEL
The Angel Centre
FINSBURY
CITY UNI
ST PANCRAS
WC1
CORAM'S FIELDS
MOUNT PLEASANT SORTING OFFICE
FARRINGDON
CLERKENWELL
CLERKENWELL RD
A5201
ROSEBERY AVE
SKINNER ST
GOSWELL RD
CITY RD
BLOOMSBURY
THE BRITISH MUSEUM
THEOBALD'S ROAD
GRAY'S INN GDNS
GRAY'S INN ROAD
HOLBORN
HIGH HOLBORN
LINCOLN'S INN FIELDS
CHANCERY LANE
FETTER LANE
KINGSWAY
ROYAL COURTS OF JUSTICE
COVENT GARDEN
STRAND
ALDWYCH
SOMERSET HOUSE
VICTORIA EMBANKMENT
TEMPLE
BLACKFRIARS
THAMESLINK
EC4
WC2
HMS PRESIDENT
HQS WELLINGTON
RIVER TH
KING'S REACH
10
WESTMINSTER
SOUTHAMPTON ROW
BLOOMSBURY WAY
FARRINGDON ST
HOLBORN VIADUCT
NEW BR. ST
CENTRAL CRIMINAL COURT (Old Bailey)
ST BARTHOLOMEW'S HOSPITAL
Central Markets (Smithfield)
BRITISH LIBRARY

H
J
K
L
M
N
P
7
142
SHOREDITCH PARK
HOXTON
NEW NORTH ROAD
EAST RD
KINGSLAND
HACKNEY ROAD
COLUMBIA ROAD
GEFFRYE MUSEUM
HACKNEY COMM COLL
1
2
3
4
5
6
7
8
9
10
11
CITY ROAD
A501
OLD STREET
ST. LUKE'S
EC1
MOORFIELDS EYE HOSPITAL
BUNHILL FIELDS
SHOREDITCH
SHOREDITCH HIGH ST
GREAT EASTERN ST
COMMERCIAL ST
BETHNAL GREEN
ARNOLD CIRCUS
Old Spitalfields Market
BROADGATE
EC2
LIVERPOOL STREET
BARBICAN
MOORGATE
LONDON WALL
ALDERSGATE
BISHOPSGATE
HOUNDSDITCH
ALDGATE
WHITECHAPEL HIGH ST
MINORIES
ST. PAUL'S CATHEDRAL
BANK
Bank of England
MANSION HOUSE
CANNON ST
MONUMENT
EC3
FENCHURCH ST
Lloyds of London
GRACECHURCH ST
EASTCHEAP
TOWER HILL
TOWER GATEWAY
ROYAL MINT
THE TOWER
Southwark Bridge Steps
SHAKESPEARE'S GLOBE THEATRE AND EXHIBITION
Bankside Jetty
Swan Lane Pier
Custom House

8
A
B
C
D
E
F
G
BAYSWATER ROAD
LANCASTER GATE
Victoria Gate
Marble Arch
Speaker's Corner
NORTH CARRIAGE DRIVE
4
OXFORD STREET where marked is closed to through traffic (except buses & taxis) from 7a.m. - 7p.m. Monday - Saturday
Marlborough Gate
The Fountains
1
76
2
Peter Pan
Speke's Monument
Physical Energy Statue
THE LONG WATER
WEST CARRIAGE DRIVE
Bird Sanctuary
HYDE PARK
KENSINGTON GARDENS
3
SERPENTINE GALLERY
THE SERPENTINE
The Lido
Clubhouse
Pier
SERPENTINE ROAD
PARK LANE
A4202
Grosvenor Gate
Brook Gate
Stanhope Gate
Curzon Gate
Achilles Statue
Bandstand
War Memorial
Queen Elizabeth Gate
ROTTEN ROW
CYCLE PATH
4
PITCH 'N' PUTT
Bowling Green
Tennis Courts
Albert Memorial
Alexandra Gate
Coalbrookdale Gate
Prince of Wales Gate
Rutland Gate
Edinburgh Gate
Albert Gate
SOUTH CARRIAGE DRIVE
HYDE PARK BARRACKS
APSLEY HOUSE WELLINGTON MUS
HYDE PARK CORNER
KNIGHTSBRIDGE
A315
A4
KENSINGTON GORE
Royal Geographical Society
5
ROYAL ALBERT HALL
ROYAL COLL OF ART
SW7
PRINCES GATE
ENNISMORE GARDENS
6
IMPERIAL COLLEGE
GOETHE INSTITUTE
PRINCE CONSORT RD
EXHIBITION ROAD
BROMPTON
Brompton Oratory
Holy Trinity
HARRODS
BROMPTON ROAD
7
SCIENCE MUSEUM
NATURAL HISTORY MUSEUM (EARTH GALLERIES)
VICTORIA & ALBERT MUSEUM
90
CROMWELL ROAD
CROMWELL GDNS PLACE
THURLOE PLACE
8
SOUTH KENSINGTON
PELHAM STREET
BEAUCHAMP PL
PONT STREET
B319
SLOANE STREET
A3216
CADOGAN PLACE
BELGRAVE SQUARE
B310
GROSVENOR PLACE
A3217
EATON SQUARE
9
CHRISTIES FINE ART SCH
DAVID GAME COLLEGE
ONSLOW SQ
A308
FULHAM ROAD
SW3
SLOANE SQUARE
LOWER SLOANE ST
DUKE OF YORK'S HEADQUARTERS
KING'S ROAD
SUTTON ESTATE
10
ROYAL MARSDEN HOSP
ROYAL BROMPTON & NAT HEART INST
B304
SYDNEY STREET
St. Luke
CHELSEA
PIMLICO ROAD
A3214
CHELSEA BRIDGE ROAD
CHELSEA BARRACKS
ROYAL HOSPITAL MUSEUM
RANELAGH GARDENS
BURTON'S COURT
B302
A
B
C
D
E
F
G

9
H
J
K
L
M
N
P
SOHO
MAYFAIR
STRAND
WC2
NATIONAL GALLERY
PICCADILLY CIR.
TRAFALGAR
CHARING CROSS
ROYAL ACAD. OF ARTS
GREEN PARK
ST. JAMES'S
ST. JAMES'S PARK
PALL MALL
THE MALL
CONSTITUTION HILL
Closed to Traffic on Sundays
Queen Victoria Memorial
BUCKINGHAM PALACE GARDENS
BUCKINGHAM PALACE
THE QUEEN'S GALLERY
THE ROYAL MEWS
BIRDCAGE WALK
HORSE GUARDS RD
WHITEHALL
PARLIAMENT ST
DOWNING ST
FOREIGN OFFICE
HM TREASURY
MINISTRY OF DEFENCE
CABINET WAR ROOMS
WESTMINSTER
WESTMINSTER ABBEY
HOUSES OF PARLIAMENT
10
VICTORIA TOWER GARDENS
MILLBANK
VICTORIA EMBANKMENT
ALBERT EMBANKMENT
WESTMINSTER BRIDGE
LAMBETH BRI
SW1
VICTORIA
VICTORIA ST
WESTMINSTER CATH (RC)
BUCKINGHAM PALACE ROAD
VAUXHALL BRIDGE ROAD
BELGRAVE ROAD
GRAVIA
PIMLICO
TATE GALLERY
MILLBANK TOWER
GROSVENOR ESTATE
CHURCHILL GARDENS
DOLPHIN SQUARE
TACHBROOK ESTATE
RIVERSIDE GARDENS
VAUXHALL BRIDGE
EBURY BRIDGE ESTATE
COACH STA
91
1
2
3
4
5
6
7
8
9
10

10
A
B
C
D
E
F
G
1
2
3
4
5
6
7
8
9
10
6
9
91
STRAND
WC2
EC4
SE11
CHARING CROSS
EMBANKMENT
TEMPLE
BLACKFRIARS
WATERLOO
WATERLOO INTERNATIONAL
WATERLOO EAST
WESTMINSTER
LAMBETH N
SOUTHWARK
KENNINGTON
LAMBETH
SOUTHWARK
ALBERTA
RIVER THAMES
KING'S REACH
VICTORIA EMBANKMENT
ALBERT EMBANKMENT
MILLBANK
WATERLOO BRI
HUNGERFORD BRI
WESTMINSTER BRI
LAMBETH BRI
VAUXHALL BRI
BLACKFRIARS BRI
STAMFORD STREET
UPPER GROUND
THE CUT
WATERLOO RD
BLACKFRIARS ROAD
WESTMINSTER BRI ROAD
LAMBETH PALACE RD
LAMBETH ROAD
KENNINGTON LANE
KENNINGTON RD
KENNINGTON PARK ROAD
NEWINGTON BUTTS
LONDON ROAD
ST. GEORGE'S ROAD
BOROUGH ROAD
WHITEHALL
PARLIAMENT ST
BRIDGE ST
A4
A3211
A301
A3200
A302
A3212
A3036
A3203
A23
A201
A3204
A3
B302
B308
B323
HMS PRESIDENT
HQS WELLINGTON
SOMERSET HOUSE
ROYAL NATIONAL THEATRE
QUEEN ELIZABETH HALL AND PURCELL ROOM
ROYAL FESTIVAL HALL
HAYWARD GALLERY
BRITISH AIRWAYS LONDON EYE
LONDON AQUARIUM
COUNTY HALL
JUBILEE GDNS
FLORENCE NIGHTINGALE MUSEUM
ST. THOMAS' HOSP
HOUSES OF PARLIAMENT
VICTORIA TOWER GARDENS
LAMBETH PALACE GDNS
ARCHBISHOP'S PARK
IMPERIAL WAR MUS
GERALDINE MARY HARMSWORTH PARK
ST. GEORGE'S CATHEDRAL
MORLEY COLLEGE
THE YOUNG VIC
THE OLD VIC
PEABODY SQUARE
TANSWELL ESTATE
LONDON NAUTICAL SCH
MINISTRY OF DEFENCE
FOREIGN OFFICE
HM TREASURY
CABINET OFFICE
MIN OF AG FISH & FOOD
TATE GALL
MILLBANK TOWER
LAMBETH WALK
PEDLARS PARK
VAUXHALL GDNS EST
SPRING GDNS
SOUTH BANK UNIVERSITY
LON. COLL OF PRINTING & DISTRIBUTIVE TRADES
CITY AND GUILDS LONDON ART SCHOOL
DRAW DOCK
GOVERNMENT OFFICE

H
J
K
L
M
N
P
11
EC3
FENCHURCH
HIGH TIMBER ST
City of Lon Sch
CANNON ST
Southwark Bridge Steps
Fire Station
MONUMENT
The Monument
EASTCHEAP
GREAT TOWER ST
TOWER HILL
PEPYS STREET
Trinity Ho
Sch of Nav
ROYAL MINT
ROYAL MINT CT
MANSELL
St. Magnus the Martyr
Site of Old Billingsgate Mkt
Custom House
LOWER THAMES ST
All Hallows by the Tower and Brass Rub. Cen
TOWER PO
THE TOWER
Tower Pier
SUGAR QUAY WK
Swan Lane Pier
SHAKESPEARE'S GLOBE THEATRE AND EXHIBITION
Bankside Jetty
BANKSIDE
Financial Times
ANCHOR INN
CLINK ST
CLINK PRISON MUS
PARK STREET
Glaziers Hall
LONDON BRIDGE HOSPITAL
London Bridge City Pier
HMS BELFAST
CITY
TOWER HAMLETS
SOUTHWARK
SOUTHWARK CATHEDRAL
TOOLEY ST
Hay's Galleria
SOUTHWARK CROWN COURT
THE QUEENS WALK
TOWER BRIDGE APPR
TOWER BRI
London Commodity Exchange
78
Tower Thistle
Ivory House
St. Katharine's Pier
Alderman Stairs
1
2
3
4
5
6
7
8
9
10
92
SOUTHWARK BRI
QUEEN ST
A300
SOUTHWARK BRIDGE ROAD
SUMNER ST
PEABODY TRUST
THRALE ST
A3200
B300
Most Precious Blood (RC)
Borough Mkt
LONDON BRI
KING WILLIAM ST
A200
ST THOMAS ST
LONDON BRIDGE
TOWER BRIDGE EXPERIENCE
SOUTHWARK COLL
BRIDGE HO PH
MAGGIE BLAKE'S CAUSE
Butlers Wharf
BRAMAH TEA & COFFEE MUS
DESIGN MUS
GREAT MAZE POND
GREENWOOD THEA
GUY'S HOSP
NEWCOMEN STREET
MERMAID CT
Prim Schs
L DORRIT CT
St. George the Martyr
THE BOROUGH
BOROUGH
Fire Sta & London Fire Brigade Mus
LOCKYER EST
PORLOCK ST
La Salette Presbytery (RC)
TYERS EST
BLACK SWAN YD
WHITES GRDS EST
CRUCIFIX LA
BERMONDSEY STREET
DRUID ST
ST. OLAVE'S EST
A100
TOM BLAU GALL
Millennium Square
ST. JOHN'S EST
TANNER STREET
REC GRD
Tenn Cts
LEATHERMARKET ST
GARDENS
KIPLING EST
LONG LANE
A2198
St. Hugh
Beormund Sch
Bermondsey Leather Mkt
SOUTHWARK COLLEGE Bermondsey Centre
PURBROOK EST
ST. SAVIOUR'S ESTATE
ABBEY STREET
B202
St. Mary Magdalen
ELIM EST
CLUNY EST
Methodist
MEAKIN EST
AYLWYN ESTATE
BERMONDSEY
TOWN HALL
GRANGE CENTRE
GRANGE WALK
GRANGE ROAD
A2206
SPA ROAD
BERMONDSEY SPA
VAUBAN ESTATE
TABARD GARDEN ESTATE
TABARD GARDENS
REC GRD
GREAT DOVER ST
A2
Holy Trinity
SE1
INNER LONDON CROWN COURT
NEWINGTON GARDENS
ROCKINGHAM ESTATE
Salvation Army
LAWSON ESTATE
SOUTH BANK UNIVERSITY Rachel McMillan Annexe
Geoffrey Chaucer Sec Sch
SOUTHWARK COLL
St. Saviour's & St. Olave's Sec Sch
Bricklayer's Arms
HAROLD ESTATE
CREASY EST
GUINNESS BLDGS
Offices
NEW KENT A201 ROAD
ELEPHANT & CASTLE
NEWINGTON
Brotherhood of the Cross & Star
St. Matthew
CORONET
Shopping Centre
OLD KENT ROAD
MANDELA WAY
LORRY PARK
DUNTON ROAD
B203
LONGFIELD ESTATE
Superstore
ROLLS
Aylwin Sc School
HEYGATE STREET
CUMING MUSEUM & Lib
St. John the Evangelist
WALWORTH
SE17
A215
BROWNING EST
EAST STREET
Walworth Lower School
Health Centre
Primary School
DAWES HOUSE
English Martyrs (RC)
ALVEY EST
SURREY SQUARE PARK
KINGLAKE EST
FARADAY GDNS
MICHAEL FARADAY HOUSE
AYLESBURY EST
PENROSE HOUSE
Walworth Sch
Fire Sta
Methodist

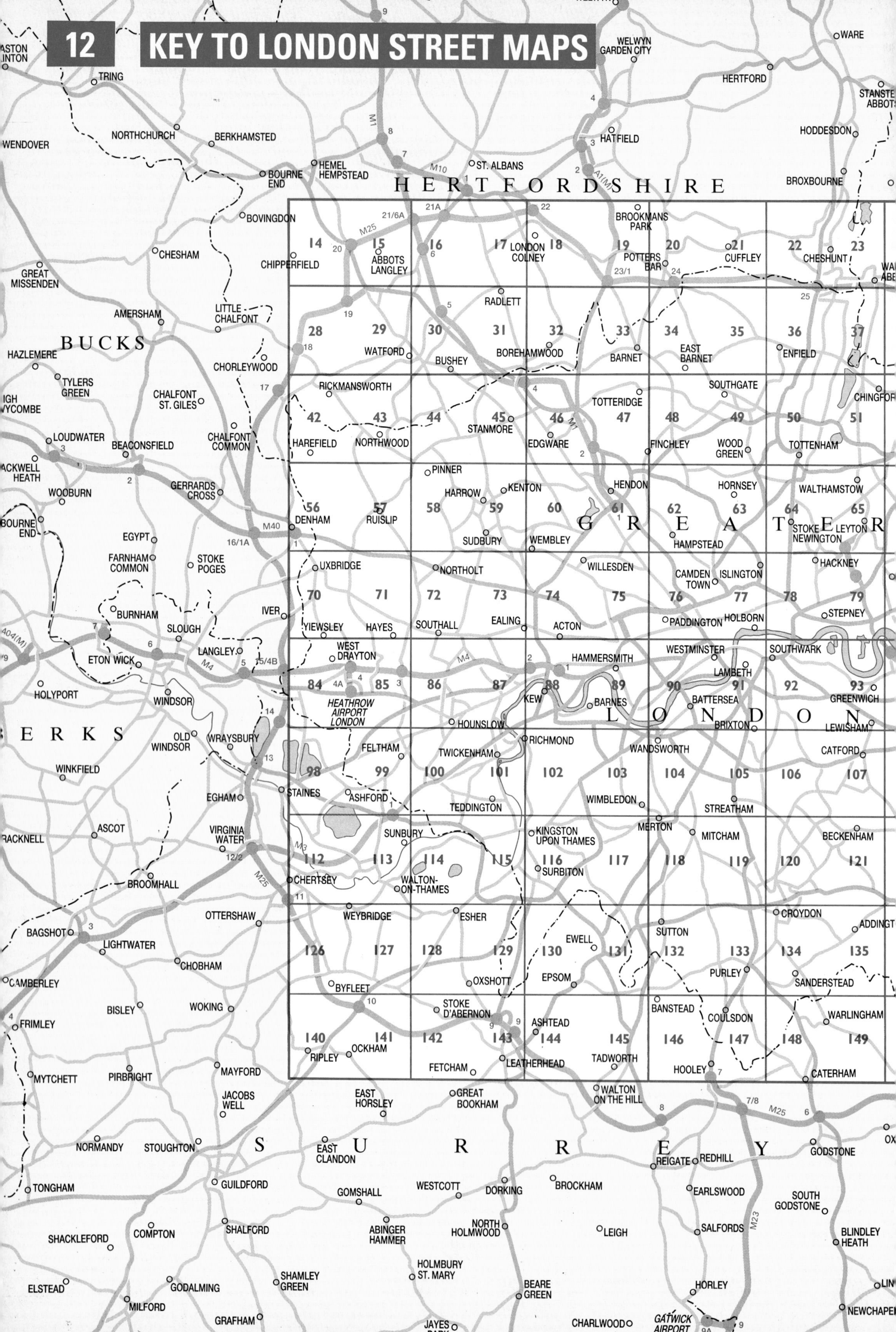

WIDFORD, SAWBRIDGEWORTH, SHEERING, LEADEN RODING, HUNSDON, OLD HARLOW, HARLOW, DON, POTTER STREET, ROXWELL, WER ZEING, 7, FYFIELD, NORTH WEALD BASSETT, CHIPPING ONGAR, BLACKMORE, 4, 25, 26, 27, EPPING, 27/6, THEYDON BOIS, M25, KELVEDON HATCH, 26, E S S E X, 8, 39, 40, 41, UGHTON, 5, ABRIDGE, STAPLEFORD ABBOTTS, M11, CHIGWELL, 28, BRENTWOOD, 2, 53, 54, 55, WOODFORD, COLLIER ROW, HAROLD HILL, 4, 29, WANSTEAD, ROMFORD, 6, 67, 68, 69, HORNCHURCH, UPMINSTER, BULPHAN, ILFORD, BARKING, DAGENHAM, ST HAM, 0, 81, 82, 83, RAINHAM, SOUTH OCKENDON, CANNING TOWN, 30, AVELEY, 31, GRAYS, WOOLWICH, ERITH, PURFLEET, 94, 95, 96, 97, TILBURY, BEXLEYHEATH, 1A, DARTFORD, ELTHAM, BEXLEY, 1B, NORTHFLEET, GRAVESEND, 08, 109, 110, 111, 2, SIDCUP, HEXTABLE, DARENTH, BROMLEY, CHISLEHURST, SWANLEY, SOUTH DARENTH, LONGFIELD, 22, 123, 124, 125, 3/1, M25, ORPINGTON, FARNINGHAM, HARTLEY, CHELSFIELD, M20, FARNBOROUGH, 4, MEOPHAM, 36, 137, 138, 139, WEST KINGSDOWN, CULVERSTONE GREEN, DOWNE, HALSTEAD, 2, BIGGIN HILL, OTFORD, KEMSING, K E N T, 2, 3, 50, 151, 152, 153, KNOCKHOLT, M25, WROTHAM, M26, 2A, TSFIELD, 5, RIVERHEAD, IGHTHAM, BOROUGH GREEN, WESTERHAM, 154, 155, SEVENOAKS, MEREWORTH, SHIPBOURNE, SEVENOAKS WEALD, HILDENBOROUGH, EAST PECKHAM, MARLPIT HILL, D, EDENBRIDGE, LEIGH, TONBRIDGE, IELD, COWDEN POUND, SOUTHBOROUGH, LOWER GREEN

KEY TO MAP SYMBOLS

M41 motorway	leisure & tourism
Dual A4 primary route	shopping
Dual A40 'A' road	administration & law
B504 'B' road	health & welfare
other road/ one way street	education
toll	industry & commerce
street market	cemetery
restricted access road	golf course
pedestrian street	public open space/ allotments
cycle path	park/garden/sports ground
track/footpath	wood/forest
level crossing LC	orchard
pedestrian ferry P	embassy USA
vehicle ferry V	Pol police station
county/borough boundary	Fire Sta fire station
postal district boundary	PO post office
main railway station	Lib library
other railway station	tourist information centre
London Underground station	youth hostel
light railway / tramway station	tower block
bus/coach station	windmill
heliport H	church
car park P	mosque
public toilet WC	synagogue

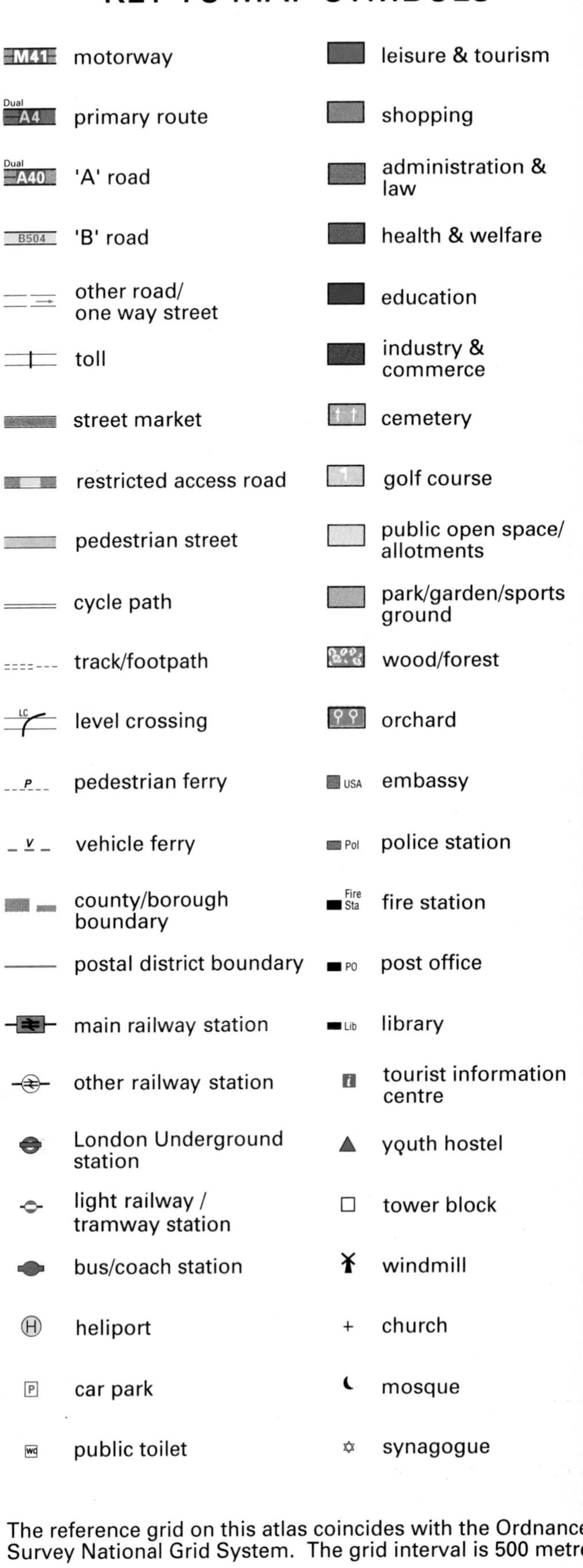

The reference grid on this atlas coincides with the Ordnance Survey National Grid System. The grid interval is 500 metre

Page Continuation Number 100   AT Grid Reference   OS National Grid Kilometre Square 03

Scale 1:20,000 (3.2 inches to 1 mile)

0   0.25   0.50   0.75   1 kilometre
0   ¼   ½ mile

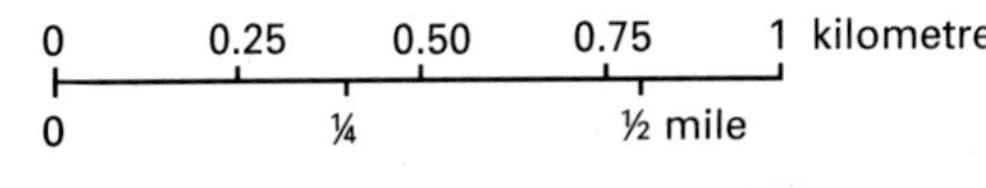

BG
BH
BJ
BK
BL
BM
BN
APSLEY
HP3
SHENDISH HOUSE GOLF COURSE
GREAT WOOD
PHASELS WOOD
Phasels Wood Activity Centre
SHENDISH HOUSE CONF CENTRE
SHEETHANGER COMMON
Felden Lodge
Felden Manor
Felden Grange
Tower Farm
Three Fields Farm
Howe's Retreat
OLD DEAN
BUCKLERS WOOD
MERCEYS WOOD
DARK WOOD
THE NUCKET
THE HANGINGS
ROUND WOOD
Barnes Lodge
Barnes Farm
Badgerdell
SCATTERDELLS WOOD
THE GROVE
THE WINGS
KINGS LANGLEY
KINGS LANGLEY COMMON
Hill Farm
Ballspond Farm
Bulstrode Farm
Tenements Farm
Tuffs Farm
Chipperfield House
Chipperfield Garden Centre
Meggacres Farm
Whippendell Farm
Whippendell Bottom
Whippendell Hill
Kings Langley Riding School
CHIPPERFIELD
WD4
ROOKERY WOOD
Rose Farm
Manor Farm
CHIPPERFIELD COMMON
Berrybush Farm
Sunbury Hill Farm
Langley Lodge
Langley Lodge Farm
Burlew Farm
Middle Farm
Wayside Farm
DACORUM
THREE RIVERS
PENMAN'S GREEN
Hillmeads Farm
Callipers Hall
Callipers Hall Farm
Cart and Horses PH
QUICKMOOR LANE
Baytree Farm
Commonwood
DEBARDINE WOOD
PLOUGH WOOD
HILLMEADS SPRING
Deliffield
Great Sarratt Hall Farm
COMMONWOOD COMMON
Bucks Hill Farm
Bucks Hill
Little Westwood Farm
BERRYBUSHES WOOD
Model Farm
HAWK SPRING
BEECHEN BOTTOM
DELLSHOT SPRING
SHEEPCOTE SPRING
NORTH GROVE WOOD
SARRATT
HIGH SPRING
JUNIPER
KINGS LANGLEY BYPASS
A41
A4251
GRAND UNION CANAL
HEMPSTEAD ROAD
LOWER ROAD
HIGH ST
WATFORD ROAD
25
26
27
28
29
30
31
32
33
34
01
02
03
04
05
06
07

28

BP
BQ
BR
BS
BT
BU
BV
08
09
10
Potters C
HP3
WD5
WD2
25
26
27
28
29
30
31
32
33
34
04
03
02
01
16
POTTERS CROUCH PLANTATION
LONG DEANS
Highwood Hall Farm
High Herts Farm
The Swan PH
Bedmond Hill
Rose Acre
Radio Station
Hyde Meadow Farm
Hyde Springs
Hyde Farm
Hyde Lane Farm
Hart Hall Farm
Pimlico House
NEW PLANTATION
Little Abbots
Hart Hall
Green End Farm
White House Farm
Woodlands Poultry Farm
Leewood Farm
Verulam Farm
NEWLANDS MOBILE HOME PARK
DEADMAN WOOD
BEDMOND WOOD
WELLFIELD SPRING
Serge Hill
Whitehouse Farm
White Hart PH
PIECORNER WOOD
HANGING WOOD
FURZEFIELD WOOD
JOB'S WOOD
Ninnings Farm
Millhouse Farm
Searches Farm
Poultry Farm
Tenements Farm
BEDMOND
Hilltop Farm
ASH VIEW MOBILE HOME PARK
MOOR WOOD
BEDMOND PLAYING FIELDS
Bell Inn PH
LONG SPRING
Benmore Farm
Glasshouse
GREAT NOTLEY
SHEPPEYS LANE
DACORUM
THREE RIVERS
M25
Junction 21 M25
Junction 6a M1
STOWES WOOD
Ovaltine Dairy Farm
Numbers Farm
LITTLE NOTLEY
Mansion House Farm
COV RES
LONG WOOD
ROUND WOOD
ST. ALBANS
Clubhouse
Works
Depot
KINGS LANGLEY
CEM
ALLOT
Fortunes Farm
SPORTS GRD
BLOOM WOOD
LEAVESDEN HOSPITAL (Closed)
ABBOTS LANGLEY
MANOR HOUSE GROUNDS
Youth Cen
Clinic
TANNERS WOOD
Garston Manor
LEAVESDEN PARK
Junction 20
GRAND UNION CANAL
WATFORD ROAD
Hunton Bridge
HUNTON BRIDGE IND EST
SOUTH WAY PLAYING FLD
Tennis Cts
Bowl Grn
Hazelwood
THE ROOKERY
Home Farm
WOODSIDE
WOODSIDE STADIUM
WATFORD PLAYING FIELDS
ALBAN WOOD
Cricket Ground
Leisure Park
NORTH ORBITAL
A405
Leavesden Studios
LEAVESDEN GREEN
Kingswood
KINGSWAY
GARSTON
NORTH WATFORD CEMETERY
STANBOROUGH PARK
NORTH WESTERN AVENUE
BRICKFIELD SPRING

Potters Crouch
CHISWELL GREEN
HOW WOOD
BRICKET WOOD
Junction 21a
Junction 21 M25
Junction 6a M1
Junction 6
M25
M1
NORTH ORBITAL ROAD
A405
WD5
WD2
ST. ALBANS
THREE RIVERS
HERTSMERE
WATFORD
BUILDING RESEARCH ESTABLISHMENT
PENFOLD PARK GOLF COURSE
GARSTON PARK
BRICKET WOOD COMMON
WOODSIDE STADIUM
WATFORD PLAYING FIELDS
KYTES ESTATE
THE GARDENS OF THE ROSE
THE NOKE THISTLE HOTEL
Noke Lane Business Cen
SMUG OAK BUSINESS PARK
Management Training College
GREENWOOD PARK
WATLING STREET CARAVAN SITE (TRAVELLERS)
GRAVEL PIT
BLOOM WOOD
WINCH HILL WOOD
HOLT WOOD
BLACKGREEN WOOD
BIRCH WOOD
NOTTLERS WOOD
MUTCHETTS WOOD
COLDHABOUR PLANTATION
PEARTREE WOOD
CRAB WOOD
FOUR ACRE PLANTATION
NEW PLANTATION
JACK WILLIAM'S WOOD
MUNDEN SPRING
SQUARE WOOD
SCRUBBS WOOD
PARK WOOD
LONG SPRING
WELLFIELD SPRING
FURZEFIELD WOOD
JOB'S WOOD
Kingswood
GARSTON
STANBOROUGH PARK
NORTH WATFORD CEMETERY
WOODSIDE
BW BX BY BZ CA CB CC
25 26 27 28 29 30 31 32 33 34
15
30
12 13 14
01 02 03 04

17
CD
CE
CF
CG
CH
CJ
CK
AL1
AL2
NORTH ORBITAL ROAD
A414
A1081
LONDON COLNEY
Park Street
RADLETT AERODROME (DISUSED)
FROGMORE
COLNEY STREET
NAPSBURY HOSPITAL
HARPERBURY HOSPITAL
SHENLEY HOSPITAL
BROAD COLNEY NATURE RESERVE
ALL SAINTS PASTORAL CENTRE
QUARRY
COLNEY PARK
HARPER LANE RAIL DEPOT
PORTERS PARK GOLF COURSE
VERULAM GOLF COURSE
Sopwell House Hotel
M25
18
25
26
27
28
29
30
31
32
33
34
RADLETT
WD7

CL
CM
CN
CP
CQ
CR
CS
19
20
21
SAND AND GRAVEL PIT
THE WARREN
Warren Farm
FREDERICK'S WOOD
COPPICE WOOD
GARDEN WOOD
Tyttenhanger House
Tyttenhanger Farm
THE NEW PLANTATION
Coursers Farm
WELWYN HATFIELD
HERTSMERE
ST. ALBANS
BIG MAYFIELD WOOD
Bowmansgreen Farm
WALSINGHAM WOOD
MORRIS PLAYING FIELD
LONDON COLNEY IND EST
AL4
AL2
BROAD COLNEY NATURE RESERVE
Broad Colney Bridge
Superstore
The Bull PH
Junction 22
COLNEY BYPASS
COBS ASH
ROUND WOOD
SPORTS GRD
UNIVERSITY COLLEGE LONDON SPORTS GROUNDS
Tennis Courts
Salisbury Hall
Salisbury Hall Farm
AIRCRAFT MUSEUM
REDWELL WOOD
Redwell Wood Farm
M25
17
DELL GROVE
RSPCA Animal Centre
SHENLEYBURY COTTAGES
COMBE WOOD
Rectory Farm
Rabley Park Farm
Rabley Park
Shenley Hill Stud Farm
Shenley Hill
Catherine Bourne Farm
Ravenscroft Farm
COW BANKS
SHENLEY HOSPITAL (Closed)
SHENLEY PARK
SHENLEY
LITTLERIDGE WOOD
BIGPURSLEY WOOD
Ridge Farm
SAND PLANTATION
Cricket Ground
SPORTS PITCH
WD7
WD6
BIRCH WOOD
Nursery
Pursley Farm
ALLOT
Football Ground
LITTLEPURSLEY WOOD
Crossoaks Farm
CROSSOAKS WOOD
THE GORSE
Auriol Farm
Wood Hall
25
26
27
28
29
30
31
32
33
34
04
03
02
01

32

19
CT
CU
CV
CW
CX
CY
CZ
22
23
24
NORTH MYMMS PARK
North Mymms Park Training Centre
Clubhouse
Cricket Ground
Home Farm
Water End
BRICK KILN WOOD
Pumping Station
PELPIN'S WOOD
BROOKMANS PARK GOLF COURSE
BROOKMANS PARK
ROUND WOOD
Clubhouse
PLAYING FIELDS
Tennis Cts
Home Farm
GOBIONS OPEN SPACE
GOBIONS GARDEN
GOBIONS POND
AL9
Blue Bridge
Deep Bottom
Swallow Hole
GOBIONS WOOD
25
26
27
28
29
30
31
32
33
34
ROYAL VETERINARY COLLEGE
CANGSLEY WOOD
HAWKSHEAD WOOD
MYMMSHALL WOOD
WELWYN HATFIELD
HERTSMERE
Hawkshead Bridge
Tennis Courts
Pav
SPORTS GROUND
PILVAGE WOOD
POTTERS BAR GOLF COURSE
20
Cricket Ground
Depot
Works
FURZEFIELD WOOD
CRANBORNE INDUSTRIAL EST
Warrengate Farm
KING GEORGE V PLAYING FIELD
Sports Cen
Mimms Hall Farm
Widmore Hall
Youth & Comm Cen
Lib & Clinic
Sch
PLAYING FLD
Town Farm
POTTERS BAR
Wyllyotts Cen
Superstore
South Mimms
Bridgefoot
Bridgefoot House
Dugdale Hill
PLAYING FIELD
Rydal Mount
Rydal Mount Stables
Bignell's Corner
Forte Posthouse
Depot
EN6
South Mimms Services
Imperial Cancer Research Centre
Tennis Courts
Blanche Farm
Works
Junction 23 (M25)
Junction 1 A1(M)
A1(M)
M25
Elm Farm
Bentley Heath Farm
Garden Centre
Bentley Heath
The Duke of York PH
Amb Sta
Fire Sta
War Meml
CEM
Schs
01
02
03
04

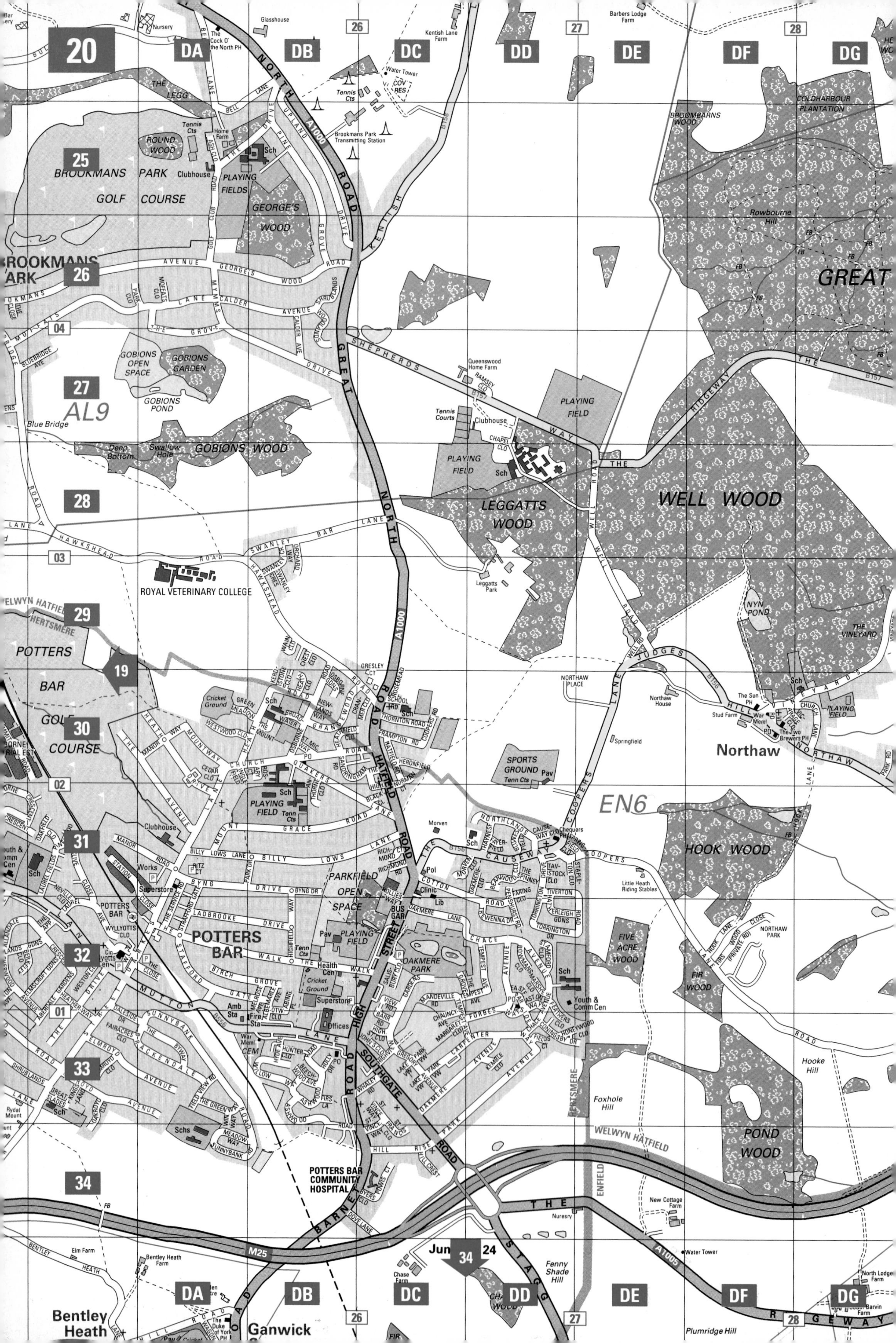

CUFFLEY
Cattlegate
Goffs Oak
CHESHUNT COMMON
SG13
EN7
EN2
HOME WOOD
WORMLEY WOOD
CATTLEGATE WOOD
NURSERY PLANTATION
CATTLINS
HERTFORDSHIRE
WELWYN HATFIELD
BROXBOURNE
M25
CREWS HILL
KING GEORGE'S FIELD
Newgate Street Bridge
Soper's Viaduct
22
35

22
DQ
DR
DS
DT
DU
DV
DW
33
34
35
Hammond Street
Flamstead End
Goffs Oak
BURY GREEN
BULLS CROSS
EN10
EN7
EN2
CHESHUNT PARK
CHESHUNT GOLF COURSE
HERTFORDSHIRE
BROXBOURNE
M25
Junction 25
CATTLINS
HOME WOOD
HANGING PLANTATION
BURYGREEN PLANTATION
ADATH YISROEL CEMETERY
BULLS CROSS RIDE CEMETERY
Capel Manor Horticultural & Environmental Centre
THEOBALDS PARK
GREAT CAMBRIDGE ROAD
A10
A121
B156
B198
04
03
02
01
21
36

23
DX
DY
DZ
EA
EB
EC
ED
36
37
38
NAZEING MARSH
Clayton Hill
King's Weir
LEE VALLEY PARK
TURNFORD MARSH
PLAYING FIELDS
HOLYFIELD LAKE
Clubhouse
Aquaduct Lock
Turnford
ALLOT
Turnford Place
Cheshunt Marriott Hotel
HALFHIDE LANE
BROOKFIELD CENTRE
HOLYFIELD MARSH
Holyfield Hill Farm
Elec Sta
THE NIGHTLEYS
NORTH METROPOLITAN PIT
SEVENTY ACRES
Cheshunt Lock
Hayes Hill Farm
Hayes Hill
Holyfield
GALLEYHILL WOOD
STUBBINS HALL LANE
Nursery
Grubbs Hill
HOLYFIELD
CHESHUNT LAKE
TURNERSHILL MARSH
HOOKS MARSH
Mariners Base
HOMEFIELD WOOD
Holyfield Farm
Monkham's Hall
KENNEL WOOD
24
PLAYING FIELD
WINDMILL LANE
CHESHUNT
THISTLY MARSH
CORNMILL
CLAYGATE
Leisure Cen
GRUNDY PARK
Cheshunt Junction
Waltham Common Lock
Sluice
HORSEMILL STREAM
EN8
CHESHUNT
LEE VALLEY PARK
HALL MARSH
ALLOT
Mile Nursery
Langley Nursery
BOWYER'S WATER
HOLYFIELD ROAD
CROOKED MILE
B194
ST. LEONARDS ROAD
MARSH LANE
COLEMAN'S SHAW
The Coach & Horses PH
Denver Lodge Farm
Peartree Farm
North Lodge Farm
Nightingales
Poultry Farm
25
26
27
28
29
30
31
32
33
34
04
03
02
01
BROXBOURNE
EPPING FOREST
RIVER LEE NAVIGATION
SMALL RIVER LEA
OLD RIVER LEA OR LEE
THE CEDARS PARK
THEOBALDS GROVE
WALTHAM MARSH
HERTFORDSHIRE
ESSEX
CHESHUNT MARSH
WALTHAM CROSS
Britannia Nursery
Marsh Bridge
Waltham Lock
HIGHBRIDGE ST
ABBEY VIEW
Lea Valley Countryside Centre
Harold's Bridge
WALTHAM ABBEY (Ruins)
ABBEY GARDENS
TOWN MEAD
RUNNING TRACK
LOWER ISLAND
Superstore
Holdbrook
Fowley Mead Caravan Park
LEA ROAD TRD EST
ELEANOR CROSS RD
STATION RD
A121
MONARCHS WAY
Pavilion Shopping Centre
Works
Depot
Pitches
M25
37
WALTHAM ABBEY CEM
LARSEN'S REC GRD
KING GEORGE'S FIELD
REC GRD
PARKLANDS
FARM HILL RD
HONEY LANE
MONKSWOOD AVENUE
ROUNDHILLS
Freezy Water
MOLLISON AVENUE
A1055
A105
A10
HODDESDON ROAD
GREAT CAMBRIDGE RD
HIGH ROAD
TURNERS HILL
RAMMEY
Quinton Hill Farm

24
EE
EF
EG
EH
EJ
EK
EL
Bumbles Green
Nazeing Gate
NAZEINGWOOD COMMON
Copthall Green
Upshire
WALTHAM ABBEY
EN9
23
38
25
26
27
28
29
30
31
32
33
34
40
41
42
04
03
02
01

Epping Green
Epping Long Green
Cobbin's Brook
Hayleys Manor Farm
Upland Road
Pinch Timber Farm
Epping Bury Farm Centre
EPPING BURY FARM CENTRE NATURE TRAIL
Hunters Hall Farm
Chambers Manor Farm
NABHILL GROVE
BALLHILL WOOD
ORANGE WOOD
Gills Farm
ORANGE FIELD PLANTATION
ORANGE PEEL
GILLS PLANTATION
Cobbin's Bridge
CM16
Lindsey Street
Bury Farm
Shaftesbury Farm
SPRATT'S HEDGEROW WOOD
SPRATT'S HEDGEROW
POND FIELD PLANTATION
JENKINS'S PLANTATION
LITTLE ROOKERY WOOD
ROOKERY WOOD
FITCHES PLANTATION
Bury Lane
The White House
Home Farm
Wood House
New Farm
Paris Hall
COPPED HALL GARDENS
Copped Hall (Ruins)
GRIFFIN'S WOOD
Griffin's Wood
Creeds Farm
Post House Hotel
Bell Common
Ivy Chimneys
EPPING
Bower Hill
THEYDON BOWER
BOWER COURT
Epping Sports Centre
THE SELVAGE
M25
BELL COMMON TUNNEL
THE WARREN
Warren Wood
Warren Lodge
EPPING THICKS
LORENTO CONVENT
Great Gregories Farm
Crown Hill Farm
Ambresbury Banks
EPPING FOREST
THEYDON BOIS GOLF COURSE
Little Bronx Stables
Piercing Hill
Gardners Farm
Long Running
Forest Lodge Stables
39

EU
EV
EW
EX
EY
EZ
FA
47
48
49
25
26
27
28
29
30
31
32
33
34
04
03
02
01
THORNWOOD
NORTH WEALD
AIRFIELD
EPPING
COOPERSALE
Bower Hill
Fiddlers Hamlet
Mount End
Theydon Mount
CM16
WINTRY WOOD
THE LOWER FOREST
EPPING PLAIN
ROUGHTALLEY'S WOOD
GERNON BUSHES
BIRCHING COPPICE
POSTERNIANE SPRING
HAWKSHILL WOOD
MOUNT WOOD
FORTY ACRES
REDYN'S WOOD
MOUNT QUARTER
ONGAR DOWN
GRAVELPIT WOOD
BEACHET WOOD
BARBER'S WOOD
THE ROUGH PATCH
ICEHOUSE PLANTATION
LONG PLANTATION
ST. MARGARET'S HOSPITAL
SPENCER CLOSE HOSP
WOODSIDE COMMERCIAL ESTATE
NORTH WEALD GOLF COURSE
HOBBS CROSS GOLF CENTRE
DRIVING RANGE
RUGBY GROUND
Golf Range
Esgors Farm
Rose Farm
Hayleys Manor Farm
Nursery
Bird Centre
Sewage Works
Weald Hall
Weald Hall Farm
The Carpenters Arms PH
Blacksmith's Arms PH
Hangar
Hangars
Clubhouse
Warehouse
NORTH WEALD IND EST
Superstore
Norway House
Piggery
Wintry Park Farm
Shaftesbury Farm
Carisbrooke Farm
Coopersale Farm
Coopersale House
Stonards Farm
Theydon Oak PH
Gaynes Park House
Gaynes Park
High Warren
Home Farm
The Merry Fiddlers PH
Masons Bridge Farm
Hornes Farm
Searles Hall
Sawkins Farm
Little Thorn Hall Farm
Gardners Farm
Farm Buildings
North House
Mount Hill Farm
Garnish Hall
Junction 40
M11
M25
UPLAND ROAD
WEALD HALL LANE
EPPING ROAD
WOODSIDE
HIGH ROAD
THORNWOOD ROAD
COOPERSALE STREET
BANKS LANE
MOUNT ROAD
GREEN ROAD
STEWARDS GREEN ROAD
HOBBS CROSS ROAD
HIGH STREET
ESSEX WAY
STEWARDS ESSEX GREEN WAY LANE
TAWNEY ROAD
NEW ROAD
LINDSEY ST
HEMNALL ST
BOWER HILL
THEYDON BOWER
BOWER COURT
STATION ROAD
EPPING

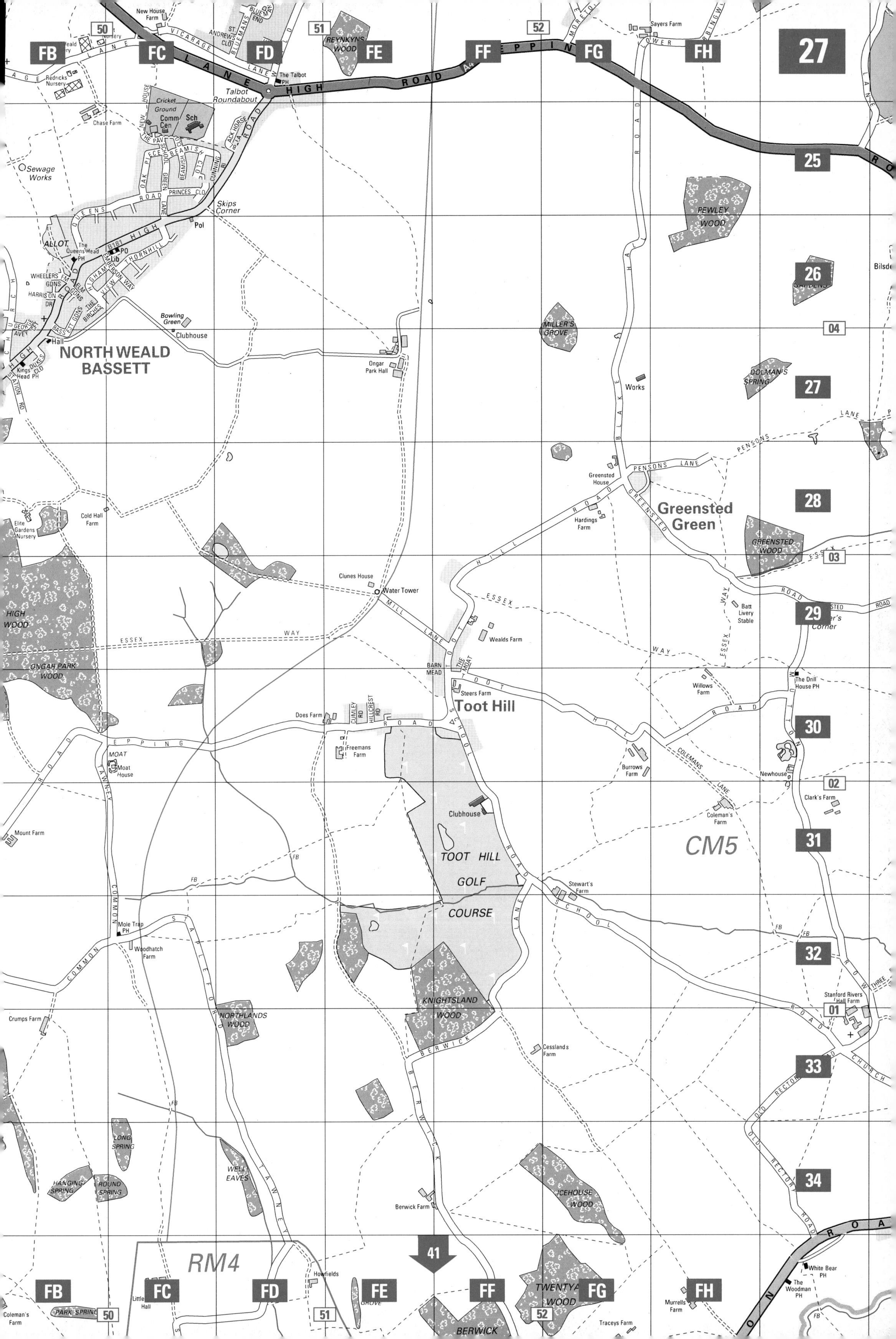
27
FB
FC
FD
FE
FF
FG
FH
50
51
52
25
26
04
27
28
03
29
30
02
31
32
01
33
34
41
NORTH WEALD BASSETT
Greensted Green
Toot Hill
TOOT HILL GOLF COURSE
CM5
RM4
HIGH ROAD
VICARAGE LANE
Talbot Roundabout
The Talbot PH
New House Farm
Redricks Nursery
Chase Farm
Sewage Works
Cricket Ground
Comm Cen
Sch
Skips Corner
Pol
ALLOT
The Queens Head PH
PO
Lib
Bowling Green
Clubhouse
Hall
Kings Head PH
Ongar Park Hall
Sayers Farm
PEWLEY WOOD
MILLER'S GROVE
DOLMAN'S SPRING
Works
Greensted House
Hardings Farm
GREENSTED WOOD
REYNKYNS WOOD
Cold Hall Farm
Elite Gardens Nursery
HIGH WOOD
ONGAR PARK WOOD
Clunes House
Water Tower
ESSEX WAY
MILL LANE
Wealds Farm
BARN MEAD
Steers Farm
Does Farm
Freemans Farm
EPPING ROAD
Moat House
Mount Farm
Clubhouse
Batt Livery Stable
Willows Farm
The Drill House PH
Burrows Farm
COLEMANS LANE
Coleman's Farm
Newhouse
Clark's Farm
Stewart's Farm
SCHOOL ROAD
Mole Trap PH
Woodhatch Farm
Crumps Farm
NORTHLANDS WOOD
KNIGHTSLAND WOOD
BERWICK LANE
Cesslands Farm
Stanford Rivers Hall Farm
CHURCH ROAD
OLD RECTORY ROAD
LONG SPRING
HANGING SPRING
ROUND SPRING
WELL EAVES
ICEHOUSE WOOD
Berwick Farm
Howfields
Little Hall
Coleman's Farm
PARK SPRING
TWENTYACRE WOOD
BERWICK
Murrells Farm
Traceys Farm
White Bear PH
The Woodman PH
FB

28
BG
BH
BJ
BK
BL
BM
BN
05
06
07
14
Bucks Hill
Commonwood
PLOUGH WOOD
HILLMEADS SPRING
Dellfield
COMMONWOOD
COMMON
Baytree Farm
Bucks Hill Farm
CONF CEN
Little Westwood Farm
Great Westwood Farm
HIGH SPRING
SHEEPCOTE SPRING
BEECHEN BOTTOM
JUNIPER HILL
WD4
35
36
37
38
39
40
41
42
43
44
99
98
97
96
SARRATT
The Boot PH
Tennis Ct
REC GRD
Pav
PO
Sch
Cricketers Inn PH
The Village Hall
Ward's Nurseries
SANDFIELD WOOD
Adams Nurseries
ALLOT
Green End Farm
Poultry Houses
Newhall Farm
Buckshill
Junction 19
TEMPLEPAN WOOD
GRAVEL
M25
TEMPLEPAN LANE
White House
Yew Court Farm
Potten's Farm
BIRCH SPRING
DARTPATH WOOD
WHITE SHACK LANE
Steven's Nurseries
The Grove Lodge
Chandler's Farm
Clarendon Arms PH
GREAT WOOD
Mickleford Green Farm
SHEEPYARD SPRING
SAWPIT SPRING
Coltspring Riding School
Coltyard Farm
Cottage Farm
Country Place
Blacketts Nurseries
New Model Farm
Sarratt Bottom Cottages
RIVER CHESS
Weir
SCRUBBS WOOD
BLUNTS WOOD
Sarrattmill Bridge
Water Works
MEAD SPRING
WILLOW WOOD
WD3
HARROCKS WOOD
Redhall Farm
WELLING GROVE
Micklefield Hall Farm
Micklefield Hall
MERLIN'S WOOD
MERLIN'S SPRING
ROUND NEWLAND'S SPRING
WATERDELL SPRING
LONG NEWLAND'S SPRING
Beechen Hill
BEECHENGROVE WOOD
MILLFIELD PLANTATION
LONG SPRING
UPPER PLANTATION
ROUND SPRING
PLAYING FIELD
Tennis Ct
Model Farm
Solesbridge Mill Water Gardens
LOUDWATER
Waterdell House
Croxley House
Thurlwood House
Killingdown Farm
PLAYING FIELD
Whitestocks Farm
PARROT'S DELL
Walden Lodge
Loudwater Ho
Mont Au Source
Glen Chess
Loudwater Farm
CHENIES RD
Cricket Ground
RICKMANSWORTH RD
A404
CHORLEYWOOD RD
White Horse PH
The Cedars
LITTLE LADY'S WOOD
Junction 18
HOME WOOD
COPTHORNE WOOD
CROXLEY GREEN
RECREATION GROUND
Tennis Cts
SPORTS GRD
Bowl Grn
Coach & Horses PH
The Artichoke PH
Comm Cen
PLAYING FIELDS
Pav
Watercress Beds
The Rickmansworth Masonic School
Nurseries
ROUND SPRING
Berry Farm
THE SCREEN
West Herts Riding School
SOLOMON'S WOOD
PHEASANT'S WOOD
ALLOT
Sch
Pumping Station
Tennis Cts
HOCKEY GRD
PLAYING FIELDS
CRICKET GRD
Clubhouse
Scotsbridge Mill PH
Scots Bridge
FORTUNE COMMON
PLAYING FIELD
PARK ROAD
SCOTS HILL
WATFORD
PLAYING FIELD
CROXLEY HALL WOOD
RICKMANSWORTH PARK
RICKMANSWORTH
PLAYING FIELD
Tenn Cts
Comet House
Croxley

BP
BQ
BR
BS
BT
BU
BV
08
09
10
15
LEAVESDEN GREEN
Kingswood
GARSTON
35
36
37
38
39
40
41
42
43
44
30
STANBOROUGH PARK
NORTH WATFORD CEMETERY
NORTH WESTERN AVENUE
KINGSWAY
Hunton Bridge Interchange
M25 LINK ROAD
HEATH WOOD
THE GROVE PARK
WD2
NORTH WATFORD
West Herts College
Bill Everett Sports Complex
Watford Tunnels
HEMPSTEAD ROAD
A411
ST ALBANS ROAD
A412
CHARLOTTE'S VALE
ROUGH WOOD
SPORTS GROUND
WHIPPENDELL WOOD
WEST HERTS GOLF COURSE
RIVER GADE
GRAND UNION CANAL
NASCOT LAWN
CASSIOBURY PARK
PADDLING POOLS
WATFORD JUNCTION
WATFORD
COLOSSEUM
TOWN HALL
DURRANTS SPORTS GROUND
RICKMANSWORTH ROAD
WEST WATFORD
VICARAGE RD CEMETERY
WATFORD GENERAL HOSPITAL
WATFORD FC
PLAYING FIELDS
CROXLEY GREEN
WATFORD WEST
HOLYWELL
HOLYWELL IND EST
LONG VALLEY WOOD
COMMON MOOR
WD1
GEORGE V PLAYING FIELDS
Power Station
Wiggenhall Bridge
SPORTS GROUND
OXHEY PARK
OXHEY
EASTBURY ROAD
WATFORD HIGH ST
BEECHEN GROVE
LOWER HIGH ST
WIGGENHALL ROAD
THE EBURY WAY CYCLE PATH

30
BW
BX
BY
BZ
CA
CB
CC
16
12
13
14
NORTH ORBITAL A405
GARSTON
Meriden
STANBOROUGH PARK
NORTH WATFORD CEMETERY
NORTH WESTERN AVENUE
NORTH WATFORD
ST ALBANS ROAD A412
A41 NORTH WESTERN AVE
(COLNE WAY)
GREYCAINE INDUSTRIAL ESTATE
WATFORD NORTH
JACK NICKLAUS GOLF CENTRE
Colne Bridge
Junction 5
Berrygrove Interchange
ALDENHAM GOLF COURSE
Aldenham
University of Hertfordshire
RIVER COLNE
HERTSMERE
WATFORD
MUNDEN SPRING
Munden House
Bushey Hall Farm
Busheymill Bridge
A4008 WAY
OTTERSPOOL WAY
EMPIRE CENTRE
WATFORD JUNCTION
The Watford Hilton National Hotel
WINFIELD MOBILE (HOME) PARK
The Three Compasses PH
Hartspring Leisure Cen
The David Lloyd Club
WD2
M1
NORTH WESTERN AVENUE (ELTON WAY)
SCOTTS WOOD
BUSHEY HALL GOLF COURSE
RADLETT ROAD PLAYING FIELDS
West Herts College
The Lincolnsfields Centre
METROPOLITAN POLICE SPORTS GROUND
BUSHEY JEWISH CEMETERY
The US International University (Europe)
ICEDALE WOODS
TOWN HALL
Palace Theatre
Harlequin Centre
BEECHEN GROVE
WATFORD HIGH ST
LOWER HIGH STREET
VICARAGE RD CEMETERY
WATFORD GENERAL HOSPITAL
WIGGENHALL ROAD
Wiggenhall Bridge
SPORTS GROUND
Power Station
WD1
OXHEY PARK
OXHEY
LONDON ROAD
HIGH STREET
MOAT FIELD REC GRD
BUSHEY
BUSHEY GOLF AND COUNTRY CLUB GOLF COURSE
KING GEORGE REC GROUND
Haydon Hill House
Watford Equestrian Centre
Watford Borough Council Nursery
35
36
37
38
39
40
41
42
43
44
29
44

31
CD
CE
CF
CG
CH
CJ
CK
15
16
17
PARK
GOLF COURSE
Clubhouse
SAND PLANTATION
Cricket Ground
Pav
SPORTS PITCH
Filter Beds
Depot
Sewerage Works
High Bridge
TYKES WATER
Fire Sta
Pol
Hall
Starveacres
RADLETT
WD7
THE GORSE
Blackbirds Farm
BLACKBIRDS LANE
OAKRIDGE LANE
Garden Centre
Kemprow Farm
KEMPROW
WATFORD ROAD
ALDENHAM ROAD
SHENLEY ROAD
SHENLEY HILL
THEOBALD STREET
WOODHALL LANE
Sch
Lib
PO
War Meml
PLAYING FLD
Bowl Grn
FIR SPRING
ALLOT
PLAYING FIELD
Tennis Cts
WATLING STREET
COBDEN HILL
A5183
Cat & Fiddle PH
Cobden Hill
RUGBY GROUND
Clubhouses
Cricket Ground
WELLHOUSE DELL
COBDENHILL DELL
MOSES DELL
KENDAL WOOD
FISH POND
Lido
Pav
Kendal Hall Farm
Country Club
Little Kendals Farm
LITTLE KENDALS WOOD
TYKES WATER
Organ Hall Farm
35
36
37
38
39
40
41
42
43
44
45
32
99
98
97
96
Battlers Green Farm
Home Farm
The Round Bush PH
The Fruit Farm
Letchmore Heath
Aldenham Grange
Aldenham Cottage
The Three Horseshoes PH
War Memorial
Bhaktivedanta Manor
Medburn Cottages
Aldenham Sports Centre
Aldenham School
PLAYING FIELDS Boydens Hill
Electricity Transfer Station
Letchmore Lodge
Slades Farm
North Medburn Farm
North Medburn Stables
Waggon & Horses PH
ELSTREE
DRIVING RANGE
Clubhouse
GOLF
COURSE
Medburn Bridge
South Medburn Farm
The Battle Axes PH
BUTTERFLY LANE
MOATS
ALDENHAM PARK WOODLAND
PLAYING FIELDS
PLAYING FIELD
TYKES WATER LAKE
ALDENHAM PARK
WD6
ALLOT
Hilfield Farm
ELSTREE AERODROME
Flying School
Club
Hangars
HOGG LANE
Boathouse
Hilfield Castle
HILFIELD PARK RESERVOIR
DAM
Pumping Sta
Pages Farm
Sewage Works
LISTER INSTITUTE
DAGGER LANE
ALDENHAM COUNTRY PARK
Pumping Station
ALDENHAM RESERVOIR
Boathouse
Clubhouse
SPORTS GROUND
Tyler's Farm
Works
Hart's Farm Riding Stables
WESTERN AVENUE A41 (TYLERS WAY)
HILFIELD LANE
Caldecote Farm
Berkeley Cottage
Gas Works
ELSTREE ROAD
WATFORD ROAD
A411
ELSTREE HILL OPEN SPACE
Comm Cen
ALLUM LANE
ELSTREE HILL NORTH
ELSTREE HILL SOUTH
HIGH STREET
BARNET LANE
Works
The Edgwarebury Hotel
ELSTREE OPEN SPACE
PLAYING FIELD
Tennis Courts
A41 BYPASS
Sparrows Herne
Heath House
Coll
Conv
ALLOT
A409
Tenn Cts

32
WD7
CL
CM
CN
CP
CQ
CR
CS
19
20
21
18
BIGPURSLEY WOOD
LITTLEPURSLEY WOOD
CROSSOAKS WOOD
Crossoaks Farm
CROSSOAKS LANE
SUMMERSWOOD LANE
Ridge Farm
THE
35
36
37
38
39
40
41
42
43
44
31
46
99
98
97
96
Auriol Farm
WOODHALL
Wood Hall Farm
Wood Hall
WOODHALL LANE
Kitwells Farm
Villa Scalabrini
Lyndhurst
ALLOT
Football Ground
Cricket Ground
Pav
LONDON ROAD
GREEN STREET
CATHARINE BOURNE
BIRCH WOOD
Purslev Farm
High Canons
Holmshill House
High Canons Farm
Buckettsland Farm
Wheatsheaf Farm
Maxwelton Nurseries
Well End Farm
Holly Cottage
Well End
Green Street
Cowleyhill Farm
COWLEY HILL
TYKES WATER
Organ Hall Farm
THEOBALD STREET
Health Cen
AYCLIFFE ROAD PITCHES
PLAYING FIELD
ABERFORD LAKE
ABERFORD PARK
Comm Cen
SPORTS GROUND
MEADOW PARK
PLAYING FLD
Sports Cen
ROWLEY LANE
Rowley Farm
Mops & Brooms PH
Strangeways Farm
BOREHAMWOOD IND PARK
De Havilland College
Swim Pool
Health Clinic
CIVIC OFFS
Lib
Amb Sta
Fire Sta
War Memorial
ELSTREE WAY A5135
Warehouses
Works
Depots
GEC SPORTS GROUND
Elstree Moat House
ARKLEY GOLF DRIVING RANGE
Clubhouse
Elstree Studios
Canterbury House
Boulevard 25
Superstore
MAXWELL PARK
BOREHAMWOOD
KING GEORGES PLAYING FIELD
TEMPSFORD GREEN
LAINGS PLAYING FIELD
ARKLEY GOLF COURSE
RIPON PARK
DRIVING RANGE
Waggon & Horses PH
Medburn Bridge
North Medburn Stables
South Medburn Farm
WD6
GOLF COURSE
ALDENHAM PARK
WATLING STREET
ELSTREE AND BOREHAMWOOD
Gas Works
ALLOT
Furze Hill
HERTSMERE BOROUGH COUNCIL CEMETERY
ELSTREE
Elli Dani Farm
ELSTREE HILL NORTH
BARNET LANE
A411
Deacons Hill
Airshafts
Woodcock Hill Farm
Tunnel
Elstree
DEACONS HILL OPEN SPACE
SCRATCH WOOD
NW7
FROGHALL WOOD
BOYS HILL WOOD
ELSTREE PARK
ARKLEY PARK
Hyver Hall
GRAVEL PIT WOOD
THISTLE WOOD
BARNET WAY
A1
ELSTREE HILL SOUTH
Elstree Manor
Penniwells Farm
The Leys
ELSTREE OPEN SPACE
PLAYING FIELD
HERTS

33
CT
CU
CV
CW
CX
CY
CZ
19
South Mimms
Junction 23 (M25)
Junction 1 A1(M)
M25
A1(M)
A1 BY-PASS
Bentley Heath
Dancers Hill
35
36
37
38
39
40
41
42
43
44
34
47
DYRHAM PARK GOLF COURSE
Dyrham Park Country Club
DYRHAM PARK
BRIDGEDOWN GOLF COURSE
WROTHAM PARK
Kitt's End
EN4
EN5
N20
OLD FOLD MANOR GOLF COURSE
MONKEN HADLEY
HADLEY GREEN
HIGH BARNET
HADLEY
BARNET
CHIPPING BARNET
ARKLEY
Barnet Gate
Ducks Island
Underhill
WROTHAM PARK OPEN SPACE
ARKLEY LANE OPEN SPACE
ARKLEY OPEN SPACE
ARKLEY GOLF COURSE
ARKLEY RISE ESTATE OPEN SPACE
Rowley Green
WHITINGS HILL OPEN SPACE
WHALEBONE PARK
BARNET GENERAL HOSP
GRANGE PLAYING FIELDS
OLD ELIZABETHANS (BARNET) MEMORIAL PLAYING FIELD
KING GEORGE'S FIELD
SOUTH HERTS GOLF COURSE
POOR CLARE MONASTERY
HERTFORDSHIRE
BARNET
HERTSMERE
ST. ALBANS ROAD
GREAT NORTH ROAD
HIGH STREET
WOOD STREET
BARNET ROAD
BARNET HILL
A1081
A411
A1000
A1000
22
23
24
97
98
99
96
Deadman's Botton
WINIFRED HOUSE HOSP

34
DA
DB
DC
DD
DE
DF
DG
M25
Junction 24
20
Bentley Heath
Ganwick Corner
Wrotham Park
WROTHAM PARK
HERTFORDSHIRE
HERTSMERE
ENFIELD
HADLEY WOOD
HADLEY WOOD GOLF COURSE
MONKEN HADLEY COMMON
MONKEN HADLEY
HADLEY
EN4
EN5
NEW BARNET
COCKFOSTERS
EAST BARNET
OAK HILL PARK
BARNET
CHIPPING BARNET
Underhill
SOUTH HERTS GOLF COURSE
KING GEORGE V PLAYING FIELD
BARNET PLAYING FIELDS
THE TUDOR GOLF COURSE
VICTORIA REC GROUND
BEECH HILL LAKE
Oak Hill Theological College
48
33
35
36
37
38
39
40
41
42
43
44
26
27
28
99
98
97
96
1. - LOCKSWOOD CLO
2. - CHERITON CLO
3. - OSBORNE CLO
4. - LICHFIELD CLO
5. - OAKHAM CLO

35
Crews Hills
CREWS HILL GOLF COURSE
Botany Bay
CHASE
TRENT PARK
TRENT PARK GOLF COURSE
Middlesex University
CHASE FARM & ENFIELD TRUST (CHASE FARM HOSPITAL)
EN2
Clay Hill
HILLYFIELDS PARK
LAVENDER HILL CEMETERY
World's End
ENFIELD GOLF COURSE
GRANGE PARK
BUSH HILL PARK GOLF COURSE
OAKWOOD
OAKWOOD PARK
N21
N14

36
DQ
DR
DS
DT
DU
DV
DW
EN7
22
BULLS CROSS RIDE CEMETERY
Theobalds Park Camping and Caravan Site
Junction 25
BULLS CROSS
Capel Manor Horticultural & Environmental Centre
WHITEWEBBS WOOD
WHITEWEBBS PARK
WHITE WEBBS GOLF COURSE
SPORTS GROUND
COUNTRY PARK
Bullsmoor
CEMETERY
Forty Hill
FORTY HALL
GOUGH PARK
BRAMLEY HOUSE
Kingswood
Rendlesham Viaduct
EN2
HILLYFIELDS PARK
CEMETERY
QUEEN ELIZABETH STADIUM
EN1
ENFIELD
ENFIELD PLAYING FIELDS
BASEBALL GROUND
MARTIN DALE INDUSTRIAL ESTATE
Enfield Highway
ENFIELD TOWN
ENFIELD CHASE
TOWN PARK
BUSH HILL PARK GOLF COURSE
BUSH HILL PARK
GRANGE PARK
N21
N9
JUBILEE PARK
KING GEORGE'S FIELD
GREAT CAMBRIDGE ROAD
A10
A110
A1010
HERTFORD ROAD
SOUTHBURY
Middlesex University
50
33
34
35
96
97
98
99

EN8
EN9
EN3
IG10
E4
Holdbrook
Freezy Water
RAMMEY MARSH
Enfield Lock
Enfield Wash
LEE VALLEY PARK
SEWARDSTONE
KING GEORGE'S RESERVOIR
Brimsdown
BRIMSDOWN INDUSTRIAL ESTATE
LEA SIDE INDUSTRIAL ESTATE
CENTENARY TRADING ESTATE
PONDERS END IND EST
THE HAWK WOOD
CHINGFORD GOLF COURSE
CHINGFORD PLAIN
WEST ESSEX GOLF COURSE
GILWELL PARK
BANCHET FIELD
Barn Hill
Yardley Hill
MOLLISON AVENUE
SEWARDSTONE ROAD
MOLLISON WAY
LEA VALLEY ROAD
M25
A1055
A110
A112
A105
A1010
23
51
38

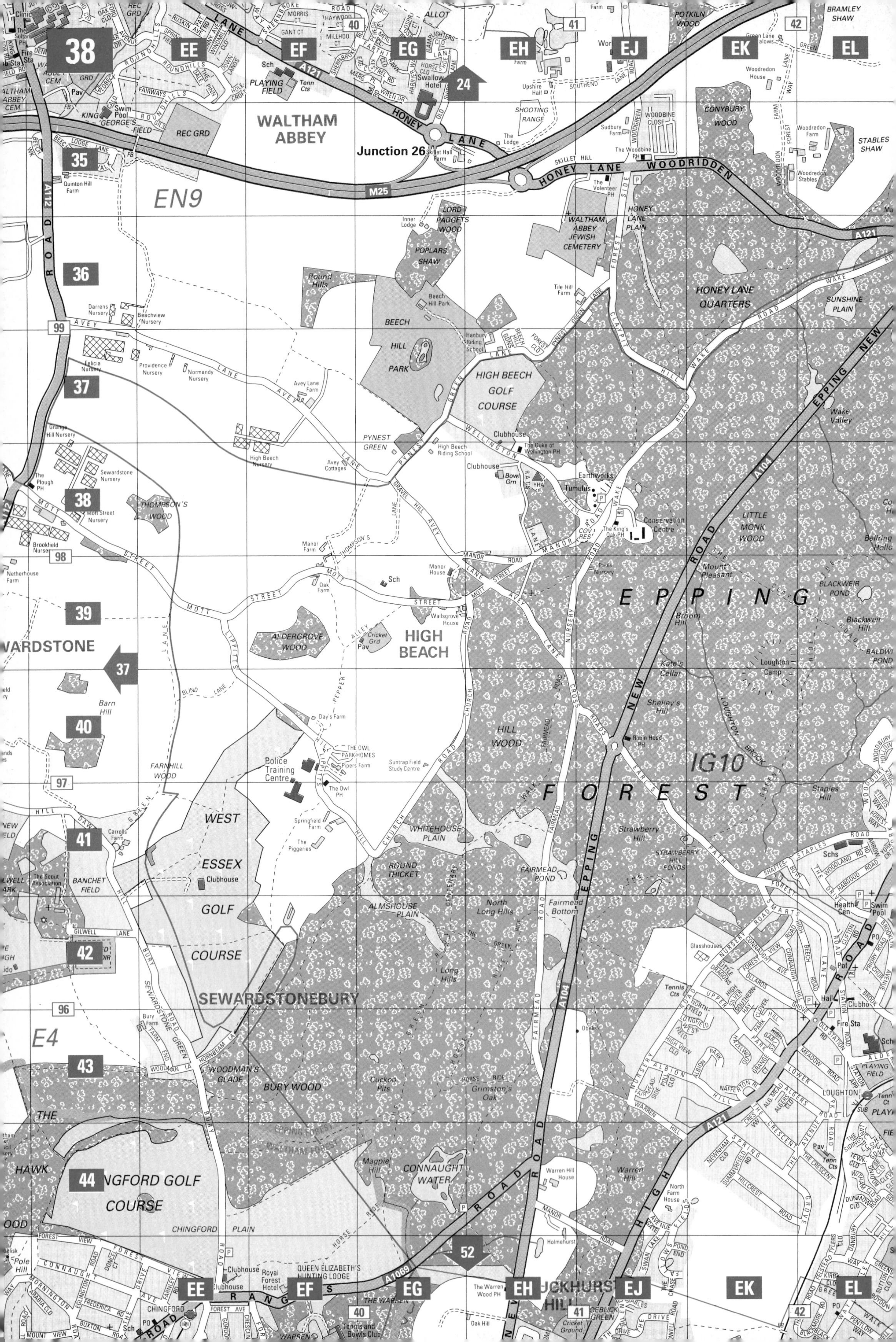

WALTHAM ABBEY
Junction 26
EN9
HIGH BEECH GOLF COURSE
BEECH HILL PARK
HIGH BEACH
EPPING FOREST
IG10
WEST ESSEX GOLF COURSE
SEWARDSTONEBURY
E4
CHINGFORD
LOUGHTON

39
EM
EN
EP
EQ
ER
ES
ET
43
44
45
25
53
40
35
36
37
38
39
40
41
42
43
44
99
98
97
96
EPPING FOREST
THEYDON BOIS
GOLF COURSE
ST. THOMAS'S QUARTERS
Long Running
Jacks Hill
Oak Hill
Dulsmead Hollow
COPLEY PLAIN
FURZE GROUND
BROADSTROOD PLAIN
GOLDING'S HILL PONDS
LOUGHTON GOLF COURSE
BIRCH WOOD
RED OAK WOOD
GAUNT'S WOOD
Debden Green
Ripley Grange
THEYDON PLAIN
THE COPPICE
QUEEN MARY & WESTFIELD COLLEGE SPORTS GROUND
THEYDON BOIS
THEYDON BOIS CEMETERY
CM16
RM4
IG7
THEYDON MEAD
LONG SHAW
BROADFIELD SHAW
Debden
HILLYFIELDS OPEN SPACE
PLAYING FIELD
CEM
DEBDEN INDUSTRIAL GROUP
PRINTING WORKS
SPORTS GROUND
OAKWOOD HILL INDUSTRIAL ESTATE
LORRY PARK
Junction 5
EPPING FOREST GOLF COURSE
DRIVING RANGE
Open Air Pool
RECREATION GROUND
SPORTS GROUND
ALLOTMENTS
OUGHTON
ABRIDGE PARK
Great Downs Farm
Turnours Hall
Maylings Farm
Taylor May's Farm
Pettits Hall
Home Farm
Rolls Park Farm
Blunts Farm
Parsonage Farm
Thrifts Hall Farm
Theydon Hall Farm
Little Bronx Stables
Birch Hall
Birch Hall Farm
Oak Hill Farm
The Sixteen String Jack PH
Forest Lodge Stables
M11
A121
A1168
A113
A1112
B172
B1393
GOLDINGS HILL
EPPING ROAD
COPPICE ROW
RECTORY LANE
CHIGWELL LANE
ABRIDGE ROAD
LONDON ROAD
GRAVEL LANE
PUDDING LANE
THEYDON PARK ROAD
LOUGHTON LANE
DEBDEN LANE
CLAY'S LANE
ENGLANDS LANE
HILLYFIELDS
BORDERS LANE
OAKWOOD HILL
RIVERSIDE WALK
RIVER RODING
LANGSTON ROAD
DEBDEN
Corbett Theatre
The Sir Winston Churchill PH
Plume of Feathers PH

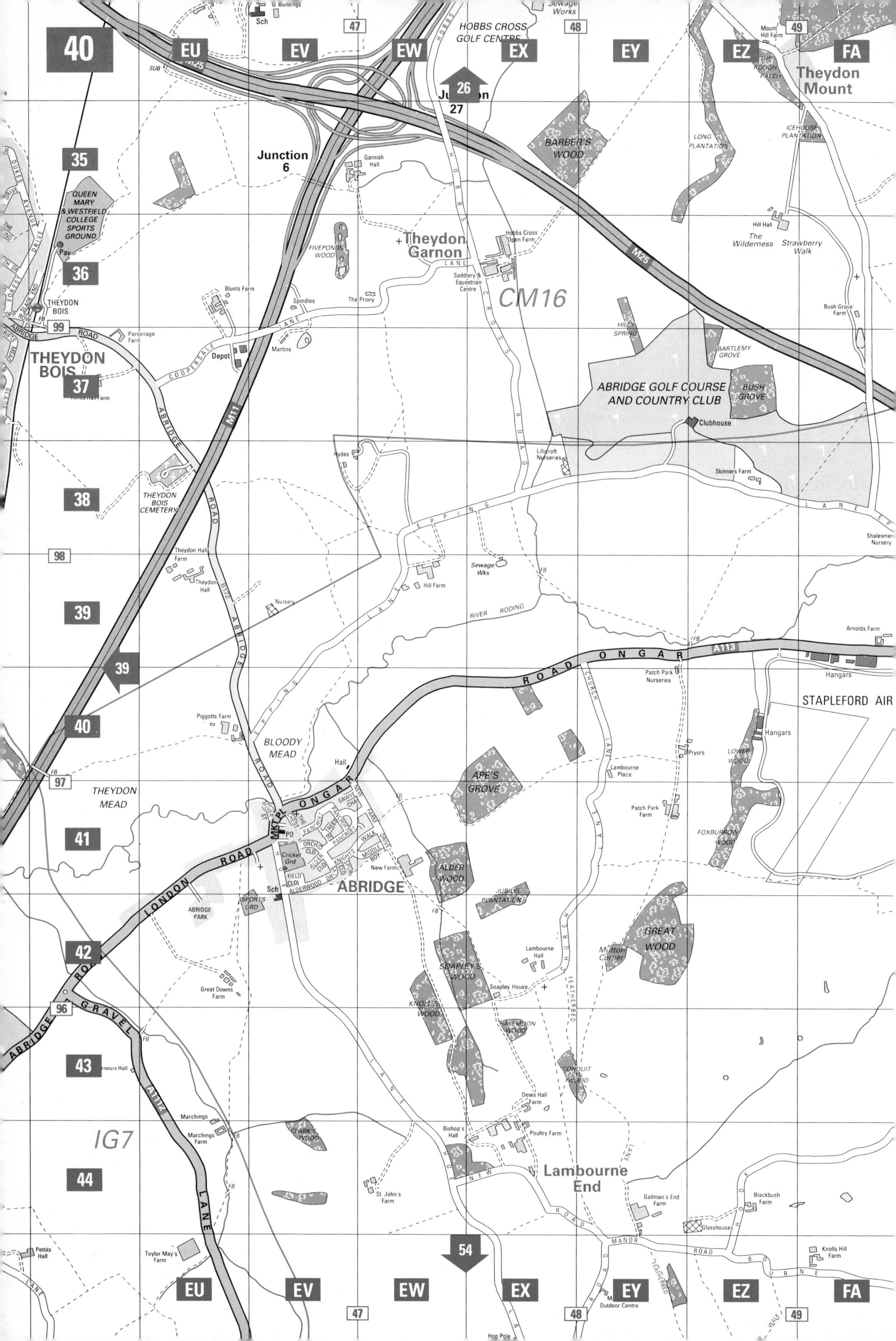

EU
EV
EW
EX
EY
EZ
FA
47
48
49
26
54
39
HOBBS CROSS GOLF CENTRE
Junction 27
Junction 6
M25
M11
Theydon Mount
THE ROUGH PATCH
Mount Hill Farm
ICEHOUSE PLANTATION
LONG PLANTATION
BARBER'S WOOD
Garnish Hall
QUEEN MARY & WESTFIELD COLLEGE SPORTS GROUND
Pav
THEYDON BOIS
Theydon Garnon
FIVEPONDS WOOD
Hobbs Cross Open Farm
Saddlery & Equestrian Centre
Hill Hall
The Wilderness
Strawberry Walk
CM16
Blunts Farm
Spindles
The Priory
Bush Grove Farm
HILLY SPRING
BARTLEMY GROVE
Parsonage Farm
Martins
Depot
COOPERSALE LANE
ABRIDGE GOLF COURSE AND COUNTRY CLUB
BUSH GROVE
Clubhouse
Lillicroft Nurseries
Skinners Farm
Hydes
THEYDON BOIS CEMETERY
EPPING LANE
Shalesmere Nursery
Theydon Hall Farm
Theydon Hall
Sewage Wks
Hill Farm
Nursery
RIVER RODING
Arnolds Farm
ONGAR ROAD
A113
Patch Park Nurseries
Hangars
STAPLEFORD AIR
Piggotts Farm
BLOODY MEAD
Pryors
LOWER WOOD
Lambourne Place
APE'S GROVE
THEYDON MEAD
Hall
Patch Park Farm
FOXBURROW WOOD
MKT PL
PO
Cricket Grd
New Farm
ALDER WOOD
ABRIDGE
Sch
SPORTS GRD
ABRIDGE PARK
LONDON ROAD
JUBILEE PLANTATION
GREAT WOOD
Mutton Corner
Lambourne Hall
SOAPLEY'S WOOD
Soapley House
Great Downs Farm
KNOLL'S WOOD
HALFMOON WOOD
GRAVEL
ABRIDGE
A1112
CONDUIT WOOD
FEATHERBED
Dews Hall Farm
Marchings
Marchings Farm
IG7
CLARK'S WOOD
Bishop's Hall
Poultry Farm
Lambourne End
St. John's Farm
Gallman's End Farm
Blackbush Farm
Glasshouses
MANOR ROAD
Knolls Hill Farm
Pettits Hall
Taylor May's Farm
Outdoor Centre
Hop Pole
35
36
37
38
39
40
41
42
43
44
96
97
98
99

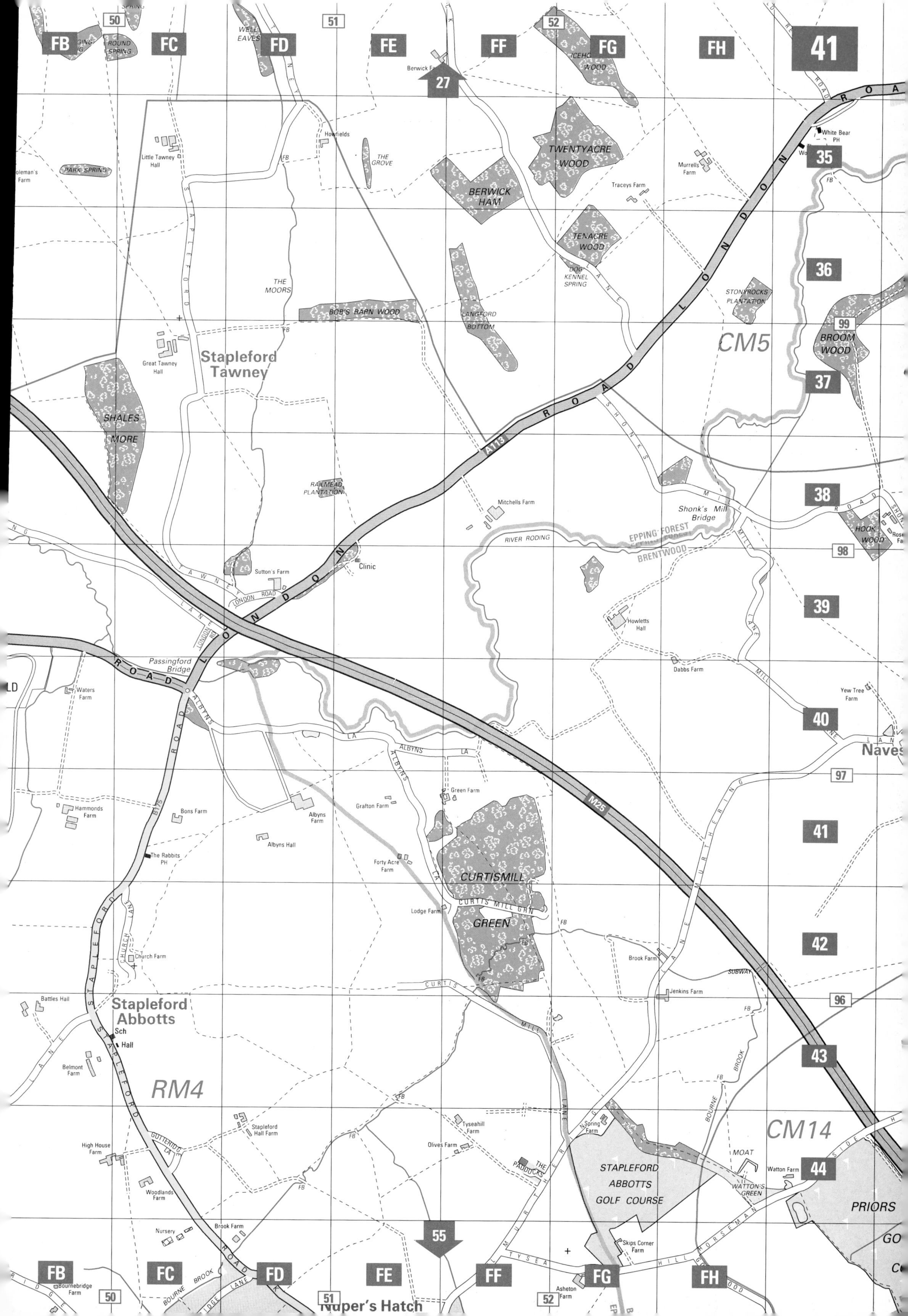
41
FB
FC
FD
FE
FF
FG
FH
50
51
52
27
55
35
36
37
38
39
40
41
42
43
44
99
98
97
96
Stapleford Tawney
Stapleford Abbotts
Navestock
Nuper's Hatch
RM4
CM5
CM14
SHALES MORE
TWENTYACRE WOOD
BERWICK HAM
TENACRE WOOD
BOB'S BARN WOOD
CURTISMILL GREEN
STAPLEFORD ABBOTTS GOLF COURSE
BROOM WOOD
HOOK WOOD
ICEHO WOOD
PARK SPRING
ROUND SPRING
WELL EAVES
THE GROVE
THE MOORS
LANGFORD BOTTOM
DOG KENNEL SPRING
STONYROCKS PLANTATION
RAILMEAD PLANTATION
Little Tawney Hall
Great Tawney Hall
Howfields
Berwick Farm
Murrells Farm
Traceys Farm
White Bear PH
Mitchells Farm
Shonk's Mill Bridge
RIVER RODING
EPPING FOREST
BRENTWOOD
Sutton's Farm
Clinic
Howletts Hall
Dabbs Farm
Yew Tree Farm
Passingford Bridge
Waters Farm
Hammonds Farm
Bons Farm
Albyns Farm
Albyns Hall
Grafton Farm
Green Farm
Forty Acre Farm
The Rabbits PH
Lodge Farm
Church Farm
Brook Farm
Jenkins Farm
Battles Hall
Sch
Hall
Belmont Farm
Stapleford Hall Farm
Tyseahill Farm
Olives Farm
High House Farm
Woodlands Farm
Nursery
Spring Farm
THE PADDOCKS
MOAT
Watton Farm
WATTON'S GREEN
Skips Corner Farm
Asheton Farm
Bournebridge Farm
PRIORS
LONDON ROAD
A113
M25
B175
SHONKS MILL ROAD
MILL LANE
MURTHERING LANE
ALBYNS LA
CURTIS MILL GRN
CURTIS MILL LANE
STAPLEFORD ROAD
STAPLEFORD LANE
CHURCH LANE
GUTTERIDGE LA
TAWNEY LANE
TYSEA HILL
HORSEMAN SIDE
BOURNE BROOK
LODGE LANE
SUBWAY
FB

42
BG
BH
BJ
BK
BL
BM
BN
28
45
46
47
48
49
50
51
52
53
54
56
05
06
07
94
93
92
91
Mill End
Moneyhill
RICKMANSWORTH
BATCHWORTH
WD3
UB9
HAREFIELD
Hill End
SOLOMON'S WOOD
PHEASANT'S WOOD
West Herts Riding School
CHORLEYWOOD ROAD CEMETERY
CHORLEYWOOD PLAYING FIELD
PLAYING FIELDS
CRICKET GRD
FORTUNE COMMON
Scots Bridge
PLAYING FIELD
CROXLEY HALL WOOD
RICKMANSWORTH PARK
SCOTS HILL
WATFORD RD
PARK ROAD
PARK RD
RECTORY RD
HIGH ST
CHURCH ST
Leisure Centre
Swim Pool
SPORTS GRD
Halfway House PH
Clinic
Boathouse
RIVERSIDE DRIVE
A404
A412
A405
UXBRIDGE ROAD
BATCHWORTH ROUNDABOUT
BATCHWORTH LAKE
THE AQUADROME
BURY LAKE
Three Valleys Water Offices
White Bear PH
Superstore
MOOR LANE
Clubhouse
RICKMANSWORTH
MOOR PARK GOLF COURSE
MOOR PARK MANSION
GARDENS
BATCHWORTH PARK GOLF COURSE
GRAND UNION CANAL
Stocker's Lock
STOCKER'S LAKE (NATURE RESERVE)
Stocker's Farm
Pumping Station
Depot
LONDON ROAD
BATCHWORTH HILL
Moor Park Farm
Whip and Collar PH
Drayton Ford
Froghall Farm
MAPLE CROSS IND. ESTATE
Works
Maple Lodge Sewage Treatment Works
Sludge Drying Beds
Watercress Beds
Lock
SPRINGWELL CHALK PIT
SPRINGWELL LAKE
CHALK PIT
GARRETT WOOD
HIGH WOOD
HERTFORDSHIRE
COCKS WOOD
THREE RIVERS
Andrews Ley Farm
WOODCOCK HILL CEMETERY
Juniper Dell
Greenbroom Spring
Sandfield Spring
WOODCOCK HILL TRADING ESTATE
Pipers Farm
Bush Spring
Home Farm House
BATCHWORTH HEATH
Batchworth Heath Farm
Rose and Crown PH
LONG SPRING
PARK WOOD
BISHOP'S WOOD
POORFIELD
LOCKWELL WOOD
Woodcock Hill Farm
PEARSON'S WOOD
WHITE HILL
HAREFIELD COVERED RESERVOIR
Battlerswells Farm
FRENCH GROVE
BATTLERS WELLS WOOD
Little Bourne Farm Equestrian Stables
Cripps House Farm
Waybeards Farm
White Heath Farm
Plough PH
ALLOT
Harefield Grove
WATTS COMMON
TAYLORS MEADOW
Bowling Green
Harefield Grove Farm
Lynsters Farm
Filter Beds
Sludge Beds
RIVER COLNE
HILLINGDON
LYNSTERS LAKE
SUMMERHOUSE LANE INDUSTRIAL ESTATE
PARK WOOD
NATURE RESERVE
COPPERMILL
PYNESFIELD LAKE
SPORTS GROUND
HAREFIELD HOSPITAL
PLAYING FIELD
Sports Cen
Tenn Cts
Shepherds Hill Farm
Shepherds Hill House
NORTHWOOD ROAD
Horseshoe Bay
Weir
Clubhouse
Colney Farm
THE GREEN
Health Cen
Swan PH
Cricket Ground
Football Ground
BREAKSPEAR ROAD
ASHAIN SPRING
KILN POND CLAYPITS
Knightscote Farm
Langley Farm
FURZEFIELD
DEADMAN'S GROVE
SCARLET SPRING
DUCKS
RAVENERS SPRING
DELL
Shooting School
HIGHBONES
Bourne Farm
DENHAM WAY
NORTH ORBITAL ROAD
OLD UXBRIDGE ROAD
TOWING PATH
GRAND UNION CANAL

43
BP
BQ
BR
BS
BT
BU
BV
08
09
10
HOLYWELL
WD1
29
LONG VALLEY WOOD
COMMON MOOR
HOLYWELL IND EST
KING GEORGE V PLAYING FIELDS
MOOR PARK INDUSTRIAL CENTRE
Moor Park Crossing
TOLPITS LANE
VALE INDUSTRIAL PARK
Tolpits House
RIVER COLNE
Brightwells Spring
HAMPERMILL LAKE
RUNNING TRACK
PLAYING FIELDS
Merchant Taylors School
SPORTS GRD
Oxhey Hall
MOAT
Power Station
45
46
47
48
49
50
51
52
53
54
44
57
93
94
92
91
HAMPERMILL WOOD
BIG WOOD
SOUTH OXHEY PLAYING F
OXHEY PARK GOLF COURSE
GOLF COURSE
SANDY LODGE GOLF COURSE
MOOR PARK
MOOR PARK ESTATE
BATHEND CLUMP
EASTBURY
OXHEY
OXHEY WOOD
THE PLANTATION
BECK MASON'S WOOD
H.M.S. Warrior
OLD FURZE FIELD
YOUNG HANGINGS
OLD HANGINGS
SOUTH OXHEY
WILD WOODS
NORTHWOOD
MOUNT VERNON HOSPITAL
THREE RIVERS
HILLINGDON
HA6
HA5
THE GRAVEL PITS
Northwood Coll
NORTHWOOD GOLF COURSE
PINNER HILL GOLF COURSE
Pinnerwood Park
NORTHWOOD & PINNER COTTAGE HOSP
NORTHWOOD HILLS
RECREATION GROUND
HASTE HILL GOLF COURSE
RUISLIP NATURE RESERVE
COPSE WOOD
HILL
PINNER GREEN
HOG'S BACK OPEN SPACE
PLAYING FIELDS
POOR'S FIELD
ST. VINCENT'S HOSPITAL
RICKMANSWORTH ROAD
PINNER ROAD
SANDY LANE
WATFORD ROAD
HIGH STREET
DUCKS HILL ROAD
EASTBURY ROAD
HAMPERMILL LANE
SANDY LODGE ROAD

WD1
BW
BX
BY
BZ
CA
CB
CC
12
13
14
30
OXHEY PARK
SPORTS GROUND
CHALK HILL
LONDON ROAD
HIGH STREET
BUSHEY
BUSHEY GOLF AND COUNTRY CLUB GOLF COURSE
Haydon Hill House
Watford Equestrian Centre
Watford Borough Council Nursery
RUNNING TRACK
Merry Hill
ALLOTMENTS
WD2
Watford Heath
SHERWOODS WOOD
MARGEHOLES WOOD
OXHEY LANE
THREE RIVERS
CARPENDERS PARK
Carpenders Park Farm
HARTSBOURNE GOLF AND COUNTRY CLUB GOLF COURSE
HERTSMERE
SPOILBANKS
GOLF DRIVING RANGE
OXHEY PARK GOLF COURSE
Warren Dell
Ox Pasture Spring
OXHEY PLAYING FIELDS
EASTBURY ROAD
BROOKDENE AVENUE
PRESTWICK ROAD
SOUTH OXHEY
OXHEY POND WOOD
SANDPIT WOOD
CARPENDERS PARK CEMETERY
WOODWALKS
MUTTON WOOD
LEVELS WOOD
GRIMSDYKE LAKE
Grims Dyke House Hotel
HARROW WEALD COMMON
GRIMS DYKE GOLF COURSE
WEALD WOOD
STONY WOOD
Grimswood House
Highcroft
OXHEY
BECK MASON'S WOOD
OXHEY WOOD
43
HERTFORDSHIRE
HARROW
Swimming Pool
PLAYING FIELD
Electricity Sub Station
NANSCOT WOOD
Oxhey Lane Farm
Pinnerwood Farm
SADDLERS MEAD REC GROUND
SPORTS GROUND
BANISTER ATHLETICS STADIUM
HATCH END
PINNER HILL GOLF COURSE
Pinnerwood Park
UXBRIDGE ROAD
A410
HARROW ARTS CENTRE
Superstore
RAGHUVANSHI CHARITABLE TRUST SPORTS GROUND
HATCH END PLAYING FIELDS
THE CEDARS
HA5
PINNER PARK
Pinner Park Farm
ST. THOMAS' DRIVE
GEORGE V AVENUE
PINNER GREEN
RICKMANSWORTH ROAD
LITTLE COMMON
HEADSTONE LANE
HEADSTONE MANOR
HA2
58
44
45
46
47
48
49
50
51
52
53
54
91
92
93
94
A4125
A4008
A411
A4140
A404
B4542

45
CD
CE
CF
CG
CH
CJ
CK
15
16
17
31
RESERVOIR
SPORTS GROUND
HILL OPEN SPACE
ELSTREE OPEN SPACE
WD6
Junction 4
M1
A41 BYPASS
WATFORD BYPASS
ELSTREE ROAD
WATFORD ROAD
BARNET ROAD
ELSTREE HILL SOUTH
BUSHEY HEATH
BUPA HOSPITAL
HEATHBOURNE ROAD
STANMORE COMMON
ROYAL NATIONAL ORTHOPAEDIC HOSPITAL
Site of Sulloniace Roman Settlement
BROCKLEY HILL
EDGWARE WAY (WATFORD BYPASS)
PEAR WOOD
GROVE FIELDS
LITTLE COMMON
CLOISTERS WOOD
BENTLEY PRIORY
HARROW WEALD COMMON
COMMON ROAD
THE COMMON
BENTLEY PRIORY OPEN SPACE
BENTLEY PRIORY NATURE RESERVE
HA7
STANMORE HILL
STANMORE
LONDON ROAD
HARROW WEALD CEMETERY
HARROW WEALD LAKE
Weald College
UXBRIDGE ROAD
BROOKSHILL
STANMORE PARK
Stanmore College
STANMORE GOLF COURSE
HONEYPOT LANE
STANMORE MARSH
SPORTS GROUND
HA8
CANONS PARK
PRINCE EDWARD PLAYING FIELD
HARROW WEALD
HA3
HIGH STREET
BELMONT
CENTENARY PARK
QUEENSBURY
WEALDSTONE
KODAK WORKS
46
47
48
49
50
51
52
53
54
59
91
92
93
94

46
CL
CM
CN
CP
CQ
CR
CS
19
20
21
32
45
46
47
48
49
50
51
52
53
54
60
94
93
92
91
DEACONS HILL
OPEN SPACE
Deacons Hill
Elstree Manor
The Edgwarebury Hotel
Penniwells Farm
SCRATCH WOOD
FROGHALL WOOD
BOYS HILL WOOD
THISTLE WOOD
GRAVEL PIT WOOD
CLUMP OF TREES WOOD
TARGET WOOD
LEG OF MUTTON POND
NUT WOOD
ELSTREE OPEN SPACE
WD6
M1
HERTSMERE
BARNET
Brockley Grange
Site of Sulloniace Roman Settl
Bury Farm
Scratchwood Services
MILL HILL
GOLF COURSE
MOAT
OPEN
HEMMINGS WOOD
STONEY WOOD LAKE
STONEY WOOD
Travelodge Hotel
EDGEWAREBURY CEMETERY
EDGWAREBURY PARK
EDGWAREBURY GOLF COURSE
EDGWARE WAY (WATFORD BYPASS)
BROCKLEY HILL
SPUR ROAD
STONEGROVE
STONEGROVE PARK
JOHN GROOM'S ESTATE
CONVENT
EDGWARE
HA8
HA7
STANMORE
CANONS PARK
THE LAKE
THE BASIN
CHANDOS RECREATION GROUND
PRINCE EDWARD PLAYING FIELD
SPORTS GROUND
EDGWARE COMMUNITY HOSPITAL
BURNT OAK
WATLING PARK
SILKSTREAM PARK
MONTROSE PLAYING FIELDS
COLINDALE HOSPITAL
COLINDALE BUSINESS PARK
BRIXTON EST
QUEENSBURY
HONEYPOT LANE
STATION ROAD
HIGH STREET
BURNT OAK BROADWAY
EDGWARE ROAD
DEANSBROOK ROAD
HALE LANE
SELVAGE LANE
WATFORD WAY
MARSH LANE
LYNDHURST PARK
MILL HILL BROADWAY
ADASTRAL ESTATE
GRAHAME PARK
NEWSPAPER COLLECTION
WOODCROFT PARK
GOVT OFF
GOVT BLDGS

CT
CU
CV
CW
CX
CY
CZ
47
22
23
24
33
EN5
Barnet Gate
Ducks Island
GRANGE PLAYING FIELDS
OLD ELIZABETHANS (BARNET) MEMORIAL PLAYING FIELD
MOUNT SPACE
45
SOUTH HERTS GOLF COURSE
N20
46
OLD CHOLELEIAN SPORTS GROUND
TOTTERIDGE FIELDS NATURE RESERVE
TOTTERIDGE PARK
TOTTERIDGE COMMON
TOTTERIDGE
TOTTERIDGE VILLAGE
A5109
94
TOTTERIDGE HILL
HIGHWOOD HILL
Highwood Hill
HIGHWOOD LANE
NW7
Ellern Mede Nursing Home
The Lynch House
Fairlawn
The Warren
TOTTERIDGE GREEN
47
Consolata Missionary College
DARLANDS LAKE NATURE RESERVE
FOLLY BROOK
48
93
49
N12
50
92
SPORTS GROUND
Burtonhole Farm
National Inst. For Medical Research
CONVENT
THE RIDGEWAY
MILL HILL
ABBEY GROUNDS
COLLEGE GROUNDS
THE MILL FIELD
ARRANDENE OPEN SPACE
Featherstone Hill
MILL HILL PARK
MILL HILL CEMETERY
INGLIS BARRACKS
FINCHLEY GOLF COURSE
BITTACY HILL PARK
51
52
91
53
MILL HILL EAST
Gas Works
CHASE LODGE PLAYING FIELD
COPTHALL STADIUM
COPTHALL SPORTS CENTRE
HENDON GOLF COURSE
HENDON CEMETERY
Junction 2
BARNET BY-PASS
WATFORD WAY
M1
A41
RAF MUSEUMS
RAF HENDON
SUNNY HILL PARK
NW4
61
HOLDERS HILL
WINDSOR OPEN SPACE
CHURCH END
FINCHLEY CENTRAL
54
AVENUE HOUSE GROUND
EAST END ROAD
N3
GREAT NORTH WAY
A504
A598
REGENTS PARK ROAD
(Police Training School)

48
DA
DB
DC
DD
DE
DF
DG
34
26
27
28
EAST BARNET
OAK HILL PARK
EN4
Oak Hill Theological College
SOUTH HERTS GOLF COURSE
N20
BROOK FARM OPEN SPACE
WYATTS FARM OPEN SPACE
BARNET PLAYING FIELD
KING GEORGE V PLAYING FIELD
SPRINGDENE HOSP
DAME ALICE OWEN'S GRD
OAKLEIGH PARK
TOTTERIDGE LANE
TOTTERIDGE & WHETSTONE
WHETSTONE
WHETSTONE STRAY
SWAN LANE OPEN SPACE
Consolata Missionary College
NORTH MIDDLESEX GOLF COURSE
BETHUNE GOLF COURSE
BRUNSWICK PARK
NEW SOUTHGATE REC GRD
FRIARY PARK
FRIERN BARNET
WOODSIDE PARK
N12
HOSP (Closed)
NORTH FINCHLEY
FINCHLEY
COPPETTS WOOD
FINCHLEY MEMORIAL HOSPITAL
GLEBELANDS OPEN SPACE
FINCHLEY LEISURE COMPLEX
NORTH CIRCULAR ROAD
ST. PANCRAS AND ISLINGTON CEMETERY
MUSWELL HILL SPORTS GROUND
COPPETTS WOOD HOSP
COLDFALL WOOD
N10
VICTORIA PARK
FINCHLEY CENTRAL
CHURCH END
AVENUE HOUSE GROUNDS
EAST END ROAD
N3
EAST FINCHLEY CEMETERY
Christ's College
62
45
46
47
48
49
50
51
52
53
54
91
92
93
94
A1000
A5109
A109
A1003
A598
A504

DH
DJ
DK
DL
DM
DN
DP
49
29
30
31
35
OAKWOOD
OAKWOOD PARK
N21
N14
WINCHMORE HILL
GROVELANDS PARK
GROVELANDS PRIORY HOSP
BOATING LAKE
WOODCROFT SPORTS GROUND
OSIDGE
SOUTHGATE
Southgate Technical College
SOUTHGATE CEMETERY
PALMERS GREEN
45
46
47
48
49
50
51
52
53
54
THE PAULIN GROUND
BARROWELL GREEN OPEN SPACE
CLOWES SPORTS GROUND
TATEM PARK REC
HOLLY-WOOD GDNS
ARNOS PARK
NEW SOUTHGATE
BROOMFIELD PARK
HAZELWOOD SPORTS GROUND
NORTH CIRCULAR ROAD
BOWES ROAD
N13
N11
New Southgate Shopping Centre
TOTTENHALL SPORTS GROUND
BOUNDARY PLAYING FIELDS
BOWES PARK
BOUNDS GREEN
MUSWELL HILL GOLF COURSE
ALLOTMENTS
SCOUT PARK
SPORTS GROUND
NEW RIVER SPORTS CENTRE
ST. GEORGES INDUSTRIAL ESTATE
WOODSIDE PARK
RECREATION GROUND
PLAYING FIELDS
N22
WOOD GREEN
NOEL PARK
LORDSHIP LANE
WOOD GRN COMMON
ALEXANDRA PALACE
ALEXANDRA PARK
SPORTS GROUND
BELMONT REC GRD
DOWNHILLS PARK
HORNSEY
63

50
DQ
DR
DS
DT
DU
DV
DW
33
34
35
36
N21
N1
N9
N18
N13
N22
N17
45
46
47
48
49
50
51
52
53
54
91
92
93
94
64
LOWER EDMONTON
EDMONTON
UPPER EDMONTON
TOTTENHAM
TOTTENHAM HALE
WINCHMORE HILL
JUBILEE PARK
RECREATION GROUND
THE PAULIN GROUND
EDMONTON CEMETERY
CHURCH STREET RECREATION GROUND
FIRS FARM PLAYING FIELDS
CLOWES SPORTS GROUND
BARROWELL GREEN OPEN SPACE
TATEM PARK REC GRD
HAZELWOOD SPORTS
PYMMES PARK
EDMONTON FEDERATION CEMETERY
TOTTENHAM PARK CEMETERY
MONTAGU RECREATION GROUND
WESTERN SYNAGOGUE CEMETERY
NORTH MIDDLESEX HOSPITAL
TOTTENHALL SPORTS GROUND
BOUNDARY PLAYING FIELDS
NEW RIVERS SPORTS CENTRE
ST GEORGES INDUSTRIAL ESTATE
TOTTENHAM CEMETERY
BRUCE CASTLE PARK
BRUCE CASTLE MUS
PEABODY ESTATE
LORDSHIP RECREATION GROUND
BELMONT REC GRD
DOWNHILLS PARK
TOTTENHAM HOTSPUR FC
SOMERFORD GROVE
THE ROYAL LONDON ESTATE
WINGATE TRADING ESTATE
LANGHEDGE LANE INDUSTRIAL ESTATE
MOWLEM TRADING ESTATE
ANGEL ROAD WORKS
MONTAGU INDUSTRIAL ESTATE
MILL MEAD IND CEN
LOCKWOOD RESERVOIR
TOTTENHAM MARSHES
LRT DEPOT
HARTINGTON PARK
CRAIG PARK
DOWN LANE REC GRD
HARINGEY ARTS COUNCIL
College of North East London
GREAT CAMBRIDGE ROAD
A10
A406
NORTH CIRCULAR ROAD
STERLING WAY
ANGEL ROAD
MERIDIAN WAY
WATERMEAD WAY
NORTH SOUTH ROUTE
HERTFORD ROAD
FORE STREET
HIGH ROAD
THE BROADWAY
LORDSHIP LANE
A109
A1080
THE ROUNDWAY
BRUCE GROVE
GREEN LANES
HEDGE LANE
A111
RIDGE AVENUE
CHURCH STREET
WHITE HART LANE
CONDUIT LANE
SILVER STREET
EDMONTON GREEN
WHITE HART LANE

51
DX
DY
DZ
EA
EB
EC
ED
36
37
38
CHINGFORD
SOUTH CHINGFORD
CHINGFORD HATCH
FRIDAY HILL
HIGHAMS PARK
HALE END
HIGHAM HILL
WALTHAMSTOW
E4
E17
IG8
LEE VALLEY LEISURE
WILLIAM GIRLING RESERVOIR
LEE VALLEY PARK
BANBURY RESERVOIR
DEEPHAMS SEWAGE WORKS
CHINGFORD MOUNT CEMETERY
LARKS WOOD
LARKSWOOD PLAYING FIELDS
MANSFIELD PARK
RIDGEWAY PARK
CHINGFORD HALL PARK
LLOYD PARK
WADHAM LODGE SPORTS GROUND
Walthamstow Greyhound Stadium
EPPING FOREST
WALTHAMSTOW FOREST
HIGHAMS PARK
THE HIGHAMS PARK
RUGBY GROUND
LEA VALLEY VIADUCT
SOUTHEND ROAD
NORTH CIRCULAR RD
WALTHAM WAY
NEW ROAD
HALL LANE
OLD CHURCH ROAD
CHINGFORD MOUNT ROAD
CHINGFORD ROAD
KINGS HEAD HILL
STATION ROAD
NEW ROAD HATCH LA
LARKSHALL RD
WADHAM RD
FOREST ROAD
MERIDIAN ROUTE
A1009
A112
A406
A110
A1037
A503
A104
A1055
B179
B160
45
46
47
48
49
50
51
52
53
54
65
91
92
93
94

52
EE
EF
EG
EH
EJ
EK
EL
40
41
42
38
CHINGFORD GOLF COURSE
CHINGFORD PLAIN
CONNAUGHT WATER
RANGERS ROAD
A1069
QUEEN ELIZABETH'S HUNTING LODGE
Royal Forest Hotel
THE WARREN
Chingford Green
BUCKHURST HILL
IG10
IG9
IG8
E4
E17
E18
45
46
47
48
49
50
51
52
53
54
91
92
93
94
CHINGFORD
STATION ROAD
KINGS ROAD
WHITEHALL ROAD
WHITEHALL PLAIN
FRIDAY HILL
HATCH FOREST
HATCH GROVE
BLUEHOUSE GROVE
PLAYING FIELD
NEW ROAD
HATCH LA
CHINGFORD LANE
WOODFORD GOLF COURSE
HIGHAMS PARK
THE HIGHAMS PARK
BOATING LAKE
WOODFORD GREEN
REED'S FOREST
LORD'S BUSHES
Knighton Wood
WOODFORD WELLS
HOLLY HOUSE HOSP
EPPING NEW ROAD
HIGH ROAD
A104
A121
A110
A1009
A113
A11
A503
A406
M11
PALMERSTON ROAD
B170
RECREATION GROUND
PLAYING FIELDS
LOUGHTON RUGBY GROUND
BANCROFT RUGBY GROUND
CITY OF LONDON POLY SPORTS GRD
RIVER RODING
RAY PARK
Filter Beds
LUXBOROUGH LANE TREATMENT WORKS
ASHTON PLAYING FIELDS
SPORTS PITCH
RUNNING TRACK
Gas Works
WOODFORD
BROADMEAD ROAD
BROADMEAD ESTATE
CHIGWELL ROAD
DARTNALLS PLAYING FIELD
Roding Valley Park
ALLOTMENTS
OLD MONOVIANS SPORTS GRD
WANSTEAD RUGBY CLUB
EPPING FOREST
SPORTS GROUND
RUGBY GROUND
HIGHAMS PARK
HALE END
SOUTHEND ROAD
WALTHAMSTOW FOREST
SOUTH WOODFORD
NORTH CIRCULAR RD
Gates Corner
WOODFORD TRADING ESTATE
Superstore
Warehouses
SOUTH WOODFORD
66

EM
EN
EP
EQ
ER
ES
ET
39
67
FOREST GOLF COURSE
ABRIDGE ROAD
ROLLS PARK
RECREATION GROUND
SPORTS GROUND
RIVER RODING
The David Lloyd Club
M11
PLAYING FIELD
METROPOLITAN POLICE SPORTS GROUND
Chigwell Hall
CEM
IG7
CHIGWELL ROW WATER WORKS
RESERVOIR
Chigwell Row
CHIGWELL
GAS TRANSMISSION STATION
CHIGWELL GOLF COURSE
CHIGWELL CEMETERY
GRANGE HILL
LAMBOURNE ROAD
MANFORD WAY
CONVENT OF THE SACRED HEART
HAINAULT ROAD
FOREST ROAD PLAYING FIELD
HAINAULT
FAIRLOP OAK PLAYING FIELD
HAINAULT RECREATION GROUND
RUGBY GROUND
SPORTS GROUND
BRACKEN INDUSTRIAL ESTATE
FOREST INDUSTRIAL PARK
WOODFORD BRIDGE
CLAYBURY HOSPITAL (Closed)
HOSPITAL HILL WOOD
COCKED HAT PLANTATION
FAIRLOP WATER
FULLWELL CROSS
IG6
FAIRLOP WATERS GOLF COURSE
IG5
CLAYHALL
GARDEN of REST
BARK. CEM
BARKINGSIDE
ALDBOROUGH HATCH
IG2
PAINTERS ROAD
45
46
47
48
49
50
51
52
53
54
91
92
93
94
43
44
45

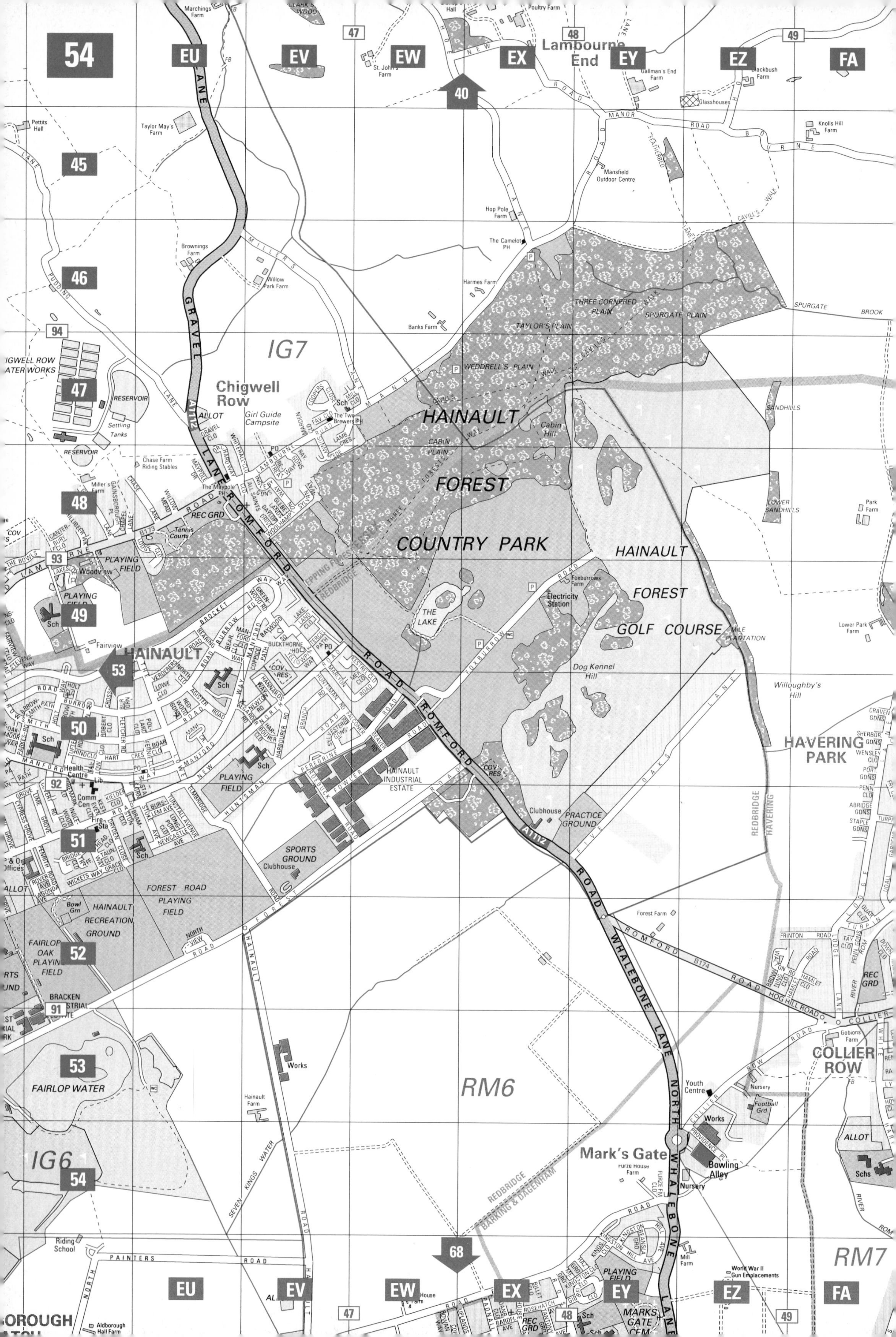
EU
EV
EW
EX
EY
EZ
FA
47
48
49
40
Lambourne End
Marchings Farm
Poultry Farm
Gallman's End Farm
Blackbush Farm
Glasshouses
Knolls Hill Farm
St. John's Farm
Pettits Hall
Taylor May's Farm
Mansfield Outdoor Centre
Hop Pole Farm
The Camelot PH
Brownings Farm
Willow Park Farm
Harmes Farm
Banks Farm
45
46
47
48
49
50
51
52
53
54
94
93
92
91
IG7
Chigwell Row
Girl Guide Campsite
RESERVOIR
Settling Tanks
Chase Farm Riding Stables
Miller's Farm
The Maypole PH
The Two Brewers PH
REC GRD
Tennis Courts
PLAYING FIELD
Woodview
Fairview
HAINAULT
HAINAULT FOREST COUNTRY PARK
THREE CORNERED PLAIN
SPURGATE PLAIN
TAYLOR'S PLAIN
WEDDRELL'S PLAIN
CABIN PLAIN
Cabin Hill
SPURGATE BROOK
SANDHILLS
LOWER SANDHILLS
Park Farm
THE LAKE
Foxburrows Farm
Electricity Station
HAINAULT FOREST GOLF COURSE
MILE PLANTATION
Lower Park Farm
Dog Kennel Hill
Willoughby's Hill
HAVERING PARK
HAINAULT INDUSTRIAL ESTATE
Clubhouse
PRACTICE GROUND
SPORTS GROUND
FOREST ROAD PLAYING FIELD
HAINAULT RECREATION GROUND
FAIRLOP OAK PLAYING FIELD
BRACKEN INDUSTRIAL ESTATE
FAIRLOP WATER
IG6
Works
Hainault Farm
RM6
Forest Farm
Gobions Farm
COLLIER ROW
Youth Centre
Nursery
Football Grd
Works
ALLOT
Bowling Alley
Mark's Gate
Furze House Farm
Nursery
Schs
Riding School
Mill Farm
World War II Gun Emplacements
RM7
REDBRIDGE
HAVERING
BARKING & DAGENHAM
68
MARKS GATE
Aldborough Hall Farm
GRAVEL LANE
ROMFORD ROAD
WHALEBONE LANE NORTH
MANOR ROAD
HOG HILL ROAD
FIVE OAKS LANE
SEVEN KINGS WATER
PAINTERS ROAD
A1112
B174
B173

FB
FC
FD
FE
FF
FG
FH
41
Nuper's Hatch
CM14
45
46
47
48
49
50
51
52
53
54
RM4
RM5
RM1
RM3
RM2
HAVERING-ATTE-BOWER
PYRGO PARK
HAVERING COUNTRY PARK
BEDFORDS PARK
CHASE CROSS
RISEBRIDGE GOLF COURSE
ROMFORD GOLF COURSE
STAPLEFORD ABBOTTS GOLF COURSE
GIDEA PARK
RAPHAEL PARK
RISE PARK
LAWNS REC GRD
GIDEA PARK SPORTS GRD
FOXBURROW WOOD
BOWER WOOD
LARCH WOOD
NURSERY WOOD
STRAIGHTS PLANTATION
PALACE PLANTATION
SANDPITS PLANTATION
TRENCH POND PLANTATION
SOUTH PARK PLANTATION
WITCH HILL PLANTATION
HILLY PARK
PHEASANT WOOD
AVENUE WOOD
DELL POND
FURRY FIELD
AVENUE NATURE RESERVE
PINE WOOD
KILN WOOD
ROUND WOOD
BEAN FIELD
BIG FIELD
OSIER BED
EPPING FOREST
ESSEX
HAVERING
BRENTWOOD
PRIORS
Stapleford Hall Farm
Woodlands Farm
Brook Farm
Bournebridge Farm
Crown Park Farm
Olives Farm
Tyseahill Farm
Skips Corner Farm
Asheton Farm
Home Farm
Widdrington Farm
Bower Farm
Round House Farm
Water Tower
St. Francis Hospice
Bower House
The Orange Tree PH
Pinewood Poultry Farm
Upper Bedfords Farm
Chase End
Foxes Hill
BEDFORDS LAKE
COV RES
North Lodge
Boyland's Oak Farm
Hillside Livery Stables
The Willows PH
Havering Park Riding School
A12
EASTERN AVENUE
MAIN ROAD
B175
B1459
HAVERING ROAD
NORTH HILL
ORANGE TREE HILL
LOWER BEDFORDS ROAD
BROXHILL ROAD
TYSEA HILL
NOAK HILL ROAD
CHASE CROSS ROAD
COLLIER ROW ROAD
69
FB
FC
FD
FE
FF
FG
FH
50
51
52
91
92
93
94

56
BG
BH
BJ
BK
BL
BM
BN
05
06
07
42
55
56
57
58
59
60
61
62
63
64
70
89
88
87
86
GRAND UNION CANAL
RIVER COLNE
SOUTH HAREFIELD
NORTH ORBITAL ROAD
A412
BATTLESFORD WOOD
RANSTON COVERT
Rank Film Laboratories
Broadwater Park
Widewater Lock
HAREFIELD MOOR
Horse & Barge PH
Pumping Station
MOORHALL ROAD
Savay Farm
SOUTH BUCKS
HILLINGDON
UB9
DENHAM
ALTCAR COVERT
CRUISE COVERT
BUCKINGHAMSHIRE GOLF COURSE
DENHAM COUNTRY PARK
HAREFIELD PLACE GOLF COURSE
FLAGMOOR COVERT
COWMOOR COVERT
ST JOHN'S COVERT
DENHAM COUNTRY PARK
Denham Lock
FRAY'S RIVER
HAREFIELD HOSP
Clubhouse
Harvil Farm
WEATHERLYS COVERT
Hillingdon Outdoor Activities Centre
Dews Farm
Park Lodge Farm Centre
RECYCLING CENTRE
Highway Farm
NEW YEARS GREEN LANE
NEWYEARS GREEN
NEWYEARS GREEN COVERT
BAYHURST WOOD COUNTRY PARK
Warren Farm
NORTH RIDING WOOD
BREAKSPEAR ROAD NORTH
Bourne Farm
Knightscote Farm
Langley Farm
Shooting School
HIGHBONES
SCARLET SPRING
ASHAIN SPRING
CLAYPITS
DELL
St. Leonard's Farm
Pylon Farm
Elm Tree Farm
High View Farm
Crows Nest Farm
Braemer Farm
Pitman Moore European HQ
COPTHALL COVERT
MOAT
Copthall Farm
Works
SKIP LANE
Depot
SWAKELEYS ROAD
SWAKELEYS DRIVE
THE CLUMP
SPORTS GRD
PLAYING FIELD
Common Plantation
PARK WOOD
HILLINGDON HOUSE FARM SPORTS GRO
UB10
UB8
Hillingdon Ski Slope
Hillingdon Ski Centre
UXBRIDGE STADIUM
UXBRIDGE COMMON
Pavilion
Open Air Pool
Uxbridge Coll
WESTERN AVENUE
A40
M40
Junction 1
SHIRE DITCH
Fray's Farm
Fray's Bridge
OXFORD ROAD
A4020
A412
DENHAM ROAD
Depot
ALLOT
Ivy House Farm
Oxford Road Nursery
Football Ground
Dog and Duck PH
PLAYING FIELD
Brickfield Farm
Osborne Farm
Kingcup Farm
Cornerfields
New House Farm
Copse Hill Farm
Southlands Manor
Glasshouses
Little Acres Farm
DENHAM
PLAYING FLD
REC GRD
Wellers Mead
Denham Place
Hall
The Prescotts
MISBOURNE
RECTORY LANE
TILEHOUSE
Health Centre
MARYNFIELD SPORTS GROUND
Clubho
DENHAM GREEN
EWSTEAD WOOD
WADLEY COVERT
HOLLY HILL WOOD
NORTHMOOR WOOD
Wyatt's Covert Caravan Site
Lea Cottage
The Lea
Denham Court
PRIORY COVERT
Mill
Lock

COPSE WOOD
MAD BESS WOOD
RUISLIP NATURE RESERVE
POOR'S FIELD
ST. VINCENT'S HOSPITAL (ORTHOPAEDIC)
RUISLIP LIDO
PARK WOOD
RUISLIP COMMON
BREAKSPEAR CREMATORIUM
EASTCOTE VILLAGE
HAYDON HALL PARK
GOVERNMENT OFFICES
KINGS COLLEGE PLAYING FIELDS
RUISLIP
EASTCOTE
RUISLIP MANOR
RUISLIP PUBLIC GOLF COURSE
WEST RUISLIP
ICKENHAM
RUISLIP GARDENS
NORTHOLT AERODROME
BESSINGBY FIELD
NEW POND FARM FIELDS
HA4
HA5
HA6

BW
BX
BY
BZ
CA
CB
CC
12
13
14
44
PINNER GREEN
PINNER
HA5
PINNER NEW CEMETERY
HEADSTONE MANOR
HEADSTONE
EASTCOTE VILLAGE
EASTCOTE
NORTH HARROW
WEST HARROW
RAYNERS LANE
ROXBOURNE PARK
HA4
HA2
SOUTH HARROW
ALEXANDRA PARK
SOUTH RUISLIP
VICTORIA RETAIL PARK
UB5
NORTHOLT RECREATION GRD
55
56
57
58
59
60
61
62
63
64
89
88
87
86
72

59
CD
CE
CF
CG
CH
CJ
CK
15
16
17
45
55
56
57
58
59
60
61
62
63
64
73
86
87
88
89
BELMONT
HA7
QUEENSBURY
WEALDSTONE
WEALDSTONE CEM
HARROW & WEALDSTONE
KENTON
KENTON RECREATION GROUND
HA3
HARROW
HA1
NORTHWICK PARK
Univ of Westminster (Harrow Campus)
NORTHWICK PARK & ST. MARK'S HOSPITAL
HARROW SCHOOL PLAYING FIELDS
NORTHWICK PARK GOLF COURSE
HARROW ON THE HILL
ROXETH
ST. ANDREW'S AT HARROW HOSP
HARROW SCHOOL GOLF COURSE
CLEMENTINE CHURCHILL HOSPITAL
NORTH WEMBLEY
SOUTH KENTON
PRESTON
PRESTON PARK
JOHN BILLHAM SPORTS GRD
WOODCOCK PARK
HA9
GEC SPORTS GROUND
GEC ESTATE
WEMBLEY COMMERCIAL CENTRE
VALE FARM SPORTS GROUND
WASPS RUGBY GROUND
KING EDWARD VII PARK
FORTY FARM SPORTS GRD
SUDBURY
SUDBURY HILL HARROW
UB6
BARHAM PARK
HA0
WEMBLEY HOSPITAL
WEMBLEY CENTRAL
SUDBURY TOWN
KODAK WORKS
WAVERLEY INDUSTRIAL ESTATE
HARROW REC
CHRISTCHURCH IND CENTRE
HAWTHORN CENTRE
DRIVING CENTRE
KENTON ROAD A4006
WATFORD ROAD A404
SHEEPCOTE ROAD A409
HARROW ROAD A404
EAST LANE A4088
GREENFORD ROAD A4127
WHITTON AVENUE WEST A4090

60
CL
CM
CN
CP
CQ
CR
CS
19
20
21
HA8
46
QUEENSBURY
55
56
57
58
59
60
61
62
63
64
89
88
87
86
COLINDALE HOSPITAL
BRIT LIB NEWSPAPER COLLECTION
COLINDALE BUSINESS PARK
CAPITOL IND EST
KINGSBURY HOSPITAL
QUEENSBURY PARK
ETON GROVE OPEN SPACE
ROE GREEN PARK
KENTON ROAD
A4006
KINGSBURY
HONEYPOT LANE
EDGWARE ROAD
COLINDEEP LANE
NW9
KINGSBURY
FRYENT COUNTRY PARK
FRYENT COUNTRY PARK
BARN HILL OPEN SPACE
FRYENT WAY
A4140
WOODCOCK PARK
HA3
JOHN BILLHAM SPORTS GRD
PRESTON
PRESTON PARK
KINGSBURY TRADING EST
RECREATION GROUND
WEST HENDON PLAYING FIELDS
SILVER JUBILEE PARK
WEST
WOODFIELD PARK
WELSH HARP OPEN SPACE
WELSH
NEASDEN REC GROUND
SALMON STREET
BRENT TOWN HALL
FORTY LANE
A4088
BLACKBIRD HILL
NEASDEN LANE
WEMBLEY PARK
FORTY FARM SPORTS GRD
GEC SPORTS GROUND
WEMBLEY COMMERCIAL CENTRE
GEC ESTATE
HA9
NW10
WEMBLEY RETAIL PARK
WEMBLEY ARENA
WEMBLEY CONFERENCE CENTRE
WEMBLEY STADIUM
KING EDWARD VII PARK
WEMBLEY
HIGH ROAD
HARROW ROAD
SHERRINS FARM OPEN SPACE
DRURY INDUSTRIAL ESTATE
BRENT PARK
GREAT CENTRAL WAY
NORTH CIRCULAR ROAD
74
KYNGTON
WEMBLEY HOSPITAL
CHURCH END
GIBBONS REC GRD
SWAMINARAYAN HINDU MISSION (TEMPLE)
A404
A406
A4089
B4557

CT
CU
CV
CW
CX
CY
CZ
61
22
23
24
47
55
56
57
58
59
60
61
62
63
64
75
87
88
89
86
HILL
NW4
N3
NW11
NW2
THE GARDEN HOSP
Peel Centre (Police Training School)
SPORTS GRD
RAF MUSEUM
SUNNY HILL PARK
CHURCH FARM HOUSE MUS
Sports Cen Middlesex University
HENDON
THE HYDE
WELSH HARP
BRENT RESERVOIR
HENDON PARK
HENDON CENTRAL
Brent Cross Shopping Centre
BRENT CROSS
CARMELITE MONASTERY
PRINCES PARK
GOLDERS GREEN
LUL DEPOT
Golders Green Hippodrome
LONDON SYNAGOGUE CEMETERY
REMEMBRANCE
Junction 1
Staples Corner
STAPLES CORNER BUSINESS PARK
ELDONWALL TRADING ESTATE
WELLINGTON PARK IND EST
CLITTERHOUSE PLAYING FIELDS
BASING HILL PK
CHILDS HILL PK
CHILDS HILL
ALLOTMENTS
CRICKLEWOOD TRADING EST
CRICKLEWOOD
DOLLIS HILL
GLADSTONE PARK
Coll of NW London
College of North West London
UNIVERSITY COLLEGE SPORTS GROUND
HAMPSTEAD CEMETERY
BRONDESBURY
KILBURN
WILLESDEN
WEST HAMPSTEAD (THAMESLINK)
WEST HAMPSTEAD
Open University Regional Centre
WATFORD WAY
HENDON WAY
EDGWARE ROAD
CRICKLEWOOD BROADWAY
SHOOT UP HILL
NORTH CIRCULAR ROAD
FINCHLEY ROAD
GOLDERS GREEN ROAD
HENDON WAY
BRENT STREET
CHURCH ROAD
THE BURROUGHS
A41
A5
A406
A407
A502
A504
A598
A5150
M1

62
DA
DB
DC
DD
DE
DF
DG
26
27
28
48
N10
N3
N2
N6
NW11
NW3
NW2
NW6
55
56
57
58
59
60
61
62
63
64
76
89
88
87
86
EAST FINCHLEY
EAST FINCHLEY CEMETERY
HAMPSTEAD GARDEN SUBURB
BIG WOOD
LITTLE WOOD
GOLDERS GREEN
HAMPSTEAD HEATH EXTENSION
HAMPSTEAD GOLF CLUB
HIGHGATE GOLF COURSE
HIGHGATE WOOD
COLDFALL WOOD
NAT HOSP FOR NEUROLOGY & NEUROSURGERY
ST LUKES WOODSIDE HOSP
ATHLONE HOUSE
THE IVEAGH BEQUEST KENWOOD HOUSE
KENWOOD
SANDY HEATH
GOLDERS HILL PARK
CHILDS HILL
WEST HEATH
HAMPSTEAD
PARLIAMENT HILL
HEATH
QUEEN MARY'S HOSP
HAMPSTEAD PONDS
HIGHGATE PONDS
ROYAL FREE HOSPITAL
WEST HAMPSTEAD
HAMPSTEAD CEMETERY
MANOR HOUSE HOSP
WEST LONDON SYNAGOGUE CEMETERY
GARDEN OF REMEMBRANCE
FALLODEN WAY
LYTTELTON ROAD
AYLMER ROAD
NORTH END ROAD
FINCHLEY ROAD
GREAT NORTH ROAD
ARCHWAY ROAD
FORTIS GREEN
EAST END ROAD
NORTH CIRCULAR ROAD
REGENTS PARK ROAD
HAMPSTEAD LANE
SPANIARDS ROAD
HAVERSTOCK HILL
ROSSLYN HILL
HAMP HIGH ST
KINGSLEY WAY
BISHOPS AVENUE
WINNINGTON ROAD
HENDON WAY
HAMPSTEAD WAY
RUNNING TRACK
COVERED RESERVOIR
SPORTS GROUND
ALLOTMENTS
CAMDEN
BARNET
HARINGEY

63
DH
DJ
DK
DL
DM
DN
DP
29
30
31
49
55
56
57
58
59
60
61
62
63
64
77
86
87
88
89
NOEL PARK
ALEXANDRA PALACE
ALEXANDRA PARK
SPORTS GROUND
RESERVOIR
N22
MUSWELL HILL
THE GROVE
HORNSEY
WOOD GRN COMMON
Gas Works
TURNPIKE LANE
WEST GREEN
BELMONT REC GRD
DOWNHILLS PARK
QUEEN'S WOOD
HORNSEY CENTRAL HOSPITAL
N8
PRIORY PARK
CROUCH END PLAYING FLDS
CROUCH END
HARRINGAY
STATIONERS PARK
CHESTNUTS REC GRD
ST ANN'S HOSPITAL
STROUD GREEN
N4
FINSBURY PARK
HIGHGATE
WATERLOW PARK
WHITTINGTON HOSPITAL
HIGHGATE CEMETERY
ELTHORNE PARK
HILLSIDE PK
SIX ACRES ESTATE
N19
UPPER HOLLOWAY
WHITTINGTON PARK
DARTMOUTH PARK
TUFNELL PARK
NW5
H.M. PRISON HOLLOWAY
HOLLOWAY
LOWER HOLLOWAY
N7
HIGHBURY ARSENAL
HIGHBURY
N5
University of North London
KENTISH TOWN
PARADISE PARK
PENTONVILLE PRISON
SPORTS GROUND
Disused Water Works
WEST RESERVOIR
A504
A1201
A103
A105
A503
A1
A400
A5200
A1199
A10
A5203

64
NOEL PARK
LORDSHIP RECREATION GROUND
THE MOSELLE
DQ
DR
DS
DT
DU
DV
DW
33
34
35
50
LOCKWOOD RESERVOIR
BELMONT REC GRD
N17
DOWNHILLS PARK
DOWNHILLS REC GRD
WEST GREEN
BRUCE GROVE
TOTTENHAM HALE
LOCKWOOD IND PK
DOWN LANE REC GRD
LEE VALLEY TECHNO-PARK
MILL MEAD IND CEN
MONUMENT WAY
FERRY LANE
LOW MAYNARD RESERVOIR
HIGH MAYNARD RESERVOIR
Tottenham Lock
TOWN HALL
Coll of N E London
Bowling Alley
HIGH CROSS CEN
Shopping Centre
RESERVOIR No 1
RESERVOIR No 2
RESERVOIR No 3
RESERVOIR No 4
55
56
57
58
59
60
61
62
63
64
86
87
88
89
TURNPIKE LANE
HARRINGAY
N15
SEVEN SISTERS
CHESTNUTS REC GRD
ST. ANN'S HOSPITAL
SOUTH TOTTENHAM
MARKFIELD REC GRD
Markfield Beam Engine
WARWICK RESERVOIR (EAST)
WARWICK RESERVOIR (WEST)
HARRINGAY GREEN LANES
N4
HARINGEY
HACKNEY
STAMFORD HILL
AMHURST PARK
SPRINGHILL SPORTS GRD
PLAYING FIELD
Seven Sisters Bridge
Springfield Marina
WALTHAMSTOW MARSHES NATURE RESERVE
SPRINGFIELD PARK
FINSBURY PARK
MANOR HOUSE
EAST RESERVOIR
WEST RESERVOIR
N16
UPPER CLAPTON
ABNEY PARK CEMETERY
STOKE NEWINGTON
WATER WORKS (DISUSED)
CLISSOLD PARK
SPORTS GROUND
NORTH MILLFIELDS RECREATION GROUND
E5
SHACKLEWELL
HACKNEY DOWNS
SPORTS GRD
N5
University of North London
HIGHBURY
E8
BUTTERFIELD GRN
DALSTON KINGSLAND
HACKNEY DOWNS
HACKNEY CENTRAL
78
BALLS POND ROAD
ST PAUL'S ROAD
DALSTON LANE
GRAHAM ROAD
HIGHBURY & ISLINGTON
HACKNEY

DX
DY
DZ
EA
EB
EC
ED
36
37
38
HIGHAM HILL
LLOYD PARK
WALTHAMSTOW
51
THORPE COOMBE HOSP
EPPING
55
FOREST
UPPER WALTHAMSTOW
56
89
57
HOLLOW POND
WHIPPS CROSS HOSPITAL
58
88
59
E17
DOUGLAS EYRE PLAYING FIELDS
WALTHAMSTOW CENTRAL
WALTHAMSTOW QUEENS ROAD
ST. JAMES STREET
WALTHAMSTOW CEM
ST. JAMES'S PARK
LOW HALL SPORTS GROUND
FOREST BUS PK
ALLOTMENTS
CROMWELL IND.EST
DORMA TRADING EST
Lea Valley Riding Centre
LEYTON MARSHES
Lea Valley Ice Centre
E11
LEYTONSTONE
66
E10
LEYTON
60
87
61
LEYTON MIDLAND ROAD
SEYMOUR ROAD PLAYING FIELD
MARSH LANE PLAYING FIELD
MINIATURE GOLF COURSE
LEA BRIDGE
RIVER LEE or LEA
SIDMOUTH PARK
ST. PATRICK'S RC CEMETERY
62
HACKNEY
LEYTON ORIENT F.C.
LANGTHORNE HOSP
86
CLAPTON PARK
RECREATION GROUND
MARSH
E9
ETON MANOR SPORTS GRD
Lea Valley Sports Centre
63
JEWISH CEM
WICK FIELD
EASTWAY CYCLE CIRCUIT
MABLEY GREEN
HOMERTON
64
E15
HACKNEY WICK
79
HOSPITAL (closed)
STRATFORD
INTERNATIONAL FREIGHT TERMINAL
EASTWAY
A503
A104
A112
A106
A12
A11
A102
A114

66
EE
EF
EG
EH
EJ
EK
EL
52
WOODFORD
SOUTH WOODFORD
E18
EPPING FOREST
SNARESBROOK
SNARESBROOK CROWN COURT
EAGLE POND
HOLLOW POND (Boating Lake)
WHIPPS CROSS HOSPITAL
E11
WANSTEAD
WANSTEAD FLATS
LEYTONSTONE
65
Junction 4
M11
RODING HOSPITAL
RECREATION GROUND
IG4
WANSTEAD GOLF COURSE
WANSTEAD PARK
ORNAMENTAL WATERS
HERONRY POND
PERCH POND
THE BASIN (Fish Pond)
SHOULDER OF MUTTON POND
BUSH WOOD
RESERVOIR WOOD
ALDERSBROOK
CITY OF LONDON CEMETERY
Crematorium
MANOR PARK
MANOR PARK CEMETERY
E7
WEST HAM CEMETERY
JEWISH CEM
E15
FOREST GATE
WOODGRANGE PARK CEM
PLASHET CEMETERY
LANGTHORNE HOSP
ST. PATRICK'S CEM
STRATFORD
55
56
57
58
59
60
61
62
63
64
80
40
41
42
86
87
88
89

67
EM
EN
EP
EQ
ER
ES
ET
43
44
45
53
55
56
57
58
59
60
61
62
63
64
68
81
86
87
88
89
IG5
IG6
IG2
IG3
IG1
E12
CLAYHALL
CLAYHALL PARK
FAIRLOP WATERS GOLF COURSE
ALDBOROUGH HATCH
BARKINGSIDE
BARKINGSIDE REC GRD
GARDEN of REST
BARK. CEM
GANTS HILL
NEWBURY PARK
BARLEY MOW SPORTS GRD
KING GEORGE HOSP
GOODMAYES HOSPITAL
FORD'S SPORTS GROUND
SEVEN KINGS PARK
SEVEN KINGS
REDBRIDGE
VALENTINES PARK
VALENTINES MANSION
MELBOURNE FIELD
THE LAKE
CRANBROOK
ILFORD
SOUTH PARK
KNOX SPORTS FIELD
LOXFORD
LOXFORD PARK
LITTLE ILFORD PARK
BARKING PARK
BARKING PARK REC GRD
BARRINGTON PLAYING FIELDS
MAYESBROOK PARK SPORTS GROUND
GOODMAYES PARK
BOATING LAKE
EASTERN AVENUE
WOODFORD AVENUE
CRANBROOK ROAD
HIGH ROAD
GREEN LANE
ILFORD LANE
NORTH CIRCULAR ROAD
SOUTH WOODFORD TO BARKING RELIEF ROAD
RIVER RODING
ALDBOROUGH ROAD
PAINTERS ROAD
LONGBRIDGE ROAD
A12
A123
A118
A1083
A406
A124

EU
EV
EW
EX
EY
EZ
FA
47
48
49
54
55
56
57
58
59
60
61
62
63
64
67
82
86
87
88
89
IG2
IG3
IG11
RM6
RM8
RM9
EASTERN AVENUE
A12
KING GEORGE HOSPITAL
GOODMAYES HOSPITAL
Redbridge College
CHADWELL HEATH
MARKS GATE CEM
GOLF DRIVING RANGE
WESTLANDS PLAYING FIELDS
TRAINING GROUND
HIGH ROAD
A118
GREEN LANE
A1083
GOODMAYES
GOODMAYES PARK
VALENCE PARK
BEACONTREE
WOOD LANE
A124
LONGBRIDGE ROAD
University of East London
PARSLOES PARK
MAYESBROOK PARK
BOATING LAKE
HEATHWAY
A1240
WHALEBONE LANE NORTH
A1112
WHALEBONE LANE SOUTH
A1153
PORTERS AVENUE
BARLEY LANE
B177
BARKING AND DAGENHAM
PAINTERS ROAD
HAINAULT ROAD
SEVEN KINGS WATER
Barking College
Barking Coll
Valence Ho Mus
DAGENHAM HEATHWAY

69
FB
FC
FD
FE
FF
FG
FH
50
51
52
55
56
57
58
59
60
61
62
63
64
83
86
87
88
89
ROMFORD GOLF COURSE
RAPHAEL PARK
GIDEA PARK
RM1
RM2
RM7
RM10
RM11
RM12
RM13
ROMFORD
VICTORIA HOSP
KING GEORGE'S PLAYING FIELDS
HUBBINET IND EST
COTTONS PARK
SPRING GDNS IND EST
ROMFORD STADIUM
OLDCHURCH HOSPITAL
Romford Ice Rink
OLDCHURCH PARK
ROMFORD CEMETERY
RUSH GREEN
CROWLANDS REC GRD
FORD SPORTS GROUND
DAGENHAM CIVIC CENTRE
CENTRAL PARK
Barking College of Technology
RUSH GREEN HOSPITAL (Closed)
EASTBROOKEND COUNTRY PARK
STERLING INDUSTRIAL ESTATE
RHONE-POULENC
DAGENHAM EAST
PONDFIELD PARK
HARROW LODGE PARK
Havering College
HYLANDS PARK
LODGE FARM PARK
ELM PARK
HORNCHURCH
Ardleigh Green
SPORTS GROUNDS
RIVER ROM
RIVER BEAM
A118
A124
A125
A112
WEST EASTERN
NORTH STREET
MAIN ROAD
HORNCHURCH ROAD
RUSH GREEN ROAD
RAINHAM ROAD

70
BG
BH
BJ
BK
BL
BM
BN
05
06
07
56
65
66
67
68
69
70
71
72
73
74
81
82
83
84
UB9
UB10
UB8
UB7
SL0
UXBRIDGE
UXBRIDGE MOOR
UXBRIDGE COMMON
HILLINGDON HOUSE FARM SPORTS GROUND
HILLINGDON COURT PARK
HILLINGDON GOLF COURSE
HILLINGDON
HILLINGDON AND UXBRIDGE CEMETERY
HILLINGDON HOSPITAL
COLHAM GREEN REC GRD
CIVIC CENTRE
ROCKINGHAM REC GROUND
GRAND UNION CANAL
COWLEY
COWLEY HALL REC GRD
Brunel University
UNIVERSITY PLAYING FIELDS
ALLOTMENTS
HUNTSMOOR PARK
COWLEY LAKE
LITTLE BRITAIN LAKE
FARLOWS LAKE
GRAND UNION CANAL (SLOUGH ARM)
IVER
RIDGEWAY INDUSTRIAL ESTATE
Sewage Works
Coal Depot
YIEWSLEY
WEST DRAYTON
STOCKLEY
STOCKLE GOLF
RECREATION GROUND
LAWN FIELDS
HORTON IND PARK
RAINBOW INDUSTRIAL ESTATE
RIVER COLNE
BUCKINGHAMSHIRE
HILLINGDON
SOUTH BUCKS
M25
A4007
A412
A4020
A408
UXBRIDGE ROAD
HIGH STREET
COWLEY ROAD
OXFORD RD
HILLINGDON RD
FALLING LANE
PARK VW RD
HARLINGTON ROAD
AVENUE
Electricity Sub Station
SARUM COMPLEX
UXBRIDGE BUSINESS PARK
UXBRIDGE IND EST
MIDAS IND EST
Uxbridge Coll
RAF Uxbridge
RIFLE RANGES
UXBRIDGE STADIUM
Hillingdon Ski Centre

71
NORTHOLT AERODROME
HA4
NORTH HILLINGDON
WESTERN AVENUE
A40
UB5
WEST LONDON SHOOTING GROUNDS
UB4
UB3
UB11
YEADING
HAYES END
HAYES
HAYES TOWN
HAYES PARK
HAYES SHRUB
THE GORSE
TEN ACRES
GUTTERIDGE WOOD
NATURE RESERVE
RECREATION GROUND
HOME COVERT
POLE HILL OPEN SPACE
YEADING BROOK MEADOWS (NATURE RESERVE)
GROSVENOR PLAYING FIELD
BELMORE PLAYING FIELDS
BARRA HALL PARK
HAYES STADIUM
STOCKLEY PARK BUSINESS PARK
PARK COURSE
GRAND UNION CANAL
UXBRIDGE ROAD
A4020
DAWLEY ROAD
A437
HAYES BY-PASS
A312
THE PARKWAY
A4180
HAYES COTTAGE HOSP
Uxbridge Coll
HILLINGDON
EALING
BP BQ BR BS BT BU BV
08 09 10
57 65 66 67 68 69 70 71 72 73 74 85

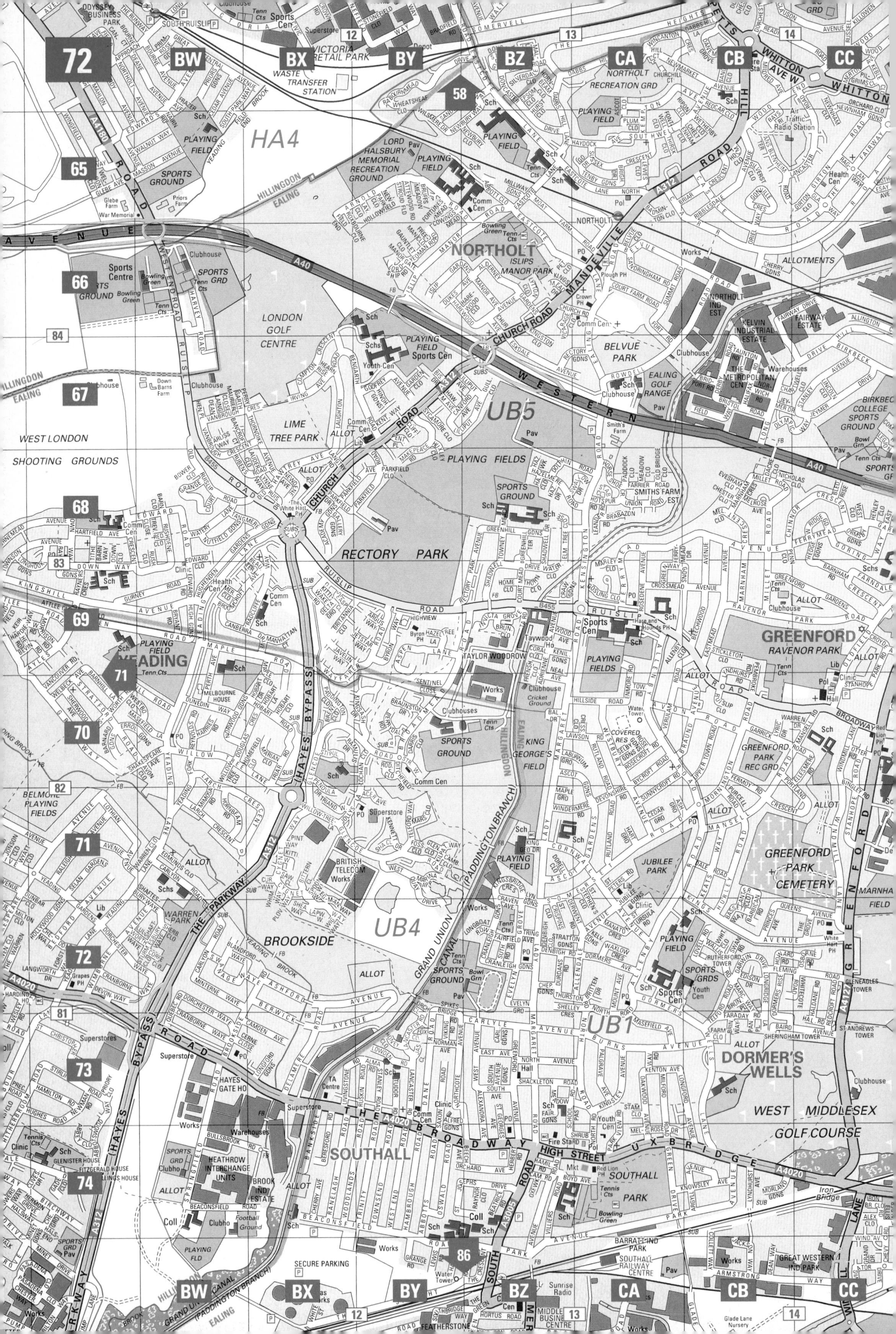
BW
BX
BY
BZ
CA
CB
CC
58
65
66
67
68
69
70
71
72
73
74
86
84
83
82
81
12
13
14
ODYSSEY BUSINESS PARK
SOUTH RUISLIP
VICTORIA RETAIL PARK
WASTE TRANSFER STATION
NORTHOLT RECREATION GRD
WHITTON AVE W
HA4
HILLINGDON
EALING
LORD HALSBURY MEMORIAL RECREATION GROUND
PLAYING FIELD
SPORTS GROUND
NORTHOLT
ISLIPS MANOR PARK
MANDEVILLE ROAD
CHURCH ROAD
WESTERN AVENUE
A40
A312
A4180
LONDON GOLF CENTRE
BELVUE PARK
EALING GOLF RANGE
NORTHOLT IND EST
KELVIN INDUSTRIAL ESTATE
FAIRWAY ESTATE
THE METROPOLITAN CEN
BIRKBECK COLLEGE SPORTS GROUND
ALLOTMENTS
UB5
WEST LONDON SHOOTING GROUNDS
LIME TREE PARK
PLAYING FIELDS
RECTORY PARK
SMITHS FARM EST
RUISLIP ROAD
GREENFORD
RAVENOR PARK
YEADING
TAYLOR WOODROW
KING GEORGE'S FIELD
GRAND UNION CANAL (PADDINGTON BRANCH)
HAYES BYPASS
THE PARKWAY
BELMORE PLAYING FIELDS
BRITISH TELECOM Works
UB4
BROOKSIDE
WARREN PARK
JUBILEE PARK
GREENFORD PARK CEMETERY
GREENFORD PARK REC GRD
UB1
DORMER'S WELLS
WEST MIDDLESEX GOLF COURSE
HAYES GATE HO
HEATHROW INTERCHANGE UNITS
SOUTHALL
THE BROADWAY
HIGH STREET
UXBRIDGE ROAD
A4020
A4127
SOUTHALL PARK
SOUTHALL RAILWAY CENTRE
GREAT WESTERN IND PARK
SOUTH ROAD
A3005
SECURE PARKING
Sunrise Radio
MIDDLESEX BUSINESS CENTRE
Glade Lane Nursery
GREENFORD ROAD

73
CD
CE
CF
CG
CH
CJ
CK
15
16
17
59
65
66
67
68
69
70
71
72
73
74
81
82
83
84
87
SUDBURY
HA0
UB6
W13
W7
W5
PERIVALE
ALPERTON
EALING
HANWELL
WEMBLEY HOSPITAL
SPORTS GROUND
BERKELEY FIELDS
GREAT BRAMSTONES
HOME MEAD
HORSENDEN WOOD
HORSENDEN HILL GOLF COURSE
HORSENDEN HILL
SUDBURY GOLF COURSE
GRAND UNION CANAL (PADDINGTON BRANCH)
PERIVALE WOOD
PERIVALE INDUSTRIAL PARK
PERIVALE NEW BUSINESS CENTRE
WADSWORTH BUSINESS CEN
FLEETWAY WEST BUSINESS PARK
SHERATON BUSINESS CENTRE
ALPERTON CEMETERY
ONE TREE HILL RECREATION GROUND
ALPERTON SPORTS GROUND
METROPOLITAN POLICE TRAFFIC UNIT
OLDFIELD REC GRD
SPORTS GROUND
PLAYING FIELD
EALING CENTRAL SPORTS GRD
ATHLETICS STADIUM
PERIVALE PARK SPORTS GROUND
PERIVALE PARK GOLF COURSE
EALING GOLF COURSE
ST. BENEDICT'S PLAYING FIELDS
PITSHANGER PARK
ALLOTMENTS
HANGER HILL PARK
OLD COURT HOSP
MONTPELIER PARK
CLEVELAND PARK
CUCKOO PARK
BRENT VALLEY PARK
BRENT VALLEY GOLF COURSE
DRAYTON GREEN
CHURCHFIELDS RECREATION GROUND
KENSINGTON & CHELSEA CEM
HANWELL CEMETERY
ST BERNARD'S HOSPITAL
EALING HOSPITAL TRUST
WALPOLE PARK
PITSHANGER MANOR MUS
Ealing Tertiary Coll
Thames Valley Uni
EALING COMMON
EALING BROADWAY
BARCLAYS BANK SPORTS GROUND
WHITTON AVENUE WEST
WHITTON AVENUE EAST
A4090
A4005
A404
A4127
A40
A4020
B452
B455
B456
WESTERN AVENUE
GREENFORD ROAD
EALING ROAD
HANGER LANE
BRIDGEWATER ROAD
UXBRIDGE ROAD
THE BROADWAY
NEW BROADWAY
CASTLEBAR ROAD
LOWER BOSTON RD
RIVER BRENT
Wharncliffe Viaduct

74
CL
CM
CN
CP
CQ
CR
CS
19
20
21
60
WEMBLEY
WEMBLEY HOSPITAL
TOKYNGTON
TOKYNGTON REC GRD
CHURCH END
HA0
HA9
ALPERTON
ONE TREE HILL RECREATION GROUND
STONEBRIDGE
STONEBRIDGE PARK
PRINCESS ROYAL DISTRIBUTION CENTRE
NORTHFIELDS INDUSTRIAL ESTATE
ABBEY MANUFACTURING ESTATE
GRAND UNION CANAL
NORTH CIRCULAR ROAD
METROPOLITAN POLICE TRAFFIC UNIT
TWYFORD ABBEY
PARK ROYAL
GUINNESS SPORTS GRD
GRAND UNION INDUSTRIAL ESTATE
TUDOR ESTATE
CENTRAL MIDDLESEX HOSPITAL
TOWNSEND INDUSTRIAL ESTATE
HARLESDEN
THE MILL TRADING ESTATE
BUSH INDUSTRIAL ESTATE
WESTERN TRADING ESTATE
WESTPOINT TRADING ESTATE
WESTERN AVENUE
A40
A406
A404
A4020
A4000
HANGER LANE
HANGER HILL PARK
NORTH ACTON
NORTH ACTON PLAYING FIELDS
VICTORIA ROAD
WALES FARM RD
ACTON CEMETERY
W5
W3
WEST ACTON
NORTH EALING
EALING
EALING BROADWAY
EALING COMMON
UXBRIDGE ROAD
GUNNERSBURY LANE
ACTON
ACTON CENTRAL
ACTON MAIN LINE
ACTON TOWN
ACTON PARK
EAST ACTON
HIGH STREET
THE VALE
NORTH THAMES GAS BOARD SPORTS GROUND
SPRINGFIELD GARDENS
88

CT
CU
CV
CW
CX
CY
CZ
22
23
24
61
65
66
67
68
69
70
71
72
73
74
76
81
82
83
84
89
WILLESDEN
WILLESDEN CEMETERY
WILLESDEN JEWISH CEMETERY
LIBERAL JEWISH CEM
ROUNDWOOD PARK
WILLESDEN GENERAL HOSP
WILLESDEN GREEN
STADIUM
KING EDWARD VII SPORTS GRD
NW2
NW6
NW10
BRONDESBURY
BRONDESBURY PARK
KILBURN GRANGE PARK
KILBURN
PADDINGTON OLD CEMETERY
QUEEN'S PARK
KENSAL RISE
KENSAL GREEN
KENSAL GREEN CEMETERY
ST. MARY'S RC CEMETERY
GRAND UNION CANAL (Paddington Branch)
KENSAL TOWN
WEST KILBURN
MAIDA HILL
W9
W10
WORMWOOD SCRUBS
OLD OAK COMMON
LITTLE WORMWOOD SCRUBS REC GRD
ST. CHARLES HOSP
PRINCESS LOUISE HOSPITAL
LINFORD CHRISTIE STADIUM
HAMMERSMITH HOSPITAL
H.M. PRISON WORMWOOD SCRUBS
NORTH KENSINGTON
WESTWAY
A40(M)
WESTBOURNE GRE
NOTTING HILL
W11
WHITE CITY
WORMHOLT PARK
HAMMERSMITH PARK
BBC TV Centre
WHITE CITY Daytona Raceway
RANGERS STADIUM QPR FC
SHEPHERD'S BUSH
W12
AVONDALE PARK
LADBROKE SQUARE GARDENS
NOTTING HILL GATE
HOLLAND PARK
KENSINGTON
W8
WEST HAMPSTEAD
WILLESDEN JUNCTION
CAR BREAKING PLANT
GATEWAY INDUSTRIAL ESTATE
SHEPHERDS BUSH GRN
UXBRIDGE ROAD
HOLLAND PARK AVE
HARROW ROAD
KILBURN HIGH ROAD
WEST CROSS ROUTE

DA
DB
DC
DD
DE
DF
DG
26
27
28
62
65
66
67
68
69
70
71
72
73
74
75
81
82
83
84
90
WEST HAMPSTEAD
SOUTH HAMPSTEAD
BELSIZE PARK
PRIMROSE HILL
NW6
NW8
KILBURN
WEST KILBURN
MAIDA VALE
MAIDA HILL
W9
ST. JOHN'S WOOD
LORD'S CRICKET GROUND
REGENT'S PARK
LONDON ZOO
QUEEN MARY'S GARDENS
BOATING LAKE
MARYLEBONE
PADDINGTON
WESTBOURNE GREEN
BAYSWATER
W2
KENSINGTON GARDENS
ROUND POND
KENSINGTON PALACE
HYDE PARK
THE SERPENTINE
THE LONG WATER
BIRD SANCTUARY
KENSINGTON
W8
HOLLAND PARK
HOLLAND HOUSE
NOTTING HILL
PADDINGTON RECREATION GROUND
ROYAL FREE HOSPITAL
FREUD MUSEUM
SAATCHI COLLECTION
HOSPITAL OF ST. JOHN & ST. ELIZ
WELLINGTON HOSP
ST. MARY'S HOSP
MARBLE ARCH
SPEAKER'S CORNER
SHERLOCK HOLMES
MADAME TUSSAUD'S
PLANETARIUM
WALLACE COLLECTION
Regent's College
LONDON CENTRAL MOSQUE
WEST HAMPSTEAD (THAMESLINK)
FINCHLEY ROAD
SWISS COTTAGE
KILBURN HIGH ROAD
MAIDA VALE
EDGWARE ROAD
WESTWAY
A40(M)
BAYSWATER ROAD
KNIGHTSBRIDGE
KENSINGTON GORE
PARK LANE
PRINCE ALBERT ROAD
ST. JOHN'S WOOD ROAD
OXFORD STREET where marked is closed to through traffic (except buses & taxis) from 7a.m.-7p.m. Monday - Saturday.

DH
DJ
DK
DL
DM
DN
DP
77
N5
30
31
63
N7
KENTISH TOWN
CALEDONIAN PARK
PENTONVILLE PRISON
BARNSBURY
HIGHBURY & ISLINGTON
65
66
67
68
69
70
71
72
73
74
78
81
82
83
84
KING'S CROSS
ST. PANCRAS HOSP & HOSP FOR TROPICAL DISEASES
CAMDEN TOWN
NW1
ISLINGTON
N1
CAMLEY ST NATURAL PARK
PENTONVILLE
SOMERS TOWN
BRITISH LIB
ST PANCRAS
REGENT'S PARK
NATIONAL TEMPERANCE HOSP
EUSTON
FINSBURY
CLERKENWELL
EC1
ST. LUKE'S
EASTMAN DENTAL HOSP
CORAM'S FIELDS
WC1
BLOOMSBURY
BRITISH MUSEUM
FITZROVIA
HOLBORN
SOHO
W1
MAYFAIR
STRAND
WC2
EC4
ST. PAUL'S CATH
BARBICAN
MUSEUM OF LONDON
ST. BART'S HOSP
SOUTHWARK
SE1
RIVER
EMBANKMENT
BLACKFRIARS
WATERLOO
ST. JAMES'S
GREEN PARK
ST. JAMES'S PARK
BUCKINGHAM PALACE
THE BOROUGH
91
29

78
DQ
DR
DS
DT
DU
DV
DW
33
34
35
64
65
66
67
68
69
70
71
72
73
74
77
81
82
83
84
92
N5
N1
E8
E2
E1
EC1
EC4
EC3
SE1
HIGHBURY
DALSTON
HACKNEY
HOXTON
HAGGERSTON
BETHNAL GREEN
SHOREDITCH
FINSBURY
CLERKENWELL
ST. LUKE'S
WHITECHAPEL
WAPPING
SHADWELL
SOUTHWARK
THE BOROUGH
LONDON FIELDS
HAGGERSTON PARK
SHOREDITCH PARK
ROSEMARY GDNS
WEAVERS FIELDS
BUNHILL FLDS
RIVER THAMES
THE TOWER
TOWER HILL
LIVERPOOL ST
BROADGATE
FENCHURCH ST
LONDON BRIDGE
GUY'S HOSPITAL
LONDON BRIDGE HOSP
ST. PAUL'S CATH
ST. BART'S HOSP
MOORFIELDS EYE HOSP
ROYAL LONDON HOSP TRUST
LONDON CHEST HOSP
MILDMAY MISS HOSP
BARBICAN
MUSEUM OF LONDON
The Guildhall
The Monument
Tower Pier
HMS BELFAST
Hay's Galleria
DESIGN MUSEUM
TOWER BRIDGE EXPERIENCE
News International
Tobacco Dock
Shakespeare's Globe Thea & Exhib
KINGSLAND ROAD
BALLS POND RD
GRAHAM RD
ESSEX ROAD
NEW NORTH ROAD
CITY ROAD
OLD STREET
GREAT EASTERN ST
COMMERCIAL ST
COMMERCIAL ROAD
WHITECHAPEL RD
MILE END RD
BETHNAL GREEN RD
HACKNEY RD
CAMBRIDGE HEATH RD
MARE ST
VICTORIA PARK RD
REGENT'S CANAL
THE HIGHWAY
EAST SMITHFIELD
BISHOPSGATE
HOUNDSDITCH
LONDON WALL
MOORGATE
ALDERSGATE ST
NEWGATE ST
HOLBORN VIADUCT
FARRINGDON RD
UPPER STREET
SOUTHWARK ST
TOOLEY ST
BOROUGH HIGH ST
BLACKFRIARS RD
UPPER POOL
LOWER POOL

DX
DY
DZ
EA
EB
EC
ED
36
37
38
65
HOMERTON
MABLEY GREEN
WICK FIELD
HACKNEY WICK
LONDON STADIUM (closed)
STRATFORD
LONDON INTERNATIONAL FREIGHT TERMINAL
E15
E9
VICTORIA PARK
OLD FORD
E3
BOW
MILE END
LONDON HOSPITAL (Mile End)
Queen Mary College (Univ of Lon)
LONDON HOSPITAL (St Clement's)
TOWER HAMLETS CEMETERY PARK
BROMLEY
BOW CHURCH
BROMLEY-BY-BOW
MEMORIAL GDNS
THE LONDON GAS MUSEUM
WEST HAM
STEPNEY GREEN
LIMEHOUSE
POPLAR
E14
CANARY WHARF
ISLE
WEST INDIA DOCKS
CANNING TOWN
EAST INDIA
BLACKWALL
MILLENNIUM EXPERIENCE
NORTH GREENWICH
BLACKWALL TUNNEL
ROTHERHITHE TUNNEL
LIMEHOUSE REACH
BOW CREEK
RIVER LEA
65
66
67
68
69
70
71
72
73
74
80
81
82
83
84
93
DX
DY
DZ
EA
EB
EC
ED
36
37
38

EE
EF
EG
EH
EJ
EK
EL
40
41
42
66
FOREST GATE
WOODGRANGE PARK CEM
PLASHET CEMETERY
ROMFORD ROAD
A118
MARYLAND
STRATFORD
65
66
67
68
69
70
71
72
73
74
79
94
84
83
82
81
WEST HAM PARK
WEST HAM
UPTON
PLASHET
EAST HAM MEML HOSP
UPTON PARK
PRIORY PARK
WEST HAM UTD FC
BARKING ROAD
A124
E13
PLAISTOW
PLAISTOW HOSP
EAST LONDON CEMETERY
MEMORIAL REC GRD
HERMIT RD REC GRD
EAST HAM JEWISH CEMETERY
E6
NEWHAM GENERAL HOSPITAL
TERENCE McMILLAN STADIUM
PLAYING FIELDS
BECKTON DISTRICT PARK NORTH
NEWHAM WAY
A13
CANNING TOWN REC GRD
CUSTOM HOUSE
KING GEORGE V PARK
BECKTON DISTRICT PARK
CANNING TOWN
E16
ROYAL VICTORIA DOCK
ROYAL ALBERT
CONNAUGHT BRIDGE
LOWER LEA CROSSING
BOW CREEK
EAST INDIA DOCK BASIN
Gas Works
MEMORIAL GDNS
THE LONDON GAS MUSEUM
RIVER
BLACKWALL REACH
BLACKWALL TUNNEL
MILLENNIUM EXPERIENCE
NORTH GREENWICH
Skyscape
Thames Wharf
London City Airport Pier
NORTH WOOLWICH ROAD
A1020
SILVERTOWN
SILVERTOWN & LONDON CITY AIRPORT
THAMES FLOOD BARRIER
WOOLWICH REACH
Tate & Lyle Jetty
Greenwich Yacht Club
PONTOON DOCK
MANOR ROAD
PRINCE REGENT LANE
HIGH ST
GREENGATE STREET
STOPFORD
A114
SILVERTOWN WAY
ROYAL DOCKS ROAD
MANOR
MANOR ROAD
NEW PLAISTOW ROAD
A112

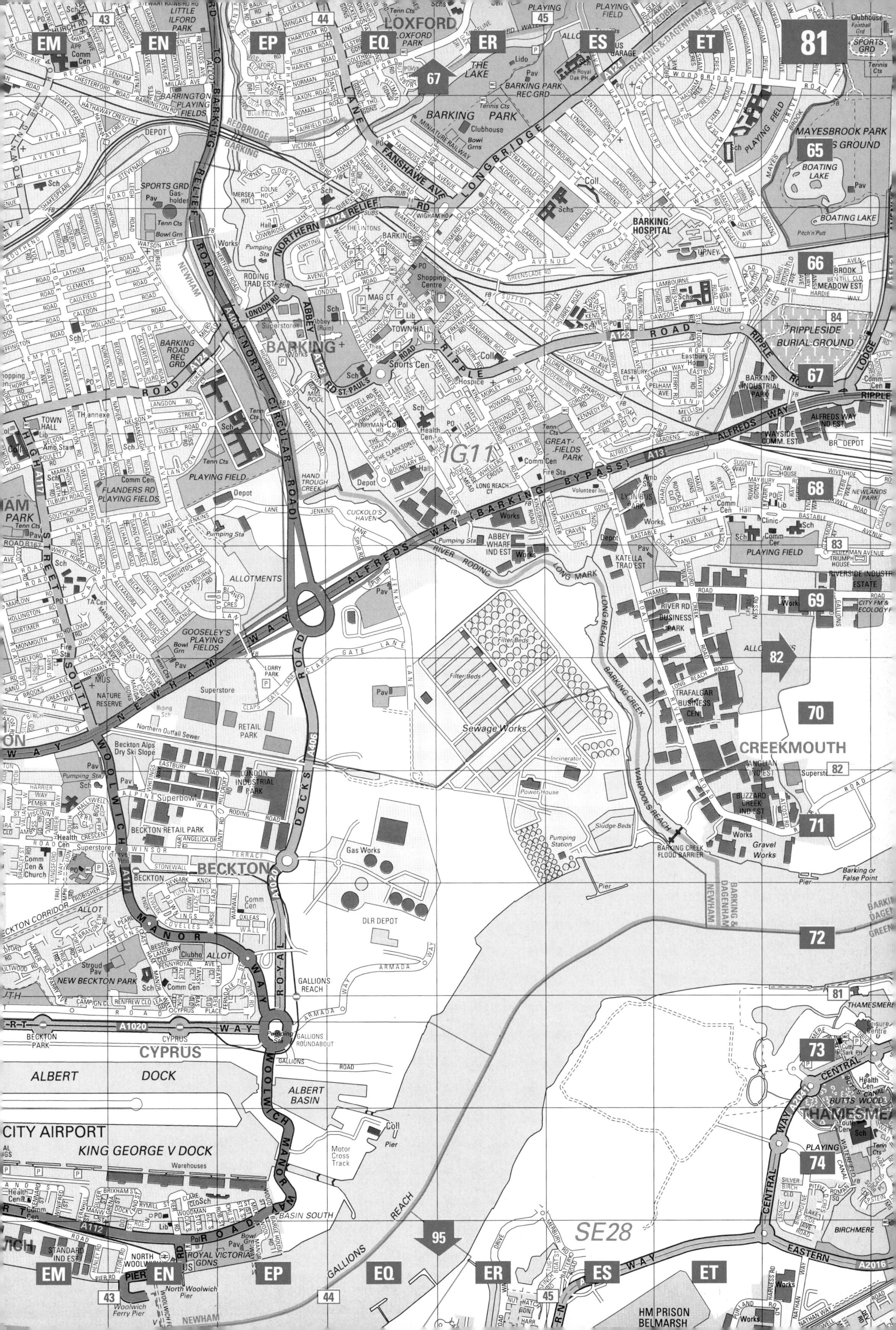

81
EM
EN
EP
EQ
ER
ES
ET
LOXFORD
LITTLE ILFORD PARK
THE LAKE
BARKING PARK
BARKING PARK REC GRD
MAYESBROOK PARK
BOATING LAKE
BARKING HOSPITAL
BARKING
IG11
RIPPLESIDE BURIAL GROUND
BARKING INDUSTRIAL PARK
ALFREDS WAY IND EST
GREATFIELDS PARK
FLANDERS RD PLAYING FIELDS
GOOSELEY'S PLAYING FIELDS
ALLOTMENTS
RIVER RODING
LONG REACH
BARKING CREEK
Sewage Works
Filter Beds
RIVER RD BUSINESS PARK
TRAFALGAR BUSINESS CEN
CREEKMOUTH
BUZZARD CREEK IND EST
BARKING CREEK FLOOD BARRIER
BECKTON
BECKTON RETAIL PARK
LONDON INDUSTRIAL PARK
NEW BECKTON PARK
Gas Works
DLR DEPOT
CYPRUS
ALBERT DOCK
ALBERT BASIN
CITY AIRPORT
KING GEORGE V DOCK
GALLIONS ROUNDABOUT
GALLIONS REACH
ROYAL VICTORIA GDNS
North Woolwich Pier
Woolwich Ferry Pier
SE28
THAMESMEAD
BIRCHMERE
HM PRISON BELMARSH
A13
A406
A124
A123
A117
A1020
A112
A2016
A2041
NEWHAM
BARKING & DAGENHAM

EU
EV
EW
EX
EY
EZ
FA
47
48
49
68
65
66
67
68
69
70
71
72
73
74
81
82
83
84
96
RM8
RM9
IG11
SE2
SE28
DA18
PARSLOES PARK
MAYESBROOK PARK SPORTS GROUND
BOATING LAKE
BARKING HOSPITAL
RIPPLESIDE BURIAL GROUND
BARKING INDUSTRIAL PARK
CASTLE GREEN
SPORTS GROUND
GORESBROOK PARK
ALLOTMENTS
DAGENHAM
Dagenham Heathway
Becontree
FORD MOTOR WORKS
DAGENHAM DOCK
Due open 1999
COAL DEPOT
Freightliner Terminal
RIVERSIDE INDUSTRIAL ESTATE
CITY FM & ECOLOGY PK
Power Station
Horse Shoe Corner
OIL STORAGE DEPOT
RIVER THAMES
BARKING AND DAGENHAM
GREENWICH
BEXLEY
BARKING CREEK FLOOD BARRIER
Barking or False Point
Cross Ness
CROSSNESS LIGHTHOUSE
ECOLOGY STUDY AREA
THAMESMEAD NORTH
CROSSWAY LAKE
Riverside Golf Course
COVERED RESERVOIRS
CROSSNESS SEWAGE TREATMENT WORKS
THAMESMERE
Leisure Centre
THAMESMEAD
BUTTS WOOD
CROSSWAY PARK
SOUTHMERE PARK
LAKESIDE CENTRE
SOUTHMERE
BIRCHMERE PARK
ERITH MARSHES
HM PRISON BELMARSH
EASTERN WAY
A2016
A13
A123
A1153
A1240
A2041
RIPPLE ROAD
ALFREDS WAY
AVENUE PORTERS
HEATHWAY
CARLYLE ROAD
MANORWAY
CENTRAL WAY

FB
FC
FD
FE
FF
FG
FH
50
51
52
69
ELM PARK
RM10
RM12
RM13
DAGENHAM EAST
PONDFIELD PARK
OLD DAGENHAM PARK
THE LEYS
SPORTS GROUNDS
Bretons Sports Club
BRITTONS PLAYING FIELDS
PLAYING FIELDS
SOUTH HORNCHURCH
RAINHAM ROAD SOUTH
DAGENHAM ROAD
RAINHAM ROAD
NEW ROAD
A1306
A125
A1311
BEAM RIVER
INGREBOURNE RIVER
HORNCHURCH COUNTRY PARK
AIRFIELD WOOD
FLIGHT WOOD
FARMFIELD WOOD
LOWFIELD WOOD
RAINHAM
Dovers Corner
Beam Bridge
Newtons Corner
CAR COMPOUND
MOTOR WORKS
HORNCHURCH MARSHES
Sewage Works
FAIRVIEW IND PARK
ALBRIGHT IND EST
DENVER IND EST
CONTAINER DEPOT
Hornchurch Shoot
Old Man's Head
RAINHAM MARSHES
Silt Lagoons
JENNINGTREE POINT LIGHTHOUSE
Jenningtree Point
Belvedere Power Station (Disused)
WENNINGTON MARSHES
Southall Bridge
65
66
67
68
69
70
71
72
73
74
84
83
82
81
97

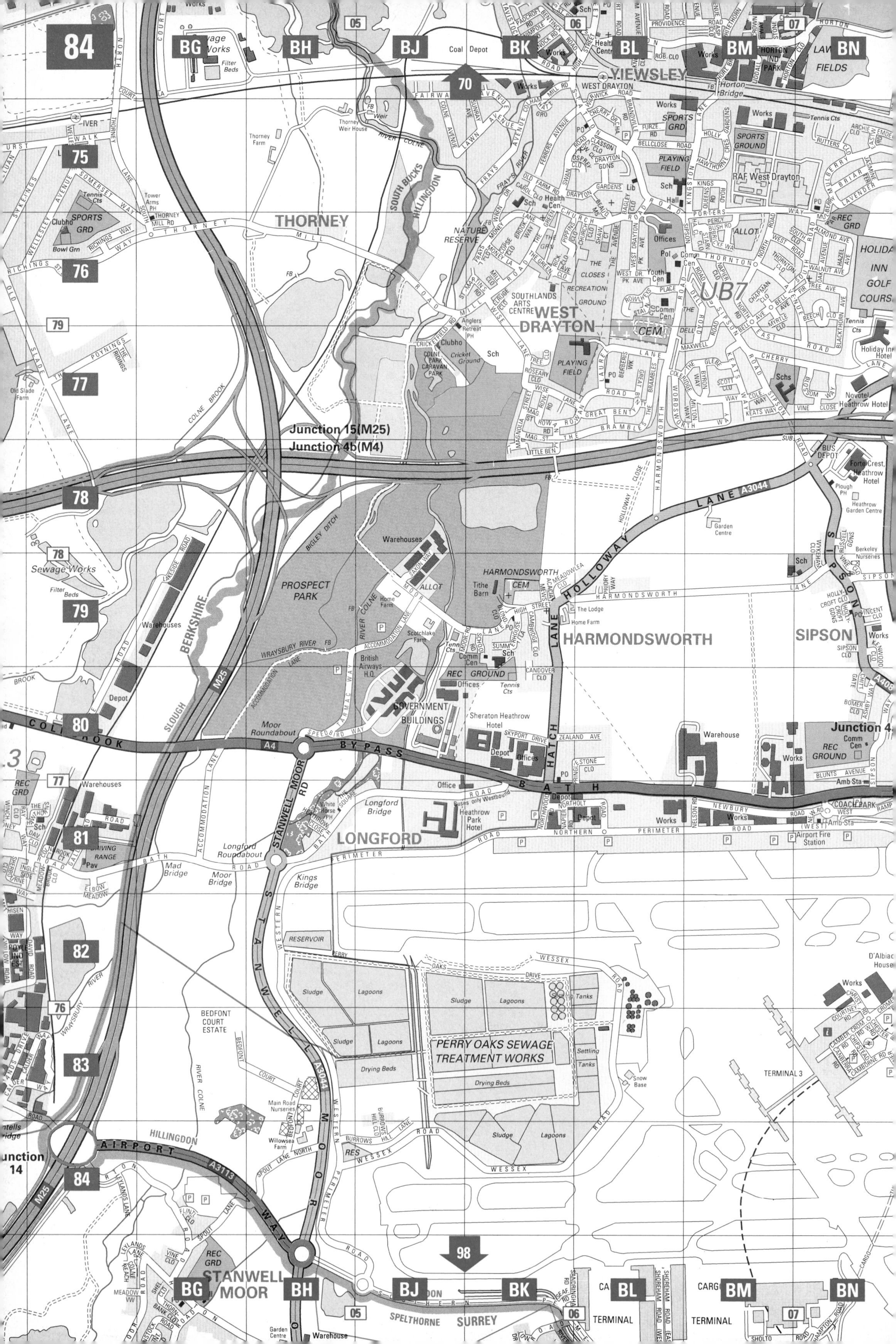

THORNEY
YIEWSLEY
WEST DRAYTON
UB7
HARMONDSWORTH
SIPSON
LONGFORD
STANWELL MOOR
PROSPECT PARK
PERRY OAKS SEWAGE TREATMENT WORKS
Junction 15(M25)
Junction 4b(M4)
BERKSHIRE
SOUTH BUCKS
HILLINGDON
SPELTHORNE
SURREY
TERMINAL 3
GOVERNMENT BUILDINGS
British Airways H.Q.
Sheraton Heathrow Hotel
Heathrow Park Hotel
Novotel Heathrow Hotel
Holiday Inn Hotel
Forte Crest, Heathrow Hotel
BG
BH
BJ
BK
BL
BM
BN
70
98
75
76
77
78
79
80
81
82
83
84

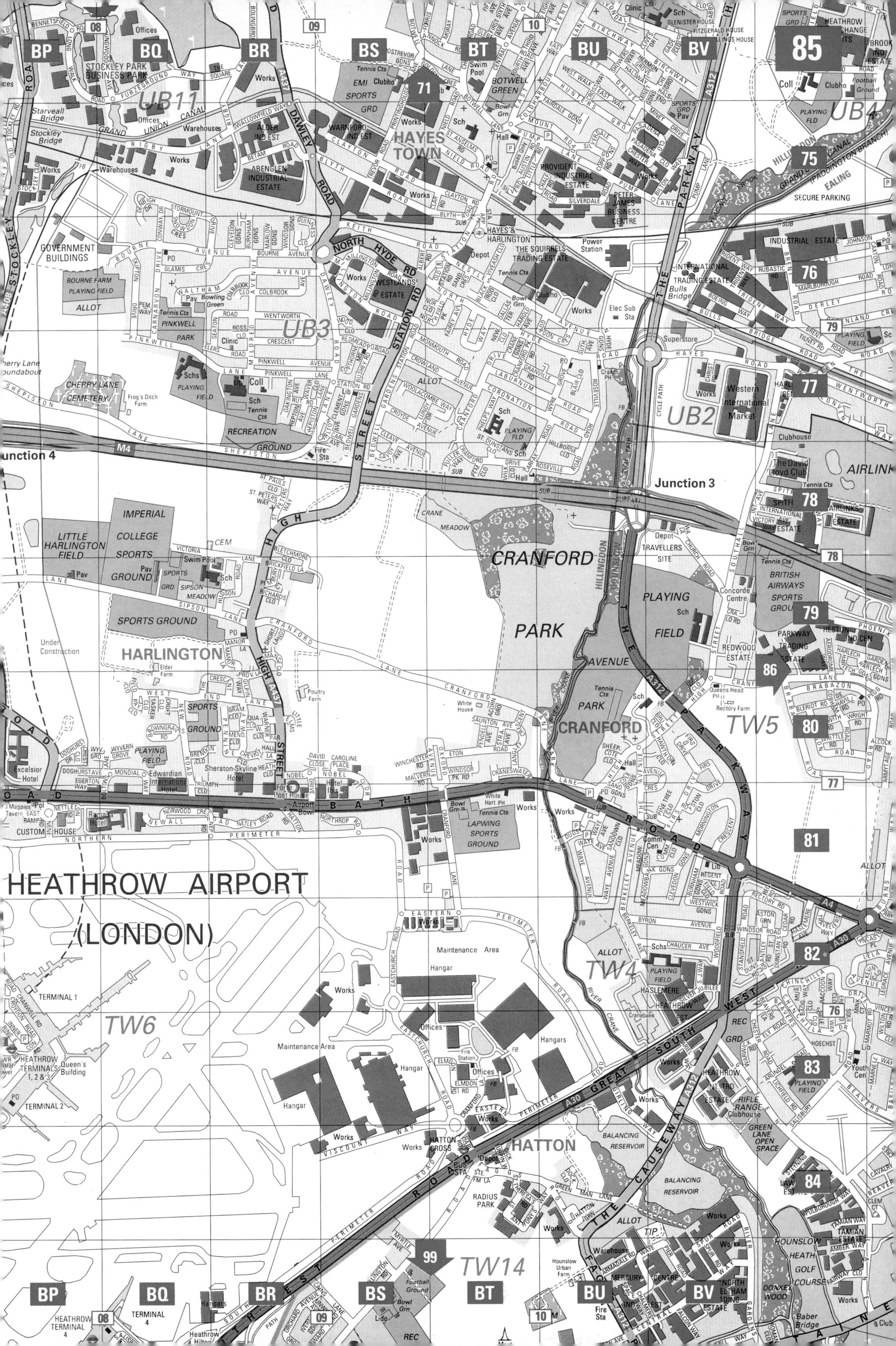

BP
BQ
BR
BS
BT
BU
BV
85
71
75
76
77
78
79
86
80
81
82
83
84
99
STOCKLEY PARK BUSINESS PARK
UB11
GRAND UNION CANAL
HAYES TOWN
BOTWELL GREEN
EMI SPORTS GRD
ALDER IND EST
ABENGLEN INDUSTRIAL ESTATE
PROVIDENT INDUSTRIAL ESTATE
PETER JAMES BUSINESS CENTRE
HAYES & HARLINGTON
THE SQUIRRELS TRADING ESTATE
INTERNATIONAL TRADING ESTATE
INDUSTRIAL ESTATE
UB4
UB3
UB2
WESTLANDS' ESTATE
GOVERNMENT BUILDINGS
BOURNE FARM PLAYING FIELD
PINKWELL PARK
CHERRY LANE CEMETERY
RECREATION GROUND
Western International Market
Junction 4
Junction 3
M4
IMPERIAL COLLEGE SPORTS GROUND
LITTLE HARLINGTON FIELD
SPORTS GROUND
HARLINGTON
CRANFORD PARK
PLAYING FIELD
CRANFORD
BRITISH AIRWAYS SPORTS GROUND
PARKWAY TRADING ESTATE
TW5
LAPWING SPORTS GROUND
BATH ROAD
HEATHROW AIRPORT (LONDON)
TERMINAL 1
HEATHROW TERMINALS 1, 2 & 3
TERMINAL 2
TW6
TW4
Maintenance Area
Hangar
Hangars
HATTON
HATTON CROSS
RADIUS PARK
BALANCING RESERVOIR
HASLEMERE HEATHROW EST
HEATHROW INT TRD ESTATE
GREEN LANE OPEN SPACE
GREAT SOUTH WEST ROAD
THE CAUSEWAY
THE PARKWAY
TW14
HOUNSLOW HEATH GOLF COURSE
DONKEY WOOD
NORTH FELTHAM TRADING ESTATE
HEATHROW TERMINAL 4

86
SOUTHALL
UB1
UB2
UB3
UB4
TW3
TW4
TW5
BW
BX
BY
BZ
CA
CB
CC
72
75
76
77
78
79
80
81
82
83
84
85
100
12
13
14
UXBRIDGE ROAD
HIGH STREET
SOUTHALL PARK
GRAND UNION CANAL (PADDINGTON BRANCH)
HILLINGDON
EALING
HOUNSLOW
SECURE PARKING
Gas Works
SOUTHALL RAILWAY CENTRE
GREAT WESTERN IND PARK
MIDDLESEX BUSINESS CENTRE
FEATHERSTONE IND EST
FOUR SEASONS IND EST
INDUSTRIAL ESTATE
CEMETERY
NORWOOD GREEN
Western International Market
HARLEQUIN CENTRE
AIRLINKS GOLF COURSE
The David Lloyd Club
Junction 3
Heston Services
NORTH HYDE
BRITISH AIRWAYS SPORTS GROUND
PLAYING FIELD
PARKWAY TRADING ESTATE
OSTERLEY PARK HOUSE
SPORTS GROUND
HESTON
HESTON PARK
SUTTON PLAYING FIELD
GREAT WEST ROAD
LAMPTON
LAMPTON PARK
HOUNSLOW CIVIC CENTRE
HOUNSLOW WEST
HOUNSLOW WEST Cavalry Barracks
BEAVERSFIELD PARK
HOUNSLOW
HOUNSLOW CENTRAL
HOUNSLOW EAST
INWOOD PARK
HOUNSLOW HEATH GOLF
GREEN LANE OPEN SPACE
NORTH FELTHAM TRADING ESTATE
CENTRAL PARK ESTATE
Heath Nurseries
Police Training Centre
BUS GARAGE
SOUTH WEST ROAD
THE PARKWAY
STAINES ROAD
WELLINGTON ROAD N
WELLINGTON ROAD S
BATH ROAD
HANWORTH RD
LAMPTON ROAD
HESTON ROAD
NORWOOD ROAD
WINDMILL LANE
CHURCH ROAD
SUTTON LANE
A312
A4
A30
A315
A3005
A3006
A3063
A4020
A4127

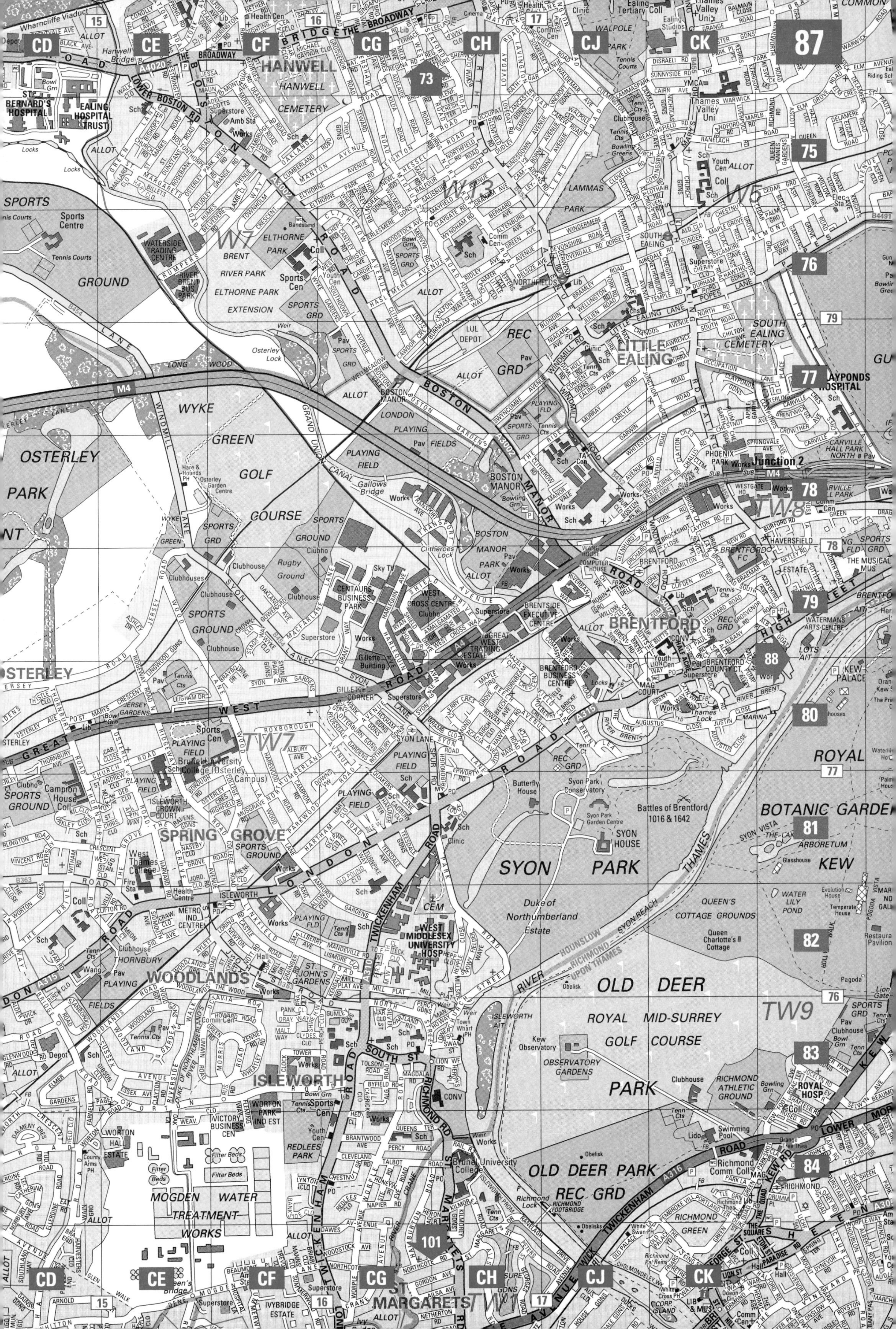

87
73
75
76
77
78
79
88
80
81
82
83
84
101
15
16
17
CD
CE
CF
CG
CH
CJ
CK
HANWELL
HANWELL CEMETERY
W13
W5
W7
TW7
TW8
TW9
TW1
LAMMAS PARK
SOUTH EALING
SOUTH EALING CEMETERY
LITTLE EALING
NORTHFIELDS
BRENT RIVER PARK
ELTHORNE PARK
ELTHORNE PARK EXTENSION
REC GRD
LUL DEPOT
LONDON PLAYING FIELDS
BOSTON MANOR
BOSTON MANOR PARK
WYKE GREEN GOLF COURSE
OSTERLEY PARK
SPORTS GROUND
M4
Junction 2
GRAND UNION CANAL
Gallows Bridge
Clitheroes Lock
Osterley Lock
CENTAURS BUSINESS PARK
WEST CROSS CENTRE
Gillette Building
GILLETTE CORNER
BRENTSIDE EXECUTIVE CENTRE
GREAT WEST TRADING ESTATE
BRENTFORD BUSINESS CENTRE
BRENTFORD
BRENTFORD FC
PHOENIX PARK
HAVERSFIELD ESTATE
THE MUSICAL MUS
WATERMANS ARTS CENTRE
LOTS AIT
KEW PALACE
BRENTFORD COUNTY CT
Thames Lock
GREAT WEST ROAD
LONDON ROAD
TWICKENHAM ROAD
SYON LANE
SYON PARK
SYON HOUSE
Butterfly House
Syon Park Conservatory
Syon Park Garden Centre
Battles of Brentford 1016 & 1642
Duke of Northumberland Estate
RIVER THAMES
ROYAL BOTANIC GARDENS
KEW
ARBORETUM
SYON VISTA
QUEEN'S COTTAGE GROUNDS
Queen Charlotte's Cottage
WATER LILY POND
Pagoda
OLD DEER PARK
ROYAL MID-SURREY GOLF COURSE
Kew Observatory
OBSERVATORY GARDENS
RICHMOND ATHLETIC GROUND
OLD DEER PARK REC GRD
Richmond Lock
RICHMOND FOOTBRIDGE
RICHMOND
RICHMOND GREEN
Richmond Comm Coll
ROYAL HOSP
Brunel University College
Brunel University College (Osterley Campus)
SPRING GROVE
ISLEWORTH
ISLEWORTH CROWN COURT
West Thames College
ISLEWORTH AIT
WEST MIDDLESEX UNIVERSITY HOSP
CEM
WOODLANDS
THORNBURY
ST. JOHN'S GARDENS
WORTON PARK IND EST
VICTORY BUSINESS CEN
WORTON HALL ESTATE
REDLEES PARK
MOGDEN WATER TREATMENT WORKS
Filter Beds
IVYBRIDGE ESTATE
ST MARGARETS
METRO IND CENTRE
ST. BERNARD'S HOSPITAL
EALING HOSPITAL TRUST
Wharncliffe Viaduct
WATERSIDE TRADING CENTRE
RIVER BRENT BUS PARK
CLAYPONDS HOSPITAL
CARVILLE HALL PARK NORTH
WALPOLE PARK
Ealing Tertiary Coll
Thames Valley Uni
Ealing Studios
YMCA

88
CL
CM
CN
CP
CQ
CR
CS
19
20
21
74
75
76
77
78
79
80
81
82
83
84
87
102
W5
W3
W4
TW8
TW9
SW14
ACTON
SOUTH ACTON
BEDFORD PARK
GUNNERSBURY PARK
GUNNERSBURY
SOUTH EALING CEMETERY
CLAYPONDS HOSPITAL
KENSINGTON CEMETERY
Junction 1
Junction 2
CHISWICK HIGH ROAD
CHISWICK
CHISWICK HOUSE GROUNDS
GROVE PARK
KEW
ROYAL BOTANIC GARDENS
KEW PALACE
PUBLIC RECORD OFFICE
RIVER THAMES
NORTH SHEEN
NORTH SHEEN CEMETERY
HAMMERSMITH CEMETERY
MORTLAKE
EAST SHEEN
QUEEN'S COTTAGE GROUNDS
ROYAL MID-SURREY GOLF COURSE
OLD DEER PARK
RICHMOND ATHLETIC GROUND
DUKE'S MEADOW ALLOTMENTS
CIVIL SERVICE SPORTS GROUND
THE QUINTIN HOGG MEMORIAL GROUND
SOUTHFIELDS PLAYING FIELDS
POPEFIELD PLAYING FIELDS
EAST SHEEN COMMON NT
Battles of Brentford 1016 & 1642
BRENTFORD
HIGH STREET
KEW ROAD
MORTLAKE ROAD
LOWER RICHMOND ROAD
UPPER RICHMOND ROAD WEST
CLIFFORD AVE
GREAT WEST ROAD
GUNNERSBURY AVENUE
NORTH CIRCULAR RD
SOUTH CIRCULAR RD
M4
A4
A205
A305
A315
A316
A3000
A3003

CT
CU
CV
CW
CX
CY
CZ
89
22
23
24
W12
SHEPHERD'S BUSH
75
KENSINGTON
W8
HOLLAND PARK
HOLLAND HOUSE
UXBRIDGE ROAD
A4020
A40
HOLLAND PARK
SHEPHERD'S BUSH COMMON
SHEPHERD'S BUSH GRN
GOLDHAWK ROAD
A402
Hammersmith & West London College
WENDELL PARK
RAVENSCOURT PARK
ROYAL MASONIC HOSP
QUEEN CHARLOTTE'S HOSP
STAMFORD BROOK
W6
W14
KENSINGTON (OLYMPIA)
OLYMPIA
LEIGHTON HO MUS
COMMONWEALTH INST
76
77
78
79
CROMWELL HOSP
PEMBROKE RD
WARWICK GDNS
KENSINGTON
A315
A3220
HAMMERSMITH RD
GLENTHORNE RD
KING ST
A315
GREAT WEST ROAD
A4
HAMMERSMITH FLYOVER
TALGARTH ROAD
WEST CROMWELL RD
HAMMERSMITH
HAMMERSMITH APOLLO
Novotel
HAMMERSMITH CEMETERY
THE QUEEN'S CLUB
EARLS COURT
EARLS COURT EXHIBITION CENTRE
WEST BROMPTON
CHARING CROSS HOSP
RIVERSIDE STUDIOS
CHISWICK LODGE
CHISWICK EYOT
PLAYING FIELDS
CASTELNAU
HAMMERSMITH & FULHAM
RICHMOND UPON THAMES
LEG OF MUTTON NATURE RESERVE
SW13
A306
BARN ELMS WILDFOWL RESERVE
LILLIE ROAD
LILLIE RD REC GRD
NORMAND PARK
A3218
DAWES ROAD
A3219
FULHAM CEM
FULHAM PALACE ROAD
90
80
81
FULHAM
FULHAM BROADWAY
PARSONS GREEN
SW6
82
83
SAMUEL LEWIS TRUST DWS
EEL BROOK COMMON
CRAVEN COTTAGE FULHAM FC
BISHOP'S PARK
FULHAM PALACE
ALLOTMENTS
BARN ELMS PLAYING FIELD
BARN ELMS SCHOOLS SPORTS CENTRE
QUEEN ELIZABETH WALK
CHURCH RD
A3003
BARNES
BARNES COMMON
PUTNEY HOSP
PUTNEY
LOWER RICHMOND ROAD
RIVER THAMES
HURLINGHAM PARK
HURLINGHAM CLUB GDNS
Hurlingham House
SOUTH PARK
PUTNEY BRIDGE
A304
NEW KINGS ROAD
A308
WANDSWORTH PARK
WANDSWORTH BRIDGE
84
WANDSWORTH
UPPER RICHMOND ROAD
SOUTH CIRCULAR ROAD
A205
PUTNEY HIGH STREET
PUTNEY HILL
A3209
EAST PUTNEY
ROEHAMPTON LANE
ROEHAMPTON GOLF COURSE
PRIORY HOSPITAL
ROCKS LANE
QUEENS RIDE
ROEHAMPTON
SW15
103

DA
DB
DC
DD
DE
DF
DG
KENSINGTON GARDENS
HYDE PARK
KENSINGTON
HOLLAND PARK
KENSINGTON PALACE
ROUND POND
THE SERPENTINE
SERPENTINE GALLERY
COURT DRESS COLLECTION
THE FLOWER WALK
Albert Memorial
ROTTEN ROW
KENSINGTON GORE
KNIGHTSBRIDGE
HYDE PARK CORNER
W8
SW7
SW3
SW5
SW10
SW6
SW11
COMMONWEALTH INST
LEIGHTON HO MUS
Royal Albert Hall
Royal College of Music
Imperial College
SCIENCE MUS
NAT HISTORY MUS
VICTORIA & ALBERT MUSEUM
SOUTH KENSINGTON
BROMPTON
CROMWELL HOSP
CROMWELL RD
EARLS COURT
EARLS COURT EXHIBITION CENTRE
WEST BROMPTON
BROMPTON CEMETERY
ROYAL MARSDEN HOSP
ROYAL BROMPTON HOSP
CHELSEA & WEST. HOSP
CHELSEA
FULHAM ROAD
KING'S ROAD
STAMFORD BRIDGE CHELSEA F.C.
FULHAM BROADWAY
WALHAM GREEN
SANDS END
PARSONS GREEN
EEL BROOK COMMON
ROYAL HOSPITAL CHELSEA
RANELAGH GARDENS
NAT ARMY MUS
Chelsea Barracks
Duke of York's Headquarters
SLOANE SQ
CHELSEA EMBANKMENT
CHEYNE WALK
BATTERSEA PARK
Festival Pleasure Gardens
BOATING LAKE
Peace Pagoda
CHELSEA REACH
BATTERSEA BRIDGE
ALBERT BRIDGE
Chelsea Harbour
LONDON WESTLAND HELIPORT
Royal Acad. of Dancing
Chelsea College of Art & Design
HURLINGHAM PARK
Hurlingham House
SOUTH PARK
THAMES
HAMMERSMITH & FULHAM
WANDSWORTH
WANDSWORTH BRIDGE
PUTNEY BRIDGE
CLAPHAM JUNCTION
LAVENDER HILL
ST. JOHN'S HEALTH CARE UNIT
BOLINGBROKE HOSP
CLAPHAM COMMON
WANDSWORTH HIGH ST
WANDSWORTH TOWN
BUS DEPOT
Gas Works
75
76
77
78
79
80
81
82
83
84
89
104
26
27
28

91
DH
DJ
DK
DL
DM
DN
DP
29
30
31
GREEN PARK
ST. JAMES'S PARK
ST. JAMES'S
BUCKINGHAM PALACE
SOUTHWARK
SE1
WATERLOO
WATERLOO INTERNATIONAL
London Eye
HOUSES OF PARLIAMENT
ST. THOMAS HOSPITAL
WESTMINSTER
VICTORIA
LAMBETH
SE11
THE BOROUGH
ELEPHANT & CASTLE
IMPERIAL WAR MUS
PIMLICO
TATE GALLERY
CHURCHILL GARDENS
DOLPHIN SQUARE
RIVER THAMES
VAUXHALL
NINE ELMS
Battersea Power Station (Disused)
New Covent Garden Market
THE OVAL
KENNINGTON
KENNINGTON PARK
SW8
SOUTH LAMBETH
SW9
MYATT'S FIELDS
STOCKWELL
CLAPHAM
TRINITY HOSPICE
SOUTH WESTERN HOSP
BRIXTON
CAMBERWELL
SE5
SE24
RUSKIN PARK
KING'S COLLEGE HOSPITAL
SW4
CLAPHAM COMMON
CAMBERWELL NEW ROAD
COLDHARBOUR LANE
CLAPHAM HIGH ST
WANDSWORTH ROAD
KENNINGTON ROAD
GROSVENOR ROAD
ALBERT EMBANKMENT
VAUXHALL BRI
LAMBETH BRI
WESTMINSTER BRI
77
105
92
75
76
78
79
80
81
82
83
84

92
SOUTHWARK
DQ
DR
DS
DT
DU
DV
DW
33
34
35
WAPPING
BRIDGE HOSP
Hay's Galleria
HMS BELFAST
Tower Pier
TOWER BRIDGE EXPERIENCE
DESIGN MUSEUM
THE POOL
LOWER POOL
Cherry Garden Pier
King's Stairs
Princes Stairs
Wapping Old Stairs
Wapping New Stairs
Wapping Dock Stairs
78
GUY'S HOSPITAL
LONDON BRIDGE
TOOLEY STREET
ST THOMAS ST
BERMONDSEY ST
LONG LANE
75
THE BOROUGH
BOROUGH ROAD
BOROUGH
SE1
TABARD GARDENS
GREAT DOVER STREET
TOWER BRIDGE ROAD
JAMAICA ROAD
76
NEWINGTON
BERMONDSEY
SE16
SOUTHWARK PARK
SOUTHWARK PARK ROAD
RAYMOUTH RD
KING'S STAIRS GDNS
IMPERIAL WAR MUS
79
ELEPHANT & CASTLE
NEW KENT ROAD
77
SE17
WALWORTH
WALWORTH ROAD
OLD KENT ROAD
ROTHERHITHE NEW ROAD
SOUTH BERMONDSEY
78
KENNINGTON PARK
79
BURGESS PARK
South Eastern Gas Works
91
80
CAMBERWELL
SE5
NORTH PECKHAM EST
PECKHAM
SE15
81
MYATT'S FIELDS
CAMBERWELL CHURCH ST
PECKHAM ROAD
PECKHAM HIGH ST
QUEENS ROAD
QUEENS ROAD PECKHAM
COSSALL PARK
82
THE MAUDSLEY HOSPITAL
KING'S COLLEGE HOSPITAL
LOUGHBOROUGH JUNCTION
COLDHARBOUR LANE
DENMARK HILL
PECKHAM RYE
83
RUSKIN PARK
DOG KENNEL HILL
EAST DULWICH ROAD
NUNHEAD
NUNHEAD LANE
EVELINA ROAD
84
GREENDALE PLAYING FIELDS
EAST DULWICH
KINGS COLL HOSP DULWICH
PECKHAM RYE COMMON
SE24
106
DULWICH GROVE
LORDSHIP LANE
HERNE HILL
ST. OLAVE'S REC GRD
PLAYING FIELDS
PECKHAM RYE
AQUARIUS GOLF COURSE

DX
DY
DZ
EA
EB
EC
ED
93
36
37
38
79
75
76
77
78
79
80
81
82
83
84
94
107
ISLE
OF
DOGS
WEST INDIA DOCKS
MILLENNIUM EXPERIENCE
NORTH GREENWICH
ROTHERHITHE
RUSSIA DOCK WOODLAND
SOUTHWARK PARK
CUBITT TOWN
MILLWALL
MUDCHUTE PARK
DLR stations to the south of the river are due to open early 2000
MILLWALL PARK
LONDON ARENA
DEPTFORD
DEPTFORD PARK
PEPYS PARK
SE8
SE10
SE13
SE14
SE4
GREENWICH
GREENWICH PARK
BLACKHEATH
NEW CROSS
NEW CROSS GATE
ST JOHN'S
LEWISHAM
HILLY FIELDS
BROCKLEY
BROCKLEY CEMETERY
LADYWELL CEMETERY
LADYWELL
TELEGRAPH HILL PARK
FORDHAM PARK
FOLKESTONE GDNS
CUTTY SARK
GIPSY MOTH IV
NATIONAL MARITIME MUS
QUEEN'S HOUSE
FLAMSTEED HOUSE (Old Royal Observatory)
RANGER'S HOUSE
THE WILDERNESS DEER PARK
MANOR HOUSE GARDENS
MANOR PARK
Goldsmiths College (Uni of London)
Lewisham Coll
University of Greenwich
ROYAL NAVAL YARD
GREENWICH REACH
LIMEHOUSE REACH
BLACKWALL TUNNEL
EVELYN STREET
REDRIFF ROAD
WESTFERRY ROAD
MANCHESTER ROAD
PRESTONS RD
ROMNEY ROAD
TRAFALGAR ROAD
CREEK ROAD
DEPTFORD CHURCH STREET
GREENWICH HIGH ROAD
BLACKHEATH HILL
SHOOTER'S HILL
NEW CROSS ROAD
LEWISHAM WAY
LOAMPIT HILL
LOAMPIT VALE
LEE HIGH ROAD
BROOKMILL ROAD
ADELAIDE AVENUE

94
EE
EF
EG
EH
EJ
EK
EL
40
41
42
LONDON
MILLENNIUM EXPERIENCE
Blackwall Point
RIVER
London City Airport Pier
NORTH WOOLWICH ROAD
A1020
SILVERTOWN
SILVERTOWN & LONDON CITY AIRPORT
THAMES RD IND EST
THAMESIDE IND EST
SHIELD IND EST
LYLE PARK
Skyscape
NORTH GREENWICH
COACH STATION
Manhattan Wharf
Greenwich Yacht Club
WOOLWICH
THAMES FLOOD BARRIER
REACH
Tate & Lyle Jetty
THAMES
NEWHAM
GREENWICH
Barrier Gdns Pier
Russian Submarine
WOOLWICH DOCKYARD IND EST
BLACKWALL TUNNEL APPROACH
A102
A2203
BUGSBY'S WAY
SOUTH EASTERN GAS BOARD SPORTS GROUND
MERIDIAN TRADING ESTATE
RAMAC INDUSTRIAL ESTATE
GREENWICH INDUSTRIAL ESTATE
NEW CHARLTON
Woolwich College
MARYON PARK
WOOLWICH ROAD
A206
CHARLTON ATHLETIC FC
MARYON WILSON PARK
GREENWICH DISTRICT HOSP
EAST GREENWICH PLEASAUNCE
WESTCOMBE PARK
TRAFALGAR ROAD
ROMNEY ROAD
NATIONAL MARITIME MUS
CHARLTON
SE7
CHARLTON PARK
CHARLTON PARK ROAD
Community Centre
WOODLANDS LOCAL HIST CEN
GREENWICH
SE10
GREENWICH PARK
93
One Tree Hill
RECTORY FIELD
THE WILDERNESS DEER PARK
Blackheath Gate
Ranger's House
HORNFAIR PARK SPORTS GROUND
SHOOTER'S HILL ROAD
A2
A207
ROCHESTER WAY RELIEF RD
KIDBROOKE PARK ROAD
A2213
BLACKHEATH
SE3
Morden College
BROOK GENERAL HOSPITAL (closed)
KIDBROOKE
PLAYING FIELDS
GREENWICH CEMETERY
KIDBROOKE GREEN NATURE RESERVE
MINI TOWN HALL
BLACKHEATH HOSPITAL
BLACKHEATH CONCERT HALLS
BLACKHEATH PARK
ROCHESTER WAY
UNIVERSITY OF GREENWICH SPORTS GROUND
MANOR HOUSE GARDENS
MANOR PARK
SUTCLIFFE PARK
108
LEE HIGH ROAD
ELTHAM ROAD
A20
A210
BURNT ASH
75
76
77
78
79
80
81
82
83
84

95
EM
EN
EP
EQ
ER
ES
ET
81
ITY AIRPORT
KING GEORGE V DOCK
GALLIONS
REACH
SE28
NORTH WOOLWICH
ROYAL VICTORIA GDNS
North Woolwich Pier
Woolwich Ferry Pier
NEWHAM
GREENWICH
WOOLWICH FREE FERRY
SE London Aquatic Cen
THAMESMEAD WEST
HM PRISON BELMARSH
EASTERN WAY
WESTERN WAY
75
76
77
78
79
80
81
82
83
84
96
109
WOOLWICH
CHURCH STREET
BERESFORD ST
PLUMSTEAD ROAD
PLUMSTEAD HIGH STREET
PLUMSTEAD
PLUMSTEAD GARDENS
PLUMSTEAD COMMON
WINN'S COMMON
WOOLWICH ARSENAL
ARTILLERY PLACE
Barracks
BARRACK FIELD
GRAND DEPOT RD
JOHN WILSON ST
WOOLWICH COMMON
ROTUNDA MUSEUM
QUEEN ELIZABETH HOSPITAL
RUGBY GROUND
Royal Military Academy
WOOLWICH COMMON
SE18
SHREWSBURY PARK
SHOOTER'S HILL GOLF COURSE
SHOOTER'S HILL
EAGLESFIELD REC GRD
CLOTHWORKERS WOOD
PLAYING FIELD
BOSTALL WO
WOOL. CEM
ROCK. GDNS
WOOLWICH CEMETERY
EAST WICKHAM OPEN SPACE
WICKHAM LANE
HILL-VIEW CEMETERY
GREENWICH
BEXLEY
SHOOTER'S HILL
CASTLEWOOD THERAPY CENTRE
MEMORIAL HOSPITAL
ELTHAM COMMON
KING GEORGE'S FIELD
Severndroog Castle
CASTLE WOOD
JACK WOOD
OXLEAS WOOD
OXLEAS MEADOW
BELLEGROVE ROAD
WELLING WAY
DA16
FALCONWOOD
FALCONWOOD FIELD
SPORTS GROUND
SHEPHERDLEAS WOOD
ELTHAM PARK NORTH
SE9
ELTHAM PARK SOUTH
ELTHAM CEMETERY
Crematorium
ELTHAM WARREN GOLF COURSE
ROCHESTER WAY
RELIEF ROAD
WELLING
SOUTH CIRCULAR ROAD
ACADEMY ROAD
43
44
45

96
SE28
EU
EV
EW
EX
EY
EZ
FA
47
48
49
82
75
76
77
78
79
80
81
82
83
84
95
110
HM PRISON BELMARSH
EASTERN WAY
A2016
BIRCHMERE PARK
SOUTHMERE PARK
LAKESIDE CENTRE
SOUTHMERE
ERITH MARSHES
DA18
ABBEY WOOD PARK
THISTLEBROOK INDUSTRIAL ESTATE
EASTERN INDUSTRIAL ESTATE
ABBEY WD PARK
SPORTS GRD
ABBEY WOOD
HARROW MANORWAY
WOODLAND WAY
PLAYING FIELD
YARNTON WAY
Lessness Abbey (Ruins)
PLUMSTEAD GARDENS
LESSNESS ABBEY WOOD
SE2
BOSTALL HEATH
BOSTALL WOODS
BOSTALL HILL
WOOLWICH ROAD
WEST HEATH
BELVEDERE SPORTS GROUND
CLAM FIELD RECREATION GROUND
GOLDIE LEIGH HOSPITAL
PLUMSTEAD CEMETERY
WOOL. CEM
WOOLWICH CEMETERY
COMMON
EAST WICKHAM
EAST WICKHAM OPEN SPACE
DA16
WICKHAM LANE
UPPER WICKHAM LA
STEVENS PARK
KNEE HILL
A2041
A206
A209
A207
A221
A210
DA7
WELLING
WELLING HIGH STREET
PARK VIEW ROAD
CROOK LOG
BROADWAY
BEXLEYHEATH
BEXLEYHEATH CEMETERY
DANSON PARK
ROCHESTER WAY
ALBION ROAD
ARNSBERG WAY
RUSSELL

97
FB
FC
FD
FE
FF
FG
FH
83
111
RIVER THAMES
ERITH REACH
ERITH RANDS
HAVERING
BEXLEY
WENNINGTON MARSHES
RM13
FREIGHTMASTER ESTATE
Warehouse
Coldharbour Point
Jetty
Pier
Belvedere Power Station (Disused)
Belvedere Industrial Estate
Oil Works
Depots
Silt Lagoons
BELVEDERE
FRANK'S PARK
Bexley College
Erith College of Technology
LESSNESS HEATH
ERITH CEMETERY
EUROPA TRADING ESTATE
ERITH
ERITH & DISTRICT HOSP
ERITH STADIUM
ERITH REC GRD
Landing Stage
Chalk Fm Wf
Railway Pier
The Saltings
DARENT INDUSTRIAL ESTATE
MANFORD IND EST
ANCHOR BAY IND EST
THE CHURCH TRD EST
DA8
NORTHUMBERLAND HEATH
POWER INDUSTRIAL ESTATE
SLADE GREEN
CRAYFORD MARSHES
Howbury Farm
BURSTED WOOD
BARNEHURST
BARNEHURST GOLF COURSE
RECREATION GROUND
DA1
CRAYMILL SQUARE
REFINERY
Perry Street Farm
The Grange
MARTENS GROVE PARK
SPORTS GRD
SHENSTONE PARK
ACORN INDUSTRIAL PARK
BARNES CRAY
CRAYFORD MARSHES
Geoffrey Whitworth Theatre
Adult Education Centre
WATLING STREET
BRONZE AGE WAY
FRASER ROAD
BEXLEY ROAD
NORTHEND ROAD
THAMES ROAD
PERRY STREET
CRAYFORD HIGH ST
LONDON ROAD
A2016
A206
A220
A2000
A207
A223
50
51
52
75
76
77
78
79
80
81
82
84
THURROCK
DARTFORD

BG
BH
BJ
BK
BL
BM
BN
05
06
07
84
112
85
86
87
88
89
90
91
92
93
94
74
73
72
71
Junction 14
AIRPORT WAY
A3113
PERIMETER ROAD
WESSEX
STANWELL MOOR
REC GRD
Hall
PO
HILLINGDON
SOUTHERN PERIMETER ROAD
SPELTHORNE
CARGO TERMINAL
CARGO TERMINAL
SHOREHAM ROAD (WEST)
SHOREHAM ROAD (EAST)
SOUTHAMPTON ROAD
SHORT ROAD
SOLENT ROAD
Works
Garden Centre
Warehouse
HORTON ROAD
HORTON RD
Hithermoor Farm
HAWS LANE
CHELTENHAM VILLAS
Lower Mill Farm
RIVER COLNE
GRAVEL PIT
KING GEORGE VI RESERVOIR
STAINES RESERVOIRS
TW19
MOOR ROAD
A3044
STANWELL MOOR ROAD
STAINES RESERVOIRS AQUEDUCT
PARK ROAD
B378
HIGH STREET
BEDFONT ROAD
COURT FARM INDUSTRIAL ESTATE
BLACKBURN TRADING ESTATE
CAMGATE ESTATE
BROADVIEW ESTATE
Animal Quarantine Sta
Mentone Farm
STANWELL
RECREATION GROUND
SPORTS GRD
SPORTS GRD
Football Ground
Oil Storage Depot
Storage Tanks
SURREY
Homers Farm
REC GRD
CEM
Health Cen
Comm Cen
Lib
Sch
Schs
FALCON DRIVE
HADFIELD ROAD
EVEREST ROAD
CANOPUS WAY
CRANFORD AVE
EXPLORER AVE
CLYDE ROAD
HOLYWELL WAY
KINGSWAY
SCOTTS CLO
VIOLA AVENUE
LONGFORD WAY
Amb Sta
BURIAL GROUND
Superstore
ASHFORD HOSPITAL
Fire Sta
PLAYING FIELDS
LONDON ROAD
A30
STANWELL ROAD
SEATON DR
GORDON ROAD
KENILWORTH ROAD
CUMBERLAND ROAD
New Inn Farm
Hengrove Farm
ASHFORD PARK
REC GROUND
AVONDALE
DORSET ROAD
PORTLAND ROAD
SALCOMBE ROAD
THETFORD ROAD
STATION CRESCENT
SANDRINGHAM DR
QUEENS WALK
TUDOR CLO
WEST CLOSE
WOODTHORPE ROAD
CHURCH ROAD
Clinic
Works
ASHFORD
Sch
Tennis Courts
PLAYING FIELD
Coll
COLLEGE WAY
VILLAGE WAY
PARKLAND GROVE
FELTHAM ROAD
B378
Pol
Hall
ELMSWAY
FONTMELL PARK
FAIRVIEW CT
MANOR ROAD
B377
Clubhouse
ASHFORD MANOR GOLF COURSE
KINGSTON ROAD
A308
STAINES BY-PASS
STAINES RESERVOIRS AQUEDUCT
Electricity Station
GRAVEL PIT
RIVER ASH
TW17
QUEEN MARY
A30
BY PASS
SUBWAY
Pumping Station
Billet Bridge
SUB
Crooked Billet Roundabout
A308 RD
LONDON ROAD
STAINES
Royal Mail
North Thames House
STAINES CENTRAL TRADING EST
ELMSLEIGH CENTRE
HIGH ST
THAMES ST
SOUTH ST
TOWN HALL
BUS STA
Lib
Mkt
STATION PATH
KINGS ROAD
GREENLANDS ROAD
Sports Cen
LEACROFT
GEORGIAN CLO
SHORTWOOD POND
SHORTWOOD COMMON
SUBWAY
ALLOT
CEM
ROMAN WAY
Shortwood Farm
ALLOT
SHORTWOOD COMMON
STAINES ROAD
PRIORY GREEN
MILLBANK
KNOWLE GREEN
Health Cen
MAG CT
COUNTY CT
FAIR CLO
Clinic
KINGSTON ROAD
WORPLE AVENUE
STAINES PARK
MINI RAILWAY
ALLOT
COMMERCIAL ROAD
Works
PLAYING FIELDS
Tennis Courts
TEMPLEDENE AVE
PAVILION GARDENS
NURSERY GDNS
BERRYSCROFT ROAD
ARNOLD ROAD
REC GRD
SHAFTESBURY CRESCENT
FORDBRIDGE PARK
Ford Bridge
FORDBRIDGE ROAD
Bowl Grn
Community Cen
SPORTS GRD
Clubho
Boatho
Youth Cen
Works
Bowl Grn
CARLYLE ROAD
MEADWAY
WHEATSHEAF LANE
Clubhouse
Sweep's Bridge
Football Grd
SPORTS GROUND
Clubho
TW18
REC GRD
Penton Hook Farm
SWEEP'S DITCH
Nursery
Penton Hook Lock
FISHING TEMPLE MOBILE HOME PARK
TEMPLE GARDENS
RIVERSIDE DRIVE
TRUSS'S IS.
CHERTSEY LANE
A320
RUNNYMEDE
SPELTHORNE

99
HATTON
TW6
TW14
TW13
TW15
TW16
HEATHROW TERMINAL 4
EAST BEDFONT
LOWER FELTHAM
FELTHAM
FELTHAMHILL
H.M. YOUNG OFFENDER INSTITUTION AND REMAND CENTRE
ASHFORD INDUSTRIAL ESTATE
LAKESIDE SPORTS GRD
KING GEORGE'S FIELD
FELTHAM ARENAS
GROSVENOR PARK
BEDFONT LANE REC GRD
NORTH FELTHAM TRADING ESTATE
HOUNSLOW HEATH GOLF COURSE
RESERVOIR
KEMPTON PARK (Only Open On Race Days)
RACECOURSE
ASHFORD COMMON WATER TREATMENT WORKS
Junction 1
STAINES ROAD
GREAT SOUTH-WEST ROAD
STAINES ROAD WEST
CHERTSEY ROAD
HARLINGTON ROAD WEST
HARLINGTON ROAD EAST
HOUNSLOW ROAD
HIGH STREET
ASHFORD RD
SUNBURY WAY
COUNTRY WAY
A30
A315
A244
A308
A312
A316
M3
B377
B3003
85
86
87
88
89
90
91
92
93
94
100
113
BP
BQ
BR
BS
BT
BU
BV
08
09
10
71
72
73
74

BW
BX
BY
BZ
CA
CB
CC
12
13
14
86
85
87
88
89
90
91
92
93
94
99
114
74
73
72
71
TW3
TW4
TW14
TW13
TW12
TW16
HOUNSLOW
HEATH
HOUNSLOW HEATH GOLF COURSE
WHITTON
FELTHAM
HANWORTH PARK
HANWORTH
CRANE PARK
TWICKENHAM CEMETERY
TWICKENHAM GOLF COURSE
FULWELL PARK
FULWELL GOLF COURSE
KEMPTON PARK
RACECOURSE
HAMPTON
RESERVOIR
BOROUGH CEMETERY
HEATHFIELD REC GRD
RECTORY MEADOW
STAINES RESERVOIRS AQUEDUCT
HALF MOON COVERT
HYDES FIELD
CARLISLE PARK
SPORTS GROUND
PLAYING FIELDS
UXBRIDGE ROAD
STAINES ROAD
HANWORTH ROAD
HARLINGTON ROAD WEST
HARLINGTON ROAD EAST
HOUNSLOW ROAD
GREAT CHERTSEY RD
HAMPTON ROAD WEST
SWIFT WAY
COUNTRY WAY
UPPER SUNBURY ROAD
HIGH STREET
CHURCH ST
NELSON ROAD
HOSPITAL BRIDGE ROAD
PARK ROAD
FELTHAMBROOK
TWICKENHAM RD
Leisure West
Police Training Centre
APEX RETAIL PARK
HANWORTH TRADING ESTATE
KINGSWAY BUSINESS PARK
Grandstands
Garden Centre
Clubhouse

CD
CE
CF
CG
CH
CJ
CK
15
16
17
87
TW9
OLD DEER PARK
REC GRD
MOGDEN WATER TREATMENT WORKS
TW6
Queen's Bridge
IVYBRIDGE ESTATE
ST. MARGARETS
TWICKENHAM TRADING ESTATE
THE RUGBY FOOTBALL UNION TWICKENHAM
Royal Military School of Music
SPORTS GRD
PLAYING FIELD
RICHMOND GREEN
RICHMOND
CORP ISLAND
LIB & MUS
85
86
87
88
89
90
91
92
93
94
102
115
74
73
72
71
MARBLE HILL
MARBLE HILL HOUSE
TW1
PARK
PETERSHAM MEADOWS
GLOVER'S ISLAND
MEADOWBANK CLUB
RICHMOND UPON THAMES COLLEGE
HARLEQUINS FC (RUGBY)
KNELLER GDNS
TW2
ALLOT
EEL PIE ISLAND
ORLEANS HOUSE GALLERY
YORK HOUSE
HAM HOUSE NT
HAM HOUSE GARDENS NT
POLO GROUND
The German School
KING GEORGE'S FIELD
HAM PLAYING FIELD
TWICKENHAM
THE COPSE
SANDY LANE EST
TW10
HAM
ST. MICHAEL'S CONVENT
RICHMOND GOLF COURSE
SUDBROOK
PETERSHAM
HAM COMMON
STRAWBERRY HILL
STRAWBERRY HILL GOLF COURSE
St. Mary's Training College
Thames Young Mariners Base
TEDDINGTON CEM
THE CASSEL HOSPITAL
Teddington Lock
Teddington Weir
Thames TV Studios
The Lensbury Club
SHELL SPORTS GRD
TROWLOCK ISLAND
KT2
TEDDINGTON
NATIONAL PHYSICAL LABORATORY
BUSHY HOUSE
NORMANSFIELD HOSPITAL (closed)
BROOM ROAD REC GRD
STEVEN'S EYOT
Kingston Canoe & Sailing Cen
Ariel Sailing Centre
TW11
BUSHY PARK
HAMPTON HILL
HAMPTON WICK
Kingston College of F E
CANAL PLANTATION
ROUND PLANTATION
LEG OF MUTTON POND
HERON POND
OVAL PLANTATION
WOODLAND GARDEN
WATERHOUSE POND
Open during daylight hours only

102
CL
CM
CN
CP
CQ
CR
CS
88
19
20
21
NORTH SHEEN
UPPER RICHMOND ROAD
EAST SHEEN
EAST SHEEN COMMON NT
EAST SHEEN CEMETERY
RICHMOND CEMETERY
PESTHOUSE COMMON
SW14
Sports Centre
BANK OF ENGLAND SPORTS GRD
PALEWELL COMMON
PALEWELL PARK PLAYING FLDS
SHEEN WOOD
Teck Plantation
Bog Gate
The Bog
ADAM'S POND
East Sheen Gate
Roehampton Gate
Tennis & Squash Club
PLAYING FIELD
RICHMOND
RICHMOND GREEN
85
86
87
88
89
90
91
92
93
94
74
73
72
71
101
TW1
TW10
KT12
POPPY FACTORY MUS
TERRACE GDNS
TERRACE FLD
Richmond College
Richmond Hill Hotel
Richmond Gate
Royal Star & Garter Home
PETERSHAM COMN
PETERSHAM MEADOWS
GLOVER'S ISLAND
PETERSHAM
PETERSHAM PARK
KING HENRY VIII MOUND
Cambrian Gate
BISHOP'S POND
CONDUIT WOOD
SHEEN CROSS WOOD
POLO FIELD
BARN WOOD POND
SAW PIT PLANTATION
JUBILEE PLANTATION
DUCHESS WOOD
WHITE LODGE PLANTATION
White Lodge (The Royal Ballet School)
KIDNEY WOOD
SIDMOUTH WOOD
RICHMOND
DEER PARK
QUEEN ELIZABETH'S PLANTATION
LEG OF MUTTON POND
PEN PONDS
KING GEORGE V PLANTATION
LAWN PLANTATION
TREEBOX WOOD
SPANKER'S HILL WOOD
POND PLANTATION
CYCLE PATH
Pond Slade
Tercentenary Plantation
MARTIN'S POND
Stag Lodge Stables
Robin Hood Gate
PARK
PRINCE CHARLES'S SPINNEY
GIBBET WOOD
HAM CROSS PLANTATION
ISABELLA PLANTATION
PEG'S POND
THOMSON'S POND
Broomfield Hill
BROOMFIELD HILL PLANTATION
HIGH WOOD
STILL POND
Deer Fold
Ham Bottom
Ham Cross
Ham Dip
Ham Gate
HAM GATE AVENUE
HAM COMMON
Parkgate House
RICHMOND GOLF COURSE
The Wilderness
SUDBROOK PARK
Ormeley Lodge
SPORTS GRD
Ham Polo Club
POLO GROUND
German School
THE COPSE
SANDY LANE EST
HAM
CORONATION PLANTATION
The Flat
Thatchedhouse Lodge
DANN'S POND
GALLOW'S POND
Kings Clump
Dark Hill
Ladderstile Gate
Kingston Gate
KINGSTON VALE
ROBIN HOOD WAY
Kingston University
Coombehurst
COOMBE HILL GOLF COURSE
THE WATERGARDENS
COOMBE WOOD GOLF COURSE
COOMBE
KINGSTON PARK ESTATE
The Kingston Riding Centre
REMAND CENTRE
Barnfield Riding School
Kingston Canoe & Sailing Cen
Ariel Sailing Centre
BROOM ROAD REC GRD
STEVEN'S FYOT
TROWLOCK ISLAND
CANBURY GARDENS
116
KINGSTON HOSP
Telephone Exchange
A238
NEW VICTORIA HOSP

103
CT
CU
CV
CW
CX
CY
CZ
22
23
24
89
85
86
87
88
89
90
91
92
93
94
104
117
74
73
72
71
WANDSWORTH
PRIORY HOSPITAL
ROEHAMPTON GOLF COURSE
ROEHAMPTON
Roehampton Institute of Higher Ed
Froebel Institute
QUEEN MARY'S UNI HOSP
ROEHAMPTON PLAYING FIELDS
Uni of Greenwich
MARYFIELD CONVENT
RICHMOND PARK (PUBLIC)
GOLF COURSE
Kingsfarm Plantation
Chohole Gate
Silver Hill
PUTNEY
SW15
South Thames Coll
EAST PUTNEY
COUNTY CT
PUTNEY HEATH
Tibbet's Corner
KING'S MERE
SCIO POND
Jerry's Hill
PUTNEY VALE CEMETERY
PUTNEY VALE
PUTNEY VALE PLAYING FIELDS
ROYAL HOSPITAL
Whitelands Training College
SW18
SOUTHFIELDS
WIMBLEDON PARK EST
Southlands College
Roehampton Institute of Adult Ed
QUEEN'S MERE
WIMBLEDON WINDMILL MUSEUM
PARKSIDE HOSPITAL
WIMBLEDON PARK
ATHLETICS TRACK
GOLF COURSE
ALL ENGLAND LAWN TENNIS & CROQUET CLUB
SW19
Indoor Tennis Cts
KING GEORGE'S PARK
Silent Pools
Stag Bog
LONDON
WIMBLEDON
Queen's Butt (Site of)
Gravelly Hill
HOOKHAMSLADE POND
BLUEGATE GRAVEL PIT (DISUSED)
SCOTTISH
White Cottage
Thatched Cottage
Springwell Cottage
COMMON
GOLF COURSE
Farm Bog
Farm Ravine
Caesar's Camp
Warren Farm
NATURE RESERVE
Mill Corner
ROYAL WIMBLEDON GOLF COURSE
Shadwell Wood
RUSHMERE POND
CANNIZARO PARK
Cannizaro House (Hotel)
LADY JANE'S WOOD
MUSEUM OF LOCAL HISTORY
HIGH ST WIMBLEDON
WIMBLEDON
WIMBLEDON HILL
King's College School
WOLFSON MED. REHAB CENTRE
ATKINSON MORLEY'S HOSP
COPSE HILL
OBERON PLAYING FIELD
HOLLAND GDNS
COTTENHAM PARK
SW20
DUNDONALD REC GRD
PLAYING FIELD
WIMBLEDON CEMETERY
SOUTH PARK GDNS
THE BROADWAY
SOUTH WIMBLEDON
MERTON PARK
MERTON PLAYING FIELDS
SPORTS GRD
KINGSTON ROAD
ROEHAMPTON LANE
PUTNEY HILL
UPPER RICHMOND ROAD
WEST HILL
WIMBLEDON PARK SIDE
PARKSIDE
DURNSFORD ROAD
A3
A205
A219
A306
A3209
A218

104
DA
DB
DC
DD
DE
DF
DG
26
27
28
90
85
86
87
88
89
73
74
72
71
103
91
92
93
94
118
WANDSWORTH
WANDSWORTH HIGH ST
ST. JOHN'S HEALTH CARE UNIT
SPENCER PARK
PLAYING FIELDS
WANDSWORTH COMMON
BOLINGBROKE HOSP
SW18
SW11
SW17
SW19
CR4
Arndale Shopping Centre
KING GEORGE'S PARK
SPORTS GROUND
H.M. PRISON WANDSWORTH
WANDSWORTH CEMETERY
EARLSFIELD
SOUTHFIELDS
BALHAM
Whitelands Training College
WIMBLEDON PARK
ATHLETICS TRACK
CENTRAL LONDON GOLF CENTRE
SPRINGFIELD UNIVERSITY HOSPITAL
GARRATT GREEN
TOOTING BEC
UPPER TOOTING
STREATHAM CEMETERY
SUMMERSTOWN
Wimbledon Stadium
WIMBLEDON CEMETERY
LAMBETH CEMETERY
ST. GEORGE'S HOSPITAL
TOOTING BROADWAY
TOOTING GRAVENEY
WIMBLEDON
SOUTH WIMBLEDON
COLLIER'S WOOD
WANDLE PARK
GREENLEA TRADING PARK
LONDON ROAD CEMETERY
FIGGE'S MARSH
DUNDONALD REC GRD
MERTON ABBEY REC GRD
MERTON HIGH STREET
MERANTUN WAY

105
DH
DJ
DK
DL
DM
DN
DP
29
30
31
91
85
86
87
88
89
90
91
92
93
94
106
119
74
73
72
71
CLAPHAM COMMON
SW4
CLAPHAM PARK
SW2
TULSE HILL ESTATE
BROCKWELL PARK
HERNE HILL
SE24
SE21
TULSE HILL
STREATHAM HILL
TOOTING BEC COMMON
TOOTING GRAVENEY COMMON
STREATHAM
STREATHAM PARK
SE27
WEST NORWOOD
WEST NORWOOD CEMETERY
STREATHAM COMMON
SW16
NORWOOD GROVE RECREATION GROUND
NORWOOD NEW TOWN
SE19
STREATHAM VALE
NORBURY PARK
NORBURY
BIGGIN WOOD
H.M. PRISON BRIXTON
SACKVILLE ESTATE
PALACE ROAD EST
ST. MARTINS EST
YORK HILL EST
PEABODY ESTATE
ST. MICHAEL'S CONVENT
THE ROOKERY
NATIONAL WESTMINSTER BANK SPORTS GROUND
BRIXTON HILL
STREATHAM HILL
STREATHAM HIGH ROAD
CHRISTCHURCH ROAD (SOUTH CIRCULAR ROAD)
POYNDERS ROAD
ATKINS ROAD
TOOTING BEC ROAD
STREATHAM COMMON NORTH
CROWN LANE
BEULAH HILL
NORWOOD ROAD
KNIGHTS HILL
DULWICH ROAD
TULSE HILL
THURLOW PARK ROAD
HALF MOON LANE
ACRE LANE
CLAPHAM PARK ROAD
SOUTH SIDE
BALHAM HILL
CAVENDISH ROAD
MITCHAM ROAD
LONDON ROAD
CROXTED ROAD
COLDHARBOUR LANE

106
DQ
DR
DS
DT
DU
DV
DW
33
34
35
92
85
86
87
88
89
90
91
92
93
94
105
120
74
73
72
71
SE24
SE15
SE22
SE21
SE27
SE26
SE19
SE20
HERNE HILL
EAST DULWICH
DULWICH
DULWICH PARK
TULSE HILL
WEST DULWICH
WEST NORWOOD
WEST NORWOOD CEMETERY
UPPER SYDENHAM
SYDENHAM
NORWOOD
NORWOOD NEW TOWN
UPPER NORWOOD
PENGE
CRYSTAL PALACE PARK
BROCKWELL PARK
PECKHAM RYE COMMON
PECKHAM RYE PARK
CAMBERWELL OLD CEMETERY
DULWICH & SYDENHAM HILL GOLF COURSE
SYDENHAM HILL WOOD (NATURE RESERVE)
DULWICH WOOD
NORWOOD PARK
HORNIMAN GDNS
DULWICH COMMON
HALF MOON LANE
LORDSHIP LANE
CROXTED ROAD
THURLOW PARK ROAD
KNIGHTS HILL
BEULAH HILL
WESTOW HILL
ANERLEY HILL
CRYSTAL PALACE PARADE
CRYSTAL PALACE PARK ROAD
CROWN DALE
CENTRAL HILL
DULWICH WOOD PARK
SYDENHAM HILL
LONDON ROAD
DARTMOUTH ROAD
KIRKDALE
WESTWOOD HILL
COLLEGE ROAD
EAST DULWICH GROVE
SOUTH BANK UNIVERSITY SPORTS GROUND
DULWICH PICTURE GALL
Dulwich College
CRYSTAL PALACE ATHLETICS STADIUM
CRYSTAL PALACE MUSEUM
STAMBOURNE WOODLAND

107
DX
DY
DZ
EA
EB
EC
ED
36
37
38
SE4
HILLY FIELDS
BROCKLEY
BROCKLEY CEMETERY
LADYWELL CEMETERY
LADYWELL
LEWISHAM HOSPITAL
MANOR PARK
MANOR HOUSE GARDENS
HONOR OAK SPORTS GROUND
CAMBERWELL NEW CEMETERY
SE13
HITHER GREEN
LEWISHAM PARK
HONOR OAK PARK
CATFORD GREYHOUND STADIUM
LADYWELL FIELDS
BLYTHE HILL FIELDS
BROCKLEY HILL PARK
SE23
MOUNTSFIELD PARK REC GRD
LEWISHAM TOWN HALL
CATFORD
BROWNHILL ROAD A205 (SOUTH CIRCULAR)
STANSTEAD ROAD A205 (SOUTH CIRCULAR ROAD)
PRIVATE BANKS SPORTS GROUND
FOREST HILL
SE6
BROMLEY ROAD
BELL GREEN
BELLINGHAM
FORSTER MEMORIAL PARK
MAYOW PARK
LOWER SYDENHAM
SOUTHEND
SOUTHEND LANE A2218
SOUTHEND PARK
HOME PARK
SYDENHAM
BR1
ALEXANDRA RECREATION GROUND
NEW BECKENHAM
BECKENHAM PLACE PARK
PUBLIC GOLF COURSE
ASH PLANTATION
LEWISHAM BOROUGH SPORTS GRD
SUMMERHOUSE HILL WOOD
MIDLAND BANK SPORTS GROUND
WARREN AVE PLAYING FIELDS
CATOR PARK
BR3
RAVENSBOURNE
NEW BECKENHAM
BR2
SHORTLANDS GOLF COURSE
BROMLEY PARK
BECKENHAM
THE SLOANE HOSPITAL
93
85
86
87
88
89
90
91
92
94
108
121
71
72
73
74

108
EE
EF
EG
EH
EJ
EK
EL
40
41
42
94
85
86
87
88
89
90
91
92
93
107
122
74
73
72
71
HIGH ROAD
ELTHAM ROAD
SIDCUP ROAD
WESTHORNE AVENUE
ELTHAM HILL
SIDCUP ROAD
A20
A210
A205
A2212
A213
A21
BURNT ASH ROAD
BURNT ASH HILL
BARING ROAD
BURNT ASH LANE
ST. MILDREDS ROAD
A205 (SOUTH CIRCULAR ROAD)
BROMLEY ROAD
BROMLEY HILL
LONDON ROAD
KIDBROOKE PARK ROAD
SE13
SE12
SE6
BR1
HITHER GREEN
LEE
GROVE PARK
MOTTINGHAM
ELTHAM
DOWNHAM
PLAISTOW
SUNDRIDGE
ELMSTEAD
MANOR PARK
MANOR HOUSE GARDENS
SUTCLIFFE PARK
OLD COLFEIAN'S SPORTS GROUND
MIDDLE PARK FIELD
QUEENSCROFT REC GROUND
UNIVERSITY OF GREENWICH SPORTS GRD
CIVIL SERVICE SPORTS GROUND
ELTHAM PALACE
KING JOHN PLAYING FIELDS
NORTHBROOK PARK
HITHER GREEN CEMETERY
Crematorium
UNIVERSITY OF WESTMINSTER SPORTS GROUND
CETYMA SPORTS GRD
MOTTINGHAM SPORTS GROUND
CHINBROOK MEADOWS
LOWER MARVELS WOOD
MARVELS WOOD
GROVE PARK CEMETERY
ELMSTEAD WOOD
SUNDRIDGE PARK GOLF COURSE
Sundridge Park Management Centre
ROCKPIT WOOD
LOGSHILL WOOD
DOWNHAM FIELDS
DOWNHAM PLAYING FIELDS
SHAFTESBURY PARK REC GRD
KING'S MEADOW PLAYING FIELDS
MIDLAND BANK SPORTS GROUND
WARREN AVE PLAYING FIELDS
SHORTLANDS GOLF COURSE
BROMLEY PARK
THE SLOANE HOSPITAL
CHILTONIAN IND. ESTATE
Sports Centre
MacIntyre Mottingham Garden Cen
Mottingham Farm
Eltham Coll Jun Sch
Eltham College
QUAGGY RIVER

EM
EN
EP
EQ
ER
ES
ET
43
44
45
95
85
86
87
88
89
90
91
92
93
94
110
123
74
73
72
71
SE9
DA16
DA15
DA14
BR7
ELTHAM PARK SOUTH
ELTHAM WARREN GOLF COURSE
ELTHAM CEMETERY
Crematorium
ROCHESTER WAY RELIEF ROAD
AVERY HILL
AVERY HILL PARK
University of Greenwich Avery Hill Campus
CAMBRIDGE MISSION SPORTS GROUND
CHARLTON ATHLETIC FC TRAIN. GROUND
MILLWALL TRAINING GRD
FOOTSCRAY PLAYING FIELDS
ROYAL BLACKHEATH GOLF COURSE
BIRD SANCTUARY
THE TARN
FAIRY HILL REC GRD
NEW ELTHAM
BLACKFEN
HOLLY OAK WOOD PARK
WILLERSLEY PARK
MARLBOROUGH PARK
LAMORBEY
OLD FARM PARK
KING GEORGE'S REC GROUND
LONGLANDS
JACK NICKLAUS GOLF CEN.
LONGLANDS REC GRL
SIDCUP
BELMONT LANE OPEN SPACE
DOG RACING TRACK
CHISLEHURST CEMETERY
OLD ELTHAMIANS SPORTS GRD
CHISLEHURST WEST
WHYTE'S WOODLAND REC GRD
CHISLEHURST
CAMDEN PARK
CHISLEHURST GOLF COURSE
CHISLEHURST COMMON
SCADBURY PARK NATURE RESERVE
PARK WOOD
QUEEN MARY'S HOSP
BLACKFEN ROAD
BEXLEY ROAD
SIDCUP ROAD
SIDCUP BY PASS
FOOTSCRAY ROAD
HALFWAY STREET
MAIN ROAD
PERRY STREET
FROGNAL AVENUE
BROMLEY LANE
WHITE HORSE HILL
RED HILL
ELTHAM HIGH ST
COURT ROAD
A2
A20
A208
A210
A211
A222
B2214

110
EU
EV
EW
EX
EY
EZ
FA
BEXLEY
DANSON
96
DA16
PARK
THE LAKE
The Boathouse Function Suite
BEXLEYHEATH
BROADWAY
ROCHESTER WAY
BLACKFEN ROAD
BLACKFEN
BEXLEYHEATH GOLF COURSE
PENHILL PARK
BEXLEY PARK WOOD
RIVERSIDE WALK
SIDCUP GOLF COURSE
MARLBOROUGH PARK
Rose Bruford College
LAMORBEY PARK
MORBEY
DA15
HURST ROAD
ALBANY PARK
SIDCUP CEM
KING GEORGE'S REC GROUND
109
SIDCUP
Sidcup Arts Cen
WARING PARK
STATION ROAD
SIDCUP HIGH ST
THE GREEN
SIDCUP PLACE
QUEEN MARY'S HOSP
NORTH CRAY
NORTH CRAY WOOD
FOOTS CRAY MEADOWS
STABLE MEADOW
Five Arch Bridge
GATTONS PLANTATION
GATTONS WOOD
DA14
FOOTS CRAY
DAVID LLOYD CLUB
SIDCUP TECHNOLOGY CENTRE
MAIDSTONE ROAD
NORTH CRAY ROAD
RUXLEY CORNER INDUSTRIAL ESTATE
RUXLEY WOOD
CHALK WOOD
SCADBURY PARK NATURE RESERVE
LITTLE WOOD
SIDCUP BYPASS
EDGINGTON WAY
SEVENOAKS
BR5
124
RUXLEY PARK GOLF COURSE
DRIVING RANGE
A20
A222
A223
A211
A2
85
86
87
88
89
90
91
92
93
94
71
72
73
74
47
48
49

111
FB
FC
FD
FE
FF
FG
FH
50
51
52
97
CRAYFORD
CRAYFORD MARSHES
DA1
ACORN INDUSTRIAL PARK
SPORTS GRD
SHENSTONE PARK
MARTENS GROVE
GROVE PARK
WATLING STREET
LONDON ROAD
A207
CRAYFORD HIGH ST
CRAYFORD WAY
ROMAN WAY
RIVER CRAY
STANHAM RIVER
DA6
BOURNE ROAD
BOURNE MEAD
A223
CRAYFORD STADIUM
RECREATION GROUND
HALL PLACE
HALL PLACE GARDENS
RUGBY GRD
ST. MARY'S REC GRD
OLD BEXLEY
DARTFORD ROAD
A226
85
86
87
88
89
90
91
92
93
94
74
73
72
71
North West Kent College of Technology
PLAYING FIELDS
QUARRY
ROCHESTER WAY
CHURCHFIELD WOOD
THE OLD ORCHARD
DARTFORD HEATH
SHEPHERDS LANE
OLD BEXLEY LANE
PRINCES ROAD
DARTFORD GOLF COURSE
BRICKHILL WOOD
University of Greenwich
DA5
NATURE AREA
VICARAGE ROAD
A2018
COLDBLOW
BEXLEY HOSPITAL
Broomhills
Clubhouse
ALLOT
JOYDEN'S WOOD
JOYDENS WOOD
Hook Green
HOOK GREEN LANE
DA2
ROWHILL WOOD
Rowhill Grange
DARTFORD
SEVENOAKS
BR8
Cricket Ground
Swanley Bottom
THE BIRCHWOOD PARK GOLF COURSE
Stonehill Woods Caravan Park
BIRCHWOOD ROAD
PUDDLEDOCK LANE
HEXTABLE
RECREATION GROUND
COLLEGE ROAD
TOURIST RAILWAY
125
Swanley Village

QUEEN MARY RESERVOIR
TW18
LALEHAM
KT16
KT15
CHERTSEY
CHERTSEY MEADS
ADDLESTONE MOOR
WEYBRIDGE
Penton Hook Island
Laleham Golf Course
Laleham Burway
Laleham Park
Abbey Lake
Fleet Lake
Penton Park Caravan Park
Penton Park Estate
Yacht Basin
Penton Hook Marina
Penton Hook Lock
Sweep's Bridge
Sports Ground
Round Copse
Gas Pipeline Station
Pumping Station
Gravel Pit
Lee International Studios, Shepperton
Laleham Abbey
Water Works
Reservoir
Chertsey Lock
Chertsey Bridge Road
Recreation Ground
Dumsey Eyot
Dockett Eddy
Dockett Point
Pharaoh's Island
Hamhaugh Island
Hamhaugh Point
Lock Island
Shepperton Lock
Charlton Quarry
Squires Bridge
Abbey Bridge
Abbey River
Abbey Chase House
Earthworks
Chertsey Mus
Cricket Ground
Gogmore Park
Woburn Park
St. George's College
Meadowlands Park
Abbey Moor Golf Course
Addlestone Cemetery
Fordwater Trading Est
Fordwater Bridge
Woburn Hill
Weybridge Road
Addlestone
Victory Park
Weybridge Business Park
Black Boy Bridge
Weybridge Lock
The Bull Dogs
Hamm Court Farm
Simplemarsh Farm
Junction 11
M3
M25
A320
A317
A318
B375
B376
B377
Staines Road
Chertsey Lane
Ashford Road
Shepperton Road
Laleham Road
Guildford Road
Eastworth Road
Woburn Way
Chertsey Road
High Street
St. Peter's Way
River Thames
Spelthorne
Runnymede
05
06
07
BG
BH
BJ
BK
BL
BM
BN
95
96
97
98
99
100
101
102
103
104
69
68
67
66
126

113
BP
BQ
BR
BS
BT
BU
BV
08
09
10
A308
99
Junction 1
ASHFORD COMMON
WATER TREATMENT
WORKS
95
RACECOURSE
PARK
96
97
98
99
100
101
102
103
104
114
127
LITTLETON
TW17
TW16
SUNBURY
KT12
KT13
M3
UPPER
HALLIFORD
SUNBURY
GOLF
COURSE
HAZELWOOD
GOLF COURSE
SUNBURY CEMETERY
GAFLAC SPORTS GRD
RUGBY GROUND LONDON IRISH RUFC
CEDARS REC GRD
SHEPPERTON
SHEPPERTON BUSINESS PARK
DESBOROUGH ISLAND
THAMES MEADOW
SHEPPERTON MARINA
BISHOP DUPPA'S REC GRD
WALTON BRIDGE RD
A244
A3050
B375
B376
B3366
WALTON-ON-THAMES
ASHLEY PARK
BROAD WATER
Oatlands Park Hotel
OATLANDS PARK
GRAVEL PIT
APPS COURT GREEN
WATER TREATMENT WORKS
Gas Works
Oil Terminal
Sports Centre
Shepperton Moat House
ELM GROVE REC GRD
NEW ZEALAND AVENUE
HEPWORTH WAY
BRIDGE STREET
HERSHAM ROAD
QUEENS ROAD
A317
RYDE
68
67
66
69
PLAYING FIELD

114
BW
BX
BY
BZ
CA
CB
CC
12
13
14
HAMPTON
RACECOURSE
PARK
TW16
SUNBURY
TW12
MOLESEY RESERVOIRS
BESSBOROUGH RESERVOIR
KNIGHTS RESERVOIR
QUEEN ELIZABETH II RESERVOIR
ISLAND BARN RESERVOIR
WEST MOLESEY
KT12
KT10
RIVER THAMES
RIVER EMBER
RIVER MOLE
STAIN HILL RESERVOIRS
KENTON COURT MEADOW
LOWER GREEN
SANDOWN PARK GOLF COURSE
RYDENS
HERSHAM
HERSHAM TRADING ESTATE
SANDOWN INDUSTRIAL PARK
ESHER
113
128
100
95
96
97
98
99
101
102
103
104

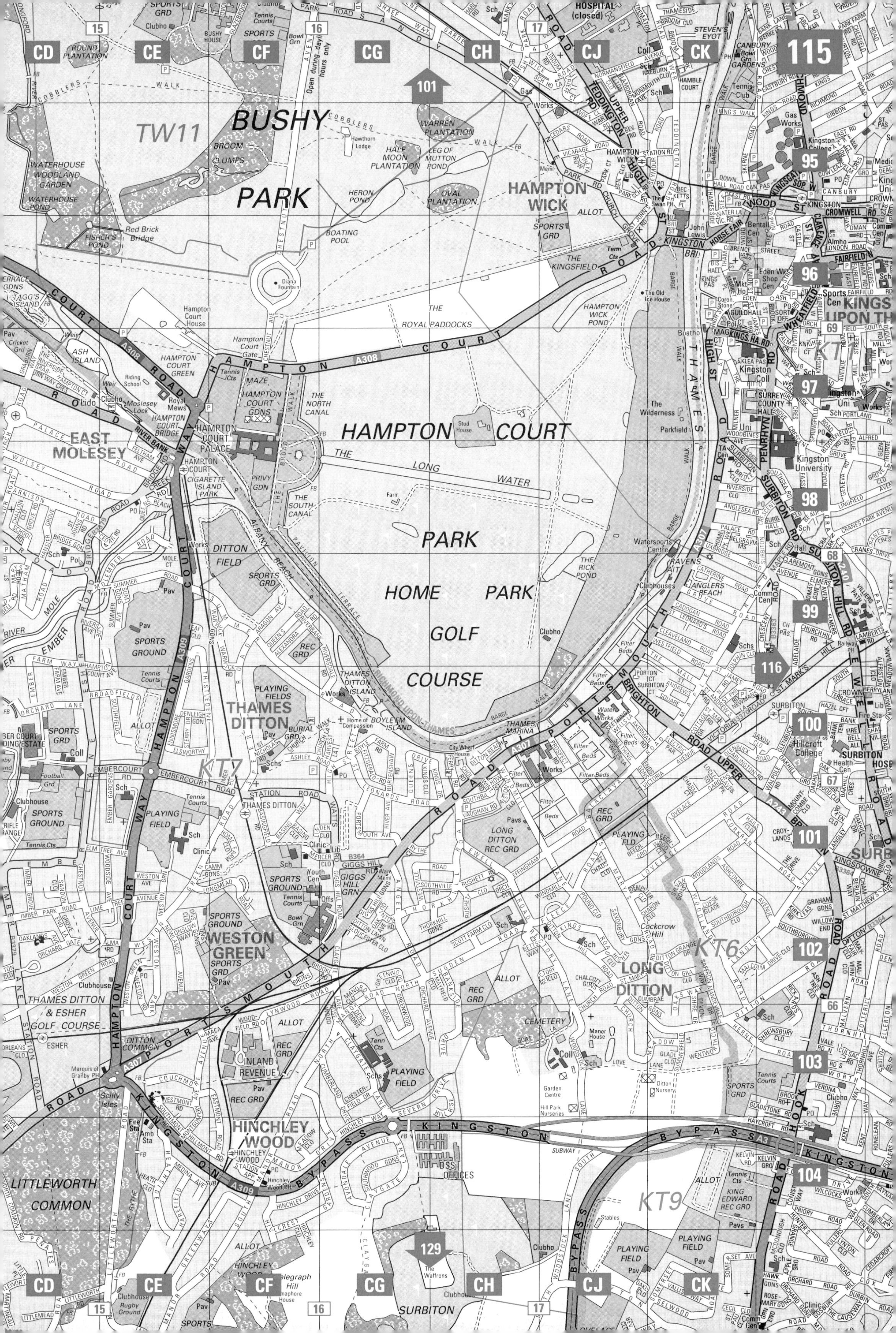
CD
CE
CF
CG
CH
CJ
CK
15
16
17
101
BUSHY
PARK
TW11
WATERHOUSE WOODLAND GARDEN
ROUND PLANTATION
BROOM CLUMPS
WARREN PLANTATION
HALF MOON PLANTATION
LEG OF MUTTON POND
HERON POND
OVAL PLANTATION
BOATING POOL
FISHER'S POND
Red Brick Bridge
Diana Fountain
HAMPTON WICK
HAMPTON WICK POND
THE KINGSFIELD
THE ROYAL PADDOCKS
HAMPTON COURT
A308
HAMPTON COURT GREEN
HAMPTON COURT GDNS
HAMPTON COURT PALACE
MAZE
PRIVY GDN
THE NORTH CANAL
THE SOUTH CANAL
THE LONG WATER
HAMPTON COURT
PARK
HOME PARK GOLF COURSE
THE RICK POND
The Wilderness
Parkfield
RIVER THAMES
ASH ISLAND
TAGG'S ISLAND
EAST MOLESEY
DITTON FIELD
SPORTS GROUND
THAMES DITTON
THAMES DITTON ISLAND
BOYLE FARM ISLAND
THAMES MARINA
RAVENS AIT
ANGLERS REACH
KINGSTON UPON THAMES
KT1
Kingston Coll
Kingston University
SURREY COUNTY HALL
95
96
97
98
99
100
101
102
103
104
116
69
68
67
66
KT7
KT6
KT9
A309
A307
A3
LONG DITTON
LONG DITTON REC GRD
WESTON GREEN
GIGGS HILL GRN
CEMETERY
THAMES DITTON & ESHER GOLF COURSE
ESHER
DITTON COMMON
INLAND REVENUE
HINCHLEY WOOD
KINGSTON BYPASS
LITTLEWORTH COMMON
DSS OFFICES
KING EDWARD REC GRD
PLAYING FIELD
SURBITON
129
Telegraph Hill
The Waffrons
CD
CE
CF
CG
CH
CJ
CK
15
16
17

116
CL
CM
CN
CP
CQ
CR
CS
19
20
21
102
COOMBE
COOMBE WOOD GOLF COURSE
KINGSTON HOSPITAL
KT2
NEW VICTORIA HOSPITAL
95
96
97
98
99
100
101
102
103
104
115
130
69
68
67
66
KINGSTON UPON THAMES
KT1
NORBITON
KINGSTON CEMETERY
Sewage Works
SURBITON CEMETERY
Kingston Uni Halls of Residence
Kingston University
SURREY COUNTY HALL
The Wilderness
Parkfield
RIVER THAMES
KT3
NEW MALDEN
PLAYING FIELD
KINGSTON ROAD REC GRD
GREEN LANE REC GROUND
SPORTS GROUND
BERRYLANDS
HOGSMILL OPEN SPACE
KT5
SURBITON
SURBITON HOSP
Hillcroft College
FISHPONDS OPEN SPACE
ALLOTMENTS
ALEXANDRA REC GRD
KT6
TOLWORTH
TOLWORTH HOSP
KINGSTON BYPASS
OLD MALDEN
MAORI SPORTS GROUND
RIVERHILL SPORTS GRD
ATHLETICS GROUND
KING GEORGE'S FIELD
KING GEORGE'S TRADING ESTATE
HOOK RISE BUS CEN
KT9
Tolworth Ct Bridge
KING EDWARD REC GRD
SURREY
A307
A308
A238
A240
A243
A3
B3363
B3364
B3370
B284

117
CT
CU
CV
CW
CX
CY
CZ
22
23
24
103
95
96
97
98
99
118
100
101
102
103
104
131
69
68
67
66
WOLFSON MED. REHAB. CENTRE
ATKINSON MORLEY'S HOSP
COPSE HILL
OBERON PLAYING FIELD
ALLOTMENTS
COTTENHAM PK REC GRD
HOLLAND GDNS
COTTENHAM PARK
PLAYING FIELDS
SPORTS GROUND
SW20
SW19
DUNDONALD REC GRD
NELSON HOSP
WIMBLEDON CHASE
JOHN INNES REC GRD
MERTON PARK
MALDEN
GOLF COURSE
RAYNES PARK SPORTS GRD
RAYNES PARK
PRINCE GEORGE'S PLAYING FIELD
The David Lloyd Club
BUSHEY MEAD
MESSINES PLAYING FLD
JOSEPH HOOD RECREATION GROUND
SOUTH MERTON
MOSTYN GARDENS
MORDEN
BEVERLEY PARK
KINGSTON UPON THAMES
MERTON
CANNON HILL COMMON
WEST BARNES
CHERRY WOOD
SM4
MORDEN PLAYING FIELDS
RAYNES PARK PLAYING FIELDS
MOTSPUR PARK
UNIVERSITY OF LONDON ATHLETICS GROUND
THE SIR JOSEPH HOOD MEMORIAL PLAYING FIELDS
BBC SPORTS GROUND
MORDEN CEMETERY
Crematorium
MERTON & SUTTON JOINT CEMETERY
MORDEN PARK
MORDEN PARK SPORTS GROUND
Merton College
Swimming Pool
MANOR PARK REC GRD
PLAYING FIELDS
KING GEORGE'S FIELD
Sewage Works
PUBLIC RUBBISH TIP
GARTH ROAD IND EST
KT4
REC GRD WORCESTER PARK
ST. ANTHONY'S HOSP
REIGATE AVENUE REC GRD
SUTTON CEMETERY
KIMPTON INDUSTRIAL ESTATE
WORCESTER PARK
SM3
NORTH CHEAM
CUDDINGTON RECREATION GROUND
COLLINGWOOD PARK
EPSOM & EWELL
SUTTON
A3
A238
A298
A24
A2043
B282
B286
B279
KINGSTON BY PASS
BEVERLEY WAY
KINGSTON ROAD
BUSHEY ROAD
CENTRAL ROAD
MALDEN ROAD
LONDON ROAD
STONECOT HILL
EPSOM ROAD
CHEAM COMMON ROAD
ST. DUNSTAN'S HILL
LOWER MORDEN LANE

DA
DB
DC
DD
DE
DF
DG
SOUTH WIMBLEDON
COLLIER'S WOOD
MERTON HIGH STREET
104
LONDON ROAD CEMETERY
FIGGE'S MARSH
STREATHAM
95
MERTON
NELSON TRADING ESTATE
MERTON INDUSTRIAL PARK
ABBEY REC GRD
PLAYING FIELDS
MERANTUN WAY
WESTERN ROAD
NELSON HOSP
96
MERTON PARK
LOMBARD BUSINESS PARK
ROCK TERRACE REC GRD
GREENLEA TRADING PARK
MORDEN HALL PARK
97
MORDEN
MOSTYN GARDENS
PHIPPS BRIDGE
BURIAL GROUND
MITCHAM
CR4
98
MORDEN HALL ROAD
SPORTS CEN
RAVENSBURY PARK
MADEIRA RD
CRANMER ROAD
CARSHALTON ROAD
SPORTS GROUND
MORDEN SOUTH
MORDEN PLAYING FIELDS
99
BROOKMEADS
WATERMEADS
GROVE FARM IND EST
MITCHAM JUNCTION
117
MORDEN PARK SPORTS GROUND
MORDEN REC GROUND
POULTER PARK
WILLOW LANE IND EST
JOHN DEED IND EST
100
SM4
PLAYING FIELDS
ST. HELIER
BEDDINGTON CORNER
101
REC GRD
THOMAS WALL PARK
CARSHALTON SPORTS ARENA
ST. HELIER AVENUE
BISHOPSFORD ROAD
EPSOM ROAD
102
ROSEHILL
REIGATE AVENUE REC GRD
ST. HELIER OPEN SPACE
ST. HELIER HOSPITAL
SM5
ROSEHILL RECREATION GROUND
ROSEHILL PARK EAST
QUEEN MARY'S HOSP FOR CHILDREN
SUTTON CEMETERY
SM3
103
BENHILTON
DALE PARK
FELNEX TRADING ESTATE
SUTTON COMMON
THE WRYTHE
WILDERNESS ISLAND
104
ROYSTON PARK
SM1
THE WRYTHE REC GRD
COLLINGWOOD PARK
132
CARSHALTON
ST. DUNSTAN'S HILL
OLDFIELDS
66
67
68
69
26
27
28

DH
DJ
DK
DL
DM
DN
DP
STREATHAM VALE
NORBURY PARK
NORBURY
SE19
NATIONAL WESTMINSTER BANK SPORTS GROUND
STREATHAM PARK CEMETERY
SW16
POLLARDS HILL
CR7
THORNTON HEATH
MITCHAM
MITCHAM (PUBLIC) GOLF COURSE
COMMON
CROYDON CEMETERY
MAYDAY HOSPITAL
QUEEN'S ROAD CEMETERY
BROAD GREEN
HACKBRIDGE
SM6
BEDDINGTON
BEDDINGTON PARK
WADDON
WANDLE PARK
CR0
DUPPAS HILL
LONDON ROAD
MITCHAM ROAD
PURLEY WAY
CROYDON ROAD
Sewage Works
Electricity Switching Station
Whitgift Shopping Centre
Drummond Shopping Centre
29
30
31
95
96
97
98
99
100
101
102
103
104
105
120
133
66
67
68
69

DQ
DR
DS
DT
DU
DV
DW
33
34
35
106
UPPER NORWOOD
WESTOW PARK
SYDENHAM WOODLAND
PENGE
THE LAWNS
ALLOTMENTS
BEAULIEU HEIGHTS
SOUTH NORWOOD GROUNDS
SYLVAN ESTATE
ORCHARD SCHOOL SPORTS CENTRE
SE20
BETTS PARK
ANERLEY
SOUTH NORWOOD LAKE
PLAYING FIELD
GRANGEWOOD PARK
SOUTH NORWOOD
BECKENHAM CEMETERY
CR7
THORNTON HEATH
SE25
SELHURST PARK
SOUTH NORWOOD COUNTRY PARK
SOUTH NORWOOD REC GRD
CROYDON AND RYLANDS FIELDS
CROYDON SPORTS ARENA
NORWOOD JUNCTION
GOLF DRIVING RANGE
WOODSIDE
SELHURST
QUEEN'S ROAD CEMETERY
QUEEN'S HOSPITAL (closed)
MAYDAY HOSPITAL
ASHBURTON PARK
SHIRLEY OAKS HOSPITAL
ROAD GREEN
ADDISCOMBE
CROYDON
WANDLE PARK
WHITGIFT PLAYING FIELDS
SHIRLEY PARK GOLF COURSE
LLOYD PARK
PARK HILL
DUPPAS HILL
CR0
95
96
97
98
99
100
101
102
103
104
119
134
66
67
68
69

DX
DY
DZ
EA
EB
EC
ED
36
37
38
107
CATOR PARK
NEW BECKENHAM
RAVENSBOURNE
WARREN AVE PLAYING FIELDS
SHORTLANDS GOLF COURSE
BROMLEY PARK
95
THE SLOANE HOSPITAL
BECKENHAM
BR3
BECKENHAM JUNCTION
KENT HOUSE
ALLOTMENTS
BECKENHAM ROAD
BECKENHAM ROAD
A234
A2015
A222
BROMLEY ROAD
SHORTLANDS
96
BR2
69
97
BECKENHAM HOSPITAL
CROYDON RD REC GROUND
ALLOTMENTS
ELMERS END
CROYDON ROAD
ELGOOD PLAYING FIELD
KELSEY PARK
HAYES LANE
B251
CREASE PARK
HARVINGTON PLAYING FIELD
EDEN PARK
SPORTS GROUND
PLAYING FIELDS
Langley Court (Research Laboratories)
98
68
99
UPPER ELMERS END
A214
PARK LANGLEY
SPORTS GROUND
122
CROUCH OAK WOOD
LINKS WAY
SOUTH EDEN PARK RD
LANGLEY PARK SPORTS GRD
LANGLEY PARK GOLF COURSE
100
67
MONKS ORCHARD
HIGH BROOM WOOD
BETHLEM ROYAL HOSPITAL
BLAKE REC GRD
THE ROOKERY
BECKENHAM ROAD
WEST WICKHAM
101
PLAYING FIELD
PARKFIELDS REC GRD
WICKHAM ROAD
A232
HIGH STREET
STATION RD
GLEBE WAY
SPORTS GRDS
102
PLAYING FIELD
66
103
SPRING PARK WOOD
WEST WICKHAM
SPORTS GRD
SHIRLEY
REC GRD
FOXES WOOD
PLAYING FIELDS
SPARROWS DEN PLAYING FIELDS
104
REC GRD
SPRING PARK
A2022
ADDINGTON
BR4
Schiller International University
EMMAUS CONF CENTRE
KENNEL WOOD
135
PINEWOODS
ADDINGTON GOLF COURSE
DX
DY
DZ
EA
EB
EC
ED
36
37
38

EE
EF
EG
EH
EJ
EK
EL
40
41
42
108
WARREN AVE PLAYING FIELDS
SHORTLANDS GOLF COURSE
BROMLEY PARK
THE SLOANE HOSPITAL
Clubhouse
SHORTLANDS
BECKENHAM ROAD
BROMLEY
QUEEN'S MEAD REC GRD
MARTINS HILL
CHURCH HOUSE GDNS
The Glades Shop Cen
Pavilion Sports Cen
CIVIC CENTRE
BR1
BR2
SHORTLANDS
WIDMORE
WIDMORE ROAD
CHISLEHURST ROAD
BICKLEY
BROMLEY SOUTH
MASONS HILL
BROMLEY HOSP
HAVELOCK REC GRD
WHITEHALL REC GRD
SOUTH HILL WOOD
PARK LANGLEY
121
95
96
97
98
99
100
101
102
103
104
69
68
67
66
NORMAN PARK RECREATION GROUND
SCROGGINHALL WOOD
Bromley College of Technology
Bromley F C
Fishers Wood
CUPOLA WOOD
REC GRD
PLAYING FIELDS
LANGLEY PARK GOLF COURSE
HAYES
BROOK WOOD
LORDS WOOD
MAZZARDS WOOD
WOODCOCK GROVE
BOLDS WOOD
THE GROVE SPORTS GRD
RECREATION GROUND
HASTINGS ROAD
COMMON ROAD
SPORTS GRDS
HAYES
THE KNOLL
HAYES GROVE PRIORY HOSPITAL
BARNET WOOD
SPORTS GROUNDS
Rugby Ground
WEST WICKHAM COMMON
HAYES COMMON
COLYERS WOOD
CROYDON ROAD
PADMALL WOOD
SPARROWS DEN PLAYING FIELDS
BR4
Schiller Internat Univers
EMMAUS CONF CENTRE
HOLLYDALE REC GRD
OAKLEY ROAD
136
Keston Court Riding Stables

123
EM
EN
EP
EQ
ER
ES
ET
43
44
45
CAMDEN PARK
CHISLEHURST GOLF COURSE
CHISLEHURST COMMON
NATURE RESERVE
PARK WOOD
109
95
96
97
98
99
100
101
102
103
104
124
137
66
67
68
69
CHISLEHURST
CHALKPIT WOOD
BANSOME WOOD
BR7
PLAYING FIELD
BIRCH WOOD
GOSHILL WOOD
POND WOOD
HAWKWOOD ESTATE NT
ST. PAUL'S CRAY COMMON
HOBLINGWELL WOOD
ST. PAUL'S CRAY
PETTS WOOD NT
Edlmann Memorial Wood
Willett Memorial Wood
Holbrook Wood
The Larches
BICKLEY
Bickley Junction
Chislehurst Junction
Piggeries
GREAT THRIFT
MOD
Bickley Manor Hotel
BLACKBROOK WOOD
THORNET WOOD
Petts Wood Junction
JUBILEE COUNTRY PARK
PETTS WOOD
BR5
SOUTHBOROUGH OPEN SPACE
SOUTHBOROUGH
BROMLEY PUBLIC GOLF COURSE
PARKFIELD RECREATION GROUND
BROMLEY COMMON
SPARROW WOOD
SPARROW COMMON
ROUNDABOUT WOOD
CROFTON HEATH
CLAY WOOD
NOBODY'S WOOD
POKERIDDEN WOOD
KNOWLEHILL WOOD
PETTS WOOD REC GRD
COVET WOOD
POVEREST REC GRD
ORPINGTON
GUMPING COMMON
CROFTON ROAD A232
BR6
NEWSTEAD WOOD
DARRICK WOOD
FARNBOROUGH REC GRD
FARNBOROUGH HOSPITAL
FARNBOROUGH ROAD
ORPINGTON HOSPITAL
SPORTS GRD
ORPINGTON ROAD A208
CHISLEHURST ROAD
SPUR ROAD A232
STATION ROAD
HIGH STREET
PERRY HALL ROAD

124
NATURE RESERVE
WOOD
EU
EV
EW
EX
EY
EZ
FA
47
48
49
110
BYPASS
A20
MAIDSTONE ROAD
SEVENOAKS WAY
A224
PLAYING FIELD
Field Study Cen
Youth Centre
Plantation
RUXLEY WOOD
Garden Centre
Profiles Ski Centre
Sports Club
RUXLEY PARK GOLF COURSE
DRIVING RANGE
Golf Centre
The Small House
CRAY VALLEY GOLF COURSE
Pilgrim Hill
Barnfield Bank
CHAPMANS LANE
Lower Hockenden Farm
Simon's Field Shaw
95
96
97
98
99
100
101
102
103
104
HOBLINGWELL WOOD
ST. PAUL'S CRAY
Superstore
CRAYFIELD IND PARK
REC GRD
BR7
BR5
BR6
PAULS CRAY HILL PARK
HIGHLANDS WOOD
HOCKENDEN WOOD
Hogspring Cottages
MURRAY BUS CEN
Gas Works
ST. MARY CRAY
STAR LANE
CEM
Comm Cen
SANDWAY PK
NUGENT IND PK
THE WARREN
Sheepcote Farm
Ringland Farm
CHILD'S WOOD
POVEREST
123
ST. MARY CRAY REC GRD
Bowl Grn
Youth Cen
B258
CROCKENHILL ROAD
Blueberry Farm
Kevington Farm
DERRY DOWNS
KYNASTON WOOD
Waldens Farm
COVET
POVEREST REC GRD
Bowling Green
ALLOT
Pumping Sta
Elec Sub Sta
Grigg's Cross
Walden Manor
Depot
A208
PRIORY GDNS
BROMLEY MUS
BURIAL GROUND
GRASSMEADE RECREATION GROUND
Heather's Holding
Bleak House Farm
ORPINGTON
Shopping Centre
Mkt
Sports Cen
Coll
RAMSDEN
PLAYING FIELD
Eastwood Farm
GRIFF'S WOOD
HOLLINGBOURNE TOWER
BEKESBOURNE TOWER
Piggery
A232
SPUR ROAD
Fire Sta
Schs
SAGE WENTS
Byways Nurseries
Crownwood Farm
Cookham Hill Farm
Cookham Farm
GODDINGTON
GODDINGTON PARK
Goddington House
ROUNDS SMALLAMS
Bowling Grn
138
LILLY'S WOOD
BLACK BUSH WOOD
ORPINGTON HOSPITAL
SPORTS GRD
Tennis Cts
Clubhouse
A223

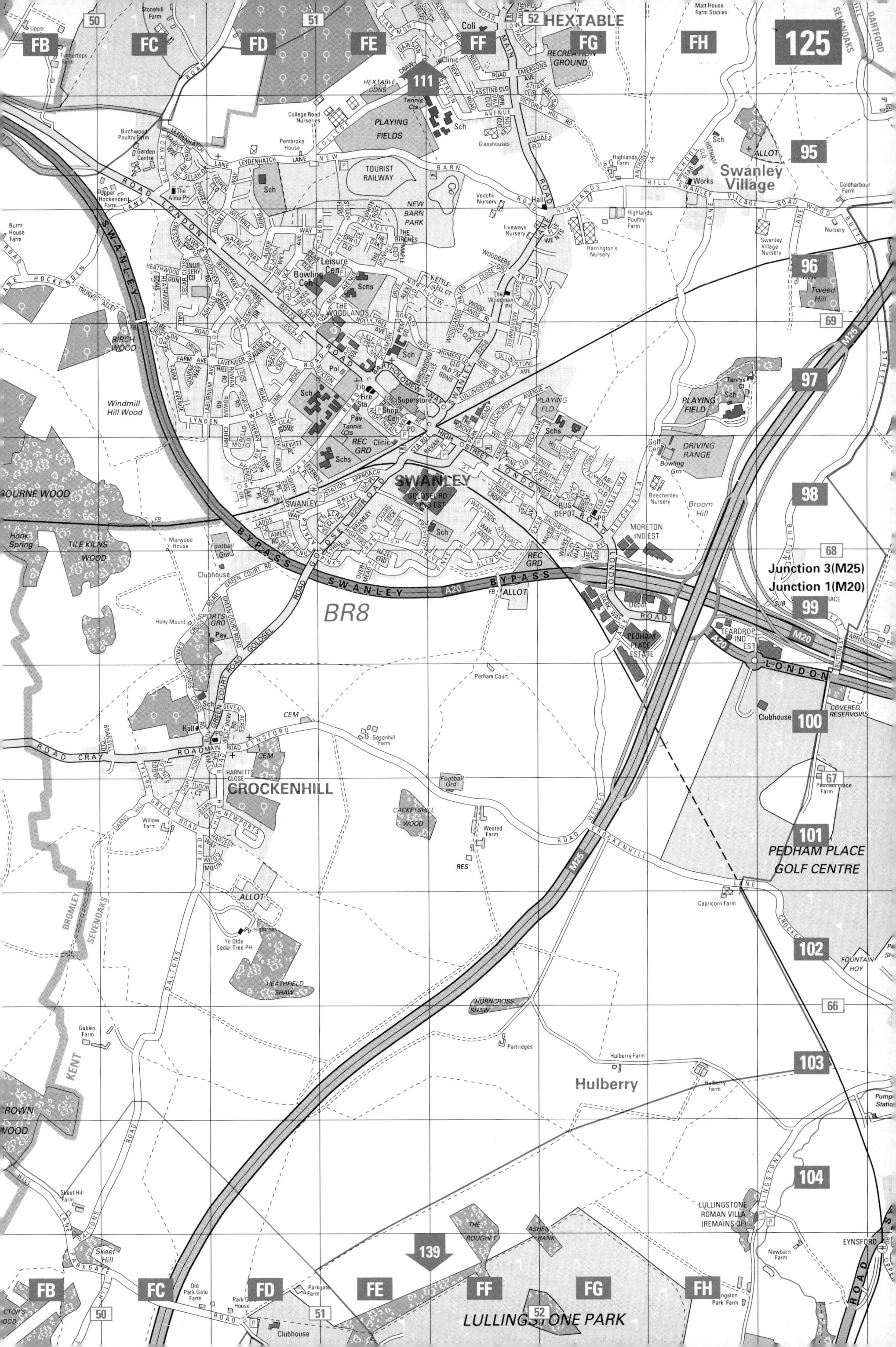

125
HEXTABLE
RECREATION GROUND
Swanley Village
SWANLEY
BR8
CROCKENHILL
Hulberry
LULLINGSTONE PARK
PEDHAM PLACE GOLF CENTRE
Junction 3(M25)
Junction 1(M20)
SWANLEY BY-PASS
M25
M20
A20
B2173
B258
TOURIST RAILWAY
PLAYING FIELDS
NEW BARN PARK
BIRCH WOOD
Windmill Hill Wood
BOURNE WOOD
TILE KILNS WOOD
Hook Spring
CACKETSHILL WOOD
HEATHFIELD SHAW
HORNCROSS SHAW
THE ROUGHET
ASHEN BANK
LULLINGSTONE ROMAN VILLA (REMAINS OF)
MORETON IND EST
PEDHAM PLACE ESTATE
TEARDROP IND EST
DRIVING RANGE
Broom Hill
Tweed Hill
Skeet Hill
BROMLEY
SEVENOAKS
KENT
DARTFORD
EYNSFORD
FB
FC
FD
FE
FF
FG
FH
95
96
97
98
99
100
101
102
103
104
50
51
52
66
67
68
69
111
139

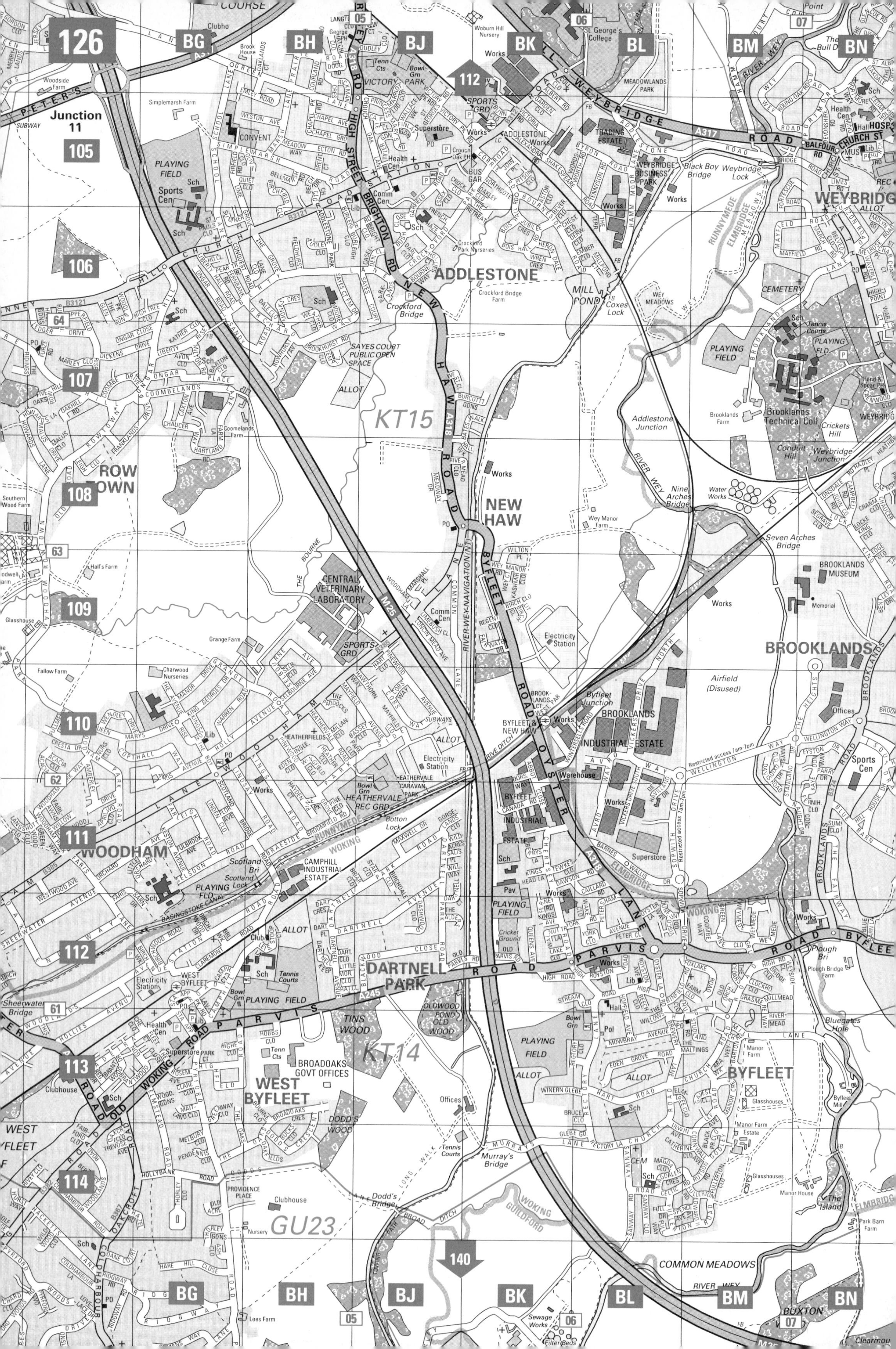

127
BP
BQ
BR
BS
BT
BU
BV
08
09
10
113
105
106
107
108
109
110
111
112
113
114
128
141
64
63
62
61
OATLANDS PARK
ASHLEY PARK
BURWOOD PARK
KT12
KT13
KT11
ST. GEORGE'S HILL
WHITELEY VILLAGE
PAINSHILL PARK
COBHAM
WALTON-ON-THAMES
BURHILL GOLF COURSE
ST. GEORGE'S HILL GOLF COURSE
SILVERMERE GOLF COURSE
WALTON COMMON
UPPER COMMON
OLD COMMON
SEVEN HILLS ROAD
QUEENS ROAD
OATLANDS DRIVE
MONUMENT HILL
BYFLEET ROAD
PORTSMOUTH ROAD
ESHER ROAD
HERSHAM ROAD
BURWOOD ROAD
Oatlands Park Hotel
Flagstaff House Conference Centre
Notre Dame Convent
Seven Hills Estate
Walton Firs Scout Camp
Heyswood Girl Guide Camp
Hilton National Cobham
Cobham Bus Mus
River Mole
The Lake
Wheel Island
Cobham Court
Norwood Farm
Hook's Corner
Chestnut Lodge Farm
Dick Turpin's Cottage
Burhill Kennels
Burvale Farm Garden Centre
Rabbit Lane House
Covered Reservoirs
Water Tower
Warren Pond
Upper Pond
Manor Pond
Beards Hill
Strawberry Hill
Long Orchard Farm
Bramble Hedge Farm
Foxwarren Park
Red Hill
Oak Pollard
Foxholm Covert
Sports Ground
Driving Range
Cobham Hosp
Rose Lodge Wood
Running Mare PH

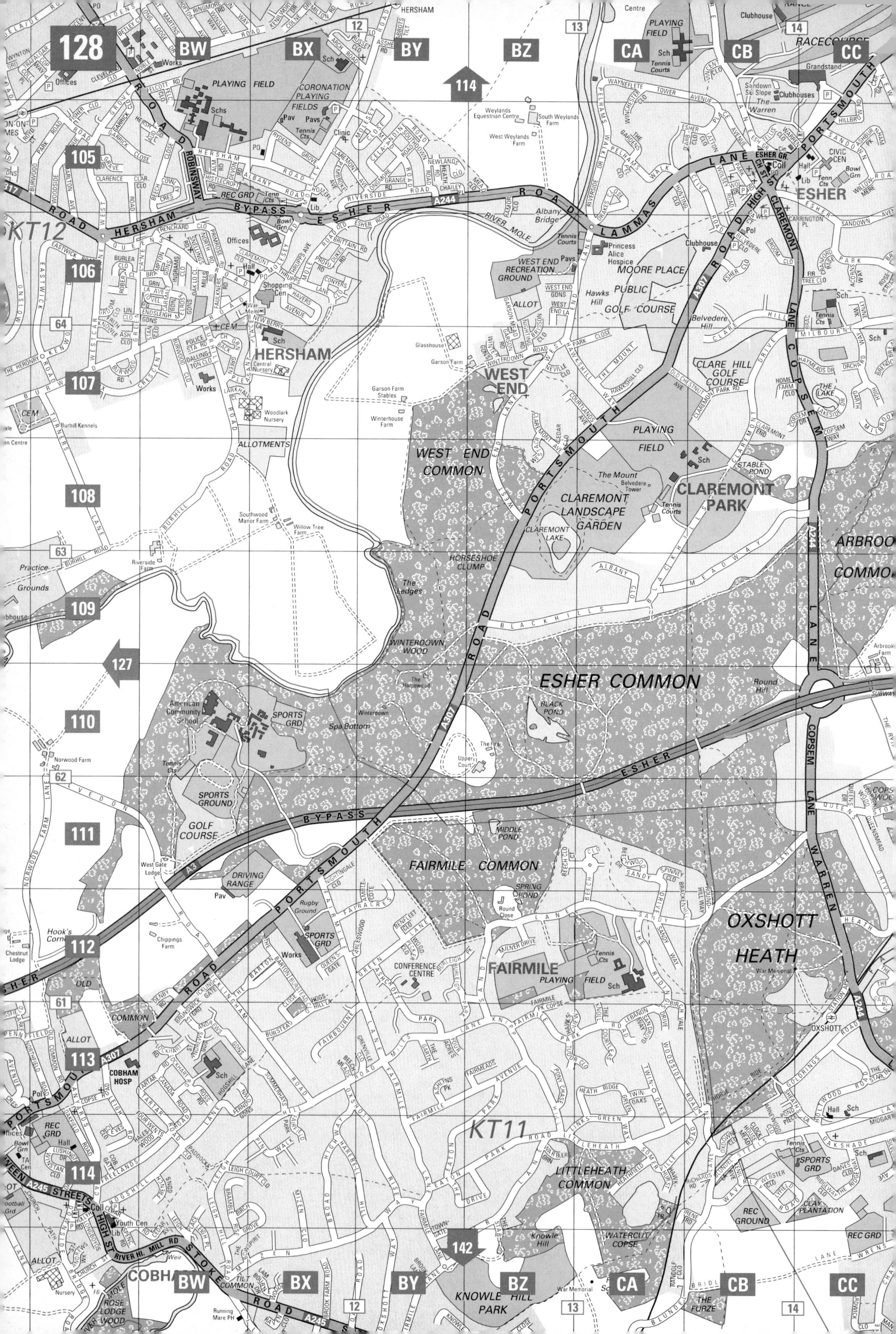

128
BW
BX
BY
BZ
CA
CB
CC
114
127
142
105
106
107
108
109
110
111
112
113
114
12
13
14
61
62
63
64
KT12
KT11
HERSHAM
ESHER
WEST END
CLAREMONT PARK
CLAREMONT LANDSCAPE GARDEN
ESHER COMMON
WEST END COMMON
FAIRMILE COMMON
FAIRMILE
OXSHOTT HEATH
LITTLEHEATH COMMON
KNOWLE HILL PARK
COBHAM
OXSHOTT
MOORE PLACE PUBLIC GOLF COURSE
CLARE HILL GOLF COURSE
WEST END RECREATION GROUND
PLAYING FIELD
CORONATION PLAYING FIELDS
SPORTS GRD
SPORTS GROUND
GOLF COURSE
DRIVING RANGE
American Community School
Princess Alice Hospice
Horseshoe Clump
Winterdown Wood
Black Pond
Middle Pond
Spring Pond
Claremont Lake
The Mount
Belvedere Tower
Stable Pond
Conference Centre
Watercut Copse
The Furze
Clay Plantation
Rec Ground
Cobham Hosp
Racecourse
Grandstand
Civic Cen
HERSHAM ROAD
HERSHAM BYPASS
ESHER ROAD
A244
A307
A3
A245
PORTSMOUTH ROAD
ESHER BYPASS
LAMMAS LANE
COPSEM LANE
WARREN LANE
CLAREMONT LANE
BLACKHILLS
STOKE ROAD
RIVER MOLE

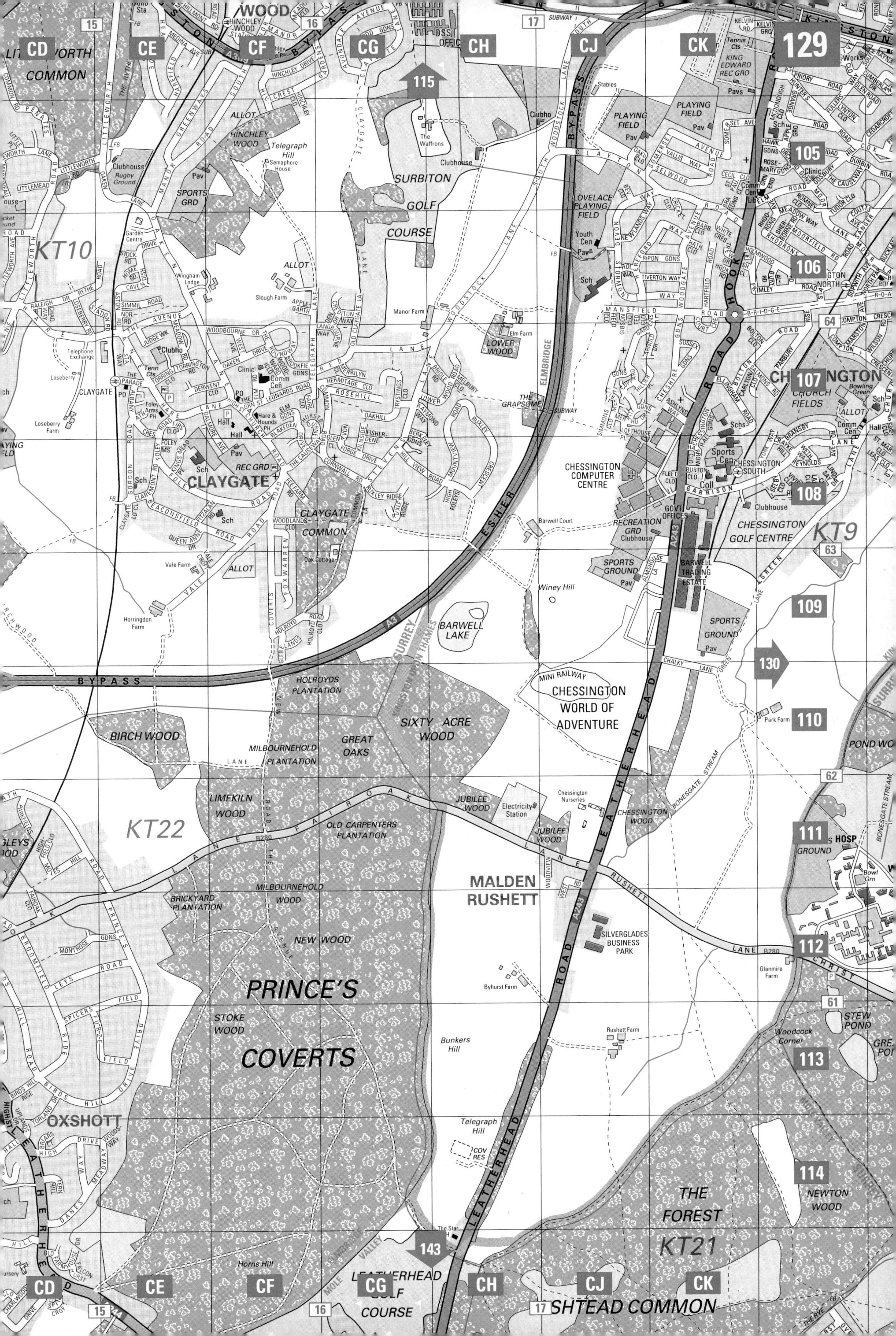

129
115
130
143
105
106
107
108
109
110
111
112
113
114
CD
CE
CF
CG
CH
CJ
CK
15
16
17
KT10
KT22
KT9
KT21
CLAYGATE
OXSHOTT
CHESSINGTON
MALDEN RUSHETT
SURBITON GOLF COURSE
CLAYGATE COMMON
PRINCE'S COVERTS
CHESSINGTON WORLD OF ADVENTURE
BARWELL LAKE
SIXTY ACRE WOOD
GREAT OAKS
BIRCH WOOD
LIMEKILN WOOD
HOLROYDS PLANTATION
MILBOURNEHOLD PLANTATION
OLD CARPENTERS PLANTATION
MILBOURNEHOLD WOOD
NEW WOOD
BRICKYARD PLANTATION
STOKE WOOD
JUBILEE WOOD
CHESSINGTON WOOD
THE FOREST
NEWTON WOOD
STEW POND
LEATHERHEAD GOLF COURSE
ASHTEAD COMMON
CHESSINGTON GOLF CENTRE
CHESSINGTON COMPUTER CENTRE
BARWELL TRADING ESTATE
SILVERGLADES BUSINESS PARK
LOVELACE PLAYING FIELD
LOWER WOOD
HINCHLEY WOOD
LITTLEWORTH COMMON
ESHER BYPASS
LEATHERHEAD ROAD
ELMBRIDGE
KINGSTON UPON THAMES
SURREY

CHESSINGTON
CHESSINGTON NORTH
CHESSINGTON SOUTH
HORTON COUNTRY PARK
HORTON PARK COUNTRY CLUB GOLF COURSE
WEST EWELL
HORTON
KT9
KT19
KT18
KT21
EPSOM COMMON
EPSOM
THE FOREST
ST. EBBA'S HOSPITAL
HORTON HOSPITAL
WEST PARK HOSPITAL
THE MANOR HOSPITAL (closed)
HOSP (disused)
HOGSMILL RIVERSIDE OPEN SPACE
NONSUCH INDUSTRIAL ESTATE
KINGSTON BYPASS
CL
CM
CN
CP
CQ
CR
CS
19
20
21
61
62
63
64
105
106
107
108
109
110
111
112
113
114
116
129
144

131
CT
CU
CV
CW
CX
CY
CZ
22
23
24
117
NORTH CHEAM
KT4
CUDDINGTON RECREATION GROUND
STONELEIGH
NONSUCH PARK
NONSUCH MANSION HOUSE
OAK PLANTATION
Diana's Dyke
SM3
CHEAM RECREATION GROUND
CHEAM PARK
CHEAM
SM1
PERRETS FIELD
COLLINGWOOD PARK
105
106
107
108
109
110
111
112
113
114
132
145
64
63
62
61
SM2
OVERTON PARK
WEST SUTTON
EWELL
EAST EWELL
NESCOT
Priest Hill
KT17
PLAYING FIELD
RECREATION GROUND
CUDDINGTON GOLF COURSE
NORTH LOOE
SURREY
EPSOM & EWELL
SM7
BANSTEAD
BANSTEAD DOWNS GOLF COURSE
ALEXANDRA REC GROUND
SPORTS GROUND
Epsom College
EPSOM DOWNS
Drift Bridge
A24
A240
A232
A2043
A217
A2022
B2200
EWELL BYPASS
LONDON ROAD
REIGATE ROAD
CHEAM ROAD
BRIGHTON ROAD
COLLEGE ROAD
FIR TREE ROAD
WINKWORTH ROAD
BELMONT RISE
ST DUNSTAN'S HILL
MALDEN ROAD
BURDON LANE

132
DA
DB
DC
DD
DE
DF
DG
26
27
28
118
SM1
SM2
SM5
SM7
CR5
COLLINGWOOD PARK
ROYSTON PARK
SUTTON
WEST SUTTON
CARSHALTON
CARSHALTON ROAD
CARSHALTON PARK
CARSHALTON BEECHES
CARSHALTON ON THE HILL
HIGH STREET
OVERTON PARK
HOSPITAL
SUTTON HOSPITAL
THE ROYAL MARSDEN HOSPITAL
MEDICAL RESEARCH COUNCIL (Closed)
HOSPITAL (closed)
WELLFIELD PLANTATION
BELMONT
BANSTEAD DOWNS
BANSTEAD COMMON
BANSTEAD DOWNS GOLF COURSE
DOWNVIEW PRISON
HIGHDOWN PRISON
OAKS SPORTS CENTRE GOLF COURSE
THE OAKS PARK
LITTLE WOODCOTE
WOODMANSTERNE LANE
WOODMANSTERNE PARK RECREATION GROUND
SPORTS GROUND
RIFFET WOOD
BIG WOOD
CLOCKHOUSE REC GRD
WOODMANSTERNE
PROSPECT PLANTATION
BRIGHTON ROAD
CROYDON ROAD
WINKWORTH ROAD
ST. DUNSTAN'S HILL
BELMONT RISE
A217
A232
A2022
B278
SURREY
SUTTON
REIGATE & BANSTEAD
105
106
107
108
109
110
111
112
113
114
131
146
61
62
63
64

133
DH
DJ
DK
DL
DM
DN
DP
29
30
31
119
BEDDINGTON
WALLINGTON
SOUTH BEDDINGTON
BANDON HILL CEMETERY
SM6
DUPPAS HILL
CR0
MELLOWS PARK
STAFFORD CROSS IND EST
ROUNDSHAW PLAYING FIELD
ROUNDSHAW OPEN SPACE
ROUNDSHAW PARK
PURLEY WAY PLAYING FIELDS
SOUTH CROYDON
HALING PARK
CR2
SPORTS GROUND
WOODCOTE
PURLEY
PURLEY HOSP
CR8
FOXLEY WOOD
HIGHER GROVE REC GRD
WOODCOTE PARK GOLF COURSE
WOODCOTE GROVE REC GRD
PLAYING FIELD
RESERVOIR
Market Garden
Surrey Tennis & Country Club
Croydon Indoor Bowling Club
Hilton National Croydon
Sports Centre
Swimming Pool
Superstore
REEDHAM
KENLEY
SMITHAM
RIDDLESDOWN
COOMBES WOOD
SUTTON
CROYDON
105
106
107
108
109
110
111
112
113
114
134
147
64
63
62
61
A232
A23
A235
A2022
A237
B272
B271
B275
B2050
DUPPAS HILL RD
PURLEY WAY
BRIGHTON ROAD
FOXLEY LANE
WOODCOTE ROAD
STAFFORD ROAD
BOTTOM LANE
GODSTONE RD
DOWNS COURT ROAD

134
DQ
DR
DS
DT
DU
DV
DW
33
34
35
120
148
133
105
106
107
108
109
110
111
112
113
114
64
63
62
61
CR0
CR2
CR8
DUPPAS HILL
PURLEY WAY PLAYING FIELDS
SOUTH CROYDON
HALING PARK
HALING GROVE
PARK HILL
LLOYD PARK
SHIRLEY GOLF COURSE
WHITGIFT PLAYING FIELDS
COOMBE PARK
PLAYING FIELD
ADDINGTON HILLS
COOMBE WOOD
BALLARDS PLANTATION
RECREATION GROUND
CROHAM HURST
CROHAM HURST GOLF COURSE
THRIFT WOOD
LITTLEHEATH WOODS
SELSDON
SANDERSTEAD
SANDERSTEAD PLANTATION
PURLEY BEECHES
PURLEY DOWNS GOLF COURSE
SELSDON PARK HOTEL GOLF COURSE
Selsdon Park Hotel
NEWLANDS WOOD
KINGS WOOD
MITCHLEY WOOD
RAGGED GROVE
AINSLEY BERRY SHAW
RIDDLESDOWN
FOXLEY WOOD
HIGHER GROVE REC GRD
COOMBES WOOD
SOUTH CROYDON REC GRD
PURLEY
KENLEY
SPORTS GROUND
HIGH ST
BRIGHTON ROAD
COOMBE ROAD
PARK LANE
SELSDON ROAD
ADDINGTON ROAD
LIMPSFIELD ROAD
MITCHLEY AVENUE
RECTORY PARK
GODSTONE ROAD
DOWNS COURT ROAD
PURLEY WAY
CROYDON
TANDRIDGE
DISPLEY'S WOOD

SHIRLEY
DX
DY
DZ
EA
EB
EC
ED
36
37
38
121
FOXES WOOD
PLAYING FIELDS
PINEWOODS
SPARROWS DEN PLAYING FIELDS
SPRING PARK
PLAYING FIELD
BR4
105
Schiller International University
EMMAUS CONF CENTRE
KENNEL WOOD
Clubhouse
ADDINGTON GOLF COURSE
THREEHALFPENNY WOOD
ADDINGTON
ADDINGTON PALACE GOLF COURSE
Addington Palace (Royal School of Church Music)
ADDINGTON PARK
ADDINGTON VILLAGE
KENT GATE WAY
A2022
A212
Fox Hill
FOXHILL SHAW
ROWDOWN FIELDS
BIRCH WOOD
106
64
107
CASTLE HILL RUFFS
BRADMANSH WOOD
GRAVEL HILL
PLAYING FIELDS
Sports Centre
108
ALLOT
ADDINGTON COURT (PUBLIC) GOLF COURSES
63
ROWDOWN WOOD
NEW ADDINGTON
109
FORESTDALE
Pumping Station
RECREATION GROUND
KING HENRY'S DRIVE
NORTH DOWN REC GRD
ADDINGTON VALE
136
110
Works
Health Centre
Clubhouse
62
SELSDON WOOD NT
STEVEN'S LARCH
BEARS WOOD (Scout Camp)
CROYDON
TANDRIDGE
111
MILNE PARK
FRITH WOOD
GREENHILL SHAW
PUPLET WOOD
BIRCHEN SHAW
FRYLANDS WOOD Scout Camp
THREECORNER GROVE
112
PLAYING FIELDS
HILLOCKS WOOD
BROOM WOOD
Haggler's Dean
CR0
Farleigh Dean
SURREY
FARLEIGH COURT GOLF COURSE
61
DUMPSEY DERRY
CRAB WOOD
CHAPEL HILL
113
BEECHES SHAW
HODGE GROVE
LINEKILN SHAW
COLDBLOW SHAW
BOGRAMS WOOD
WELLS SHAW
Elm Farm
Farleigh House Farm
HOGCROFT SHAW
Fairchildes Farm
MOSSYHILL SHAW
White Bear Inn
Fickleshole Farm
114
FARLEIGH
Farleigh Cottages
Farleigh Court Manor House
Little Farleigh Green Farm
LITTLE FARLEIGH GREEN
LITTLE GREAT HILL
OAKEN SHAW
Kingswood Lodge
Scotshall Farm
CR6
MOSESHILL SHAW
149
GREATPARK WOOD
FIVE ACRE SHAW
The Harrow Inn
WARLINGHAM PARK HOSPITAL

136
EE
EF
EG
EH
EJ
EK
EL
40
41
42
122
BR4
BR2
105
106
107
108
109
110
111
112
113
114
135
64
63
62
61
PLAYING FIELDS
Schiller International University
EMMAUS CONF CENTRE
WICKHAM COMMON
HAYES COMMON
COLYERS WOOD
CROYDON ROAD
KESTON
WELL WOOD
Rouse Farm
PADMALL WOOD
REVENSBOURNE OPEN SPACE
SOUTH PARK
KESTON COMMON
LEAFY GROVE
Caesar's Camp
Seismograph Service Co. HQ
LONG SHAW
COOPER'S WOOD
North Pole Farm
FULLER'S WOOD
JAMES'S WOOD
Nash Farm
Fortune Bank Farm
Elm Farm
Foxhill Farm
Raithes Worm Farm
War Bank
BRADMANSHILL WOOD
Electricity Station
Five Oaks Equestrian Centre
RUSHFIELD SHAW
BROOMFIELDBANK SHAW
Metropolitan Police Dog Training Centre
Keston Court Farm
Scout Camp
Milchden
Keston Fruit Farm
Glebe Farm
Holwood Farm
NEW ADDINGTON
ADDINGTON VALE
ROWDOWN WOOD
Layham's Farm
Racing Circuit
FURZE BOTTOM
Kimberley Farm
Gas Works
Works
Schs
SPORTS GRD
Clubhouse
Holmshaw Farm
Greyhound Training Kennels
HOPPERSNATCH SHAW
The Vale Farm
Crown Inn
Bradmore
High House Farm
Greenacres Riding School
Colinette Farm
Milking Lane Farm
The Kings Arms PH
MILNE PARK
Higham's Hill
Highams Hill Farm
SPORTS GRD
PLAYING FIELDS
THREECORNER GROVE
CHAPEL HILL
BOGRAMS WOOD
JEWELS WOOD
HELIPAD
Barracks (disused)
Hangars
REC GRD
BIGGIN HILL CIVIL AIRPORT
CUDHAM LODGE WOODS
North Lodge
South Lodge
Fairchildes Farm
White Bear Inn
Coxs Cottage
Blackmans Cottages
TANDRIDGE
BROMLEY
SURREY
CR6
150
TN16
Skid Hill House
GREATHILL SHAW
FIVE ACRE SHAW
AIRPORT IND EST
BIGGIN HILL BUS
A232
A233
A2022
B265
MAIN ROAD
LEAVES GREEN ROAD
WESTERHAM ROAD
SALT BOX HILL
SKID HILL LANE
JEWELS HILL
SHEEPBARN LANE
FAIRCHILDES LANE
BLACKMAN'S LANE
OAKLANDS LANE
NASH LANE
JACKASS LANE
CHURCH LANE
DOWNE ROAD
LAYHAMS ROAD
NORTH POLE LANE

137
123
138
151
105
106
107
108
109
110
111
112
113
114
EM
EN
EP
EQ
ER
ES
ET
43
44
45
61
62
63
64
FARNBOROUGH HOSPITAL
Superstore
FARNBOROUGH ROAD
CROFTON
BASSETTS CENTRE
COMMON
FARNBOROUGH
DARRICK WOOD
PLAYING FIELD
NEWSTEAD WOOD
ORPINGTON HOSPITAL
SPORTS GRD
WARREN ROAD
SEVENOAKS ROAD
A21
A223
A232
B2158
HIGH STREET
FARNBOROUGH
Clubhouse
PLAYING FLD
ALLOT
CHURCH FIELD PLANTATION
BR6
NINHAMS WOOD
LAKE WOOD
FARNBOROUGH RESERVOIRS
BROOM BANK
MILL HILL
GLENTRAMMON REC GRD
GREEN STREET GREEN
RAMUS WOOD
COCKSETT PLANTATION
Cocksett Hill
Rose and Crown PH
Chelsfield Hall Farm
FARNBOROUGH WAY
SEVENOAKS WAY
ROUNDS WOOD
Sevenoaks Lodge
SHIRE LANE
Lower Hook Farm
North End Farm
High Elms Nature Centre
Woodpiece
Clubhouse
WHITELANDS WOOD
Denbarn Farm
NORTH END LANE
High Elms Clockhouse
BLACKLANDS
HIGH ELMS GOLF COURSE
THE ROOKERY
North End Farm Cottages
BOGEY LANE
FARTHING STREET
Farthing Street Farm
Farthings
Orange Court
ORANGE COURT LANE
Meadow Cottage
Green Acres
NATURE FIELD
HIGH ELMS ROAD
Cuckoo Lodge
CUCKOO WOOD
LITTLE MOLLOMS WOOD
GREAT MOLLOMS WOOD
Hazels
Little Crowhill
ROOKERY ROAD
The Rookery
MILL LANE
STANDARD RD
Gorringes Farm
CUDHAM PARK RD
BURNT GORSE
Grasslands Farm
Avondale Farm
Long Acre
DOWNE
Sch
PO
Petleys Farm
Petleys
Downe Hall
Hall
The Shack
White Earth
Snag Farm
Endsleigh
SNAG LANE
Southfields
Rose Cottage
HOMEFIELD SPRING
NORSTED
Christmas Tree Farm
CUDHAM ROAD
SQUARE SHAW
Hang Grove Farm
HAZEL WOOD
SPINNEY WAY
FOXBERRY WOOD
The Oaks
Snag Lane Farm
Downe Lodge
THOMPSON WOOD
DARWIN MUS
Downe Court Manor
Downe Court Farm
LUXTED ROAD
WEST KENT GOLF COURSE
Buxton Browne Research Institute
Cricket Ground
DOWNE BANK (NATURE RESERVE)
LORDFIELD SHAW
The Shaws (Girl Guide Camp)
Mace Farm
Mace Farm Cottages
BROOM WOOD
HIGH WOOD
HANG GROVE
Beechwood
The Boundary
Hostye Farm
MACE LANE
KANGLES WOOD
DOWNE ROAD
CUDHAM LANE
LADIES WOOD
SPENCERS GROVE
Luxted Farm
Church Hill Farm
FOXBURROW WOOD
NEW YEARS WOOD
NEWLANDS WOOD
Down Scout Camp
BIRD HOUSE WOOD
TWENTY ACRE SHAW
HOOK WOOD
Angas Home
TN14
New Years Cottage
BIRCHES CROFT
LEASONS WOOD
Clock Tower
BIRDHOUSE LANE
BROMLE CROFT
SINGLE STREET
Bottom Farm
CHURCH HILL
Blacksmiths Arms
REC GRD
Tennis Cts
PLAYING FIELD
JOCKEY'S WOOD
Cudham
WASHNECK LANE

EU
EV
EW
EX
EY
EZ
FA
47
48
49
124
105
106
107
108
109
110
111
112
113
114
64
63
62
61
137
152
ORPINGTON BYPASS
ORPINGTON ROAD
COURT ROAD
SEVENOAKS ROAD
SEVENOAKS WAY
FARNBOROUGH HILL
FARNBOROUGH WAY
HIGH STREET
A21
A223
A224
BR6
CHELSFIELD
PLAYING FIELD
SPORTS GRD
CHELSFIELD PARK HOSPITAL
Maypole
GLENTRAMMON REC GRD
HIGH BEECHES
ELEVEN OAKS
CHELSFIELD HILL WOOD
ROUNDS WOOD
CHELSFIELD DOWN GOLF COURSE
BROKE HILL GOLF COURSE
KNOCKHOLT
PRATT'S BOTTOM
CHARM WOOD
PRATTS GROVE
RUSHMOOR HILL WOOD
BIRTHDAY WOOD
PRATTS BOTTOM WOOD
HOOK WOOD
LITTLE MOLLOMS WOOD
HOMEFIELD SPRING
FOXBERRY WOOD
BROOM WOOD
HIGH WOOD
LOWER BROOMS WOOD
UPPER BROOMS WOOD
LATTICE COPPICE
BIRCHINGBANK WOOD
PERRY WOOD
LOWER RANDLE'S WOOD
DEERLEAP WOOD
HALSTEAD
KANGLES WOOD
NEW YEARS WOOD
NEWLANDS WOOD
HAYMAN'S WOOD
PIECE WOOD
HAWFIELD WOOD
BIRCHES CROFT
LONG BOTTOM SHAW
JOCKEY'S WOOD
Knockholt Pound
CHAPEL CROFT
BROOMFIELD WOOD
CHALKHURST WOOD
WATERCROFTS WOOD
GOSS BUSHES
CONEYEARTH WOOD
LILLY'S WOOD
BLACK BUSH WOOD
ROCK-FIELD SHAW
ROUNDS SMALLAMS
GODDINGTON PARK
KENT

139
FB
FC
FD
FE
FF
FG
FH
50
51
52
125
153
105
106
107
108
109
110
111
112
113
114
64
63
62
61
DA4
TN14
LULLINGSTONE PARK
GOLF COURSE
LULLINGSTONE ROMAN VILLA (REMAINS OF)
LULLINGSTONE CASTLE
Lullingstone Park Visitor Centre
Lullingston Park Farm
Gatehouse
Newbarn Farm
EYNSFORD
THE ROUGHET
ASHEN BANK
Clubhouse
Parkgate Farm
Park Gate House
Old Park Gate Farm
Skeet Hill Farm
Skeet Hill
PARKGATE ROAD
DALTONS LANE
WELL HILL
FIRMINGERS ROAD
Deans Piggery
The Kent Hounds PH
Owen Farm
Well Hill Nursery
Well Hill
ROCK HILL
Works
Westwood Farm
WEST WOOD
UPPER BEECHEN WOOD
LOWER BEECHEN WOOD
HOME WOOD
The Baron's
REDMANS ROAD
Great Cockerhurst Farm
COCKERHURST
Ridge Farm
Brent Farm
Castle Farm
CASTLE LANE
FARM ROAD
CASTLE ROAD
DARENT VALLEY PATH
Pumping Station
Electricity Station
RIVER DARENT
Preston Farm
THE BIRCHES
PRESTON HILL PLANTATION
RIFLE RANGE
DANGER AREA
EYNSFORD ROAD
A225
SHOREHAM ROAD
Junction 4
M25
LONGSPRING WOOD
CHELSFIELD LANE
SAUNDER'S SPRING WOOD
BARNETT'S WOOD
BADGERS MOUNT
BADGERS RD
HIGHLAND ROAD
CHARLES RD
AVENUE
SHACKLANDS ROAD
Timberdine Farm
JENKIN'S NECK WOOD
ANDREW'S WOOD
ANDREWS WOOD
ROBSACK WOOD
The Polhill Centre
Widhurst Farm
LONDON ROAD
BYPASS
A224
MEENFIELD WOOD
HIGH STREET
Oxbourne House
Oxbourne Farm
MILL LA
Crown Inn PH
CROWN RD
ALLOT
War Memorial
PO
Hall
Tennis Cts
SHOREHAM
CHURCH STREET
Sch
PLAYING FIELD
MESNE WAY
STATION ROAD
SHOREHAM PLACE
Clubhouse
Little Copt Farm
GOLD HILL
Dunstall Priory
DUNSTALL WOODS
WHITE HILL
FACKENDEN LANE
Whitehill Farm
Warren Farm
FILSTON LANE
WATER LANE
Filston Hall
Filston Farm
PILOTS WOOD
Home Farm
Cricket Ground
Pav
DARENTH VALLEY GOLF COURSE
Works
Polhill Arms PH
POLHILL
Lip Lap Farm
Polhill Riding Centre
Fayell Farm
Danehill Farm
Electricity Station
Sepham Farm
Lower Barn
BROOK
TWITTON
BECKMAN CLO
FORT RD
GREENHILL ROAD
HILLYDEAL ROAD
Cricket Ground
Clubhouse
Tennis Cts
REC
Park

140
BG
BH
BJ
BK
BL
BM
BN
126
05
06
07
KT14
GU22
GU23
Pyrford Green
Pyrford Village
Wisley
WISLEY COMMON
THE WISLEY GOLF COURSE
PYRFORD GOLF COURSE
WISLEY GARDEN (RHS)
OCKHAM COMMON
Elm Corner
DISUSED AIRFIELD
RIPLEY GREEN
RIPLEY SEWAGE WORKS
WALSHAM MEADOW
Ripley
OCKHAM PARK
PARK WOOD
Send Marsh
LOVELAND'S COPSE
ROBOROW WOOD
BRAMBLERIDE COPSE
BACHELOR'S COPSE
PEATMOOR WOOD
BUXTON WOOD
COMMON MEADOWS
RIVER WEY
M25
PORTSMOUTH ROAD
RIPLEY BYPASS
A3
Newark Lock
Walsham Lock
Pyrford Lock
Newark Mill Bri
Stratford Bridge
Murray's Bridge
Wisley Bridge
GARLICK'S ARCH COPSE
Ockham Mill
Papercourt Weir
The Jovial Sailor PH
The Anchor PH
The Half Moon PH
Services
59
58
57
56
115
116
117
118
119
120
121
122
123
124

141
127
142
KT11
KT24
PAINSHILL PARK
THE LAKE
COBHAM
Downside
OCKHAM COMMON
CHATLEY WOOD
CHATLEY HEATH
HATCHFORD WOOD
HATCHFORD PARK
Junction 10
PORTSMOUTH ROAD
RIVER MOLE
Martyr's Green
ELMBRIDGE
GUILDFORD
HOOK WOOD
CHAFFERS COPSE
STUMPS GROVE
DRIFT GOLF COURSE
BARNSTHORNS WOOD
EFFINGHAM COMMON
EFFINGHAM JUNCTION
DOWNSIDE COMMON
BOLDER MERE
OLD OAK COMMON
THE NEW PRESERVE
ROUNDABOUT
CLAMP ROUGH
GALLOWS GROVE
BUSHY THICKET
THICKET COPSE
NEW BARN WOOD
EVEN WOOD
115
116
117
118
119
120
121
122
123
124
BP
BQ
BR
BS
BT
BU
BV
08
09
10
56
57
58
59

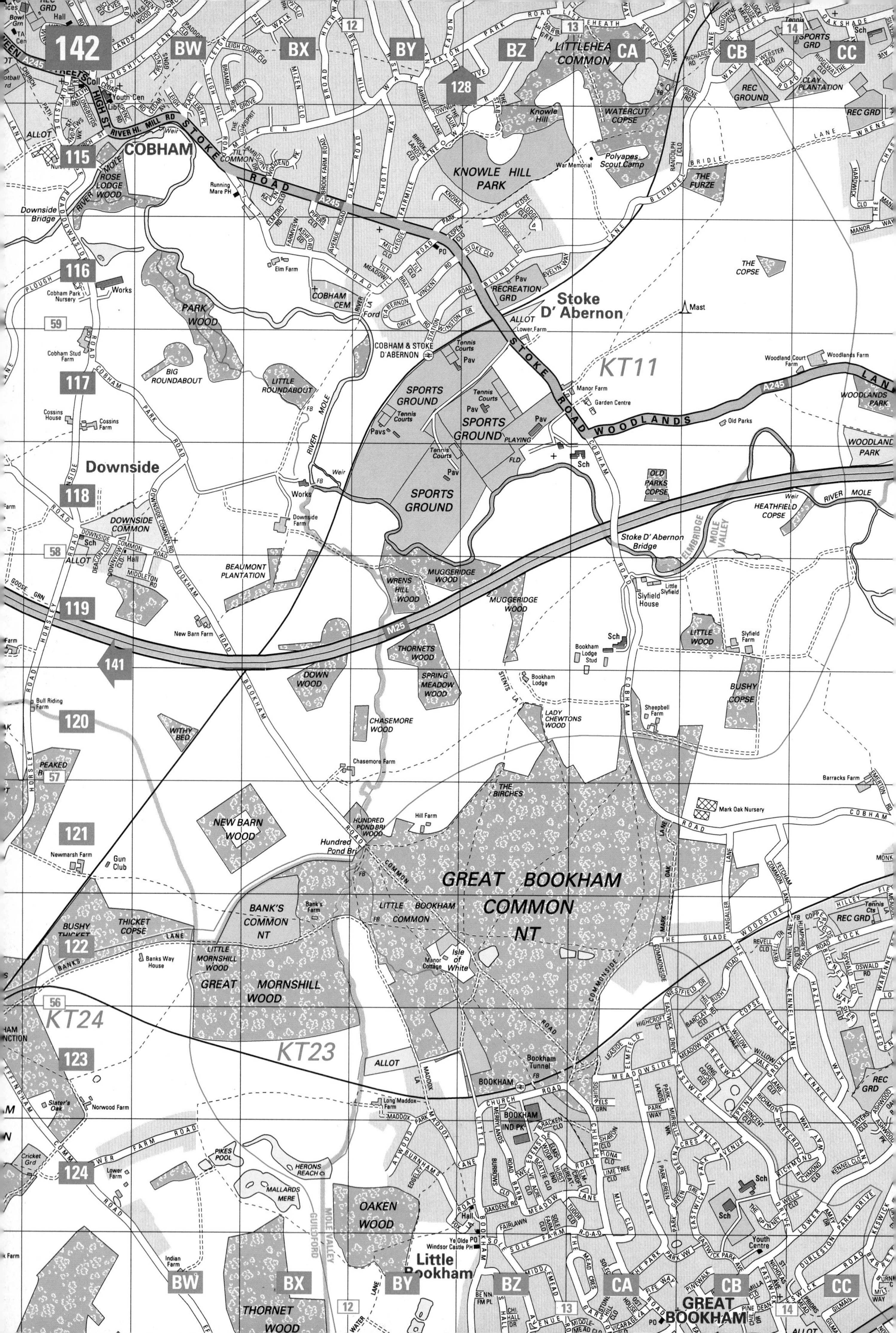
BW
BX
BY
BZ
CA
CB
CC
12
13
14
128
141
115
116
117
118
119
120
121
122
123
124
59
58
57
56
COBHAM
Stoke D' Abernon
Downside
KT11
KT24
KT23
STOKE ROAD
A245
M25
RIVER MOLE
KNOWLE HILL PARK
Knowle Hill
WATERCUT COPSE
LITTLEHEATH COMMON
Polyapes Scout Camp
War Memorial
THE FURZE
THE COPSE
Mast
REC GROUND
CLAY PLANTATION
SPORTS GRD
REC GRD
ROSE LODGE WOOD
Downside Bridge
Running Mare PH
TILT COMMON
Elm Farm
COBHAM CEM
Ford
PO
RECREATION GRD
Pav
ALLOT
Lower Farm
COBHAM & STOKE D'ABERNON
Tennis Courts
SPORTS GROUND
PLAYING FLD
Manor Farm
Garden Centre
WOODLANDS
Woodland Court Farm
Woodlands Farm
WOODLANDS PARK
Old Parks
WOODLAND PARK
OLD PARKS COPSE
HEATHFIELD COPSE
Weir
Stoke D' Abernon Bridge
ELMBRIDGE
MOLE VALLEY
Works
Cobham Park Nursery
Cobham Stud Farm
PARK WOOD
BIG ROUNDABOUT
LITTLE ROUNDABOUT
COBHAM PARK ROAD
Cossins House
Cossins Farm
DOWNSIDE COMMON
Downside Farm
BEAUMONT PLANTATION
WRENS HILL WOOD
MUGGERIDGE WOOD
Little Slyfield
Slyfield House
Sch
Hall
New Barn Farm
Bookham Lodge Stud
LITTLE WOOD
Slyfield Farm
THORNETS WOOD
SPRING MEADOW WOOD
DOWN WOOD
STENTS LA
Bookham Lodge
BUSHY COPSE
Bull Riding Farm
WITHY BED
CHASEMORE WOOD
LADY CHEWTONS WOOD
Sheepbell Farm
Chasemore Farm
PEAKED
THE BIRCHES
Barracks Farm
NEW BARN WOOD
HUNDRED POND BRI WOOD
Hill Farm
Hundred Pond Bri
Mark Oak Nursery
Newmarsh Farm
Gun Club
GREAT BOOKHAM COMMON NT
LITTLE BOOKHAM COMMON
BANK'S COMMON NT
Bank's Farm
BUSHY THICKET
THICKET COPSE
Banks Way House
LITTLE MORNSHILL WOOD
GREAT MORNSHILL WOOD
Manor Cottage
Isle of White
Bookham Tunnel
BOOKHAM
BOOKHAM IND. PK
ALLOT
Slater's Oak
Norwood Farm
Long Maddox Farm
Cricket Grd
Lower Farm
PIKES POOL
HERONS REACH
MALLARDS MERE
OAKEN WOOD
Indian Farm
Ye Olde Windsor Castle PH
Little Bookham
THORNET WOOD
GREAT BOOKHAM
Youth Centre
REC GRD
Tennis Cts

LEATHERHEAD GOLF COURSE
ASHTEAD COMMON
Pachesham Park
WOODLANDS PARK
TEAZLE WOOD
PACHESHAM GOLF COURSE
Leatherhead Common
Lower Ashtead
ASHTEAD
ASHTEAD HOSPITAL
LEATHERHEAD
FETCHAM
Junction 9
KT9
KT21
KT22
OXSHOTT ROAD
KINGSTON ROAD
RANDALLS ROAD
LEATHERHEAD BYPASS ROAD
GUILDFORD ROAD
YOUNG STREET
REIGATE ROAD
WOOD FIELD
Beaverbrook Roundabout
RANDALLS PARK CEMETERY
Esso House

EPSOM COMMON
CL
CM
CN
CP
CQ
CR
CS
NEWTON WOOD
FOREST
130
EPSOM
CONVENT
EPSOM GENERAL HOSP
DORKING ROAD
A24
115
116
117
118
119
120
121
122
123
124
WOOD FIELD
ASHTEAD
ASHTEAD PARK
Cottage in the Park
Woodcote
WORLDS END
FISH POND
Woodcote Stud Farm
Woodcote Park Hotel
WOODCOTE PARK GOLF COURSE
THE GROVE
The Durdans
Marsden Nursery and Garden Centre
Farm Lane Nurseries
Ashtead Ho
PLAYING FIELDS
Ashtead Park
Clubhouse
Sports Hall
BURIAL GRD
City of London Freemen's School
ASHTEAD REC GRD
Cricket Ground
Bowling Green
Brewery Inn
KT21
143
ASHTEAD HOSPITAL
ALLOT
Esso House
Chance Farm Stud
Larchfield
Stables
LANGLEY BOTTOM WOOD
Langley Bottom Farm
Langley Vale
THE WARREN
The Downs House Riding Stables
KT18
MOLE VALLEY
EPSOM & EWELL
ADDLESTEAD WOOD
Addlestead Farm
M25
Highlands Farm
COVERED RESERVOIR
Tyrrell's Wood
TYRRELL'S WOOD
HAMBLETON WOOD
HEADLEY COURT
SPORTS GRD
Clubhouse
Court Farm
COVERED RES
PIGNUT WOOD
LITTLE HURST WOOD
HOOK WOOD
GREAT HURST WOOD
COSTAL WOOD
Beaverbrook Roundabout
LEATHERHEAD BYPASS RD
KT22
TYRRELL'S WOOD GOLF COURSE
NOWER WOOD
OYSTER HILL NT
Headley
Glasshouses
19
20
21
56
57
58
59

CT
CU
CV
CW
CX
CY
CZ
22
23
24
131
KT17
SM7
KT20
115
116
117
118
119
120
121
122
123
124
146
59
58
57
56
SPORTS GROUND
Epsom College
EPSOM DOWNS
Clubhouse
South Hatch Stables
EPSOM GOLF COURSE
BUCKLE'S GAP
Derby Stables
EPSOM RACE COURSE
EPSOM DOWNS
The Hill
Race Stables
Tattenham Corner
TATTENHAM CORNER
LANGLEY VALE
WALTON DOWNS
EPSOM & EWELL
REIGATE & BANSTEAD
NORK
PARK WOOD
NORK PARK
PLAYING FIELD
Nork Park Farm
Works
TATTENHAM WAY RECREATION GROUND
PARK WOOD
ALLOT
PAGES ACRE
RUFFETT WOOD
CANONS WOOD
Superstore
COVERED RESERVOIRS
Burgh Heath
BURGH HEATH
Canons Farm
PLAYING FIELD
REC GRD
Football Ground
Comm Cen
Youth Cen
Sports Cen
PIT WOOD
Legal and General House
SPORTS GROUND
BUPA WINSCOMBE
Garden Farm
KINGSWOOD
THE CHILDRENS TRUST TADWORTH
TADWORTH
Tumble Beacon PH
WORKHOUSE POND
Kingswood Warren
KINGSWOOD
Cricket Ground
Police Training School
SPORTS GRD
Wingfield Stud Farm
MERE POND
BANSTEAD HEATH
Ebbisham Farm
SANDHILL WOOD
Walton Manor
Walton Manor Farm
WALTON ON THE HILL
War Memorial
The Clock Tower Riding Centre
Clubhouse
BEECHEN
SPORTS GROUND
BANSTEAD
COLLEGE ROAD
REIGATE ROAD
BRIGHTON ROAD
A217
A240
A2022
B290
B284
B2221
B2220
TATTENHAM CORNER RD
YEW TREE BOTTOM ROAD
BONSOR
WATERHOUSE LANE
MILL ROAD
NEW ROAD
DORKING ROAD
CHIPSTEAD

146
DA
DB
DC
DD
DE
DF
DG
132
145
115
116
117
118
119
120
121
122
123
124
26
27
28
56
57
58
59
WINKWORTH ROAD
BANSTEAD
REC GRD
SM7
THE SHRUBBERY
SCRATCH WOOD
WOODMANSTERNE
Banstead Place
Mint Farm
The Mint PH
Courtlands Farm
Tall Trees
New Place
Little Haugh
Home
Roseacre
GREAT SOLOM'S WOOD
CHALK WORKS
PARK DOWNS
HOLLY LANE
PAGES ACRE
RUFFETT WOOD
CANONS WOOD
SURREY HEARTLANDS QUEEN ELIZABETH HOSPITAL
DEPOT
NATURE RESERVE
BANSTEAD WOOD
CHIPSTEAD GOLF COURSE
CHIPSTEAD
COVERED RESERVOIR
Canons Farm
Perrotts Farm
LUNCH WOOD
FAMES ROUGH
CHIPSTEAD BOTTOM
CHIPHOUSE WOOD
WELL COPSE
OUTWOOD SHAW
Chipstead Bottom
SPORTS GROUND
Legal and General House
Tennis Courts
TUPA WINSCOMBE
St. Monica's
KINGSWOOD
KT20
OUTWOOD
POORFIELD WOOD
CHIPSTEAD MEADS REC GRD
Clubhouses
Bowling Green
EMBERS SHAW
STARROCK SHAW
Court Lodge
War Memorial
BURIAL GRD
Hooley
FOURTEEN ACRE SHAW
Noke Farm
THE GROVE
THE BELT
Shabden Park
Eyhurst Farm
Eyhurst Court
THE LONG PLANTATION
KINGSWOOD GOLF COURSE
Kingswood Warren
KINGSWOOD
THE RUFFETT
ROUND WOOD
RUFFETTS WOOD
COALROAS SHAW
HEDGELAND SHAW
WHITE HILL
Pigeonhouse Farm
TOP SHAW
ROUND WOOD
Manor Park
South Lodge
Reeves Rest
Well House PH
SMUGGLERS PIT PLANTATION
Clubhouse
Southerns Farm
BEECHEN COPSE
SPORTS GROUND
MILLFIELD WOOD
Mugswell
Park Farm
FOX SHAW
HARPS OAK SHAW
CLOCKHOUSE REC GRD
BIG WOOD
PROSPECT PLANTATION
How Hills
Longshaw
Elmore
Hengest Farm
Nicola Farm
The Manor House
Manor Cottage Farm

147
DH
DJ
DK
DL
DM
DN
DP
29
30
31
133
115
116
117
118
119
120
121
122
123
124
148
WOODCOTE PARK GOLF COURSE
CR8
HIGHER GROVE REC GRD
KENLEY
COULSDON
COULSDON SOUTH
SMITHAM
ULLSWATER CRESCENT TRADING ESTATE
COULSDON COURT PUBLIC GOLF COURSE
HARTLEY BUSHES
STONYFIELD SHAW
POSTERN WOOD
FARTHING OR FAIRDEAN DOWNS
MARLFIELD SHAW
GRANGE PARK
BETTS MEAD RECREATION GROUND
The Wattenden Arms
Old Coulsdon
CR5
CROYDON
REIGATE & BANSTEAD
STAR SHAW
THREE CORNERED SHAW
SPORTS GRD
REC GRD
BOXERS WOOD
DITCHES SHAW
DEVILSDEN WOOD
THE DEVILS DEN
SPARKLIE WOOD
HAPPY VALLEY PARK
REC GROUND
COULSDON COMMON
The Fox PH
SPORTS GROUND
Star Bridge
PETERSHOLE SHAW
SURREY
Forge Bridge
HOSPITAL (closed)
THE GULLET
FIGGS WOOD
TANDRIDGE
RIFLE RANGES
Caterham Barracks (closed)
HAPPY VALLEY GOLF COURSE
NETHERNE WOOD
Netherne Farm
SPORTS GROUND
Bowling Green
GRASSCUTS SHAW
LORD'S WOOD
BROAD WOOD
PILES WOOD
CHURCH GREEN
LIFECARE TRUST
HOME WOOD
RH1
Dean Farm
Court Farm
CARAVAN PARK
FURZEFIELD WOOD
ALDERSTEAD HEATH
FRYERN BROOM WOOD
Fryern Farm
Chaldon Mead
Chaldon
Rook Hill
CR3
WILLEY BROOM WOOD
SPARTICLES WOOD
Merstham Tunnel
Airshafts
COVERED RESERVOIR
Alderstead Farm
Upland Farm
BROTHERS FIELD
HIGH STANDING
BADGERS WOOD
Junction 7
BRIGHTON ROAD

DQ
DR
DS
DT
DU
DV
DW
33
34
35
134
147
115
116
117
118
119
120
121
122
123
124
59
58
57
56
KENLEY
Whyteleafe
Old Coulsdon
Caterham-on-the-Hill
CATERHAM
Hamsey Green
KINGS WOOD
RIDDLESDOWN WOOD
KENLEY AERODROME
KENLEY COMMON
COULSDON COMMON
WESTWAY COMMON
CR2
CR3
CR5
CR8
CROYDON
TANDRIDGE
SURREY
A21 ROAD
GODSTONE ROAD
CATERHAM BY-PASS A22
AINSLEY BERRY SHAW
RAGGED GROVE
DISPLEY'S WOOD
THE DOBBIN
TITHEPIT SHAW
WHYTELEAFE RECREATION GROUND
UPPER WARLINGHAM
BETTS MEAD RECREATION GROUND
The Wattenden Arms
Surrey Hill Gliding Club
Air Training Corp
COXES WOOD
BLIZE WOOD
Joysons Hill
BURIAL GRD
WHYTELEAFE SOUTH
Whyteleafe Football Club
MANOR PARK
Burntwood Hill
ROUND SHAW
Birchwood House Farm
Birchwood House
Stony Hill
BIRCH WOOD
WINDMILL SHAW
RYDON'S WOOD
Caterham Barracks (Closed)
RIFLE RANGES
MAGAZINE
Cricket Ground
LIFECARE NHS TRUST
HOME WOOD
Fryern Farm
Chaldon Mead
FRYERN BROOM WOOD
Rook Hill
WILLEY BROOM WOOD
BROAD WOOD
CATERHAM DENE HOSP
HOSP
THE NORTH DOWNS HOSP
Adult Education Inst
Tillingdown Farm
PARK SHAW
COV RES
The Miller Centre
Raglan Precinct
QUEENS PARK
Rugby Ground
SPORTS GROUND
PLAYING FIELDS
Gas Works
Rose & Crown PH
Warlingham Court Farm

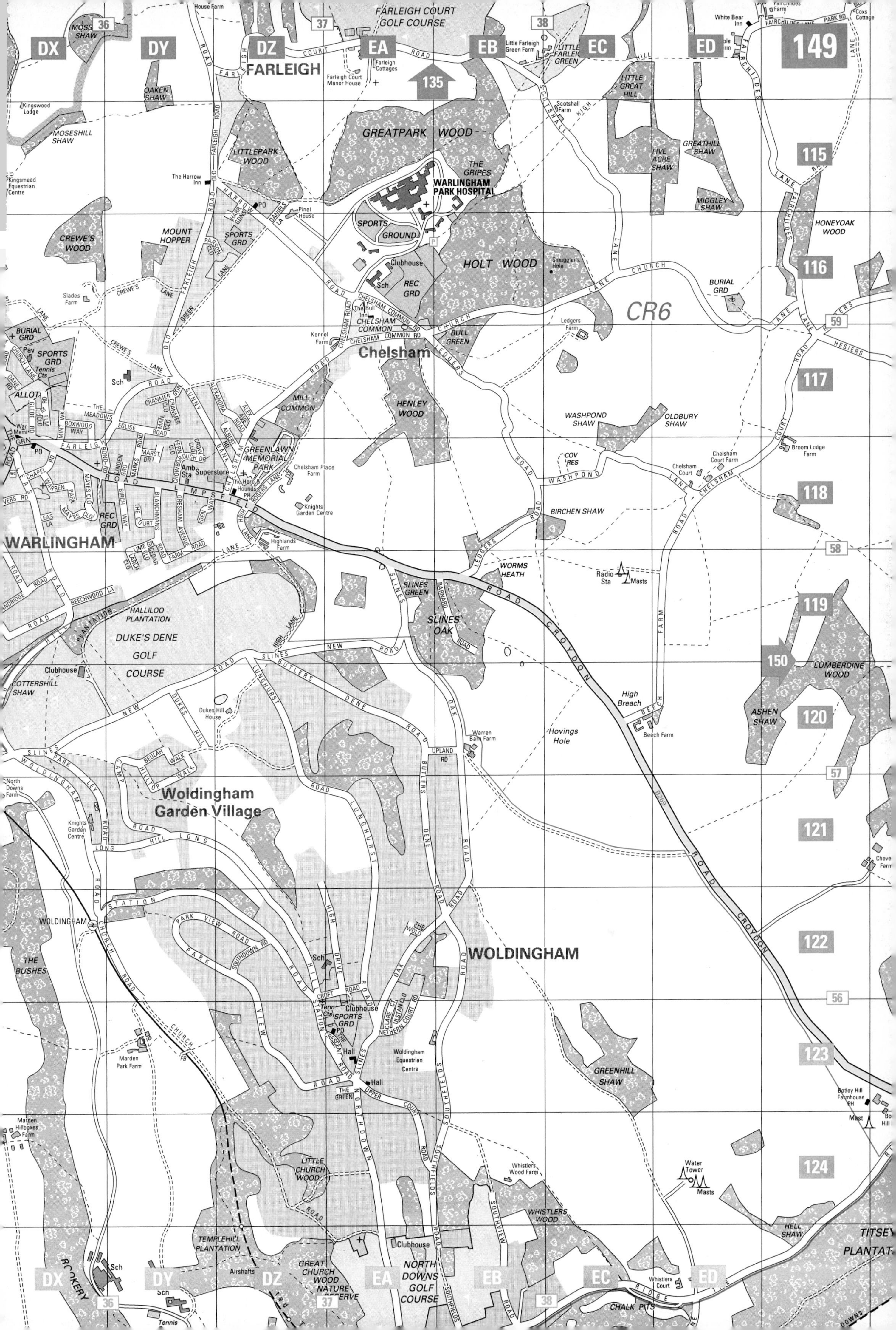
149
135
150
115
116
117
118
119
120
121
122
123
124
DX
DY
DZ
EA
EB
EC
ED
36
37
38
59
58
57
56
FARLEIGH
FARLEIGH COURT GOLF COURSE
GREATPARK WOOD
WARLINGHAM PARK HOSPITAL
HOLT WOOD
CR6
Chelsham
WARLINGHAM
Woldingham Garden Village
WOLDINGHAM
DUKE'S DENE GOLF COURSE
NORTH DOWNS GOLF COURSE
CROYDON ROAD
LIMPSFIELD ROAD
HONEYOAK WOOD
LUMBERDINE WOOD
ASHEN SHAW
GREENHILL SHAW
WHISTLERS WOOD
LITTLE CHURCH WOOD
GREAT CHURCH WOOD NATURE RESERVE
TEMPLEHILL PLANTATION
THE BUSHES
CREWE'S WOOD
MOUNT HOPPER
LITTLEPARK WOOD
HENLEY WOOD
WORMS HEATH
SLINES OAK
BIRCHEN SHAW
WASHPOND SHAW
OLDBURY SHAW
GREATHILL SHAW
FIVE ACRE SHAW
MIDGLEY SHAW
LITTLE GREAT HILL
HALLILOO PLANTATION
COTTERSHILL SHAW
MOSESHILL SHAW
OAKEN SHAW
MOSS SHAW
HELL SHAW
CHALK PITS
Woldingham Equestrian Centre
Marden Park Farm
Beech Farm
Broom Lodge Farm
Chelsham Court Farm
Ledgers Farm
Radio Sta
Masts
Water Tower
Hovings Hole
High Breach
Warren Barn Farm
Dukes Hill House
Knights Garden Centre
GREENLAWN MEMORIAL PARK
The Harrow Inn
Kingsmead Equestrian Centre
Kingswood Lodge
Slades Farm
House Farm
Farleigh Court Manor House
Farleigh Cottages
Little Farleigh Green Farm
LITTLE FARLEIGH GREEN
Scotshall Farm
White Bear Inn
Coxs Cottage
Botley Hill Farmhouse PH
Whistlers Wood Farm
Whistlers Court
TITSEY PLANTAT

150
EE
EF
EG
EH
EJ
EK
EL
136
149
115
116
117
118
119
120
121
122
123
124
40
41
42
59
58
57
56
BIGGIN HILL CIVIL AIRPORT
BIGGIN HILL
Tatsfield
Titsey
CR6
CR3
RH8
SURREY
BROMLEY
TANDRIDGE
MOLLARDS WOOD
OWLS WOOD
HONEYOAK WOOD
LUMBERDINE WOOD
ASHEN SHAW
PITCHERS WOOD
TITSEY PLANTATION
TITSEY PLACE GARDENS
PARK WOOD GOLF COURSE
LONG COPPICE
ROUND WOOD
HOME WOOD
ISLE SHAW
PARSONS SHAW
CHERRY TREE SHAW
SHEPHERDS SHAW
LONGLANDS SHAW
JERRY REDDINGS SHAW
COWYARD SHAW
WHITE BANK
CONY CROOK
OLDBURY SHAW
FIVE ACRE SHAW
MIDGLEY SHAW
HELL SHAW
CLARKSLANE SHAW
CHURCH WOOD
CLACKET WOOD
BARTON SHAW
WESTMORE GREEN
LIMEHOUSE BOTTOM
COLDHARBOUR BEECHES
BEAVER WATER WORLD
SPORTS GRD
Botley Hill
CROYDON ROAD
CLARKS LANE
MAIN ROAD
HESIERS ROAD
BEDDLESTEAD LANE
NORHEADS LANE
LUSTED HALL LANE
PILGRIMS LANE

151
137
152
BR6
TN14
TN16
Single Street
Cudham
Berry's Green
Horns Green
Aperfield
South Street
CHERRY LODGE GOLF COURSE
CUDHAM FRITH
NEW YEARS WOOD
BLACKBUSH SHAW
THE GROVE
THE NOWER
WESTERHAM WOOD
HARTLEY WOOD
HOLYWELL SHAW
PARK WOOD
KNOCKHOLT WOOD
BASTON WOOD
GREATER LONDON
KENT
BROMLEY
SEVENOAKS
M25
A233
A25

EU
EV
EW
EX
EY
EZ
FA
47
48
49
138
151
115
116
117
118
119
120
121
122
123
124
59
58
57
56
NEW YEARS WOOD
NEWLANDS WOOD
HAYMAN'S WOOD
New Years Cottage
BIRCHES CROFT
LONG BOTTOM SHAW
JOCKEY'S WOOD
HAWFIELD WOOD
Singles Cross
Blueberry Farm
The Spinney Nurseries
Whitelegg's Garden Centre
New Stables Farm
HUNTERS WALK
Warehouses
Knockholt Pound
WAYLANDS CLO
CHAPEL CROFT
Curry Farm
BROOMFIELD WOOD
Works
Harrow PH
Meadow Fm
Aldwyn House
Warren Farm
Rose Cottage Farm
BOND CLO
Clinic
Comm Cen
IVY LANE
Ivy Farm
Bowl Grn
The Grange
Football Ground
The Mill House
LEES WOOD
DUTCHMORE WOOD
Chine Farm
COPHALL WOOD
Shelleys
Letts Green
BROOM WOOD
Homefield
Court Lodge
Knockholt
COOPER'S WOOD
BASTON WOOD
War Meml
Sch
The Crown PH
LITTLE JOCKEYS WOOD
ASH PLATT
KNOCKHOLT BEECHES
ASHFIELD WOOD
STAR HILL WOOD
Masts
KNOCKHOLT WOOD
SAND BANKS
MINNY WOOD
COV RES
Keepers Cottage
Beeches Farm
Mountross Farm
The Tally Ho PH
SUMMERHOUSE WOOD
CHEVENING PARK
PARK WOOD
Sundridge Hill
Hazlet Wood Farm
THE SPINNEY
Chevening
ROUGHFIELDS WOOD
HAGBUSH WOOD
Chevening House
Well
BURIAL GROUND
Shootfield
TN14
KENT
BROMLEY
SEVENOAKS
Home Farm
Brasted Hill Farm
SHOOTFIELD WOOD
THE NOWER
HOME WOOD
JOELAND'S WOOD
Chevening Cross
Grove House
CLAYPIT SHAW
Oveny Green Farm
Farm
Combe Bank Farm
Ovenden Lodge
Junction 5
Hogtrough Hill
M25
Court Lodge Farm
Combe Bank Wood
COMBEBANK WOOD
COMBE WOOD
Willow Farm
TN16
B2211
PLAYING FLD
Sch
Pav
SPORTS GROUND
Pumping Station
Council Yard
PARK WOOD
ST MARTINS MEADOW
Tanners
Little Coombe Bank
Offices
Glasshouses
Mill Farm
The Stanhope Arms PH
The Old Rectory
PYM ORCHARD
Warren Farm
The Lamb PH
Brasted
Depots
Mill
Hall
Bowl Grn
The White Horse PH
Sunridge
The Old Rectory
Park Farm
Bull Inn
White Hart Inn
THE CARRIAGEWAY
Charmans Farm
REC GRD
Orchard Farm
Brasted Place
Sch
THE WARREN
THE ROOKERIES
Horizons Centre
Works
Mountwood
Fountain Cottages
Brasted Place Farm
Long Barn
RIVER DARENT
NORTH DOWNS WAY
PILGRIMS WAY
HIGH STREET
MAIN ROAD
CHEVENING ROAD
OVENDEN ROAD
COMBE BANK DRIVE

FB
FC
FD
FE
FF
FG
FH
139
Twitton
OTFORD
Dunton Green
Longford
Chipstead
Riverhead
Bessels Green
TN13
SEVENOAKS WILDFOWL RESERVE
EAST LAKE
WEST LAKE
LONGFORD LAKE
DEFENCE RESEARCH AGENCY
CHALK PIT
OLD GROVE
OTFORD CEMETERY
GRAVEL PIT
MONTREAL PARK
RIVERHEAD PARKLAND
CHIPSTEAD COMMON
COLD ARBOR WOOD
ASH PLAT WOOD
OBELISK WOOD
RAKEFIELD WOOD
ALDER SHAW
EDWARD SHAW
HOME WOOD
RYE WOOD
BLUEBELL WOOD
LITTLE BRITAIN'S WOOD
MIDDLINGS WOOD
KNOLE PADDOCK
KNOLE ENVIRONMENTAL PARK
SEVENOAKS HOSP
Morants Court Cross
Donnington Manor Hotel
Great Dunton Farm
Rye House Farm
Homestead Farm
Hopgarden Farm
Bradbourne Farm & Riding Centre
Montreal Park Farm
Salters Heath Farm
Brittains Farm
Smarts Garden Centre
Windmill Farm
Froghole
Otford Junction
115
116
117
118
119
120
121
122
123
124
154
155
50
51
52
56
57
58
59

154
FA
FB
FC
FD
FE
FF
FG
153
152
Longford
EAST LAKE
SEVENOAKS WILDFOWL
TN14
WEST LAKE
LONGFORD LAKE
Junction 5
Chevening Cross
CLAYPIT SHAW
RAKEFIELD WOOD
HELIPORT
Chipstead
Riverhead
Sunridge
Bessels Green
MONTREAL PARK
TN13
RIVERHEAD PARKLAND
ANT WOOD
ASH PLAT WOOD
OBELISK WOOD
COLD ARBOR WOOD
THE WARREN
CODS CORNER
LITTLE BRITAIN'S WOOD
MIDDLINGS WOOD
SEVENOAKS
Kippington
RED GROVE
GREAT BRITAIN'S WOOD
TN14
GREENLANE WOOD
FURZEFIELD WOOD
MILL WATER BOTTOM WOOD
MILDRIDGE WOOD
PLAYING FIELD
MILL BANK WOOD
WHITLEY FOREST
Seven Wents
HYDE'S FOREST
DUST WOOD
BARN WOOD
Goathurst Common
SHEEPHILL WOOD
PITFIELD WOOD
Douglas Hill
KEATING WOOD
ROUNDABOUT WOOD
LONGSPRINGS WOOD
Bayley's Hill
STUBBS WOOD
BROCKHOULT MOUNT
SEVENOAKS BYPASS
WESTERHAM ROAD
BRADBOURNE VALE
121
122
123
124
125
126
127
128
129
130
50
51
52
53
54
55
56

FH
FJ
FK
FL
FM
FN
FP
53
54
55
Greatness
Works
Gas Wks
Superstores
SEVENOAKS BUSINESS CEN
GREATNESS PARK PLAYING FIELDS
GREATNESS CEMETERY
Penfield
Tanners Cross
Stonepit Farm
Money Shaw
Fullers Hill Farm
Seal
121
TN15
A25
PINEWOOD AVE
Tumulus
MILLPOND WOOD
SEVENOAKS HOSP
PLAYING FIELD
Sports Centre
SUMMERHOUSE WOOD
WILDERNESSE AVENUE
Wilderness
Waterden
122
The Grove
COV RES
56
Clubhouse
CHANCE WOOD
WILDERNESSE GOLF COURSE
123
SEAL CHART
CHAPEL WOOD
RICHARDSON'S WOOD
GUY'S WOOD
APP'S WOOD
STONE STREET
HANGER WOOD
LITTLE ROGER'S WOOD
124
ALLOTMENTS
SPORTS GRD
Bowls Centre
Cricket Grd
Blackhall
Blackhall Farm
Clubhouse
DUCHESS PLANTATION
GODDEN WOOD
The Post House
The Bucks Head PH
Godden Green
HALL WOOD
Clinic
Stormont Court
125
PLAYING FIELD
KNOLE PADDOCK
SEVENOAKS
KNOLE ENVIRONMENTAL PARK
KNOLE PARK GOLF COURSE
LORD'S SPRING WOOD
DIANTSHATCH WOOD
SOUTH FIELD SHAW
RAMBLES WOOD
BAKER'S WOOD
126
NT
Knole
THE WILDERNESS
RUNNING TRACK
SPORTS GROUND
Tennis Centre
Cedarholme
Keepers Cottages
The Kennels
54
Lower Fawke Farm
BITCHET COMMMON
127
FAWKE COMMON
FAWKE WOOD
KNOLE PARK
DEER PARK
PLAYING FIELD
REDLANDS WOOD
CLACKETTS WOOD
One Tree Hill NT
128
White Rocks
Rooks Hill
Carter's Hill
CHESTNUT PLANTATION
53
BADCOCK WOOD
Sevenoaks Common
THE SEVEN OAKS
The White Hart PH
QUARRY SHAW
BROADFIELD SHAW
RUMSHOTT WOOD
129
Kettleshill Farm
Rumshott Manor
St. Julians
Well
BRIMSTONEWELL WOOD
COVERED RESERVOIR
Underriver Vineyard
Absalom's Farm
Black Charles Barn
Valley Farm
SEVENOAKS COMMON
CHESTNUT PLANTATION
BEECHMONT BANK
River Hill
PARK WOOD
Riverhill House
ASH PLAT
130
Underriver
White Rock PH
Hubbard's Hill
Weald Place
Airshaft
Hall
BURIAL GRD
GEORGE'S SHAW
Underriver Farm
Panthurst Farm
RIVER HILL
A225
TONBRIDGE ROAD

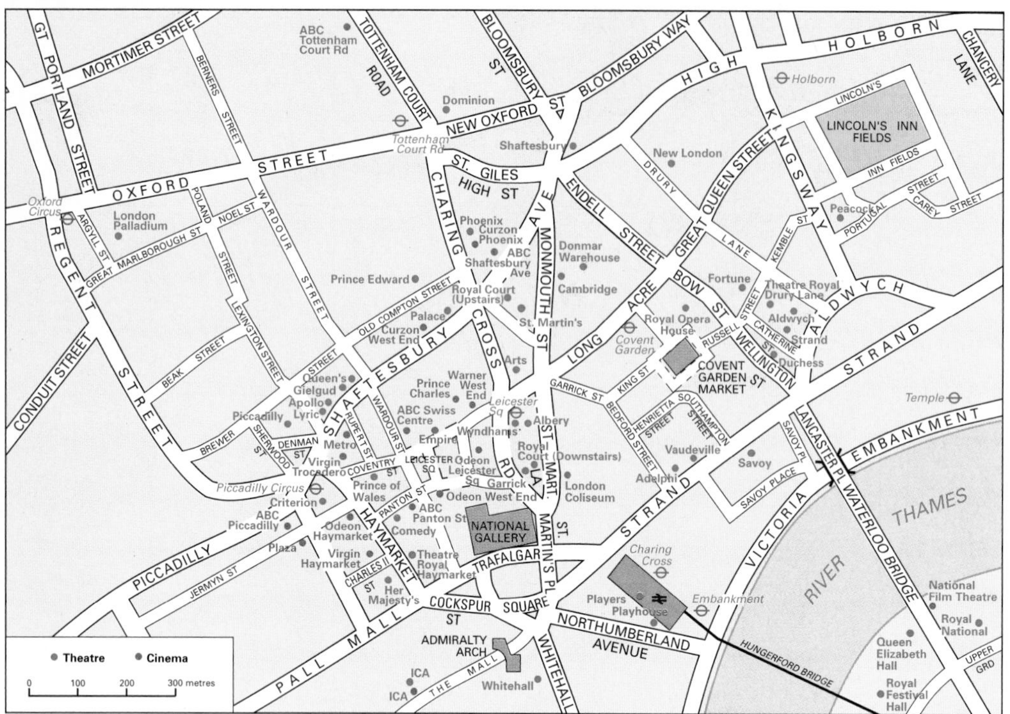

THEATRES

Adelphi 020 7344 0055
Albery 020 7369 1730
Aldwych 020 7416 6003
Apollo 020 7416 6022
Arts 020 7836 2132
Cambridge 020 7494 5054
Comedy 020 7369 1731
Criterion 020 7369 1747
Dominion 020 7656 1888
Donmar Warehouse 020 7369 1732
Duchess 020 7494 5075
Fortune 020 7836 2238
Garrick 020 7494 5085
Gielgud 020 7494 5065
Her Majesty's 020 7494 5400
ICA 020 7930 3647
London Coliseum 020 7632 8300
London Palladium 020 7494 5020
Lyric 020 7494 5045
New London 020 7405 0072
Palace 020 7434 0909
Peacock 020 7314 8800
Phoenix 020 7369 1733
Piccadilly 020 7369 1734
Players 020 7839 1134
Playhouse 020 7839 4401
Prince Edward 020 7734 8951
Prince of Wales 020 7839 5987
Queen Elizabeth Hall
 020 7960 4242
Queen's 020 7494 5041
Royal Court Theatre Downstairs
 020 7565 5000
Royal Court Theatre Upstairs
 020 7565 5000
Royal Festival Hall
 020 7960 4242
Royal National 020 7452 3000
Royal Opera House (CLOSED)
 020 7304 4000
St. Martin's 020 7836 1443
Savoy 020 7836 8888
Shaftesbury 020 7379 5399
Strand 020 7930 8800
Theatre Royal, Drury Lane
 020 7494 5550
Theatre Royal, Haymarket
 020 7930 8800
Vaudeville 020 7836 9987
Whitehall 020 7369 1735
Wyndhams 020 7369 1736

CINEMAS

ABC Panton St 020 7930 0631
ABC Piccadilly 020 7437 3561
ABC ShaftesburyAvenue
 020 7836 6279
ABC Swiss Centre
 020 7439 4470
ABC Tottenham Court Rd
 020 7636 6148
Curzon Phoenix 020 7369 1721

Curzon West End 020 7369 1722
Empire 020 7437 1234
ICA 020 7930 3647
Metro 020 7437 0757
National Film Theatre
 020 7928 3232
Odeon Haymarket
 0426 915353
Odeon Leicester Sq
 020 8315 4215

Odeon Mezzanine
(Odeon Leicester Sq)
 020 8315 4215
Odeon West End
 020 8315 4221
Plaza 020 7437 1234
Prince Charles 020 7437 8181
Virgin Haymarket 0870 907 0712
Virgin Trocadero 0870 907 0716
Warner West End 020 7437 4347

WEST END SHOPPING

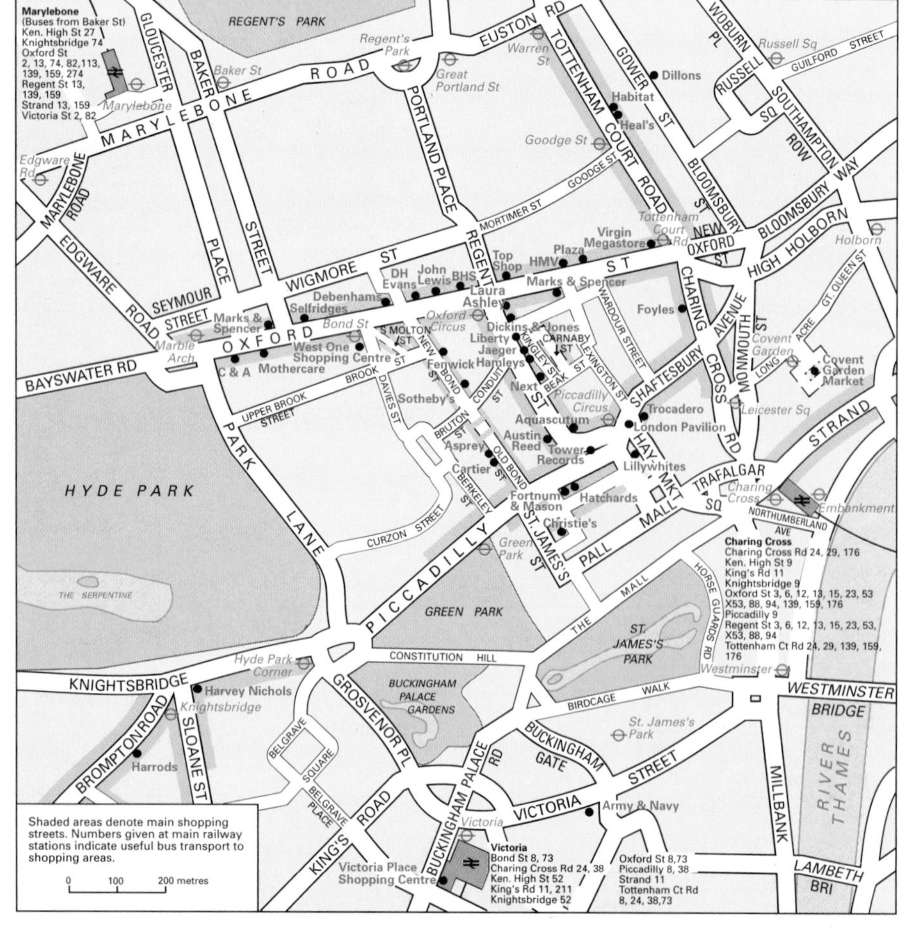

SHOPS

Aquascutum 020 7734 6090
Army & Navy 020 7834 1234
Asprey 020 7493 6767
Austin Reed 020 7734 6789
BHS (Oxford St) 020 7629 2011
C & A 020 7629 7272
Cartier 020 7493 6962
Christie's 020 7839 9060
Covent Garden Market 020 7836 9137
DH Evans 020 7629 8800
Debenhams 020 7580 3000
Dickins & Jones 020 7734 7070
Dillons 020 7636 1577
Fenwick 020 7629 9161
Fortnum & Mason 020 7734 8040
Foyles 020 7437 5660
Habitat (Tottenham Court Rd)
 020 7631 3880
Hamleys 020 7734 3161
Harrods 020 7730 1234
Harvey Nichols 020 7235 5000
Hatchards 020 7439 9921
Heal's 020 7636 1666
HMV 020 7631 3423
Jaeger 020 7200 4000
John Lewis 020 7629 7711
Laura Ashley (Regent St) 020 7355 1363
Liberty 020 7734 1234
Lillywhites 020 7930 3181
London Pavilion 020 7437 1838
Marks & Spencer
 (Marble Arch) 020 7935 7954
Marks & Spencer (Oxford St)
 020 7437 7722
Mothercare 020 7580 1688
Next (Regent St) 020 7434 2515
Plaza on Oxford St 020 7637 8811
Selfridges 020 7629 1234
Sotheby's 020 7493 8080
Top Shop & Top Man 020 7636 7700
Tower Records 020 7439 2500
Trocadero 020 7439 1791
Victoria Place Shopping Centre
 020 7931 8811
Virgin Megastore 020 7580 5822

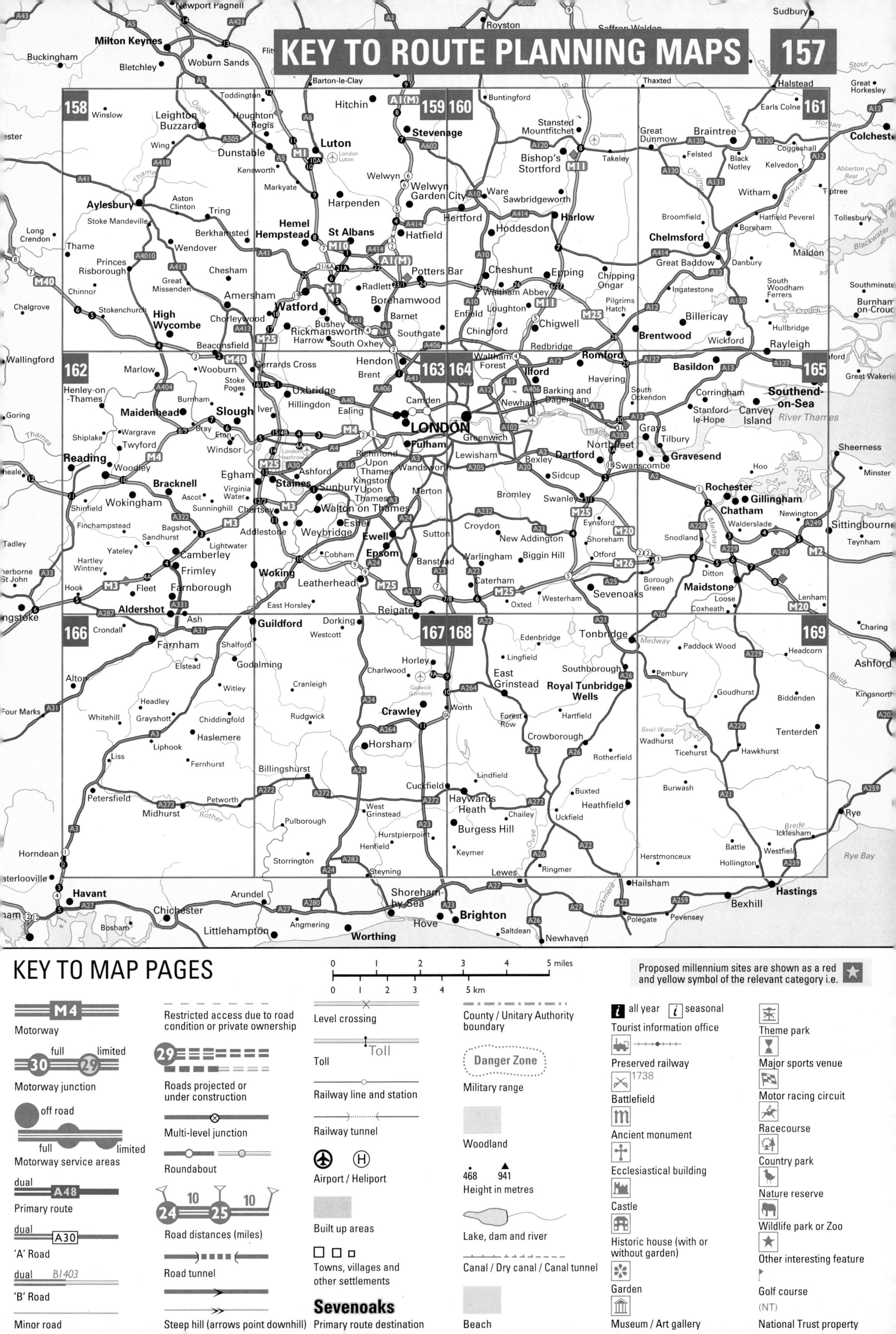

KEY TO ROUTE PLANNING MAPS

157

158 | **159 160** | **161**

162 | **163 164** | **165**

166 | **167 168** | **169**

KEY TO MAP PAGES

M4 Motorway

30 — 29 Motorway junction
full / limited

Motorway service areas (off road) full / limited

dual **A48** Primary route

dual **A30** 'A' Road

dual *B1403* 'B' Road

Minor road

Restricted access due to road condition or private ownership

29 Roads projected or under construction

Multi-level junction

Roundabout

24 — 10 — 25 — 10 Road distances (miles)

Road tunnel

Steep hill (arrows point downhill)

Sevenoaks Primary route destination

Level crossing

Toll Toll

Railway line and station

Railway tunnel

✈ / Ⓗ Airport / Heliport

County / Unitary Authority boundary

Danger Zone Military range

Woodland

468 / ▲ **941** Height in metres

Lake, dam and river

Canal / Dry canal / Canal tunnel

Built up areas

□ ▢ ▫ Towns, villages and other settlements

Beach

ⓘ all year **ⓘ** seasonal
Tourist information office

Preserved railway
1738

Battlefield

Ⓜ Ancient monument

Ecclesiastical building

Castle

Historic house (with or without garden)

Garden

Museum / Art gallery

Proposed millennium sites are shown as a red and yellow symbol of the relevant category i.e. ★

Theme park

Major sports venue

Motor racing circuit

Racecourse

Country park

Nature reserve

Wildlife park or Zoo

Other interesting feature

Golf course

(NT) National Trust property

158
A
B
C
1
2
3
4
AYLESBURY
HIGH WYCOMBE
AMERSHAM
CHESHAM
Leighton Buzzard
Winslow
Thame
Tring
Wendover
Princes Risborough
Great Missenden
Beaconsfield
Marlow
Hazlemere
Tylers Green
Wooburn
Waddesdon
Stokenchurch
Watlington
Chinnor
Haddenham
Long Crendon
Stoke Mandeville
Bierton
Wing
Ledburn
Soulbury
Stewkley
Swanbourne
Padbury
Steeple Claydon
Quainton
Whitchurch
Hardwick
Weedon
Aston Clinton
Halton
Wigginton
Northchurch
Cholesbury
Chartridge
Prestwood
Naphill
Downley
West Wycombe
Lane End
Fingest
Turville
Ibstone
Christmas Common
Pyrton
Shirburn
Chiltern Hills
The Three Hundreds of Aylesbury

159
LETCHWORTH
Hitchin
STEVENAGE
LUTON
London Luton
HARPENDEN
WELWYN GARDEN CITY
HERTFORD
HEMEL HEMPSTEAD
ST ALBANS
Hatfield
WATFORD
Borehamwood
BARNET
ENFIELD
HARROW
HARINGEY
Rickmansworth
Abbots Langley
Radlett
Potters Bar
Bushey
South Oxhey
Westoning
Apsley End
Higham Gobion
Barton-le-Clay
Hexton
Sharpenhoe
Harlington
Barton Hills
Sundon Hills
Toddington
Streatley
Fancott
Upper Sundon
Lower Sundon
Chalton
Sundon Park
Warden Hill
Lilley
Limbury
Leagrave
Stopsley
Houghton Regis
Dunstable
Stockwood Craft Mus & Gdns
Mus. & Art Gallery
Pirton
Holwell
Icklefield
Walsworth
Charlton
Great Offley
Gosmore
Preston
Ley Green
Cockernhoe
King's Walden
Breachwood Green
St Paul's Walden
Langley
Whitwell
Knebworth House
Bendish
Great Wymondley
St Ippollitts
Little Wymondley
William
Weston
Graveley
Clothall
Walllington
Hall's Green
Cromer
Hare Street
Ardeley
Walkern
Aston End
Benington Lordship
Benington
Shephall Aston
Hebing End
Broadwater
Bragbury End
Haultwick
Knebworth
Old Knebworth
The Node
Datchworth
Woolmer Green
Datchworth Green
Oaklands
Bull's Green
Burnham Green
Harmer Green
Digswell
Tewin
Bramfield
Sacombe
Watton at Stone
Stapleford
Tonwell
Chapmore End
Waterford
Bengeo
Codicote
Ayot St Lawrence
Shaw's Corner (NT)
Welwyn
Ayot St Peter
Kimpton
Peter's Green
New Mill End
Luton Hoo
Caddington
Slip End
Kensworth
Kensworth Common
Whipsnade Wild Animal Park
Woodside Farm
Studham
Markyate
Cheverell's Green
Flamstead
Trowley Bottom
East Hyde
Kinsbourne Green
Blackmore End
The Folly
Marshall's Heath
Hatching Green
Wheathampstead
Gaddesden Row
Great Gaddesden
Nettleden
Water End
Redbourn
Church End
Potten End
Piccotts End
Childwick Green
Sandridge
Cromer Hyde
Lemsford
Stanborough
Activity World
Hatfield Hyde
Mill Green Museum
Hatfield House
Cole Green
Hertingfordbury
Letty Green
Essendon
Bayford
Little Berkhamsted
Epping Green
Woodside
Wildhill
Welham Green
Water End
Bell Bar
Brookmans Park
Newgate Street
Great Wood
Hammond Street
Goff's Oak
Cuffley
Northaw
Verulamium Roman Town
Verulamium Museum
Gorhambury
Colney Heath
Bowmans Farm
Boxmoor
Leverstock Green
St Stephens
Apsley
Potters Crouch
Chiswell Green
Park Street
Frogmore
London Colney
Felden
Bovingdon
Bedmond
Kings Langley
Chipperfield
Flaunden
Huntonbridge
Bucks Hill
Smug Oak
Bricket Wood
Colney Street
Shenleybury
Shenley
South Mimms
Ridge
Green Street
Sarratt
Chenies
Chandler's Cross
Cassiobury Park
Aldenham
Letchmore Heath
Elstree
Aldenham Reservoir
Arkley
Wrotham Park
Enfield Chase
Hadley Wood
Monken Hadley
Barnet 1471
Trent Park
Botany Bay
Forty Hill
Cockfosters
New Barnet
East Barnet
Winchmore Hill
Southgate
Croxley Green
Merry Hill
Bushey Heath
Batchworth
Maple Cross
Moor Park
Batchworth Heath
Eastbury
Stanmore
Hatch End
Edgware
London Gateway
Totteridge
Mill Hill
Friern Barnet
Wood Green
West Hyde
Northwood
Pinner Green
Harrow Weald
Wealdstone
Harrow Museum
Harefield
Ruislip Common
Bayhurst Wood
Pinner
Eastcote
Kingsbury
R.A.F. Mus
Hendon
Finchley
Tottenham
Hornsey
Golders Green
Kenwood
Ruislip
Greenhill
Denham
Harrow
Wembley
Watling Street
M1
M10
M25
A1(M)
A5120
A6141
A600
A507
A6
A505
A5065
A5
A1072
A1155
A602
A1081
A5183
A6129
A414
A4147
A1057
A4251
A405
A411
A412
A404
A4145
A4125
A4008
A409
A5109
A1000
A1005
A110
A41
A4140
A4180
A598
A504
A4006
A502
A103
A406
A109
A10
A40
Chess
Grand Union Canal

A B C

Wallington Roe Green Mill End Quin Anstey Wicken Bonhunt Debden Debden Green
Chipping Wyddial Meesden Clavering Rickling Wendens Ambo Prior's Hall Barn Mole Hall
Rushden Throcking Brent Pelham Starling's Green Quendon
Buntingford B1038 Great Hormead Stocking Pelham Berden Rickling Green
Cromer Cottered Hare Street Little Hormead Barleycroft End Ugley Henham Chickney
Hare Street Ardeley Aspenden Furneux Pelham East End Ugley Green B1051 Broxted
Westmill B1368 Hay Street Manuden Elsenham
Walkern Wood End Patmore Heath Farnham Green Farnham
Benington Lordship Benington Great Munden Nasty Braughing Albury Hazel End Stansted Mountfitchet Molehill Green
Haultwick Puckeridge Birchanger Stansted Bamber's Green
Hebing End Green End Standon A120 Little Hadham Takeley Street Takeley
Bragbury End Collier's End Hadham Ford BISHOP'S STORTFORD Birchanger Green A120
A602 Dane End Bury Green Smith's Green
Datchworth Sacombe Much Hadham Thorley Street Hope End
Datchworth Green Watton at Stone High Cross B1004 Great Hallingbury Hatfield Forest (NT) Bacon End
Bull's Green Stapleford Tonwell Wadesmill Hadham Cross Thorley Little Hallingbury
Burnham Green Chapmore End Thundridge Perry Green Green Tye Spellbrook Great Canfield
Baker's End Allen's Green Adventure Island Playbarn Hatfield Broad Oak
A119 Paynes Hall A1170 Widford Sawbridgeworth A1060 Hatfield Heath
Tewin Bramfield Bengeo Ware B1004 Wareside Hunsdon Aythorpe Roding Keeres Green
Waterford B1000 Great Amwell High Wych A1184 Sheering
HERTFORD A119 Stanstead Abbotts Gilston Park Pye Corner Churchgate Street White Roding Leaden Roding
Cole Green A414 St Margarets Eastwick A414 Matching M11
Hertingfordbury Little Amwell A1170 Hailey Roydon HARLOW Matching Green Abbess Roding
Letty Green Hertford Heath A1169 Matching Tye
Bayfordbury B1197 Rye Park Little Parndon A1025 Church Langley Threshers Bush Beauchamp Roding
Essendon Hoddesdon Great Parndon Foster Street Magdalen Laver Little Laver
Bayford Little Berkhamsted Broxbourne Spitalbrook Roydon Hamlet A1169 Potter Street Hastingwood High Laver Pickerells
Epping Green Newgate Street Paradise Wildlife Park A10 Broxbourne Broadley Common North Weald Airfield Moreton Fyfield Willingale
Wormley Lower Nazeing Nazeing Epping Green B181 B1393 Bovinger Bobbingworth Clatterford End
Great Wood Turnford Bumble's Green Thornwood Common Tylers Green Shelley Norton Mandeville
Hammond Street Flamstead End Epping Upland North Weald Bassett Chipping Ongar Norton Heath
Goff's Oak Cheshunt Coopersale Common A414
Cuffley B156 Churchgate Lee Valley Cobbin's Brook Toot Hill Greensted High Ongar
Potters Bar B156 Waltham Cross Upshire Epping Fiddlers Hamlet A128 Stondon Massey
M25 Waltham Abbey Stanford Rivers
A1005 Enfield Chase Botany Bay Capel Manor 25 26 6/27 Stapleford Tawney Little End Kelvedon Hatch
Hadley Wood Forty Hill A1010 Sewardstone Epping Forest B172 Theydon Bois A113 Doddinghurst
A111 Trent Park ENFIELD A1055 High Beach Loughton Navestock
A110 Ponders End A1168 M11 Passingford Bridge Abridge Navestock Side Pilgrims Hatch
A105 Winchmore Hill A104 A121 Stapleford Abbotts M25 Coxtie Green
Chingford A1069 Buckhurst Hill A113 A1112 Weald Park
A1010 B154 A110 Hainault Forest Lambourne End Bournebridge South Weald
Southgate A10 B160 Chigwell Noak Hill Havering-atte-Bower
A109 Friern Barnet Edmonton A1037 A1009 Chigwell Row Havering A1023
Woodford Green B173 Grange Hill Hainault Harold Hill 28 Brook Street
A109 Wood Green A406 Woodford Woodford Bridge Fairlop Waters Collier Row Roman Road Great Warley
A406 Tottenham WALTHAM FOREST A11 A113 Barkingside A12 Gidea Park Harold Wood
A504 Hornsey A1055 B179 A503 A112 10 Marks Gate A127
HARINGEY Walthamstow A1400 REDBRIDGE Seven Kings A118 ROMFORD 29
Kenwood A103 A107 Wanstead A406 A123 Rush Green Cranham
Kenwood House A104 A12 A114 Leyton ILFORD Ilford A1083 A124 Hornchurch A125 Upminster B187

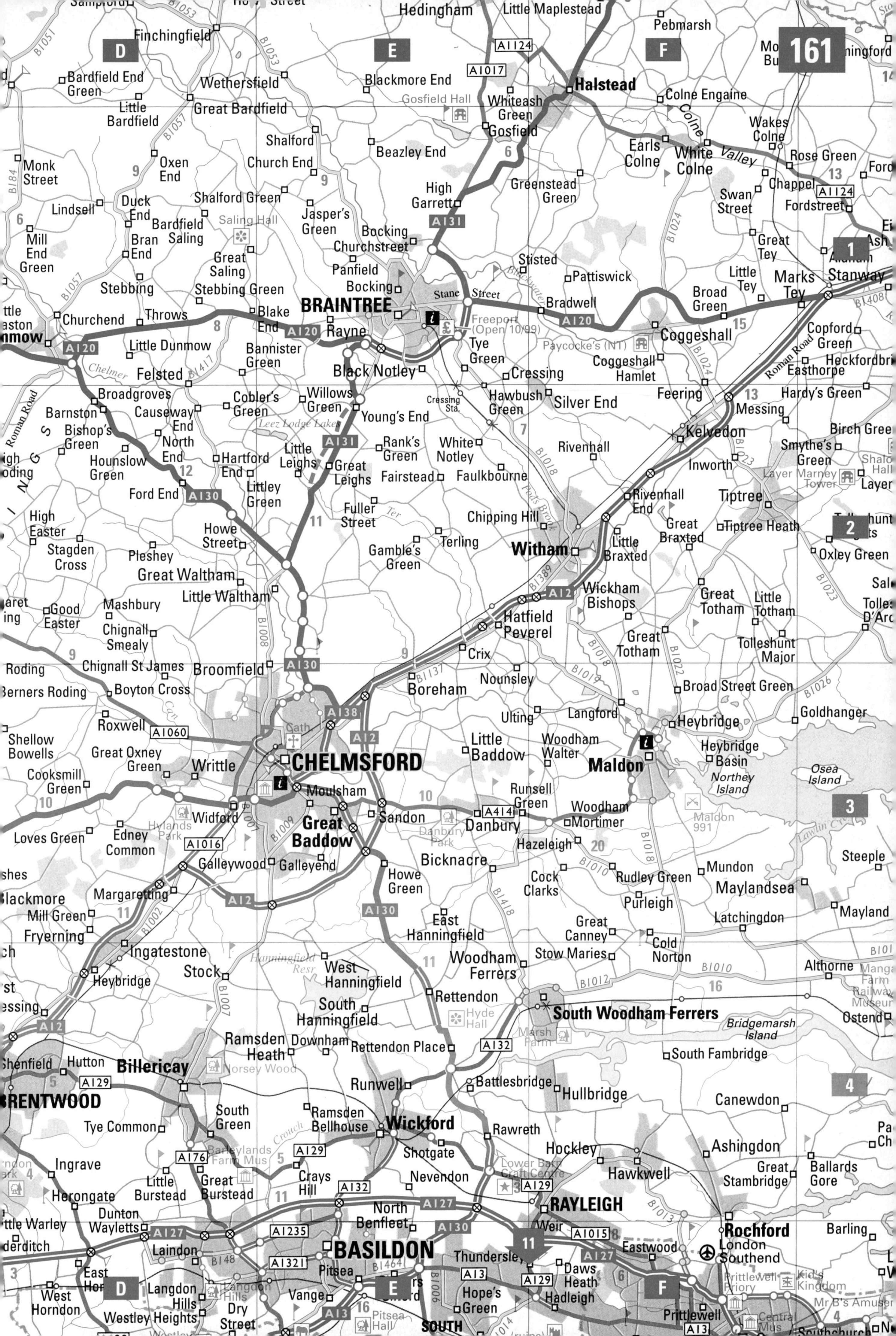

161
D
E
F
Hedingham
Little Maplestead
Pebmarsh
Finchingfield
B1053
B1051
A1124
A1017
Bardfield End Green
Wethersfield
Blackmore End
Halstead
Colne Engaine
Little Bardfield
Great Bardfield
Gosfield Hall
Whiteash Green
Gosfield
Colne Valley
Wakes Colne
B1057
Shalford
Beazley End
Earls Colne
White Colne
Rose Green
Monk Street
Oxen End
Church End
6
Greenstead Green
13
Chappel
Swan Street
A1124
Fordstreet
B184
9
Duck End
Shalford Green
Jasper's Green
High Garrett
A131
Lindsell
Bardfield Saling
Saling Hall
Bocking Churchstreet
Mill End Green
Bran End
Great Saling
B1024
Great Tey
1
Panfield
Stisted
Pattiswick
Little Tey
Marks Tey
Stanway
Stebbing
Stebbing Green
Bocking
Blackwater
Broad Green
Churchend
Throws
Blake End
BRAINTREE
Stane Street
Bradwell
B1408
A120
Rayne
Freeport (Open 10/99)
A120
15
Copford Green
A120
Little Dunmow
Bannister Green
Tye Green
Paycocke's (NT)
Coggeshall
Roman Road
Chelmer
Felsted
B1417
Black Notley
Cressing
Coggeshall Hamlet
Heckfordbridge
Easthorpe
Broadgroves
Barnston
Causeway End
Cobler's Green
Willows Green
Cressing Sta.
Hawbush Green
Silver End
Feering
13
Messing
Hardy's Green
Roman Road
Bishop's Green
Leez Lodge Lakes
Young's End
7
Kelvedon
Birch Green
North End
Hartford End
Little Leighs
A131
Rank's Green
White Notley
Rivenhall
Smythe's Green
Hounslow Green
12
Great Leighs
Fairstead
Faulkbourne
B1018
B1023
Inworth
Layer Marney Tower
Layer
Littley Green
Rivenhall End
Tiptree
Ford End
A130
High Easter
Fuller Street
Chipping Hill
Great Braxted
Tiptree Heath
2
Howe Street
11
Ter
Pods Brook
Terling
Stagden Cross
Gamble's Green
Witham
Little Braxted
Oxley Green
Pleshey
Great Waltham
B1389
A12
Wickham Bishops
Great Totham
Little Totham
Little Waltham
B1023
Good Easter
Mashbury
Hatfield Peverel
Chignall Smealy
B1008
Great Totham
Tolleshunt Major
9
Crix
B1018
B1022
Roding
Chignall St James
Broomfield
A130
B1137
Nounsley
B1019
Broad Street Green
B1026
Berners Roding
Boyton Cross
Boreham
Roxwell
A1060
A138
Ulting
Langford
Heybridge
Goldhanger
Shellow Bowells
Cath
A12
Little Baddow
Woodham Walter
Heybridge Basin
Great Oxney Green
Writtle
CHELMSFORD
Maldon
Osea Island
Cooksmill Green
Northey Island
Moulsham
Runsell Green
10
10
Widford
Sandon
A414
Danbury
Woodham Mortimer
Maldon 991
3
Hylands Park
Great Baddow
Danbury Park
Loves Green
Edney Common
B1009
Hazeleigh
20
B1018
A1016
Bicknacre
Steeple
Galleywood
Galleyend
Howe Green
Cock Clarks
B1010
Rudley Green
Mundon
Margaretting
A12
Maylandsea
Blackmore
11
Purleigh
Mill Green
A130
B1418
Mayland
East Hanningfield
Great Canney
Latchingdon
Fryerning
B1002
Cold Norton
Ingatestone
Hanningfield Resr
Woodham Ferrers
Stow Maries
11
B1010
Althorne
Stock
West Hanningfield
B1012
16
Mangapps Farm Railway Museum
Heybridge
B1007
Rettendon
South Hanningfield
Hyde Hall
South Woodham Ferrers
Bridgemarsh Island
Ostend
A12
Ramsden Heath
Downham
Marsh Farm
Rettendon Place
A132
South Fambridge
Shenfield
Hutton
Billericay
Norsey Wood
A129
5
Battlesbridge
4
BRENTWOOD
Runwell
Hullbridge
Canewdon
South Green
Ramsden Bellhouse
Tye Common
Crouch
Wickford
Rawreth
Barleylands Farm Mus
Hockley
Ashingdon
Ingrave
A176
A129
5
Shotgate
Great Stambridge
Ballards Gore
4
Little Burstead
Great Burstead
Crays Hill
Nevendon
Lower Barn Craft Centre
Hawkwell
Herongate
A132
A129
11
North Benfleet
A127
RAYLEIGH
B1013
Dunton Wayletts
A127
A1235
A130
Weir
A1015
Rochford
Barling
Laindon
BASILDON
11
Eastwood
London Southend
Langdon Hills
B148
A1321
Thundersley
A127
Pitsea
B1464
A13
Daws Heath
Prittlewell Priory
Kid's Kingdom
East Horndon
D
E
F
West Horndon
Langdon Hills
Dry Street
Vange
B1006
Hope's Green
A129
Hadleigh
Mr B's Amusements
3
Westley Heights
16
Pitsea Hall
A13
SOUTH
Prittlewell
Central Mus
A13
Southchurch

162
A
B
C
HIGH WYCOMBE
M40
Christmas Common
Northend
Ibstone
Cadmore End
Bolter End
Lane End
Fingest
Frieth
Skirmett
Turville Heath
Turville
Greenfield
Pishill
Russell's Water
Stonor Park
Stonor
Park Corner
Maidensgrove
Huntercombe End
Fawley
Middle Assendon
Nettlebed
Hambleden
Rockwell End
Lower Woodend
Marlow
Booker
Handy Cross
Wycombe Marsh
Loudwater
Flackwell Heath
Little Marlow
Well End
Wooburn
Wooburn Green
Bourne End
Hedsor
Penn
Knotty Green
Forty Green
Bekonscot Model Village
Holtspur
Beaconsfield
Milton's Cottage
Seer Green
Jordans
Chalfont St Peter
Odds Farm Park
Hedgerley
Farnham Common
Dropmore
Cliveden (NT)
Burnham Beeches
Stoke Poges
Farnham Royal
Burnham
Cookham
Bisham
Bisham Abbey N.S.C.
Cookham Dean
Cookham Rise
Furze Platt
Hurley
Medmenham
Hurley Bottom
Mill End
Greenlands
Bix
Lower Assendon
Fawley Court
Aston
Remenham
Remenham Hill
Greys Court (NT)
Greys Green
Henley-on-Thames
River & Rowing Mus
Thames or Isis
Stoke Row
Shepherd's Green
Highmoor Cross
Rotherfield Greys
Rotherfield Peppard
Harpsden
Sonning Common
Kidmore End
Burchett's Green
Cockpole Green
Ashley Hill
Crazies Hill
Warren Row
Knowl Hill
Pinkneys Green
Taplow
MAIDENHEAD
SLOUGH
Salt Hill
Upton
Bray Wick
Bray
Dorney
Eton Wick
Eton
Dorney Court
Boveney
Windsor
Clewer Village
WINDSOR
A404(M)
Littlewick Green
Woodlands Park
White Waltham
Wargrave
Kiln Green
Hare Hatch
Lower Shiplake
Shiplake
Tokers Green
Binfield Heath
Dunsden Green
Mapledurham
Mapledurham House &
Emmer Green
Caversham
Sonning Eye
Play Hatch
Museum of Reading
READING
Sonning
Woodley
Twyford
Ruscombe
Waltham St Lawrence
Paley Street
Stud Green
Holyport
Touchen-End
Fifield
Oakley Green
Spital
Legoland
Hawthorn Hill
Whistley Green
Shurlock Row
Hurst
Dinton Pastures
Warfield
Maiden's Green
Winkfield
Cranbourne
Windsor Forest
Windsor Great Park
Cooper's Hill
Englefield Green
Savill
Woodside
Winkfield Row
Binfield
Newell Green
Winnersh
A329(M)
Whitley
Shinfield
Burghfield
Sindlesham
Wokingham
Popeswood
BRACKNELL
North Ascot
Ascot
Burleigh
Cheapside
Virginia Water
Sunninghill
Sunningdale
South Ascot
Easthampstead
Eastheath
Arborfield
Arborfield Cross
Arborfield Garrison
Barkham
Three Mile Cross
Grazeley
Spencers Wood
Swallowfield Park
Swallowfield
Wokefield Park
Beech Hill
Stratfield Mortimer
Farley Hill
Riseley
Wellington
Stratfield Saye
Look Out Discovery Park
Surrey Hill
California
Wick Hill
Crowthorne
Bagshot
Windlesham
Longcross
Chobham Common
Finchampstead
Eversley
Eversley Cross
Sandhurst
Yateley
CAMBERLEY
Blackwater
Darby Green
Frogmore
Bramshill
Bramshill Forest
Heckfield
Stratfield Turgis
Turgis Green
Hound Green
Hazeley
Mattingley
Hartley Wespall
Sherfield on Loddon
Church End
Rotherwick
West Green
West Green House (NT)
Phoenix Green
Hartfordbridge
Hartley Wintney
Minley Manor
Hawley
Hawley Lake
Fox Lane
West Heath
Cove
FRIMLEY
Frimley Green
Farnborough Green
Deepcut
Mytchett
Bagshot Heath
Chobham Ridges
Danger Zone
Donkey Town
Lightwater
West End
Chobham
Burrowhill
Bisley
Knaphill
St John's
Horsell
Brookwood
Pirbright
Henley Park
Worplesdon
Pitch Place
Stoughton
Wood Street
Normandy
Ash Vale
Ash
Wanborough
Flexford
Tongham
Hog's Back
Onslow Village
Compton
Puttenham
Seale
Loseley
FARNBOROUGH
Army Mus
North Town
ALDERSHOT
Heath End
Badshot Lea
Runfold
Hale
FARNHAM
Dippenhall
Ewshot
Crondall
Church Crookham
Crookham Village
FLEET
Fleet Pond
Winchfield
Dogmersfield
Long Valley
Mill Lane
Hook
Newnham
Nately Scures
Old Basing
Hatch
Up Nately
Greywell
Odiham
North Warnborough
Mapledurwell
Upton Grey
South Warnborough
Sutton
Well
Weston Corbett
Weston Patrick
NORTH DOWNS

Rickmansworth
South Oxhey
Edgware
Totteridge
Southgate
Mill Hill
Northwood
Harefield
Pinner
HARROW
Wealdstone
Harrow Weald
Kingsbury
Finchley
Hendon
Golders Green
Hornsey
HARINGEY
Tottenham
Denham
Ruislip
Eastcote
Greenhill
Harrow on the Hill
Sudbury
BRENT
Wembley
Hampstead
ISLINGTON
CAMDEN
HACKNEY
UXBRIDGE
HILLINGDON
Ickenham
Northolt
Greenford
Perivale
Willesden
Harlesden
Paddington
Marylebone
Finsbury
Shoreditch
Cowley
Yeading
Hayes
Southall
EALING
Hanwell
Acton
HAMMERSMITH & FULHAM
CITY OF WESTMINSTER
Hyde Park
Iver
Yiewsley
West Drayton
Norwood Green
Heston
Brentford
Chiswick
KENSINGTON & CHELSEA
Colnbrook
Sipson
Harmondsworth
Longford
Cranford
Osterley
Barnes
Fulham
Battersea
SOUTHWARK
London Heathrow
Hatton
Isleworth
Kew
Mortlake
Putney
Roehampton
WANDSWORTH
Clapham
Stanwell Moor
Stanwell
East Bedfont
HOUNSLOW
Twickenham
RICHMOND UPON THAMES
LAMBETH
Dulwich
Wraysbury
Feltham
Ham
Wimbledon
West Norwood
Ashford
Teddington
KINGSTON UPON THAMES
Upper Tooting
Streatham
STAINES
Hanworth
Wimbledon
Sunbury
West Molesey
Hampton
Norbiton
Mitcham
Littleton
Laleham
East Molesey
Surbiton
New Malden
MERTON
Morden
Upper Halliford
Shepperton
WALTON-ON-THAMES
Thames Ditton
Long Ditton
Worcester Park
Malden
Beddington Corner
Chertsey
Weybridge
Hersham
ESHER
Tolworth
Hook
Carshalton
Wallington
Beddington
Addlestone
New Haw
West End
Claygate
Chessington
Ewell
Cheam
SUTTON
South Beddington
Row Town
Woodham
Whiteley Village
Belmont
Purley
Byfleet
Oxshott
Malden Rushett
EPSOM
Woodmansterne
West Byfleet
Cobham
Stoke D'Abernon
BANSTEAD
Chipstead
Wisley
Pyrford
WOKING
Downside
Ashtead
Burgh Heath
Coulsdon
Martyr's Green
Ripley
LEATHERHEAD
Old Woking
Ockham
Send Marsh
Send
Fetcham
Tadworth
Kingswood
Hooley
Chaldon
Headley
Walton on the Hill
Little Bookham
Great Bookham
Effingham
Givons Grove
Mickleham
The Hermitage
West Clandon
East Horsley
West Horsley
Pebble Coombe
Merstham
Burpham
Merrow
East Clandon
Westhumble
Buckland
Nutfield
Newland's Corner
Dorking
Brockham
Betchworth
REIGATE
Redhill
South Park
GUILDFORD
Shere
Gomshall
Wotton
Dover
Albury
Abinger Hammer
Leigh
Sidlowbridge
Chilworth
North Holmwood
Salfords
M25
M41
A40(M)

164
A
B
C
Southgate
Edmonton
Wood Green
Tottenham
WALTHAM FOREST
Chigwell
Chigwell Row
Havering
Havering-atte-Bower
Noak Hill
Harold Hill
Brook Street
Woodford
Woodford Green
Woodford Bridge
Grange Hill
Hainault
Fairlop Waters
Collier Row
Gidea Park
Roman Road
Harold Wood
Barkingside
Marks Gate
REDBRIDGE
Seven Kings
ROMFORD
Hornsey
HARINGEY
Walthamstow
Wanstead
Rush Green
Cranham
Hornchurch
Upminster
Leyton
ILFORD
Ilford
Becontree
BARKING & DAGENHAM
Elm Park
HAVERING
Stoke Newington
ISLINGTON
Hampstead
CAMDEN
HACKNEY
Bethnal Green
Forest Gate
Barking
Dagenham
South Hornchurch
London Zoo
Regents Park
Shoreditch
Finsbury
West Ham
East Ham
Rainham
Belhus Wood
Marylebone
British Mus
Great Ct
Stepney
Mile End Park
TOWER HAMLETS
NEWHAM
Creekmouth
Wennington
Poplar
Beckton
Thamesmead
CITY OF WESTMINSTER
CITY OF LONDON
Millennium Experience
London Arena
London City
Erith Marshes
Danger Zone
Aveley
Purfleet
Thurrock Lakeside
Bermondsey
Woolwich
Abbey Wood
Belvedere
Oval
Camberwell
Deptford
Rangers House
Charlton
Plumstead
Erith
Battersea Park
Children's Zoo
SOUTHWARK
GREENWICH
Shooter's Hill
East Wickham
Slade Green
West Thurrock
Dartford Tunnel & Bridge
Blackheath
Kidbrooke
Welling
Bexleyheath
DARTFORD
Toll
Greenhithe
Clapham
LEWISHAM
Eltham
Hall Place
Crayford
Stone
Hither Green
Eltham Palace
BEXLEY
Horniman Museum
LAMBETH
Dulwich
Catford
Upper Tooting
West Norwood
Sydenham
Grove Park
Mottingham
New Eltham
Coldblow
Wilmington
Hawley
Lane End
North Cray
Streatham
Crystal Palace Park
Crystal Palace
Farmyard
Crystal Palace N.S.C.
Sidcup
Foots Cray
Darenth
Upper Norwood
Penge
Chislehurst
Chislehurst Caves
Hextable
Sutton at Hone
Green Street Green
South Darenth
Beckenham
Bickley
St Paul's Cray
Swanley
Farningham Rd Sta.
Horton Kirby
Mitcham
South Norwood
BROMLEY
St Mary Cray
Crockenhill
Farningham
Fawkham Green
Beddington Corner
Fairfield Halls
Croydon Skyline
Eden Park
West Wickham
Bromley Common
Hayes
Orpington
Roman Villa (ruins)
Eynsford
Lullingstone
Beddington
Shirley
Locksbottom
Addington
Keston
Farnborough
Green Street Green
Chelsfield
Knockholt Sta.
Well Hill
Brands Hatch
Wallington
CROYDON
South Beddington
New Addington
Leaves Green
Downe
Pratt's Bottom
Badgers Mount
Shoreham
West Kingsdown
Purley
Selsdon
London Biggin Hill
Hazelwood
Down House
Halstead
Romney Street
Sanderstead
Farleigh
Cudham
Knockholt Pound
Kenley
Coulsdon
Biggin Hill
Otford
Kemsing
Heaverham
Whyteleafe
Whyteleafe Sta.
Chelsham
Warlingham
Knockholt
Chevening
Dunton Green
Seal
Oldbury
Chaldon
Hooley
Tatsfield
Quebec House (NT)
Riverhead
Woldingham
Chipstead
Stone Street
Ivy Hatch
Caterham
Clacket Lane
Titsey
Brasted
Sundridge
Sevenoaks
Ightham Mote (NT)
Merstham
Limpsfield
Westerham
Emmetts (NT)
Knole (NT)
Underriver
Oxted
Squerryes Court
Brasted Chart
Ide Hill
Whitley Row
Shipbourne
Godstone
Hurst Green
Toy's Hill
Sevenoaks Weald
Nutfield
Tandridge
Holland
Chartwell (NT)
Nizels
Bletchingley
Crockham Hill
Redhill
South Nutfield
Godstone Farm
Cooper's Corner
Hildenborough
14
Ridge Green
South Godstone
Godstone
Marlpit Hill
Four Elms
Bough Beech Resr
Redhill Aerodrome & Heliport
Crowhurst Lane End
Crowhurst
Bough Beech
Chiddingstone Causeway
Hall Place
Hilden Park
The Grange
Blindley
Haxted
Hever Castle
Penshurst
Leigh
M25
M20
M26
A1037
A1009
A406
A1055
A503
A112
A113
A1400
A123
A118
A12
A127
A504
A103
A107
A104
A114
A1083
A124
A125
A1112
A1201
A10
A11
A115
A1153
A1240
A5203
A1205
A1306
A13
A1020
A2016
A206
A102
A1206
A200
A215
A2
A3212
A3036
A202
A3
A207
A209
A220
A282
A1090
A205
A210
A2018
A226
A296
A214
A20
A211
A222
A223
A217
A2212
A208
A21
A224
A225
A236
A212
A232
A237
A235
A2022
A23
A233
A22
A25
A2044
B2027
B269
B2026
B2042
B245
267

Tye Common
Ingrave
Herongate
Little Burstead
Great Burstead
Barleylands Farm Mus
Crays Hill
Ramsden Bellhouse
Wickford
Shotgate
Nevendon
Rawreth
Hockley
Lower Barn Craft Centre
Hawkwell
Ashingdon
Stambridge
Dunton Wayletts
Laindon
North Benfleet
BASILDON
RAYLEIGH
Weir
Eastwood
Rochford
Barling
London Southend
Thundersley
Daws Heath
Hadleigh
Hope's Green
East Horndon
West Horndon
Langdon Hills
Dry Street
Westley Heights
Pitsea
Vange
Bowers Gifford
Pitsea Hall
Waf Tyler
SOUTH BENFLEET
(ruins)
Leigh-on-Sea
Westcliff-on-Sea
Peter Pan's Playground
Southend Pier
Prittlewell Priory
Prittlewell
Kid's Kingdom
Central Mus
Southchurch
Sea Life Centre
Bulphan
Zoo
One Tree Hill
Horndon on the Hill
Orsett
Corringham
Fobbing
Stanford-le-Hope
Coryton
Thames Haven
Mucking
Baker Street
Leigh Beck
CANVEY ISLAND
Chapman Sands
SOUTHEND-ON-SEA
THAMES
Blythe Sands
Linford
Chadwell St Mary
Little Thurrock
West Tilbury
GRAYS
Tilbury
East Tilbury
Fort
Halstow Marshes
St Mary's Marshes
Allhallows-on-Sea
Allhallows
St Mary's Hoo
Isle of Grain
Cliffe
Cooling
Northward Hill
Lower Stoke
Grain
Church Street
High Halstow
Stoke
Stoke Saltings
Wallend
Swanscombe
GRAVESEND
M.V. Princess Pocahontas
Danger Zone
Milton Chantry
Chalk
Lower Higham
Cliffe Woods
Chattenden
Kingsnorth Power Station
Hoo
Queenborough
Perry Street
Betsham
Southfleet
Singlewell or Ifield
Shorne
Thong
Shorne Ridgeway
Higham
Wainscott
Upnor
Upper Upnor
Frindsbury
Medway
Chetney Marshes
Hook Green
Longfield
Istead Rise
Owletts (NT)
Guildhall Mus
Chatham Historic Dockyard & Lifeboat Collection
Cobham
Cobham Hall
Strood
ROCHESTER
Manor
Rochester Cath
Brompton
GILLINGHAM
Grange
Upchurch
Iwade
Swale Sta.
Longfield Hill
Camer
Sole Street
New College
CHATHAM
Luton
Lower Halstow
Kemsley
Hook Green
Camer
Cuxton
Luddesdown
Borstal
Rainham
Bobbing
Meopham
Capstone
Wigmore
Newington
Milton Regis
Meopham Green
Halling
Wouldham
Walderslade
Hartlip
Upper Halling
Medway
SITTINGBOURNE
Ridley
South Street
Harvel
Holborough
Snodland
Blue Bell Hill
Lidsing
Borden
Oad Street
Culverstone Green
Burham
Bredhurst
Stockbury
Bapchild
Tunstall
Trosley
Fairseat
Vigo Village
Coldrum Long Barrow (NT)
Birling
Ham Hill
Eccles
Kit's Coty House
Little Kit's Coty House
Bredgar
Highsted
Ryarsh
Trottiscliffe
Addington
New Hythe
The Friars
Aylesford
Abbey
Boxley
Bicknor
Wrotham Heath
Leybourne
Ditton
Sandling
Allington
Detling
Hucking
Milstead
West Malling
Abbey
East Malling
Royal British Legion Village
Barming Sta.
Thurnham
Wormshill
Offham
St Leonard's Tower
Manor
Broad Street
Frinsted
Platt
Great Comp
St Leonard's Street
Mus & Art Gall
MAIDSTONE
Bearsted
Maidstone
Eyhorne Manor
Hollingbourne
Eyhorne Street
Wichling
Crouch
Old Soar Manor (NT)
Kent Street
East Barming
Tovil
Stoneacre (NT)
Leeds
West Street
Mereworth
Waterinbury
Teston
Shepway
Otham
Harrietsham
Warren Street
Dunk's Green
West Peckham
Nettlestead Green
West Farleigh
Nettlestead
East Farleigh
Dean Street
Leeds Castle & Gdns
Langley
Langley Heath
Broomfield
Kingswood
Lenham
Loose
Boughton Green
Sandway
Lenham Heath
Goose Green
Coxheath
Chart Corner
Five Wents
Hadlow
Hale Street
Yalding
Linton
Boughton Monchelsea Place
Liverton Street
Higham Wood
East Peckham
Hunton
Sutton Valence
Ulcombe
Grafty Green
Boughton Malherbe
Benover
Gold Green
Beltring
Beult
Laddingford
Mockbeggar
Cross-at-Hand
Egerton
D
E
F
1
2
3
4
7
15

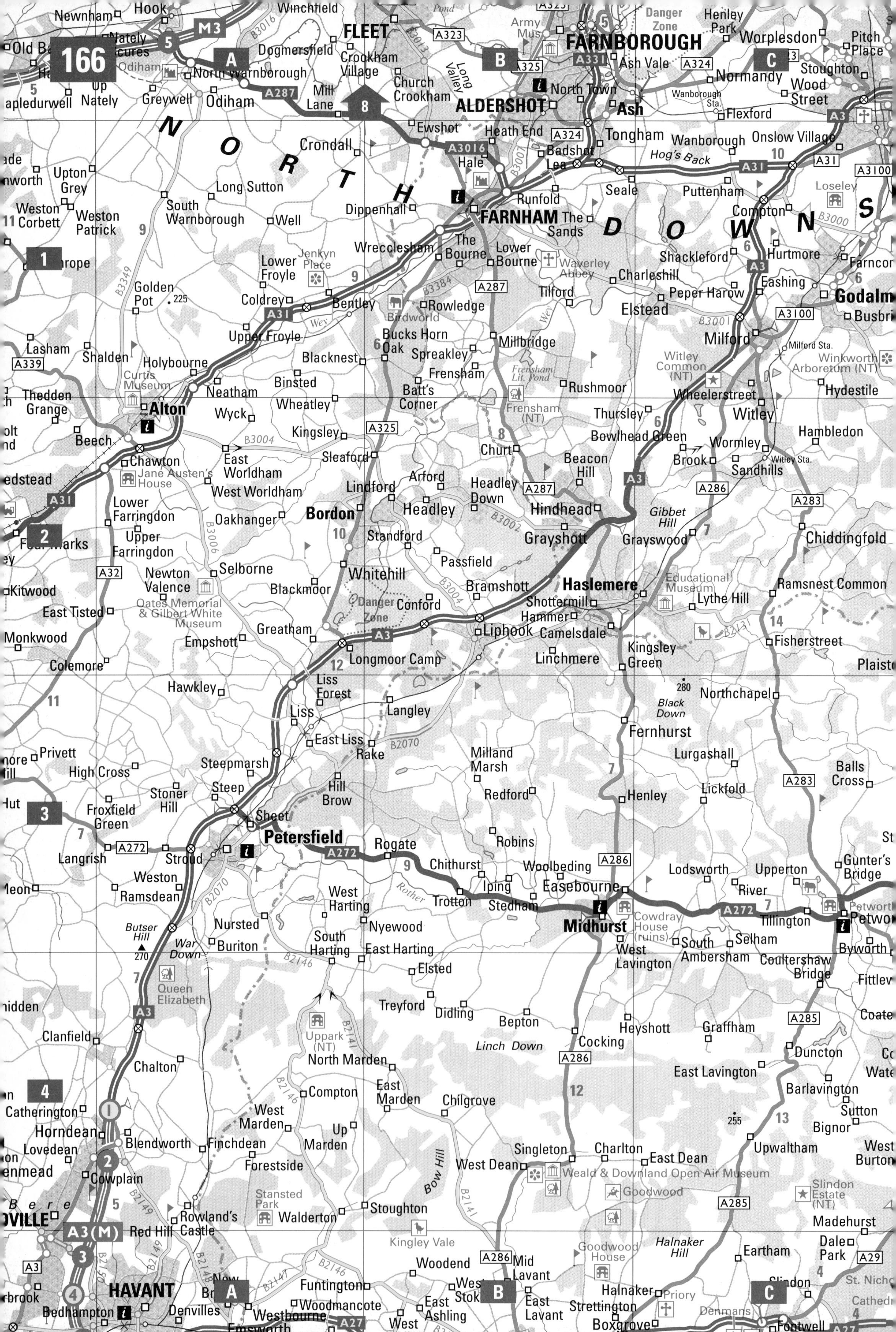
166
NORTH DOWNS
FLEET
FARNBOROUGH
ALDERSHOT
FARNHAM
Alton
Bordon
Haslemere
Petersfield
Midhurst
HAVANT
Godalming
Liphook
Odiham
Crondall
Hindhead
Grayshott
Milford
Fernhurst
Liss
Emsworth
Westbourne
Singleton
Weald & Downland Open Air Museum
Goodwood
Halnaker
Boxgrove
Cowplain
Horndean
Rowland's Castle

167
GUILDFORD
Dorking
REIGATE
Redhill
Horley
CRAWLEY
HORSHAM
Cranleigh
Burgess Hill
Storrington
Pulborough
Steyning
Billingshurst
Arundel
East Horsley
West Horsley
Effingham
Mickleham
West Clandon
Burpham
Merrow
East Clandon
Newland's Corner
Shere
Gomshall
Albury
Chilworth
Shalford
Wonersh
Bramley
Blackheath
Farley Green
Shamley Green
Westcott
Wotton
Abinger Hammer
Brockham
Betchworth
Buckland
Merstham
Nutfield
South Park
Doversgreen
Leigh
Sidlowbridge
Salfords
North Holmwood
South Holmwood
Friday Street
Abinger Common
Sutton
Peaslake
Holmbury St Mary
Hurtwood Common
Leith Hill
Coldharbour
Beare Green
Newdigate
Capel
Parkgate
Norwood Hill
Hookwood
Charlwood
Gatwick (London)
Tinsley Green
Lowfield Heath
County Oak
Ifield
Three Bridges
Pound Hill
Worth
Ifieldwood
Rusper
Lambs Green
Gossops Green
Faygate
Holmbush
Colgate
Roffey
Pease Pottage
St Leonard's Forest
Handcross
Staplefield
Slaugham
Warninglid
Lower Beeding
Mannings Heath
Monk's Gate
Nuthurst
Copsale
Maplehurst
Cowfold
Bolney
Ansty
Cuckfield
Hickstead
Twineham
Wineham
Henfield
Albourne
Sayers Common
Hurstpierpoint
Hassocks
Keymer
Ditchling
Clayton
Pyecombe
Poynings
Fulking
Edburton
Small Dole
Woodmancote
Blackstone
Upper Beeding
Bramber
Botolphs
Coombes
Patcham
Hollingbury
Preston
Hangleton
Kingston
Findon
Washington
Ashington
Ashurst
Partridge Green
West Grinstead
Dial Post
Shipley
Coolham
Southwater
Brooks Green
Coneyhurst Common
The Bar
Broadbridge Heath
Warnham
Kingsfold
Oakwoodhill
Walliswood
Ewhurst Green
Ockley
Jayes Park
Forest Green
Ewhurst
Rudgwick
Bucks Green
Ellen's Green
Rowhook
Slinfold
Itchingfield
Barns Green
Five Oaks
Buckman Corner
Newpound Common
The Haven
Alfold
Alfold Crossways
Dunsfold
Loxwood
Ifold
Kirdford
Roundstreet Common
Wisborough Green
Adversane
Broadford Bridge
North Heath
Gay Street
Codmore Hill
Stopham
Nutbourne
West Chiltington
Thakeham
Warminghurst
Abingworth
Hardham
Wiggonholt
Greatham
Rackham
Cootham
Parham
Sullington
Kithurst Hill
Bury
Amberley
Houghton
North Stoke
South Stoke
Burpham
Warningcamp
Harrow Hill
North End
Patching
Clapham
Stroud Common
Rowly
Grafham
Holmwood Sta.
Denne Park
Christ's Hosp. Sta.
Gatwick Zoo
Redhill Aerodrome & Heliport
Wakehurst Place (NT)
High Beeches
Nymans (NT)
Leonardslee
Brook Street
Whitemans Green
Crabtree
Ditchling Beacon
Pulborough Brooks R.S.P.B. Nature Reserve
Amberley Museum
Amberley Sta.
Wildfowl Trust
Fishers Farm Park
Stane Street
A24
A23
A29
A264
A272
A281
A283
A25
M23

168
M25
Limpsfield
Oxted
Hurst Green
Tandridge
Holland
10
Westerham
Brasted Chart
Emmetts (NT)
Toy's Hill
Chartwell (NT)
Crockham Hill
Ide Hill
Whitley Row
Knole (NT)
Ightham Mote (NT)
Underriver
Shipbourne
Sevenoaks Weald
Nizels
Cooper's Corner
Hildenborough
Nutfield
Redhill
Godstone
Bletchingley
South Nutfield
Godstone Farm
South Godstone
Godstone Sta.
Ridge Green
Redhill Aerodrome & Heliport
Crowhurst Lane End
Crowhurst
The Grange
Blindley Heath
Marlpit Hill
Four Elms
Bough Beech Resr
Bough Beech
Chiddingstone Causeway
Hall Place
Hilden Park
Leigh
Leigh Sta.
Penshurst Sta.
Hever Castle
Haxted
Edenbridge
Chiddingstone
Hever
Penshurst Place
Outwood
Horne
Mill & Museum
Marsh Green
Bidborough
Horley
Smallfield
Lingfield
Markbeech
Penshurst
Southborough
Povey Cross
Burstow
Newchapel
Felcourt
Dormansland
Greathed Manor
Cowden Pound
Cowden Sta.
Chiddingstone Hoath
Poundsbridge
Speldhurst
Shipley Bridge
Tinsley Green
Dormans Park
Claydene
Cowden
Fordcombe
Copthorne
Felbridge
Blackham
Rusthall
Hammerwood
Holtye Common
Ashurst
Stone Cross
Langton Green
Three Bridges
East Grinstead
Sackville College
Brockhurst
Hammerwood Park
Crawley Down
Sunnyside
Groombridge
Pound Hill
Crabbet Park
Forest Way
Hartwell
Hartfield
Withyham
Spa Valley Rly
Eridge Sta.
CRAWLEY
Worth
Saint Hill
Brambletye
Ashurstwood
Forest Row
Frant
Eridge Green
Tilgate Forest
Turners Hill
Standen (NT)
Upper Hartfield
Selsfield Common
Weir Wood Resr
Spring Hill Wildfowl Park
Kidbrooke Park
Coleman's Hatch
Pease Pottage
Millennium Seed Bank
Friar's Gate
Boarshead
Wakehurst Place (NT)
Priest House
West Hoathly
Sharpthorne
Mark Cross
High Beeches
Wych Cross
Crowborough
Steel Cross
Balcombe
Highbrook
Ashdown Forest
Town Row
Handcross
Nymans (NT)
Horsted Keynes Sta.
Chelwood Gate
Jarvis Brook
Rotherfield
Horsted Keynes
Duddleswell
Poundgate
Ardingly
Ardingly Resr
Staplefield
Danehill
Nutley
Heron's Ghyll
Brook Street
Borde Hill
Paxhill Park
Fairwarp
High Hurstwood
Lindfield
Bluebell Railway
Sheffield Green
Five Ashes
Butcher's Cross
Cuckfield
Haywards Heath
Sheffield Park (NT)
Maresfield
Five Ash Down
Ansty
Scayne's Hill
Sheffield Park Sta.
Fletching
Hadlow Down
Pound Green
Buxted
Ringles Cross
Piltdown
Sandrocks
North Chailey
Newick
Cross in Hand
Uckfield
Blackboys
Possingworth Park
New Town
Framfield
Stonebridge
Little London
Wivelsfield
Wivelsfield Sta.
Beeches Farm
Chailey
Ridgewood
Waldron
Wivelsfield Green
Burgess Hill
Ditchling Common
South Street
Newick Park
Horsted Place
Mayn Green
Vine's Cross
Little Horsted
Plumpton Green
South Common
Spithurst
Isfield
Foxhunt Green
Horam
Halland
Bentley Motor Museum
Hurstpierpoint
Plumpton
Barcombe Cross
East Hoathly
Burlow
Keymer
Hassocks
Streat
Shortgate
Ditchling
East Chiltington
Barcombe
Wildfowl Park
Whitesmith
Chiddingly
Clayton
Westmeston
Cooksbridge
Laughton
Muddles Green
Pyecombe
Plumpton
Ouse
Holme's Hill
Golden Cross
Lealar
Ditchling Beacon
Mount Harry
Offham
Hamsey
Ringmer
Hellingly
South Malling
Lower Dicker
Lewes 1264
Cliffe Hill
Glyndebourne
Upper Dicker
Lewes
Stanmer
Mount Caburn
Glynde Place
Ripe
The Dicker
Michelham Priory
Patcham
Glynde
Middle Farm & English Farm Cider Centre
Chalvington
Coldean
Falmer
Mus. of Sussex Archaeology
Hollingbury
Kingston near Lewes
Beddingham
British Engineerium
Moulsecoomb
Iford
West Firle
Firle Place
Arlington Resr
Berwick Sta.
Arlington
Preston
Bevendean
Newmarket Hill
Rodmell
Charleston
Selmeston

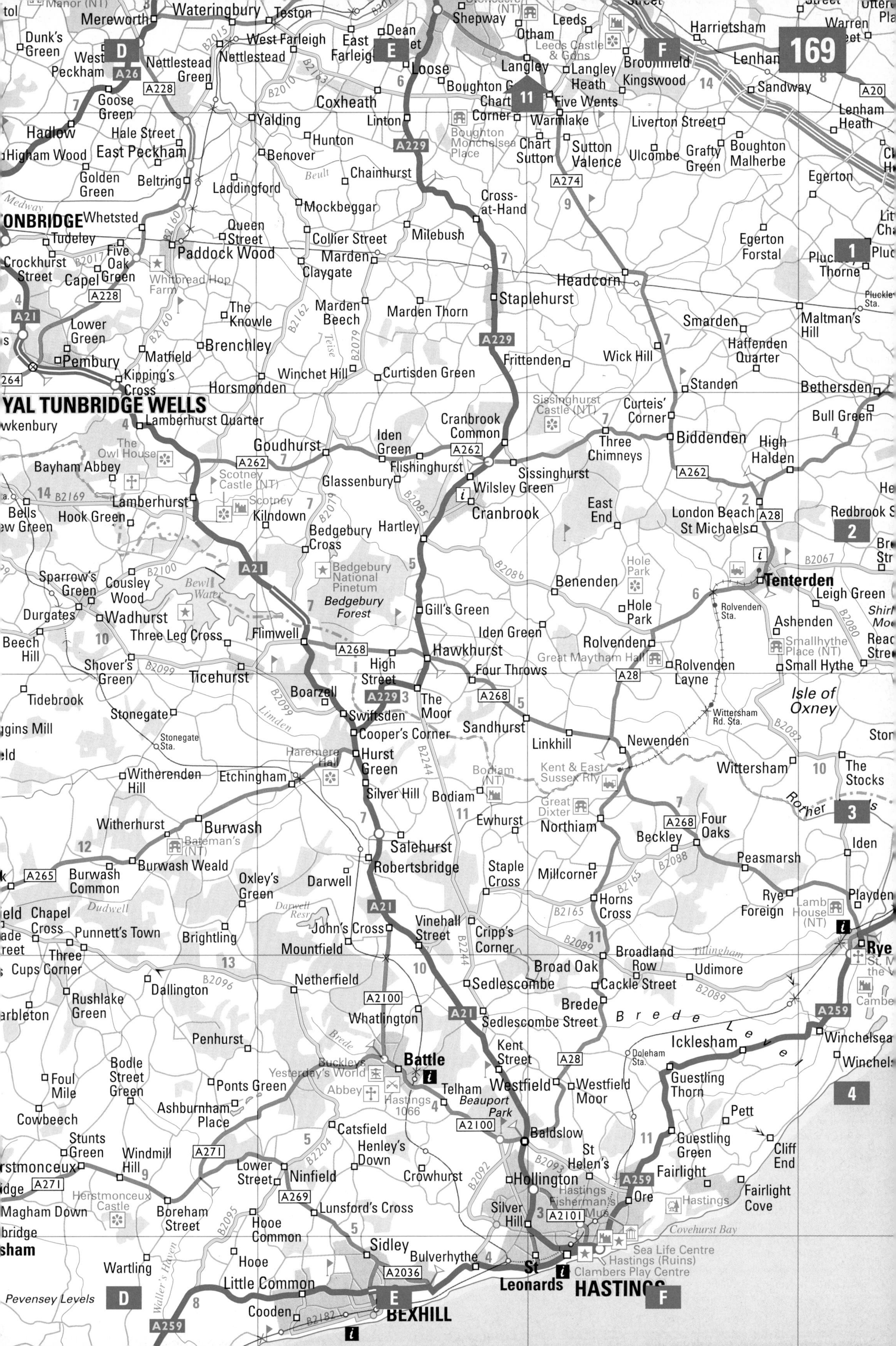

169
Wateringbury
Teston
Mereworth
Dunk's Green
West Peckham
Nettlestead Green
Nettlestead
West Farleigh
East Farleigh
Dean Street
Loose
Shepway
Otham
Leeds
Leeds Castle & Gdns
Harrietsham
Warren Street
Lenham
Broomfield
Kingswood
Langley
Langley Heath
Boughton Green
Chart Corner
Five Wents
Sandway
Lenham Heath
Goose Green
Coxheath
Linton
Hadlow
Hale Street
Yalding
Hunton
Warmlake
Liverton Street
Higham Wood
East Peckham
Benover
Boughton Monchelsea Place
Chart Sutton
Sutton Valence
Ulcombe
Grafty Green
Boughton Malherbe
Egerton
Golden Green
Beltring
Laddingford
Chainhurst
Beult
Medway
Cross-at-Hand
TONBRIDGE
Whetsted
Queen Street
Mockbeggar
Tudeley
Collier Street
Milebush
Egerton Forstal
Crockhurst Street
Five Oak Green
Paddock Wood
Marden
Claygate
Capel
Whitbread Hop Farm
Headcorn
Pluckley Thorne
Pluckley Sta.
Staplehurst
Smarden
Maltman's Hill
The Knowle
Marden Beech
Marden Thorn
Teise
Lower Green
Brenchley
Haffenden Quarter
Wick Hill
Matfield
Frittenden
Pembury
Kipping's Cross
Winchet Hill
Curtisden Green
Standen
Bethersden
Horsmonden
ROYAL TUNBRIDGE WELLS
Sissinghurst Castle (NT)
Curteis' Corner
Lamberhurst Quarter
Cranbrook Common
Bull Green
Hawkenbury
The Owl House
Goudhurst
Iden Green
Three Chimneys
Biddenden
High Halden
Bayham Abbey
Flishinghurst
Sissinghurst
Scotney Castle (NT)
Glassenbury
Wilsley Green
Lamberhurst
Bells Yew Green
Hook Green
Kilndown
Cranbrook
East End
London Beach
St Michaels
Redbrook Street
Bedgebury Cross
Hartley
Hole Park
Tenterden
Sparrow's Green
Cousley Wood
Bewl Water
Bedgebury National Pinetum
Bedgebury Forest
Benenden
Leigh Green
Durgates
Wadhurst
Gill's Green
Rolvenden Sta.
Ashenden
Beech Hill
Three Leg Cross
Flimwell
Iden Green
Rolvenden
Smallhythe Place (NT)
Shover's Green
Ticehurst
High Street
Hawkhurst
Great Maytham Hall
Four Throws
Rolvenden Layne
Small Hythe
Tidebrook
Boarzell
The Moor
Isle of Oxney
Stonegate
Swiftsden
Sandhurst
Wittersham Rd. Sta.
Limden
Cooper's Corner
Stonegate Sta.
Linkhill
Newenden
Haremere Hall
Hurst Green
Wittersham
The Stocks
Witherenden Hill
Etchingham
Bodiam (NT)
Kent & East Sussex Rly
Silver Hill
Bodiam
Ewhurst
Great Dixter
Northiam
Rother
Witherhurst
Burwash
Bateman's (NT)
Salehurst
Four Oaks
Beckley
Iden
Burwash Weald
Robertsbridge
Staple Cross
Peasmarsh
Burwash Common
Oxley's Green
Darwell
Millcorner
Horns Cross
Rye Foreign
Playden
Lamb House (NT)
Chapel Cross
Dudwell
Darwell Resr.
John's Cross
Vinehall Street
Cripp's Corner
Rye
Punnett's Town
Brightling
Mountfield
Three Cups Corner
Broad Oak
Broadland Row
Udimore
Tillingham
Dallington
Netherfield
Sedlescombe
Cackle Street
Rushlake Green
Brede
Whatlington
Sedlescombe Street
Winchelsea
Penhurst
Kent Street
Icklesham
Doleham Sta.
Buckleys Yesterday's World
Battle
Bodle Street Green
Foul Mile
Ponts Green
Abbey
Hastings 1066
Telham
Beauport Park
Westfield
Westfield Moor
Guestling Thorn
Ashburnham Place
Pett
Cowbeech
Catsfield
Stunts Green
Windmill Hill
Henley's Down
Baldslow
Guestling Green
Cliff End
Lower Street
Ninfield
Crowhurst
St Helen's
Fairlight
Herstmonceux
Hollington
Ore
Herstmonceux Castle
Boreham Street
Lunsford's Cross
Hastings Fisherman's Mus
Hastings
Fairlight Cove
Magham Down
Hooe Common
Silver Hill
Covehurst Bay
Sidley
Bulverhythe
St Leonards
Sea Life Centre
Hastings (Ruins)
Clambers Play Centre
HASTINGS
Wartling
Hooe
Little Common
Pevensey Levels
Waller's Haven
Cooden
BEXHILL
A21
A26
A228
A229
A262
A268
A28
A274
A20
A265
A271
A259
A269
A2100
A2036
A2101
A21
B2015
B2010
B2163
B2160
B2017
B2162
B2079
B2085
B2086
B2067
B2080
B2169
B2100
B2099
B2244
B2082
B2088
B2165
B2089
B2096
B2204
B2092
B2093
B2095
B2182

General Abbreviations

All	Alley	Conv	Convent	Gar	Garage	Ms	Mews	St.	Saint
Allot	Allotments	Cor	Corner	Gdn	Garden	Mt	Mount	Sta	Station
Amb	Ambulance	Cors	Corners	Gdns	Gardens	Mus	Museum	Sts	Streets
App	Approach	Coron	Coroners	Govt	Government	N	North	Sub	Subway
Arc	Arcade	Cotts	Cottages	Gra	Grange	PH	Public House	Swim	Swimming
Ave	Avenue	Cov	Covered	Grd	Ground	Par	Parade	TA	Territorial Army
Bdy	Broadway	Crem	Crematorium	Grds	Grounds	Pas	Passage	Tenn	Tennis
Bldgs	Buildings	Cres	Crescent	Grn	Green	Pav	Pavilion	Ter	Terrace
Boul	Boulevard	Ct	Court	Grns	Greens	Pk	Park	Thea	Theatre
Bowl	Bowling	Ctyd	Courtyard	Gro	Grove	Pl	Place	Trd	Trading
Bri	Bridge	Dep	Depot	Gros	Groves	Prec	Precinct	Twr	Tower
C of E	Church of England	Dr	Drive	Ho	House	Prom	Promenade	Twrs	Towers
Cath	Cathedral	Dws	Dwellings	Hos	Houses	Pt	Point	Vill	Villas
Cem	Cemetery	E	East	Hosp	Hospital	Quad	Quadrant	Vw	View
Cen	Central, Centre	Ed	Education	Ind	Industrial	RC	Roman Catholic	W	West
Cft	Croft	Elec	Electricity	Junct	Junction	Rd	Road	Wd	Wood
Cfts	Crofts	Embk	Embankment	La	Lane	Rds	Roads	Wds	Woods
Ch	Church	Est	Estate	Las	Lanes	Rec	Recreation	Wf	Wharf
Chyd	Churchyard	Ex	Exchange	Lo	Lodge	Res	Reservoir	Wk	Walk
Cin	Cinema	FB	Footbridge	Lwr	Lower	Ri	Rise	Wks	Walks
Circ	Circus	FC	Football Club	Mag	Magistrates	S	South	Yd	Yard
Clo	Close	Fld	Field	Mans	Mansions	Sch	School		
Co	County	Flds	Fields	Meml	Memorial	Shop	Shopping		
Coll	College	Fm	Farm	Mkt	Market	Sq	Square		
Comm	Community	Gall	Gallery	Mkts	Markets	St	Street		

Post Town Abbreviations

Abb.L.	Abbots Langley	Dag.	Dagenham	Nthlt.	Northolt	Sutt.	Sutton
Add.	Addlestone	Dart.	Dartford	Nthwd.	Northwood	Swan.	Swanley
Ash.	Ashtead	E.Mol.	East Molesey	Ong.	Ongar	T.Ditt.	Thames Ditton
Ashf.	Ashford	Edg.	Edgware	Orp.	Orpington	Tad.	Tadworth
Bans.	Banstead	Enf.	Enfield	Oxt.	Oxted	Tedd.	Teddington
Bark.	Barking	Epp.	Epping	Pnr.	Pinner	Th.Hth.	Thornton Heath
Barn.	Barnet	Felt.	Feltham	Pot.B.	Potters Bar	Twick.	Twickenham
Beck.	Beckenham	Grnf.	Greenford	Pur.	Purley	Uxb.	Uxbridge
Belv.	Belvedere	Har.	Harrow	Rad.	Radlett	W.Byf.	West Byfleet
Bex.	Bexley	Hat.	Hatfield	Rain.	Rainham	W.Mol.	West Molesey
Bexh.	Bexleyheath	Hem.H.	Hemel Hempstead	Red.	Redhill	W.Wick.	West Wickham
Borwd.	Borehamwood	Hert.	Hertford	Rich.	Richmond	Wal.Abb.	Waltham Abbey
Brent.	Brentford	Hmptn.	Hampton	Rick.	Rickmansworth	Wal.Cr.	Waltham Cross
Brom.	Bromley	Horn.	Hornchurch	Rom.	Romford	Wall.	Wallington
Brox.	Broxbourne	Houns.	Hounslow	Ruis.	Ruislip	Walt.	Walton-on-Thames
Brwd.	Brentwood	Ilf.	Ilford	S.Croy.	South Croydon	Warl.	Warlingham
Buck.H.	Buckhurst Hill	Islw.	Isleworth	Sev.	Sevenoaks	Wat.	Watford
Cars.	Carshalton	Ken.	Kenley	Shep.	Shepperton	Wdf.Grn.	Woodford Green
Cat.	Caterham	Kes.	Keston	Sid.	Sidcup	Well.	Welling
Cher.	Chertsey	Kings L.	Kings Langley	Slou.	Slough	Wem.	Wembley
Chess.	Chessington	Kings.T.	Kingston upon Thames	St.Alb.	St. Albans	West Dr.	West Drayton
Chig.	Chigwell	Loug.	Loughton	Stai.	Staines	West.	Westerham
Chis.	Chislehurst	Lthd.	Leatherhead	Stan.	Stanmore	Wey.	Weybridge
Cob.	Cobham	Mitch.	Mitcham	Sthl.	Southall	Whyt.	Whyteleafe
Couls.	Coulsdon	Mord.	Morden	Sun.	Sunbury-on-Thames	Wok.	Woking
Croy.	Croydon	N.Mal.	New Malden	Surb.	Surbiton	Wor.Pk.	Worcester Park

Notes

A strict word-by-word alphabetical order is followed in the index whereby generic terms such as Avenue, Close, Gardens etc., although abbreviated, are ordered in their expanded form. So, for example, Abbot St. comes before Abbots Ave., and Abbots Ri. comes before Abbots Rd.

Street names preceded by a definite article (i.e. The) are indexed from their second word onwards with the article being placed at the end of the name,
e.g. Avenue, The, or Long Walk, The

The alphabetical order extends to include postal information so that where two or more streets have exactly the same name, London post town references are given first in alpha-numeric order and are followed by non-London post town references in alphabetic order,
e.g. Abbey Rd. SE2 is followed by Abbey Rd. SW19 and then Abbey Rd., Barking.

In some cases there are two or more streets of the same name in the same postal area. In order to aid correct location, extra information will be given in brackets,
e.g. High St., Epsom and High St. (Ewell), Epsom.

The street name and postal district or post town of an entry is followed by the page number and grid reference on which the name will be found, e.g. Abbey Road SW19 will be found on page 104 and in square DC94. Likewise, Norfolk Crescent, Sidcup will be found on page 109 and in square ES87 (within postal district DA15).

All streets within the Central London enlarged-scale section (pages 4-11) are shown in **bold type** when named in the index, e.g. **Abbey St. SE1** will be found on page **11** and in square **N6**. Certain streets may also be duplicated on parts of pages 76-78 and 90-92. In these cases the Central London section reference is always given first in bold type, followed by the same name in standard type, e.g.

Abbey Orchard St. SW1   9   M6
Abbey Orchard St. SW1   91   DK76

The index also contains some roads for which there is insufficient space to name on the map. The adjoining, or nearest named thoroughfare to such roads is shown in *italics*, and the reference indicates where the unnamed road is located off the named thoroughfare,
e.g. Oyster Catchers Close E16 is off *Freemasons Road* and is located off this road on page 80 in square EH72.

A.C. Ct., T.Ditt. 115 CG100
Harvest La.
Abberley Ms. SW4 91 DH83
Cedars Rd.
Abberton Wk., Rain. 83 FE66
Ongar Way
Abbess Clo. E6 80 EL71
Oliver Gdns.
Abbess Clo. SW2 105 DN88
Abbeville Rd. N8 63 DK56
Barrington Rd.
Abbeville Rd. SW4 105 DJ86
Abbey Ave., Wem. 74 CL68
Abbey Clo., Hayes 71 BV74
Abbey Clo., Nthlt. 72 BZ69
Invicta Gro.
Abbey Clo., Pnr. 57 BV55
Abbey Clo., Rom. 69 FG58
Abbey Ct., Wal.Abb. 23 EB34
Abbey Cres., Belv. 96 FA77
Abbey Dr. SW17 104 DG92
Church La.
Abbey Dr., Abb.L. 15 BU32
Abbey Dr., Stai. 112 BJ97
Abbey Gdns. NW8 76 DC68
Abbey Gdns. SE16 92 DU77
Southwark Pk. Rd.
Abbey Gdns. W6 89 CY79
Abbey Gdns., Cher. 112 BG100
Abbey Grn., Cher. 112 BG100
Abbey Gro. SE2 96 EV77
Abbey La. E15 79 EC68
Abbey La., Beck. 107 EA94
Abbey Manufacturing Est., Wem. 74 CM67
Abbey Ms. E17 65 EA57
Leamington Ave.
Abbey Orchard St. SW1 9 M6
Abbey Orchard St. SW1 91 DK76
Abbey Par. W5 74 CM69
Hanger La.
Abbey Pk., Beck. 107 EA94
Abbey Rd. E15 79 ED68
Abbey Rd. NW6 76 DB66
Abbey Rd. NW8 76 DB67
Abbey Rd. NW10 74 CP68
Abbey Rd. SE2 96 EX77
Abbey Rd. SW19 104 DC94
Abbey Rd., Bark. 81 EP66
Abbey Rd., Belv. 96 EX77
Abbey Rd., Bexh. 96 EY84
Abbey Rd., Cher. 112 BH101
Abbey Rd., Croy. 119 DP104
Abbey Rd., Enf. 36 DS43
Abbey Rd., Ilf. 67 ER57
Abbey Rd., Shep. 112 BN102
Abbey Rd., S.Croy. 135 DX110
Abbey Rd., Wal.Cr. 23 DY34
Abbey Rd. Est. NW8 76 DB67
Abbey St. E13 80 EG70
Abbey St. SE1 11 N6
Abbey St. SE1 92 DT76
Abbey Ter. SE2 96 EW77
Abbey Vw. NW7 47 CT48
Abbey Vw., Wal.Abb. 23 EB33
Abbey Vw., Wat. 30 BX36
Abbey Wk., W.Mol. 114 CB97
Abbey Way SE2 96 EX75
Wolvercote Rd.
Abbey Wf. Ind. Est., Bark. 81 ER68
Abbey Wd. Rd. SE2 96 EV77
Abbeydale Rd., Wem. 74 CN67
Abbeyfield Est. SE16 92 DW77
Abbeyfield Rd.
Abbeyfield Rd. SE16 92 DW77
Abbeyfields Clo. NW10 74 CN69
Abbeyhill Rd., Sid. 110 EW89
Abbot Clo., Stai. 98 BK94
Abbot Clo., W.Byf. 126 BK110
Abbot St. E8 78 DT65
Abbots Clo. N1 78 DQ65
Alwyne Rd.
Abbots Clo., Orp. 123 EQ102
Abbots Clo., Ruis. 58 BX62
Abbots Clo., Uxb. 70 BK71
Abbots Cres., Enf. 35 DP40
Abbots Dr., Har. 58 CA61
Abbots Gdns. N2 62 DD56
Abbots Gdns. W8 90 DB76
St. Mary's Pl.
Abbots Grn., Croy. 135 DX107
Abbots La. SE1 11 N3
Abbots La., Ken. 148 DQ116
Abbots Manor Est. SW1 9 H10
Abbots Pk. SW2 105 DN88
Abbot's Pl. NW6 76 DB67
Abbots Ri., Kings L. 14 BM26
Abbot's Rd. E6 80 EK67
Abbots Rd., Abb.L. 15 BQ31
Abbots Rd., Edg. 46 CQ52
Abbots Ter. N8 63 DL58
Abbots Tilt, Walt. 114 BY104
Abbots Vw., Kings L. 14 BM27
Abbots Wk. W8 90 DB76
St. Mary's Pl.
Abbots Wk., Cat. 148 DU122
Tillingdown Hill
Abbots Way, Beck. 121 DY99
Abbotsbury Clo. E15 79 EC68
Abbotsbury Clo. W14 89 CZ75
Abbotsbury Rd.
Abbotsbury Gdns., Pnr. 58 BW58
Abbotsbury Ms. SE15 92 DW83
Abbotsbury Rd. W14 89 CY75
Abbotsbury Rd., Brom. 122 EF103
Abbotsbury Rd., Mord. 118 DB99
Abbotsford Ave. N15 64 DQ56
Abbotsford Gdns., Wdf.Grn. 52 EG52
Abbotsford Lo., Nthwd. 43 BS50
Abbotsford Rd., Ilf. 68 EU61
Abbotshade Rd. SE16 79 DX74
Abbotshall Ave. N14 49 DJ48
Abbotshall Rd. SE6 107 ED88
Abbotsleigh Clo., Sutt. 132 DB108
Abbotsleigh Rd. SW16 105 DJ91
Abbotsmede Clo., Twick. 101 CF89
Abbotstone Rd. SW15 89 CW83
Abbotswell Rd. SE4 107 DZ85
Abbotswood Clo., Belv. 96 EY76
Coptefield Dr.
Abbotswood Dr., Wey. 127 BR110
Abbotswood Gdns., Ilf. 67 EM55
Abbotswood Rd. SE22 92 DS84
Abbotswood Rd. SW16 105 DK90
Abbotswood Way, Hayes 71 BV74
Abbott Ave. SW20 117 CX95
Abbott Clo., Hmptn. 100 BY93
Abbott Clo., Nthlt. 72 BZ65
Abbott Rd. E14 79 EC72
Abbotts Clo. SE28 82 EW73
Abbotts Clo., Rom. 69 FB55
Abbotts Clo., Swan. 125 FG98
Abbotts Cres. E4 51 ED49
Abbotts Dr., Wal.Abb. 24 EG33
Abbotts Dr., Wem. 59 CH61
Abbotts Pk. Rd. E10 65 EC59
Abbotts Rd., Barn. 34 DB42
Abbotts Rd., Mitch. 119 DJ98
Abbotts Rd., Sthl. 72 BY74
Abbotts Rd., Sutt. 131 CY105
Abbotts Wk., Bexh. 96 EX80
Abchurch La. EC4 7 L10
Abchurch La. EC4 78 DR73
Abchurch Yd. EC4 7 K10
Abdale Rd. W12 75 CV74
Abenglen Ind. Est., Hayes 85 BR75
Aberavon Rd. E3 79 DY69
Abercairn Rd. SW16 105 DJ94
Aberconway Rd., Mord. 118 DB97
Abercorn Clo. NW7 47 CY52
Abercorn Clo. NW8 76 DC69
Abercorn Clo., S.Croy. 135 DX112
Abercorn Cres., Har. 58 CB61
Abercorn Gdns., Har. 59 CK59
Abercorn Gdns., Rom. 68 EV58
Abercorn Gro., Ruis. 57 BR56
Abercorn Pl. NW8 76 DC69
Abercorn Rd. NW7 47 CY52
Abercorn Rd., Stan. 45 CJ52
Abercorn Way SE1 92 DU78
Abercrombie Dr., Enf. 36 DU39
Abercrombie St. SW11 90 DE82
Aberdale Gdns., Pot.B. 19 CY32
Aberdare Clo., W.Wick. 121 EC103
Aberdare Gdns. NW6 76 DB66
Aberdare Gdns. NW7 47 CX52
Aberdare Rd., Enf. 36 DW42
Aberdeen La. N5 64 DQ64
Aberdeen Par. N18 50 DV50
Angel Rd.
Aberdeen Pk. N5 64 DQ64
Aberdeen Pk. Ms. N5 64 DQ63
Aberdeen Pl. NW8 76 DD70
Aberdeen Rd. N5 64 DQ63
Aberdeen Rd. N18 50 DV50
Aberdeen Rd. NW10 61 CT64
Aberdeen Rd., Croy. 134 DQ105
Aberdeen Rd., Har. 45 CF54
Aberdeen Sq. E14 79 DZ74
Westferry Circ.
Aberdeen Ter. SE3 93 ED82
Aberdour Rd., Ilf. 68 EV62
Aberdour St. SE1 11 M8
Aberdour St. SE1 92 DS77
Aberfeldy St. E14 79 EC72
Aberford Gdns. SE18 94 EL81
Aberford Rd., Borwd. 32 CN40
Aberfoyle Rd. SW16 105 DK93
Abergeldie Rd. SE12 108 EH86
Abernethy Rd. SE13 94 EE84
Abersham Rd. E8 64 DT64
Abery St. SE18 95 ES77
Abingdon Clo. NW1 77 DK65
Camden Sq.
Abingdon Clo. SE1 92 DT77
Bushwood Dr.
Abingdon Clo. SW19 104 DC93
Abingdon Clo., Uxb. 70 BM67
Abingdon Pl., Pot.B. 20 DB32
Abingdon Rd. N3 48 DC54
Abingdon Rd. SW16 119 DL96
Abingdon Rd. W8 90 DA76
Abingdon St. SW1 9 P6
Abingdon St. SW1 91 DL76
Abingdon Vill. W8 90 DA76
Abingdon Way, Orp. 138 EV105
Abinger Ave., Sutt. 131 CW109
Abinger Clo., Bark. 68 EU63
Abinger Clo., Brom. 122 EL97
Abinger Clo., Wall. 133 DL106
Garden Clo.
Abinger Gdns., Islw. 87 CE83
Sussex Ave.
Abinger Gro. SE8 93 DZ79
Abinger Ms. W9 76 DA70
Warlock Rd.
Abinger Rd. W4 88 CS76
Ablett St. SE16 92 DW78
Abney Gdns. N16 64 DT61
Stoke Newington High St.
Aboyne Dr. SW20 117 CU96
Aboyne Est. SW17 104 DD90
Aboyne Rd. NW10 60 CR62
Aboyne Rd. SW17 104 DD90
Abridge Clo., Wal.Cr. 37 DX35
Abridge Gdns., Rom. 54 FA51
Abridge Pk. (Abridge), Rom. 40 EU42
Abridge Rd., Chig. 39 ER44
Abridge Rd., Epp. 39 ES36
Abridge Rd. (Abridge), Rom. 40 EU39
Abridge Way, Bark. 82 EV68
Abyssinia Clo. SW11 90 DE84
Cairns Rd.
Acacia Ave. N17 50 DR52
Acacia Ave., Brent. 87 CH80
Acacia Ave., Hayes 71 BT72
Acacia Ave., Horn. 69 FF61
Acacia Ave., Mitch. 119 DH96
Acacia Ave., Ruis. 57 BU60
Acacia Ave., Shep. 112 BN99
Acacia Ave., Wem. 60 CL64
Acacia Ave., West Dr. 70 BM73
Acacia Clo. SE20 120 DU96
Selby Rd.
Acacia Clo., Orp. 123 ER99
Acacia Clo., Stan. 45 CE51
Acacia Clo., Wal.Cr. 22 DS27
Acacia Dr., Bans. 131 CX114
Acacia Dr., Sutt. 117 CZ102
Acacia Gdns. NW8 76 DD68
Acacia Rd.
Acacia Gdns., W.Wick. 121 EC103
Acacia Gro. SE21 106 DR89
Acacia Gro., N.Mal. 116 CS97
Acacia Ms., West Dr. 84 BK79
Acacia Pl. NW8 76 DD68
Acacia Rd. E11 66 EE61
Acacia Rd. E17 65 DY58
Acacia Rd. N22 49 DN53
Acacia Rd. NW8 76 DD68
Acacia Rd. SW16 119 DL95
Acacia Rd. W3 74 CQ73
Acacia Rd., Beck. 121 DZ97
Acacia Rd., Enf. 36 DR39
Acacia Rd., Hmptn. 100 CA93
Acacia Rd., Mitch. 118 DG96
Acacia Rd., Stai. 98 BH92
Acacia Wk., Swan. 125 FD96
Walnut Way
Acacia Way, Sid. 109 ET88
Academy Gdns., Croy. 120 DT102
Academy Gdns., Nthlt. 72 BX68
Academy Pl. SE18 95 EM81
Academy Rd. SE18 95 EM81
Acanthus Dr. SE1 92 DU78
Acanthus Rd. SW11 90 DG83
Accommodation La., West Dr. 84 BG81
Accommodation Rd. NW11 61 CZ59
Acer Ave., Hayes 72 BY71
Acer Rd., West. 150 EK116
Acers, St.Alb. 16 CC28
Acfold Rd. SW6 90 DB81
Achilles Clo. SE1 92 DU78
Achilles Rd. NW6 62 DA64
Achilles St. SE14 93 DY80
Achilles Way W1 8 G3
Acklam Rd. W10 75 CZ71
St. Ervans Rd.
Acklington Dr. NW9 46 CS53
Ackmar Rd. SW6 90 DA81
Ackroyd Dr. E3 79 DZ71
Ackroyd Rd. SE23 107 DX87
Ackworth Clo. N9 50 DW45
Turin Rd.
Acland Clo. SE18 95 ER80
Clothworkers Rd.
Acland Cres. SE5 92 DR84
Acland Rd. NW2 75 CV65
Acme Rd., Wat. 29 BU38
Acol Cres., Ruis. 57 BV64
Acol Rd. NW6 76 DA66
Aconbury Rd., Dag. 82 EV67
Acorn Clo. E4 51 EB50
The Lawns
Acorn Clo., Chis. 109 EQ92
Acorn Clo., Enf. 35 DP39
Acorn Clo., Stan. 45 CH52
Acorn Ct., Ilf. 67 ES58
Acorn Gdns. SE19 120 DT95
Acorn Gdns. W3 74 CR71
Acorn Gro., Hayes 85 BT80
Acorn Gro., Ruis. 57 BT63
Acorn Gro., Tad. 145 CY124
Warren Lo. Dr.
Acorn Ind. Pk., Dart. 111 FG85
Acorn La. (Cuffley), Pot.B. 21 DL29
Acorn Par. SE15 92 DV80
Carlton Gro.
Acorn Pl., Wat. 29 BU37
Acorn Rd., Dart. 111 FF85
Acorn Wk. SE16 79 DY74
Acorn Way SE23 107 DX90
Acorn Way, Orp. 137 EP105
Acorns, The, Chig. 53 ES49
Acorns Clo., Hmptn. 100 CB93
Acorns Way, Esher 128 CC106
Acre La. SW2 91 DL84
Acre La., Cars. 132 DG105
Acre La., Wall. 132 DG105
Acre Path, Nthlt. 72 BY65
Arnold Rd.
Acre Rd. SW19 104 DD93
Acre Rd., Dag. 83 FB66
Acre Rd., Kings.T. 116 CL95
Acre Way, Nthwd. 43 BT53
Acres Gdns., Tad. 145 CX119
Acris St. SW18 104 DC85
Acton Clo. N9 50 DU47
Acton Clo. (Cheshunt), Wal.Cr. 23 DY31
Acton La. NW10 74 CQ69
Acton La. W3 88 CQ75
Acton La. W4 88 CQ77
Acton Ms. E8 78 DT67
Acton Pk. Ind. Est. W3 88 CR75
Acton St. WC1 6 B3
Acton St. WC1 77 DM69
Acuba Rd. SW18 104 DB88
Acworth Clo. N9 50 DW45
Turin Rd.
Ada Gdns. E14 79 ED72
Ada Gdns. E15 80 EF67
Ada Pl. E2 78 DU67
Ada Rd. SE5 92 DS80
Ada Rd., Wem. 59 CJ62
Ada St. E8 78 DV67
Adair Clo. SE25 120 DV97
Adair Rd. W10 75 CY70
Adair Twr. W10 75 CY70
Appleford Rd.
Adam & Eve Ct. W1 5 L8
Adam & Eve Ms. W8 90 DA76
Adam Ct. SW7 90 DC77
Gloucester Rd.
Adam Pl. N16 64 DT61
Stoke Newington High St.
Adam Rd. E4 51 DZ51
Adam St. WC2 10 A1
Adam St. WC2 77 DL73
Adam Wk. SW6 89 CW80
Adams Clo. N3 48 DA52
Falkland Ave.
Adams Clo. NW9 60 CP61
Adams Clo., Surb. 116 CM100
Adams Ct. EC2 7 L8
Adams Gdns. Est. SE16 92 DW75
St. Marychurch St.
Adams Pl. E14 79 EB74
North Colonnade
Adams Pl. N7 63 DM64
George's Rd.
Adams Rd. N17 50 DR54
Adams Rd., Beck. 121 DY99
Adams Row W1 8 G1
Adams Row W1 76 DG73
Adams Sq., Bexh. 96 EY83
Regency Way
Adams Way, Croy. 120 DT100
Adamsfield, Wal.Cr. 22 DT26
Adamson Rd. E16 80 EG72
Adamson Rd. NW3 76 DD66
Adamsrill Clo., Enf. 36 DR43
Adamsrill Rd. SE26 107 DY91
Adare Wk. SW16 105 DM90
Adastral Est. NW9 46 CS53
Adcock Wk., Orp. 137 ET105
Borkwood Pk.
Adderley Gdns. SE9 109 EN91
Adderley Gro. SW11 104 DG85
Culmstock Rd.
Adderley Rd., Har. 45 CF53
Adderley St. E14 79 EC72
Addington Border, Croy. 135 DY110
Addington Ct. SW14 88 CR83
Addington Dr. N12 48 DC51
Addington Gro. SE26 107 DY91
Addington Rd. E3 79 EA69
Addington Rd. E16 80 EE70
Addington Rd. N4 63 DN58
Addington Rd., Croy. 119 DN102
Addington Rd., S.Croy. 134 DU112
Addington Rd., W.Wick. 135 EC105
Addington Sq. SE5 92 DR79
Addington St. SE1 10 C5
Addington Village Rd., Croy. 135 DZ107
Addis Clo., Enf. 37 DX39
Addiscombe Ave., Croy. 120 DU101
Addiscombe Clo., Har. 59 CJ57
Addiscombe Ct. Rd., Croy. 120 DS102
Addiscombe Gro., Croy. 120 DS103
Addiscombe Rd., Croy. 120 DS103
Addiscombe Rd., Wat. 29 BV42
Addison Ave. N14 35 DH44
Addison Ave. W11 75 CY74
Addison Ave., Houns. 86 CC81
Addison Bri. Pl. W14 89 CZ77
Addison Clo., Cat. 148 DR122
Addison Clo., Nthwd. 43 BU53
Addison Clo., Orp. 123 EQ100
Addison Cres. W14 89 CY76
Addison Dr. SE12 108 EH85
Eltham Rd.
Addison Gdns. W14 89 CX76
Addison Gdns., Surb. 116 CM98
Addison Gro. W4 88 CS76
Addison Pl. W11 75 CY74
Addison Pl., Sthl. 72 CA73
Longford Ave.
Addison Rd. E11 66 EG58
Addison Rd. E17 65 EB57
Addison Rd. SE25 120 DU98
Addison Rd. W14 89 CY76
Addison Rd., Brom. 122 EJ99
Addison Rd., Cat. 148 DR121
Addison Rd., Enf. 36 DW39
Addison Rd., Ilf. 53 EQ53
Addison Rd., Tedd. 101 CH93
Addison Way NW11 61 CZ56
Addison Way, Hayes 71 BU72
Addison Way, Nthwd. 43 BT53
Addison's Clo., Croy. 121 DZ103
Addle Hill EC4 6 G9
Addle St. EC2 7 J7
Addlestone Moor, Add. 112 BJ103
Addlestone Pk., Add. 126 BH106
Addlestone Rd., Add. 126 BL105
Adecroft Way, W.Mol. 114 CC97
Adela Ave., N.Mal. 117 CV99
Adela St. W10 75 CY70
Kensal Rd.
Adelaide Ave. SE4 93 DZ84
Adelaide Clo., Enf. 36 DS38
Adelaide Clo., Stan. 45 CG49
Adelaide Cotts. W7 87 CF75
Adelaide Gdns., Rom. 68 EY57
Adelaide Gro. W12 75 CU74
Adelaide Pl., Wey. 127 BR105
Adelaide Rd. E10 65 EC62
Adelaide Rd. NW3 76 DD66
Adelaide Rd. SW18 104 DA85
Putney Bri. Rd.
Adelaide Rd. W13 73 CG74
Adelaide Rd., Ashf. 98 BK92
Adelaide Rd., Chis. 109 EP92
Adelaide Rd., Houns. 86 BY81
Adelaide Rd., Ilf. 67 EP61
Adelaide Rd., Rich. 88 CM84
Adelaide Rd., Sthl. 86 BY77
Adelaide Rd., Surb. 116 CL99
Adelaide Rd., Tedd. 101 CF93
Adelaide Rd., Walt. 113 BU104
Adelaide St. WC2 9 P1
Adelaide Ter., Brent. 87 CK78
Adelaide Wk. SW9 91 DN84
Sussex Wk.
Adelina Gro. E1 78 DW71
Adelina Ms. SW12 105 DK88
King's Ave.
Adeline Pl. WC1 5 N7
Adeline Pl. WC1 77 DK71
Adelphi Cres., Hayes 71 BT69
Adelphi Cres., Horn. 69 FG61
Adelphi Rd., Epsom 130 CR113
Adelphi Ter. WC2 10 A1
Adelphi Ter. WC2 77 DL73
Adelphi Way, Hayes 71 BT69
Aden Gro. N16 64 DR63
Aden Rd., Enf. 37 DY42
Aden Rd., Ilf. 67 EP59
Aden Ter. N16 64 DR63
Adeney Clo. W6 89 CX79
Adenmore Rd. SE6 107 EA87
Adie Rd. W6 89 CW76
Adine Rd. E13 80 EH70
Adler St. E1 78 DU72
Adley St. E5 65 DY63
Adlington Clo. N18 50 DS50
Admaston Rd. SE18 95 EQ79
Admiral Clo., Orp. 124 EX98
Admiral Pl. SE16 79 DY74
Admiral Seymour Rd. SE9 95 EM84
Admiral Sq. SW10 90 DC81
Admiral St. SE8 93 EA81
Admirals Clo. E18 66 EH56
Admirals Wk. NW3 62 DC62
Admiral's Wk., The, Couls. 147 DM120
Goodenough Way
Admirals Way E14 93 EA75
Admiralty Clo. SE8 93 EA80
Reginald Sq.
Admiralty Rd., Tedd. 101 CF93
Adnams Wk., Rain. 83 FF65
Lovell Wk.
Adolf St. SE6 107 EB91
Adolphus Rd. N4 63 DP61
Adolphus St. SE8 93 DZ80
Adomar Rd., Dag. 68 EX62
Adpar St. W2 76 DD71
Adrian Ave. NW2 61 CV60
North Circular Rd.
Adrian Clo., Uxb. 42 BK53
Adrian Ms. SW10 90 DB79
Adrian Rd., Abb.L. 15 BS31
Adrienne Ave., Sthl. 72 BZ69
Advance Rd. SE27 106 DQ91
Advent Way N18 51 DX50
Eley Rd.
Adys Rd. SE15 92 DT83
Aerodrome Rd. NW4 61 CU55
Aerodrome Rd. NW9 61 CT55
Aerodrome Way, Houns. 86 BW79
Aeroville NW9 46 CS54
Affleck St. N1 6 C1
Afghan Rd. SW11 90 DE82
Aftab Ter. E1 78 DV70
Tent St.
Agamemnon Rd. NW6 61 CZ64
Agar Clo., Surb. 116 CM103
Agar Gro. NW1 77 DJ66
Agar Gro. Est. NW1 77 DJ66
Agar Pl. NW1 77 DJ66
Agar St. WC2 9 P1
Agar St. WC2 77 DL73
Agate Clo. E16 80 EK72
Agate Rd. W6 89 CW76
Agates La., Ash. 143 CK118
Agatha Clo. E1 78 DV74
Prusom St.
Agaton Rd. SE9 109 EQ89
Agave Rd. NW2 61 CW63
Agdon St. EC1 6 F4
Agdon St. EC1 77 DP70
Agincourt Rd. NW3 62 DF63
Agister Rd., Chig. 54 EU50

Agnes Ave., Ilf. 67 EP63
Agnes Clo. E6 81 EN73
Agnes Gdns., Dag. 68 EX63
Agnes Rd. W3 75 CT74
Agnes Scott Ct., Wey. 113 BP104
Palace Dr.
Agnes St. E14 79 DZ72
Agnesfield Clo. N12 48 DE51
Agnew Rd. SE23 107 DX87
Agricola Pl., Enf. 36 DT43
Aidan Clo., Dag. 68 EY63
Aileen Wk. E15 80 EF66
Devenay Rd.
Ailsa Ave., Twick. 101 CG85
Ailsa Rd., Twick. 101 CH85
Ailsa St. E14 79 EC71
Ainger Ms. NW3 76 DF66
Ainger Rd.
Ainger Rd. NW3 76 DF66
Ainsdale Clo., Orp. 123 ER102
Ainsdale Cres., Pnr. 58 CA55
Ainsdale Rd. W5 73 CK70
Ainsdale Rd., Wat. 44 BW48
Ainsley Ave., Rom. 69 FB58
Ainsley Clo. N9 50 DS46
Ainsley St. E2 78 DV69
Ainslie Wk. SW12 105 DH87
Balham Gro.
Ainslie Wd. Cres. E4 51 EB50
Ainslie Wd. Gdns. E4 51 EB50
Ainslie Wd. Rd. E4 51 EA50
Ainsty Est. SE16 93 DX75
Needleman St.
Ainsworth Clo. NW2 61 CU62
Ainsworth Rd. E9 78 DW66
Ainsworth Rd., Croy. 119 DP103
Ainsworth Way NW8 76 DC67
Aintree Ave. E6 80 EL67
Aintree Clo., Uxb. 71 BP72
Craig Dr.
Aintree Cres., Ilf. 53 EQ54
Aintree Est. SW6 89 CY80
Dawes Rd.
Aintree Rd., Grnf. 73 CH68
Aintree St. SW6 89 CY80
Air St. W1 9 L1
Air St. W1 77 DJ73
Airdrie Clo. N1 77 DM66
Airdrie Clo., Hayes 72 BY71
Glencoe Rd.
Airedale Ave. W4 89 CT77
Airedale Ave. S. W4 89 CT78
Netheravon Rd. S.
Airedale Rd. SW12 104 DF87
Airedale Rd. W5 87 CJ76
Airfield Way, Horn. 83 FH65
Airlie Gdns. W8 76 DA74
Campden Hill Rd.
Airlie Gdns., Ilf. 67 EP60
Airlinks Est., Houns. 86 BW78
Airport Ind. Est., West. 150 EK115
Airport Roundabout E16 80 EK74
Connaught Bri.
Airthrie Rd., Ilf. 68 EV61
Aisgill Ave. W14 89 CZ78
Aisher Rd. SE28 82 EW73
Aisher Way, Sev. 153 FD119
London Rd.
Aislibie Rd. SE12 94 EE84
Aitken Clo. E8 78 DU67
Pownall Rd.
Aitken Clo., Mitch. 118 DF101
Aitken Rd. SE6 107 EB89
Aitken Rd., Barn. 33 CW43
Ajax Ave. NW9 60 CS55
Ajax Rd. NW6 61 CZ64
Akabusi Clo., Croy. 120 DU100
Akehurst La., Sev. 155 FJ125
Akehurst St. SW15 103 CU86
Akenside Rd. NW3 62 DD64
Akerman Rd. SW9 91 DP82
Akerman Rd., Surb. 115 CJ100
Alabama St. SE18 95 ER80
Alacross Rd. W5 87 CJ75
Alan Dr., Barn. 33 CY44
Alan Gdns., Rom. 68 FA59
Alan Hocken Way E15 80 EE68
Alan Rd. SW19 103 CY92
Alandale Dr., Pnr. 43 BV54
Alanthus Clo. SE12 108 EF85
Alaska St. SE1 10 D3
Alba Clo., Hayes 72 BX70
Ramulis Dr.
Alba Gdns. NW11 61 CY58
Alba Pl. W11 75 CZ72
Portobello Rd.
Albacore Cres. SE13 107 EB86
Albain Cres., Ashf. 98 BL89
Alban Cres., Borwd. 32 CN39
Alban Highwalk EC2 78 DQ71
London Wall
Albans Vw., Wat. 15 BV33
Albany, The W1 9 K1
Albany, The, Wdf.Grn. 52 EF49
Albany Clo. N15 63 DP56
Albany Clo. SW14 88 CP84
Albany Clo., Bex. 110 EW87
Albany Clo., Esher 128 CA109
Albany Clo., Uxb. 56 BN64
Albany Clo. (Bushey), Wat. 31 CD44
Albany Ct. E4 37 EB44
Chelwood Clo.
Albany Ct., Epp. 25 ET30
Albany Ctyd. W1 9 L1
Albany Cres., Edg. 46 CN52
Albany Cres., Esher 129 CE107
Albany Mans. SW11 90 DE80
Albert Bri. Rd.
Albany Ms. N1 77 DN66
Barnsbury Pk.
Albany Ms. SE5 92 DQ79
Albany Rd.
Albany Ms., Brom. 108 EG93
Avondale Rd.
Albany Ms., Kings.T. 101 CK93
Albany Ms., St.Alb. 16 CA27
North Orbital Rd.
Albany Ms., Sutt. 132 DB106
Camden Rd.
Albany Pk. Ave., Enf. 36 DW39
Albany Pk. Rd., Kings.T. 101 CK93
Albany Pk. Rd., Lthd. 143 CG119
Albany Pas., Rich. 102 CM85
Albany Pl. N7 63 DN63
Benwell Rd.
Albany Pl., Brent. 88 CL79
Albany Rd. E10 65 EA59
Albany Rd. E12 66 EK63
Albany Rd. E17 65 DY58
Albany Rd. N4 63 DM58
Albany Rd. N18 50 DV50
Albany Rd. SE5 92 DR79
Albany Rd. SW19 104 DB92
Albany Rd. W13 73 CH73
Albany Rd., Belv. 96 EZ79
Albany Rd., Bex. 110 EW87
Albany Rd., Brent. 87 CK79
Albany Rd., Chis. 109 EP92
Albany Rd., Enf. 37 DX37
Albany Rd., Horn. 69 FG60
Albany Rd., N.Mal. 116 CR98
Albany Rd., Rich. 102 CM85
Albert Rd.
Albany Rd., Rom. 68 EZ58
Albany Rd., Walt. 128 BW105
Albany St. NW1 77 DH68
Albany Ter. NW1 77 DH70
Marylebone Rd.
Albany Vw., Buck.H. 52 EG46
Albatross Gdns., S.Croy. 135 DX111
Albatross St. SE18 95 ES80
Albatross Way SE16 93 DX75
Needleman St.
Albemarle SW19 103 CX89
Albemarle App., Ilf. 67 EP58
Albemarle Ave., Pot.B. 20 DB33
Albemarle Ave., Twick. 100 BZ88
Albemarle Ave. (Cheshunt), Wal.Cr. 22 DW28
Albemarle Gdns., Ilf. 67 EP58
Albemarle Gdns., N.Mal. 116 CR98
Albemarle Pk., Stan. 45 CJ50
Albemarle Rd., Barn. 48 DE45
Albemarle Rd., Beck. 121 EB95
Albemarle St. W1 9 J1
Albemarle St. W1 77 DH73
Albemarle Way EC1 6 F5
Alberon Gdns. NW11 61 CZ56
Albert Ave. E4 51 EA49
Albert Ave. SW8 91 DM80
Albert Ave., Cher. 112 BG97
Albert Bri. SW3 90 DE79
Albert Bri. SW11 90 DE80
Albert Bri. Rd. SW11 90 DE80
Albert Carr Gdns. SW16 105 DL92
Albert Clo. E9 78 DV67
Northiam St.
Albert Clo. N22 49 DK53
Albert Ct. SW7 90 DD75
Albert Cres. E4 51 EA49
Albert Dr. SW19 103 CY89
Albert Embk. SE1 91 DL78
Albert Gdns. E1 79 DX72
Albert Gate SW1 8 E4
Albert Gate SW1 90 DF75
Albert Gro. SW20 117 CX95
Albert Hall Mans. SW7 90 DD75
Kensington Gore
Albert Mans. SW11 90 DF81
Albert Bri. Rd.
Albert Ms. E14 79 DY73
Narrow St.
Albert Ms. W8 90 DC76
Victoria Gro.
Albert Pl. N3 48 DA53
Albert Pl. N17 64 DT55
High Rd.
Albert Pl. W8 90 DB75
Albert Rd. E10 65 EC61
Albert Rd. E16 80 EL74
Albert Rd. E17 65 EA57
Albert Rd. E18 66 EH55
Albert Rd. N4 63 DM60
Albert Rd. N15 64 DS58
Albert Rd. N22 49 DJ53
Albert Rd. NW4 61 CX56
Albert Rd. NW6 75 CZ68
Albert Rd. NW7 47 CT50
Albert Rd. SE9 108 EL90
Albert Rd. SE20 107 DX93
Albert Rd. SE25 120 DU98
Albert Rd. W5 73 CH70
Albert Rd., Add. 112 BK104
Albert Rd., Ashf. 98 BM92
Albert Rd., Ash. 144 CM118
Albert Rd., Barn. 34 DD42
Albert Rd., Belv. 96 EZ78
Albert Rd., Bex. 110 FA86
Albert Rd., Brom. 122 EK99
Albert Rd., Buck.H. 52 EK47
Albert Rd., Dag. 68 FA60
Albert Rd., Epsom 131 CT113
Albert Rd., Hmptn. 100 CC92
Albert Rd., Har. 58 CC55
Albert Rd., Hayes 85 BS76
Albert Rd., Houns. 86 CA84
Albert Rd., Ilf. 67 EP62
Albert Rd., Kings.T. 116 CM96
Albert Rd., Mitch. 118 DF97
Albert Rd., N.Mal. 117 CT98
Albert Rd., Orp. 138 EU106
Albert Rd. (St. Mary Cray), Orp. 124 EV100
Albert Rd., Rich. 102 CL85
Albert Rd., Rom. 69 FF57
Albert Rd., Sthl. 86 BX76
Albert Rd., Sutt. 132 DD106
Albert Rd., Tedd. 101 CF93
Albert Rd., Twick. 101 CF88
Albert Rd., Warl. 149 DZ117
Albert Rd., West Dr. 70 BL74
Albert Rd. Est., Belv. 96 EZ78
Albert Rd. N., Wat. 29 BV41
Albert Rd. S., Wat. 29 BV41
Albert Sq. E15 66 EE64
Albert Sq. SW8 91 DM80
Albert St. N12 48 DC50
Albert St. NW1 77 DH67
Albert Ter. NW1 76 DG67
Albert Ter. NW10 74 CR67
Albert Ter., Buck.H. 52 EK47
Albert Ter. Ms. NW1 76 DG67
Regents Pk. Rd.
Albert Wk. E16 95 EN75
Pier Rd.
Alberta Ave., Sutt. 131 CY105
Alberta Est. SE17 10 G10
Alberta Est. SE17 91 DP78
Alberta Rd., Enf. 36 DT44
Alberta Rd., Erith 97 FC81
Alberta St. SE17 10 F10
Alberta St. SE17 91 DP78
Albertine Clo., Epsom 145 CV116
Rose Bushes
Albion Ave. N10 48 DG53
Albion Ave. SW8 91 DK82
Albion Bldgs. EC1 78 DQ71
Bartholomew Clo.
Albion Clo. W2 4 C10
Albion Clo., Rom. 69 FD58
Albion Dr. E8 78 DT66
Albion Est. SE16 92 DW75
Albion Gdns. W6 89 CV77
Albion Gro. N16 64 DS63
Albion Hill SE13 93 EB82
Albion Hill, Loug. 38 EJ43
Albion Ms. N1 77 DN66
Albion Ms. NW6 75 CZ66
Kilburn High Rd.
Albion Ms. W2 4 C10
Albion Ms. W2 76 DE72
Albion Par. N16 64 DR63
Albion Rd.
Albion Pk., Loug. 38 EK43
Albion Pl. EC1 6 F6
Albion Pl. EC1 77 DP71
Albion Pl. SE25 120 DU97
High St.
Albion Pl. W6 89 CV77
Albion Rd. E17 65 EC55
Albion Rd. N16 64 DR63
Albion Rd. N17 50 DU54
Albion Rd., Bexh. 96 EZ84
Albion Rd., Hayes 71 BS72
Albion Rd., Houns. 86 CA84
Albion Rd., Kings.T. 116 CQ95
Albion Rd., Sutt. 132 DD107
Albion Rd., Twick. 101 CE88
Albion Sq. E8 78 DT66
Albion St. SE16 92 DW75
Albion St. W2 4 C9
Albion St. W2 76 DE72
Albion St., Croy. 119 DP102
Albion Ter. E8 78 DT66
Albion Vill. Rd. SE26 106 DW90
Albion Way EC1 7 H7
Albion Way SE13 93 EC84
Albion Way, Wem. 60 CP62
North End Rd.
Albion Yd. E1 78 DV71
Albright Ind. Est., Rain. 83 FF71
Albrighton Rd. SE22 92 DS83
Albuhera Clo., Enf. 35 DN39
Albury Ave., Bexh. 96 EY82
Albury Ave., Islw. 87 CF80
Albury Ave., Sutt. 131 CW109
Albury Clo., Hmptn. 100 CA93
Albury Dr., Pnr. 44 BW53
Albury Gro. Rd. (Cheshunt), Wal.Cr. 23 DX30
Albury Ms. E12 66 EJ60
Albury Ride (Cheshunt), Wal.Cr. 23 DX31
Albury Rd., Chess. 130 CL106
Albury Rd., Walt. 127 BS107
Albury St. SE8 93 EA79
Albury Wk. (Cheshunt), Wal.Cr. 22 DW30
Albyfield, Brom. 123 EM97
Albyn Rd. SE8 93 EA81
Albyns Clo., Rain. 83 FG66
South End Rd.
Albyns La., Rom. 41 FC40
Alcester Cres. E5 64 DV61
Alcester Rd., Wall. 133 DH105
Alcock Clo., Wall. 133 DK108
Alcock Rd., Houns. 86 BX80
Alcocks Clo., Tad. 145 CY120
Alcocks La., Tad. 145 CY121
Alconbury Rd. E5 64 DU61
Alcorn Clo., Sutt. 118 DA103
Alcott Clo. W7 73 CF71
Westcott Cres.
Alcuin Ct., Stan. 45 CJ51
Aldborough Rd., Dag. 83 FC65
Aldborough Rd. N., Ilf. 67 ET57
Aldborough Rd. S., Ilf. 67 ES60
Aldbourne Rd. W12 75 CT74
Aldbridge St. SE17 11 N10
Aldbridge St. SE17 92 DS78
Aldburgh Ms. W1 4 G8
Aldbury Ave., Wem. 74 CP66
Aldbury Clo., Wat. 30 BX36
Aldbury Ms. N9 50 DR45
Aldebert Ter. SW8 91 DL80
Aldeburgh Clo. E5 64 DV61
Southwold Rd.
Aldeburgh Pl., Wdf.Grn. 52 EG49
Aldeburgh St. SE10 94 EG78
Alden Ave. E15 80 EF70
Aldenham Ave., Rad. 31 CG36
Aldenham Dr., Uxb. 71 BP70
Aldenham Gro., Rad. 17 CG34
Aldenham Rd., Borwd. 31 CG41
Aldenham Rd., Rad. 31 CG35
Aldenham Rd., Wat. 30 BX44
Aldenham Rd. (Bushey), Wat. 30 BY44
Aldenham Rd. (Letchmore Heath), Wat. 31 CE39
Aldenham St. NW1 5 L1
Aldenham St. NW1 77 DJ68
Aldenholme, Wey. 127 BS107
Aldensley Rd. W6 89 CV76
Alder Clo. SE15 92 DT79
Alder Clo., St.Alb. 16 CB28
Alder Cft., Couls. 147 DM116
Alder Gro. NW2 61 CU61
Alder Ind. Est., Hayes 85 BR75
Alder Ms. N19 63 DJ61
Bredgar Rd.
Alder Rd. SW14 88 CR83
Alder Rd., Sid. 109 ET90
Alder Rd., Uxb. 70 BJ65
Alder Wk., Ilf. 67 EQ64
Loxford La.
Alder Wk., Wat. 29 BV35
Aspen Pk. Dr.
Alder Way, Swan. 125 FD96
Alderbrook Rd. SW12 105 DH86
Alderbury Rd. SW13 89 CU79
Aldercroft, Couls. 147 DM116
Aldergrove Gdns., Houns. 86 BY82
Bath Rd.
Alderholt Way SE15 92 DT80
Daniel Gdns.
Alderman Ave., Bark. 82 EU69
Alderman Judge Mall, Kings.T. 116 CL96
Eden St.
Aldermanbury EC2 7 J8
Aldermanbury EC2 78 DQ72
Aldermanbury Sq. EC2 7 J7
Aldermans Hill N13 49 DL49
Alderman's Wk. EC2 7 M7
Aldermary Rd., Brom. 122 EG95
Aldermoor Rd. SE6 107 DZ90
Alderney Ave., Houns. 86 CB80
Alderney Gdns., Nthlt. 72 BZ66
Alderney Rd. E1 79 DX70
Alderney Rd., Erith 97 FG80
Alderney St. SW1 9 J10
Alderney St. SW1 91 DH77
Alders, The N21 35 DN44
Alders, The, Felt. 100 BY91
Alders, The, Houns. 86 BZ79
Alders, The, W.Byf. 126 BJ112
Alders, The, W.Wick. 121 EB102
Alders Ave., Wdf.Grn. 52 EE51
Alders Clo. E11 66 EH61
Aldersbrook Rd.
Alders Clo. W5 87 CK76
Alders Clo., Edg. 46 CQ50
Alders Gro., E.Mol. 115 CD99
Esher Rd.
Alders Rd., Edg. 46 CQ50
Aldersbrook Ave., Enf. 36 DS40
Aldersbrook Dr., Kings.T. 102 CM93
Aldersbrook La. E12 67 EM62
Aldersbrook Rd. E11 66 EH61
Aldersbrook Rd. E12 66 EH61
Aldersey Gdns., Bark. 81 ER65
Aldersford Clo. SE4 107 DX85
Aldersgate St. EC1 7 H6
Aldersgate St. EC1 78 DQ71
Aldersgrove, Wal.Abb. 24 EE34
Roundhills
Aldersgrove Ave. SE9 108 EJ90
Aldershot Rd. NW6 75 CZ67
Aldersmead Ave., Croy. 121 DX100
Aldersmead Rd., Beck. 107 DY94
Alderson Pl., Sthl. 72 CC74
Alderson St. W10 75 CY70
Kensal Rd.
Alderstead Heath, Red. 147 DK124
Alderton Clo. NW10 60 CR62
Alderton Clo., Loug. 39 EN42
Alderton Cres. NW4 61 CV57
Alderton Hall La., Loug. 39 EN42
Alderton Hill, Loug. 38 EL43
Alderton Ri., Loug. 39 EN42
Alderton Rd. SE24 92 DQ83
Alderton Rd., Croy. 120 DT101
Alderton Way NW4 61 CV57
Alderton Way, Loug. 39 EM43
Alderville Rd. SW6 89 CZ82
Alderwick Dr., Houns. 87 CD83
Alderwood Clo., Rom. 40 EV41
Alderwood Dr., Rom. 40 EV41
Alderwood Rd. SE9 109 ER86
Aldford St. W1 8 F2
Aldford St. W1 76 DG74
Aldgate EC3 7 N9
Aldgate EC3 78 DS72
Aldgate Ave. E1 7 P8
Aldgate High St. EC3 7 P9
Aldgate High St. EC3 78 DT72
Aldine Ct. W12 75 CW74
Aldine St.
Aldine Pl. W12 75 CW74
Uxbridge Rd.
Aldine St. W12 75 CW74
Aldingham Ct., Horn. 69 FG64
Easedale Dr.
Aldingham Gdns., Horn. 69 FG64
Aldington Clo., Dag. 68 EW59
Aldington Rd. SE18 94 EK76
Aldis Ms. SW17 104 DE92
Aldis St.
Aldis St. SW17 104 DE92
Aldred Rd. NW6 62 DA64
Aldren Rd. SW17 104 DC90
Aldrich Cres., Croy. 135 EC109
Aldrich Gdns., Sutt. 117 CZ104
Aldrich Ter. SW18 104 DC89
Lidiard Rd.
Aldriche Way E4 51 EC51
Aldridge Ave., Edg. 46 CP48
Aldridge Ave., Enf. 37 EA38
Aldridge Ave., Ruis. 58 BX61
Aldridge Ave., Stan. 46 CL53
Aldridge Ri., N.Mal. 116 CS101
Aldridge Rd. Vill. W11 75 CZ71
Aldridge Wk. N14 49 DL45
Aldrington Rd. SW16 105 DJ91
Aldsworth Clo. W9 76 DB70
Aldwick Clo. SE9 109 ER90
Aldwick Rd., Croy. 119 DM104
Aldworth Gro. SE13 107 EC86
Aldworth Rd. E15 80 EE66
Aldwych WC2 6 B10
Aldwych WC2 77 DM73
Aldwych Ave., Ilf. 67 EQ56
Aldwych Clo., Horn. 69 FG61
Alers Rd., Bexh. 110 EX85
Aleston Beck Rd. E16 80 EK72
Fulmer Rd.
Alexa Ct. W8 90 DA77
Lexham Gdns.
Alexander Ave. NW10 75 CV66
Alexander Clo., Barn. 34 DD42
Alexander Clo., Brom. 122 EG102
Alexander Clo., Sid. 109 ES86
Alexander Clo., Sthl. 72 CC74
Alexander Clo., Twick. 101 CF89
Alexander Ct., Wal.Cr. 23 DX30
Alexander Evans Ms. SE23 107 DX88
Sunderland Rd.
Alexander Godley Clo., Ash. 144 CM119
Alexander Ms. W2 76 DB72
Alexander St.
Alexander Pl. SW7 8 B8
Alexander Pl. SW7 90 DE77
Alexander Rd. N19 63 DL62
Alexander Rd., Bexh. 96 EX82
Alexander Rd., Chis. 109 EP92
Alexander Rd., Couls. 147 DH115
Alexander Rd., St.Alb. 17 CJ25
Alexander Sq. SW3 8 B8
Alexander Sq. SW3 90 DE77
Alexander St. W2 76 DA72
Alexandra Ave. N22 49 DK53
Alexandra Ave. SW11 90 DG81
Alexandra Ave. W4 88 CR80
Alexandra Ave., Har. 58 BZ60
Alexandra Ave., Sthl. 72 BZ73
Alexandra Ave., Sutt. 118 DA104
Alexandra Ave., Warl. 149 DZ117
Alexandra Clo., Ashf. 99 BR94
Alexandra Rd.
Alexandra Clo., Har. 58 CA62
Alexandra Ave.
Alexandra Clo., Stai. 98 BK93
Alexandra Clo., Swan. 125 FE96
Alexandra Clo., Walt. 113 BU103
Alexandra Cotts. SE14 93 DZ81
Alexandra Ct. N14 35 DJ43
Alexandra Ct., Ashf. 99 BR93
Alexandra Rd.
Alexandra Ct., Wem. 60 CM63
Alexandra Cres., Brom. 108 EF93
Alexandra Dr. SE19 106 DS92
Alexandra Dr., Surb. 116 CN101
Alexandra Est. NW8 76 DB67
Alexandra Gdns. N10 63 DH56
Alexandra Gdns. W4 88 CS80
Alexandra Gdns., Cars. 132 DG109
Alexandra Gdns., Houns. 86 CB82
Alexandra Gro. N4 63 DP60
Alexandra Gro. N12 48 DB50
Alexandra Ms. N2 62 DF55
Fortis Grn.
Alexandra Ms. SW19 104 DA93
Alexandra Rd.
Alexandra Palace N22 63 DK55
Alexandra Palace Way N22 63 DJ56
Alexandra Pk. Rd. N10 49 DH54
Alexandra Pk. Rd. N22 49 DJ53
Alexandra Pl. NW8 76 DC67
Alexandra Pl. SE25 120 DR99

Alexandra Pl., Croy. 120 DS102
Alexandra Rd.
Alexandra Rd. E6 81 EN69
Alexandra Rd. E10 65 EC62
Alexandra Rd. E17 65 DZ58
Alexandra Rd. E18 66 EH55
Alexandra Rd. N8 63 DN55
Alexandra Rd. N9 50 DV45
Alexandra Rd. N10 49 DH53
Alexandra Rd. N15 64 DR57
Alexandra Rd. NW4 61 CX56
Alexandra Rd. NW8 76 DC66
Alexandra Rd. SE26 107 DX93
Alexandra Rd. SW14 88 CR83
Alexandra Rd. SW19 103 CZ93
Alexandra Rd. W4 88 CR75
Alexandra Rd., Add. 126 BK105
Alexandra Rd., Ashf. 99 BR94
Alexandra Rd., Borwd. 32 CR38
Alexandra Rd., Brent. 87 CK79
Alexandra Rd., Croy. 120 DS102
Alexandra Rd., Enf. 37 DX42
Alexandra Rd., Epsom 131 CT113
Alexandra Rd., Erith 97 FF79
Alexandra Rd., Houns. 86 CB82
Alexandra Rd., Kings L. 14 BN29
Alexandra Rd. 14 BG30
(Chipperfield), Kings L.
Alexandra Rd., Kings.T. 102 CN94
Alexandra Rd., Mitch. 104 DE94
Alexandra Rd., Rain. 83 FF67
Alexandra Rd., Rich. 88 CM82
Alexandra Rd., Rick. 28 BG36
Alexandra Rd., Rom. 69 FF58
Alexandra Rd. 68 EX58
(Chadwell Heath), Rom.
Alexandra Rd., T.Ditt. 115 CF99
Alexandra Rd., Twick. 101 CJ86
Alexandra Rd., Uxb. 70 BK68
Alexandra Rd., Warl. 149 DY117
Alexandra Rd., Wat. 29 BU40
Alexandra Rd., West. 150 EH119
Alexandra Sq., Mord. 118 DA99
Alexandra St. E16 80 EG71
Alexandra St. SE14 93 DY80
Alexandra Wk. SE19 106 DS92
Alexandra Way, Wal.Cr. 23 DZ34
Alexandria Rd. W13 73 CG73
Alexis St. SE16 92 DU77
Alfan La., Dart. 111 FD92
Alfearn Rd. E5 64 DW63
Alford Grn., Croy. 135 ED107
Alford Pl. N1 7 J1
Alford Rd. SW8 91 DK81
Alford Rd., Erith 97 FC78
Alfoxton Ave. N15 63 DP56
Alfred Gdns., Sthl. 72 BY73
Alfred Ms. W1 5 M6
Alfred Ms. W1 77 DK71
Alfred Pl. WC1 5 M6
Alfred Pl. WC1 77 DK71
Alfred Prior Ho. E12 67 EN63
Alfred Rd. E15 66 EF64
Alfred Rd. SE25 120 DU99
Alfred Rd. W2 76 DA71
Alfred Rd. W3 74 CQ74
Alfred Rd., Belv. 96 EZ78
Alfred Rd., Buck.H. 52 EK47
Alfred Rd., Felt. 100 BW89
Alfred Rd., Kings.T. 116 CL97
Alfred Rd., Sutt. 132 DC106
Alfred St. E3 79 DZ69
Alfred St. E16 80 EF73
Alfreda St. SW11 91 DH81
Alfred's Gdns., Bark. 81 ES68
Alfreds Way, Bark. 81 EQ69
Alfreds Way Ind. Est., 82 EU67
Bark.
Alfreton Clo. SW19 103 CX90
Alfriston Ave., Croy. 119 DL101
Alfriston Ave., Har. 58 CA58
Alfriston Clo., Surb. 116 CM99
Alfriston Rd. SW11 104 DF85
Algar Clo., Islw. 87 CG83
Algar Rd.
Algar Clo., Stan. 45 CF50
Algar Rd., Islw. 87 CG83
Algarve Rd. SW18 104 DB88
Algernon Rd. NW4 61 CU58
Algernon Rd. NW6 76 DA67
Algernon Rd. SE13 93 EB83
Algers Clo., Loug. 38 EK43
Algers Mead, Loug. 38 EK43
Algers Rd., Loug. 38 EK43
Algiers Rd. SE13 93 EA84
Alibon Gdns., Dag. 68 FA64
Alibon Rd., Dag. 68 EZ64
Alice Gilliatt Ct. W14 89 CZ78
Alice La. E3 79 DZ67
Alice Ms., Tedd. 101 CF92
Luther Rd.
Alice St. SE1 11 M7
Alice St. SE1 92 DS76
Alice Thompson Clo. 108 EJ89
SE12
Alice Walker Clo. SE24 91 DP84
Shakespeare Rd.
Alice Way, Houns. 86 CB84
Alicia Ave., Har. 59 CH56
Alicia Clo., Har. 59 CJ56
Alicia Gdns., Har. 59 CH56
Alie St. E1 78 DT72
Alington Cres. NW9 60 CQ60
Alington Gro., Wall. 133 DJ109
Alison Clo. E6 81 EN72
Alison Clo., Croy. 121 DX102
Shirley Oaks Rd.
Aliwal Rd. SW11 90 DE84
Alkerden Rd. W4 88 CS78
Alkham Rd. N16 64 DT60
All Hallows Rd. N17 50 DS53
All Saints Clo. N9 50 DU47
All Saints Clo., Chig. 54 EV48
All Saints Cres., Wat. 16 BX33
All Saints Dr. SE3 94 EE82
All Saints Dr., S.Croy. 134 DT112
All Saints La., Rick. 28 BN44
All Saints Ms., Har. 45 CE51
All Saints Pas. SW18 104 DB85
Wandsworth High St.
All Saints Rd. SW19 104 DC94
All Saints Rd. W3 88 CQ76
All Saints Rd. W11 75 CZ72
All Saints Rd., Sutt. 118 DB104
All Saints St. N1 77 DM68
All Saints Twr. E10 65 EB59
All Souls Ave. NW10 75 CV68
All Souls Pl. W1 5 J7
Allan Barclay Clo. N15 64 DT58
High Rd.
Allan Clo., N.Mal. 116 CR99
Allan Way W3 74 CQ71
Allandale Ave. N3 61 CY55
Allandale Cres., Pot.B. 19 CZ32
Allandale Pl., Orp. 124 EX104
Allandale Rd., Enf. 37 DX36
Allandale Rd., Horn. 69 FF59
Allard Clo., Orp. 124 EW101
Allard Clo. (Cheshunt), 22 DT27
Wal.Cr.
Allard Cres. (Bushey), 44 CC46
Wat.
Allard Gdns. SW4 105 DK85
Allardyce St. SW4 91 DM84
Allbrook Clo., Tedd. 101 CE92
Allcot Clo., Felt. 99 BT88
Allcroft Rd. NW5 62 DG64
Allen Clo., Mitch. 119 DH95
Allen Clo., Rad. 18 CL32
Russet Dr.
Allen Clo., Sun. 113 BV95
Allen Ct., Grnf. 59 CF64
Allen Edwards Dr. SW8 91 DL81
Allen Pl., Twick. 101 CG88
Church St.
Allen Rd. E3 79 DZ68
Allen Rd. N16 64 DS63
Allen Rd., Beck. 121 DX96
Allen Rd., Croy. 119 DM102
Allen Rd., Sun. 113 BV95
Allen St. W8 90 DA76
Allenby Ave., S.Croy. 134 DQ109
Allenby Clo., Grnf. 72 CA69
Allenby Rd. SE23 107 DY90
Allenby Rd., Sthl. 72 CA69
Allenby Rd., West. 150 EL117
Allendale Ave., Sthl. 72 CA72
Allendale Clo. SE5 92 DR81
Daneville Rd.
Allendale Clo. SE26 107 DX92
Allendale Rd., Grnf. 73 CH65
Allens Rd., Enf. 36 DW43
Allensbury Pl. NW1 77 DK66
Allenswood Rd. SE9 94 EL83
Allerford Ct., Har. 58 CB57
Allerford Rd. SE6 107 EB90
Allerton Clo., Borwd. 32 CM38
Allerton Rd. N16 64 DQ61
Allerton Rd., Borwd. 32 CL38
Allerton Wk. N7 63 DM61
Durham Rd.
Allestree Rd. SW6 89 CY80
Alleyn Cres. SE21 106 DR89
Alleyn Pk. SE21 106 DR89
Alleyn Pk., Sthl. 86 CA78
Alleyn Rd. SE21 106 DR90
Alleyndale Rd., Dag. 68 EW61
Allfarthing La. SW18 104 DB86
Allgood Clo., Mord. 117 CX100
Allgood St. E2 78 DT68
Allhallows La. EC4 11 K1
Allhallows Rd. E6 80 EL71
Alliance Clo., Wem. 59 CK63
Milford Gdns.
Alliance Rd. E13 80 EJ70
Alliance Rd. SE18 96 EU79
Alliance Rd. W3 74 CP70
Allied Ind. Est. W3 88 CS75
Allied Way W3 88 CS75
Larden Rd.
Allingham Clo. W7 73 CF73
Allingham St. N1 78 DQ68
Allington Ave. N17 50 DS51
Allington Clo. SW19 103 CX92
High St. Wimbledon
Allington Clo., Grnf. 72 CC66
Allington Ct. SW19 103 CX92
High St. Wimbledon
Allington Ct., Enf. 37 DX43
Allington Rd. NW4 61 CV57
Allington Rd. W10 75 CY68
Allington Rd., Har. 58 CC57
Allington Rd., Orp. 123 ER103
Allington St. SW1 9 J7
Allington St. SW1 91 DH76
Allison Clo. SE10 93 EC81
Dartmouth Hill
Allison Clo., Wal.Abb. 24 EG33
Allison Gro. SE21 106 DS88
Allison Rd. N8 63 DN57
Allison Rd. W3 74 CQ72
Allitsen Rd. NW8 4 B1
Allitsen Rd. NW8 76 DE68
Allmains Clo., Wal.Abb. 24 EH25
Allnutt Way SW4 105 DK85
Allnutts Rd., Epp. 26 EU33
Alloa Rd. SE8 93 DY78
Alloa Rd., Ilf. 68 EU61
Allonby Dr., Ruis. 57 BP59
Allonby Gdns., Wem. 59 CJ60
Allotment La., Sev. 155 FJ122
Alloway Rd. E3 79 DY69
Allsop Pl. NW1 4 E5
Allsop Pl. NW1 76 DF70
Allum Clo., Borwd. 32 CL42
Allum Gro., Tad. 145 CV121
Preston La.
Allum La., Borwd. 31 CK43
Allum Way N20 48 DC46
Allwood Clo. SE26 107 DX91
Allwood Rd., Wal.Cr. 22 DT27
Alma Ave. E4 51 EC52
Alma Cres., Sutt. 131 CY106
Alma Gro. SE1 92 DT77
Alma Pl. NW10 75 CV69
Harrow Rd.
Alma Pl. SE19 106 DT94
Alma Pl., Th.Hth. 119 DN99
Alma Rd. N10 49 DH52
Alma Rd. SW18 90 DC84
Alma Rd., Cars. 132 DE106
Alma Rd., Enf. 37 DY41
Alma Rd., Esher 115 CE102
Alma Rd., Orp. 124 EX103
Alma Rd., Sid. 110 EU90
Alma Rd., Sthl. 72 BY73
Alma Row, Har. 45 CD53
Alma Sq. NW8 76 DC69
Alma St. E15 79 ED65
Alma St. NW5 77 DH65
Alma Ter. SW18 104 DD87
Almack Rd. E5 64 DW63
Almeida St. N1 77 DP66
Almer Rd. SW20 103 CU94
Almeric Rd. SW11 90 DF84
Almington St. N4 63 DL60
Almond Ave. W5 88 CL76
Almond Ave., Cars. 118 DF103
Almond Ave., Uxb. 57 BP62
Almond Ave., West Dr. 84 BN76
Almond Clo. SE15 92 DU82
Almond Clo., Brom. 123 EN101
Almond Clo., Hayes 71 BS73
Almond Clo., Ruis. 57 BT62
The Roundways
Almond Clo., Shep. 113 BQ96
Almond Dr., Swan. 125 FD96
Almond Gro., Brent. 87 CH80
Almond Rd. N17 50 DU52
Almond Rd. SE16 92 DV77
Almond Rd., Epsom 130 CR111
Almond Way, Borwd. 32 CP42
Almond Way, Brom. 123 EN101
Almond Way, Har. 44 CB54
Almond Way, Mitch. 119 DK99
Almonds Ave., Buck.H. 52 EG47
Almorah Rd. N1 78 DR66
Almorah Rd., Houns. 86 BX81
Alms Heath, Wok. 141 BP121
Almshouse La., 129 CJ109
Chess.
Almshouse La., Enf. 36 DV37
Alnwick Gro., Mord. 118 DB98
Bordesley Rd.
Alnwick Rd. E16 80 EJ72
Alnwick Rd. SE12 108 EH87
Alperton La., Grnf. 73 CK68
Alperton La., Wem. 73 CK68
Alperton St. W10 75 CY70
Alpha Clo. NW1 4 C3
Alpha Ct., Whyt. 148 DU118
Alpha Gro. E14 93 EA75
Alpha Pl. NW6 76 DA68
Alpha Pl. SW3 90 DE79
Alpha Rd. E4 51 EA48
Alpha Rd. N18 50 DU51
Alpha Rd. SE14 93 DZ81
Alpha Rd., Croy. 120 DS102
Alpha Rd., Enf. 37 DY42
Alpha Rd., Surb. 116 CM100
Alpha Rd., Tedd. 101 CD92
Alpha Rd., Uxb. 71 BP70
Alpha St. SE15 92 DU82
Alphabet Gdns., Cars. 118 DD100
Alphabet Sq. E3 79 EA71
Hawgood St.
Alphea Clo. SW19 104 DE94
Courtney Rd.
Alpine Ave., Surb. 116 CQ103
Alpine Clo., Croy. 120 DS104
Alpine Copse, Brom. 123 EN96
Alpine Rd. SE16 92 DW77
Alpine Rd., Walt. 113 BU101
Alpine Vw., Cars. 132 DE106
Alpine Wk., Stan. 45 CE47
Alpine Way E6 81 EN71
Alric Ave. NW10 74 CR66
Alric Ave., N.Mal. 116 CS97
Alroy Rd. N4 63 DN59
Alsace Rd. SE17 11 M10
Alsace Rd. SE17 92 DS78
Alscot Rd. SE1 92 DT77
Alscot Way SE1 11 P8
Alscot Way SE1 92 DT77
Alsike Rd. SE2 96 EX76
Alsike Rd., Erith 96 EY76
Alsom Ave., Wor.Pk. 131 CT105
Alston Clo., Surb. 115 CH101
Alston Rd. N18 50 DV50
Alston Rd. SW17 104 DD91
Alston Rd., Barn. 33 CY41
Alt Gro. SW19 103 CZ94
St. George's Rd.
Altair Clo. N17 50 DT51
Altair Way, Nthwd. 43 BT50
Altash Way SE9 109 EM89
Altenburg Ave. W13 87 CH76
Altenburg Gdns. SW11 90 DF84
Altham Rd., Pnr. 44 BY52
Althea St. SW6 90 DB82
Althorne Gdns. E18 66 EF56
Althorne Way, Dag. 68 FA61
Althorp Rd. SW17 104 DF88
Althorpe Gro. SW11 90 DD81
Westbridge Rd.
Althorpe Ms. SW11 90 DD81
Westbridge Rd.
Althorpe Rd., Har. 58 CC57
Altmore Ave. E6 81 EM66
Alton Ave., Stan. 45 CF52
Alton Clo., Bex. 110 EY88
Alton Clo., Islw. 87 CF82
Alton Gdns., Beck. 107 EA94
Alton Gdns., Twick. 101 CD86
Alton Rd. N17 64 DR55
Alton Rd. SW15 103 CU88
Alton Rd., Croy. 119 DN104
Alton Rd., Rich. 88 CL84
Alton St. E14 79 EB71
Altyre Clo., Beck. 121 DZ99
Altyre Rd., Croy. 120 DR103
Altyre Way, Beck. 121 DZ100
Alva Way, Wat. 44 BX47
Alvanley Gdns. NW6 62 DB64
Alverston Gdns. SE25 120 DS99
Alverstone Ave. SW19 104 DA89
Alverstone Ave., Barn. 48 DE45
Alverstone Gdns. SE9 109 EQ88
Alverstone Rd. E12 67 EN63
Alverstone Rd. NW2 75 CW66
Alverstone Rd., N.Mal. 117 CT98
Alverstone Rd., Wem. 60 CM60
Alverton St. SE8 93 DZ78
Alveston Ave., Har. 59 CH55
Alvey Est. SE17 11 M9
Alvey St. SE17 11 M10
Alvey St. SE17 92 DS78
Alvia Gdns., Sutt. 132 DC105
Alvington Cres. E8 64 DT64
Alway Ave., Epsom 130 CQ106
Alwold Cres. SE12 108 EH86
Alwyn Ave. W4 88 CR78
Alwyn Clo., Borwd. 32 CM44
Alwyn Clo., Croy. 135 EB108
Alwyn Gdns. NW4 61 CU56
Alwyn Gdns. W3 74 CP72
Alwyne La. N1 77 DP66
Alwyne Vill.
Alwyne Pl. N1 78 DQ65
Alwyne Rd. N1 78 DQ66
Alwyne Rd. SW19 103 CZ93
Alwyne Rd. W7 73 CE73
Alwyne Sq. N1 78 DQ65
Alwyne Vill. N1 77 DP66
Alyth Gdns. NW11 62 DA58
Alzette Ho. E2 79 DX68
Mace St.
Amalgamated Dr., Brent. 87 CG79
Amanda Clo., Chig. 53 ER51
Amazon St. E1 78 DV72
Hessel St.
Ambassador Clo., Houns. 86 BY82
Ambassador Gdns. E6 81 EM71
Ambassador Sq. E14 93 EB77
Ambassador's Ct. SW1 9 L3
Amber Ave. E17 51 DY53
Amber Gro. NW2 61 CX60
Prayle Gro.
Amber St. E15 79 ED65
Salway Rd.
Ambercroft Way, Couls. 147 DP119
Amberden Ave. N3 62 DA55
Ambergate St. SE17 10 G10
Ambergate St. SE17 91 DP78
Amberley Clo., Orp. 137 ET106
Warnford Rd.
Amberley Clo., Pnr. 58 BZ55
Amberley Ct., Sid. 110 EW92
Amberley Gdns., Enf. 50 DS45
Amberley Gdns., Epsom 131 CT105
Amberley Gro. SE26 106 DV92
Amberley Gro., Croy. 120 DT101
Amberley Rd. E10 65 EA59
Amberley Rd. N13 49 DM47
Amberley Rd. SE2 96 EX79
Amberley Rd. W9 76 DA71
Amberley Rd., Buck.H. 52 EJ46
Amberley Rd., Enf. 50 DT45
Amberley Way, Houns. 100 BW85
Amberley Way, Mord. 117 CZ101
Amberley Way, Rom. 69 FB56
Amberley Way, Uxb. 70 BL69
Amberside Clo., Islw. 101 CD86
Amberwood Ri., N.Mal. 116 CS100
Amblecote, Cob. 128 BY112
Amblecote Clo. SE12 108 EH90
Amblecote Meadows 108 EH90
SE12
Amblecote Rd. SE12 108 EH90
Ambler Rd. N4 63 DP62
Ambleside, Brom. 107 ED93
Ambleside, Epp. 26 EU31
Ambleside Ave. SW16 105 DK91
Ambleside Ave., Beck. 121 DY99
Ambleside Ave., Horn. 69 FH64
Ambleside Ave., Walt. 114 BW102
Ambleside Clo. E9 64 DW64
Churchill Wk.
Ambleside Clo. E10 65 EB59
Ambleside Cres., Enf. 37 DX41
Ambleside Dr., Felt. 99 BT88
Ambleside Gdns., Ilf. 66 EL56
Ambleside Gdns., 135 DX109
S.Croy.
Ambleside Gdns., Sutt. 132 DC107
Ambleside Gdns., Wem. 59 CK60
Ambleside Rd. NW10 75 CT66
Ambleside Rd., Bexh. 96 FA82
Ambrey Way, Wall. 133 DK109
Ambrooke Rd., Belv. 96 FA76
Ambrosden Ave. SW1 9 L7
Ambrosden Ave. SW1 91 DJ76
Ambrose Ave. NW11 61 CY59
Ambrose Clo. E6 80 EL71
Lovage App.
Ambrose Clo., Dart. 97 FF84
Ambrose Clo., Orp. 123 ET104
Stapleton Rd.
Ambrose Ms. SW11 90 DF82
Abercrombie St.
Ambrose St. SE16 92 DV77
Ambrose Wk. E3 79 EA68
Malmesbury Rd.
Amelia St. SE17 11 H10
Amelia St. SE17 91 DP78
Amen Cor. EC4 6 G9
Amen Cor. SW17 104 DF93
Amen Ct. EC4 6 G8
Amenity Way, Mord. 117 CW101
America Sq. EC3 7 P10
America St. SE1 11 H3
Amerland Rd. SW18 103 CZ85
Amersham Ave. N18 50 DR51
Amersham Gro. SE14 93 DZ80
Amersham Rd. SE14 93 DZ81
Amersham Rd., Croy. 120 DQ100
Amersham Vale SE14 93 DZ80
Amery Gdns. NW10 75 CV67
Amery Rd., Har. 59 CG61
Amesbury, Wal.Abb. 24 EG32
Amesbury Ave. SW2 105 DL89
Amesbury Clo., Epp. 25 ET31
Amesbury Rd.
Amesbury Clo., Wor.Pk. 117 CW102
Amesbury Dr. E4 37 EB44
Amesbury Rd., Brom. 122 EK97
Amesbury Rd., Dag. 82 EX66
Amesbury Rd., Epp. 25 ET31
Amesbury Rd., Felt. 100 BX89
Amethyst Rd. E15 65 ED63
Amey Dr., Lthd. 142 CC124
Amherst Ave. W13 73 CJ72
Amherst Clo., Orp. 124 EU98
Amherst Dr., Orp. 123 ET98
Amherst Hill, Sev. 154 FE122
Amherst Rd. W13 73 CJ72
Amherst Rd., Sev. 155 FH122
Amhurst Gdns., Islw. 87 CF81
Amhurst Par. N16 64 DT59
Amhurst Pk.
Amhurst Pk. N16 64 DR59
Amhurst Pas. E8 64 DU64
Amhurst Rd. E8 64 DV64
Amhurst Rd. N16 64 DT63
Amhurst Ter. E8 64 DU63
Amhurst Wk. SE28 82 EU74
Pitfield Cres.
Amidas Gdns., Dag. 68 EV63
Amiel St. E1 78 DW70
Amies St. SW11 90 DF83
Amina Way SE16 92 DU76
Yalding Rd.
Amis Ave., Add. 126 BG110
Amis Ave., Epsom 130 CN107
Amity Gro. SW20 117 CW95
Amity Rd. E15 80 EF67
Ammanford Gdn. NW9 60 CS58
Ruthin Clo.
Amner Rd. SW11 104 DG86
Amoco Ho. W5 74 CL69
Amor Rd. W6 89 CW76
Amott Rd. SE15 92 DU83
Amoy Pl. E14 79 EA72
Ampere Way, Croy. 119 DL101
Ampleforth Rd. SE2 96 EV75
Ampthill Sq. Est. NW1 5 L1
Ampton Pl. WC1 6 B3
Ampton Pl. WC1 77 DM69
Ampton St. WC1 6 B3
Ampton St. WC1 77 DM69
Amroth Clo. SE23 106 DV88
Amsterdam Rd. E14 93 EC76
Amwell Clo., Enf. 36 DR43
Amwell Clo., Wat. 30 BY35
Phillipers
Amwell Ct., Wal.Abb. 24 EE33
Amwell Ct. Est. N4 64 DQ60
Amwell St. EC1 6 D2
Amwell St. EC1 77 DN69
Amy Warne Clo. E6 80 EL70
Evelyn Denington Rd.
Amyand Cotts., Twick. 101 CH86
Amyand Pk. Rd.
Amyand La., Twick. 101 CH87
Marble Hill Gdns.
Amyand Pk. Gdns., 101 CH87
Twick.
Amyand Pk. Rd.
Amyand Pk. Rd., Twick. 101 CG87
Amyruth Rd. SE4 107 EA85
Anatola Rd. N19 63 DH61
Dartmouth Pk. Hill
Ancaster Cres., N.Mal. 117 CU100
Ancaster Ms., Beck. 121 DX97
Ancaster Rd.

Ancaster Rd., Beck. 121 DX97
Ancaster St. SE18 95 ES80
Anchor & Hope La. SE7 94 EJ77
Anchor Clo. (Cheshunt), Wal.Cr. 23 DX28
Anchor Dr., Rain. 83 FH69
Anchor Ms. SW12 105 DH86
Hazelbourne Rd.
Anchor St. SE16 92 DV77
Anchor Wf. E3 79 EB71
Watts Gro.
Anchor Yd. EC1 7 J4
Anchorage Clo. SW19 104 DA92
Ancill Clo. W6 89 CY79
Ancona Rd. NW10 75 CU68
Ancona Rd. SE18 95 ER78
Andace Pk. Gdns., Brom. 122 EJ95
Andalus Rd. SW9 91 DL83
Ander Clo., Wem. 59 CK63
Anderson Clo. N21 35 DM43
Worlds End La.
Anderson Clo. W3 74 CR72
Anderson Clo., Epsom 130 CP112
Anderson Clo., Uxb. 42 BG53
Anderson Dr., Ashf. 99 BQ91
Anderson Ho., Bark. 81 ER68
The Coverdales
Anderson Pl., Houns. 86 CB84
Anderson Rd. E9 79 DX65
Anderson Rd., Rad. 18 CN33
Anderson Rd., Wey. 113 BR104
Anderson Rd., Wdf.Grn. 66 EK55
Anderson St. SW3 8 D10
Anderson St. SW3 90 DF78
Anderson Way, Belv. 97 FB75
Anderton Clo. SE5 92 DR83
Andover Ave. E16 80 EK72
King George Ave.
Andover Clo., Epsom 130 CR111
Andover Clo., Felt. 99 BT88
Andover Clo., Grnf. 72 CB70
Ruislip Rd.
Andover Clo., Uxb. 70 BH68
Andover Pl. NW6 76 DB68
Andover Rd. N7 63 DM61
Andover Rd., Orp. 123 ES103
Andover Rd., Twick. 101 CD88
Andre St. E8 64 DU64
Andrew Borde St. WC2 5 N8
Andrew Clo., Bex. 111 FD85
Andrew Clo., Dart. 111 FD85
Andrew Clo., Ilf. 53 ER51
Andrew Pl. SW8 91 DK81
Cowthorpe Rd.
Andrew St. E14 79 EC72
Andrewes Gdns. E6 80 EL72
Andrewes Ho. EC2 78 DQ71
Fore St.
Andrews Clo. E6 80 EL72
Linton Gdns.
Andrews Clo., Buck.H. 52 EJ47
Andrews Clo., Epsom 131 CT114
Andrews Clo., Har. 59 CD59
Bessborough Rd.
Andrews Clo., Orp. 124 EX97
Andrews Clo., Wor.Pk. 117 CW103
Andrews Crosse WC2 6 D9
Andrews La. (Cheshunt), Wal.Cr. 22 DS28
Andrews Pl. SE9 109 EP86
Andrew's Rd. E8 78 DV67
Andrews Wk. SE17 91 DP79
Dale Rd.
Andwell Clo. SE2 96 EV75
Anerley Gro. SE19 106 DT94
Anerley Hill SE19 106 DT93
Anerley Pk. SE20 106 DU94
Anerley Pk. Rd. SE20 106 DV94
Anerley Rd. SE19 106 DU94
Anerley Rd. SE20 106 DU94
Anerley Sta. Rd. SE20 120 DV95
Anerley St. SW11 90 DF82
Anerley Vale SE19 106 DT94
Anfield Clo. SW12 105 DJ87
Belthorn Cres.
Angas Ct., Wey. 127 BQ106
Angel All. E1 78 DU72
Whitechapel Rd.
Angel Clo. N18 50 DT50
Angel Ct. EC2 7 L8
Angel Ct. SW1 9 L3
Angel Ct. SW17 104 DF91
Angel Hill, Sutt. 118 DB104
Sutton Common Rd.
Angel Hill Dr., Sutt. 118 DB104
Angel La. E15 79 ED65
Angel La., Hayes 71 BR71
Angel Ms. N1 6 E1
Angel Ms. N1 77 DN68
Angel Pas. EC4 11 K1
Angel Pl. N18 50 DU50
Angel Clo.
Angel Pl. SE1 11 K4
Angel Rd. N18 50 DU50
Angel Rd., Har. 59 CE58
Angel Rd., T.Ditt. 115 CG101
Angel Rd. Wks. N18 50 DW50
Angel Sq. EC1 77 DN68
Islington High St.
Angel St. EC1 7 H8
Angel St. EC1 78 DQ72
Angel Wk. W6 89 CW78
Angel Way, Rom. 69 FE57
Angelfield, Houns. 86 CB84
Angelica Dr. E6 81 EN71
Angelica Gdns., Croy. 121 DX102
Angell Pk. Gdns. SW9 91 DN83
Angell Rd. SW9 91 DN83
Angerstein La. SE3 94 EF81
Angle Clo., Uxb. 70 BN67
Angle Grn., Dag. 68 EW60
Burnside Rd.
Anglers Clo., Rich. 101 CJ91
Locksmeade Rd.
Angler's La. NW5 77 DH65
Angles Rd. SW16 105 DL91
Anglesea Ave. SE18 95 EP77
Anglesea Rd. SE18 95 EP77
Anglesea Rd., Kings.T. 115 CK98
Anglesea Rd., Orp. 124 EW100
Anglesea Ter. W6 89 CV76
Wellesley Ave.
Anglesey Clo., Ashf. 98 BN91
Anglesey Ct. Rd., Cars. 132 DG107
Anglesey Dr., Rain. 83 FG70
Anglesey Gdns., Cars. 132 DG107
Anglesey Rd., Enf. 36 DV42
Anglesey Rd., Wat. 44 BW50
Anglesmede Cres., Pnr. 58 BY55
Anglesmede Way, Pnr. 58 BY55
Anglia Clo. N17 50 DV52
Park La.
Anglia Ho. E14 79 DY72
Anglia Wk. E6 81 EM67
Napier Rd.
Anglian Clo., Wat. 30 BW40
Anglian Ind. Est., Bark. 82 EU71
Anglian Rd. E11 65 ED62
Anglo Rd. E3 79 DZ68
Angrave Ct. E8 78 DT67
Angrave Pas. E8 78 DT67
Haggerston Rd.
Angus Clo., Chess. 130 CN106
Angus Dr., Ruis. 58 BW63
Angus Gdns. NW9 46 CR53
Angus Rd. E13 80 EJ69
Angus St. SE14 93 DY80
Anhalt Rd. SW11 90 DE80
Ankerdine Cres. SE18 95 EP81
Anlaby Rd., Tedd. 101 CE92
Anley Rd. W14 89 CX75
Anmersh Gro., Stan. 45 CK53
Ann La. SW10 90 DD80
Ann Moss Way SE16 92 DW76
Ann St. SE18 95 EQ78
Anna Clo. E8 78 DT67
Anna Neagle Clo. E7 66 EG63
Dames Rd.
Annabel Clo. E14 79 EB72
Annan Way, Rom. 55 FD53
Annandale Gro., Uxb. 57 BQ62
Thorpland Ave.
Annandale Rd. SE10 94 EF78
Annandale Rd. W4 88 CS78
Annandale Rd., Croy. 120 DU103
Annandale Rd., Sid. 109 ES87
Anne Boleyn's Wk., Kings.T. 102 CL92
Anne Boleyn's Wk., Sutt. 131 CX108
Anne Case Ms., N.Mal. 116 CR97
Sycamore Gro.
Anne St. E13 80 EG70
Anne Way, Ilf. 53 EQ51
Anne Way, W.Mol. 114 CB98
Anne's Wk., Cat. 148 DS120
Annesley Ave. NW9 60 CR55
Annesley Clo. NW10 60 CS62
Annesley Dr., Croy. 135 DZ105
Annesley Rd. SE3 94 EH81
Annesley Wk. N19 63 DJ61
Macdonald Rd.
Annett Clo., Shep. 113 BS98
Annett Rd., Walt. 113 BU101
Annette Clo., Har. 45 CE54
Spencer Rd.
Annette Cres. N1 78 DQ66
Essex Rd.
Annette Rd. N7 63 DM62
Annie Besant Clo. E3 79 DZ67
Anning St. EC2 7 N4
Annington Rd. N2 62 DF55
Annis Rd. E9 79 DY65
Ann's Clo. SW1 8 E5
Ann's Pl. E1 7 P7
Annsworthy Ave., Th.Hth. 120 DR97
Grange Pk. Rd.
Annsworthy Cres. SE25 120 DR96
Grange Rd.
Ansdell Rd. SE15 92 DW82
Ansdell St. W8 90 DB76
Ansdell Ter. W8 90 DB76
Ansdell St.
Ansell Gro., Cars. 118 DG102
Ansell Rd. SW17 104 DE90
Anselm Clo., Croy. 120 DT104
Park Hill Ri.
Anselm Rd. SW6 90 DA79
Anselm Rd., Pnr. 44 BZ52
Ansford Rd., Brom. 107 EC92
Ansleigh Pl. W11 75 CX73
Ansley Clo., S.Croy. 134 DV114
Anson Clo., Ken. 148 DR120
Anson Clo., Rom. 55 FB54
Anson Rd. N7 63 DJ63
Anson Rd. NW2 61 CV64
Anson Ter., Nthlt. 72 CB65
Anson Wk., Nthwd. 43 BP49
Anstead Dr., Rain. 83 FG68
Anstey Rd. SE15 92 DU83
Anstey Wk. N15 63 DP56
Anstice Clo. W4 88 CS80
Anstridge Path SE9 109 ER86
Anstridge Rd.
Anstridge Rd. SE9 109 ER86
Antelope Rd. SE18 95 EM76
Anthony Clo. NW7 46 CS49
Anthony Clo., Sev. 154 FE121
Anthony Clo., Wat. 44 BW46
Anthony La., Swan. 125 FG95
Anthony Rd. SE25 120 DU100
Anthony Rd., Borwd. 32 CM40
Anthony Rd., Grnf. 73 CE68
Anthony Rd., Well. 96 EU81
Anthony St. E1 78 DV72
Commercial Rd.
Anthorne Clo., Pot.B. 20 DB31
Anthus Ms., Nthwd. 43 BS52
Antigua Clo. SE19 106 DR92
Salters Hill
Antigua Wk. SE19 106 DR92
Salters Hill
Antill Rd. E3 79 DY69
Antill Rd. N15 64 DU56
Antill Ter. E1 79 DX72
Antlers Hill E4 37 EB42
Antoinette Ct., Abb.L. 15 BT29
Anton Cres., Sutt. 118 DA104
Anton St. E8 64 DU64
Antoneys Clo., Pnr. 44 BX54
Antrim Gro. NW3 76 DF65
Antrim Mans. NW3 76 DF65
Antrim Rd.
Antrim Rd. NW3 76 DF65
Antrobus Clo., Sutt. 131 CZ106
Antrobus Rd. W4 88 CQ77
Anvil La., Cob. 127 BU114
Anvil Rd., Sun. 113 BU98
Anworth Clo., Wdf.Grn. 52 EH51
Anyards Rd., Cob. 127 BV113
Apeldoorn Dr., Wall. 133 DL109
Aperdele Rd., Lthd. 143 CG118
Aperfield Rd., Erith 97 FF79
Aperfield Rd., West. 150 EL117
Apex Clo., Beck. 121 EB95
Apex Clo., Wey. 113 BR104
Apex Cor. NW7 46 CR49
Apex Twr., N.Mal. 116 CS97
Aplin Way, Islw. 87 CE81
Apollo Ave., Brom. 122 EH95
Rodway Rd.
Apollo Ave., Nthwd. 43 BU50
Apollo Clo., Horn. 69 FH61
Apollo Pl. E11 66 EE62
Apollo Pl. SW10 90 DD80
Riley St.
Apollo Way SE28 95 ER76
Broadwater Rd.
Apostle Way, Th.Hth. 119 DP96
Apothecary St. EC4 6 F9
Appach Rd. SW2 105 DN85
Apple Garth, Brent. 87 CK77
Apple Gro., Chess. 130 CL105
Apple Gro., Enf. 36 DS41
Apple Mkt., Kings.T. 115 CK96
Eden St.
Apple Orchard, Swan. 125 FD98
Apple Rd. E11 66 EE62
Apple Tree Ave., Uxb. 70 BM72
Apple Tree Ave., West Dr. 70 BM72
Apple Tree Yd. SW1 9 L2
Appleby Clo. E4 51 EB51
Appleby Clo. N15 64 DR57
Appleby Clo., Twick. 101 CD89
Appleby Gdns., Felt. 99 BT88
Appleby Rd. E8 78 DU66
Appleby Rd. E16 80 EF72
Appleby St. E2 7 P1
Appleby St. E2 78 DT68
Appleby St. (Cheshunt), Wal.Cr. 22 DR25
Applecroft, St.Alb. 16 CB28
Appledore Ave., Bexh. 97 FC81
Appledore Ave., Ruis. 58 BW62
Appledore Clo. SW17 104 DF89
Appledore Clo., Brom. 122 EF99
Appledore Clo., Edg. 46 CN53
Appledore Cres., Sid. 109 ES90
Appledown Ri., Couls. 147 DJ115
Appleford Rd. W10 75 CY70
Applegarth, Croy. 135 EB108
Applegarth, Esher 129 CF106
Applegarth Dr., Ilf. 67 ET56
Applegarth Rd. SE28 82 EV74
Applegarth Rd. W14 89 CX76
Appleton Gdns., N.Mal. 117 CU100
Appleton Rd. SE9 94 EL83
Appleton Rd., Loug. 39 EP41
Appleton Sq., Mitch. 118 DE95
Appletree Clo. SE20 120 DV95
Jasmine Gro.
Appletree Clo., Lthd. 142 CC122
Kennel La.
Appletree Gdns., Barn. 34 DE42
Appletree Wk., Wat. 15 BV34
Applewood Clo. N20 48 DE46
Applewood Clo. NW2 61 CV62
Appold St. EC2 7 M6
Appold St. EC2 78 DS71
Appold St., Erith 97 FF79
Apprentice Way E5 64 DV63
Clarence Rd.
Approach, The NW4 61 CX57
Approach, The W3 74 CR72
Approach, The, Enf. 36 DV40
Approach, The, Lthd. 142 BY123
Maddox La.
Approach, The, Orp. 123 ET103
Approach, The, Pot.B. 19 CZ32
Approach Clo. N16 64 DS64
Cowper Rd.
Approach Rd. E2 78 DW68
Approach Rd. SW20 117 CW96
Approach Rd., Ashf. 99 BQ93
Approach Rd., Barn. 34 DC42
Approach Rd., Pur. 133 DP112
Approach Rd., W.Mol. 114 CA99
Aprey Gdns. NW4 61 CW56
April Clo. W7 73 CE73
April Clo., Ash. 144 CM117
April Clo., Felt. 99 BU90
April Clo., Orp. 137 ET106
Briarswood Way
April Glen SE23 107 DX90
April St. E8 64 DT63
Apsley Clo., Har. 58 CC57
Apsley Rd. SE25 120 DV98
Apsley Rd., N.Mal. 116 CQ97
Apsley Way NW2 61 CU61
Apsley Way W1 8 G4
Aquarius Way, Nthwd. 43 BU50
Aquila Clo., Lthd. 144 CL121
Aquila St. NW8 76 DD68
Aquinas St. SE1 10 E3
Arabella Dr. SW15 88 CS84
Arabia Clo. E4 51 EC45
Arabin Rd. SE4 93 DY84
Aragon Ave., Epsom 131 CV109
Aragon Ave., T.Ditt. 115 CF99
Aragon Clo., Brom. 123 EM102
Seymour Dr.
Aragon Clo., Croy. 136 EE110
Aragon Clo., Enf. 35 DM38
Aragon Clo., Loug. 38 EL44
Aragon Clo., Rom. 55 FB51
Aragon Clo., Sun. 99 BT94
Aragon Dr., Ilf. 53 EQ52
Aragon Dr., Ruis. 58 BX60
Aragon Ms. E1 78 DU74
Thomas More St.
Aragon Rd., Kings.T. 102 CL92
Aragon Rd., Mord. 117 CX100
Aragon Wk., W.Byf. 126 BM113
Aran Ct., Wey. 113 BR103
Mallards Reach
Aran Dr., Stan. 45 CJ49
Arandora Cres., Rom. 68 EV59
Arbery Rd. E3 79 DY69
Arbor Clo., Beck. 121 EB96
Arbor Ct. N16 64 DR61
Lordship Rd.
Arbor Rd. E4 51 ED48
Arbour Clo., Lthd. 143 CF123
Arbour Rd., Enf. 37 DX42
Arbour Sq. E1 79 DX72
Arbour Way, Horn. 69 FH64
Arbroath Grn., Wat. 43 BU48
Arbroath Rd. SE9 94 EL83
Arbrook Clo., Orp. 124 EU97
Arbrook La., Esher 128 CC107
Arbury Ter. SE26 106 DV90
Oaksford Ave.
Arbuthnot La., Bex. 110 EY86
Arbuthnot Rd. SE14 93 DX82
Arbutus St. E8 78 DT67
Arcade, The EC2 7 M7
Arcade Pl., Rom. 69 FE57
Arcadia Ave. N3 48 DA53
Arcadia Clo., Cars. 132 DG105
Arcadia St. E14 79 EA72
Arcadian Ave., Bex. 110 EY86
Arcadian Clo., Bex. 110 EY86
Arcadian Gdns. N22 49 DM52
Arcadian Rd., Bex. 110 EY86
Arch Rd., Walt. 114 BX104
Arch St. SE1 11 H7
Arch St. SE1 92 DQ76
Archangel St. SE16 93 DX75
Archbishops Pl. SW2 105 DM86
Archdale Pl., N.Mal. 116 CP97
Archdale Rd. SE22 106 DT85
Archel Rd. W14 89 CZ79
Archer Clo., Kings L. 14 BM29
Archer Clo., Kings.T. 102 CL94
Archer Ho. SW11 90 DD81
Vicarage Cres.
Archer Ms., Hmptn. 100 CC93
Windmill Rd.
Archer Rd. SE25 120 DV98
Archer Rd., Orp. 124 EU99
Archer St. W1 5 M10
Archer Ter., West Dr. 70 BL73
Yew Ave.
Archer Way, Swan. 125 FF96
Archers Dr., Enf. 36 DW40
Archers Wk. SE15 92 DT81
Exeter Rd.
Archery Clo. W2 4 C9
Archery Clo. W2 76 DE72
Archery Clo., Har. 59 CF55
Archery Rd. SE9 109 EM85
Arches, The SW6 89 CZ82
Munster Rd.
Arches, The WC2 10 A2
Arches, The, Har. 58 CB61
Archibald Ms. W1 9 H1
Archibald Ms. W1 76 DG73
Archibald Rd. N7 63 DK63
Archibald St. E3 79 EA70
Archie Clo., West Dr. 84 BN75
Archway, Rom. 55 FH51
Archway Clo. N19 63 DJ61
St. Johns Way
Archway Clo. SW19 104 DB91
Archway Clo., Wall. 119 DK104
Archway Mall N19 63 DJ61
Magdala Ave.
Archway Rd. N6 62 DF57
Archway Rd. N19 63 DJ60
Archway St. SW13 88 CS83
Arcola St. E8 64 DT64
Arctic St. NW5 62 DG64
Gillies St.
Arcus Rd., Brom. 108 EE93
Ardbeg Rd. SE24 106 DR85
Arden Clo., Har. 59 CD62
Arden Clo. (Bushey), Wat. 45 CF45
Arden Ct. Gdns. N2 62 DD58
Arden Cres. E14 93 EA77
Arden Cres., Dag. 82 EW66
Arden Est. N1 7 M1
Arden Est. N1 78 DS68
Arden Gro., Orp. 137 EP105
Arden Ms. E17 65 EB57
Arden Mhor, Pnr. 57 BV56
Arden Rd. N3 61 CY55
Arden Rd. W13 73 CJ73
Ardent Clo. SE25 120 DS97
Ardesley Wd., Wey. 127 BS105
Ardfern Ave. SW16 119 DN97
Ardfillan Rd. SE6 107 ED88
Ardgowan Rd. SE6 108 EE87
Ardilaun Rd. N5 64 DQ63
Ardingly Clo., Croy. 121 DX104
Ardleigh Gdns., Sutt. 118 DA101
Ardleigh Ho., Bark. 81 EQ67
St. Ann's
Ardleigh Ms., Ilf. 67 EP62
Bengal Rd.
Ardleigh Rd. E17 51 DZ53
Ardleigh Rd. N1 78 DS65
Ardleigh Ter. E17 51 DZ53
Ardley Clo. NW10 60 CS62
Ardley Clo. SE6 107 DY90
Ardley Clo., Ruis. 57 BQ59
Ardlui Rd. SE27 106 DQ89
Ardmay Gdns., Surb. 116 CL99
Ardmere Rd. SE13 107 ED86
Ardmore La., Buck.H. 52 EH45
Ardmore Pl., Buck.H. 52 EH45
Ardoch Rd. SE6 107 ED89
Ardra Rd. N9 51 DX48
Ardross Ave., Nthwd. 43 BS50
Ardrossan Gdns., Wor.Pk. 117 CU104
Ardshiel Clo. SW15 89 CX83
Bemish Rd.
Ardwell Ave., Ilf. 67 EQ57
Ardwell Rd. SW2 105 DL89
Ardwick Rd. NW2 62 DA63
Arena Ind. Est., Enf. 37 DZ38
Argall Ave. E10 65 DX59
Argent St. SE1 10 G4
Argenta Way NW10 74 CP66
Argon Ms. SW6 90 DA80
Argon Rd. N18 51 DX50
Harbet Rd.
Argosy La., Stai. 98 BK87
Argus Clo., Rom. 55 FB53
Argus Way W3 88 CP76
Argus Way, Nthlt. 72 BY69
Argyle Ave., Houns. 100 CA86
Argyle Clo. W13 73 CG70
Argyle Pas. N17 50 DT53
Argyle Rd.
Argyle Pl. W6 89 CV77
Argyle Rd. E1 79 DX70
Argyle Rd. E15 66 EE64
Argyle Rd. E16 80 EH72
Argyle Rd. N12 48 DA50
Argyle Rd. N17 50 DU53
Argyle Rd. N18 50 DU49
Argyle Rd. W13 73 CG71
Argyle Rd., Barn. 33 CW42
Argyle Rd., Grnf. 73 CF69
Argyle Rd., Har. 58 CB58
Argyle Rd., Houns. 100 CB85
Argyle Rd., Ilf. 67 EN61
Argyle Rd., Sev. 155 FH125
Argyle Rd., Tedd. 101 CE92
Argyle Sq. WC1 6 A2
Argyle Sq. WC1 77 DL69
Argyle St. WC1 5 P2
Argyle St. WC1 77 DL69
Argyle Wk. WC1 5 P3
Argyle Way SE16 92 DU78
Argyll Ave., Sthl. 72 CB74
Argyll Clo. SW9 91 DM83
Dalyell Rd.
Argyll Gdns., Edg. 46 CP54
Argyll Rd. W8 90 DA75
Argyll St. W1 5 K9
Argyll St. W1 77 DJ72
Arica Rd. SE4 93 DY84
Ariel Rd. NW6 76 DA65
Ariel Way W12 75 CW74
Ariel Way, Houns. 85 BV83
Aristotle Rd. SW4 91 DK83
Arkell Gro. SE19 105 DP94
Arkindale Rd. SE6 107 EC90
Arkley Cres. E17 65 DZ57
Arkley Dr., Barn. 33 CU42
Arkley La., Barn. 33 CU41
Arkley Rd. E17 65 DZ57
Arkley Vw., Barn. 33 CV42
Arklow Ms., Surb. 116 CL103
Vale Rd. S.
Arklow Rd. SE14 93 DZ79
Arkwright Rd. NW3 62 DC64
Arkwright Rd., S.Croy. 134 DT110
Arlesey Clo. SW15 103 CY86
Lytton Gro.
Arlesford Rd. SW9 91 DL83
Arlingford Rd. SW2 105 DN85
Arlington N12 48 DA48

Arlington Ave. N1 78 DQ67
Arlington Clo., Sid. 109 ES87
Arlington Clo., Sutt. 118 DA103
Arlington Clo., Twick. 101 CJ86
Arlington Ct., Hayes 85 BR78
Shepiston La.
Arlington Cres., Wal.Cr. 23 DY34
Arlington Dr., Cars. 118 DF103
Arlington Dr., Ruis. 57 BR58
Arlington Gdns. W4 88 CQ78
Arlington Gdns., Ilf. 67 EN60
Arlington Lo. SW2 91 DM84
Arlington Lo., Wey. 127 BP105
Arlington Ms., Twick. 101 CH86
Arlington Rd.
Arlington Pl. SE10 93 EC80
Greenwich S. St.
Arlington Rd. N14 49 DH47
Arlington Rd. NW1 77 DH67
Arlington Rd. W13 73 CH72
Arlington Rd., Ashf. 98 BM92
Arlington Rd., Rich. 101 CK89
Arlington Rd., Surb. 115 CK100
Arlington Rd., Tedd. 101 CF91
Arlington Rd., Twick. 101 CJ86
Arlington Rd., Wdf.Grn. 52 EG52
Arlington Sq. N1 78 DQ67
Arlington St. SW1 9 K2
Arlington St. SW1 77 DJ74
Arlington Way EC1 6 E2
Arlington Way EC1 77 DN69
Arliss Way, Nthlt. 72 BW67
Arlow Rd. N21 49 DN46
Armada Ct. SE8 93 EA79
Watergate St.
Armada St. SE8 93 EA79
Armada Way E6 81 EQ73
Armadale Clo. N17 64 DV56
Armadale Rd. SW6 90 DA80
Armadale Rd., Felt. 99 BU85
Armagh Rd. E3 79 DZ67
Armand Clo., Wat. 29 BT38
Armfield Clo., W.Mol. 114 BZ99
Armfield Cres., Mitch. 118 DF96
Armfield Rd., Enf. 36 DR39
Arminger Rd. W12 75 CV74
Armitage Clo., Rick. 28 BK42
Armitage Rd. NW11 61 CY60
Armitage Rd. SE10 94 EF78
Armour Clo. N7 77 DM65
Roman Way
Armoury Rd. SE8 93 EB82
Armoury Way SW18 104 DA85
Armstead Wk., Dag. 82 FA66
Armstrong Ave., Wdf.Grn. 52 EE51
Armstrong Clo. E6 81 EM72
Porter Rd.
Armstrong Clo., Dag. 68 EX60
Palmer Rd.
Armstrong Clo., Pnr. 57 BU58
Armstrong Clo., Sev. 153 FB115
Armstrong Clo., Walt. 113 BU100
Sunbury La.
Armstrong Cres., Barn. 34 DD41
Armstrong Gdns., Rad. 18 CL32
Armstrong Rd. SW7 90 DD76
Armstrong Rd. W3 75 CT74
Armstrong Rd., Felt. 100 BY92
Armstrong Way, Sthl. 86 CB75
Armytage Rd., Houns. 86 BX80
Arnal Cres. SW18 103 CY87
Arncroft Ct., Bark. 82 EV69
Renwick Rd.
Arndale Cen., The SW18 104 DB86
Arndale Wk. SW18 104 DB85
Garratt La.
Arne Gro., Orp. 123 ET104
Arne St. WC2 6 A9
Arne St. WC2 77 DL72
Arne Wk. SE3 94 EF84
Arnett Clo., Rick. 28 BG44
Arnett Sq. E4 51 DZ51
Silver Birch Ave.
Arnett Way, Rick. 28 BG44
Arneway St. SW1 9 N7
Arneways Ave., Rom. 68 EX56
Arnewood Clo. SW15 103 CU88
Arnewood Clo., Lthd. 128 CB113
Arney's La., Mitch. 118 DG100
Arngask Rd. SE6 107 ED87
Arnhem Dr., Croy. 135 ED111
Arnhem Pl. E14 93 EA76
Arnhem Way SE22 106 DS85
East Dulwich Gro.
Arnison Rd., E.Mol. 115 CD98
Arnold Ave. E., Enf. 37 EA38
Arnold Ave. W., Enf. 37 DZ38
Arnold Circ. E2 7 P3
Arnold Circ. E2 78 DT69
Arnold Clo., Har. 60 CM59
Arnold Cres., Islw. 101 CD85
Arnold Dr., Chess. 129 CK107
Arnold Est. SE1 92 DT75
Arnold Gdns. N13 49 DP50
Arnold Rd. E3 79 EA69
Arnold Rd. N15 64 DT55
Arnold Rd. SW17 104 DF94
Arnold Rd., Dag. 82 EZ66
Arnold Rd., Nthlt. 72 BX65
Arnold Rd., Stai. 98 BJ94
Arnos Gro. N14 49 DK49
Arnos Rd. N11 49 DJ50
Arnott Clo. SE28 82 EW73
Applegarth Rd.
Arnott Clo. W4 88 CR77
Fishers La.
Arnould Ave. SE5 92 DR84
Arnsberg Way, Bexh. 96 FA84
Arnside Gdns., Wem. 59 CK60
Arnside Rd., Bexh. 96 FA81
Arnside St. SE17 92 DQ79
Arnulf St. SE6 107 EB91
Arnulls Rd. SW16 105 DN93
Arodene Rd. SW2 105 DM86
Arosa Rd., Twick. 101 CK86
Arragon Gdns. SW16 105 DL94
Arragon Gdns., W.Wick. 121 EB104
Arragon Rd. E6 80 EK67
Arragon Rd. SW18 104 DA88
Bodmin St.
Arragon Rd., Twick. 101 CG87
Arran Clo., Erith 97 FD79
Arran Clo., Wall. 133 DJ105
Arran Dr. E12 66 EK60
Arran Ms. W5 74 CM74
Arran Rd. SE6 107 EB89
Arran Wk. N1 78 DQ66
Arran Way, Esher 114 CB103
Arranmore Ct. (Bushey), Wat. 30 BY42
Bushey Hall Rd.
Arras Ave., Mord. 118 DC99
Arrol Rd., Beck. 120 DW97
Arrow Rd. E3 79 EB69
Arrowscout Wk., Nthlt. 72 BY69
Argus Way
Arrowsmith Clo., Chig. 53 ET50
Arrowsmith Path, Chig. 53 ES50
Arrowsmith Rd., Chig. 53 ES50
Arrowsmith Rd., Loug. 38 EL41
Arsenal Rd. SE9 95 EM82
Arterberry Rd. SW20 103 CW94
Arterial Ave., Rain. 83 FH70
Artesian Clo. NW10 74 CR66
Artesian Clo., Horn. 69 FF58
Artesian Gro., Barn. 34 DC42
Artesian Rd. W2 76 DA72
Artesian Wk. E11 66 EE62
Arthingworth St. E15 80 EE67
Arthur Ct. W2 76 DB72
Queensway
Arthur Gro. SE18 95 EQ77
Arthur Henderson Ho. SW6 89 CZ82
Arthur Rd. E6 81 EM68
Arthur Rd. N7 63 DM63
Arthur Rd. N9 50 DT47
Arthur Rd. SW19 103 CY92
Arthur Rd., Kings.T. 102 CN94
Arthur Rd., N.Mal. 117 CV99
Arthur Rd., Rom. 68 EX58
Arthur Rd., West. 150 EJ115
Arthur St. EC4 7 L10
Arthur St., Erith 97 FF80
Arthur St. (Bushey), Wat. 30 BX42
Arthurdon Rd. SE4 107 EA85
Artichoke Hill E1 78 DV73
Pennington St.
Artichoke Pl. SE5 92 DR81
Camberwell Ch. St.
Artillery Clo., Ilf. 67 EQ58
Horns Rd.
Artillery La. E1 7 N7
Artillery La. E1 78 DS71
Artillery La. W12 75 CU72
Artillery Pas. E1 7 N7
Artillery Pl. SE18 95 EM77
Artillery Pl. SW1 9 M7
Artillery Row SW1 9 M7
Artillery Row SW1 91 DK76
Artington Clo., Orp. 137 EQ105
Artisan Clo. E6 81 EP72
Ferndale St.
Artizan St. E1 7 N8
Arundel Ave., Epsom 131 CV110
Arundel Ave., Mord. 117 CZ98
Arundel Ave., S.Croy. 134 DU110
Arundel Clo. E15 66 EE63
Arundel Clo. SW11 104 DE85
Chivalry Rd.
Arundel Clo., Bex. 110 EZ86
Arundel Clo., Croy. 119 DP104
Arundel Clo., Hmptn. 100 CB92
Arundel Clo. (Cheshunt), Wal.Cr. 22 DV28
Arundel Ct. N12 48 DE51
Arundel Ct., Har. 58 CA63
Arundel Dr., Borwd. 32 CP43
Arundel Dr., Har. 58 BZ63
Arundel Dr., Orp. 138 EV106
Arundel Dr., Wdf.Grn. 52 EG52
Arundel Gdns. N21 49 DN46
Arundel Gdns. W11 75 CZ73
Arundel Gdns., Edg. 46 CR52
Arundel Gdns., Ilf. 68 EU61
Arundel Great Ct. WC2 6 C10
Arundel Gro. N16 64 DS64
Arundel Pl. N1 77 DN65
Arundel Rd., Barn. 34 DE41
Arundel Rd., Croy. 120 DR100
Arundel Rd., Houns. 86 BW83
Arundel Rd., Kings.T. 116 CP96
Arundel Rd., Sutt. 131 CY108
Arundel Rd., Uxb. 70 BH68
Arundel Sq. N7 77 DN65
Arundel St. WC2 6 C10
Arundel St. WC2 77 DM73
Arundel Ter. SW13 89 CV79
Arundell Rd., Abb.L. 15 BU32
Arvon Rd. N5 63 DN64
Asbaston Ter., Ilf. 67 EQ64
Loxford La.
Ascalon St. SW8 91 DJ80
Ascension Rd., Rom. 55 FC51
Ascham Dr. E4 51 EB52
Rushcroft Rd.
Ascham End E17 51 DY53
Ascham St. NW5 63 DJ64
Aschurch Rd., Croy. 120 DT101
Ascot Clo., Borwd. 32 CN43
Ascot Clo., Ilf. 53 ES51
Ascot Clo., Nthlt. 72 CA65
Ascot Gdns., Enf. 36 DW37
Ascot Gdns., Sthl. 72 BZ70
Ascot Ms., Wall. 133 DJ109
Ascot Rd. E6 81 EM69
Ascot Rd. N15 64 DR57
Ascot Rd. N18 50 DU49
Ascot Rd. SW17 104 DG93
Ascot Rd., Felt. 98 BN89
Ascot Rd., Orp. 123 ET98
Ascot Rd., Wat. 29 BS43
Ascott Ave. W5 88 CL75
Ash Clo. SE20 120 DW96
Ash Clo., Abb.L. 15 BR32
Ash Clo., Cars. 118 DF103
Ash Clo., Edg. 46 CQ49
Ash Clo., Hat. 20 DA25
Ash Clo., N.Mal. 116 CR96
Ash Clo., Orp. 123 ER99
Ash Clo., Rom. 55 FB52
Ash Clo., Sid. 110 EV90
Ash Clo., Stan. 45 CG51
Ash Clo., Swan. 125 FC96
Ash Clo., Uxb. 42 BK53
Ash Clo., Wat. 29 BV35
Cedar Wd. Dr.
Ash Clo. (Pyrford), Wok. 140 BG115
Ash Copse, St.Alb. 16 BZ31
Ash Ct., Epsom 130 CQ105
Ash Grn., Uxb. 70 BH65
Ash Gro. E8 78 DV67
Ash Gro. N13 50 DQ48
Ash Gro. NW2 61 CX63
Ash Gro. SE20 120 DW96
Ash Gro. W5 88 CL75
Ash Gro., Enf. 50 DS45
Ash Gro., Felt. 99 BS88
Ash Gro., Hayes 71 BR73
Ash Gro., Houns. 86 BX81
Ash Gro., Sthl. 72 CA71
Ash Gro., Stai. 98 BJ93
Ash Gro., Uxb. 42 BK53
Ash Gro., Wem. 59 CG63
Ash Gro., West Dr. 70 BM73
Ash Gro., W.Wick. 121 EC103
Ash Hill Clo. (Bushey), Wat. 44 CB46
Ash Hill Dr., Pnr. 58 BW55
Ash Island, E.Mol. 115 CD97
Ash La., Croy. 133 DP105
Ash La., Rom. 55 FG51
Ash Ms., Epsom 130 CS113
Ash Platt, The, Sev. 155 FL121
Ash Platt Rd., Sev. 155 FL121
Ash Ride, Enf. 35 DN35
Ash Rd. E15 66 EE64
Ash Rd., Croy. 121 EA103
Ash Rd., Orp. 137 ET108
Ash Rd., Shep. 112 BN98
Ash Rd., Sutt. 117 CY101
Ash Row, Brom. 123 EN101
Ash Tree Clo., Croy. 121 DY100
Ash Tree Clo., Surb. 116 CL102
Ash Tree Dell NW9 60 CR57
Ash Tree Rd., Wat. 29 BV36
Ash Tree Way, Croy. 121 DY99
Ash Vw. Clo., Ashf. 98 BL93
Ash Vw. Gdns., Ashf. 98 BL92
Ash Vw. Mobile Home Pk., Kings L. 15 BQ28
Ash Wk. SW2 105 DM88
Ash Wk., Wem. 59 CJ62
Ashan Ct., Ashf. 99 BS94
Ashbourne Ave. E18 66 EH56
Ashbourne Ave. N20 48 DF47
Ashbourne Ave. NW11 61 CZ57
Ashbourne Ave., Bexh. 96 EY80
Ashbourne Ave., Har. 59 CD61
Ashbourne Clo. N12 48 DB49
Ashbourne Clo. W5 74 CN71
Ashbourne Clo., Couls. 147 DJ118
Ashbourne Ct. E5 65 DY63
Daubeney Rd.
Ashbourne Gro. NW7 46 CR50
Ashbourne Gro. SE22 106 DT85
Ashbourne Gro. W4 88 CS78
Ashbourne Ri., Orp. 137 ER105
Ashbourne Rd. W5 74 CM70
Ashbourne Rd., Mitch. 104 DG93
Ashbourne Sq., Nthwd. 43 BS51
Ashbourne Ter. SW19 104 DA94
Ashbourne Way NW11 61 CZ57
Ashbourne Ave.
Ashbridge Rd. E11 66 EE59
Ashbridge St. NW8 4 B5
Ashbridge St. NW8 76 DE70
Ashbrook Rd. N19 63 DK60
Ashbrook Rd., Dag. 69 FB62
Ashburn Gdns. SW7 90 DC77
Ashburn Pl. SW7 90 DC77
Ashburnham Ave., Har. 59 CF58
Ashburnham Clo. N2 62 DD55
Ashburnham Clo., Sev. 155 FJ127
Fiennes Way
Ashburnham Clo., Wat. 43 BU48
Ashburnham Dr.
Ashburnham Dr., Wat. 43 BU48
Ashburnham Gdns., Har. 59 CF59
Ashburnham Gro. SE10 93 EB80
Ashburnham Pk., Esher 128 CC105
Ashburnham Pl. SE10 93 EB80
Ashburnham Retreat SE10 93 EB80
Ashburnham Rd. NW10 75 CW69
Ashburnham Rd. SW10 90 DC80
Ashburnham Rd., Belv. 97 FC77
Ashburnham Rd., Rich. 101 CH89
Ashburton Ave., Croy. 120 DV102
Ashburton Ave., Ilf. 67 ES63
Ashburton Clo., Croy. 120 DU102
Ashburton Ct., Pnr. 58 BX55
Ashburton Gdns., Croy. 120 DU103
Ashburton Gro. N7 63 DN63
Ashburton Rd. E16 80 EG72
Ashburton Rd., Croy. 120 DU103
Ashburton Rd., Ruis. 57 BU61
Ashburton Ter. E13 80 EG68
Grasmere Rd.
Ashbury Dr., Uxb. 57 BP61
Ashbury Gdns., Rom. 68 EX57
Ashbury Rd. SW11 90 DF83
Ashby Ave., Chess. 130 CN107
Ashby Gro. N1 78 DQ66
Ashby Ms. SE4 93 DZ82
Ashby Rd. N15 64 DU57
Ashby Rd. SE4 93 DZ82
Ashby Rd., Wat. 29 BU38
Ashby St. EC1 6 G3
Ashby Wk., Croy. 120 DQ100
Ashby Way, West Dr. 84 BN80
Ashchurch Gro. W12 89 CU76
Ashchurch Pk. Vill. W12 89 CU76
Ashchurch Ter. W12 89 CU76
Ashcombe Ave., Surb. 115 CK101
Ashcombe Gdns., Edg. 46 CN49
Ashcombe Pk. NW2 60 CS62
Ashcombe Rd. SW19 104 DA92
Ashcombe Rd., Cars. 132 DG107
Ashcombe Sq., N.Mal. 116 CQ97
Ashcombe St. SW6 90 DB82
Ashcombe Ter., Tad. 145 CV120
Ashcroft, Pnr. 44 CA51
Ashcroft Ave., Sid. 110 EU86
Ashcroft Cres., Sid. 110 EU86
Ashcroft Pk., Cob. 128 BY112
Ashcroft Ri., Couls. 147 DL116
Ashcroft Rd. E3 79 DY69
Ashcroft Rd., Chess. 116 CM104
Ashcroft Sq. W6 89 CW77
King St.
Ashdale Clo., Stai. 98 BL89
Ashdale Clo., Twick. 100 CC87
Ashdale Gro., Stan. 45 CF51
Ashdale Rd. SE12 108 EH88
Ashdale Way, Twick. 100 CC87
Ashdale Clo.
Ashdene SE15 92 DV81
Carlton Gro.
Ashdene, Pnr. 58 BW55
Ashdene Clo., Ashf. 99 BQ94
Ashdon Clo., Wdf.Grn. 52 EH51
Ashdon Rd. NW10 75 CT67
Ashdon Rd. (Bushey), Wat. 30 BX41
Ashdown Clo., Beck. 121 EB96
Ashdown Clo., Bex. 111 FC87
Ashdown Cres. NW5 62 DG64
Queens Cres.
Ashdown Cres. (Cheshunt), Wal.Cr. 23 DY28
Ashdown Dr., Borwd. 32 CM40
Ashdown Est. E11 66 EE63
High Rd. Leytonstone
Ashdown Gdns., S.Croy. 148 DV115
Ashdown Rd., Enf. 36 DW41
Ashdown Rd., Epsom 131 CT113
Ashdown Rd., Kings.T. 116 CL96
Ashdown Rd., Uxb. 70 BN68
Ashdown Wk. E14 93 EA77
Charnwood Gdns.
Ashdown Wk., Rom. 55 FB54
Ashdown Way SW17 104 DG89
Ashen E6 81 EN72
Downings
Ashen Dr., Dart. 111 FG86
Ashen Gro. SW19 104 DA90
Ashen Vale, S.Croy. 135 DX109
Ashenden Rd. E5 65 DY64
Asher Way E1 78 DU74
Ashfield Ave., Felt. 99 BV88
Ashfield Ave. (Bushey), Wat. 30 CB44
Ashfield Clo., Beck. 107 EA94
Brackley Rd.
Ashfield Clo., Rich. 102 CL88
Ashfield La., Chis. 109 EQ93
Ashfield Par. N14 49 DK46
Ashfield Rd. N4 64 DQ58
Ashfield Rd. N14 49 DJ48
Ashfield Rd. W3 75 CT74
Ashfield St. E1 78 DV71
Ashfields, Loug. 39 EM40
Ashfields, Wat. 29 BT35
Ashford Ave. N8 63 DL56
Ashford Ave., Ashf. 99 BP93
Ashford Ave., Hayes 72 BX72
Ashford Clo. E17 65 DZ58
Ashford Clo., Ashf. 98 BL91
Ashford Cres., Ashf. 98 BL90
Ashford Cres., Enf. 36 DW40
Ashford Gdns., Cob. 142 BX116
Ashford Grn., Wat. 44 BX50
Ashford Ind. Est., Ashf. 99 BQ91
Ashford Rd. E6 81 EN65
Ashford Rd. E18 52 EH54
Ashford Rd. NW2 61 CX63
Ashford Rd., Ashf. 99 BP94
Ashford Rd., Felt. 99 BR91
Ashford Rd., Stai. 112 BK95
Ashford St. N1 7 M2
Ashgrove Rd., Ashf. 99 BQ92
Ashgrove Rd., Brom. 107 ED93
Ashgrove Rd., Ilf. 67 ET60
Ashgrove Rd., Sev. 154 FG127
Ashingdon Clo. E4 51 EC48
Ashington Rd. SW6 89 CZ82
Ashlake Rd. SW16 105 DL91
Ashland Pl. W1 4 F6
Ashland Pl. W1 76 DG71
Ashlar Pl. SE18 95 EP77
Masons Hill
Ashleigh Gdns., Sutt. 118 DB103
Ashleigh Rd. SE20 120 DV97
Ashleigh Rd. SW14 88 CS83
Ashley Ave., Epsom 130 CR113
Ashley Ave., Ilf. 53 EP54
Ashley Ave., Mord. 118 DA99
Chalgrove Ave.
Ashley Cen., Epsom 130 CR113
Ashley Clo. NW4 47 CW54
Ashley Clo., Pnr. 43 BV54
Ashley Clo., Sev. 155 FH124
Ashley Clo., Walt. 113 BS102
Ashley Ct., Epsom 130 CR113
Ashley Cres. N22 49 DN54
Ashley Cres. SW11 90 DG83
Ashley Dr., Bans. 132 DA114
Ashley Dr., Borwd. 32 CQ43
Ashley Dr., Islw. 87 CE79
Ashley Dr., Twick. 100 CB88
Ashley Dr., Walt. 113 BU104
Ashley Gdns. N13 50 DQ49
Ashley Gdns. SW1 9 L7
Ashley Gdns., Orp. 137 ES106
Ashley Gdns., Rich. 101 CK89
Ashley Gdns., Wem. 60 CL61
Ashley Gro., Loug. 38 EL41
Staples Rd.
Ashley La. NW4 47 CW54
Ashley La., Croy. 133 DP105
Ashley Pk. Ave., Walt. 113 BT103
Ashley Pk. Cres., Walt. 113 BT102
Ashley Pk. Rd., Walt. 113 BU103
Ashley Pl. SW1 9 K7
Ashley Pl. SW1 91 DJ76
Ashley Ri., Walt. 127 BT105
Ashley Rd. E4 51 EA50
Ashley Rd. E7 80 EJ66
Ashley Rd. N17 64 DU55
Ashley Rd. N19 63 DL60
Ashley Rd. SW19 104 DB93
Ashley Rd., Enf. 36 DW40
Ashley Rd., Epsom 130 CR113
Ashley Rd., Hmptn. 114 CA95
Ashley Rd., Rich. 88 CL83
Jocelyn Rd.
Ashley Rd., Sev. 155 FH124
Ashley Rd., T.Ditt. 115 CF100
Ashley Rd., Th.Hth. 119 DM98
Ashley Rd., Uxb. 70 BH68
Ashley Rd., Walt. 113 BU102
Ashley Wk. NW7 47 CW52
Ashlin Rd. E15 65 ED63
Ashling Rd., Croy. 120 DU102
Ashlone Rd. SW15 89 CW83
Ashlyn Clo. (Bushey), Wat. 30 BY41
Ashlyns Pk., Cob. 128 BY113
Ashlyns Rd., Epp. 25 ET30
Ashlyns Way, Chess. 129 CK107
Ashmead N14 35 DJ43
Ashmead Dr., Uxb. 56 BG61
Ashmead Gate, Brom. 122 EJ95
Ashmead La., Uxb. 56 BG61
Ashmead Rd. SE8 93 EA82
Ashmead Rd., Felt. 99 BU88
Ashmeads Ct., Rad. 17 CK33
Ashmere Ave., Beck. 121 ED96
Ashmere Clo., Sutt. 131 CW106
Ashmere Gro. SW2 91 DL84
Ashmill St. NW1 4 B6
Ashmill St. NW1 76 DE71
Ashmole Pl. SW8 91 DM79
Ashmole St. SW8 91 DM79
Ashmore Ct., Houns. 86 CA79
Wheatlands
Ashmore Gro., Well. 95 ER83
Ashmore La., Kes. 136 EJ111
Ashmore Rd. W9 75 CZ68
Ashmount Rd. N15 64 DT57
Ashmount Rd. N19 63 DJ59
Ashmount Ter. W5 87 CK77
Murray Rd.
Ashmour Gdns., Rom. 55 FD54
Ashneal Gdns., Har. 59 CD62
Ashness Gdns., Grnf. 73 CH65
Ashness Rd. SW11 104 DF85
Ashridge Clo., Har. 59 CJ58
Ashridge Cres. SE18 95 EQ80
Ashridge Dr., St.Alb. 16 BY30
Ashridge Dr., Wat. 43 BV50
Ashridge Gdns. N13 49 DK50
Ashridge Gdns., Pnr. 58 BY56
Ashridge Way, Mord. 117 CZ97
Ashridge Way, Sun. 99 BU93
Ashtead Gap, Lthd. 143 CG116
Kingston Rd.
Ashtead Rd. E5 64 DU59
Ashtead Wds. Rd., Ash. 143 CJ116
Ashton Clo., Sutt. 132 DA105
Ashton Clo., Walt. 127 BV107
Ashton Gdns., Houns. 86 BZ84
Ashton Gdns., Rom. 68 EY58
Ashton Rd. E15 65 ED64

Ashton Rd., Enf. 37 DY36
Ashton St. E14 79 EC73
Ashtree Ave., Mitch. 118 DD96
Ashtree Clo., Orp. 137 EP105
Broadwater Gdns.
Ashurst Clo. SE20 120 DV95
Ashurst Clo., Dart. 97 FF83
Ashurst Clo., Ken. 148 DR115
Ashurst Clo., Nthwd. 43 BS52
Ashurst Dr., Ilf. 67 EP58
Ashurst Dr., Shep. 112 BL99
Ashurst Rd. N12 48 DE50
Ashurst Rd., Barn. 34 DF43
Ashurst Rd., Tad. 145 CV121
Ashurst Wk., Croy. 120 DV103
Ashvale Gdns., Rom. 55 FD50
Ashvale Rd. SW17 104 DF92
Ashville Rd. E11 65 ED61
Ashwater Rd. SE12 108 EG88
Ashwell Clo. E6 80 EL72
Northumberland Rd.
Ashwin St. E8 78 DT65
Ashwood, Warl. 148 DW120
Ashwood Ave., Rain. 83 FH69
Ashwood Ave., Uxb. 70 BN72
Ashwood Gdns., Croy. 135 EB107
Ashwood Gdns., Hayes 85 BT77
Cranford Dr.
Ashwood Pk., Lthd. 142 CC123
Ashwood Rd. E4 51 ED48
Ashwood Rd., Pot.B. 20 DB33
Ashworth Clo. SE5 92 DR82
Denmark Hill
Ashworth Rd. W9 76 DB69
Aske St. N1 7 M2
Askern Clo., Bexh. 96 EX84
Askew Cres. W12 89 CT75
Askew Rd. W12 75 CT74
Askew Rd., Nthwd. 43 BR47
Askham Ct. W12 75 CU74
Askham Rd. W12 75 CU74
Askill Dr. SW15 103 CY85
Keswick Rd.
Askwith Rd., Rain. 83 FD69
Asland Rd. E15 79 ED67
Aslett St. SW18 104 DB87
Asmar Clo., Couls. 147 DL115
Asmara Rd. NW2 61 CY64
Asmuns Hill NW11 62 DA57
Asmuns Pl. NW11 61 CZ57
Aspen Clo. N19 63 DJ61
Hargrave Pk.
Aspen Clo. W5 88 CM75
Aspen Clo., Cob. 142 BY116
Aspen Clo., Orp. 138 EU106
Aspen Clo., St.Alb. 16 BY30
Aspen Clo., Swan. 125 FD95
Aspen Clo., West Dr. 70 BM74
Aspen Copse, Brom. 123 EM96
Aspen Ct., Hayes 85 BS77
Clement Gdns.
Aspen Dr., Wem. 59 CG63
Aspen Gdns. W6 89 CV78
Aspen Gdns., Mitch. 118 DG99
Aspen Grn., Erith 96 EZ76
Aspen La., Nthlt. 72 BY69
Aspen Pk. Dr., Wat. 29 BV35
Aspen Sq., Wey. 113 BR104
Oatlands Dr.
Aspen Way E14 79 ED73
Aspen Way, Bans. 131 CX114
Aspen Way, Enf. 37 DX35
Aspen Way, Felt. 99 BV90
Aspenlea Rd. W6 89 CX79
Aspern Gro. NW3 62 DE64
Aspinall Rd. SE4 93 DX83
Aspinden Rd. SE16 92 DV77
Aspley Rd. SW18 104 DB85
Aspley Way NW2 61 CU61
Asplins Rd. N17 50 DU53
Asquith Clo., Dag. 68 EW60
Crystal Way
Ass Ho. La., Har. 44 CB49
Assam St. E1 78 DU72
White Ch. La.
Assata Ms. N1 77 DP65
St. Paul's Rd.
Assembly Pas. E1 78 DW71
Assembly Wk., Cars. 118 DE101
Assher Rd., Walt. 114 BY104
Assurance Cotts., Belv. 96 EZ78
Heron Hill
Astall Clo., Har. 45 CE53
Sefton Ave.
Astbury Rd. SE15 92 DW81
Aste St. E14 93 EC75
Astell St. SW3 8 C10
Astell St. SW3 90 DE78
Asteys Row N1 77 DP66
River Pl.
Asthall Gdns., Ilf. 67 EQ56
Astle St. SW11 90 DG82
Astleham Rd., Shep. 112 BL97
Astley Ave. NW2 61 CW64
Aston Ave., Har. 59 CJ59
Aston Clo., Ash. 143 CJ118
Aston Clo., Sid. 110 EU90
Aston Clo., Wat. 30 BW40
Aston Clo. (Bushey), Wat. 30 CC44
Aston Grn., Houns. 86 BW82
Aston Ms., Rom. 68 EW59
Reynolds Ave.
Aston Rd. SW20 117 CW96
Aston Rd. W5 73 CK72
Aston Rd., Esher 129 CE106
Aston St. E14 79 DY72
Aston Way, Epsom 145 CT116
Aston Way, Pot.B. 20 DD32
Astons Rd., Nthwd. 43 BQ48
Astonville St. SW18 104 DA88
Astor Ave., Rom. 69 FC58
Astor Clo., Add. 126 BK105
Astor Clo., Kings.T. 102 CP93
Astoria Wk. SW9 91 DN83
Astra Clo., Horn. 83 FH65
Astrop Ms. W6 89 CW76
Astrop Ter. W6 89 CW75
Astwood Ms. SW7 90 DB77
Asylum Rd. SE15 92 DV80
Atalanta Clo., Pur. 133 DN110
Atalanta St. SW6 89 CX81
Atbara Ct., Tedd. 101 CH93
Atbara Rd., Tedd. 101 CH93
Atcham Rd., Houns. 86 CC84
Atcost Rd., Bark. 82 EU71
Atheldene Rd. SW18 104 DC87
Athelney St. SE6 107 EA90
Athelstan Rd., Kings.T. 116 CM98
Athelstan Way, Orp. 124 EU95
Athelstane Gro. E3 79 DZ68
Athelstane Ms. N4 63 DN60
Stroud Grn. Rd.
Athelstone Rd., Har. 45 CD54
Athena Clo., Har. 59 CE61
Byron Hill Rd.
Athena Clo., Kings.T. 116 CM97
Athena Pl., Nthwd. 43 BT53
The Dr.
Athenaeum Pl. N10 63 DH55
Fortis Grn. Rd.
Athenaeum Rd. N20 48 DC46
Athenlay Rd. SE15 107 DX85
Athens Gdns. W9 76 DA70
Elgin Ave.
Atherden Rd. E5 64 DW63
Atherfold Rd. SW9 91 DL83
Atherley Way, Houns. 100 BZ87
Atherstone Ms. SW7 90 DC77
Atherton Clo., Stai. 98 BK86
Atherton Dr. SW19 103 CX91
Atherton Heights, Wem. 73 CJ65
Atherton Ms. E7 80 EF65
Atherton Pl., Har. 59 CD55
Atherton Pl., Sthl. 72 CB73
Longford Ave.
Atherton Rd. E7 80 EF65
Atherton Rd. SW13 89 CU80
Atherton Rd., Ilf. 52 EL54
Atherton St. SW11 90 DE82
Athlon Rd., Wem. 73 CK68
Athlone, Esher 129 CE107
Athlone Clo. E5 64 DV63
Goulton Rd.
Athlone Clo., Rad. 31 CG36
Athlone Rd. SW2 105 DM87
Athlone St. NW5 76 DG65
Athol Clo., Pnr. 43 BV53
Athol Gdns., Pnr. 43 BV53
Athol Rd., Erith 97 FC78
Athol Sq. E14 79 EC72
Athol Way, Uxb. 70 BN69
Athole Gdns., Enf. 36 DS43
Atholl Rd., Ilf. 68 EU59
Atkins Dr., W.Wick. 121 ED103
Atkins Rd. E10 65 EB58
Atkins Rd. SW12 105 DK87
Atkinson Clo., Orp. 138 EU106
Martindale Ave.
Atkinson Rd. E16 80 EJ71
Atlanta Boul., Rom. 69 FE58
Atlantic Rd. SW9 91 DN84
Atlas Gdns. SE7 94 EJ77
Atlas Ms. E8 78 DT65
Tyssen St.
Atlas Ms. N7 77 DM65
Atlas Rd. E13 80 EG68
Atlas Rd. NW10 74 CS69
Atlas Rd., Wem. 60 CQ63
Atley Rd. E3 79 EA67
Atlip Rd., Wem. 74 CL67
Atney Rd. SW15 89 CY84
Atria Rd., Nthwd. 43 BU50
Attenborough Clo., Wat. 44 BY48
Harrow Way
Atterbury Rd. N4 63 DN58
Atterbury St. SW1 9 P9
Atterbury St. SW1 91 DL77
Attewood Ave. NW10 60 CS62
Attewood Rd., Nthlt. 72 BY65
Attfield Clo. N20 48 DD47
Attle Clo., Uxb. 70 BN68
Attlee Clo., Hayes 71 BV69
Attlee Clo., Th.Hth. 120 DQ100
Attlee Rd. SE28 82 EV73
Attlee Rd., Hayes 71 BU69
Attlee Ter. E17 65 EB56
Attneave St. WC1 6 D3
Attwood Clo., S.Croy. 134 DV114
Atwater Clo. SW2 105 DN88
Atwell Clo. E10 65 EB58
Belmont Pk. Rd.
Atwell Rd. SE15 92 DU82
Rye La.
Atwood, Lthd. 142 BY124
Atwood Ave., Rich. 88 CN82
Atwood Rd. W6 89 CV77
Aubert Pk. N5 63 DN63
Aubert Rd. N5 63 DP63
Aubrey Ave., St.Alb. 17 CJ26
Aubrey Pl. NW8 76 DC68
Violet Hill
Aubrey Rd. E17 65 EA55
Aubrey Rd. N8 63 DL57
Aubrey Rd. W8 75 CZ74
Aubrey Wk. W8 75 CZ74
Aubyn Hill SE27 106 DQ91
Aubyn Sq. SW15 89 CU84
Auckland Ave., Rain. 83 FF69
Auckland Clo. SE19 120 DT95
Auckland Clo., Enf. 36 DV37
Auckland Gdns. SE19 120 DS95
Auckland Hill SE27 106 DQ91
Auckland Ri. SE19 120 DS95
Auckland Rd. E10 65 EB62
Auckland Rd. SE19 120 DT95
Auckland Rd. SW11 90 DE84
Auckland Rd., Cat. 148 DS122
Auckland Rd., Ilf. 67 EP60
Auckland Rd., Kings.T. 116 CM98
Auckland Rd., Pot.B. 19 CX32
Auckland St. SE11 91 DM78
Kennington La.
Auden Pl. NW1 76 DG67
Manley St.
Audleigh Pl., Chig. 53 EN51
Audley Clo. N10 49 DH52
Audley Clo. SW11 90 DG83
Audley Clo., Add. 126 BH106
Audley Clo., Borwd. 32 CN41
Audley Ct. E18 66 EF56
Audley Ct., Pnr. 44 BW54
Audley Dr., Warl. 148 DW115
Audley Firs, Walt. 128 BW105
Audley Gdns., Ilf. 67 ET61
Audley Gdns., Loug. 39 EQ40
Audley Gdns., Wal.Abb. 23 EC34
Audley Pl., Sutt. 132 DB108
Audley Rd. NW4 61 CU58
Audley Rd. W5 74 CM71
Audley Rd., Enf. 35 DP40
Audley Rd., Rich. 102 CM85
Audley Sq. W1 8 G2
Audley Wk., Orp. 124 EW100
Audrey Clo., Beck. 121 EB100
Audrey Gdns., Wem. 59 CH61
Audrey Rd., Ilf. 67 EP62
Audrey St. E2 78 DU68
Audric Clo., Kings.T. 116 CN95
Audwick Clo. (Cheshunt), Wal.Cr. 23 DY28
Augurs La. E13 80 EH69
Augusta Clo., W.Mol. 114 BZ97
Freeman Dr.
Augusta Rd., Twick. 100 CC89
Augusta St. E14 79 EB72
Augustine Rd. W14 89 CX76
Augustine Rd., Har. 44 CB53
Augustine Rd., Orp. 124 EX97
Augustus Clo., Brent. 87 CK80
Augustus La., Orp. 124 EU103
Augustus Rd. SW19 103 CX88
Augustus St. NW1 5 J1
Augustus St. NW1 77 DH68
Aulton Pl. SE11 91 DN78
Milverton St.
Aultone Way, Cars. 118 DF104
Aultone Way, Sutt. 118 DB103
Aurelia Gdns., Croy. 119 DM99
Aurelia Rd., Croy. 119 DL100
Auriel Ave., Dag. 83 FD65
Auriga Ms. N16 64 DR64
Auriol Clo., Wor.Pk. 116 CS104
Auriol Pk. Rd.
Auriol Dr., Grnf. 73 CD66
Auriol Dr., Uxb. 71 BP65
Auriol Pk. Rd., Wor.Pk. 116 CS104
Auriol Rd. W14 89 CY77
Austell Gdns. NW7 46 CS48
Austen Clo. SE28 82 EV74
Austen Clo., Loug. 39 ER41
Austen Ho. NW6 76 DA69
Austen Rd., Erith 97 FB81
Belmont Rd.
Austen Rd., Har. 58 CB61
Austin Ave., Brom. 122 EL99
Austin Clo. SE23 107 DZ87
Austin Clo., Couls. 147 DP118
Austin Clo., Twick. 101 CJ85
Austin Ct. E6 80 EJ67
Kings Rd.
Austin Friars EC2 7 L8
Austin Friars EC2 78 DR72
Austin Friars Pas. EC2 7 L8
Austin Friars Sq. EC2 7 L8
Austin Rd. SW11 90 DG81
Austin Rd., Hayes 85 BT75
Austin Rd., Orp. 124 EU100
Austin St. E2 7 P3
Austin St. E2 78 DT69
Austin Waye, Uxb. 70 BJ67
Austin's La., Uxb. 57 BQ62
Austral Clo., Sid. 109 ET90
Austral St. SE11 10 F8
Austral St. SE11 91 DP77
Australia Rd. W12 75 CV73
Austyn Gdns., Surb. 116 CP102
Autumn Clo., Enf. 36 DU39
Autumn Dr., Sutt. 132 DB109
Autumn St. E3 79 EA67
Avalon Clo. SW20 117 CY96
Avalon Clo. W13 73 CG71
Avalon Clo., Enf. 35 DN40
Avalon Clo., Orp. 124 EX104
Avalon Clo., Wat. 16 BY32
Avalon Rd. SW6 90 DB81
Avalon Rd. W13 73 CG70
Avalon Rd., Orp. 124 EV103
Avard Gdns., Orp. 137 EQ105
Isabella Dr.
Avarn Rd. SW17 104 DF93
Ave Maria La. EC4 6 G9
Ave Maria La. EC4 77 DP72
Avebury Ct. N1 78 DR67
Poole St.
Avebury Pk., Surb. 115 CK101
Avebury Rd. E11 65 ED60
Southwest Rd.
Avebury Rd. SW19 117 CZ95
Avebury Rd., Orp. 123 ER104
Avebury St. N1 78 DR67
Poole St.
Aveley Clo., Erith 97 FF79
Aveley Rd., Rom. 69 FD56
Aveline St. SE11 91 DN78
Aveling Clo., Pur. 133 DM113
Aveling Pk. Rd. E17 51 EA54
Avelon Rd., Rain. 83 FG67
Avelon Rd., Rom. 55 FD51
Avenell Rd. N5 63 DP62
Avening Rd. SW18 104 DA87
Brathway Rd.
Avening Ter. SW18 104 DA86
Avenons Rd. E13 80 EG70
Avenue, The E4 51 ED51
Avenue, The (Leytonstone) E11 66 EF61
Avenue, The (Wanstead) E11 66 EH58
Avenue, The N3 48 DA54
Sylvan Ave.
Avenue, The N8 63 DN55
Avenue, The N10 49 DJ54
Avenue, The N11 49 DH50
Avenue, The N17 50 DS54
Avenue, The NW6 75 CX67
Avenue, The SE7 94 EJ80
Avenue, The SE10 93 ED80
Avenue, The SW4 104 DG85
Avenue, The SW11 104 DF87
Bellevue Rd.
Avenue, The SW18 104 DE87
Avenue, The W4 88 CS76
Avenue, The W13 73 CH73
Avenue, The, Add. 126 BG110
Avenue, The, Barn. 33 CY41
Avenue, The, Beck. 121 EB95
Avenue, The, Bex. 110 EX86
Avenue, The, Brom. 122 EK97
Avenue, The, Cars. 132 DG108
Avenue, The, Couls. 147 DK115
Avenue, The, Croy. 120 DS104
Avenue, The, Epsom 131 CV108
Avenue, The, Esher 129 CE107
Avenue, The, Hmptn. 100 BZ93
Avenue, The, Har. 45 CF53
Avenue, The, Houns. 100 CB85
Avenue, The (Cranford), Houns. 85 BU81
Avenue, The, Islw. 87 CD80
Jersey Rd.
Avenue, The, Kes. 122 EK104
Avenue, The, Lthd. 129 CF112
Avenue, The, Loug. 38 EK44
Avenue, The, Nthwd. 43 BQ51
Avenue, The, Orp. 123 ET103
Avenue, The (St. Paul's Cray), Orp. 110 EV94
Avenue, The, Pnr. 58 BZ58
Avenue, The (Hatch End), Pnr. 44 BZ51
Avenue, The, Pot.B. 19 CZ30
Avenue, The, Rad. 17 CG33
Avenue, The, Rich. 88 CM82
Avenue, The, Rom. 69 FD56
Avenue, The, Stai. 112 BH95
Avenue, The, Sun. 113 BV95
Avenue, The, Surb. 116 CM100
Avenue, The, Sutt. 131 CY109
Avenue, The (Cheam), Sutt. 131 CV108
Avenue, The, Tad. 145 CV122
Avenue, The, Twick. 101 CH85
Avenue, The (Cowley), Uxb. 70 BK70
Avenue, The (Ickenham), Uxb. 56 BN63
Avenue, The, Wal.Abb. 24 EJ25
Avenue, The, Wat. 29 BU40
Avenue, The (Bushey), Wat. 30 BZ42
Avenue, The, Wem. 60 CL60
Avenue, The, West Dr. 84 BL76
Avenue, The, W.Wick. 121 EC101
Avenue, The, West. 151 EM122
Avenue, The, Whyt. 148 DU119
Avenue, The, Wor.Pk. 117 CT103
Avenue App., Kings L. 14 BN30
Avenue Clo. N14 35 DJ44
Avenue Clo. NW8 76 DE67
Avenue Clo., Houns. 85 BU81
The Ave.
Avenue Clo., Tad. 145 CV122
Avenue Clo., West Dr. 84 BK76
Avenue Cres. W3 88 CP75
Avenue Cres., Houns. 85 BV80
Avenue Elmers, Surb. 116 CL99
Avenue Gdns. SE25 120 DU97
Avenue Gdns. SW14 88 CS83
Avenue Gdns. W3 88 CP75
Avenue Gdns., Houns. 85 BU80
The Ave.
Avenue Gdns., Tedd. 101 CF94
Avenue Gate, Loug. 38 EJ44
Avenue Ind. Est. E4 51 DZ51
Avenue Ms. N10 63 DH55
Avenue Pk. Rd. SE27 105 DP89
Avenue Ri. (Bushey), Wat. 30 CA43
Avenue Rd. E7 66 EH63
Avenue Rd. N6 63 DJ59
Avenue Rd. N12 48 DC49
Avenue Rd. N14 49 DH45
Avenue Rd. N15 64 DR57
Avenue Rd. NW3 76 DD66
Avenue Rd. NW8 76 DD66
Avenue Rd. NW10 75 CT68
Avenue Rd. SE20 120 DW95
Avenue Rd. SE25 120 DT96
Avenue Rd. SW16 119 DK96
Avenue Rd. SW20 117 CV96
Avenue Rd. W3 88 CP75
Avenue Rd., Bans. 146 DB115
Avenue Rd., Beck. 121 DX95
Avenue Rd., Belv. 97 FC77
Avenue Rd., Bexh. 96 EY84
Avenue Rd., Brent. 87 CJ78
Avenue Rd., Cat. 148 DR122
Avenue Rd., Cob. 142 BX116
Avenue Rd., Epp. 39 ER36
Avenue Rd., Epsom 130 CR114
Avenue Rd., Erith 97 FC80
Avenue Rd., Felt. 99 BT90
Avenue Rd., Hmptn. 114 CB95
Avenue Rd., Islw. 87 CF81
Avenue Rd., Kings.T. 116 CL97
Avenue Rd., N.Mal. 116 CS98
Avenue Rd., Pnr. 58 BY55
Avenue Rd. (Chadwell Heath), Rom. 68 EV60
Avenue Rd., Sev. 155 FJ124
Avenue Rd., Sthl. 86 BZ75
Avenue Rd., Sutt. 132 DA110
Avenue Rd., Tedd. 101 CG94
Avenue Rd., Wall. 133 DJ108
Avenue Rd., West. 150 EL120
Avenue Rd., Wdf.Grn. 52 EJ51
Avenue S., Surb. 116 CM101
Avenue Ter., N.Mal. 116 CQ97
Kingston Rd.
Avenue Ter., Wat. 30 BY44
Averil Gro. SW16 105 DP93
Averill St. W6 89 CX79
Avern Gdns., W.Mol. 114 CB98
Avern Rd., W.Mol. 114 CB98
Avery Fm. Row SW1 9 H9
Avery Gdns., Ilf. 67 EM57
Avery Hill Rd. SE9 109 ER86
Avery Row W1 5 J10
Avery Row W1 77 DH73
Avey La., Loug. 38 EH39
Avey La., Wal.Abb. 37 ED36
Aviary Clo. E16 80 EF71
Aviary Rd., Wok. 140 BG116
Aviemore Clo., Beck. 121 DZ99
Aviemore Way, Beck. 121 DY99
Avignon Rd. SE4 93 DX83
Avington Ct. SE1 92 DS77
Old Kent Rd.
Avington Gro. SE20 106 DW94
Avington Way SE15 92 DT80
Daniel Gdns.
Avior Dr., Nthwd. 43 BT49
Avis Gro., Croy. 135 DY111
Avis Sq. E1 79 DX72
Avoca Rd. SW17 104 DG91
Avocet Ms. SE28 95 ER76
Avon Clo., Add. 126 BG107
Avon Clo., Hayes 72 BW70
Avon Clo., Sutt. 132 DC105
Avon Clo., Wat. 16 BW34
Avon Clo., Wor.Pk. 117 CU103
Avon Ct., Grnf. 72 CB70
Braund Ave.
Avon Ms., Pnr. 44 BZ53
Avon Path, S.Croy. 134 DQ107
Avon Pl. SE1 11 J5
Avon Rd. E17 65 ED55
Avon Rd. SE4 93 EA83
Avon Rd., Grnf. 72 CA70
Avon Rd., Sun. 99 BT94
Avon Way E18 66 EG55
Avondale Ave. N12 48 DB50
Avondale Ave. NW2 60 CS62
Avondale Ave., Barn. 48 DF46
Avondale Ave., Esher 115 CG104
Avondale Ave., Wor.Pk. 117 CT102
Avondale Clo., Loug. 53 EM45
Avondale Clo., Walt. 128 BW106
Pleasant Pl.
Avondale Ct. E11 66 EE60
Avondale Ct. E16 80 EE71
Avondale Rd.
Avondale Ct. E18 52 EH53
Avondale Cres., Enf. 37 DY41
Avondale Cres., Ilf. 66 EK57
Avondale Dr., Hayes 71 BU74
Avondale Dr., Loug. 53 EM45
Avondale Gdns., Houns. 100 BZ85
Avondale Ms., Brom. 108 EG93
Avondale Rd.
Avondale Pk. Gdns. W11 75 CY73
Avondale Pk. Rd. W11 75 CY73
Avondale Pavement SE1 92 DU78
Avondale Sq.
Avondale Ri. SE15 92 DT83
Avondale Rd. E16 80 EE71
Avondale Rd. E17 65 EA59
Avondale Rd. N3 48 DC53
Avondale Rd. N13 49 DN47
Avondale Rd. N15 63 DP57
Avondale Rd. SE9 108 EL89
Avondale Rd. SW14 88 CR83
Avondale Rd. SW19 104 DB92
Avondale Rd., Ashf. 98 BK90
Avondale Rd., Brom. 108 EE93

Avondale Rd., Har. 59 CF55
Avondale Rd., S.Croy. 134 DQ108
Avondale Rd., Well. 96 EW82
Avondale Sq. SE1 92 DU78
Avonley Rd. SE14 92 DW80
Avonmore Gdns. W14 89 CY77
Avonmore Rd.
Avonmore Pl. W14 89 CY77
Avonmore Rd.
Avonmore Rd. W14 89 CY77
Avonmouth St. SE1 11 H6
Avonmouth St. SE1 92 DQ76
Avonwick Rd., Houns. 86 CB82
Avril Way E4 51 EC50
Avro Way, Wall. 133 DL108
Avro Way, Wey. 126 BL111
Award Gdns., Orp. 137 EQ105
Awlfield Ave. N17 50 DR53
Awliscombe Rd., Well. 95 ET82
Axe St., Bark. 81 EQ67
Axholme Ave., Edg. 46 CN53
Axminster Cres., Well. 96 EW81
Axminster Rd. N7 63 DL62
Axtaine Rd., Orp. 124 EX101
Axwood, Epsom 144 CQ115
Aybrook St. W1 4 F7
Aybrook St. W1 76 DG71
Aycliffe Clo., Brom. 123 EM98
Aycliffe Rd. W12 75 CT74
Aycliffe Rd., Borwd. 32 CL39
Aylands Clo., Wem. 60 CL61
Preston Rd.
Aylands Rd., Enf. 37 DX36
Ayles Rd., Hayes 71 BV69
Aylesbury Clo. E7 80 EF65
Atherton Rd.
Aylesbury Est. SE17 92 DR78
Villa St.
Aylesbury Rd. SE17 92 DR78
Aylesbury Rd., Brom. 122 EG97
Aylesbury St. EC1 6 F5
Aylesbury St. EC1 77 DP70
Aylesbury St. NW10 60 CR62
Aylesford Ave., Beck. 121 DY99
Aylesford St. SW1 91 DK78
Aylesham Clo. NW7 47 CU52
Aylesham Rd., Orp. 123 ET101
Aylestone Ave. NW6 75 CX66
Aylett Rd. SE25 120 DV98
Belfast Rd.
Aylett Rd., Islw. 87 CE82
Ayley Cft., Enf. 36 DU43
Ayliffe Clo., Kings.T. 116 CN96
Cambridge Gdns.
Aylmer Clo., Stan. 45 CG49
Aylmer Dr., Stan. 45 CG49
Aylmer Par. N2 62 DF57
Aylmer Rd.
Aylmer Rd. E11 66 EF60
Aylmer Rd. N2 62 DE57
Aylmer Rd. W12 89 CT75
Aylmer Rd., Dag. 68 EY62
Ayloffe Rd., Dag. 82 EZ65
Aylsham Dr., Uxb. 57 BQ61
Aylton Est. SE16 92 DW75
Renforth St.
Aylward Rd. SE23 107 DX89
Aylward Rd. SW20 117 CZ96
Aylward St. E1 78 DW72
Aylwards Ri., Stan. 45 CG49
Aylwyn Est. SE1 11 N6
Aylwyn Est. SE1 92 DS76
Aynho St., Wat. 29 BV43
Aynhoe Rd. W14 89 CX77
Aynscombe Angle, Orp. 124 EU101
Aynscombe La. SW14 88 CQ83
Aynscombe Path SW14 88 CQ82
Thames Bank
Ayot Path, Borwd. 32 CN38
Walshford Way
Ayr Ct. W3 74 CN71
Monks Dr.
Ayr Grn., Rom. 55 FE52
Ayr Way, Rom. 55 FE52
Ayres Clo. E13 80 EG69
Ayres Cres. NW10 74 CR66
Ayres St. SE1 11 J4
Ayres St. SE1 92 DQ75
Ayrsome Rd. N16 64 DS62
Ayrton Rd. SW7 90 DD76
Wells Way
Aysgarth Rd. SE21 106 DS86
Aytoun Pl. SW9 91 DM82
Aytoun Rd. SW9 91 DM82
Azalea Clo. W7 73 CF74
Azalea Clo., Ilf. 67 EP64
Lavender Pl.
Azalea Ct., Wdf.Grn. 52 EE52
Bridle Path
Azalea Dr., Swan. 125 FD98
Azalea Wk., Pnr. 57 BV57
Azalea Wk., Sthl. 86 CC75
Navigator Dr.
Azenby Rd. SE15 92 DT82
Azile Everitt Ho. SE18 95 EQ78
Vicarage Pk.
Azof St. SE10 94 EE77

B

Baalbec Rd. N5 63 DP64
Babbacombe Clo., Chess. 129 CK106
Babbacombe Gdns., Ilf. 66 EL56
Babbacombe Rd., Brom. 122 EG95
Baber Dr., Felt. 100 BW86
Babington Ri., Wem. 74 CN65
Babington Rd. NW4 61 CV56
Babington Rd. SW16 105 DK92
Babington Rd., Dag. 68 EW64
Babington Rd., Horn. 69 FH60
Babmaes St. SW1 9 M2
Bacchus Wk. N1 7 M1
Bachelor's La., Wok. 140 BM124
Baches St. N1 7 L3
Baches St. N1 78 DR69
Back Ch. La. E1 78 DU73
Back Grn., Walt. 128 BW107
Back Hill EC1 6 D5
Back Hill EC1 77 DN70
Back La. N8 63 DL57
Back La. NW3 62 DC63
Heath St.
Back La., Bex. 110 FA87
Back La., Brent. 87 CK79
Back La., Edg. 46 CQ53
Back La., Rich. 101 CJ90
Back La., Rom. 68 EY59
St. Chad's Rd.
Back La. (Godden Grn.), Sev. 155 FN124
Back La. (Ide Hill), Sev. 154 FB128
Back La., Wat. 31 CE39
Back Rd., Sid. 110 EU91
Backhouse Pl. SE17 11 N9
Backley Gdns. SE25 120 DU100
Bacon Gro. SE1 11 P7
Bacon Gro. SE1 92 DT76
Bacon La. NW9 60 CP56
Bacon La., Edg. 46 CN53
Bacon Link, Rom. 55 FB51
Bacon St. E1 78 DT70
Bacon St. E2 78 DT70
Bacon Ter., Dag. 68 EV64
Fitzstephen Rd.
Bacons Dr. (Cuffley), Pot.B. 21 DL29
Bacons La. N6 62 DG60
Bacons Mead, Uxb. 56 BG61
Bacton NW5 62 DG64
Bacton St. E2 78 DW69
Roman Rd.
Badburgham Ct., Wal.Abb. 24 EF33
Baddow Clo., Dag. 82 FA67
Baddow Clo., Wdf.Grn. 52 EK51
Baden Clo., Stai. 98 BG94
Baden Pl. SE1 11 K4
Baden Powell Clo., Surb. 116 CM103
Baden Powell Rd., Sev. 154 FE122
Baden Rd. N8 63 DK56
Baden Rd., Ilf. 67 EP64
Bader Clo., Ken. 148 DR115
Bader Way, Rain. 83 FG65
Badger Clo., Felt. 99 BU90
Sycamore Clo.
Badger Clo., Houns. 86 BW83
Badger Clo., Ilf. 67 EQ59
Badgers Clo., Ashf. 98 BM92
Fordbridge Rd.
Badgers Clo., Borwd. 32 CM40
Kingsley Ave.
Badgers Clo., Enf. 35 DP41
Badgers Clo., Har. 59 CD58
Badgers Clo., Hayes 71 BS74
Badgers Copse, Orp. 123 ET103
Badgers Copse, Wor.Pk. 117 CT103
Badgers Cft. N20 47 CY46
Badgers Cft. SE9 109 EN90
Badgers Hole, Croy. 135 DX105
Badgers La., Warl. 148 DW119
Badgers Ri., Sev. 138 FA110
Badgers Rd., Sev. 139 FB110
Badgers Wk., N.Mal. 116 CS96
Badgers Wk., Pur. 133 DJ111
Badgers Wk., Whyt. 148 DT119
Badingham Dr., Lthd. 143 CE123
Badlis Rd. E17 51 EA54
Badlow Clo., Erith 97 FE80
Badminton Clo., Borwd. 32 CN40
Badminton Clo., Har. 59 CE56
Badminton Clo., Nthlt. 72 CA66
Badminton Ms. E16 80 EG74
Silvertown Way
Badminton Rd. SW12 104 DG86
Badsworth Rd. SE5 92 DQ81
Baffin Way E14 79 ED73
Prestons Rd.
Bagley Clo., West Dr. 84 BL75
Bagley's La. SW6 90 DB81
Bagleys Spring, Rom. 68 EY56
Bagot Clo., Ash. 144 CM116
Bagshot Ct. SE18 95 EN81
Prince Imperial Rd.
Bagshot Rd., Enf. 50 DT45
Bagshot St. SE17 92 DS78
Bahram Rd., Epsom 130 CR110
Baildon St. SE8 93 EA80
Watson's St.
Bailey Clo. E4 51 EC49
Bailey Pl. SE26 107 DX93
Baillie Clo., Rain. 83 FH70
Baillies Wk. W5 87 CK75
Liverpool Rd.
Bainbridge Rd., Dag. 68 EZ63
Bainbridge St. WC1 5 N8
Bainbridge St. WC1 77 DK72
Baird Ave., Sthl. 72 CB73
Baird Clo. NW9 60 CQ58
Baird Clo. (Bushey), Wat. 30 CB44
Ashfield Ave.
Baird Gdns. SE19 106 DS91
Baird Rd., Enf. 36 DV42
Baird St. EC1 7 J4
Bairstow Clo., Borwd. 32 CL39
Baizdon Rd. SE3 94 EE82
Baker Boy La., Croy. 135 DZ112
Baker La., Mitch. 118 DG96
Baker Pas. NW10 74 CS67
Acton La.
Baker Rd. NW10 74 CS67
Baker Rd. SE18 94 EL81
Baker St. NW1 4 E5
Baker St. NW1 76 DF70
Baker St. W1 4 E6
Baker St. W1 76 DF71
Baker St., Enf. 36 DR41
Baker St., Pot.B. 33 CY36
Baker St., Wey. 126 BN105
Bakers Ave. E17 65 EB58
Bakers Ct. SE25 120 DS97
Bakers End SW20 117 CY96
Bakers Fld. N7 63 DK63
Crayford Rd.
Bakers Gdns., Cars. 118 DE103
Bakers Hill E5 64 DV60
Bakers Hill, Barn. 34 DB40
Bakers La. N6 62 DF58
Bakers La., Epp. 25 ET30
Baker's Ms. W1 4 F8
Bakers Ms., Orp. 137 ET107
Bakers Pas. NW3 62 DC63
Heath St.
Baker's Rents E2 7 P3
Bakers Rd., Uxb. 70 BK66
Bakers Rd. (Cheshunt), Wal.Cr. 22 DV30
Bakers Row E15 80 EE68
Baker's Row EC1 6 D5
Baker's Row EC1 77 DN70
Baker's Yd. EC1 77 DN70
Baker's Row
Baker's Yd., Uxb. 70 BK66
Bakers Rd.
Bakery Clo. SW9 91 DM81
Bakery Path, Edg. 46 CP51
Station Rd.
Bakery Pl. SW11 90 DF84
Altenburg Gdns.
Bakewell Way, N.Mal. 116 CS96
Bala Gdn. NW9 60 CS58
Snowdon Dr.
Balaam St. E13 80 EG70
Balaams La. N14 49 DK47
Balaclava Rd. SE1 92 DT77
Balaclava Rd., Surb. 115 CJ101
Balben Path E9 79 DX66
Speldhurst Rd.
Balcaskie Rd. SE9 109 EM85
Balchen Rd. SE3 94 EK82
Balchier Rd. SE22 106 DV86
Balcombe Clo., Bexh. 96 EX84
Balcombe St. NW1 4 D4
Balcombe St. NW1 76 DF70
Balcon Way, Borwd. 32 CQ39
Balcorne St. E9 78 DW66
Balder Ri. SE12 108 EH89
Balderton St. W1 4 G9
Balderton St. W1 76 DG72
Baldock St. E3 79 EB68
Baldock Way, Borwd. 32 CM39
Baldocks Rd., Epp. 39 ES35
Baldry Gdns. SW16 105 DL93
Baldwin Cres. SE5 92 DQ81
Baldwin St. EC1 7 K3
Baldwin Ter. N1 78 DQ68
Baldwin's Gdns. EC1 6 D6
Baldwin's Gdns. EC1 77 DN71
Baldwins Hill, Loug. 39 EM40
Baldwins La., Rick. 28 BN42
Baldwyn Gdns. W3 74 CR73
Baldwyns Pk., Bex. 111 FD89
Baldwyns Rd., Bex. 111 FD89
Balfe St. N1 6 A1
Balfe St. N1 77 DL68
Balfern Gro. W4 88 CS78
Balfern St. SW11 90 DE82
Balfont Clo., S.Croy. 134 DU113
Balfour Ave. W7 73 CF74
Balfour Gro. N20 48 DF48
Balfour Ho. W10 75 CX71
St. Charles Sq.
Balfour Ms. N9 50 DU48
The Bdy.
Balfour Ms. W1 8 G2
Balfour Pl. SW15 89 CV84
Balfour Pl. W1 8 G1
Balfour Rd. N5 64 DQ63
Balfour Rd. SE25 120 DU99
Balfour Rd. SW19 104 DB94
Balfour Rd. W3 74 CQ71
Balfour Rd. W13 87 CG75
Balfour Rd., Brom. 122 EK99
Balfour Rd., Cars. 132 DF108
Balfour Rd., Har. 59 CD57
Balfour Rd., Houns. 86 CB83
Balfour Rd., Ilf. 67 EP61
Balfour Rd., Sthl. 86 BX76
Balfour Rd., Wey. 126 BN105
Balfour St. SE17 11 K8
Balfour St. SE17 92 DR77
Balgonie Rd. E4 51 ED46
Balgores Cres., Rom. 69 FH55
Balgores La., Rom. 69 FH55
Balgores Sq., Rom. 69 FH56
Balgowan Clo., N.Mal. 116 CS98
Balgowan Rd., Beck. 121 DY97
Balgowan St. SE18 95 ET77
Balham Continental Mkt. SW12 105 DH88
Balham Gro. SW12 104 DG87
Balham High Rd. SW12 104 DG90
Balham High Rd. SW17 104 DG90
Balham Hill SW12 105 DH87
Balham New Rd. SW12 105 DH87
Balham Pk. Rd. SW12 104 DF88
Balham Rd. N9 50 DU47
Balham Sta. Rd. SW12 105 DH88
Balkan Wk. E1 78 DV73
Pennington St.
Balladier Wk. E14 79 EB71
Morris Rd.
Ballamore Rd., Brom. 108 EG90
Ballance Rd. E9 79 DX65
Ballands N., The, Lthd. 143 CE122
Ballands S., The, Lthd. 143 CE123
Ballantine St. SW18 90 DC84
Ballantyne Dr., Tad. 145 CZ121
Ballard Clo., Kings.T. 102 CR94
Ballards Clo., Dag. 83 FB67
Ballards Fm. Rd., Croy. 134 DU107
Ballards Fm. Rd., S.Croy. 134 DU107
Ballards Grn., Tad. 145 CY119
Ballards La. N3 48 DA53
Ballards La. N12 48 DC51
Ballards Ms., Edg. 46 CN51
Ballards Ri., S.Croy. 134 DU107
Ballards Rd. NW2 61 CU61
Ballards Rd., Dag. 83 FB68
Ballards Way, Croy. 134 DV107
Ballards Way, S.Croy. 134 DU107
Ballast Quay SE10 93 ED78
Ballater Clo., Wat. 44 BW49
Ballater Rd. SW2 91 DL84
Ballater Rd., S.Croy. 134 DT106
Ballenger Ct., Wat. 29 BV41
Ballina St. SE23 107 DX87
Ballingdon Rd. SW11 104 DG86
Ballinger Pt. E3 79 EB69
Bromley High St.
Balliol Ave. E4 52 EE49
Balliol Rd. N17 50 DS53
Balliol Rd. W10 75 CX72
Balliol Rd., Well. 96 EV82
Balloch Rd. SE6 107 ED88
Ballogie Ave. NW10 60 CS63
Ballow Clo. SE5 92 DS80
Harris St.
Balls Pond Pl. N1 78 DR65
Balls Pond Rd.
Balls Pond Rd. N1 78 DR65
Balmain Clo. W5 73 CK74
Balmer Rd. E3 79 DZ68
Balmes Rd. N1 78 DR67
Balmoral Ave. N11 48 DG50
Balmoral Ave., Beck. 121 DY98
Balmoral Clo. SW15 103 CX86
Westleigh Ave.
Balmoral Cres., W.Mol. 114 CA97
Balmoral Dr., Borwd. 32 CR43
Balmoral Dr., Hayes 71 BS70
Balmoral Dr., Sthl. 72 BZ70
Balmoral Gdns. W13 87 CG76
Balmoral Gdns., Bex. 110 EZ87
Balmoral Gdns., Ilf. 67 ET60
Balmoral Gro. N7 77 DM65
Balmoral Ms. W12 89 CT76
Balmoral Rd. E7 66 EJ63
Balmoral Rd. E10 65 EB61
Balmoral Rd. NW2 75 CV65
Balmoral Rd., Abb.L. 15 BU32
Balmoral Rd., Enf. 37 DX36
Balmoral Rd., Har. 58 CA63
Balmoral Rd., Kings.T. 116 CM98
Balmoral Rd., Rom. 69 FH57
Balmoral Rd., Wat. 30 BW38
Balmoral Rd., Wor.Pk. 117 CV104
Balmoral Way, Sutt. 132 DA110
Balmore Cres., Barn. 34 DG43
Balmore St. N19 63 DH61
Balmuir Gdns. SW15 89 CW84
Balnacraig Ave. NW10 60 CS63
Balniel Gate SW1 9 N10
Balniel Gate SW1 91 DK78
Balquhain Clo., Ash. 143 CK117
Baltic Clo. SW19 104 DD94
Baltic Ct. SE16 93 DX75
Timber Pond Rd.
Baltic St. E. EC1 7 H5
Baltic St. E. EC1 78 DQ70
Baltic St. W. EC1 7 H5
Baltic St. W. EC1 78 DQ70
Baltimore Pl., Well. 95 ET82
Balvernie Gro. SW18 103 CZ87
Bamber Ho., Bark. 81 EQ67
St. Margarets
Bamborough Gdns. W12 89 CW75
Bamford Ave., Wem. 74 CM67
Bamford Ct. E15 65 EB64
Clays La.
Bamford Rd., Bark. 81 EQ65
Bamford Rd., Brom. 107 EC92
Bamford Way, Rom. 55 FB50
Bampfylde Clo., Wall. 119 DJ104
Bampton Rd. SE23 107 DX90
Banavie Gdns., Beck. 121 EC95
Banbury Clo., Enf. 35 DP39
Holtwhites Hill
Banbury Ct. WC2 5 P10
Banbury Ct., Sutt. 132 DA108
Banbury Enterprise Cen., Croy. 119 DP103
Factory La.
Banbury Rd. E9 79 DX66
Banbury Rd. E17 51 DY53
Banbury St. SW11 90 DE82
Banbury St., Wat. 29 BU43
Banbury Wk., Nthlt. 72 CA68
Brabazon Rd.
Banchory Rd. SE3 94 EH80
Bancroft Ave. N2 62 DE57
Bancroft Ave., Buck.H. 52 EG47
Bancroft Clo., Ashf. 98 BN92
Feltham Hill Rd.
Bancroft Ct., Nthlt. 72 BW67
Bancroft Gdns., Har. 44 CC53
Bancroft Gdns., Orp. 123 ET102
Bancroft Rd. E1 79 DX69
Bancroft Rd., Har. 44 CC53
Bandon Ri., Wall. 133 DK106
Bangalore St. SW15 89 CW83
Bangor Clo., Nthlt. 58 CB64
Banim St. W6 89 CV77
Banister Rd. W10 75 CX69
Bank, The N6 63 DH60
Cholmeley Pk.
Bank Ave., Mitch. 118 DD96
Bank End SE1 11 J2
Bank End SE1 78 DQ74
Bank La. SW15 102 CS85
Bank La., Kings.T. 102 CL94
Bank Ms., Sutt. 132 DA111
Sutton Ct. Rd.
Bank St., Sev. 155 FH125
Bankfoot Rd., Brom. 108 EE91
Bankhurst Rd. SE6 107 DZ87
Banks La., Bexh. 96 EZ84
Banks La., Epp. 26 EY33
Bank's La., Lthd. 141 BV122
Banks Rd., Borwd. 32 CQ40
Banksia Rd. N18 50 DW50
Banksian Wk., Islw. 87 CE81
The Gro.
Bankside SE1 11 H1
Bankside SE1 78 DQ73
Bankside, Enf. 35 DP39
Bankside, Sev. 154 FE121
Bankside, S.Croy. 134 DT107
Bankside, Sthl. 72 BX74
Bankside Ave., Nthlt. 71 BU68
Townson Ave.
Bankside Clo., Bex. 111 FD91
Bankside Clo., Cars. 132 DE107
Bankside Clo., Islw. 87 CF84
Bankside Clo., West. 150 EJ118
Bankside Dr., T.Ditt. 115 CH102
Bankside Way SE19 106 DS93
Lunham Rd.
Bankton Rd. SW2 91 DN84
Bankwell Rd. SE13 94 EE84
Banner St. EC1 7 J5
Banner St. EC1 78 DQ70
Bannerman Ho. SW8 91 DM79
Banning St. SE10 94 EE78
Bannister Clo. SW2 105 DN88
Ewen Cres.
Bannister Clo., Grnf. 59 CD64
Bannister Gdns., Orp. 124 EW97
Main Rd.
Bannister Ho. E9 65 DX64
Homerton High St.
Bannockburn Rd. SE18 95 ES77
Banstead Gdns. N9 50 DS48
Banstead Rd., Bans. 131 CX112
Banstead Rd., Cars. 132 DE107
Banstead Rd., Cat. 148 DR122
Banstead Rd., Epsom 131 CV110
Banstead Rd., Pur. 133 DN111
Banstead Rd. S., Sutt. 132 DC111
Banstead St. SE15 92 DW83
Banstead Way, Wall. 133 DL106
Banstock Rd., Edg. 46 CP51
Banting Dr. N21 35 DM43
Banton Clo., Enf. 36 DV40
Central Ave.
Bantry St. SE5 92 DR80
Banwell Rd., Bex. 110 EX86
Woodside La.
Banyard Rd. SE16 92 DV76
Southwark Pk. Rd.
Bapchild Pl., Orp. 124 EW98
Okemore Gdns.
Baptist Gdns. NW5 76 DG65
Queens Cres.
Barandon Wk. W11 75 CX73
Whitchurch Rd.
Barb Ms. W6 89 CW76
Barbara Brosnan Ct. NW8 76 DD68
Grove End Rd.
Barbara Clo., Shep. 113 BP99
Barbara Hucklesby Clo. N22 49 DP54
The Sandlings
Barbauld Rd. N16 64 DS62
Barbel Clo., Wal.Cr. 23 EA34
Barber Clo. N21 49 DN45
Barber's All. E13 80 EH69
Greengate St.
Barbers Rd. E15 79 EB68
Barbican, The EC2 7 H6
Barbican, The EC2 78 DQ71
Barbican Rd., Grnf. 72 CB72
Barbon Clo. WC1 6 A6
Barbot Clo. N9 50 DU48
Barchard St. SW18 104 DB85
Barchester Clo. W7 73 CF74
Barchester Clo., Uxb. 70 BJ70
Barchester Rd., Har. 45 CD54
Barchester St. E14 79 EB71
Barclay Clo. SW6 90 DA80
Barclay Clo., Lthd. 142 CB123
Barclay Clo., Wat. 29 BU44
Barclay Oval, Wdf.Grn. 52 EG49

Barclay Path E17 65 EC57
Grove Rd.
Barclay Rd. E11 66 EE60
Barclay Rd. E13 80 EJ70
Barclay Rd. E17 65 EC57
Barclay Rd. N18 50 DR51
Barclay Rd. SW6 90 DA80
Barclay Rd., Croy. 120 DR104
Barclay Way SE22 106 DU87
Lordship La.
Barcombe Ave. SW2 105 DL89
Barcombe Clo., Orp. 124 EU97
Bard Rd. W10 75 CX73
Barden Clo., Uxb. 42 BJ52
Barden St. SE18 95 ES80
Bardfield Ave., Rom. 68 EX55
Bardney Rd., Mord. 118 DB98
Bardolph Ave., Croy. 135 DY109
Bardolph Rd. N7 63 DL63
Bardolph Rd., Rich. 88 CM83
St. Georges Rd.
Bardsey Pl. E1 78 DW71
Bardsey Wk. N1 78 DQ65
Clephane Rd.
Bardsley Clo., Croy. 120 DT104
Bardsley La. SE10 93 EC79
Barfett St. W10 75 CZ70
Barfield Ave. N20 48 DF47
Barfield Rd. E11 66 EF60
Barfield Rd., Brom. 123 EN97
Barfields, Loug. 39 EN42
Barfields Gdns., Loug. 39 EN42
Barfields
Barfields Path, Loug. 39 EN42
Barford Clo. NW4 47 CU53
Barford St. N1 77 DN67
Barforth Rd. SE15 92 DV83
Barfreston Way SE20 120 DV95
Bargate Clo. SE18 95 ET78
Bargate Clo., N.Mal. 117 CU101
Barge Ho. Rd. E16 95 EP75
Barge Ho. St. SE1 10 E2
Barge Wk., E.Mol. 115 CD97
Barge Wk., Kings.T. 115 CK96
Barge Wk., Walt. 114 BW97
Bargery Rd. SE6 107 EB88
Bargrove Clo. SE20 106 DU94
Bargrove Cres. SE6 107 DZ89
Elm La.
Barham Ave., Borwd. 32 CM41
Barham Clo., Brom. 122 EL102
Barham Clo., Chis. 109 EP92
Barham Clo., Rom. 55 FB54
Barham Clo., Wem. 73 CH65
Barham Clo., Wey. 127 BQ105
Barham Rd. SW20 103 CU94
Barham Rd., Chis. 109 EP92
Barham Rd., S.Croy. 134 DQ105
Baring Clo. SE12 108 EG89
Baring Rd. SE12 108 EG87
Baring Rd., Barn. 34 DD42
Baring Rd., Croy. 120 DU102
Baring St. N1 78 DR67
Bark Hart Rd., Orp. 124 EV102
Bark Pl. W2 76 DB73
Barker Dr. NW1 77 DJ66
Barker Ms. SW4 91 DH84
Barker St. SW10 90 DC79
Barker Wk. SW16 105 DK90
Mount Ephraim Rd.
Barker Way SE22 106 DU88
Dulwich Common
Barkham Rd. N17 50 DR52
Barking Ind. Pk., Bark. 81 ET67
Barking Rd. E6 80 EK68
Barking Rd. E13 80 EG70
Barking Rd. E16 80 EE71
Barkis Way SE16 92 DV78
Egan Way
Barkston Gdns. SW5 90 DB77
Barkston Path, Borwd. 32 CN37
Walshford Way
Barkway Ct. N4 64 DQ62
Queens Dr.
Barkwood Clo., Rom. 69 FC57
Barkworth Rd. SE16 92 DV78
Credon Rd.
Barlborough St. SE14 93 DX80
Barlby Gdns. W10 75 CX70
Barlby Rd. W10 75 CW71
Barlee Cres., Uxb. 70 BJ71
Barley Clo. (Bushey), Wat. 30 CB43
Barley La., Ilf. 68 EU59
Barley La., Rom. 68 EV58
Barley Mow Pas. EC1 6 G7
Barley Mow Pas. W4 88 CR78
Heathfield Ter.
Barley Mow Way, Shep. 112 BN98
Barley Shotts Business Pk. W10 75 CZ71
St. Ervans Rd.
Barleycorn Way E14 79 DZ73
Barleyfields Clo., Rom. 68 EV58
Barlow Clo., Wall. 133 DL107
Cobham Clo.
Barlow Pl. W1 9 J1
Barlow Rd. NW6 75 CZ65
Barlow Rd. W3 74 CP74
Barlow Rd., Hmptn. 100 CA94
Barlow St. SE17 11 L9
Barlow Way, Rain. 83 FD71
Barmeston Rd. SE6 107 EB89
Barmor Clo., Har. 44 CB54
Barmouth Ave., Grnf. 73 CF68
Barmouth Rd. SW18 104 DC86
Barmouth Rd., Croy. 121 DX103
Barn Clo., Ashf. 99 BP92
Barn Clo., Bans. 146 DD115
Barn Clo., Epsom 144 CQ115
Barn Clo., Nthlt. 72 BW68
Barn Clo., Rad. 31 CG35
Barn Cres., Pur. 134 DR113
Barn Cres., Stan. 45 CJ51
Barn Elms Pk. SW15 89 CW82
Barn Hill, Wem. 60 CN60
Barn Lea, Rick. 42 BG46
Barn Mead, Epp. 39 ES36
Barn Mead, Ong. 27 FE29
Barn Meadow La., Lthd. 142 BZ124
Barn Ms., Har. 58 CA62
Barn Ri., Wem. 60 CN60
Barn St. N16 64 DS62
Stoke Newington Ch. St.
Barn Way, Wem. 60 CN60
Barnabas Ct. N21 35 DN43
Cheyne Wk.
Barnabas Rd. E9 65 DX64
Barnaby Clo., Har. 58 CC61
Barnaby Pl. SW7 90 DD77
Barnaby Way, Chig. 53 EN48
Barnacre Clo., Uxb. 70 BK72
New Peachey La.
Barnacres Rd., Hem.H. 14 BM25
Barnard Clo. SE18 95 EN76
Barnard Clo., Chis. 123 ER95
Barnard Clo., Sun. 99 BV94
Oak Gro.
Barnard Clo., Wall. 133 DK108
Barnard Gdns., Hayes 71 BV70
Barnard Gdns., N.Mal. 117 CU98
Barnard Gro. E15 80 EF66
Vicarage La.
Barnard Hill N10 49 DH53
Barnard Ms. SW11 90 DE84
Barnard Rd. SW11 90 DE84
Barnard Rd., Enf. 36 DV40
Barnard Rd., Mitch. 118 DG97
Barnard Rd., Warl. 149 EB119
Barnardo Dr., Ilf. 67 EQ56
Civic Way
Barnardo St. E1 79 DX72
Devonport St.
Barnard's Inn EC1 6 D8
Barnards Pl., S.Croy. 133 DP109
Barnato Clo., W.Byf. 126 BL112
Viscount Gdns.
Barnby Sq. E15 80 EE67
Barnby St.
Barnby St. E15 80 EE67
Barnby St. NW1 5 L2
Barnby St. NW1 77 DJ69
Barncroft Clo., Loug. 39 EM43
Barncroft Clo., Uxb. 71 BP71
Harlington Rd.
Barncroft Grn., Loug. 39 EN43
Barncroft Rd., Loug. 39 EN43
Barnehurst Ave., Bexh. 97 FC81
Barnehurst Ave., Erith 97 FC81
Barnehurst Clo., Erith 97 FC81
Barnehurst Rd., Bexh. 97 FC82
Barnes All., Hmptn. 114 CC96
Hampton Ct. Rd.
Barnes Ave. SW13 89 CU80
Barnes Ave., Sthl. 86 BZ77
Barnes Bri. SW13 88 CS82
Barnes Bri. W4 88 CS82
Barnes Clo. E12 66 EK63
Barnes Ct. E16 80 EJ71
Ridgwell Rd.
Barnes Ct., Wdf.Grn. 52 EK50
Barnes Cray Cotts., Dart. 111 FG85
Maiden La.
Barnes Cray Rd., Dart. 97 FG84
Barnes End, N.Mal. 117 CU99
Barnes High St. SW13 89 CT82
Barnes Ho., Bark. 81 ER67
St. Marys
Barnes La., Kings L. 14 BH27
Barnes Ri., Kings L. 14 BM27
Barnes Rd. N18 50 DW49
Barnes Rd., Ilf. 67 EQ64
Barnes St. E14 79 DY72
Barnes Ter. SE8 93 DZ78
Barnes Wallis Dr., Wey. 126 BL111
Barnesbury Ho. SW4 105 DK86
Barnesdale Cres., Orp. 124 EU100
Barnet Bypass, Barn. 32 CS39
Barnet Dr., Brom. 122 EL103
Barnet Gate La., Barn. 33 CT44
Barnet Gro. E2 78 DU69
Barnet Hill, Barn. 33 CZ42
Barnet Ho. N20 48 DC47
Barnet La. N20 47 CZ46
Barnet La., Barn. 34 DA44
Barnet La., Borwd. 31 CK44
Barnet Rd. (Arkley), Barn. 32 CR44
Barnet Rd., Pot.B. 20 DB34
Barnet Rd., St.Alb. 18 CL27
Barnet Trd. Est., Barn. 33 CZ41
Barnet Way NW7 46 CR48
Barnet Wd. Rd., Brom. 122 EH103
Barnett Clo., Erith 97 FF82
Barnett Clo., Lthd. 143 CH119
Barnett St. E1 78 DV72
Cannon St. Rd.
Barnett Wd. La., Ash. 143 CJ118
Barnett Wd. La., Lthd. 143 CH120
Barney Clo. SE7 94 EJ78
Barnfield, Bans. 132 DB114
Barnfield, Epp. 26 EU28
Barnfield, N.Mal. 116 CS100
Barnfield Ave., Croy. 120 DW103
Barnfield Ave., Kings.T. 102 CL92
Barnfield Ave., Mitch. 119 DH98
Barnfield Clo. N4 63 DL59
Crouch Hill
Barnfield Clo. SW17 104 DC90
Barnfield Clo., Couls. 148 DQ119
Barnfield Clo., Swan. 125 FC101
Barnfield Gdns. SE18 95 EP79
Plumstead Common Rd.
Barnfield Gdns., Kings.T. 102 CL92
Barnfield Pl. E14 93 EA77
Barnfield Rd. SE18 95 EP79
Barnfield Rd. W5 73 CJ70
Barnfield Rd., Belv. 96 EZ79
Barnfield Rd., Edg. 46 CQ53
Barnfield Rd., Orp. 124 EX97
Barnfield Rd., Sev. 154 FD123
Barnfield Rd., S.Croy. 134 DS109
Barnfield Rd., West. 150 EK120
Barnfield Wd. Clo., Beck. 121 ED100
Barnfield Wd. Rd., Beck. 121 ED100
Barnham Rd., Grnf. 72 CC69
Barnham St. SE1 11 N4
Barnham St. SE1 92 DS75
Barnhill, Pnr. 58 BW57
Barnhill Ave., Brom. 122 EF99
Barnhill La., Hayes 71 BV70
Barnhill Rd., Hayes 71 BV70
Barnhill Rd., Wem. 60 CQ62
Barnhurst Path, Wat. 44 BW50
Barningham Way NW9 60 CR58
Barnlea Clo., Felt. 100 BY89
Barnmead Gdns., Dag. 68 EZ64
Barnmead Rd., Beck. 121 DY95
Barnmead Rd., Dag. 68 EZ64
Barnsbury Clo., N.Mal. 116 CQ98
Barnsbury Cres., Surb. 116 CP102
Barnsbury Est. N1 77 DN67
Barnsbury Rd.
Barnsbury Gro. N7 77 DM65
Barnsbury La., Surb. 116 CP103
Barnsbury Pk. N1 77 DN66
Barnsbury Rd. N1 77 DN68
Barnsbury Sq. N1 77 DN66
Barnsbury St. N1 77 DN66
Barnsbury Ter. N1 77 DM66
Barnscroft SW20 117 CV97
Barnsdale Ave. E14 93 EB77
Barnsdale Clo., Borwd. 32 CM39
Barnsdale Rd. W9 75 CZ70
Barnsfield Pl., Uxb. 70 BJ67
Barnsley St. E1 78 DV70
Barnstaple Rd., Ruis. 58 BW62
Barnston Wk. N1 78 DQ67
Popham St.
Barnsway, Kings L. 14 BL28
Barnwell Rd. SW2 105 DN85
Barnwood Clo. W9 76 DB70
Barnwood Clo., Ruis. 57 BR61
Lysander Rd.
Barnwood Ct. E16 80 EG74
North Woolwich Rd.
Barnyard, The, Tad. 145 CU124
Baron Clo. N11 48 DG50
Balmoral Ave.
Baron Clo., Sutt. 132 DB110
Baron Gdns., Ilf. 67 EQ55
Baron Gro., Mitch. 118 DE98
Baron Rd., Dag. 68 EX60
Baron St. N1 6 D1
Baron St. N1 77 DN68
Baron Wk. E16 80 EF71
Baron Wk., Mitch. 118 DE98
Baroness Rd. E2 78 DT69
Diss St.
Baronet Gro. N17 50 DU53
St. Paul's Rd.
Baronet Rd. N17 50 DU53
Barons, The, Twick. 101 CH86
Barons Ct., Wall. 119 DK104
Whelan Way
Barons Ct. Rd. W14 89 CY78
Barons Gate, Barn. 34 DE44
Barons Hurst, Epsom 144 CQ116
Barons Keep W14 89 CY78
Barons Mead, Har. 59 CE56
Barons Pl. SE1 10 E5
Barons Pl. SE1 91 DN75
Barons Wk., Croy. 121 DY100
Baronsfield Rd., Twick. 101 CH86
Baronsmead Rd. SW13 89 CU81
Baronsmede W5 88 CM75
Baronsmere Rd. N2 62 DE56
Barque Ms. SE8 93 EA79
Watergate St.
Barr Rd., Pot.B. 20 DC33
Barra Hall Circ., Hayes 71 BS72
Barra Hall Rd., Hayes 71 BS73
Barrack Rd., Houns. 86 BX84
Barracks La., Barn. 33 CY41
High St.
Barratt Ave. N22 49 DM54
Barratt Ind. Pk., Sthl. 86 CA75
Barratt Way, Har. 59 CD55
Tudor Rd.
Barrenger Rd. N10 48 DF53
Barrett Clo., Rom. 55 FH52
Barrett Rd. E17 65 EC56
Barrett Rd., Lthd. 143 CD124
Barrett St. W1 4 G9
Barrett St. W1 76 DG72
Barretts Grn. Rd. NW10 74 CQ69
Barretts Gro. N16 64 DS64
Barretts Rd., Sev. 153 FD120
Barrhill Rd. SW2 105 DL89
Barrie Clo., Couls. 147 DJ115
Barrie Est. W2 76 DD73
Craven Ter.
Barrie Twr. W3 88 CQ75
Barriedale SE14 93 DY82
Barrier App. SE7 94 EK76
Barringer Sq. SW17 104 DG91
Barrington Clo. NW5 62 DG64
Grafton Rd.
Barrington Clo., Ilf. 53 EM53
Hurstleigh Gdns.
Barrington Clo., Loug. 39 EQ42
Barrington Rd.
Barrington Dr., Uxb. 42 BG52
Park La.
Barrington Grn., Loug. 39 EQ42
Barrington Lo., Wey. 127 BQ106
Barrington Rd. E12 81 EN65
Barrington Rd. N8 63 DK57
Barrington Rd. SW9 91 DP83
Barrington Rd., Bexh. 96 EX82
Barrington Rd., Loug. 39 EQ42
Barrington Rd., Pur. 133 DJ112
Barrington Rd., Sutt. 118 DA102
Barrington Vill. SE18 95 EN81
Barrow Ave., Cars. 132 DF108
Barrow Clo. N21 49 DP48
Barrow Hedges Clo., Cars. 132 DE108
Barrow Hedges Way, Cars. 132 DE108
Barrow Hill, Wor.Pk. 116 CS103
Barrow Hill Clo., Wor.Pk. 116 CS103
Barrow Hill
Barrow Hill Rd. NW8 4 B1
Barrow Hill Rd. NW8 76 DE68
Barrow La. (Cheshunt), Wal.Cr. 22 DT30
Barrow Pt. Ave., Pnr. 44 BY54
Barrow Pt. La., Pnr. 44 BY54
Barrow Rd. SW16 105 DK93
Barrow Rd., Croy. 133 DN106
Barrow Wk., Brent. 87 CJ78
Glenhurst Rd.
Barrow Way N7 63 DM62
Barrowdene Clo., Pnr. 44 BY54
Paines La.
Barrowell Grn. N21 49 DP47
Barrowfield Clo. N9 50 DV48
Barrowgate Rd. W4 88 CQ78
Barrowsfield, S.Croy. 134 DT112
Barrs Rd. NW10 74 CR66
Barry Ave. N15 64 DT58
Craven Pk. Rd.
Barry Ave., Bexh. 96 EY80
Barry Clo., Orp. 123 ES104
Barry Clo., St.Alb. 16 CB25
Barry Rd. E6 80 EL72
Barry Rd. NW10 74 CQ66
Barry Rd. SE22 106 DU86
Barset Rd. SE15 92 DW83
Barson Clo. SE20 106 DW94
Barston Rd. SE27 106 DQ89
Barstow Cres. SW2 105 DM88
Barter St. WC1 6 A7
Barter St. WC1 77 DL71
Barters Wk., Pnr. 58 BY55
High St.
Barth Rd. SE18 95 ES77
Bartholomew Clo. EC1 7 H7
Bartholomew Clo. EC1 78 DQ71
Bartholomew Clo. SW18 90 DC84
Bartholomew La. EC2 7 L9
Bartholomew Pl. EC1 7 H7
Bartholomew Rd. NW5 77 DJ65
Bartholomew Sq. E1 78 DV70
Coventry Rd.
Bartholomew Sq. EC1 7 J4
Bartholomew Sq. EC1 78 DQ70
Bartholomew St. SE1 11 L7
Bartholomew St. SE1 92 DR76
Bartholomew Vill. NW5 77 DJ65
Bartholomew Way, Swan. 125 FE97
Bartle Ave. E6 80 EL68
Bartle Rd. W11 75 CY72
Bartlett Clo. E14 79 EA72
Bartlett Ct. EC4 6 E8
Bartlett St., S.Croy. 134 DR106
Bartlow Gdns., Rom. 55 FD53
Barton, The, Cob. 128 BW112
Barton Ave., Rom. 69 FB60
Barton Clo. E6 81 EM72
Brandreth Rd.
Barton Clo. E9 64 DW64
Churchill Wk.
Barton Clo. SE15 92 DV83
Kirkwood Rd.
Barton Clo., Add. 126 BG107
Barton Clo., Bexh. 110 EY85
Barton Clo., Chig. 53 EQ47
Barton Clo., Shep. 113 BP100
Barton Grn., N.Mal. 116 CR96
Barton Meadows, Ilf. 67 EP56
Barton Rd. W14 89 CY78
Barton Rd., Horn. 69 FG60
Barton Rd., Sid. 110 EY93
Barton St. SW1 9 P6
Barton Way, Borwd. 32 CN40
Barton Way, Rick. 29 BP43
Bartons, The, Borwd. 31 CK44
Bartonway NW8 76 DD68
Queen's Ter.
Bartram Clo., Uxb. 71 BP70
Lees Rd.
Bartram Rd. SE4 107 DY85
Bartrams La., Barn. 34 DC38
Bartrop Clo., Wal.Cr. 22 DR28
Poppy Wk.
Barville Clo. SE4 93 DY84
St. Norbert Rd.
Barwell Trd. Est., Chess. 129 CK109
Barwick Rd. E7 66 EH63
Barwood Ave., W.Wick. 121 EB102
Basden Gro., Felt. 100 CA89
Basedale Rd., Dag. 82 EV66
Baseing Clo. E6 81 EN73
Bashley Rd. NW10 74 CR70
Basil Ave. E6 80 EL68
Basil Gdns., Croy. 121 DX102
Primrose La.
Basil St. SW3 8 D6
Basil St. SW3 90 DF76
Basildene Rd., Houns. 86 BX83
Basildon Ave., Ilf. 53 EN53
Basildon Clo., Sutt. 132 DB109
Basildon Rd. SE2 96 EU78
Basildon Rd., Bexh. 96 EY82
Basin S. E16 81 EP74
Basing Clo., T.Ditt. 115 CF101
Basing Ct. SE15 92 DT81
Basing Dr., Bex. 110 EZ86
Basing Hill NW11 61 CZ60
Basing Hill, Wem. 60 CM61
Basing Ho., Bark. 81 ER67
St. Margarets
Basing Ho. Yd. E2 7 N2
Basing Pl. E2 7 N2
Basing Rd., Bans. 131 CZ114
Basing St. W11 75 CZ72
Basing Way N3 62 DA55
Basing Way, T.Ditt. 115 CF101
Basingdon Way SE5 92 DR84
Basingfield Rd., T.Ditt. 115 CF101
Basinghall Ave. EC2 7 K7
Basinghall Ave. EC2 78 DR71
Basinghall Gdns., Sutt. 132 DB109
Basinghall St. EC2 7 K8
Basinghall St. EC2 78 DQ71
Basire St. N1 78 DQ67
Baskerville Rd. SW18 104 DE87
Basket Gdns. SE9 108 EL85
Baslow Clo., Har. 45 CD53
Baslow Wk. E5 65 DX63
Overbury St.
Basnett Rd. SW11 90 DG83
Basque Ct. SE16 93 DX75
Poolmans St.
Bassano St. SE22 106 DT85
Bassant Rd. SE18 95 ET79
Bassein Pk. Rd. W12 89 CT75
Basset Clo., Add. 126 BH110
Basset Ho., Dag. 82 EV67
Bassett Clo., Sutt. 132 DB109
Bassett Gdns., Epp. 27 FB26
Bassett Gdns., Islw. 86 CC80
Bassett Rd. W10 75 CX72
Bassett Rd., Uxb. 70 BJ66
New Windsor St.
Bassett St. NW5 76 DG65
Bassett Way, Grnf. 72 CB72
Bassetts Clo., Orp. 123 EP104
Bassetts Way, Orp. 137 EP105
Bassingham Rd. SW18 104 DC87
Bassingham Rd., Wem. 73 CK65
Bassishaw Highwalk EC2 78 DQ71
London Wall
Basswood Clo. SE15 92 DV83
Linden Gro.
Bastable Ave., Bark. 81 ES68
Bastion Highwalk EC2 78 DQ71
London Wall
Bastion Ho. EC2 78 DQ71
London Wall
Bastion Rd. SE2 96 EU78
Baston Manor Rd., Brom. 122 EH104
Baston Rd., Brom. 122 EH102
Bastwick St. EC1 7 H4
Bastwick St. EC1 78 DQ70
Basuto Rd. SW6 90 DA81
Bat & Ball Rd., Sev. 155 FJ121
Batavia Clo., Sun. 114 BW95
Batavia Ms. SE14 93 DY80
Goodwood Rd.
Batavia Rd. SE14 93 DY80
Batavia Rd., Sun. 113 BV95
Batchelor St. N1 77 DN68
Batchwood Grn., Orp. 124 EU97
Batchworth Heath Hill, Rick. 42 BN49
Batchworth Hill, Rick. 42 BM48
Batchworth La., Nthwd. 43 BP50
Batchworth Roundabout, Rick. 42 BK46
Bate St. E14 79 DZ73
Three Colt St.
Bateman Clo., Bark. 81 EQ65
Glenny Rd.
Bateman Ho. SE17 91 DP79
Otto St.
Bateman Rd. E4 51 EA51
Bateman Rd., Rick. 28 BN44
Bateman St. W1 5 M9
Bateman's Bldgs. W1 5 M9
Bateman's Row EC2 7 N4
Bateman's Row EC2 78 DS70
Bates Cres. SW16 105 DJ94
Bates Cres., Croy. 133 DN106
Bates Wk., Add. 126 BJ107
Bateson St. SE18 95 ES77
Gunning St.
Bath Clo. SE15 92 DV80
Asylum Rd.
Bath Ct. EC1 6 D5
Bath Ho. Rd., Croy. 119 DL102

Bath Pas., Kings.T. 115 CK96
St. James Rd.
Bath Pl. EC2 78 DS69
Rivington St.
Bath Pl., Barn. 33 CZ41
Bath Rd. E7 80 EK65
Bath Rd. N9 50 DV47
Bath Rd. W4 88 CS77
Bath Rd., Dart. 111 FH87
Bath Rd., Hayes 85 BS81
Bath Rd., Houns. 86 BX82
Bath Rd., Mitch. 118 DD97
Bath Rd., Rom. 68 EY58
Bath Rd. (Poyle), Slou. 84 BG81
Bath Rd., West Dr. 84 BK81
Bath St. EC1 7 J3
Bath St. EC1 78 DQ69
Bath Ter. SE1 11 H7
Bath Ter. SE1 92 DQ76
Bathgate Rd. SW19 103 CX90
Baths Rd., Brom. 122 EK98
Bathurst Ave. SW19 118 DB95
Brisbane Ave.
Bathurst Gdns. NW10 75 CV68
Bathurst Ms. W2 4 A10
Bathurst Rd., Ilf. 67 EP60
Bathurst St. W2 4 A10
Bathurst St. W2 76 DD73
Bathway SE18 95 EN77
Batley Clo., Mitch. 118 DF101
Batley Pl. N16 64 DT62
Batley Rd. N16 64 DT62
Stoke Newington High St.
Batley Rd., Enf. 36 DR39
Batman Clo. W12 75 CV74
Batoum Gdns. W6 89 CW76
Batson St. W12 89 CU75
Batsworth Rd., Mitch. 118 DD97
Batten Clo. E6 81 EM72
Savage Gdns.
Batten St. SW11 90 DE83
Battenburg Wk. SE19 106 DS92
Brabourne Clo.
Battersby Rd. SE6 107 ED89
Battersea Bri. SW3 90 DD80
Battersea Bri. SW11 90 DE80
Battersea Bri. Rd. SW11 90 DE80
Battersea Ch. Rd. SW11 90 DD81
Battersea High St. SW11 90 DD81
Battersea Pk. SW11 90 DF80
Battersea Pk. Rd. SW8 91 DH81
Battersea Pk. Rd. SW11 90 DE82
Battersea Ri. SW11 104 DD85
Battersea Sq. SW11 90 DD81
Battersea High St.
Battery Rd. SE28 95 ES75
Battis, The, Rom. 69 FE58
Waterloo Rd.
Battishill Gdns. N1 77 DP66
Waterloo Ter.
Battishill St. N1 77 DP66
Waterloo Ter.
Battle Bri. La. SE1 11 M3
Battle Bri. La. SE1 78 DS74
Battle Bri. Rd. NW1 5 P1
Battle Bri. Rd. NW1 77 DL68
Battle Clo. SW19 104 DC93
North Rd.
Battle Rd., Belv. 97 FC77
Battle Rd., Erith 97 FC77
Battledean Rd. N5 63 DP64
Battlers Grn. Dr., Rad. 31 CE37
Batty St. E1 78 DU72
Baudwin Rd. SE6 108 EE89
Baugh Rd., Sid. 110 EW92
Baulk, The SW18 104 DA87
Bavant Rd. SW16 119 DM96
Bavaria Rd. N19 63 DL61
Bavent Rd. SE5 92 DQ82
Bawdale Rd. SE22 106 DT85
Bawdsey Ave., Ilf. 67 ET56
Bawtree Clo., Sutt. 132 DC110
Bawtree Rd. SE14 93 DY80
Bawtree Rd., Uxb. 70 BK65
Bawtry Rd. N20 48 DF48
Baxendale N20 48 DC47
Baxendale St. E2 78 DU69
Baxter Clo., Uxb. 71 BP69
Baxter Rd. E16 80 EJ72
Baxter Rd. N1 78 DR65
Baxter Rd. N18 50 DV49
Baxter Rd. NW10 74 CS70
Baxter Rd., Ilf. 67 EP64
Bay Ct. W5 88 CL76
Popes La.
Bay Tree Clo., Brom. 122 EJ95
Bay Tree Wk., Wat. 29 BT38
Bayards, Warl. 148 DW118
Baydon Ct., Brom. 122 EF97
Bayeaux, Tad. 145 CX122
Heathcote
Bayes Clo. SE26 106 DW92
Bayfield Rd. SE9 94 EK84
Bayford Ms. E8 78 DV66
Bayford St.
Bayford Rd. NW10 75 CX69
Bayford St. E8 78 DV66
Bayham Pl. NW1 77 DJ67
Bayham Rd. W4 88 CR76
Bayham Rd. W13 73 CH73
Bayham Rd., Mord. 118 DB98
Bayham Rd., Sev. 155 FJ123
Bayham St. NW1 77 DJ67
Bayhurst Dr., Nthwd. 43 BT51
Bayley St. WC1 5 M7
Bayley St. WC1 77 DK71
Bayley Wk. SE2 96 EY78
Woolwich Rd.
Baylin Rd. SW18 104 DB86
Garratt La.
Baylis Rd. SE1 10 D5
Baylis Rd. SE1 91 DN75
Bayliss Ave. SE28 82 EX73
Bayliss Clo. N21 35 DL43
Macleod Rd.
Bayne Clo. E6 81 EM72
Savage Gdns.
Baynes Clo., Enf. 36 DU39
Baynes Ms. NW3 76 DD65
Belsize La.
Baynes St. NW1 77 DJ66
Baynham Clo., Bex. 110 EZ86
Bayonne Rd. W6 89 CY79
Bayshill Ri., Nthlt. 72 CB65
Bayston Rd. N16 64 DT62
Bayswater Rd. W2 76 DB73
Baythorne St. E3 79 DZ71
Baytree Clo., Sid. 109 ET88
Baytree Clo., Wal.Cr. 22 DT27
Baytree Rd. SW2 91 DM84
Baywood Sq., Chig. 54 EV49
Bazalgette Clo., N.Mal. 116 CR99
Bazalgette Gdns., N.Mal. 116 CR99
Bazely St. E14 79 EC73
Bazile Rd. N21 35 DN44
Beach Gro., Felt. 100 CA89
Beacham Clo. SE7 94 EK78
Beachborough Rd., Brom. 107 EC91
Beachcroft Rd. E11 66 EE62
Beachcroft Way N19 63 DK60
Beachy Rd. E3 79 EA66
Beacon Clo., Bans. 145 CX116
Beacon Clo., Uxb. 56 BK64
Beacon Gate SE14 93 DX82
Beacon Gro., Cars. 132 DG105
Beacon Hill N7 63 DL64
Beacon Ri., Sev. 154 FG126
Beacon Rd. SE13 107 ED86
Beacon Rd., Erith 97 FH80
Beacon Rd., Houns. 98 BN86
Beacon Way, Bans. 145 CX116
Beacon Way, Rick. 42 BG45
Beaconfield Ave., Epp. 25 ET29
Beaconfield Rd., Epp. 25 ET29
Beaconfield Way, Epp. 25 ET29
Beaconfields, Sev. 154 FF126
Beacons, The, Loug. 39 EN38
Beacons Clo. E6 80 EL71
Oliver Gdns.
Beaconsfield Clo. N11 48 DG50
Beaconsfield Clo. SE3 94 EG79
Beaconsfield Clo. W4 88 CQ78
Beaconsfield Par. SE9 108 EL91
Beaconsfield Rd.
Beaconsfield Pl., Epsom 130 CS112
Beaconsfield Rd. E10 65 EC61
Beaconsfield Rd. E16 80 EF70
Beaconsfield Rd. E17 65 DZ58
Beaconsfield Rd. N9 50 DU48
Beaconsfield Rd. N11 48 DG48
Beaconsfield Rd. N15 64 DS56
Beaconsfield Rd. NW10 75 CT65
Beaconsfield Rd. SE3 94 EF80
Beaconsfield Rd. SE9 108 EL89
Beaconsfield Rd. SE17 92 DR79
Beaconsfield Rd. W4 88 CR76
Beaconsfield Rd. W5 87 CJ75
Beaconsfield Rd., Bex. 111 FD89
Beaconsfield Rd., Brom. 122 EK97
Beaconsfield Rd., Croy. 120 DR100
Beaconsfield Rd., Enf. 37 DX37
Beaconsfield Rd., Epsom 144 CR119
Beaconsfield Rd., Esher 129 CE108
Beaconsfield Rd., Hayes 72 BW74
Beaconsfield Rd., N.Mal. 116 CR96
Beaconsfield Rd., Sthl. 72 BX74
Beaconsfield Rd., Surb. 116 CM101
Beaconsfield Rd., Twick. 101 CH86
Beaconsfield Ter., Rom. 68 EX58
Beaconsfield Ter. Rd. W14 89 CY76
Beaconsfield Wk. E6 81 EN72
East Ham Manor Way
Beaconsfield Wk. SW6 89 CZ81
Parsons Grn. La.
Beacontree Ave. E17 51 ED53
Beacontree Rd. E11 66 EF59
Beadlow Clo., Cars. 118 DD100
Olveston Wk.
Beadman Pl. SE27 105 DP91
Norwood High St.
Beadman St. SE27 105 DP91
Beadnell Rd. SE23 107 DX88
Beadon Rd. W6 89 CW77
Beadon Rd., Brom. 122 EG98
Beaford Gro. SW20 117 CY97
Beagle Clo., Felt. 99 BV91
Beagle Clo., Rad. 31 CF37
Beagles Clo., Orp. 124 EX103
Beak St. W1 5 L10
Beak St. W1 77 DJ73
Beal Clo., Well. 96 EU81
Beal Rd., Ilf. 67 EN61
Beale Clo. N13 49 DP50
Beale Pl. E3 79 DZ68
Beale Rd. E3 79 DZ67
Beales La., Wey. 112 BN104
Beam Ave., Dag. 83 FB67
Beam Way, Dag. 83 FD66
Beaminster Gdns., Ilf. 53 EP54
Beamish Clo., Epp. 27 FC25
Beamish Dr. (Bushey), Wat. 44 CC46
Beamish Rd. N9 50 DU46
Beamish Rd., Orp. 124 EW101
Bean Rd., Bexh. 96 EX84
Beanacre Clo. E9 79 DZ65
Beanshaw SE9 109 EN91
Beansland Gro., Rom. 54 EY54
Bear All. EC4 6 F8
Bear Clo., Rom. 69 FB58
Bear Gdns. SE1 11 H2
Bear Gdns. SE1 78 DQ74
Bear La. SE1 10 G3
Bear La. SE1 77 DP74
Bear Rd., Felt. 100 BX92
Bear St. WC2 5 N10
Beard Rd., Kings.T. 102 CM92
Beardell St. SE19 106 DT93
Beardow Gro. N14 35 DJ44
Beard's Hill, Hmptn. 114 CA95
Beard's Hill Clo., Hmptn. 114 CA95
Beard's Hill
Beards Rd., Ashf. 99 BS93
Beardsfield E13 80 EG67
Valetta Gro.
Beardsley Ter., Dag. 68 EV64
Fitzstephen Rd.
Beardsley Way W3 88 CR75
Bearfield Rd., Kings.T. 102 CL94
Bearing Clo., Chig. 54 EU49
Bearing Way, Chig. 54 EU49
Bears Den, Tad. 145 CZ122
Bearstead Ri. SE4 107 DZ85
Bearstead Ter., Beck. 121 EA95
Copers Cope Rd.
Bearwood Clo., Add. 126 BG107
Ongar Pl.
Bearwood Clo., Pot.B. 20 DD31
Beasley's Ait La., Sun. 113 BT100
Beasleys Yd., Uxb. 70 BJ66
Warwick Pl.
Beatrice Ave. SW16 119 DM96
Beatrice Ave., Wem. 60 CL64
Beatrice Clo. E13 80 EG70
Chargeable La.
Beatrice Clo., Pnr. 57 BU56
Reid Clo.
Beatrice Ct., Buck.H. 52 EK47
Beatrice Pl. W8 90 DB76
Beatrice Rd. E17 65 EA57
Beatrice Rd. N4 63 DN59
Beatrice Rd. N9 50 DW45
Beatrice Rd. SE1 92 DU77
Beatrice Rd., Rich. 102 CM85
Albert Rd.
Beatrice Rd., Sthl. 72 BZ74
Beatson Wk. SE16 79 DY74
Beattie Clo., Lthd. 142 BZ124
Beattock Ri. N10 63 DH56
Beatty Rd. N16 64 DS63
Beatty Rd., Stan. 45 CJ51
Beatty St. NW1 77 DJ68
Beattyville Gdns., Ilf. 67 EN55
Beauchamp Clo. W4 88 CQ76
Church Path
Beauchamp Gdns., Rick. 42 BG46
Beauchamp Pl. SW3 8 C6
Beauchamp Pl. SW3 90 DE76
Beauchamp Rd. E7 80 EH66
Beauchamp Rd. SE19 120 DR95
Beauchamp Rd. SW11 90 DE84
Beauchamp Rd., E.Mol. 114 CB99
Beauchamp Rd., Sutt. 132 DA105
Beauchamp Rd., Twick. 101 CG87
Beauchamp Rd., W.Mol. 114 CB99
Beauchamp St. EC1 6 D7
Beauchamp Ter. SW15 89 CV83
Dryburgh Rd.
Beauclare Clo., Lthd. 143 CK121
Hatherwood
Beauclerc Rd. W6 89 CV76
Beauclerk Clo., Felt. 99 BV88
Florence Rd.
Beaudesert Ms., West Dr. 84 BL75
Beaufort E6 81 EN71
Newark Knok
Beaufort Ave., Har. 59 CG56
Beaufort Clo. E4 51 EB51
Higham Sta. Ave.
Beaufort Clo. SW15 103 CV87
Beaufort Clo. W5 74 CM71
Beaufort Clo., Epp. 26 FA26
Beaufort Clo., Rom. 69 FC56
Beaufort Ct., Rich. 101 CJ91
Beaufort Rd.
Beaufort Dr. NW11 62 DA56
Beaufort Gdns. NW4 61 CW58
Beaufort Gdns. SW3 8 C6
Beaufort Gdns. SW3 90 DE76
Beaufort Gdns. SW16 105 DM94
Beaufort Gdns., Houns. 86 BY81
Beaufort Gdns., Ilf. 67 EN60
Beaufort Ms. SW6 89 CZ79
Lillie Rd.
Beaufort Pk. NW11 62 DA56
Beaufort Rd. W5 74 CM71
Beaufort Rd., Kings.T. 116 CL98
Beaufort Rd., Rich. 101 CJ91
Beaufort Rd., Ruis. 57 BR61
Lysander Rd.
Beaufort Rd., Twick. 101 CJ87
Beaufort St. SW3 90 DD79
Beaufort Way, Epsom 131 CU108
Beaufoy Rd. N17 50 DS52
Beaufoy Wk. SE11 10 C9
Beaufoy Wk. SE11 91 DM77
Beaulieu Ave. SE26 106 DV91
Beaulieu Clo. NW9 60 CS55
Beaulieu Clo. SE5 92 DR83
Beaulieu Clo., Houns. 100 BZ85
Beaulieu Clo., Mitch. 118 DG95
Beaulieu Clo., Twick. 101 CK86
Beaulieu Clo., Wat. 44 BW46
Beaulieu Dr., Pnr. 58 BX58
Beaulieu Gdns. N21 50 DQ45
Beaulieu Pl. W4 88 CQ76
Rothschild Rd.
Beauly Way, Rom. 55 FE53
Beaumanor Gdns. SE9 109 EN91
Beanshaw
Beaumaris Dr., Wdf.Grn. 52 EK52
Beaumont Ave. W14 89 CZ78
Beaumont Ave., Har. 58 CB58
Beaumont Ave., Rich. 88 CM83
Beaumont Ave., Wem. 59 CJ64
Beaumont Clo., Kings.T. 102 CN94
Beaumont Cres. W14 89 CZ78
Beaumont Cres., Rain. 83 FG65
Beaumont Dr., Ashf. 99 BR92
Beaumont Gdns. NW3 62 DA62
Beaumont Gate, Rad. 31 CH35
Shenley Hill
Beaumont Gro. E1 79 DX70
Beaumont Ms. W1 4 G6
Beaumont Pl. W1 5 L4
Beaumont Pl. W1 77 DJ70
Beaumont Pl., Barn. 33 CZ39
Beaumont Pl., Islw. 101 CF85
Beaumont Ri. N19 63 DK59
Beaumont Rd. E10 65 EB59
Beaumont Rd. E13 80 EH69
Beaumont Rd. SE19 106 DQ93
Beaumont Rd. SW19 103 CY87
Beaumont Rd. W4 88 CQ76
Beaumont Rd., Orp. 123 ER100
Beaumont Rd., Pur. 133 DN113
Beaumont Sq. E1 79 DX70
Beaumont St. W1 4 G6
Beaumont St. W1 76 DG71
Beaumont Vw. (Cheshunt), Wal.Cr. 22 DR26
Beaumont Wk. NW3 76 DF66
Beauvais Ter., Nthlt. 72 BX69
Beauval Rd. SE22 106 DT86
Beaver Clo. SE20 106 DU94
Lullington Rd.
Beaver Clo., Hmptn. 114 CB95
Beaver Gro., Nthlt. 72 BY69
Jetstar Way
Beaver Rd., Ilf. 54 EW50
Beaverbank Rd. SE9 109 ER88
Beaverbrook Roundabout, Lthd. 143 CK123
Beavers Cres., Houns. 86 BX84
Beavers La., Houns. 86 BW82
Beavers La. Camp, Houns. 86 BW83
Beaverwood Rd., Chis. 109 ES93
Beavor Gro. W6 89 CU77
Beavor La.
Beavor La. W6 89 CU77
Bebbington Rd. SE18 95 ES77
Bebletts Clo., Orp. 137 ET106
Bec Clo., Ruis. 58 BX62
Beccles Dr., Bark. 81 ES65
Beccles St. E14 79 DZ73
Beck Clo. SE13 93 EB81
Beck Ct., Beck. 121 DX97
Beck La., Beck. 121 DX97
Beck River Pk., Beck. 121 EA95
Rectory Rd.
Beck Rd. E8 78 DV67
Beck Way, Beck. 121 DZ97
Beckenham Gdns. N9 50 DS48
Beckenham Gro., Brom. 121 ED96
Beckenham Hill Rd. SE6 107 EC92
Beckenham Hill Rd., Beck. 107 EB92
Beckenham La., Brom. 122 EE96
Beckenham Pl. Pk., Beck. 107 EB94
Beckenham Rd., Beck. 121 DX95
Beckenham Rd., W.Wick. 121 EB101
Beckenshaw Gdns., Bans. 146 DD115
Beckers, The N16 64 DU62
Rectory Rd.
Becket Ave. E6 81 EN69
Becket Clo. SE25 120 DU100
Becket Fold, Har. 59 CF57
Courtfield Cres.
Becket Rd. N18 50 DW49
Becket St. SE1 11 K6
Beckett Ave., Ken. 147 DP115
Beckett Clo. NW10 74 CR65
Beckett Clo. SW16 105 DK89
Beckett Clo., Belv. 96 EY76
Tunstock Way
Beckett Wk., Beck. 107 DY93
Becketts Clo., Felt. 99 BV86
Becketts Clo., Orp. 123 ET104
Becketts Pl., Kings.T. 115 CK95
Beckford Dr., Orp. 123 ER101
Beckford Pl. SE17 92 DQ78
Walworth Rd.
Beckford Rd., Croy. 120 DT100
Becklow Gdns. W12 89 CU75
Becklow Rd.
Becklow Rd. W12 89 CT75
Beckman Clo., Sev. 153 FC115
Becks Rd., Sid. 110 EU90
Beckton Pk. Roundabout E16 94 EK76
Royal Albert Way
Beckton Retail Pk. E6 81 EN71
Beckton Rd. E16 80 EF71
Beckway Rd. SW16 119 DK96
Beckway St. SE17 11 M9
Beckway St. SE17 92 DR77
Beckwith Rd. SE24 106 DR86
Beclands Rd. SW17 104 DG93
Becmead Ave. SW16 105 DK91
Becmead Ave., Har. 59 CH57
Becondale Rd. SE19 106 DS92
Becontree Ave., Dag. 68 EV63
Bective Pl. SW15 89 CZ84
Bective Rd.
Bective Rd. E7 66 EG63
Bective Rd. SW15 89 CY84
Becton Pl., Erith 97 FB80
Bedale Rd., Enf. 36 DQ38
Bedale St. SE1 11 K3
Bedale St. SE1 78 DR74
Beddington Fm. Rd., Croy. 119 DL101
Beddington Gdns., Cars. 132 DG107
Beddington Gdns., Wall. 133 DH107
Beddington Grn., Orp. 123 ET95
Beddington Gro., Wall. 133 DK106
Beddington La., Croy. 119 DJ99
Beddington Path, Orp. 123 ET95
Beddington Rd., Ilf. 67 ET59
Beddington Rd., Orp. 123 ES95
Beddington Trd. Pk. W., Croy. 119 DL102
Beddington Fm. Rd.
Beddlestead La., Warl. 150 EF117
Bede Clo., Pnr. 44 BX53
Bede Rd., Rom. 68 EW58
Bedenham Way SE15 92 DT80
Daniel Gdns.
Bedens Rd., Sid. 110 EY93
Bedfont Clo., Felt. 99 BQ86
Bedfont Clo., Mitch. 118 DG96
Bedfont Ct., Stai. 84 BH84
Bedfont Ct. Est., Stai. 84 BG83
Bedfont Grn. Clo., Felt. 99 BQ88
Bedfont La., Felt. 99 BS87
Bedfont Rd., Felt. 99 BQ88
Bedfont Rd., Stai. 98 BL86
Bedford Ave. WC1 5 N7
Bedford Ave. WC1 77 DK71
Bedford Ave., Barn. 33 CZ43
Bedford Ave., Hayes 71 BV72
Bedford Clo. N10 48 DG52
Bedford Clo. W4 88 CS79
Bedford Cor. W4 88 CS77
The Ave.
Bedford Ct. WC2 9 P1
Bedford Cres., Enf. 37 DY35
Bedford Gdns. W8 76 DA74
Bedford Hill SW12 105 DH88
Bedford Hill SW16 105 DH88
Bedford Ho. SW4 91 DL84
Bedford Pk., Croy. 120 DQ102
Bedford Pas. SW6 89 CY80
Dawes Rd.
Bedford Pl. W1 77 DJ71
Charlotte St.
Bedford Pl. WC1 5 P6
Bedford Pl. WC1 77 DL71
Bedford Pl., Croy. 120 DR102
Bedford Rd. E6 81 EN67
Bedford Rd. E17 51 EA54
Bedford Rd. E18 52 EG54
Bedford Rd. N2 62 DE55
Bedford Rd. N8 63 DK58
Bedford Rd. N9 50 DV45
Bedford Rd. N15 64 DS56
Bedford Rd. N22 49 DL53
Bedford Rd. NW7 46 CS47
Bedford Rd. SW4 91 DL83
Bedford Rd. W4 88 CR76
Bedford Rd. W13 73 CH73
Bedford Rd., Har. 58 CC58
Bedford Rd., Ilf. 67 EP62
Bedford Rd., Nthwd. 43 BQ48
Bedford Rd., Orp. 124 EV103
Bedford Rd., Ruis. 57 BT63
Bedford Rd., Sid. 109 ES90
Bedford Rd., Twick. 101 CD90
Bedford Rd., Wor.Pk. 117 CW103
Bedford Row WC1 6 C6
Bedford Row WC1 77 DM71
Bedford Sq. WC1 5 N7
Bedford Sq. WC1 77 DK71
Bedford St. WC2 5 P10
Bedford St. WC2 77 DL73
Bedford St., Wat. 29 BV39
Bedford Ter. SW2 105 DL85
Lyham Rd.
Bedford Way WC1 5 N5
Bedford Way WC1 77 DK70
Bedfordbury WC2 9 P1
Bedgebury Gdns. SW19 103 CY89
Bedgebury Rd. SE9 94 EK84
Bedivere Rd., Brom. 108 EG90
Bedlow Way, Croy. 133 DM105
Bedmond Grn., Abb.L. 15 BT27
Bedmond La., Abb.L. 15 BV25
Bedmond Rd., Abb.L. 15 BT29
Bedonwell Rd. SE2 96 EY79
Bedonwell Rd., Belv. 96 EY79
Bedonwell Rd., Bexh. 96 EZ81
Bedser Clo. SE11 91 DM79
Harleyford Rd.
Bedser Clo., Th.Hth. 120 DQ97
Bedser Dr., Grnf. 59 CD64
Bedster Gdns., W.Mol. 114 CB96
Bedwardine Rd. SE19 106 DS94
Bedwell Gdns., Hayes 85 BS78
Bedwell Rd. N17 50 DS53

Bedwell Rd., Belv. 96 FA78
Bedwin Way SE16 92 DV78
Catlin St.
Beeby Rd. E16 80 EH71
Beech Ave. N20 48 DE46
Beech Ave. W3 74 CS74
Beech Ave., Brent. 87 CH80
Beech Ave., Buck.H. 52 EH47
Beech Ave., Enf. 35 DN35
Beech Ave., Rad. 17 CG33
Beech Ave., Ruis. 57 BV60
Beech Ave., Sid. 110 EU87
Beech Ave., S.Croy. 134 DR111
Beech Ave., Swan. 125 FF98
Beech Ave., West. 150 EK119
Westmore Rd.
Beech Clo. N9 36 DU44
Beech Clo. SE8 93 DZ79
Clyde St.
Beech Clo. SW15 103 CU87
Beech Clo. SW19 103 CW93
Beech Clo., Ashf. 99 BR92
Beech Clo., Cars. 118 DF103
Beech Clo., Cob. 128 CA112
Beech Clo., Horn. 69 FH62
Beech Clo., Stai. 98 BK87
St. Marys Cres.
Beech Clo., Sun. 114 BX96
Harfield Rd.
Beech Clo., Walt. 128 BW105
Beech Clo., W.Byf. 126 BL112
Beech Clo., West Dr. 84 BN76
Beech Clo. Ct., Cob. 128 BZ111
Beech Copse, Brom. 123 EM96
Beech Copse, S.Croy. 134 DS106
Beech Ct. E17 65 ED55
Beech Ct. SE9 108 EL86
Beech Ct., Ilf. 67 EN62
Riverdene Rd.
Beech Dell, Kes. 137 EM105
Beech Dr. N2 48 DF54
Beech Dr., Borwd. 32 CM40
Beech Dr., Tad. 145 CZ122
Beech Dr., Wok. 140 BG124
Beech Fm. Rd., Warl. 149 EC120
Beech Gdns. EC2 78 DQ71
Aldersgate St.
Beech Gdns. W5 88 CL75
Beech Gdns., Dag. 83 FB66
Beech Gro., Add. 126 BH105
Beech Gro., Croy. 135 DY110
Beech Gro., Epsom 145 CV117
Beech Gro., Ilf. 53 ES51
Beech Gro., Mitch. 119 DK99
Beech Gro., N.Mal. 116 CR97
Beech Hall Cres. E4 51 ED52
Beech Hall Rd. E4 51 EC52
Beech Hill, Barn. 34 DD38
Beech Hill Ave., Barn. 34 DC39
Beech Hill Gdns., Wal.Abb. 38 EH37
Beech Holt, Lthd. 143 CJ122
Beech Ho., Croy. 135 EB107
Beech Ho. Rd., Croy. 120 DR104
Beech La., Buck.H. 52 EH47
Beech Lawns N12 48 DD50
Beech Pl., Epp. 25 ET31
Beech Rd. N11 49 DL51
Beech Rd. SW16 119 DL96
Beech Rd., Epsom 145 CT115
Beech Rd., Felt. 99 BS87
Beech Rd., Orp. 138 EU108
Beech Rd., Sev. 155 FH125
Victoria Rd.
Beech Rd., Wat. 29 BU37
Beech Rd., West. 150 EH118
Beech Rd., Wey. 127 BR105
Beech Row, Rich. 102 CL91
Beech St. EC2 7 H6
Beech St. EC2 78 DQ71
Beech St., Rom. 69 FC56
Beech Tree Glade E4 52 EF46
Forest Side
Beech Wk. NW7 46 CS51
Beech Wk., Dart. 97 FG84
Beech Wk., Epsom 131 CU111
Beech Way NW10 74 CR66
Beech Way, Epsom 145 CT115
Beech Way, S.Croy. 135 DX113
Beech Way, Twick. 100 CA90
Beechcroft, Ash. 144 CM119
Beechcroft, Chis. 109 EN94
Beechcroft Ave. NW11 61 CZ59
Beechcroft Ave., Bexh. 97 FD81
Beechcroft Ave., Har. 58 CA59
Beechcroft Ave., Ken. 148 DR115
Beechcroft Ave., N.Mal. 116 CQ95
Beechcroft Ave., Rick. 29 BQ44
Beechcroft Ave., Sthl. 72 BZ74
Beechcroft Clo., Houns. 86 BY80
Beechcroft Clo., Orp. 137 ER105
Beechcroft Gdns., Wem. 60 CM62
Beechcroft Manor, Wey. 113 BR104
Beechcroft Rd. E18 52 EH54
Beechcroft Rd. SW14 88 CQ83
Elm Rd.
Beechcroft Rd. SW17 104 DE89
Beechcroft Rd., Chess. 130 CM105
Beechcroft Rd., Orp. 137 ER105
Beechcroft Rd. (Bushey), Wat. 30 BY43
Beechdale N21 49 DM47
Beechdale Rd. SW2 105 DM86
Beechdene, Tad. 145 CV122
Beechen Cliff Way, Islw. 87 CF81
Henley Clo.
Beechen Gro., Pnr. 58 BZ55
Beechen Gro., Wat. 29 BV41
Beechenlea La., Swan. 125 FG98
Beeches, The, Bans. 146 DB116
Beeches, The, Houns. 86 CB81
Beeches, The, Lthd. 143 CE124
Beeches, The, St.Alb. 17 CD27
Beeches Ave., Cars. 132 DE108
Beeches Clo. SE20 120 DW95
Genoa Rd.
Beeches Clo., Tad. 146 DA123
Beeches Ct., Brom. 108 EG93
Avondale Rd.
Beeches Rd. SW17 104 DE90
Beeches Rd., Sutt. 117 CY102
Beeches Wk., Cars. 132 DD109
Beeches Wd., Tad. 146 DA122
Beechfield, Bans. 132 DB113
Beechfield, Kings L. 14 BM30
Beechfield Cotts., Brom. 122 EJ96
Widmore Rd.
Beechfield Gdns., Rom. 69 FC59
Beechfield Rd. N4 64 DQ58
Beechfield Rd. SE6 107 DZ88
Beechfield Rd., Brom. 122 EJ96
Beechfield Rd., Erith 97 FE80
Beechfield Wk., Wal.Abb. 37 ED35
Beechhill Rd. SE9 109 EN85
Beechmeads, Cob. 128 BX113
Beechmont Clo., Brom. 108 EE92
Beechmont Rd., Sev. 155 FH129
Beechmore Gdns., Sutt. 117 CX103
Beechmore Rd. SW11 90 DF81
Beechmount Ave. W7 73 CD71
Beecholm Ms., Wal.Cr. 23 DX28
Beecholme, Bans. 131 CY114
Beecholme Ave., Mitch. 119 DH95
Beecholme Est. E5 64 DV62
Prout Rd.
Beechpark Way, Wat. 29 BS37
Beechtree Clo., Stan. 45 CJ50
Beechtree Pl., Sutt. 132 DB106
St. Nicholas Way
Beechvale Clo. N12 48 DE50
Beechway, Bex. 110 EX86
Beechway, S.Croy. 135 DX113
Beechwood Ave. N3 61 CZ55
Beechwood Ave., Couls. 147 DH115
Beechwood Ave., Grnf. 72 CB69
Beechwood Ave., Har. 58 CB62
Beechwood Ave., Hayes 71 BR73
Beechwood Ave., Orp. 137 ES106
Beechwood Ave., Pot.B. 20 DB33
Beechwood Ave., Rich. 88 CN81
Beechwood Ave., Ruis. 57 BT61
Beechwood Ave., Stai. 98 BH93
Beechwood Ave., Sun. 99 BU93
Beechwood Ave., Tad. 146 DA121
Beechwood Ave., Th.Hth. 119 DP98
Beechwood Ave., Uxb. 70 BM72
Beechwood Ave., Wey. 127 BS105
Beechwood Clo. NW7 46 CR50
Beechwood Clo., Surb. 115 CK101
Beechwood Clo. (Cheshunt), Wal.Cr. 22 DS26
Beechwood Clo., Wey. 127 BS105
Beechwood Ct., Cars. 132 DF105
Beechwood Ct., Sun. 99 BU93
Beechwood Cres., Bexh. 96 EX83
Beechwood Dr., Cob. 128 CA111
Beechwood Dr., Kes. 136 EK105
Beechwood Dr., Wdf.Grn. 52 EF50
Beechwood Gdns. NW10 74 CM69
St. Annes Gdns.
Beechwood Gdns., Cat. 148 DU122
Beechwood Gdns., Har. 58 CB62
Beechwood Gdns., Ilf. 67 EM57
Beechwood Gdns., Rain. 83 FH71
Beechwood Gro. W3 74 CS73
East Acton La.
Beechwood Gro., Surb. 115 CJ101
Beechwood La., Warl. 149 DX119
Beechwood Manor, Wey. 127 BS105
Beechwood Ms. N9 50 DU47
Beechwood Pk. E18 66 EG55
Beechwood Pk., Lthd. 143 CJ123
Beechwood Ri., Chis. 109 EP91
Beechwood Ri., Wat. 29 BV36
Beechwood Rd. E8 78 DT65
Beechwood Rd. N8 63 DK56
Beechwood Rd., Cat. 148 DU122
Beechwood Rd., S.Croy. 134 DS110
Beechwoods Ct. SE19 106 DT92
Crystal Palace Par.
Beechworth Clo. NW3 62 DA61
Beecot La., Walt. 114 BW103
Beecroft Rd. SE4 107 DY85
Beehive Clo. E8 78 DT66
Beehive Clo., Borwd. 31 CK44
Beehive Clo., Uxb. 70 BM66
Honey Hill
Beehive La., Ilf. 67 EM57
Beehive Pas. EC3 7 M9
Beehive Pl. SW9 91 DN83
Beehive Rd. (Cheshunt), Wal.Cr. 21 DP28
Beeken Dene, Orp. 137 EQ105
Isabella Dr.
Beeleigh Rd., Mord. 118 DB98
Beeston Clo. E8 64 DU64
Ferncliff Rd.
Beeston Clo., Wat. 44 BX49
Beeston Dr., Wal.Cr. 23 DX27
Beeston Pl. SW1 9 J7
Beeston Pl. SW1 91 DH76
Beeston Rd., Barn. 34 DD44
Beeston Way, Felt. 100 BW86
Beethoven Rd., Borwd. 31 CJ44
Beethoven St. W10 75 CY69
Beeton Clo., Pnr. 44 CA52
Begbie Rd. SE3 94 EJ81
Beggars Bush La., Wat. 29 BR43
Beggars Hill, Epsom 130 CS107
Beggars Hollow, Enf. 36 DR37
Beggars Roost La., Sutt. 132 DA107
Begonia Clo. E6 80 EL71
Begonia Pl., Hmptn. 100 CA93
Gresham Rd.
Begonia Wk. W12 75 CT72
Du Cane Rd.
Beira St. SW12 105 DH87
Beken Ct., Wat. 30 BW35
Bekesbourne St. E14 79 DY72
Ratcliffe La.
Bekesbourne Twr., Orp. 124 EX102
Belcroft Clo., Brom. 108 EF94
Hope Pk.
Beldam Haw, Sev. 138 FA112
Beldham Gdns., W.Mol. 114 CB97
Belfairs Dr., Rom. 68 EW59
Belfairs Grn., Wat. 44 BX50
Heysham Dr.
Belfast Rd. N16 64 DT61
Belfast Rd. SE25 120 DV98
Belfield Rd., Epsom 130 CR109
Belfont Wk. N7 63 DL63
Belford Gro. SE18 95 EN77
Belford Rd., Borwd. 32 CM38
Belfort Rd. SE15 92 DW82
Belfry Ave., Uxb. 42 BG53
Belfry La., Rick. 42 BJ46
Belgrade Rd. N16 64 DS63
Belgrade Rd., Hmptn. 114 CB95
Belgrave Ave., Wat. 29 BT43
Belgrave Clo. N14 35 DJ43
Prince George Ave.
Belgrave Clo. W3 88 CQ75
Avenue Rd.
Belgrave Clo., Orp. 124 EW98
Belgrave Clo., Walt. 127 BV105
Belgrave Cres., Sun. 113 BV95
Belgrave Dr., Kings L. 15 BQ28
Belgrave Gdns. N14 35 DK43
Belgrave Gdns. NW8 76 DB67
Belgrave Gdns., Stan. 45 CJ50
Copley Rd.
Belgrave Ms., Uxb. 70 BK70
Belgrave Ms. N. SW1 8 F5
Belgrave Ms. N. SW1 90 DG76
Belgrave Ms. S. SW1 8 G6
Belgrave Ms. S. SW1 90 DG76
Belgrave Ms. W. SW1 8 F6
Belgrave Ms. W. SW1 90 DG76
Belgrave Pl. SW1 8 G6
Belgrave Pl. SW1 90 DG76
Belgrave Rd. E10 65 EC60
Belgrave Rd. E11 66 EG61
Belgrave Rd. E13 80 EJ69
Belgrave Rd. E17 65 EA57
Belgrave Rd. SE25 120 DU98
Belgrave Rd. SW1 9 K9
Belgrave Rd. SW1 91 DH77
Belgrave Rd. SW13 89 CT80
Belgrave Rd., Houns. 86 BZ83
Belgrave Rd., Ilf. 67 EM60
Belgrave Rd., Mitch. 118 DD97
Belgrave Rd., Sun. 113 BV95
Belgrave Sq. SW1 8 F6
Belgrave Sq. SW1 90 DG76
Belgrave St. E1 79 DX71
Belgrave Ter., Wdf.Grn. 52 EG48
Belgrave Wk., Mitch. 118 DD97
Belgrave Yd. SW1 9 H7
Belgravia Gdns., Brom. 108 EE93
Belgravia Ho. SW4 105 DK86
Belgravia Ms., Kings.T. 115 CK98
Belgrove St. WC1 6 A2
Belgrove St. WC1 77 DL69
Belham Rd., Kings L. 14 BM28
Belham Wk. SE5 92 DR81
D'Eynsford Rd.
Belhaven Ct., Borwd. 32 CM39
Belinda Rd. SW9 91 DP83
Belitha Vill. N1 77 DM66
Bell Ave., Rom. 55 FH53
Bell Ave., West Dr. 84 BM76
Bell Clo., Abb.L. 15 BT27
Bell Clo., Pnr. 44 BW54
Bell Clo., Ruis. 57 BT62
Bell Common, Epp. 25 ES32
Bell Ct., Surb. 116 CP103
Barnsbury La.
Bell Cres., Couls. 147 DH121
Maple Way
Bell Dr. SW18 103 CY87
Bell Fm. Ave., Dag. 69 FC62
Bell Gdns. E17 65 DZ57
Markhouse Rd.
Bell Gdns., Orp. 124 EW99
Bell Grn. SE26 107 DZ90
Bell Grn. La. SE26 107 DZ92
Bell Hill, Croy. 120 DQ104
Surrey St.
Bell Ho. Rd., Rom. 69 FC60
Bell Inn Yd. EC3 7 L9
Bell La. E1 7 P7
Bell La. E1 78 DT71
Bell La. E16 80 EG74
Bell La. NW4 61 CW56
Bell La., Abb.L. 15 BT27
Bell La., Enf. 37 DX38
Bell La., Hat. 20 DA25
Bell La., Lthd. 143 CD123
Bell La., St.Alb. 18 CL29
Bell La., Twick. 101 CG88
The Embk.
Bell La., Wem. 59 CK61
Magnet Rd.
Bell La. Clo., Lthd. 143 CD123
Bell Meadow SE19 106 DS91
Dulwich Wd. Ave.
Bell Rd., E.Mol. 115 CD99
Bell Rd., Enf. 36 DR39
Bell Rd., Houns. 86 CB83
Bell St. NW1 4 B6
Bell St. NW1 76 DE71
Bell Water Gate SE18 95 EN76
Bell Wf. La. EC4 7 J10
Bell Yd. WC2 6 D9
Bell Yd. WC2 77 DN72
Bellamy Clo. W14 89 CZ78
Aisgill Ave.
Bellamy Clo., Edg. 46 CQ48
Bellamy Clo., Uxb. 56 BN62
Bellamy Clo., Wat. 29 BU39
Bellamy Dr., Stan. 45 CH53
Bellamy Rd. E4 51 EB51
Bellamy Rd., Enf. 36 DR40
Bellamy Rd. (Cheshunt), Wal.Cr. 23 DY29
Bellamy St. SW12 105 DH87
Bellasis Ave. SW2 105 DL89
Bellclose Rd., West Dr. 84 BL75
Belle Staines Pleasaunce E4 51 EA47
Belle Vue, Grnf. 73 CD67
Belle Vue Clo., Stai. 112 BG95
Belle Vue Est. NW4 61 CW56
Bell La.
Belle Vue La. (Bushey), Wat. 45 CD46
Belle Vue Rd. E17 51 ED54
Belle Vue Rd. NW4 61 CW56
Bell La.
Belle Vue Rd., Orp. 137 EN110
Standard Rd.
Bellefield Rd., Orp. 124 EV99
Bellefields Rd. SW9 91 DM83
Bellegrove Clo., Well. 95 ET82
Bellegrove Rd., Well. 95 ES82
Bellenden Rd. SE15 92 DT83
Belleville Rd. SW11 104 DE85
Bellevue Ms. N11 48 DG50
Bellevue Rd.
Bellevue Par. SW17 104 DE88
Bellevue Rd.
Bellevue Pk., Th.Hth. 120 DQ97
Bellevue Pl. E1 78 DW70
Bellevue Rd. N11 48 DG49
Bellevue Rd. SW13 89 CU82
Bellevue Rd. SW17 104 DE88
Bellevue Rd. W13 73 CH70
Bellevue Rd., Bexh. 110 EZ85
Bellevue Rd., Kings.T. 116 CL97
Bellevue Rd., Rom. 55 FC51
Bellew St. SW17 104 DC90
Bellfield, Croy. 135 DZ108
Bellfield Ave., Har. 45 CD50
Bellflower Clo. E6 80 EL71
Sorrel Gdns.
Bellgate Ms. NW5 63 DH62
York Ri.
Bellingham Ct., Bark. 82 EV69
Renwick Rd.
Bellingham Grn. SE6 107 EA90
Bellingham Rd. SE6 107 EC90
Bellmarsh Rd., Add. 126 BH105
Bellmount Wd. Ave., Wat. 29 BS39
Bello Clo. SE24 105 DP87
Bellot Gdns. SE10 94 EE78
Bellot St. SE10 94 EE78
Bellring Clo., Belv. 96 FA79
Bells All. SW6 90 DA82
Bells Gdn. Est. SE15 92 DU80
Buller Clo.
Bells Hill, Barn. 33 CX43
Belltrees Gro. SW16 105 DM92
Bellwood Rd. SE15 93 DX84
Belmarsh Rd. SE28 95 ES75
Western Way
Belmont Ave. N9 50 DU46
Belmont Ave. N13 49 DL50
Belmont Ave. N17 64 DQ55
Belmont Ave., Barn. 34 DF43
Belmont Ave., N.Mal. 117 CU99
Belmont Ave., Sthl. 86 BY76
Belmont Ave., Well. 95 ES82
Belmont Ave., Wem. 74 CM67
Belmont Circle, Har. 45 CH54
Kenton La.
Belmont Clo. E4 51 ED50
Belmont Clo. N20 48 DB46
Belmont Clo. SW4 91 DJ83
Belmont Clo., Barn. 34 DF42
Belmont Clo., Uxb. 70 BK65
Belmont Clo., Wdf.Grn. 52 EH49
Belmont Ct. NW11 61 CZ57
Belmont Gro. SE13 93 ED83
Belmont Hall Ct. SE13 93 ED83
Belmont Gro.
Belmont Hill SE13 93 EC83
Belmont La., Chis. 109 ER92
Belmont La., Stan. 45 CJ52
Belmont Pk. SE13 93 ED84
Belmont Pk. Clo. SE13 93 ED84
Belmont Pk.
Belmont Pk. Rd. E10 65 EB58
Belmont Ri., Sutt. 131 CZ107
Belmont Rd. N15 64 DQ56
Belmont Rd. N17 64 DQ55
Belmont Rd. SE25 120 DV99
Belmont Rd. SW4 91 DJ83
Belmont Rd. W4 88 CR77
Belmont Rd., Beck. 121 DZ96
Belmont Rd., Chis. 109 EP92
Belmont Rd., Erith 96 FA80
Belmont Rd., Har. 59 CF55
Belmont Rd., Ilf. 67 EQ62
Belmont Rd., Lthd. 143 CG122
Belmont Rd., Sutt. 132 DA110
Belmont Rd., Twick. 101 CD89
Belmont Rd., Uxb. 70 BK66
Belmont Rd., Wall. 133 DH106
Belmont Rd. (Bushey), Wat. 30 BY43
Belmont St. NW1 76 DG66
Belmont Ter. W4 88 CR77
Belmont Rd.
Belmor, Borwd. 32 CN43
Belmore Ave., Hayes 71 BU72
Belmore La. N7 63 DK64
Belmore St. SW8 91 DK81
Beloe Clo. SW15 89 CU83
Belper Ct. E5 65 DX63
Pedro St.
Belsham St. E9 78 DW65
Belsize Ave. N13 49 DM51
Belsize Ave. NW3 76 DD65
Belsize Ave. W13 87 CH76
Belsize Cres. NW3 62 DD64
Belsize Gdns., Sutt. 132 DB105
Belsize Gro. NW3 76 DE65
Belsize La. NW3 76 DD65
Belsize Ms. NW3 76 DD65
Belsize La.
Belsize Pk. NW3 76 DD65
Belsize Pk. Gdns. NW3 76 DE65
Belsize Pk. Ms. NW3 76 DD65
Belsize La.
Belsize Pl. NW3 76 DD65
Belsize La.
Belsize Rd. NW6 76 DB67
Belsize Rd., Har. 45 CD52
Belsize Sq. NW3 76 DD65
Belsize Ter. NW3 76 DD65
Belson Rd. SE18 95 EM77
Beltane Dr. SW19 103 CX90
Belthorn Cres. SW12 105 DJ87
Belton Rd. E7 80 EH66
Belton Rd. E11 66 EE63
Belton Rd. N17 64 DS55
Belton Rd. NW2 75 CU65
Belton Rd., Sid. 110 EU91
Belton Way E3 79 EA71
Beltona Gdns. (Cheshunt), Wal.Cr. 23 DX27
Beltran Rd. SW6 90 DB82
Beltwood Rd., Belv. 97 FC77
Belvedere Ave. SW19 103 CY92
Belvedere Ave., Ilf. 53 EP54
Belvedere Bldgs. SE1 10 G5
Belvedere Clo., Esher 128 CB106
Belvedere Clo., Tedd. 101 CE92
Belvedere Clo., Wey. 126 BN106
Belvedere Ct. N2 62 DD57
Belvedere Dr. SW19 103 CY92
Belvedere Gdns., St.Alb. 16 CA27
Belvedere Gdns., W.Mol. 114 BZ99
Belvedere Gro. SW19 103 CY92
Belvedere Ho., Felt. 99 BU88
Belvedere Ind. Est., Belv. 97 FC76
Crabtree Manorway S.
Belvedere Ms. SE15 92 DW83
Belvedere Pl. SE1 10 G5
Belvedere Rd. E10 65 DY60
Belvedere Rd. SE1 10 C4
Belvedere Rd. SE1 91 DM75
Belvedere Rd. SE2 82 EX74
Belvedere Rd. SE19 106 DT94
Belvedere Rd. W7 87 CE76
Belvedere Rd., Bexh. 96 EZ83
Belvedere Rd., West. 151 EM118
Belvedere Sq. SW19 103 CY92
Belvedere Strand NW9 47 CT54
Belvedere Way, Har. 60 CL58
Belvoir Clo. SE9 108 EL90
Belvoir Rd. SE22 106 DU87
Belvue Clo., Nthlt. 72 CA66
Belvue Rd., Nthlt. 72 CA66
Bembridge Clo. NW6 75 CY66
Bembridge Gdns., Ruis. 57 BR61
Bemerton Est. N1 77 DL66
Bemerton St. N1 77 DM67
Bemish Rd. SW15 89 CX83
Bempton Dr., Ruis. 57 BV61
Bemsted Rd. E17 65 DZ55
Ben Hale Clo., Stan. 45 CH49
Ben Jonson Rd. E1 79 DX71
Ben Smith Way SE16 92 DU76
Jamaica Rd.
Ben Tillet Clo. E16 81 EM74
Newland St.
Ben Tillet Clo., Bark. 82 EU66
Benares Rd. SE18 95 ET77
Benbow Rd. W6 89 CV76
Benbow St. SE8 93 EA79
Benbow Waye, Uxb. 70 BJ71
Benbury Clo., Brom. 107 EC92
Bench Fld., S.Croy. 134 DT107
Bencombe Rd., Pur. 133 DN114
Bencroft (Cheshunt), Wal.Cr. 22 DU26
Bencroft Rd. SW16 105 DJ94
Bencurtis Pk., W.Wick. 121 ED104
Bendall Ms. NW1 4 C6
Bendemeer Rd. SW15 89 CX83
Bendish Rd. E6 80 EL66

Bendmore Ave. SE2 96 EU78
Bendon Valley SW18 104 DB87
Bendysh Rd. (Bushey), Wat. 30 BY41
Benedict Clo., Belv. 96 EY76
Tunstock Way
Benedict Clo., Orp. 123 ES104
Benedict Dr., Felt. 99 BR87
Benedict Rd. SW9 91 DM83
Benedict Rd., Mitch. 118 DD97
Benedict Way N2 62 DC55
Benedictine Gate, Wal.Cr. 23 DY27
Benenden Grn., Brom. 122 EF99
Benett Gdns. SW16 119 DL96
Benfleet Clo., Cob. 128 BY112
Benfleet Clo., Sutt. 118 DC104
Bengal Ct. EC3 78 DR72
Birchin La.
Bengal Rd., Ilf. 67 EP63
Bengarth Dr., Har. 45 CD54
Bengarth Rd., Nthlt. 72 BX67
Bengeworth Rd. SE5 92 DQ83
Bengeworth Rd., Har. 59 CG61
Benham Clo. SW11 90 DD83
Benham Clo., Chess. 129 CJ107
Merritt Gdns.
Benham Clo., Couls. 147 DP118
Benham Gdns., Houns. 86 BZ84
Benham Rd. W7 73 CE71
Benhams Pl. NW3 62 DC63
Holly Wk.
Benhill Ave., Sutt. 132 DB105
Benhill Rd. SE5 92 DR80
Benhill Rd., Sutt. 118 DC104
Benhill Wd. Rd., Sutt. 132 DC105
Benhilton Gdns., Sutt. 118 DB104
Benhurst Ave., Horn. 69 FH63
Benhurst Clo., S.Croy. 135 DX110
Benhurst Ct. SW16 105 DN92
Benhurst Gdns., S.Croy. 134 DW110
Benhurst La. SW16 105 DN92
Benin St. SE13 107 ED87
Benjafield Clo. N18 50 DV49
Brettenham Rd.
Benjamin Clo. E8 78 DU67
Benjamin Clo., Horn. 69 FG58
Benjamin St. EC1 6 F6
Benjamin St. EC1 77 DP71
Benledi St. E14 79 ED72
Benn St. E9 79 DY65
Bennerley Rd. SW11 104 DE85
Bennet's Hill EC4 6 G10
Bennetsfield Rd., Uxb. 71 BP74
Bennett Clo., Cob. 127 BU113
Bennett Clo., Kings.T. 115 CJ95
Bennett Clo., Nthwd. 43 BT52
Bennett Clo., Well. 96 EU82
Bennett Gro. SE13 93 EB81
Bennett Pk. SE3 94 EF83
Bennett Rd. E13 80 EJ70
Bennett Rd. N16 64 DS63
Bennett Rd., Rom. 68 EY58
Bennett St. SW1 9 K2
Bennett St. W4 88 CS79
Bennetts Ave., Croy. 121 DY103
Bennetts Ave., Grnf. 73 CE67
Bennetts Castle La., Dag. 68 EW63
Bennetts Clo. N17 50 DT51
Bennetts Clo., Mitch. 119 DH95
Bennetts Copse, Chis. 108 EL93
Bennetts Way, Croy. 121 DY103
Bennetts Yd. SW1 9 N7
Benningholme Rd., Edg. 46 CS51
Bennington Rd. N17 50 DS53
Bennington Rd., Wdf.Grn. 52 EE52
Benn's Wk., Rich. 88 CL84
Rosedale Rd.
Benrek Clo., Ilf. 53 EQ53
Bensbury Clo. SW15 103 CW87
Bensham Clo., Th.Hth. 120 DQ98
Bensham Gro., Th.Hth. 120 DQ96
Bensham La., Croy. 119 DP101
Bensham La., Th.Hth. 119 DP98
Bensham Manor Rd., Th.Hth. 120 DQ98
Bensington Ct., Felt. 99 BR86
Benskin Rd., Wat. 29 BU43
Bensley Clo. N11 48 DF50
Benson Ave. E6 80 EJ68
Benson Clo., Houns. 86 CA84
Benson Clo., Uxb. 70 BL71
Benson Quay E1 78 DW73
Garnet St.
Benson Rd. SE23 106 DW88
Benson Rd., Croy. 119 DN104
Bentfield Gdns. SE9 108 EJ90
Aldersgrove Ave.
Benthal Rd. N16 64 DU61
Benthall Gdns., Ken. 148 DQ116
Bentham Rd. E9 79 DX65
Bentham Rd. SE28 82 EV73
Bentham Wk. NW10 60 CQ64
Bentinck Ms. W1 4 G8
Bentinck Pl. NW8 4 B1
Bentinck Rd., West Dr. 70 BK74
Bentinck St. W1 4 G8
Bentinck St. W1 76 DG72
Bentley Dr., Ilf. 67 EQ58
Bentley Dr., Wey. 126 BN109
Bentley Heath La., Barn. 33 CZ35
Bentley Rd. N1 78 DS65
Tottenham Rd.
Bentley Way, Stan. 45 CG50
Bentley Way, Wdf.Grn. 52 EG48
Benton Rd., Ilf. 67 ER60
Benton Rd., Wat. 44 BX50
Bentons La. SE27 106 DQ91
Bentons Ri. SE27 106 DR92
Bentry Clo., Dag. 68 EY61
Bentry Rd., Dag. 68 EY61
Bentworth Rd. W12 75 CV72
Benwell Ct., Sun. 113 BU95
Benwell Rd. N7 63 DN63
Benwick Clo. SE16 92 DV77
Benworth St. E3 79 DZ69
Benyon Rd. N1 78 DR67
Southgate Rd.
Beomonds Row, Cher. 112 BG101
Berber Rd. SW11 104 DF85
Berberis Wk., West Dr. 84 BL77
Berceau Wk., Wat. 29 BS39
Bercta Rd. SE9 109 EQ89
Bere St. E1 79 DX73
Cranford St.
Berenger Wk. SW10 90 DD80
Blantyre St.
Berens Rd. NW10 75 CX69
Berens Rd., Orp. 124 EX99
Berens Way, Chis. 123 ET98
Beresford Ave. N20 48 DF47
Beresford Ave. W7 73 CD71
Beresford Ave., Surb. 116 CP102
Beresford Ave., Twick. 101 CJ86
Beresford Ave., Wem. 74 CM67
Beresford Dr., Brom. 122 EL97
Beresford Dr., Wdf.Grn. 52 EJ49
Beresford Gdns., Enf. 36 DS42
Beresford Gdns., Houns. 100 BZ85
Beresford Gdns., Rom. 68 EY57
Beresford Rd. E4 52 EE46
Beresford Rd. E17 51 EB53
Beresford Rd. N2 62 DE55
Beresford Rd. N5 64 DR64
Beresford Rd. N8 63 DN57
Beresford Rd., Har. 59 CD57
Beresford Rd., Kings.T. 116 CM95
Beresford Rd., N.Mal. 116 CQ98
Beresford Rd., Sthl. 72 BX74
Beresford Rd., Sutt. 131 CZ108
Beresford Sq. SE18 95 EP77
Beresford St. SE18 95 EP76
Beresford Ter. N5 64 DQ64
Berestede Rd. W6 89 CT78
Bergen Sq. SE16 93 DY76
Norway Gate
Berger Clo., Orp. 123 ER100
Berger Rd. E9 79 DX65
Berghem Ms. W14 89 CX76
Blythe Rd.
Bergholt Ave., Ilf. 66 EL57
Bergholt Cres. N16 64 DS59
Bergholt Ms. NW1 77 DJ66
Rossendale Way
Bering Wk. E16 80 EK72
Berisford Ms. SW18 104 DC86
Berkeley Ave., Bexh. 96 EX81
Berkeley Ave., Grnf. 73 CE65
Berkeley Ave., Houns. 85 BU81
Berkeley Ave., Ilf. 53 EN54
Berkeley Ave., Rom. 55 FC52
Berkeley Clo., Abb.L. 15 BT32
Berkeley Clo., Borwd. 32 CN43
Berkeley Clo., Kings.T. 102 CL94
Berkeley Clo., Orp. 123 ES101
Berkeley Clo., Pot.B. 19 CY32
Berkeley Clo., Ruis. 57 BU62
Berkeley Ct. N14 35 DJ44
Berkeley Ct., Wall. 119 DJ104
Berkeley Ct., Wey. 113 BR103
Berkeley Cres., Barn. 34 DD43
Berkeley Gdns. N21 50 DR45
Berkeley Gdns. W8 76 DA74
Brunswick Gdns.
Berkeley Gdns., Esher 129 CG107
Berkeley Gdns., Walt. 113 BT101
Berkeley Ho. E3 79 EA69
Wellington Way
Berkeley Ms. W1 4 E9
Berkeley Pl. SW19 103 CX93
Berkeley Pl., Epsom 144 CR115
Berkeley Rd. E12 66 EL64
Berkeley Rd. N8 63 DK57
Berkeley Rd. N15 64 DR58
Berkeley Rd. NW9 60 CN56
Berkeley Rd. SW13 89 CU81
Berkeley Rd., Uxb. 71 BQ66
Berkeley Sq. W1 9 J1
Berkeley Sq. W1 77 DH73
Berkeley St. W1 9 J2
Berkeley St. W1 77 DH74
Berkeley Wk. N7 63 DM61
Durham Rd.
Berkeley Waye, Houns. 86 BX80
Berkeleys, The, Lthd. 143 CE124
Berkhampstead Rd., Belv. 96 FA78
Berkhamsted Ave., Wem. 74 CM65
Berkley Ave., Wal.Cr. 23 DX34
Berkley Ct., Rick. 29 BR43
Mayfare
Berkley Dr., W.Mol. 114 BZ97
Berkley Gro. NW1 76 DF66
Berkley Rd.
Berkley Rd. NW1 76 DF66
Berkshire Clo., Cat. 148 DR122
Berkshire Gdns. N13 49 DN51
Berkshire Gdns. N18 50 DV50
Berkshire Rd. E9 79 DZ65
Berkshire Sq., Mitch. 119 DL98
Berkshire Way
Berkshire Way, Mitch. 119 DL98
Bermans Way NW10 60 CS63
Bermondsey Sq. SE1 11 N6
Bermondsey St. SE1 11 M3
Bermondsey St. SE1 92 DS75
Bermondsey Wall E. SE16 92 DU75
Bermondsey Wall W. SE16 92 DU75
Bernal Clo. SE28 82 EX73
Haldane Rd.
Bernard Ashley Dr. SE7 94 EH78
Bernard Ave. W13 87 CH76
Bernard Cassidy St. E16 80 EF71
Bernard Gdns. SW19 103 CZ92
Bernard Rd. N15 64 DT57
Bernard Rd., Rom. 69 FC59
Bernard Rd., Wall. 133 DH106
Bernard St. WC1 5 P5
Bernard St. WC1 77 DL70
Bernards Clo., Ilf. 53 EQ52
Bernato Clo., W.Byf. 126 BL112
Viscount Gdns.
Bernays Clo., Stan. 45 CJ51
Bernays Gro. SW9 91 DM84
Berne Rd., Th.Hth. 119 DP99
Bernel Dr., Croy. 121 DZ104
Berners Dr. W13 73 CG72
Berners Ms. W1 5 L7
Berners Ms. W1 77 DJ71
Berners Pl. W1 5 L8
Berners Pl. W1 77 DJ72
Berners Rd. N1 77 DN67
Berners Rd. N22 49 DN53
Berners St. W1 5 L7
Berners St. W1 77 DJ71
Bernersmede SE3 94 EG83
Blackheath Pk.
Berney Rd., Croy. 120 DR101
Bernville Way, Har. 60 CM57
Kenton Rd.
Bernwell Rd. E4 52 EE48
Berridge Grn., Edg. 46 CP52
Berridge Rd. SE19 106 DS92
Berriman Rd. N7 63 DM62
Berrington Dr., Lthd. 141 BT124
Berriton Rd., Har. 58 BZ60
Berry Ave., Wat. 29 BU36
Berry Clo. N21 49 DP46
Berry Clo. NW10 74 CS66
Berry Clo., Rick. 42 BH45
Berry Ct., Houns. 100 BZ85
Berry Gro. La. (Bushey), Wat. 30 BY38
Berry Hill, Stan. 45 CK49
Berry La. SE21 106 DR91
Berry La., Rick. 42 BH45
Berry Meade, Ash. 144 CM117
Berry Pl. EC1 6 G3
Berry St. EC1 6 G4
Berry St. EC1 77 DP70
Berry Wk., Ash. 144 CM119
Berry Way W5 88 CL76
Berry Way, Rick. 42 BH45
Berrybank Clo. E4 51 EC47
Greenbank Clo.
Berrydale Rd., Hayes 72 BY70
Berryfield Clo. E17 65 EB56
Berryfield Clo., Brom. 122 EL95
Berryfield Rd. SE17 10 G10
Berryfield Rd. SE17 91 DP78
Berryhill SE9 95 EP84
Berryhill Gdns. SE9 95 EP84
Berrylands SW20 117 CW97
Berrylands, Orp. 124 EW104
Berrylands, Surb. 116 CM100
Berrylands Rd., Surb. 116 CM100
Berryman Clo., Dag. 68 EW62
Bennetts Castle La.
Berrymans La. SE26 107 DX91
Berrymead Gdns. W3 88 CQ75
Berrymede Rd. W4 88 CR76
Berrys Grn. Rd., West. 151 EP115
Berrys Hill, West. 151 EP115
Berrys La., W.Byf. 126 BK111
Berryscroft Ct., Stai. 98 BJ94
Berryscroft Rd.
Berryscroft Rd., Stai. 98 BJ94
Bert Rd., Th.Hth. 120 DQ99
Bertal Rd. SW17 104 DD91
Berthon St. SE8 93 EA80
Bertie Rd. NW10 75 CU65
Bertie Rd. SE26 107 DX93
Bertram Cotts. SW19 104 DA94
Hartfield Rd.
Bertram Rd. NW4 61 CU58
Bertram Rd., Enf. 36 DU42
Bertram Rd., Kings.T. 102 CN94
Bertram St. N19 63 DH61
Bertram Way, Enf. 36 DT42
Bertrand St. SE13 93 EB83
Bertrand Way SE28 82 EV73
Berwick Ave., Hayes 72 BX72
Berwick Clo., Stan. 45 CF52
Gordon Ave.
Berwick Clo., Wal.Cr. 23 EA34
Berwick Cres., Sid. 109 ES86
Berwick La., Ong. 27 FE33
Berwick Rd. E16 80 EH72
Berwick Rd. N22 49 DP53
Berwick Rd., Borwd. 32 CL38
Berwick Rd., Well. 96 EV81
Berwick St. W1 5 L8
Berwick St. W1 77 DJ72
Berwick Way, Orp. 124 EU102
Berwick Way, Sev. 155 FH121
Berwyn Ave., Houns. 86 CB81
Berwyn Rd. SE24 105 DP88
Berwyn Rd., Rich. 88 CP84
Beryl Ave. E6 80 EL71
Beryl Rd. W6 89 CX78
Berystede, Kings.T. 102 CP94
Besant Ct. N1 64 DR64
Newington Grn. Rd.
Besant Rd. NW2 61 CY63
Besant Wk. N7 63 DM61
Newington Barrow Way
Besant Way NW10 60 CQ64
Besley St. SW16 105 DJ94
Bessant Dr., Rich. 88 CP81
Bessborough Gdns. SW1 9 N10
Bessborough Gdns. SW1 91 DK78
Bessborough Pl. SW1 9 M10
Bessborough Pl. SW1 91 DK78
Bessborough Rd. SW15 103 CU88
Bessborough Rd., Har. 59 CD60
Bessborough St. SW1 9 M10
Bessborough St. SW1 91 DK78
Bessels Grn. Rd., Sev. 154 FD123
Bessels Meadow, Sev. 154 FD124
Bessels Way, Sev. 154 FC124
Bessemer Rd. SE5 92 DQ82
Bessie Lansbury Clo. E6 81 EN72
Bessingby Rd., Ruis. 57 BV61
Bessingham Wk. SE4 93 DX84
Frendsbury Rd.
Besson St. SE14 92 DW81
Bessy St. E2 78 DW69
Roman Rd.
Bestwood St. SE8 93 DX77
Beswick Ms. NW6 76 DB65
Lymington Rd.
Betam Rd., Hayes 85 BR75
Betchworth Clo., Sutt. 132 DD106
Turnpike La.
Betchworth Rd., Ilf. 67 ES61
Betchworth Way, Croy. 135 EC109
Betenson Ave., Sev. 154 FF122
Betham Rd., Grnf. 73 CD69
Bethany Waye, Felt. 99 BS87
Bethecar Rd., Har. 59 CE57
Bethel Rd., Sev. 155 FJ123
Bethel Rd., Well. 96 EW83
Bethell Ave. E16 80 EF70
Bethell Ave., Ilf. 67 EN59
Bethersden Clo., Beck. 107 DZ94
Bethnal Grn. Rd. E1 7 P4
Bethnal Grn. Rd. E1 78 DT70
Bethnal Grn. Rd. E2 78 DT70
Bethune Ave. N11 48 DF49
Bethune Rd. N16 64 DR59
Bethune Rd. NW10 74 CR70
Bethwin Rd. SE5 91 DP80
Betjeman Clo., Couls. 147 DM117
Betjeman Clo., Pnr. 58 CA56
Betjeman Clo., Wal.Cr. 22 DU28
Rosedale Way
Betley Ct., Walt. 113 BV104
Betony Clo., Croy. 121 DX102
Primrose La.
Betoyne Ave. E4 52 EE49
Betsham Rd., Erith 97 FF80
Betstyle Rd. N11 49 DH49
Betterton Dr., Sid. 110 EY89
Betterton Rd., Rain. 83 FE69
Betterton St. WC2 5 P9
Betterton St. WC2 77 DL72
Bettles Clo., Uxb. 70 BJ68
Westcott Way
Bettons Pk. E15 80 EE67
Bettridge Rd. SW6 89 CZ82
Betts Clo., Beck. 121 DY96
Kendall Rd.
Betts Ms. E17 65 DZ58
Queen's Rd.
Betts Rd. E16 80 EH73
Victoria Dock Rd.
Betts St. E1 78 DV73
The Highway
Betts Way SE20 120 DV95
Betts Way, Surb. 115 CH102
Betula Clo., Ken. 148 DR115
Between Sts., Cob. 127 BU114
Beulah Ave., Th.Hth. 119 DM98
Beulah Rd.
Beulah Clo., Edg. 46 CP48
Beulah Cres., Th.Hth. 120 DQ96
Beulah Gro., Croy. 120 DQ100
Beulah Hill SE19 105 DP93
Beulah Path E17 65 EB57
Addison Rd.
Beulah Rd. E17 65 EB57
Beulah Rd. SW19 103 CZ94
Beulah Rd., Epp. 26 EU29
Beulah Rd., Sutt. 132 DA105
Beulah Rd., Th.Hth. 120 DQ97
Beulah Wk., Cat. 149 DY120
Beult Rd., Dart. 97 FG83
Bev Callender Clo. SW8 91 DH83
Daley Thompson Way
Bevan Ave., Bark. 82 EU66
Bevan Ct., Croy. 133 DN106
Bevan Pl., Swan. 125 FE98
Bevan Rd. SE2 96 EV78
Bevan Rd., Barn. 34 DF42
Bevan St. N1 78 DQ67
Bevenden St. N1 7 L2
Bevenden St. N1 78 DR69
Bevercote Wk., Belv. 96 EZ79
Osborne Rd.
Beveridge Rd. NW10 74 CS66
Curzon Cres.
Beverley NW8 4 B3
Beverley Ave. SW20 117 CT95
Beverley Ave., Houns. 86 BZ84
Beverley Ave., Sid. 109 ET87
Beverley Clo. N21 50 DQ46
Beverley Clo. SW11 90 DD84
Maysoule Rd.
Beverley Clo. SW13 89 CT82
Beverley Clo., Add. 126 BK106
Beverley Clo., Chess. 129 CJ105
Beverley Clo., Enf. 36 DS42
Beverley Clo., Epsom 131 CW111
Beverley Clo., Wey. 113 BS103
Beverley Cotts. SW15 102 CR91
Kingston Vale
Beverley Ct. N14 49 DJ45
Beverley Ct. SE4 93 DZ83
Beverley Cres., Wdf.Grn. 52 EH53
Beverley Dr., Edg. 60 CN55
Beverley Gdns. NW11 61 CY59
Beverley Gdns. SW13 89 CT83
Beverley Gdns., Stan. 45 CG53
Beverley Gdns. (Cheshunt), Wal.Cr. 22 DT30
Beverley Gdns., Wem. 60 CM60
Beverley Gdns., Wor.Pk. 117 CU102
Green La.
Beverley La. SW15 103 CT90
Beverley La., Kings.T. 102 CS94
Beverley Ms. E4 51 ED51
Beverley Rd.
Beverley Path SW13 89 CT82
Beverley Rd. E4 51 ED51
Beverley Rd. E6 80 EK69
Beverley Rd. SE20 120 DV96
Wadhurst Clo.
Beverley Rd. SW13 89 CT83
Beverley Rd. W4 89 CT78
Beverley Rd., Bexh. 97 FC82
Beverley Rd., Brom. 122 EL103
Beverley Rd., Dag. 68 EY63
Beverley Rd., Kings.T. 115 CJ95
Beverley Rd., Mitch. 119 DK98
Beverley Rd., N.Mal. 117 CU98
Beverley Rd., Ruis. 57 BU61
Beverley Rd., Sthl. 86 BY77
Beverley Rd., Sun. 113 BT95
Beverley Rd., Whyt. 148 DS116
Beverley Rd., Wor.Pk. 117 CW103
Beverley Way SW20 117 CT95
Beverley Way, N.Mal. 117 CT95
Beversbrook Rd. N19 63 DK62
Beverston Ms. W1 4 D7
Beverstone Rd. SW2 105 DM85
Beverstone Rd., Th.Hth. 119 DN98
Bevill Allen Clo. SW17 104 DF92
Bevill Clo. SE25 120 DU97
Bevin Clo. SE16 79 DY74
Bevin Ct. WC1 77 DN69
Holford St.
Bevin Rd., Hayes 71 BU69
Bevin Way WC1 6 D2
Bevington Rd. W10 75 CY71
Bevington Rd., Beck. 121 EB96
Bevington St. SE16 92 DU75
Bevis Marks EC3 7 N8
Bevis Marks EC3 78 DS72
Bewcastle Gdns., Enf. 35 DL42
Bewdley St. N1 77 DN66
Bewick St. SW8 91 DH82
Bewley Clo. (Cheshunt), Wal.Cr. 23 DX31
Bewley St. E1 78 DV73
Bewlys Rd. SE27 105 DP92
Bexhill Clo., Felt. 100 BY89
Bexhill Rd. N11 49 DK50
Bexhill Rd. SE4 107 DZ86
Bexhill Rd. SW14 88 CQ83
Bexhill Wk. E15 80 EE68
Mitre Rd.
Bexley Clo., Dart. 111 FE85
Bexley Gdns. N9 50 DR48
Bexley Gdns., Rom. 68 EV57
Bexley High St., Bex. 110 FA87
Bexley La., Dart. 111 FE85
Bexley La., Sid. 110 EW91
Bexley Rd. SE9 109 EP85
Bexley Rd., Erith 97 FC80
Beynon Rd., Cars. 132 DF106
Bianca Ho. N1 78 DS68
Crondall St.
Bianca Rd. SE15 92 DT79
Bibsworth Rd. N3 47 CZ54
Bibury Clo. SE15 92 DS79
Bicester Rd., Rich. 88 CN83
Bickenhall St. W1 4 E6
Bickenhall St. W1 76 DF71
Bickersteth Rd. SW17 104 DF93
Bickerton Rd. N19 63 DJ61
Bickley Cres., Brom. 122 EL98
Bickley Pk. Rd., Brom. 122 EL97
Bickley Rd. E10 65 EB59
Bickley Rd., Brom. 122 EK96
Bickley St. SW17 104 DE92
Bicknell Rd. SE5 92 DQ83
Bickney Way, Lthd. 142 CC122
Bicknoller Clo., Sutt. 132 DB110
Bicknoller Rd., Enf. 36 DS39
Bicknor Rd., Orp. 123 ES101
Bidborough Clo., Brom. 122 EF99
Bidborough St. WC1 5 P3
Bidborough St. WC1 77 DL69
Biddenden Way SE9 109 EN91
Biddenham Turn, Wat. 30 BW35
Bidder St. E16 80 EE71
Biddestone Rd. N7 63 DM63
Biddulph Rd. W9 76 DB69
Biddulph Rd., S.Croy. 134 DQ109
Bideford Ave., Grnf. 73 CH68
Bideford Clo., Edg. 46 CN53
Bideford Clo., Felt. 100 BZ90
Bideford Gdns., Enf. 50 DS45
Bideford Rd., Brom. 108 EF90
Bideford Rd., Enf. 37 DZ38

Bideford Rd., Ruis. 57 BV62
Bideford Rd., Well. 96 EV80
Bidhams Cres., Tad. 145 CW121
Bidwell Gdns. N11 49 DJ52
Bidwell St. SE15 92 DV81
Big Hill E5 64 DV60
Bigbury Clo. N17 50 DR52
Weir Hall Rd.
Bigbury Rd. N17 50 DS52
Barkham Rd.
Biggerstaff Rd. E15 79 EC67
Biggerstaff St. N4 63 DN61
Biggin Ave., Mitch. 118 DF95
Biggin Hill SE19 119 DP95
Biggin Hill Clo., Kings.T. 101 CJ92
Biggin Way SE19 105 DP94
Bigginwood Rd. SW16 105 DP94
Biggs Row SW15 89 CX83
Felsham Rd.
Bigland St. E1 78 DV72
Bignell Rd. SE18 95 EP78
Bignold Rd. E7 66 EG63
Bigwood Rd. NW11 62 DB57
Biko Clo., Uxb. 70 BJ72
Sefton Way
Bill Hamling Clo. SE9 109 EM89
Billet Clo., Rom. 68 EX55
Billet Rd. E17 51 DX53
Billet Rd., Rom. 68 EV56
Billet Rd., Stai. 98 BG90
Farnell Rd.
Billets Hart Clo. W7 87 CE75
Billing Pl. SW10 90 DB80
Billing Rd. SW10 90 DB80
Billing St. SW10 90 DB80
Billingford Clo. SE4 93 DX84
Billington Rd. SE14 93 DX80
Billiter Sq. EC3 7 N9
Billiter St. EC3 7 N9
Billiter St. EC3 78 DS72
Billockby Clo., Chess. 130 CM107
Billson St. E14 93 EC77
Billy Lows La., Pot.B. 20 DA31
Bilsby Gro. SE9 108 EK91
Bilton Rd., Erith 97 FG80
Bilton Rd., Grnf. 73 CG67
Bilton Way, Enf. 37 DY39
Bilton Way, Hayes 85 BV75
Bina Gdns. SW5 90 DC77
Bincote Rd., Enf. 35 DM41
Binden Rd. W12 89 CT76
Bindon Grn., Mord. 118 DB98
Bayham Rd.
Binfield Rd. SW4 91 DL81
Binfield Rd., S.Croy. 134 DT106
Binfield Rd., W.Byf. 126 BL112
Bingfield St. N1 77 DL67
Bingham Dr., Stai. 98 BK94
Bingham Pl. W1 4 F6
Bingham Rd., Croy. 120 DU102
Bingham St. N1 78 DR65
Bingley Rd. E16 80 EJ72
Bingley Rd., Grnf. 72 CC70
Bingley Rd., Sun. 99 BU94
Binney St. W1 4 G9
Binney St. W1 76 DG72
Binns Rd. W4 88 CS78
Binns Ter. W4 88 CS78
Binns Rd.
Binsey Wk. SE2 96 EW75
Binyon Cres., Stan. 45 CF50
Birbeck Gdns., Wdf.Grn. 52 EF47
Birbetts Rd. SE9 109 EM89
Birch Ave. N13 50 DQ48
Birch Ave., Cat. 148 DR124
Birch Ave., Lthd. 143 CF120
Birch Ave., West Dr. 70 BM72
Birch Clo. E16 80 EE71
Birch Clo. N19 63 DJ61
Hargrave Pk.
Birch Clo. SE15 92 DU82
Birch Clo., Add. 126 BK109
Birch Clo., Brent. 87 CH80
Birch Clo., Buck.H. 52 EK48
Birch Clo., Houns. 87 CD83
Birch Clo., Rom. 69 FB55
Birch Clo., Sev. 155 FH123
Birch Clo., Tedd. 101 CG92
Birch Copse, St.Alb. 16 BY30
Birch Ct., Nthwd. 43 BQ51
Rickmansworth Rd.
Birch Cres., Uxb. 70 BM67
Birch Gdns., Dag. 69 FC62
Birch Grn. NW9 46 CS52
Clayton Fld.
Birch Gro. E11 66 EE62
Birch Gro. SE12 108 EF87
Birch Gro. W3 74 CN74
Birch Gro., Cob. 128 BW114
Birch Gro., Pot.B. 20 DA32
Birch Gro., Shep. 113 BS96
Birch Gro., Tad. 145 CY124
Birch Gro., Well. 96 EU84
Birch Hill, Croy. 135 DX106
Birch La., Pur. 133 DL111
Birch Mead, Orp. 123 EN103
Birch Pk., Har. 44 CC52
Birch Rd., Felt. 100 BX92
Birch Rd., Rom. 69 FB55
Birch Row, Brom. 123 EN101
Birch Tree Ave., W.Wick. 136 EF106
Birch Tree Wk., Wat. 29 BT37
Birch Tree Way, Croy. 120 DV103
Birch Vale, Cob. 128 CA113
Birch Vw., Epp. 26 EV29
Birch Wk., Borwd. 32 CN39
Grove Rd.
Birch Wk., Erith 97 FC79
Birch Wk., Mitch. 119 DH95
Birch Wk., W.Byf. 126 BG112
Birch Way, St.Alb. 17 CK27
Birch Way, Warl. 149 DY118
Birch Wd., Rad. 18 CN34
Bircham Path SE4 93 DX84
St. Norbert Rd.
Birchanger Rd. SE25 120 DU99
Birchdale Clo., W.Byf. 126 BJ111
Birchdale Gdns., Rom. 68 EX59
Birchdale Rd. E7 66 EJ64
Birchdene Dr. SE28 82 EU74
Birchen Clo. NW9 60 CR61
Birchen Gro. NW9 60 CR61
Birchend Clo., S.Croy. 134 DR107
Sussex Rd.
Birches, The N21 35 DM44
Birches, The SE7 94 EH79
Birches, The, Epp. 27 FB26
Birches, The, Orp. 137 EN105
Birches, The, Swan. 125 FE96
Birches, The (Bushey), Wat. 30 CC43
Birches Clo., Epsom 144 CS115
Birches Clo., Mitch. 118 DF97
Birches Clo., Pnr. 58 BY57
Birchfield Clo., Add. 126 BH105
Birchfield Clo., Couls. 147 DM116
Birchfield Gro., Epsom 131 CW110
Birchfield Rd. (Cheshunt), Wal.Cr. 22 DV29
Birchfield St. E14 79 EA73
Birchgate Ms., Tad. 145 CW121
Bidhams Cres.
Birchin La. EC3 7 L9
Birchin La. EC3 78 DR72
Birchington Clo., Bexh. 97 FB81
Birchington Clo., Orp. 124 EW102
Hart Dyke Rd.
Birchington Rd. N8 63 DK58
Birchington Rd. NW6 76 DA67
Birchington Rd., Surb. 116 CM101
Birchlands Ave. SW12 104 DF87
Birchmead, Wat. 29 BT38
Birchmead Ave., Pnr. 58 BW56
Birchmere Row SE3 94 EF82
Birchmore Wk. N5 64 DQ62
Highbury Quad.
Birchville Ct. (Bushey), Wat. 45 CE46
Heathbourne Rd.
Birchway, Hayes 71 BU74
Birchwood, Wal.Abb. 24 EE34
Roundhills
Birchwood Ave. N10 62 DG55
Birchwood Ave., Beck. 121 DZ98
Birchwood Ave., Sid. 110 EV89
Birchwood Ave., Wall. 118 DG104
Birchwood Clo., Mord. 118 DB98
Birchwood Ct. N13 49 DP50
Birchwood Ct., Edg. 46 CQ54
Birchwood Dr. NW3 62 DB62
Birchwood Dr., Dart. 111 FE91
Birchwood Dr., W.Byf. 126 BG112
Birchwood Gro., Hmptn. 100 CA93
Birchwood La., Esher 129 CD109
Birchwood La., Lthd. 129 CF110
Birchwood La., Sev. 152 EZ115
Birchwood Pk. Ave., Swan. 125 FE97
Birchwood Rd. SW17 105 DH92
Birchwood Rd., Dart. 111 FD93
Birchwood Rd., Orp. 123 ER98
Birchwood Rd., Swan. 125 FC95
Birchwood Rd., W.Byf. 126 BG112
Birchwood Ter., Swan. 125 FC95
Birchwood Rd.
Birchwood Way, St.Alb. 16 CB28
Bird in Bush Rd. SE15 92 DU80
Bird La., Uxb. 42 BJ54
Bird St. W1 4 G9
Bird Wk., Twick. 100 BZ88
Bird-in-Hand La., Brom. 122 EK96
Bird-in-Hand Pas. SE23 106 DW89
Dartmouth Rd.
Birdbrook Clo., Dag. 83 FC66
Birdbrook Rd. SE3 94 EJ83
Birdcage Wk. SW1 9 L5
Birdcage Wk. SW1 91 DJ75
Birdham Clo., Brom. 122 EL99
Birdhouse La., Orp. 151 EN115
Birdhurst Ave., S.Croy. 134 DR105
Birdhurst Gdns., S.Croy. 134 DR105
Birdhurst Ri., S.Croy. 134 DS106
Birdhurst Rd. SW18 90 DC84
Birdhurst Rd. SW19 104 DE93
Birdhurst Rd., S.Croy. 134 DS106
Birdlip Clo. SE15 92 DS79
Birds Fm. Ave., Rom. 55 FB53
Birds Hill Dr., Lthd. 129 CD113
Birds Hill Ri., Lthd. 129 CD113
Birds Hill Rd., Lthd. 129 CD112
Birdsfield La. E3 79 DZ67
Birdwood Clo., S.Croy. 134 DW111
Birdwood Clo., Tedd. 101 CE91
Birkbeck Ave. W3 74 CQ73
Birkbeck Ave., Grnf. 72 CC67
Birkbeck Gdns., Wdf.Grn. 52 EF47
Birkbeck Gro. W3 88 CR75
Birkbeck Hill SE21 105 DP89
Birkbeck Ms. E8 64 DT64
Sandringham Rd.
Birkbeck Pl. SE21 106 DQ88
Birkbeck Rd. E8 64 DT64
Birkbeck Rd. N8 63 DL56
Birkbeck Rd. N12 48 DC50
Birkbeck Rd. N17 50 DT53
Birkbeck Rd. NW7 47 CT50
Birkbeck Rd. SW19 104 DB92
Birkbeck Rd. W3 74 CR74
Birkbeck Rd. W5 87 CJ77
Birkbeck Rd., Beck. 120 DW96
Birkbeck Rd., Enf. 36 DR39
Birkbeck Rd., Ilf. 67 ER57
Birkbeck Rd., Rom. 69 FD60
Birkbeck Rd., Sid. 110 EU90
Birkbeck St. E2 78 DV69
Cambridge Heath Rd.
Birkbeck Way, Grnf. 72 CC67
Birkdale Ave., Pnr. 58 CA55
Birkdale Clo., Orp. 123 ER101
Birkdale Gdns., Croy. 135 DX105
Birkdale Gdns., Wat. 44 BX48
Birkdale Rd. SE2 96 EU77
Birkdale Rd. W5 74 CL70
Birken Ms., Nthwd. 43 BP50
Birkenhead Ave., Kings.T. 116 CM96
Birkenhead St. WC1 6 A2
Birkenhead St. WC1 77 DL69
Birkhall Rd. SE6 107 ED88
Birkwood Clo. SW12 105 DK87
Birley Rd. N20 48 DC47
Birley St. SW11 90 DG82
Birling Rd., Erith 97 FD80
Birnam Clo., Wok. 140 BG124
Birnam Rd. N4 63 DM61
Birse Cres. NW10 60 CS63
Birstall Grn., Wat. 44 BX49
Birstall Rd. N15 64 DS57
Birtley Path, Borwd. 32 CL39
Darrington Rd.
Biscay Rd. W6 89 CX78
Biscoe Clo., Houns. 86 CA79
Biscoe Way SE13 93 ED83
Bisenden Rd., Croy. 120 DS103
Bisham Clo., Cars. 118 DF101
Bisham Gdns. N6 62 DG60
Bishop Butt Clo., Orp. 123 ET104
Stapleton Rd.
Bishop Duppa's Pk., Shep. 113 BR101
Bishop Fox Way, W.Mol. 114 BZ98
Bishop Ken Rd., Har. 45 CF54
Bishop Kings Rd. W14 89 CY77
Bishop Rd. N14 49 DH45
Bishop St. N1 78 DQ67
Bishop Way NW10 74 CS66
Bishop Wilfred Wd. Clo. SE15 92 DU82
Moncrieff St.
Bishop's Ave. E13 80 EH67
Bishop's Ave. SW6 89 CX82
Bishops Ave., Borwd. 32 CM43
Bishops Ave., Brom. 122 EJ96
Bishops Ave., Nthwd. 43 BS49
Bishops Ave., Rom. 68 EW58
Bishops Ave., The N2 62 DD59
Bishops Bri. W2 76 DC71
Bishops Bri. Rd. W2 76 DB72
Bishops Clo. E17 65 EB56
Bishops Clo. N19 63 DJ62
Wyndham Cres.
Bishops Clo. SE9 109 EQ89
Bishops Clo., Barn. 33 CX44
Bishop's Clo., Couls. 147 DN118
Bishops Clo., Enf. 36 DV40
Central Ave.
Bishops Clo., Rich. 101 CK90
Bishops Clo., Sutt. 118 DA104
Bishops Clo., Uxb. 70 BN68
Bishop's Ct. EC4 6 F8
Bishop's Ct. WC2 6 D8
Bishops Dr., Felt. 99 BR86
Bishops Dr., Nthlt. 72 BY67
Bishops Gro. N2 62 DD58
Bishops Gro., Hmptn. 100 BZ91
Bishop's Hall, Kings.T. 115 CK96
Bishops Hill, Walt. 113 BU101
Bishop's Pk. SW6 89 CX82
Bishop's Pk. Rd. SW6 89 CX82
Bishops Pk. Rd. SW16 119 DL95
Bishops Rd. N6 62 DG58
Bishops Rd. SW6 89 CY81
Bishops Rd. W7 87 CE75
Bishops Rd., Croy. 119 DP101
Bishops Rd., Hayes 71 BQ71
Bishops Ter. SE11 10 E8
Bishops Ter. SE11 91 DN77
Bishops Wk., Chis. 123 EQ95
Bishops Wk., Croy. 135 DX106
Bishop's Wk., Pnr. 58 BY55
High St.
Bishops Way E2 78 DV68
Bishopsford Rd., Mord. 118 DC101
Bishopsgate EC2 7 M9
Bishopsgate EC2 78 DS72
Bishopsgate Arc. EC2 7 N7
Bishopsgate Chyd. EC2 7 M8
Bishopsthorpe Rd. SE26 107 DX91
Bishopswood Rd. N6 62 DF59
Biskra, Wat. 29 BU39
Bisley Clo., Wal.Cr. 23 DX33
Bisley Clo., Wor.Pk. 117 CW102
Bispham Rd. NW10 74 CM69
Bisson Rd. E15 79 EC68
Bisterne Ave. E17 65 ED55
Bitchet Rd., Sev. 155 FP127
Bittacy Clo. NW7 47 CX51
Bittacy Hill NW7 47 CX51
Bittacy Pk. Ave. NW7 47 CX51
Bittacy Ri. NW7 47 CW51
Bittacy Rd. NW7 47 CX51
Bittern Clo., Hayes 72 BX71
Bittern St. SE1 11 H5
Bittoms, The, Kings.T. 115 CK97
Bixley Clo., Sthl. 86 BZ77
Black Boy La. N15 64 DQ57
Black Boy Wd., St.Alb. 16 CA30
Black Fan Clo., Enf. 36 DQ39
Black Friars Ct. EC4 6 F10
Black Friars La. EC4 6 F10
Black Friars La. EC4 77 DP72
Black Gates, Pnr. 58 BZ55
Church La.
Black Horse Ct. SE1 11 L6
Black Lion Hill, Rad. 18 CL32
Black Lion La. W6 89 CU77
Black Path E10 65 DX59
Black Prince Clo., W.Byf. 126 BM114
Black Prince Rd. SE1 10 A9
Black Prince Rd. SE1 91 DM77
Black Prince Rd. SE11 10 C9
Black Prince Rd. SE11 91 DM77
Black Rod Clo., Hayes 85 BT76
Black Swan Yd. SE1 11 M4
Black Thorne Rd., West. 150 EK115
Blackacre Rd., Epp. 39 ER37
Blackall St. EC2 7 M4
Blackberry Clo., Shep. 113 BS98
Cherry Way
Blackberry Fm. Clo., Houns. 86 BY80
Blackberry Fld., Orp. 124 EU95
Blackbird Hill NW9 60 CQ61
Blackbird Yd. E2 78 DT69
Ravenscroft St.
Blackbirds La., Wat. 31 CD35
Blackborne Rd., Dag. 82 FA65
Blackbrook La., Brom. 123 EN97
Blackburn, The, Lthd. 142 BZ124
Little Bookham St.
Blackburn Rd. NW6 76 DB65
Blackburn Trd. Est., Stai. 98 BM86
Blackburne's Ms. W1 4 F10
Blackburne's Ms. W1 76 DG73
Blackbury Clo., Pot.B. 20 DC31
Blackbush Ave., Rom. 68 EX57
Blackbush Clo., Sutt. 132 DB108
Blackdale (Cheshunt), Wal.Cr. 22 DU27
Blackdown Clo. N2 48 DC54
Blackdown Ter. SE18 95 EN80
Prince Imperial Rd.
Blackett St. SW15 89 CX83
Blackfen Rd., Sid. 109 ES86
Blackford Clo., S.Croy. 133 DP109
Blackford Rd., Wat. 44 BX50
Blackford's Path SW15 103 CU87
Roehampton High St.
Blackfriars Bri. EC4 10 F1
Blackfriars Bri. EC4 77 DP73
Blackfriars Bri. SE1 10 F1
Blackfriars Bri. SE1 77 DP73
Blackfriars Pas. EC4 6 F10
Blackfriars Rd. SE1 10 F2
Blackfriars Rd. SE1 77 DP74
Blackhall La., Sev. 155 FK123
Blackhall Pl., Sev. 155 FL124
Blackhall La.
Blackheath Ave. SE10 93 ED80
Blackheath Gro. SE3 94 EF82
Blackheath Hill SE10 93 EC81
Blackheath Pk. SE3 94 EF83
Blackheath Ri. SE13 93 EC82
Blackheath Rd. SE10 93 EB81
Blackheath Vale SE3 94 EE82
Blackheath Village SE3 94 EF82
Blackhills, Esher 128 BZ109
Blackhorse La. E17 65 DX56
Blackhorse La., Croy. 120 DU101
Blackhorse La., Epp. 27 FD25
Blackhorse La., Pot.B. 18 CS30
Blackhorse Ms. E17 65 DX55
Blackhorse Rd.
Blackhorse Rd. E17 65 DX56
Blackhorse Rd. SE8 93 DY78
Blackhorse Rd., Sid. 110 EU91
Blacklands Dr., Hayes 71 BQ70
Blacklands Rd. SE6 107 EC91
Blacklands Ter. SW3 8 D9
Blacklands Ter. SW3 90 DF77
Blackley Clo., Wat. 29 BT37
Blackmans La., Warl. 136 EE114
Blackmans Yd. E2 78 DU70
Cheshire St.
Blackmead, Sev. 153 FD119
London Rd.
Blackmoor La., Wat. 29 BQ44
Blackmore Ave., Sthl. 73 CD74
Blackmore Ct., Wal.Abb. 24 EG33
Blackmore Rd., Buck.H. 52 EL45
Blackmore Way, Uxb. 70 BK65
Blackmores Gro., Tedd. 101 CG93
Blackness La., Kes. 136 EK108
Blackpool Gdns., Hayes 71 BS70
Blackpool Rd. SE15 92 DV82
Blacks Rd. W6 89 CW77
Queen Caroline St.
Blackshaw Pl. N1 78 DS66
Hertford Rd.
Blackshaw Rd. SW17 104 DC91
Blacksmith Clo., Ash. 144 CM119
Rectory La.
Blacksmiths Clo., Rom. 68 EW58
Blacksmiths Hill, S.Croy. 134 DU113
Blacksmiths La., Cher. 112 BG101
Blacksmiths La., Orp. 124 EW99
Blacksmiths La., Rain. 83 FF67
Blacksmiths La., Stai. 112 BH97
Blackstock Ms. N4 63 DP61
Blackstock Rd.
Blackstock Rd. N4 63 DP61
Blackstock Rd. N5 63 DP61
Blackstone Est. E8 78 DU66
Blackstone Rd. NW2 61 CW64
Blackthorn Ave., West Dr. 84 BN77
Blackthorn Clo., Wat. 15 BV32
Blackthorn Ct., Houns. 86 BY80
Blackthorn Gro., Bexh. 96 EY83
Blackthorn St. E3 79 EA70
Blackthorne Ave., Croy. 120 DW102
Blackthorne Dr. E4 51 ED49
Blacktree Ms. SW9 91 DN83
Blackwall La. SE10 94 EE78
Blackwall Pier E14 80 EE73
Blackwall Tunnel E14 79 ED74
Blackwall Tunnel App. SE10 94 EE75
Blackwall Tunnel Northern App. E3 79 EA68
Blackwall Tunnel Northern App. E14 79 EC70
Blackwall Way E14 79 EC73
Blackwater Clo. E7 66 EF64
Tower Hamlets Rd.
Blackwater Clo., Rain. 83 FD71
Blackwater Rd., Sutt. 132 DB105
High St.
Blackwater St. SE22 106 DT85
Blackwell Clo. E5 65 DY63
Blackwell Clo., Har. 45 CD52
Blackwell Dr., Wat. 30 BW44
Blackwell Gdns., Edg. 46 CN48
Blackwell Rd., Kings L. 14 BN29
Blackwood Clo., W.Byf. 126 BJ112
Blackwood St. SE17 11 K10
Blackwood St. SE17 92 DR78
Blade Ms. SW15 89 CZ84
Deodar Rd.
Bladen Clo., Wey. 127 BR107
Blades Clo., Lthd. 143 CK120
Bladindon Dr., Bex. 110 EW87
Bladon Gdns., Har. 58 CB58
Blagdens Clo. N14 49 DJ47
Blagdens La. N14 49 DK47
Blagdon Rd. SE13 107 EB86
Blagdon Rd., N.Mal. 117 CT98
Blagdon Wk., Tedd. 101 CJ93
Blagrove Rd. W10 75 CY71
Blair Ave. NW9 60 CS59
Blair Ave., Esher 114 CC103
Blair Clo. N1 78 DQ65
Blair Clo., Hayes 85 BU77
Blair Clo., Sid. 109 ES85
Blair Dr., Sev. 155 FH123
Blair St. E14 79 EC72
Blairderry Rd. SW2 105 DL89
Blairhead Dr., Wat. 43 BV48
Blake Ave., Bark. 81 ES67
Blake Clo. W10 75 CW71
Blake Clo., Cars. 118 DE101
Blake Clo., Rain. 83 FF67
Blake Clo., Well. 95 ES81
Blake Gdns. SW6 90 DB81
Blake Hall Cres. E11 66 EG60
Blake Hall Rd. E11 66 EG59
Blake Hall Rd., Ong. 27 FG27
Blake Ho., Beck. 107 EA93
Blake Rd. E16 80 EF70
Blake Rd. N11 49 DJ52
Blake Rd., Croy. 120 DS103
Blake Rd., Mitch. 118 DE97
Blake St. SE8 93 EA79
Watergate St.
Blakeden Dr., Esher 129 CF107
Blakehall Rd., Cars. 132 DF107
Blakeley Cotts. SE10 93 ED75
Tunnel Ave.
Blakemore Rd. SW16 105 DL90
Blakemore Rd., Th.Hth. 119 DM99
Blakemore Way, Belv. 96 EY76
Blakeney Ave., Beck. 121 DZ95
Blakeney Clo. E8 64 DU64
Ferncliff Rd.
Blakeney Clo. N20 48 DC46
Blakeney Clo. NW1 77 DK66
Rossendale Way
Blakeney Clo., Epsom 130 CR111
Blakeney Rd., Beck. 121 DZ95
Blakenham Rd. SW17 104 DF91
Blaker Ct. SE7 94 EJ80
Fairlawn
Blaker Rd. E15 79 EC67
Blakes Ave., N.Mal. 117 CT99
Blake's Grn., W.Wick. 121 EC102
Blakes La., N.Mal. 117 CT99
Blakes Rd. SE15 92 DS80
Blakes Ter., N.Mal. 117 CU99
Blakesley Ave. W5 73 CJ72
Blakesley Wk. SW20 117 CZ96
Kingston Rd.
Blakesware Gdns. N9 50 DR45
Blakewood Clo., Felt. 100 BW91
Blanch Clo. SE15 92 DW80
Culmore Rd.
Blanchard Clo. SE9 108 EL90
Blanchard Way E8 78 DU65
Blanche La., Pot.B. 19 CU32
Blanche St. E16 80 EF70
Blanchedowne SE5 92 DR84
Blanchland Rd., Mord. 118 DB99
Blanchmans Rd., Warl. 149 DY118
Bland St. SE9 94 EK84
Blandfield Rd. SW12 104 DG86
Blandford Ave., Beck. 121 DY96
Blandford Ave., Twick. 100 CB88

Blandford Clo. N2 62 DC57
Blandford Clo., Croy. 119 DL104
Blandford Clo., Rom. 69 FB56
Blandford Cres. E4 51 EC45
Blandford Rd. W4 88 CS76
Blandford Rd. W5 87 CK75
Blandford Rd., Beck. 120 DW96
Blandford Rd., Sthl. 86 CA77
Blandford Rd., Tedd. 101 CD92
Blandford Sq. NW1 4 C5
Blandford Sq. NW1 76 DE70
Blandford St. W1 4 E8
Blandford St. W1 76 DF72
Blandford Waye, Hayes 72 BW72
Blaney Cres. E6 81 EP69
Blanmerle Rd. SE9 109 EP88
Blann Clo. SE9 108 EK86
Blantyre St. SW10 90 DD80
Blantyre Wk. SW10 90 DD80
Blantyre St.
Blashford NW3 76 DF66
Blashford St. SE13 107 ED87
Blasker Wk. E14 93 EA78
Blattner Clo., Borwd. 32 CL42
Blawith Rd., Har. 59 CE56
Blaydon Clo. N17 50 DV52
Blaydon Clo., Ruis. 57 BS59
Blaydon Wk. N17 50 DV52
Bleak Hill La. SE18 95 ET79
Blean Gro. SE20 106 DW94
Bleasdale Ave., Grnf. 73 CG68
Blechynden St. W10 75 CX73
Bramley Rd.
Bleddyn Clo., Sid. 110 EW86
Bledlow Clo. SE28 82 EW73
Bledlow Ri., Grnf. 72 CC68
Bleeding Heart Yd. EC1 6 E7
Blegborough Rd. SW16 105 DJ93
Blendon Dr., Bex. 110 EX86
Blendon Path, Brom. 108 EF94
Hope Pk.
Blendon Rd., Bex. 110 EW86
Blendon Ter. SE18 95 EQ78
Blendworth Way SE15 92 DS80
Daniel Gdns.
Blenheim Ave., Ilf. 67 EN58
Blenheim Clo. N21 50 DQ46
Elm Pk. Rd.
Blenheim Clo. SW20 117 CW97
Blenheim Clo., Grnf. 73 CD68
Leaver Gdns.
Blenheim Clo., Rom. 69 FC56
Blenheim Clo., Wall. 133 DJ108
Blenheim Clo., Wat. 44 BX45
Blenheim Ct. N19 63 DL61
Marlborough Rd.
Blenheim Ct., Sid. 109 ER90
Blenheim Cres. W11 75 CY73
Blenheim Cres., Ruis. 57 BR61
Blenheim Cres., S.Croy. 134 DQ108
Blenheim Dr., Well. 95 ET81
Blenheim Gdns. NW2 75 CW65
Blenheim Gdns. SW2 105 DM86
Blenheim Gdns., Kings.T. 102 CP94
Blenheim Gdns., S.Croy. 134 DU112
Blenheim Gdns., Wall. 133 DJ107
Blenheim Gdns., Wem. 60 CL62
Blenheim Gro. SE15 92 DU82
Blenheim Pk. Rd., S.Croy. 134 DQ109
Blenheim Pas. NW8 76 DC68
Blenheim Ter.
Blenheim Ri. N15 64 DT56
Talbot Rd.
Blenheim Rd. E6 80 EK69
Blenheim Rd. E15 66 EE63
Blenheim Rd. E17 65 DX55
Blenheim Rd. NW8 76 DC68
Blenheim Rd. SE20 106 DW94
Maple Rd.
Blenheim Rd. SW20 117 CW97
Blenheim Rd. W4 88 CS76
Blenheim Rd., Abb.L. 15 BU32
Blenheim Rd., Barn. 33 CX41
Blenheim Rd., Brom. 122 EL98
Blenheim Rd., Epsom 130 CR111
Blenheim Rd., Har. 58 CB58
Blenheim Rd., Nthlt. 72 CB65
Blenheim Rd., Orp. 124 EW103
Blenheim Rd., Sid. 110 EW88
Blenheim Rd., Sutt. 118 DA104
Blenheim St. W1 5 H9
Blenheim Ter. NW8 76 DC68
Blenheim Way, Epp. 26 FA27
Blenheim Way, Islw. 87 CG81
Blenkarne Rd. SW11 104 DF86
Bleriot Rd., Houns. 86 BW80
Blessbury Rd., Edg. 46 CQ53
Blessing Way, Bark. 82 EW69
Blessington Clo. SE13 93 ED83
Blessington Rd. SE13 93 ED84
Bletchingley Clo., Th.Hth. 119 DP98
Bletchley Ct. N1 7 K1
Bletchley St. N1 7 J1
Bletchley St. N1 78 DQ68
Bletchmore Clo., Hayes 85 BR78
Bletsoe Wk. N1 78 DQ68
Cropley St.
Blighs Rd., Sev. 155 FH125
Blincoe Clo. SW19 103 CX89
Blind La., Bans. 146 DE115
Blind La., Loug. 38 EE40
Blind La., Wal.Abb. 24 EJ33
Blindman's La. (Cheshunt), Wal.Cr. 23 DX30
Bliss Cres. SE13 93 EB82
Coldbath St.
Blissett St. SE10 93 EC81
Blisworth Clo., Hayes 72 BY70
Braunston Dr.
Blithbury Rd., Dag. 82 EV65
Blithdale Rd. SE2 96 EU77
Blithfield St. W8 90 DB76
Blockley Rd., Wem. 59 CH61
Bloemfontein Ave. W12 75 CV74
Bloemfontein Rd. W12 75 CV73
Blomfield Rd. W9 76 DB71
Blomfield St. EC2 7 L7
Blomfield St. EC2 78 DR71
Blomfield Vill. W2 76 DB71
Blomville Rd., Dag. 68 EY62
Blondel St. SW11 90 DG82
Blondell Clo., West Dr. 84 BK79
Blondin Ave. W5 87 CJ77
Blondin St. E3 79 EA68
Bloom Gro. SE27 105 DP90
Bloom Pk. Rd. SW6 89 CZ80
Bloomburg St. SW1 9 L9
Bloomfield Cres., Ilf. 67 EP58
Bloomfield Pl. W1 5 J10
Bloomfield Rd. N6 62 DG58
Bloomfield Rd. SE18 95 EP78
Bloomfield Rd., Brom. 122 EK99
Bloomfield Rd., Kings.T. 116 CL98
Bloomfield Ter. SW1 8 G10
Bloomfield Ter. SW1 90 DG78
Bloomhall Rd. SE19 106 DR92
Bloomsbury Clo. W5 74 CM73
Bloomsbury Clo., Epsom 130 CR110
Bloomsbury Ct. WC1 6 A7
Bloomsbury Ct., Pnr. 58 BZ55
Bloomsbury Ho. SW4 105 DK86
Bloomsbury Pl. SW18 104 DC85
Fullerton Rd.
Bloomsbury Pl. WC1 6 A6
Bloomsbury Sq. WC1 6 A7
Bloomsbury Sq. WC1 77 DL71
Bloomsbury St. WC1 5 N7
Bloomsbury St. WC1 77 DK71
Bloomsbury Way WC1 5 P8
Bloomsbury Way WC1 77 DL71
Blore Clo. SW8 91 DK81
Thessaly Rd.
Blore Ct. W1 5 M10
Blossom Clo. W5 88 CL75
Almond Ave.
Blossom Clo., Dag. 82 EZ67
Blossom Clo., S.Croy. 134 DT106
Melville Ave.
Blossom La., Enf. 36 DQ39
Blossom St. E1 7 N5
Blossom St. E1 78 DS70
Blossom Way, Uxb. 70 BM66
Blossom Way, West Dr. 84 BN77
Blossom Waye, Houns. 86 BY80
Blount St. E14 79 DY71
Bloxam Gdns. SE9 108 EL85
Bloxhall Rd. E10 65 DZ60
Bloxham Cres., Hmptn. 100 BZ94
Bloxworth Clo., Wall. 119 DJ104
Blucher Rd. SE5 92 DQ80
Blue Anchor All., Rich. 88 CL84
Kew Rd.
Blue Anchor La. SE16 92 DU77
Blue Anchor Yd. E1 78 DU73
Blue Ball Yd. SW1 9 K3
Blue Barn La., Wey. 126 BN111
Blue Cedars, Bans. 131 CX114
Bluebell Ave. E12 66 EL64
Bluebell Clo. SE26 106 DT91
Bluebell Clo., Orp. 123 EQ103
Bluebell Clo., Wall. 119 DH102
Bluebell Dr., Abb.L. 15 BT27
Bluebell Dr., Wal.Cr. 22 DR28
St. James Rd.
Bluebell Way, Ilf. 81 EP65
Blueberry Gdns., Couls. 147 DM116
Blueberry La., Sev. 152 EW116
Bluebridge Ave., Hat. 19 CY27
Bluebridge Rd., Hat. 19 CY26
Bluefield Clo., Hmptn. 100 CA92
Bluegates, Epsom 131 CU108
Bluehouse Rd. E4 52 EE48
Bluett Rd., St.Alb. 17 CK27
Blundel La., Cob. 142 BZ116
Blundell Rd., Edg. 46 CR53
Blundell St. N7 77 DL66
Blunden Clo., Dag. 68 EW60
Blunesfield, Pot.B. 20 DD31
Blunt Rd., S.Croy. 134 DR106
Blunts Ave., West Dr. 84 BN80
Blunts La., St.Alb. 16 BW27
Blunts Rd. SE9 109 EN85
Blurton Rd. E5 64 DW63
Blyth Clo. E14 93 ED77
Manchester Rd.
Blyth Clo., Borwd. 32 CM39
Blyth Clo., Twick. 101 CF86
Grimwood Rd.
Blyth Rd. E17 65 DZ59
Blyth Rd. SE28 82 EW73
Blyth Rd., Brom. 122 EF95
Blyth Rd., Hayes 85 BS75
Blythe Clo. SE6 107 DZ87
Blythe Hill SE6 107 DZ87
Blythe Hill, Orp. 123 ET95
Blythe Hill La. SE6 107 DZ87
Blythe Rd. W14 89 CX76
Blythe St. E2 78 DV69
Blythe Vale SE6 107 DZ88
Blythswood Rd., Ilf. 68 EU60
Blythwood Rd. N4 63 DL59
Blythwood Rd., Pnr. 44 BX53
Boades Ms. NW3 62 DD63
New End
Boadicea St. N1 77 DM67
Copenhagen St.
Boakes Clo. NW9 60 CQ56
Roe Grn.
Boakes Meadow, Sev. 139 FF111
Boar Clo., Chig. 54 EU50
Boardman Ave. E4 37 EB43
Boardman Clo., Barn. 33 CY43
Boar's Head Yd., Brent. 87 CK80
Brent Way
Boat Lifter Way SE16 93 DY77
Sweden Gate
Boathouse Wk. SE15 92 DT80
Boathouse Wk., Rich. 87 CK81
Kew Rd.
Bob Anker Clo. E13 80 EG69
Chesterton Rd.
Bob Marley Way SE24 91 DN84
Mayall Rd.
Bobbin Clo. SW4 91 DJ83
Bobs La., Rom. 55 FF53
Bocketts La., Lthd. 143 CF124
Bockhampton Rd., Kings.T. 102 CM94
Bocking St. E8 78 DV67
Boddicott Clo. SW19 103 CY89
Bodiam Clo., Enf. 36 DR40
Bodiam Rd. SW16 105 DK94
Bodley Clo., Epp. 25 ET30
Bodley Clo., N.Mal. 116 CS99
Bodley Manor Way SW2 105 DN87
Papworth Way
Bodley Rd., N.Mal. 116 CR100
Bodmin Clo., Har. 58 BZ62
Bodmin Clo., Orp. 124 EW102
Bodmin Gro., Mord. 118 DB98
Bodmin St. SW18 104 DA88
Bodnant Gdns. SW20 117 CV97
Bodney Rd. E8 64 DV64
Boeing Way, Sthl. 85 BV76
Boevey Path, Belv. 96 EZ78
Orchard Ave.
Bogey La., Orp. 137 EM108
Bognor Gdns., Wat. 44 BW50
Bowring Grn.
Bognor Rd., Well. 96 EX81
Bohemia Pl. E8 78 DW65
Bohun Gro., Barn. 34 DE44
Boileau Par. W5 74 CM72
Boileau Rd.
Boileau Rd. SW13 89 CU80
Boileau Rd. W5 74 CM72
Bois Hall Rd., Add. 126 BK106
Bolden St. SE8 93 EB82
Bolderwood Way, W.Wick. 121 EB103
Boldmere Rd., Pnr. 58 BW59
Boleyn Ave., Enf. 36 DV39
Boleyn Ave., Epsom 131 CU110
Boleyn Clo. E17 65 EA56
Boleyn Clo., Loug. 38 EL44
Roding Gdns.
Boleyn Ct., Buck.H. 52 EG46
Boleyn Dr., Ruis. 58 BX61
Boleyn Dr., W.Mol. 114 BZ97
Boleyn Gdns., Dag. 83 FC66
Boleyn Gdns., W.Wick. 121 EB103
Boleyn Gro., W.Wick. 121 EC103
Boleyn Rd. E6 80 EK68
Boleyn Rd. E7 80 EG66
Boleyn Rd. N16 64 DS64
Boleyn Wk., Lthd. 143 CF120
Boleyn Way, Barn. 34 DC41
Boleyn Way, Ilf. 53 EQ51
Bolina Rd. SE16 92 DW78
Bolingbroke Gro. SW11 104 DF86
Bolingbroke Rd. W14 89 CX76
Bolingbroke Wk. SW11 90 DD81
Bolingbroke Way, Hayes 71 BR74
Bolliger Ct. NW10 74 CQ70
Park Royal Rd.
Bollo Bri. Rd. W3 88 CP76
Bollo La. W3 88 CP75
Bollo La. W4 88 CQ77
Bolney St. SW8 91 DM80
Bolney Way, Felt. 100 BY90
Bolsover St. W1 5 J5
Bolsover St. W1 77 DH70
Bolstead Rd., Mitch. 119 DH95
Bolt Cellar La., Epp. 25 ES30
Bolt Ct. EC4 6 E9
Bolters La., Bans. 131 CZ114
Boltmore Clo. NW4 61 CX55
Bolton Clo. SE20 120 DU96
Selby Rd.
Bolton Clo., Chess. 129 CK107
Bolton Cres. SE5 91 DP79
Bolton Gdns. NW10 75 CX68
Bolton Gdns. SW5 90 DB78
Bolton Gdns., Brom. 108 EF93
Bolton Gdns., Tedd. 101 CG93
Bolton Gdns. Ms. SW10 90 DB78
Bolton Rd. E15 80 EF65
Bolton Rd. N18 50 DT50
Bolton Rd. NW8 76 DB67
Bolton Rd. NW10 74 CS67
Bolton Rd. W4 88 CQ80
Bolton Rd., Chess. 129 CK107
Bolton Rd., Har. 58 CC56
Bolton St. W1 9 J2
Bolton St. W1 77 DH74
Bolton Wk. N7 63 DM61
Durham Rd.
Boltons, The SW10 90 DC78
Boltons, The, Wem. 59 CF63
Boltons, The, Wdf.Grn. 52 EG49
Boltons Clo., Wok. 140 BG116
Boltons La., Hayes 85 BQ81
Boltons La., Wok. 140 BG116
Boltons Pl. SW5 90 DC78
Bombay St. SE16 92 DV77
Bombers La., West. 151 ES120
Grays Rd.
Bomer Clo., West Dr. 84 BN80
Bomore Rd. W11 75 CY73
Bon Marche Ter. SE27 106 DS91
Gipsy Rd.
Bonar Pl., Chis. 108 EL94
Bonar Rd. SE15 92 DU80
Bonchester Clo., Chis. 109 EN94
Bonchurch Clo., Sutt. 132 DB108
Bonchurch Rd. W10 75 CY71
Bonchurch Rd. W13 73 CH74
Bond Clo., Sev. 152 EX115
Bond Clo., West Dr. 70 BM72
Bond Ct. EC4 7 K9
Bond Gdns., Wall. 133 DJ105
Bond Rd., Mitch. 118 DE96
Bond Rd., Surb. 116 CM102
Bond Rd., Warl. 149 DX118
Bond St. E15 66 EE64
Bond St. W4 88 CS77
Chiswick Common Rd.
Bond St. W5 73 CK73
Bondfield Rd. E6 80 EL71
Lovage App.
Bondfield Rd., Hayes 71 BU69
Bonding Yd. Wk. SE16 93 DY76
Finland St.
Bondway SW8 91 DL79
Boneta Rd. SE18 95 EM76
Bonfield Rd. SE13 93 EC84
Bonham Gdns., Dag. 68 EX61
Bonham Rd. SW2 105 DM85
Bonham Rd., Dag. 68 EX61
Bonheur Rd. W4 88 CR75
Bonhill St. EC2 7 L5
Bonhill St. EC2 78 DR70
Boniface Gdns., Har. 44 CB52
Boniface Rd., Uxb. 57 BP62
Boniface Wk., Har. 44 CB52
Bonner Hill Rd., Kings.T. 116 CM97
Bonner Rd. E2 78 DW68
Bonner St. E2 78 DW68
Bonnersfield Clo., Har. 59 CF58
Bonnersfield La., Har. 59 CF58
Bonneville Gdns. SW4 105 DJ86
Bonney Gro. (Cheshunt), Wal.Cr. 22 DU30
Bonney Way, Swan. 125 FE96
Bonnington Sq. SW8 91 DM79
Bonnington Twr., Brom. 122 EL100
Bonny St. NW1 77 DJ66
Bonser Rd., Twick. 101 CF89
Bonsor Dr., Tad. 145 CY122
Bonsor St. SE5 92 DS80
Bonville Gdns. NW4 61 CU56
Handowe Clo.
Bonville Rd., Brom. 108 EF92
Book Ms. WC2 5 N9
Booker Clo. E14 79 DZ71
Wallwood St.
Booker Rd. N18 50 DU50
Bookham Ct., Lthd. 142 BZ123
Church Rd.
Bookham Ind. Pk., Lthd. 142 BZ123
Bookham Rd., Cob. 142 BW119
Boone Ct. N9 50 DW48
Boone St. SE13 94 EE84
Boones Rd. SE13 94 EE84
Boord St. SE10 94 EE76
Boot St. N1 7 M3
Boot St. N1 78 DS69
Booth Clo. SE28 82 EV73
Booth Dr., Stai. 98 BK93
Booth Rd. NW9 46 CR54
Booth Rd., Croy. 119 DP103
Waddon New Rd.
Boothby Rd. N19 63 DK61
Booth's Pl. W1 5 L7
Bordars Rd. W7 73 CE71
Bordars Wk. W7 73 CE71
Borden Ave., Enf. 36 DR44
Border Cres. SE26 106 DV92
Border Gdns., Croy. 135 EB105
Border Rd. SE26 106 DV92
Bordergate, Mitch. 118 DF95
Borders La., Loug. 39 EN42
Bordesley Rd., Mord. 118 DB98
Bordon Wk. SW15 103 CU87
Boreas Wk. N1 6 G1
Boreham Ave. E16 80 EG72
Boreham Clo. E11 65 EC60
Hainault Rd.
Boreham Holt, Borwd. 32 CM42
Boreham Rd. N22 50 DQ54
Borehamwood Ind. Pk., Borwd. 32 CR40
Borer's Pas. E1 7 N8
Borgard Rd. SE18 95 EM77
Borkwood Pk., Orp. 137 ET105
Borkwood Way, Orp. 137 ES105
Borland Rd. SE15 92 DW84
Borland Rd., Tedd. 101 CH93
Bornedene, Pot.B. 19 CY31
Borneo St. SW15 89 CW83
Borough High St. SE1 11 J5
Borough High St. SE1 92 DQ75
Borough Hill, Croy. 119 DP104
Borough Rd. SE1 10 G6
Borough Rd. SE1 91 DP76
Borough Rd., Islw. 87 CE81
Borough Rd., Kings.T. 116 CN95
Borough Rd., Mitch. 118 DE96
Borough Rd., West. 150 EK121
Borough Sq. SE1 11 H5
Borough Way, Pot.B. 19 CY32
Borrett Clo. SE17 92 DQ78
Penrose St.
Borrodaile Rd. SW18 104 DB86
Borrowdale Ave., Har. 45 CG54
Borrowdale Clo., Ilf. 66 EL56
Borrowdale Clo., S.Croy. 134 DT113
Borrowdale Ct., Enf. 36 DQ39
Borrowdale Dr., S.Croy. 134 DT112
Borthwick Ms. E15 66 EE63
Borthwick Rd.
Borthwick Rd. E15 66 EE63
Borthwick Rd. NW9 61 CT58
West Hendon Bdy.
Borthwick St. SE8 93 EA78
Borwick Ave. E17 65 DZ55
Bosanquet Clo., Uxb. 70 BK70
Bosbury Rd. SE6 107 EC90
Boscastle Rd. NW5 63 DH62
Bosco Clo., Orp. 137 ET105
Strickland Way
Boscobel Pl. SW1 8 G8
Boscobel Pl. SW1 90 DG77
Boscobel St. NW8 4 A5
Boscobel St. NW8 76 DD70
Boscombe Ave. E10 65 ED59
Boscombe Clo. E5 65 DY64
Boscombe Gdns. SW16 105 DL93
Boscombe Rd. SW17 104 DG93
Boscombe Rd. SW19 118 DA95
Boscombe Rd. W12 75 CU74
Boscombe Rd., Wor.Pk. 117 CW102
Bosgrove E4 51 EC46
Boss St. SE1 11 P4
Bostal Row, Bexh. 96 EZ83
Harlington Rd.
Bostall Heath SE2 96 EV78
Bostall Hill SE2 96 EU78
Bostall La. SE2 96 EV78
Bostall Manorway SE2 96 EV77
Bostall Pk. Ave., Bexh. 96 EY80
Bostall Rd., Orp. 110 EV94
Boston Gdns. W4 88 CS79
Boston Gdns. W7 87 CG77
Boston Rd.
Boston Gdns., Brent. 87 CG77
Boston Gro., Ruis. 57 BQ58
Boston Manor Rd., Brent. 87 CH77
Boston Pk. Rd., Brent. 87 CJ78
Boston Pl. NW1 4 D5
Boston Pl. NW1 76 DF70
Boston Rd. E6 80 EL69
Boston Rd. E17 65 EA58
Boston Rd. W7 73 CE74
Boston Rd., Croy. 119 DM100
Boston Rd., Edg. 46 CQ52
Boston St. E2 78 DU68
Audrey St.
Boston Vale W7 87 CG77
Bostonthorpe Rd. W7 87 CE75
Bosville Ave., Sev. 154 FG123
Bosville Dr., Sev. 154 FG123
Bosville Rd., Sev. 154 FG123
Boswell Clo., Orp. 124 EW100
Killewarren Way
Boswell Ct. WC1 6 A6
Boswell Path, Hayes 85 BT77
Croyde Ave.
Boswell Rd., Th.Hth. 120 DQ98
Boswell St. WC1 6 A6
Boswell St. WC1 77 DL71
Bosworth Clo. E17 51 DZ53
Bosworth Rd. N11 49 DK51
Bosworth Rd. W10 75 CY70
Bosworth Rd., Barn. 34 DA41
Bosworth Rd., Dag. 68 FA62
Botany Bay La., Chis. 123 EQ96
Botany Clo., Barn. 34 DE42
Boteley Clo. E4 51 ED47
Botha Rd. E13 80 EH71
Botham Clo., Edg. 46 CQ52
Pavilion Way
Bothwell Clo. E16 80 EF71
Bothwell Rd., Croy. 135 EC110
Bothwell St. W6 89 CX79
Delorme St.
Botolph All. EC3 7 M10
Botolph La. EC3 7 M10
Botsford Rd. SW20 117 CY96
Bottom La., Kings L. 28 BH35
Botts Ms. W2 76 DA72
Chepstow Rd.
Botts Pas. W2 76 DA72
Chepstow Rd.
Botwell Common Rd., Hayes 71 BR73
Botwell Cres., Hayes 71 BS72
Botwell La., Hayes 71 BS73
Boucher Clo., Tedd. 101 CF92
Bouchier Wk., Rain. 83 FG65
Deere Ave.
Boughton Ave., Brom. 122 EF101
Boughton Rd. SE28 95 ES76
Boulcott St. E1 79 DX72
Boulevard, The SW17 104 DG89
Balham High Rd.
Boulevard, The, Pnr. 58 CA56
Pinner Rd.
Boulevard, The, Wat. 29 BR43
Boulmer Rd., Uxb. 70 BJ69
Boulogne Rd., Croy. 120 DQ100
Boulter Gdns., Rain. 83 FG65

Bou–Bra This index reads in the sequence: Street Name / Postal District or Post Town / Map Page Number / Grid Reference

Boulton Ho., Brent. 88 CL78
Green Dragon La.
Boulton Rd., Dag. 68 EY62
Boultwood Rd. E6 81 EM72
Bounce Hill (Navestock), Rom. 41 FH38
Mill La.
Bounces La. N9 50 DV47
Bounces Rd. N9 50 DV47
Boundaries Rd. SW12 104 DF89
Boundaries Rd., Felt. 100 BW88
Boundary Ave. E17 65 DZ59
Boundary Rd.
Boundary Clo. SE20 120 DU96
Haysleigh Gdns.
Boundary Clo., Ilf. 67 ES63
Loxford La.
Boundary Clo., Kings.T. 116 CP97
Boundary Clo., Sthl. 86 CA78
Boundary La. E13 80 EK69
Boundary La. SE17 92 DQ79
Boundary Par. N8 63 DL58
Boundary Pas. E2 7 P4
Boundary Rd. E13 80 EJ68
Boundary Rd. E17 65 DZ59
Boundary Rd. N9 36 DW44
Boundary Rd. N22 63 DP55
Boundary Rd. NW8 76 DC67
Boundary Rd. SW19 104 DD93
Boundary Rd., Ashf. 98 BJ92
Boundary Rd., Bark. 81 ER67
Boundary Rd., Cars. 132 DG108
Boundary Rd., Pnr. 58 BX59
Boundary Rd., Rom. 69 FG58
Boundary Rd., Sid. 109 ES85
Boundary Rd., Wall. 133 DH107
Boundary Rd., Wem. 60 CL62
Boundary Row SE1 10 F4
Boundary St. E2 7 P3
Boundary St. E2 78 DT70
Boundary St., Erith 97 FF80
Boundary Way, Croy. 135 EA106
Boundary Way, Wat. 15 BV32
Boundfield Rd. SE6 108 EE90
Bounds Grn. Rd. N11 49 DJ51
Bounds Grn. Rd. N22 49 DL52
Bourchier Clo., Sev. 155 FH126
Bourchier St. W1 5 M10
Bourdon Pl. W1 5 J10
Bourdon Rd. SE20 120 DW96
Bourdon St. W1 9 H1
Bourdon St. W1 77 DH73
Bourke Clo. NW10 74 CS65
Mayo Rd.
Bourke Clo. SW4 105 DL86
Bourke Hill, Couls. 146 DF118
Bourlet Clo. W1 5 K7
Bourn Ave. N15 64 DR56
Bourn Ave., Barn. 34 DD43
Bourn Ave., Uxb. 70 BN70
Bournbrook Rd. SE3 94 EK83
Bourne, The N14 49 DK46
Bourne Ave. N14 49 DL47
Bourne Ave., Cher. 112 BG97
Eastern Ave.
Bourne Ave., Hayes 85 BQ76
Bourne Ave., Ruis. 58 BW64
Bourne Bri. La., Rom. 54 EZ45
Bourne Clo., W.Byf. 126 BH113
Bourne Ct., Ruis. 57 BV64
Bourne Dr., Mitch. 118 DD96
Bourne End Rd., Nthwd. 43 BS49
Bourne Est. EC1 6 D6
Bourne Est. EC1 77 DN71
Bourne Gdns. E4 51 EB49
Bourne Gro., Ash. 143 CK119
Bourne Hill N13 49 DM47
Bourne Ind. Pk., Dart. 111 FE85
Bourne Rd.
Bourne La., Cat. 148 DR121
Bourne Mead, Bex. 111 FC85
Bourne Pk. Clo., Ken. 148 DS116
Bourne Pl. W4 88 CR78
Dukes Ave.
Bourne Rd. E7 66 EF62
Bourne Rd. N8 63 DL58
Bourne Rd., Bex. 111 FB87
Bourne Rd., Brom. 122 EK98
Bourne Rd., Dart. 111 FD85
Bourne Rd. (Bushey), Wat. 30 CA43
Bourne St. SW1 8 F9
Bourne St. SW1 90 DG77
Bourne St., Croy. 119 DP103
Waddon New Rd.
Bourne Ter. W2 76 DB71
Bourne Vale, Brom. 122 EF102
Bourne Vw., Grnf. 73 CF65
Bourne Vw., Ken. 148 DR115
Bourne Way, Add. 126 BJ106
Bourne Way, Brom. 122 EE103
Bourne Way, Epsom 130 CQ105
Bourne Way, Sutt. 131 CZ106
Bourne Way, Swan. 125 FC97
Bournefield Rd., Whyt. 148 DT118
Godstone Rd.
Bournehall Ave. (Bushey), Wat. 30 CA43
Bournehall La. (Bushey), Wat. 30 CA44
Bournehall Rd. (Bushey), Wat. 30 CA44
Bournemead Ave., Nthlt. 71 BU68
Bournemead Clo., Nthlt. 71 BU69
Bournemead Way, Nthlt. 71 BV68
Bournemouth Rd. SE15 92 DU82
Bournemouth Rd. SW19 118 DA95
Bourneside Cres. N14 49 DK46
Bourneside Gdns. SE6 107 EC92
Bourneside Rd., Add. 126 BK105
Bournevale Rd. SW16 105 DL91
Bournewood Rd. SE18 96 EU80
Bournewood Rd., Orp. 124 EV101
Bournville Rd. SE6 107 EA87
Bournwell Clo., Barn. 34 DF41
Bourton Clo., Hayes 71 BU74
Avondale Dr.
Bousfield Rd. SE14 93 DX82
Boutflower Rd. SW11 90 DE84
Bouverie Gdns., Har. 59 CK58
Bouverie Ms. N16 64 DS61
Bouverie Rd.
Bouverie Pl. W2 4 A8
Bouverie Pl. W2 76 DD72
Bouverie Rd. N16 64 DS60
Bouverie Rd., Couls. 146 DG118
Bouverie Rd., Har. 58 CC58
Bouverie St. EC4 6 E9
Bouverie St. EC4 77 DN72
Bouvier Rd., Enf. 36 DW38
Boveney Rd. SE23 107 DX87
Bovill Rd. SE23 107 DX87
Bovingdon Ave., Wem. 74 CN65
Bovingdon Clo. N19 63 DJ61
Junction Rd.
Bovingdon Cres., Wat. 16 BX34
Bovingdon La. NW9 46 CS53
Bovingdon Rd. SW6 90 DB81
Bovingdon Sq., Mitch. 119 DL98
Leicester Ave.
Bow Bri. Est. E3 79 EB68
Bow Chyd. EC4 7 J9
Bow Common La. E3 79 DY70
Bow Ind. Est. E15 79 EB66
Bow La. EC4 7 J9
Bow La. EC4 78 DQ72
Bow La. N12 48 DC52
Bow La., Mord. 117 CY100
Bow Rd. E3 79 DZ69
Bow St. E15 66 EE64
Bow St. WC2 6 A9
Bow St. WC2 77 DL72
Bowater Clo. NW9 60 CR57
Bowater Clo. SW2 105 DL86
Bowater Pl. SE3 94 EH80
Bowater Ridge, Wey. 127 BR110
Bowater Rd. SE18 94 EK76
Bowden Clo., Felt. 99 BS88
Bowden St. SE11 10 E10
Bowden St. SE11 91 DN78
Bowditch SE8 93 DZ78
Bowdon Rd. E17 65 EA59
Bowen Dr. SE21 106 DS90
Bowen Rd., Har. 58 CC59
Bowen St. E14 79 EB72
Bowens Wd., Croy. 135 DZ109
Bower Ave. SE10 94 EE81
Bower Clo., Nthlt. 72 BW68
Bower Clo., Rom. 55 FD52
Bower Ct., Epp. 26 EU32
Bower Fm. Rd. Rom. (Havering-atte-Bower) 55 FC48
Bower Hill, Epp. 26 EU32
Bower Rd., Swan. 111 FG94
Bower St. E1 79 DX72
Bower Ter., Epp. 26 EU32
Bower Hill
Bower Vale, Epp. 26 EU32
Bowerdean St. SW6 90 DB81
Bowerman Ave. SE14 93 DY79
Bowers Rd., Sev. 139 FF111
Bowers Wk. E6 81 EM72
Northumberland Rd.
Bowes Clo., Sid. 110 EV86
Bowes Rd. N11 49 DH50
Bowes Rd. N13 49 DL50
Bowes Rd. W3 74 CS73
Bowes Rd., Dag. 68 EW63
Bowes Rd., Walt. 113 BV103
Bowfell Rd. W6 89 CW79
Bowford Ave., Bexh. 96 EY81
Bowhill Clo. SW9 91 DN80
Bowie Clo. SW4 105 DK87
Bowl Ct. EC2 7 N5
Bowl Ct. EC2 78 DS70
Bowland Rd. SW4 91 DK84
Bowland Rd., Wdf.Grn. 52 EJ51
Bowland Yd. SW1 8 E5
Bowles Grn., Enf. 36 DV36
Bowles Rd. SE1 92 DU79
Old Kent Rd.
Bowley Clo. SE19 106 DT93
Bowley La. SE19 106 DT92
Bowling Ct., Wat. 29 BU42
Bowling Grn. Clo. SW15 103 CV87
Bowling Grn. La. EC1 6 E4
Bowling Grn. La. EC1 77 DN70
Bowling Grn. Pl. SE1 11 K4
Bowling Grn. Pl. SE1 92 DR75
Bowling Grn. Row SE18 95 EM76
Samuel St.
Bowling Grn. St. SE11 91 DN79
Bowling Grn. Wk. N1 7 M2
Bowls, The, Chig. 53 ES48
Bowls Clo., Stan. 45 CH50
Bowman Ave. E16 80 EF73
Bowman Ms. SW18 103 CZ88
Bowmans Clo. W13 73 CH74
Bowmans Clo., Pot.B. 20 DD32
Bowmans Grn., Wat. 30 BX36
Bowmans Lea SE23 106 DW87
Bowmans Meadow, Wall. 119 DH104
Bowmans Ms. E1 78 DU72
Hooper St.
Bowmans Ms. N7 63 DL62
Seven Sisters Rd.
Bowmans Pl. N7 63 DL62
Holloway Rd.
Bowmans Rd., Dart. 111 FF87
Bowman's Trd. Est. NW9 60 CM55
Westmoreland Rd.
Bowmead SE9 109 EM89
Bowmore Wk. NW1 77 DK66
St. Paul's Cres.
Bowness Clo. E8 78 DT65
Beechwood Rd.
Bowness Cres. SW15 102 CS92
Bowness Dr., Houns. 86 BY84
Bowness Rd. SE6 107 EB87
Bowness Rd., Bexh. 97 FB82
Bowness Way, Horn. 69 FG64
Bowood Rd. SW11 104 DG85
Bowood Rd., Enf. 37 DX40
Bowring Grn., Wat. 44 BW50
Bowrons Ave., Wem. 73 CK66
Bowsprit, The, Cob. 142 BW115
Bowyer Clo. E6 81 EM71
Bowyer Pl. SE5 92 DQ80
Bowyer St. SE5 92 DQ80
Bowyers Clo., Ash. 144 CM118
Box La., Bark. 82 EV68
Box Ridge Ave., Pur. 133 DM112
Boxall Rd. SE21 106 DS86
Boxford Clo., S.Croy. 135 DX112
Boxgrove Rd. SE2 96 EV75
Boxley Rd., Mord. 118 DC98
Boxley St. E16 80 EH74
Boxmoor Rd., Har. 59 CH56
Boxmoor Rd., Rom. 55 FC50
Boxoll Rd., Dag. 68 EZ63
Boxted Clo., Buck.H. 52 EL46
Boxtree La., Har. 44 CC53
Boxtree Rd., Har. 45 CD52
Boxtree Wk., Orp. 124 EX102
Eldred Dr.
Boxwood Clo., West Dr. 84 BM75
Hawthorne Cres.
Boxwood Way, Warl. 149 DX117
Boxworth Clo. N12 48 DD50
Boxworth Gro. N1 77 DM67
Richmond Ave.
Boyard Rd. SE18 95 EP78
Boyce Clo., Borwd. 32 CL39
Boyce St. SE1 10 B3
Boyce Way E13 80 EG70
Boycroft Ave. NW9 60 CQ58
Boyd Ave., Sthl. 72 BZ74
Boyd Clo., Kings.T. 102 CN94
Crescent Rd.
Boyd Rd. SW19 104 DD93
Boyd St. E1 78 DU72
Boydell Ct. NW8 76 DD66
St. John's Wd. Pk.
Boyfield St. SE1 10 G5
Boyfield St. SE1 91 DP75
Boyland Rd., Brom. 108 EF92
Boyle Ave., Stan. 45 CG51
Boyle Fm. Rd., T.Ditt. 115 CG100
Boyle St. W1 5 K10
Boyne Ave. NW4 61 CX56
Boyne Rd. SE13 93 EC83
Boyne Rd., Dag. 68 FA62
Boyne Ter. Ms. W11 75 CZ74
Boyseland Ct., Edg. 46 CQ47
Boyson Rd. SE17 92 DR79
Boythorn Way SE16 92 DV78
Credon Rd.
Boyton Clo. E1 79 DX70
Stayner's Rd.
Boyton Clo. N8 63 DL55
Boyton Rd. N8 63 DL55
Brabant Ct. EC3 7 M10
Brabant Rd. N22 49 DM54
Brabazon Ave., Wall. 133 DL108
Brabazon Rd., Houns. 86 BW80
Brabazon Rd., Nthlt. 72 CA68
Brabazon St. E14 79 EB72
Brabourn Gro. SE15 92 DW82
Brabourne Clo. SE19 106 DS92
Brabourne Cres., Bexh. 96 EZ79
Brabourne Heights NW7 46 CS48
Brabourne Ri., Beck. 121 EC99
Bracewell Ave., Grnf. 73 CG65
Bracewell Rd. W10 75 CW71
Bracewood Gdns., Croy. 120 DT104
Bracey Ms. N4 63 DL61
Bracey St.
Bracey St. N4 63 DL61
Bracken, The E4 51 EC47
Hortus Rd.
Bracken Ave. SW12 104 DG86
Bracken Ave., Croy. 121 EA104
Bracken Clo. E6 81 EM71
Bracken Clo., Borwd. 32 CN40
Hartforde Rd.
Bracken Clo., Lthd. 142 BZ124
Bracken Clo., Sun. 99 BT93
Cavendish Rd.
Bracken Clo., Twick. 100 CA87
Hedley Rd.
Bracken Dr., Chig. 53 EP51
Bracken End, Islw. 101 CD85
Bracken Gdns. SW13 89 CU82
Bracken Hill Clo., Brom. 122 EF95
Bracken Hill La.
Bracken Hill La., Brom. 122 EF95
Bracken Ind. Est., Ilf. 53 ET52
Bracken Ms. E4 51 EC47
Hortus Rd.
Bracken Ms., Rom. 69 FB58
Bracken Path, Epsom 130 CN113
Brackenbridge Dr., Ruis. 58 BX62
Brackenbury Gdns. W6 89 CV76
Brackenbury Rd. N2 62 DC55
Brackenbury Rd. W6 89 CV76
Brackendale N21 49 DM47
Brackendale, Pot.B. 20 DA33
Brackendale Clo., Houns. 86 CB81
Brackendene, Dart. 111 FE91
Brackendene, St.Alb. 16 BZ30
Brackenfield Clo. E5 64 DV63
Tiger Way
Brackenhill, Cob. 128 CA111
Brackens, The, Enf. 50 DS45
Brackens, The, Orp. 138 EU106
Brackenwood, Sun. 113 BU95
Brackley, Wey. 127 BR106
Brackley Clo., Wall. 133 DL108
Brackley Rd. W4 88 CS78
Brackley Rd., Beck. 107 DZ94
Brackley Sq., Wdf.Grn. 52 EK52
Brackley St. EC1 7 J6
Brackley Ter. W4 88 CS78
Bracklyn Clo. N1 78 DR68
Parr St.
Bracklyn Ct. N1 78 DR68
Wimbourne St.
Bracklyn St. N1 78 DR68
Bracknell Clo. N22 49 DN53
Bracknell Gdns. NW3 62 DB63
Bracknell Gate NW3 62 DB64
Bracknell Way NW3 62 DB63
Bracondale, Esher 128 CC107
Bracondale Rd. SE2 96 EU77
Brad St. SE1 10 E3
Bradbourne Pk. Rd., Sev. 154 FG123
Bradbourne Rd., Bex. 110 FA87
Bradbourne Rd., Sev. 155 FH122
Bradbourne St. SW6 90 DA82
Bradbourne Vale Rd., Sev. 154 FF122
Bradbury Clo., Borwd. 32 CP39
Bradbury Clo., Sthl. 86 BZ77
Bradbury Ms. N16 64 DS64
Bradbury St.
Bradbury St. N16 64 DS64
Braddock Clo., Islw. 87 CF83
Braddon Rd., Rich. 88 CM83
Braddyll St. SE10 94 EE78
Braden St. W9 76 DB70
Shirland Rd.
Bradenham Ave., Well. 96 EU84
Bradenham Clo. SE17 92 DR79
Bradenham Rd., Har. 59 CH56
Bradenham Rd., Hayes 71 BS69
Bradfield Dr., Bark. 68 EU64
Bradfield Rd. E16 94 EG75
Bradfield Rd., Ruis. 58 BY64
Bradford Clo. SE26 106 DV91
Coombe Rd.
Bradford Clo., Brom. 123 EM102
Bradford Dr., Epsom 131 CT107
Bradford Rd. W3 88 CS75
Warple Way
Bradford Rd., Ilf. 67 ER60
Bradgate (Cuffley), Pot.B. 21 DK27
Bradgate Clo. (Cuffley), Pot.B. 21 DK28
Bradgate Rd. SE6 107 EA86
Brading Cres. E11 66 EH61
Brading Rd. SW2 105 DM87
Brading Rd., Croy. 119 DM100
Bradiston Rd. W9 75 CZ69
Bradley Clo. N7 77 DM65
Sutterton St.
Bradley Clo., Sutt. 132 DA110
Station Rd.
Bradley Gdns. W13 73 CH72
Bradley Ms. SW17 104 DF88
Bellevue Rd.
Bradley Rd. N22 49 DM54
Bradley Rd. SE19 106 DQ93
Bradley Rd., Enf. 37 DY37
Bradley Stone Rd. E6 81 EM71
Bradley's Clo. N1 77 DN68
White Lion St.
Bradman Row, Edg. 46 CQ52
Pavilion Way
Bradmead SW8 91 DH80
Bradmore Grn., Couls. 147 DM118
Coulsdon Rd.
Bradmore Grn., Hat. 19 CY26
Bradmore Ho. E1 78 DW71
Jamaica St.
Bradmore La., Hat. 19 CW27
Bradmore Pk. Rd. W6 89 CV77
Bradmore Way, Couls. 147 DL117
Bradmore Way, Hat. 19 CY26
Bradshaw Clo. SW19 104 DA93
Bradshaw Rd., Wat. 30 BW39
Bradshawe Waye, Uxb. 70 BL71
Bradshaws Clo. SE25 120 DU97
Bradstock Rd. E9 79 DX65
Bradstock Rd., Epsom 131 CU106
Bradwell Ave., Dag. 68 FA61
Bradwell Clo. E18 66 EF56
Bradwell Clo., Horn. 83 FH65
Bradwell Ms. N18 50 DU49
Lyndhurst Rd.
Bradwell Rd., Buck.H. 52 EL46
Bradwell St. E1 79 DX69
Brady Ave., Loug. 39 EQ40
Brady St. E1 78 DV70
Bradymead E6 81 EP72
Warwall
Braemar Ave. N22 49 DL53
Braemar Ave. NW10 60 CR62
Braemar Ave. SW19 104 DA89
Braemar Ave., Bexh. 97 FC84
Braemar Ave., S.Croy. 134 DQ110
Braemar Ave., Th.Hth. 119 DN97
Braemar Ave., Wem. 73 CK66
Braemar Gdns. NW9 46 CR53
Braemar Gdns., Sid. 109 ER90
Braemar Gdns., W.Wick. 121 EC102
Braemar Rd. E13 80 EF70
Braemar Rd. N15 64 DS57
Braemar Rd., Brent. 87 CK79
Braemar Rd., Wor.Pk. 117 CV104
Braes St. N1 77 DP66
Braeside, Add. 126 BH111
Braeside, Beck. 107 EA92
Braeside Ave. SW19 117 CY95
Braeside Ave., Sev. 154 FF124
Braeside Clo., Pnr. 44 CA52
The Ave.
Braeside Clo., Sev. 154 FF123
Braeside Cres., Bexh. 97 FC84
Braeside Rd. SW16 105 DJ94
Braesyde Clo., Belv. 96 EZ77
Brafferton Rd., Croy. 134 DQ105
Braganza St. SE17 91 DP78
Braham St. E1 78 DT72
Braid Ave. W3 74 CS72
Braid Clo., Felt. 100 BZ89
Braidwood Rd. SE6 107 ED88
Braidwood St. SE1 11 M3
Brailsford Clo., Mitch. 104 DE94
Brailsford Rd. SW2 105 DN85
Brainton Ave., Felt. 99 BV87
Braintree Ave., Ilf. 66 EL56
Braintree Rd., Dag. 68 FA62
Braintree Rd., Ruis. 57 BV63
Braintree St. E2 78 DW70
Braithwaite Ave., Rom. 68 FA59
Braithwaite Gdns., Stan. 45 CJ53
Braithwaite Rd., Enf. 37 DZ41
Bramah Grn. SW9 91 DN81
Bramalea Clo. N6 62 DG58
Bramall Clo. E15 66 EF64
Idmiston Rd.
Bramber Ct., Brent. 88 CL77
Sterling Pl.
Bramber Rd. N12 48 DE50
Bramber Rd. W14 89 CZ79
Bramble Banks, Cars. 132 DG109
Bramble Clo., Cat. 148 DS122
Burntwood La.
Bramble Clo., Croy. 135 EA105
Bramble Clo., Shep. 113 BR98
Halliford Clo.
Bramble Clo., Stan. 45 CK52
Bramble Clo., Uxb. 70 BM71
Bramble Clo., Wat. 15 BU34
Bramble Cft., Erith 97 FC77
Bramble Gdns. W12 75 CT73
Wallflower St.
Bramble La., Hmptn. 100 BZ93
Bramble La., Sev. 155 FH128
Bramble Ri., Cob. 128 BW114
Bramble Wk., Epsom 130 CP114
Brambleacres Clo., Sutt. 132 DA108
Bramblebury Rd. SE18 95 EQ78
Brambledown, Stai. 112 BH95
Brambledown Clo., W.Wick. 122 EE99
Brambledown Rd., Cars. 132 DG108
Brambledown Rd., S.Croy. 134 DS108
Brambledown Rd., Wall. 133 DH108
Brambles, The, Chig. 53 EQ51
Brambles, The, Wal.Cr. 23 DX31
Brambles, The, West Dr. 84 BK77
Brambles Clo., Cat. 148 DS122
Brambles Clo., Islw. 87 CH80
Brambles Fm. Dr., Uxb. 70 BN69
Bramblewood Clo., Cars. 118 DF102
Brambling Clo., Wat. 30 BY42
Bramblings, The E4 51 ED49
Bramcote Ave., Mitch. 118 DF98
Bramcote Gro. SE16 92 DW78
Bramcote Rd. SW15 89 CV84
Bramdean Cres. SE12 108 EG88
Bramdean Gdns. SE12 108 EG88
Bramerton Rd., Beck. 121 DZ97
Bramerton St. SW3 90 DE79
Bramfield, Wat. 16 BY34
Garston La.
Bramfield Ct. N4 64 DQ61
Queens Dr.
Bramfield Rd. SW11 104 DE86
Bramford Ct. N14 49 DK47
Bramford Rd. SW18 90 DC84
Bramham Gdns. SW5 90 DB78
Bramham Gdns., Chess. 129 CK105
Bramhope La. SE7 94 EH79
Bramlands Clo. SW11 90 DE83
Bramleas, Wat. 29 BT42
Bramley Ave., Couls. 147 DJ115
Bramley Clo. E17 51 DY54
Bramley Clo. N14 35 DH43
Bramley Clo., Cher. 112 BH102
Bramley Clo., Hayes 71 BU73
Orchard Rd.
Bramley Clo., Orp. 123 EP102
Bramley Clo., S.Croy. 133 DP106
Bramley Clo., Stai. 98 BJ93
Bramley Clo., Swan. 125 FE98
Bramley Clo., Twick. 100 CC86
Bramley Ct., Wat. 15 BV31
Orchard Ave.
Bramley Ct., Well. 96 EV81
Bramley Cres. SW8 91 DK80
Pascal St.

Bramley Cres., Ilf. 67 EN58
Bramley Gdns., Wat. 44 BW50
Bramley Hill, S.Croy. 133 DP106
Bramley Pl., Dart. 97 FG84
Bramley Rd. N14 35 DH43
Bramley Rd. W5 87 CJ76
Bramley Rd. W10 75 CX73
Bramley Rd., Sutt. 132 DD106
Bramley Rd. (Cheam), Sutt. 131 CX109
Bramley Shaw, Wal.Abb. 24 EF33
Bramley Way, Ash. 144 CM117
Bramley Way, Houns. 100 BZ85
Bramley Way, W.Wick. 121 EB103
Brampton Clo. E5 64 DV61
Brampton Clo. (Cheshunt), Wal.Cr. 22 DU28
Brampton Gdns. N15 64 DQ57
Brampton Rd.
Brampton Gdns., Walt. 128 BW106
Brampton Gro. NW4 61 CV56
Brampton Gro., Har. 59 CG56
Brampton Gro., Wem. 60 CM60
Brampton La. NW4 61 CW56
Brampton Pk. Rd. N22 63 DN55
Brampton Rd. E6 80 EK70
Brampton Rd. N15 64 DQ57
Brampton Rd. NW9 60 CN56
Brampton Rd. SE2 96 EW79
Brampton Rd., Bexh. 96 EX83
Brampton Rd., Croy. 120 DT101
Brampton Rd., Uxb. 71 BP68
Brampton Rd., Wat. 43 BU48
Brampton Ter., Borwd. 32 CN38
Bramsham Gdns., Wat. 44 BX50
Bramshaw Ri., N.Mal. 116 CS100
Bramshaw Rd. E9 79 DX65
Bramshill Clo., Chig. 53 ES50
Tine Rd.
Bramshill Gdns. NW5 63 DH62
Bramshill Rd. NW10 74 CS68
Bramshot Ave. SE7 94 EG79
Bramshot Way, Wat. 43 BU47
Bramston Clo., Ilf. 53 ET51
Bramston Rd. NW10 75 CU68
Bramston Rd. SW17 104 DC90
Bramwell Clo., Sun. 114 BX96
Bramwell Ms. N1 77 DM67
Brancaster Dr. NW7 47 CU52
Brancaster La., Pur. 134 DQ110
Brancaster Pl., Loug. 39 EM41
Brancaster Rd. E12 67 EM63
Brancaster Rd. SW16 105 DL90
Brancaster Rd., Ilf. 67 ER58
Brancepeth Gdns., Buck.H. 52 EG47
Branch Hill NW3 62 DC62
Branch Pl. N1 78 DR67
Branch Rd. E14 79 DY73
Branch Rd., Ilf. 54 EV50
Branch Rd. (Park St.), St.Alb. 17 CD27
Branch St. SE15 92 DS80
Brancker Clo., Wall. 133 DL108
Brown Clo.
Brancker Rd., Har. 59 CK55
Brancroft Way, Enf. 37 DY39
Brand St. SE10 93 EC80
Brandlehow Rd. SW15 89 CZ84
Brandon Clo. (Cheshunt), Wal.Cr. 22 DS26
Brandon Est. SE17 91 DP79
Brandon Ms. EC2 78 DR71
Moor La.
Brandon Rd. E17 65 EC55
Brandon Rd. N7 77 DL66
Brandon Rd., Sthl. 86 BZ78
Brandon Rd., Sutt. 132 DB105
Brandon St. SE17 11 J9
Brandon St. SE17 92 DQ77
Brandram Rd. SE13 94 EE83
Brandreth Rd. E6 81 EM72
Brandreth Rd. SW17 105 DH89
Brandries, The, Wall. 119 DK104
Brandville Gdns., Ilf. 67 EP56
Brandville Rd., West Dr. 84 BL75
Brandy Way, Sutt. 132 DA108
Brangbourne Rd., Brom. 107 EC92
Brangton Rd. SE11 91 DM78
Brangwyn Cres. SW19 118 DC96
Branksea St. SW6 89 CY80
Branksome Ave. N18 50 DT51
Branksome Clo., Walt. 114 BX103
Branksome Rd. SW2 91 DL84
Branksome Rd. SW19 118 DA95
Branksome Way, Har. 60 CL58
Branksome Way, N.Mal. 116 CQ95
Bransby Rd., Chess. 130 CL108
Branscombe Gdns. N21 49 DN45
Branscombe St. SE13 93 EB83
Bransdale Clo. NW6 76 DB67
West End La.
Bransell Clo., Swan. 125 FC100
Bransgrove Rd., Edg. 46 CM53
Branston Cres., Orp. 123 ER102
Branstone Rd., Rich. 88 CM81
Brants Wk. W7 73 CE70
Brantwood Ave., Erith 97 FC80
Brantwood Ave., Islw. 87 CG84
Brantwood Clo. E17 65 EB55
Brantwood Gdns., Enf. 35 DL42
Brantwood Gdns., Ilf. 66 EL56
Brantwood Rd. N17 50 DT51
Brantwood Rd. SE24 106 DQ85
Brantwood Rd., Bexh. 97 FB82
Brantwood Rd., S.Croy. 134 DQ109
Brantwood Way, Orp. 124 EW97
Brasenose Dr. SW13 89 CV79
Trinity Ch. Rd.
Brasher Clo., Grnf. 59 CD64
Brass Tally All. SE16 93 DX75
Middleton Dr.
Brassey Clo., Felt. 99 BT88
Brassey Rd. NW6 75 CZ65
Brassey Sq. SW11 90 DG83
Brassie Ave. W3 74 CS72
Brasted Clo. SE26 106 DW91
Brasted Clo., Bexh. 110 EX85
Brasted Clo., Orp. 124 EU103
Brasted Clo., Sutt. 132 DA110
Brasted Hill, Sev. 152 EU120
Brasted Hill Rd., West. 152 EV121
Brasted La., Sev. 152 EU119
Brasted Rd., Erith 97 FF78
Brathway Rd. SW18 104 DA87
Bratley St. E1 78 DU70
Weaver St.
Brattle Wd., Sev. 155 FH129
Braund Ave., Grnf. 72 CB70
Braundton Ave., Sid. 109 ET88
Braunston Dr., Hayes 72 BY70
Bravington Clo., Shep. 112 BM99
Bravington Pl. W9 75 CZ70
Bravington Rd.
Bravington Rd. W9 75 CZ69
Brawne Ho. SE17 91 DP79
Hillingdon St.
Braxfield Rd. SE4 93 DY84
Braxted Pk. SW16 105 DM93
Bray NW3 76 DE66
Bray Clo., Borwd. 32 CQ39
Bray Cres. SE16 93 DX75
Marlow Way
Bray Dr. E16 80 EF73
Bray Pas. E16 80 EF73
Bowman Ave.
Bray Pl. SW3 8 D9
Bray Pl. SW3 90 DF77
Bray Rd. NW7 47 CX52
Bray Rd., Cob. 142 BY116
Brayards Rd. SE15 92 DV82
Brayards Rd. Est. SE15 92 DV82
Brayards Rd.
Braybourne Clo., Uxb. 70 BJ65
Braybourne Dr., Islw. 87 CF80
Braybrook St. W12 75 CT71
Braybrooke Gdns. SE19 106 DT94
Fox Hill
Brayburne Ave. SW4 91 DJ82
Braycourt Ave., Walt. 113 BV101
Braydon Rd. N16 64 DU59
Brayfield Ter. N1 77 DN66
Lofting Rd.
Brayford Sq. E1 79 DY72
Summercourt Rd.
Brayton Gdns., Enf. 35 DK42
Braywood Rd. SE9 95 ER84
Brazil Clo., Croy. 119 DL101
Breach La., Dag. 82 FA69
Bread St. EC4 7 J10
Bread St. EC4 78 DQ73
Breakfield, Couls. 147 DL116
Breakspear Ct., Abb.L. 15 BT30
The Cres.
Breakspear Rd., Ruis. 57 BP59
Breakspear Rd. N., Uxb. 42 BJ53
Breakspear Rd. S., Uxb. 56 BM62
Breakspeare Clo., Wat. 29 BV38
Breakspeare Rd., Abb.L. 15 BS31
Breakspears Dr., Orp. 124 EU95
Breakspears Ms. SE4 93 EA82
Breakspears Rd.
Breakspears Rd. SE4 93 DZ83
Bream Clo. N17 64 DV56
Bream Gdns. E6 81 EN69
Bream St. E3 79 EA66
Breamore Clo. SW15 103 CU88
Breamore Rd., Ilf. 67 ET61
Bream's Bldgs. EC4 6 D8
Bream's Bldgs. EC4 77 DN72
Breamwater Gdns., Rich. 101 CH90
Brearley Clo., Edg. 46 CQ52
Pavilion Way
Brearley Clo., Uxb. 70 BL65
Breasley Clo. SW15 89 CV84
Brechin Pl. SW7 90 DC77
Rosary Gdns.
Brecknock Rd. N7 63 DK64
Brecknock Rd. N19 63 DJ63
Brecknock Rd. Est. N7 63 DJ63
Brecon Clo., Mitch. 119 DL97
Brecon Clo., Wor.Pk. 117 CW103
Cotswold Way
Brecon Rd. W6 89 CY79
Brecon Rd., Enf. 36 DW42
Brede Clo. E6 81 EN69
Bredgar Rd. N19 63 DJ61
Bredhurst Clo. SE20 106 DW93
Bredon Rd. SE5 92 DQ83
Bredon Rd., Croy. 120 DT101
Bredune, Ken. 148 DR115
Church Rd.
Breech La., Tad. 145 CU124
Breer St. SW6 90 DB83
Breezers Hill E1 78 DU73
Pennington St.
Brember Rd., Har. 58 CC61
Bremer Ms. E17 65 EB56
Church La.
Bremer Rd., Stai. 98 BG90
Bremner Clo., Swan. 125 FG98
Bremner Rd. SW7 90 DC76
Queen's Gate
Brenchley Clo., Brom. 122 EF100
Brenchley Clo., Chis. 123 EN95
Brenchley Gdns. SE23 106 DW86
Brenchley Rd., Orp. 123 ES95
Brenda Rd. SW17 104 DF89
Brende Gdns., W.Mol. 114 CB98
Brendon Ave. NW10 60 CS63
Brendon Clo., Erith 97 FE81
Brendon Clo., Esher 128 CC107
Brendon Clo., Hayes 85 BQ80
Brendon Ct., Rad. 17 CH34
The Ave.
Brendon Dr., Esher 128 CC107
Brendon Gdns., Har. 58 CB63
Brendon Gdns., Ilf. 67 ES57
Brendon Gro. N2 48 DC54
Brendon Rd. SE9 109 ER89
Brendon Rd., Dag. 68 EZ60
Brendon St. W1 4 C8
Brendon St. W1 76 DE72
Brendon Way, Enf. 50 DS45
Brenley Clo., Mitch. 118 DG97
Brenley Gdns. SE9 94 EK84
Brent Clo., Bex. 110 EY88
Brent Cres. NW10 74 CM68
Brent Cross Gdns. NW4 61 CX58
Haley Rd.
Brent Cross Shop. Cen. NW4 61 CW59
Brent Grn. NW4 61 CW57
Brent Grn. Wk., Wem. 60 CQ62
Brent Lea, Brent. 87 CJ80
Brent Pk. NW10 60 CR64
Brent Pk. Rd. NW4 61 CV59
Brent Pk. Rd. NW9 61 CV59
Brent Pl., Barn. 34 DA43
Brent Rd. E16 80 EG71
Brent Rd. SE18 95 EP80
Brent Rd., Brent. 87 CJ79
Brent Rd., S.Croy. 134 DV109
Brent Rd., Sthl. 86 BW76
Brent St. NW4 61 CW56
Brent Ter. NW2 61 CW60
Brent Vw. Rd. NW9 61 CU58
Brent Way N3 48 DA51
Brent Way, Brent. 87 CK80
Brent Way, Wem. 74 CP65
Brentcot Clo. W13 73 CH70
Brentfield NW10 74 CP66
Brentfield Clo. NW10 74 CR65
Normans Mead
Brentfield Gdns. NW2 61 CX59
Hendon Way
Brentfield Rd. NW10 74 CR65
Brentford Business Cen., Brent. 87 CJ80
Brentford Clo., Hayes 72 BX70
Brentham Way W5 73 CK70
Brenthouse Rd. E9 78 DW65
Brenthurst Rd. NW10 75 CT65
Brentmead Clo. W7 73 CE73
Brentmead Gdns. NW10 74 CM68
Brentmead Pl. NW11 61 CX58
North Circular Rd.
Brenton St. E14 79 DY72
Brentside, Brent. 87 CJ79
Brentside Clo. W13 73 CG70
Brentside Executive Cen., Brent. 87 CH79
Brentvale Ave., Sthl. 73 CD74
Brentvale Ave., Wem. 74 CM67
Brentwick Gdns., Brent. 88 CL77
Brentwood Clo. SE9 109 EQ88
Brentwood Ct., Add. 126 BH105
Brentwood Ho. SE18 94 EK80
Shooter's Hill Rd.
Brentwood Rd., Rom. 69 FF58
Brereton Rd. N17 50 DT52
Bressenden Pl. SW1 9 J6
Bressenden Pl. SW1 91 DH76
Bressey Ave., Enf. 36 DU39
Bressey Gro. E18 52 EF54
Brett Clo. N16 64 DS61
Yoakley Rd.
Brett Clo., Nthlt. 72 BX69
Broomcroft Ave.
Brett Ct. N9 50 DW47
Brett Cres. NW10 74 CR66
Brett Gdns., Dag. 82 EY66
Brett Ho. Clo. SW15 103 CX86
Putney Heath La.
Brett Pas. E8 64 DV64
Kenmure Rd.
Brett Pl., Wat. 29 BU37
The Harebreaks
Brett Rd. E8 64 DV64
Brett Rd., Barn. 33 CW43
Brettell St. SE17 92 DR78
Merrow St.
Brettenham Ave. E17 51 EA53
Penrhyn Ave.
Brettenham Rd. E17 51 EA54
Brettenham Rd. N18 50 DU49
Brettgrave, Epsom 130 CQ111
Brewer St. W1 5 L10
Brewer St. W1 77 DJ73
Brewer's Grn. SW1 9 L6
Brewers Hall Gdns. EC2 7 J7
Brewers La., Rich. 101 CK85
George St.
Brewery Clo., Wem. 59 CG64
Brewery La., Sev. 155 FJ125
High St.
Brewery La., Twick. 101 CF87
Brewery La., W.Byf. 126 BL113
Brewery Rd. N7 77 DL66
Brewery Rd. SE18 95 ER78
Brewery Rd., Brom. 122 EL102
Brewery Sq. SE1 78 DT74
Horselydown La.
Brewhouse La. E1 78 DV74
Brewhouse Rd. SE18 95 EM77
Brewhouse St. SW15 89 CY83
Brewhouse Wk. SE16 79 DY74
Brewhouse Yd. EC1 6 F4
Brewood Rd., Dag. 82 EV65
Brewster Gdns. W10 75 CW71
Brewster Ho. E14 79 DZ73
Brewster Rd. E10 65 EB60
Breycaine Ind. Est., Wat. 30 BX37
Brian Ave., S.Croy. 134 DS112
Brian Clo., Horn. 69 FH63
Brian Rd., Rom. 68 EW57
Briane Rd., Epsom 130 CQ110
Briant St. SE14 93 DX81
Briants Clo., Pnr. 44 BZ54
Briar Ave. SW16 105 DM94
Briar Banks, Cars. 132 DG109
Briar Clo. N2 48 DB54
Briar Clo. N13 50 DQ48
Briar Clo., Buck.H. 52 EK47
Briar Clo., Hmptn. 100 BZ92
Briar Clo., Islw. 101 CF85
Briar Clo. (Cheshunt), Wal.Cr. 22 DW29
Briar Clo., W.Byf. 126 BH111
Briar Ct., Sutt. 131 CW105
Briar Cres., Nthlt. 72 CB65
Briar Gdns., Brom. 122 EF102
Briar Gro., S.Croy. 134 DU113
Briar Hill, Pur. 133 DL111
Briar La., Cars. 132 DG109
Briar La., Croy. 135 EB105
Briar Pas. SW16 119 DL97
Pollards Cres.
Briar Pl. SW16 119 DM97
Briar Rd.
Briar Rd. NW2 61 CW63
Briar Rd. SW16 119 DL97
Briar Rd., Bex. 111 FD90
Briar Rd., Har. 59 CJ57
Briar Rd., Shep. 112 BM99
Briar Rd., Twick. 101 CE88
Briar Rd., Wat. 15 BU34
Briar Wk. SW15 89 CV84
Briar Wk. W10 75 CY70
Droop St.
Briar Wk., Edg. 46 CQ52
Briar Wk., W.Byf. 126 BG112
Briar Way, West Dr. 84 BN75
Briarbank Rd. W13 73 CG72
Briardale Gdns. NW3 62 DA62
Briarfield Ave. N3 48 DB54
Briaris Clo. N17 50 DV52
Briars, The, Rick. 28 BH36
Briars, The (Cheshunt), Wal.Cr. 23 DY31
Briars, The (Bushey), Wat. 45 CE45
Briars Ct., Lthd. 129 CD114
Briarswood Way, Orp. 137 ET106
Briarwood Clo. NW9 60 CQ58
Briarwood Clo., Felt. 99 BS90
Briarwood Dr., Nthwd. 43 BU54
Briarwood Rd. SW4 105 DK85
Briarwood Rd., Epsom 131 CU107
Briary Clo. NW3 76 DE66
Fellows Rd.
Briary Ct., Sid. 110 EV92
Briary Gdns., Brom. 108 EH92
Briary Gro., Edg. 46 CP54
Briary La. N9 50 DT48
Brick Ct. EC4 6 D9
Brick Fm. Clo., Rich. 88 CP81
Brick Kiln Clo., Wat. 30 BY44
Brick La. E1 78 DT70
Brick La. E2 78 DT69
Brick La., Enf. 36 DV40
Brick La., Stan. 45 CK52
Honeypot La.
Brick St. W1 9 H3
Brick St. W1 77 DH74
Brickcroft, Brox. 23 DY26
Brickenden Ct., Wal.Abb. 24 EF33
Brickett Clo., Ruis. 57 BQ57
Brickfield Clo., Brent. 87 CJ80
Brickfield Cotts. SE18 95 ET79
Brickfield Fm. Gdns., Orp. 137 EQ105
Brickfield La., Barn. 33 CT44
Brickfield La., Hayes 85 BR79
Brickfield Rd. SW19 104 DB91
Brickfield Rd., Epp. 26 EX29
Brickfield Rd., Th.Hth. 119 DP95
Brickfields, Har. 59 CD61
Brickfields La., Epp. 26 EX29
Brickfield Rd.
Brickfields Way, West Dr. 84 BM76
Bricklayer's Arms SE1 11 N8
Brickwall La., Ruis. 57 BS60
Brickwood Clo. SE26 106 DV90
Brickwood Rd., Croy. 120 DS103
Bride Ct. EC4 6 F9
Bride La. EC4 6 F9
Bride St. N7 77 DM65
Brideale Clo. SE15 92 DT80
Colegrove Rd.
Bridewain St. SE1 11 P6
Bridewain St. SE1 92 DT76
Bridewell Pl. E1 78 DV74
Brewhouse La.
Bridewell Pl. EC4 6 F9
Bridford Ms. W1 5 J6
Bridge, The, Har. 59 CE55
Bridge App. NW1 76 DG66
Bridge Ave. W6 89 CV78
Bridge Ave. W7 73 CD71
Bridge Clo. W10 75 CX72
Kingsdown Clo.
Bridge Clo., Enf. 36 DV40
Bridge Clo., Rom. 69 FE58
Bridge Clo., Walt. 113 BT101
Bridge Clo., W.Byf. 126 BM112
Bridge Dr. N13 49 DM50
Bridge End E17 51 EC53
Bridge Gdns., Ashf. 99 BQ94
Bridge Gdns., E.Mol. 115 CD98
Bridge Gate N21 50 DQ45
Ridge Ave.
Bridge Hill, Epp. 25 ET33
Bridge Ho. Quay E14 79 EC74
Prestons Rd.
Bridge La. NW11 61 CY56
Bridge La. SW11 90 DE81
Bridge Meadows SE14 93 DX79
Bridge Pk. SW18 104 DA85
Bridge Pl. SW1 9 J8
Bridge Pl. SW1 91 DH77
Bridge Pl., Croy. 120 DR102
Bridge Pl., Wat. 30 BX43
Bridge Rd. E6 81 EM66
Bridge Rd. E15 79 ED67
Bridge Rd. E17 65 DZ59
Bridge Rd. N9 50 DU48
The Bdy.
Bridge Rd. N22 49 DL53
Bridge Rd. NW10 74 CS65
Bridge Rd., Beck. 107 DZ94
Bridge Rd., Bexh. 96 EY82
Bridge Rd., Cher. 112 BH101
Bridge Rd., Chess. 129 CK106
Bridge Rd., Croy. 120 DQ104
Duppas Hill Rd.
Bridge Rd., E.Mol. 115 CD99
Bridge Rd., Epsom 131 CT112
Bridge Rd., Erith 97 FF82
Bridge Rd., Houns. 87 CD83
Bridge Rd., Islw. 87 CD83
Bridge Rd., Kings L. 15 BQ33
Bridge Rd., Orp. 124 EV100
Bridge Rd., Rain. 83 FG70
Bridge Rd., Sthl. 86 BZ75
Bridge Rd., Sutt. 132 DB107
Bridge Rd., Twick. 101 CH86
Bridge Rd., Uxb. 70 BJ67
Bridge Rd., Wall. 133 DH106
Bridge Rd., Wem. 60 CN62
Bridge Rd., Wey. 126 BM105
Bridge Row, Croy. 120 DR102
Cross Rd.
Bridge St. SW1 9 P5
Bridge St. SW1 91 DL75
Bridge St. W4 88 CR77
Bridge St., Lthd. 143 CG122
Bridge St., Pnr. 58 BY55
Bridge St., Rich. 101 CK85
Bridge St., Walt. 113 BS102
Bridge Ter. E15 79 ED66
Bridge Vw. W6 89 CW78
Bridge Way N11 49 DJ48
Pymmes Grn. Rd.
Bridge Way NW11 61 CZ57
Bridge Way, Cob. 127 BT113
Bridge Way, Couls. 146 DE119
Bridge Way, Twick. 100 CC87
Bridge Way, Uxb. 57 BP64
Bridge Way, Wem. 74 CL66
Bridge Wf., Cher. 112 BJ102
Bridge Wf. Rd., Islw. 87 CH83
Church St.
Bridge Wks. Ind. Est., Uxb. 70 BJ70
Bridge Yd. SE1 11 L2
Bridgefield Clo., Bans. 145 CW115
Bridgefield Rd., Sutt. 132 DA107
Bridgefoot SE1 91 DL78
Bridgefoot La., Pot.B. 19 CX33
Bridgeham Clo., Wey. 126 BN106
Mayfield Rd.
Bridgeland Rd. E16 80 EG73
Bridgeman Rd. N1 77 DM66
Bridgeman Rd. W4 88 CQ76
Bridgeman Rd., Tedd. 101 CG93
Bridgeman St. NW8 4 B1
Bridgeman St. NW8 76 DE68
Bridgen Rd., Bex. 110 EY86
Bridgend Rd. SW18 90 DC84
Bridgend Rd., Enf. 36 DW35
Bridgenhall Rd., Enf. 36 DT39
Bridgeport Pl. E1 78 DU74
Kennet St.
Bridger Clo., Wat. 16 BX33
Bridges Ct. SW11 90 DD83
Bridges La., Croy. 133 DL105
Bridges Ms. SW19 104 DB93
Bridges Rd.
Bridges Pl. SW6 89 CZ81
Bridges Rd. SW19 104 DB93
Bridges Rd., Stan. 45 CF50
Bridges Rd. Ms. SW19 104 DB93
Bridges Rd.
Bridgetown Clo. SE19 106 DS92
St. Kitts Ter.
Bridgeview Ct., Ilf. 53 ER51
Bridgewater Clo., Chis. 123 ES97
Bridgewater Gdns., Edg. 46 CM54
Bridgewater Rd., Ruis. 57 BU63
Bridgewater Rd., Wem. 73 CJ65
Bridgewater Rd., Wey. 127 BR107
Bridgewater Sq. EC2 7 H6
Bridgewater St. EC2 7 H6
Bridgewater Way (Bushey), Wat. 30 CB44

Bridgeway, Bark. 81 ET66
Bridgeway St. NW1 5 L1
Bridgeway St. NW1 77 DJ68
Bridgewood Clo. SE20 106 DV94
Bridgewood Rd. SW16 105 DK94
Bridgewood Rd., Wor.Pk. 117 CU104
Bridgford St. SW18 104 DC90
Bridgwater Rd. E15 79 EC67
Bridle Clo., Enf. 37 DZ37
Bridle Clo., Epsom 130 CR106
Bridle Clo., Kings.T. 115 CK98
Bridle Clo., Sun. 113 BU97
Forge La.
Bridle End, Epsom 131 CT113
Bridle La. W1 5 L10
Bridle La., Cob. 142 CB115
Bridle La., Lthd. 142 CC115
Bridle La., Rick. 28 BJ41
Bridle La., Twick. 101 CH86
Crown Rd.
Bridle Path, Croy. 119 DL104
Bridle Path, Wat. 29 BV40
Station Rd.
Bridle Path, Wdf.Grn. 52 EE52
Bridle Path, The, Epsom 131 CV110
Bridle Rd., Croy. 121 EA104
Bridle Rd., Epsom 131 CT113
Bridle Rd., Esher 129 CH107
Bridle Rd., Pnr. 58 BW58
Bridle Rd., The, Pur. 133 DL110
Bridle Way, Croy. 135 EA106
Bridle Way, Orp. 137 EQ105
Bridle Way, The, Croy. 135 DY110
Bridle Way, The, Wall. 133 DJ105
Bridlepath Way, Felt. 99 BS87
Bridleway Clo., Epsom 131 CW110
Bridlington Clo., West. 150 EH119
Bridlington Rd. N9 50 DV45
Bridlington Rd., Wat. 44 BX48
Bridport Ave., Rom. 69 FB58
Bridport Pl. N1 78 DR67
Bridport Rd. N18 50 DS50
Bridport Rd., Grnf. 72 CB67
Bridport Rd., Th.Hth. 119 DN97
Bridport Ter. SW8 91 DK81
Wandsworth Rd.
Bridstow Pl. W2 76 DA72
Talbot Rd.
Brief St. SE5 91 DP81
Brier Rd., Tad. 145 CV119
Brierley, Croy. 135 EB107
Brierley Ave. N9 50 DW46
Brierley Clo. SE25 120 DU98
Brierley Rd. E11 65 ED63
Brierley Rd. SW12 105 DJ89
Brierly Gdns. E2 78 DW68
Royston St.
Briery Fld., Rick. 28 BG42
Brig Ms. SE8 93 EA79
Watergate St.
Brigade Clo., Har. 59 CD61
Brigade St. SE3 94 EF82
Royal Par.
Brigadier Ave., Enf. 36 DQ38
Brigadier Hill, Enf. 36 DQ38
Briggeford Clo. E5 64 DU61
Geldeston Rd.
Briggs Clo., Mitch. 119 DH95
Bright Clo., Belv. 96 EX77
Bright St. E14 79 EB72
Brightfield Rd. SE12 108 EF85
Brightling Rd. SE4 107 DZ86
Brightlingsea Pl. E14 79 DZ73
Brightman Rd. SW18 104 DD88
Brighton Ave. E17 65 DZ57
Brighton Clo., Add. 126 BJ106
Brighton Clo., Uxb. 71 BP66
Brighton Dr., Nthlt. 72 CA65
Brighton Gro. SE14 93 DY81
New Cross Rd.
Brighton Rd. E6 81 EN69
Brighton Rd. N2 48 DC54
Brighton Rd. N16 64 DS63
Brighton Rd., Add. 126 BJ105
Brighton Rd., Bans. 145 CZ116
Brighton Rd., Couls. 147 DH121
Brighton Rd., Pur. 133 DN111
Brighton Rd., S.Croy. 134 DQ106
Brighton Rd., Surb. 115 CJ100
Brighton Rd., Sutt. 132 DC108
Brighton Rd., Tad. 145 CY122
Brighton Rd., Wat. 29 BU38
Brighton Ter. SW9 91 DM84
Brights Ave., Rain. 83 FH70
Brightside, The, Enf. 37 DX39
Brightside Ave., Stai. 98 BJ94
Brightside Rd. SE13 107 ED86
Brightview Clo., St.Alb. 16 BY29
Brightwell Clo., Croy. 119 DN102
Sumner Rd.
Brightwell Cres. SW17 104 DF92
Brightwell Rd., Wat. 29 BU43
Brigstock Rd., Belv. 97 FB77
Brigstock Rd., Couls. 147 DH115
Brigstock Rd., Th.Hth. 119 DN99
Brill Pl. NW1 5 N1
Brill Pl. NW1 77 DK68
Brim Hill N2 62 DC56
Brimpsfield Clo. SE2 96 EV76
Brimsdown Ave., Enf. 37 DY40
Brimsdown Ind. Est., Enf. 37 DZ40
Brimstone Clo., Orp. 138 EW108
Brindle Gate, Sid. 109 ES88
Brindles, The, Bans. 145 CZ117
Brindley Clo., Bexh. 97 FB83
Brindley St. SE14 93 DZ81
Brindley Way, Brom. 108 EG92
Brindley Way, Sthl. 72 CB73
Brindwood Rd. E4 51 DZ48
Brinkburn Clo. SE2 96 EU77
Brinkburn Clo., Edg. 46 CP54
Brinkburn Gdns., Edg. 60 CN55
Brinkley Rd., Wor.Pk. 117 CV103
Brinklow Cres. SE18 95 EP80
Brinklow Ho. W2 76 DB71
Brinkworth Rd., Ilf. 66 EL55
Brinkworth Way E9 79 DZ65
Brinley Clo. (Cheshunt), Wal.Cr. 23 DX31
Brinsdale Rd. NW4 61 CX55
Brinsley Rd., Har. 45 CD54
Brinsley St. E1 78 DV72
Watney St.
Brinsmead (Park St.), St.Alb. 17 CD27
Brinsworth Clo., Twick. 101 CD88
Brinton Wk. SE1 10 F3
Brion Pl. E14 79 EC71
Brisbane Ave. SW19 118 DB95
Brisbane Ct. N10 49 DH52
Sydney Rd.
Brisbane Rd. E10 65 EB61
Brisbane Rd. W13 87 CG75
Brisbane Rd., Ilf. 67 EP59
Brisbane St. SE5 92 DR80
Briscoe Clo. E11 66 EF61
Briscoe Rd. SW19 104 DD93
Briset Rd. SE9 94 EK83
Briset St. EC1 6 F6
Briset Way N7 63 DM61
Brisson Clo., Esher 128 BZ107
Bristol Clo., Stai. 98 BL86
Bristol Gdns. W9 76 DB70
Bristol Ms. W9 76 DB70
Bristol Gdns.
Bristol Pk. Rd. E17 65 DY56
Hervey Pk. Rd.
Bristol Rd. E7 80 EJ65
Bristol Rd., Grnf. 72 CB67
Bristol Rd., Mord. 118 DC99
Briston Gro. N8 63 DL58
Briston Ms. NW7 47 CU52
Bristow Rd. SE19 106 DS92
Bristow Rd., Bexh. 96 EY81
Bristow Rd., Croy. 133 DL105
Bristow Rd., Houns. 86 CB83
Britannia Clo. SW4 91 DK84
Bowland Rd.
Britannia Clo., Nthlt. 72 BX69
Britannia Gate E16 80 EG74
Silvertown Way
Britannia La., Twick. 100 CC87
Britannia Rd. E14 93 EA77
Britannia Rd. N12 48 DC48
Britannia Rd. SW6 90 DB80
Britannia Rd., Ilf. 67 EP62
Britannia Rd., Surb. 116 CM101
Britannia Rd., Wal.Cr. 23 DZ34
Britannia Row N1 77 DP67
Britannia St. WC1 6 B2
Britannia St. WC1 77 DM69
Britannia Wk. N1 7 K2
Britannia Way NW10 74 CP70
Britannia Way SW6 90 DB81
Britannia Rd.
Britannia Way, Stai. 98 BK87
British Gro. W4 89 CT78
British Gro. Pas. W4 89 CT78
British Gro. S. W4 89 CT78
British Gro. Pas.
British Legion Rd. E4 52 EF47
British St. E3 79 DZ69
Briton Clo., S.Croy. 134 DS111
Briton Cres., S.Croy. 134 DS111
Briton Hill Rd., S.Croy. 134 DS110
Brittain Rd., Dag. 68 EY62
Brittain Rd., Walt. 128 BX106
Brittains La., Sev. 154 FF123
Britten Clo. NW11 62 DB60
Britten Clo., Borwd. 31 CK44
Rodgers Clo.
Britten Dr., Sthl. 72 CA72
Britten St. SW3 90 DE78
Brittenden Clo., Orp. 137 ES107
Britten's Ct. E1 78 DV73
The Highway
Britton Clo. SE6 107 ED87
Brownhill Rd.
Britton St. EC1 6 F5
Britton St. EC1 77 DP70
Brixham Cres., Ruis. 57 BU60
Brixham Gdns., Ilf. 67 ES64
Brixham Rd., Well. 96 EX81
Brixham St. E16 81 EM74
Brixton Est., Edg. 46 CP54
Brixton Hill SW2 105 DL87
Brixton Hill Pl. SW2 105 DL87
Brixton Hill
Brixton Oval SW2 91 DN84
Brixton Rd. SW9 91 DN83
Brixton Rd., Wat. 29 BV39
Brixton Sta. Rd. SW9 91 DN83
Brixton Water La. SW2 105 DN85
Broad Acre, St.Alb. 16 BY30
Broad Clo., Walt. 114 BX104
Broad Ct. WC2 6 A9
Broad Grn. Ave., Croy. 119 DP101
Broad Highway, Cob. 128 BX114
Broad La. EC2 7 M7
Broad La. EC2 78 DS71
Broad La. N8 63 DM57
Tottenham La.
Broad La. N15 64 DT56
Broad La., Dart. 111 FG89
Broad La., Hmptn. 100 BZ94
Broad Lawn SE9 109 EN89
Broad Mead, Ash. 144 CM117
Broad Oak, Wdf.Grn. 52 EH50
Broad Oak Clo. E4 51 EA50
Royston Ave.
Broad Oak Clo., Orp. 124 EU96
Broad Sanctuary SW1 9 N5
Broad Sanctuary SW1 91 DK75
Broad St., Dag. 82 FA66
Broad St., Tedd. 101 CF93
Broad St. Ave. EC2 7 M7
Broad St. Pl. EC2 7 L7
Broad Vw. NW9 60 CN58
Broad Wk. N21 49 DM47
Broad Wk. NW1 76 DG68
Broad Wk. SE3 94 EJ82
Broad Wk. W1 8 F2
Broad Wk. W1 76 DG74
Broad Wk., Cat. 148 DT122
Broad Wk., Couls. 146 DG123
Broad Wk., Epsom 144 CS117
Chalk La.
Broad Wk. (Burgh Heath), Epsom 145 CX119
Broad Wk., Houns. 86 BX81
Broad Wk., Orp. 124 EX104
Broad Wk., Rich. 88 CM80
Broad Wk., Sev. 155 FL128
Broad Wk., The W8 76 DC74
Broad Wk., The, E.Mol. 115 CF98
Broad Wk., The, Nthwd. 43 BQ54
Broad Wk. La. NW11 61 CZ59
Broad Water Cres., Wey. 113 BQ104
Churchill Dr.
Broad Yd. EC1 6 F5
Broadacre, Stai. 98 BG92
Broadacre Clo., Uxb. 57 BP62
Broadbent Clo. N6 63 DH60
Broadbent St. W1 5 H10
Broadberry Ct. N18 50 DV51
Alston Rd.
Broadbridge Clo. SE3 94 EG80
Broadcoombe, S.Croy. 134 DW108
Broadcroft Ave., Stan. 45 CK54
Broadcroft Rd., Orp. 123 ER101
Broadfield Clo. NW2 61 CW62
Broadfield Clo., Croy. 119 DM103
Progress Way
Broadfield Clo., Rom. 69 FF57
Broadfield Clo., Tad. 145 CW120
Broadfield Ct. (Bushey), Wat. 45 CE47
Broadfield La. NW1 77 DL66
Broadfield Rd. SE6 108 EE87
Broadfield Sq., Enf. 36 DV40
Broadfield Way, Buck.H. 52 EJ48
Broadfields, E.Mol. 115 CD100
Broadfields, Har. 44 CB53
Broadfields (Cheshunt), Wal.Cr. 21 DP29
Broadfields Ave. N21 49 DN45
Broadfields Ave., Edg. 46 CP49
Broadfields Heights, Edg. 46 CP49
Broadfields La., Wat. 43 BV46
Broadfields Way NW10 61 CT64
Broadgate E13 80 EJ68
Broadgate EC2 78 DS71
Liverpool St.
Broadgate, Wal.Abb. 24 EF33
Broadgate Circle EC2 7 M6
Broadgate Rd. E16 80 EK72
Fulmer Rd.
Broadgates Ave., Barn. 34 DB39
Broadgates Rd. SW18 104 DD88
Ellerton Rd.
Broadhead Strand NW9 47 CT53
Broadheath Dr., Chis. 109 EM92
Broadhinton Rd. SW4 91 DH83
Broadhurst, Ash. 144 CL116
Broadhurst Ave., Edg. 46 CP49
Broadhurst Ave., Ilf. 67 ET63
Broadhurst Clo. NW6 76 DC65
Broadhurst Gdns.
Broadhurst Clo., Rich. 102 CM85
Lower Gro. Rd.
Broadhurst Gdns. NW6 76 DB65
Broadhurst Gdns., Chig. 53 EQ49
Broadhurst Gdns., Ruis. 58 BW61
Broadhurst Wk., Rain. 83 FG65
Tuck Rd.
Broadlake Clo., St.Alb. 17 CK27
Broadlands, The, Felt. 100 BZ90
Broadlands Ave. SW16 105 DL89
Broadlands Ave., Enf. 36 DV41
Broadlands Ave., Shep. 113 BQ100
Broadlands Clo. N6 62 DG59
Broadlands Clo. SW16 105 DL89
Broadlands Clo., Enf. 36 DW41
Broadlands Clo., Wal.Cr. 23 DX34
Broadlands Dr., Warl. 148 DW119
Broadlands Rd. N6 62 DF59
Broadlands Rd., Brom. 108 EH91
Broadlands Way, N.Mal. 117 CT100
Broadlawns Ct., Har. 45 CF53
Broadley St. NW8 4 A6
Broadley St. NW8 76 DD71
Broadley Ter. NW1 4 C5
Broadley Ter. NW1 76 DE70
Broadmayne SE17 11 K10
Broadmead SE6 107 EA90
Broadmead Ave., Wor.Pk. 117 CU101
Broadmead Clo., Hmptn. 100 CA93
Broadmead Clo., Pnr. 44 BY52
Broadmead Est., Wdf.Grn. 52 EJ52
Broadmead Rd., Hayes 72 BY70
Broadmead Rd., Nthlt. 72 BY70
Broadmead Rd., Wdf.Grn. 52 EG51
Broadoak Ave., Enf. 37 DX35
Broadoak Rd., Erith 97 FD80
Broadoaks, Epp. 25 ET32
Broadoaks, Surb. 116 CP102
Broadoaks Cres., W.Byf. 126 BH113
Broadoaks Way, Brom. 122 EF99
Broadstone Pl. W1 4 F7
Broadstone Rd., Horn. 69 FG61
Broadstrood, Loug. 39 EN38
Broadview Est., Stai. 98 BN86
Broadview Rd. SW16 105 DK94
Broadwalk E18 66 EF55
Broadwalk, Croy. 135 DY111
Broadwalk, Har. 58 CA57
Broadwall SE1 10 E2
Broadwall SE1 77 DN74
Broadwater, Pot.B. 20 DB30
Broadwater Clo., Walt. 127 BU106
Broadwater Gdns., Orp. 137 EP105
Broadwater Gdns., Uxb. 56 BH56
Broadwater La., Uxb. 56 BH56
Broadwater Rd. N17 50 DS53
Broadwater Rd. SE28 95 EQ76
Broadwater Rd. SW17 104 DE91
Broadwater Rd. N., Walt. 127 BT106
Broadwater Rd. S., Walt. 127 BT106
Broadway E15 79 ED66
Broadway N20 48 DC47
Broadway SW1 9 M6
Broadway SW1 91 DK76
Broadway, Bark. 81 EQ66
Broadway, Bexh. 96 EY84
Broadway, Grnf. 72 CC70
Broadway, Rain. 83 FG70
Broadway, Rom. 55 FG54
Broadway, Stai. 98 BH92
Broadway, Surb. 116 CP102
Broadway, Swan. 125 FC100
Broadway, The E4 51 EC51
Broadway, The E13 80 EH68
Broadway, The N8 63 DL58
Broadway, The N9 50 DU48
Broadway, The N14 49 DK46
Winchmore Hill Rd.
Broadway, The N22 49 DN54
Broadway, The NW7 46 CS50
Broadway, The SW13 88 CS82
The Ter.
Broadway, The SW19 104 DA94
Broadway, The W5 73 CK73
Broadway, The W7 73 CE74
Broadway, The W13 73 CG74
Broadway, The, Add. 126 BG110
Broadway, The, Croy. 133 DL105
Croydon Rd.
Broadway, The, Dag. 68 EZ61
Whalebone La. S.
Broadway, The, Epsom 131 CU106
Broadway, The, Har. 45 CE54
Broadway, The, Horn. 69 FH63
Broadway, The, Loug. 39 EQ42
Broadway, The, Pnr. 44 BZ52
Broadway, The, Sthl. 72 BX73
Broadway, The, Stai. 112 BJ97
Broadway, The, Stan. 45 CJ50
Broadway, The, Sutt. 131 CY107
Broadway, The, T.Ditt. 115 CE102
Hampton Ct. Way
Broadway, The, Wat. 30 BW41
Broadway, The, Wem. 60 CL62
East La.
Broadway, The, Wdf.Grn. 52 EH51
Broadway Ave., Croy. 120 DR99
Broadway Ave., Twick. 101 CH86
Broadway Clo., S.Croy. 134 DV114
Broadway Clo., Wdf.Grn. 52 EH51
Broadway Ct. SW19 104 DA93
The Bdy.
Broadway E., Uxb. 56 BG59
Broadway Gdns., Mitch. 118 DE98
Broadway Mkt. E8 78 DV67
Broadway Mkt. Ms. E8 78 DU67
Brougham Rd.
Broadway Ms. E5 64 DT59
Broadway Ms. N13 49 DM50
Elmdale Rd.
Broadway Ms. N21 49 DP46
Compton Rd.
Broadway Par. N8 63 DL58
Broadway Pl. SW19 103 CZ93
Hartfield Rd.
Broadwick St. W1 5 L10
Broadwick St. W1 77 DJ72
Broadwood Ave., Ruis. 57 BS58
Brocas Clo. NW3 76 DE66
Fellows Rd.
Brock Pl. E3 79 EB70
Brock Rd. E13 80 EH71
Brock St. SE15 92 DW83
Evelina Rd.
Brockdish Ave., Bark. 67 ET64
Brockenhurst, W.Mol. 114 BZ100
Brockenhurst Ave., Wor.Pk. 116 CS102
Brockenhurst Gdns. NW7 46 CS51
Brockenhurst Gdns., Ilf. 67 EQ64
Brockenhurst Rd., Croy. 120 DV101
Brockenhurst Way SW16 119 DK96
Brocket Clo., Chig. 53 ET50
Burrow Rd.
Brocket Way, Chig. 53 ES50
Brockham Clo. SW19 103 CZ92
Brockham Cres., Croy. 135 ED108
Brockham Dr. SW2 105 DM87
Fairview Pl.
Brockham Dr., Ilf. 67 EP58
Brockham St. SE1 11 J6
Brockham St. SE1 92 DQ76
Brockhurst Clo., Stan. 45 CF51
Brockill Cres. SE4 93 DY84
Brocklebank Ct., Whyt. 148 DU118
Brocklebank Rd. SE7 94 EH77
Brocklebank Rd. SW18 104 DC87
Brocklehurst St. SE14 93 DX80
Brocklesbury Clo., Wat. 30 BW41
Brocklesby Rd. SE25 120 DV98
Brockley Ave., Stan. 46 CL48
Brockley Clo., Stan. 46 CL49
Brockley Combe, Wey. 127 BR105
Brockley Cres., Rom. 55 FC52
Brockley Cross SE4 93 DY83
Endwell Rd.
Brockley Footpath SE15 92 DW84
Brockley Gdns. SE4 93 DZ82
Brockley Gro. SE4 107 DZ85
Brockley Hall Rd. SE4 107 DY85
Brockley Hill, Stan. 45 CJ46
Brockley Ms. SE4 107 DY85
Brockley Pk. SE23 107 DY87
Brockley Ri. SE23 107 DY87
Brockley Rd. SE4 93 DZ83
Brockley Vw. SE23 107 DY87
Brockley Way SE4 107 DX85
Brockleyside, Stan. 46 CL49
Brockman Ri., Brom. 107 ED91
Brocks Dr., Sutt. 117 CY104
Brockshot Clo., Brent. 87 CK78
Brockton Clo., Rom. 69 FF56
Brockway Clo. E11 66 EE61
Brockwell Clo., Orp. 123 ET98
Brockwell Pk. Gdns. SE24 105 DN87
Brockworth Clo. SE15 92 DS79
Brodewater Rd., Borwd. 32 CP40
Brodia Rd. N16 64 DS62
Brodie Rd. E4 51 EC46
Brodie Rd., Enf. 36 DQ38
Brodie St. SE1 92 DT78
Coopers Rd.
Brodlove La. E1 79 DX73
Brodrick Gro. SE2 96 EV77
Brodrick Rd. SW17 104 DE89
Brograve Gdns., Beck. 121 EB96
Broke Fm. Dr., Orp. 138 EX109
Broke Wk. E8 78 DU67
Marlborough Ave.
Broken Wf. EC4 7 H10
Brokesley St. E3 79 DZ69
Bromar Rd. SE5 92 DS83
Bromborough Grn., Wat. 44 BW50
Brome Rd. SE9 95 EM83
Bromefield, Stan. 45 CJ53
Bromefield Ct., Wal.Abb. 24 EG33
Bromehead Rd. E1 78 DW72
Commercial Rd.
Bromell's Rd. SW4 91 DJ84
Bromet Clo., Wat. 29 BT38
Hempstead Rd.
Bromfelde Rd. SW4 91 DK83
Bromfelde Wk. SW4 91 DL82
Bromfield St. N1 77 DN68
Bromhall Rd., Dag. 82 EV65
Bromhedge SE9 109 EM90
Bromholm Rd. SE2 96 EV76
Bromleigh Clo. (Cheshunt), Wal.Cr. 23 DY28
Martins Dr.
Bromleigh Ct. SE23 106 DV89
Lapse Wd. Wk.
Bromley Ave., Brom. 108 EE94
Bromley Common, Brom. 122 EJ98
Bromley Cres., Brom. 122 EF97
Bromley Cres., Ruis. 57 BT63
Bromley Gdns., Brom. 122 EF97
Bromley Gro., Brom. 121 ED96
Bromley Hall Rd. E14 79 EC71
Bromley High St. E3 79 EB69
Bromley Hill, Brom. 108 EE93
Bromley La., Chis. 109 EQ94
Bromley Pl. W1 5 K6
Bromley Rd. E10 65 EB58
Bromley Rd. E17 51 EA54
Bromley Rd. N17 50 DT53
Bromley Rd. N18 50 DR48
Bromley Rd. SE6 107 EB89
Bromley Rd., Beck. 121 EB96
Bromley Rd., Brom. 121 EB96
Bromley Rd. (Downham), Brom. 107 ED91
Bromley Rd., Chis. 123 EP95
Bromley St. E1 79 DX71
Brompton Arc. SW3 8 D5
Brompton Clo. SE20 120 DU96
Selby Rd.
Brompton Clo., Houns. 100 BZ85
Brompton Dr., Erith 97 FH80
Brompton Gro. N2 62 DE56
Brompton Pk. Cres. SW6 90 DB79
Brompton Pl. SW3 8 C6
Brompton Pl. SW3 90 DE76
Brompton Rd. SW1 8 D5
Brompton Rd. SW1 90 DF75
Brompton Rd. SW3 8 B8
Brompton Rd. SW3 90 DE77
Brompton Rd. SW7 8 B7
Brompton Rd. SW7 90 DE76
Brompton Sq. SW3 8 B6
Brompton Sq. SW3 90 DE76
Brompton Ter. SE18 95 EN81
Prince Imperial Rd.

Buckhurst Rd., West. 151 EP121
Buckhurst St. E1 78 DV70
Buckhurst Way, Buck.H. 52 EK49
Buckingham Arc. WC2 10 A1
Buckingham Ave. N20 48 DC45
Buckingham Ave., Felt. 99 BV86
Buckingham Ave., Grnf. 73 CG67
Buckingham Ave., Th.Hth. 119 DN95
Buckingham Ave., Well. 95 ES84
Buckingham Ave., W.Mol. 114 CB97
Buckingham Clo. W5 73 CJ71
Buckingham Clo., Enf. 36 DS40
Buckingham Clo., Hmptn. 100 BZ92
Buckingham Clo., Orp. 123 ES101
Buckingham Ct. NW4 61 CU55
Buckingham Dr., Chis. 109 EP92
Buckingham Gdns., Edg. 46 CL52
Buckingham Gdns., Th.Hth. 119 DN96
Buckingham Gdns., W.Mol. 114 CB96
Buckingham Ave.
Buckingham Gate SW1 9 K5
Buckingham Gate SW1 91 DH76
Buckingham Gro., Uxb. 70 BN68
Buckingham La. SE23 107 DY87
Buckingham Ms. NW10 75 CT68
Buckingham Rd.
Buckingham Ms. SW1 9 K6
Buckingham Palace Rd. SW1 9 H9
Buckingham Palace Rd. SW1 91 DH77
Buckingham Pl. SW1 9 K6
Buckingham Rd. E10 65 EB62
Buckingham Rd. E11 66 EJ57
Buckingham Rd. E15 66 EF64
Buckingham Rd. E18 52 EF53
Buckingham Rd. N1 78 DS65
Buckingham Rd. N22 49 DL53
Buckingham Rd. NW10 75 CT68
Buckingham Rd., Borwd. 32 CR42
Buckingham Rd., Edg. 46 CM52
Buckingham Rd., Hmptn. 100 BZ91
Buckingham Rd., Har. 59 CD57
Buckingham Rd., Ilf. 67 ER61
Buckingham Rd., Kings.T. 116 CM98
Buckingham Rd., Mitch. 119 DL99
Buckingham Rd., Rich. 101 CK89
Buckingham Rd., Wat. 29 BV37
Buckingham St. WC2 10 A1
Buckingham Way, Wall. 133 DJ109
Buckland Cres. NW3 76 DD66
Buckland Ri., Pnr. 44 BW53
Buckland Rd. E10 65 EC61
Buckland Rd., Chess. 130 CM106
Buckland Rd., Orp. 137 ES105
Buckland Rd., Sutt. 131 CW110
Buckland St. N1 7 L1
Buckland St. N1 78 DR68
Buckland Wk., Mord. 118 DC98
Buckland Way, Wor.Pk. 117 CW102
Bucklands Rd., Tedd. 101 CJ93
Buckle St. E1 78 DT72
Leman St.
Buckleigh Ave. SW20 117 CY97
Buckleigh Rd. SW16 105 DK93
Buckleigh Way SE19 120 DT95
Buckler Gdns. SE9 109 EM90
Southold Ri.
Bucklers All. SW6 90 DA79
Haldane Rd.
Bucklers Way, Cars. 118 DF104
Bucklersbury EC4 7 K9
Bucklersbury EC4 78 DR72
Bucklersbury Pas. EC4 77 DP73
Queen Victoria St.
Buckles Ct., Belv. 96 EX76
Fendyke Rd.
Buckles Way, Bans. 145 CY116
Buckley Clo., Dart. 97 FF82
Buckley Rd. NW6 75 CZ66
Buckley St. SE1 10 B3
Buckmaster Rd. SW11 90 DE84
Bucknall St. WC2 5 N8
Bucknall St. WC2 77 DK72
Bucknalls Clo., Wat. 16 BY32
Bucknalls Dr., St.Alb. 16 BZ31
Bucknalls La., Wat. 16 BX32
Bucknell Clo. SW2 91 DM84
Buckner Rd. SW2 91 DM84
Bucknills Clo., Epsom 130 CQ114
Buckrell Rd. E4 51 ED47
Bucks Ave., Wat. 44 BY45
Bucks Clo., W.Byf. 126 BH114
Bucks Cross Rd., Orp. 138 EY106
Bucks Hill, Kings L. 14 BJ33
Buckstone Clo. SE23 106 DW86
Buckstone Rd. N18 50 DU50
Buckters Rents SE16 79 DY74
Buckthorne Ho., Chig. 54 EV49
Buckthorne Rd. SE4 107 DY86
Buckton Rd., Borwd. 32 CM38
Budd Clo. N12 48 DB49
Buddings Circle, Wem. 60 CQ62
Budd's All., Twick. 101 CJ85
Arlington Clo.
Budebury Rd., Stai. 98 BG92
Budge La., Mitch. 118 DF101
Budge Row EC4 7 K10
Budge's Wk. W2 76 DD73
Budgin's Hill, Orp. 138 EV112
Budich Ct., Ilf. 68 EU61
Budleigh Cres., Well. 96 EW81
Budoch Dr., Ilf. 68 EU61
Buer Rd. SW6 89 CY82
Buff Ave., Bans. 132 DB114
Bug Hill, Warl. 149 DX120
Bugsby's Way SE7 94 EG77
Bugsby's Way SE10 94 EF77
Bulganak Rd., Th.Hth. 120 DQ98
Bulinga St. SW1 9 P9
Bulinga St. SW1 91 DK77
Bull All., Well. 96 EV83
Welling High St.
Bull Hill, Lthd. 143 CG121
Bull Inn Ct. WC2 10 A1
Bull La. N18 50 DS50
Bull La., Chis. 109 ER94
Bull La., Dag. 69 FB62
Bull Rd. E15 80 EF68
Bull Wf. La. EC4 7 J10
Bull Yd. SE15 92 DU81
Peckham High St.
Bullace Row SE5 92 DQ81
Camberwell Rd.
Bullards Pl. E2 79 DX69
Bullbanks Rd., Belv. 97 FC77
Bullen St. SW11 90 DE82
Buller Clo. SE15 92 DU80
Buller Rd. N17 50 DU54
Buller Rd. N22 49 DN54
Buller Rd. NW10 75 CX69
Chamberlayne Rd.
Buller Rd., Bark. 81 ES66
Buller Rd., Th.Hth. 120 DR96
Bullers Clo., Sid. 110 EY92
Bullers Wd. Dr., Chis. 109 EM94
Bullescroft Rd., Edg. 46 CN48
Bullfinch Clo., Sev. 154 FD122
Bullfinch Dene, Sev. 154 FD122
Bullfinch La., Sev. 154 FD122
Bullfinch Rd., S.Croy. 135 DX110
Bullhead Rd., Borwd. 32 CQ40
Bullied Way SW1 9 J9
Bullivant St. E14 79 EC72
Bullrush Gro., Uxb. 70 BJ70
Bull's All. SW14 88 CR82
Bulls Bri. Ind. Est., Sthl. 85 BV76
Bulls Bri. Rd., Sthl. 85 BV76
Bulls Cross, Enf. 36 DU37
Bulls Cross Ride, Wal.Cr. 36 DU35
Bulls Gdns. SW3 8 C8
Bull's Head Pas. EC3 7 M9
Bullsbrook Rd., Hayes 72 BW74
Bullsmoor Clo., Wal.Cr. 36 DW35
Bullsmoor Gdns., Wal.Cr. 36 DV35
Bullsmoor La., Enf. 36 DW35
Bullsmoor La., Wal.Cr. 36 DU35
Bullsmoor Ride, Wal.Cr. 36 DW35
Bullsmoor Way, Wal.Cr. 36 DV35
Bullwell Cres. (Cheshunt), Wal.Cr. 23 DY29
Bulmer Gdns., Har. 59 CK59
Bulmer Ms. W11 76 DA73
Ladbroke Rd.
Bulmer Pl. W11 76 DA74
Bulow Est. SW6 90 DB82
Broughton Rd.
Bulstrode Ave., Houns. 86 BZ82
Bulstrode Gdns., Houns. 86 BZ83
Bulstrode La., Hem.H. 14 BG27
Bulstrode Pl. W1 4 G7
Bulstrode Rd., Houns. 86 CA83
Bulstrode St. W1 4 G8
Bulstrode St. W1 76 DG72
Bulwer Ct. Rd. E11 65 ED60
Bulwer Gdns., Barn. 34 DC42
Bulwer Rd.
Bulwer Rd. E11 65 ED59
Bulwer Rd. N18 50 DS49
Bulwer Rd., Barn. 34 DB42
Bulwer St. W12 75 CW74
Bumbles Grn. La., Wal.Abb. 24 EH25
Bunbury Way, Epsom 145 CV116
Bunce Dr., Cat. 148 DQ121
Coulsdon Rd.
Bunces La., Wdf.Grn. 52 EF52
Bungalow Rd. SE25 120 DS98
Bungalow Rd., Wok. 141 BQ124
Bungalows, The SW16 105 DH94
Bungalows, The, Wall. 133 DH106
Bunhill Row EC1 7 K4
Bunhill Row EC1 78 DR70
Bunhouse Pl. SW1 8 F10
Bunhouse Pl. SW1 90 DG78
Bunkers Hill NW11 62 DC59
Bunkers Hill, Belv. 96 FA77
Bunkers Hill, Sid. 110 EZ90
Bunkers La., Hem.H. 14 BN25
Bunning Way N7 77 DL66
Bunns La. NW7 46 CS51
Bunsen St. E3 79 DY68
Kenilworth Rd.
Bunting Clo. N9 51 DX46
Dunnock Clo.
Bunting Clo., Mitch. 118 DF99
Buntingbridge Rd., Ilf. 67 ER57
Bunton St. SE18 95 EN76
Creton St.
Bunyan Ct. EC2 78 DQ71
Beech St.
Bunyan Rd. E17 65 DY55
Buonaparte Ms. SW1 9 M10
Burbage Clo. SE1 11 K7
Burbage Clo. SE1 92 DR76
Burbage Clo. (Cheshunt), Wal.Cr. 23 DY31
Burbage Rd. SE21 106 DR87
Burbage Rd. SE24 106 DQ86
Burberry Clo., N.Mal. 116 CS96
Burbidge Rd., Shep. 112 BN98
Burbridge Way N17 50 DT54
Burcham St. E14 79 EB72
Burcharbro Rd. SE2 96 EX79
Burchell Ct. (Bushey), Wat. 44 CC45
Catsey La.
Burchell Rd. E10 65 EB60
Burchell Rd. SE15 92 DV81
Burchett Way, Rom. 68 EZ58
Burchetts Way, Shep. 113 BP100
Burchwall Clo., Rom. 55 FC52
Burcote, Wey. 127 BR107
Burcote Rd. SW18 104 DD87
Burcott Gdns., Add. 126 BJ107
Burcott Rd., Pur. 133 DN114
Burden Clo., Brent. 87 CJ78
Burden Way E11 66 EH61
Brading Cres.
Burdenshott Ave., Rich. 88 CP84
Burder Clo. N1 78 DS65
Burder Rd. N1 78 DS65
Balls Pond Rd.
Burdett Ave. SW20 117 CU95
Burdett Clo., Sid. 110 EY92
Burdett Ms. NW3 76 DD65
Belsize Cres.
Burdett Ms. W2 76 DB72
Hatherley Gro.
Burdett Rd. E3 79 DY70
Burdett Rd. E14 79 DZ71
Burdett Rd., Croy. 120 DR100
Burdett Rd., Rich. 88 CM82
Burdett St. SE1 10 D6
Burdetts Rd., Dag. 82 EZ67
Burdock Clo., Croy. 121 DX102
Burdock Rd. N17 64 DU55
Burdon La., Sutt. 131 CY108
Burdon Pk., Sutt. 131 CZ109
Burfield Clo. SW17 104 DD91
Burfield Dr., Warl. 148 DW119
Burford Clo., Dag. 68 EW62
Burford Clo., Ilf. 67 EQ56
Burford Clo., Uxb. 56 BL63
Burford Gdns. N13 49 DM48
Burford La., Epsom 131 CW111
Burford Rd. E6 80 EL69
Burford Rd. E15 79 ED66
Burford Rd. SE6 107 DZ89
Burford Rd., Brent. 88 CL78
Burford Rd., Brom. 122 EL98
Burford Rd., Sutt. 118 DA103
Burford Rd., Wor.Pk. 117 CT101
Burford Wk. SW6 90 DB80
Cambria St.
Burford Way, Croy. 135 EC107
Burgate Clo., Dart. 97 FF83
Burge St. SE1 11 L7
Burge St. SE1 92 DR76
Burges Ct. E6 81 EN66
Burges Gro. SW13 89 CV80
Burges Rd. E6 80 EL66
Burges Way, Stai. 98 BG92
Burgess Ave. NW9 60 CR58
Burgess Clo., Felt. 100 BY91
Burgess Ct., Borwd. 32 CM38
Belford Rd.
Burgess Hill NW2 62 DA63
Burgess Rd. E15 66 EE63
Burgess Rd., Sutt. 132 DB105
Burgess St. E14 79 EA71
Burgh Heath Rd., Epsom 130 CS114
Burgh Mt., Bans. 145 CZ115
Burgh St. N1 77 DP68
Burgh Wd., Bans. 145 CY115
Burghfield, Epsom 145 CT115
Burghill Rd. SE26 107 DY91
Burghley Ave., Borwd. 32 CQ43
Burghley Ave., N.Mal. 116 CR95
Burghley Pl., Mitch. 118 DF99
Burghley Rd. E11 66 EE60
Burghley Rd. N8 63 DN55
Burghley Rd. NW5 63 DH63
Burghley Rd. SW19 103 CX91
Burghley Twr. W3 75 CT73
Burgon St. EC4 6 G9
Burgos Gro. SE10 93 EB81
Burgoyne Rd. N4 63 DP58
Burgoyne Rd. SE25 120 DT98
Burgoyne Rd. SW9 91 DM83
Burgoyne Rd., Sun. 99 BS93
Burham Clo. SE20 106 DW94
Maple Rd.
Burhill Gro., Pnr. 44 BY54
Burhill Rd., Walt. 127 BV109
Burke Clo. SW15 88 CS84
Burke St. E16 80 EF72
Burket Clo., Sthl. 86 BZ77
Kingsbridge Rd.
Burland Rd. SW11 104 DF85
Burland Rd., Rom. 55 FC51
Burlea Clo., Walt. 127 BV106
Burleigh Ave., Sid. 109 ET85
Burleigh Ave., Wall. 118 DG104
Burleigh Clo., Add. 126 BH106
Burleigh Gdns. N14 49 DJ46
Burleigh Gdns., Ashf. 99 BQ92
Burleigh Ho. W10 75 CX71
St. Charles Sq.
Burleigh Pk., Cob. 128 BY112
Burleigh Pl. SW15 103 CX85
Burleigh Pl., Mitch. 118 DF99
Burleigh Rd., Add. 126 BH106
Burleigh Rd., Enf. 36 DS42
Burleigh Rd., Sutt. 117 CY102
Burleigh Rd., Uxb. 71 BP67
Burleigh Rd. (Cheshunt), Wal.Cr. 23 DY32
Burleigh St. WC2 6 A10
Burleigh Wk. SE6 107 EC88
Muirkirk Rd.
Burleigh Way, Enf. 36 DR41
Church St.
Burleigh Way (Cuffley), Pot.B. 21 DL30
Burley Clo. E4 51 EA50
Burley Clo. SW16 119 DK96
Burley Orchard, Cher. 112 BG100
Burley Rd. E16 80 EJ71
Burlings La., Sev. 151 ET118
Burlington Arc. W1 9 K1
Burlington Ave., Rich. 88 CN81
Burlington Ave., Rom. 69 FB58
Burlington Clo. E6 80 EL72
Northumberland Rd.
Burlington Clo. W9 75 CZ70
Burlington Clo., Felt. 99 BR87
Burlington Clo., Orp. 123 EP103
Burlington Clo., Pnr. 57 BV55
Tolcarne Dr.
Burlington Gdns. W1 9 K1
Burlington Gdns. W1 77 DJ73
Burlington Gdns. W3 74 CQ74
Burlington Gdns. W4 88 CQ78
Burlington Gdns., Rom. 68 EY59
Burlington La. W4 88 CS80
Burlington Ms. W3 74 CQ74
Burlington Pl. SW6 89 CY82
Burlington Rd.
Burlington Pl., Wdf.Grn. 52 EH48
Burlington Ri., Barn. 48 DE46
Burlington Rd. N10 48 DG54
Tetherdown
Burlington Rd. N17 50 DU53
Burlington Rd. SW6 89 CY82
Burlington Rd. W4 88 CQ78
Burlington Rd., Enf. 36 DR39
Burlington Rd., Islw. 87 CD81
Burlington Rd., N.Mal. 117 CT98
Burlington Rd., Th.Hth. 120 DQ96
Burma Rd. N16 64 DR63
Burmester Rd. SW17 104 DC90
Burn Clo., Add. 126 BK105
Burn Side N9 50 DW48
Burnaby Cres. W4 88 CQ79
Burnaby Gdns. W4 88 CP79
Burnaby St. SW10 90 DC80
Burnbrae Clo. N12 48 DB51
Burnbury Rd. SW12 105 DJ88
Burncroft Ave., Enf. 36 DW40
Burne Jones Ho. W14 89 CZ77
Burne St. NW1 4 B6
Burne St. NW1 76 DE71
Burnell Ave., Rich. 101 CJ92
Burnell Ave., Well. 96 EU82
Burnell Gdns., Stan. 45 CK53
Burnell Rd., Sutt. 132 DB105
Burnell Wk. SE1 92 DT78
Cadet Dr.
Burnels Ave. E6 81 EN69
Burness Clo. N7 77 DM65
Roman Way
Burness Clo., Uxb. 70 BK68
Whitehall Rd.
Burnet Gro., Epsom 130 CQ113
Burnett Clo. E9 64 DW64
Burney Ave., Surb. 116 CM99
Burney Dr., Loug. 39 EP40
Burney St. SE10 93 EC80
Burnfoot Ave. SW6 89 CY81
Burnfoot Ct. SE22 106 DV88
Burnham NW3 76 DE66
Burnham Ave., Uxb. 57 BQ63
Burnham Clo. NW7 47 CU52
Burnham Clo. SE1 92 DT77
Cadet Dr.
Burnham Clo., Enf. 36 DS38
Burnham Ct. NW4 61 CW56
Burnham Cres. E11 66 EJ56
Burnham Dr., Wor.Pk. 117 CX103
Burnham Gdns., Croy. 120 DT101
Burnham Gdns., Hayes 85 BR76
Burnham Gdns., Houns. 85 BV81
Burnham Rd. E4 51 DZ50
Burnham Rd., Dag. 82 EV66
Burnham Rd., Mord. 118 DB99
Burnham Rd., Rom. 69 FD55
Burnham Rd., Sid. 110 EY89
Burnham St. E2 78 DW69
Burnham St., Kings.T. 116 CN95
Burnham Way SE26 107 DZ92
Burnham Way W13 87 CH77
Burnhams Rd., Lthd. 142 BY124
Burnhill Rd., Beck. 121 EA96
Burnley Clo., Wat. 44 BW50
Burnley Rd. NW10 61 CT64
Burnley Rd. SW9 91 DM82
Burns Ave., Felt. 99 BU86
Burns Ave., Rom. 68 EW59
Burns Ave., Sid. 110 EU86
Burns Ave., Sthl. 72 CA73
Burns Clo. SW19 104 DD93
North Rd.
Burns Clo., Erith 97 FF81
Burns Clo., Hayes 71 BT71
Burns Clo., Well. 95 ET81
Burns Dr., Bans. 131 CY114
Burns Rd. NW10 75 CT67
Burns Rd. SW11 90 DF82
Burns Rd. W13 87 CH75
Burns Rd., Wem. 74 CL68
Burns Way, Houns. 86 BX82
Burnsall St. SW3 8 C10
Burnsall St. SW3 90 DE78
Burnside, Ash. 144 CM118
Burnside Ave. E4 51 DZ51
Burnside Clo. SE16 79 DX74
Burnside Clo., Barn. 34 DA41
Burnside Clo., Twick. 101 CG86
Burnside Cres., Wem. 73 CK67
Burnside Rd., Dag. 68 EW61
Burnt Ash Hill SE12 108 EF86
Burnt Ash La., Brom. 108 EG94
Burnt Ash Rd. SE12 108 EF85
Burnt Fm. Ride, Enf. 21 DP34
Burnt Fm. Ride, Wal.Cr. 21 DP31
Burnt Oak Bdy., Edg. 46 CP52
Burnt Oak Flds., Edg. 46 CQ53
Burnt Oak La., Sid. 110 EU89
Burnthwaite Rd. SW6 89 CZ80
Burntwood Clo. SW18 104 DD88
Burntwood Clo., Cat. 148 DU121
Burntwood Gra. Rd. SW18 104 DD88
Burntwood Gro., Sev. 155 FH127
Burntwood La. SW17 104 DC90
Burntwood La., Cat. 148 DS122
Burntwood Rd., Sev. 155 FH128
Burntwood Vw. SE19 106 DT92
Bowley La.
Buross St. E1 78 DV72
Commercial Rd.
Burr Clo. E1 78 DU74
Burr Clo., Bexh. 96 EZ83
Burr Clo., St.Alb. 18 CL27
Burr Rd. SW18 104 DA88
Burrage Gro. SE18 95 EQ77
Burrage Pl. SE18 95 EP78
Burrage Rd. SE18 95 EQ77
Burrard Rd. E16 80 EH72
Burrard Rd. NW6 62 DA64
Burrell Clo., Croy. 121 DY100
Burrell Clo., Edg. 46 CP47
Burrell Row, Beck. 121 EA96
High St.
Burrell St. SE1 10 F2
Burrell St. SE1 77 DP74
Burrell Twr. E10 65 EA59
Burrells Wf. Sq. E14 93 EB78
Burrfield Dr., Orp. 124 EX99
Burritt Rd., Kings.T. 116 CN96
Burroughs, The NW4 61 CV56
Burroughs Gdns. NW4 61 CV56
Burrow Clo., Chig. 53 ET50
Burrow Rd.
Burrow Grn., Chig. 53 ET50
Burrow Rd. SE22 92 DS84
Burrow Rd., Chig. 53 ET50
Burrow Wk. SE21 106 DQ87
Rosendale Rd.
Burrows Clo., Lthd. 142 BZ124
Burrows Hill Clo., Houns. 84 BJ84
Burrows Hill La., Houns. 84 BH84
Burrows Ms. SE1 10 F4
Burrows Rd. NW10 75 CW69
Bursdon Clo., Sid. 109 ET89
Bursland Rd., Enf. 37 DX42
Burslem Ave., Ilf. 54 EU51
Burslem St. E1 78 DU72
Burstead Clo., Cob. 128 BX112
Burstock Rd. SW15 89 CY84
Burston Dr., St.Alb. 16 CC28
Burston Rd. SW15 103 CX85
Burston Vill. SW15 103 CX85
St. John's Ave.
Burstow Rd. SW20 117 CY95
Burt Rd. E16 80 EJ74
Burtenshaw Rd., T.Ditt. 115 CG101
Burtley Clo. N4 64 DQ60
Burton Ave., Wat. 29 BU42
Burton Clo., Chess. 129 CK108
Burton Ct. SW3 90 DF78
Franklin's Row
Burton Gdns., Houns. 86 BZ81
Burton Gro. SE17 92 DR78
Portland St.
Burton La. SW9 91 DN82
Burton La. (Cheshunt), Wal.Cr. 22 DS29
Burton Ms. SW1 8 G9
Burton Pl. WC1 5 N3
Burton Rd. E18 66 EH55
Burton Rd. NW6 75 CZ66
Burton Rd. SW9 91 DP82
Burton Rd., Kings.T. 102 CL94
Burton Rd., Loug. 39 EQ42
Burton St. WC1 5 N3
Burton St. WC1 77 DK69
Burtonhole Clo. NW7 47 CX49
Burtonhole La. NW7 47 CW50
Burtons Rd., Hmptn. 100 CB91
Burtwell La. SE27 106 DR91
Burwash Ct., Orp. 124 EW99
Rookery Gdns.
Burwash Ho. SE1 11 L5
Burwash Rd. SE18 95 ER78
Burway Cres., Cher. 112 BG97
Burwell Ave., Grnf. 73 CE65
Burwell Clo. E1 78 DV72
Bigland St.
Burwell Rd. E10 65 DY60
Burwell Wk. E3 79 EA70
Burwood Ave., Brom. 122 EH103
Burwood Ave., Ken. 133 DP114
Burwood Ave., Pnr. 57 BV57
Burwood Clo., Surb. 116 CN102
Burwood Clo., Walt. 128 BW107
Burwood Gdns., Rain. 83 FF69
Burwood Pk. Rd., Walt. 127 BV105
Burwood Pl. W2 4 C8

Street	Page	Grid
Burwood Pl. W2	76	DE72
Burwood Rd., Walt.	127	BS108
Bury Ave., Hayes	71	BS68
Bury Ave., Ruis.	57	BQ58
Bury Clo. SE16	79	DX74
Rotherhithe St.		
Bury Ct. EC3	**7**	**N8**
Bury Grn. Rd. (Cheshunt), Wal.Cr.	22	DU31
Bury Gro., Mord.	118	DB99
Bury La., Epp.	25	ER28
Bury La., Rick.	42	BK46
Bury Meadows, Rick.	42	BK46
Bury Pl. WC1	**5**	**P7**
Bury Pl. WC1	77	DL71
Bury Rd. E4	38	EE42
Bury Rd. N22	63	DN55
Bury Rd., Dag.	69	FB64
Bury Rd., Epp.	25	ES31
Bury St. EC3	**7**	**N9**
Bury St. EC3	78	DS72
Bury St. N9	50	DT45
Bury St. SW1	**9**	**K2**
Bury St. SW1	77	DJ74
Bury St., Ruis.	57	BQ57
Bury St. W. N9	50	DR45
Bury Wk. SW3	**8**	**B9**
Bury Wk. SW3	90	DE77
Burydell La., St.Alb.	17	CD27
Busbridge Ho. E14	79	EA71
Brabazon St.		
Busby Ms. NW5	77	DK65
Busby Pl. NW5	77	DK65
Busby St. E2	78	DT70
Chilton St.		
Bush Clo., Add.	126	BJ106
Bush Clo., Ilf.	67	ER57
Bush Cotts. SW18	104	DA85
Putney Bri. Rd.		
Bush Ct. W12	89	CX75
Bush Elms Rd., Horn.	69	FG59
Bush Gro. NW9	60	CQ59
Bush Gro., Stan.	45	CK52
Bush Hill N21	50	DQ45
Bush Hill Rd. N21	36	DR44
Bush Hill Rd., Har.	60	CM58
Bush Ind. Est. NW10	74	CR70
Bush La. EC4	**7**	**K10**
Bush Rd. E8	78	DV67
Bush Rd. E11	66	EF59
Bush Rd. SE8	93	DX77
Bush Rd., Buck.H.	52	EK49
Bush Rd., Rich.	88	CM79
Bush Rd., Shep.	112	BM99
Bushbaby Clo. SE1	**11**	**M7**
Bushbarns (Cheshunt), Wal.Cr.	22	DU29
Bushberry Rd. E9	79	DY65
Bushell Clo. SW2	105	DM89
Bushell Grn. (Bushey), Wat.	45	CD47
Bushell St. E1	78	DU74
Hermitage Wall		
Bushell Way, Chis.	109	EN92
Bushey Ave. E18	66	EF55
Bushey Ave., Orp.	123	ER101
Bushey Clo. E4	51	EC48
Bushey Clo., Ken.	148	DS116
Bushey Clo., Uxb.	56	BN61
Bushey Ct. SW20	117	CV97
Bushey Down SW12	105	DH89
Bedford Hill		
Bushey Gro. Rd. (Bushey), Wat.	30	BX42
Bushey Hall Dr. (Bushey), Wat.	30	BY42
Bushey Hall Rd. (Bushey), Wat.	30	BX42
Bushey Hill Rd. SE5	92	DS81
Bushey La., Sutt.	118	DA104
Bushey Lees, Sid.	109	ET86
Fen Gro.		
Bushey Mill Cres., Wat.	30	BW37
Bushey Mill La., Wat.	30	BW37
Bushey Mill La. (Bushey), Wat.	30	BY38
Bushey Rd. E13	80	EJ68
Bushey Rd. N15	64	DS58
Bushey Rd. SW20	117	CV97
Bushey Rd., Croy.	121	EA103
Bushey Rd., Hayes	85	BS77
Bushey Rd., Sutt.	132	DA105
Bushey Rd., Uxb.	56	BN61
Bushey Shaw, Ash.	143	CH117
Bushey Vw. Wk., Wat.	30	BW40
Raphael Dr.		
Bushey Way, Beck.	121	ED100
Bushfield Clo., Edg.	46	CP47
Bushfield Cres., Edg.	46	CP47
Bushfields, Loug.	39	EN43
Bushgrove Rd., Dag.	68	EX63
Bushmead Clo. N15	64	DT56
Copperfield Dr.		
Bushmoor Cres. SE18	95	EQ80
Bushnell Rd. SW17	105	DH89
Bushrise, Wat.	29	BU36
Bushway, Dag.	68	EX63
Bushwood E11	66	EF60
Bushwood Dr. SE1	92	DT77
Bushwood Rd., Rich.	88	CN79
Bushy Pk., Hmptn.	115	CF95
Bushy Pk., Tedd.	115	CF95
Bushy Pk. Gdns., Tedd.	101	CD92
Bushy Pk. Rd., Tedd.	101	CH94
Bushy Rd., Lthd.	142	CB122
Bushy Rd., Tedd.	101	CF93
Butcher Row E1	79	DX73
Butcher Row E14	79	DX73
Butchers Rd. E16	80	EG72
Bute Ave., Rich.	102	CL89
Bute Ct., Wall.	133	DJ106
Bute Rd.		
Bute Gdns. W6	89	CX77
Bute Gdns., Wall.	133	DJ106
Bute Gdns. W., Wall.	133	DJ106
Bute Rd., Croy.	119	DN102
Bute Rd., Ilf.	67	EP57
Bute Rd., Wall.	133	DJ105
Bute St. SW7	90	DD77
Bute Wk. N1	78	DR65
Marquess Rd.		
Butler Ave., Har.	59	CD59
Butler Pl. SW1	**9**	**M6**
Butler Rd. NW10	75	CT66
Curzon Cres.		
Butler Rd., Dag.	68	EV63
Butler Rd., Har.	58	CC59
Butler St. E2	78	DW69
Knottisford St.		
Butler St., Uxb.	71	BP70
Butlers Dene Rd., Cat.	149	DZ119
Butlers Dr. E4	37	EC38
Butlers Wf. SE1	92	DT75
Lafone St.		
Butter Hill, Cars.	118	DG104
Butter Hill, Wall.	118	DG104
Buttercross La., Epp.	26	EU30
Buttercup Sq., Stai.	98	BK88
Diamedes Ave.		
Butterfield Clo. SE16	92	DV75
Wilson Gro.		
Butterfield Clo., Twick.	101	CF86
Rugby Rd.		
Butterfield Sq. E6	81	EM72
Harper Rd.		
Butterfields E17	65	EC57
Butterfly La. SE9	109	EP86
Butterfly La., Borwd.	31	CH41
Butterfly Wk. SE5	92	DR81
Denmark Hill		
Butterfly Wk., Warl.	148	DW120
Butteridges Clo., Dag.	82	EZ67
Buttermere Clo. SE1	**11**	**P9**
Buttermere Clo., Felt.	99	BT88
Buttermere Clo., Mord.	117	CX100
Buttermere Dr. SW15	103	CY85
Buttermere Gdns., Pur.	134	DR113
Buttermere Rd., Orp.	124	EX98
Buttermere Wk. E8	78	DT65
Butterwick W6	89	CW77
Butterwick, Wat.	30	BY36
Butterworth Gdns., Wdf.Grn.	52	EG50
Harts Gro.		
Buttesland St. N1	**7**	**L2**
Buttesland St. N1	78	DR69
Buttfield Clo., Dag.	83	FB65
Buttmarsh Clo. SE18	95	EP78
Butts, The, Brent.	87	CJ79
Butts, The, Sev.	153	FH116
Butts, The, Sun.	114	BW97
Elizabeth Gdns.		
Butts Cotts., Felt.	100	BZ90
Butts Cres., Felt.	100	CA90
Butts Piece, Nthlt.	71	BV68
Longhook Gdns.		
Butts Rd., Brom.	108	EE92
Buttsbury Rd., Ilf.	67	EQ64
Buttsmead, Nthwd.	43	BQ52
Buxted Rd. E8	78	DT66
Buxted Rd. N12	48	DE50
Buxted Rd. SE22	92	DS84
Buxton Ave., Cat.	148	DS121
Buxton Clo., Wdf.Grn.	52	EK51
Buxton Ct. N1	**7**	**J2**
Buxton Cres., Sutt.	131	CY105
Buxton Dr. E11	66	EE56
Buxton Dr., N.Mal.	116	CR96
Buxton Gdns. W3	74	CP73
Buxton La., Cat.	148	DR120
Buxton Path, Wat.	44	BW48
Buxton Rd. E4	51	ED45
Buxton Rd. E6	80	EL69
Buxton Rd. E15	66	EE64
Buxton Rd. E17	65	DY56
Buxton Rd. N19	63	DK60
Buxton Rd. NW2	75	CV65
Buxton Rd. SW14	88	CS83
Buxton Rd., Ashf.	98	BK92
Buxton Rd., Epp.	39	ES36
Buxton Rd., Erith	97	FD80
Buxton Rd., Ilf.	67	ES58
Buxton Rd., Th.Hth.	119	DP99
Buxton Rd., Wal.Abb.	24	EG33
Buxton St. E1	78	DT70
Buzzard Creek Ind. Est., Bark.	81	ET71
By the Wd., Wat.	44	BX47
Byam St. SW6	90	DC82
Byards Cft. SW16	119	DK95
Byatt Wk., Hmptn.	100	BY93
Victors Dr.		
Bychurch End, Tedd.	101	CF92
Church Rd.		
Bycroft Rd., Sthl.	72	CA70
Bycroft St. SE20	107	DX94
Parish La.		
Bycullah Ave., Enf.	35	DP41
Bycullah Rd., Enf.	35	DP40
Bye, The W3	74	CS72
Bye Way, The, Har.	45	CF53
Bye Ways, Twick.	100	CB90
Byegrove Rd. SW19	104	DD93
Byers Clo., Pot.B.	20	DC34
Byeway, The SW14	88	CQ83
Byeway, The, Epsom	131	CT105
Byeway, The, Rick.	42	BL47
Byeways, The, Ash.	143	CK118
Skinners La.		
Byeways, The, Surb.	116	CN99
Byfeld Gdns. SW13	89	CU81
Byfield Clo. SE16	93	DY75
Byfield Rd., Islw.	87	CG83
Byfleet Ind. Est., W.Byf.	126	BK111
Byfleet Rd., Add.	126	BK109
Byfleet Rd., Cob.	126	BN112
Byford Clo. E15	80	EE66
Bygrove, Croy.	135	EB107
Bygrove St. E14	79	EB72
Byland Clo. N21	49	DM45
Bylands Clo. SE2	96	EV76
Finchale Rd.		
Bylands Clo. SE16	79	DX74
Rotherhithe St.		
Byne Rd. SE26	106	DW93
Byne Rd., Cars.	118	DE103
Bynes Rd., S.Croy.	134	DR108
Byng Dr., Pot.B.	20	DA31
Byng Pl. WC1	**5**	**M5**
Byng Pl. WC1	77	DK70
Byng Rd., Barn.	33	CX41
Byng St. E14	93	EA75
Bynon Ave., Bexh.	96	EZ83
Byre, The N14	35	DH44
Farm La.		
Byre Rd. N14	34	DG44
Farm La.		
Byrne Rd. SW12	105	DH88
Byron Ave. E12	80	EL65
Byron Ave. E18	66	EF55
Byron Ave. NW9	60	CP56
Byron Ave., Borwd.	32	CN43
Byron Ave., Couls.	147	DL115
Byron Ave., Houns.	85	BU82
Byron Ave., N.Mal.	117	CU99
Byron Ave., Sutt.	132	DD105
Byron Ave., Wat.	30	BX39
Byron Ave. E., Sutt.	132	DD105
Byron Clo. E8	78	DU67
Byron Clo. SE26	107	DY91
Porthcawe Rd.		
Byron Clo. SE28	82	EW74
Byron Clo., Hmptn.	100	BZ91
Byron Clo., Wal.Cr.	22	DT27
Allard Clo.		
Byron Clo., Walt.	114	BY102
Byron Ct. W9	76	DA70
Lanhill Rd.		
Byron Ct., Enf.	35	DP40
Bycullah Rd.		
Byron Dr. N2	62	DD58
Byron Dr., Erith	97	FB81
Belmont Rd.		
Byron Gdns., Sutt.	132	DD105
Byron Hill Rd., Har.	59	CD60
Byron Ho., Beck.	107	EB93
Byron Ms. NW3	62	DE63
Byron Ms. W9	76	DA70
Shirland Rd.		
Byron Pl., Lthd.	143	CH122
Byron Rd. E10	65	EB60
Byron Rd. E17	65	EA55
Byron Rd. NW2	61	CV61
Byron Rd. NW7	47	CU50
Byron Rd. W5	74	CM74
Byron Rd., Add.	126	BK105
Byron Rd., Har.	59	CE58
Byron Rd. (Wealdstone), Har.	45	CF54
Byron Rd., S.Croy.	134	DV110
Byron Rd., Wem.	59	CJ61
Byron St. E14	79	EC72
St. Leonards Rd.		
Byron Ter. N9	50	DW45
Byron Way, Hayes	71	BS70
Byron Way, Nthlt.	72	BY69
Byron Way, West Dr.	84	BM77
Bysouth Clo., Ilf.	53	EP53
Bythorn St. SW9	91	DM84
Byton Rd. SW17	104	DF93
Byward Ave., Felt.	100	BW86
Byward St. EC3	**11**	**N1**
Byward St. EC3	78	DS73
Bywater Pl. SE16	79	DY74
Bywater St. SW3	**8**	**D10**
Bywater St. SW3	90	DF78
Byway, The, Pot.B.	20	DA33
Byway, The, Sutt.	132	DD109
Bywell Pl. W1	**5**	**K7**
Bywood Ave., Croy.	120	DW100
Bywood Clo., Ken.	147	DP115
Byworth Wk. N19	63	DK60
Courtauld Rd.		
C		
C.I. Twr., N.Mal.	116	CS97
Cabbell Pl., Add.	126	BJ105
Cabbell St. NW1	**4**	**B7**
Cabbell St. NW1	76	DE71
Cabinet Way E4	51	DZ51
Cable Pl. SE10	93	EC81
Diamond Ter.		
Cable St. E1	78	DU73
Cabot Sq. E14	79	EA74
Cabot Way E6	80	EK67
Parr Rd.		
Cabul Rd. SW11	90	DE82
Cackets La., Sev.	151	ER115
Cactus Wk. W12	75	CT73
Du Cane Rd.		
Cadbury Clo., Islw.	87	CG81
Cadbury Clo., Sun.	99	BS94
Cadbury Rd., Sun.	99	BS94
Cadbury Way SE16	92	DU76
Yalding Rd.		
Caddington Clo., Barn.	34	DE43
Caddington Rd. NW2	61	CY62
Caddis Clo., Stan.	45	CF52
Daventer Dr.		
Cade La., Sev.	155	FJ128
Cade Rd. SE10	93	ED81
Cadell Clo. E2	78	DT69
Shipton St.		
Cader Rd. SW18	104	DC86
Cadet Dr. SE1	92	DT78
Cadet Pl. SE10	94	EE78
Cadiz Rd., Dag.	83	FC66
Cadiz St. SE17	92	DQ78
Cadley Ter. SE23	106	DW89
Cadlocks Hill, Sev.	138	EZ110
Cadmer Clo., N.Mal.	116	CS98
Cadmore La. (Cheshunt), Wal.Cr.	23	DX28
Cadmus Clo. SW4	91	DK83
Aristotle Rd.		
Cadogan Clo., Beck.	121	ED95
Albemarle Rd.		
Cadogan Clo., Har.	58	CB63
Cadogan Clo., Tedd.	101	CE92
Cadogan Ct., Sutt.	132	DB107
Cadogan Gdns. E18	66	EH55
Cadogan Gdns. N3	48	DB53
Cadogan Gdns. N21	35	DN43
Cadogan Gdns. SW3	**8**	**E8**
Cadogan Gdns. SW3	90	DF77
Cadogan Gate SW1	**8**	**E8**
Cadogan Gate SW1	90	DF77
Cadogan La. SW1	**8**	**F7**
Cadogan La. SW1	90	DG76
Cadogan Pl. SW1	**8**	**E6**
Cadogan Pl. SW1	90	DF76
Cadogan Rd., Surb.	115	CK99
Cadogan Sq. SW1	**8**	**E7**
Cadogan Sq. SW1	90	DF76
Cadogan St. SW3	**8**	**D9**
Cadogan St. SW3	90	DF77
Cadogan Ter. E9	79	DZ65
Cadoxton Ave. N15	64	DT58
Cadwallon Rd. SE9	109	EP89
Caedmon Rd. N7	63	DM63
Caen Wd. Rd., Ash.	143	CJ118
Caenshill Rd., Wey.	126	BN108
Caenwood Clo., Wey.	126	BN107
Caerleon Clo., Sid.	110	EW92
Caerleon Ter. SE2	96	EV77
Blithdale Rd.		
Caernarvon Clo., Mitch.	119	DL97
Caernarvon Dr., Ilf.	53	EN53
Caesars Wk., Mitch.	118	DF99
Caesars Way, Shep.	113	BR100
Cage Pond Rd., Rad.	18	CM33
Cage Rd. E16	80	EE71
Malmesbury Rd.		
Cahill St. EC1	**7**	**J5**
Cahir St. E14	93	EB77
Caillard Rd., W.Byf.	126	BL111
Cains La., Felt.	99	BR85
Caird St. W10	75	CY69
Cairn Ave. W5	73	CK74
Cairn Way, Stan.	45	CF51
Cairndale Clo., Brom.	108	EF94
Cairnfield Ave. NW2	60	CS62
Cairngorm Clo., Tedd.	101	CG92
Vicarage Rd.		
Cairns Ave., Wdf.Grn.	52	EL51
Cairns Rd. SW11	104	DE85
Cairo New Rd., Croy.	119	DP103
Cairo Rd. E17	65	EA56
Caishowe Rd., Borwd.	32	CP39
Caistor Ms. SW12	105	DH87
Caistor Rd.		
Caistor Pk. Rd. E15	80	EF67
Caistor Rd. SW12	105	DH87
Caithness Gdns., Sid.	109	ET86
Caithness Rd. W14	89	CX76
Caithness Rd., Mitch.	105	DH94
Calabria Rd. N5	77	DP65
Calais Gate SE5	91	DP81
Calais St.		
Calais St. SE5	91	DP81
Calbourne Ave., Horn.	69	FH64
Calbourne Rd. SW12	104	DF87
Calcott Wk. SE9	108	EL91
Caldbeck, Wal.Abb.	23	ED34
Caldbeck Ave., Wor.Pk.	117	CU103
Caldecot Ave., Wal.Cr.	22	DT29
Caldecot Rd. SE5	92	DQ82
Caldecote Gdns. (Bushey), Wat.	31	CE44
Caldecote La. (Bushey), Wat.	45	CF45
Caldecott Way E5	65	DX62
Calder Ave., Grnf.	73	CF68
Calder Ave., Hat.	20	DA26
Calder Clo., Enf.	36	DS41
Calder Gdns., Edg.	60	CN55
Calder Rd., Mord.	118	DC99
Calderon Pl. W10	75	CW71
St. Quintin Gdns.		
Calderon Rd. E11	65	EC63
Caldervale Rd. SW4	105	DK85
Calderwood St. SE18	95	EN77
Caldicot Grn. NW9	60	CS58
Snowdon Dr.		
Caldwell Rd., Wat.	44	BX49
Caldwell St. SW9	91	DM80
Caldwell Yd. EC4	78	DQ73
Upper Thames St.		
Caldy Rd., Belv.	97	FB76
Caldy Wk. N1	78	DQ65
Clephane Rd.		
Cale St. SW3	**8**	**B10**
Cale St. SW3	90	DE78
Caleb St. SE1	**11**	**H4**
Caledon Rd. E6	80	EL67
Caledon Rd., St.Alb.	17	CJ26
Caledon Rd., Wall.	132	DG105
Caledonia Rd., Stai.	98	BL87
Caledonia St. N1	**6**	**A1**
Caledonia St. N1	77	DL68
Caledonian Clo., Ilf.	68	EV60
Caledonian Rd. N1	**6**	**A1**
Caledonian Rd. N1	77	DL68
Caledonian Rd. N7	63	DM63
Caledonian Wf. Rd. E14	93	ED77
Caletock Way SE10	94	EF78
Calico Row SW11	90	DC83
York Pl.		
Calidore Clo. SW2	105	DM86
Endymion Rd.		
California La. (Bushey), Wat.	45	CD46
California Rd., N.Mal.	116	CQ97
Callaby Ter. N1	78	DR65
Wakeham St.		
Callaghan Clo. SE13	94	EE84
Glenton Rd.		
Callander Rd. SE6	107	EB89
Callard Ave. N13	49	DP50
Callcott Rd. NW6	75	CZ66
Callcott St. W8	76	DA74
Hillgate Pl.		
Callendar Rd. SW7	90	DD76
Calley Down Cres., Croy.	135	ED110
Callingham Clo. E14	79	DZ71
Wallwood St.		
Callis Fm. Clo., Stai.	98	BL86
Bedfont Rd.		
Callis Rd. E17	65	DZ58
Callow Fld., Pur.	133	DN113
Callow St. SW3	90	DD79
Callowland Clo., Wat.	29	BV38
Calmington Rd. SE5	92	DS78
Calmont Rd., Brom.	107	ED93
Calne Ave., Ilf.	53	EP53
Calonne Rd. SW19	103	CX91
Calshot Rd., Houns.	84	BN82
Calshot St. N1	77	DM68
Calshot Way, Enf.	35	DP41
Calthorpe Gdns., Edg.	46	CL50
Jesmond Way		
Calthorpe Gdns., Sutt.	118	DC104
Calthorpe St. WC1	**6**	**C4**
Calthorpe St. WC1	77	DM70
Calton Ave. SE21	106	DS86
Calton Rd., Barn.	34	DC44
Calverley Clo., Beck.	107	EB93
Calverley Cres., Dag.	68	FA61
Calverley Gdns., Har.	59	CK59
Calverley Gro. N19	63	DK60
Calverley Rd., Epsom	131	CU107
Calvert Ave. E2	**7**	**N3**
Calvert Ave. E2	78	DS69
Calvert Clo., Belv.	96	FA77
Calvert Clo., Sid.	110	EY93
Calvert Rd. SE10	94	EF78
Calvert Rd., Barn.	33	CX40
Calvert St. NW1	76	DG67
Chalcot Rd.		
Calverton SE5	92	DS79
Albany Rd.		
Calverton Rd. E6	81	EN67
Calvert's Bldgs. SE1	**11**	**K3**
Calvin Clo., Orp.	124	EX97
Calvin St. E1	**7**	**P5**
Calvin St. E1	78	DT70
Calydon Rd. SE7	94	EH78
Calypso Way SE16	93	DZ77
Cam Rd. E15	79	ED67
Camac Rd., Twick.	101	CD88
Cambalt Rd. SW15	103	CX85
Camberley Ave. SW20	117	CV96
Camberley Ave., Enf.	36	DS42
Camberley Clo., Sutt.	117	CX104
Camberley Rd., Houns.	84	BN83
Cambert Way SE3	94	EH84
Camberwell Ch. St. SE5	92	DR81
Camberwell Glebe SE5	92	DS81
Camberwell Grn. SE5	92	DR81
Camberwell Gro. SE5	92	DR81
Camberwell New Rd. SE5	91	DN79
Camberwell Pas. SE5	92	DQ81
Camberwell Grn.		
Camberwell Rd. SE5	92	DQ79
Camberwell Sta. Rd. SE5	92	DQ81
Cambeys Rd., Dag.	69	FB64
Camborne Ave. W13	87	CH75
Camborne Ms. W11	75	CY72
St. Marks Rd.		
Camborne Rd. SW18	104	DA87
Camborne Rd., Croy.	120	DU101
Camborne Rd., Houns.	84	BN83
Camborne Rd., Mord.	117	CX99
Camborne Rd., Sid.	110	EW90
Camborne Rd., Sutt.	132	DA108
Camborne Rd., Well.	95	ET82
Camborne Way, Houns.	86	CA81
Cambourne Ave. N9	51	DX45
Cambray Rd. SW12	105	DJ88
Cambray Rd., Orp.	123	ET101
Cambria Clo., Houns.	86	CA84
Cambria Clo., Sid.	109	ER88

Catlin Cres., Shep. 113 BR99
Catlin St. SE16 92 DU78
Catling Clo. SE23 106 DW90
Catlins La., Pnr. 57 BV55
Cato Rd. SW4 91 DK83
Cato St. W1 4 C7
Cator Clo., Croy. 136 EE111
Cator Cres., Croy. 136 EE111
Cator La., Beck. 121 DZ95
Rectory Grn.
Cator Rd. SE26 107 DX93
Cator Rd., Cars. 132 DF106
Cator St. SE15 92 DT79
Catsey La. (Bushey), Wat. 44 CC45
Catsey Wds. (Bushey), Wat. 44 CC45
Catterick Way, Borwd. 32 CM39
Cattistock Rd. SE9 108 EL92
Cattlegate Rd., Enf. 21 DL34
Cattlegate Rd., Pot.B. 21 DK31
Cattley Clo., Barn. 33 CY42
Wood St.
Cattlins Clo., Wal.Cr. 22 DT29
Catton St. WC1 6 B7
Catton St. WC1 77 DM71
Caulfield Rd. E6 80 EL67
Caulfield Rd. SE15 92 DV82
Causeway, The N2 62 DE56
Causeway, The SW18 104 DB85
Causeway, The SW19 103 CW92
Causeway, The, Cars. 118 DG104
Causeway, The, Chess. 130 CL105
Causeway, The, Esher 129 CF108
Causeway, The, Felt. 85 BU84
Causeway, The, Pot.B. 20 DC31
Causeway, The, Sutt. 132 DC109
Causeway, The, Tedd. 101 CF93
Broad St.
Causeway Clo., Pot.B. 20 DD31
Causeyware Rd. N9 50 DV45
Causton Rd. N6 63 DH59
Causton St. SW1 9 N9
Causton St. SW1 91 DK77
Cautley Ave. SW4 105 DJ85
Cavalier Clo., Rom. 68 EX56
Cavalier Gdns., Hayes 71 BR72
Hanover Circle
Cavalry Barracks, Houns. 86 BX83
Cavalry Cres., Houns. 86 BX84
Cavalry Gdns. SW15 103 CZ85
Upper Richmond Rd.
Cavaye Pl. SW10 90 DC78
Fulham Rd.
Cave Rd. E13 80 EH68
Cave Rd., Rich. 101 CJ91
Cave St. N1 77 DM68
Carnegie St.
Cavell Dr., Enf. 35 DN40
Cavell Rd. N17 50 DR52
Cavell Rd. (Cheshunt), Wal.Cr. 22 DT27
Cavell St. E1 78 DV71
Cavendish Ave. N3 48 DA54
Cavendish Ave. NW8 4 A1
Cavendish Ave. NW8 76 DD68
Cavendish Ave. W13 73 CG71
Cavendish Ave., Erith 97 FC80
Cavendish Ave., Har. 59 CD63
Cavendish Ave., Horn. 83 FH65
Cavendish Ave., N.Mal. 117 CU99
Cavendish Ave., Ruis. 57 BV64
Cavendish Ave., Sev. 154 FG122
Cavendish Ave., Sid. 110 EU87
Cavendish Ave., Well. 95 ET83
Cavendish Ave., Wdf.Grn. 52 EH53
Cavendish Clo. N18 50 DV50
Cavendish Rd.
Cavendish Clo. NW6 75 CZ66
Cavendish Rd.
Cavendish Clo. NW8 4 A2
Cavendish Clo. NW8 76 DD69
Cavendish Clo., Hayes 71 BS71
Westacott
Cavendish Clo., Sun. 99 BT93
Cavendish Ct. EC3 7 N8
Cavendish Ct., Rick. 29 BR43
Mayfare
Cavendish Ct., Sun. 99 BT93
Cavendish Cres., Borwd. 32 CN42
Cavendish Cres., Horn. 83 FH65
Cavendish Dr. E11 65 ED60
Cavendish Dr., Edg. 46 CM51
Cavendish Dr., Esher 129 CE106
Cavendish Gdns., Bark. 67 ES64
Cavendish Gdns., Ilf. 67 EN60
Cavendish Gdns., Rom. 68 EY57
Cavendish Ms. N. W1 5 J6
Cavendish Ms. S. W1 5 J7
Cavendish Pl. W1 5 J8
Cavendish Pl. W1 77 DH72
Cavendish Rd. E4 51 EC52
Cavendish Rd. N4 63 DN58
Cavendish Rd. N18 50 DV50
Cavendish Rd. NW6 75 CY66
Cavendish Rd. SW12 105 DH86
Cavendish Rd. SW19 104 DD94
Cavendish Rd. W4 88 CQ81
Cavendish Rd., Barn. 33 CW41
Cavendish Rd., Croy. 119 DP102
Cavendish Rd., N.Mal. 116 CS99
Cavendish Rd., Sun. 99 BT93
Cavendish Rd., Sutt. 132 DC108
Cavendish Rd., Wey. 127 BP109
Cavendish Sq. W1 5 J8
Cavendish Sq. W1 77 DH72
Cavendish St. N1 7 K1
Cavendish St. N1 78 DR68

Cavendish Ter., Felt. 99 BU89
High St.
Cavendish Way, W.Wick. 121 EB102
Cavenham Gdns., Ilf. 67 ER62
Caverleigh Way, Wor.Pk. 117 CU102
Caversham Ave. N13 49 DN48
Caversham Ave., Sutt. 117 CY103
Caversham Flats SW3 90 DF79
Caversham St.
Caversham Rd. N15 64 DQ56
Caversham Rd. NW5 77 DJ65
Caversham Rd., Kings.T. 116 CM96
Caversham St. SW3 90 DF79
Caverswall St. W12 75 CW72
Caveside Clo., Chis. 123 EN95
Cavill's Wk., Rom. 54 EW47
Cawdor Cres. W7 87 CG77
Cawnpore St. SE19 106 DS92
Caxton Ave., Add. 126 BG107
Caxton Dr., Uxb. 70 BK68
Chiltern Vw. Rd.
Caxton Gro. E3 79 EA69
Caxton Ms., Brent. 87 CK79
The Butts
Caxton Rd. N22 49 DM54
Caxton Rd. SW19 104 DC92
Caxton Rd. W12 75 CX74
Caxton Rd., Sthl. 86 BX76
Caxton St. SW1 9 L6
Caxton St. SW1 91 DJ76
Caxton St. N. E16 80 EF73
Victoria Dock Rd.
Caxton Way, Wat. 43 BR45
Caygill Clo., Brom. 122 EF98
Cayley Clo., Wall. 133 DL108
Brabazon Ave.
Cayton Pl. EC1 7 K3
Cayton Rd., Grnf. 73 CE68
Cayton St. EC1 7 K3
Cazenove Rd. E17 51 EA53
Cazenove Rd. N16 64 DT61
Cearn Way, Couls. 147 DM115
Cearns Ho. E6 80 EK67
Cecil Ave., Bark. 81 ER66
Cecil Ave., Enf. 36 DT42
Cecil Ave., Wem. 60 CM64
Cecil Clo. W5 73 CJ71
Mount Ave.
Cecil Clo., Ashf. 99 BQ93
Cecil Clo., Chess. 129 CK105
Cecil Ct. WC2 9 P1
Cecil Ct., Barn. 33 CX41
Cecil Pk., Pnr. 58 BY56
Cecil Pl., Mitch. 118 DF99
Cecil Rd. E11 66 EE62
Cecil Rd. E13 80 EG67
Cecil Rd. E17 51 EA53
Cecil Rd. N10 49 DH54
Cecil Rd. N14 49 DJ46
Cecil Rd. NW9 60 CR55
Cecil Rd. NW10 74 CS67
Cecil Rd. SW19 104 DB94
Cecil Rd. W3 74 CQ71
Cecil Rd., Ashf. 99 BQ94
Cecil Rd., Croy. 119 DL100
Cecil Rd., Enf. 36 DQ42
Cecil Rd., Har. 59 CE55
Cecil Rd., Houns. 86 CC82
Cecil Rd., Ilf. 67 EP63
Cecil Rd., Pot.B. 19 CU32
Cecil Rd., Rom. 68 EX59
Cecil Rd., Sutt. 131 CZ107
Cecil Rd. (Cheshunt), Wal.Cr. 23 DX32
Cecil St., Wat. 29 BV38
Cecil Way, Brom. 122 EG102
Cecile Pk. N8 63 DL58
Cecilia Clo. N2 62 DC55
Cecilia Rd. E8 64 DT64
Cedar Ave., Barn. 48 DE45
Cedar Ave., Cob. 142 BW115
Cedar Ave., Enf. 36 DW40
Cedar Ave., Hayes 71 BU72
Acacia Ave.
Cedar Ave., Rom. 68 EY57
Cedar Ave., Ruis. 72 BW65
Cedar Ave., Sid. 110 EU87
Cedar Ave., Twick. 100 CB86
Cedar Ave., Wal.Cr. 23 DX33
Cedar Ave., West Dr. 70 BM74
Cedar Clo. SE21 106 DQ88
Cedar Clo. SW15 102 CR91
Cedar Clo., Borwd. 32 CP42
Cedar Clo., Brom. 122 EL104
Cedar Clo., Buck.H. 52 EK47
Cedar Clo., Cars. 132 DF107
Cedar Clo., E.Mol. 115 CE98
Cedar Rd.
Cedar Clo., Epsom 131 CT114
Cedar Clo., Esher 128 BZ108
Cedar Clo., Pot.B. 20 DA30
Cedar Clo., Rom. 69 FC56
Cedar Clo., Stai. 112 BJ96
Cedar Clo., Swan. 125 FC96
Cedar Clo., Warl. 149 DY118
Cedar Copse, Brom. 123 EM96
Cedar Ct. E8 78 DT66
Cedar Ct. N1 78 DQ66
Essex Rd.
Cedar Ct. SE9 108 EL86
Cedar Ct. SW19 103 CX90
Cedar Ct., Epp. 26 EU31
Cedar Cres., Brom. 122 EL104
Cedar Dr. N2 62 DE56
Cedar Dr., Lthd. 143 CE122
Cedar Dr., Pnr. 44 CA52
Cedar Gdns., Sutt. 132 DC107

Cedar Gro. W5 88 CL76
Cedar Gro., Bex. 110 EW86
Cedar Gro., Sthl. 72 CA71
Cedar Gro., Wey. 127 BQ105
Cedar Heights, Rich. 102 CL88
Cedar Hill, Epsom 144 CQ116
Cedar Ho., Croy. 135 EB107
Cedar Ho., Sun. 99 BT94
Cedar Lawn Ave., Barn. 33 CY43
Cedar Mt. SE9 108 EK88
Cedar Pk. Gdns., Rom. 68 EX59
Cedar Pk. Rd., Enf. 36 DQ38
Cedar Pl. SE7 94 EJ78
Floyd Rd.
Cedar Pl., Nthwd. 43 BQ51
Cedar Ri. N14 48 DG45
Cedar Rd. N17 50 DT53
Cedar Rd. NW2 61 CW63
Cedar Rd., Brom. 122 EJ96
Cedar Rd., Cob. 127 BV114
Cedar Rd., Croy. 120 DR103
Cedar Rd., E.Mol. 115 CE98
Cedar Rd., Enf. 35 DP38
Cedar Rd., Erith 97 FG81
Cedar Rd., Felt. 99 BR88
Cedar Rd., Houns. 86 BW82
Cedar Rd., Rom. 69 FC56
Cedar Rd., Sutt. 132 DC107
Cedar Rd., Tedd. 101 CG92
Cedar Rd., Wat. 30 BW44
Cedar Rd., Wey. 126 BN105
Cedar Ter., Rich. 88 CL84
Cedar Ter. Rd., Sev. 155 FJ123
Cedar Tree Gro. SE27 105 DP92
Cedar Vista, Rich. 88 CL81
Kew Rd.
Cedar Wk., Ken. 148 DQ116
Cedar Wk., Tad. 145 CY120
Cedar Wk., Wal.Abb. 23 ED34
Cypress Clo.
Cedar Way NW1 77 DK66
Cedar Way, Sun. 99 BS94
Cedar Wd. Dr., Wat. 29 BV35
Cedarcroft Rd., Chess. 130 CM105
Cedarhurst, Brom. 108 EE94
Elstree Hill
Cedarhurst Dr. SE9 108 EJ85
Cedarne Rd. SW6 90 DB80
Cedars, Bans. 132 DF114
Cedars, The E15 80 EF67
Portway
Cedars, The W13 73 CJ72
Heronsforde
Cedars, The, Buck.H. 52 EG46
Cedars, The, Lthd. 143 CK121
Cedars, The, Tedd. 101 CF93
Adelaide Rd.
Cedars, The, W.Byf. 126 BM112
Cedars Ave. E17 65 EA57
Cedars Ave., Mitch. 118 DG98
Cedars Ave., Rick. 42 BJ46
Cedars Clo. NW4 61 CX55
Cedars Ct. N9 50 DS47
Church St.
Cedars Dr., Uxb. 70 BM68
Cedars Ms. SW4 91 DH84
Cedars Rd.
Cedars Pl. SE7 94 EJ78
Floyd Rd.
Cedars Rd. E15 80 EE65
Cedars Rd. N9 50 DU47
Church St.
Cedars Rd. N21 49 DP47
Cedars Rd. SW4 91 DH83
Cedars Rd. SW13 89 CT82
Cedars Rd. W4 88 CQ79
Cedars Rd., Beck. 121 DY96
Cedars Rd., Croy. 119 DL104
Cedars Rd., Kings.T. 115 CJ95
Cedars Rd., Mord. 118 DA98
Cedarville Gdns. SW16 105 DM93
Cedra Ct. N16 64 DU60
Cedric Ave., Rom. 69 FE55
Cedric Rd. SE9 109 EQ90
Celadon Clo., Enf. 37 DY41
Celandine Clo. E14 79 EA71
Celandine Dr. SE28 82 EV74
Celandine Rd., Walt. 128 BY105
Celandine Way E15 80 EE69
Celbridge Ms. W2 76 DB72
Porchester Rd.
Celestial Gdns. SE13 93 ED84
Celia Cres., Ashf. 98 BK93
Celia Rd. N19 63 DJ63
Celtic Ave., Brom. 122 EE97
Celtic Rd., W.Byf. 126 BL114
Celtic St. E14 79 EB71
Cemetery La. SE7 94 EL79
Cemetery La., Shep. 113 BP101
Cemetery La., Wal.Abb. 24 EF25
Cemetery Rd. E7 66 EF63
Cemetery Rd. N17 50 DS52
Cemetery Rd. SE2 96 EV80
Cenacle Clo. NW3 62 DA62
Centaur St. SE1 10 C6
Centaur St. SE1 91 DM76
Centaurs Business Pk., Islw. 87 CG79
Centenary Rd., Enf. 37 DZ42
Centenary Trd. Est., Enf. 37 DZ42
Central Ave. E11 65 ED61
Central Ave. N2 48 DD54
Central Ave. N9 50 DS48
Central Ave. SW11 90 DF80
Central Ave., Enf. 36 DV40
Central Ave., Hayes 71 BT74
Central Ave., Houns. 86 CC84

Central Ave., Pnr. 58 BZ58
Central Ave., Wall. 133 DL106
Central Ave., Wal.Cr. 23 DY33
Central Ave., Well. 95 ET82
Central Ave., W.Mol. 114 BZ98
Central Circ. NW4 61 CV57
Hendon Way
Central Gdns., Mord. 118 DC99
Central Hill SE19 106 DR92
Central Mkts. EC1 6 G7
Central Mkts. EC1 78 DQ71
Central Par., Croy. 135 EC110
Central Par., Felt. 100 BW87
Sparrow Fm. Dr.
Central Par., Surb. 116 CL100
St. Mark's Hill
Central Pk. Ave., Dag. 69 FB62
Central Pk. Est., Houns. 100 BX85
Central Pk. Rd. E6 80 EK68
Central Pl. SE25 120 DV98
Portland Rd.
Central Rd., Mord. 118 DA100
Central Rd., Wem. 59 CH64
Central Rd., Wor.Pk. 117 CU102
Central Sq. NW11 62 DA57
Central Sq., Wem. 60 CL64
Station Gro.
Central Sq., W.Mol. 114 BZ98
Central St. EC1 7 H2
Central St. EC1 78 DQ69
Central Way NW10 74 CQ69
Central Way SE28 82 EU74
Central Way, Cars. 132 DE108
Central Way, Felt. 99 BU85
Centre, The, Felt. 99 BU89
Highfield Rd.
Centre, The, Walt. 113 BU102
Hepworth Way
Centre Ave. W3 74 CR74
Centre Ave. W10 75 CW69
Harrow Rd.
Centre Ave., Epp. 25 ET32
Centre Clo., Epp. 25 ET32
Centre Ave.
Centre Common Rd., Chis. 109 EQ93
Centre Dr., Epp. 25 ET32
Centre Grn., Epp. 25 ET32
Centre Ave.
Centre Rd. E7 66 EG61
Centre Rd. E11 66 EG61
Centre Rd., Dag. 83 FB68
Centre St. E2 78 DV68
Centre Way E17 51 EC52
Centre Way N9 50 DW47
Centreway NW7 47 CU52
Centreway, Ilf. 67 EQ61
Centric Clo. NW1 77 DH67
Oval Rd.
Centurion Clo. N7 77 DM66
Centurion Ct., Wall. 119 DH103
Wandle Rd.
Centurion La. E3 79 DZ68
Libra Rd.
Centurion Way, Erith 96 FA76
Century Rd. E17 65 DY55
Cephas Ave. E1 78 DW70
Cephas St. E1 78 DW70
Ceres Rd. SE18 95 ET77
Cerise Rd. SE15 92 DU81
Cerne Clo., Hayes 72 BW73
Cerne Rd., Mord. 118 DC100
Cerney Ms. W2 76 DD73
Gloucester Ter.
Cervantes Ct. W2 76 DB72
Inverness Ter.
Cervantes Ct., Nthwd. 43 BT52
Cester St. E2 78 DU67
Whiston Rd.
Ceylon Rd. W14 89 CX76
Chace Ave., Pot.B. 20 DD32
Chadacre Ave., Ilf. 67 EM55
Chadacre Rd., Epsom 131 CV107
Chadbourn St. E14 79 EB71
Chadd Dr., Brom. 122 EL97
Chadd Grn. E13 80 EG67
Chadview Ct., Rom. 68 EX59
Chadville Gdns., Rom. 68 EX57
Chadway, Dag. 68 EW60
Chadwell Ave., Rom. 68 EV59
Chadwell Ave. (Cheshunt), Wal.Cr. 22 DW28
Chadwell Heath La., Rom. 68 EV56
Chadwell St. EC1 6 E2
Chadwell St. EC1 77 DN69
Chadwick Ave. E4 51 ED49
Chadwick Ave. SW19 104 DA93
Chadwick Clo., Tedd. 101 CG93
Chadwick Rd. E11 66 EE59
Chadwick Rd. NW10 75 CT67
Chadwick Rd. SE15 92 DT82
Chadwick Rd., Ilf. 67 EP62
Chadwick St. SW1 9 M7
Chadwick St. SW1 91 DK76
Chadwick Way SE28 82 EX73
Chadwin Rd. E13 80 EH71
Chadworth Way, Esher 129 CD106
Chaffers Mead, Ash. 144 CM116
Chaffinch Ave., Croy. 121 DX100
Chaffinch Clo. N9 51 DX46
Chaffinch Clo., Croy. 121 DX99
Chaffinch Clo., Surb. 116 CN104
Chaffinch La., Wat. 43 BT45
Chaffinch Rd., Beck. 121 DY95
Chafford Way, Rom. 68 EW56
Chagford St. NW1 4 D5
Chagford St. NW1 76 DF70

Chailey Ave., Enf. 36 DT40
Chailey Clo., Houns. 86 BX81
Springwell Rd.
Chailey Pl., Walt. 128 BY105
Chailey St. E5 64 DW62
Chalcombe Rd. SE2 96 EV76
Chalcot Clo., Sutt. 132 DA108
Chalcot Cres. NW1 76 DF67
Chalcot Gdns. NW3 76 DF65
Chalcot Ms. SW16 105 DL90
Chalcot Rd. NW1 76 DG66
Chalcot Sq. NW1 76 DG66
Chalcott Gdns., Surb. 115 CJ102
Chalcroft Rd. SE13 108 EE85
Chaldon Common Rd., Cat. 148 DQ124
Chaldon Path, Th.Hth. 119 DP98
Chaldon Rd. SW6 89 CY80
Chaldon Rd., Cat. 148 DR124
Chaldon Way, Couls. 147 DL117
Chale Rd. SW2 105 DL86
Chale Wk., Sutt. 132 DB109
Hulverston Clo.
Chalet Clo., Bex. 111 FD91
Chalet Est. NW7 47 CU49
Chalfont Ave., Wem. 74 CP65
Chalfont Ct. NW9 61 CT55
Chalfont Grn. N9 50 DS48
Chalfont Rd. N9 50 DS48
Chalfont Rd. SE25 120 DT97
Chalfont Rd., Hayes 85 BU75
Chalfont Wk., Pnr. 44 BW54
Willows Clo.
Chalfont Way W13 87 CH76
Chalford Clo., W.Mol. 114 CA98
Chalford Rd. SE21 106 DR90
Chalford Wk., Wdf.Grn. 52 EK53
Chalforde Gdns., Rom. 69 FH56
Chalgrove Ave., Mord. 118 DA99
Chalgrove Cres., Ilf. 52 EL54
Chalgrove Gdns. N3 61 CY55
Chalgrove Rd. E9 78 DW65
Morning La.
Chalgrove Rd. N17 50 DV53
Chalgrove Rd., Sutt. 132 DD108
Chalice Clo., Wall. 133 DK107
Lavender Vale
Chalk Cres. SE12 108 EH90
Chalk Fm. Rd. NW1 76 DG66
Chalk Hill, Wat. 30 BX44
Chalk Hill Rd. W6 89 CX77
Shortlands
Chalk La., Ash. 144 CM119
Chalk La., Barn. 34 DF41
Chalk La., Epsom 144 CR115
Chalk Paddock, Epsom 144 CR115
Chalk Pit Ave., Orp. 124 EW97
Chalk Pit Rd., Bans. 146 DA117
Chalk Pit Rd., Epsom 144 CQ119
Chalk Pit Way, Sutt. 132 DC106
Chalk Rd. E13 80 EH71
Chalk Wk., Sutt. 132 DB109
Hulverston Clo.
Chalkenden Clo. SE20 106 DV94
Chalkhill Rd., Wem. 60 CN62
Chalklands, The, Wem. 60 CQ62
Chalkley Clo., Mitch. 118 DF96
Chalkmill Rd., Enf. 36 DV41
Crown Rd.
Chalkstone Clo., Well. 96 EU81
Chalkwell Pk. Ave., Enf. 36 DS42
Chalky La., Chess. 129 CK109
Challenge Rd., Ashf. 99 BR90
Challice Way SW2 105 DM88
Challin St. SE20 120 DW95
Challis Rd., Brent. 87 CK78
Challock Clo., West. 150 EJ116
Challoner Clo. N2 48 DD54
Challoner Cres. W14 89 CZ78
Challoner St.
Challoner St. W14 89 CZ78
Challoners Clo., E.Mol. 115 CD98
Chalmers Ct., Rick. 42 BM45
Chalmers Rd., Ashf. 99 BP91
Chalmers Rd., Bans. 146 DD115
Chalmers Rd. E., Ashf. 99 BP91
Chalmers Wk. SE17 91 DP79
Hillingdon St.
Chalmers Way, Felt. 99 BU85
Chaloner Ct. SE1 11 K4
Chalsey Rd. SE4 93 DZ84
Chalton Dr. N2 62 DC58
Chalton St. NW1 77 DJ68
Chamber St. E1 78 DT73
Chamberlain Clo. SE28 95 ER76
Broadwater Rd.
Chamberlain Cotts. SE5 92 DR81
Camberwell Gro.
Chamberlain Cres., W.Wick. 121 EB102
Chamberlain La., Pnr. 57 BU56
Chamberlain Pl. E17 65 DY55
Chamberlain Rd. N2 48 DC54
Chamberlain Rd. N9 50 DU48
Chamberlain Rd. W13 87 CG75
Midhurst Rd.
Chamberlain St. NW1 76 DF66
Regents Pk. Rd.
Chamberlain Wk., Felt. 100 BY91
Burgess Clo.
Chamberlain Way, Pnr. 57 BV55
Chamberlain Way, Surb. 116 CL101
Chamberlayne Rd. NW10 75 CW67
Chambers Gdns. N2 48 DD53
Strawberry Vale
Chambers La. NW10 75 CV66
Chambers Rd. N7 63 DL63

Chambers St. SE16 92 DU75
Chambord St. E2 78 DT69
Champion Cres. SE26 107 DY91
Champion Gro. SE5 92 DR83
Champion Hill SE5 92 DR83
Champion Hill Est. SE5 92 DS83
Champion Pk. SE5 92 DR82
Champion Pk. Est. SE5 92 DR83
Denmark Hill
Champion Rd. SE26 107 DY91
Champness Clo. SE27 106 DR91
Rommany Rd.
Champneys Clo., Sutt. 131 CZ108
Chance St. E1 7 P4
Chance St. E1 78 DT70
Chance St. E2 7 P4
Chance St. E2 78 DT70
Chancel St. SE1 10 F3
Chancel St. SE1 77 DP74
Chancellor Gdns., S.Croy. 133 DP109
Chancellor Gro. SE21 106 DQ89
Chancellor Pas. E14 79 EA74
South Colonnade
Chancellor Pl. NW9 47 CT54
Chancellor Way, Sev. 154 FG122
Chancellors Rd. W6 89 CW78
Chancellors St. W6 89 CW78
Chancelot Rd. SE2 96 EV77
Chancery La. WC2 6 D8
Chancery La. WC2 77 DN72
Chancery La., Beck. 121 EB96
Chanctonbury Clo. SE9 109 EP90
Chanctonbury Gdns., Sutt. 132 DB108
Chanctonbury Way N12 48 DA49
Chandler Ave. E16 80 EG71
Chandler Clo., Hmptn. 114 CA95
Chandler Rd., Loug. 39 EP39
Chandler St. E1 78 DV74
Wapping La.
Chandler Way SE15 92 DT80
Chandlers Clo., Felt. 99 BT87
Chandlers Dr., Erith 97 FD77
West St.
Chandler's La., Rick. 28 BL36
Chandlers Ms. E14 93 EA75
Chandlers Way SW2 105 DN87
Chandlers Way, Rom. 69 FE57
Chandos Ave. E17 51 EA54
Chandos Ave. N14 49 DJ48
Chandos Ave. N20 48 DC46
Chandos Ave. W5 87 CK77
Chandos Clo., Buck.H. 52 EH47
Chandos Cres., Edg. 46 CM52
Chandos Par., Edg. 46 CM52
Chandos Pl. WC2 9 P1
Chandos Pl. WC2 77 DL73
Chandos Rd. E15 65 ED64
Chandos Rd. N2 48 DD54
Chandos Rd. N17 50 DS54
Chandos Rd. NW2 61 CW64
Chandos Rd. NW10 74 CS70
Chandos Rd., Borwd. 32 CM40
Chandos Rd., Har. 58 CC57
Chandos Rd., Pnr. 58 BX59
Chandos St. W1 5 J7
Chandos St. W1 77 DH71
Chandos Way NW11 62 DB60
Change All. EC3 7 L9
Channel Clo., Houns. 86 CA81
Channel Gate Rd. NW10 75 CT69
Old Oak La.
Channelsea Rd. E15 79 ED67
Chant Sq. E15 79 EE66
Chant St. E15 79 EE66
Chanton Dr., Sutt. 131 CW110
Chantress Clo., Dag. 83 FC67
Leys Ave.
Chantrey Clo., Ash. 143 CJ119
Chantrey Rd. SW9 91 DM83
Chantry, The, Uxb. 70 BM69
Chantry Clo., Enf. 36 DQ38
Bedale Rd.
Chantry Clo., Har. 60 CM57
Chantry Clo., Kings L. 14 BN29
Chantry Clo., Sid. 110 EY92
Ellenborough Rd.
Chantry Clo., West Dr. 70 BK73
Chantry Hurst, Epsom 144 CR115
Chantry La., Brom. 122 EK99
Bromley Common
Chantry La., St.Alb. 17 CK26
Chantry Pl., Har. 44 CB53
Chantry Pt. W9 75 CZ70
Chantry Rd., Cher. 112 BJ101
Chantry Rd., Chess. 130 CM106
Chantry Rd., Har. 44 CB53
Chantry St. N1 77 DP67
Chantry Way, Mitch. 118 DD97
Chantry Way, Rain. 83 FD68
Chapel Ave., Add. 126 BH105
Chapel Clo., Dart. 111 FE85
Chapel Clo., Hat. 20 DD27
Chapel Clo., Wat. 15 BT34
Chapel Ct. N2 62 DE55
Chapel Ct. SE1 11 K4
Chapel Cft., Kings L. 14 BG31
Chapel Fm. Rd. SE9 109 EM90
Chapel Gro., Add. 126 BH105
Chapel Gro., Epsom 145 CW119
Chapel Hill, Dart. 111 FE85
Chapel Ho. St. E14 93 EB78
Chapel La., Chig. 53 ET48
Chapel La., Pnr. 58 BX55
Chapel La., Rom. 68 EX59
Chapel La., Uxb. 70 BN72
Chapel Mkt. N1 77 DN68
Chapel Pk. Rd., Add. 126 BH105
Chapel Path E11 66 EH58
Chapel Pl. EC2 7 M3
Chapel Pl. N1 77 DN68
Chapel Mkt.
Chapel Pl. N17 50 DT52
White Hart La.
Chapel Pl. W1 5 H9
Chapel Pl. W1 77 DH72
Chapel Rd. SE27 105 DP91
Chapel Rd. W13 73 CH74
Chapel Rd., Bexh. 96 FA84
Chapel Rd., Epp. 25 ET30
Chapel Rd., Houns. 86 CB83
Chapel Rd., Ilf. 67 EN62
Chapel Rd., Tad. 145 CW123
Chapel Rd., Twick. 101 CH87
Orleans Rd.
Chapel Rd., Warl. 149 DX118
Chapel Row, Uxb. 42 BJ53
Chapel Side W2 76 DB73
Chapel Stones N17 50 DT53
King's Rd.
Chapel St. E15 79 ED66
Chapel St. NW1 4 B7
Chapel St. NW1 76 DE71
Chapel St. SW1 8 G5
Chapel St. SW1 90 DG76
Chapel St., Enf. 36 DR41
Chapel St., Uxb. 70 BJ67
Trumper Way
Chapel Ter., Loug. 38 EL42
Forest Rd.
Chapel Vw., S.Croy. 134 DW107
Chapel Wk. NW4 61 CV56
Chapel Wk., Croy. 120 DQ103
Wellesley Rd.
Chapel Way N7 63 DM62
Sussex Way
Chapel Way, Epsom 145 CW119
Chapel Yd. SW18 104 DA85
Wandsworth High St.
Chapelmount Rd., Wdf.Grn. 53 EM51
Chaplin Clo. SE1 10 E4
Chaplin Clo. SE1 91 DN75
Chaplin Cres., Sun. 99 BS93
Chaplin Rd. E15 80 EE67
Chaplin Rd. N17 64 DT55
Chaplin Rd. NW2 75 CU65
Chaplin Rd., Dag. 82 EY66
Chaplin Rd., Wem. 73 CJ65
Chaplin Sq. N12 48 DD52
Chapman Clo., West Dr. 84 BM76
Chapman Cres., Har. 60 CL57
Chapman Rd. E9 79 DZ65
Chapman Rd., Belv. 96 FA78
Chapman Rd., Croy. 119 DN102
Chapman St. E1 78 DV73
Chapman's La. SE2 96 EW77
Chapmans La., Belv. 96 EX77
Chapmans La., Orp. 124 EW96
Chapmans Pk. Ind. Est. NW10 75 CT65
Chapmans Rd., Sev. 152 EY124
Chapmans Yd., Wat. 30 BW42
New Rd.
Chapone Pl. W1 5 M9
Chapter Clo. W4 88 CQ76
Beaumont Rd.
Chapter Clo., Uxb. 70 BM66
Chapter Ho. Ct. EC4 6 G9
Chapter Rd. NW2 61 CU64
Chapter Rd. SE17 91 DP78
Chapter St. SW1 9 M9
Chapter St. SW1 91 DK77
Chapter Way, Hmptn. 100 CA91
Chara Pl. W4 88 CR79
Charcroft Gdns., Enf. 37 DX42
Chardin Rd. W4 88 CS77
Elliott Rd.
Chardmore Rd. N16 64 DU60
Chardwell Clo. E6 80 EL72
Northumberland Rd.
Charecroft Way W12 89 CX75
Charfield Ct. W9 76 DB70
Shirland Rd.
Charford Rd. E16 80 EG71
Chargate Clo., Walt. 127 BT107
Chargeable La. E13 80 EF70
Chargeable St. E16 80 EF70
Chargrove Clo. SE16 93 DX75
Marlow Way
Charing Clo., Orp. 137 ET105
Charing Cross SW1 9 P2
Charing Cross Rd. WC2 5 N9
Charing Cross Rd. WC2 77 DK72
Charlbert St. NW8 76 DE68
Charlbury Ave., Stan. 45 CK50
Charlbury Gdns., Ilf. 67 ET61
Charlbury Gro. W5 73 CJ72
Charlbury Rd., Uxb. 56 BM62
Charldane Rd. SE9 109 EP90
Charlecote Gro. SE26 106 DV90
Charlecote Rd., Dag. 68 EY62
Charlemont Rd. E6 81 EM69
Charles Barry Clo. SW4 91 DJ83
Charles Burton Ct. E5 65 DY64
Ashenden Rd.
Charles Clo., Sid. 110 EV91
Charles Coveney Rd. SE15 92 DT81
Southampton Way
Charles Cres., Har. 59 CD59
Charles Dickens Ho. E2 78 DV69
Charles Grinling Wk. SE18 95 EN77
Charles Ho. N17 50 DT52
Charles La. NW8 76 DD68
St. John's Wd. High St.
Charles Pl. NW1 5 L3
Charles Rd. E7 80 EJ66
Lens Rd.
Charles Rd. SW19 118 DA95
Charles Rd. W13 73 CG72
Charles Rd., Dag. 83 FD65
Charles Rd., Rom. 68 EX59
Charles Rd., Sev. 139 FB110
Charles Rd., Stai. 98 BK93
Charles II St. SW1 9 M2
Charles II St. SW1 77 DK74
Charles Sevright Dr. NW7 47 CX50
Charles Sq. N1 7 L3
Charles Sq. Est. N1 78 DR69
Pitfield St.
Charles St. E16 80 EK74
Charles St. SW13 88 CS82
Charles St. W1 9 H2
Charles St. W1 77 DH74
Charles St., Croy. 120 DQ104
Charles St., Enf. 36 DT43
Charles St., Epp. 26 EU32
Charles St., Houns. 86 BY82
Charles St., Uxb. 71 BP70
Charlesfield SE9 108 EJ90
Charleston Clo., Felt. 99 BU90
Charleston St. SE17 11 J9
Charleston St. SE17 92 DQ77
Charleville Circ. SE26 106 DU92
Charleville Rd. W14 89 CY78
Charlieville Rd., Erith 97 FC80
Northumberland Pk.
Charlmont Rd. SW17 104 DF93
Charlock Way, Wat. 29 BT44
Charlotte Clo., Bexh. 110 EY85
Charlotte Despard Ave. SW11 90 DG81
Charlotte Gdns., Rom. 55 FB51
Charlotte Ms. W1 5 L6
Charlotte Ms. W14 89 CY77
Munden St.
Charlotte Pl. NW9 60 CQ57
Uphill Dr.
Charlotte Pl. SW1 9 K9
Charlotte Pl. W1 5 L7
Charlotte Rd. EC2 7 M3
Charlotte Rd. EC2 78 DS70
Charlotte Rd. SW13 89 CT81
Charlotte Rd., Dag. 83 FB65
Charlotte Rd., Wall. 133 DJ107
Charlotte Row SW4 91 DJ83
North St.
Charlotte Sq., Rich. 102 CM86
Greville Rd.
Charlotte St. W1 5 L6
Charlotte St. W1 77 DJ71
Charlotte Ter. N1 77 DM67
Charlow Clo. SW6 90 DC82
Townmead Rd.
Charlton Ave., Walt. 127 BV105
Charlton Ch. La. SE7 94 EJ78
Charlton Clo., Uxb. 57 BP61
Charlton Cres., Bark. 81 ET68
Charlton Dene SE7 94 EJ80
Charlton Dr., West. 150 EK117
Charlton Gdns., Couls. 147 DJ118
Charlton Kings, Wey. 113 BS104
Charlton Kings Rd. NW5 63 DK64
Charlton La. SE7 94 EK78
Charlton La., Shep. 113 BQ97
Charlton Pk. La. SE7 94 EK80
Charlton Pk. Rd. SE7 94 EK79
Charlton Pl. N1 77 DP68
Charlton Rd. N9 51 DX46
Charlton Rd. NW10 74 CS67
Charlton Rd. SE3 94 EH80
Charlton Rd. SE7 94 EJ79
Charlton Rd., Har. 59 CK57
Charlton Rd., Shep. 113 BQ97
Charlton Rd., Wem. 60 CM60
Charlton Way SE3 94 EE81
Charlwood, Croy. 135 DZ109
Charlwood Clo., Har. 45 CE52
Kelvin Cres.
Charlwood Dr., Lthd. 143 CD115
Charlwood Pl. SW1 9 L9
Charlwood Pl. SW1 91 DJ77
Charlwood Rd. SW15 89 CX84
Charlwood Sq., Mitch. 118 DD97
Charlwood St. SW1 9 L10
Charlwood St. SW1 91 DJ78
Charlwood Ter. SW15 89 CX84
Cardinal Pl.
Charmian Ave., Stan. 59 CK55
Charminster Ave. SW19 118 DA96
Charminster Ct., Surb. 115 CK100
Charminster Rd. SE9 108 EK91
Charminster Rd., Wor.Pk. 117 CX102
Charmouth Rd., Well. 96 EV81
Charmwood La., Orp. 138 EV109
Charne, The, Sev. 153 FG117
Charnock, Swan. 125 FE98
Charnock Rd. E5 64 DV62
Charnwood Ave. SW19 118 DA96
Charnwood Clo., N.Mal. 116 CS98
Charnwood Dr. E18 66 EH55
Charnwood Gdns. E14 93 EA77
Charnwood Pl. N20 48 DC48
Charnwood Rd. SE25 120 DR99
Charnwood Rd., Enf. 36 DV36
Charnwood Rd., Uxb. 70 BN69
Charnwood St. E5 64 DV61
Charrington Rd., Croy. 119 DP103
Drayton Rd.
Charrington St. NW1 77 DK68
Charsley Rd. SE6 107 EB89
Chart Clo., Brom. 122 EE95
Chart Clo., Croy. 120 DW100
Stockbury Rd.
Chart St. N1 7 L2
Chart St. N1 78 DR69
Charter Ave., Ilf. 67 ER60
Charter Ct., N.Mal. 116 CS97
Charter Cres., Houns. 86 BY84
Charter Dr., Bex. 110 EY87
Charter Pl., Uxb. 70 BJ66
Charter Pl., Wat. 30 BW41
Beechen Gro.
Charter Rd., Kings.T. 116 CP97
Charter Rd., The, Wdf.Grn. 52 EE51
Charter Sq., Kings.T. 116 CP96
Charter Way N3 61 CZ56
Regents Pk. Rd.
Charter Way N14 35 DJ44
Charterhouse Ave., Wem. 59 CJ63
Charterhouse Bldgs. EC1 6 G5
Charterhouse Dr., Sev. 154 FG123
Charterhouse Ms. EC1 6 G6
Charterhouse Rd., Orp. 124 EU104
Charterhouse Sq. EC1 6 G6
Charterhouse Sq. EC1 77 DP71
Charterhouse St. EC1 6 F7
Charterhouse St. EC1 77 DN71
Charteris Rd. N4 63 DN60
Charteris Rd. NW6 75 CZ67
Charteris Rd., Wdf.Grn. 52 EH52
Charters Clo. SE19 106 DS92
Chartfield Ave. SW15 103 CV85
Chartfield Sq. SW15 103 CX85
Chartfield Ave.
Chartham Gro. SE27 105 DN90
Royal Circ.
Chartham Rd. SE25 120 DV97
Chartley Ave. NW2 60 CS62
Chartley Ave., Stan. 45 CF51
Charton Clo., Belv. 96 EZ79
Chartridge Clo., Barn. 33 CU43
Chartridge Clo. (Bushey), Wat. 30 CC44
Chartway, Sev. 155 FJ124
Chartwell Clo. SE9 109 EQ89
Chartwell Clo., Croy. 120 DR102
Tavistock Rd.
Chartwell Clo., Grnf. 72 CB67
Chartwell Clo., Wal.Abb. 24 EE33
Chartwell Dr., Orp. 137 ER106
Chartwell Gdns., Sutt. 131 CY105
Chartwell Pl., Epsom 130 CS114
Chartwell Pl., Har. 59 CD60
Chartwell Pl., Sutt. 117 CZ104
Chartwell Rd., Nthwd. 43 BT51
Chartwell Way SE20 120 DV95
Charville La., Hayes 71 BQ69
Charville La. W., Uxb. 71 BP69
Charwood SW16 105 DN91
Chase, The E12 66 EK63
Chase, The SW4 91 DH83
Chase, The SW16 105 DM94
Chase, The SW20 117 CY95
Chase, The, Ash. 143 CJ118
Chase, The, Bexh. 97 FB83
Chase, The, Brom. 122 EH97
Chase, The, Chig. 53 EQ49
Chase, The, Couls. 133 DJ114
Chase, The, Edg. 46 CP53
Chase, The, Horn. 69 FF62
Chase, The (Oxshott), Lthd. 142 CC115
Chase, The, Loug. 52 EJ45
Chase, The, Pnr. 58 BZ56
Chase, The (Eastcote), Pnr. 58 BW58
Chase, The, Rad. 31 CF35
Chase, The, Rom. 69 FE55
Chase, The (Chadwell Heath), Rom. 68 EY58
Chase, The (Rush Grn.), Rom. 69 FD62
Chase, The, Stan. 45 CG50
Chase, The, Sun. 113 BV95
Chase, The, Tad. 146 DA122
Chase, The, Uxb. 56 BN64
Chase, The, Wall. 133 DL106
Chase, The (Cheshunt), Wal.Cr. 21 DP28
Chase, The, Wat. 29 BS42
Chase Ct. Gdns., Enf. 36 DQ41
Chase Cross Rd., Rom. 55 FC52
Chase End, Epsom 130 CR112
Chase Gdns. E4 51 EA49
Chase Gdns., Twick. 101 CD86
Chase Grn., Enf. 36 DQ41
Chase Grn. Ave., Enf. 35 DP40
Chase Hill, Enf. 36 DQ41
Chase La., Chig. 53 ET48
Chase La., Ilf. 67 ER57
Chase Ridings, Enf. 35 DN40
Chase Rd. N14 35 DJ43
Chase Rd. NW10 74 CR70
Chase Rd. W3 74 CR70
Chase Rd., Epsom 130 CR112
Chase Side N14 34 DG43
Chase Side, Enf. 36 DQ41
Chase Side Ave. SW20 117 CY96
Chase Side Ave., Enf. 36 DQ40
Chase Side Cres., Enf. 36 DQ39
Chase Side Pl., Enf. 36 DQ41
Chase Side
Chase Way N14 49 DH47
Chasefield Rd. SW17 104 DF91
Chaseley Dr. W4 88 CP81
Wellesley Rd.
Chaseley Dr., S.Croy. 134 DR110
Chaseley St. E14 79 DY72
Chasemore Clo., Mitch. 118 DF101
Chasemore Gdns., Croy. 133 DP106
Thorneloe Gdns.
Chaseside Clo., Rom. 55 FE51
Chaseside Gdns., Cher. 112 BH101
Chaseville Pk. Rd. N21 35 DL43
Chasewood Ave., Enf. 35 DP40
Chastilian Rd., Dart. 111 FF87
Chatfield Ct., Cat. 148 DR122
York Gate
Chatfield Rd. SW11 90 DC83
Chatfield Rd., Croy. 119 DP102
Chatham Ave., Brom. 122 EF101
Chatham Clo. NW11 62 DA57
Chatham Clo., Sutt. 117 CZ101
Chatham Hill Rd., Sev. 155 FJ121
Chatham Pl. E9 78 DW65
Chatham Rd. E17 65 DY55
Chatham Rd. E18 52 EF54
Grove Hill
Chatham Rd. SW11 104 DF86
Chatham Rd., Kings.T. 116 CN96
Chatham Rd., Orp. 137 EQ106
Chatham St. SE17 11 K8
Chatham St. SE17 92 DR77
Chatsfield, Epsom 131 CU110
Chatsfield Pl. W5 74 CL72
Chatsworth Ave. NW4 47 CW54
Chatsworth Ave. SW20 117 CY95
Chatsworth Ave., Brom. 108 EH92
Chatsworth Ave., Sid. 110 EU88
Chatsworth Ave., Wem. 60 CM64
Chatsworth Clo. NW4 47 CW54
Chatsworth Clo., Borwd. 32 CN41
Chatsworth Clo., W.Wick. 122 EF103
Chatsworth Ct. W8 90 DA77
Pembroke Rd.
Chatsworth Cres., Houns. 87 CD84
Chatsworth Dr., Enf. 50 DU45
Chatsworth Est. E5 65 DX63
Elderfield Rd.
Chatsworth Gdns. W3 74 CP74
Chatsworth Gdns., Har. 58 CB60
Chatsworth Gdns., N.Mal. 117 CT99
Chatsworth Pl., Lthd. 129 CD113
Chatsworth Pl., Mitch. 118 DF97
Chatsworth Pl., Tedd. 101 CG91
Chatsworth Ri. W5 74 CM70
Chatsworth Rd. E5 64 DW62
Chatsworth Rd. E15 66 EF64
Chatsworth Rd. NW2 75 CX65
Chatsworth Rd. W4 88 CQ79
Chatsworth Rd. W5 74 CM70
Chatsworth Rd., Croy. 134 DR105
Chatsworth Rd., Hayes 71 BV70
Chatsworth Rd., Sutt. 131 CX106
Chatsworth Way SE27 105 DP90
Chattern Hill, Ashf. 99 BP91
Chattern Rd., Ashf. 99 BQ91
Chatterton Rd. N4 63 DP62
Chatterton Rd., Brom. 122 EK98
Chatto Rd. SW11 104 DF85
Chaucer Ave., Hayes 71 BU71
Chaucer Ave., Houns. 85 BV82
Chaucer Ave., Rich. 88 CN83
Chaucer Ave., Wey. 126 BN108
Chaucer Clo. N11 49 DJ50
Chaucer Clo., Bans. 131 CY114
Chaucer Ct. N16 64 DS63
Chaucer Dr. SE1 92 DT77
Chaucer Gdns., Sutt. 118 DA104
Chaucer Grn., Croy. 120 DW101
Chaucer Rd. E7 80 EG65
Chaucer Rd. E11 66 EG58
Chaucer Rd. E17 51 EC54
Chaucer Rd. SE24 105 DN85
Chaucer Rd. W3 74 CQ74
Chaucer Rd., Ashf. 98 BL91
Chaucer Rd., Rom. 55 FH52
Chaucer Rd., Sid. 110 EW88
Chaucer Rd., Sutt. 132 DA105
Chaucer Rd., Well. 95 ET81
Chaucer Way SW19 104 DD93
Chaucer Way, Add. 126 BG107
Chauncey Clo. N9 50 DU48
Chauncy Ave., Pot.B. 20 DC33
Chaundrye Clo. SE9 108 EL86
Chauntler Clo. E16 80 EH72
Chavecroft Ter., Epsom 145 CW119
Cheam Clo., Tad. 145 CV121
Waterfield
Cheam Common Rd., Wor.Pk. 117 CV103
Cheam Mans., Sutt. 131 CY108
Cheam Pk. Way, Sutt. 131 CY107
Cheam Rd., Epsom 131 CU110
Cheam Rd., Sutt. 131 CZ107
Cheam Rd. (East Ewell), Sutt. 131 CX110
Cheam St. SE15 92 DV83
Evelina Rd.
Cheapside EC2 7 H9
Cheapside EC2 78 DQ72
Cheddar Rd., Houns. 84 BN82
Cromer Rd.
Cheddar Waye, Hayes 71 BV72
Cheddington Rd. N18 50 DS48
Chedworth Clo. E16 80 EF72
Hallsville Rd.
Cheeseman Clo., Hmptn. 100 BY93
Cheesemans Ter. W14 89 CZ78
Chelford Rd., Brom. 107 ED92

Chelmer Cres., Bark. 82 EV68
Chelmer Rd. E9 65 DX64
Chelmsford Ave., Rom. 55 FD52
Chelmsford Clo. E6 81 EM72
Guildford Rd.
Chelmsford Clo. W6 89 CX79
Chelmsford Clo., Sutt. 132 DA109
Chelmsford Gdns., Ilf. 66 EL59
Chelmsford Rd. E11 65 ED60
Chelmsford Rd. E17 65 EA58
Chelmsford Rd. E18 52 EF53
Chelmsford Rd. N14 49 DJ45
Chelmsford Sq. NW10 75 CW67
Chelsea Bri. SW1 91 DH79
Chelsea Bri. SW8 91 DH79
Chelsea Bri. Rd. SW1 8 F10
Chelsea Bri. Rd. SW1 90 DG78
Chelsea Cloisters SW3 90 DE77
Lucan Pl.
Chelsea Clo. NW10 74 CR67
Winchelsea Rd.
Chelsea Clo., Edg. 46 CN54
Chelsea Clo., Hmptn. 100 CC93
Chelsea Embk. SW3 90 DE79
Chelsea Gdns., Sutt. 131 CY105
Chelsea Harbour SW10 90 DD81
Chelsea Harbour Dr. SW10 90 DC81
Chelsea Manor Gdns. SW3 90 DE78
Chelsea Manor St. SW3 90 DE78
Chelsea Pk. Gdns. SW3 90 DD79
Chelsea Sq. SW3 8 A10
Chelsea Sq. SW3 90 DD78
Chelsea Wf. SW10 90 DD80
Lots Rd.
Chelsfield Ave. N9 51 DX45
Chelsfield Gdns. SE26 106 DW90
Chelsfield Grn. N9 51 DX45
Chelsfield Ave.
Chelsfield Hill, Orp. 138 EW109
Chelsfield La., Orp. 138 FA108
Chelsfield La. (Chelsfield), Orp. 124 EX101
Chelsfield La., Sev. 139 FC109
Chelsfield Rd., Orp. 124 EW100
Chelsham Clo., Warl. 149 DY118
Limpsfield Rd.
Chelsham Common Rd., Warl. 149 EA117
Chelsham Ct. Rd., Warl. 149 ED118
Chelsham Rd. SW4 91 DK83
Chelsham Rd., S.Croy. 134 DR107
Chelsham Rd., Warl. 149 DZ118
Chelston App., Ruis. 57 BU61
Chelston Rd., Ruis. 57 BU60
Chelsworth Dr. SE18 95 ER79
Cheltenham Ave., Twick. 101 CG87
Cheltenham Clo., N.Mal. 116 CQ97
Northcote Rd.
Cheltenham Clo., Nthlt. 72 CB65
Cheltenham Gdns. E6 80 EL68
Cheltenham Gdns., Loug. 38 EL44
Cheltenham Pl. W3 74 CP74
Cheltenham Pl., Har. 60 CL56
Cheltenham Rd. E10 65 EC58
Cheltenham Rd. SE15 92 DW84
Cheltenham Rd., Orp. 124 EU104
Cheltenham Ter. SW3 8 E10
Cheltenham Ter. SW3 90 DF78
Chelverton Rd. SW15 89 CX84
Chelwood Clo. E4 37 EB44
Chelwood Clo., Epsom 131 CT112
Chelwood Clo., Nthwd. 43 BQ52
Chelwood Gdns., Rich. 88 CN82
Chelwood Wk. SE4 93 DY84
Chenappa Clo. E13 80 EG69
Chenduit Way, Stan. 45 CF50
Cheney Rd. NW1 5 P1
Cheney Rd. NW1 77 DL68
Cheney Row E17 51 DZ53
Cheney St., Pnr. 58 BW57
Cheneys Rd. E11 66 EE62
Chenies, The, Dart. 111 FE91
Chenies, The, Orp. 123 ES100
Chenies Ms. WC1 5 M5
Chenies Pl. NW1 77 DK68
Chenies St. WC1 5 M6
Chenies St. WC1 77 DK71
Chenies Way, Wat. 43 BS45
Cheniston Gdns. W8 90 DB76
Chepstow Clo. SW15 103 CY86
Lytton Gro.
Chepstow Cres. W11 76 DA73
Chepstow Cres., Ilf. 67 ES58
Chepstow Gdns., Sthl. 72 BZ72
Chepstow Pl. W2 76 DA72
Chepstow Ri., Croy. 120 DS104
Chepstow Rd. W2 76 DA72
Chepstow Rd. W7 87 CG76
Chepstow Rd., Croy. 120 DS104
Chepstow Vill. W11 75 CZ73
Chepstow Way SE15 92 DT80
Exeter Rd.
Chequer St. EC1 7 J5
Chequers Clo., Orp. 123 ET98
Chequers Gdns. N13 49 DP50
Chequers La., Dag. 82 EZ71
Chequers La., Wat. 16 BW30
Chequers Par. SE9 109 EM86
Eltham High St.
Chequers Rd., Loug. 39 EN43
Chequers Sq., Uxb. 70 BJ66
High St.
Chequers Wk., Wal.Abb. 24 EF33
Chartwell Clo.
Chequers Way N13 49 DP50
Cherbury Clo. SE28 82 EX72
Cherbury Ct. N1 78 DR68
Cherbury St.
Cherbury St. N1 7 L1
Cherbury St. N1 78 DR68
Cherchefelle Ms., Stan. 45 CH50
Cherimoya Gdns., W.Mol. 114 CB97
Kelvinbrook
Cherington Rd. W7 73 CF74
Cheriton Ave., Brom. 122 EF99
Cheriton Ave., Ilf. 53 EM54
Cheriton Clo. W5 73 CJ71
Cheriton Clo., Barn. 34 DG41
Cheriton Ct., Walt. 114 BW102
St. Johns Dr.
Cheriton Dr. SE18 95 ER80
Cheriton Sq. SW17 104 DG89
Cherry Ave., Sthl. 72 BX74
Cherry Ave., Swan. 125 FD97
Cherry Clo. E17 65 EB57
Eden Rd.
Cherry Clo. SW2 105 DN87
Tulse Hill
Cherry Clo. W5 87 CK76
Cherry Clo., Bans. 131 CX114
Cherry Clo., Cars. 118 DF103
Cherry Clo., Mord. 117 CY98
Cherry Clo., Ruis. 57 BT62
The Roundways
Cherry Cres., Brent. 87 CH80
Cherry Gdn. St. SE16 92 DV75
Cherry Gdns., Dag. 68 EZ64
Cherry Gdns., Nthlt. 72 CB66
Cherry Garth, Brent. 87 CK78
Cherry Gro., Hayes 71 BV74
Cherry Gro., Uxb. 71 BP71
Cherry Hill, Barn. 34 DB44
Cherry Hill, Har. 45 CE52
Cherry Hill, Rick. 28 BH41
Cherry Hill, St.Alb. 16 CA25
Cherry Hill Gdns., Croy. 133 DM105
Cherry Hollow, Abb.L. 15 BT31
Cherry La., West Dr. 84 BM77
Cherry Laurel Wk. SW2 105 DM86
Beechdale Rd.
Cherry Orchard, Ash. 144 CP118
Cherry Orchard, Stai. 98 BG92
Cherry Orchard, West Dr. 84 BL75
Cherry Orchard Clo., Orp. 124 EW99
Cherry Orchard Gdns., Croy. 120 DR103
Oval Rd.
Cherry Orchard Gdns., W.Mol. 114 BZ97
Cherry Orchard Rd., Brom. 122 EL103
Cherry Orchard Rd., Croy. 120 DR103
Cherry Orchard Rd., W.Mol. 114 BZ97
Cherry Rd., Enf. 36 DW38
Cherry St., Rom. 69 FD57
Cherry Tree Ave., St.Alb. 17 CK26
Cherry Tree Ave., Stai. 98 BH93
Cherry Tree Ave., West Dr. 70 BM72
Cherry Tree Clo., Rain. 83 FG68
Cherry Tree Clo., Wem. 59 CF63
Cherry Tree Ct. NW9 60 CQ56
Cherry Tree Ct., Couls. 147 DM117
Cherry Tree Dr. SW16 105 DL90
Cherry Tree Grn., S.Croy. 134 DV114
Cherry Tree La., Dart. 111 FF90
Cherry Tree La., Pot.B. 20 DB34
Ashwood Rd.
Cherry Tree La., Rain. 83 FE69
Cherry Tree Ri., Buck.H. 52 EJ49
Cherry Tree Rd. E15 66 EE63
Wingfield Rd.
Cherry Tree Rd. N2 62 DF56
Cherry Tree Rd., Wat. 29 BV36
Cherry Tree Wk. EC1 78 DQ70
Whitecross St.
Cherry Tree Wk., Beck. 121 DZ98
Cherry Tree Wk., W.Wick. 136 EF105
Cherry Tree Way, Stan. 45 CH51
Cherry Wk., Brom. 122 EG102
Cherry Wk., Rain. 83 FF68
Cherry Wk., Rick. 28 BJ40
Cherry Way, Epsom 130 CR107
Cherry Way, Shep. 113 BR98
Cherry Wd. Way W5 74 CN71
Hanger Vale La.
Cherrycot Hill, Orp. 137 ER105
Cherrycot Ri., Orp. 137 EQ105
Cherrycroft Gdns., Pnr. 44 BZ52
Westfield Pk.
Cherrydale, Wat. 29 BT42
Cherrydown Ave. E4 51 DZ48
Cherrydown Clo. E4 51 DZ48
Cherrydown Rd., Sid. 110 EX89
Cherrydown Wk., Rom. 55 FB54
Cherrytree La., Iver 70 BG67
Cherrywood Clo. E3 79 DY69
Cherrywood Clo., Kings.T. 102 CN94
Cherrywood Dr. SW15 103 CX85
Cherrywood La., Mord. 117 CY98
Cherston Gdns., Loug. 39 EN42
Cherston Rd.
Cherston Rd., Loug. 39 EN42
Chertsey Bri. Rd., Cher. 112 BK101
Chertsey Clo., Ken. 147 DP115
Chertsey Cres., Croy. 135 EC110
Chertsey Dr., Sutt. 117 CY103
Chertsey Rd. E11 65 ED61
Chertsey Rd., Add. 112 BH103
Chertsey Rd., Ashf. 99 BR94
Chertsey Rd., Felt. 99 BS92
Chertsey Rd., Ilf. 67 ER63
Chertsey Rd., Shep. 112 BK101
Chertsey Rd., Sun. 99 BR94
Chertsey Rd., Twick. 101 CF86
Chertsey Rd., W.Byf. 126 BK111
Chertsey St. SW17 104 DG92
Chervil Clo., Felt. 99 BU90
Chervil Ms. SE28 82 EV74
Cherwell Clo., Rick. 28 BN43
Cherwell Ct., Epsom 130 CQ105
Cherwell Way, Ruis. 57 BQ58
Cheryls Clo. SW6 90 DB81
Cheseman St. SE26 106 DV90
Chesfield Rd., Kings.T. 102 CL94
Chesham Ave., Orp. 123 EP100
Chesham Clo. SW1 8 F7
Chesham Clo., Rom. 69 FD56
Chesham Clo., Sutt. 131 CY110
Chesham Ct., Nthwd. 43 BT51
Frithwood Ave.
Chesham Cres. SE20 120 DW96
Chesham Ms. SW1 8 F6
Chesham Ms. SW1 90 DG76
Chesham Pl. SW1 8 F7
Chesham Pl. SW1 90 DG76
Chesham Rd. SE20 120 DW96
Chesham Rd. SW19 104 DD92
Chesham Rd., Kings.T. 116 CN96
Chesham St. NW10 60 CR62
Chesham St. SW1 8 F7
Chesham St. SW1 90 DG76
Chesham Ter. W13 87 CH75
Chesham Way, Wat. 29 BS44
Cheshire Clo. SE4 93 DZ82
Cheshire Clo., Mitch. 119 DL97
Cheshire Gdns., Chess. 129 CK107
Cheshire Rd. N22 49 DM51
Cheshire St. E2 78 DT70
Chesholm Rd. N16 64 DS62
Cheshunt Pk. (Cheshunt), Wal.Cr. 22 DV26
Cheshunt Rd. E7 80 EH65
Cheshunt Rd., Belv. 96 FA78
Cheshunt Wash (Cheshunt), Wal.Cr. 23 DY27
Chesil Ct. E2 78 DW68
Bonner Rd.
Chesil Way, Hayes 71 BT69
Chesilton Rd. SW6 89 CZ81
Chesley Gdns. E6 80 EK68
Cheslyn Gdns., Wat. 29 BT37
Chesney Cres., Croy. 135 EC108
Chesney St. SW11 90 DG81
Chesnut Est. N17 64 DT55
Chesnut Rd.
Chesnut Gro. N17 64 DT55
Chesnut Rd.
Chesnut Rd. N17 64 DT55
Chess Clo., Rick. 28 BK42
Chess Hill, Rick. 28 BK42
Chess La., Rick. 28 BK42
Chess Vale Ri., Rick. 28 BM44
Chess Way, Rick. 28 BG41
Chessholme Ct., Sun. 99 BS94
Scotts Ave.
Chessholme Rd., Ashf. 99 BQ93
Chessington Ave. N3 61 CY55
Chessington Ave., Bexh. 96 EY80
Chessington Clo., Epsom 130 CQ107
Chessington Ct., Pnr. 58 BZ56
Chessington Hall Gdns., Chess. 129 CK108
Chessington Hill Pk., Chess. 130 CN106
Chessington Lo. N3 61 CZ55
Chessington Rd., Epsom 130 CP107
Chessington Way, W.Wick. 121 EB103
Chesson Rd. W14 89 CZ79
Chesswood Way, Pnr. 44 BX54
Chester Ave., Rich. 102 CM86
Chester Ave., Twick. 100 BZ88
Chester Clo. SW1 9 H5
Chester Clo. SW1 91 DH75
Chester Clo. SW13 89 CV83
Chester Clo., Ashf. 99 BR92
Chester Clo., Loug. 39 EQ39
Chester Clo., Pot.B. 20 DB29
Chester Clo., Sutt. 118 DA103
Broomloan La.
Chester Clo., Uxb. 71 BP72
Dawley Ave.
Chester Clo. N. NW1 5 J2
Chester Clo. S. NW1 5 J3
Chester Cotts. SW1 8 F9
Chester Ct. NW1 5 J2
Chester Ct. SE5 92 DR80
Chester Cres. E8 78 DT65
Ridley Rd.
Chester Dr., Har. 58 BZ58
Chester Gdns. W13 73 CH72
Chester Gdns., Enf. 36 DV44
Chester Gdns., Mord. 118 DC100
Chester Gate NW1 5 H3
Chester Gate NW1 77 DH69
Chester Grn., Loug. 39 EQ39
Chester Ms. SW1 9 H6
Chester Ms. SW1 91 DH76
Chester Path, Loug. 39 EQ39
Chester Pl. NW1 5 H2
Chester Rd. E7 80 EK66
Chester Rd. E11 66 EH58
Chester Rd. E16 80 EE70
Chester Rd. E17 65 DX57
Chester Rd. N9 50 DV46
Chester Rd. N17 64 DR55
Chester Rd. N19 63 DH61
Chester Rd. NW1 4 G3
Chester Rd. NW1 76 DG69
Chester Rd. SW19 103 CW93
Chester Rd., Borwd. 32 CQ41
Chester Rd., Chig. 53 EN47
Chester Rd., Houns. 85 BV83
Chester Rd. (Heathrow Airport), Houns. 84 BN83
Chester Rd., Ilf. 67 ET60
Chester Rd., Loug. 39 EP40
Chester Rd., Nthwd. 43 BS52
Chester Rd., Sid. 109 ES85
Chester Rd., Wat. 29 BU43
Chester Row SW1 8 F9
Chester Row SW1 90 DG77
Chester Sq. SW1 8 G8
Chester Sq. SW1 90 DG77
Chester Sq. Ms. SW1 9 H7
Chester St. E2 78 DU70
Chester St. SW1 8 G6
Chester St. SW1 90 DG76
Chester Ter. NW1 5 H2
Chester Way SE11 10 E9
Chester Way SE11 91 DN77
Chesterfield Clo., Orp. 124 EX98
Chesterfield Dr., Dart. 111 FH85
Chesterfield Dr., Esher 115 CG103
Chesterfield Dr., Sev. 154 FD122
Chesterfield Gdns. N4 63 DP57
Chesterfield Gdns. SE10 93 ED80
Crooms Hill
Chesterfield Gdns. W1 9 H2
Chesterfield Gdns. W1 77 DH74
Chesterfield Gro. SE22 106 DT85
Chesterfield Hill W1 9 H2
Chesterfield Hill W1 77 DH74
Chesterfield Ms. N4 63 DP57
Chesterfield Gdns.
Chesterfield Ms., Ashf. 98 BL91
Chesterfield Rd.
Chesterfield Rd. E10 65 EC58
Chesterfield Rd. N3 48 DA51
Chesterfield Rd. W4 88 CQ79
Chesterfield Rd., Ashf. 98 BL91
Chesterfield Rd., Barn. 33 CX43
Chesterfield Rd., Enf. 37 DY37
Chesterfield Rd., Epsom 130 CR108
Chesterfield St. W1 9 H2
Chesterfield St. W1 77 DH74
Chesterfield Wk. SE10 93 ED81
Chesterfield Way SE15 92 DW80
Chesterfield Way, Hayes 85 BU75
Chesterford Gdns. NW3 62 DB63
Chesterford Ho. SE18 94 EK80
Shooter's Hill Rd.
Chesterford Rd. E12 67 EM64
Chesters, The, N.Mal. 116 CS95
Chesterton Clo. SW18 104 DA85
Ericcson Clo.
Chesterton Clo., Grnf. 72 CB68
Chesterton Dr., Stai. 98 BM88
Chesterton Rd. E13 80 EG69
Chesterton Rd. W10 75 CX71
Chesterton Ter. E13 80 EG69
Chesterton Ter., Kings.T. 116 CN96
Chesthunte Rd. N17 50 DQ53
Chestnut All. SW6 89 CZ79
Lillie Rd.
Chestnut Ave. E7 66 EH63
Chestnut Ave. N8 63 DL57
Chestnut Ave. SW14 88 CR83
Thornton Rd.
Chestnut Ave., Brent. 87 CK77
Chestnut Ave., Buck.H. 52 EK48
Chestnut Ave., E.Mol. 115 CF97
Chestnut Ave., Edg. 46 CL51
Chestnut Ave., Epsom 130 CS105
Chestnut Ave., Esher 115 CD101
Chestnut Ave., Hmptn. 100 CA94
Chestnut Ave., Horn. 69 FF61
Chestnut Ave., Nthwd. 43 BT54
Chestnut Ave., Rick. 28 BG43
Chestnut Ave., Tedd. 115 CF96
Chestnut Ave., Walt. 127 BS110
Chestnut Ave., Wem. 59 CH64
Chestnut Ave., West Dr. 70 BM73
Chestnut Ave., W.Wick. 136 EE106
Chestnut Ave., West. 150 EK123
Chestnut Ave., Wey. 127 BQ108
Chestnut Ave. N. E17 65 EC56
Chestnut Ave. S. E17 65 EC56
Chestnut Clo. N14 35 DJ43
Chestnut Clo. N16 64 DR61
Lordship Gro.
Chestnut Clo. SE6 107 EC92
Chestnut Clo. SE14 93 DZ83
Shardeloes Rd.
Chestnut Clo. SW16 105 DN91
Chestnut Clo., Add. 126 BK106
Chestnut Clo., Ashf. 99 BP91
Chestnut Clo., Buck.H. 52 EK48
Chestnut Clo., Cars. 118 DF102
Chestnut Clo., Hayes 71 BS73
Chestnut Clo., Orp. 138 EU106
Chestnut Clo., Sid. 110 EU88
Chestnut Clo., Sun. 99 BT93
Chestnut Clo., Tad. 146 DA123
Chestnut Clo., West Dr. 85 BP80
Chestnut Clo., Wok. 140 BG124
Chestnut Ct. SW6 89 CZ79
North End Rd.
Chestnut Dr. E11 66 EG58
Chestnut Dr., Bexh. 96 EX83
Chestnut Dr., Har. 45 CF52
Chestnut Dr., Pnr. 58 BX58
Chestnut Glen, Horn. 69 FG61
Chestnut Gro. SE20 106 DV94
Hawthorn Gro.
Chestnut Gro. SW12 104 DG87
Chestnut Gro. W5 87 CK76
Chestnut Gro., Barn. 34 DF43
Chestnut Gro., Dart. 111 FD91
Chestnut Gro., Ilf. 53 ES51
Chestnut Gro., Islw. 87 CG84
Chestnut Gro., Mitch. 119 DK99
Chestnut Gro., N.Mal. 116 CR97
Chestnut Gro., S.Croy. 134 DV108
Chestnut Gro., Stai. 98 BJ93
Chestnut Gro., Wem. 59 CH64
Chestnut La. N20 47 CY46
Chestnut La., Sev. 155 FH124
Chestnut La., Wey. 127 BP106
Chestnut Manor Clo., Stai. 98 BH92
Chestnut Pl., Ash. 144 CL119
Chestnut Ri. SE18 95 ES78
Chestnut Ri. (Bushey), Wat. 44 CB45
Chestnut Rd. SE27 105 DP90
Chestnut Rd. SW20 117 CX96
Chestnut Rd., Ashf. 99 BP91
Chestnut Rd., Enf. 37 DY36
Chestnut Rd., Kings.T. 102 CL94
Chestnut Rd., Twick. 101 CE89
Chestnut Wk., Sev. 155 FL129
Chestnut Wk., Shep. 113 BS99
Chestnut Wk., Walt. 127 BS109
Octagon Rd.
Chestnut Wk., Wat. 29 BU37
Chestnut Wk., W.Byf. 126 BL112
Royston Rd.
Chestnut Wk., Wdf.Grn. 52 EG50
Chestnut Way, Felt. 99 BV90
Chestnuts, The, Rom. 40 EV41
Chestnuts, The, Walt. 113 BU103
Cheston Ave., Croy. 121 DY103
Chestwood Gro., Uxb. 70 BM66
Cheswick Clo., Dart. 97 FF84
Chesworth Clo., Erith 97 FE81
Chettle Clo. SE1 11 K6
Chettle Ct. N8 63 DN58
Chetwode Dr., Epsom 145 CX118
Chetwode Rd. SW17 104 DF90
Chetwode Rd., Tad. 145 CW119
Chetwood Wk. E6 80 EL71
Oliver Gdns.
Chetwynd Ave., Barn. 48 DF46
Chetwynd Dr., Uxb. 70 BM68
Chetwynd Rd. NW5 63 DH63
Cheval Pl. SW7 8 C6
Cheval Pl. SW7 90 DE76
Cheval St. E14 93 EA76
Chevely Clo., Epp. 26 EX29
Cheveney Wk., Brom. 122 EG97
Marina Clo.
Chevening La., Sev. 152 EY116
Chevening Rd. NW6 75 CX68
Chevening Rd. SE10 94 EF78
Chevening Rd. SE19 106 DR93
Chevening Rd., Sev. 152 EZ119
Chevenings, The, Sid. 110 EW90
Cheverton Rd. N19 63 DK60
Chevet St. E9 65 DY64
Kenworthy Rd.
Cheviot Clo., Bans. 146 DB115
Cheviot Clo., Bexh. 97 FE82
Cheviot Clo., Enf. 36 DR40
Cheviot Clo., Hayes 85 BR80
Cheviot Clo., Sutt. 132 DD109
Cheviot Clo. (Bushey), Wat. 30 CC44
Cheviot Gdns. NW2 61 CX61
Cheviot Gate NW2 61 CY61
Cheviot Rd. SE27 105 DN92
Cheviot Rd., Horn. 69 FG59
Cheviot Way, Ilf. 67 ES56
Chevron Clo. E16 80 EG72
Chevy Rd., Sthl. 86 CC75
Chewton Rd. E17 65 DY56
Cheyham Gdns., Sutt. 131 CX110
Cheyham Way, Sutt. 131 CY110
Cheyne Ave. E18 66 EF55
Cheyne Ave., Twick. 100 BZ88
Cheyne Clo. NW4 61 CW58
Cheyne Wk.
Cheyne Clo., Brom. 122 EL104
Cedar Cres.
Cheyne Ct. SW3 90 DF79
Flood St.
Cheyne Ct., Bans. 146 DB115
Park Rd.
Cheyne Gdns. SW3 90 DE79
Cheyne Hill, Surb. 116 CM98
Cheyne Ms. SW3 90 DE79
Cheyne Wk.
Cheyne Path W7 73 CF72
Copley Clo.
Cheyne Pl. SW3 90 DF79
Royal Hospital Rd.
Cheyne Rd., Ashf. 99 BR93
Cheyne Row SW3 90 DE79
Cheyne Wk. N21 35 DP43
Cheyne Wk. NW4 61 CW58
Cheyne Wk. SW3 90 DE79
Cheyne Wk. SW10 90 DD80
Cheyne Wk., Croy. 120 DU103
Cheyney Rd., Ashf. 99 BR93
Cheyneys Ave., Edg. 45 CK51
Chichele Gdns., Croy. 134 DT105
Brownlow Rd.
Chichele Rd. NW2 61 CX64
Chicheley Gdns., Har. 44 CC52
Chicheley Rd., Har. 44 CC52

Chicheley St. SE1 10 C4
Chicheley St. SE1 91 DM75
Chichester Ave., Ruis. 57 BR61
Chichester Clo. E6 80 EL72
Chichester Clo. SE3 94 EJ81
Chichester Clo., Hmptn. 100 BZ93
Maple Clo.
Chichester Ct., Epsom 131 CT109
Chichester Ct., Stan. 60 CL55
Chichester Dr., Pur. 133 DM112
Chichester Dr., Sev. 154 FF125
Chichester Gdns., Ilf. 66 EL59
Chichester Ms. SE27 105 DN91
Chichester Rents WC2 6 D8
Chichester Rd. E11 66 EE62
Chichester Rd. N9 50 DU47
Chichester Rd. NW6 76 DA68
Chichester Rd. W2 76 DB71
Chichester Rd., Croy. 120 DS104
Chichester St. SW1 91 DJ78
Chichester Way E14 93 ED77
Chichester Way, Felt. 100 BW87
Chichester Way, Wat. 16 BY33
Chicksand St. E1 78 DT71
Chiddingfold N12 48 DA48
Chiddingstone Ave., Bexh. 96 EZ80
Chiddingstone Clo., Sutt. 132 DA110
Chiddingstone St. SW6 90 DA82
Chieveley Rd., Bexh. 97 FB84
Chignell Pl. W13 73 CG74
The Bdy.
Chigwell Hill E1 78 DV73
Pennington St.
Chigwell Hurst Ct., Pnr. 44 BX54
Chigwell La., Loug. 39 EQ42
Chigwell Pk. Dr., Chig. 53 EN48
Chigwell Ri., Chig. 53 EN47
Chigwell Rd. E18 66 EH55
Chigwell Rd., Wdf.Grn. 52 EK52
Chigwell Vw., Rom. 54 FA51
Lodge La.
Chilbrook Rd., Cob. 141 BU118
Chilcot Clo. E14 79 EB72
Grundy St.
Chilcott Rd., Wat. 29 BS36
Childebert Rd. SW17 105 DH89
Childeric Rd. SE14 93 DY80
Childerley St. SW6 89 CX81
Fulham Palace Rd.
Childers, The, Wdf.Grn. 53 EM50
Childers St. SE8 93 DY79
Childs Ave., Uxb. 42 BJ54
Childs Hill Wk. NW2 61 CZ62
Church Wk.
Childs La. SE19 106 DS93
Westow St.
Child's Pl. SW5 90 DA77
Child's St. SW5 90 DA77
Child's Wk. SW5 90 DA77
Child's Pl.
Childs Way NW11 61 CZ57
Chilham Clo., Bex. 110 EZ87
Chilham Clo., Grnf. 73 CG68
Chilham Rd. SE9 108 EL91
Chilham Way, Brom. 122 EG101
Chillerton Rd. SW17 104 DG92
Chillingworth Gdns., Twick. 101 CF90
Tower Rd.
Chillingworth Rd. N7 63 DN64
Liverpool Rd.
Chilmark Gdns., N.Mal. 117 CT101
Chilmark Rd. SW16 119 DK96
Chiltern Ave., Twick. 100 CA88
Chiltern Ave. (Bushey), Wat. 30 CC44
Chiltern Clo., Bexh. 97 FE81
Cumbrian Ave.
Chiltern Clo., Borwd. 32 CM40
Chiltern Clo., Croy. 120 DS104
Chiltern Clo., Uxb. 56 BN61
Chiltern Clo. (Cheshunt), Wal.Cr. 21 DP27
Chiltern Clo. (Bushey), Wat. 30 CB44
Chiltern Clo., Wor.Pk. 117 CW103
Cotswold Way
Chiltern Dene, Enf. 35 DM42
Chiltern Dr., Surb. 116 CN100
Chiltern Gdns. NW2 61 CX62
Chiltern Gdns., Brom. 122 EF98
Chiltern Rd. E3 79 EA70
Knapp Rd.
Chiltern Rd., Ilf. 67 ES56
Chiltern Rd., Pnr. 58 BW57
Chiltern Rd., Sutt. 132 DB109
Chiltern St. W1 4 F6
Chiltern St. W1 76 DG71
Chiltern Vw. Rd., Uxb. 70 BJ68
Chiltern Way, Wdf.Grn. 52 EG48
Chilterns, The, Sutt. 132 DB109
Gatton Clo.
Chilthorne Clo. SE6 107 DZ87
Ravensbourne Pk. Cres.
Chilton Ave. W5 87 CK77
Chilton Ct., Walt. 127 BU105
Chilton Gro. SE8 93 DX77
Chilton Rd., Edg. 46 CN51
Manor Pk. Cres.
Chilton Rd., Rich. 88 CN83
Chilton St. E2 78 DT70
Chiltonian Ind. Est. SE12 108 EF86
Chiltons, The E18 52 EG54
Grove Hill
Chiltons Clo., Bans. 146 DB115
High St.
Chilver St. SE10 94 EF78
Chilwell Gdns., Wat. 44 BW49
Chilworth Ct. SW19 103 CX88
Chilworth Gdns., Sutt. 118 DC104
Chilworth Ms. W2 76 DD72
Chilworth St. W2 76 DC72
Chimes Ave. N13 49 DN50
Chinbrook Cres. SE12 108 EH90
Chinbrook Rd.
Chinbrook Est. SE9 108 EK90
Chinbrook Rd. SE12 108 EH90
Chinchilla Dr., Houns. 86 BW82
Chine, The N10 63 DJ56
Chine, The N21 35 DP44
Chine, The, Wem. 59 CH64
Ching Ct. WC2 5 P9
Ching Way E4 51 DZ51
Chingdale Rd. E4 52 EE48
Chingford Ave. E4 51 EA48
Chingford Hall Est. E4 51 DZ51
Chingford Ind. Est. E4 51 DY50
Chingford La., Wdf.Grn. 52 EE49
Chingford Mt. Rd. E4 51 EA49
Chingford Rd. E4 51 EA51
Chingford Rd. E17 51 EB53
Chingley Clo., Brom. 108 EE93
Chinnery Clo., Enf. 36 DT39
Garnault Rd.
Chinnor Cres., Grnf. 72 CB68
Chip St. SW4 91 DK84
Prescott Pl.
Chipka St. E14 93 EC75
Chipley St. SE14 93 DY79
Nynehead St.
Chipmunk Gro., Nthlt. 72 BY69
Argus Way
Chippendale All., Uxb. 70 BK66
Chippendale Waye
Chippendale St. E5 65 DX62
Chippendale Waye, Uxb. 70 BK66
Chippenham Ave., Wem. 60 CP64
Chippenham Clo., Pnr. 57 BT56
Chippenham Gdns. NW6 76 DA69
Chippenham Ms. W9 76 DA70
Chippenham Rd. W9 76 DA70
Chipperfield Rd., Kings L. 14 BJ30
Chipperfield Rd., Orp. 124 EU95
Chipping Clo., Barn. 33 CY41
St. Albans Rd.
Chipstead Ave., Th.Hth. 119 DP98
Chipstead Clo. SE19 106 DT94
Chipstead Clo., Couls. 146 DG116
Chipstead Clo., Sutt. 132 DB109
Chipstead Gdns. NW2 61 CV61
Chipstead Gate, Couls. 147 DJ119
Woodfield Clo.
Chipstead La., Couls. 146 DB124
Chipstead La., Sev. 154 FC122
Chipstead Pk., Sev. 154 FD122
Chipstead Pk. Clo., Sev. 154 FC122
Chipstead Pl. Gdns., Sev. 154 FC122
Chipstead Rd., Bans. 145 CZ117
Chipstead Rd., Erith 97 FE80
Chipstead Rd., Houns. 84 BN83
Chipstead Sta. Par., Couls. 146 DF118
Station App.
Chipstead St. SW6 90 DA81
Chipstead Valley Rd., Couls. 146 DG116
Chipstead Way, Bans. 146 DF115
Chirk Clo., Hayes 72 BY70
Braunston Dr.
Chisenhale Rd. E3 79 DY68
Chisholm Rd., Croy. 120 DS103
Chisholm Rd., Rich. 102 CM86
Chisledon Wk. E9 79 DZ65
Osborne Rd.
Chislehurst Ave. N12 48 DC52
Chislehurst Rd., Brom. 122 EK96
Chislehurst Rd., Chis. 122 EK96
Chislehurst Rd., Orp. 123 ES100
Chislehurst Rd., Rich. 102 CL85
Chislehurst Rd., Sid. 110 EU92
Chislet Clo., Beck. 107 EA94
Abbey La.
Chisley Rd. N15 64 DS58
Chiswell Ct., Wat. 30 BW38
Chiswell Grn. La., St.Alb. 16 BY25
Chiswell Sq. SE3 94 EH82
Brook La.
Chiswell St. EC1 7 K6
Chiswell St. EC1 78 DR71
Chiswick Bri. SW14 88 CQ82
Chiswick Bri. W4 88 CQ82
Chiswick Clo., Croy. 119 DM104
Chiswick Common Rd. W4 88 CR77
Chiswick Ct., Pnr. 58 BZ55
Chiswick Gdns. W4 88 CQ81
Hartington Rd.
Chiswick High Rd. W4 88 CN78
Chiswick High Rd., Brent. 88 CN78
Chiswick Ho. Grds. W4 88 CR79
Chiswick La. W4 88 CS78
Chiswick La. S. W4 89 CT78
Chiswick Mall W4 89 CT79
Chiswick Mall W6 89 CU78
Chiswick Quay W4 88 CQ81
Chiswick Rd. N9 50 DU47
Chiswick Rd. W4 88 CQ77
Chiswick Sq. W4 88 CS79
Hogarth Roundabout
Chiswick Staithe W4 88 CQ81
Chiswick Ter. W4 88 CQ77
Acton La.
Chiswick Village W4 88 CP79
Chiswick Wf. W4 89 CT79
Chittenden Cotts., Wok. 140 BL116
Chitterfield Gate, West Dr. 84 BN80
Chitty St. W1 5 L6
Chitty St. W1 77 DJ71
Chitty's La., Dag. 68 EX61
Chivalry Rd. SW11 104 DE85
Chivenor Gro., Kings.T. 101 CK92
Chivers Rd. E4 51 EB49
Choats Manor Way, Bark. 82 EV70
Renwick Rd.
Choats Rd., Bark. 82 EW68
Choats Rd., Dag. 82 EY69
Chobham Gdns. SW19 103 CX89
Chobham Rd. E15 65 ED64
Cholmeley Cres. N6 63 DH59
Cholmeley Pk. N6 63 DH60
Cholmley Gdns. NW6 62 DA64
Fortune Grn. Rd.
Cholmley Rd., T.Ditt. 115 CH100
Cholmondeley Ave. NW10 75 CU68
Cholmondeley Wk., Rich. 101 CJ85
Choppins Ct. E1 78 DV74
Wapping La.
Chopwell Clo. E15 79 ED66
Bryant St.
Chorleywood Clo., Rick. 42 BK45
Chorleywood Cres., Orp. 123 ET96
Chorleywood Rd., Rick. 28 BG42
Choumert Gro. SE15 92 DU82
Choumert Rd. SE15 92 DT83
Choumert Sq. SE15 92 DU82
Chow Sq. E8 64 DT64
Arcola St.
Chrislaine Clo. (Stanwell), Stai. 98 BK86
High St.
Chrisp St. E14 79 EB71
Christ Ch. Ave., Erith 97 FD79
Christ Ch. Pas. EC1 6 G8
Christ Ch. Rd. SW14 102 CP85
Christ Ch. Rd., Beck. 121 EA96
Fairfield Rd.
Christ Ch. Rd., Epsom 130 CL112
Christ Ch. Rd., Surb. 116 CM101
Christchurch Ave. N12 48 DC51
Christchurch Ave. NW6 75 CX67
Christchurch Ave., Har. 59 CF56
Christchurch Ave., Rain. 83 FF68
Christchurch Ave., Tedd. 101 CG92
Christchurch Ave., Wem. 74 CL65
Christchurch Clo. SW19 104 DD94
Christchurch Cres., Rad. 31 CG36
Christchurch Gdns., Epsom 130 CP111
Christchurch Gdns., Har. 59 CG56
Christchurch Grn., Wem. 74 CL65
Christchurch Hill NW3 62 DD62
Christchurch Ind. Cen., Har. 59 CF56
Christchurch La., Barn. 33 CY40
Christchurch Mt., Epsom 130 CP112
Christchurch Pk., Sutt. 132 DC108
Christchurch Pas. NW3 62 DD62
Christchurch Hill
Christchurch Pas., Barn. 33 CY41
Christchurch La.
Christchurch Rd. N8 63 DL58
Christchurch Rd. SW2 105 DM88
Christchurch Rd. SW19 118 DD95
Christchurch Rd., Houns. 84 BN82
Christchurch Rd., Ilf. 67 EP60
Christchurch Rd., Pur. 133 DP110
Christchurch Rd., Sid. 109 ET91
Christchurch Sq. E9 78 DW67
Victoria Pk. Rd.
Christchurch St. SW3 90 DF79
Christchurch Ter. SW3 90 DF79
Christchurch St.
Christchurch Way SE10 94 EE78
Christian Ct. SE16 79 DZ74
Christian Flds. SW16 105 DN94
Christian St. E1 78 DU72
Christie Dr., Croy. 120 DT100
Christie Gdns., Rom. 68 EV58
Christie Rd. E9 79 DY65
Christie Wk., Cat. 148 DQ121
Coulsdon Rd.
Christies Ave., Sev. 138 FA110
Christina Sq. N4 63 DP60
Adolphus Rd.
Christina St. EC2 7 M4
Christopher Ave. W7 87 CG76
Christopher Clo. SE16 93 DX75
Christopher Clo., Sid. 109 ET85
Christopher Clo., Tad. 145 CW123
High St.
Christopher Ct., Tad. 145 CW123
Christopher Gdns., Dag. 68 EX64
Wren Rd.
Christopher Pl. NW1 5 N3
Christopher Rd., Sthl. 85 BV77
Christopher St. EC2 7 L5
Christopher St. EC2 78 DR70
Christopher's Ms. W11 75 CY74
Penzance St.
Christy Rd., West. 150 EJ115
Chryssell Rd. SW9 91 DN80
Chubworthy St. SE14 93 DY79
Chucks La., Tad. 145 CV124
Chudleigh Cres., Ilf. 67 ES63
Chudleigh Gdns., Sutt. 118 DC104
Chudleigh Rd. NW6 75 CX66
Chudleigh Rd. SE4 107 DZ85
Chudleigh Rd., Twick. 101 CE86
Chudleigh St. E1 79 DX72
Chudleigh Way, Ruis. 57 BU60
Chulsa Rd. SE26 106 DV92
Chumleigh St. SE5 92 DS79
Chumleigh Wk., Surb. 116 CM98
Church All., Croy. 119 DP101
Handcroft Rd.
Church All., Wat. 30 CC38
Church App. SE21 106 DR90
Church App., Sev. 151 EQ115
Cudham La. S.
Church App., Stai. 98 BK86
Church Ave. E4 51 ED51
Church Ave. NW1 77 DH65
Kentish Town Rd.
Church Ave. SW14 88 CR83
Church Ave., Beck. 121 EA95
Church Ave., Nthlt. 72 BZ66
Church Ave., Pnr. 58 BY58
Church Ave., Ruis. 57 BR60
Church Ave., Sid. 110 EU92
Church Ave., Sthl. 86 BY76
Church Clo. N20 48 DE48
Church Clo. W8 90 DB75
Kensington Ch. St.
Church Clo., Add. 126 BH105
Church Clo., Edg. 46 CQ50
Church Clo., Hayes 71 BR71
Church Clo., Lthd. 143 CD124
Church Clo., Loug. 39 EM40
Church Clo., Nthwd. 43 BT52
Church Clo. (Cuffley), Pot.B. 21 DL29
Church Clo., Rad. 31 CG36
Church Clo., Stai. 112 BJ97
The Bdy.
Church Clo., Uxb. 70 BH68
Church Clo., West Dr. 84 BL76
Church Ct., Rich. 101 CK85
George St.
Church Cres. E9 79 DX66
Church Cres. N3 47 CZ53
Church Cres. N10 63 DH56
Church Cres. N20 48 DE48
Church Dr. NW9 60 CR60
Church Dr., Har. 58 BZ58
Church Dr., W.Wick. 122 EE104
Church Elm La., Dag. 82 FA65
Church End E17 65 EB56
Church End NW4 61 CV55
Church Entry EC4 77 DP72
Carter La.
Church Fm. Clo., Swan. 125 FC100
Church Fm. La., Sutt. 131 CY107
Church Fld., Epp. 26 EU29
Church Fld., Rad. 31 CG36
Church Fld., Sev. 154 FE122
Church Gdns. W5 87 CK75
Church Gdns., Wem. 59 CG63
Church Gate SW6 89 CY83
Church Grn., Hayes 71 BT72
Church Grn., Walt. 128 BW107
Church Gro. SE13 93 EB84
Church Gro., Kings.T. 115 CJ95
Church Hill E17 65 EA56
Church Hill N21 49 DM45
Church Hill SE18 95 EM76
Church Hill SW19 103 CZ92
Church Hill, Abb.L. 15 BT26
Church Hill, Cars. 132 DF106
Church Hill, Cat. 148 DT124
Church Hill (Crayford), Dart. 97 FE84
Church Hill, Epp. 26 EU30
Church Hill, Har. 59 CE60
Church Hill, Loug. 39 EM41
Church Hill, Orp. 124 EU101
Church Hill, Pur. 133 DL110
Church Hill, Sev. 151 EQ115
Church Hill, Uxb. 56 BJ55
Church Hill, West. 150 EK122
Church Hill Rd. E17 65 EB56
Church Hill Rd., Barn. 34 DE44
Church Hill Rd., Surb. 116 CL99
Church Hill Rd., Sutt. 131 CX105
Church Hill Wd., Orp. 124 EU99
Church Hyde SE18 95 ES79
Old Mill Rd.
Church La. E11 66 EE60
Church La. E17 65 EB56
Church La. N2 62 DC55
Church La. N8 63 DM56
Church La. N9 50 DU47
Church La. N17 50 DS53
Church La. NW9 60 CQ58
Church La. SW17 105 DH92
Church La. SW19 117 CZ95
Church La. W5 87 CJ75
Church La. (Nork), Bans. 145 CX117
Reigate Rd.
Church La., Brom. 122 EL102
Church La., Cat. 147 DN123
Church La., Chess. 130 CM107
Church La., Chis. 123 EQ95
Church La., Couls. 146 DG122
Church La., Dag. 83 FB65
Church La., Enf. 36 DR41
Church La., Epp. 27 FB27
Church La., Epsom 145 CX117
Reigate Rd.
Church La. (Headley), Epsom 144 CQ124
Church La., Har. 45 CF53
Church La., Kings L. 14 BN29
Church La., Loug. 39 EM41
Church La., Pnr. 58 BY55
Church La., Pot.B. 20 DG30
Church La., Rich. 102 CL88
Petersham Rd.
Church La. (Mill End), Rick. 42 BG46
Church La., Rom. 69 FE56
Church La. (Abridge), Rom. 40 EY40
Church La. (Stapleford Abbotts), Rom. 41 FC42
Church La., Tedd. 101 CF92
Church La., T.Ditt. 115 CF100
Church La., Twick. 101 CG88
Church La., Uxb. 70 BH68
Church La., Wall. 119 DK104
Church La. (Cheshunt), Wal.Cr. 22 DV29
Church La., Warl. 149 DX117
Church La. (Chelsham), Warl. 149 EB117
Church La., Wat. 30 CB38
Church La., West. 150 EK122
Church La. Ave., Couls. 147 DH122
Church La. Dr., Couls. 147 DH122
Church Manor Est. SW9 91 DN80
Vassall Rd.
Church Manorway SE2 96 EU78
Church Manorway, Erith 97 FD76
Church Meadow, Surb. 115 CJ103
Church Mt. N2 62 DD57
Church Pas. EC2 78 DQ72
Gresham St.
Church Pas., Barn. 33 CZ42
Wood St.
Church Pas., Surb. 116 CL99
Adelaide Rd.
Church Path E11 66 EG57
Church Path E17 65 EB56
St. Mary Rd.
Church Path N12 48 DC50
Church Path N17 50 DS52
White Hart La.
Church Path N20 48 DC49
Church Path NW10 74 CS66
Church Path SW14 88 CR83
North Worple Way
Church Path SW19 117 CZ96
Church Path W4 88 CQ76
Church Path W7 73 CE74
Station Rd.
Church Path, Cob. 127 BU114
Church Path, Couls. 147 DN118
Canon's Hill
Church Path, Croy. 120 DQ103
Keeley Rd.
Church Path, Mitch. 118 DE97
Church Path, Sthl. 86 BZ76
Church Pl. SW1 9 L1
Church Pl. W5 87 CK75
Church Pl., Mitch. 118 DE97
Church Pl., Twick. 101 CH88
Church St.
Church Pl., Uxb. 57 BQ62
Church Ri. SE23 107 DX89
Church Ri., Chess. 130 CM107
Church Rd. E10 65 EA60
Church Rd. E12 66 EL64
Church Rd. E17 51 DY54
Church Rd. N6 62 DG58
Church Rd. N17 50 DS53
Church Rd. NW4 61 CV56
Church Rd. NW10 74 CS66
Church Rd. SE19 120 DS95
Church Rd. SW13 89 CT82
Church Rd. (Wimbledon) SW19 103 CY92
Church Rd. W3 74 CQ74
Church Rd. W7 73 CD73
Church Rd., Add. 126 BG106
Church Rd., Ashf. 98 BM90
Church Rd., Ash. 143 CK117
Church Rd., Bark. 81 EQ65
Church Rd., Bexh. 96 EZ83
Church Rd., Brom. 122 EG96
Church Rd. (Shortlands), Brom. 122 EE97
Church Rd., Buck.H. 52 EH46
Church Rd., Cat. 148 DT123
Church Rd. (Woldingham), Cat. 149 DX122
Church Rd., Croy. 119 DP103
Church Rd., E.Mol. 115 CD98
Church Rd., Enf. 36 DW44
Church Rd., Epsom 130 CS112
Church Rd. (West Ewell), Epsom 130 CR108
Church Rd., Erith 97 FC78
Church Rd., Esher 129 CF107
Church Rd., Felt. 100 BX92
Church Rd., Hayes 71 BT74
Church Rd. (Cranford), Houns. 85 BV78
Church Rd. (Heston), Houns. 86 CA80
Church Rd., Ilf. 67 ES58
Church Rd., Islw. 87 CD81
Church Rd., Ken. 148 DR115
Church Rd., Kes. 136 EK108
Church Rd., Kings.T. 116 CM96
Church Rd., Lthd. 143 CH122
Church Rd. (Great Bookham), Lthd. 142 BZ123
Church Rd., Loug. 38 EG41
Church Rd., Mitch. 118 DD97
Church Rd., Nthlt. 72 BX68
Church Rd., Nthwd. 43 BT52
Church Rd. (Chelsfield), Orp. 138 EW108
Church Rd. (Farnborough), Orp. 137 EQ106

Church Rd., Pot.B. 20 DA30
Church Rd., Pur. 133 DL110
Church Rd., Rich. 88 CL84
Church Rd. (Ham), Rich. 101 CK91
Church Rd. (Halstead), Sev. 138 EY111
Church Rd. (Seal), Sev. 155 FM121
Church Rd., Shep. 113 BP101
Church Rd., Sid. 110 EU91
Church Rd., Sthl. 86 BZ76
Church Rd., Stan. 45 CH50
Church Rd., Surb. 115 CJ102
Church Rd., Sutt. 131 CY107
Church Rd. (Crockenhill), Swan. 125 FD101
Church Rd., Tedd. 101 CE91
Church Rd. (Cowley), Uxb. 70 BK70
Church Rd. (Harefield), Uxb. 56 BJ55
Church Rd., Wall. 119 DJ104
Church Rd., Warl. 149 DX117
Church Rd., Wat. 29 BU39
Church Rd., Well. 96 EV82
Church Rd., W.Byf. 126 BL114
Church Rd., West Dr. 84 BK76
Church Rd. (Biggin Hill), West. 150 EK117
Church Rd. (Brasted), West. 152 EV124
Church Rd., Whyt. 148 DT118
Church Rd., Wor.Pk. 116 CS103
Church Rd. Merton SW19 118 DD95
Church Row NW3 62 DC63
Church Row, Chis. 123 EQ95
Church Side, Epsom 130 CP113
Church Sq., Shep. 113 BP101
Church St. E15 80 EE68
Church St. E16 81 EP74
Church St. N9 50 DT47
Church St. NW8 4 A6
Church St. NW8 76 DD71
Church St. W2 4 A6
Church St. W2 76 DD71
Church St. W4 89 CT79
Church St., Cob. 141 BV115
Church St., Croy. 120 DQ103
Church St., Dag. 83 FB65
Church St., Enf. 36 DQ41
Church St., Epsom 130 CS113
Church St. (Ewell), Epsom 131 CU109
Church St., Esher 128 CB105
Church St., Hmptn. 114 CC96
Church St., Islw. 87 CH83
Church St., Kings.T. 115 CK96
Church St., Lthd. 143 CH122
Church St., Rick. 42 BL46
Church St. (Seal), Sev. 155 FN121
Church St. (Shoreham), Sev. 139 FF111
Church St., Sun. 113 BU97
Church St., Sutt. 132 DB106
High St.
Church St., Twick. 101 CG88
Church St., Wal.Abb. 23 EC33
Church St., Walt. 113 BU102
Church St., Wat. 30 BW42
Church St., Wey. 126 BN105
Church St. Est. NW8 4 A5
Church St. Est. NW8 76 DD70
Church St. N. E15 80 EE67
Church St. Pas. E15 80 EE67
Church St.
Church Stretton Rd., Houns. 100 CC85
Church Ter. NW4 61 CV55
Church Ter. SE13 94 EE83
Church Ter. SW8 91 DK82
Church Ter., Rich. 101 CK85
Church Vale N2 62 DF55
Church Vale SE23 106 DW89
Church Vw., Swan. 125 FD97
Lime Rd.
Church Vill., Sev. 154 FE122
Church Fld.
Church Wk. N6 62 DG62
Swains La.
Church Wk. N16 64 DR63
Church Wk. NW2 61 CZ62
Church Wk. NW4 61 CW55
Church Wk. NW9 60 CR61
Church Wk. SW13 89 CU81
Church Wk. SW15 103 CV85
St. Margarets Cres.
Church Wk. SW16 119 DJ96
Church Wk. SW20 117 CW97
Church Wk., Brent. 87 CJ79
Church Wk., Cat. 148 DU124
Church Wk., Cher. 112 BG100
Church Wk., Hayes 71 BS72
Church Wk., Lthd. 143 CH122
The Cres.
Church Wk., Rich. 101 CK85
Red Lion St.
Church Wk., T.Ditt. 115 CF100
Church Wk., Walt. 113 BU102
Church Wk., Wey. 113 BP103
Beales La.
Church Way N20 48 DD48
Church Way, Barn. 34 DF42
Mount Pleasant
Church Way, Edg. 46 CN51
Station Rd.
Church Way, S.Croy. 134 DT110
Churchbury Clo., Enf. 36 DS40
Churchbury La., Enf. 36 DR41
Churchbury Rd. SE9 108 EK87
Churchbury Rd., Enf. 36 DR40
Churchcroft Clo. SW12 104 DG87
Endlesham Rd.
Churchdown, Brom. 108 EE91
Churchfield Ave. N12 48 DC51
Churchfield Clo., Har. 58 CC56
Churchfield Clo., Hayes 71 BT73
West Ave.
Churchfield Path (Cheshunt), Wal.Cr. 22 DW29
Churchfield Rd. W3 74 CQ74
Churchfield Rd. W7 87 CE75
Churchfield Rd. W13 73 CH74
Churchfield Rd., Walt. 113 BU102
Churchfield Rd., Well. 96 EU83
Churchfield Rd., Wey. 126 BN105
Churchfields E18 52 EG53
Churchfields SE10 93 EC79
Roan St.
Churchfields, Loug. 38 EL42
Churchfields, W.Mol. 114 CA97
Churchfields Ave., Felt. 100 BZ90
Churchfields Ave., Wey. 127 BP105
Churchfields Rd., Beck. 121 DX96
Churchfields Rd., Wat. 29 BT36
Churchgate (Cheshunt), Wal.Cr. 22 DV30
Churchgate Rd. (Cheshunt), Wal.Cr. 22 DV29
Churchill Ave., Har. 59 CH58
Churchill Ave., Uxb. 71 BP69
Churchill Clo., Felt. 99 BT88
Churchill Clo., Lthd. 143 CE123
Churchill Clo., Uxb. 71 BP69
Churchill Clo., Warl. 148 DW117
Churchill Ct. W5 74 CM70
Churchill Ct., Nthlt. 58 CA64
Churchill Ct., Stai. 98 BJ93
Churchill Dr., Wey. 113 BQ104
Churchill Gdns. SW1 91 DJ78
Churchill Gdns. W3 74 CN72
Churchill Gdns. Rd. SW1 91 DH78
Churchill Ms., Wdf.Grn. 52 EF51
High Rd. Woodford Grn.
Churchill Pl. E14 79 EB74
Churchill Pl., Har. 59 CE56
Sandridge Clo.
Churchill Rd. E16 80 EJ72
Churchill Rd. NW2 75 CV65
Churchill Rd. NW5 63 DH63
Churchill Rd., Edg. 46 CM51
Churchill Rd., S.Croy. 134 DQ109
Churchill Ter. E4 51 EA49
Churchill Wk. E9 64 DW64
Churchill Way, Brom. 122 EG97
Ethelbert Rd.
Churchill Way, Sun. 99 BU92
Churchill Way, West. 150 EK115
Churchley Rd. SE26 106 DV91
Churchmead Clo., Barn. 34 DE44
Churchmead Rd. NW10 75 CU65
Churchmore Rd. SW16 119 DJ95
Churchside Clo., West. 150 EJ117
Churchview Rd., Twick. 101 CD88
Churchway NW1 5 N2
Churchway NW1 77 DK69
Churchwell Path E9 78 DW65
Morning La.
Churchwood Gdns., Wdf.Grn. 52 EG49
Churchyard Row SE11 10 G8
Churston Ave. E13 80 EH67
Churston Clo. SW2 105 DP88
Tulse Hill
Churston Dr., Mord. 117 CX99
Churston Gdns. N11 49 DJ51
Churton Pl. SW1 9 L9
Churton St. SW1 9 L9
Churton St. SW1 91 DJ77
Chusan Pl. E14 79 DZ72
Commercial Rd.
Chuters Clo., W.Byf. 126 BL112
Chuters Gro., Epsom 131 CT112
Chyngton Clo., Sid. 109 ET90
Cibber Rd. SE23 107 DX89
Cicada Rd. SW18 104 DC86
Cicely Rd. SE15 92 DU81
Cinderford Way, Brom. 108 EE91
Cinema Par. W5 74 CM70
Ashbourne Rd.
Cinnamon Clo., Croy. 119 DL101
Cinnamon Row SW11 90 DC83
Cinnamon St. E1 78 DV74
Cintra Pk. SE19 106 DT94
Circle, The NW2 60 CS62
Circle, The NW7 46 CR50
Circle Gdns. SW19 118 DA96
Circle Gdns., W.Byf. 126 BM112
High Rd.
Circle Rd., Walt. 127 BS110
Circuits, The, Pnr. 58 BW56
Circular Rd. N17 64 DT55
Circular Way SE18 95 EM79
Circus Ms. W1 4 D6
Circus Pl. EC2 7 L7
Circus Rd. NW8 76 DD69
Circus St. SE10 93 EC80
Cirencester St. W2 76 DB71
Cissbury Ring N. N12 47 CZ50
Cissbury Ring S. N12 47 CZ50
Cissbury Rd. N15 64 DR57
Citadel Pl. SE11 10 B10
Citizen Rd. N7 63 DN62
Citron Ter. SE15 92 DV83
Nunhead La.
City Gdn. Row N1 6 G1
City Gdn. Row N1 77 DP68
City Rd. EC1 6 F1
City Rd. EC1 77 DP68
Civic Way, Ilf. 67 EQ56
Civic Way, Ruis. 58 BX64
Clabon Ms. SW1 8 D7
Clabon Ms. SW1 90 DF76
Clack St. SE16 92 DW75
Clacket La., West. 150 EL124
Clacton Rd. E6 80 EK69
Clacton Rd. E17 65 DY58
Clacton Rd. N17 50 DT54
Sperling Rd.
Claigmar Gdns. N3 48 DB53
Claire Ct. N12 48 DC48
Claire Ct., Pnr. 44 BZ52
Westfield Pk.
Claire Ct., Wat. 45 CD46
Claire Pl. E14 93 EA76
Clairvale Rd., Houns. 86 BX81
Clairview Rd. SW16 105 DH92
Clairville Gdns. W7 73 CE74
Clairville Pt. SE23 107 DX90
Clammas Way, Uxb. 70 BJ71
Clamp Hill, Stan. 45 CD49
Clancarty Rd. SW6 90 DA82
Clandon Clo. W3 88 CP75
Avenue Rd.
Clandon Clo., Epsom 131 CT107
Clandon Gdns. N3 62 DA55
Clandon Rd., Ilf. 67 ES61
Clandon St. SE8 93 EA82
Clanfield Way SE15 92 DS80
Diamond St.
Clanricarde Gdns. W2 76 DA73
Clap La., Dag. 69 FB62
Clapgate Rd. (Bushey), Wat. 30 CB44
Clapham Common N. Side SW4 90 DF84
Clapham Common S. Side SW4 105 DH86
Clapham Common W. Side SW4 90 DF84
Clapham Cres. SW4 91 DK84
Clapham High St. SW4 91 DK84
Clapham Junct. Est. SW11 90 DE84
Clapham Manor St. SW4 91 DJ83
Clapham Pk. Est. SW4 105 DK86
Clapham Pk. Rd. SW4 91 DK84
Clapham Rd. SW9 91 DL83
Clapham Rd. Est. SW4 91 DK83
Claps Gate La. E6 81 EP70
Royal Docks Rd.
Claps Gate La., Bark. 81 EP70
Royal Docks Rd.
Clapton Common E5 64 DT59
Clapton Pk. Est. E5 65 DY63
Blackwell Clo.
Clapton Pas. E5 64 DW64
Lower Clapton Rd.
Clapton Sq. E5 64 DW64
Clapton Ter. N16 64 DU60
Oldhill St.
Clapton Way E5 64 DU63
Clara Pl. SE18 95 EN77
Clare Clo. N2 62 DC55
Thomas More Way
Clare Clo., Borwd. 32 CM44
Clare Clo., W.Byf. 126 BG113
Clare Cor. SE9 109 EP87
Clare Ct., Cat. 149 EA123
Clare Ct., Nthwd. 43 BS50
Clare Cres., Lthd. 143 CG119
Clare Gdns. E7 66 EG63
Clare Gdns. W11 75 CY72
Westbourne Pk. Rd.
Clare Gdns., Bark. 81 ET65
Clare Gdns., Stan. 45 CJ50
Clare Hill, Esher 128 CB107
Clare La. N1 78 DQ66
Clare Lawn Ave. SW14 102 CR85
Clare Mkt. WC2 6 B9
Clare Ms. SW6 90 DB80
Waterford Rd.
Clare Pl. SW15 103 CT86
Minstead Gdns.
Clare Rd. E11 65 ED58
Clare Rd. NW10 75 CU66
Clare Rd. SE14 93 DZ82
Clare Rd., Grnf. 73 CD65
Clare Rd., Houns. 86 BZ83
Clare Rd., Stai. 98 BK88
Clare St. E2 78 DV68
Clare Way, Bexh. 96 EY81
Clare Way, Sev. 155 FJ128
Clare Wd., Lthd. 143 CH118
Claredale St. E2 78 DV68
Claremont, St.Alb. 16 CA31
Claremont (Cheshunt), Wal.Cr. 22 DT29
Claremont Ave., Esher 128 BZ107
Claremont Ave., Har. 60 CL57
Claremont Ave., N.Mal. 117 CV99
Claremont Ave., Sun. 113 BV95
Claremont Ave., Walt. 128 BX105
Claremont Clo. E16 81 EN74
Claremont Clo. N1 6 D1
Claremont Clo. N1 77 DN68
Claremont Clo. SW2 105 DL88
Streatham Hill
Claremont Clo., Orp. 137 EN105
Claremont Clo., S.Croy. 148 DV115
Claremont Clo., Walt. 128 BW106
Claremont Cres., Dart. 97 FE84
Claremont Cres., Rick. 29 BQ43
Claremont Dr., Esher 128 CB108
Claremont Dr., Shep. 113 BP100
Claremont End, Esher 128 CB107
Claremont Gdns., Ilf. 67 ES61
Claremont Gdns., Surb. 116 CL99
Claremont Gro. W4 88 CS80
Edensor Gdns.
Claremont Gro., Wdf.Grn. 52 EJ51
Claremont La., Esher 128 CB105
Claremont Pk. N3 47 CY53
Claremont Pk. Rd., Esher 128 CB107
Claremont Rd. E7 66 EH64
Claremont Rd. E17 51 DY54
Claremont Rd. N6 63 DH59
Claremont Rd. NW2 61 CW59
Claremont Rd. W9 75 CZ68
Claremont Rd. W13 73 CG71
Claremont Rd., Barn. 34 DD37
Claremont Rd., Brom. 122 EL98
Claremont Rd., Croy. 120 DU102
Claremont Rd., Esher 129 CE108
Claremont Rd., Har. 45 CE54
Claremont Rd., Horn. 69 FG58
Claremont Rd., Surb. 116 CL100
Claremont Rd., Swan. 111 FE94
Claremont Rd., Tedd. 101 CF92
Claremont Rd., Twick. 101 CH86
Claremont Rd., W.Byf. 126 BG112
Claremont Sq. N1 6 D1
Claremont Sq. N1 77 DN68
Claremont St. E16 81 EN74
Claremont St. N18 50 DU51
Claremont St. SE10 93 EB79
Claremont Way NW2 61 CW60
Claremount Clo., Epsom 145 CW117
Claremount Gdns., Epsom 145 CW117
Clarence Ave. SW4 105 DK87
Clarence Ave., Brom. 122 EL98
Clarence Ave., Ilf. 67 EN58
Clarence Ave., N.Mal. 116 CQ96
Clarence Clo., Walt. 127 BV105
Clarence Clo. (Bushey), Wat. 45 CF45
Clarence Cres. SW4 105 DK86
Clarence Cres., Sid. 110 EV90
Clarence Gdns. NW1 5 J3
Clarence Gdns. NW1 77 DH69
Clarence La. SW15 102 CS86
Clarence Ms. E5 64 DV64
Clarence Ms. SE16 79 DX74
Clarence Pas. NW1 5 P1
Clarence Pl. E5 64 DV64
Clarence Rd. E5 64 DV63
Clarence Rd. E12 66 EK64
Clarence Rd. E16 80 EE70
Clarence Rd. E17 51 DX54
Clarence Rd. N15 64 DQ57
Clarence Rd. N22 49 DL52
Clarence Rd. NW6 75 CZ66
Clarence Rd. SE9 108 EL89
Clarence Rd. SW19 104 DB93
Clarence Rd. W4 88 CN78
Clarence Rd., Bexh. 96 EY84
Clarence Rd., Brom. 122 EK97
Clarence Rd., Croy. 120 DR101
Clarence Rd., Enf. 36 DV43
Clarence Rd., Rich. 88 CM81
Clarence Rd., Sid. 110 EV90
Clarence Rd., Sutt. 132 DB105
Clarence Rd., Tedd. 101 CF93
Clarence Rd., Wall. 133 DH106
Clarence Rd., Walt. 127 BV105
Clarence Rd., West. 151 EM118
Clarence St., Kings.T. 116 CL96
Clarence St., Rich. 88 CL84
Clarence St., Sthl. 86 BX76
Clarence Ter. NW1 4 E4
Clarence Ter., Houns. 86 CB84
Clarence Wk. SW4 91 DL82
Clarence Way NW1 77 DH66
Clarence Way Est. NW1 77 DH66
Clarenden Pl., Dart. 111 FE92
Clarendon Clo. W2 4 B10
Clarendon Clo., Orp. 124 EU97
Clarendon Cres. W11 75 CY73
Clarendon Rd.
Clarendon Cres., Twick. 101 CD90
Clarendon Cross W11 75 CY73
Portland Rd.
Clarendon Dr. SW15 89 CW83
Clarendon Gdns. NW4 61 CU55
Clarendon Gdns. W9 76 DC70
Clarendon Gdns., Ilf. 67 EM60
Clarendon Gdns., Wem. 59 CK62
Clarendon Grn., Orp. 124 EU97
Clarendon Gro. NW1 5 M2
Clarendon Gro., Mitch. 118 DF97
Clarendon Gro., Orp. 124 EU98
Clarendon Ms. W2 4 B10
Clarendon Ms., Bex. 111 FB88
Clarendon Ms., Borwd. 32 CN41
Clarendon Rd.
Clarendon Path, Orp. 124 EU97
Clarendon Pl. W2 4 B10
Clarendon Pl. W2 76 DE73
Clarendon Ri. SE13 93 EC83
Clarendon Rd. E11 65 ED60
Clarendon Rd. E17 65 EB58
Clarendon Rd. E18 66 EG55
Clarendon Rd. N8 63 DM55
Clarendon Rd. N15 63 DP56
Clarendon Rd. N18 50 DU51
Clarendon Rd. N22 49 DM54
Clarendon Rd. SW19 104 DE94
Clarendon Rd. W5 74 CL70
Clarendon Rd. W11 75 CY73
Clarendon Rd., Ashf. 98 BM91
Clarendon Rd., Borwd. 32 CN41
Clarendon Rd., Croy. 119 DP103
Clarendon Rd., Har. 59 CE58
Clarendon Rd., Hayes 85 BT75
Clarendon Rd., Sev. 154 FG124
Clarendon Rd., Wall. 133 DJ107
Clarendon Rd. (Cheshunt), Wal.Cr. 23 DX29
Clarendon Rd., Wat. 29 BV40
Clarendon St. SW1 9 J10
Clarendon St. SW1 91 DH78
Clarendon Ter. W9 76 DC70
Lanark Pl.
Clarendon Wk. W11 75 CY72
Lancaster Rd.
Clarendon Way N21 36 DQ44
Clarendon Way, Chis. 123 ET97
Clarendon Way, Orp. 124 EU97
Clarens St. SE6 107 DZ89
Clares, The, Cat. 148 DU124
Clareville Rd.
Claret Gdns. SE25 120 DS98
Clareville Gro. SW7 90 DC77
Clareville Rd., Cat. 148 DU124
Clareville Rd., Orp. 123 EQ103
Clareville St. SW7 90 DC77
Clarewood Wk. SW9 91 DN84
Somerleyton Rd.
Clarges Ms. W1 9 H2
Clarges Ms. W1 77 DH74
Clarges St. W1 9 J2
Clarges St. W1 77 DH74
Claribel Rd. SW9 91 DP82
Clarice Way, Wall. 133 DL109
Claridge Rd., Dag. 68 EX60
Clarina Rd. SE20 107 DX94
Evelina Rd.
Clarissa Rd., Rom. 68 EX59
Clarissa St. E8 78 DT67
Clark Clo., Erith 97 FG81
Forest Rd.
Clark St. E1 78 DV71
Clark Way, Houns. 86 BX80
Clarke Grn., Wat. 29 BU35
Clarke Path N16 64 DU60
Braydon Rd.
Clarke Way, Wat. 29 BU35
Clarkes Ave., Wor.Pk. 117 CX102
Clarkes Dr., Uxb. 70 BL71
Clarke's Ms. W1 4 G6
Clarkfield, Rick. 42 BH46
Clarks La., Epp. 25 ET31
Clarks La., Sev. 138 EZ112
Clarks La., Warl. 150 EF123
Clarks La., West. 150 EJ123
Clarks Mead (Bushey), Wat. 44 CC45
Clarks Pl. EC2 7 M8
Clarks Pl. EC2 78 DS72
Clarks Rd., Ilf. 67 ER61
Clarkson Rd. E16 80 EF72
Clarkson St. E2 78 DV69
Clarksons, The, Bark. 81 EQ68
Classon Clo., West Dr. 84 BL75
Claston Clo., Dart. 97 FE84
Iron Mill La.
Claude Rd. E10 65 EC61
Claude Rd. E13 80 EH67
Claude Rd. SE15 92 DV82
Claude St. E14 93 EA77
Claudia Jones Way SW2 105 DL86
Claudia Pl. SW19 103 CY88
Claughton Rd. E13 80 EJ68
Clauson Ave., Nthlt. 58 CB64
Clave St. E1 78 DV74
Cinnamon St.
Clavell St. SE10 93 EC79
Claverdale Rd. SW2 105 DM87
Claverhambury Rd., Wal.Abb. 24 EF29
Clavering Ave. SW13 89 CV79
Clavering Clo., Twick. 101 CG91
Clavering Rd. E12 66 EK60
Claverings Ind. Est. N9 51 DX47
Claverley Gro. N3 48 DB53
Claverley Vill. N3 48 DB52
Claverley Gro.
Claverton St. SW1 91 DJ78
Claxton Gro. W6 89 CX78
Clay Ave., Mitch. 119 DH96
Clay Hill, Enf. 35 DP37
Clay La., Edg. 46 CP47
Clay La., Epsom 144 CP124
Clay La., Stai. 98 BM87
Clay La. (Bushey), Wat. 45 CE45
Clay Rd., The, Loug. 38 EK39
Clay St. W1 4 E7
Claybank Gro. SE13 93 EB83
Algernon Rd.
Claybourne Ms. SE19 106 DS94
Church Rd.
Claybridge Rd. SE12 108 EJ91
Claybrook Clo. N2 62 DD55
Long La.
Claybrook Rd. W6 89 CX79
Claybury (Bushey), Wat. 44 CB45
Claybury Bdy., Ilf. 66 EL55
Claybury Rd., Wdf.Grn. 52 EL52
Claydon Dr., Croy. 133 DL105
Clayfarm Rd. SE9 109 EQ89
Claygate Clo., Horn. 69 FG63
Claygate Cres., Croy. 135 EC107
Claygate La., Esher 115 CG104
Claygate La., T.Ditt. 115 CG102
Claygate La., Wal.Abb. 23 EC30
Claygate Lo. Clo., Esher 129 CE108
Claygate Rd. W13 87 CH76

Common, The, Kings L. 14 BG32
Common, The, Rich. 101 CK90
Common, The, Sthl. 86 BW77
Common, The, Stan. 45 CE47
Common La., Add. 126 BJ109
Common La., Dart. 111 FG89
Common La., Esher 129 CG108
Common La., Kings L. 14 BM28
Common La., Rad. 31 CF37
Common La., Wat. 31 CE39
Common Rd. SW13 89 CU83
Common Rd., Esher 129 CG107
Common Rd., Lthd. 142 BY121
Common Rd., Stan. 45 CD48
Commondale SW15 89 CW83
Commonfield La. SW17 104 DE92
Tooting Gro.
Commonfield Rd., Bans. 132 DA114
Commonmeadow La., Wat. 16 CB33
Commonside, Epsom 144 CN115
Commonside, Kes. 136 EJ105
Commonside, Lthd. 142 CA122
Commonside Clo., Couls. 147 DP120
Coulsdon Rd.
Commonside Clo., Sutt. 132 DB111
Downs Rd.
Commonside E., Mitch. 118 DG97
Commonside W., Mitch. 118 DF97
Commonwealth Ave. W12 75 CV73
Commonwealth Ave., Hayes 71 BR72
Commonwealth Rd. N17 50 DU52
Commonwealth Rd., Cat. 148 DU123
Commonwealth Way SE2 96 EW78
Commonwood La., Kings L. 14 BH34
Community Clo., Houns. 85 BV81
Community Clo., Uxb. 57 BQ62
Community La. N7 63 DK64
Hilldrop Rd.
Community Rd. E15 65 ED64
Community Rd., Grnf. 72 CC67
Community Way, Rick. 29 BP43
Barton Way
Como Rd. SE23 107 DY89
Como St., Rom. 69 FD57
Compass Hill, Rich. 101 CK86
Compayne Gdns. NW6 76 DB66
Comport Grn., Croy. 136 EE112
Compton Ave. E6 80 EK68
Compton Ave. N1 77 DP65
Compton Ave. N6 62 DE59
Compton Ave., Rom. 69 FH55
Compton Clo. E3 79 EA71
Compton Clo. NW1 5 J3
Compton Clo. W13 73 CG72
Compton Clo., Edg. 46 CQ52
Pavilion Way
Compton Clo., Esher 128 CC106
Compton Ct. SE19 106 DS92
Victoria Cres.
Compton Cres. N17 50 DQ52
Compton Cres. W4 88 CQ79
Compton Cres., Chess. 130 CL107
Compton Cres., Nthlt. 72 BX67
Compton Gdns., Add. 126 BH106
Monks Cres.
Compton Gdns., St.Alb. 16 CB26
Compton Pas. EC1 6 G4
Compton Pl. WC1 5 P4
Compton Pl., Erith 97 FF79
Compton Pl., Wat. 44 BY48
Compton Ri., Pnr. 58 BY57
Compton Rd. N1 77 DP65
Compton Rd. N21 49 DN46
Compton Rd. NW10 75 CX69
Compton Rd. SW19 103 CZ93
Compton Rd., Croy. 120 DV102
Compton Rd., Hayes 71 BS73
Compton St. EC1 6 F4
Compton St. EC1 77 DP70
Compton Ter. N1 77 DP65
Comreddy Clo., Enf. 35 DP39
Comus Pl. SE17 11 M9
Comus Pl. SE17 92 DS77
Comyn Rd. SW11 90 DE84
Comyne Rd., Wat. 29 BT36
Comyns, The (Bushey), Wat. 44 CC46
Comyns Clo. E16 80 EF71
Comyns Rd., Dag. 82 FA66
Conant Ms. E1 78 DU73
Back Ch. La.
Conaways Clo., Epsom 131 CU110
Concanon Rd. SW2 91 DM84
Concert Hall App. SE1 10 C3
Concert Hall App. SE1 77 DM74
Concord Clo., Nthlt. 72 BX69
Britannia Clo.
Concord Rd. W3 74 CP70
Concord Rd., Enf. 36 DV43
Concorde Clo., Houns. 86 CB82
Lampton Rd.
Concorde Clo., Uxb. 70 BL68
Concorde Dr. E6 81 EM71
Concourse, The N9 50 DU47
New Rd.
Concourse, The NW9 47 CT53
Long Mead
Condell Rd. SW8 91 DJ81
Conder St. E14 79 DY72
Conderton Rd. SE5 92 DQ83
Condor Path, Nthlt. 72 CA68
Brabazon Rd.
Condor Rd., Stai. 112 BH97
Condor Wk., Horn. 83 FH66
Heron Flight Ave.
Condover Cres. SE18 95 EP80
Condray Pl. SW11 90 DE80
Conduit Ct. WC2 5 P10
Conduit La. N18 50 DW50
Conduit La., Croy. 134 DU106
Conduit La., Enf. 37 DY44
Morson Rd.
Conduit La., S.Croy. 134 DU106
Conduit Ms. W2 76 DD72
Conduit Pas. W2 76 DD72
Conduit Pl.
Conduit Pl. W2 76 DD72
Conduit Rd. SE18 95 EP78
Conduit St. W1 5 J10
Conduit St. W1 77 DH73
Conduit Way NW10 74 CQ66
Conewood St. N5 63 DP62
Coney Acre SE21 106 DQ88
Coney Burrows E4 52 EE47
Wyemead Cres.
Coney Gro., Uxb. 70 BN69
Coney Hill Rd., W.Wick. 122 EE103
Coney Way SW8 91 DM79
Coneybury Clo., Warl. 148 DV119
Coneygrove Path, Nthlt. 72 BY65
Arnold Rd.
Conference Clo. E4 51 EC47
Greenbank Clo.
Conference Rd. SE2 96 EW77
Congleton Gro. SE18 95 EQ78
Congo Rd. SE18 95 ER78
Congress Rd. SE2 96 EW77
Congreve Rd. SE9 95 EM83
Congreve Rd., Wal.Abb. 24 EE33
Congreve St. SE17 11 M9
Congreve St. SE17 92 DS77
Congreve Wk. E16 80 EK71
Fulmer Rd.
Conical Cor., Enf. 36 DQ40
Conifer Ave., Rom. 55 FB50
Conifer Clo., Orp. 137 ER105
Conifer Clo., Wal.Cr. 22 DT29
Conifer Gdns. SW16 105 DL90
Conifer Gdns., Enf. 36 DR44
Conifer Gdns., Sutt. 118 DB104
Conifer Way, Hayes 71 BU73
Conifer Way, Swan. 125 FC95
Conifer Way, Wem. 59 CJ62
Conifers, Wey. 113 BS104
Conifers, The, Wat. 30 BW35
Conifers Clo., Tedd. 101 CJ94
Coniger Rd. SW6 90 DA82
Coningesby Dr., Wat. 29 BS39
Coningham Ms. W12 75 CU74
Percy Rd.
Coningham Rd. W12 75 CV74
Coningsby Cotts. W5 87 CK75
Coningsby Rd.
Coningsby Dr., Pot.B. 20 DD33
Coningsby Gdns. E4 51 EB51
Coningsby Rd. N4 63 DP59
Coningsby Rd. W5 87 CK75
Coningsby Rd., S.Croy. 134 DQ109
Conington Rd. SE13 93 EB82
Conisbee Ct. N14 35 DJ43
Conisborough Cres. SE6 107 EC90
Coniscliffe Rd. N13 50 DQ48
Coniston Ave., Bark. 81 ES66
Coniston Ave., Grnf. 73 CH69
Coniston Ave., Well. 95 ES83
Coniston Clo. N20 48 DC48
Coniston Clo. SW13 89 CT80
Lonsdale Rd.
Coniston Clo. SW20 117 CX100
Coniston Clo. W4 88 CQ80
Coniston Clo., Bark. 81 ES66
Coniston Ave.
Coniston Clo., Bexh. 97 FC81
Coniston Clo., Dart. 111 FH88
Coniston Clo., Erith 97 FE80
Coniston Gdns. N9 50 DW46
Coniston Gdns. NW9 60 CR57
Coniston Gdns., Ilf. 66 EL56
Coniston Gdns., Pnr. 57 BU56
Coniston Gdns., Sutt. 132 DD107
Coniston Gdns., Wem. 59 CJ60
Coniston Ho. SE5 92 DQ80
Wyndham Rd.
Coniston Rd. N10 49 DH54
Coniston Rd. N17 50 DU51
Coniston Rd., Bexh. 97 FC81
Coniston Rd., Brom. 107 ED93
Coniston Rd., Couls. 147 DJ116
Coniston Rd., Croy. 120 DU101
Coniston Rd., Kings L. 14 BM28
Coniston Rd., Twick. 100 CB86
Coniston Wk. E9 64 DW64
Clifden Rd.
Coniston Way, Chess. 116 CL104
Coniston Way, Horn. 69 FG64
Conistone Way N7 77 DL66
Conlan St. W10 75 CY70
Conley Rd. NW10 74 CS65
Conley St. SE10 94 EE78
Pelton Rd.
Connaught Ave. E4 51 ED45
Connaught Ave. SW14 88 CQ83
Connaught Ave., Ashf. 98 BL91
Connaught Ave., Barn. 48 DF46
Connaught Ave., Enf. 36 DS40
Connaught Ave., Houns. 100 BY85
Connaught Ave., Loug. 38 EK42
Connaught Bri. E16 80 EK73
Connaught Clo. E10 65 DY61
Connaught Clo. W2 4 B9
Connaught Clo., Enf. 36 DS40
Connaught Clo., Sutt. 132 DD107
Connaught Clo., Uxb. 71 BQ70
New Rd.
Connaught Dr. NW11 62 DA56
Connaught Dr., Wey. 126 BN111
Connaught Gdns. N10 63 DH57
Connaught Gdns. N13 49 DP49
Connaught Gdns., Mord. 118 DC98
Connaught Hill, Loug. 38 EK42
Connaught La., Ilf. 67 ER61
Connaught Rd.
Connaught Ms. SE18 95 EN78
Woolwich New Rd.
Connaught Ms. W2 4 D9
Connaught Ms., Ilf. 67 ER61
Connaught Rd.
Connaught Pl. W2 4 D9
Connaught Pl. W2 76 DF73
Connaught Rd. E4 52 EE45
Connaught Rd. E11 65 ED60
Connaught Rd. E17 65 EA57
Connaught Rd. N4 63 DN59
Connaught Rd. NW10 74 CS67
Connaught Rd. SE18 95 EN78
Connaught Rd. W13 73 CH73
Connaught Rd., Barn. 33 CX44
Connaught Rd., Har. 45 CF53
Connaught Rd., Ilf. 67 ER61
Connaught Rd., N.Mal. 116 CS98
Connaught Rd., Rich. 102 CM85
Albert Rd.
Connaught Rd., Sutt. 118 DD103
Connaught Rd., Tedd. 101 CD92
Connaught Roundabout E16 80 EK73
Connaught Bri.
Connaught Sq. W2 4 D9
Connaught Sq. W2 76 DF72
Connaught St. W2 4 C9
Connaught St. W2 76 DE72
Connaught Way N13 49 DP49
Connell Cres. W5 74 CM70
Connemara Clo., Borwd. 32 CR44
Percheron Rd.
Connington Cres. E4 51 ED48
Connop Rd., Enf. 37 DX38
Connor Rd., Dag. 68 EZ63
Connor St. E9 79 DX67
Lauriston Rd.
Conolly Rd. W7 73 CE74
Conquest Rd., Add. 126 BG106
Conrad Dr., Wor.Pk. 117 CW102
Conrad Ho. N16 64 DS64
Cons St. SE1 10 E4
Consfield Ave., N.Mal. 117 CU98
Consort Ms., Islw. 101 CD85
Consort Rd. SE15 92 DV81
Constable Clo. NW11 62 DB58
Constable Clo., Hayes 71 BQ69
Charville La.
Constable Cres. N15 64 DU57
Constable Gdns., Edg. 46 CN53
Constable Gdns., Islw. 101 CD85
Constable Ms., Dag. 68 EV63
Stonard Rd.
Constable Wk. SE21 106 DT90
Ferrings
Constance Cres., Brom. 122 EF101
Constance Rd., Croy. 119 DP101
Constance Rd., Enf. 36 DS44
Constance Rd., Sutt. 132 DC105
Constance Rd., Twick. 100 CB87
Constance St. E16 80 EL74
Albert Rd.
Constantine Rd. NW3 62 DE63
Constitution Hill SW1 9 H4
Constitution Hill SW1 91 DH75
Constitution Ri. SE18 95 EN81
Consul Ave., Dag. 83 FC69
Consul Gdns., Swan. 111 FG93
Princes Rd.
Content St. SE17 11 J9
Content St. SE17 92 DQ77
Contessa Clo., Orp. 137 ES106
Control Twr. Rd., Houns. 84 BN83
Convair Wk., Nthlt. 72 BX69
Kittiwake Rd.
Convent Clo., Beck. 107 EC94
Convent Gdns. W5 87 CJ77
Convent Gdns. W11 75 CZ72
Kensington Pk. Rd.
Convent Hill SE19 106 DQ93
Convent La., Cob. 127 BS111
Seven Hills Rd.
Convent Rd., Ashf. 98 BN92
Convent Way, Sthl. 86 BW77
Conway Clo., Rain. 83 FG66
Conway Clo., Stan. 45 CG51
Conway Cres., Grnf. 73 CE68
Conway Cres., Rom. 68 EW58
Conway Dr., Ashf. 99 BQ93
Conway Dr., Hayes 85 BQ76
Conway Dr., Sutt. 132 DB107
Conway Gdns., Enf. 36 DS38
Conway Gdns., Mitch. 119 DK98
Conway Gdns., Wem. 59 CJ59
Conway Gro. W3 74 CR71
Conway Ms. W1 5 K5
Conway Rd. N14 49 DL48
Conway Rd. N15 63 DP57
Conway Rd. NW2 61 CW61
Conway Rd. SE18 95 ER77
Conway Rd. SW20 117 CW95
Conway Rd., Felt. 100 BX92
Conway Rd., Houns. 100 BZ87
Conway Rd. (Heathrow Airport), Houns. 85 BP83
Conway St. E13 80 EG70
Conway St. W1 5 K5
Conway St. W1 77 DJ70
Conway Wk., Hmptn. 100 BZ93
Fearnley Cres.
Conybeare NW3 76 DE66
King Henry's Rd.
Conybury Clo., Wal.Abb. 24 EG32
Conyer St. E3 79 DY68
Conyers Clo., Walt. 128 BX106
Conyers Clo., Wdf.Grn. 52 EE51
Conyers Rd. SW16 105 DK92
Conyers Way, Loug. 39 EP41
Cooden Clo., Brom. 108 EH94
Plaistow La.
Cooderidge Clo. N17 50 DT51
Brantwood Rd.
Cook Ct. SE16 78 DW74
Rotherhithe St.
Cook Rd., Dag. 82 EY67
Cook Sq., Erith 97 FF80
Cooke Clo. E14 79 EA74
Cabot Sq.
Cookes Clo. E11 66 EF61
Cookes La., Sutt. 131 CY107
Cookham Cres. SE16 93 DX75
Marlow Way
Cookham Dene Clo., Chis. 123 ER95
Cookham Hill, Orp. 124 FA104
Cookham Rd., Sid. 124 FA95
Cookham Rd., Swan. 124 FA95
Cookhill Rd. SE2 96 EV75
Cooks Clo., Rom. 55 FC53
Cook's Hole Rd., Enf. 35 DP38
Cooks Mead (Bushey), Wat. 30 CB44
Cook's Rd. E15 79 EB68
Cooks Rd. SE17 91 DP79
Cookson Gro., Erith 97 FB80
Sussex Rd.
Cool Oak La. NW9 60 CS59
Coolfin Rd. E16 80 EG72
Coolgardie Ave. E4 51 ED50
Coolgardie Ave., Chig. 53 EN48
Coolgardie Rd., Ashf. 99 BQ92
Coolhurst Rd. N8 63 DK58
Coomassie Rd. W9 75 CZ70
Bravington Rd.
Coombe Ave., Croy. 134 DS105
Coombe Ave., Sev. 153 FH120
Coombe Bank, Kings.T. 116 CS95
Coombe Clo., Edg. 46 CM54
Coombe Clo., Houns. 86 CA84
Coombe Cor. N21 49 DP46
Coombe Cres., Hmptn. 100 BY94
Coombe Dr., Kings.T. 102 CR94
Coombe Dr., Ruis. 57 BV60
Coombe End, Kings.T. 102 CR94
Coombe Gdns. SW20 117 CU96
Coombe Gdns., N.Mal. 117 CT98
Coombe Heights, Kings.T. 102 CS94
Coombe Hill Glade, Kings.T. 102 CS94
Coombe Hill Rd., Kings.T. 102 CS94
Coombe Hill Rd., Rick. 42 BG45
Coombe Ho. Chase, N.Mal. 116 CR95
Coombe La. SW20 117 CT95
Coombe La., Croy. 134 DV106
Coombe La. W., Kings.T. 116 CP95
Coombe Lea, Brom. 122 EL97
Coombe Neville, Kings.T. 102 CR94
Coombe Pk., Kings.T. 102 CR92
Coombe Ridings, Kings.T. 102 CQ92
Coombe Ri., Kings.T. 116 CQ95
Coombe Rd. N22 49 DN54
Coombe Rd. NW10 60 CR62
Coombe Rd. SE26 106 DV91
Coombe Rd. W4 88 CS78
Coombe Rd. W13 87 CH76
Northcroft Rd.
Coombe Rd., Croy. 134 DQ105
Coombe Rd., Hmptn. 100 BZ93
Coombe Rd., Kings.T. 116 CN95
Coombe Rd., N.Mal. 116 CS96
Coombe Rd. (Bushey), Wat. 44 CC45
Coombe Wk., Sutt. 118 DB104
Coombe Way, W.Byf. 126 BM112
Coombe Wd. Hill, Pur. 134 DQ112
Coombe Wd. Rd., Kings.T. 102 CQ92
Coombefield Clo., N.Mal. 116 CS99
Coombehurst Clo., Barn. 34 DF40
Coombelands La., Add. 126 BG107
Coomber Way, Croy. 119 DK101
Coombes Rd., Dag. 82 EZ67
Coombes Rd., St.Alb. 17 CJ26
Coombewood Dr., Rom. 68 FA58
Coombs St. N1 6 G1
Coombs St. N1 77 DP68
Coomer Ms. SW6 89 CZ79
Coomer Pl.
Coomer Pl. SW6 89 CZ79
Coomer Rd. SW6 89 CZ79
Coomer Pl.
Cooms Wk., Edg. 46 CQ53
East Rd.
Cooper Ave. E17 51 DY53
Cooper Clo. SE1 10 E5
Cooper Ct. E15 65 EB64
Clays La.
Cooper Cres., Cars. 118 DF104
Cooper Rd. NW10 61 CU64
Cooper Rd., Croy. 133 DP105
Cooper St. E16 80 EF71
Lawrence St.
Cooperage Clo. N17 50 DT51
Brantwood Rd.
Coopers Clo. E1 78 DW70
Coopers Clo., Chig. 54 EV47
Coopers Clo., Dag. 83 FB65
Coopers Cres., Borwd. 32 CQ39
Coopers La. E10 65 EB60
Coopers La. NW1 5 N1
Coopers La. NW1 77 DK68
Cooper's La. SE12 108 EH89
Coopers La., Pot.B. 20 DD31
Coopers La. Rd., Pot.B. 20 DE31
Coopers Rd. SE1 92 DT78
Coopers Rd., Pot.B. 20 DC30
Cooper's Row EC3 7 P10
Coopers Wk. (Cheshunt), Wal.Cr. 23 DX28
Cooper's Yd. SE19 106 DS93
Westow Hill
Coopersale Clo., Wdf.Grn. 52 EJ52
Navestock Cres.
Coopersale Common, Epp. 26 EX28
Coopersale La., Epp. 40 EU37
Coopersale Rd. E9 65 DX64
Coopersale St., Epp. 26 EW32
Coote Gdns., Dag. 68 EZ62
Nicholas Rd.
Coote Rd., Bexh. 96 EZ81
Coote Rd., Dag. 68 EZ62
Cope Pl. W8 90 DA76
Cope St. SE16 93 DX77
Copeland Dr. E14 93 EA77
Copeland Rd. E17 65 EB57
Copeland Rd. SE15 92 DU82
Copeman Clo. SE26 106 DW92
Copenhagen Gdns. W4 88 CR75
Copenhagen Pl. E14 79 DZ72
Copenhagen St. N1 77 DL67
Copenhagen Way, Walt. 113 BV104
Copers Cope Rd., Beck. 107 DZ94
Copeswood Rd., Wat. 29 BV39
Copford Clo., Wdf.Grn. 52 EL51
Copford Wk. N1 78 DQ67
Popham St.
Copinger Wk., Edg. 46 CP53
North Rd.
Copland Ave., Wem. 59 CK64
Copland Clo., Wem. 59 CJ64
Copland Ms., Wem. 74 CL65
Copland Rd.
Copland Rd., Wem. 74 CL65
Copleigh Dr., Tad. 145 CY120
Copleston Ms. SE15 92 DT82
Copleston Rd.
Copleston Pas. SE15 92 DT82
Copleston Rd. SE15 92 DT83
Copley Clo. SE17 91 DP79
Hillingdon St.
Copley Clo. W7 73 CF70
Copley Dene, Brom. 122 EK95
Copley Pk. SW16 105 DM93
Copley Rd., Stan. 45 CJ50
Copley St. E1 79 DX71
Stepney Grn.
Copley Way, Tad. 145 CX120
Copnor Way SE15 92 DS80
Diamond St.
Coppard Gdns., Chess. 129 CJ107
Copped Hall SE21 106 DR89
Glazebrook Clo.
Coppelia Rd. SE3 94 EF84
Coppen Rd., Dag. 68 EZ59
Copper Beech Clo. NW3 76 DD65
Daleham Ms.
Copper Beech Clo., Ilf. 53 EN53
Copper Beech Clo., Orp. 124 EW99
Rookery Gdns.
Copper Beech Ct., Loug. 39 EN39
Copper Beeches, Islw. 87 CD81
Eversley Cres.
Copper Clo. SE19 106 DT94
Copper Mead Clo. NW2 61 CW62
Copper Mill Dr., Islw. 87 CF82
Copper Mill La. SW17 104 DC91
Copper Row SE1 78 DT74
Horselydown La.
Copperas St. SE8 93 EB79
Copperbeech Clo. NW3 62 DD64
Akenside Rd.
Copperdale Rd., Hayes 85 BU75
Copperfield, Chig. 53 ER50
Copperfield App., Chig. 53 ER51
Copperfield Ave., Uxb. 70 BN71
Copperfield Clo., S.Croy. 134 DQ111
Copperfield Ct., Lthd. 143 CG121
Kingston Rd.
Copperfield Ct., Pnr. 58 BZ56
Copperfield Dr. N15 64 DT56
Copperfield Ms. N18 50 DS50
Copperfield Rd. E3 79 DY70
Copperfield Rd. SE28 82 EW72
Copperfield St. SE1 10 G4
Copperfield St. SE1 91 DP75
Copperfield Way, Chis. 109 EQ93
Copperfield Way, Pnr. 58 BZ56
Copperfields, Lthd. 142 CC122
Coppergate Clo., Brom. 122 EH95
Coppermill La. E17 64 DW58
Coppetts Clo. N12 48 DE52
Coppetts Rd. N10 48 DF52
Coppice, The, Ashf. 99 BP93
School Rd.

Coppice, The, Enf. 35 DP42
Coppice, The, Wat. 30 BW44
Coppice, The, West Dr. 70 BL72
Coppice Clo. SW20 117 CW97
Coppice Clo., Ruis. 57 BR58
Coppice Clo., Stan. 45 CF51
Coppice Dr. SW15 103 CU86
Coppice Path, Chig. 54 EV49
Coppice Row, Epp. 39 EN36
Coppice Wk. N20 48 DA48
Coppice Way E18 66 EF56
Coppies Gro. N11 49 DH49
Copping Clo., Croy. 134 DS105
Tipton Dr.
Coppins, The, Croy. 135 EB107
Coppins, The, Har. 45 CE51
Coppock Clo. SW11 90 DE82
Coppsfield, W.Mol. 114 CA97
Hurst Rd.
Copse, The E4 52 EF46
Copse, The, Lthd. 142 CB123
Copse Ave., W.Wick. 121 EB104
Copse Clo. SE7 94 EH79
Copse Clo., Nthwd. 43 BQ54
Copse Clo., West Dr. 84 BK76
Copse Edge Ave., Epsom 131 CT113
Copse Glade, Surb. 115 CK102
Copse Hill SW20 117 CU95
Copse Hill, Pur. 133 DL113
Copse Hill, Sutt. 132 DB108
Copse Rd., Cob. 127 BV113
Copse Vw., S.Croy. 135 DX109
Copse Wd. Way, Nthwd. 43 BP53
Copsem Dr., Esher 128 CB107
Copsem La., Esher 128 CB107
Copsem La., Lthd. 128 CC111
Copsem Way, Esher 128 CC107
Copsen Wd., Lthd. 128 CC111
Copsewood Clo., Sid. 109 ES86
Parish Gate Dr.
Copt Hill La., Tad. 145 CY120
Coptefield Dr., Belv. 96 EX76
Copthall Ave. EC2 7 L8
Copthall Ave. EC2 78 DR72
Copthall Bldgs. EC2 7 L8
Copthall Clo. EC2 7 K8
Copthall Dr. NW7 47 CU52
Copthall Gdns. NW7 47 CU52
Copthall Gdns., Twick. 101 CF88
Copthall Rd. E., Uxb. 56 BN61
Copthall Rd. W., Uxb. 56 BN61
Copthorne Ave. SW12 105 DK87
Copthorne Ave., Brom. 123 EM103
Copthorne Ave., Ilf. 53 EP51
Copthorne Chase, Ashf. 98 BM91
Ford Rd.
Copthorne Clo., Rick. 28 BM43
Copthorne Clo., Shep. 113 BQ100
Copthorne Ms., Hayes 85 BS77
Copthorne Ri., S.Croy. 134 DR113
Copthorne Rd., Lthd. 143 CH120
Copthorne Rd., Rick. 28 BM44
Coptic St. WC1 5 P7
Coptic St. WC1 77 DL71
Copwood Clo. N12 48 DD49
Coral Clo., Rom. 68 EW55
Coral Row SW11 90 DC83
Gartons Way
Coral St. SE1 10 E5
Coral St. SE1 91 DN75
Coraline Clo., Sthl. 72 BZ69
Coralline Wk. SE2 96 EW75
Coram St. WC1 5 P5
Coram St. WC1 77 DL70
Coran Clo. N9 51 DX45
Corban Rd., Houns. 86 CA83
Corbar Clo., Barn. 34 DD39
Corbet Clo., Wall. 118 DG102
Corbet Ct. EC3 7 L9
Corbet Pl. E1 7 P6
Corbet Rd., Epsom 130 CS110
Corbett Clo., Croy. 135 ED112
Corbett Gro. N22 49 DL52
Bounds Grn. Rd.
Corbett Ho., Wat. 44 BW48
Corbett Rd. E11 66 EJ58
Corbett Rd. E17 65 EC55
Corbetts La. SE16 92 DW77
Rotherhithe New Rd.
Corbetts Pas. SE16 92 DW77
Rotherhithe New Rd.
Corbicum E11 66 EE59
Corbiere Ct. SW19 103 CX93
Thornton Rd.
Corbiere Ho. N1 78 DS67
Corbins La., Har. 58 CB62
Corbridge Cres. E2 78 DV68
Corby Clo., St.Alb. 16 CA25
Corby Cres., Enf. 35 DL42
Corby Rd. NW10 74 CR68
Corby Way E3 79 EA70
Knapp Rd.
Corbylands Rd., Sid. 109 ES87
Corbyn St. N4 63 DL60
Cord Way E14 93 EA76
Mellish St.
Cordelia Clo. SE24 91 DP84
Cordelia Gdns., Stai. 98 BL87
Cordelia Rd., Stai. 98 BL87
Cordelia St. E14 79 EB72
Cordell Clo. (Cheshunt), Wal.Cr. 23 DY28
Cording St. E14 79 EB71
Chrisp St.
Cordingley Rd., Ruis. 57 BR61
Cordova Rd. E3 79 DY69
Cordrey Gdns., Couls. 147 DL115
Cordwainers Wk. E13 80 EG68
Clegg St.
Cordwell Rd. SE13 108 EE85
Corelli Rd. SE3 94 EL81
Corfe Ave., Har. 58 CA63
Corfe Clo., Ash. 143 CJ118
Corfe Clo., Hayes 72 BW72
Corfe Twr. W3 88 CQ75
Corfield Rd. N21 35 DM43
Corfield St. E2 78 DV69
Corfton Rd. W5 74 CL72
Coriander Ave. E14 79 ED72
Cories Clo., Dag. 68 EX61
Corinium Clo., Wem. 60 CM63
Corinne Rd. N19 63 DJ63
Corinth Par., Hayes 71 BT71
Corinthian Manorway, Erith 97 FD77
Corinthian Rd., Erith 97 FD77
Cork Sq. E1 78 DV74
Smeaton St.
Cork St. W1 9 K1
Cork St. W1 77 DJ73
Cork St. Ms. W1 9 K1
Cork Tree Way E4 51 DY50
Corker Wk. N7 63 DM61
Corkran Rd., Surb. 115 CK101
Corkscrew Hill, W.Wick. 121 EC103
Corlett St. NW1 4 B6
Cormont Rd. SE5 91 DP81
Cormorant Clo. E17 51 DX53
Banbury Rd.
Cormorant Rd. E7 66 EF64
Cormorant Wk., Horn. 83 FH65
Heron Flight Ave.
Corn Mill Dr., Orp. 124 EU101
Corn Way E11 65 ED62
Cornbury Rd., Edg. 45 CK52
Cornelia Pl., Erith 97 FE79
Queen St.
Cornelia St. N7 77 DM65
Cornell Clo., Sid. 110 EY93
Cornell Way, Rom. 54 FA50
Corner Grn. SE3 94 EG82
Corner Ho. St. WC2 9 P2
Corner Mead NW9 47 CT52
Cornerside, Ashf. 99 BQ94
Corney Reach Way W4 88 CS80
Corney Rd. W4 88 CS79
Cornfield Clo., Uxb. 70 BK68
The Greenway
Cornfield Rd. (Bushey), Wat. 30 CB42
Cornflower La., Croy. 121 DX102
Cornflower Ter. SE22 106 DV86
Cornford Clo., Brom. 122 EG99
Cornford Gro. SW12 105 DH89
Cornhill EC3 7 L9
Cornhill EC3 78 DR72
Cornhill Clo., Add. 112 BH103
Cornhill Dr., Enf. 37 DX37
Ordnance Rd.
Cornish Ct. N9 50 DV45
Cornish Gro. SE20 120 DV95
Cornish Ho. SE17 91 DP79
Otto St.
Cornish Ho., Brent. 88 CM78
Green Dragon La.
Cornmill, Wal.Abb. 23 EB33
Cornmill La. SE13 93 EC83
Cornmow Dr. NW10 61 CU63
Cornshaw Rd., Dag. 68 EX60
Cornthwaite Rd. E5 64 DW62
Cornwall Ave. E2 78 DW69
Cornwall Ave. N3 48 DA52
Cornwall Ave. N22 49 DL53
Cornwall Ave., Esher 129 CF108
The Causeway
Cornwall Ave., Sthl. 72 BZ71
Cornwall Ave., Well. 95 ES83
Cornwall Ave., W.Byf. 126 BM114
Cornwall Clo., Bark. 81 ET65
Cornwall Clo., Wal.Cr. 23 DY33
Cornwall Cres. W11 75 CY72
Cornwall Dr., Orp. 110 EW94
Cornwall Gdns. NW10 75 CV65
Cornwall Gdns. SW7 90 DB76
Cornwall Gdns. Wk. SW7 90 DB76
Cornwall Gdns.
Cornwall Gro. W4 88 CS78
Cornwall Ms. S. SW7 90 DC76
Cornwall Ms. W. SW7 90 DB76
Cornwall Gdns.
Cornwall Rd. N4 63 DN59
Cornwall Rd. N15 64 DR57
Cornwall Rd. N18 50 DU50
Fairfield Rd.
Cornwall Rd. SE1 10 D2
Cornwall Rd. SE1 77 DN74
Cornwall Rd., Croy. 119 DP103
Cornwall Rd., Esher 129 CG108
Cornwall Rd., Har. 58 CC58
Cornwall Rd., Pnr. 44 BZ52
Cornwall Rd., Ruis. 57 BT62
Cornwall Rd., Sutt. 131 CZ108
Cornwall Rd., Twick. 101 CG87
Cornwall Rd., Uxb. 70 BK65
Cornwall St. E1 78 DV73
Watney St.
Cornwall Ter. NW1 4 E5
Cornwall Ter. Ms. NW1 4 E5
Cornwallis Ave. N9 50 DV47
Cornwallis Ave. SE9 109 ER89
Cornwallis Clo., Erith 97 FF79
Cornwallis Gro. N9 50 DV47
Cornwallis Rd. E17 65 DX56
Cornwallis Rd. N9 50 DV47
Cornwallis Rd. N19 63 DL61
Cornwallis Rd., Dag. 68 EX63
Cornwallis Sq. N19 63 DL61
Cornwallis Wk. SE9 95 EM83
Cornwood Clo. N2 62 DD57
Cornwood Dr. E1 78 DW72
Cornworthy Rd., Dag. 68 EW64
Corona Rd. SE12 108 EG87
Corfield Rd. N21 35 DM43
Coronation Ave. N16 64 DT62
Victorian Rd.
Coronation Clo., Bex. 110 EX86
Coronation Clo., Ilf. 67 EQ56
Coronation Dr., Horn. 69 FH63
Coronation Hill, Epp. 25 ET30
Coronation Rd. E13 80 EJ69
Coronation Rd. NW10 74 CM69
Coronation Rd., Hayes 85 BT77
Coronation Wk., Twick. 100 CA88
Coronet St. N1 7 M3
Coronet St. N1 78 DS69
Corporation Ave., Houns. 86 BY84
Corporation Row EC1 6 E4
Corporation Row EC1 77 DN70
Corporation St. E15 80 EE68
Corporation St. N7 63 DL64
Corrance Rd. SW2 91 DL84
Corri Ave. N14 49 DK49
Corrib Dr., Sutt. 132 DE106
Corrie Rd., Add. 126 BK105
Corrigan Ave., Couls. 132 DG114
Corringham Ct. NW11 62 DB59
Corringham Rd.
Corringham Rd. NW11 62 DA59
Corringham Rd., Wem. 60 CN61
Corringway NW11 62 DB59
Corringway W5 74 CM71
Corsair Clo., Stai. 98 BK87
Corsair Rd., Stai. 98 BL87
Corscombe Clo., Kings.T. 102 CQ92
Corsehill St. SW16 105 DJ93
Corsham St. N1 7 L3
Corsham St. N1 78 DR69
Corsica St. N5 77 DP65
Corsley Way E9 79 DZ65
Osborne Rd.
Cortayne Rd. SW6 89 CZ82
Cortis Rd. SW15 103 CV86
Cortis Ter. SW15 103 CV86
Corunna Rd. SW8 91 DJ81
Corunna Ter. SW8 91 DJ81
Corvette Sq. SE10 93 ED79
Feathers Pl.
Corwell Gdns., Uxb. 71 BQ72
Corwell La., Uxb. 71 BQ72
Coryton Path W9 75 CZ70
Ashmore Rd.
Cosbycote Ave. SE24 106 DQ85
Cosdach Ave., Wall. 133 DK108
Cosedge Cres., Croy. 133 DN106
Cosgrove Clo. N21 50 DQ47
Cosgrove Clo., Hayes 72 BY70
Kingsash Dr.
Cosmo Pl. WC1 6 A6
Cosmur Clo. W12 89 CT76
Cossall Wk. SE15 92 DV81
Cosser St. SE1 10 D6
Cosser St. SE1 91 DN76
Costa St. SE15 92 DU82
Coston Wk. SE4 93 DX84
Frendsbury Rd.
Costons Ave., Grnf. 73 CD69
Costons La., Grnf. 73 CD69
Cosway St. NW1 4 C6
Cosway St. NW1 76 DE71
Cotall St. E14 79 EA72
Coteford Clo., Loug. 39 EP40
Coteford Clo., Pnr. 57 BU57
Coteford St. SW17 104 DF91
Cotelands, Croy. 120 DS104
Cotesbach Rd. E5 64 DW62
Cotesmore Gdns., Dag. 68 EW63
Cotford Rd., Th.Hth. 120 DQ98
Cotham St. SE17 11 J9
Cotherstone, Epsom 130 CR110
Cotherstone Rd. SW2 105 DM88
Cotlandswick, St.Alb. 17 CJ25
Cotleigh Ave., Bex. 110 EX89
Cotleigh Rd. NW6 76 DA66
Cotleigh Rd., Rom. 69 FD58
Cotman Clo. NW11 62 DC58
Cotman Clo. SW15 103 CW86
Westleigh Ave.
Cotman Gdns., Edg. 46 CN54
Cotman Ms., Dag. 68 EW64
Highgrove Rd.
Cotmandene Cres., Orp. 124 EU96
Cotmans Clo., Hayes 71 BU74
Coton Rd., Well. 96 EU83
Cotsford Ave., N.Mal. 116 CQ99
Cotswold Ave. (Bushey), Wat. 30 CC44
Cotswold Clo., Bexh. 97 FE82
Cotswold Clo., Kings.T. 102 CP93
Cotswold Clo., Stai. 98 BG92
Cotswold Clo., Uxb. 70 BJ67
Cotswold Ct. N11 48 DG49
Cotswold Gdns. E6 80 EK69
Cotswold Gdns. NW2 61 CX61
Cotswold Gdns., Ilf. 67 ER59
Cotswold Gate NW2 61 CY60
Cotswold Gdns.
Cotswold Grn., Enf. 35 DM42
Cotswold Way
Cotswold Ms. SW11 90 DD81
Battersea High St.
Cotswold Ri., Orp. 123 ET100
Cotswold Rd., Hmptn. 100 CA93
Cotswold Rd., Sutt. 132 DB110
Cotswold St. SE27 105 DP91
Norwood High St.
Cotswold Way, Enf. 35 DM41
Cotswold Way, Wor.Pk. 117 CW103
Cottage Ave., Brom. 122 EL102
Cottage Clo., Rick. 28 BM44
Scots Hill
Cottage Clo., Ruis. 57 BR60
Cottage Clo., Wat. 29 BT40
Cottage Fld. Clo., Sid. 110 EW88
Cottage Grn. SE5 92 DR80
Cottage Gro. SW9 91 DL83
Cottage Gro., Surb. 115 CK100
Cottage Homes NW7 47 CU49
Cottage Homes Chalet Est. NW7 47 CU49
Cottage Pl. SW3 8 B7
Cottage Pl. SW3 90 DE76
Cottage Rd., Epsom 130 CR108
Cottage St. E14 79 EB73
Cottage Wk. N16 64 DT62
Smalley Clo.
Cottage Wk. SE15 92 DT80
Sumner Est.
Cottenham Dr. NW9 61 CT55
Cottenham Dr. SW20 103 CV94
Cottenham Par. SW20 117 CV96
Durham Rd.
Cottenham Pk. Rd. SW20 117 CV95
Cottenham Pl. SW20 103 CV94
Cottenham Rd. E17 65 DZ56
Cotterill Rd., Surb. 116 CL103
Cottesbrook St. SE14 93 DY80
Nynehead St.
Cottesloe Ms. SE1 91 DN76
Pearman St.
Cottesmore Ave., Ilf. 53 EN54
Cottesmore Gdns. W8 90 DB76
Cottimore Ave., Walt. 113 BV102
Cottimore Cres., Walt. 113 BV101
Cottimore La., Walt. 113 BV101
Cottimore Ter., Walt. 113 BV101
Cottingham Chase, Ruis. 57 BU62
Cottingham Rd. SE20 107 DX94
Cottingham Rd. SW8 91 DM80
Cottington Rd., Felt. 100 BX91
Cottington St. SE11 10 E10
Cottle St. SE16 92 DW75
St. Marychurch St.
Cotton Ave. W3 74 CR72
Cotton Hill, Brom. 107 ED91
Cotton Rd., Pot.B. 20 DC31
Cotton Row SW11 90 DD83
Cotton St. E14 79 EC73
Cottongrass Clo., Croy. 121 DX102
Cornflower La.
Cottons App., Rom. 69 FD57
Cottons Ct., Rom. 69 FD57
Cottons Gdns. E2 7 N2
Cottons La. SE1 11 L2
Couchmore Ave., Esher 115 CE103
Couchmore Ave., Ilf. 53 EM54
Coulgate St. SE4 93 DY83
Coulsdon Common, Cat. 148 DQ120
Coulsdon Ct. Rd., Couls. 147 DM116
Coulsdon La., Couls. 146 DF119
Coulsdon Pl., Cat. 148 DR122
Coulsdon Ri., Couls. 147 DL117
Coulsdon Rd., Cat. 148 DQ121
Coulsdon Rd., Couls. 147 DM115
Coulson Clo., Dag. 68 EW59
Coulson St. SW3 8 D10
Coulson St. SW3 90 DF78
Coulter Clo. (Cuffley), Pot.B. 21 DK27
Coulter Rd. W6 89 CV76
Coultree Clo., Hayes 72 BY70
Berrydale Rd.
Councillor St. SE5 92 DQ80
Counter Ct. SE1 11 K3
Counter St. SE1 11 M3
Countess Clo., Uxb. 42 BJ54
Countess Rd. NW5 63 DJ64
Countisbury Ave., Enf. 50 DT45
Countisbury Gdns., Add. 126 BH106
Addlestone Pk.
Country Way, Felt. 99 BV93
Country Way, Sun. 99 BU94
County Gdns., Bark. 81 ES68
River Rd.
County Gate SE9 109 EQ90
County Gate, Barn. 34 DB44
County Gro. SE5 92 DQ81
County Rd. E6 81 EP71
County Rd., Th.Hth. 119 DP96
County St. SE1 11 J7
County St. SE1 92 DQ76
Coupland Pl. SE18 95 EQ78
Courcy Rd. N8 63 DN55
Courier Rd., Dag. 83 FC70
Courland Gro. SW8 91 DK82
Courland Rd., Add. 112 BH104
Courland St. SW8 91 DK81
Course, The SE9 109 EN90
Coursers Rd., St.Alb. 18 CN27
Court, The, Ruis. 58 BY63
Court, The, Warl. 149 DY118
Court Ave., Belv. 96 EZ78
Court Ave., Couls. 147 DN118
Court Bushes Rd., Whyt. 148 DU119
Court Clo., Har. 59 CK55
Court Clo., Twick. 100 CB90
Court Clo., Wall. 133 DK108
Court Clo. Ave., Twick. 100 CB90
Court Cres., Chess. 129 CK106
Court Cres., Swan. 125 FE98
Court Downs Rd., Beck. 121 EB96
Court Dr., Croy. 133 DM105
Court Dr., Stan. 46 CL49
Court Dr., Sutt. 132 DE105
Court Dr., Uxb. 70 BM67
Court Fm. Ave., Epsom 130 CR106
Court Fm. Ind. Est., Stai. 98 BM86
Court Fm. Rd. SE9 108 EK89
Court Fm. Rd., Nthlt. 72 CA66
Court Fm. Rd., Warl. 148 DU118
Court Gdns. N7 77 DN65
Highbury Cor.
Court Haw, Bans. 146 DE115
Court Hill, Couls. 146 DE118
Court Hill, S.Croy. 134 DS112
Court Ho. Gdns. N3 48 DA51
Court La. SE21 106 DS86
Court La., Epsom 130 CQ113
Court La., Iver 70 BG74
Court La. Gdns. SE21 106 DS87
Court Mead, Nthlt. 72 BZ69
Court Par., Wem. 59 CH62
Court Rd. SE9 109 EM86
Court Rd. SE25 120 DT96
Court Rd., Bans. 146 DA116
Court Rd., Cat. 148 DR123
Court Rd., Orp. 124 EV101
Court Rd., Sthl. 86 BZ77
Court Rd., Uxb. 57 BP64
Court St. E1 78 DV71
Durward St.
Court St., Brom. 122 EG96
Court Way NW9 60 CS56
Court Way W3 74 CQ71
Court Way, Ilf. 67 EQ55
Court Way, Twick. 101 CF87
Court Wd. Dr., Sev. 154 FG124
Court Wd. Gro., Croy. 135 DY111
Court Wd. La., Croy. 135 DZ110
Court Yd. SE9 109 EM86
Courtauld Clo. SE28 82 EU74
Pitfield Cres.
Courtauld Rd. N19 63 DK60
Courtaulds, Kings L. 14 BH30
Courtenay Ave. N6 62 DE59
Courtenay Ave., Har. 44 CC52
Courtenay Ave., Sutt. 132 DA109
Courtenay Dr., Beck. 121 ED96
Courtenay Gdns., Har. 44 CC54
Courtenay Ms. E17 65 DY57
Cranbrook Ms.
Courtenay Pl. E17 65 DY57
Cranbrook Ms.
Courtenay Rd. E11 66 EF62
Courtenay Rd. E17 65 DX56
Courtenay Rd. SE20 107 DX94
Courtenay Rd., Wem. 59 CK62
Courtenay Rd., Wor.Pk. 117 CW104
Courtenay Sq. SE11 91 DN78
Courtenay St.
Courtenay St. SE11 10 D10
Courtenay St. SE11 91 DN78
Courtens Ms., Stan. 45 CJ52
Courtfield W5 73 CJ71
Courtfield Ave., Har. 59 CF57
Courtfield Cres., Har. 59 CF57
Courtfield Gdns. SW5 90 DB77
Courtfield Gdns. W13 73 CG72
Courtfield Gdns., Ruis. 57 BT61
Courtfield Gdns., Uxb. 56 BG62
Courtfield Ms. SW5 90 DB77
Courtfield Gdns.
Courtfield Ri., W.Wick. 121 ED104
Courtfield Rd. SW7 90 DC77
Courtfield Rd., Ashf. 99 BP93
Courthill Rd. SE13 93 EC84
Courthope Rd. NW3 62 DF63
Courthope Rd. SW19 103 CY92
Courthope Rd., Grnf. 73 CD68
Courthope Vill. SW19 103 CY94
Courthouse Rd. N12 48 DB51
Courtland Ave. E4 52 EF47
Courtland Ave. NW7 46 CR48
Courtland Ave. SW16 105 DM94
Courtland Ave., Ilf. 67 EM61
Courtland Dr., Chig. 53 EP48
Courtland Gro. SE28 82 EX73
Courtland Rd. E6 80 EL67
Harrow Rd.
Courtlands, Rich. 102 CN85
Courtlands Ave. SE12 108 EH85
Courtlands Ave., Brom. 122 EE102
Courtlands Ave., Esher 128 BZ107
Courtlands Ave., Hmptn. 100 BZ93
Courtlands Ave., Rich. 88 CP82
Courtlands Clo., Ruis. 57 BT59
Courtlands Clo., S.Croy. 134 DT110
Courtlands Clo., Wat. 29 BS35
Courtlands Cres., Bans. 146 DA115
Courtlands Dr., Epsom 130 CS107
Courtlands Dr., Wat. 29 BS37
Courtlands Rd., Surb. 116 CN101
Courtleas, Cob. 128 CA113
Courtleet Dr., Erith 97 FB81
Courtleigh Ave., Barn. 34 DD38
Courtleigh Gdns. NW11 61 CY56
Courtman Rd. N17 50 DQ52
Courtmead Clo. SE24 106 DQ86
Courtnell St. W2 76 DA72
Courtney Clo. SE19 106 DS93
Courtney Cres., Cars. 132 DF108
Courtney Pl., Croy. 119 DN104
Courtney Rd.
Courtney Rd. N7 63 DN64
Bryantwood Rd.
Courtney Rd. SW19 104 DE94
Courtney Rd., Croy. 119 DN104

Courtney Rd., Houns. 84 BN83
Courtrai Rd. SE23 107 DY86
Courtside N8 63 DK58
Courtway, Wdf.Grn. 52 EJ50
Courtway, The, Wat. 44 BY47
Courtyard, The N1 77 DM66
Barnsbury Ter.
Cousin La. EC4 11 K1
Cousins Clo., West Dr. 70 BL73
Couthurst Rd. SE3 94 EH79
Coutts Ave., Chess. 130 CL106
Coutts Cres. NW5 62 DG62
Coval Gdns. SW14 88 CP84
Coval La. SW14 88 CP84
Coval Rd. SW14 88 CP84
Coveham Cres., Cob. 127 BU113
Covelees Wall E6 81 EN72
Covell Ct. SE8 93 EA80
Reginald Sq.
Covent Gdn. WC2 6 A10
Covent Gdn. WC2 77 DL73
Coventry Clo. E6 81 EM72
Harper Rd.
Coventry Clo. NW6 76 DA67
Kilburn High Rd.
Coventry Cross E3 79 EC70
Gillender St.
Coventry Rd. E1 78 DV70
Coventry Rd. E2 78 DV70
Coventry Rd. SE25 120 DU98
Coventry Rd., Ilf. 67 EP61
Coventry St. W1 9 M1
Coventry St. W1 77 DK73
Coverack Clo. N14 35 DJ44
Coverack Clo., Croy. 121 DY101
Coverdale Clo., Stan. 45 CH50
Coverdale Ct., Enf. 37 DY37
Raynton Rd.
Coverdale Gdns., Croy. 120 DT104
Park Hill Ri.
Coverdale Rd. NW2 75 CX66
Coverdale Rd. W12 89 CV75
Coverdales, The, Bark. 81 ER68
Coverley Clo. E1 78 DU71
Covert, The, Nthwd. 43 BQ52
Covert, The, Orp. 123 ES100
Covert Rd., Ilf. 53 ET51
Covert Way, Barn. 34 DC40
Coverton Rd. SW17 104 DE92
Coverts Rd., Esher 129 CF109
Covet Wd. Clo., Orp. 123 ET100
Lockesley Dr.
Covington Gdns. SW16 105 DP94
Covington Way SW16 105 DM93
Cow La., Grnf. 73 CD68
Oldfield La. S.
Cow La., Wat. 30 BW36
Cow Leaze E6 81 EN72
Cowan Clo. E6 80 EL71
Oliver Gdns.
Cowbridge La., Bark. 81 EP66
Cowbridge Rd., Har. 60 CM56
Cowcross St. EC1 6 F6
Cowcross St. EC1 77 DP71
Cowden Rd., Orp. 123 ET101
Cowden St. SE6 107 EA91
Cowdenbeath Path N1 77 DM67
Bingfield St.
Cowdray Rd., Uxb. 71 BQ67
Cowdray Way, Horn. 69 FF63
Cowdrey Clo., Enf. 36 DS40
Cowdrey Ct., Dart. 111 FH87
Cowdrey Rd. SW19 104 DB92
Cowdry Rd. E9 79 DY65
Wick Rd.
Cowen Ave., Har. 58 CC61
Cowgate Rd., Grnf. 73 CD68
Cowick Rd. SW17 104 DF91
Cowings Mead, Nthlt. 72 BY65
Cowland Ave., Enf. 36 DW42
Cowleaze Rd., Kings.T. 116 CL95
Cowles (Cheshunt), Wal.Cr. 22 DT27
Cowley Clo., S.Croy. 134 DW109
Cowley Cres., Uxb. 70 BJ71
Cowley Cres., Walt. 128 BW105
Cowley Hill, Borwd. 32 CP37
Cowley La. E11 66 EE62
Cathall Rd.
Cowley Mill Rd., Uxb. 70 BH68
Cowley Pl. NW4 61 CW57
Cowley Rd. E11 66 EH57
Cowley Rd. SW9 91 DN81
Cowley Rd. SW14 88 CS83
Cowley Rd. W3 75 CT74
Cowley Rd., Ilf. 67 EM59
Cowley Rd., Rom. 55 FH52
Cowley Rd., Uxb. 70 BJ67
Cowley St. SW1 9 P6
Cowling Clo. W11 75 CY74
Wilsham St.
Cowper Ave. E6 80 EL66
Cowper Ave., Sutt. 132 DD105
Cowper Clo., Brom. 122 EK98
Cowper Clo., Well. 110 EU85
Cowper Ct., Wat. 29 BU37
Cowper Gdns. N14 35 DH44
Cowper Gdns., Wall. 133 DJ107
Cowper Rd. N14 49 DH46
Cowper Rd. N16 64 DS64
Cowper Rd. N18 50 DU50
Cowper Rd. SW19 104 DC93
Cowper Rd. W3 74 CR74
Cowper Rd. W7 73 CF73
Cowper Rd., Belv. 96 FA77
Cowper Rd., Brom. 122 EK98
Cowper Rd., Kings.T. 102 CM92
Cowper Rd., Rain. 83 FG70
Cowper St. EC2 7 L4
Cowper St. EC2 78 DR70
Cowper Ter. W10 75 CX71
St. Marks Rd.
Cowslip Clo., Uxb. 70 BL66
Cowslip Rd. E18 52 EH54
Cowthorpe Rd. SW8 91 DK81
Cox Clo., Rad. 18 CM32
Cox La., Chess. 130 CL105
Cox La., Epsom 130 CP105
Coxdean, Epsom 145 CW119
Coxley Ri., Pur. 134 DQ113
Coxmount Rd. SE7 94 EK78
Cox's Wk. SE21 106 DU88
Coxson Pl. SE1 11 P5
Coxwell Rd. SE18 95 ER78
Coxwell Rd. SE19 106 DS94
Coxwold Path, Chess. 130 CL108
Garrison La.
Crab Hill, Beck. 107 ED94
Crab La., Wat. 30 CB35
Crabbs Cft. Clo., Orp. 137 EQ106
Ladycroft Way
Crabtree Ave., Rom. 68 EX56
Crabtree Ave., Wem. 74 CL68
Crabtree Clo. E2 78 DT68
Crabtree Clo. (Bushey), Wat. 30 CB43
Crabtree Ct. E15 65 EB64
Clays La.
Crabtree La. SW6 89 CX80
Crabtree Manorway N., Belv. 97 FC75
Crabtree Manorway S., Belv. 97 FC76
Crabtree Wk. SE15 92 DT81
Lisford St.
Crace St. NW1 5 M2
Craddock Rd., Enf. 36 DT41
Craddock St. NW5 76 DG65
Prince of Wales Rd.
Craddocks Ave., Ash. 144 CL117
Craddocks Par., Ash. 144 CL117
Cradley Rd. SE9 109 ER88
Cragg Ave., Rad. 31 CF36
Craig Dr., Uxb. 71 BP72
Craig Gdns. E18 52 EF54
Craig Mt., Rad. 31 CH35
Craig Pk. Rd. N18 50 DV50
Craig Rd., Rich. 101 CJ91
Craigdale Rd., Horn. 69 FF58
Craigen Ave., Croy. 120 DV102
Craigerne Rd. SE3 94 EH80
Craigholm SE18 95 EN82
Craigmuir Pk., Wem. 74 CM67
Craignair Rd. SW2 105 DN87
Craignish Ave. SW16 119 DM96
Craigs Ct. SW1 9 P2
Craigs Wk. (Cheshunt), Wal.Cr. 23 DX28
Davison Dr.
Craigton Rd. SE9 95 EM84
Craigweil Clo., Stan. 45 CK50
Craigweil Dr., Stan. 45 CK50
Craigwell Ave., Felt. 99 BU90
Craigwell Ave., Rad. 31 CH35
Craik Ct. NW6 75 CZ68
Carlton Vale
Crail Row SE17 11 L9
Cramer St. W1 4 G7
Crammerville Wk., Rain. 83 FH70
Baillie Clo.
Cramond Clo. W6 89 CY79
Cramond Ct., Felt. 99 BR88
Kilross Rd.
Crampshaw La., Ash. 144 CM119
Crampton Rd. SE20 106 DW93
Crampton St. SE17 11 H9
Crampton St. SE17 92 DQ77
Cramptons Rd., Sev. 153 FH120
Cranberry Clo., Nthlt. 72 BX68
Parkfield Ave.
Cranberry La. E16 80 EE70
Cranborne Ave., Sthl. 86 CA77
Cranborne Clo., Pot.B. 19 CY31
Cranborne Cres., Pot.B. 19 CY31
Cranborne Ind. Est., Pot.B. 19 CY30
Cranborne Rd., Bark. 81 ER67
Cranborne Rd., Pot.B. 19 CY31
Cranborne Rd. (Cheshunt), Wal.Cr. 23 DX32
Cranborne Waye, Hayes 71 BV72
Cranbourn All. WC2 5 N10
Cranbourn Pas. SE16 92 DV75
Marigold St.
Cranbourn St. WC2 5 N10
Cranbourn St. WC2 77 DK73
Cranbourne Ave. E11 66 EH56
Cranbourne Ave., Surb. 116 CN104
Cranbourne Clo. SW16 119 DL97
Cranbourne Dr., Pnr. 58 BX57
Cranbourne Gdns. NW11 61 CY57
Cranbourne Gdns., Ilf. 67 EQ55
Cranbourne Rd. E12 66 EL64
High St. N.
Cranbourne Rd. E15 65 EC63
Cranbourne Rd. N10 49 DH54
Cranbourne Rd., Nthwd. 57 BT55
Cranbrook Clo., Brom. 122 EG100
Cranbrook Dr., Esher 114 CC102
Cranbrook Dr., Rom. 69 FH56
Cranbrook Dr., Twick. 100 CB88
Cranbrook Est. E2 79 DX68
Cranbrook Ms. E17 65 DZ57
Cranbrook Pk. N22 49 DM53
Cranbrook Pt. E16 80 EG74
Cranbrook Ri., Ilf. 67 EM58
Cranbrook Rd. SE8 93 EA81
Cranbrook Rd. SW19 103 CY94
Cranbrook Rd. W4 88 CS78
Cranbrook Rd., Barn. 34 DD44
Cranbrook Rd., Bexh. 96 EZ81
Cranbrook Rd., Houns. 86 BZ84
Cranbrook Rd., Ilf. 67 EN57
Cranbrook Rd., Th.Hth. 120 DQ96
Cranbrook St. E2 79 DX68
Roman Rd.
Cranbury Rd. SW6 90 DB82
Crane Ave. W3 74 CQ73
Crane Ave., Islw. 101 CG85
Crane Clo., Dag. 82 FA65
Crane Clo., Har. 58 CC62
Crane Ct. EC4 6 E9
Crane Ct., Epsom 130 CQ105
Crane Gdns., Hayes 85 BT77
Crane Gro. N7 77 DN65
Crane Lo. Rd., Houns. 85 BV79
Crane Mead SE16 93 DX77
Crane Pk. Rd., Twick. 100 CB89
Crane Rd., Twick. 101 CE88
Crane St. SE10 93 ED78
Crane St. SE15 92 DT81
Southampton Way
Crane Way, Twick. 100 CC87
Cranebrook, Twick. 100 CC89
Manor Rd.
Craneford Clo., Twick. 101 CF87
Craneford Way, Twick. 101 CE87
Cranes Dr., Surb. 116 CL98
Cranes Pk., Surb. 116 CL98
Cranes Pk. Ave., Surb. 116 CL98
Cranes Pk. Cres., Surb. 116 CM98
Cranes Way, Borwd. 32 CQ43
Craneswater, Hayes 85 BT80
Craneswater Pk., Sthl. 86 BZ78
Cranfield Clo. SE27 106 DQ90
Dunelm Gro.
Cranfield Cres. (Cuffley), Pot.B. 21 DL29
Cranfield Dr. NW9 46 CS52
Cranfield Dr., Wat. 16 BY32
Cranfield Rd. SE4 93 DZ83
Cranfield Rd. E., Cars. 132 DG109
Cranfield Rd. W., Cars. 132 DF109
Cranfield Row SE1 10 E6
Cranford Ave. N13 49 DL50
Cranford Ave., Stai. 98 BL87
Cranford Clo. SW20 103 CV94
Cranford Clo., Pur. 134 DQ113
Cranford Clo., Stai. 98 BL87
Canopus Way
Cranford Cotts. E1 79 DX73
Cranford St.
Cranford Dr., Hayes 85 BT77
Cranford La., Hayes 85 BR79
Cranford La. (Cranford), Houns. 85 BT81
Cranford La. (Hatton Cross), Houns. 85 BT83
Cranford La. (Heston), Houns. 85 BV80
Cranford Pk. Rd., Hayes 85 BT77
Cranford Ri., Esher 128 CC106
Cranford St. E1 79 DX73
Cranford Way N8 63 DM57
Cranham Rd., Horn. 69 FH58
Cranhurst Rd. NW2 61 CW64
Cranleigh Clo. SE20 120 DV96
Cranleigh Clo., Bex. 111 FB86
Cranleigh Clo., Orp. 124 EU104
Cranleigh Clo., S.Croy. 134 DU112
Cranleigh Clo. (Cheshunt), Wal.Cr. 22 DU28
Cranleigh Dr., Swan. 125 FE99
Cranleigh Gdns. N21 35 DN43
Cranleigh Gdns. SE25 120 DS97
Cranleigh Gdns., Bark. 81 ER66
Cranleigh Gdns., Har. 60 CL57
Cranleigh Gdns., Kings.T. 102 CM93
Cranleigh Gdns., Loug. 39 EM44
Cranleigh Gdns., S.Croy. 134 DU112
Cranleigh Gdns., Sthl. 72 BZ72
Cranleigh Gdns., Sutt. 118 DB103
Cranleigh Ms. SW11 90 DE82
Cranleigh Rd. N15 64 DQ57
Cranleigh Rd. SW19 117 CZ97
Cranleigh Rd., Esher 114 CC102
Cranleigh Rd., Felt. 99 BT91
Cranleigh St. NW1 5 L1
Cranleigh St. NW1 77 DJ68
Cranley Dene Ct. N10 63 DH56
Cranley Dr., Ilf. 67 EQ59
Cranley Dr., Ruis. 57 BT61
Cranley Gdns. N10 63 DH56
Cranley Gdns. N13 49 DM48
Cranley Gdns. SW7 90 DC78
Cranley Gdns., Wall. 133 DJ108
Cranley Ms. SW7 90 DC78
Cranley Par. SE9 108 EL91
Beaconsfield Rd.
Cranley Pl. SW7 90 DD77
Cranley Rd. E13 80 EH71
Cranley Rd., Ilf. 67 EQ58
Cranley Rd., Walt. 127 BS106
Cranmer Ave. W13 87 CH76
Cranmer Clo., Mord. 117 CX100
Cranmer Clo., Pot.B. 20 DB30
Cranmer Clo., Ruis. 58 BX60
Cranmer Clo., Stan. 45 CJ52
Cranmer Clo., Warl. 149 DY117
Cranmer Clo., Wey. 127 BR108
Cranmer Ct. SW3 8 C9
Cranmer Ct. SW4 91 DK83
Cranmer Ct., Hmptn. 100 CB92
Cranmer Rd.
Cranmer Fm. Clo., Mitch. 118 DF98
Cranmer Gdns., Dag. 69 FC63
Cranmer Gdns., Warl. 149 DY117
Cranmer Rd. E7 66 EH63
Cranmer Rd. SW9 91 DN80
Cranmer Rd., Croy. 119 DP104
Cranmer Rd., Edg. 46 CP48
Cranmer Rd., Hmptn. 100 CB92
Cranmer Rd., Hayes 71 BR72
Cranmer Rd., Kings.T. 102 CL92
Cranmer Rd., Mitch. 118 DF98
Cranmer Rd., Sev. 154 FE123
Cranmer Ter. SW17 104 DD92
Cranmore Ave., Islw. 86 CC80
Cranmore Rd., Brom. 108 EF90
Cranmore Rd., Chis. 109 EM92
Cranmore Way N10 63 DJ56
Cranston Clo., Houns. 86 BY82
Cranston Clo., Uxb. 57 BR61
Cranston Est. N1 7 L1
Cranston Est. N1 78 DR68
Cranston Gdns. E4 51 EB50
Cranston Rd. SE23 107 DY88
Cranswick Rd. SE16 92 DV78
Crantock Rd. SE6 107 EB89
Cranwell Clo. E3 79 EB70
Cranwell Gro., Shep. 112 BM98
Cranwell Rd., Houns. 85 BP82
Cranwich Ave. N21 50 DR45
Cranwich Rd. N16 64 DR59
Cranwood St. EC1 7 L3
Cranwood St. EC1 78 DR69
Cranworth Cres. E4 51 ED46
Cranworth Gdns. SW9 91 DN81
Craster Rd. SW2 105 DM87
Crathie Rd. SE12 108 EH86
Crathorn St. SE13 93 EC83
Loampit Vale
Cravan Ave., Felt. 99 BU89
Craven Ave. W5 73 CJ73
Craven Ave., Sthl. 72 BZ71
Craven Clo., Hayes 71 BU72
Craven Gdns. SW19 104 DA92
Craven Gdns., Bark. 81 ES68
Craven Gdns., Ilf. 53 ER54
Craven Gdns. (Collier Row), Rom. 54 FA50
Craven Hill W2 76 DC73
Craven Hill Gdns. W2 76 DC73
Craven Hill Ms. W2 76 DC73
Craven Ms. SW11 90 DG83
Taybridge Rd.
Craven Pk. NW10 74 CS67
Craven Pk. Ms. NW10 74 CS67
Craven Pk. Rd. N15 64 DT58
Craven Pk. Rd. NW10 74 CS67
Craven Pas. WC2 9 P2
Craven Rd. NW10 74 CR67
Craven Rd. W2 76 DC72
Craven Rd. W5 73 CJ73
Craven Rd., Croy. 120 DV102
Craven Rd., Kings.T. 116 CM95
Craven Rd., Orp. 124 EX104
Craven St. WC2 9 P2
Craven St. WC2 77 DL74
Craven Ter. W2 76 DC73
Craven Wk. N16 64 DU59
Crawford Ave., Wem. 59 CK64
Crawford Clo., Islw. 87 CE82
Crawford Est. SE5 92 DQ82
Crawford Gdns. N13 49 DP48
Crawford Gdns., Nthlt. 72 BZ69
Crawford Ms. W1 4 D7
Crawford Pas. EC1 6 D5
Crawford Pl. W1 4 C8
Crawford Pl. W1 76 DE72
Crawford Rd. SE5 92 DQ81
Crawford St. W1 4 C7
Crawford St. W1 76 DF71
Crawfords, Swan. 111 FE94
Crawley Rd. E10 65 EB60
Crawley Rd. N22 50 DQ54
Crawley Rd., Enf. 50 DS45
Crawshaw Ct. SW9 91 DN81
Eythorne Rd.
Crawshay Clo., Sev. 154 FG123
Crawthew Gro. SE22 92 DT84
Cray Ave., Ash. 144 CL116
Cray Ave., Orp. 124 EV100
Cray Clo., Dart. 97 FG84
Cray Riverway, Dart. 111 FF85
Cray Rd., Belv. 96 FA79
Cray Rd., Sid. 110 EW94
Cray Rd., Swan. 125 FB100
Cray Valley Rd., Orp. 124 EU99
Craybrooke Rd., Sid. 110 EV91
Craybury End SE9 109 EQ89
Craydene Rd., Erith 97 FF81
Crayford Clo. E6 80 EL71
Neatscourt Rd.
Crayford High St., Dart. 111 FE85
Crayford Rd. N7 63 DK63
Crayford Rd., Dart. 111 FE85
Crayford Way, Dart. 111 FF85
Crayke Hill, Chess. 130 CL108
Craylands, Orp. 124 EW97
Craymill Sq., Dart. 97 FG83
Norris Way
Crayonne Clo., Sun. 113 BS95
Crayside Ind. Est., Dart. 97 FH84
Thames Rd.
Crealock Gro., Wdf.Grn. 52 EF50
Crealock St. SW18 104 DB86
Creasey Clo., Horn. 69 FH61
St. Leonards Way
Creasy Clo., Abb.L. 15 BT31
Creasy Est. SE1 11 M7
Crebor St. SE22 106 DU86
Credenhall Dr., Brom. 123 EM102
Credenhill St. SW16 105 DJ93
Crediton Hill NW6 62 DB64
Crediton Rd. E16 80 EG72
Pacific Rd.
Crediton Rd. NW10 75 CX67
Crediton Way, Esher 129 CG106
Credon Rd. E13 80 EJ68
Credon Rd. SE16 92 DV78
Cree Way, Rom. 55 FE52
Creechurch La. EC3 7 N9
Creechurch La. EC3 78 DS72
Creechurch Pl. EC3 7 N9
Creed Ct. EC4 77 DP72
Ludgate Hill
Creed La. EC4 6 G9
Creek, The, Sun. 113 BU99
Creek Rd. SE8 93 EA79
Creek Rd. SE10 93 EB79
Creek Rd., Bark. 81 ET69
Creek Rd., E.Mol. 115 CE98
Creekside SE8 93 EB80
Creekside, Rain. 83 FE70
Creeland Gro. SE6 107 DZ88
Catford Hill
Crefeld Clo. W6 89 CX79
Creffield Rd. W3 74 CM73
Creffield Rd. W5 74 CM73
Creighton Ave. E6 80 EK68
Creighton Ave. N2 62 DE55
Creighton Ave. N10 48 DF54
Creighton Clo. W12 75 CV73
Bloemfontein Rd.
Creighton Rd. N17 50 DS52
Creighton Rd. NW6 75 CX68
Creighton Rd. W5 87 CK76
Cremer St. E2 7 P1
Cremer St. E2 78 DT68
Cremorne Est. SW10 90 DD79
Milman's St.
Cremorne Gdns., Epsom 130 CR109
Cremorne Rd. SW10 90 DC80
Crescent, The E17 65 DY57
Crescent, The EC3 7 P10
Crescent, The N11 48 DG49
Crescent, The NW2 61 CV62
Crescent, The SW13 89 CT82
Crescent, The SW19 104 DA90
Crescent, The W3 74 CS72
Crescent, The, Abb.L. 15 BT30
Crescent, The, Ashf. 98 BM92
Crescent, The, Barn. 34 DB41
Crescent, The, Beck. 121 EA95
Crescent, The, Bex. 110 EW87
Crescent, The, Cat. 149 EA123
Crescent, The, Cher. 112 BG97
Western Ave.
Crescent, The, Croy. 120 DR99
Crescent, The, Epp. 25 ET32
Crescent, The, Epsom 130 CN114
Crescent, The, Har. 58 CC60
Crescent, The, Hayes 85 BQ80
Crescent, The, Ilf. 67 EN58
Crescent, The, Lthd. 143 CH122
Crescent, The, Loug. 38 EK43
Crescent, The, N.Mal. 116 CQ96
Crescent, The, Rick. 29 BP44
Crescent, The, St.Alb. 16 CA30
Crescent, The, Sev. 155 FK121
Crescent, The, Shep. 113 BT101
Crescent, The, Sid. 109 ET91
Crescent, The, Sthl. 86 BZ75
Crescent, The, Surb. 116 CL99
Crescent, The, Sutt. 132 DD106
Crescent, The (Belmont), Sutt. 132 DA111
Crescent, The, Wat. 30 BW42
Crescent, The (Aldenham), Wat. 44 CB47
Crescent, The, Wem. 59 CG61
Crescent, The, W.Mol. 114 CA98
Crescent, The, W.Wick. 122 EE100
Crescent, The, Wey. 112 BN104
Crescent Ave., Horn. 69 FF61
Crescent Cotts., Sev. 153 FE120
Crescent Dr., Orp. 123 EP100
Crescent E., Barn. 34 DC38
Crescent Gdns. SW19 104 DA90
Crescent Gdns., Ruis. 57 BV59
Crescent Gdns., Swan. 125 FC96
Crescent Gro. SW4 91 DJ84
Crescent Gro., Mitch. 118 DE98
Crescent La. SW4 91 DJ84
Crescent Pl. SW3 8 B8
Crescent Pl. SW3 90 DE77
Crescent Ri. N22 49 DK53
Crescent Ri., Barn. 34 DE43
Crescent Rd. E4 52 EE45
Crescent Rd. E6 80 EJ67
Crescent Rd. E10 65 EB61
Crescent Rd. E13 80 EG67
Crescent Rd. E18 52 EJ54
Crescent Rd. N3 47 CZ53
Crescent Rd. N8 63 DK58
Crescent Rd. N9 50 DU46
Crescent Rd. N11 48 DF49
Crescent Rd. N15 63 DP55
Carlingford Rd.
Crescent Rd. N22 49 DK53
Crescent Rd. SE18 95 EP78
Crescent Rd. SW20 117 CX95
Crescent Rd., Barn. 34 DD42
Crescent Rd., Beck. 121 EB96
Crescent Rd., Brom. 108 EG94

Crescent Rd., Cat. 148 DU124
Crescent Rd., Dag. 69 FB62
Crescent Rd., Enf. 35 DP42
Crescent Rd., Erith 97 FF79
Crescent Rd., Kings.T. 102 CN94
Crescent Rd., Shep. 113 BQ99
Crescent Rd., Sid. 109 ET90
Crescent Row EC1 7 H5
Crescent Stables SW15 89 CY84
Upper Richmond Rd.
Crescent St. N1 77 DM66
Crescent Vw., Loug. 38 EK43
Crescent Way N12 48 DE51
Crescent Way SE4 93 EA83
Crescent Way SW16 105 DM93
Crescent Way, Orp. 137 ES106
Crescent W., Barn. 34 DC39
Crescent Wd. Rd. SE26 106 DU90
Cresford Rd. SW6 90 DB81
Crespigny Rd. NW4 61 CV58
Cress End, Rick. 42 BG46
Springwell Ave.
Cressage Clo., Sthl. 72 CA70
Cressall Clo., Lthd. 143 CH120
Cresset Rd. E9 78 DW65
Cresset St. SW4 91 DK83
Cressfield Clo. NW5 62 DG64
Cressida Rd. N19 63 DJ60
Cressingham Gro., Sutt. 132 DC105
Cressingham Rd. SE13 93 EC83
Cressingham Rd., Edg. 46 CR51
Cressington Clo. N16 64 DS64
Wordsworth Rd.
Cresswell Gdns. SW5 90 DC78
Cresswell Pk. SE3 94 EF83
Cresswell Pl. SW10 90 DC78
Cresswell Rd. SE25 120 DU98
Cresswell Rd., Felt. 100 BY91
Cresswell Rd., Twick. 101 CK86
Cresswell Way N21 49 DN45
Cressy Ct. E1 78 DW71
Cressy Pl.
Cressy Ct. W6 89 CV76
Cressy Pl. E1 78 DW71
Cressy Rd. NW3 62 DF64
Crest, The N13 49 DN49
Crest, The NW4 61 CW57
Crest, The, Surb. 116 CN99
Crest, The (Cheshunt), Wal.Cr. 21 DP27
Orchard Way
Crest Clo., Sev. 139 FB111
Crest Dr., Enf. 36 DW38
Crest Gdns., Ruis. 58 BW62
Crest Rd. NW2 61 CT62
Crest Rd., Brom. 122 EF101
Crest Rd., S.Croy. 134 DV108
Crest Vw., Pnr. 58 BX56
Crest Vw. Dr., Orp. 123 EP99
Crestbrook Ave. N13 49 DP48
Crestfield St. WC1 6 A2
Crestfield St. WC1 77 DL69
Creston Way, Wor.Pk. 117 CX102
Crestway SW15 103 CU86
Crestwood Way, Houns. 100 BZ85
Creswick Rd. W3 74 CP73
Creswick Wk. E3 79 EA69
Malmesbury Rd.
Creswick Wk. NW11 61 CZ56
Creton St. SE18 95 EN76
Crewdson Rd. SW9 91 DN80
Crewe Pl. NW10 75 CT69
Crewe's Ave., Warl. 148 DW116
Crewe's Clo., Warl. 148 DW117
Crewe's La., Warl. 148 DW117
Crews St. E14 93 EA77
Crewys Rd. NW2 61 CZ61
Crewys Rd. SE15 92 DV82
Crichton Ave., Wall. 133 DK106
Crichton Rd., Cars. 132 DF108
Cricket Fld. Rd., Uxb. 70 BK67
Cricket Grn., Mitch. 118 DF97
Cricket Grd. Rd., Chis. 123 EP95
Cricket La., Beck. 107 DY92
Cricket Way, Wey. 113 BS103
Cricketers Arms Rd., Enf. 36 DQ40
Cricketers Clo. N14 49 DJ45
Cricketers Clo., Chess. 129 CK105
Cricketers Clo., Erith 97 FE78
Cricketers Ct. SE11 10 F9
Cricketers Ter., Cars. 118 DE104
Wrythe La.
Cricketfield Rd. E5 64 DV63
Cricketfield Rd., West Dr. 84 BJ77
Cricklade Ave. SW2 105 DL89
Cricklewood Bdy. NW2 61 CW62
Cricklewood La. NW2 61 CX63
Cricklewood Trd. Est. NW2 61 CY62
Cridland St. E15 80 EF67
Church St.
Crieff Ct., Tedd. 101 CJ94
Crieff Rd. SW18 104 DC86
Criffel Ave. SW2 105 DK89
Crimscott St. SE1 11 N7
Crimscott St. SE1 92 DS76
Crimsworth Rd. SW8 91 DK81
Crinan St. N1 77 DL68
Cringle St. SW8 91 DJ80
Cripplegate St. EC2 7 H6
Crisp Rd. W6 89 CW78
Crispe Ho., Bark. 81 ER68
Dovehouse Mead
Crispen Rd., Felt. 100 BY91
Crispian Clo. NW10 60 CS63
Crispin Clo., Ash. 144 CM118
Crispin Clo., Croy. 119 DL103
Harrington Clo.
Crispin Cres., Croy. 119 DK103
Crispin Rd., Edg. 46 CQ51
Crispin St. E1 7 P7
Crispin St. E1 78 DT71
Cristowe Rd. SW6 89 CZ82
Criterion Ms. N19 63 DK61
Crockenhill La., Swan. 125 FG101
Crockenhill Rd., Orp. 124 EX99
Crockenhill Rd., Swan. 124 EZ100
Crockerton Rd. SW17 104 DF89
Crockford Clo., Add. 126 BJ105
Crockford Pk. Rd., Add. 126 BJ106
Crockham Way SE9 109 EN91
Crocus Clo., Croy. 121 DX102
Cornflower La.
Crocus Fld., Barn. 33 CZ44
Croffets, Tad. 145 CX121
Croft, The NW10 75 CT68
Croft, The W5 74 CL71
Croft, The, Barn. 33 CY42
Croft, The, Houns. 86 BY79
Croft, The, Loug. 39 EN40
Croft, The, Pnr. 58 BZ59
Rayners La.
Croft, The, Ruis. 58 BW63
Croft, The, St.Alb. 16 CA25
Croft, The, Swan. 125 FC97
Croft, The, Wem. 59 CJ64
Croft Ave., W.Wick. 121 EC102
Croft Clo. NW7 46 CS48
Croft Clo., Belv. 96 EZ78
Croft Clo., Chis. 109 EM91
Croft Clo., Hayes 85 BQ80
Croft Clo., Kings L. 14 BG30
Croft Clo., Uxb. 70 BN66
Croft End Rd., Kings L. 14 BG30
Croft Fld., Kings L. 14 BG30
Croft Gdns. W7 87 CG75
Croft Gdns., Ruis. 57 BS60
Croft La., Kings L. 14 BG30
Croft Lo. Clo., Wdf.Grn. 52 EH51
Croft Meadow, Kings L. 14 BG30
Croft Ms. N12 48 DC48
Croft Rd. SW16 119 DN95
Croft Rd. SW19 104 DC94
Croft Rd., Brom. 108 EG93
Croft Rd., Cat. 149 DZ122
Croft Rd., Enf. 37 DY39
Croft Rd., Sutt. 132 DE106
Croft St. SE8 93 DY77
Croft Way NW3 62 DA63
Ferncroft Ave.
Croft Way, Sev. 154 FF125
Croft Way, Sid. 109 ES90
Croftdown Rd. NW5 62 DG62
Crofters Clo., Islw. 101 CD85
Ploughmans End
Crofters Ct. SE8 93 DY77
Crofters Mead, Croy. 135 DZ109
Crofters Rd., Nthwd. 43 BS49
Crofters Way NW1 77 DK67
Croftleigh Ave., Pur. 147 DP116
Crofton, Ash. 144 CL118
Crofton Ave. W4 88 CQ80
Crofton Ave., Bex. 110 EX87
Crofton Ave., Orp. 123 EQ103
Crofton Ave., Walt. 114 BW104
Crofton Gro. E4 51 ED49
Crofton La., Orp. 123 ER103
Crofton Pk. Rd. SE4 107 DZ86
Crofton Rd. E13 80 EH70
Crofton Rd. SE5 92 DS81
Crofton Rd., Orp. 123 EN104
Crofton Ter. E5 65 DY64
Studley Clo.
Crofton Ter., Rich. 88 CM84
Crofton Way, Barn. 34 DB44
Wycherley Cres.
Crofton Way, Enf. 35 DN40
Croftongate Way SE4 107 DY85
Crofts, The, Shep. 113 BS98
Crofts La. N22 49 DN52
Glendale Ave.
Crofts Rd., Har. 59 CG58
Crofts St. E1 78 DU73
Croftside SE25 120 DU97
Sunny Bank
Croftway NW3 62 DA63
Croftway, Rich. 101 CH90
Crogsland Rd. NW1 76 DG66
Croham Clo., S.Croy. 134 DS108
Croham Manor Rd., S.Croy. 134 DS108
Croham Mt., S.Croy. 134 DS108
Croham Pk. Ave., S.Croy. 134 DS106
Croham Rd., S.Croy. 134 DR106
Croham Valley Rd., S.Croy. 134 DT107
Croindene Rd. SW16 119 DL95
Cromartie Rd. N19 63 DK59
Cromarty Rd., Edg. 46 CP47
Crombie Clo., Ilf. 67 EM57
Crombie Rd., Sid. 109 ER88
Cromer Clo., Uxb. 71 BQ72
Dawley Ave.
Cromer Pl., Orp. 123 ER102
Andover Rd.
Cromer Rd. E10 65 ED58
James La.
Cromer Rd. N17 50 DU54
Cromer Rd. SE25 120 DV97
Cromer Rd. SW17 104 DG93
Cromer Rd., Barn. 34 DC42
Cromer Rd., Houns. 84 BN83
Cromer Rd., Rom. 69 FC58
Cromer Rd. (Chadwell Heath), Rom. 68 EY58
Cromer Rd., Wat. 30 BW38
Cromer Rd., Wdf.Grn. 52 EG49
Cromer Rd. W., Houns. 84 BN83
Cromer St. WC1 6 A3
Cromer St. WC1 77 DL69
Cromer Ter. E8 64 DU64
Ferncliff Rd.
Cromer Vill. Rd. SW18 103 CZ86
Cromford Clo., Orp. 123 ES104
Cromford Path E5 65 DX63
Overbury St.
Cromford Rd. SW18 104 DA85
Cromford Way, N.Mal. 116 CR95
Cromlix Clo., Chis. 123 EP96
Crompton St. W2 76 DD70
Cromwell Ave. N6 63 DH60
Cromwell Ave. W6 89 CV77
Cromwell Ave., Brom. 122 EH97
Cromwell Ave., N.Mal. 117 CT99
Cromwell Ave. (Cheshunt), Wal.Cr. 22 DU30
Cromwell Clo. E1 78 DU74
Vaughan Way
Cromwell Clo. N2 62 DD56
Cromwell Clo. W3 74 CQ74
High St.
Cromwell Clo., Brom. 122 EH98
Cromwell Clo., Walt. 113 BV102
Cromwell Cres. SW5 90 DA77
Cromwell Gdns. SW7 8 A7
Cromwell Gdns. SW7 90 DD76
Cromwell Gro. W6 89 CW76
Cromwell Gro., Cat. 148 DQ121
Cromwell Ind. Est. E10 65 DY60
Cromwell Ms. SW7 8 A8
Cromwell Ms. SW7 90 DD77
Cromwell Pl. N6 63 DH60
Cromwell Ave.
Cromwell Pl. SW7 8 A8
Cromwell Pl. SW7 90 DD77
Cromwell Pl. SW14 88 CQ83
Cromwell Pl. W3 74 CQ74
Grove Pl.
Cromwell Rd. E7 80 EJ66
Cromwell Rd. E17 65 EC57
Cromwell Rd. N3 48 DC54
Cromwell Rd. N10 48 DG52
Cromwell Rd. SW5 90 DB77
Cromwell Rd. SW7 90 DB77
Cromwell Rd. SW9 91 DP81
Cromwell Rd. SW19 104 DA92
Cromwell Rd., Beck. 121 DY96
Cromwell Rd., Borwd. 32 CL39
Cromwell Rd., Cat. 148 DQ121
Cromwell Rd., Croy. 120 DR101
Cromwell Rd., Felt. 99 BV88
Cromwell Rd., Hayes 71 BR72
Cromwell Rd., Houns. 86 CA84
Cromwell Rd., Kings.T. 116 CL95
Cromwell Rd., Tedd. 101 CG93
Cromwell Rd. (Cheshunt), Wal.Cr. 22 DV28
Cromwell Rd., Walt. 114 BW102
Cromwell Rd., Wem. 74 CL68
Cromwell Rd., Wor.Pk. 116 CR104
Cromwell St., Houns. 86 CA84
Cromwell Twr. EC2 78 DQ71
Whitecross St.
Cromwells Mere, Rom. 55 FD51
Havering Rd.
Crondace Rd. SW6 90 DA81
Crondall St. N1 7 M1
Crondall St. N1 78 DR68
Crook Log, Bexh. 96 EX83
Crooke Rd. SE8 93 DY78
Crooked Billet SW19 103 CW93
Woodhayes Rd.
Crooked Billet Roundabout E17 51 EA52
Crooked Billet Yd. E2 78 DS69
Kingsland Rd.
Crooked Mile, Wal.Abb. 23 EC33
Crooked Usage N3 61 CY55
Crookham Rd. SW6 89 CZ81
Crookston Rd. SE9 95 EN83
Croombs Rd. E16 80 EJ71
Crooms Hill SE10 93 EC80
Crooms Hill Gro. SE10 93 EC80
Cropley Ct. N1 78 DR68
Cropley St.
Cropley St. N1 78 DR68
Croppath Rd., Dag. 68 FA63
Cropthorne Ct. W9 76 DC69
Maida Vale
Crosby Clo., Felt. 100 BY91
Crosby Ct. SE1 11 K4
Crosby Rd. E7 80 EG65
Crosby Rd., Dag. 83 FB68
Crosby Row SE1 11 K4
Crosby Row SE1 92 DR75
Crosby Sq. EC3 7 M9
Crosby Wk. E8 78 DT65
Laurel St.
Crosby Wk. SW2 105 DN87
Crosier Rd., Uxb. 57 BQ63
Crosier Way, Ruis. 57 BS62
Crosland Pl. SW11 90 DG83
Taybridge Rd.
Cross Ave. SE10 93 ED79
Cross Deep, Twick. 101 CF90
Cross Deep Gdns., Twick. 101 CF89
Cross Keys Clo. W1 4 G7
Cross Keys Clo., Sev. 154 FG127
Brittains La.
Cross Keys Sq. EC1 7 H7
Cross Lances Rd., Houns. 86 CB84
Cross La. EC3 11 M1
Cross La. N8 63 DM55
Cross La., Bex. 110 EZ87
Cross Rd. E4 52 EE46
Cross Rd. N11 49 DH50
Cross Rd. N22 49 DN52
Cross Rd. SE5 92 DS82
Cross Rd. SW19 104 DA94
Cross Rd., Brom. 122 EL103
Cross Rd., Croy. 120 DR102
Cross Rd., Enf. 36 DT42
Cross Rd., Felt. 100 BY91
Cross Rd., Har. 59 CD56
Cross Rd. (South Harrow), Har. 58 CB62
Cross Rd. (Wealdstone), Har. 45 CG54
Cross Rd., Kings.T. 102 CM94
Cross Rd., Orp. 124 EV99
Cross Rd., Pur. 133 DP113
Cross Rd., Rom. 68 FA56
Cross Rd. (Chadwell Heath), Rom. 68 EW59
Cross Rd., Sid. 110 EV91
Sidcup Hill
Cross Rd., Sutt. 132 DD106
Cross Rd. (Belmont), Sutt. 132 DA110
Cross Rd., Tad. 145 CW122
Cross Rd., Uxb. 70 BJ66
New Windsor St.
Cross Rd., Wal.Cr. 23 DY33
Cross Rd., Wat. 30 BY44
Cross Rd., Wey. 113 BR104
Cross Rd., Wdf.Grn. 53 EM51
Cross Rds., Loug. 38 EH40
Cross St. N1 77 DP67
Cross St. SW13 88 CS82
Cross St., Erith 97 FE78
Bexley Rd.
Cross St., Hmptn. 100 CC92
Cross St., Uxb. 70 BJ66
Cross St., Wat. 30 BW41
Cross Way, Pnr. 43 BV54
Cross Way, The, Har. 45 CE54
Crossbow Rd., Chig. 53 ET50
Crossbrook Rd. SE3 94 EL82
Crossbrook St. (Cheshunt), Wal.Cr. 23 DX31
Crossfield Pl., Wey. 127 BP108
Crossfield Rd. N17 64 DQ55
Crossfield Rd. NW3 76 DD65
Crossfield St. SE8 93 EA80
Crossfields, Loug. 39 EP43
Crossford St. SW9 91 DL82
Crossgate, Edg. 46 CN48
Crossgate, Grnf. 73 CH65
Crossing Rd., Epp. 26 EU32
Crossland Rd., Th.Hth. 119 DP99
Crosslands Ave. W5 74 CM74
Crosslands Ave., Sthl. 86 BZ78
Crosslands Rd., Epsom 130 CR107
Crosslet St. SE17 11 L8
Crosslet Vale SE10 93 EB81
Blackheath Rd.
Crossley Clo., West. 150 EK115
Crossley St. N7 77 DN65
Crossmead SE9 109 EM88
Crossmead, Wat. 29 BV44
Crossmead Ave., Grnf. 72 CA69
Crossmount Ho. SE5 92 DQ80
Bowyer St.
Crossness La. SE28 82 EX73
Bayliss Ave.
Crossness Rd., Bark. 81 ET69
Crossoaks La., Borwd. 32 CR35
Crossoaks La. (South Mimms), Pot.B. 18 CS34
Crosspath, The, Rad. 31 CG35
Crossthwaite Ave. SE5 92 DR84
Crosswall EC3 7 P10
Crosswall EC3 78 DT73
Crossway N12 48 DD51
Crossway N16 64 DS64
Crossway N22 49 DP52
Crossway NW9 61 CT56
Crossway SE28 82 EW72
Crossway SW20 117 CW98
Crossway W13 73 CG70
Crossway, Dag. 68 EW62
Crossway, Enf. 50 DS45
Crossway, Hayes 71 BU74
Crossway, Orp. 123 ER98
Crossway, Ruis. 58 BW63
Crossway, Walt. 113 BV103
Crossway, Wdf.Grn. 52 EJ49
Crossway, The SE9 108 EK89
Crossway, The, Uxb. 70 BM68
Crossways N21 36 DQ44
Crossways, Rom. 69 FH55
Crossways, S.Croy. 135 DY108
Crossways, Sun. 99 BT94
Crossways, Sutt. 132 DD109
Crossways, West. 150 EJ120
Crossways, The, Couls. 147 DM119
Crossways, The, Houns. 86 BZ80
Crossways, The, Wem. 60 CN61
Crossways Rd., Beck. 121 EA98
Crossways Rd., Mitch. 119 DH97
Crosswell Clo., Shep. 113 BQ96
Croston St. E8 78 DU67
Crothall Clo. N13 49 DM48
Crouch Ave., Bark. 82 EV68
Crouch Clo., Beck. 107 EA93
Abbey La.
Crouch Cft. SE9 109 EN90
Crouch End Hill N8 63 DK59
Crouch Hall Rd. N8 63 DK58
Crouch Hill N4 63 DL59
Crouch Hill N8 63 DL58
Crouch La. (Cheshunt), Wal.Cr. 22 DQ28
Crouch Oak La., Add. 126 BJ105
Crouch Rd. NW10 74 CR66
Crouchman's Clo. SE26 106 DT90
Crow Clo., Warl. 149 DY118
Crow Dr., Sev. 153 FC115
Crow La., Rom. 68 EZ59
Crowborough Clo., Warl. 149 DY118
Crowborough Dr., Warl. 149 DY118
Crowborough Path, Wat. 44 BX49
Prestwick Rd.
Crowborough Rd. SW17 104 DG93
Crowden Way SE28 82 EW73
Crowder St. E1 78 DV73
Crowfoot Clo. E9 65 DZ64
Lee Conservancy Rd.
Crowhurst Clo. SW9 91 DN82
Crowhurst Way, Orp. 124 EW99
Crowland Ave., Hayes 85 BS77
Crowland Gdns. N14 49 DL45
Crowland Rd. N15 64 DT57
Crowland Rd., Th.Hth. 120 DR98
Crowland Ter. N1 78 DR66
Crowland Wk., Mord. 118 DB100
Crowlands Ave., Rom. 69 FB58
Crowley Cres., Croy. 133 DN106
Crowline Wk. N1 78 DR65
Clephane Rd.
Crowmarsh Gdns. SE23 106 DW87
Tyson Rd.
Crown Arc., Kings.T. 115 CK96
Union St.
Crown Ash Hill, West. 136 EH114
Crown Ash La., West. 150 EG116
Crown Clo. E3 79 EA67
Crown Clo. NW6 76 DB65
Crown Clo. NW7 47 CT47
Crown Clo., Hayes 85 BT75
Station Rd.
Crown Clo., Orp. 138 EU105
Crown Clo., Walt. 114 BW101
Crown Ct. EC2 7 J9
Crown Ct. SE12 108 EH86
Crown Ct. WC2 6 A9
Crown Ct., Brom. 122 EK99
Victoria Rd.
Crown Dale SE19 105 DP93
Crown Hill, Croy. 120 DQ103
Crown Hill, Epp. 25 EN34
Crown Hill, Wal.Abb. 24 EL33
Crown La. N14 49 DJ46
Crown La. SW16 105 DN92
Crown La., Brom. 122 EK99
Crown La., Chis. 123 EQ95
Crown La., Mord. 118 DA97
Crown La. Gdns. SW16 105 DN92
Crown La.
Crown La. Spur, Brom. 122 EK100
Crown Ms. E13 80 EJ67
Waghorn Rd.
Crown Ms. W6 89 CU77
Crown Office Row EC4 6 D10
Crown Par., Hayes 71 BT71
Crown Pas. SW1 9 L3
Crown Pas., Wat. 30 BW42
The Cres.
Crown Pl. NW5 77 DH65
Kentish Town Rd.
Crown Pt. Par. SE19 105 DP93
Beulah Hill
Crown Ri., Wat. 16 BW34
Crown Rd. N10 48 DG52
Crown Rd., Borwd. 32 CN39
Crown Rd., Enf. 36 DU41
Crown Rd., Ilf. 67 ER56
Crown Rd., Mord. 118 DA98
Crown Rd., N.Mal. 116 CQ95
Crown Rd., Orp. 138 EU106
Crown Rd., Ruis. 58 BX64
Crown Rd., Sev. 139 FF110
Crown Rd., Sutt. 132 DA105
Crown Rd., Twick. 101 CH86
Crown St. SE5 92 DQ80
Crown St. W3 74 CP74
Crown St., Dag. 83 FC65
Crown St., Har. 59 CD60
Crown Ter., Rich. 88 CM84
Crown Wk., Uxb. 70 BJ66
Oxford Rd.
Crown Wk., Wem. 60 CM62
Crown Way, West Dr. 70 BM74
Crown Wds. La. SE9 95 EQ82
Crown Wds. La. SE18 95 EP82
Crown Wds. Way SE9 109 ER85
Crown Yd., Houns. 86 CC83
High St.
Crowndale Rd. NW1 77 DJ68
Crownfield Ave., Ilf. 67 ES58
Crownfield Rd. E15 65 ED63
Crownfields, Sev. 155 FH125
Crownhill Rd. NW10 75 CT67
Crownhill Rd., Wdf.Grn. 52 EL52
Crownmead Way, Rom. 69 FB56
Crownstone Rd. SW2 105 DN85
Crowntree Clo., Islw. 87 CF79
Crows Rd. E15 79 ED69
Crows Rd., Epp. 25 ET30
Crowshott Ave., Stan. 45 CJ54
Crowther Ave., Brent. 88 CL77
Crowther Rd. SE25 120 DU98
Crowthorne Clo. SW18 103 CZ88
Crowthorne Rd. W10 75 CX72
Croxdale Rd., Borwd. 32 CM40
Croxden Clo., Edg. 60 CM55
Croxden Wk., Mord. 118 DC100

Dallington St. EC1 77 DP70
Dalmain Rd. SE23 107 DX88
Dalmally Rd., Croy. 120 DT101
Dalmeny Ave. N7 63 DK63
Dalmeny Ave. SW16 119 DN96
Dalmeny Clo., Wem. 73 CJ65
Dalmeny Cres., Houns. 87 CD84
Dalmeny Rd. N7 63 DK62
Dalmeny Rd., Barn. 34 DC44
Dalmeny Rd., Cars. 132 DG108
Dalmeny Rd., Erith 97 FB81
Dalmeny Rd., Wor.Pk. 117 CV104
Dalmeyer Rd. NW10 75 CT65
Dalmore Ave., Esher 129 CF107
Dalmore Rd. SE21 106 DQ89
Dalrymple Clo. N14 49 DK45
Dalrymple Rd. SE4 93 DY84
Dalston Cross Shop. Cen. E8 78 DT65
Kingsland High St.
Dalston Gdns., Stan. 46 CL53
Dalston La. E8 78 DT65
Dalton Ave., Mitch. 118 DE96
Dalton Clo., Hayes 71 BR70
Dalton Clo., Orp. 123 ES104
Dalton Clo., Pur. 134 DQ112
Dalton Rd., Har. 45 CD54
Athelstone Rd.
Dalton St. SE27 105 DP89
Daltons Rd., Orp. 139 FB105
Daltons Rd., Swan. 125 FC102
Dalwood St. SE5 92 DS81
Daly Ct. E15 65 EC64
Clays La.
Dalyell Rd. SW9 91 DM83
Damascene Wk. SE21 106 DQ88
Lovelace Rd.
Damask Cres. E16 80 EE70
Cranberry La.
Dame St. N1 78 DQ68
Damer Ter. SW10 90 DC80
Tadema Rd.
Dames Rd. E7 66 EG62
Dameswick Vw., St.Alb. 16 CA27
Damien St. E1 78 DV72
Damon Clo., Sid. 110 EV90
Damson Ct., Swan. 125 FD98
Damson Way, Cars. 132 DF110
Damsonwood Rd., Sthl. 86 CA76
Dan Leno Wk. SW6 90 DB80
Britannia Rd.
Danbrook Rd. SW16 119 DL95
Danbury Clo., Rom. 68 EX55
Danbury Ms., Wall. 133 DH105
Danbury Rd., Loug. 52 EL45
Danbury Rd., Rain. 83 FF67
Danbury St. N1 77 DP68
Danbury Way, Wdf.Grn. 52 EJ51
Danby St. SE15 92 DT83
Dancer Rd. SW6 89 CZ81
Dancer Rd., Rich. 88 CN83
Dancers Hill Rd., Barn. 33 CW36
Dancers La., Barn. 33 CW35
Dando Cres. SE3 94 EH83
Dandridge Clo. SE10 94 EF78
Dane Clo., Bex. 110 FA87
Dane Clo., Orp. 137 ER106
Dane Pl. E3 79 DY68
Roman Rd.
Dane Rd. N18 50 DW49
Dane Rd. SW19 118 DC95
Dane Rd. W13 73 CJ74
Dane Rd., Ashf. 99 BQ93
Dane Rd., Ilf. 67 EQ64
Dane Rd., Sev. 153 FE117
Dane Rd., Sthl. 72 BY73
Dane Rd., Warl. 149 DX117
Dane St. WC1 6 B7
Danebury, Croy. 135 EB107
Danebury Ave. SW15 102 CS86
Daneby Rd. SE6 107 EB90
Danecourt Gdns., Croy. 120 DT104
Danecroft Rd. SE24 106 DQ85
Danehill Wk., Sid. 110 EU90
Hatherley Rd.
Danehurst Gdns., Ilf. 66 EL57
Danehurst St. SW6 89 CY81
Daneland, Barn. 34 DF43
Danemead Gro., Nthlt. 58 CB64
Danemere St. SW15 89 CW83
Danes, The, St.Alb. 16 CC28
Danes Clo., Lthd. 128 CC114
Danes Ct., Wem. 60 CP62
Danes Gate, Har. 59 CE55
Danes Rd., Rom. 69 FC59
Danes Way, Lthd. 129 CD114
Danesbury Rd., Felt. 99 BV88
Danescombe SE12 108 EG88
Winn Rd.
Danescourt Cres., Sutt. 118 DC103
Danescroft NW4 61 CX57
Danescroft Ave. NW4 61 CX57
Danescroft Gdns. NW4 61 CX57
Danesdale Rd. E9 79 DY65
Danesfield SE5 92 DS79
Albany Rd.
Daneswood Ave. SE6 107 EC90
Daneswood Clo., Wey. 127 BP106
Danethorpe Rd., Wem. 73 CK65
Danetree Clo., Epsom 130 CQ108
Danetree Rd., Epsom 130 CQ108
Danette Gdns., Dag. 68 EZ61
Daneville Rd. SE5 92 DR81
Dangan Rd. E11 66 EG58
Daniel Bolt Clo. E14 79 EB71
Uamvar St.
Daniel Clo. N18 50 DW49
Daniel Clo. SW17 104 DE93
Daniel Gdns. SE15 92 DT80
Daniel Pl. NW4 61 CV58
Daniel Rd. W5 74 CM73
Daniel Way, Bans. 132 DB114
Daniell Way, Croy. 119 DM102
Daniels La., Warl. 149 DZ116
Daniels Ms. SE4 93 DZ84
Daniels Rd. SE15 92 DW83
Dansey Pl. W1 5 M10
Dansington Rd., Well. 96 EU84
Danson Cres., Well. 96 EV83
Danson La., Well. 96 EU84
Danson Mead, Well. 96 EW83
Danson Pk., Bexh. 96 EW84
Danson Rd., Bex. 110 EX85
Danson Rd., Bexh. 110 EX85
Dante Pl. SE11 10 G9
Dante Rd. SE11 10 F8
Dante Rd. SE11 91 DP77
Danube St. SW3 8 C10
Danvers Rd. N8 63 DK56
Danvers St. SW3 90 DD79
Danvers Way, Cat. 148 DQ121
Coulsdon Rd.
Danziger Way, Borwd. 32 CQ39
Daphne Gdns. E4 51 EC48
Gunners Gro.
Daphne St. SW18 104 DC86
Daplyn St. E1 78 DU71
Hanbury St.
D'Arblay St. W1 5 L9
D'Arblay St. W1 77 DJ72
Darby Clo., Cat. 148 DQ122
Fairbourne La.
Darby Cres., Sun. 114 BW96
Darby Dr., Wal.Abb. 23 EC33
Darby Gdns., Sun. 114 BW96
Darcy Ave., Wall. 133 DJ105
Darcy Clo. N20 48 DD47
Darcy Clo., Couls. 147 DP119
Darcy Clo. (Cheshunt), Wal.Cr. 23 DY31
D'Arcy Dr., Har. 59 CK56
Darcy Gdns., Dag. 82 EZ67
D'Arcy Gdns., Har. 60 CL56
D'Arcy Pl., Ash. 144 CM117
Darcy Rd. SW16 119 DL96
D'Arcy Rd., Ash. 144 CM117
Darcy Rd., Islw. 87 CG81
London Rd.
D'Arcy Rd., Sutt. 131 CX105
Dare Gdns., Dag. 68 EY62
Grafton Rd.
Darell Rd., Rich. 88 CN83
Darent Valley Path, Sev. 154 FC121
Darenth Clo., Sev. 154 FC122
Darenth La., Sev. 154 FE121
Darenth Rd. N16 64 DT59
Darenth Rd., Well. 96 EU81
Darenth Way, Sev. 139 FG111
Darfield Rd. SE4 107 DZ85
Darfield Way W10 75 CX72
Darfur St. SW15 89 CX83
Dargate Clo. SE19 106 DT94
Chipstead Clo.
Darien Rd. SW11 90 DD83
Dark La. (Cheshunt), Wal.Cr. 22 DU31
Darkes La., Pot.B. 19 CZ32
Darlan Rd. SW6 89 CZ80
Darlaston Rd. SW19 103 CX94
Darley Clo., Add. 126 BJ106
Darley Clo., Croy. 121 DY100
Darley Dr., N.Mal. 116 CR96
Darley Gdns., Mord. 118 DC100
Darley Rd. N9 50 DT46
Darley Rd. SW11 104 DF86
Darling Rd. SE4 93 EA83
Darling Row E1 78 DV70
Darlington Rd. SE27 105 DP92
Darlton Clo., Dart. 97 FF83
Darmaine Clo., S.Croy. 134 DQ108
Churchill Rd.
Darndale Clo. E17 51 DZ54
Darnets Fld., Sev. 153 FF117
Darnhills, Rad. 31 CF35
Darnicle Hill (Cheshunt), Wal.Cr. 21 DM25
Darnley Ho. E14 79 DY72
Camdenhurst St.
Darnley Pk., Wey. 113 BP104
Darnley Rd. E9 78 DW65
Darnley Rd., Wdf.Grn. 52 EG53
Darnley Ter. W11 75 CY74
St. James Gdns.
Darns Hill, Swan. 125 FC101
Darrell Rd. SE22 106 DU85
Darren Clo. N4 63 DM59
Darrick Wd. Rd., Orp. 123 ER103
Darrington Rd., Borwd. 32 CL39
Darris Clo., Hayes 72 BY70
Darsley Dr. SW8 91 DL81
Dart St. W10 75 CY69
Dartford Ave. N9 36 DW44
Dartford Rd., Bex. 111 FC88
Dartford Rd., Dart. 111 FG86
Dartford Rd. (Wilmington), Dart. 111 FH93
Dartford Rd., Sev. 155 FJ124
Dartford St. SE17 92 DQ79
Dartmoor Wk. E14 93 EA77
Charnwood Gdns.
Dartmouth Clo. W11 76 DA72
Dartmouth Gro. SE10 93 EC81
Dartmouth Hill SE10 93 EC81
Dartmouth Pk. Ave. NW5 63 DH62
Dartmouth Pk. Hill N19 63 DH60
Dartmouth Pk. Hill NW5 63 DJ62
Dartmouth Pk. Rd. NW5 63 DH63
Dartmouth Pl. SE23 106 DW89
Dartmouth Rd.
Dartmouth Pl. W4 88 CS79
Dartmouth Rd. E16 80 EG72
Fords Pk. Rd.
Dartmouth Rd. NW2 75 CX65
Dartmouth Rd. NW4 61 CU58
Dartmouth Rd. SE23 106 DW89
Dartmouth Rd. SE26 106 DV90
Dartmouth Rd., Brom. 122 EG101
Dartmouth Rd., Ruis. 57 BU62
Dartmouth Row SE10 93 EC81
Dartmouth St. SW1 9 N5
Dartmouth St. SW1 91 DK75
Dartmouth Ter. SE10 93 ED81
Dartnell Ave., W.Byf. 126 BH112
Dartnell Clo., W.Byf. 126 BH112
Dartnell Ct., W.Byf. 126 BJ112
Dartnell Cres., W.Byf. 126 BH112
Dartnell Keep, W.Byf. 126 BH112
Dartnell Pk. Rd., W.Byf. 126 BH112
Dartnell Pl., W.Byf. 126 BH112
Dartnell Rd., Croy. 120 DT101
Dartrey Wk. SW10 90 DD80
World's End Est.
Darville Rd. N16 64 DT62
Darwell Clo. E6 81 EN68
Darwin Clo. N11 49 DH48
Darwin Clo., Orp. 137 ER106
Darwin Dr., Sthl. 72 CB72
Darwin Gdns., Wat. 44 BW50
Darwin Rd. N22 49 DP53
Darwin Rd. W5 87 CJ78
Darwin Rd., Well. 95 ET83
Darwin St. SE17 11 L8
Darwin St. SE17 92 DR77
Daryngton Dr., Grnf. 73 CD68
Dashwood Clo., Bexh. 110 FA85
Dashwood Clo., W.Byf. 126 BJ112
Dashwood Rd. N8 63 DM58
Dassett Rd. SE27 105 DP92
Datchelor Pl. SE5 92 DR81
Datchet Rd. SE6 107 DZ90
Datchworth Ct. N4 64 DQ62
Queens Dr.
Date St. SE17 92 DQ78
Daubeney Gdns. N17 50 DQ52
Daubeney Rd. E5 65 DY63
Daubeney Rd. N17 50 DQ52
Daubeney Twr. SE8 93 DZ77
Dault Rd. SW18 104 DC86
Davema Clo., Chis. 123 EN95
Davenant Rd. N19 63 DK61
Davenant Rd., Croy. 133 DP105
Duppas Hill Rd.
Davenant St. E1 78 DU71
Davenham Ave., Nthwd. 43 BT49
Davenport Clo., Tedd. 101 CG93
Davenport Rd. SE6 107 EC86
Davenport Rd., Sid. 110 EX89
Daventer Dr., Stan. 45 CF52
Daventry Ave. E17 65 EA57
Daventry St. NW1 4 B6
Daventry St. NW1 76 DE71
Davern Clo. SE10 94 EF77
Davey Clo. N7 77 DM65
Davey Rd. E9 79 EA66
Davey St. SE15 92 DT79
David Ave., Grnf. 73 CE69
David Clo., Hayes 85 BR80
David Ms. W1 4 F6
David Rd., Dag. 68 EY61
David St. E15 79 ED65
Davidge St. SE1 10 G5
Davidge St. SE1 91 DP75
Davids Rd. SE23 106 DW88
David's Way, Ilf. 53 ES52
Davidson Gdns. SW8 91 DL80
Davidson La., Har. 59 CF59
Grove Hill
Davidson Rd., Croy. 120 DS102
Davidson Way, Rom. 69 FE58
Davies Clo., Croy. 120 DT100
Davies La. E11 66 EE61
Davies Ms. W1 5 H10
Davies St. W1 5 H10
Davies St. W1 77 DH73
Davington Gdns., Dag. 68 EV64
Davington Rd., Dag. 82 EV65
Davinia Clo., Wdf.Grn. 53 EM51
Deacon Way
Davis Clo., Sev. 155 FJ122
Davis Rd. W3 75 CT74
Davis Rd., Chess. 130 CN105
Davis Rd., Wey. 126 BM110
Davis St. E13 80 EH68
Davison Clo., Wal.Cr. 23 DX28
Davison Dr. (Cheshunt), Wal.Cr. 23 DX28
Davisville Rd. W12 89 CU75
Dawell Dr., West. 150 EJ117
Dawes Ave., Islw. 101 CG85
Dawes Ct., Esher 128 CB105
Dawes Ho. SE17 11 K9
Dawes Rd. SW6 89 CY80
Dawes Rd., Uxb. 70 BL68
Dawes St. SE17 11 L10
Dawes St. SE17 92 DR78
Dawley Ave., Uxb. 71 BQ72
Dawley Par., Hayes 71 BQ73
Dawley Rd.
Dawley Rd., Hayes 71 BQ73
Dawlish Ave. N13 49 DL49
Dawlish Ave. SW18 104 DB89
Dawlish Ave., Grnf. 73 CG68
Dawlish Dr., Ilf. 67 ES63
Dawlish Dr., Pnr. 58 BY57
Dawlish Dr., Ruis. 57 BU61
Dawlish Rd. E10 65 EC60
Dawlish Rd. N17 64 DU55
Dawlish Rd. NW2 75 CX65
Dawn Clo., Houns. 86 BY83
Dawnay Gdns. SW18 104 DD89
Dawnay Rd. SW18 104 DC89
Dawpool Rd. NW2 61 CT61
Daws Hill E4 37 EC40
Daws La. NW7 47 CT50
Dawson Ave., Bark. 81 ET66
Dawson Ave., Orp. 124 EV96
Dawson Clo. SE18 95 EQ77
Dawson Clo., Hayes 71 BR71
Dawson Dr., Rain. 83 FH66
Dawson Dr., Swan. 111 FE93
Dawson Gdns., Bark. 81 ET66
Dawson Ave.
Dawson Heights Est. SE22 106 DU87
Dawson Pl. W2 76 DA73
Dawson Rd. NW2 61 CW64
Dawson Rd., Kings.T. 116 CM97
Dawson Rd., W.Byf. 126 BK111
Dawson St. E2 78 DT68
Dax Ct., Sun. 114 BW97
Thames St.
Daybrook Rd. SW19 118 DB96
Daylesford Ave. SW15 89 CU84
Daylop Dr., Chig. 54 EV48
Daymer Gdns., Pnr. 57 BV56
Daymerslea Ridge, Lthd. 143 CJ121
Days Acre, S.Croy. 134 DT110
Days La., Sid. 109 ES87
Daysbrook Rd. SW2 105 DM89
Dayton Gro. SE15 92 DW81
De Barowe Ms. N5 63 DP63
Leigh Rd.
De Beauvoir Cres. N1 78 DS67
De Beauvoir Est. N1 78 DR67
De Beauvoir Rd. N1 78 DS67
De Beauvoir Sq. N1 78 DS66
De Bohun Ave. N14 35 DH44
De Brome Rd., Felt. 100 BW88
De Burgh Pk., Bans. 146 DB115
De Crespigny Pk. SE5 92 DR82
De Frene Rd. SE26 107 DX91
De Havilland Ct., Rad. 18 CL32
Armstrong Gdns.
De Havilland Dr., Wey. 126 BL111
De Havilland Rd., Edg. 46 CN54
De Havilland Rd., Houns. 86 BW80
De Havilland Rd., Wall. 133 DL108
De Havilland Way, Abb.L. 15 BT32
De Havilland Way, Stai. 98 BK86
De Lapre Clo., Orp. 124 EX101
De Laune St. SE17 91 DP78
De Luci Rd., Erith 97 FC78
De Lucy St. SE2 96 EV77
De Mandeville Gate, Enf. 36 DU42
Southbury Rd.
De Montfort Rd. SW16 105 DL90
De Morgan Rd. SW6 90 DB83
De Quincey Ms. E16 80 EG74
Silvertown Way
De Quincey Rd. N17 50 DR53
De Salis Rd., Uxb. 71 BQ70
De Vere Cotts. W8 90 DC76
Canning Pl.
De Vere Gdns. W8 90 DC75
De Vere Gdns., Ilf. 67 EM61
De Vere Ms. W8 90 DC76
Canning Pl.
De Vere Wk., Wat. 29 BS40
De Walden St. W1 4 G7
Deacon Clo., Cob. 141 BV119
Deacon Clo., Pur. 133 DL109
Deacon Ms. N1 78 DR66
Deacon Pl., Cat. 148 DQ121
Coulsdon Rd.
Deacon Rd. NW2 61 CU64
Deacon Rd., Kings.T. 116 CM95
Deacon Way SE17 11 H8
Deacon Way SE17 92 DQ77
Deacon Way, Wdf.Grn. 53 EM52
Deacons Clo., Borwd. 32 CN42
Deacons Clo., Pnr. 43 BV54
Deacons Hill, Wat. 30 BW44
Deacon's Hill Rd., Borwd. 32 CM42
Deacons Leas, Orp. 137 ER105
Deacons Wk., Hmptn. 100 BZ91
Bishops Gro.
Deadman's Ash La., Rick. 28 BH36
Deakin Clo., Wat. 43 BS45
Chenies Way
Deal Porters Way SE16 92 DW76
Deal Rd. SW17 104 DG93
Deal St. E1 78 DU71
Deal's Gateway SE10 93 EB81
Blackheath Rd.
Dealtry Rd. SW15 89 CW84
Dean Bradley St. SW1 9 P7
Dean Bradley St. SW1 91 DL76
Dean Clo. E9 64 DW64
Churchill Wk.
Dean Clo. SE16 79 DX74
Surrey Water Rd.
Dean Clo., Uxb. 70 BM66
Dean Ct., Wem. 59 CH62
Dean Dr., Stan. 46 CL54
Dean Farrar St. SW1 9 N6
Dean Farrar St. SW1 91 DK76
Dean Gdns. E17 65 ED56
Dean Gdns. W13 73 CH74
Northfield Ave.
Dean La., Red. 147 DH123
Dean Rd. NW2 75 CW65
Dean Rd., Croy. 134 DR105
Dean Rd., Hmptn. 100 BZ92
Dean Rd., Houns. 100 CB85
Dean Ryle St. SW1 9 P8
Dean Ryle St. SW1 91 DL77
Dean Stanley St. SW1 9 P7
Dean Stanley St. SW1 91 DL76
Dean St. E7 66 EG64
Dean St. W1 5 M8
Dean St. W1 77 DK72
Dean Trench St. SW1 9 P7
Dean Wk., Edg. 46 CQ51
Deansbrook Rd.
Dean Way, Sthl. 86 CB75
Deancross St. E1 78 DW72
Deane Ave., Ruis. 57 BV64
Deane Cft. Rd., Pnr. 58 BW58
Deane Way, Ruis. 57 BV58
Deanery Clo. N2 62 DE56
Deanery Ms. W1 8 G2
Deanery Rd. E15 80 EE65
Deanery St. W1 8 G2
Deanery St. W1 76 DG74
Deanhill Rd. SW14 88 CP84
Deans Bldgs. SE17 11 L9
Deans Bldgs. SE17 92 DR77
Deans Clo. W4 88 CP79
Deans Clo., Abb.L. 15 BR32
Dean's Clo., Croy. 120 DT104
Deans Clo., Edg. 46 CQ51
Deans Clo., Tad. 145 CV124
Deans La.
Deans Ct. EC4 6 G9
Deans Dr. N13 49 DP51
Deans Dr., Edg. 46 CR50
Dean's Gate Clo. SE23 107 DX90
Deans La., Edg. 46 CQ51
Deans La., Tad. 145 CV124
Deans Ms. W1 5 J8
Dean's Pl. SW1 9 M10
Dean's Pl. SW1 91 DK78
Deans Rd. W7 73 CF74
Deans Rd., Sutt. 118 DB104
Deans Wk., Couls. 147 DN118
Deans Way, Edg. 46 CQ50
Dean's Yd. SW1 9 N6
Deansbrook Clo., Edg. 46 CQ51
Deansbrook Rd., Edg. 46 CP52
Deanscroft Ave. NW9 60 CQ61
Deansway N2 62 DD56
Deansway N9 50 DS48
Dearn Gdns., Mitch. 118 DE97
Dearne Clo., Stan. 45 CG50
Dearsley Ho., Rain. 83 FD68
Dearsley Rd., Enf. 36 DV41
Baird Rd.
Deason St. E15 79 EC67
High St.
Debden Clo., Kings.T. 101 CK92
Debden Clo., Wdf.Grn. 52 EK52
Debden Ind. Group, Loug. 39 ER42
Debden La., Loug. 39 EP38
Debden Rd., Loug. 39 EP38
Debden Wk., Horn. 83 FH65
Tangmere Cres.
Debenham Rd. (Cheshunt), Wal.Cr. 22 DV27
Debnams Rd. SE16 92 DW77
Rotherhithe New Rd.
Deborah Clo., Islw. 87 CE81
Deborah Cres., Ruis. 57 BR59
Debrabant Clo., Erith 97 FD79
Deburgh Rd. SW19 104 DC94
Decima St. SE1 11 M6
Decima St. SE1 92 DS76
Deck Clo. SE16 93 DX75
Thame Rd.
Decoy Ave. NW11 61 CY57
Dee Rd., Rich. 88 CM84
Dee St. E14 79 EC72
Dee Way, Epsom 130 CS110
Dee Way, Rom. 55 FE52
Deeley Rd. SW8 91 DK81
Deena Clo. W3 74 CM72
Deepdale SW19 103 CX91
Deepdale Ave., Brom. 122 EF98
Deepdene W5 74 CM70
Deepdene, Pot.B. 19 CX31
Deepdene Ave., Croy. 120 DT104
Deepdene Clo. E11 66 EG56
Deepdene Ct. N21 35 DP44
Deepdene Gdns. SW2 105 DM87
Deepdene Path, Loug. 39 EN42
Deepdene Rd. SE5 92 DR84
Deepdene Rd., Loug. 39 EN42
Deepdene Rd., Well. 96 EU83
Deepfield Way, Couls. 147 DL116
Deepwell Clo., Islw. 87 CG81
Deepwood La., Grnf. 73 CD69
Cowgate Rd.
Deer Pk. Clo., Kings.T. 102 CP94
Deer Pk. Gdns., Mitch. 118 DD97
Deer Pk. Rd. SW19 118 DB96
Deer Pk. Way, W.Wick. 122 EE103
Deerbrook Rd. SE24 105 DP88
Deerdale Rd. SE24 92 DQ84
Deere Ave., Rain. 83 FG65
Deerhurst Clo., Felt. 99 BU91
Deerhurst Cres., Hmptn. 100 CC92
Deerhurst Rd. NW2 75 CX65
Deerhurst Rd. SW16 105 DM92
Deerings Dr., Pnr. 57 BU57
Deerleap Gro. E4 37 EB43
Deerleap La., Sev. 138 EX113
Deers Fm. Clo., Wok. 140 BL116

Dibden Row SE1 91 DN76
Gerridge St.
Dibden St. N1 78 DQ67
Dibdin Clo., Sutt. 118 DA104
Dibdin Rd., Sutt. 118 DA104
Diceland Rd., Bans. 145 CZ116
Dicey Ave. NW2 61 CW63
Dick Turpin Way, Felt. 85 BT84
Dickens Ave. N3 48 DC53
Dickens Ave., Uxb. 71 BP72
Dickens Clo., Erith 97 FB81
Belmont Rd.
Dickens Clo., Hayes 85 BS77
Croyde Ave.
Dickens Clo., Rich. 102 CL89
Dickens Clo., Wal.Cr. 22 DU26
Dickens Dr., Chis. 109 EQ93
Dickens Est. SE1 92 DT75
Dickens Est. SE16 92 DT75
Dickens La. N18 50 DS50
Dickens Ri., Chig. 53 EP48
Dickens Rd. E6 80 EK68
Dickens Sq. SE1 11 J6
Dickens Sq. SE1 92 DQ76
Dickens St. SW8 91 DH82
Dickenson Clo. N9 50 DU46
Croyland Rd.
Dickenson Rd. N8 63 DL59
Dickenson Rd., Felt. 100 BX92
Dickenson St. NW5 77 DH65
Dalby St.
Dickensons La. SE25 120 DU99
Dickensons Pl. SE25 120 DU100
Dickerage La., N.Mal. 116 CQ97
Dickerage Rd., Kings.T. 116 CQ95
Dickerage Rd., N.Mal. 116 CQ95
Dickinson Ave., Rick. 28 BN44
Dickinson Sq., Rick. 28 BN44
Dickson (Cheshunt), Wal.Cr. 22 DT27
Dickson Fold, Pnr. 58 BX56
Dickson Rd. SE9 94 EL83
Didsbury Clo. E6 81 EM67
Barking Rd.
Dig Dag Hill (Cheshunt), Wal.Cr. 22 DT27
Digby Cres. N4 64 DQ61
Digby Gdns., Dag. 82 FA67
Digby Pl., Croy. 120 DT104
Digby Rd. E9 65 DX64
Digby Rd., Bark. 81 ET66
Digby St. E2 78 DW69
Digby Way, W.Byf. 126 BM112
High Rd.
Digdens Ri., Epsom 144 CQ115
Dighton Ct. SE5 92 DQ79
Hillingdon St.
Dighton Rd. SW18 104 DC85
Digswell Clo., Borwd. 32 CN38
Digswell St. N7 77 DN65
Holloway Rd.
Dilhorne Clo. SE12 108 EH90
Dilke St. SW3 90 DF79
Dillwyn Clo. SE26 107 DY91
Dilston Clo., Nthlt. 72 BW69
Yeading La.
Dilston Gro. SE16 92 DW77
Abbeyfield Rd.
Dilston Rd., Lthd. 143 CG119
Dilton Gdns. SW15 103 CV88
Dimes Pl. W6 89 CV77
King St.
Dimmock Dr., Grnf. 59 CD64
Dimmocks La., Rick. 28 BH36
Dimond Clo. E7 66 EG63
Dimsdale Dr. NW9 60 CQ60
Dimsdale Dr., Enf. 36 DU44
Dimsdale Wk. E13 80 EG67
Stratford Rd.
Dimson Cres. E3 79 EA70
Wellington Way
Dingle, The, Uxb. 71 BP69
Dingle Clo., Barn. 33 CT44
Dingle Gdns. E14 79 EA73
Dingle Rd., Ashf. 99 BP92
Dingley La. SW16 105 DK89
Dingley Pl. EC1 7 J3
Dingley Pl. EC1 78 DQ69
Dingley Rd. EC1 7 H3
Dingley Rd. EC1 78 DQ69
Dingwall Ave., Croy. 120 DQ103
Dingwall Gdns. NW11 62 DA58
Dingwall Pl., Croy. 120 DR103
Dingwall Rd.
Dingwall Rd. SW18 104 DC87
Dingwall Rd., Cars. 132 DF109
Dingwall Rd., Croy. 120 DR102
Dinmont St. E2 78 DV68
Coate St.
Dinsdale Gdns. SE25 120 DS99
Dinsdale Gdns., Barn. 34 DB43
Dinsdale Rd. SE3 94 EF79
Dinsmore Rd. SW12 105 DH87
Dinton Rd. SW19 104 DD93
Dinton Rd., Kings.T. 102 CM94
Diploma Ave. N2 62 DE56
Dirdene Clo., Epsom 131 CT112
Dirdene Gdns., Epsom 131 CT112
Dirdene Gro., Epsom 131 CT112
Dirleton Rd. E15 80 EF67
Disbrowe Rd. W6 89 CY79
Discovery Wk. E1 78 DV74
Wapping La.
Dishforth La. NW9 46 CS53
Disney Ms. N4 63 DP57
Chesterfield Gdns.
Disney Pl. SE1 11 J4
Disney St. SE1 11 J4
Dison Clo., Enf. 37 DX39
Disraeli Clo. SE28 82 EW74
Disraeli Clo. W4 88 CR77
Acton La.
Disraeli Gdns. SW15 89 CZ84
Fawe Pk. Rd.
Disraeli Rd. E7 80 EG65
Disraeli Rd. NW10 74 CR68
Disraeli Rd. SW15 89 CY84
Disraeli Rd. W5 73 CK74
Diss St. E2 7 P2
Diss St. E2 78 DT69
Distaff La. EC4 7 H10
Distaff La. EC4 78 DQ73
Distillery La. W6 89 CW78
Fulham Palace Rd.
Distillery Rd. W6 89 CW78
Distillery Wk., Brent. 88 CL79
Pottery Rd.
Distin St. SE11 10 D9
District Rd., Wem. 59 CH64
Ditch All. SE10 93 EB81
Ditchburn St. E14 79 EC73
Ditches La., Couls. 147 DL120
Ditchfield Rd., Hayes 72 BY70
Dittisham Rd. SE9 108 EL91
Ditton Clo., T.Ditt. 115 CG101
Watts Rd.
Ditton Gra. Clo., Surb. 115 CK102
Ditton Gra. Dr., Surb. 115 CK102
Ditton Hill, Surb. 115 CJ102
Ditton Hill Rd., Surb. 115 CJ102
Ditton Lawn, T.Ditt. 115 CG102
Ditton Pl. SE20 120 DV95
Hartfield Gro.
Ditton Reach, T.Ditt. 115 CH100
Ditton Rd., Bexh. 110 EX85
Ditton Rd., Sthl. 86 BZ78
Ditton Rd., Surb. 115 CK103
Divis Way SW15 103 CV86
Dover Pk. Dr.
Dixon Clark Ct. N1 77 DP65
Canonbury Rd.
Dixon Clo. E6 81 EM72
Brandreth Rd.
Dixon Dr., Wey. 126 BM110
Dixon Pl., W.Wick. 121 EB102
Dixon Rd. SE14 93 DY81
Dixon Rd. SE25 120 DS97
Dixon's All. SE16 92 DV75
West La.
Dixons Hill Clo., Hat. 19 CV25
Dixons Hill Rd., Hat. 19 CU25
Dobbin Clo., Har. 45 CG54
Dobell Rd. SE9 109 EM85
Dobree Ave. NW10 75 CV66
Dobson Clo. NW6 76 DD66
Dock Hill Ave. SE16 93 DX75
Dock Rd. E16 80 EF73
Dock Rd., Brent. 87 CK80
Dock St. E1 78 DU73
Dockers Tanner Rd. E14 93 EA77
Dockett Eddy La., Shep. 112 BM102
Dockhead SE1 92 DT75
Dockland St. E16 81 EN74
Dockley Rd. SE16 92 DU76
Dockwell Clo., Felt. 85 BU84
Doctor Johnson Ave. SW17 105 DH90
Doctors Clo. SE26 106 DW92
Doctors La., Cat. 147 DN123
Docwra's Bldgs. N1 78 DS65
Dod St. E14 79 EA72
Dodbrooke Rd. SE27 105 DN90
Doddington Gro. SE17 91 DP79
Doddington Pl. SE17 91 DP79
Dodd's Cres., W.Byf. 126 BH114
Dodd's La., Wok. 126 BG114
Dodsley Pl. N9 50 DW48
Dodson St. SE1 10 E5
Dodson St. SE1 91 DN75
Doebury Wk. SE18 96 EU79
Prestwood Clo.
Doel Clo. SW19 104 DC94
Dog Kennel Hill SE22 92 DS83
Dog Kennel Hill Est. SE22 92 DS83
Dog La. NW10 60 CS63
Doggets Ct., Barn. 34 DE43
Doggett Rd. SE6 107 EA87
Doghurst Ave., Hayes 85 BP80
Doghurst Dr., West Dr. 85 BP80
Doghurst La., Couls. 146 DF120
Doherty Rd. E13 80 EG70
Dolben St. SE1 10 G3
Dolben St. SE1 77 DP74
Dolby Ct. EC4 78 DQ73
Garlick Hill
Dolby Rd. SW6 89 CZ82
Dolland St. SE11 91 DM78
Dollis Ave. N3 47 CZ53
Dollis Brook Wk., Barn. 33 CY44
Dollis Cres., Ruis. 58 BW60
Dollis Hill Ave. NW2 61 CV62
Dollis Hill Est. NW2 61 CU62
Dollis Hill La. NW2 61 CT63
Dollis Ms. N3 47 CZ53
Dollis Pk.
Dollis Pk. N3 47 CZ53
Dollis Rd. N3 47 CY53
Dollis Rd. NW7 47 CY52
Dollis Valley Grn. Wk. N20 48 DC47
Totteridge La.
Dollis Valley Grn. Wk., Barn. 33 CY44
Leeside
Dollis Valley Way, Barn. 33 CZ43
Dolman Clo. N3 48 DC54
Avondale Rd.
Dolman Rd. W4 88 CR77
Dolman St. SW4 91 DM84
Dolphin App., Rom. 69 FF56
Dolphin Clo. SE16 93 DX75
Kinburn St.
Dolphin Clo. SE28 82 EX72
Dolphin Clo., Surb. 115 CK100
Dolphin Ct. NW11 61 CY58
Dolphin Ct., Stai. 98 BG90
Bremer Rd.
Dolphin Ct. N., Stai. 98 BG90
Bremer Rd.
Dolphin Est., The, Sun. 113 BS95
Dolphin La. E14 79 EB73
Dolphin Rd., Nthlt. 72 BZ67
Dolphin Rd., Sun. 113 BS95
Dolphin Rd. N., Sun. 113 BS95
Dolphin Rd. S., Sun. 113 BR95
Dolphin Rd. W., Sun. 113 BS95
Dolphin Sq. SW1 91 DJ78
Dolphin Sq. W4 88 CS80
Dolphin St., Kings.T. 116 CL95
Dombey St. WC1 6 B6
Dombey St. WC1 77 DM71
Dome Hill Pk. SE26 106 DT91
Domett Clo. SE5 92 DR84
Domfe Pl. E5 64 DW63
Rushmore Rd.
Domingo St. EC1 7 H4
Dominion Dr., Rom. 55 FB51
Dominion Rd., Croy. 120 DT101
Dominion Rd., Sthl. 86 BY76
Dominion St. EC2 7 L6
Dominion Way, Rain. 83 FG69
Domonic Dr. SE9 109 EP91
Domville Clo. N20 48 DD47
Don Phelan Clo. SE5 92 DR81
Don Way, Rom. 55 FE52
Donald Dr., Rom. 68 EW57
Donald Rd. E13 80 EH67
Donald Rd., Croy. 119 DM100
Donald Wds. Gdns., Surb. 116 CP103
Donaldson Rd. NW6 75 CZ67
Donaldson Rd. SE18 95 EN81
Doncaster Dr., Nthlt. 58 BZ64
Doncaster Gdns. N4 64 DQ58
Stanhope Gdns.
Doncaster Gdns., Nthlt. 58 BZ64
Doncaster Grn., Wat. 44 BW50
Doncaster Rd. N9 50 DV45
Doncel Ct. E4 51 ED45
Donegal St. N1 6 C1
Donegal St. N1 77 DM68
Doneraile St. SW6 89 CX82
Dongola Rd. E13 80 EH69
Dongola Rd. N17 64 DS55
Dongola Rd. W. E13 80 EH69
Balaam St.
Donington Ave., Ilf. 67 EQ57
Donkey All. SE22 106 DU87
Donkey La., Enf. 36 DU40
Donne Ct. SE24 106 DQ86
Donne Pl. SW3 8 C8
Donne Pl. SW3 90 DE77
Donne Pl., Mitch. 119 DH98
Donne Rd., Dag. 68 EW61
Donnefield Ave., Edg. 46 CL52
Donnington Rd. NW10 75 CV66
Donnington Rd., Har. 59 CJ57
Donnington Rd., Sev. 153 FD120
Donnington Rd., Wor.Pk. 117 CU103
Donnybrook Rd. SW16 105 DJ94
Donovan Ave. N10 63 DH55
Donovan Clo., Epsom 130 CR110
Nimbus Rd.
Doon St. SE1 10 D2
Doone Clo., Tedd. 101 CG93
Dora Rd. SW19 104 DA92
Dora St. E14 79 DZ72
Dorado Gdns., Orp. 124 EX104
Doral Way, Cars. 132 DF106
Doran Gro. SE18 95 ES80
Doran Mans. N2 62 DF57
Great N. Rd.
Doran Wk. E15 79 EC66
Dorchester Ave. N13 50 DQ49
Dorchester Ave., Bex. 110 EX88
Dorchester Ave., Har. 58 CC58
Dorchester Clo., Nthlt. 58 CB64
Dorchester Clo., Orp. 110 EU94
Grovelands Rd.
Dorchester Ct. N14 49 DH45
Dorchester Ct. SE24 106 DQ85
Dorchester Ct., Rick. 29 BR43
Mayfare
Dorchester Dr. SE24 106 DQ85
Dorchester Dr., Felt. 99 BS86
Dorchester Gdns. E4 51 EA49
Dorchester Gdns. NW11 62 DA56
Dorchester Gro. W4 88 CS78
Dorchester Ms., N.Mal. 116 CR98
Elm Rd.
Dorchester Ms., Twick. 101 CJ87
Dorchester Rd., Mord. 118 DB101
Dorchester Rd., Nthlt. 58 CB64
Dorchester Rd., Wey. 113 BP104
Dorchester Rd., Wor.Pk. 117 CW102
Dorchester Way, Har. 60 CM58
Dorchester Waye, Hayes 71 BV72
Dorcis Ave., Bexh. 96 EY82
Dordrecht Rd. W3 74 CS74
Dore Ave. E12 67 EN64
Dore Gdns., Mord. 118 DB101
Doreen Ave. NW9 60 CR60
Dorell Clo., Sthl. 72 BZ71
Doria Rd. SW6 89 CZ82
Dorian Rd., Horn. 69 FG60
Doric Dr., Tad. 145 CZ120
Doric Way NW1 5 M2
Doric Way NW1 77 DK69
Dorien Rd. SW20 117 CX96
Doris Ave., Erith 97 FC81
Doris Rd. E7 80 EG66
Doris Rd., Ashf. 99 BR93
Dorking Clo. SE8 93 DZ79
Dorking Clo., Wor.Pk. 117 CX103
Dorking Rd., Epsom 144 CN116
Dorking Rd., Lthd. 143 CH122
Dorking Rd., Tad. 145 CX123
Dorlcote Rd. SW18 104 DE87
Dorling Dr., Epsom 131 CT112
Dorly Clo., Shep. 113 BS98
Dorma Trd. Est. E10 65 DX60
Dorman Pl. N9 50 DU47
Balham Rd.
Dorman Wk. NW10 60 CR64
Garden Way
Dorman Way NW8 76 DD67
Dormans Clo., Nthwd. 43 BR52
Dormay St. SW18 104 DB85
Dormer Clo. E15 80 EF65
Dormer Clo., Barn. 33 CX43
Dormers Ave., Sthl. 72 CA72
Dormers Ri., Sthl. 72 CB73
Dormers Wells La., Sthl. 72 CA72
Dormywood, Ruis. 57 BT57
Dornberg Clo. SE3 94 EG80
Dornberg Rd. SE3 94 EH80
Banchory Rd.
Dorncliffe Rd. SW6 89 CY82
Dorney NW3 76 DE66
Dorney Gro., Wey. 113 BP103
Dorney Ri., Orp. 123 ET98
Dorney Way, Houns. 100 BY85
Dornfell St. NW6 61 CZ64
Dornford Gdns., Couls. 148 DQ119
Dornton Rd. SW12 105 DH89
Dornton Rd., S.Croy. 134 DR106
Dorothy Ave., Wem. 74 CL66
Dorothy Evans Clo., Bexh. 97 FB84
Dorothy Gdns., Dag. 68 EV63
Dorothy Rd. SW11 90 DF83
Dorrell Pl. SW9 91 DN84
Brixton Rd.
Dorrien Wk. SW16 105 DK89
Dingley La.
Dorrington Ct. SE25 120 DS96
Dorrington Pt. E3 79 EB69
Bromley High St.
Dorrington St. EC1 6 D6
Dorrington St. EC1 77 DN71
Dorrit Ms. N18 50 DS50
Dorrit Way, Chis. 109 EQ93
Dorrofield Clo., Rick. 29 BQ43
Dors Clo. NW9 60 CR60
Dorset Ave., Hayes 71 BS69
Dorset Ave., Rom. 69 FD56
Dorset Ave., Sthl. 86 CA77
Dorset Ave., Well. 95 ET84
Dorset Bldgs. EC4 6 F9
Dorset Clo. NW1 4 D6
Dorset Clo., Hayes 71 BS69
Dorset Dr., Edg. 46 CM51
Dorset Est. E2 78 DT69
Dorset Gdns., Mitch. 119 DM98
Dorset Ms. N3 48 DA53
Dorset Ms. SW1 9 H6
Dorset Pl. E15 79 ED65
Dorset Pl. SW1 9 M10
Dorset Ri. EC4 6 F9
Dorset Ri. EC4 77 DP72
Dorset Rd. E7 80 EJ66
Dorset Rd. N15 64 DR56
Dorset Rd. N22 49 DL53
Dorset Rd. SE9 108 EL89
Dorset Rd. SW8 91 DL80
Dorset Rd. SW19 118 DA95
Dorset Rd. W5 87 CJ76
Dorset Rd., Ashf. 98 BK90
Dorset Rd., Beck. 121 DX97
Dorset Rd., Har. 58 CC58
Dorset Rd., Mitch. 118 DE96
Dorset Rd., Sutt. 132 DA110
Dorset Sq. NW1 4 D5
Dorset Sq. NW1 76 DF70
Dorset Sq., Epsom 130 CR110
Dorset St. W1 4 E7
Dorset St. W1 76 DF71
Dorset St., Sev. 155 FH125
High St.
Dorset Way, Twick. 101 CD88
Dorset Way, Uxb. 70 BM68
Dorset Way, W.Byf. 126 BK110
Dorset Waye, Houns. 86 BZ80
Dorton Dr., Sev. 155 FM122
Dorville Cres. W6 89 CV76
Dorville Rd. SE12 108 EF85
Dothill Rd. SE18 95 ER80
Douai Gro., Hmptn. 114 CC95
Doubleday Rd., Loug. 39 EQ41
Doughty Ms. WC1 6 B5
Doughty Ms. WC1 77 DM70
Doughty St. WC1 6 B4
Doughty St. WC1 77 DM70
Douglas Ave. E17 51 EA53
Douglas Ave., N.Mal. 117 CV98
Douglas Ave., Wat. 30 BX37
Douglas Ave., Wem. 74 CL66
Douglas Clo., Stan. 45 CG50
Douglas Clo., Wall. 133 DL107
Douglas Ct., Cat. 148 DQ122
Fairbourne La.
Douglas Ct., West. 150 EL117
Douglas Cres., Hayes 72 BW70
Douglas Dr., Croy. 121 EA104
Douglas Est. N1 78 DQ65
Douglas Ms. NW2 61 CY62
Douglas Pl. E14 93 EC78
Manchester Rd.
Douglas Rd. E4 52 EE45
Douglas Rd. E16 80 EG71
Douglas Rd. N1 78 DQ66
Douglas Rd. N22 49 DN53
Douglas Rd. NW6 75 CZ67
Douglas Rd., Add. 112 BH104
Douglas Rd., Esher 114 CB103
Douglas Rd., Horn. 69 FF58
Douglas Rd., Houns. 86 CB83
Douglas Rd., Ilf. 68 EU59
Douglas Rd., Kings.T. 116 CP96
Douglas Rd., Stai. 98 BK86
Douglas Rd., Surb. 116 CM103
Douglas Rd., Well. 96 EV81
Douglas Sq., Mord. 118 DA100
Douglas St. SW1 9 M9
Douglas St. SW1 91 DK77
Douglas Ter. E17 51 EA53
Douglas Ave.
Douglas Way SE8 93 DZ80
Doulton Ms. NW6 76 DB65
Lymington Rd.
Doultons, The, Stai. 98 BG94
Dounesforth Gdns. SW18 104 DB88
Douro Pl. W8 90 DB76
Douro St. E3 79 EA68
Douthwaite Sq. E1 78 DU74
Torrington Pl.
Dove App. E6 80 EL71
Dove Clo., Nthlt. 72 BX70
Wayfarer Rd.
Dove Clo., S.Croy. 135 DX111
Dove Ct. EC2 7 K9
Dove Ho. Gdns. E4 51 EA47
Dove La., Pot.B. 20 DB34
Dove Ms. SW5 90 DC77
Dove Pk., Pnr. 44 CA52
Dove Rd. N1 78 DR65
Dove Row E2 78 DU67
Dove Wk. SW1 8 F10
Dove Wk., Horn. 83 FH65
Heron Flight Ave.
Dovecot Clo., Pnr. 57 BV57
Dovecote Ave. N22 63 DN55
Dovecote Clo., Wey. 113 BP104
Dovecote Gdns. SW14 88 CR83
Avondale Rd.
Dovecott Gdns. SW14 88 CR83
North Worple Way
Dovedale Ave., Har. 59 CJ58
Dovedale Ave., Ilf. 53 EN54
Dovedale Clo., Uxb. 42 BJ54
Dovedale Clo., Well. 96 EU81
Dovedale Ri., Mitch. 104 DF94
Dovedale Rd. SE22 106 DV85
Dovedon Clo. N14 49 DL47
Dovehouse Grn., Wey. 127 BR105
Rosslyn Pk.
Dovehouse Mead, Bark. 81 ER68
Dovehouse St. SW3 8 B10
Dovehouse St. SW3 90 DD78
Doveney Clo., Orp. 124 EW97
Dover Clo. NW2 61 CX61
Brent Ter.
Dover Clo., Rom. 55 FC54
Dover Flats SE1 92 DS77
Old Kent Rd.
Dover Gdns., Cars. 118 DF104
Dover Ho. Rd. SW15 89 CU84
Dover Pk. Dr. SW15 103 CV86
Dover Rd. E12 66 EJ61
Dover Rd. N9 50 DW47
Dover Rd. SE19 106 DR93
Dover Rd., Rom. 68 EY58
Dover St. W1 9 J1
Dover St. W1 77 DH73
Dover Way, Rick. 29 BQ42
Dover Yd. W1 9 J2
Dovercourt Ave., Th.Hth. 119 DN99
Dovercourt Est. N1 78 DR65
Balls Pond Rd.
Dovercourt Gdns., Stan. 46 CL50
Dovercourt La., Sutt. 118 DC104
Dovercourt Rd. SE22 106 DS86
Doverfield, Wal.Cr. 22 DQ29
Doverfield Rd. SW2 105 DL86
Doveridge Gdns. N13 49 DP49
Doves Clo., Brom. 122 EL103
Doveton Rd., S.Croy. 134 DR106
Doveton St. E1 78 DW70
Malcolm Rd.
Dowanhill Rd. SE6 107 ED88
Dowdeswell Clo. SW15 88 CS84
Dowding Pl., Stan. 45 CG51
Dowding Rd., Uxb. 70 BM66
Dowding Rd., West. 150 EK115
Dowding Way, Horn. 83 FH66
Dower Ave., Wall. 133 DH109
Dowgate Hill EC4 7 K10
Dowgate Hill EC4 78 DR73
Dowland St. W10 75 CY69
Dowlas Est. SE5 92 DS80
Dowlas St.
Dowlas St. SE5 92 DS80
Dowlerville Rd., Orp. 137 ET107
Dowman Clo. SW19 118 DB95
Nelson Gro. Rd.
Down Clo., Nthlt. 71 BV68
Down Hall Rd., Kings.T. 115 CK95
Down Pl. W6 89 CV78

Duncan Gro. W3 74 CS72
Duncan Rd. E8 78 DV67
Duncan Rd., Rich. 88 CL84
Duncan Rd., Tad. 145 CY119
Duncan St. N1 77 DP68
Duncan Ter. N1 6 F1
Duncan Ter. N1 77 DP68
Duncan Way (Bushey), Wat. 30 BZ40
Duncannon St. WC2 9 P1
Duncannon St. WC2 77 DL73
Dunch St. E1 78 DV72
Watney St.
Duncombe Hill SE23 107 DY87
Duncombe Rd. N19 63 DK60
Duncrievie Rd. SE13 107 ED86
Duncroft SE18 95 ES80
Dundalk Rd. SE4 93 DY83
Dundas Gdns., W.Mol. 114 CB97
Dundas Rd. SE15 92 DW82
Dundee Rd. E13 80 EH68
Dundee Rd. SE25 120 DV99
Dundee St. E1 78 DV74
Dundela Gdns., Wor.Pk. 131 CV105
Dundonald Clo. E6 80 EL72
Northumberland Rd.
Dundonald Rd. NW10 75 CX67
Dundonald Rd. SW19 103 CY94
Dunedin Rd. E10 65 EB62
Dunedin Rd., Ilf. 67 EQ60
Dunedin Rd., Rain. 83 FE69
Dunedin Way, Hayes 72 BW70
Dunelm Gro. SE27 106 DQ91
Dunelm St. E1 79 DX72
Dunfee Way, W.Byf. 126 BL112
Dunfield Gdns. SE6 107 EB92
Dunfield Rd. SE6 107 EB92
Dunford Rd. N7 63 DM63
Dungarvan Ave. SW15 89 CU84
Dunheved Clo., Th.Hth. 119 DN100
Dunheved Rd. N., Th.Hth. 119 DN100
Dunheved Rd. S., Th.Hth. 119 DN100
Dunheved Rd. W., Th.Hth. 119 DN100
Dunholme Grn. N9 50 DT48
Dunholme La. N9 50 DT48
Dunholme Rd.
Dunholme Rd. N9 50 DT48
Dunkeld Rd. SE25 120 DR98
Dunkeld Rd., Dag. 68 EV61
Dunkery Rd. SE9 108 EK91
Dunkirk St. SE27 106 DQ91
Waring St.
Dunlace Rd. E5 64 DW63
Dunleary Clo., Houns. 100 BZ87
Dunley Dr., Croy. 135 EB108
Dunlin Ho. W13 73 CF70
Dunloe Ave. N17 64 DR55
Dunloe St. E2 78 DT68
Dunlop Pl. SE16 92 DT76
Spa Rd.
Dunlop Pt. E16 80 EG74
Dunmail Dr., Pur. 134 DS114
Dunmore Pt. E2 7 P3
Dunmore Rd. NW6 75 CY67
Dunmore Rd. SW20 117 CW95
Dunmow Clo., Felt. 100 BX91
Dunmow Clo., Loug. 38 EL44
Dunmow Clo., Rom. 68 EW57
Dunmow Dr., Rain. 83 FF67
Dunmow Ho., Dag. 82 EV67
Dunmow Rd. E15 65 ED63
Dunmow Wk. N1 78 DQ67
Popham St.
Dunn Mead NW9 47 CT52
Field Mead
Dunn St. E8 64 DT64
Dunnale Cres. SE16 93 DY77
Plough Way
Dunningford Clo., Horn. 69 FF64
Dunnock Clo. N9 51 DX46
Dunnock Clo., Borwd. 32 CN42
Dunnock Rd. E6 80 EL72
Dunns Pas. WC1 6 A8
Dunnymans Rd., Bans. 145 CZ115
Dunollie Pl. NW5 63 DJ64
Dunollie Rd.
Dunollie Rd. NW5 63 DJ64
Dunoon Rd. SE23 106 DW87
Dunraven Dr., Enf. 35 DN40
Dunraven Rd. W12 75 CU74
Dunraven St. W1 4 E10
Dunsany Rd. W14 89 CX76
Dunsborough Pk., Wok. 140 BJ120
Dunsbury Clo., Sutt. 132 DB109
Nettlecombe Clo.
Dunsfold Ri., Couls. 133 DK113
Dunsfold Way, Croy. 135 EB108
Dunsford Way SW15 103 CV86
Dover Pk. Dr.
Dunsmore Clo., Hayes 72 BY70
Kingsash Dr.
Dunsmore Clo. (Bushey), Wat. 31 CD44
Dunsmore Rd., Walt. 113 BV100
Dunsmore Way (Bushey), Wat. 31 CD44
Dunsmure Rd. N16 64 DS60
Dunspring La., Ilf. 53 EP54
Dunstable Ms. W1 4 G6
Dunstable Rd., Rich. 88 CL84
Dunstable Rd., W.Mol. 114 BZ98
Dunstall Rd. SW20 103 CV93
Dunstall Way, W.Mol. 114 CB97
Dunstan Clo. N2 62 DC55
Thomas More Way
Dunstan Rd. NW11 61 CZ60
Dunstan Rd., Couls. 147 DK117
Dunstans Gro. SE22 106 DV86
Dunstans Rd. SE22 106 DU87
Dunster Ave., Mord. 117 CX102
Dunster Clo., Barn. 33 CX42
Dunster Clo., Rom. 55 FC54
Dunster Clo., Uxb. 42 BH53
Dunster Ct. EC3 7 M10
Dunster Dr. NW9 60 CQ60
Dunster Gdns. NW6 75 CZ66
Dunster Way, Har. 58 BY62
Dunsterville Way SE1 11 L5
Dunston Rd. E8 78 DT67
Dunston Rd. SW11 90 DG83
Dunston St. E8 78 DT67
Dunton Clo., Surb. 116 CL102
Dunton Rd. E10 65 EB59
Dunton Rd. SE1 11 P9
Dunton Rd. SE1 92 DT77
Dunton Rd., Rom. 69 FE56
Duntshill Rd. SW18 104 DB88
Dunvegan Clo., W.Mol. 114 CB98
Dunvegan Rd. SE9 95 EM84
Dunwich Rd., Bexh. 96 EZ81
Dunworth Ms. W11 75 CZ72
Portobello Rd.
Duplex Ride SW1 8 E5
Dupont Rd. SW20 117 CX96
Dupont St. E14 79 DY71
Maroon St.
Duppas Ave., Croy. 133 DP105
Violet La.
Duppas Clo., Shep. 113 BR99
Green La.
Duppas Hill La., Croy. 133 DP105
Duppas Hill Rd.
Duppas Hill Rd., Croy. 133 DN105
Duppas Hill Ter., Croy. 119 DP104
Duppas Rd., Croy. 119 DN104
Dupree Rd. SE7 94 EH78
Dura Den Clo., Beck. 107 EB94
Durand Clo., Cars. 118 DF102
Durand Gdns. SW9 91 DM81
Durand Way NW10 74 CQ66
Durands Wk. SE16 93 DY75
Salter Rd.
Durant Rd., Swan. 111 FG93
Durant St. E2 78 DU69
Durants Pk. Ave., Enf. 37 DX42
Durants Rd., Enf. 36 DW42
Durban Gdns., Dag. 83 FC66
Durban Rd. E15 80 EE69
Durban Rd. E17 51 DZ53
Durban Rd. N17 50 DS51
Durban Rd. SE27 106 DQ91
Durban Rd., Beck. 121 DZ96
Durban Rd., Ilf. 67 ES60
Durban Rd. E., Wat. 29 BU42
Durban Rd. W., Wat. 29 BU42
Durbin Rd., Chess. 130 CL105
Durdans Rd., Sthl. 72 BZ72
Durell Gdns., Dag. 68 EX64
Durell Rd., Dag. 68 EX64
Durford Cres. SW15 103 CV88
Durham Ave., Brom. 122 EF98
Durham Ave., Houns. 86 BZ79
Durham Ave., Wdf.Grn. 52 EK50
Durham Clo. SW20 117 CV96
Durham Rd.
Durham Hill, Brom. 108 EF91
Durham Ho. St. WC2 10 A1
Durham Pl. SW3 90 DF78
Smith St.
Durham Pl., Ilf. 67 EQ63
Eton Rd.
Durham Ri. SE18 95 EQ78
Durham Rd. E12 66 EK63
Durham Rd. E16 80 EE70
Durham Rd. N2 62 DE55
Durham Rd. N7 63 DM61
Durham Rd. N9 50 DU47
Durham Rd. SW20 117 CV95
Durham Rd. W5 87 CK76
Durham Rd., Borwd. 32 CQ41
Durham Rd., Brom. 122 EF97
Durham Rd., Dag. 69 FC64
Durham Rd., Felt. 100 BW87
Durham Rd., Har. 58 CB57
Durham Rd., Sid. 110 EV92
Durham Row E1 79 DY71
Durham St. SE11 91 DM78
Durham Ter. W2 76 DB72
Durham Wf., Brent. 87 CJ80
High St.
Durham Yd. E2 78 DV69
Teesdale St.
Duriun Way, Erith 97 FH80
Durley Ave., Pnr. 58 BY59
Durley Gdns., Orp. 138 EV105
Durley Rd. N16 64 DS59
Durlston Rd. E5 64 DU61
Durlston Rd., Kings.T. 102 CL93
Durnell Way, Loug. 39 EN41
Durnford St. N15 64 DS57
Durnford St. SE10 93 EC79
Greenwich Ch. St.
Durning Rd. SE19 106 DR92
Durnsford Ave. SW19 104 DA89
Durnsford Rd. N11 49 DK53
Durnsford Rd. SW19 104 DA89
Durrant Way, Orp. 137 ER106
Durrants Dr., Rick. 29 BQ41
Durrell Rd. SW6 89 CZ81
Durrell Way, Shep. 113 BR100
Durrington Ave. SW20 117 CW95
Durrington Pk. Rd. SW20 117 CW95
Durrington Rd. E5 65 DY63
Dursley Clo. SE3 94 EJ82
Dursley Gdns. SE3 94 EK81
Dursley Rd. SE3 94 EJ82
Durward St. E1 78 DV71
Durweston Ms. W1 4 E6
Durweston St. W1 4 E7
Dury Rd., Barn. 33 CZ40
Dutch Barn Clo., Stai. 98 BK86
Dutch Gdns., Kings.T. 102 CP93
Windmill Ri.
Dutch Yd. SW18 104 DA85
Wandsworth High St.
Duthie St. E14 79 EC73
Prestons Rd.
Dutton St. SE10 93 EC81
Duxberry Clo., Brom. 122 EL99
Southborough La.
Duxford Clo., Horn. 83 FH65
Dwight Ct. SW6 89 CY82
Burlington Rd.
Dwight Rd., Wat. 43 BR45
Dye Ho. La. E3 79 EA67
Dyer's Bldgs. EC1 6 D7
Dyers Hall Rd. E11 66 EE61
Dyers La. SW15 89 CV84
Dyers Way, Rom. 55 FH52
Dyke Dr., Orp. 124 EW102
Dykes Way, Brom. 122 EF97
Dykewood Clo., Bex. 111 FE90
Dylan Clo., Borwd. 45 CK45
Coates Rd.
Dylan Rd. SE24 91 DP84
Dylan Rd., Belv. 96 FA76
Dylan Thomas Ho. N8 63 DM56
Dylways SE5 92 DR84
Dymchurch Clo., Ilf. 67 EN55
Dymchurch Clo., Orp. 137 ES105
Dymes Path SW19 103 CX89
Queensmere Rd.
Dymock St. SW6 90 DB83
Dymoke Rd., Horn. 69 FF59
Dymond Est. SW17 104 DE90
Glenburnie Rd.
Dyne Rd. NW6 75 CY66
Dyneley Rd. SE12 108 EJ91
Dynevor Rd. N16 64 DT62
Dynevor Rd., Rich. 102 CL85
Dynham Rd. NW6 76 DA66
Dyott St. WC1 5 N8
Dyott St. WC1 77 DK72
Dyrham La., Barn. 33 CU36
Dysart Ave., Kings.T. 101 CJ92
Dysart St. EC2 7 M5
Dyson Rd. E11 66 EE58
Dyson Rd. E15 80 EF65
Dysons Clo., Wal.Cr. 23 DX33
Dysons Rd. N18 50 DV50

E

Eade Rd. N4 64 DQ59
Eagans Clo. N2 62 DE55
Market Pl.
Eagle Ave., Rom. 68 EY58
Eagle Clo. SE16 92 DW78
Varcoe Rd.
Eagle Clo., Enf. 36 DW42
Eagle Clo., Horn. 83 FH65
Eagle Clo., Wall. 133 DL107
Eagle Clo., Wal.Abb. 24 EG34
Eagle Ct. EC1 6 F6
Eagle Ct. EC1 77 DP71
Eagle Dr. NW9 46 CS54
Eagle Hill SE19 106 DR93
Eagle La. E11 66 EG56
Eagle Ms. N1 78 DS65
Tottenham Rd.
Eagle Pl. SW1 9 L1
Eagle Pl. SW7 90 DC78
Old Brompton Rd.
Eagle Rd., Wem. 73 CK66
Eagle St. WC1 6 B7
Eagle St. WC1 77 DM71
Eagle Ter., Wdf.Grn. 52 EH52
Eagle Wf. E14 79 EB71
Broomfield St.
Eagle Wf. Rd. N1 78 DQ68
Eagles Dr., West. 150 EK118
Eaglesfield Rd. SE18 95 EP82
Ealdham Sq. SE9 94 EJ84
Ealing Clo., Borwd. 32 CR39
Ealing Downs Ct., Grnf. 73 CG69
Perivale La.
Ealing Grn. W5 73 CK74
Ealing Pk. Gdns. W5 87 CJ77
Ealing Rd., Brent. 87 CK77
Ealing Rd., Nthlt. 72 CA67
Ealing Rd., Wem. 74 CL65
Ealing Village W5 74 CL72
Eamont Clo., Ruis. 57 BP59
Allonby Dr.
Eamont St. NW8 76 DE68
Eardemont Clo., Dart. 97 FF84
Eardley Cres. SW5 90 DA78
Eardley Pt. SE18 95 EP77
Wilmount St.
Eardley Rd. SW16 105 DJ92
Eardley Rd., Belv. 96 FA78
Eardley Rd., Sev. 155 FH124
Earl Clo. N11 49 DH50
Earl Ri. SE18 95 ER77
Earl Rd. SE1 11 P10
Earl Rd. SE1 92 DT78
Earl Rd. SW14 88 CQ84
Elm Rd.
Earl St. EC2 7 L6
Earl St. EC2 78 DR71
Earl St., Wat. 30 BW41
Earldom Rd. SW15 89 CW84
Earle Gdns., Kings.T. 102 CL94
Earleswood, Cob. 128 BX112
Earlham Gro. E7 66 EF64
Earlham Gro. N22 49 DM52
Earlham St. WC2 5 N9
Earlham St. WC2 77 DK72
Earls Ct. Gdns. SW5 90 DB77
Earls Ct. Rd. SW5 90 DA77
Earls Ct. Rd. W8 90 DA77
Earls Ct. Sq. SW5 90 DB78
Earls Cres., Har. 59 CE56
Earls La., Pot.B. 18 CS32
Earl's Path, Loug. 38 EJ40
Earls Ter. W8 89 CZ76
Earls Wk. W8 90 DA76
Earls Wk., Dag. 68 EV63
Earls Way, Orp. 123 ET103
Station Rd.
Earlsdown Ho., Bark. 81 ER68
Wheelers Cross
Earlsferry Way N1 77 DM66
Earlsfield Rd. SW18 104 DC88
Earlshall Rd. SE9 95 EM84
Earlsmead, Har. 58 BZ63
Earlsmead Rd. N15 64 DT57
Earlsmead Rd. NW10 75 CW69
Earlsthorpe Ms. SW12 104 DG86
Earlsthorpe Rd. SE26 107 DX91
Earlstoke St. EC1 6 F2
Earlston Gro. E9 78 DV67
Earlswood Ave., Th.Hth. 119 DN99
Earlswood Clo. SE10 94 EE78
Earlswood St.
Earlswood Gdns., Ilf. 67 EN55
Earlswood St. SE10 94 EE78
Early Ms. NW1 77 DH67
Arlington Rd.
Earnshaw St. WC2 5 N8
Earnshaw St. WC2 77 DK72
Earsby St. W14 89 CY77
Easby Cres., Mord. 118 DB100
Easebourne Rd., Dag. 68 EW64
Easedale Dr., Horn. 69 FG64
Easedale Ho., Islw. 101 CF85
Easley's Ms. W1 4 G8
East Acton La. W3 74 CS73
East Arbour St. E1 79 DX72
East Ave. E12 80 EL66
East Ave. E17 65 EB56
East Ave., Hayes 85 BT75
East Ave., Sthl. 72 BZ73
East Ave., Wall. 133 DM106
East Ave., Walt. 127 BT110
Octagon Rd.
East Bank N16 64 DS59
East Barnet Rd., Barn. 34 DD42
East Churchfield Rd. W3 74 CR74
East Clo. W5 74 CN70
East Clo., Barn. 34 DG42
East Clo., Grnf. 72 CC68
East Clo., Rain. 83 FH70
East Clo., St.Alb. 16 CB25
East Ct., Wem. 59 CJ61
East Cres. N11 48 DF49
East Cres., Enf. 36 DS43
East Cross Route E3 79 DZ66
East Dr., Cars. 132 DE109
East Dr., Nthwd. 43 BS47
East Dr., Orp. 124 EV100
East Dr., Wat. 29 BV35
East Duck Lees La., Enf. 37 DY42
Duck Lees La.
East Dulwich Gro. SE22 106 DS85
East Dulwich Rd. SE15 92 DU84
East Dulwich Rd. SE22 92 DT84
East End Rd. N2 62 DB55
East End Rd. N3 47 CZ54
East End Way, Pnr. 58 BY55
East Entrance, Dag. 83 FB68
East Ferry Rd. E14 93 EB77
East Gdns. SW17 104 DE93
East Gorse, Croy. 135 DY112
East Grn., Hem.H. 14 BM25
East Hall Rd., Orp. 124 EY101
East Ham Ind. Est. E6 80 EK70
East Ham Manor Way E6 81 EN72
East Harding St. EC4 6 E8
East Heath Rd. NW3 62 DC62
East Hill SW18 104 DB85
East Hill, S.Croy. 134 DS110
East Hill, Wem. 60 CN61
East Hill, West. 150 EH118
East Holme, Erith 97 FD81
East Holme, Hayes 71 BU74
East India Dock Rd. E14 79 EA72
East India Dock Wall Rd. E14 79 ED73
East La. SE16 92 DU75
East La., Abb.L. 15 BT28
East La., Kings.T. 115 CK97
East La., Wem. 59 CH62
East Lo. La., Enf. 35 DK36
East Mascalls SE7 94 EJ79
Mascalls Rd.
East Mead, Ruis. 58 BX62
East Mt. St. E1 78 DV71
East Pk. Clo., Rom. 68 EX57
East Pas. EC1 7 H6
East Pier E1 78 DV74
Wapping High St.
East Pl. SE27 106 DQ91
Pilgrim Hill
East Poultry Ave. EC1 6 F7
East Ramp, Houns. 85 BP81
East Ridgeway (Cuffley), Pot.B. 21 DL28
East Rd. E15 80 EG67
East Rd. N1 7 L2
East Rd. N1 78 DR69
East Rd. SW19 104 DC93
East Rd., Barn. 48 DG46
East Rd., Edg. 46 CP53
East Rd., Enf. 36 DW38
East Rd., Felt. 99 BR87
East Rd., Kings.T. 116 CL95
East Rd. (Chadwell Heath), Rom. 68 EY57
East Rd. (Rush Grn.), Rom. 69 FD59
East Rd., Well. 96 EV82
East Rd., West Dr. 84 BM77
East Rd., Wey. 127 BR108
East Rochester Way SE9 95 ER84
East Rochester Way, Bex. 110 EX86
East Rochester Way, Sid. 95 ER84
East Row E11 66 EG58
East Row W10 75 CY70
East Sheen Ave. SW14 102 CR85
East Smithfield E1 78 DT73
East St. SE17 11 J10
East St. SE17 92 DQ78
East St., Bexh. 96 FA84
East St., Brent. 87 CJ80
East St., Brom. 122 EG96
East St., Cher. 112 BG101
East St., Epsom 130 CS113
East Surrey Gro. SE15 92 DT80
East Tenter St. E1 78 DT72
East Twrs., Pnr. 58 BX57
East Vw. E4 51 EC50
East Vw., Barn. 33 CZ40
East Wk. NW7 47 CU52
Northway
East Wk., Barn. 48 DG45
East Wk., Hayes 71 BU74
East Way E11 66 EH57
East Way, Brom. 122 EG101
East Way, Croy. 121 DY103
East Way, Hayes 71 BU74
East Way, Ruis. 57 BU60
East Woodside, Bex. 110 EY88
Maiden Erlegh Ave.
Eastbank Rd., Hmptn. 100 CC92
Eastbourne Ave. W3 74 CR72
Eastbourne Gdns. SW14 88 CQ83
Eastbourne Ms. W2 76 DC72
Eastbourne Rd. E6 81 EN69
Eastbourne Rd. E15 80 EE67
Eastbourne Rd. N15 64 DS58
Eastbourne Rd. SW17 104 DG93
Eastbourne Rd. W4 88 CQ79
Eastbourne Rd., Brent. 87 CK78
Eastbourne Rd., Felt. 100 BX89
Eastbourne Ter. W2 76 DC72
Eastbournia Ave. N9 50 DV48
Eastbrook Ave. N9 50 DW45
Eastbrook Ave., Dag. 69 FC63
Eastbrook Dr., Rom. 69 FE62
Eastbrook Rd. SE3 94 EH81
Eastbrook Rd., Wal.Abb. 24 EE33
Eastbury Ave., Bark. 81 ES67
Eastbury Ave., Enf. 36 DS39
Eastbury Ave., Nthwd. 43 BS50
Eastbury Clo., Nthwd. 43 BT50
Eastbury Ave.
Eastbury Ct., Bark. 81 ES67
Eastbury Gro. W4 88 CS78
Eastbury Ho., Bark. 81 ET67
Eastbury Pl., Nthwd. 43 BT50
Eastbury Ave.
Eastbury Rd. E6 81 EN70
Eastbury Rd., Kings.T. 102 CL94
Eastbury Rd., Nthwd. 43 BS50
Eastbury Rd., Orp. 123 ER100
Eastbury Rd., Rom. 69 FD58
Eastbury Rd., Wat. 43 BV45
Eastbury Sq., Bark. 81 ET67
Eastbury Ter. E1 79 DX70
Eastcastle St. W1 5 K8
Eastcastle St. W1 77 DJ72
Eastcheap EC3 7 L10
Eastcheap EC3 78 DR73
Eastchurch Rd., Houns. 85 BS82
Eastcombe Ave. SE7 94 EH79
Eastcote, Orp. 123 ET102
Eastcote Ave., Grnf. 73 CG65
Eastcote Ave., Har. 58 CB61
Eastcote Ave., W.Mol. 114 BZ99
Eastcote High Rd., Pnr. 57 BU58
Eastcote La., Har. 58 BY63
Eastcote La., Nthlt. 58 BZ64
Eastcote La. N., Nthlt. 72 BZ65
Eastcote Rd., Har. 58 CC62
Eastcote Rd., Pnr. 58 BX57
Eastcote Rd., Ruis. 57 BS59
Eastcote Rd., Well. 95 ER82
Eastcote St. SW9 91 DM82
Eastcote Vw., Pnr. 58 BW56
Eastcroft Rd., Epsom 130 CS108
Eastdean Ave., Epsom 130 CP113
Eastdown Pk. SE13 93 ED84
Eastern Ave. E11 66 EH58
Eastern Ave., Cher. 112 BG97
Eastern Ave., Ilf. 67 EP58
Eastern Ave., Pnr. 58 BX59
Eastern Ave., Rom. 68 EW56
Eastern Ave., Wal.Cr. 23 DY33
Eastern Ave. E., Rom. 69 FD55
Eastern Ave. W., Rom. 68 EY56
Eastern Ind. Est., Erith 96 EZ75

Eastern Perimeter Rd., Houns. 85 BS82
Eastern Rd. E13 80 EH68
Eastern Rd. E17 65 EC57
Eastern Rd. N2 62 DF55
Eastern Rd. N22 49 DL53
Eastern Rd. SE4 93 EA84
Eastern Rd., Rom. 69 FE57
Eastern Vw., West. 150 EJ117
Eastern Way SE2 82 EY74
Eastern Way SE28 96 EU75
Eastern Way, Erith 82 EY74
Easternville Gdns., Ilf. 67 EQ58
Eastfield Ave., Wat. 30 BX39
Eastfield Cotts., Hayes 85 BR78
Bletchmore Clo.
Eastfield Gdns., Dag. 68 FA63
Eastfield Par., Pot.B. 20 DD32
Eastfield Rd. E17 65 EA56
Eastfield Rd. N8 63 DL55
Eastfield Rd., Dag. 68 EZ63
Eastfield Rd., Enf. 37 DX38
Eastfield Rd., Wal.Cr. 23 DY32
Eastfields, Pnr. 58 BW57
Eastfields Rd. W3 74 CQ71
Eastfields Rd., Mitch. 118 DG96
Eastgate, Bans. 131 CZ114
Eastgate Clo. SE28 82 EX72
Eastglade, Nthwd. 43 BT50
Eastglade, Pnr. 58 BZ55
Eastham Clo., Barn. 33 CY43
Eastholm NW11 62 DB56
Eastlake Rd. SE5 92 DQ82
Eastlands Cres. SE21 106 DT86
Eastlea Ave., Wat. 30 BY37
Eastleigh Ave., Har. 58 CB61
Eastleigh Clo. NW2 60 CS62
Eastleigh Clo., Sutt. 132 DB108
Eastleigh Rd. E17 51 DZ54
Eastleigh Rd., Bexh. 97 FC82
Eastleigh Rd., Houns. 85 BT83
Cranford La.
Eastleigh Wk. SW15 103 CU87
Alton Rd.
Eastleigh Way, Felt. 99 BU88
Eastman Rd. W3 88 CR75
Eastmead Ave., Grnf. 72 CB69
Eastmead Clo., Brom. 122 EL96
Eastmearn Rd. SE21 106 DQ89
Eastmont Rd., Esher 115 CF103
Eastmoor Pl. SE7 94 EK76
Eastmoor St.
Eastmoor St. SE7 94 EK76
Eastney Rd., Croy. 119 DP102
Eastney St. SE10 93 ED78
Eastnor Rd. SE9 109 EQ88
Easton Gdns., Borwd. 32 CR42
Easton St. WC1 6 D3
Eastry Ave., Brom. 122 EF100
Eastry Rd., Erith 96 FA79
Eastside Rd. NW11 61 CZ56
Eastview Ave. SE18 95 ES80
Eastville Ave. NW11 61 CZ58
Eastway E9 79 DZ65
Eastway E10 65 EA63
Eastway, Epsom 130 CQ112
Eastway, Mord. 117 CX99
Eastway, Wall. 133 DJ105
Eastwell Clo., Beck. 107 DY94
Eastwick Dr., Lthd. 142 CB122
Eastwick Pk. Ave., Lthd. 142 CB124
Eastwick Rd., Walt. 127 BV106
Eastwood Clo. E18 52 EG54
George La.
Eastwood Clo. N17 50 DV52
Northumberland Gro.
Eastwood Dr., Rain. 83 FH72
Eastwood Rd. E18 52 EG54
Eastwood Rd. N10 48 DG54
Eastwood Rd., Ilf. 68 EU59
Eastwood Rd., West Dr. 84 BN75
Eastwood St. SW16 105 DJ93
Eastworth Rd., Cher. 112 BG102
Eatington Rd. E10 65 ED57
Eaton Clo. SW1 8 F9
Eaton Clo. SW1 90 DG77
Eaton Clo., Stan. 45 CH49
Eaton Dr. SW9 91 DP84
Eaton Dr., Kings.T. 102 CN94
Eaton Dr., Rom. 55 FB52
Eaton Gdns., Dag. 82 EY66
Eaton Gate SW1 8 F8
Eaton Gate SW1 90 DG77
Eaton Gate, Nthwd. 43 BQ51
Eaton La. SW1 9 J7
Eaton La. SW1 91 DH76
Eaton Ms. N. SW1 8 F7
Eaton Ms. N. SW1 90 DG76
Eaton Ms. S. SW1 9 H7
Eaton Ms. S. SW1 90 DG77
Eaton Ms. W. SW1 8 G8
Eaton Ms. W. SW1 90 DG77
Eaton Pk., Cob. 128 BY114
Eaton Pk. Rd. N13 49 DN47
Eaton Pk. Rd., Cob. 128 BY114
Eaton Pl. SW1 8 F7
Eaton Pl. SW1 90 DG76
Eaton Ri. E11 66 EJ57
Eaton Ri. W5 73 CJ71
Eaton Rd. NW4 61 CW57
Eaton Rd., Enf. 36 DS41
Eaton Rd., Houns. 87 CD84
Eaton Rd., Sid. 110 EX89
Eaton Rd., Sutt. 132 DD107
Eaton Row SW1 9 H7
Eaton Row SW1 91 DH76
Eaton Sq. SW1 8 G8
Eaton Sq. SW1 90 DG77
Eaton Ter. SW1 8 F8
Eaton Ter. SW1 90 DG77
Eaton Ter. Ms. SW1 8 F8
Eaton Wk. SE15 92 DT80
Sumner Est.
Eatons Mead E4 51 EA47
Eatonville Rd. SW17 104 DF89
Eatonville Vill. SW17 104 DF89
Eatonville Rd.
Ebbas Way, Epsom 144 CP115
Ebbisham Dr. SW8 91 DM79
Ebbisham La., Tad. 145 CU123
Ebbisham Rd., Epsom 130 CP114
Ebbisham Rd., Wor.Pk. 117 CW103
Ebbsfleet Rd. NW2 61 CY64
Ebdon Way SE3 94 EH83
Ebenezer St. N1 7 K2
Ebenezer St. N1 78 DR69
Ebenezer Wk. SW16 119 DJ95
Ebley Clo. SE15 92 DT79
Ebner St. SW18 104 DB85
Ebor St. E1 7 P4
Ebor St. E1 78 DT70
Ebrington Rd., Har. 59 CJ58
Ebsworth St. SE23 107 DX87
Eburne Rd. N7 63 DL62
Ebury Bri. SW1 9 H10
Ebury Bri. SW1 91 DH78
Ebury Bri. Est. SW1 9 H10
Ebury Bri. Est. SW1 91 DH78
Ebury Bri. Rd. SW1 90 DG78
Ebury Clo., Kes. 122 EL104
Ebury Clo., Nthwd. 43 BQ50
Ebury Ms. SE27 105 DP90
Ebury Ms. SW1 9 H8
Ebury Ms. SW1 91 DH77
Ebury Ms. E. SW1 9 H7
Ebury Rd., Rick. 42 BK46
Ebury Rd., Wat. 30 BW41
Ebury Sq. SW1 8 G9
Ebury Sq. SW1 90 DG77
Ebury St. SW1 8 G9
Ebury St. SW1 90 DG77
Ebury Way, The, Rick. 42 BN46
Ebury Way, The, Wat. 43 BS45
Eccles Rd. SW11 90 DF84
Ecclesbourne Clo. N13 49 DN50
Ecclesbourne Gdns. N13 49 DN50
Ecclesbourne Rd. N1 78 DQ66
Ecclesbourne Rd., Th.Hth. 120 DQ99
Eccleston Bri. SW1 9 J8
Eccleston Bri. SW1 91 DH77
Eccleston Clo., Barn. 34 DF42
Eccleston Clo., Orp. 123 ER102
Eccleston Cres., Rom. 68 EU59
Eccleston Ms. SW1 8 G7
Eccleston Ms. SW1 90 DG76
Eccleston Pl. SW1 9 H8
Eccleston Pl. SW1 91 DH77
Eccleston Rd. W13 73 CG73
Eccleston Sq. SW1 9 J9
Eccleston Sq. SW1 91 DH77
Eccleston Sq. Ms. SW1 9 J9
Eccleston St. SW1 8 G7
Eccleston St. SW1 91 DH77
Ecclestone Ct., Wem. 60 CL64
St. John's Rd.
Ecclestone Pl., Wem. 60 CM64
Echelforde Dr., Ashf. 98 BN91
Echo Heights E4 51 EB46
Mount Echo Dr.
Eckersley St. E1 78 DU70
Buxton St.
Eckford St. N1 77 DN68
Eckstein Rd. SW11 90 DE84
Eclipse Rd. E13 80 EH71
Ecton Rd., Add. 126 BH105
Ector Rd. SE6 108 EE89
Edbrooke Rd. W9 76 DA70
Eddiscombe Rd. SW6 89 CZ82
Eddy Clo., Rom. 69 FB58
Eddystone Rd. SE4 107 DY85
Eddystone Wk., Stai. 98 BL87
Clare Rd.
Ede Clo., Houns. 86 BZ83
Eden Clo. W8 90 DA76
Adam & Eve Ms.
Eden Clo., Add. 126 BH110
Eden Clo., Bex. 111 FD91
Eden Clo., Wem. 73 CK67
Eden Gro. E17 65 EB57
Eden Gro. N7 63 DM64
Eden Gro. Rd., W.Byf. 126 BL113
Eden Ms. SW17 104 DC90
Huntspill St.
Eden Pk. Ave., Beck. 121 DY98
Eden Rd. E17 65 EB57
Eden Rd. SE27 105 DP92
Eden Rd., Beck. 121 DY98
Eden Rd., Bex. 111 FC91
Eden Rd., Croy. 134 DR105
Eden St., Kings.T. 115 CK96
Eden Wk., Kings.T. 116 CL96
Eden St.
Eden Way, Beck. 121 DZ99
Eden Way, Warl. 149 DY118
Edenbridge Clo., Orp. 124 EX98
Edenbridge Rd. E9 79 DX66
Edenbridge Rd., Enf. 36 DS44
Edencourt Rd. SW16 105 DH93
Edendale Rd., Bexh. 97 FD81
Edenfield Gdns., Wor.Pk. 117 CT104
Edenham Way W10 75 CZ71
Elkstone Rd.
Edenhurst Ave. SW6 89 CZ83
Edenside Rd., Lthd. 142 BZ124
Edensor Gdns. W4 88 CS80
Edensor Rd. W4 88 CS80
Edenvale Rd., Mitch. 104 DG94
Edenvale St. SW6 90 DB82
Ederline Ave. SW16 119 DM97
Edgar Clo., Swan. 125 FF97
Edgar Kail Way SE22 92 DS84
Edgar Rd. E3 79 EB69
Edgar Rd., Houns. 100 BZ87
Edgar Rd., Rom. 68 EX59
Edgar Rd., S.Croy. 134 DR110
Edgar Rd., West Dr. 70 BL73
Edgar Rd., West. 150 EK121
Edgarley Ter. SW6 89 CY81
Edgbaston Dr., Rad. 18 CL32
Edgbaston Rd., Wat. 43 BV48
Holmside Ri.
Edge Clo., Wey. 126 BN108
Edge Hill SE18 95 EP79
Edge Hill SW19 103 CX94
Edge Hill Ave. N3 62 DA56
Edge Hill Ct. SW19 103 CX94
Edge St. W8 76 DA74
Kensington Ch. St.
Edgeborough Way, Brom. 108 EK94
Edgebury, Chis. 109 EP91
Edgebury Wk., Chis. 109 EQ91
Edgehill Rd.
Edgecombe Ho. SW19 103 CY88
Edgecoombe, S.Croy. 134 DW108
Edgecoombe Clo., Kings.T. 102 CR94
Edgecot Gro. N15 64 DR57
Oulton Rd.
Edgecote Clo. W3 74 CQ74
Cheltenham Pl.
Edgefield Ave., Bark. 81 ET66
Edgehill Ct., Walt. 114 BW102
St. Johns Dr.
Edgehill Gdns., Dag. 68 FA63
Edgehill Rd. W13 73 CJ71
Edgehill Rd., Chis. 109 EQ90
Edgehill Rd., Mitch. 119 DH95
Edgehill Rd., Pur. 133 DN110
Edgel St. SW18 90 DB84
Ferrier St.
Edgeley, Lthd. 142 BY124
Edgeley La. SW4 91 DK83
Edgeley Rd.
Edgeley Rd. SW4 91 DK83
Edgepoint Clo. SE27 105 DP92
Knights Hill
Edgewood Dr., Orp. 137 ET106
Edgewood Grn., Croy. 121 DX102
Edgeworth Ave. NW4 61 CU57
Edgeworth Clo. NW4 61 CU57
Edgeworth Clo., Whyt. 148 DU118
Edgeworth Cres. NW4 61 CU57
Edgeworth Rd. SE9 94 EJ84
Edgeworth Rd., Barn. 34 DE42
Edgington Rd. SW16 105 DK93
Edgington Way, Sid. 110 EW94
Edgware Ct., Edg. 46 CN51
Cavendish Dr.
Edgware Rd. NW2 61 CV60
Edgware Rd. NW9 46 CQ54
Edgware Rd. W2 76 DD70
Edgware Way, Edg. 46 CM49
Edgwarebury Gdns., Edg. 46 CN50
Edgwarebury La., Borwd. 46 CL45
Edgwarebury La., Edg. 46 CN47
Edinburgh Ave., Rick. 28 BG44
Edinburgh Clo. E2 78 DW68
Russia La.
Edinburgh Clo., Uxb. 57 BP63
Edinburgh Ct. SW20 117 CX99
Edinburgh Cres., Wal.Cr. 23 DY33
Edinburgh Dr., Abb.L. 15 BU32
Edinburgh Dr., Rom. 69 FC56
Eastern Ave. W.
Edinburgh Dr., Stai. 98 BK93
Edinburgh Dr. (Ickenham), Uxb. 57 BP63
Edinburgh Gate SW1 8 D5
Edinburgh Gate SW1 90 DF75
Edinburgh Ho. W9 76 DB69
Edinburgh Rd. E13 80 EH68
Edinburgh Rd. E17 65 EA57
Edinburgh Rd. N18 50 DU50
Edinburgh Rd. W7 87 CF75
Edinburgh Rd., Sutt. 118 DC103
Edington Rd. SE2 96 EV76
Edington Rd., Enf. 36 DW40
Edis St. NW1 76 DG67
Edison Ave., Horn. 69 FF60
Edison Clo. E17 65 EA57
Exeter Rd.
Edison Clo., Horn. 69 FF60
Edison Ave.
Edison Dr., Sthl. 72 CB72
Edison Gro. SE18 95 ET80
Edison Rd. N8 63 DK58
Edison Rd., Brom. 122 EG96
Edison Rd., Enf. 37 DZ40
Edison Rd., Well. 95 ET81
Edith Cavell Clo. N19 63 DK59
Hornsey Ri. Gdns.
Edith Gdns., Surb. 116 CP101
Edith Gro. SW10 90 DC79
Edith Rd. E6 80 EK66
Edith Rd. E15 65 ED64
Chandos Rd.
Edith Rd. N11 49 DK52
Edith Rd. SE25 120 DR99
Edith Rd. SW19 104 DB93
Edith Rd. W14 89 CY77
Edith Rd., Orp. 138 EU106
Edith Rd., Rom. 68 EX58
Edith Row SW6 90 DB81
Edith St. E2 78 DT68
Queensbridge Rd.
Edith Ter. SW10 90 DC80
Edith Turbeville Ct. N19 63 DL59
Hillrise Rd.
Edith Vill. W14 89 CZ78
Edith Yd. SW10 90 DC80
World's End Est.
Edithna St. SW9 91 DL83
Edmansons Clo. N17 50 DS53
Bruce Gro.
Edmeston Clo. E9 79 DY65
Edmonds Ct., W.Mol. 114 CB98
Avern Rd.
Edmonton Grn. N9 50 DV47
Hertford Rd.
Edmund Rd., Mitch. 118 DE97
Edmund Rd., Orp. 124 EW100
Edmund Rd., Rain. 83 FE68
Edmund Rd., Well. 96 EU83
Edmund St. SE5 92 DR80
Edmunds Ave., Orp. 124 EX97
Edmunds Clo., Hayes 72 BW71
Edmunds Wk. N2 62 DE56
Edna Rd. SW20 117 CX96
Edna St. SW11 90 DE81
Edric Rd. SE14 93 DX80
Edrich Ho. SW4 91 DL81
Edrick Rd., Edg. 46 CQ51
Edrick Wk., Edg. 46 CQ51
Edridge Clo. (Bushey), Wat. 30 CC43
Edridge Rd., Croy. 120 DQ104
Edulf Rd., Borwd. 32 CP39
Edward Amey Clo., Wat. 30 BW36
Edward Ave. E4 51 EB51
Edward Ave., Mord. 118 DD99
Edward Clo. N9 50 DT45
Edward Clo., Abb.L. 15 BT32
Edward Clo., Hmptn. 100 CC92
Edward Rd.
Edward Clo., Nthlt. 72 BW68
Edward Ct. E16 80 EG71
Alexandra St.
Edward Ct., Stai. 98 BJ93
Elizabeth Ave.
Edward Ct., Wal.Abb. 24 EF33
Edward Gro., Barn. 34 DD43
Edward Rd.
Edward Ms. NW1 5 J1
Edward Pauling Ho., Felt. 99 BT87
Edward Pl. SE8 93 DZ79
Edward Rd. E17 65 DX56
Edward Rd. SE20 107 DX94
Edward Rd., Barn. 34 DD43
Edward Rd., Brom. 108 EH94
Edward Rd., Chis. 109 EP92
Edward Rd., Couls. 147 DK115
Edward Rd., Croy. 120 DS101
Edward Rd., Felt. 99 BR85
Edward Rd., Hmptn. 100 CC92
Edward Rd., Har. 58 CC55
Edward Rd., Nthlt. 72 BW68
Edward Rd., Rom. 68 EX58
Edward Rd., West. 150 EL118
Edward II Ave., W.Byf. 126 BM114
Edward Sq. N1 77 DM67
Caledonian Rd.
Edward Sq. SE16 79 DY74
Rotherhithe St.
Edward St. E16 80 EG70
Edward St. SE8 93 DZ79
Edward St. SE14 93 DY80
Edward Temme Ave. E15 80 EF66
Edward Tyler Rd. SE12 108 EJ89
Edward Way, Ashf. 98 BM89
Edwardes Sq. W8 89 CZ76
Edward's Ave., Ruis. 71 BV65
Edwards Clo., Wor.Pk. 117 CX103
Edwards Cotts. N1 77 DP65
Compton Ave.
Edwards Dr. N11 49 DK52
Gordon Rd.
Edwards Gdns., Swan. 125 FD98
Ladds Way
Edwards La. N16 64 DR61
Edwards Ms. N1 77 DP66
Edwards Ms. W1 4 F9
Edwards Ms. W1 76 DG72
Edwards Rd., Belv. 96 FA77
Edwin Ave. E6 81 EN68
Edwin Clo., Bexh. 96 EZ79
Edwin Clo., Rain. 83 FF69
Edwin Pl., Croy. 120 DR102
Cross Rd.
Edwin Rd., Dart. 111 FH90
Edwin Rd., Edg. 46 CR51
Edwin Rd., Twick. 101 CE88
Edwin St. E1 78 DW70
Edwin St. E16 80 EG71
Edwina Gdns., Ilf. 66 EL57
Edwins Mead E9 65 DY63
Lindisfarne Way
Edwyn Clo., Barn. 33 CW44
Eel Brook Studios SW6 90 DA80
Moore Pk. Rd.
Eel Pie Island, Twick. 101 CG88
Effie Pl. SW6 90 DA80
Effie Rd. SW6 90 DA80
Effingham Clo., Sutt. 132 DB108
Effingham Common Rd., Lthd. 141 BU123
Effingham Rd. N8 63 DN57
Effingham Rd. SE12 108 EE85
Effingham Rd., Croy. 119 DM101
Effingham Rd., Surb. 115 CH101
Effort St. SW17 104 DE92
Effra Par. SW2 105 DN85
Effra Rd. SW2 91 DN84
Effra Rd. SW19 104 DA93
Egan Way SE16 92 DV78
Egan Way, Hayes 71 BS73
Egbert St. NW1 76 DG67
Egdean Wk., Sev. 155 FJ123
Egerton Ave., Swan. 111 FF94
Egerton Clo., Dart. 111 FH88
Egerton Clo., Pnr. 43 BU54
Egerton Cres. SW3 8 C8
Egerton Cres. SW3 90 DE77
Egerton Dr. SE10 93 EB81
Egerton Gdns. NW4 61 CV56
Egerton Gdns. NW10 75 CW67
Egerton Gdns. SW3 8 B7
Egerton Gdns. SW3 90 DE77
Egerton Gdns. W13 73 CH72
Egerton Gdns., Ilf. 67 ET62
Egerton Gdns. Ms. SW3 8 C7
Egerton Gdns. Ms. SW3 90 DE76
Egerton Pl. SW3 8 C7
Egerton Pl. SW3 90 DE76
Egerton Pl., Wey. 127 BQ107
Egerton Rd. N16 64 DT59
Egerton Rd. SE25 120 DS97
Egerton Rd., N.Mal. 117 CT98
Egerton Rd., Twick. 101 CE87
Egerton Rd., Wem. 74 CM66
Egerton Rd., Wey. 127 BQ107
Egerton Ter. SW3 8 C7
Egerton Ter. SW3 90 DE76
Egerton Way, Hayes 85 BP80
Egg Hall, Epp. 26 EU29
Egham Clo. SW19 103 CY89
Winterfold Clo.
Egham Clo., Sutt. 117 CY103
Egham Cres., Sutt. 117 CX104
Egham Rd. E13 80 EH71
Eglantine Rd. SW18 104 DC85
Egleston Rd., Mord. 118 DB100
Eglington Ct. SE17 92 DQ79
Carter St.
Eglington Rd. E4 51 ED45
Eglinton Hill SE18 95 EP79
Eglinton Rd. SE18 95 EP79
Eglise Rd., Warl. 149 DY117
Egliston Ms. SW15 89 CW83
Egliston Rd. SW15 89 CW83
Eglon Ms. NW1 76 DF66
Berkley Rd.
Egmont Ave., Surb. 116 CM102
Egmont Rd., N.Mal. 117 CT98
Egmont Rd., Surb. 116 CM102
Egmont Rd., Sutt. 132 DC108
Egmont Rd., Walt. 113 BV101
Egmont St. SE14 93 DX80
Egmont Way, Tad. 145 CY119
Oatlands Rd.
Egremont Rd. SE27 105 DN90
Egret Way, Hayes 72 BX71
Eider Clo. E7 66 EF64
Cormorant Rd.
Eider Clo., Hayes 72 BX71
Cygnet Way
Eighteenth Rd., Mitch. 119 DL98
Eighth Ave. E12 67 EM63
Eighth Ave., Hayes 71 BU74
Eileen Rd. SE25 120 DR99
Eindhoven Clo., Cars. 118 DG102
Eisenhower Dr. E6 80 EL71
Elaine Gro. NW5 62 DG64
Elam Clo. SE5 91 DP82
Elam St. SE5 91 DP82
Eland Rd. SW11 90 DF83
Eland Rd., Croy. 119 DP104
Elba Pl. SE17 11 J8
Elbe St. SW6 90 DC82
Elberon Ave., Croy. 119 DJ100
Elborough Rd. SE25 120 DU99
Elborough St. SW18 104 DA88
Elbury Dr. E16 80 EG72
Elcho St. SW11 90 DE80
Elcot Ave. SE15 92 DU80
Elder Ave. N8 63 DL57
Elder Clo., West Dr. 70 BL73
Yew Ave.
Elder Ct. (Bushey), Wat. 45 CE47
Elder Oak Clo. SE20 120 DV95
Elder Rd. SE27 106 DQ92
Elder St. E1 7 P5
Elder St. E1 78 DT71
Elder Wk. N1 77 DP67
Essex Rd.
Elderbeck Clo., Wal.Cr. 22 DU28
Elderberry Gro. SE27 106 DQ92
Linton Gro.
Elderberry Rd. W5 88 CL75
Elderberry Way, Wat. 29 BV35
Elderfield Rd. E5 65 DX63
Elderfield Wk. E11 66 EH57
Elderflower Way E15 80 EE66
Elderslie Clo., Beck. 121 EA99
Elderslie Rd. SE9 109 EN85
Elderton Rd. SE26 107 DY91
Eldertree Pl., Mitch. 119 DJ95
Eldertree Way
Eldertree Way, Mitch. 119 DJ95
Elderwood Pl. SE27 106 DQ92
Elder Rd.
Eldon Ave., Borwd. 32 CN40
Eldon Ave., Croy. 120 DW103
Eldon Ave., Houns. 86 CA80

Eldon Gro. NW3 62 DD64
Eldon Pk. SE25 120 DV98
Eldon Rd. E17 65 DZ56
Eldon Rd. N9 50 DW47
Eldon Rd. N22 49 DP53
Eldon Rd. W8 90 DB76
Eldon Rd., Cat. 148 DR121
Eldon St. EC2 7 L7
Eldon St. EC2 78 DR71
Eldon Way NW10 74 CP68
Eldonwall Trd. Est. NW2 61 CU60
Eldred Dr., Orp. 124 EW102
Eldred Rd., Bark. 81 ES67
Eldrick Ct., Felt. 99 BR88
Kilross Rd.
Eldridge Clo., Felt. 99 BU88
Eleanor Ave., Epsom 130 CR110
Eleanor Clo. N15 64 DT55
Eleanor Clo. SE16 93 DX75
Eleanor Cres. NW7 47 CX49
Eleanor Cross Rd., Wal.Cr. 23 DY34
Eleanor Gdns., Barn. 33 CX43
Chesterfield Rd.
Eleanor Gdns., Dag. 68 EZ62
Nicholas Rd.
Eleanor Gro. SW13 88 CS83
Eleanor Gro., Uxb. 57 BP62
Eleanor Rd. E8 78 DV65
Eleanor Rd. E15 80 EF65
Eleanor Rd. N11 49 DL51
Eleanor Rd., Wal.Cr. 23 DY33
Eleanor St. E3 79 EA69
Eleanor Wk. SE18 95 EM77
Samuel St.
Eleanor Way, Wal.Cr. 23 DZ34
Electric Ave. SW9 91 DN84
Electric La. SW9 91 DN84
Electric Par., Surb. 115 CK100
Elephant & Castle SE1 10 G8
Elephant & Castle SE1 91 DP76
Elephant La. SE16 92 DW75
Elephant Rd. SE17 11 H8
Elephant Rd. SE17 92 DQ77
Elers Rd. W13 87 CJ75
Elers Rd., Hayes 85 BR77
Eleven Acre Ri., Loug. 39 EM41
Eley Est. N18 50 DW49
Eley Rd. N18 50 DW49
Elf Row E1 78 DW73
Elfin Gro., Tedd. 101 CF92
Broad St.
Elfindale Rd. SE24 106 DQ85
Elford Clo. SE3 94 EJ84
Elfort Rd. N5 63 DN63
Elfrida Cres. SE6 107 EA91
Elfrida Rd., Wat. 30 BW43
Elfwine Rd. W7 73 CE71
Elgal Clo., Orp. 137 EP106
Orchard Rd.
Elgar Ave. NW10 74 CR65
Mitchellbrook Way
Elgar Ave. SW16 119 DL97
Elgar Ave. W5 88 CL75
Elgar Ave., Surb. 116 CN102
Elgar Clo. E13 80 EJ68
Bushey Rd.
Elgar Clo. SE8 93 EA80
Comet St.
Elgar Clo., Borwd. 45 CJ45
Elgar Clo., Buck.H. 52 EK47
Elgar Clo., Uxb. 56 BN61
Elgar St. SE16 93 DY75
Elgin Ave. W9 76 DA70
Elgin Ave., Ashf. 99 BQ93
Elgin Ave., Har. 45 CH54
Elgin Cres. W11 75 CY73
Elgin Cres., Cat. 148 DU122
Elgin Cres., Houns. 85 BS82
Eastern Perimeter Rd.
Elgin Dr., Nthwd. 43 BS52
Elgin Est. W9 76 DA70
Elgin Ms. W11 75 CY72
Ladbroke Gro.
Elgin Ms. N. W9 76 DB69
Randolph Ave.
Elgin Ms. S. W9 76 DB69
Randolph Ave.
Elgin Rd. N22 49 DJ54
Elgin Rd., Croy. 120 DT103
Elgin Rd., Ilf. 67 ES60
Elgin Rd., Sutt. 118 DC104
Elgin Rd., Wall. 133 DJ107
Elgin Rd. (Cheshunt), Wal.Cr. 22 DW30
Elgin Rd., Wey. 126 BN106
Elgood Ave., Nthwd. 43 BT51
Elgood Clo. W11 75 CY73
Avondale Pk. Rd.
Elham Clo., Brom. 108 EK94
Elia Ms. N1 6 F1
Elia Ms. N1 77 DP68
Elia St. N1 6 F1
Elia St. N1 77 DP68
Elias Pl. SW8 91 DN79
Elibank Rd. SE9 95 EM84
Elim Est. SE1 11 M6
Elim Est. SE1 92 DR76
Elim Way E13 80 EF69
Eliot Bank SE23 106 DV89
Eliot Cotts. SE3 94 EE82
Eliot Pl.
Eliot Dr., Har. 58 CB61
Eliot Gdns. SW15 89 CU84
Eliot Hill SE13 93 EC82
Eliot Ms. NW8 76 DC68
Eliot Pk. SE13 93 EC82
Eliot Pl. SE3 94 EE82
Eliot Rd., Dag. 68 EX63
Eliot Vale SE3 93 ED82
Elizabeth Ave. N1 78 DQ66
Elizabeth Ave., Enf. 35 DP41
Elizabeth Ave., Ilf. 67 ER61
Elizabeth Ave., Stai. 98 BJ93
Elizabeth Blackwell Ho. N22 49 DN53
Progress Way
Elizabeth Bri. SW1 9 H9
Elizabeth Bri. SW1 91 DH77
Elizabeth Clo. E14 79 EB72
Grundy St.
Elizabeth Clo. W9 76 DC70
Randolph Ave.
Elizabeth Clo., Barn. 33 CX41
Elizabeth Clo., Rom. 55 FB53
Elizabeth Clo., Sutt. 131 CZ105
Sunningdale Rd.
Elizabeth Clyde Clo. N15 64 DS56
Elizabeth Cotts., Rich. 88 CM81
Elizabeth Ct. SW1 9 N7
Elizabeth Ct., Wat. 29 BT38
Elizabeth Dr., Epp. 39 ES36
Elizabeth Est. SE17 92 DR79
Elizabeth Fry Rd. E8 78 DV66
Lamb La.
Elizabeth Gdns. W3 75 CT74
Elizabeth Gdns., Stan. 45 CJ51
Elizabeth Gdns., Sun. 114 BW97
Elizabeth Ms. NW3 76 DF65
Elizabeth Pl. N15 64 DR56
Elizabeth Ride N9 50 DV45
Elizabeth Rd. E6 80 EK67
Elizabeth Rd. N15 64 DS57
Elizabeth Rd., Rain. 83 FH71
Elizabeth Sq. SE16 79 DY73
Rotherhithe St.
Elizabeth St. SW1 8 G8
Elizabeth St. SW1 90 DG77
Elizabeth Ter. SE9 109 EM86
Elizabeth Way SE19 106 DR94
Elizabeth Way, Felt. 100 BW91
Elizabeth Way, Orp. 124 EW99
Elizabethan Clo., Stai. 98 BK87
Elizabethan Way
Elizabethan Way, Stai. 98 BK87
Elkington Rd. E13 80 EH70
Elkins, The, Rom. 55 FE54
Elkstone Rd. W10 75 CZ71
Ella Rd. N8 63 DL59
Ellaline Rd. W6 89 CX79
Ellanby Cres. N18 50 DV49
Elland Rd. SE15 92 DW84
Elland Rd., Walt. 114 BX103
Ellement Clo., Pnr. 58 BX57
Ellen Clo., Brom. 122 EK97
Ellen Ct. N9 50 DW47
Densworth Gro.
Ellen St. E1 78 DU72
Ellen Webb Dr., Har. 59 CE55
Ellenborough Pl. SW15 89 CU84
Ellenborough Rd. N22 50 DQ53
Ellenborough Rd., Sid. 110 EX92
Ellenbridge Way, S.Croy. 134 DS109
Ellenbrook Clo., Wat. 29 BV39
Hatfield Rd.
Elleray Rd., Tedd. 101 CF93
Ellerby St. SW6 89 CX81
Ellerdale Clo. NW3 62 DC63
Ellerdale Rd.
Ellerdale Rd. NW3 62 DC64
Ellerdale St. SE13 93 EB84
Ellerdine Rd., Houns. 87 CD84
Ellerker Gdns., Rich. 102 CL85
Ellerman Ave., Twick. 100 BZ88
Ellerslie Gdns. NW10 75 CU67
Ellerslie Rd. W12 75 CV74
Ellerslie Sq. Ind. Est. SW2 91 DL84
Ellerton Gdns., Dag. 82 EW66
Ellerton Rd. SW13 89 CU81
Ellerton Rd. SW18 104 DD88
Ellerton Rd. SW20 103 CU94
Ellerton Rd., Dag. 82 EW66
Ellerton Rd., Surb. 116 CM103
Ellery Rd. SE19 106 DR94
Ellery St. SE15 92 DV82
Ellesborough Clo., Wat. 44 BW50
Ellesmere Ave. NW7 46 CR48
Ellesmere Ave., Beck. 121 EB96
Ellesmere Clo. E11 66 EF57
Ellesmere Clo., Ruis. 57 BQ59
Ellesmere Dr., S.Croy. 134 DV114
Ellesmere Gdns., Ilf. 66 EL57
Ellesmere Gro., Barn. 33 CZ43
Ellesmere Rd. E3 79 DY68
Ellesmere Rd. NW10 61 CU64
Ellesmere Rd. W4 88 CR79
Ellesmere Rd., Grnf. 72 CC70
Ellesmere Rd., Twick. 101 CJ86
Ellesmere Rd., Wey. 127 BS108
Ellesmere St. E14 79 EB72
Ellingfort Rd. E8 78 DV66
Ellingham Rd. E15 65 ED63
Ellingham Rd. W12 89 CU75
Ellingham Rd., Chess. 129 CK107
Ellington Rd. N10 63 DH56
Ellington Rd., Felt. 99 BT91
Ellington Rd., Houns. 86 CB82
Ellington St. N7 77 DN65
Ellington Way, Epsom 145 CV117
Elliot Clo. E15 80 EE66
Elliot Rd. NW4 61 CV58
Elliot Rd., Stan. 45 CG51
Elliott Ave., Ruis. 57 BV61
Elliott Clo., Wem. 60 CM62
Elliott Gdns., Rom. 55 FH53
Elliott Gdns., Shep. 112 BN98
Elliott Rd. SW9 91 DP80
Elliott Rd. W4 88 CS77
Elliott Rd., Brom. 122 EK98
Elliott Rd., Th.Hth. 119 DP98
Elliott Sq. NW3 76 DE66
Elliotts Clo., Uxb. 70 BJ71
Elliotts La., Sev. 152 EW124
Elliott's Pl. N1 77 DP67
St. Peters St.
Elliotts Row SE11 10 F8
Elliotts Row SE11 91 DP77
Ellis Ave., Rain. 83 FG71
Ellis Clo. SE9 109 EQ89
Ellis Clo., Couls. 147 DM120
Ellis Ct. W7 73 CF71
Ellis Ms. SE7 94 EJ79
Ellis Rd., Couls. 147 DM120
Ellis Rd., Mitch. 118 DF100
Ellis Rd., Sthl. 72 CC74
Ellis St. SW1 8 E8
Ellis St. SW1 90 DF77
Elliscombe Rd. SE7 94 EJ78
Ellisfield Dr. SW15 103 CT87
Ellison Gdns., Sthl. 86 BZ77
Ellison Rd. SW13 89 CT82
Ellison Rd. SW16 105 DK94
Ellison Rd., Sid. 109 ER88
Elliston Ho. SE18 95 EN77
Wellington St.
Ellmore Clo., Rom. 55 FH53
Ellora Rd. SW16 105 DK92
Ellsworth St. E2 78 DV69
Ellwood Ct. W9 76 DB70
Clearwell Dr.
Ellwood Gdns., Wat. 15 BV34
Elm Ave. W5 74 CL74
Elm Ave., Cars. 132 DF110
Elm Ave., Ruis. 57 BU60
Elm Ave., Wat. 44 BY45
Elm Bank N14 49 DL45
Elm Bank, Brom. 122 EK96
Elm Bank Gdns. SW13 88 CS82
Elm Clo. E11 66 EH58
Elm Clo. N19 63 DJ61
Hargrave Pk.
Elm Clo. NW4 61 CX57
Elm Clo. SW20 117 CW98
Grand Dr.
Elm Clo., Buck.H. 52 EK47
Elm Clo., Cars. 118 DF102
Elm Clo., Har. 58 CB58
Elm Clo., Hayes 71 BU72
Elm Clo., Lthd. 143 CH122
Elm Clo., Rom. 55 FB53
Elm Clo., S.Croy. 134 DS107
Elm Clo., Stai. 98 BK88
Elm Clo., Surb. 116 CQ101
Elm Clo., Twick. 100 CB89
Elm Clo., Wal.Abb. 23 ED34
Elm Clo., Warl. 149 DX117
Elm Clo. (Send Marsh), Wok. 140 BG124
Elm Ct. EC4 6 D10
Elm Ct., Mitch. 118 DF96
Armfield Cres.
Elm Ct., Sun. 99 BT94
Elm Cres. W5 74 CL74
Elm Cres., Kings.T. 116 CL95
Elm Cft., Sutt. 117 CX104
Elm Dr., Har. 58 CB58
Elm Dr., Lthd. 143 CH123
Elm Dr., Sun. 114 BW96
Elm Dr., Swan. 125 FD96
Elm Dr. (Cheshunt), Wal.Cr. 23 DY28
Elm Friars Wk. NW1 77 DK66
Maiden La.
Elm Gdns. N2 62 DC55
Elm Gdns., Enf. 36 DR38
Elm Gdns., Epp. 27 FB26
Elm Gdns., Epsom 145 CW119
Elm Gdns., Esher 129 CF107
Elm Gdns., Mitch. 119 DK98
Elm Grn. W3 74 CS72
Elm Gro. N8 63 DL58
Elm Gro. NW2 61 CX63
Elm Gro. SE15 92 DT82
Elm Gro. SW19 103 CY94
Elm Gro., Cat. 148 DS122
Elm Gro., Epsom 130 CQ114
Elm Gro., Erith 97 FD80
Elm Gro., Har. 58 CA59
Elm Gro., Kings.T. 116 CL95
Elm Gro., Orp. 123 ET102
Elm Gro., Sutt. 132 DB105
Elm Gro., Wat. 29 BU37
Elm Gro., West Dr. 70 BM73
Willow Ave.
Elm Gro., Wdf.Grn. 52 EF50
Elm Gro. Par., Wall. 118 DG104
Butter Hill
Elm Gro. Rd. SW13 89 CU82
Elm Gro. Rd. W5 88 CL75
Elm Gro. Rd., Cob. 142 BX116
Elm Hall Gdns. E11 66 EH58
Elm La. SE6 107 DZ89
Elm La., Wok. 140 BM118
Elm Lawn Clo., Uxb. 70 BL66
Park Rd.
Elm Ms., Rich. 102 CM86
Grove Rd.
Elm Pk. SW2 105 DM86
Elm Pk., Stan. 45 CH50
Elm Pk. Ave. N15 64 DT57
Elm Pk. Ave., Horn. 69 FG63
Elm Pk. Ct., Pnr. 58 BW55
Elm Pk. Gdns. NW4 61 CX57
Elm Pk. Gdns. SW10 90 DD78
Elm Pk. La. SW3 90 DD78
Elm Pk. Mans. SW10 90 DC79
Park Wk.
Elm Pk. Rd. E10 65 DY60
Elm Pk. Rd. N3 47 CZ52
Elm Pk. Rd. N21 50 DQ45
Elm Pk. Rd. SE25 120 DT97
Elm Pk. Rd. SW3 90 DD79
Elm Pk. Rd., Pnr. 44 BW54
Elm Pl. SW7 90 DD78
Elm Quay Ct. SW8 91 DK79
Elm Rd. E7 80 EF65
Elm Rd. E11 65 ED61
Elm Rd. E17 65 EC57
Elm Rd. N22 49 DP53
Granville Rd.
Elm Rd. SW14 88 CQ83
Elm Rd., Barn. 33 CZ42
Elm Rd., Beck. 121 DZ96
Elm Rd., Chess. 130 CL105
Elm Rd., Epsom 131 CT107
Elm Rd., Erith 97 FG81
Elm Rd., Esher 129 CF107
Elm Rd., Felt. 99 BR88
Elm Rd., Kings.T. 116 CM95
Elm Rd., Lthd. 143 CH122
Elm Rd., N.Mal. 116 CR97
Elm Rd., Orp. 138 EU108
Elm Rd., Pur. 133 DP113
Elm Rd., Rom. 55 FB54
Elm Rd., Sid. 110 EU91
Elm Rd., Th.Hth. 120 DR98
Elm Rd., Wall. 118 DG102
Elm Rd., Warl. 149 DX117
Elm Rd., Wem. 60 CL64
Elm Rd. W., Sutt. 117 CZ101
Elm Row NW3 62 DC62
Elm St. WC1 6 C5
Elm St. WC1 77 DM70
Elm Ter. NW2 62 DA62
Elm Ter. NW3 62 DE63
Constantine Rd.
Elm Ter. SE9 109 EN86
Elm Ter., Har. 45 CD53
Elm Tree Ave., Esher 115 CD101
Elm Tree Clo. NW8 76 DD69
Elm Tree Clo., Ashf. 99 BP92
Convent Rd.
Elm Tree Clo., Nthlt. 72 BZ68
Elm Tree Rd. NW8 76 DD69
Elm Wk. NW3 62 DA61
Elm Wk. SW20 117 CW98
Elm Wk., Orp. 123 EM104
Elm Wk., Rad. 31 CF36
Elm Wk., Rom. 69 FG55
Elm Way N11 48 DG51
Elm Way NW10 60 CS63
Elm Way, Epsom 130 CR106
Elm Way, Rick. 42 BH46
Elm Way, Wor.Pk. 117 CW104
Elmar Rd. N15 64 DR56
Elmbank Ave., Barn. 33 CW42
Elmbank Way W7 73 CD71
Elmbourne Dr., Belv. 97 FB77
Elmbourne Rd. SW17 104 DG90
Elmbridge Ave., Surb. 116 CP99
Elmbridge Clo., Ruis. 57 BU58
Elmbridge Dr., Ruis. 57 BT57
Elmbridge Rd., Ilf. 54 EU51
Elmbridge Wk. E8 78 DU66
Wilman Gro.
Elmbrook Clo., Sun. 113 BV95
Elmbrook Gdns. SE9 94 EL84
Elmbrook Rd., Sutt. 131 CZ105
Elmcote Way, Rick. 28 BM44
Elmcourt Rd. SE27 105 DP89
Elmcroft, Lthd. 142 CA124
Elmcroft Ave. E11 66 EH57
Elmcroft Ave. N9 36 DV44
Elmcroft Ave. NW11 61 CZ59
Elmcroft Ave., Sid. 109 ET87
Elmcroft Clo. E11 66 EH56
Elmcroft Clo. N8 63 DM57
Elmcroft Clo. W5 73 CK72
Elmcroft Clo., Chess. 116 CL104
Elmcroft Clo., Felt. 99 BT86
Elmcroft Cres. NW11 61 CX59
Elmcroft Cres., Har. 58 CA55
Elmcroft Dr., Ashf. 98 BN92
Elmcroft Dr., Chess. 116 CL104
Elmcroft Gdns. NW9 60 CN57
Elmcroft Rd., Orp. 124 EU101
Elmcroft St. E5 64 DW63
Elmdale Rd. N13 49 DM50
Elmdene, Surb. 116 CQ102
Elmdene Clo., Beck. 121 DZ99
Elmdene Rd. SE18 95 EP78
Elmdon Rd., Houns. 86 BX82
Elmdon Rd. (Hatton Cross), Houns. 85 BT83
Elmer Ave., Rom. (Havering-atte-Bower) 55 FE48
Elmer Clo., Enf. 35 DM41
Elmer Cotts., Lthd. 143 CG123
Elmer Gdns., Edg. 46 CP52
Elmer Gdns., Islw. 87 CD83
Elmer Gdns., Rain. 83 FG66
Elmer Ms., Lthd. 143 CG122
Elmer Rd. SE6 107 EC87
Elmers Dr., Tedd. 101 CH93
Kingston Rd.
Elmers End Rd. SE20 120 DW96
Elmers End Rd., Beck. 120 DW96
Elmers Rd. SE25 120 DU101
Elmerside Rd., Beck. 121 DY98
Elmfield, Lthd. 142 CA123
Elmfield Ave. N8 63 DL57
Elmfield Ave., Mitch. 118 DG95
Elmfield Ave., Tedd. 101 CF92
Elmfield Clo., Har. 59 CE61
Elmfield Clo., Pot.B. 19 CY33
Elmfield Pk., Brom. 122 EG97
Elmfield Rd. E4 51 EC47
Elmfield Rd. E17 65 DX57
Elmfield Rd. N2 62 DD55
Elmfield Rd. SW17 104 DG89
Elmfield Rd., Brom. 122 EG97
Elmfield Rd., Pot.B. 19 CY32
Elmfield Rd., Sthl. 86 BY76
Elmfield Way W9 76 DA71
Elmfield Way, S.Croy. 134 DT109
Elmgate Ave., Felt. 99 BV90
Elmgate Gdns., Edg. 46 CR50
Elmgreen Clo. E15 80 EE67
Church St. N.
Elmgrove Cres., Har. 59 CF57
Elmgrove Gdns., Har. 59 CG57
Elmgrove Rd., Croy. 120 DV101
Elmgrove Rd., Har. 59 CF57
Elmgrove Rd., Wey. 126 BN105
Elmhurst, Belv. 96 EY79
Elmhurst Ave. N2 62 DD55
Elmhurst Ave., Mitch. 104 DG94
Elmhurst Dr. E18 52 EG54
Elmhurst Gdns. E18 52 EH53
Elmhurst Rd. E7 80 EH66
Elmhurst Rd. N17 50 DS54
Elmhurst Rd. SE9 108 EL89
Elmhurst Rd., Enf. 36 DW37
Elmhurst St. SW4 91 DK83
Elmhurst Way, Loug. 53 EM45
Elmington Clo., Bex. 111 FB86
Elmington Est. SE5 92 DR80
Elmington Rd. SE5 92 DR81
Elmira St. SE13 93 EB83
Elmlea Dr., Hayes 71 BS71
Grange Rd.
Elmlee Clo., Chis. 109 EM93
Elmley Clo. E6 80 EL71
Northumberland Rd.
Elmley St. SE18 95 ER77
Elmore Clo., Wem. 74 CL68
Elmore Rd. E11 65 EC62
Elmore Rd., Couls. 146 DF121
Elmore Rd., Enf. 37 DX38
Elmore St. N1 78 DR66
Elmores, Loug. 39 EN41
Elmpark Gdns., S.Croy. 134 DW110
Elmroyd Ave., Pot.B. 19 CZ33
Elmroyd Clo., Pot.B. 19 CZ33
Elms, The SW13 89 CT83
Elms Ave. N10 63 DH55
Elms Ave. NW4 61 CX57
Elms Ct., Wem. 59 CG63
Elms Cres. SW4 105 DJ86
Elms Gdns., Dag. 68 EZ63
Elms Gdns., Wem. 59 CG63
Elms La., Wem. 59 CG62
Elms Ms. W2 76 DD73
Elms Pk. Ave., Wem. 59 CG63
Elms Rd. SW4 105 DJ85
Elms Rd., Har. 45 CE52
Elms Wk. SE3 94 EF84
Elmscott Gdns. N21 36 DQ44
Elmscott Rd., Brom. 108 EE92
Elmscroft N8 63 DM57
Tottenham La.
Elmscroft Gdns., Pot.B. 19 CZ32
Elmsdale Rd. E17 65 DZ56
Elmshaw Rd. SW15 103 CU85
Elmshorn, Epsom 145 CW116
Elmshurst Cres. N2 62 DC56
Elmside, Croy. 135 EB107
Elmside Rd., Wem. 60 CN62
Elmsleigh Ave., Har. 59 CH56
Elmsleigh Rd., Twick. 101 CD89
Elmslie Clo., Epsom 130 CQ114
Elmslie Clo., Wdf.Grn. 53 EM51
Gwynne Pk. Ave.
Elmslie Pt. E3 79 DZ71
Ackroyd Dr.
Elmstead Ave., Chis. 109 EM92
Elmstead Ave., Wem. 60 CL60
Elmstead Clo. N20 48 DA47
Elmstead Clo., Epsom 130 CS106
Elmstead Clo., Sev. 154 FE122
Elmstead Cres., Well. 96 EW79
Elmstead Gdns., Wor.Pk. 117 CU104
Elmstead Glade, Chis. 109 EM93
Elmstead La., Chis. 108 EL94
Elmstead Rd., Erith 97 FE81
Elmstead Rd., Ilf. 67 ES61
Elmstead Rd., W.Byf. 126 BG113
Elmstone Rd. SW6 90 DA81
Elmsway, Ashf. 98 BM92
Elmswood, Lthd. 142 BZ124
Elmsworth Ave., Houns. 86 CB82
Elmton Way E5 64 DU62
Rendlesham Rd.
Elmtree Clo., W.Byf. 126 BL113
Elmtree Rd., Tedd. 101 CE91
Elmwood Ave. N13 49 DL50
Elmwood Ave., Borwd. 32 CP42
Elmwood Ave., Felt. 99 BU89
Elmwood Ave., Har. 59 CG57
Elmwood Clo., Ash. 143 CK117
Elmwood Clo., Epsom 131 CU108
Elmwood Clo., Wall. 118 DG103
Elmwood Ct., Ash. 143 CK117
Elmwood Clo.

Elmwood Ct., Wem. 59 CG62
Elmwood Cres. NW9 60 CQ56
Elmwood Dr., Bex. 110 EY87
Elmwood Dr., Epsom 131 CU107
Elmwood Gdns. W7 73 CE72
Elmwood Rd. SE24 106 DR85
Elmwood Rd. W4 88 CQ79
Elmwood Rd., Croy. 119 DP101
Elmwood Rd., Mitch. 118 DF97
Elmworth Gro. SE21 106 DR89
Elnathan Ms. W9 76 DB70
Shirland Rd.
Elphinstone Rd. E17 51 DZ54
Elphinstone St. N5 63 DP63
Avenell Rd.
Elrick Clo., Erith 97 FE79
Elrington Rd. E8 78 DU65
Elrington Rd., Wdf.Grn. 52 EG50
Elruge Clo., West Dr. 84 BK76
Elsa Rd., Well. 96 EV82
Elsa St. E1 79 DY71
Elsdale St. E9 78 DW65
Elsden Ms. E2 78 DW68
Old Ford Rd.
Elsden Rd. N17 50 DT53
Elsenham Rd. E12 67 EN64
Elsenham St. SW18 103 CZ88
Elsham Rd. E11 66 EE62
Elsham Rd. W14 89 CY75
Elsham Ter. W14 89 CY75
Elsie Rd. SE22 92 DT84
Elsiedene Rd. N21 50 DQ45
Elsiemaud Rd. SE4 107 DZ85
Elsinge Rd., Enf. 36 DV36
Elsinore Ave., Stai. 98 BL87
Elsinore Gdns. NW2 61 CY62
Elsinore Rd. SE23 107 DY88
Elsinore Way, Rich. 88 CP83
Lower Richmond Rd.
Elsley Rd. SW11 90 DF83
Elspeth Rd. SW11 90 DF84
Elspeth Rd., Wem. 60 CL64
Elsrick Ave., Mord. 118 DA99
Chalgrove Ave.
Elstan Way, Croy. 121 DY101
Elsted St. SE17 11 L9
Elsted St. SE17 92 DR77
Elston La., Sev. 153 FF117
Elstow Clo. SE9 109 EN85
Elstow Clo., Ruis. 58 BX59
Elstow Gdns., Dag. 82 EY67
Elstow Rd., Dag. 82 EY66
Elstree Gdns. N9 50 DV46
Elstree Gdns., Belv. 96 EY77
Elstree Gdns., Ilf. 67 EQ64
Elstree Hill, Brom. 108 EE94
Elstree Hill N., Borwd. 31 CK44
Elstree Hill S., Borwd. 45 CJ45
Elstree Rd., Borwd. 31 CH44
Elstree Rd. (Bushey), Wat. 45 CD45
Elstree Way, Borwd. 32 CP41
Elswick Rd. SE13 93 EB82
Elswick St. SW6 90 DC82
Elsworth Clo., Felt. 99 BS88
Elsworthy, T.Ditt. 115 CE100
Elsworthy Ri. NW3 76 DE66
Elsworthy Rd. NW3 76 DD67
Elsworthy Ter. NW3 76 DE66
Elsynge Rd. SW18 104 DD85
Eltham Grn. SE9 108 EJ85
Eltham Grn. Rd. SE9 94 EJ84
Eltham High St. SE9 109 EM86
Eltham Hill SE9 108 EK85
Eltham Palace Rd. SE9 108 EJ86
Eltham Pk. Gdns. SE9 95 EN84
Eltham Rd. SE9 108 EJ85
Eltham Rd. SE12 108 EG85
Elthiron Rd. SW6 90 DA81
Elthorne Ave. W7 87 CF75
Elthorne Ct., Felt. 100 BW88
Elthorne Pk. Rd. W7 87 CF75
Elthorne Rd. N19 63 DK61
Elthorne Rd. NW9 60 CR59
Elthorne Rd., Uxb. 70 BK68
Elthorne Way NW9 60 CR58
Elthruda Rd. SE13 107 ED86
Eltisley Rd., Ilf. 67 EP63
Elton Ave., Barn. 33 CZ43
Elton Ave., Grnf. 73 CE65
Elton Ave., Wem. 59 CH64
Elton Clo., Kings.T. 101 CJ94
Elton Ho. E3 79 DZ67
Elton Pk., Wat. 29 BV40
Elton Pl. N16 64 DS64
Elton Rd., Kings.T. 116 CM95
Elton Rd., Pur. 133 DJ112
Elton Way (Bushey), Wat. 30 CB40
Eltringham St. SW18 90 DC84
Elvaston Ms. SW7 90 DC76
Elvaston Pl. SW7 90 DC76
Elveden Clo., Wok. 140 BH117
Elveden Pl. NW10 74 CN68
Elveden Rd. NW10 74 CN68
Elvedon Rd., Cob. 127 BV111
Elvendon Rd. N13 49 DL51
Elver Gdns. E2 78 DU68
St. Peter's Clo.
Elverson Rd. SE8 93 EB82
Elverton St. SW1 9 M8
Elverton St. SW1 91 DK77
Elvington Grn., Brom. 122 EF99
Elvington La. NW9 46 CS53
Elvino Rd. SE26 107 DX92
Elvis Rd. NW2 75 CW65
Elwill Way, Beck. 121 EC98
Elwin St. E2 78 DU69
Elwood St. N5 63 DP62
Elwyn Gdns. SE12 108 EG87
Ely Clo., Erith 97 FF82
Ely Clo., N.Mal. 117 CT96
Ely Ct. EC1 6 E7
Ely Gdns., Borwd. 32 CR43
Ely Gdns., Dag. 69 FC62
Ely Gdns., Ilf. 66 EL59
Canterbury Ave.
Ely Pl. EC1 6 E7
Ely Pl., Wdf.Grn. 53 EN51
Ely Rd. E10 65 EC59
Ely Rd., Croy. 120 DR99
Ely Rd. 85 BT82
(Heathrow Airport), Houns.
Eastern Perimeter Rd.
Ely Rd. (Hounslow W.), 86 BW83
Houns.
Elyne Rd. N4 63 DN58
Elysian Ave., Orp. 123 ES100
Elysium Pl. SW6 89 CZ82
Fulham Pk. Gdns.
Elysium St. SW6 89 CZ82
Fulham Pk. Gdns.
Elystan Clo., Wall. 133 DH109
Elystan Pl. SW3 8 C10
Elystan Pl. SW3 90 DE78
Elystan St. SW3 8 B9
Elystan St. SW3 90 DE77
Elystan Wk. N1 77 DN67
Cloudesley Rd.
Emanuel Ave. W3 74 CQ72
Emanuel Dr., Hmptn. 100 BZ92
Emba St. SE16 92 DU75
Embankment SW15 89 CX82
Embankment, The, 101 CG88
Twick.
Embankment Gdns. SW3 90 DF79
Embankment Pl. WC2 10 A2
Embankment Pl. WC2 77 DL74
Embassy Ct., Sid. 110 EV90
Embassy Ct., Well. 96 EV83
Ember Clo., Add. 126 BK106
Ember Clo., Orp. 123 EQ101
Ember Fm. Ave., E.Mol. 115 CD100
Ember Fm. Way, E.Mol. 115 CD100
Ember Gdns., T.Ditt. 115 CE101
Ember La., E.Mol. 115 CD100
Ember La., Esher 115 CD101
Embercourt Rd., T.Ditt. 115 CE100
Emberson Way, Epp. 27 FC26
Emberton SE5 92 DS79
Albany Rd.
Embleton Rd. SE13 93 EB84
Embleton Rd., Wat. 43 BU48
Embleton Wk., Hmptn. 100 BZ93
Fearnley Cres.
Embley Pt. E5 64 DV63
Tiger Way
Embry Clo., Stan. 45 CG49
Embry Dr., Stan. 45 CG51
Embry Way, Stan. 45 CG49
Emden Clo., West Dr. 84 BN75
Emden St. SW6 90 DB81
Emerald Clo. E16 80 EL72
Emerald Gdns., Dag. 68 FA60
Emerald St. WC1 6 B6
Emerald St. WC1 77 DM71
Emerson Gdns., Har. 60 CM58
Emerson Rd., Ilf. 67 EN59
Emerson St. SE1 11 H2
Emerson St. SE1 78 DQ74
Emersons Ave., Swan. 111 FF94
Emerton Clo., Bexh. 96 EY84
Emerton Rd., Lthd. 142 CC120
Emery Hill St. SW1 9 L7
Emery Hill St. SW1 91 DJ76
Emery St. SE1 10 E6
Emes Rd., Erith 97 FC80
Emily Jackson Clo., Sev. 155 FH124
Emily Pl. N7 63 DN63
Emley Rd., Add. 112 BG104
Emlyn Gdns. W12 88 CS75
Emlyn La., Lthd. 143 CG122
Emlyn Rd. W12 88 CS75
Emma Rd. E13 80 EF68
Emma St. E2 78 DV68
Emmanuel Clo., Nthwd. 43 BT52
Emmanuel Rd.
Emmanuel Lo., Wal.Cr. 22 DW30
College Rd.
Emmanuel Rd. SW12 105 DJ88
Emmanuel Rd., Nthwd. 43 BT52
Emmaus Way, Chig. 53 EN50
Emmott Ave., Ilf. 67 EQ57
Emmott Clo. E1 79 DY70
Emmott Clo. NW11 62 DC58
Emms Pas., Kings.T. 115 CK96
High St.
Emperor's Gate SW7 90 DB76
Empire Ave. N18 50 DQ50
Empire Cen., Wat. 30 BW39
Empire Ct., Wem. 60 CP62
Empire Rd., Grnf. 73 CH67
Empire Way, Wem. 60 CM63
Empire Wf. Rd. E14 93 ED77
Empire Yd. N7 63 DL62
Holloway Rd.
Empress Ave. E4 51 EB52
Empress Ave. E12 66 EJ61
Empress Ave., Ilf. 67 EM61
Empress Ave., Wdf.Grn. 52 EF52
Empress Dr., Chis. 109 EP93
Empress Pl. SW6 90 DA78
Empress St. SE17 92 DQ79
Empson St. E3 79 EB70
Emsworth Clo. N9 50 DW46
Emsworth Rd., Ilf. 53 EP54
Emsworth St. SW2 105 DL89
Emu Rd. SW8 91 DH82
Ena Rd. SW16 119 DL97
Enbrook St. W10 75 CY69
End Way, Surb. 116 CN101
Endale Clo., Cars. 118 DF103
Endeavour Rd. 23 DY27
(Cheshunt), Wal.Cr.
Endeavour Way SW19 104 DB91
Endeavour Way, Bark. 82 EU68
Endeavour Way, Croy. 119 DK101
Endell St. WC2 5 P8
Endell St. WC2 77 DL72
Enderby St. SE10 94 EE78
Enderley Clo., Har. 45 CE53
Enderley Rd., Har. 45 CE53
Endersby Rd., Barn. 33 CW43
Endersleigh Gdns. NW4 61 CU56
Endlebury Rd. E4 51 EC47
Endlesham Rd. SW12 104 DG87
Endsleigh Clo., S.Croy. 134 DW110
Endsleigh Gdns. WC1 5 M4
Endsleigh Gdns. WC1 77 DK70
Endsleigh Gdns., Ilf. 67 EM61
Endsleigh Gdns., Surb. 115 CJ100
Endsleigh Gdns., Walt. 128 BW106
Endsleigh Pl. WC1 5 N4
Endsleigh Pl. WC1 77 DK70
Endsleigh Rd. W13 73 CG73
Endsleigh Rd., Sthl. 86 BY77
Endsleigh St. WC1 5 N4
Endsleigh St. WC1 77 DK70
Endwell Rd. SE4 93 DY82
Endymion Rd. N4 63 DN59
Endymion Rd. SW2 105 DM86
Enfield Clo., Uxb. 70 BK68
Villier St.
Enfield Retail Pk., Enf. 36 DU41
Crown Rd.
Enfield Rd. N1 78 DS66
Enfield Rd. W3 88 CP75
Enfield Rd., Brent. 87 CK78
Enfield Rd., Enf. 35 DL42
Enfield Rd., Houns. 85 BS82
Eastern Perimeter Rd.
Enfield Wk., Brent. 87 CK78
Enfield Rd.
Enford St. W1 4 D6
Enford St. W1 76 DF71
Engadine Clo., Croy. 120 DT104
Engadine St. SW18 103 CZ88
Engate St. SE13 93 EC84
Engel Pk. NW7 47 CW51
Engineer Clo. SE18 95 EN79
Engineers Way, Wem. 60 CN63
Englands La. NW3 76 DF65
Englands La., Loug. 39 EN40
Englefield Clo., Croy. 120 DQ100
Queen's Rd.
Englefield Clo., Enf. 35 DN40
Englefield Clo., Orp. 123 ET98
Englefield Cres., Orp. 123 ET98
Englefield Path, Orp. 124 EU98
Englefield Rd. N1 78 DR66
Englefield Rd., Orp. 124 EU98
Engleheart Dr., Felt. 99 BT86
Engleheart Rd. SE6 107 EB87
Englewood Rd. SW12 105 DH86
English Grds. SE1 11 M3
English St. E3 79 DZ70
Enid Clo., St.Alb. 16 BZ31
Enid St. SE16 92 DT76
Enmore Ave. SE25 120 DU99
Enmore Gdns. SW14 102 CR85
Enmore Rd. SE25 120 DU99
Enmore Rd. SW15 89 CW84
Enmore Rd., Sthl. 72 CA70
Ennerdale Ave., Horn. 69 FG64
Ennerdale Ave., Stan. 59 CJ55
Ennerdale Clo., Felt. 99 BT88
Ennerdale Clo. (Cheam), 131 CZ105
Sutt.
Ennerdale Dr. NW9 60 CS57
Ennerdale Gdns., Wem. 59 CJ60
Ennerdale Ho. E3 79 DZ70
Ennerdale Rd., Bexh. 96 FA81
Ennerdale Rd., Rich. 88 CM82
Ennersdale Rd. SE13 107 ED85
Ennis Rd. N4 63 DN60
Ennis Rd. SE18 95 EQ79
Ennismore Ave. W4 89 CT77
Ennismore Ave., Grnf. 73 CE65
Ennismore Gdns. SW7 8 B6
Ennismore Gdns. SW7 90 DE75
Ennismore Gdns., T.Ditt. 115 CE100
Ennismore Gdns. Ms. 8 B6
SW7
Ennismore Gdns. Ms. 90 DE76
SW7
Ennismore Ms. SW7 8 B6
Ennismore Ms. SW7 90 DE76
Ennismore St. SW7 8 B6
Ennismore St. SW7 90 DE76
Ensign Clo., Pur. 133 DN110
Ensign Clo., Stai. 98 BL88
Ensign Dr. N13 50 DQ48
Ensign St. E1 78 DU73
Ensign Way, Stai. 98 BK88
Enslin Rd. SE9 109 EN87
Ensor Ms. SW7 90 DD78
Cranley Gdns.
Enstone Rd., Enf. 37 DY41
Enstone Rd., Uxb. 56 BM62
Enterprise Clo., Croy. 119 DN102
Enterprise Way NW10 75 CU69
Enterprise Way SW18 90 DA84
Enterprise Way, Tedd. 101 CF92
Enterprize Way SE8 93 DZ77
Epirus Ms. SW6 90 DA80
Epirus Rd.
Epirus Rd. SW6 89 CZ80
Epping Clo. E14 93 EA77
Epping Clo., Rom. 69 FB55
Epping Glade E4 37 EC44
Epping La., Rom. 40 EV40
Epping New Rd., Buck.H. 52 EG48
Epping New Rd., Loug. 38 EJ41
Epping Pl. N1 77 DN65
Liverpool Rd.
Epping Rd., Epp. 39 EM35
Epping Rd. (Epping Grn.), 25 ER26
Epp.
Epping Rd., Epp. 26 EW28
(North Weald Bassett)
Epping Rd. (Toot Hill), 27 FC30
Ong.
Epping Way E4 37 EB44
Epple Rd. SW6 89 CZ81
Epsom Clo., Bexh. 97 FB83
Epsom Clo., Nthlt. 58 BZ64
Epsom Downs, Epsom 145 CT118
Epsom Gap, Lthd. 143 CH115
Kingston Rd.
Epsom La. N., Epsom 145 CV118
Epsom La. S., Tad. 145 CW121
Epsom Rd. E10 65 EC58
Epsom Rd., Ash. 144 CM118
Epsom Rd., Croy. 133 DN105
Epsom Rd., Epsom 131 CT111
Epsom Rd., Ilf. 67 ET58
Epsom Rd., Lthd. 143 CH121
Epsom Rd., Mord. 118 DA100
Epsom Rd., Sutt. 117 CZ101
Epsom Sq., Houns. 85 BT82
Eastern Perimeter Rd.
Epstein Rd. SE28 82 EU74
Epworth Rd., Islw. 87 CH81
Epworth St. EC2 7 L5
Epworth St. EC2 78 DR70
Equity Sq. E2 78 DT69
Shacklewell St.
Erasmus St. SW1 9 N9
Erasmus St. SW1 91 DK77
Erconwald St. W12 75 CT72
Eresby Dr., Beck. 121 EA102
Eresby Pl. NW6 76 DA66
Eric Clo. E7 66 EG63
Eric Rd. E7 66 EG63
Eric Rd. NW10 75 CT65
Church Rd.
Eric Rd., Rom. 68 EX59
Eric Steele Ho., St.Alb. 16 CB27
Eric St. E3 79 DZ70
Erica Ct., Swan. 125 FE98
Azalea Dr.
Erica Gdns., Croy. 121 EA104
Erica St. W12 75 CU73
Ericcson Clo. SW18 104 DA85
Eridge Grn. Clo., Orp. 124 EW102
Petten Gro.
Eridge Rd. W4 88 CR76
Erin Clo., Brom. 108 EE94
Erindale SE18 95 ER79
Erindale Ter. SE18 95 ER79
Eriswell Cres., Walt. 127 BS107
Eriswell Rd., Walt. 127 BT105
Erith Cres., Rom. 55 FC53
Erith High St., Erith 97 FE78
Erith Rd., Belv. 96 FA78
Erith Rd., Bexh. 97 FB84
Erith Rd., Erith 97 FC81
Erlanger Rd. SE14 93 DX81
Erlesmere Gdns. W13 87 CG76
Ermine Clo., Houns. 86 BW82
Ermine Clo. (Cheshunt), 22 DV31
Wal.Cr.
Ermine Ho. N17 50 DT52
Ermine Rd. N15 64 DT58
Ermine Rd. SE13 93 EB84
Ermine Side, Enf. 36 DU43
Ermington Rd. SE9 109 EQ89
Ermyn Clo., Lthd. 143 CK121
Ermyn Way, Lthd. 143 CK121
Ernald Ave. E6 80 EL68
Erncroft Way, Twick. 101 CF86
Ernest Ave. SE27 105 DP91
Ernest Clo., Beck. 121 EA99
Ernest Gdns. W4 88 CP79
Ernest Gro., Beck. 121 DZ99
Ernest Rd., Kings.T. 116 CP96
Ernest Sq., Kings.T. 116 CP96
Ernest St. E1 79 DX70
Ernle Rd. SW20 103 CV94
Ernshaw Pl. SW15 103 CY85
Carlton Dr.
Erpingham Rd. SW15 89 CW83
Erridge Rd. SW19 118 DA96
Errington Rd. W9 75 CZ70
Errol Gdns., Hayes 71 BV70
Errol Gdns., N.Mal. 117 CU98
Errol St. EC1 7 J5
Errol St. EC1 78 DQ70
Erroll Rd., Rom. 69 FF56
Erskine Clo., Sutt. 118 DE104
Erskine Cres. N17 64 DV56
Erskine Hill NW11 62 DA57
Erskine Ms. NW3 76 DF66
Erskine Rd.
Erskine Rd. E17 65 DZ56
Erskine Rd. NW3 76 DF66
Erskine Rd., Sutt. 132 DD105
Erskine Rd., Wat. 44 BW48
Erwood Rd. SE7 94 EL78
Esam Way SW16 105 DN92
Escot Way, Barn. 33 CW43
Escott Gdns. SE9 108 EL91
Escreet Gro. SE18 95 EN77
Esher Ave., Rom. 69 FC58
Esher Ave., Sutt. 117 CX104
Esher Ave., Walt. 113 BU100
Esher Bypass, Chess. 129 CJ105
Esher Bypass, Cob. 127 BU112
Esher Bypass, Esher 129 CH108
Esher Clo., Bex. 110 EY88
Esher Clo., Esher 128 CB106
Esher Cres., Houns. 85 BS82
Eastern Perimeter Rd.
Esher Gdns. SW19 103 CX89
Esher Grn., Esher 128 CB105
Esher Ms., Mitch. 118 DF97
Esher Pk. Ave., Esher 128 CC105
Esher Pl. Ave., Esher 128 CA105
Esher Rd., E.Mol. 115 CD100
Esher Rd., Ilf. 67 ES62
Esher Rd., Walt. 128 BX106
Esk Rd. E13 80 EG70
Esk Way, Rom. 55 FD52
Eskdale, St.Alb. 18 CM27
Eskdale Ave., Nthlt. 72 BZ67
Eskdale Clo., Wem. 59 CK61
Eskdale Gdns., Pur. 134 DR114
Eskdale Rd., Bexh. 96 FA82
Eskdale Rd., Uxb. 70 BH68
Eskmont Ridge SE19 106 DS94
Esmar Cres. NW9 61 CU59
Esme Ho. SW15 89 CT84
Ludovick Wk.
Esmeralda Rd. SE1 92 DU77
Esmond Clo., Rain. 83 FH66
Dawson Dr.
Esmond Rd. NW6 75 CZ67
Esmond Rd. W4 88 CR77
Esmond St. SW15 89 CY84
Esparto St. SW18 104 DB87
Essenden Rd., Belv. 96 FA78
Essenden Rd., S.Croy. 134 DS108
Essendene Clo., Cat. 148 DS123
Essendene Rd., Cat. 148 DS123
Essendine Rd. W9 76 DA69
Essex Ave., Islw. 87 CE83
Essex Clo. E17 65 DY56
Essex Clo., Add. 126 BJ105
Essex Clo., Mord. 117 CX101
Essex Clo., Rom. 69 FB56
Essex Clo., Ruis. 58 BX60
Essex Ct. EC4 6 D9
Essex Ct. SW13 89 CT82
Essex Gdns. N4 63 DP58
Essex Gro. SE19 106 DR93
Essex Ho. E14 79 EB72
Giraud St.
Essex La., Kings L. 15 BR33
Essex Pk. N3 48 DB51
Essex Pk. Ms. W3 74 CS74
Essex Pl. W4 88 CQ77
Essex Rd. E4 52 EE46
Essex Rd. E10 65 EC58
Essex Rd. E12 66 EL64
Essex Rd. E17 65 DY58
Essex Rd. E18 52 EH54
Essex Rd. N1 77 DP67
Essex Rd. NW10 74 CS66
Essex Rd. W3 74 CQ73
Essex Rd. W4 88 CR77
Belmont Rd.
Essex Rd., Bark. 81 ER66
Essex Rd., Borwd. 32 CN41
Essex Rd., Dag. 69 FC64
Essex Rd., Enf. 36 DR42
Essex Rd., Rom. 68 FA56
Essex Rd. 68 EW59
(Chadwell Heath), Rom.
Essex Rd., Wat. 29 BU40
Essex Rd. S. E11 65 ED59
Essex St. E7 66 EG64
Essex St. WC2 6 D10
Essex Twr. SE20 120 DV95
Essex Vill. W8 90 DA75
Essex Way, Epp. 26 EV32
Essex Way, Ong. 27 FF29
Essex Wf. E5 64 DW61
Essian St. E1 79 DY71
Essoldo Way, Edg. 60 CM55
Estate Way E10 65 DZ60
Estcourt Rd. SE25 120 DV100
Estcourt Rd. SW6 89 CZ80
Estcourt Rd., Wat. 30 BW41
Este Rd. SW11 90 DE83
Estella Ave., N.Mal. 117 CV98
Estelle Rd. NW3 62 DF63
Esterbrooke St. SW1 9 M9
Esterbrooke St. SW1 91 DK77
Esther Clo. N21 49 DN45
Esther Rd. E11 66 EE59
Estoria Clo. SW2 105 DM87
Upper Tulse Hill
Estreham Rd. SW16 105 DK93
Estridge Clo., Houns. 86 CA84
Estuary Clo., Bark. 82 EV69
Eswyn Rd. SW17 104 DF91
Etchingham Pk. Rd. N3 48 DB52
Etchingham Rd. E15 65 EC63
Eternit Wk. SW6 89 CW81
Etfield Gro., Sid. 110 EV92
Ethel Rd. E16 80 EH72
Ethel Rd., Ashf. 98 BL92
Ethel St. SE17 11 J9
Ethel Ter., Orp. 138 EW109
Ethelbert Clo., Brom. 122 EG97
Ethelbert Gdns., Ilf. 67 EM57
Ethelbert Rd. SW20 117 CX95

Eth–Fai This index reads in the sequence: Street Name / Postal District or Post Town / Map Page Number / Grid Reference

Ethelbert Rd., Brom. 122 EG97
Ethelbert Rd., Erith 97 FC80
Ethelbert Rd., Orp. 124 EX97
Ethelbert St. SW12 105 DH88
Fernlea Rd.
Ethelburga St. SW11 90 DE81
Ethelden Rd. W12 75 CV74
Etheldene Ave. N10 63 DJ56
Ethelwine Pl., Abb.L. 15 BT30
The Cres.
Etheridge Grn., Loug. 39 EQ41
Etheridge Rd.
Etheridge Rd. NW2 61 CW59
Etheridge Rd., Loug. 39 EP40
Etherley Rd. N15 64 DQ57
Etherow St. SE22 106 DU86
Etherstone Grn. SW16 105 DN91
Etherstone Rd.
Etherstone Rd. SW16 105 DN91
Ethnard Rd. SE15 92 DV79
Ethronvi Rd., Bexh. 96 EY83
Etloe Rd. E10 65 EA61
Eton Ave. N12 48 DC52
Eton Ave. NW3 76 DD66
Eton Ave., Barn. 34 DE44
Eton Ave., Houns. 86 BZ79
Eton Ave., N.Mal. 116 CR99
Eton Ave., Wem. 59 CH64
Eton College Rd. NW3 76 DF65
Eton Ct. NW3 76 DD66
Eton Ave.
Eton Ct., Wem. 59 CJ63
Eton Ave.
Eton Garages NW3 76 DE65
Lambolle Pl.
Eton Gro. NW9 60 CN55
Eton Gro. SE13 94 EE83
Eton Hall NW3 76 DF65
Eton College Rd.
Eton Pl. NW3 76 DG66
Haverstock Hill
Eton Ri. NW3 76 DF65
Eton College Rd.
Eton Rd. NW3 76 DF66
Eton Rd., Hayes 85 BT80
Eton Rd., Ilf. 67 EQ64
Eton Rd., Orp. 138 EV105
Eton St., Rich. 102 CL85
Eton Vill. NW3 76 DF65
Etta St. SE8 93 DY79
Ettrick St. E14 79 EC72
Etwell Pl., Surb. 116 CM100
Eugenia Rd. SE16 92 DW77
Eureka Rd., Kings.T. 116 CN96
Washington Rd.
Europa Pl. EC1 7 H3
Europe Rd. SE18 95 EM76
Eustace Rd. E6 80 EL69
Eustace Rd. SW6 90 DA80
Eustace Rd., Rom. 68 EX59
Euston Ave., Wat. 29 BT43
Euston Cen. NW1 5 K4
Euston Gro. NW1 5 M3
Euston Gro. NW1 77 DK69
Euston Rd. N1 77 DH70
Euston Rd. NW1 5 J5
Euston Rd. NW1 77 DH70
Euston Rd., Croy. 119 DN102
Euston Sq. NW1 5 M3
Euston Sq. NW1 77 DK69
Euston Sta. Colonnade NW1 5 M3
Euston St. NW1 5 L3
Euston St. NW1 77 DJ69
Eva Rd., Rom. 68 EW59
Evandale Rd. SW9 91 DN82
Evangelist Rd. NW5 63 DH63
Evans Ave., Wat. 29 BT35
Evans Clo. E8 78 DT65
Buttermere Wk.
Evans Clo., Rick. 28 BN43
New Rd.
Evans Gro., Felt. 100 CA89
Evans Rd. SE6 108 EE89
Evansdale, Rain. 83 FF69
New Zealand Way
Evanston Ave. E4 51 EC52
Evanston Gdns., Ilf. 66 EL58
Eve Rd. E11 66 EE63
Eve Rd. E15 80 EE68
Eve Rd. N17 64 DS55
Eve Rd., Islw. 87 CG84
Evelina Rd. SE15 92 DW83
Evelina Rd. SE20 107 DX94
Eveline Lowe Est. SE16 92 DU76
Eveline Rd., Mitch. 118 DF95
Evelyn Ave. NW9 60 CR55
Evelyn Ave., Ruis. 57 BT59
Evelyn Clo., Twick. 100 CB87
Evelyn Ct. N1 7 K1
Evelyn Cres., Sun. 113 BT95
Evelyn Denington Rd. E6 81 EM71
Evelyn Dr., Pnr. 44 BX52
Evelyn Fox Ct. W10 75 CW71
Evelyn Gdns. SW7 90 DD78
Evelyn Gdns., Rich. 88 CL84
Kew Rd.
Evelyn Gro. W5 74 CM74
Evelyn Gro., Sthl. 72 BZ72
Evelyn Rd. E16 80 EH74
Evelyn Rd. E17 65 EC56
Evelyn Rd. SW19 104 DB92
Evelyn Rd. W4 88 CR76
Evelyn Rd., Barn. 34 DF42
Evelyn Rd., Rich. 88 CL83
Evelyn Rd. (Ham), Rich. 101 CJ90
Evelyn St. SE8 93 DY78
Evelyn Ter., Rich. 88 CL83
Evelyn Wk. N1 7 K1
Evelyn Wk. N1 78 DR68
Evelyn Way, Cob. 142 BZ116
Evelyn Way, Sun. 113 BT95
Evelyn Way, Wall. 133 DK105
Evelyn Yd. W1 5 M8
Evelyns Clo., Uxb. 70 BN72
Evening Hill, Beck. 107 EC94
Evenwood Clo. SW15 103 CY85
Everard Ave., Brom. 122 EG102
Everard La., Cat. 148 DU122
Tillingdown Hill
Everard Way, Wem. 60 CL62
Everatt Clo. SW18 103 CZ86
Amerland Rd.
Everdon Rd. SW13 89 CU79
Everest Pl. E14 79 EC71
Everest Pl., Swan. 125 FD98
Everest Rd. SE9 109 EM85
Everest Rd., Stai. 98 BK87
Everett Clo., Pnr. 57 BT55
Everett Clo., Wat. 45 CE46
Everett Wk., Belv. 96 EZ78
Osborne Rd.
Everglade, West. 150 EK118
Everglade Strand NW9 47 CT53
Evergreen Ct., Stai. 98 BK87
Evergreen Way, Hayes 71 BT73
Evergreen Way, Stai. 98 BK87
Everilda St. N1 77 DM67
Evering Rd. E5 64 DU62
Evering Rd. N16 64 DU62
Everington Rd. N10 48 DF54
Everington St. W6 89 CX79
Everitt Rd. NW10 74 CR69
Everleigh St. N4 63 DM60
Eversfield Gdns. NW7 46 CS51
Eversfield Rd., Rich. 88 CM82
Evershed Wk. W4 88 CR76
Eversholt St. NW1 77 DJ68
Evershot Rd. N4 63 DM60
Eversleigh Rd. E6 80 EK67
Eversleigh Rd. N3 47 CZ52
Eversleigh Rd. SW11 90 DF83
Eversleigh Rd., Barn. 34 DC43
Eversley Ave., Bexh. 97 FD82
Eversley Ave., Wem. 60 CN61
Eversley Clo. N21 35 DM44
Eversley Cres. N21 35 DM44
Eversley Cres., Islw. 87 CD81
Eversley Cres., Ruis. 57 BS61
Eversley Cross, Bexh. 97 FE82
Eversley Mt. N21 35 DM44
Eversley Pk. SW19 103 CV92
Eversley Pk. Rd. N21 35 DM44
Eversley Rd. SE7 94 EH79
Eversley Rd. SE19 106 DR94
Eversley Rd., Surb. 116 CM98
Eversley Way, Croy. 135 EA105
Everthorpe Rd. SE15 92 DT83
Everton Bldgs. NW1 5 K3
Everton Dr., Stan. 60 CM55
Everton Rd., Croy. 120 DU102
Evesham Ave. E17 51 EA54
Evesham Clo., Grnf. 72 CB68
Evesham Clo., Sutt. 132 DA108
Evesham Grn., Mord. 118 DB100
Evesham Rd. E15 80 EF66
Evesham Rd. N11 49 DJ50
Evesham Rd., Felt. 100 BW87
Sparrow Fm. Dr.
Evesham Rd., Mord. 118 DB100
Evesham St. W11 75 CX73
Evesham Wk. SE5 92 DR82
Love Wk.
Evesham Wk. SW9 91 DN82
Evesham Way SW11 90 DG83
Evesham Way, Ilf. 67 EN55
Evry Rd., Sid. 110 EW93
Ewald Rd. SW6 89 CZ82
Ewanrigg Ter., Wdf.Grn. 52 EJ50
Ewart Gro. N22 49 DN53
Ewart Pl. E3 79 DZ68
Ewart Rd. SE23 107 DX87
Ewe Clo. N7 77 DL65
Ewell Bypass, Epsom 131 CU107
Ewell Ct. Ave., Epsom 130 CS106
Ewell Downs Rd., Epsom 131 CU111
Ewell Ho. Gro., Epsom 131 CT110
Ewell Pk. Way, Epsom 131 CU107
Ewell Rd., Surb. 116 CL99
Ewell Rd. (Long Ditton), Surb. 115 CH101
Ewell Rd., Sutt. 131 CX108
Ewellhurst Rd., Ilf. 52 EL54
Ewelme Rd. SE23 106 DW88
Ewen Cres. SW2 105 DN87
Ewer St. SE1 11 H3
Ewer St. SE1 78 DQ74
Ewhurst Ave., S.Croy. 134 DT109
Ewhurst Clo., Sutt. 131 CW109
Ewhurst Ho. E1 78 DW71
Jamaica St.
Ewhurst Rd. SE4 107 DZ86
Exbury Rd. SE6 107 EA89
Excel Ct. WC2 9 N1
Excelsior Clo., Kings.T. 116 CN96
Washington Rd.
Excelsior Gdns. SE13 93 EC82
Exchange Arc. EC2 7 N6
Exchange Arc. EC2 78 DS71
Exchange Bldgs. E1 78 DS72
Cutler St.
Exchange Ct. WC2 10 A1
Exchange Pl. EC2 7 M6
Exchange Pl. EC2 78 DS71
Exchange Rd., Wat. 29 BV41
Exchange Sq. EC2 7 M6
Exchange Sq. EC2 78 DS71
Exchange St., Rom. 69 FE57
Exeforde Ave., Ashf. 98 BN91
Exeter Clo. E6 81 EM72
Harper Rd.
Exeter Clo., Wat. 30 BW40
Exeter Gdns., Ilf. 66 EL60
Exeter Ho. SW15 103 CW86
Putney Heath
Exeter Ms. NW6 76 DB65
West Hampstead Ms.
Exeter Rd. E16 80 EG71
Exeter Rd. E17 65 EA57
Exeter Rd. N9 50 DW47
Exeter Rd. N14 49 DH46
Exeter Rd. NW2 61 CY64
Exeter Rd. SE15 92 DT81
Exeter Rd., Croy. 120 DS101
Exeter Rd., Dag. 83 FB65
Exeter Rd., Enf. 37 DX41
Exeter Rd., Felt. 100 BZ90
Exeter Rd., Har. 58 BY61
Exeter Rd., Well. 95 ET82
Exeter St. WC2 6 A10
Exeter St. WC2 77 DL73
Exeter Way SE14 93 DZ80
Exford Gdns. SE12 108 EH88
Exford Rd. SE12 108 EH89
Exhibition Clo. W12 75 CW73
Exhibition Rd. SW7 8 A6
Exhibition Rd. SW7 90 DD75
Exmoor Clo., Ilf. 53 EQ53
Exmoor St. W10 75 CX71
Exmouth Mkt. EC1 6 D4
Exmouth Mkt. EC1 77 DN70
Exmouth Ms. NW1 5 L3
Exmouth Pl. E8 78 DV66
Exmouth Rd. E17 65 DZ57
Exmouth Rd., Brom. 122 EH97
Exmouth Rd., Hayes 71 BS69
Exmouth Rd., Ruis. 58 BW62
Exmouth Rd., Well. 96 EW81
Exmouth St. E1 78 DW72
Commercial Rd.
Exning Rd. E16 80 EF70
Exon St. SE17 11 M9
Exon St. SE17 92 DS77
Explorer Ave., Stai. 98 BL87
Explorer Dr., Wat. 29 BT44
Express Dr., Ilf. 68 EV60
Exton Cres. NW10 74 CQ66
Exton Gdns., Dag. 68 EW64
Exton St. SE1 10 D3
Exton St. SE1 77 DN74
Eyebright Clo., Croy. 121 DX102
Primrose La.
Eyhurst Ave., Horn. 69 FG62
Eyhurst Clo. NW2 61 CU61
Eyhurst Clo., Tad. 145 CZ123
Eyhurst Spur, Tad. 145 CZ124
Eylewood Rd. SE27 106 DQ92
Eynella Rd. SE22 106 DT87
Eynham Rd. W12 75 CW72
Eynsford Clo., Orp. 123 EQ101
Eynsford Cres., Bex. 110 EW88
Eynsford Rd., Ilf. 67 ES61
Eynsford Rd., Sev. 139 FH110
Eynsford Rd., Swan. 125 FD100
Eynsham Dr. SE2 96 EU77
Eynswood Dr., Sid. 110 EV92
Eyot Gdns. W6 89 CT78
Eyot Grn. W4 89 CT79
Chiswick Mall
Eyre Clo., Rom. 69 FH56
Eyre Ct. NW8 76 DD68
Finchley Rd.
Eyre St. Hill EC1 6 D5
Eyston Dr., Wey. 126 BN110
Eythorne Rd. SW9 91 DN81
Ezra St. E2 78 DT69

F

Faber Gdns. NW4 61 CU57
Fabian Rd. SW6 89 CZ80
Fabian St. E6 81 EM70
Fackenden La., Sev. 139 FH113
Factory La. N17 50 DT54
Factory La., Croy. 119 DN102
Factory Pl. E14 93 EB78
Factory Rd. E16 80 EL74
Factory Sq. SW16 105 DL93
Factory Yd. W7 73 CE74
Uxbridge Rd.
Faesten Way, Bex. 111 FE90
Faggotts Clo., Rad. 31 CJ35
Faggs Rd., Felt. 99 BU85
Faints Clo., Wal.Cr. 22 DT29
Fair Acres, Brom. 122 EG99
Fair Clo. (Bushey), Wat. 44 CB45
Claybury
Fair St. SE1 11 N4
Fair St., Houns. 86 CC83
High St.
Fairacre, N.Mal. 116 CS97
Fairacres SW15 103 CU85
Fairacres, Cob. 128 BX112
Fairacres, Croy. 135 DZ109
Fairacres, Ruis. 57 BT59
Fairacres, Tad. 145 CW121
Fairacres Clo., Pot.B. 19 CZ33
Fairbairn Clo., Pur. 133 DN113
Fairbairn Grn. SW9 91 DN81
Fairbank Ave., Orp. 123 EP103
Fairbanks Rd. N17 64 DT55
Fairbourne, Cob. 128 BX113
Fairbourne La., Cat. 148 DQ122
Fairbourne Rd. N17 64 DS55
Fairbridge Rd. N19 63 DK61
Fairbrook Clo. N13 49 DN50
Fairbrook Rd. N13 49 DN51
Fairburn Clo., Borwd. 32 CN39
Fairburn Ct. SW15 103 CY85
Mercier Rd.
Fairby Rd. SE12 108 EH85
Fairchild Clo. SW11 90 DD82
Wye St.
Fairchild Pl. EC2 7 N5
Fairchild St. EC2 7 N5
Fairchildes Ave., Croy. 135 ED112
Fairchildes La., Warl. 135 ED114
Fairclough St. E1 78 DU72
Faircross Ave., Bark. 81 EQ65
Faircross Ave., Rom. 55 FD52
Fairdale Gdns. SW15 89 CV84
Fairdale Gdns., Hayes 85 BU75
Fairdene Rd., Couls. 147 DK118
Fairey Ave., Hayes 85 BT77
Fairfax Ave., Epsom 131 CV110
Fairfax Clo., Walt. 113 BV102
Fairfax Gdns. SE3 94 EJ81
Fairfax Pl. NW6 76 DC66
Fairfax Rd. N8 63 DN56
Fairfax Rd. NW6 76 DC66
Fairfax Rd. W4 88 CS76
Fairfax Rd., Tedd. 101 CG93
Fairfax Way N10 48 DG52
Cromwell Rd.
Fairfield Ave. NW4 61 CV58
Fairfield Ave., Edg. 46 CP51
Fairfield Ave., Ruis. 57 BQ59
Fairfield Ave., Twick. 100 CB88
Fairfield Ave., Wat. 44 BW48
Fairfield Clo. N12 48 DC49
Fairfield Clo., Enf. 37 DY42
Scotland Grn. Rd. N.
Fairfield Clo., Epsom 130 CS106
Fairfield Clo., Horn. 69 FG60
Fairfield Clo., Mitch. 104 DE94
Fairfield Clo., Nthwd. 43 BP50
Thirlmere Gdns.
Fairfield Clo., Rad. 31 CE37
Fairfield Clo., Sid. 109 ET86
Fairfield Ct. NW10 75 CU67
Fairfield Cres., Edg. 46 CP51
Fairfield Dr. SW18 104 DB85
Fairfield Dr., Grnf. 73 CJ67
Fairfield Dr., Har. 58 CC55
Fairfield E., Kings.T. 116 CL96
Fairfield Gdns. N8 63 DL57
Elder Ave.
Fairfield Gro. SE7 94 EK79
Fairfield Ind. Est., Kings.T. 116 CN97
Fairfield N., Kings.T. 116 CL96
Fairfield Pk., Cob. 128 BX114
Fairfield Path, Croy. 120 DR104
Fairfield Pl., Kings.T. 116 CL97
Fairfield Rd. E3 79 EA68
Fairfield Rd. E17 51 DY54
Fairfield Rd. N8 63 DL57
Fairfield Rd. N18 50 DU49
Fairfield Rd. W7 87 CG76
Southdown Ave.
Fairfield Rd., Beck. 121 EA96
Fairfield Rd., Bexh. 96 EZ82
Fairfield Rd., Brom. 108 EG94
Fairfield Rd., Croy. 120 DS104
Fairfield Rd., Epp. 26 EV29
Fairfield Rd., Ilf. 81 EP65
Fairfield Rd., Kings.T. 116 CL96
Fairfield Rd., Lthd. 143 CH121
Fairfield Rd., Orp. 123 ER100
Fairfield Rd., Sthl. 72 BZ72
Fairfield Rd., Uxb. 70 BK65
Fairfield Rd., West Dr. 70 BL73
Fairfield Rd., Wdf.Grn. 52 EG51
Fairfield S., Kings.T. 116 CL97
Fairfield St. SW18 104 DB85
Fairfield Wk., Lthd. 143 CH121
Fairfield Rd.
Fairfield Wk. (Cheshunt), Wal.Cr. 23 DY28
Martins Dr.
Fairfield Way, Barn. 34 DA43
Fairfield Way, Couls. 133 DK114
Fairfield Way, Epsom 130 CS106
Fairfield W., Kings.T. 116 CL96
Fairfields, Cher. 112 BG102
Fairfields Clo. NW9 60 CQ57
Fairfields Cres. NW9 60 CQ57
Fairfields Rd., Houns. 86 CC83
Fairfolds, Wat. 30 BY35
Fairfoot Rd. E3 79 EA70
Fairford Ave., Bexh. 97 FD81
Fairford Ave., Croy. 121 DX99
Fairford Clo., Croy. 121 DX99
Fairford Gdns., Wor.Pk. 117 CT103
Fairgreen, Barn. 34 DF41
Fairgreen E., Barn. 34 DF41
Fairgreen Rd., Th.Hth. 119 DP99
Fairhaven Ave., Croy. 121 DX100
Fairhaven Cres., Wat. 43 BU48
Fairhazel Gdns. NW6 76 DB65
Fairholme, Felt. 99 BR87
Fairholme Ave., Rom. 69 FG57
Fairholme Clo. N3 61 CY56
Fairholme Cres., Ash. 143 CJ117
Fairholme Cres., Hayes 71 BT70
Fairholme Gdns. N3 61 CY55
Fairholme Rd. W14 89 CY78
Fairholme Rd., Ashf. 98 BL92
Fairholme Rd., Croy. 119 DN101
Fairholme Rd., Har. 59 CF57
Fairholme Rd., Ilf. 67 EM59
Fairholme Rd., Sutt. 131 CZ107
Fairholt Clo. N16 64 DS60
Fairholt Rd. N16 64 DR60
Fairholt St. SW7 8 C6
Fairland Rd. E15 80 EF65
Fairlands Ave., Buck.H. 52 EG47
Fairlands Ave., Sutt. 118 DA103
Fairlands Ave., Th.Hth. 119 DM98
Fairlands Ct. SE9 109 EN86
North Pk.
Fairlawn SE7 94 EJ79
Fairlawn, Lthd. 142 BZ124
Fairlawn Ave. N2 62 DE56
Fairlawn Ave. W4 88 CQ77
Fairlawn Ave., Bexh. 96 EX82
Fairlawn Clo. N14 35 DJ44
Fairlawn Clo., Esher 129 CF107
Fairlawn Clo., Felt. 100 BZ91
Fairlawn Clo., Kings.T. 102 CQ93
Fairlawn Dr., Wdf.Grn. 52 EG52
Fairlawn Gdns., Sthl. 72 BZ73
Fairlawn Gro. W4 88 CQ77
Fairlawn Gro., Bans. 132 DD113
Fairlawn Pk. SE26 107 DY92
Fairlawn Rd. SW19 103 CZ94
Fairlawn Rd., Cars. 132 DC111
Fairlawns, Pnr. 44 BW54
Fairlawns, Sun. 113 BU97
Fairlawns, Twick. 101 CJ86
Fairlawns, Wat. 29 BT38
Langley Rd.
Fairlawns, Wey. 127 BS106
Fairlawns Clo., Stai. 98 BH93
Fairlea Pl. W5 73 CJ71
Fairley Way (Cheshunt), Wal.Cr. 22 DV28
Fairlie Gdns. SE23 106 DW87
Fairlight Ave. E4 51 ED47
Fairlight Ave. NW10 74 CS68
Fairlight Ave., Wdf.Grn. 52 EG51
Fairlight Clo. E4 51 ED47
Fairlight Clo., Wor.Pk. 131 CW105
Fairlight Dr., Uxb. 70 BK65
Fairlight Rd. SW17 104 DD91
Fairlop Clo., Horn. 83 FH65
Fairlop Gdns., Ilf. 53 EQ52
Fairlop Rd. E11 65 ED59
Fairlop Rd., Ilf. 53 EQ54
Fairmark Dr., Uxb. 70 BN65
Fairmead, Brom. 123 EM98
Fairmead, Surb. 116 CP102
Fairmead Clo., Brom. 123 EM98
Fairmead Clo., Houns. 86 BX80
Fairmead Clo., N.Mal. 116 CR97
Fairmead Cres., Edg. 46 CQ48
Fairmead Gdns., Ilf. 66 EL57
Fairmead Rd. N19 63 DK62
Fairmead Rd., Croy. 119 DM102
Fairmead Rd., Loug. 38 EH43
Fairmead Side, Loug. 38 EJ43
Fairmeads, Cob. 128 BZ113
Fairmeads, Loug. 39 EP40
Fairmile Ave. SW16 105 DK92
Fairmile Ave., Cob. 128 BY114
Fairmile La., Cob. 128 BX112
Fairmile Pk. Copse, Cob. 128 BZ112
Fairmile Pk. Rd., Cob. 128 BZ113
Fairmont Clo., Belv. 96 EZ78
Lullingstone Rd.
Fairmount Rd. SW2 105 DM86
Fairoak Clo., Ken. 147 DP115
Fairoak Clo., Lthd. 129 CD112
Fairoak Clo., Orp. 123 EP101
Fairoak Dr. SE9 109 ER85
Fairoak Gdns., Rom. 55 FE54
Fairoak La., Chess. 129 CH111
Fairoak La., Lthd. 128 CC113
Fairs Rd., Lthd. 143 CG119
Fairseat Clo. (Bushey), Wat. 45 CE47
Hive Rd.
Fairstead Wk. N1 78 DQ67
Popham Rd.
Fairthorn Rd. SE7 94 EG78
Fairtrough Rd., Orp. 138 EV113
Fairview, Epsom 131 CW111
Fairview, Erith 97 FF80
Guild Rd.
Fairview, Pot.B. 20 DB29
Hawkshead Rd.
Fairview Ave., Wem. 73 CK65
Fairview Clo. E17 51 DY53
Fairview Clo., Chig. 53 ES49
Fairview Ct., Ashf. 98 BN92
Fairview Cres., Har. 58 CA60
Fairview Dr., Chig. 53 ES49
Fairview Dr., Orp. 137 ER105
Fairview Dr., Shep. 112 BM99
Fairview Dr., Wat. 29 BS36
Fairview Gdns., Wdf.Grn. 52 EH53
Fairview Ind. Pk., Rain. 83 FD71
Fairview Pl. SW2 105 DM87
Fairview Rd. N15 64 DT57
Fairview Rd. SW16 119 DM95
Fairview Rd., Chig. 53 ES49
Fairview Rd., Enf. 35 DN39
Fairview Rd., Epsom 131 CT111
Fairview Rd., Sutt. 132 DD106
Fairview Way, Edg. 46 CN49
Fairwater Ave., Well. 96 EU84
Fairwater Dr., Add. 126 BK109
Fairway SW20 117 CW97

Fairway, Bexh. 110 EY85
Fairway, Cars. 132 DC111
Fairway, Cher. 112 BH102
Fairway, Orp. 123 ER99
Fairway, Wdf.Grn. 52 EJ50
Fairway, The N13 50 DQ48
Fairway, The N14 35 DH44
Fairway, The NW7 46 CR48
Fairway, The W3 74 CS72
Fairway, The, Abb.L. 15 BR32
Fairway, The, Barn. 34 DB44
Fairway, The, Brom. 123 EM99
Fairway, The, Lthd. 143 CG118
Fairway, The, N.Mal. 116 CR95
Fairway, The, Nthlt. 72 CC65
Fairway, The, Nthwd. 43 BS49
Fairway, The, Ruis. 58 BW63
Fairway, The, Uxb. 70 BM69
Fairway, The, Wem. 59 CH62
Fairway, The, W.Mol. 114 CB97
Fairway, The, Wey. 126 BN111
Fairway Ave. NW9 60 CP55
Fairway Ave., Borwd. 32 CP40
Fairway Ave., West Dr. 70 BJ74
Fairway Clo. NW11 62 DC59
Fairway Clo., Croy. 121 DY99
Fairway Clo., Epsom 130 CQ105
Fairway Clo., Houns. 100 BW85
Fairway Clo., St.Alb. 16 CC27
Fairway Clo., West Dr. 70 BK74
Fairway Ave.
Fairway Ct. NW7 46 CR48
The Fairway
Fairway Dr. SE28 82 EX72
Summerton Way
Fairway Dr., Grnf. 72 CB66
Fairway Est., Grnf. 72 CC66
Fairway Gdns., Beck. 121 ED100
Fairway Gdns., Ilf. 67 EQ64
Fairways, Ashf. 99 BP93
Fairways, Ken. 148 DQ117
Fairways, Stan. 46 CL54
Fairways, Tedd. 101 CK94
Fairways, Wal.Abb. 24 EE34
Fairways, Wal.Cr. 23 DX26
Fairweather Clo. N15 64 DS56
Fairweather Rd. N16 64 DU58
Fairwyn Rd. SE26 107 DY91
Fakenham Clo. NW7 47 CU52
Fakenham Clo., Nthlt. 72 CA65
Goodwood Dr.
Fakruddin St. E1 78 DU70
Falcon Ave., Brom. 122 EL98
Falcon Clo. SE1 10 G2
Falcon Clo. W4 88 CQ79
Sutton La. S.
Falcon Clo., Nthwd. 43 BS52
Falcon Clo., Wal.Abb. 24 EG34
Kestrel Rd.
Falcon Cres., Enf. 37 DX43
Falcon Dr., Stai. 98 BK86
Falcon Gro. SW11 90 DE83
Falcon Ho. W13 73 CF70
Falcon La. SW11 90 DE83
Falcon Rd. SW11 90 DE82
Falcon Rd., Enf. 37 DX43
Falcon Rd., Hmptn. 100 BZ94
Falcon St. E13 80 EF70
Falcon Ter. SW11 90 DE83
Falcon Trd. Est. NW10 60 CS63
Falcon Way E11 66 EG56
Falcon Way E14 93 EB77
Falcon Way NW9 46 CS54
Falcon Way, Felt. 99 BV85
Falcon Way, Har. 60 CL57
Falcon Way, Horn. 83 FG66
Falcon Way, Sun. 113 BS96
Falcon Way, Wat. 16 BY34
Falconberg Ct. W1 5 N8
Falconberg Ms. W1 5 M8
Falconer Rd., Ilf. 54 EV50
Falconer Rd. (Bushey), Wat. 30 BZ44
Falconer Wk. N7 63 DM61
Newington Barrow Way
Falconhurst, Lthd. 143 CD115
Falconwood, Lthd. 141 BT124
Falconwood Ave., Well. 95 ER82
Falconwood Par., Well. 95 ES84
Falconwood Rd., Croy. 135 DZ109
Falcourt Clo., Sutt. 132 DB106
Falkirk Gdns., Wat. 44 BX50
Blackford Rd.
Falkirk Ho. W9 76 DB69
Falkirk St. N1 7 N1
Falkirk St. N1 78 DS68
Falkland Ave. N3 48 DA52
Falkland Ave. N11 48 DG49
Falkland Pk. Ave. SE25 120 DS97
Falkland Pl. NW5 63 DJ64
Falkland Rd.
Falkland Rd. N8 63 DN56
Falkland Rd. NW5 63 DJ64
Falkland Rd., Barn. 33 CY40
Fallaize Ave., Ilf. 67 EP63
Riverdene Rd.
Falling La., West Dr. 70 BL73
Falloden Way NW11 62 DA56
Fallow Clo., Chig. 53 ET50
Fallow Ct. SE16 92 DU78
Argyle Way
Fallow Ct. Ave. N12 48 DC52
Fallow Flds., Loug. 38 EJ44
Fallowfield, Stan. 45 CG49
Fallowfield Clo., Uxb. 42 BJ53
Fallowfield Ct., Stan. 45 CG48
Stanmore Hill
Fallowfields Dr. N12 48 DE51
Fallows Clo. N2 48 DC54
Fallsbrook Rd. SW16 105 DH93
Falmer Rd. E17 65 EB55
Falmer Rd. N15 64 DQ57
Falmer Rd., Enf. 36 DS42
Falmouth Ave. E4 51 ED50
Falmouth Clo. N22 49 DM52
Truro Rd.
Falmouth Clo. SE12 108 EF85
Falmouth Gdns., Ilf. 66 EK56
Falmouth Rd. SE1 11 J7
Falmouth Rd. SE1 92 DQ76
Falmouth Rd., Walt. 128 BW105
Falmouth St. E15 65 ED64
Falstaff Ms., Hmptn. 101 CD92
Hampton Rd.
Fambridge Clo. SE26 107 DZ91
Fambridge Rd., Dag. 68 FA60
Famet Ave., Pur. 134 DQ113
Famet Clo., Pur. 134 DQ113
Famet Wk., Pur. 134 DQ113
Fane St. W14 89 CZ79
North End Rd.
Fann St. EC1 7 H5
Fann St. EC1 78 DQ70
Fann St. EC2 7 H5
Fann St. EC2 78 DQ70
Fanshaw St. N1 7 M2
Fanshaw St. N1 78 DS69
Fanshawe Ave., Bark. 81 EQ65
Fanshawe Cres., Dag. 68 EY64
Fanshawe Rd., Rich. 101 CJ91
Fanthorpe St. SW15 89 CW83
Faraday Ave., Sid. 110 EU89
Faraday Clo. N7 77 DM65
Bride St.
Faraday Clo., Wat. 29 BR44
Faraday Rd. E15 80 EF65
Faraday Rd. SW19 104 DA93
Faraday Rd. W3 74 CQ73
Faraday Rd. W10 75 CY71
Faraday Rd., Sthl. 72 CB73
Faraday Rd., Well. 96 EU83
Faraday Rd., W.Mol. 114 CA98
Faraday Way SE18 94 EK76
Faraday Way, Croy. 119 DM102
Ampere Way
Faraday Way, Orp. 124 EV98
Fareham Rd., Felt. 100 BW87
Fareham St. W1 5 M8
Farewell Pl., Mitch. 118 DE95
Faringdon Ave., Brom. 123 EN101
Faringford Clo., Pot.B. 20 DD31
Faringford Rd. E15 80 EE66
Farington Acres, Wey. 113 BR104
Farjeon Rd. SE3 94 EK81
Farleton Clo., Wey. 127 BR107
Farleigh Ave., Brom. 122 EF100
Farleigh Border, Croy. 135 DX112
Farleigh Ct. Rd., Warl. 135 DZ114
Farleigh Dean Cres., Croy. 135 EB111
Farleigh Pl. N16 64 DT63
Farleigh Rd.
Farleigh Rd. N16 64 DT63
Farleigh Rd., Add. 126 BG111
Farleigh Rd., Warl. 149 DX118
Farley Dr., Ilf. 67 ES60
Farley Pl. SE25 120 DU98
Farley Rd. SE6 107 EC87
Farley Rd., S.Croy. 134 DU108
Farlington Pl. SW15 103 CV87
Roehampton La.
Farlow Rd. SW15 89 CW83
Farlton Rd. SW18 104 DB87
Farm Ave. NW2 61 CY62
Farm Ave. SW16 105 DL91
Farm Ave., Har. 58 BZ59
Farm Ave., Swan. 125 FC97
Farm Ave., Wem. 73 CJ65
Farm Clo., Barn. 33 CV43
Farm Clo., Borwd. 31 CK38
Farm Clo., Buck.H. 52 EJ48
Farm Clo., Couls. 146 DF120
Farm Clo., Dag. 83 FC66
Farm Clo. (Fetcham), Lthd. 143 CD124
Farm Clo. (Cuffley), Pot.B. 21 DK27
Farm Clo., Shep. 112 BN101
Farm Clo., Sthl. 72 CB73
Farm Clo., Sutt. 132 DD108
Farm Clo., Uxb. 57 BP61
Farm Clo., Wall. 133 DJ110
Farm Clo. (Cheshunt), Wal.Cr. 22 DW30
Farm Clo., W.Byf. 126 BM112
Farm Clo., W.Wick. 122 EE104
Farm Ct. NW4 61 CU55
Farm Dr., Croy. 121 DZ103
Farm Dr., Pur. 133 DK112
Farm End E4 38 EE43
Farm End, Nthwd. 43 BP53
Drakes Dr.
Farm Fld., Wat. 29 BS38
Farm Flds., S.Croy. 134 DS111
Farm Hill Rd., Wal.Abb. 23 ED33
Farm La. N14 34 DG44
Farm La. SW6 90 DA79
Farm La., Add. 126 BG107
Farm La., Ash. 144 CN116
Farm La., Cars. 132 DF110
Farm La., Croy. 121 DZ103
Farm La., Epsom 144 CP120
Farm La., Pur. 133 DJ110
Farm La., Rick. 28 BH41
Farm Pl. W8 76 DA74
Uxbridge St.
Farm Pl., Dart. 97 FG84
Farm Rd. N21 50 DQ46
Farm Rd., Edg. 46 CP51
Farm Rd., Esher 114 CB102
Farm Rd., Houns. 100 BY88
Farm Rd., Mord. 118 DB99
Farm Rd., Nthwd. 43 BQ50
Farm Rd., Sev. 155 FJ121
Farm Rd., Stai. 98 BH93
Farm Rd., Sutt. 132 DD108
Farm Rd., Warl. 149 DY119
Farm St. W1 9 H1
Farm St. W1 77 DH73
Farm Vale, Bex. 111 FB86
Farm Wk. NW11 61 CZ57
Farm Way, Buck.H. 52 EJ49
Farm Way, Horn. 69 FH63
Farm Way, Nthwd. 43 BS49
Farm Way (Bushey), Wat. 30 CB42
Farm Way, Wor.Pk. 117 CW104
Farman Gro., Nthlt. 72 BX69
Wayfarer Rd.
Farmborough Clo., Har. 59 CD59
Pool Rd.
Farmcote Rd. SE12 108 EG88
Farmdale Rd. SE10 94 EG78
Farmdale Rd., Cars. 132 DE108
Farmer Rd. E10 65 EB60
Farmer St. W8 76 DA74
Uxbridge St.
Farmers Clo., Wat. 15 BV33
Farmers Ct., Wal.Abb. 24 EG33
Winters Way
Farmers Rd. SE5 91 DP80
Farmfield Rd., Brom. 108 EE92
Farmhouse Clo., Brox. 23 DZ25
Farmhouse Rd. SW16 105 DJ94
Farmilo Rd. E17 65 DZ59
Farmington Ave., Sutt. 118 DD104
Farmland Wk., Chis. 109 EP92
Farmlands, Enf. 35 DN39
Farmlands, Pnr. 57 BU56
Farmlands, The, Nthlt. 72 CA65
Moat Fm. Rd.
Farmleigh N14 49 DJ45
Farmleigh Gro., Walt. 127 BS106
Farmstead Rd. SE6 107 EB91
Farmstead Rd., Har. 45 CD53
Farmview, Cob. 142 BX116
Farmway, Dag. 68 EW62
Farnaby Dr., Sev. 154 FF126
Farnaby Rd. SE9 94 EJ84
Farnaby Rd., Brom. 107 ED94
Farnan Ave. E17 51 EA54
Farnan Rd. SW16 105 DL92
Farnborough Ave. E17 65 DY55
Farnborough Ave., S.Croy. 135 DX108
Farnborough Clo., Wem. 60 CP61
Chalkhill Rd.
Farnborough Common, Orp. 123 EM104
Farnborough Cres., Brom. 122 EF102
Saville Row
Farnborough Cres., S.Croy. 135 DY109
Farnborough Hill, Orp. 137 ER106
Farnborough Way SE15 92 DS80
Daniel Gdns.
Farnborough Way, Orp. 137 EP106
Farncombe St. SE16 92 DU75
Farndale Ave. N13 49 DP48
Farndale Cres., Grnf. 72 CC69
Farnell Ms. SW5 90 DB78
Earls Ct. Sq.
Farnell Rd., Islw. 87 CD84
Farnell Rd., Stai. 98 BG90
Farnham Clo. N20 48 DC45
Farnham Gdns. SW20 117 CV96
Farnham Pl. SE1 10 G3
Farnham Rd., Ilf. 67 ET59
Farnham Rd., Well. 96 EW82
Farnham Royal SE11 91 DM78
Farningham Cres., Cat. 148 DU123
Commonwealth Rd.
Farningham Rd. N17 50 DU52
Farningham Rd., Cat. 148 DU123
Farnley Rd. E4 52 EE45
Farnley Rd. SE25 120 DR98
Faro Clo., Brom. 123 EN96
Faroe Rd. W14 89 CX76
Farorna Wk., Enf. 35 DN39
Farquhar Rd. SE19 106 DT92
Farquhar Rd. SW19 104 DA90
Farquharson Rd., Croy. 120 DQ102
Farr Ave., Bark. 82 EU68
Farr Rd., Enf. 36 DR39
Farraline Rd., Wat. 29 BV42
Farrance Rd., Rom. 68 EY58
Farrance St. E14 79 EA72
Farrans Ct., Har. 59 CH59
Farrant Ave. N22 49 DN54
Farrant Clo., Orp. 138 EU108
Farrant Way, Borwd. 32 CL39
Farrell Ho. E1 78 DW72
Devonport St.
Farren Rd. SE23 107 DY89
Farrer Ms. N8 63 DJ56
Farrer Rd.
Farrer Rd. N8 63 DJ56
Farrer Rd., Har. 60 CL57
Farrer's Pl., Croy. 135 DX105
Farrier Clo., Sun. 113 BU98
Farrier Rd., Nthlt. 72 CA68
Farrier St. NW1 77 DH66
Farrier Wk. SW10 90 DC79
Farriers Clo., Epsom 130 CS112
Farriers Ct., Wat. 15 BV32
Farriers End, Brox. 23 DZ26
Farriers Rd., Epsom 130 CS111
Farriers Way, Borwd. 32 CR43
Farringdon La. EC1 6 E5
Farringdon La. EC1 77 DN70
Farringdon Rd. EC1 6 D4
Farringdon Rd. EC1 77 DN70
Farringdon St. EC4 6 F8
Farringdon St. EC4 77 DP71
Farringford Clo., St.Alb. 16 CA26
Farrington Ave., Orp. 124 EV97
Farrington Pl., Chis. 109 ER94
Farrins Rents SE16 79 DY74
Farrow La. SE14 92 DW80
Farrow Pl. SE16 93 DY76
Ropemaker Rd.
Farthing All. SE1 92 DU75
Wolseley St.
Farthing Flds. E1 78 DV74
Raine St.
Farthing St., Orp. 137 EM108
Farthingale Ct., Wal.Abb. 24 EG34
Farthingale La., Wal.Abb. 24 EG34
Farthingale Wk. E15 79 ED66
Great Eastern Rd.
Farthings, The, Kings.T. 116 CN95
Brunswick Rd.
Farthings Clo. E4 52 EE48
Farthings Clo., Pnr. 57 BV58
Farwell Rd., Sid. 110 EV90
Farwig La., Brom. 122 EF95
Fashion St. E1 78 DT71
Fashoda Rd., Brom. 122 EJ98
Fassett Rd. E8 78 DU65
Fassett Rd., Kings.T. 116 CL98
Fassett Sq. E8 78 DU65
Fassnidge Way, Uxb. 70 BJ66
Oxford Rd.
Fauconberg Rd. W4 88 CQ79
Faulkner Clo., Dag. 68 EX59
Faulkner St. SE14 92 DW81
Faulkner's All. EC1 6 F6
Faulkners Rd., Walt. 128 BW106
Fauna Clo., Rom. 68 EW58
Faunce St. SE17 91 DP78
Harmsworth St.
Favart Rd. SW6 90 DA81
Faverolle Grn., Wal.Cr. 23 DX28
Faversham Ave. E4 52 EE46
Faversham Ave., Enf. 36 DR44
Faversham Clo., Chig. 54 EV47
Faversham Rd. SE6 107 DZ87
Faversham Rd., Beck. 121 DZ96
Faversham Rd., Mord. 118 DB100
Fawcett Clo. SW11 90 DD82
Fawcett Est. E5 64 DU60
Fawcett Rd. NW10 75 CT66
Fawcett Rd., Croy. 120 DQ104
Fawcett St. SW10 90 DB79
Fawcus Clo., Esher 129 CF107
Dalmore Ave.
Fawe Pk. Rd. SW15 89 CZ84
Fawe St. E14 79 EB71
Fawke Common Rd., Sev. 155 FN126
Fawley Rd. NW6 62 DB64
Fawn Rd. E13 80 EJ68
Fawn Rd., Chig. 53 ET50
Fawnbrake Ave. SE24 105 DP85
Fawns Manor Clo., Felt. 99 BQ88
Fawns Manor Rd., Felt. 99 BR88
Fawood Ave. NW10 74 CR66
Fay Grn., Abb.L. 15 BR33
Fayerfield, Pot.B. 20 DD31
Faygate Cres., Bexh. 110 FA85
Faygate Rd. SW2 105 DM89
Fayland Ave. SW16 105 DJ92
Fearney Mead, Rick. 42 BG46
Fearnley Cres., Hmptn. 100 BY92
Fearnley St., Wat. 29 BV42
Fearon St. SE10 94 EG78
Featherbed La., Abb.L. 15 BV26
Sergehill La.
Featherbed La., Croy. 135 DZ108
Featherbed La., Hem.H. 14 BG25
Featherbed La., Rom. 40 EX42
Featherbed La., Warl. 135 EB111
Feathers Pl. SE10 93 ED79
Featherstone Ave. SE23 106 DV89
Featherstone Clo., Pot.B. 20 DD32
Featherstone Gdns., Borwd. 32 CQ42
Featherstone Ind. Est., Sthl. 86 BY75
Featherstone Rd. NW7 47 CV51
Featherstone Rd., Sthl. 86 BY76
Featherstone St. EC1 7 K4
Featherstone St. EC1 78 DR70
Featherstone Ter., Sthl. 86 BY76
Featley Rd. SW9 91 DP83
Federal Rd., Grnf. 73 CJ68
Federal Way, Wat. 30 BW39
Federation Rd. SE2 96 EV77
Fee Fm. Rd., Esher 129 CF108
Felbridge Ave., Stan. 45 CG53
Felbridge Clo. SW16 105 DN91
Felbridge Clo., Sutt. 132 DB109
Felbrigge Rd., Ilf. 67 ET61
Felcott Clo., Walt. 114 BW104
Felcott Rd., Walt. 114 BW104
Felday Rd. SE13 107 EB86
Felden Clo., Pnr. 44 BY52
Felden Clo., Wat. 16 BX34
Felden St. SW6 89 CZ81
Feldman Clo. N16 64 DU60
Felgate Ms. W6 89 CV77
Felhampton Rd. SE9 109 EP89
Felhurst Cres., Dag. 69 FB63
Felix Ave. N8 63 DL58
Felix La., Shep. 113 BS100
Felix Rd. W13 73 CG73
Felix Rd., Walt. 113 BU100
Felix St. E2 78 DV68
Hackney Rd.
Felixstowe Rd. N9 50 DU48
Felixstowe Rd. N17 64 DT55
Felixstowe Rd. NW10 75 CV69
Felixstowe Rd. SE2 96 EV76
Fell Rd., Croy. 120 DQ104
Fell Wk., Edg. 46 CP53
East Rd.
Fellbrigg Rd. SE22 106 DT85
Fellbrigg St. E1 78 DV70
Headlam St.
Fellbrook, Rich. 101 CH90
Fellowes Clo., Hayes 72 BX70
Paddington Clo.
Fellowes Rd., Cars. 118 DE104
Fellows Ct. E2 7 P1
Fellows Rd. NW3 76 DD66
Felltram Way SE7 94 EG77
Felmersham Clo. SW4 91 DK84
Haselrigge Rd.
Felmingham Rd. SE20 120 DW96
Fels Clo., Dag. 69 FB62
Fels Fm. Ave., Dag. 69 FC62
Felsberg Rd. SW2 105 DL86
Felsham Rd. SW15 89 CX83
Felspar Clo. SE18 95 ET78
Felstead Ave., Ilf. 53 EN53
Felstead Gdns. E14 93 EC78
Ferry St.
Felstead Rd. E11 66 EG59
Felstead Rd., Epsom 130 CR111
Felstead Rd., Loug. 52 EL45
Felstead Rd., Orp. 124 EU103
Felstead Rd., Rom. 55 FC51
Felstead Rd., Wal.Cr. 23 DY32
Felstead St. E9 79 DZ65
Felsted Rd. E16 80 EK72
Feltham Ave., E.Mol. 115 CE98
Feltham Hill Rd., Ashf. 99 BP92
Feltham Hill Rd., Felt. 99 BU91
Feltham Rd., Ashf. 99 BP91
Feltham Rd., Mitch. 118 DF96
Felthambrook Ind. Est., Felt. 99 BV90
Felthambrook Way, Felt. 99 BV90
Felton Clo., Borwd. 32 CL38
Felton Clo., Brox. 23 DZ25
Felton Clo., Orp. 123 EP100
Felton Gdns., Bark. 81 ES67
Sutton Rd.
Felton Lea, Sid. 109 ET92
Felton Rd. W13 87 CJ75
Camborne Ave.
Felton Rd., Bark. 81 ES68
Sutton Rd.
Felton St. N1 78 DR67
Fen Ct. EC3 7 M10
Fen Gro., Sid. 109 ET86
Fen St. E16 80 EF73
Victoria Dock Rd.
Fencepiece Rd., Chig. 53 EQ50
Fencepiece Rd., Ilf. 53 EQ51
Fenchurch Ave. EC3 7 M9
Fenchurch Ave. EC3 78 DS72
Fenchurch Bldgs. EC3 7 N9
Fenchurch Pl. EC3 7 N10
Fenchurch St. EC3 7 M10
Fenchurch St. EC3 78 DS73
Fendall Rd., Epsom 130 CQ106
Fendall St. SE1 11 N7
Fendall St. SE1 92 DS76
Fendt Clo. E16 80 EF73
Bowman Ave.
Fendyke Rd., Belv. 96 EX76
Fenelon Pl. W14 89 CZ77
Fenham Rd. SE15 92 DU80
Fenman Ct. N17 50 DV53
Shelbourne Rd.
Fenman Gdns., Ilf. 68 EV60
Fenn Clo., Brom. 108 EG93
Fenn St. E9 64 DW64
Fennel Clo. E16 80 EE70
Cranberry La.
Fennel Clo., Croy. 121 DX102
Primrose La.
Fennel St. SE18 95 EN79
Fennells Mead, Epsom 131 CT109
Fenner Clo. SE16 92 DV77
Layard Rd.
Fenner Ho., Walt. 127 BU105
Fenner Sq. SW11 90 DD83
Thomas Baines Rd.
Fenning St. SE1 11 M4
Fens Way, Swan. 111 FG93
Fenstanton Ave. N12 48 DD51
Fenswood Clo., Bex. 110 FA86
Fentiman Rd. SW8 91 DL79
Fenton Ave., Stai. 98 BJ93
Fenton Clo. E8 78 DT65
Laurel St.
Fenton Clo. SW9 91 DM82
Fenton Clo., Chis. 109 EM92
Fenton Rd. N17 50 DQ52
Fentons Ave. E13 80 EH68
Fenwick Clo. SE18 95 EN79
Ritter St.
Fenwick Gro. SE15 92 DU83

Fenwick Path, Borwd. 32 CM38
Berwick Rd.
Fenwick Pl. SW9 91 DL83
Fenwick Rd. SE15 92 DU83
Ferdinand Pl. NW1 76 DG66
Ferdinand St.
Ferdinand St. NW1 76 DG66
Fergus Rd. N5 63 DP64
Calabria Rd.
Ferguson Ave., Surb. 116 CM99
Ferguson Clo. E14 93 EA77
Ferguson Clo., Brom. 121 ED97
Ferguson Dr. W3 74 CR72
Ferme Pk. Rd. N4 63 DM59
Ferme Pk. Rd. N8 63 DL57
Fermor Rd. SE23 107 DY88
Fermoy Rd. W9 75 CZ70
Fermoy Rd., Grnf. 72 CB70
Fern Ave., Mitch. 119 DK98
Fern Clo., Erith 97 FH81
Hollywood Way
Fern Clo., Warl. 149 DY118
Fern Dene W13 73 CH71
Templewood
Fern Gro., Felt. 99 BV87
Fern Hill, Lthd. 129 CD114
Fern La., Houns. 86 BZ78
Fern St. E3 79 EA70
Fern Wk., Ashf. 98 BK92
Ferndale Rd.
Fern Way, Wat. 29 BV35
Fernbank, Buck.H. 52 EH46
Fernbank Ave., Walt. 114 BY101
Fernbank Ave., Wem. 59 CF63
Fernbank Rd., Add. 126 BG106
Fernbrook Ave., Sid. 109 ES85
Blackfen Rd.
Fernbrook Cres. SE13 108 EE86
Fernbrook Rd.
Fernbrook Dr., Har. 58 CB59
Fernbrook Rd. SE13 108 EE86
Ferncliff Rd. E8 64 DU64
Ferncroft Ave. N12 48 DE51
Ferncroft Ave. NW3 62 DA62
Ferncroft Ave., Ruis. 58 BW61
Ferndale, Brom. 122 EJ96
Ferndale Ave. E17 65 ED57
Ferndale Ave., Houns. 86 BY83
Ferndale Ct. SE3 94 EF80
Ferndale Cres., Uxb. 70 BJ69
Ferndale Rd. E7 80 EH66
Ferndale Rd. E11 66 EE61
Ferndale Rd. N15 64 DT58
Ferndale Rd. SE25 120 DV99
Ferndale Rd. SW4 91 DM84
Ferndale Rd. SW9 91 DL84
Ferndale Rd., Ashf. 98 BK92
Ferndale Rd., Bans. 145 CZ116
Ferndale Rd., Enf. 37 DY36
Ferndale Rd., Rom. 55 FC54
Ferndale St. E6 81 EP73
Ferndale Ter., Har. 59 CF56
Ferndale Way, Orp. 137 ER106
Ferndell Ave., Bex. 111 FD90
Fernden Way, Rom. 69 FB58
Ferndene, St.Alb. 16 BZ31
Ferndene Rd. SE24 92 DQ84
Ferndown, Nthwd. 43 BU54
Ferndown Ave., Orp. 123 ER102
Ferndown Clo., Pnr. 44 BY52
Ferndown Clo., Sutt. 132 DD107
Ferndown Gdns., Cob. 128 BW113
Ferndown Rd. SE9 108 EK87
Ferndown Rd., Wat. 44 BW48
Fernes Clo., Uxb. 70 BJ72
Ferney Ct., W.Byf. 126 BK112
Ferney Rd.
Ferney Meade Way, Islw. 87 CG82
Ferney Rd., Barn. 48 DG45
Ferney Rd., W.Byf. 126 BK112
Fernhall Dr., Ilf. 66 EK57
Fernhall La., Wal.Abb. 24 EK31
Fernham Rd., Th.Hth. 120 DQ97
Fernhead Rd. W9 75 CZ69
Fernheath Way, Dart. 111 FD92
Fernhill Ct. E17 51 ED54
Fernhill Gdns., Kings.T. 101 CK92
Fernhill St. E16 81 EM74
Fernhills, Kings L. 15 BR34
Fernholme Rd. SE15 107 DX85
Fernhurst Gdns., Edg. 46 CN51
Fernhurst Rd. SW6 89 CY81
Fernhurst Rd., Ashf. 99 BQ91
Fernhurst Rd., Croy. 120 DU101
Fernie Clo., Chig. 54 EU50
Fernihough Clo., Wey. 126 BN111
Fernlea, Lthd. 142 CB124
Fernlea Rd. SW12 105 DH88
Fernlea Rd., Mitch. 118 DG96
Fernleigh Clo., Croy. 133 DN105
Stafford Rd.
Fernleigh Ct., Har. 44 CB54
Fernleigh Ct., Wem. 60 CL61
Fernleigh Rd. N21 49 DN47
Ferns Clo., Enf. 37 DY36
Ferns Clo., S.Croy. 134 DV110
Ferns Rd. E15 80 EF65
Fernsbury St. WC1 6 D3
Fernshaw Rd. SW10 90 DC79
Fernside NW11 62 DA61
Finchley Rd.
Fernside, Buck.H. 52 EH46
Fernside Ave. NW7 46 CR48
Fernside Ave., Felt. 99 BV91
Fernside La., Sev. 155 FJ129
Fernside Rd. SW12 104 DF88
Fernthorpe Rd. SW16 105 DJ93
Ferntower Rd. N5 64 DR64
Fernways, Ilf. 67 EP63
Cecil Rd.
Fernwood, Croy. 135 DY109
Fernwood Ave. SW16 105 DK91
Fernwood Ave., Wem. 59 CJ64
Bridgewater Rd.
Fernwood Clo., Brom. 122 EJ96
Fernwood Cres. N20 48 DF48
Ferny Hill, Barn. 34 DF38
Ferranti Clo. SE18 94 EK76
Ferraro Clo., Houns. 86 CA79
Ferrers Ave., Wall. 133 DK105
Ferrers Ave., West Dr. 84 BK75
Ferrers Rd. SW16 105 DK92
Ferrestone Rd. N8 63 DM56
Ferriby Clo. N1 77 DN66
Bewdley St.
Ferrier Pt. E16 80 EH71
Forty Acre La.
Ferrier St. SW18 90 DB84
Ferriers Way, Epsom 145 CW118
Ferring Clo., Har. 58 CC60
Ferrings SE21 106 DS89
Ferris Ave., Croy. 121 DZ104
Ferris Rd. SE22 92 DU84
Ferron Rd. E5 64 DV62
Ferry La. N17 64 DV56
Ferry La. SW13 89 CT79
Ferry La., Brent. 88 CL79
Ferry La., Cher. 112 BG100
Ferry La., Rain. 83 FE72
Ferry La., Rich. 88 CM79
Ferry La., Shep. 112 BN102
Ferry La. (Laleham), Stai. 112 BJ97
Ferry Pl. SE18 95 EN76
Woolwich High St.
Ferry Rd. SW13 89 CU80
Ferry Rd., Tedd. 101 CH92
Ferry Rd., T.Ditt. 115 CH100
Ferry Rd., Twick. 101 CH88
Ferry Rd., W.Mol. 114 CA97
Ferry Sq., Brent. 87 CK79
Ferry Sq., Shep. 113 BP101
Ferry St. E14 93 EC78
Ferryhills Clo., Wat. 44 BW48
Ferrymead Ave., Grnf. 72 CA69
Ferrymead Dr., Grnf. 72 CA69
Ferrymead Gdns., Grnf. 72 CC68
Ferrymoor, Rich. 101 CH90
Festing Rd. SW15 89 CX83
Festival Clo., Bex. 110 EX88
Festival Clo., Erith 97 FF80
Betsham Rd.
Festival Clo., Uxb. 71 BP67
Fetcham Common La., Lthd. 142 CB121
Fetcham Pk. Dr., Lthd. 143 CE123
Fetter La. EC4 6 E9
Fetter La. EC4 77 DN72
Ffinch St. SE8 93 EA80
Fiddicroft Ave., Bans. 132 DB114
Fidler Pl. (Bushey), Wat. 30 CB44
Ashfield Ave.
Field Clo. E4 51 EB51
Field Clo., Brom. 122 EJ96
Field Clo., Buck.H. 52 EJ48
Field Clo., Chess. 129 CJ106
Field Clo., Hayes 85 BQ80
Field Clo., Houns. 85 BV81
Field Clo., Rom. 40 EV41
Field Clo., Ruis. 57 BQ60
Field Way
Field Clo., S.Croy. 134 DV114
Field Clo., W.Mol. 114 CB99
Field Ct. WC1 6 C7
Field End, Barn. 33 CV42
Field End, Couls. 133 DK114
Field End, Nthlt. 72 BX65
Field End, Ruis. 72 BW65
Field End, Twick. 101 CF91
Field End Clo., Wat. 44 BY45
Field End Rd., Pnr. 57 BV57
Field End Rd., Ruis. 58 BW60
Field La., Brent. 87 CJ80
Field La., Tedd. 101 CG92
Field Mead NW7 46 CS52
Field Mead NW9 46 CS52
Field Pl., N.Mal. 117 CT100
Field Rd. E7 66 EG63
Field Rd. N17 64 DR55
Field Rd. W6 89 CY78
Field Rd., Felt. 99 BV86
Field Rd., Wat. 30 BY44
Field St. WC1 6 B2
Field St. WC1 77 DM69
Field Vw., Felt. 99 BR91
Field Vw. Ri., St.Alb. 16 BY29
Field Vw. Rd., Pot.B. 20 DA33
Field Way NW10 74 CQ66
Twybridge Way
Field Way, Croy. 135 EB108
Field Way, Grnf. 72 CB67
Field Way, Rick. 42 BH46
Field Way, Ruis. 57 BQ60
Field Way, Uxb. 70 BK70
Fieldcommon La., Walt. 114 BY102
Fieldend Rd. SW16 119 DJ95
Fielders Clo., Enf. 36 DS42
Woodfield Clo.
Fielders Clo., Har. 58 CC60
Fieldfare Rd. SE28 82 EW73
Fieldgate La., Mitch. 118 DE97
Fieldgate St. E1 78 DU71
Fieldhouse Rd. SW12 105 DJ88
Fieldhurst Clo., Add. 126 BH106
Fielding Ave., Twick. 100 CC90
Fielding Ho. NW6 76 DA69
Fielding Ms. SW13 89 CV79
Castelnau
Fielding Rd. W4 88 CR76
Fielding Rd. W14 89 CX76
Fielding St. SE17 92 DQ79
Fieldings, The SE23 106 DW88
Fieldings Rd. (Cheshunt), Wal.Cr. 23 DZ28
Fields Ct., Pot.B. 20 DD33
Fields Est. E8 78 DU66
Fields Pk. Cres., Rom. 68 EW57
Fieldsend Rd., Sutt. 131 CY106
Fieldside Clo., Orp. 137 EQ105
State Fm. Ave.
Fieldside Rd., Brom. 107 ED92
Fieldview SW18 104 DD88
Fieldway, Dag. 68 EW62
Fieldway, Orp. 123 ER100
Fieldway Cres. N5 63 DN64
Fiennes Clo., Dag. 68 EW60
Fiennes Way, Sev. 155 FJ127
Fiesta Dr., Dag. 83 FC70
Fife Rd. E16 80 EG71
Fife Rd. N22 49 DP52
Fife Rd. SW14 102 CQ85
Fife Rd., Kings.T. 116 CL96
Fife Ter. N1 77 DM68
Wynford Rd.
Fifehead Clo., Ashf. 98 BL93
Fifield Path SE23 107 DX90
Bampton Rd.
Fifth Ave. E12 67 EM63
Fifth Ave. W10 75 CY69
Fifth Ave., Hayes 71 BT74
Fifth Ave., Wat. 30 BW35
Fifth Cross Rd., Twick. 101 CD89
Fifth Way, Wem. 60 CP63
Fig St., Sev. 154 FF129
Fig Tree Clo. NW10 74 CS67
Craven Pk.
Figges Rd., Mitch. 104 DG94
Filby Rd., Chess. 130 CM107
Filey Ave. N16 64 DU60
Filey Clo., Sutt. 132 DC108
Filey Clo., West. 150 EH119
Filey Waye, Ruis. 57 BU61
Fillebrook Ave., Enf. 36 DS40
Fillebrook Rd. E11 65 ED60
Filmer La., Sev. 155 FL121
Filmer Rd. SW6 89 CY81
Filston La., Sev. 153 FD116
Filston Rd., Erith 97 FB78
Riverdale Rd.
Finborough Rd. SW10 90 DB78
Finborough Rd. SW17 104 DF93
Finch Ave. SE27 106 DR91
Finch Clo. NW10 60 CR64
Finch Clo., Barn. 34 DA43
Brent Pl.
Finch Dr., Felt. 100 BX87
Finch La. EC3 7 L9
Finch La. (Bushey), Wat. 30 CA43
Finch Ms. SE15 92 DT81
Southampton Way
Finchale Rd. SE2 96 EU76
Fincham Clo., Uxb. 57 BQ61
Aylsham Dr.
Finchdale Rd. SE2 96 EU76
Finchdean Way SE15 92 DT80
Daniel Gdns.
Finchingfield Ave., Wdf.Grn. 52 EJ52
Finchley Ct. N3 48 DB51
Finchley La. NW4 61 CW56
Finchley Pk. N12 48 DC49
Finchley Pl. NW8 76 DD68
Finchley Rd. NW2 62 DA62
Finchley Rd. NW3 62 DB64
Finchley Rd. NW8 76 DD66
Finchley Rd. NW11 61 CZ56
Finchley Way N3 48 DA52
Finck St. SE1 10 C5
Finck St. SE1 91 DM75
Finden Rd. E7 66 EH64
Findhorn Ave., Hayes 71 BV71
Findhorn St. E14 79 EC72
Findon Clo. SW18 104 DA86
Wimbledon Pk. Rd.
Findon Clo., Har. 58 CB62
Findon Gdns., Rain. 83 FG71
Findon Rd. N9 50 DV46
Findon Rd. W12 89 CU75
Fine Bush La., Uxb. 57 BP58
Fingal St. SE10 94 EF78
Finglesham Clo., Orp. 124 EX102
Westwell Clo.
Finians Clo., Uxb. 70 BM66
Finland Quay SE16 93 DY76
Finland Rd. SE4 93 DY83
Finland St. SE16 93 DY76
Finlay Gdns., Add. 126 BJ105
Finlay St. SW6 89 CX81
Finlays Clo., Chess. 130 CN106
Finnart Clo., Wey. 127 BQ105
Finnart Ho. Dr., Wey. 127 BQ105
Vaillant Rd.
Finnis St. E2 78 DV69
Finnymore Rd., Dag. 82 EY66
Finsbury Ave. EC2 7 L7
Finsbury Circ. EC2 7 L7
Finsbury Circ. EC2 78 DR71
Finsbury Cotts. N22 49 DL52
Clarence Rd.
Finsbury Est. EC1 6 E3
Finsbury Est. EC1 77 DN69
Finsbury Ho. N22 49 DL53
Finsbury Mkt. EC2 7 M5
Finsbury Mkt. EC2 78 DS70
Finsbury Pk. Ave. N4 64 DQ58
Finsbury Pk. Rd. N4 63 DP61
Finsbury Pavement EC2 7 L6
Finsbury Pavement EC2 78 DR71
Finsbury Rd. N22 49 DM53
Finsbury Sq. EC2 7 L5
Finsbury Sq. EC2 78 DR71
Finsbury St. EC2 7 K6
Finsbury St. EC2 78 DR71
Finsbury Way, Bex. 110 EZ86
Finsen Rd. SE5 92 DQ83
Finstock Rd. W10 75 CX72
Finucane Dr., Orp. 124 EW101
Finucane Gdns., Rain. 83 FG65
Finucane Ri. (Bushey), Wat. 44 CC47
Finway Ct., Wat. 29 BT43
Whippendell Rd.
Fiona Clo., Lthd. 142 CA124
Fir Clo., Walt. 113 BU101
Fir Dene, Orp. 123 EM104
Fir Gra. Ave., Wey. 127 BP106
Fir Gro., N.Mal. 117 CT100
Fir Rd., Felt. 100 BX92
Fir Rd., Sutt. 117 CZ102
Fir Tree Ave., West Dr. 84 BN76
Fir Tree Clo. SW16 105 DJ92
Fir Tree Clo. W5 74 CL72
Fir Tree Clo., Epsom 131 CT105
Fir Tree Clo., Esher 128 CC106
Fir Tree Clo., Lthd. 143 CJ123
Fir Tree Clo., Orp. 137 ET106
Highfield Ave.
Fir Tree Clo., Rom. 69 FD55
Fir Tree Gdns., Croy. 135 EA105
Fir Tree Gro., Cars. 132 DF108
Fir Tree Hill, Rick. 28 BM38
Fir Tree Pl., Ashf. 98 BN92
Percy Ave.
Fir Tree Rd., Bans. 131 CW114
Fir Tree Rd., Epsom 145 CV116
Fir Tree Rd., Houns. 86 BY84
Fir Tree Rd., Lthd. 143 CJ123
Fir Tree Wk., Dag. 69 FC62
Wheel Fm. Dr.
Fir Tree Wk., Enf. 36 DR41
Fir Trees, Rom. 40 EV41
Fir Trees Clo. SE16 79 DY74
Firbank Clo. E16 80 EK71
Firbank Clo., Enf. 36 DQ42
Gladbeck Way
Firbank Dr., Wat. 44 BY45
Firbank Rd. SE15 92 DV82
Firbank Rd., Rom. 55 FB50
Fircroft Ave., Chess. 130 CM105
Fircroft Gdns., Har. 59 CE62
Fircroft Rd. SW17 104 DF89
Firdene, Surb. 116 CQ102
Fire Bell All., Surb. 116 CL100
Fire Sta. All., Barn. 33 CZ40
Christchurch La.
Firecrest Dr. NW3 62 DB62
Firefly Clo., Wall. 133 DL108
Defiant Way
Firefly Gdns. E6 80 EL70
Jack Dash Way
Firfield Rd., Add. 126 BG105
Firfields, Wey. 127 BP107
Firhill Rd. SE6 107 EA91
Firlands, Wey. 127 BS107
Firmingers Rd., Orp. 139 FB106
Firs, The N20 48 DD46
Firs, The W5 73 CK71
Firs, The, Bex. 111 FD88
Dartford Rd.
Firs, The, Cat. 148 DR122
York Gate
Firs, The, Wal.Cr. 22 DS27
Firs Ave. N10 62 DG55
Firs Ave. N11 48 DF51
Firs Ave. SW14 88 CQ84
Firs Clo. N10 62 DG55
Firs Ave.
Firs Clo. SE23 107 DX87
Firs Clo., Esher 129 CE107
Firs Clo., Mitch. 119 DH96
Firs Dr., Houns. 85 BV81
Firs Dr., Loug. 39 EN39
Firs La. N13 50 DQ48
Firs La. N21 50 DQ47
Firs La., Pot.B. 20 DB33
Firs Pk. Ave. N21 50 DR46
Firs Pk. Gdns. N21 50 DQ46
Firs Rd., Ken. 147 DP115
Firs Wk., Nthwd. 43 BR51
Firs Wk., Wdf.Grn. 52 EG50
Firs Wd. Clo., Pot.B. 20 DF32
Firsby Ave., Croy. 121 DX102
Firsby Rd. N16 64 DT60
Firscroft N13 50 DQ48
Firside Gro., Sid. 109 ET88
First Ave. E12 66 EL63
First Ave. E13 80 EG69
First Ave. E17 65 EA57
First Ave. N18 50 DW49
First Ave. NW4 61 CW56
First Ave. SW14 88 CS83
First Ave. W3 75 CT74
First Ave. W10 75 CZ70
First Ave., Bexh. 96 EW80
First Ave., Dag. 83 FB68
First Ave., Enf. 36 DT43
First Ave., Epsom 130 CS109
First Ave., Hayes 71 BT74
First Ave., Rom. 68 EW57
First Ave., Walt. 113 BV100
First Ave., Wat. 30 BW35
First Ave., Wem. 59 CK61
First Ave., W.Mol. 114 BZ98
First Clo., W.Mol. 114 CC97
First Cross Rd., Twick. 101 CE89
First Slip, Lthd. 143 CG118
First St. SW3 8 C8
First St. SW3 90 DE77
First Way, Wem. 60 CP63
Firstway SW20 117 CW96
Firswood Ave., Epsom 131 CT106
Firth Gdns. SW6 89 CY81
Firtree Ave., Mitch. 118 DG96
Firtree Clo. (Stoneleigh), Epsom 145 CV116
Firtree Ct., Borwd. 32 CM42
Fish St. Hill EC3 11 L1
Fish St. Hill EC3 78 DR73
Fisher Clo., Croy. 120 DT102
Grant Rd.
Fisher Clo., Grnf. 72 CA69
Gosling Clo.
Fisher Clo., Kings L. 14 BN29
Fisher Clo., Walt. 127 BV105
Fisher Rd., Har. 45 CF54
Fisher St. E16 80 EG71
Fisher St. WC1 6 B7
Fisher St. WC1 77 DM71
Fisherman Clo., Rich. 101 CJ91
Locksmeade Rd.
Fishermans Dr. SE16 93 DX75
Fisherman's Wk. E14 79 EA74
Cabot Sq.
Fishers Clo., Wal.Cr. 23 EA34
Fishers Ct. SE14 93 DX81
Besson St.
Fishers La. W4 88 CR77
Fishers La., Epp. 25 ES32
Fishers Way, Belv. 83 FC74
Fishersdene, Esher 129 CG107
Fisherton Est. NW8 4 A4
Fisherton St. NW8 76 DD70
Fisherton St. Est. NW8 76 DD70
Fishponds Rd. SW17 104 DE91
Fishponds Rd., Kes. 136 EK106
Fisons Rd. E16 80 EG74
Fitzalan Rd. N3 61 CY55
Fitzalan Rd., Esher 129 CE108
Fitzalan St. SE11 10 D8
Fitzalan St. SE11 91 DM77
Fitzgeorge Ave. W14 89 CY77
Fitzgeorge Ave., N.Mal. 116 CR95
Fitzgerald Ave. SW14 88 CS83
Fitzgerald Clo. E11 66 EG57
Fitzgerald Rd.
Fitzgerald Ho. E14 79 EB72
Kerbey St.
Fitzgerald Ho., Hayes 71 BV74
Fitzgerald Rd. E11 66 EG57
Fitzgerald Rd. SW14 88 CR83
Fitzgerald Rd., T.Ditt. 115 CG100
Fitzhardinge St. W1 4 F8
Fitzhardinge St. W1 76 DG72
Fitzhugh Gro. SW18 104 DD86
Fitzhugh Gro. Est. SW18 104 DD86
Fitzjames Ave. W14 89 CY77
Fitzjames Ave., Croy. 120 DU103
Fitzjohn Ave., Barn. 33 CY43
Fitzjohn's Ave. NW3 62 DD64
Fitzmaurice Pl. W1 9 J2
Fitzmaurice Pl. W1 77 DH74
Fitzneal St. W12 75 CT72
Fitzroy Clo. N6 62 DF60
Fitzroy Ct. W1 5 L5
Fitzroy Cres. W4 88 CR80
Fitzroy Gdns. SE19 106 DS94
Fitzroy Ms. W1 5 K5
Fitzroy Pk. N6 62 DF61
Fitzroy Rd. NW1 76 DG67
Fitzroy Sq. W1 5 K5
Fitzroy Sq. W1 77 DJ70
Fitzroy St. W1 5 K5
Fitzroy St. W1 77 DJ70
Fitzroy Yd. NW1 76 DG67
Fitzroy Rd.
Fitzstephen Rd., Dag. 68 EV64
Fitzwarren Gdns. N19 63 DJ60
Fitzwilliam Ave., Rich. 88 CM82
Fitzwilliam Ms. E16 80 EG74
Silvertown Way
Fitzwilliam Rd. SW4 91 DJ83
Fitzwygram Clo., Hmptn. 100 CC92
Five Acre NW9 47 CT53
Five Acres, Kings L. 14 BM29
Five Acres, St.Alb. 17 CK25
Five Acres Ave., St.Alb. 16 BZ29
Five Bell All. E14 79 DZ73
Three Colt St.
Five Elms Rd., Brom. 122 EH104
Five Elms Rd., Dag. 68 EZ62
Five Oaks La., Chig. 54 EY51
Five Wents, Swan. 125 FG96
Fiveacre Clo., Th.Hth. 119 DN100
Fiveways Rd. SW9 91 DN82
Fladbury Rd. N15 64 DR58
Fladgate Rd. E11 66 EE58
Flag Clo., Croy. 121 DX102
Flag Wk., Pnr. 57 BU58
Eastcote Rd.
Flagstaff Clo., Wal.Abb. 23 EB33
Flagstaff Rd., Wal.Abb. 23 EB33
Flambard Rd., Har. 59 CG58
Flamborough Clo., West. 150 EH119
Flamborough Rd., Ruis. 57 BU62
Flamborough St. E14 79 DY72

This index reads in the sequence: Street Name / Postal District or Post Town / Map Page Number / Grid Reference **Fla–Fou**

Flamingo Gdns., Nthlt. 72 BY69
Jetstar Way
Flamingo Wk., Horn. 83 FG66
Flamstead End Rd. (Cheshunt), Wal.Cr. 22 DV28
Flamstead Gdns., Dag. 82 EW66
Flamstead Rd.
Flamstead Rd., Dag. 82 EW66
Flamsted Ave., Wem. 74 CN65
Flamsteed Rd. SE7 94 EL78
Flanchford Rd. W12 89 CT76
Flanders Cres. SW17 104 DF94
Flanders Rd. E6 81 EM68
Flanders Rd. W4 88 CS77
Flanders Way E9 79 DX65
Flank St. E1 78 DU73
Dock St.
Flash La., Enf. 35 DP37
Flask Cotts. NW3 62 DD63
New End Sq.
Flask Wk. NW3 62 DC63
Flavell Ms. SE10 94 EE78
Flaxen Clo. E4 51 EB48
Flaxen Rd.
Flaxen Rd. E4 51 EB48
Flaxley Rd., Mord. 118 DB100
Flaxman Ct. W1 5 M9
Flaxman Rd. SE5 91 DP83
Flaxman Ter. WC1 5 N3
Flaxman Ter. WC1 77 DK69
Flaxmore Pl., Beck. 121 ED100
Flaxton Rd. SE18 95 ER80
Flecker Clo., Stan. 45 CF50
Fleece Dr. N9 50 DU49
Fleece Rd., Surb. 115 CJ102
Fleece Wk. N7 77 DL65
Manger Rd.
Fleeming Clo. E17 51 DZ54
Pennant Ter.
Fleeming Rd. E17 51 DZ54
Fleet Clo., Ruis. 57 BQ58
Fleet Clo., W.Mol. 114 CA99
Fleet La., W.Mol. 114 BZ100
Fleet Pl. EC4 77 DN72
Farringdon St.
Fleet Rd. NW3 62 DE64
Fleet Sq. WC1 6 C3
Fleet St. EC4 6 E9
Fleet St. EC4 77 DN72
Fleet St. Hill E1 78 DU70
Weaver St.
Fleetside, W.Mol. 114 BZ99
Fleetway W. Business Pk., Grnf. 73 CH68
Fleetwood Clo. E16 80 EK71
Fleetwood Clo., Chess. 129 CK108
Fleetwood Clo., Croy. 120 DS104
Chepstow Ri.
Fleetwood Clo., Tad. 145 CX120
Fleetwood Ct. E6 81 EM71
Evelyn Denington Rd.
Fleetwood Ct., W.Byf. 126 BG113
Fleetwood Gro. W3 74 CS73
East Acton La.
Fleetwood Rd. NW10 61 CU64
Fleetwood Rd., Kings.T. 116 CP97
Fleetwood Sq., Kings.T. 116 CP97
Fleetwood St. N16 64 DS61
Stoke Newington Ch. St.
Fleetwood Way, Wat. 44 BW49
Fleming Ave., Ruis. 57 BV61
Fleming Clo. (Cheshunt), Wal.Cr. 22 DU26
Fleming Ct. W2 76 DD71
St. Marys Ter.
Fleming Ct., Croy. 133 DN106
Fleming Mead, Mitch. 104 DE94
Fleming Rd. SE17 91 DP79
Fleming Rd., Sthl. 72 CB72
Fleming Way SE28 82 EX73
Fleming Way, Islw. 87 CF83
Flemish Flds., Cher. 112 BG101
Flempton Rd. E10 65 DY60
Fletcher Clo. E6 81 EP72
Trader Rd.
Fletcher La. E10 65 EC59
Fletcher Path SE8 93 EA80
New Butt La.
Fletcher Rd. W4 88 CQ76
Fletcher Rd., Chig. 53 ET50
Fletcher St. E1 78 DU73
Fletchers Clo., Brom. 122 EH98
Fletching Rd. E5 64 DW62
Fletching Rd. SE7 94 EJ79
Fletton Rd. N11 49 DL52
Fleur de Lis St. E1 7 N5
Fleur de Lis St. E1 78 DS70
Fleur Gates SW19 103 CX87
Princes Way
Flexmere Gdns. N17 50 DR53
Flexmere Rd.
Flexmere Rd. N17 50 DR53
Flight App. NW9 47 CT54
Lanacre Ave.
Flimwell Clo., Brom. 108 EE92
Flint Clo., Sutt. 132 DB114
Flint Down Clo., Orp. 124 EU95
Flint St. SE17 11 L9
Flint St. SE17 92 DR77
Flintlock Clo., Stai. 84 BG84
Flintmill Cres. SE3 94 EL82
Flinton St. SE17 11 N10
Flinton St. SE17 92 DS78
Flitcroft St. WC2 5 N9
Flock Mill Pl. SW18 104 DB88
Flockton St. SE16 92 DU75
George Row
Flodden Rd. SE5 92 DQ81
Flood La., Twick. 101 CG88
Church La.
Flood Pas. SE18 95 EM77
Samuel St.
Flood St. SW3 90 DE78
Flood Wk. SW3 90 DE79
Flora Clo. E14 79 EB72
Flora Clo., Croy. 135 EC111
Flora Gdns. W6 89 CV77
Ravenscourt Rd.
Flora Gdns., Rom. 68 EW58
Flora St., Belv. 96 EZ78
Victoria St.
Floral Ct., Ash. 143 CJ118
Rosedale
Floral Dr., St.Alb. 17 CK26
Floral St. WC2 5 P10
Floral St. WC2 77 DL73
Florence Ave., Add. 126 BG111
Florence Ave., Enf. 36 DQ41
Florence Ave., Mord. 118 DC99
Florence Cantwell Wk. N19 63 DL59
Hillrise Rd.
Florence Clo., Walt. 113 BV101
Florence Rd.
Florence Clo., Wat. 29 BU35
Florence Dr., Enf. 36 DQ41
Florence Gdns. W4 88 CQ79
Florence Gdns., Stai. 98 BH94
Florence Nightingale Ho. N1 78 DR65
Clephane Rd.
Florence Rd. E6 80 EJ67
Florence Rd. E13 80 EF68
Florence Rd. N4 63 DN60
Florence Rd. SE2 96 EW76
Florence Rd. SE14 93 DZ81
Florence Rd. SW19 104 DB93
Florence Rd. W4 88 CR76
Florence Rd. W5 74 CL73
Florence Rd., Beck. 121 DY96
Florence Rd., Brom. 122 EG95
Florence Rd., Felt. 99 BV88
Florence Rd., Kings.T. 102 CM94
Florence Rd., S.Croy. 134 DR109
Florence Rd., Sthl. 86 BX77
Florence Rd., Walt. 113 BV101
Florence St. E16 80 EF70
Florence St. N1 77 DP66
Florence St. NW4 61 CW56
Florence Ter. SE14 93 DZ81
Florence Way SW12 104 DF88
Florfield Pas. E8 78 DV65
Reading La.
Florfield Rd. E8 78 DV65
Reading La.
Florian Ave., Sutt. 132 DD105
Florian Rd. SW15 89 CY84
Florida Clo. (Bushey), Wat. 45 CD47
Florida Rd., Th.Hth. 119 DP95
Florida St. E2 78 DU69
Floriston Ave., Uxb. 71 BQ66
Floriston Clo., Stan. 45 CH53
Floriston Gdns., Stan. 45 CH53
Floss St. SW15 89 CW82
Flower & Dean Wk. E1 78 DT71
Thrawl St.
Flower La. NW7 47 CT50
Flower Wk., The SW7 90 DC75
Flowerfield, Sev. 153 FF117
Flowers Ms. N19 63 DJ61
Tollhouse Way
Flowersmead SW17 104 DG89
Floyd Rd. SE7 94 EJ78
Floyds La., Wok. 140 BG116
Fludyer St. SE13 94 EE84
Folair Way SE16 92 DV78
Catlin St.
Foley Ms., Esher 129 CE107
Foley Rd., Esher 129 CE108
Foley Rd., West. 150 EK118
Foley St. W1 5 K7
Foley St. W1 77 DJ71
Folgate St. E1 7 N6
Folgate St. E1 78 DS71
Foliot St. W12 75 CT72
Folkestone Rd. E6 81 EN68
Folkestone Rd. E17 65 EB56
Folkestone Rd. N18 50 DU49
Folkingham La. NW9 46 CR53
Folkington Cor. N12 47 CZ50
Follet Dr., Abb.L. 15 BT31
Follett St. E14 79 EC72
Folly Clo., Rad. 31 CF36
Folly La. E4 51 DY53
Folly La. E17 51 DY53
Folly Ms. W11 75 CZ72
Portobello Rd.
Folly Pathway, Rad. 31 CF35
Folly Wall E14 93 EC75
Follyfield Rd., Bans. 132 DA114
Font Hills N2 48 DC54
Fontaine Rd. SW16 105 DM94
Fontarabia Rd. SW11 90 DG84
Fontayne Ave., Chig. 53 EQ49
Fontayne Ave., Rain. 83 FE66
Fontayne Ave., Rom. 69 FE55
Fontenoy Rd. SW12 105 DH89
Fonteyne Gdns., Wdf.Grn. 52 EK54
Lechmere Ave.
Fonthill Clo. SE20 120 DU96
Selby Rd.
Fonthill Ms. N4 63 DN61
Lennox Rd.
Fonthill Rd. N4 63 DM60
Fontley Way SW15 103 CU87
Fontmell Clo., Ashf. 98 BN92
Fontmell Pk., Ashf. 98 BM92
Fontwell Clo., Har. 45 CE52
Fontwell Clo., Nthlt. 72 CA65
Fontwell Dr., Brom. 123 EN99
Football La., Har. 59 CE60
Footbury Hill Rd., Orp. 124 EU101
Footpath, The SW15 103 CU85
Parkstead Rd.
Foots Cray High St., Sid. 110 EW93
Foots Cray La., Sid. 110 EW88
Footscray Rd. SE9 109 EN86
Footway, The SE9 109 EQ87
Forbench Clo., Wok. 140 BH122
Forbes Ave., Pot.B. 20 DD33
Forbes Clo. NW2 61 CU61
Forbes Clo., Horn. 69 FH60
St. Leonards Way
Forbes Ct. SE19 106 DS92
Forbes St. E1 78 DU72
Ellen St.
Forbes Way, Ruis. 57 BV61
Forburg Rd. N16 64 DU60
Force Grn. La., West. 151 ER124
Ford Clo. E3 79 DY68
Roman Rd.
Ford Clo., Ashf. 98 BL93
Ford Clo., Har. 59 CD59
Ford Clo., Rain. 83 FF66
Ford Clo., Shep. 112 BN98
Ford Clo., Th.Hth. 119 DP99
Ford Clo. (Bushey), Wat. 30 CC42
Ford End, Wdf.Grn. 52 EH51
Ford La., Iver 70 BG72
Ford La., Rain. 83 FF66
Ford Rd. E3 79 DY67
Ford Rd., Ashf. 98 BM91
Ford Rd., Cher. 112 BH102
Ford Rd., Dag. 82 EZ66
Ford Sq. E1 78 DV71
Ford St. E3 79 DY67
Ford St. E16 80 EF72
Fordbridge Clo., Cher. 112 BH102
Fordbridge Rd., Ashf. 98 BL93
Fordbridge Rd., Shep. 113 BS100
Fordbridge Rd., Sun. 113 BS100
Fordcroft Rd., Orp. 124 EV99
Forde Ave., Brom. 122 EJ97
Fordel Rd. SE6 107 ED88
Fordham Clo., Barn. 34 DE41
Fordham Rd., Barn. 34 DD41
Fordham St. E1 78 DU72
Fordhook Ave. W5 74 CM73
Fordingley Rd. W9 75 CZ69
Fordington Rd. N6 62 DF57
Fordmill Rd. SE6 107 EA89
Fords Gro. N21 50 DQ46
Fords Pk. Rd. E16 80 EG72
Fordwater Rd., Cher. 112 BH102
Fordwater Trd. Est., Cher. 112 BH102
Fordwich Clo., Orp. 123 ET101
Fordwych Rd. NW2 61 CY63
Fordyce Rd. SE13 107 EC86
Fordyke Rd., Dag. 68 EZ61
Fore St. EC2 7 J7
Fore St. EC2 78 DQ71
Fore St. N9 50 DU49
Fore St. N18 50 DT51
Fore St., Pnr. 57 BU57
Fore St. Ave. EC2 7 K7
Forefield, St.Alb. 16 CA27
Foreland Ct. NW4 47 CX53
Foreland St. SE18 95 ER77
Plumstead Rd.
Foreman Ct. W6 89 CW77
Hammersmith Bdy.
Foremark Clo., Ilf. 53 ET51
Foreshore SE8 93 DZ77
Forest, The E11 66 EE56
Forest App. E4 52 EE45
Forest App., Wdf.Grn. 52 EG52
Forest Ave. E4 52 EE45
Forest Ave., Chig. 53 EN50
Forest Business Pk. E17 65 DY59
Forest Clo. E11 66 EF57
Forest Clo., Chis. 123 EN95
Forest Clo., Wal.Abb. 38 EH37
Forest Clo., Wdf.Grn. 52 EH49
Forest Ct. E4 52 EF46
Forest Ct. E11 66 EE56
Forest Cres., Ash. 144 CN116
Forest Cft. SE23 106 DV89
Forest Dr. E12 66 EK62
Forest Dr., Epp. 39 ES36
Forest Dr., Kes. 136 EL105
Forest Dr., Sun. 99 BT94
Forest Dr., Tad. 145 CY121
Forest Dr., Wdf.Grn. 51 ED52
Forest Dr. E. E11 65 ED59
Forest Dr. W. E11 65 EC59
Forest Edge, Buck.H. 52 EJ49
Forest Gdns. N17 50 DT54
Forest Gate NW9 60 CS57
Forest Glade E4 52 EE49
Forest Glade E11 66 EE58
Forest Glade, Epp. 26 EY28
Forest Gro. E8 78 DT65
Forest Heights, Buck.H. 52 EG47
Forest Hill Rd. SE22 106 DV85
Forest Hill Rd. SE23 106 DW86
Forest Ind. Est., Ilf. 53 ES53
Forest La. E7 66 EG64
Forest La. E15 80 EE65
Forest La., Chig. 53 EN50
Forest La., Lthd. 141 BT124
Forest Mt. Rd., Wdf.Grn. 51 ED52
Forest Ridge, Beck. 121 EA97
Forest Ridge, Kes. 136 EL105
Forest Ri. E17 65 ED57
Forest Rd. E7 66 EG63
Forest Rd. E8 78 DT65
Forest Rd. E11 65 ED59
Forest Rd. E17 64 DW56
Forest Rd. N9 50 DV46
Forest Rd. N17 64 DW56
Forest Rd., Enf. 37 DY36
Forest Rd., Erith 97 FG81
Forest Rd., Felt. 100 BW89
Forest Rd., Ilf. 53 ES53
Forest Rd., Lthd. 141 BU123
Forest Rd., Loug. 38 EK41
Forest Rd., Rich. 88 CN80
Forest Rd., Rom. 69 FB55
Forest Rd., Sutt. 118 DA102
Forest Rd. (Cheshunt), Wal.Cr. 23 DX29
Forest Rd., Wat. 15 BV33
Forest Rd., Wdf.Grn. 52 EG48
Forest Side E4 52 EF45
Forest Side E7 66 EH63
Capel Rd.
Forest Side, Buck.H. 52 EH46
Forest Side, Epp. 25 ER33
Forest Side, Wal.Abb. 38 EJ36
Forest Side, Wor.Pk. 117 CT102
Forest St. E7 66 EG64
Forest Vw. E4 51 ED45
Forest Vw. E11 66 EF59
Forest Vw. Ave. E10 65 ED57
Forest Vw. Rd. E12 66 EL63
Forest Vw. Rd. E17 51 EC53
Forest Vw. Rd., Loug. 38 EK42
Forest Wk. (Bushey), Wat. 30 BZ39
Millbrook Rd.
Forest Way N19 63 DJ61
Hargrave Pk.
Forest Way, Ash. 144 CM117
Forest Way, Loug. 38 EL41
Forest Way, Orp. 123 ET99
Forest Way, Sid. 109 ER87
Forest Way, Wal.Abb. 24 EK33
Forest Way, Wdf.Grn. 52 EH49
Forestdale N14 49 DK49
Forester Rd. SE15 92 DV84
Foresters Clo., Wall. 133 DK108
Foresters Clo., Wal.Cr. 22 DS27
Foresters Cres., Bexh. 97 FB84
Foresters Dr. E17 65 ED56
Foresters Dr., Wall. 133 DK107
Forestholme Clo. SE23 106 DW89
Forfar Rd. N22 49 DP53
Forfar Rd. SW11 90 DG81
Forge Ave., Couls. 147 DN120
Forge Clo., Brom. 122 EG102
Forge Clo., Hayes 85 BR79
High St.
Forge Clo., Kings L. 14 BG31
Forge Cotts. W5 73 CK74
Ealing Grn.
Forge Dr., Esher 129 CG108
Forge End, St.Alb. 16 CA26
Forge La., Felt. 100 BY92
Forge La., Nthwd. 43 BS52
Forge La., Sun. 113 BU97
Forge La., Sutt. 131 CY108
Forge Pl. NW1 76 DG65
Malden Cres.
Forge Way, Sev. 139 FF111
Forgefield, West. 150 EK116
Main Rd.
Forman Pl. N16 64 DT63
Farleigh Rd.
Formby Ave., Stan. 59 CJ55
Formosa St. W9 76 DB70
Formunt Clo. E16 80 EF71
Vincent St.
Forres Gdns. NW11 62 DA58
Forrest Gdns. SW16 119 DM97
Forrester Path SE26 106 DW91
Forris Ave., Hayes 71 BT74
Forset St. W1 4 C8
Forset St. W1 76 DE72
Forstal Clo., Brom. 122 EG97
Ridley Rd.
Forster Rd. E17 65 DY58
Forster Rd. N17 64 DT55
Forster Rd. SW2 105 DL87
Forster Rd., Beck. 121 DY97
Forster Rd., Croy. 120 DQ101
Windmill Rd.
Forsters Clo., Rom. 68 EZ58
Forsters Way, Hayes 71 BV72
Forston St. N1 78 DR68
Cropley St.
Forsyte Cres. SE19 120 DS95
Forsyth Gdns. SE17 91 DP79
Forsyth Pl., Enf. 36 DS43
Forsythia Clo., Ilf. 67 EP64
Fort Rd. SE1 92 DT77
Fort Rd., Nthlt. 72 CA66
Fort Rd., Sev. 153 FC115
Fort St. E1 7 N7
Fort St. E1 78 DS71
Fort St. E16 80 EH74
Forterie Gdns., Ilf. 68 EU62
Fortescue Ave. E8 78 DV66
Mentmore Ter.
Fortescue Ave., Twick. 100 CC90
Fortescue Rd. SW19 104 DD94
Fortescue Rd., Edg. 46 CQ53
Fortescue Rd., Wey. 126 BM105
Fortess Gro. NW5 63 DH64
Fortess Rd.
Fortess Rd. NW5 63 DH64
Fortess Wk. NW5 63 DH64
Fortess Rd.
Forthbridge Rd. SW11 90 DG84
Fortis Clo. E16 80 EJ72
Fortis Grn. N2 62 DE56
Fortis Grn. N10 62 DG55
Fortis Grn. Ave. N2 62 DF55
Fortis Grn. Rd. N10 62 DG55
Fortismere Ave. N10 62 DG55
Fortnam Rd. N19 63 DK61
Fortnums Acre, Stan. 45 CF51
Fortrose Gdns. SW2 105 DK88
New Pk. Rd.
Fortuna Clo. N7 77 DM65
Vulcan Way
Fortune Gate Rd. NW10 74 CS67
Fortune Grn. Rd. NW6 62 DA63
Fortune La., Borwd. 31 CK44
Fortune St. EC1 7 J5
Fortune St. EC1 78 DQ70
Fortune Wk. SE28 95 ER76
Broadwater Rd.
Fortune Way NW10 75 CU69
Fortunes Mead, Nthlt. 72 BY65
Forty Acre La. E16 80 EG71
Forty Ave., Wem. 60 CM62
Forty Clo., Wem. 60 CM62
Forty Hill, Enf. 36 DS38
Forty La., Wem. 60 CP61
Fortyfoot Rd., Lthd. 143 CJ121
Forum, The, W.Mol. 114 CB98
Forum Way, Edg. 46 CN51
High St.
Forumside, Edg. 46 CN51
High St.
Forval Clo., Mitch. 118 DF99
Forward Dr., Har. 59 CF56
Fosbury Ms. W2 76 DB73
Inverness Ter.
Foscote Ms. W9 76 DA71
Amberley Rd.
Foscote Rd. NW4 61 CV57
Foskett Rd. SW6 89 CZ82
Foss Ave., Croy. 133 DN106
Foss Rd. SW17 104 DD91
Fossdene Rd. SE7 94 EH78
Fossdyke Clo., Hayes 72 BY71
Fosse Way W13 73 CG71
Fossil Rd. SE13 93 EA83
Fossington Rd., Belv. 96 EX77
Fossway, Dag. 68 EW61
Foster Clo. (Cheshunt), Wal.Cr. 23 DY30
Windmill La.
Foster La. EC2 7 H8
Foster La. EC2 78 DQ72
Foster Rd. E13 80 EG70
Foster Rd. W3 74 CS73
Foster Rd. W4 88 CR78
Foster St. NW4 61 CW56
Foster Wk. NW4 61 CW56
New Brent St.
Fosters Clo. E18 52 EH53
Fosters Clo., Chis. 109 EM92
Fothergill Clo. E13 80 EG68
Fothergill Dr. N21 35 DM43
Fotheringham Rd., Enf. 36 DT42
Foubert's Pl. W1 5 K9
Foubert's Pl. W1 77 DJ72
Foulden Rd. N16 64 DT63
Foulden Ter. N16 64 DT63
Foulden Rd.
Foulis Ter. SW7 8 A10
Foulis Ter. SW7 90 DD78
Foulser Rd. SW17 104 DF90
Foulsham Rd., Th.Hth. 120 DQ97
Founder Clo. E6 81 EP72
Trader Rd.
Founders Ct. EC2 7 K8
Founders Gdns. SE19 106 DQ94
Foundry Clo. SE16 79 DY74
Foundry Ms. NW1 5 L4
Fount St. SW8 91 DK80
Fountain Clo., Uxb. 71 BQ71
New Rd.
Fountain Ct. EC4 6 D10
Fountain Dr. SE19 106 DT91
Fountain Dr., Cars. 132 DF108
Fountain Grn. Sq. SE16 92 DU75
Bermondsey Wall E.
Fountain Ms. N5 64 DQ63
Kelross Rd.
Fountain Pl. SW9 91 DN81
Fountain Pl., Wal.Abb. 23 EC34
Fountain Rd. SW17 104 DD92
Fountain Rd., Th.Hth. 120 DQ96
Fountain Sq. SW1 9 H8
Fountain St. E2 78 DT69
Columbia Rd.
Fountains Ave., Felt. 100 BZ90
Fountains Clo., Felt. 100 BZ89
Fountains Cres. N14 49 DL45
Fountayne Rd. N15 64 DU56
Fountayne Rd. N16 64 DU61
Four Acres, Cob. 128 BY113
Four Seasons Cres., Sutt. 117 CZ103
Kimpton Rd.
Four Seasons Ind. Est., Sthl. 86 CB76
Four Tubs, The (Bushey), Wat. 45 CD45
Four Wents, Cob. 128 BW114
Four Wents, The E4 51 ED47
Kings Rd.

Fouracres SW12 105 DH89
Little Dimocks
Fouracres, Enf. 37 DY39
Fourland Wk., Edg. 46 CQ51
Fournier St. E1 78 DT71
Fourth Ave. E12 67 EM63
Fourth Ave. W10 75 CY69
Fourth Ave., Hayes 71 BT74
Fourth Ave., Rom. 69 FC60
Fourth Ave., Wat. 30 BX35
Fourth Cross Rd., Twick. 101 CD89
Fourth Dr., Couls. 147 DK116
Fourth Way, Wem. 60 CQ63
Fowey Ave., Ilf. 66 EK57
Fowey Clo. E1 78 DV74
Kennet St.
Fowler Clo. SW11 90 DD83
Fowler Rd. E7 66 EG63
Fowler Rd. N1 77 DP66
Halton Rd.
Fowler Rd., Ilf. 54 EV51
Fowler Rd., Mitch. 118 DG96
Fowlers Clo., Sid. 110 EY92
Thursland Rd.
Fowlers Wk. W5 73 CK70
Fowley Clo., Wal.Cr. 23 DZ34
Fowley Mead Caravan Pk., Wal.Cr. 23 EA34
Fownes St. SW11 90 DE83
Fox and Knot St. EC1 6 G6
Fox Clo. E1 78 DW70
Fox Clo. E16 80 EG71
Fox Clo., Borwd. 31 CK44
Rodgers Clo.
Fox Clo., Orp. 138 EU106
Fox Clo., Rom. 55 FB50
Fox Clo. (Bushey), Wat. 30 CB42
Fox Clo., Wey. 127 BR106
Fox Covert, Lthd. 143 CD124
Fox Hill SE19 106 DT94
Fox Hill, Kes. 136 EH106
Fox Hill Gdns. SE19 106 DT94
Fox Hollow Dr., Bexh. 96 EX83
Fox Ho. Rd., Belv. 97 FB77
Fox La. N13 49 DL47
Fox La. W5 74 CL70
Fox La., Cat. 147 DP121
Fox La., Kes. 136 EH106
Fox La., Lthd. 142 BY124
Fox Rd. E16 80 EF71
Foxacre, Cat. 148 DS122
Town End Clo.
Foxberry Rd. SE4 93 DY83
Foxborough Gdns. SE4 107 EA86
Foxbourne Rd. SW17 104 DG89
Foxburrow Rd., Chig. 54 EX49
Foxbury Ave., Chis. 109 ER93
Foxbury Clo., Brom. 108 EH93
Foxbury Clo., Orp. 138 EU106
Foxbury Dr.
Foxbury Dr., Orp. 138 EU107
Foxbury Rd., Brom. 108 EG93
Foxcombe, Croy. 135 EB107
Foxcombe Clo. E6 80 EK68
Boleyn Rd.
Foxcombe Rd. SW15 103 CU88
Alton Rd.
Foxcote SE5 92 DS78
Albany Rd.
Foxcroft Rd. SE18 95 EP81
Foxdell, Nthwd. 43 BR51
Foxearth Clo., West. 150 EL118
Foxearth Rd., S.Croy. 134 DV110
Foxearth Spur, S.Croy. 134 DW109
Foxes Dale SE3 94 EG83
Foxes Dale, Brom. 121 ED97
Foxes Dr., Wal.Cr. 22 DU29
Foxfield Clo., Nthwd. 43 BT51
Foxfield Rd., Orp. 123 ER103
Foxglove Clo., Sthl. 72 BY73
Foxglove Clo., Stai. 98 BK88
Foxglove Gdns. E11 66 EJ56
Foxglove Gdns., Pur. 133 DL111
Foxglove La., Chess. 130 CN105
Foxglove St. W12 75 CT73
Foxglove Way, Wall. 119 DH102
Foxgrove N14 49 DL48
Foxgrove Ave., Beck. 107 EB94
Foxgrove Path, Wat. 44 BX50
Foxgrove Rd., Beck. 107 EB94
Foxham Rd. N19 63 DK62
Foxhill, Wat. 29 BU36
Foxhole Rd. SE9 108 EL85
Foxholes, Wey. 127 BR106
Foxholt Gdns. NW10 74 CQ66
Foxhome Clo., Chis. 109 EN93
Foxlake Rd., W.Byf. 126 BM112
Foxlands Clo., Wat. 15 BU34
Foxlands Cres., Dag. 69 FC64
Foxlands La., Dag. 69 FD64
Rainham Rd. S.
Foxlands Rd., Dag. 69 FC64
Foxlees, Wem. 59 CG63
Foxley Clo. E8 64 DU64
Ferncliff Rd.
Foxley Clo., Loug. 39 EP40
Foxley Gdns., Pur. 133 DP113
Foxley Hill Rd., Pur. 133 DN112
Foxley La., Pur. 133 DJ111
Foxley Rd. SW9 91 DN80
Foxley Rd., Ken. 133 DP114
Foxley Rd., Th.Hth. 119 DP98
Foxley Sq. SW9 91 DP80
Cancell Rd.
Foxleys, Wat. 44 BY47
Foxmead Clo., Enf. 35 DM41
Foxmore St. SW11 90 DF81
Foxon Clo., Cat. 148 DS121
Foxon La., Cat. 148 DR121
Foxon La. Gdns., Cat. 148 DS121
Fox's Path, Mitch. 118 DE96
Foxton Gro., Mitch. 118 DD96
Foxwarren, Esher 129 CF109
Foxwell Clo. SE4 93 DY83
Foxwell St.
Foxwell Ms. SE4 93 DY83
Foxwell St.
Foxwell St. SE4 93 DY83
Foxwood Clo. NW7 46 CS49
Foxwood Clo., Felt. 99 BV90
Foxwood Grn. Clo., Enf. 36 DS44
Foxwood Gro., Orp. 138 EW110
Foxwood Rd. SE3 94 EF84
Foyle Rd. N17 50 DU53
Foyle Rd. SE3 94 EF79
Framfield Clo. N12 48 DA48
Framfield Ct., Enf. 36 DS44
Framfield Rd. N5 63 DP64
Framfield Rd. W7 73 CF72
Framfield Rd., Mitch. 104 DG94
Framlingham Clo. E5 64 DW61
Detmold Rd.
Framlingham Cres. SE9 108 EL91
Frampton Clo., Sutt. 132 DA108
Frampton Pk. Est. E9 78 DW66
Frampton Pk. Rd. E9 78 DW65
Frampton Rd., Epp. 26 EU28
Frampton Rd., Houns. 100 BY85
Frampton Rd., Pot.B. 20 DC30
Frampton St. NW8 4 A5
Frampton St. NW8 76 DD70
Francemary Rd. SE4 107 EA85
Frances Rd. E4 51 EA51
Frances St. SE18 95 EM77
Franche Ct. Rd. SW17 104 DC90
Francis Ave., Bexh. 96 FA82
Francis Ave., Felt. 99 BU90
Francis Ave., Ilf. 67 ER61
Francis Barber Clo. SW16 105 DM91
Well Clo.
Francis Chichester Way SW11 90 DG81
Francis Clo. E14 93 ED77
Saunders Ness Rd.
Francis Clo., Epsom 130 CR105
Francis Clo., Shep. 112 BN98
Francis Gro. SW19 103 CZ93
Francis Rd. E10 65 EC60
Francis Rd. N2 62 DF56
Lynmouth Rd.
Francis Rd., Cat. 148 DR122
Francis Rd., Croy. 119 DP101
Francis Rd., Grnf. 73 CH68
Francis Rd., Har. 59 CG57
Francis Rd., Houns. 86 BX82
Francis Rd., Ilf. 67 ER61
Francis Rd., Orp. 124 EX97
Francis Rd., Pnr. 58 BW57
Francis Rd., Wall. 133 DJ107
Francis Rd., Wat. 29 BV42
Francis St. E15 66 EE64
Francis St. SW1 9 K8
Francis St. SW1 91 DJ77
Francis St., Ilf. 67 ER61
Francis Ter. N19 63 DJ62
Junction Rd.
Francis Wk. N1 77 DM67
Bingfield St.
Franciscan Rd. SW17 104 DF92
Francklyn Gdns., Edg. 46 CN48
Francombe Gdns., Rom. 69 FG58
Franconia Rd. SW4 105 DK85
Frank Bailey Wk. E12 67 EN64
Gainsborough Ave.
Frank Burton Clo. SE7 94 EH78
Victoria Way
Frank Dixon Clo. SE21 106 DS88
Frank Dixon Way SE21 106 DS88
Frank Martin Ct., Wal.Cr. 22 DU30
Frank St. E13 80 EG70
Frank Trowell Ct., Felt. 99 BU88
Frankfurt Rd. SE24 106 DQ85
Frankham St. SE8 93 EA80
Frankland Clo. SE16 92 DW77
Frankland Clo., Rick. 42 BN45
Frankland Clo., Wdf.Grn. 52 EJ50
Frankland Rd. E4 51 EA50
Frankland Rd. SW7 90 DD76
Frankland Rd., Rick. 29 BP44
Franklin Ave. (Cheshunt), Wal.Cr. 22 DU30
Franklin Clo. N20 48 DC45
Franklin Clo. SE13 93 EB81
Franklin Clo. SE27 105 DP90
Franklin Clo., Kings.T. 116 CN97
Franklin Cres., Mitch. 119 DJ98
Franklin Ho. NW9 61 CT59
Franklin Pas. SE9 94 EL83
Phineas Pett Rd.
Franklin Rd. SE20 106 DW94
Franklin Rd., Bexh. 96 EY81
Franklin Rd., Wat. 29 BV40
Franklin Sq. W14 89 CZ78
Marchbank Rd.
Franklin St. E3 79 EB69
St. Leonards St.
Franklin St. N15 64 DS58
Franklin Way, Croy. 119 DL102
Franklins Ms., Har. 58 CC61
Franklin's Row SW3 8 E10
Franklin's Row SW3 90 DF78
Franklyn Gdns., Ilf. 53 ER51
Franklyn Rd. NW10 75 CT66
Franklyn Rd., Walt. 113 BU100
Franks Ave., N.Mal. 116 CQ98
Frankswood Ave., Orp. 123 EP99
Frankswood Ave., West Dr. 70 BM72
Franlaw Cres. N13 50 DQ49
Franmil Rd., Horn. 69 FG60
Fransfield Gro. SE26 106 DV90
Frant Clo. SE20 106 DW94
Frant Rd., Th.Hth. 119 DP99
Franthorne Way SE6 107 EB89
Fraser Clo. E6 80 EL72
Linton Gdns.
Fraser Clo., Bex. 111 FC88
Dartford Rd.
Fraser Ho., Brent. 88 CM78
Green Dragon La.
Fraser Rd. E17 65 EB57
Fraser Rd. N9 50 DV48
Fraser Rd., Erith 97 FC78
Fraser Rd., Grnf. 73 CH67
Fraser Rd. (Cheshunt), Wal.Cr. 23 DY28
Fraser St. W4 88 CS78
Frating Cres., Wdf.Grn. 52 EH51
Frays Ave., West Dr. 84 BK75
Frays Clo., West Dr. 84 BK76
Frays Lea, Uxb. 70 BJ68
Frays Waye, Uxb. 70 BJ67
Frazer Ave., Ruis. 58 BW64
Frazer Clo., Rom. 69 FF59
Frazier St. SE1 10 D5
Frazier St. SE1 91 DN75
Frean St. SE16 92 DU76
Fred Wigg Twr. E11 66 EF61
Freda Corbett Clo. SE15 92 DU80
Bird in Bush Rd.
Frederic Ms. SW1 8 E5
Frederic St. E17 65 DY57
Frederica Rd. E4 51 ED45
Frederica St. N7 77 DM66
Caledonian Rd.
Frederick Clo. W2 4 C10
Frederick Clo. W2 76 DE73
Frederick Clo., Sutt. 131 CZ105
Frederick Ct. NW2 61 CY62
Douglas Ms.
Frederick Cres. SW9 91 DP80
Frederick Cres., Enf. 36 DW40
Frederick Gdns., Sutt. 131 CZ106
Frederick Pl. SE18 95 EP78
Frederick Rd. SE17 91 DP78
Chapter Rd.
Frederick Rd., Rain. 83 FD68
Frederick Rd., Sutt. 131 CZ106
Frederick Sq. SE16 79 DY73
Rotherhithe St.
Frederick St. WC1 6 B3
Frederick St. WC1 77 DM69
Frederick Ter. E8 78 DT67
Haggerston Rd.
Frederick's Pl. EC2 7 K9
Fredericks Pl. N12 48 DC49
Frederick's Row EC1 6 F2
Fredora Ave., Hayes 71 BT70
Free Prae Rd., Cher. 112 BG102
Freeborne Gdns., Rain. 83 FG65
Mungo Pk. Rd.
Freedom Clo. E17 65 DY56
Freedom Rd. N17 50 DR54
Freedom St. SW11 90 DF82
Freedown La., Sutt. 132 DB113
Freegrove Rd. N7 63 DL64
Freeland Pk. NW4 47 CY54
Freeland Rd. W5 74 CM73
Freeland Way, Erith 97 FG81
Slade Grn. Rd.
Freelands Ave., S.Croy. 135 DX109
Freelands Gro., Brom. 122 EH95
Freelands Rd., Brom. 122 EH95
Freelands Rd., Cob. 127 BV114
Freeling St. N1 77 DM66
Caledonian Rd.
Freeman Clo., Nthlt. 72 BY66
Freeman Dr., W.Mol. 114 BZ97
Freeman Rd., Mord. 118 DD99
Freemans Clo., Shep. 113 BS98
Freemans La., Hayes 71 BS73
Freemantle Ave., Enf. 37 DX43
Freemasons Rd. E16 80 EH71
Freemasons Rd., Croy. 120 DS102
Freesia Clo., Orp. 137 ET106
Briarswood Way
Freethorpe Clo. SE19 120 DS95
Freezeland Way, Uxb. 70 BN65
Western Ave.
Freke Rd. SW11 90 DG83
Fremantle Rd., Belv. 96 FA77
Fremantle Rd., Ilf. 53 EQ54
Fremantle St. SE17 11 M10
Fremantle St. SE17 92 DS78
Fremont St. E9 78 DW67
French Gdns., Cob. 128 BW114
French Ordinary Ct. EC3 78 DS73
Crutched Friars
French Pl. E1 7 N4
French St., Sun. 114 BW96
Frenchaye, Add. 126 BJ106
Frendsbury Rd. SE4 93 DY84
Frensham (Cheshunt), Wal.Cr. 22 DT27
Frensham Clo., Sthl. 72 BZ70
Frensham Ct., Mitch. 118 DD97
Phipps Bri. Rd.
Frensham Dr. SW15 103 CT90
Frensham Dr., Croy. 135 EC108
Frensham Rd. SE9 109 ER89
Frensham Rd., Ken. 133 DP114
Frensham St. SE15 92 DU79
Frensham Way, Epsom 145 CW116
Frere St. SW11 90 DE82
Fresh Wf. Rd., Bark. 81 EP67
Freshfield Ave. E8 78 DT66
Freshfield Clo. SE13 93 ED84
Marischal Rd.
Freshfield Dr. N14 49 DH45
Freshfields, Croy. 121 DZ101
Freshford St. SW18 104 DC90
Freshmount Gdns., Epsom 130 CP111
Freshwater Clo. SW17 104 DG93
Freshwater Rd. SW17 104 DG93
Freshwater Rd., Dag. 68 EX60
Freshwell Ave., Rom. 68 EW56
Freshwood Clo., Beck. 121 EB95
Freshwood Way, Wall. 133 DH109
Freston Gdns., Barn. 34 DF43
Freston Pk. N3 47 CZ54
Freston Rd. W10 75 CX73
Freston Rd. W11 75 CX73
Freta Rd., Bexh. 110 EZ85
Frewin Rd. SW18 104 DD88
Friar Ms. SE27 105 DP90
Prioress Rd.
Friar Rd., Hayes 72 BX70
Friar Rd., Orp. 124 EU99
Friar St. EC4 6 G9
Friars, The, Chig. 53 ES49
Friars Ave. N20 48 DE48
Friars Ave. SW15 103 CT90
Friars Clo. E4 51 EC48
Friars Clo. N2 62 DD56
Friars Clo., Nthlt. 72 BX69
Broomcroft Ave.
Friars Gdns. W3 74 CR72
St. Dunstans Ave.
Friars Gate Clo., Wdf.Grn. 52 EG49
Friars La., Rich. 101 CK85
Friars Mead E14 93 EC76
Friars Ms. SE9 109 EN85
Friars Orchard, Lthd. 143 CD121
Friars Pl. La. W3 74 CR73
Friars Rd. E6 80 EK67
Friars Stile Pl., Rich. 102 CL86
Friars Stile Rd.
Friars Stile Rd., Rich. 102 CL86
Friars Wk. N14 49 DH45
Friars Wk. SE2 96 EX78
Friars Way W3 74 CR72
Friars Way, Cher. 112 BG99
Friars Way, Kings L. 14 BN30
Friars Way (Bushey), Wat. 30 BZ39
Friars Wd., Croy. 135 DY109
Friary Clo. N12 48 DE50
Friary Ct. SW1 9 L3
Friary Est. SE15 92 DU79
Friary La., Wdf.Grn. 52 EG49
Friary Rd. N12 48 DD49
Friary Rd. SE15 92 DU80
Friary Rd. W3 74 CQ72
Friary Way N12 48 DE49
Friday Hill E4 52 EE47
Friday Hill E. E4 52 EE48
Friday Hill W. E4 52 EE47
Friday Rd., Erith 97 FD78
Friday Rd., Mitch. 104 DF94
Friday St. EC4 7 H9
Friday St. EC4 78 DQ73
Frideswide Pl. NW5 63 DJ64
Islip St.
Friend St. EC1 6 F2
Friend St. EC1 77 DP69
Friendly Pl. SE13 93 EB81
Lewisham Rd.
Friendly St. SE8 93 EA82
Friendly St. Ms. SE8 93 EA82
Friendly St.
Friends Ave., Wal.Cr. 23 DX31
Friends Rd., Croy. 120 DR104
Friends Rd., Pur. 133 DP112
Friends Wk., Uxb. 70 BK66
Bakers Rd.
Friendship Wk., Nthlt. 72 BX69
Wayfarer Rd.
Friern Barnet La. N11 48 DF49
Friern Barnet La. N20 48 DC47
Friern Barnet Rd. N11 48 DF50
Friern Ct. N20 48 DD48
Friern Mt. Dr. N20 48 DC45
Friern Pk. N12 48 DC50
Friern Rd. SE22 106 DU87
Friern Watch Ave. N12 48 DC49
Frigate Ms. SE8 93 EA79
Watergate St.
Frimley Ave., Wall. 133 DL106
Frimley Clo. SW19 103 CY89
Frimley Clo., Croy. 135 EC108
Frimley Ct., Sid. 110 EW92
Frimley Cres., Croy. 135 EC108
Frimley Gdns., Mitch. 118 DE97
Frimley Rd., Chess. 129 CK106
Frimley Rd., Ilf. 67 ES62
Frimley Way E1 79 DX70
Frimley Way, Wall. 133 DL106
Fringewood Clo., Nthwd. 43 BP53
Frinsted Clo., Orp. 124 EX98
Frinsted Rd., Erith 97 FD80
Frinton Clo., Wat. 43 BV47
Frinton Dr., Wdf.Grn. 51 ED52
Frinton Ms., Ilf. 67 EN58
Bramley Cres.
Frinton Rd. E6 80 EK69
Frinton Rd. N15 64 DS58
Frinton Rd. SW17 104 DG93
Frinton Rd., Rom. 54 EZ52
Frinton Rd., Sid. 110 EY89
Friston Path, Chig. 53 ES50
Manford Way
Friston St. SW6 90 DB82
Friswell Pl., Bexh. 96 FA84
Frith Ct. NW7 47 CY52
Frith Knowle, Walt. 127 BV106
Frith La. NW7 47 CY52
Frith Rd. E11 65 EC63
Frith Rd., Croy. 120 DQ103
Frith St. W1 5 M9
Frith St. W1 77 DK72
Fritham Clo., N.Mal. 116 CS100
Frithville Gdns. W12 75 CW74
Frithwood Ave., Nthwd. 43 BS51
Frizlands La., Dag. 69 FB63
Frobisher Clo., Ken. 148 DR117
Hayes La.
Frobisher Clo., Pnr. 58 BX59
Frobisher Cres., Stai. 98 BL87
Frobisher Gdns., Stai. 98 BL87
Frobisher Cres.
Frobisher Pas. E14 79 EA74
North Colonnade
Frobisher Rd. E6 81 EM72
Frobisher Rd. N8 63 DN56
Frobisher Rd., Erith 97 FF80
Frobisher St. SE10 94 EE79
Frog La., Rain. 83 FD71
Froghall La., Chig. 53 ER49
Frogley Rd. SE22 92 DT84
Frogmoor La., Rick. 42 BK47
Frogmore SW18 104 DA85
Frogmore, St.Alb. 17 CD27
Frogmore Ave., Hayes 71 BS70
Frogmore Clo., Sutt. 117 CX104
Frogmore Gdns., Hayes 71 BS70
Frogmore Gdns., Sutt. 131 CY105
Frogmore Mobile Home Pk., St.Alb. 17 CD27
Frognal NW3 62 DC64
Frognal Ave., Har. 59 CF56
Frognal Ave., Sid. 110 EU92
Frognal Clo. NW3 62 DC64
Frognal Ct. NW3 76 DC65
Frognal Gdns. NW3 62 DC63
Frognal La. NW3 62 DB64
Frognal Par. NW3 76 DC65
Frognal Ct.
Frognal Pl., Sid. 110 EU93
Frognal Ri. NW3 62 DC62
Frognal Way NW3 62 DC63
Froissart Rd. SE9 108 EK85
Frome Rd. N22 63 DP55
Westbury Ave.
Frome St. N1 78 DQ68
Fromondes Rd., Sutt. 131 CY106
Frostic Wk. E1 78 DU71
Chicksand St.
Froude St. SW8 91 DH82
Frowyke Cres., Pot.B. 19 CU32
Fruen Rd., Felt. 99 BT87
Fry Clo., Rom. 54 FA50
Fry Rd. E6 80 EK66
Fry Rd. NW10 75 CT67
Fryatt Rd. N17 50 DR52
Fryatt St. E14 80 EE72
Orchard Pl.
Fryent Clo. NW9 60 CN57
Fryent Cres. NW9 60 CS58
Fryent Flds. NW9 60 CS58
Fryent Gro. NW9 60 CS58
Fryent Way NW9 60 CN57
Fryern Wd., Cat. 148 DQ124
Frye's Bldgs. N1 77 DN68
Upper St.
Frying Pan All. E1 7 P7
Fryston Ave., Couls. 133 DH114
Fryston Ave., Croy. 120 DU103
Fuchsia St. SE2 96 EV78
Fulbeck Dr. NW9 46 CS53
Fulbeck Way, Har. 44 CC54
Fulbourne Rd. E17 51 EC53
Fulbourne St. E1 78 DV71
Durward St.
Fulbrook Ave., Add. 126 BG111
Fulbrook Ms. N19 63 DJ63
Junction Rd.
Fulbrook Rd. N19 63 DJ63
Junction Rd.
Fulbrooks Ave., Wor.Pk. 117 CT102
Fulford Gro., Wat. 43 BV47
Fulford Rd., Cat. 148 DR121
Fulford Rd., Epsom 130 CR108
Fulford St. SE16 92 DV75
Paradise St.
Fulham Bdy. SW6 90 DA80
Fulham Clo., Uxb. 71 BQ70
Uxbridge Rd.
Fulham Ct. SW6 90 DA80
Fulham Rd.
Fulham High St. SW6 89 CY82
Fulham Palace Rd. SW6 89 CX79
Fulham Palace Rd. W6 89 CW78
Fulham Pk. Gdns. SW6 89 CZ82
Fulham Pk. Rd. SW6 89 CZ82
Fulham Rd. SW3 90 DD78
Fulham Rd. SW6 89 CY82
Fulham Rd. SW10 90 DD78
Fuller Clo. E2 78 DU70
St. Matthew's Row
Fuller Clo., Orp. 137 ET106
Fuller Gdns., Wat. 29 BV37
Fuller Rd.
Fuller Rd., Dag. 68 EV62
Fuller Rd., Wat. 29 BV37
Fuller St. NW4 61 CW56

Gaunt St. SE1 10 G6
Gaunt St. SE1 92 DQ76
Gauntlet Clo., Nthlt. 72 BY66
Gauntlet Cres., Ken. 148 DR120
Gauntlett Ct., Wem. 59 CH64
Gauntlett Rd., Sutt. 132 DD106
Gautrey Rd. SE15 92 DW82
Gautrey Sq. E6 81 EM72
Truesdale Rd.
Gavel St. SE17 11 L8
Gavell Rd., Cob. 127 BU113
Gaverick St. E14 93 EA77
Gaveston Rd., Lthd. 143 CG120
Gavestone Clo., W.Byf. 126 BM113
Gavestone Cres. SE12 108 EH87
Gavestone Rd. SE12 108 EH87
Gaviller Pl. E5 64 DV63
Clarence Rd.
Gavin St. SE18 95 ES77
Gavina Clo., Mord. 118 DD99
Gawber St. E2 78 DW69
Gawsworth Clo. E15 66 EE64
Ash Rd.
Gawthorne Ave. NW7 47 CY50
Lane App.
Gawthorne Ct. E3 79 EA68
Mostyn Gro.
Gay Clo. NW2 61 CV64
Gay Gdns., Dag. 69 FC63
Gay Rd. E15 79 ED68
Gay St. SW15 89 CX83
Waterman St.
Gaydon Ho. W2 76 DB71
Gaydon La. NW9 46 CS53
Gayfere Rd., Epsom 131 CU106
Gayfere Rd., Ilf. 67 EM55
Gayfere St. SW1 9 P7
Gayfere St. SW1 91 DL76
Gayford Rd. W12 89 CT75
Gayhurst SE17 92 DR79
Hopwood Rd.
Gayhurst Rd. E8 78 DU66
Gaylor Rd., Nthlt. 58 BZ64
Gaynes Hill Rd., Wdf.Grn. 52 EL51
Gaynesford Rd. SE23 107 DX89
Gaynesford Rd., Cars. 132 DF108
Gaysham Ave., Ilf. 67 EN57
Gaysham Hall, Ilf. 67 EP55
Longwood Gdns.
Gayton Clo., Ash. 144 CL118
Gayton Ct., Har. 59 CF58
Gayton Cres. NW3 62 DD63
Gayton Rd. NW3 62 DD63
Gayton Rd. SE2 96 EW76
Florence Rd.
Gayton Rd., Har. 59 CF58
Gayville Rd. SW11 104 DF86
Gaywood Ave. (Cheshunt), Wal.Cr. 23 DX30
Gaywood Clo. SW2 105 DM88
Gaywood Est. SE1 10 G7
Gaywood Rd. E17 65 EA55
Gaywood Rd., Ash. 144 CM118
Gaywood St. SE1 10 G7
Gaza St. SE17 91 DP78
Braganza St.
Gazelda Vill., Wat. 30 BX43
Lower High St.
Geariesville Gdns., Ilf. 67 EP56
Geary Rd. NW10 61 CU64
Geary St. N7 63 DM64
GEC Est., Wem. 59 CK62
Geddes Pl., Bexh. 96 FA84
Market Pl.
Geddes Rd. (Bushey), Wat. 30 CC42
Gedeney Rd. N17 50 DQ53
Gedling Pl. SE1 92 DT76
Gee St. EC1 7 H4
Gee St. EC1 78 DQ70
Geere Rd. E15 80 EF67
Gees Ct. W1 4 G9
Geffrye Ct. N1 7 N1
Geffrye Est. N1 78 DS68
Stanway St.
Geffrye St. E2 7 P1
Geffrye St. E2 78 DT68
Geisthorp Ct., Wal.Abb. 24 EG33
Winters Way
Geldart Rd. SE15 92 DV80
Geldeston Rd. E5 64 DU61
Gell Clo., Uxb. 56 BM62
Gellatly Rd. SE14 92 DW82
Gelsthorpe Rd., Rom. 55 FB52
Gemini Gro., Nthlt. 72 BY69
Javelin Way
General Gordon Pl. SE18 95 EP77
General Wolfe Rd. SE10 93 ED81
Generals Wk., The, Enf. 37 DY37
Genesta Rd. SE18 95 EP79
Geneva Clo., Shep. 113 BS96
Geneva Dr. SW9 91 DN84
Geneva Gdns., Rom. 68 EY57
Geneva Rd., Kings.T. 116 CL98
Geneva Rd., Th.Hth. 120 DQ99
Genever Clo. E4 51 EA50
Genista Rd. N18 50 DV50
Genoa Ave. SW15 103 CW85
Genoa Rd. SE20 120 DW95
Genotin Rd., Enf. 36 DR41
Genotin Ter., Enf. 36 DR41
Genotin Rd.
Gentian Row SE13 93 EC81
Sparta St.
Gentlemans Row, Enf. 36 DQ41
Gentry Gdns. E13 80 EG70
Whitwell Rd.
Geoffrey Clo. SE5 92 DQ82
Geoffrey Gdns. E6 80 EL68
Geoffrey Rd. SE4 93 DZ83
George Avey Cft., Epp. 27 FB26
George Beard Rd. SE8 93 DZ77
George Comberton Wk. E12 67 EN64
Gainsborough Ave.
George Ct. WC2 10 A1
George Cres. N10 48 DG52
George Downing Est. N16 64 DT61
Cazenove Rd.
George V Ave., Pnr. 44 BZ53
George V Clo., Pnr. 58 CA55
George V Ave.
George V Way, Grnf. 73 CH67
George V Way, Rick. 28 BG36
George Gange Way, Har. 59 CE55
George Gro. Rd. SE20 120 DU95
George Inn Yd. SE1 11 K3
George La. E18 52 EG54
George La. SE13 107 EC86
George La., Brom. 122 EH102
George Lansbury Ho. N22 49 DN53
Progress Way
George Loveless Ho. E2 78 DT69
Diss St.
George Lowe Ct. W2 76 DB71
Bourne Ter.
George Ms. NW1 5 K3
George Ms., Enf. 36 DR41
Sydney Rd.
George Pl. N17 64 DS55
Dongola Rd.
George Rd. E4 51 EA51
George Rd., Kings.T. 102 CP94
George Rd., N.Mal. 117 CT98
George Row SE16 92 DU75
George Sq. SW19 117 CZ97
Mostyn Rd.
George St. E16 80 EF72
George St. W1 4 D8
George St. W1 76 DF72
George St. W7 73 CE74
The Bdy.
George St., Bark. 81 EQ66
George St., Croy. 120 DQ103
George St., Houns. 86 BZ82
George St., Rich. 101 CK85
George St., Rom. 69 FF58
George St., Sthl. 86 BY77
George St., Sutt. 132 DB106
George St., Uxb. 70 BK66
George St., Wat. 30 BW42
George Wyver Clo. SW19 103 CY87
Beaumont Rd.
George Yd. EC3 7 L9
George Yd. W1 4 G10
George Yd. W1 76 DG73
Georgelands (Ripley), Wok. 140 BH121
Georges Clo., Orp. 124 EW97
Georges Mead, Borwd. 31 CK44
George's Rd. N7 63 DM64
Georges Rd., Brom. 123 EM97
Georges Rd., West. 150 EK120
Georges Sq. SW6 89 CZ79
North End Rd.
Georges Ter., Cat. 148 DQ122
Coulsdon Rd.
George's Wd. Rd., Hat. 20 DA26
Georgetown Clo. SE19 106 DR92
St. Kitts Ter.
Georgette Pl. SE10 93 EC80
King George St.
Georgeville Gdns., Ilf. 67 EP56
Georgewood Rd., Hem.H. 14 BM25
Georgia Rd., N.Mal. 116 CQ98
Georgia Rd., Th.Hth. 119 DP95
Georgian Clo., Brom. 122 EH101
Georgian Clo., Stai. 98 BH91
Georgian Clo., Stan. 45 CG52
Georgian Clo., Uxb. 56 BL63
Georgian Ct. SW16 105 DL91
Gleneldon Rd.
Georgian Ct., Wem. 74 CN65
Georgian Way, Har. 59 CD61
Georgiana St. NW1 77 DJ67
Georgina Gdns. E2 78 DT69
Columbia Rd.
Geraint Rd., Brom. 108 EG91
Gerald Ms. SW1 8 G8
Gerald Rd. E16 80 EF70
Gerald Rd. SW1 8 G8
Gerald Rd. SW1 90 DG77
Gerald Rd., Dag. 68 EZ61
Gerald Sq. SW1 90 DG77
Eccleston St.
Geraldine Rd. SW18 104 DC85
Geraldine Rd. W4 88 CN79
Geraldine St. SE11 10 F7
Geraldine St. SE11 91 DP76
Geralds Gro., Bans. 131 CX114
Gerard Ave., Houns. 100 CA87
Redfern Ave.
Gerard Gdns., Rain. 83 FE68
Gerard Rd. SW13 89 CT81
Gerard Rd., Har. 59 CG58
Gerards Clo. SE16 92 DW78
Gerda Rd. SE9 109 EQ89
Germander Way E15 80 EE69
Gernon Rd. E3 79 DY68
Geron Way NW2 61 CV61
Gerrard Gdns., Pnr. 57 BU57
Gerrard Pl. W1 5 N10
Gerrard Rd. N1 77 DP68
Gerrard St. W1 5 N10
Gerrard St. W1 77 DK73
Gerrards Clo. N14 35 DJ43
Gerrards Mead, Bans. 145 CZ117
Garratts La.
Gerridge St. SE1 10 E6
Gerridge St. SE1 91 DN76
Gerry Raffles Sq. E15 79 ED65
Salway Rd.
Gertrude Rd., Belv. 96 FA77
Gertrude St. SW10 90 DC79
Gervase Clo., Wem. 60 CQ62
Gervase Rd., Edg. 46 CQ53
Gervase St. SE15 92 DV80
Gews Cor. (Cheshunt), Wal.Cr. 23 DX29
Ghent St. SE6 107 EA89
Ghent Way E8 78 DT65
Giant Arches Rd. SE24 106 DQ87
Giant Tree Hill (Bushey), Wat. 45 CD46
Gibbard Ms. SW19 103 CX92
Gibbfield Clo., Rom. 68 EY55
Gibbins Rd. E15 79 EC66
Gibbon Rd. SE15 92 DW82
Gibbon Rd. W3 74 CS73
Gibbon Rd., Kings.T. 116 CL95
Gibbon Wk. SW15 89 CU84
Swinburne Rd.
Gibbons Clo., Borwd. 32 CL39
Gibbons Rd. NW10 74 CS65
Gibbs Ave. SE19 106 DR92
Gibbs Clo. SE19 106 DR92
Gibbs Clo. (Cheshunt), Wal.Cr. 23 DX29
Gibbs Couch, Wat. 44 BX48
Gibbs Grn. W14 89 CZ78
Gibbs Grn., Edg. 46 CQ50
Gibbs Rd. N18 50 DW49
Gibbs Sq. SE19 106 DR92
Gibraltar Cres., Epsom 130 CS110
Gibraltar Wk. E2 78 DT69
Gibson Clo. E1 78 DW70
Colebert Ave.
Gibson Clo. N21 35 DN44
Gibson Clo., Chess. 129 CJ107
Gibson Clo., Epp. 27 FC25
Beamish Clo.
Gibson Clo., Islw. 87 CD83
Gibson Gdns. N16 64 DT61
Northwold Rd.
Gibson Pl., Stai. 98 BJ86
Gibson Rd. SE11 10 C9
Gibson Rd. SE11 91 DM77
Gibson Rd., Dag. 68 EW60
Gibson Rd., Sutt. 132 DB106
Gibson Rd., Uxb. 56 BM63
Gibson Sq. N1 77 DN67
Gibson St. SE10 94 EE78
Gibson's Hill SW16 105 DN94
Gidd Hill, Couls. 146 DG116
Gidea Ave., Rom. 69 FG55
Gidea Clo., Rom. 69 FG55
Gideon Clo., Belv. 97 FB77
Gideon Rd. SW11 90 DG83
Gidian Ct., St.Alb. 17 CD27
Giesbach Rd. N19 63 DJ61
Giffard Rd. N18 50 DS50
Giffin St. SE8 93 EA80
Gifford Gdns. W7 73 CD71
Gifford St. N1 77 DL66
Gift La. E15 80 EF67
Giggs Hill, Orp. 124 EU96
Giggs Hill Gdns., T.Ditt. 115 CG102
Giggs Hill Rd., T.Ditt. 115 CG101
Gilbert Clo. SE18 95 EM81
Gilbert Gro., Edg. 46 CR53
Gilbert Ho. EC2 78 DQ71
Fore St.
Gilbert Ho. SE8 93 EA79
McMillan St.
Gilbert Pl. WC1 5 P7
Gilbert Rd. SE11 10 E9
Gilbert Rd. SE11 91 DN77
Gilbert Rd. SW19 104 DC94
Gilbert Rd., Belv. 96 FA76
Gilbert Rd., Brom. 108 EG94
Gilbert Rd., Pnr. 58 BX56
Gilbert Rd., Rom. 69 FF56
Gilbert Rd., Uxb. 42 BK54
Gilbert St. E15 66 EE63
Gilbert St. W1 4 G9
Gilbert St. W1 76 DG72
Gilbert St., Enf. 36 DW37
Gilbert St., Houns. 86 CC83
High St.
Gilbey Clo., Uxb. 57 BP63
Gilbey Rd. SW17 104 DE91
Gilbeys Yd. NW1 77 DH67
Oval Rd.
Gilbourne Rd. SE18 95 ET79
Gilda Ave., Enf. 37 DY43
Gilda Cres. N16 64 DU60
Gildea St. W1 5 J7
Gilden Cres. NW5 62 DG64
Gilders Rd., Chess. 130 CM108
Gildersome St. SE18 95 EN79
Nightingale Vale
Giles Coppice SE19 106 DT91
Gilfrid Clo., Uxb. 71 BP72
Craig Dr.
Gilhams Ave., Bans. 131 CX112
Gilkes Cres. SE21 106 DS86
Gilkes Pl. SE21 106 DS86
Gill Ave. E16 80 EG72
Gill St. E14 79 DZ73
Gillam Way, Rain. 83 FG65
Gillan Grn. (Bushey), Wat. 44 CC47
Gillards Ms. E17 65 EA56
Gillards Way
Gillards Way E17 65 EA56
Gillender St. E3 79 EC70
Gillender St. E14 79 EC70
Gillespie Rd. N5 63 DN62
Gillett Ave. E6 80 EL68
Gillett Pl. N16 64 DS64
Gillett St.
Gillett Rd., Th.Hth. 120 DR98
Gillett St. N16 64 DS64
Gillfoot NW1 5 K1
Gillfoot NW1 77 DJ68
Gillham Ter. N17 50 DU51
Gilliam Gro., Pur. 133 DN110
Gillian Pk. Rd., Sutt. 117 CZ102
Gillian St. SE13 107 EB85
Gillies St. NW5 62 DG64
Gilling Ct. NW3 76 DE65
Gillingham Ms. SW1 9 K8
Gillingham Rd. NW2 61 CY62
Gillingham Row SW1 9 K8
Gillingham St. SW1 9 J8
Gillingham St. SW1 91 DJ77
Gillison Wk. SE16 92 DU76
Tranton Rd.
Gillman Dr. E15 80 EF67
Gillmans Rd., Orp. 124 EV102
Gills Hill, Rad. 31 CF35
Gills Hill La., Rad. 31 CF36
Gills Hollow, Rad. 31 CF36
Gillum Clo., Barn. 48 DF46
Gilmore Clo., Uxb. 56 BN62
Gilmore Cres., Ashf. 98 BN92
Gilmore Rd. SE13 93 ED84
Gilmour Clo., Wal.Cr. 36 DU35
Gilpin Ave. SW14 88 CR84
Gilpin Clo., Mitch. 118 DE96
Gilpin Cres. N18 50 DT50
Gilpin Cres., Twick. 100 CB87
Gilpin Rd. E5 65 DY63
Gilpin Way, Hayes 85 BR80
Gilroy Clo., Rain. 83 FF65
Gilroy Way, Orp. 124 EV101
Gilsland, Wal.Abb. 38 EE35
Gilsland Rd., Th.Hth. 120 DR98
Gilstead Ho., Bark. 82 EV68
Gilstead Rd. SW6 90 DB82
Gilston Rd. SW10 90 DC78
Gilton Rd. SE6 108 EE90
Giltspur St. EC1 6 G8
Giltspur St. EC1 77 DP72
Gilwell Clo. E4 37 EB42
Antlers Hill
Gilwell La. E4 37 ED42
Gilwell Pk. E4 37 EC41
Gimcrack Hill, Lthd. 143 CH123
Dorking Rd.
Gippeswyck Clo., Pnr. 44 BX53
Uxbridge Rd.
Gipsy Hill SE19 106 DS92
Gipsy La. SW15 89 CU83
Gipsy Rd. SE27 106 DQ91
Gipsy Rd., Well. 96 EX81
Gipsy Rd. Gdns. SE27 106 DQ91
Giralda Clo. E16 80 EK71
Fulmer Rd.
Giraud St. E14 79 EB72
Girdlers Rd. W14 89 CX77
Girdlestone Wk. N19 63 DJ61
Girdwood Rd. SW18 103 CY87
Girling Way, Felt. 85 BU83
Gironde Rd. SW6 89 CZ80
Girtin Rd. (Bushey), Wat. 30 CB43
Girton Ave. NW9 60 CN55
Girton Clo., Nthlt. 72 CC65
Girton Ct., Wal.Cr. 23 DY30
Girton Gdns., Croy. 121 EA104
Girton Rd. SE26 107 DX92
Girton Rd., Nthlt. 72 CC65
Girton Vill. W10 75 CX72
Cambridge Gdns.
Girton Way, Rick. 29 BQ43
Gisborne Gdns., Rain. 83 FF69
Gisbourne Clo., Wall. 119 DK104
Gisburn Rd. N8 63 DM56
Gisburne Ho., Wat. 29 BU37
Gisburne Way, Wat. 29 BU37
Gissing Wk. N1 77 DN66
Lofting Rd.
Gittens Clo., Brom. 108 EF91
Given Wilson Wk. E13 80 EF68
Stride Rd.
Glacier Way, Wem. 73 CK68
Gladbeck Way, Enf. 35 DP43
Gladding Rd. E12 66 EK63
Glade, The N21 35 DM44
Glade, The SE7 94 EJ80
Glade, The, Brom. 122 EK96
Glade, The, Couls. 147 DN119
Glade, The, Croy. 121 DX99
Glade, The, Enf. 35 DN41
Glade, The, Epsom 131 CU106
Glade, The, Ilf. 53 EM53
Glade, The, Lthd. 142 CA122
Glade, The, Sev. 155 FH123
Glade, The, Stai. 98 BH94
Glade, The, Sutt. 131 CY109
Glade, The, Tad. 146 DA121
Glade, The, W.Wick. 121 EB104
Glade, The, Wdf.Grn. 52 EH48
Glade Clo., Surb. 115 CK103
Glade Ct., Ilf. 53 EM53
The Glade
Glade Gdns., Croy. 121 DY101
Glade La., Sthl. 86 CB75
Glade Spur, Tad. 146 DB121
Glades Pl., Brom. 122 EG96
Glades Shop. Cen., The, Brom. 122 EG96
Gladeside N21 49 DM45
Gladeside, Croy. 121 DX101
Gladeside Clo., Chess. 129 CK108
Leatherhead Rd.
Gladeside Ct., Warl. 148 DV120
Gladesmore Rd. N15 64 DT58
Gladeswood Rd., Belv. 97 FB77
Gladeway, The, Wal.Abb. 23 ED33
Gladiator St. SE23 107 DY87
Glading Ter. N16 64 DT62
Gladioli Clo., Hmptn. 100 CA93
Gresham Rd.
Gladsdale Dr., Pnr. 57 BV56
Gladsmuir Clo., Walt. 114 BW103
Gladsmuir Rd. N19 63 DJ60
Gladsmuir Rd., Barn. 33 CY40
Gladstone Ave. E12 80 EL66
Gladstone Ave. N22 49 DN54
Gladstone Ave., Felt. 99 BU86
Gladstone Ave., Twick. 101 CD87
Gladstone Ms. NW6 75 CZ66
Cavendish Rd.
Gladstone Ms. SE20 106 DW94
Gladstone Pk. Gdns. NW2 61 CV63
Gladstone Pl. E3 79 DZ68
Roman Rd.
Gladstone Pl., Barn. 33 CX42
Gladstone Rd. SW19 104 DA94
Gladstone Rd. W4 88 CR76
Acton La.
Gladstone Rd., Ash. 143 CK118
Gladstone Rd., Buck.H. 52 EH46
Gladstone Rd., Croy. 120 DR101
Gladstone Rd., Kings.T. 116 CN97
Gladstone Rd., Orp. 137 EQ106
Gladstone Rd., Sthl. 86 BY75
Gladstone Rd., Surb. 115 CK103
Gladstone Rd., Wat. 30 BW41
Gladstone St. SE1 10 F6
Gladstone St. SE1 91 DP76
Gladstone Ter. SE27 106 DQ91
Gladstone Ter. SW8 91 DH81
Gladstone Way, Har. 59 CE55
Gladwell Rd. N8 63 DM58
Gladwell Rd., Brom. 108 EG93
Gladwyn Rd. SW15 89 CX83
Gladys Rd. NW6 76 DA66
Glaisher St. SE10 93 EC80
Straightsmouth
Glamis Clo. (Cheshunt), Wal.Cr. 22 DU29
Glamis Cres., Hayes 85 BQ76
Glamis Pl. E1 78 DW73
Glamis Rd. E1 78 DW73
Glamis Way, Nthlt. 72 CC65
Glamorgan Clo., Mitch. 119 DL97
Glamorgan Rd., Kings.T. 101 CJ94
Glanfield Rd., Beck. 121 DZ98
Glanleam Rd., Stan. 45 CK49
Glanville Rd. SW2 105 DL85
Glanville Rd., Brom. 122 EH97
Glasbrook Ave., Twick. 100 BZ88
Glasbrook Rd. SE9 108 EK87
Glaserton Rd. N16 64 DS59
Glasford St. SW17 104 DF93
Glasgow Ho. W9 76 DB68
Glasgow Rd. E13 80 EH68
Glasgow Rd. N18 50 DV50
Aberdeen Rd.
Glasgow Ter. SW1 91 DJ78
Glass St. E2 78 DV70
Coventry Rd.
Glass Yd. SE18 95 EN76
Glasse Clo. W13 73 CG73
Glasshill St. SE1 10 G4
Glasshill St. SE1 91 DP75
Glasshouse All. EC4 6 E9
Glasshouse Flds. E1 79 DX73
Glasshouse St. W1 9 L1
Glasshouse St. W1 77 DJ73
Glasshouse Wk. SE11 10 A10
Glasshouse Wk. SE11 91 DL78
Glasshouse Yd. EC1 7 H5
Glasslyn Rd. N8 63 DK57
Glassmill La., Brom. 122 EF96
Glastonbury Ave., Wdf.Grn. 52 EK52
Glastonbury Clo., Orp. 124 EW102
Glastonbury Rd. N9 50 DT46
Glastonbury Rd., Mord. 118 DA101
Glastonbury St. NW6 61 CZ64
Glaucus St. E3 79 EB71
Glazbury Rd. W14 89 CY77
Glazebrook Clo. SE21 106 DR89
Glazebrook Rd., Tedd. 101 CF94
Glebe, The SE3 94 EE83
Glebe, The SW16 105 DK91
Glebe, The, Chis. 123 EQ95
Glebe, The, Kings L. 14 BN29
Glebe, The, Wat. 16 BX33
Glebe, The, West Dr. 84 BM77
Glebe, The, Wor.Pk. 117 CT102
Glebe Ave., Enf. 35 DP41
Glebe Ave., Har. 60 CL55
Glebe Ave., Mitch. 118 DE96
Glebe Ave., Ruis. 71 BV65
Glebe Ave., Uxb. 57 BQ62
Glebe Ave., Wdf.Grn. 52 EG51
Glebe Clo. W4 88 CS78
Glebe St.
Glebe Clo., S.Croy. 134 DT111
Glebe Clo., Uxb. 57 BQ63
Glebe Cotts., Sutt. 132 DB105
Vale Rd.

Glebe Cotts., West. 152 EV123
Glebe Ct. W7 73 CD73
Glebe Ct., Mitch. 118 DF97
Glebe Ct., Stan. 45 CJ50
Glebe Rd.
Glebe Cres. NW4 61 CW56
Glebe Cres., Har. 60 CL55
Glebe Gdns., N.Mal. 116 CS101
Glebe Gdns., W.Byf. 126 BK114
Glebe Ho. Dr., Brom. 122 EH102
Glebe Hyrst SE19 106 DT91
Giles Coppice
Glebe Hyrst, S.Croy. 134 DT112
Glebe La., Barn. 33 CU43
Glebe La., Har. 60 CL56
Glebe La., Sev. 155 FH126
Glebe Path, Mitch. 118 DE97
Glebe Pl. SW3 90 DE79
Glebe Rd. E8 78 DT66
Middleton Rd.
Glebe Rd. N3 48 DC53
Glebe Rd. N8 63 DM56
Glebe Rd. NW10 75 CT65
Glebe Rd. SW13 89 CU82
Glebe Rd., Ash. 143 CK118
Glebe Rd., Brom. 122 EG95
Glebe Rd., Cars. 132 DF107
Glebe Rd., Dag. 83 FB65
Glebe Rd., Hayes 71 BT74
Glebe Rd., Rain. 83 FH69
Glebe Rd., Red. 147 DH124
Glebe Rd., Stai. 98 BH92
Glebe Rd., Stan. 45 CJ50
Glebe Rd., Sutt. 131 CY109
Glebe Rd., Uxb. 70 BJ68
Glebe Rd., Warl. 149 DX117
Glebe Side, Twick. 101 CF87
Glebe St. W4 88 CS78
Glebe Ter. E3 79 EA69
Bow Rd.
Glebe Way, Erith 97 FE79
Glebe Way, Felt. 100 CA90
Glebe Way, S.Croy. 134 DT112
Glebe Way, W.Wick. 121 EC103
Glebefield, The, Sev. 154 FF123
Glebeland Gdns., Shep. 113 BQ100
Glebelands, Chig. 54 EV48
Glebelands, Dart. 97 FF84
Glebelands, Esher 129 CF109
Glebelands, W.Mol. 114 CB99
Glebelands Ave. E18 52 EG54
Glebelands Ave., Ilf. 67 ER59
Glebelands Clo. SE5 92 DS83
Grove Hill Rd.
Glebelands Rd., Felt. 99 BU87
Glebeway, Wdf.Grn. 52 EJ50
Gledhow Gdns. SW5 90 DC77
Gledhow Wd., Tad. 146 DB121
Gledstanes Rd. W14 89 CY78
Gledwood Ave., Hayes 71 BT71
Gledwood Cres., Hayes 71 BT71
Gledwood Dr., Hayes 71 BT71
Gledwood Gdns., Hayes 71 BT71
Gleed Ave. (Bushey), Wat. 45 CD47
Gleeson Dr., Orp. 137 ET106
Glegg Pl. SW15 89 CX84
Glen, The, Brom. 122 EE96
Glen, The, Croy. 121 DX104
Glen, The, Enf. 35 DP42
Glen, The, Nthwd. 43 BR52
Glen, The, Orp. 123 EM104
Glen, The, Pnr. 58 BY59
Glen, The (Eastcote), Pnr. 57 BV57
Glen, The, Sthl. 86 BZ78
Glen, The, Wem. 59 CK63
Glen Albyn Rd. SW19 103 CX89
Glen Ave., Ashf. 98 BN91
Glen Clo., Shep. 112 BN98
Glen Clo., Tad. 145 CY123
Glen Cres., Wdf.Grn. 52 EH51
Glen Gdns., Croy. 119 DP104
Glen Ri., Wdf.Grn. 52 EH51
Glen Rd. E13 80 EJ70
Glen Rd. E17 65 DZ57
Glen Rd., Chess. 116 CL104
Glen Rd. End, Wall. 133 DH109
Glen Ter. E14 93 EC75
Manchester Rd.
Glen Wk., Islw. 101 CD85
Glen Way, Wat. 29 BS38
Glena Mt., Sutt. 132 DC105
Glenaffric Ave. E14 93 ED77
Glenalla Rd., Ruis. 57 BT59
Glenalmond Rd., Har. 60 CL56
Glenalvon Way SE18 94 EL77
Glenarm Rd. E5 64 DW64
Glenavon Clo., Esher 129 CG107
Glenavon Rd. E15 80 EE66
Glenbarr Clo. SE9 95 EP83
Dumbreck Rd.
Glenbow Rd., Brom. 108 EE93
Glenbrook N., Enf. 35 DM42
Glenbrook Rd. NW6 62 DA64
Glenbrook S., Enf. 35 DM42
Glenbuck Ct., Surb. 115 CK100
Glenbuck Rd.
Glenbuck Rd., Surb. 115 CK100
Glenburnie Rd. SW17 104 DE90
Glencairn Dr. W5 73 CJ70
Glencairn Rd. SW16 105 DL94
Glencairne Clo. E16 80 EK71
Glencoe Ave., Ilf. 67 ER59
Glencoe Dr., Dag. 68 FA63
Glencoe Rd., Hayes 72 BX70
Glencoe Rd. (Bushey), Wat. 30 CA44
Glencoe Rd., Wey. 112 BN104
Glencourse Grn., Wat. 44 BX49
Caldwell Rd.
Glendale, Swan. 125 FF99
Glendale Ave. N22 49 DN52
Glendale Ave., Edg. 46 CN49
Glendale Ave., Rom. 68 EW59
Glendale Clo. SE9 95 EN83
Dumbreck Rd.
Glendale Dr. SW19 103 CZ92
Glendale Gdns., Wem. 59 CK60
Glendale Ms., Beck. 121 EB95
Glendale Ri., Ken. 147 DP115
Glendale Rd., Erith 97 FC77
Glendale Wk. (Cheshunt), Wal.Cr. 23 DY30
Glendale Way SE28 82 EW73
Glendall St. SW9 91 DM84
Glendarvon St. SW15 89 CX83
Glendevon Clo., Edg. 46 CP48
Tayside Dr.
Glendish Rd. N17 50 DU53
Glendor Gdns. NW7 46 CR49
Glendower Cres., Orp. 124 EU100
Glendower Gdns. SW14 88 CR83
Glendower Rd.
Glendower Pl. SW7 90 DD77
Glendower Rd. E4 51 ED46
Glendower Rd. SW14 88 CR83
Glendown Rd. SE2 96 EU78
Glendun Rd. W3 74 CS73
Gleneagle Ms. SW16 105 DK92
Ambleside Ave.
Gleneagle Rd. SW16 105 DK93
Gleneagles, Stan. 45 CH51
Gleneagles Clo. SE16 92 DV78
Ryder Dr.
Gleneagles Clo., Orp. 123 ER102
Gleneagles Clo., Stai. 98 BK86
Gleneagles Clo., Stan. 45 CH51
Gleneagles Clo., Wat. 44 BX49
Gleneagles Grn., Orp. 123 ER102
Tandridge Dr.
Gleneagles Twr., Sthl. 72 CC72
Gleneldon Ms. SW16 105 DL91
Gleneldon Rd. SW16 105 DL91
Glenelg Rd. SW2 105 DL85
Glenesk Rd. SE9 95 EN83
Glenfarg Rd. SE6 107 ED88
Glenfield Cres., Ruis. 57 BR59
Glenfield Rd. SW12 105 DJ88
Glenfield Rd. W13 87 CH75
Glenfield Rd., Ashf. 99 BP93
Glenfield Rd., Bans. 146 DB115
Glenfield Ter. W13 73 CH74
Glenfinlas Way SE5 91 DP80
Glenforth St. SE10 94 EF78
Glengall Causeway E14 93 EA76
Glengall Gro. E14 93 EC76
Glengall Rd. NW6 75 CZ67
Glengall Rd. SE15 92 DT78
Glengall Rd., Bexh. 96 EY83
Glengall Rd., Edg. 46 CP48
Glengall Rd., Wdf.Grn. 52 EG51
Glengall Ter. SE15 92 DT79
Glengarnock Ave. E14 93 EC77
Glengarry Rd. SE22 106 DS85
Glenham Dr., Ilf. 67 EP57
Glenhaven Ave., Borwd. 32 CN41
Glenhead Clo. SE9 95 EP83
Dumbreck Rd.
Glenheadon Clo., Lthd. 143 CK123
Glenheadon Ri.
Glenheadon Ri., Lthd. 143 CK123
Glenhill Clo. N3 48 DA54
Glenhouse Rd. SE9 109 EN85
Glenhurst Ave. NW5 62 DG63
Glenhurst Ave., Bex. 110 EZ88
Glenhurst Ave., Ruis. 57 BQ59
Glenhurst Ct. SE19 106 DT92
Glenhurst Ri. SE19 106 DQ94
Glenhurst Rd. N12 48 DD50
Glenhurst Rd., Brent. 87 CJ79
Glenilla Rd. NW3 76 DE65
Glenister Ho., Hayes 71 BV74
Glenister Pk. Rd. SW16 105 DK94
Glenister Rd. SE10 94 EF78
Glenister St. E16 81 EN74
Glenlea Rd. SE9 109 EN85
Glenlion Ct., Wey. 113 BR104
Glenloch Rd. NW3 76 DE65
Glenloch Rd., Enf. 36 DW40
Glenluce Rd. SE3 94 EG79
Glenlyon Rd. SE9 109 EN85
Glenmere Ave. NW7 47 CU52
Glenmill, Hmptn. 100 BZ92
Glenmore Clo., Add. 112 BH104
Glenmore Gdns., Abb.L. 15 BU32
Stewart Clo.
Glenmore Rd. NW3 76 DE65
Glenmore Rd., Well. 95 ET80
Glenmore Way, Bark. 82 EU69
Glenmount Path SE18 95 EQ78
Raglan Rd.
Glenn Ave., Pur. 133 DP111
Glennie Rd. SE27 105 DN90
Glenny Rd., Bark. 81 EQ65
Glenorchy Clo., Hayes 72 BY71
Glenparke Rd. E7 80 EH65
Glenrosa St. SW6 90 DC82
Glenrose Ct., Sid. 110 EV92
Glenroy St. W12 75 CW72
Glensdale Rd. SE4 93 DZ83
Glenshee Clo., Nthwd. 43 BQ51
Merrows Clo.
Glenshiel Rd. SE9 109 EN85
Glenside, Chig. 53 EP51
Glentanner Way SW17 104 DD90
Aboyne Rd.
Glentham Gdns. SW13 89 CV79
Glentham Rd.
Glentham Rd. SW13 89 CU79
Glenthorne Ave., Croy. 120 DV102
Glenthorne Clo., Sutt. 118 DA102
Glenthorne Clo., Uxb. 70 BN69
Uxbridge Rd.
Glenthorne Gdns., Ilf. 67 EN55
Glenthorne Gdns., Sutt. 118 DA102
Glenthorne Ms. W6 89 CV77
Glenthorne Rd.
Glenthorne Rd. E17 65 DY57
Glenthorne Rd. N11 48 DF50
Glenthorne Rd. W6 89 CV77
Glenthorne Rd., Kings.T. 116 CM98
Glenthorpe Rd., Mord. 117 CX99
Glenton Clo., Rom. 55 FE51
Glenton Rd. SE13 94 EE84
Glenton Way, Rom. 55 FE52
Glentrammon Ave., Orp. 137 ET107
Glentrammon Clo., Orp. 137 ET106
Glentrammon Gdns., Orp. 137 ET107
Glentrammon Rd., Orp. 137 ET107
Glentworth St. NW1 4 E5
Glentworth St. NW1 76 DF70
Glenure Rd. SE9 109 EN85
Glenview SE2 96 EX79
Glenview Rd., Brom. 122 EK96
Glenville Ave., Enf. 36 DQ38
Glenville Gro. SE8 93 DZ80
Glenville Ms. SW18 104 DB87
Glenville Rd., Kings.T. 116 CN95
Glenwood Ave. NW9 60 CS60
Glenwood Ave., Rain. 83 FG70
Glenwood Clo., Har. 59 CF57
Glenwood Dr., Rom. 69 FG57
Glenwood Gdns., Ilf. 67 EN57
Glenwood Gro. NW9 60 CQ60
Glenwood Rd. N15 63 DP57
Glenwood Rd. NW7 46 CS48
Glenwood Rd. SE6 107 DZ88
Glenwood Rd., Epsom 131 CU107
Glenwood Rd., Houns. 87 CD83
Glenwood Way, Croy. 121 DX100
Glenworth Ave. E14 93 ED77
Gliddon Rd. W14 89 CY77
Glimpsing Grn., Erith 96 EY76
Glisson Rd., Uxb. 70 BN68
Gload Cres., Orp. 124 EX103
Global App. E3 79 EB68
Hancock Rd.
Globe Pond Rd. SE16 79 DY74
Globe Rd. E1 79 DX70
Globe Rd. E2 78 DW69
Globe Rd. E15 66 EF64
Globe Rd., Horn. 69 FG58
Globe Rd., Wdf.Grn. 52 EJ51
Globe Rope Wk. E14 93 EC77
Stebondale St.
Globe St. SE1 11 K5
Globe St. SE1 92 DR75
Globe Ter. E2 78 DW69
Globe Rd.
Globe Yd. W1 5 H9
Glossop Rd., S.Croy. 134 DR109
Gloster Rd., N.Mal. 116 CS98
Gloucester Ave. NW1 76 DG66
Gloucester Ave., Sid. 109 ES89
Gloucester Ave., Wal.Cr. 23 DY33
Gloucester Ave., Well. 95 ET84
Gloucester Circ. SE10 93 EC80
Gloucester Clo. NW10 74 CR66
Gloucester Clo., T.Ditt. 115 CG102
Gloucester Ct. EC3 11 N1
Gloucester Ct., Rich. 88 CN80
Gloucester Ct., Uxb. 56 BG58
Moorfield Rd.
Gloucester Cres. NW1 77 DH67
Gloucester Cres., Stai. 98 BK93
Gloucester Dr. N4 63 DP61
Gloucester Dr. NW11 62 DA56
Gloucester Gdns. NW11 61 CZ59
Gloucester Gdns. W2 76 DC72
Bishops Bri. Rd.
Gloucester Gdns., Barn. 34 DG42
Gloucester Gdns., Ilf. 66 EL59
Gloucester Gdns., Sutt. 118 DB103
Gloucester Gate NW1 77 DH68
Gloucester Gate Ms. NW1 77 DH68
Gloucester Gate
Gloucester Gro., Edg. 46 CR53
Gloucester Gro. Est. SE15 92 DS79
Gloucester Ho. N7 63 DL62
Gloucester Ho. NW6 76 DA68
Gloucester Ms. E10 65 EA59
Gloucester Rd.
Gloucester Ms. W2 76 DC72
Gloucester Ms. W. W2 76 DC72
Cleveland Ter.
Gloucester Par., Sid. 110 EU85
Gloucester Pl. NW1 4 D4
Gloucester Pl. NW1 76 DF70
Gloucester Pl. W1 4 E6
Gloucester Pl. W1 76 DF71
Gloucester Pl. Ms. W1 4 E7
Gloucester Rd. E10 65 EA59
Gloucester Rd. E11 66 EH57
Gloucester Rd. E12 67 EM62
Gloucester Rd. E17 51 DX54
Gloucester Rd. N17 64 DR55
Gloucester Rd. N18 50 DT50
Gloucester Rd. SW7 90 DC76
Gloucester Rd. W3 88 CQ75
Gloucester Rd. W5 87 CJ75
Gloucester Rd., Barn. 34 DB43
Gloucester Rd., Belv. 96 EZ78
Gloucester Rd., Croy. 120 DR102
Gloucester Rd., Dart. 111 FH87
Gloucester Rd., Enf. 36 DQ38
Gloucester Rd., Felt. 100 BW88
Gloucester Rd., Hmptn. 100 CB94
Gloucester Rd., Har. 58 CB57
Gloucester Rd., Houns. 86 BY84
Gloucester Rd., Kings.T. 116 CN96
Gloucester Rd., Rich. 88 CN80
Gloucester Rd., Rom. 69 FE58
Gloucester Rd., Tedd. 101 CE92
Gloucester Rd., Twick. 100 CC88
Gloucester Sq. E2 78 DU67
Whiston Rd.
Gloucester Sq. W2 4 A9
Gloucester Sq. W2 76 DD72
Gloucester St. SW1 91 DJ78
Gloucester Ter. W2 76 DB72
Gloucester Wk. W8 90 DA75
Gloucester Way EC1 6 E3
Gloucester Way EC1 77 DN69
Glover Clo. SE2 96 EW77
Glover Clo., Wal.Cr. 22 DT27
Allwood Rd.
Glover Dr. N18 50 DW51
Glover Rd., Pnr. 58 BX58
Glovers Gro., Ruis. 57 BP59
Gloxinia Wk., Hmptn. 100 CA93
The Ave.
Glycena Rd. SW11 90 DF83
Glyn Ave., Barn. 34 DD42
Glyn Clo. SE25 120 DS96
Glyn Clo., Epsom 131 CU109
Glyn Ct. SW16 105 DN90
Glyn Davies Clo., Sev. 153 FE120
Glyn Dr., Sid. 110 EV91
Glyn Rd. E5 65 DX64
Glyn Rd., Enf. 36 DW42
Glyn Rd., Wor.Pk. 117 CX103
Glyn St. SE11 91 DM78
Kennington La.
Glynde Ms. SW3 8 C7
Glynde Rd., Bexh. 96 EX83
Glynde St. SE4 107 DZ86
Glyndebourne Pk., Orp. 123 EP103
Glyndon Rd. SE18 95 EQ77
Glynfield Rd. NW10 74 CS66
Glynne Rd. N22 49 DN54
Glynwood Ct. SE23 106 DW90
Goat La., Enf. 36 DT38
Goat La., Surb. 115 CH103
Goat Rd., Mitch. 118 DF101
Goat St. SE1 11 P4
Goat Wf., Brent. 88 CL79
Goaters All. SW6 89 CZ80
Dawes Rd.
Goatsfield Rd., West. 150 EJ120
Goatswood La., Rom. 55 FH45
Gobions Ave., Rom. 55 FD52
Gobions Way, Pot.B. 20 DB28
Swanley Bar La.
Godalming Ave., Wall. 133 DL106
Godalming Rd. E14 79 EB71
Godbold Rd. E15 80 EE69
Goddard Clo., Shep. 112 BM97
Magdalene Rd.
Goddard Rd., Beck. 121 DX98
Goddards Way, Ilf. 67 ER60
Goddington Chase, Orp. 138 EV105
Goddington La., Orp. 124 EU104
Godfrey Ave., Nthlt. 72 BY67
Godfrey Ave., Twick. 101 CD87
Godfrey Hill SE18 94 EL77
Godfrey Rd. SE18 95 EM77
Godfrey St. E15 79 EC68
Godfrey St. SW3 8 C10
Godfrey St. SW3 90 DE78
Godfrey Way, Houns. 100 BZ87
Goding St. SE11 91 DL78
Godley Rd. SW18 104 DD88
Godley Rd., W.Byf. 126 BM114
Godliman St. EC4 7 H9
Godliman St. EC4 78 DQ72
Godman Rd. SE15 92 DV82
Godolphin Clo. N13 49 DP51
Godolphin Clo., Sutt. 131 CZ110
Godolphin Pl. W3 74 CR73
Vyner Rd.
Godolphin Rd. W12 75 CV74
Godolphin Rd., Wey. 127 BR107
Godric Cres., Croy. 135 ED110
Godson Rd., Croy. 119 DN104
Godson St. N1 77 DN68
White Lion St.
Godstone Rd., Cat. 148 DU124
Godstone Rd., Ken. 133 DN112
Godstone Rd., Pur. 133 DN112
Godstone Rd., Sutt. 132 DC105
Godstone Rd., Twick. 101 CG86
Godstone Rd., Whyt. 148 DT116
Godstow Rd. SE2 96 EV75
Godwin Clo. E4 37 EC38
Godwin Clo. N1 78 DQ68
Napier Gro.
Godwin Clo., Epsom 130 CQ107
Godwin Ct. NW1 77 DJ68
Crowndale Rd.
Godwin Rd. E7 66 EH63
Godwin Rd., Brom. 122 EJ97
Goffers Rd. SE3 94 EE82
Goffs Cres. (Cheshunt), Wal.Cr. 22 DQ29
Goffs La. (Cheshunt), Wal.Cr. 22 DR29
Goffs Oak Ave. (Cheshunt), Wal.Cr. 21 DP28
Goffs Rd., Ashf. 99 BR93
Goidel Clo., Wall. 133 DK105
Golborne Gdns. W10 75 CZ70
Golborne Rd.
Golborne Ms. W10 75 CY71
Portobello Rd.
Golborne Rd. W10 75 CY71
Gold Hill, Edg. 46 CR51
Gold La., Edg. 46 CR51
Golda Clo., Barn. 33 CX44
Goldbeaters Gro., Edg. 46 CS51
Goldcliff Clo., Mord. 118 DA101
Goldcrest Clo. E16 80 EK71
Sheerwater Rd.
Goldcrest Clo. SE28 82 EW73
Goldcrest Ms. W5 73 CK71
Montpelier Ave.
Goldcrest Way, Croy. 135 ED109
Goldcrest Way, Pur. 133 DK110
Goldcrest Way (Bushey), Wat. 44 CC46
Golden Ct., Rich. 101 CK85
George St.
Golden Cres., Hayes 71 BS74
Golden Cross Ms. W11 75 CZ72
Basing St.
Golden La. EC1 7 H5
Golden La. EC1 78 DQ70
Golden La. Est. EC1 7 H5
Golden Manor W7 73 CE73
Golden Plover Clo. E16 80 EH72
Maplin Rd.
Golden Sq. W1 5 L10
Golden Sq. W1 77 DJ73
Golden Yd. NW3 62 DC63
Heath St.
Golders Clo., Edg. 46 CP50
Golders Gdns. NW11 61 CY59
Golders Grn. Cres. NW11 61 CZ59
Golders Grn. Rd. NW11 61 CY58
Golders Manor Dr. NW11 61 CX58
Golders Pk. Clo. NW11 62 DA60
Golders Ri. NW4 61 CX57
Golders Way NW11 61 CZ59
Goldfinch Clo., Orp. 138 EU106
Goldfinch Rd. SE28 95 ER76
Goldfinch Rd., S.Croy. 135 DX110
Goldfinch Way, Borwd. 32 CN42
Siskin Clo.
Goldhawk Ms. W12 89 CV75
Devonport Rd.
Goldhawk Rd. W6 89 CT77
Goldhawk Rd. W12 89 CU76
Goldhaze Clo., Wdf.Grn. 52 EK52
Goldhurst Ter. NW6 76 DB66
Golding Clo., Chess. 129 CJ107
Coppard Gdns.
Golding Rd., Sev. 155 FJ122
Golding St. E1 78 DU72
Goldingham Ave., Loug. 39 EQ40
Goldings Hill, Loug. 39 EM37
Goldings Ri., Loug. 39 EN39
Goldings Rd., Loug. 39 EN39
Goldington Cres. NW1 77 DK68
Goldington Cres. Gdns. NW1 77 DK68
Goldington St. NW1 77 DK68
Goldman Clo. E2 78 DU70
Goldney Rd. W9 76 DA70
Goldrings Rd., Lthd. 128 CB113
Goldsborough Cres. E4 51 EB47
Goldsborough Rd. SW8 91 DK81
Goldsdown Clo., Enf. 37 DY40
Goldsdown Rd., Enf. 37 DX40
Goldsel Rd., Swan. 125 FD99
Goldsel Rd. Ind. Est., Swan. 125 FE98
Goldsmid St. SE18 95 ES78
Sladedale Rd.
Goldsmith Ave. E12 80 EL65
Goldsmith Ave. NW9 60 CS57
Goldsmith Ave. W3 74 CR73
Goldsmith Ave., Rom. 68 FA59
Goldsmith Clo. W3 74 CS74
East Acton La.
Goldsmith Clo., Har. 58 CB60
Goldsmith La. NW9 60 CP56
Goldsmith Rd. E10 65 EA60
Goldsmith Rd. E17 51 DX54
Goldsmith Rd. N11 48 DF50
Goldsmith Rd. SE15 92 DU81
Goldsmith Rd. W3 74 CR74
Goldsmith St. EC2 7 J8
Goldsmith's Row E2 78 DU68
Goldsmith's Sq. E2 78 DU68
Goldsworthy Gdns. SE16 92 DW77
Goldwell Rd., Th.Hth. 119 DM98
Goldwin Clo. SE14 92 DW81
Goldwing Clo. E16 80 EG72
Golf Clo., Stan. 45 CJ52
Golf Clo. (Bushey), Wat. 30 BX41
Golf Club Dr., Kings.T. 102 CR94
Golf Club Rd., Hat. 20 DA26
Golf Club Rd., Wey. 127 BP109
Golf Ride, Enf. 35 DN35
Golf Rd. W5 74 CM72
Boileau Rd.
Golf Rd., Brom. 123 EN97
Golf Rd., Ken. 148 DR118
Golf Side, Sutt. 131 CY111
Golf Side, Twick. 101 CD90
Golfe Rd., Ilf. 67 ER62
Golfside Clo. N20 48 DE48
Golfside Clo., N.Mal. 116 CS96
Goliath Clo., Wall. 133 DL108
Avro Way
Gollogly Ter. SE7 94 EJ78

Granville Rd. N22 49 DP53
Granville Rd. NW2 61 CZ61
Granville Rd. NW6 76 DA68
Granville Rd. SW18 103 CZ87
Granville Rd. SW19 104 DA94
Russell Rd.
Granville Rd., Barn. 33 CW42
Granville Rd., Epp. 26 EV29
Granville Rd., Hayes 85 BT77
Granville Rd., Ilf. 67 EP60
Granville Rd., Sev. 154 FG124
Granville Rd., Sid. 110 EU91
Granville Rd., Uxb. 71 BP65
Granville Rd., Wat. 30 BW42
Granville Rd., Well. 96 EW83
Granville Rd., Wey. 127 BQ108
Granville Sq. SE15 92 DS80
Blakes Rd.
Granville Sq. WC1 6 C3
Granville Sq. WC1 77 DM69
Granville St. WC1 6 C3
Granville St. WC1 77 DM69
Grape St. WC2 5 P8
Graphite Sq. SE11 10 B10
Grasdene Rd. SE18 96 EU80
Grasmere Ave. SW15 102 CR91
Grasmere Ave. SW19 118 DA97
Grasmere Ave. W3 74 CR73
Grasmere Ave., Houns. 100 CB86
Grasmere Ave., Orp. 123 EP104
Grasmere Ave., Ruis. 57 BQ59
Grasmere Ave., Wem. 59 CJ59
Grasmere Clo., Felt. 99 BT88
Grasmere Clo., Loug. 39 EM40
Grasmere Clo., Wat. 15 BV32
Grasmere Ct. N22 49 DM51
Palmerston Rd.
Grasmere Gdns., Har. 45 CG54
Grasmere Gdns., Ilf. 67 EM57
Grasmere Gdns., Orp. 123 EP104
Grasmere Rd. E13 80 EG68
Grasmere Rd. N10 49 DH53
Grasmere Rd. N17 50 DU51
Grasmere Rd. SE25 120 DV100
Grasmere Rd. SW16 105 DM92
Grasmere Rd., Bexh. 97 FC81
Grasmere Rd., Brom. 122 EF95
Grasmere Rd., Orp. 123 EP104
Grasmere Rd., Pur. 133 DP111
Grasmere Way, W.Byf. 126 BM112
Grass Pk. N3 47 CZ53
Grassfield Clo., Couls. 147 DJ119
Grassington Clo., St.Alb. 16 CA30
Grassington Rd., Sid. 110 EU91
Grassmount SE23 106 DV89
Grassmount, Pur. 133 DJ110
Grassway, Wall. 133 DJ105
Grassy La., Sev. 155 FH126
Grasvenor Ave., Barn. 34 DA44
Grately Way SE15 92 DT80
Daniel Gdns.
Gratton Rd. W14 89 CY76
Gratton Ter. NW2 61 CX62
Gravel Clo., Chig. 54 EU47
Gravel Hill N3 47 CZ54
Gravel Hill, Bexh. 111 FB85
Gravel Hill, Croy. 135 DX107
Gravel Hill, Lthd. 143 CH121
North St.
Gravel Hill, Loug. 38 EG38
Gravel Hill, Uxb. 56 BK64
Gravel Hill Clo., Bexh. 111 FB85
Gravel La. E1 7 P8
Gravel La., Chig. 39 ET42
Gravel Pit La. SE9 109 EQ85
Gravel Pit Way, Orp. 124 EU103
Gravel Rd., Brom. 122 EL104
Gravel Rd., Twick. 101 CE88
Graveley Ave., Borwd. 32 CQ42
Gravelly Ride SW19 103 CT91
Gravelwood Clo., Chis. 109 EQ90
Graveney Gro. SE20 106 DW94
Graveney Rd. SW17 104 DE91
Gravesend Rd. W12 75 CU73
Gray Ave., Dag. 68 EZ60
Gray Gdns., Rain. 69 FG64
Gray St. SE1 10 E5
Grayham Cres., N.Mal. 116 CR98
Grayham Rd., N.Mal. 116 CR98
Grayland Clo., Brom. 122 EK95
Graylands, Epp. 39 ER37
Grayling Clo. E16 80 EE70
Cranberry La.
Grayling Rd. N16 64 DR61
Grayling Sq. E2 78 DU69
Nelson Gdns.
Graylings, The, Abb.L. 15 BR33
Grays Fm. Rd., Orp. 124 EV95
Gray's Inn WC1 6 C6
Gray's Inn WC1 77 DM71
Gray's Inn Pl. WC1 6 C7
Gray's Inn Rd. WC1 6 A2
Gray's Inn Rd. WC1 77 DL69
Gray's Inn Sq. WC1 6 D6
Grays La., Ashf. 99 BP91
Gray's La., Ash. 144 CM119
Gray's La., Epsom 144 CP121
Shepherds' Wk.
Grays Rd., Uxb. 70 BL67
Grays Rd., West. 151 EP121
Gray's Yd. W1 4 G8
Grayscroft Rd. SW16 105 DK94
Grayshott Rd. SW11 90 DG82
Grayswood Gdns. SW20 117 CV96
Farnham Gdns.
Graywood Ct. N12 48 DC52
Grazebrook Rd. N16 64 DR61
Grazeley Clo., Bexh. 111 FC85
Grazeley Ct. SE19 106 DS91
Gipsy Hill
Great Acre Ct. SW4 91 DK84
St. Alphonsus Rd.
Great Bell All. EC2 7 K8
Great Benty, West Dr. 84 BL77
Great Brownings SE21 106 DT91
Great Bushey Dr. N20 48 DB46
Great Cambridge Rd. N9 50 DR48
Great Cambridge Rd. N17 50 DR52
Great Cambridge Rd. N18 50 DR49
Great Cambridge Rd., Brox. 23 DY26
Great Cambridge Rd., Enf. 36 DU41
Great Cambridge Rd. (Cheshunt), Wal.Cr. 22 DW32
Great Castle St. W1 5 J8
Great Castle St. W1 77 DH72
Great Cen. Ave., Ruis. 58 BW64
Great Cen. St. NW1 4 D6
Great Cen. St. NW1 76 DF71
Great Cen. Way NW10 60 CQ63
Great Cen. Way, Wem. 60 CQ63
Great Chapel St. W1 5 M8
Great Chapel St. W1 77 DK72
Great Chertsey Rd. W4 88 CQ82
Great Chertsey Rd., Felt. 100 CA90
Great Ch. La. W6 89 CX78
Great College St. SW1 9 P6
Great College St. SW1 91 DL76
Great Cross Ave. SE10 94 EE80
Great Cullings, Rom. 69 FE61
Great Cumberland Ms. W1 4 D9
Great Cumberland Pl. W1 4 E8
Great Cumberland Pl. W1 76 DF72
Great Dover St. SE1 11 K5
Great Dover St. SE1 92 DR75
Great Eastern Rd. E15 79 ED66
Great Eastern St. EC2 7 M3
Great Eastern St. EC2 78 DS69
Great Eastern Wk. EC2 7 M7
Great Ellshams, Bans. 146 DA116
Great Elms Rd., Brom. 122 EJ98
Great Fld. NW9 46 CS53
Great Fleete Way, Bark. 82 EW68
Great Galley Clo., Bark. 82 EV69
Great Gdns. Rd., Horn. 69 FH58
Great George St. SW1 9 N5
Great George St. SW1 91 DK75
Great Gregories La., Epp. 25 ES33
Great Gro. (Bushey), Wat. 30 CB42
Great Guildford St. SE1 11 H2
Great Guildford St. SE1 78 DQ74
Great Harry Dr. SE9 109 EN90
Great James St. WC1 6 B6
Great James St. WC1 77 DM71
Great Julians, Rick. 28 BN42
Grove Cres.
Great Marlborough St. W1 5 K9
Great Marlborough St. W1 77 DJ72
Great Maze Pond SE1 11 L4
Great Maze Pond SE1 78 DR74
Great New St. EC4 6 E8
Great Newport St. WC2 5 N10
Great N. Rd. N2 62 DE56
Great N. Rd. N6 62 DF57
Great N. Rd., Barn. 33 CZ40
Great N. Rd. (New Barnet), Barn. 34 DB43
Great N. Rd., Hat. 20 DB27
Great N. Rd., Pot.B. 20 DB27
Great N. Way NW4 47 CV53
Great Oaks, Chig. 53 EQ49
Great Ormond St. WC1 6 A6
Great Ormond St. WC1 77 DL71
Great Owl Rd., Chig. 53 EN48
Great Pk., Kings L. 14 BM30
Great Percy St. WC1 6 C2
Great Percy St. WC1 77 DM69
Great Peter St. SW1 9 M7
Great Peter St. SW1 91 DK76
Great Portland St. W1 5 J6
Great Portland St. W1 77 DH70
Great Pulteney St. W1 5 L10
Great Pulteney St. W1 77 DJ73
Great Queen St. WC2 6 A9
Great Queen St. WC2 77 DL72
Great Russell St. WC1 5 N8
Great Russell St. WC1 77 DK72
Great St. Helens EC3 7 M8
Great St. Thomas Apostle EC4 7 J10
Great Scotland Yd. SW1 9 P2
Great Scotland Yd. SW1 77 DL74
Great Slades, Pot.B. 19 CZ33
Great Smith St. SW1 9 N6
Great Smith St. SW1 91 DK76
Great South-West Rd., Felt. 99 BQ87
Great South-West Rd., Houns. 85 BV83
Great Spilmans SE22 106 DS85
Great Strand NW9 47 CT53
Great Suffolk St. SE1 10 G3
Great Suffolk St. SE1 77 DP74
Great Sutton St. EC1 6 G5
Great Sutton St. EC1 77 DP70
Great Swan All. EC2 7 K8
Great Tattenhams, Epsom 145 CV118
Great Thrift, Orp. 123 EQ98
Great Till Clo., Sev. 153 FE116
Great Titchfield St. W1 5 K6
Great Titchfield St. W1 77 DJ71
Great Twr. St. EC3 7 M10
Great Twr. St. EC3 78 DS73
Great Trinity La. EC4 7 J10
Great Turnstile WC1 6 C7
Great W. Rd. W4 88 CP78
Great W. Rd. W6 89 CU78
Great W. Rd., Brent. 88 CP78
Great W. Rd., Houns. 86 BY82
Great W. Rd., Islw. 87 CD80
Great Western Ind. Pk., Sthl. 86 CB75
Great Western Rd. W2 75 CZ71
Great Western Rd. W9 75 CZ71
Great Western Rd. W11 75 CZ71
Great Wf. Rd. E14 79 EB74
Churchill Pl.
Great Winchester St. EC2 7 L8
Great Winchester St. EC2 78 DR72
Great Windmill St. W1 5 M10
Great Windmill St. W1 77 DK73
Great Woodcote Dr., Pur. 133 DK110
Great Woodcote Pk., Pur. 133 DK110
Great Yd. SE1 11 N4
Greatdown Rd. W7 73 CF70
Greatfield Ave. E6 81 EM70
Greatfield Clo. N19 63 DJ63
Warrender Rd.
Greatfield Clo. SE4 93 EA84
Greatfields Dr., Uxb. 70 BN71
Greatfields Rd., Bark. 81 ER67
Greatham Rd. (Bushey), Wat. 30 BX41
Greatham Wk. SW15 103 CU88
Bessborough Rd.
Greathurst End, Lthd. 142 BZ124
Greatness La., Sev. 155 FJ121
Greatness Rd., Sev. 155 FJ121
Greatorex St. E1 78 DU71
Greatwood, Chis. 109 EN94
Greaves Clo., Bark. 81 ES66
Norfolk Rd.
Greaves Pl. SW17 104 DE91
Grebe Ave., Hayes 72 BX72
Cygnet Way
Grebe Clo. E7 66 EF64
Cormorant Rd.
Grebe Clo. E17 51 DY52
Grecian Cres. SE19 105 DP93
Gredo Ho., Bark. 82 EV69
Greek Ct. W1 5 N9
Greek St. W1 5 N9
Greek St. W1 77 DK72
Greek Yd. WC2 5 P10
Green, The E4 51 EC46
Green, The E11 66 EH58
Green, The E15 80 EE65
Green, The N9 50 DU47
Green, The N14 49 DK48
Green, The N21 49 DN45
Green, The SW14 88 CQ83
Green, The SW19 103 CX92
Green, The W3 74 CS72
Green, The W5 73 CK74
The Gro.
Green, The, Bexh. 96 FA81
Green, The, Brom. 122 EG101
Green, The, Cars. 132 DG105
Green, The, Cat. 149 EA123
Green, The, Croy. 135 DZ109
Green, The, Epp. 39 ES36
Green, The, Epsom 131 CU112
Green, The, Esher 129 CF107
Green, The, Felt. 99 BV89
Green, The, Hayes 71 BS72
Wood End
Green, The, Houns. 86 CA79
Heston Rd.
Green, The, Lthd. 143 CD124
Green, The, Mord. 117 CY98
Green, The, N.Mal. 116 CQ97
Green, The (Pratt's Bottom), Orp. 138 EW110
Rushmore Hill
Green, The (St. Paul's Cray), Orp. 110 EV94
The Ave.
Green, The, Rich. 101 CK85
Green, The (Croxley Grn.), Rick. 28 BM44
Green, The (Sarratt), Rick. 28 BG35
Green, The, Sev. 155 FK122
Green, The, Shep. 113 BS98
Green, The, Sid. 110 EU91
Green, The, Sthl. 86 BY76
Green, The, Sutt. 118 DB104
Green, The, Tad. 145 CY119
Green, The, Twick. 101 CE89
Green, The, Uxb. 57 BQ61
Green, The, Wal.Abb. 23 EC34
Sewardstone Rd.
Green, The (Cheshunt), Wal.Cr. 22 DW28
Green, The, Walt. 127 BS110
Octagon Rd.
Green, The, Warl. 149 DX117
Green, The, Wat. 31 CE39
Green, The, Well. 95 ES84
Green, The, Wem. 59 CG61
Green, The, West Dr. 84 BK76
Green, The, Wdf.Grn. 52 EG50
Green Acres, Croy. 120 DT104
Green Arbour Ct. EC1 6 F8
Green Ave. NW7 46 CR49
Green Ave. W13 87 CH76
Green Bank E1 78 DV74
Green Bank N12 48 DB49
Green Clo. NW9 60 CQ58
Green Clo. NW11 62 DC59
Green Clo., Brom. 122 EE97
Green Clo., Cars. 118 DF103
Green Clo., Felt. 100 BY92
Green Clo., Hat. 19 CY26
Station Rd.
Green Clo. (Cheshunt), Wal.Cr. 23 DY31
Green Ct. Rd., Swan. 125 FD100
Green Cft., Edg. 46 CQ50
Deans La.
Green Curve, Bans. 131 CZ114
Green Dale SE5 92 DR84
Wanley Rd.
Green Dale SE22 106 DS85
Green Dale Clo. SE22 106 DS85
Green Dale
Green Dragon Ct. SE1 11 K2
Green Dragon La. N21 35 DN43
Green Dragon La., Brent. 88 CL78
Green Dragon Yd. E1 78 DU71
Old Montague St.
Green Dr., Sthl. 72 CA74
Green End N21 49 DP47
Green End, Chess. 130 CL105
Green Gdns., Orp. 137 EQ106
Green Glade, Epp. 39 ES37
Green Hill, Buck.H. 52 EJ46
Green Hill, Orp. 137 EM112
Green Hill La., Warl. 149 DY117
Sunny Bank
Green Hill Ter. SE18 95 EM78
Green Hill Way, Croy. 135 DX112
Green Hundred Rd. SE15 92 DU79
Green La. E4 37 ED41
Green La. NW4 61 CX56
Green La. SE9 109 EP88
Green La. SE20 107 DX94
Green La. SW16 105 DM94
Green La. W7 87 CE75
Green La., Add. 112 BG104
Green La., Ash. 143 CJ117
Green La., Chess. 130 CL109
Green La., Chig. 53 EQ46
Green La., Chis. 109 EP90
Green La., Cob. 128 BY112
Green La., Dag. 68 EX61
Green La., Edg. 46 CM49
Green La., Felt. 100 BY92
Green La., Har. 59 CE62
Green La., Houns. 85 BV83
Green La., Ilf. 67 EQ61
Green La., Lthd. 143 CK121
Green La., Mord. 118 DA100
Green La., N.Mal. 116 CQ99
Green La., Nthwd. 43 BR52
Green La., Pur. 133 DJ111
Green La., Rick. 28 BM43
Green La., Shep. 113 BQ100
Green La., Stan. 45 CH49
Green La., Sun. 99 BT94
Green La., Th.Hth. 119 DP95
Green La., Uxb. 71 BQ71
Green La., Wal.Abb. 24 EJ34
Green La., Walt. 127 BV107
Green La., Warl. 149 DY116
Green La., Wat. 44 BW46
Green La., W.Byf. 126 BM112
Green La., W.Mol. 114 CB99
Green La. (Ockham), Wok. 141 BP124
Green La., Wor.Pk. 117 CU102
Green La. Ave., Walt. 128 BW106
Green La. Clo., W.Byf. 126 BM112
Green La. Gdns., Th.Hth. 119 DP96
Green Las. N4 63 DP59
Green Las. N8 63 DP55
Green Las. N13 49 DM51
Green Las. N15 63 DP55
Green Las. N16 64 DQ62
Green Las. N21 49 DP47
Green Las., Epsom 130 CS109
Green Lawns, Ruis. 58 BW60
Green Leaf Ave., Wall. 133 DK105
Ferrers Ave.
Green Leas, Sun. 99 BT94
Green Leas, Wal.Abb. 23 ED34
Roundhills
Green Leas Clo., Sun. 99 BT93
Green Leas
Green Man Gdns. W13 73 CG73
Green Man La. W13 73 CG73
Green Man La., Felt. 85 BU84
Green Mead, Esher 128 BZ107
Winterdown Gdns.
Green Meadow, Pot.B. 20 DA30
Green Moor Link N21 49 DP45
Green Pl., Dart. 111 FE85
Green Pt. E15 80 EE65
Green Pond Clo. E17 65 DY55
Green Pond Rd. E17 65 DY55
Green Ride, Epp. 39 EP35
Green Ride, Loug. 38 EG43
Green Rd. N14 35 DH44
Green Rd. N20 48 DC48
Green Shield Ind. Est. E16 80 EG74
Green St. E7 80 EH65
Green St. E13 80 EJ66
Green St. W1 4 E10
Green St. W1 76 DF73
Green St., Enf. 36 DW40
Green St., Rad. 18 CN34
Green St., Sun. 113 BU95
Green Vale W5 74 CM72
Green Vale, Bexh. 110 EX85
Green Verges, Stan. 45 CK52
Green Vw., Chess. 130 CM108
Green Wk. NW4 61 CX57
Green Wk. SE1 11 M7
Green Wk., Dart. 111 FF85
Green Wk., Hmptn. 100 BZ93
Orpwood Clo.
Green Wk., Ruis. 57 BT60
Green Wk., Sthl. 86 CA78
Green Wk., Wdf.Grn. 52 EL51
Green Wk., The E4 51 EC45
Green Way SE9 108 EK85
Green Way, Brom. 122 EL100
Green Way, Sun. 113 BU98
Green Wrythe Cres., Cars. 118 DE102
Green Wrythe La., Cars. 118 DD100
Greenacre Clo., Barn. 33 CZ38
Greenacre Clo., Swan. 125 FE98
Greenacre Gdns. E17 65 EC56
Greenacre Sq. SE16 93 DX75
Fishermans Dr.
Greenacre Wk. N14 49 DL48
Greenacres SE9 109 EN86
Greenacres, Epp. 25 ET28
Greenacres, Lthd. 142 CB124
Greenacres (Bushey), Wat. 45 CD47
Greenacres Ave., Uxb. 56 BM62
Greenacres Clo., Nthlt. 58 BZ64
Eastcote La.
Greenacres Clo., Orp. 137 EQ105
Greenacres Dr., Stan. 45 CH51
Greenall Clo. (Cheshunt), Wal.Cr. 23 DY30
Greenaway Gdns. NW3 62 DB63
Greenbank (Cheshunt), Wal.Cr. 22 DV28
Greenbank Ave., Wem. 59 CG64
Greenbank Clo. E4 51 EC47
Greenbank Cres. NW4 61 CY56
Greenbank Rd., Wat. 29 BR36
Greenbay Rd. SE7 94 EK80
Greenberry St. NW8 4 B1
Greenberry St. NW8 76 DE68
Greenbrook Ave., Barn. 34 DC39
Greencoat Pl. SW1 9 L8
Greencoat Pl. SW1 91 DJ77
Greencoat Row SW1 9 L7
Greencourt Ave., Croy. 120 DV103
Greencourt Ave., Edg. 46 CP53
Greencourt Gdns., Croy. 120 DV102
Greencourt Rd., Orp. 123 ER99
Greencrest Pl. NW2 61 CV62
Dollis Hill La.
Greencroft Ave., Ruis. 58 BW61
Greencroft Clo. E6 80 EL71
Neatscourt Rd.
Greencroft Gdns. NW6 76 DB66
Greencroft Gdns., Enf. 36 DS41
Greencroft Rd., Houns. 86 BZ81
Greene Fielde End, Stai. 98 BK94
Berryscroft Rd.
Greenend Rd. W4 88 CS75
Greenfarm Clo., Orp. 137 ET106
Greenfell St. SE10 94 EE76
Greenfield Ave., Surb. 116 CP101
Greenfield Ave., Wat. 44 BX47
Greenfield Gdns. NW2 61 CY61
Greenfield Gdns., Dag. 82 EX67
Greenfield Gdns., Orp. 123 ER101
Greenfield Link, Couls. 147 DL115
Greenfield Rd. E1 78 DU71
Greenfield Rd. N15 64 DS57
Greenfield Rd., Dag. 82 EW66
Greenfield Rd., Dart. 111 FD92
Greenfield St., Wal.Abb. 23 EC34
Greenfield Way, Har. 58 CB55
Greenfields, Loug. 39 EN42
Greenfields (Cuffley), Pot.B. 21 DL30
South Dr.
Greenfields Clo., Loug. 39 EN42
Greenford Ave. W7 73 CE70
Greenford Ave., Sthl. 72 BZ73
Greenford Gdns., Grnf. 72 CB69
Greenford Rd., Grnf. 72 CC72
Greenford Rd., Har. 59 CF63
Greenford Rd., Sthl. 72 CC72
Greenford Rd., Sutt. 132 DB105
Greengate, Grnf. 73 CH65
Greengate St. E13 80 EH68
Greenhalgh Wk. N2 62 DC56
Greenham Clo. SE1 10 D5
Greenham Clo. SE1 91 DN75
Greenham Cres. E4 51 DZ51
Greenham Rd. N10 48 DG54
Greenhayes Ave., Bans. 132 DA114
Greenhayes Gdns., Bans. 146 DA115
Greenheys Clo., Nthwd. 43 BS53
Greenheys Dr. E18 66 EF55
Greenhill NW3 62 DD63
Hampstead High St.
Greenhill SE18 95 EM78
Greenhill, Sutt. 118 DC103
Greenhill, Wem. 60 CP61
Greenhill Ave., Cat. 148 DV121
Greenhill Cres., Wat. 29 BS44
Greenhill Gdns., Nthlt. 72 BZ68
Greenhill Gro. E12 66 EL63
Greenhill Pk. NW10 74 CS67
Greenhill Pk., Barn. 34 DB43
Greenhill Rd. NW10 74 CS67
Greenhill Rd., Har. 59 CE58
Greenhill Ter., Nthlt. 72 BZ68
Greenhill Way, Har. 59 CE58
Greenhill Way, Wem. 60 CP61
Greenhills Clo., Rick. 28 BH43
Greenhill's Rents EC1 6 F6
Greenhills Ter. N1 78 DR65
Baxter Rd.

Greenhithe Clo., Sid. 109 ES87
Greenholm Rd. SE9 109 EP85
Greenhurst Rd. SE27 105 DN92
Greening St. SE2 96 EW77
Greenland Cres., Sthl. 86 BW76
Greenland Ms. SE8 93 DX78
Trundleys Rd.
Greenland Pl. NW1 77 DH67
Greenland Rd.
Greenland Quay SE16 93 DX77
Greenland Rd. NW1 77 DH67
Greenland Rd., Barn. 33 CW44
Greenland St. NW1 77 DH67
Camden High St.
Greenlands Rd., Stai. 98 BG91
Greenlands Rd., Wey. 113 BP104
Greenlaw Gdns., N.Mal. 117 CT101
Greenlaw St. SE18 95 EN76
Greenlea Trd. Pk. SW19 118 DD95
Greenleaf Clo. SW2 105 DN87
Tulse Hill
Greenleaf Rd. E6 80 EJ67
Redclyffe Rd.
Greenleaf Rd. E17 65 DZ55
Greenleafe Dr., Ilf. 67 EP55
Greenleaves Ct., Ashf. 99 BP93
Redleaves Ave.
Greenleigh Ave., Orp. 124 EV98
Greenman St. N1 78 DQ66
Greenmoor Rd., Enf. 36 DW40
Greeno Cres., Shep. 112 BN99
Greenoak Pl., Barn. 34 DF41
Cockfosters Rd.
Greenoak Ri., West. 150 EJ118
Greenoak Way SW19 103 CX91
Greenock Rd. SW16 119 DK95
Greenock Rd. W3 88 CP76
Greenock Way, Rom. 55 FE52
Greenpark Ct., Wem. 73 CJ66
Greens Clo., The, Loug. 39 EN40
Green's Ct. W1 5 M10
Green's End SE18 95 EP77
Greenshank Clo. E17 51 DY52
Banbury Rd.
Greenside, Bex. 110 EY88
Greenside, Borwd. 32 CN38
Greenside, Dag. 68 EW60
Greenside, Swan. 125 FD96
Greenside Clo. N20 48 DD47
Greenside Clo. SE6 107 ED89
Greenside Rd. W12 89 CU76
Greenside Rd., Croy. 119 DN101
Greenside Rd., Wey. 113 BP104
Greenside Wk., West. 150 EH118
Kings Rd.
Greenslade Ave., Ash. 144 CP119
Greenslade Rd., Bark. 81 ER66
Greenstead Ave., Wdf.Grn. 52 EJ52
Greenstead Clo., Wdf.Grn. 52 EJ51
Greenstead Gdns.
Greenstead Gdns. SW15 103 CU85
Greenstead Gdns., Wdf.Grn. 52 EJ51
Greensted Rd., Loug. 52 EL45
Greensted Rd., Ong. 27 FG28
Greenstone Ms. E11 66 EG58
Greensward (Bushey), Wat. 30 CB44
Greentrees, Epp. 26 EU31
Greenvale Rd. SE9 95 EM84
Greenview Ave., Beck. 121 DY100
Greenview Ave., Croy. 121 DY100
Greenview Ct., Ashf. 98 BM91
Village Way
Greenville Clo., Cob. 128 BY113
Greenway N14 49 DL47
Greenway N20 48 DA47
Greenway SW20 117 CW98
Greenway, Chis. 109 EN92
Greenway, Dag. 68 EW61
Greenway, Har. 60 CL57
Greenway, Hayes 71 BU69
Greenway, Lthd. 142 CB123
Greenway, Pnr. 43 BV54
Greenway, Wall. 133 DJ105
Greenway, West. 150 EJ120
Greenway, Wdf.Grn. 52 EJ50
Greenway, The NW9 46 CR54
Greenway, The, Enf. 37 DX35
Greenway, The, Epsom 130 CN114
Greenway, The, Har. 45 CE53
Greenway, The, Houns. 86 BZ84
Greenway, The, Orp. 124 EV100
Greenway, The, Pnr. 58 BZ58
Greenway, The, Pot.B. 20 DA33
Greenway, The, Rick. 42 BG45
Greenway, The, Uxb. 70 BK68
Greenway, The (Ickenham), Uxb. 57 BP61
Greenway Ave. E17 65 ED56
Greenway Clo. N4 64 DQ61
Greenway Clo. N11 48 DG51
Greenway Clo. N15 64 DT56
Copperfield Dr.
Greenway Clo. N20 48 DA47
Greenway Clo. NW9 46 CR54
Greenway Clo., W.Byf. 126 BG113
Greenway Dr., Stai. 112 BK95
Greenway Gdns. NW9 46 CR54
Greenway Gdns., Croy. 121 DZ104
Greenway Gdns., Grnf. 72 CA69
Greenway Gdns., Har. 45 CE54
Greenways, Abb.L. 15 BS32
Greenways, Beck. 121 EA96
Greenways, Esher 129 CE105
Greenways (Cheshunt), Wal.Cr. 21 DP29
Greenways, The, Twick. 101 CG86
Greenwell St. W1 5 J5
Greenwell St. W1 77 DH70
Greenwich Ch. St. SE10 93 EC79
Greenwich Cres. E6 80 EL71
Swan App.
Greenwich High Rd. SE10 93 EB81
Greenwich Ind. Est. SE7 94 EH77
Greenwich Mkt. SE10 93 EC79
Greenwich Pk. SE10 93 ED80
Greenwich Pk. St. SE10 93 ED78
Greenwich S. St. SE10 93 EB81
Greenwich Vw. Pl. E14 93 EB76
Greenwood Ave., Dag. 69 FB63
Greenwood Ave., Enf. 37 DY40
Greenwood Ave. (Cheshunt), Wal.Cr. 22 DV31
Greenwood Clo., Mord. 117 CY98
Greenwood Clo., Orp. 123 ES100
Greenwood Clo., Sid. 110 EU89
Hurst Rd.
Greenwood Clo., T.Ditt. 115 CG102
Greenwood Clo. (Cheshunt), Wal.Cr. 22 DV31
Greenwood Ave.
Greenwood Clo. (Bushey), Wat. 45 CE45
Langmead Dr.
Greenwood Ct. SW1 91 DJ78
Cambridge St.
Greenwood Dr. E4 51 EC50
Avril Way
Greenwood Dr., Wat. 15 BV34
Greenwood Gdns. N13 49 DP48
Greenwood Gdns., Ilf. 53 EQ52
Greenwood La., Hmptn. 100 CB92
Greenwood Pk., Kings.T. 102 CS94
Greenwood Pl. NW5 63 DH64
Highgate Rd.
Greenwood Rd. E8 78 DU65
Greenwood Rd. E13 80 EF68
Maud Rd.
Greenwood Rd., Bex. 111 FD91
Greenwood Rd., Chig. 54 EV48
Greenwood Rd., Croy. 119 DP101
Greenwood Rd., Islw. 87 CF83
Greenwood Rd., Mitch. 119 DK97
Greenwood Rd., T.Ditt. 115 CG102
Greenwood Ter. NW10 74 CR67
Greenwood Way, Sev. 154 FF125
Greenwoods, The, Har. 58 CC61
Sherwood Rd.
Greenyard, Wal.Abb. 23 EC34
Greer Rd., Har. 44 CC53
Greet St. SE1 10 E3
Greet St. SE1 77 DN74
Greg Clo. E10 65 EC58
Gregor Ms. SE3 94 EG80
Gregory Ave., Pot.B. 20 DC33
Gregory Cres. SE9 108 EK87
Gregory Pl. W8 90 DB75
Gregory Rd., Rom. 68 EX56
Gregory Rd., Sthl. 86 CA76
Gregson Clo., Borwd. 32 CQ39
Greig Clo. N8 63 DL57
Greig Ter. SE17 91 DP79
Lorrimore Sq.
Grena Gdns., Rich. 88 CM84
Grena Rd., Rich. 88 CM84
Grenaby Ave., Croy. 120 DR101
Grenaby Rd., Croy. 120 DR101
Grenada Rd. SE7 94 EJ80
Grenade St. E14 79 DZ73
Grenadier St. E16 81 EN74
Grenadine Clo., Wal.Cr. 22 DT27
Allwood Rd.
Grendon Gdns., Wem. 60 CN61
Grendon St. NW8 4 B4
Grendon St. NW8 76 DE70
Grenfell Ave., Horn. 69 FF60
Grenfell Clo., Borwd. 32 CQ39
Grenfell Gdns., Har. 60 CL59
Grenfell Rd. W11 75 CX73
Grenfell Rd., Mitch. 104 DF93
Grenfell Twr. W11 75 CX73
Grenfell Wk. W11 75 CX73
Whitchurch Rd.
Grennell Clo., Sutt. 118 DD103
Grennell Rd., Sutt. 118 DC104
Grenoble Gdns. N13 49 DN51
Grenville Clo. N3 47 CZ53
Grenville Clo., Surb. 116 CQ102
Grenville Clo., Wal.Cr. 23 DX32
Grenville Gdns., Wdf.Grn. 52 EJ53
Grenville Ms. SW7 90 DC77
Grenville Ms., Hmptn. 100 CB92
Grenville Pl. NW7 46 CR50
Grenville Pl. SW7 90 DC76
Grenville Rd. N19 63 DL60
Grenville Rd., Croy. 135 EC109
Grenville St. WC1 6 A5
Grenville St. WC1 77 DL70
Gresham Ave. N20 48 DF49
Gresham Ave., Warl. 149 DY118
Gresham Clo., Bex. 110 EY86
Gresham Clo., Enf. 36 DQ41
Gresham Dr., Rom. 68 EV57
Gresham Gdns. NW11 61 CY60
Gresham Rd. E6 81 EM68
Gresham Rd. E16 80 EH72
Gresham Rd. NW10 60 CR64
Gresham Rd. SE25 120 DU98
Gresham Rd. SW9 91 DN83
Gresham Rd., Beck. 121 DY96
Gresham Rd., Edg. 46 CM51
Gresham Rd., Hmptn. 100 CA93
Gresham Rd., Houns. 86 CC81
Gresham Rd., Uxb. 70 BN68
Gresham St. EC2 7 J8
Gresham St. EC2 78 DQ72
Gresham Way SW19 104 DA90
Gresley Clo. E17 65 DY58
Gresley Clo. N15 64 DR56
Clinton Rd.
Gresley Ct., Pot.B. 20 DC29
Gresley Rd. N19 63 DJ60
Gresse St. W1 5 M8
Gresse St. W1 77 DK71
Gressenhall Rd. SW18 103 CZ86
Gresswell Clo., Sid. 110 EU90
Greswell St. SW6 89 CX81
Gretton Rd. N17 50 DS52
Greville Ave., S.Croy. 135 DX110
Greville Clo., Ash. 144 CL119
Greville Clo., Twick. 101 CH87
Greville Hall NW6 76 DB68
Greville Ms. NW6 76 DB68
Greville Rd.
Greville Pk. Ave., Ash. 144 CL118
Greville Pk. Rd., Ash. 144 CL118
Greville Pl. NW6 76 DB68
Greville Rd. E17 65 EC56
Greville Rd. NW6 76 DB68
Greville Rd., Rich. 102 CM86
Greville St. EC1 6 E7
Greville St. EC1 77 DN71
Grey Alders, Bans. 131 CW114
High Beeches
Grey Clo. NW11 62 DC58
Grey Eagle St. E1 78 DT71
Greycaine Rd., Wat. 30 BX37
Greycoat Pl. SW1 9 M7
Greycoat Pl. SW1 91 DK76
Greycoat St. SW1 9 M7
Greycoat St. SW1 91 DK76
Greycot Rd., Beck. 107 EA92
Greyfell Clo., Stan. 45 CH50
Coverdale Clo.
Greyfields Clo., Pur. 133 DP113
Greyfriars Pas. EC1 6 G8
Greyfriars Rd., Wok. 140 BG124
Greyhound Hill NW4 61 CU55
Greyhound La. SW16 105 DK93
Greyhound La., Pot.B. 19 CU33
Greyhound Rd. N17 64 DS55
Greyhound Rd. NW10 75 CV69
Greyhound Rd. W6 89 CX79
Greyhound Rd. W14 89 CY79
Greyhound Rd., Sutt. 132 DC106
Greyhound Ter. SW16 119 DJ95
Greyhound Way, Dart. 111 FE86
Greys Pk. Clo., Kes. 136 EK106
Greystead Rd. SE23 106 DW87
Greystoke Ave., Pnr. 58 CA55
Greystoke Dr., Ruis. 57 BP58
Greystoke Gdns. W5 74 CL70
Greystoke Gdns., Enf. 35 DK42
Greystoke Pk. Ter. W5 73 CK69
Greystoke Pl. EC4 6 D8
Greystone Clo., S.Croy. 134 DW111
Greystone Gdns., Har. 59 CJ58
Greystone Gdns., Ilf. 53 EQ54
Greystone Path E11 66 EF59
Grove Rd.
Greyswood St. SW16 105 DH93
Grice Ave., West. 136 EH113
Grierson Rd. SE23 107 DY86
Griffin Clo. NW10 61 CV64
Griffin Manorway SE28 95 ER76
Griffin Rd. N17 50 DS54
Griffin Rd. SE18 95 ER78
Griffin Way, Sun. 113 BU96
Griffith Clo., Dag. 68 EW60
Gibson Rd.
Griffiths Clo., Wor.Pk. 117 CV103
Griffiths Rd. SW19 104 DA94
Griggs App., Ilf. 67 EQ61
Griggs Pl. SE1 11 N6
Griggs Rd. E10 65 EC58
Grilse Clo. N9 50 DV49
Grimsby St. E2 78 DU70
Cheshire St.
Grimsdyke Cres., Barn. 33 CW41
Grimsdyke Rd., Pnr. 44 BY52
Grimsel Path SE5 91 DP80
Laxley Clo.
Grimshaw Clo. N6 62 DG59
Grimshaw Way, Rom. 69 FF57
Grimston Rd. SW6 89 CZ82
Grimstone Clo., Rom. 55 FB51
Grimwade Ave., Croy. 120 DU104
Grimwade Clo. SE15 92 DW83
Grimwade Cres. SE15 92 DW83
Evelina Rd.
Grimwood Rd., Twick. 101 CF87
Grindal St. SE1 10 D5
Grindall Clo., Croy. 133 DP105
Hillside Rd.
Grindley Gdns., Croy. 120 DT100
Grinling Pl. SE8 93 EA79
Grinstead Rd. SE8 93 DY78
Grisedale Clo., Pur. 134 DR114
Grisedale Gdns., Pur. 134 DS114
Grittleton Ave., Wem. 74 CP65
Grittleton Rd. W9 76 DA70
Grizedale Ter. SE23 106 DV89
Eliot Bank
Grocer's Hall Ct. EC2 7 K9
Grogan Clo., Hmptn. 100 BZ93
Groom Cres. SW18 104 DD87
Groom Pl. SW1 8 G6
Groom Pl. SW1 90 DG76
Groom Rd., Brox. 23 DZ26
Groombridge Clo., Walt. 127 BV106
Groombridge Clo., Well. 110 EU85
Groombridge Rd. E9 79 DX66
Groomfield Clo. SW17 104 DG91
Grooms Dr., Pnr. 57 BU57
Grosmont Rd. SE18 95 ET79
Grosse Way SW15 103 CV86
Grosvenor Ave. N5 64 DQ64
Grosvenor Ave. SW14 88 CS83
Grosvenor Ave., Cars. 132 DF107
Grosvenor Ave., Har. 58 CB58
Grosvenor Ave., Hayes 71 BS68
Grosvenor Ave., Kings L. 15 BQ28
Grosvenor Ave., Rich. 102 CL85
Grosvenor Rd.
Grosvenor Clo., Loug. 39 EP39
Grosvenor Cotts. SW1 8 F8
Grosvenor Ct. N14 49 DJ45
Grosvenor Ct., Rick. 29 BR43
Mayfare
Grosvenor Cres. NW9 60 CN56
Grosvenor Cres. SW1 8 G5
Grosvenor Cres. SW1 90 DG75
Grosvenor Cres., Uxb. 71 BP66
Grosvenor Cres. Ms. SW1 8 F5
Grosvenor Cres. Ms. SW1 90 DG75
Grosvenor Dr., Loug. 39 EP40
Grosvenor Est. SW1 9 N8
Grosvenor Est. SW1 91 DK77
Grosvenor Gdns. E6 80 EK69
Grosvenor Gdns. N10 63 DJ55
Grosvenor Gdns. N14 35 DK42
Grosvenor Gdns. NW2 61 CW64
Grosvenor Gdns. NW11 61 CZ58
Grosvenor Gdns. SW1 9 J7
Grosvenor Gdns. SW1 91 DH76
Grosvenor Gdns. SW14 88 CS83
Grosvenor Gdns., Kings.T. 101 CK93
Grosvenor Gdns., Wall. 133 DJ108
Grosvenor Gdns., Wdf.Grn. 52 EG51
Grosvenor Gdns. Ms. E. SW1 9 J6
Grosvenor Gdns. Ms. N. SW1 9 H7
Grosvenor Gdns. Ms. S. SW1 9 J7
Grosvenor Gate W1 8 E1
Grosvenor Hill SW19 103 CY93
Grosvenor Hill W1 5 H10
Grosvenor Hill W1 77 DH73
Grosvenor Pk. SE5 92 DQ80
Grosvenor Pk. Rd. E17 65 EA57
Grosvenor Path, Loug. 39 EP39
Grosvenor Pl. SW1 8 G5
Grosvenor Pl. SW1 90 DG75
Grosvenor Pl., Wey. 113 BR104
Vale Rd.
Grosvenor Ri. E. E17 65 EB57
Grosvenor Rd. E6 80 EK67
Grosvenor Rd. E7 80 EH65
Grosvenor Rd. E10 65 EC60
Grosvenor Rd. E11 66 EG57
Grosvenor Rd. N3 47 CZ52
Grosvenor Rd. N9 50 DV46
Grosvenor Rd. N10 49 DH53
Grosvenor Rd. SE25 120 DU98
Grosvenor Rd. SW1 91 DH79
Grosvenor Rd. W4 88 CP78
Grosvenor Rd. W7 73 CG74
Grosvenor Rd., Belv. 96 FA79
Grosvenor Rd., Bexh. 110 EX85
Grosvenor Rd., Borwd. 32 CN41
Grosvenor Rd., Brent. 87 CK79
Grosvenor Rd., Dag. 68 EZ60
Grosvenor Rd., Epsom 144 CR119
Grosvenor Rd., Houns. 86 BZ83
Grosvenor Rd., Ilf. 67 EQ62
Grosvenor Rd., Nthwd. 43 BT50
Grosvenor Rd., Orp. 123 ES100
Grosvenor Rd., Rich. 102 CL85
Grosvenor Rd., Rom. 69 FD59
Grosvenor Rd., Sthl. 86 BZ76
Grosvenor Rd., Stai. 98 BG94
Grosvenor Rd., Twick. 101 CG87
Grosvenor Rd., Wall. 133 DH107
Grosvenor Rd., Wat. 30 BW41
Grosvenor Rd., W.Wick. 121 EB102
Grosvenor Sq. W1 4 G10
Grosvenor Sq. W1 76 DG73
Grosvenor St. W1 5 H10
Grosvenor St. W1 77 DH73
Grosvenor Ter. SE5 92 DQ79
Grosvenor Vale, Ruis. 57 BT61
Grosvenor Way E5 64 DW61
Grosvenor Wf. Rd. E14 93 ED77
Grote's Bldgs. SE3 94 EE82
Grote's Pl. SE3 94 EE82
Groton Rd. SW18 104 DB89
Grotto Pas. W1 4 G6
Grotto Rd., Twick. 101 CF89
Grotto Rd., Wey. 113 BP104
Grove, The E15 80 EE65
Grove, The N3 48 DA53
Grove, The N4 63 DM59
Grove, The N6 62 DG60
Grove, The N8 63 DK57
Grove, The N13 49 DN50
Grove, The N14 35 DJ43
Grove, The NW9 60 CR57
Grove, The NW11 61 CY59
Grove, The W5 73 CK74
Grove, The, Add. 126 BH106
Grove, The, Bexh. 96 EX84
Grove, The, Cat. 147 DP121
Grove, The, Couls. 147 DK115
Grove, The, Edg. 46 CP49
Grove, The, Enf. 35 DN40
Grove, The, Epsom 130 CS113
Grove, The (Ewell), Epsom 131 CT110
West St.
Grove, The, Esher 114 CB102
Grove, The, Grnf. 72 CC72
Grove, The, Hat. 20 DA26
Grove, The, Islw. 87 CE81
Grove, The, Pot.B. 20 DD32
Grove, The, Rad. 17 CG34
Grove, The, Sid. 110 EY92
Grove, The, Swan. 125 FF97
Grove, The, Tedd. 101 CG91
Grove, The, Twick. 101 CH86
Bridge Rd.
Grove, The, Uxb. 56 BN64
Grove, The, Walt. 113 BV101
Grove, The, W.Wick. 121 EB104
Grove, The, West. 150 EK118
Grove Ave. N3 48 DA52
Grove Ave. N10 49 DJ54
Grove Ave. W7 73 CE72
Grove Ave., Epsom 130 CS113
Grove Ave., Pnr. 58 BY57
Grove Ave., Sutt. 132 DA107
Grove Rd.
Grove Ave., Twick. 101 CF88
Grove Clo. N14 49 DH45
Avenue Rd.
Grove Clo. SE23 107 DY88
Grove Clo., Brom. 122 EG103
Grove Clo., Felt. 100 BY91
Grove Clo., Kings.T. 116 CM98
Grove Clo., Uxb. 56 BN64
Grove Cotts. SW3 90 DE79
Grove Ct. SE3 94 EG81
Grove Ct., E.Mol. 115 CD99
Walton Rd.
Grove Ct., Wal.Abb. 23 EB33
Grove Cres. E18 52 EF54
Grove Cres. NW9 60 CQ56
Grove Cres. SE5 92 DS82
Grove Cres., Felt. 100 BY91
Grove Cres., Kings.T. 116 CL97
Grove Cres., Rick. 28 BN42
Grove Cres., Walt. 113 BV101
Grove Cres. Rd. E15 79 ED65
Grove End E18 52 EF54
Grove Hill
Grove End La., Esher 115 CD102
Grove End Rd. NW8 76 DD68
Grove Fm. Ind. Est., Mitch. 118 DF99
Grove Fm. Pk., Nthwd. 43 BR50
Grove Footpath, Surb. 116 CL98
Grove Gdns. E15 80 EE65
Grove Gdns. NW4 61 CU57
Grove Gdns. NW8 4 C3
Grove Gdns., Dag. 69 FC62
Grove Gdns., Enf. 37 DX38
Grove Gdns., Tedd. 101 CG91
Grove Grn. Rd. E11 65 EC62
Grove Hall Ct. NW8 76 DC69
Hall Rd.
Grove Hall Rd., Wat. 30 BY42
Grove Heath Ct., Wok. 140 BJ124
Grove Heath N., Wok. 140 BH122
Grove Heath Rd. (Ripley), Wok. 140 BH123
Grove Hill E18 52 EF54
Grove Hill, Har. 59 CE59
Grove Hill Rd. SE5 92 DS83
Grove Hill Rd., Har. 59 CE59
Grove Ho. Rd. N8 63 DL56
Grove La. SE5 92 DS82
Grove La., Chig. 53 ET48
Grove La., Couls. 133 DH114
Grove La., Epp. 26 EU30
High St.
Grove La., Kings.T. 116 CL98
Grove La., Uxb. 70 BM70
Grove Mkt. Pl. SE9 109 EM86
Grove Ms. W6 89 CW76
Grove Ms. W11 75 CZ72
Portobello Rd.
Grove Mill La., Wat. 29 BP37
Grove Pk. E11 66 EH58
Grove Pk. NW9 60 CQ56
Grove Pk. SE5 92 DS82
Grove Pk. Ave. E4 51 EB52
Grove Pk. Bri. W4 88 CQ80
Grove Pk. Gdns. W4 88 CQ80
Grove Pk. Ms. W4 88 CQ80
Grove Pk. Rd. N15 64 DS56
Grove Pk. Rd. SE9 108 EJ90
Grove Pk. Rd. W4 88 CP80
Grove Pk. Rd., Rain. 83 FG67
Grove Pk. Ter. W4 88 CP80
Grove Pas. E2 78 DV68
The Oval
Grove Pas., Tedd. 101 CG92
Grove Path (Cheshunt), Wal.Cr. 22 DU31
Tudor Ave.
Grove Pl. NW3 62 DD63
Christchurch Hill
Grove Pl. W3 74 CQ74
Grove Pl. W5 73 CK74
The Gro.
Grove Pl., Bark. 81 EQ67
Clockhouse Ave.
Grove Pl., Wat. 30 CB39
Hartspring La.

Grove Pl., Wey. 127 BQ106
Princes Rd.
Grove Rd. E3 79 DX67
Grove Rd. E4 51 EC49
Grove Rd. E11 66 EF59
Grove Rd. E17 65 EB58
Grove Rd. E18 52 EF54
Grove Rd. N11 49 DH50
Grove Rd. N12 48 DD50
Grove Rd. N15 64 DS57
Grove Rd. NW2 75 CW65
Grove Rd. SW13 89 CT82
Grove Rd. SW19 104 DC94
Grove Rd. W3 74 CQ74
Grove Rd. W5 73 CK73
Grove Rd., Ash. 144 CM118
Grove Rd., Barn. 34 DE41
Grove Rd., Belv. 96 EZ79
Grove Rd., Bexh. 97 FC84
Grove Rd., Borwd. 32 CN39
Grove Rd., Brent. 87 CJ78
Grove Rd., E.Mol. 115 CD98
Grove Rd., Edg. 46 CN51
Grove Rd., Epsom 130 CS113
Grove Rd., Houns. 86 CA84
Grove Rd., Islw. 87 CE81
Grove Rd., Mitch. 118 DG97
Grove Rd., Nthwd. 43 BR50
Grove Rd., Pnr. 58 BZ57
Grove Rd., Rich. 102 CM86
Grove Rd., Rick. 42 BG47
Grove Rd., Rom. 68 EV59
Grove Rd., Sev. 155 FJ121
Grove Rd. (Seal), Sev. 155 FN122
Grove Rd., Shep. 113 BQ100
Grove Rd., Surb. 115 CK99
Grove Rd., Sutt. 132 DA107
Grove Rd., Th.Hth. 119 DN98
Grove Rd., Twick. 101 CD90
Grove Rd., Uxb. 70 BK66
Grove Rd., West. 150 EJ120
Grove Rd. W., Enf. 36 DW37
Grove Shaw, Tad. 145 CY124
Grove St. N18 50 DT50
Grove St. SE8 93 DZ77
Grove Ter. NW5 63 DH62
Grove Ter., Tedd. 101 CG91
Grove Vale SE22 92 DS84
Grove Vale, Chis. 109 EN93
Grove Vill. E14 79 EB73
Grove Way, Esher 114 CC101
Grove Way, Uxb. 70 BK66
Grove Wd. Hill, Couls. 133 DJ114
Grovebarns, Stai. 98 BG93
Grovebury Clo., Erith 97 FD79
Grovebury Gdns., St.Alb. 16 CC27
Grovebury Rd. SE2 96 EV75
Grovedale Clo. (Cheshunt), Wal.Cr. 22 DT30
Grovedale Rd. N19 63 DK61
Grovehall Rd. (Bushey), Wat. 30 BY42
Groveland Ave. SW16 105 DM94
Groveland Ct. EC4 7 J9
Groveland Rd., Beck. 121 DZ97
Groveland Way, N.Mal. 116 CQ99
Grovelands, St.Alb. 16 CB27
Grovelands, W.Mol. 114 CA98
Grovelands Clo. SE5 92 DS82
Grovelands Clo., Har. 58 CB62
Grovelands Ct. N14 49 DK45
Grovelands Rd. N13 49 DM49
Grovelands Rd. N15 64 DU58
Grovelands Rd., Orp. 110 EU94
Grovelands Rd., Pur. 133 DL112
Groveley Rd., Sun. 99 BS92
Grover Rd., Wat. 30 BX44
Groveside Clo. W3 74 CP72
Groveside Clo., Cars. 118 DE103
Groveside Rd. E4 52 EE47
Grovestile Waye, Felt. 99 BR87
Groveway SW9 91 DM81
Groveway, Dag. 68 EX63
Groveway, Wem. 60 CQ64
Grovewood, Rich. 88 CN81
Sandycoombe Rd.
Grovewood Pl., Wdf.Grn. 53 EM51
Grummant Rd. SE15 92 DT81
Grundy St. E14 79 EB72
Gruneisen Rd. N3 48 DB52
Guardian Clo., Horn. 69 FH60
Gubyon Ave. SE24 105 DP85
Guerin Sq. E3 79 DZ69
Malmesbury Rd.
Guernsey Clo., Houns. 86 CA81
Guernsey Gro. SE24 106 DQ87
Guernsey Rd. E11 65 ED60
Guibal Rd. SE12 108 EH87
Guild Rd. SE7 94 EK78
Guild Rd., Erith 97 FF80
Guildersfield Rd. SW16 105 DL94
Guildford Ave., Felt. 99 BT89
Guildford Gro. SE10 93 EB81
Guildford Rd. E6 81 EM72
Guildford Rd. E17 51 EC53
Guildford Rd. SW8 91 DL81
Guildford Rd., Croy. 120 DR100
Guildford Rd., Ilf. 67 ES61
Guildford Rd., Lthd. 143 CF123
Guildford St., Stai. 98 BG93
Guildford Way, Wall. 133 DL106
Guildhall Bldgs. EC2 7 K8
Guildhall Yd. EC2 78 DR72
Gresham St.
Guildhouse St. SW1 9 K8
Guildhouse St. SW1 91 DJ77
Guildown Ave. N12 48 DB49
Guildsway E17 51 DZ53
Guileshill La., Wok. 140 BL123
Guilford Ave., Surb. 116 CM99
Guilford Pl. WC1 6 B5
Guilford Pl. WC1 77 DM70
Guilford St. WC1 6 A5
Guilford St. WC1 77 DL70
Guilford Vill., Surb. 116 CM100
Alpha Rd.
Guilsborough Clo. NW10 74 CS66
Guinevere Gdns., Wal.Cr. 23 DX31
Guinness Bldgs. SE1 11 M7
Guinness Bldgs. SE1 92 DS77
Guinness Clo. E9 79 DY66
Guinness Clo., Hayes 85 BR76
Guinness Sq. SE1 11 M8
Guinness Trust Bldgs. SE11 10 F10
Guinness Trust Bldgs. SE11 91 DP78
Guinness Trust Bldgs. SW3 8 D9
Guinness Trust Est. N16 64 DS60
Holmleigh Rd.
Guinness Trust Est. SW9 91 DP84
Guion Rd. SW6 89 CZ82
Gull Clo., Wall. 133 DL108
Gull Wk., Horn. 83 FH66
Heron Flight Ave.
Gulland Clo. (Bushey), Wat. 30 CC43
Gulland Wk. N1 78 DQ65
Clephane Rd.
Gullet Wd. Rd., Wat. 29 BU35
Gulliver Clo., Nthlt. 72 BZ67
Gulliver Rd., Sid. 109 ES89
Gulliver St. SE16 93 DZ76
Gulston Wk. SW3 8 E9
Gumleigh Rd. W5 87 CJ77
Gumley Gdns., Islw. 87 CG83
Gumping Rd., Orp. 123 EQ102
Gun St. E1 7 P7
Gun St. E1 78 DT71
Gundulph Rd., Brom. 122 EJ97
Gunmakers La. E3 79 DY67
Gunnell Clo. SE26 106 DU91
Gunnell Clo., Croy. 120 DU100
Gunner La. SE18 95 EN78
Gunners Gro. E4 51 EC48
Gunners Rd. SW18 104 DD89
Gunnersbury Ave. W3 74 CM74
Gunnersbury Ave. W4 74 CM74
Gunnersbury Ave. W5 74 CM74
Gunnersbury Clo. W4 88 CP78
Grange Rd.
Gunnersbury Ct. W3 88 CP75
Bollo La.
Gunnersbury Cres. W3 88 CN75
Gunnersbury Dr. W5 88 CM75
Gunnersbury Gdns. W3 88 CN75
Gunnersbury La. W3 88 CN76
Gunnersbury Ms. W4 88 CP78
Chiswick High Rd.
Gunnersbury Pk. W3 88 CM77
Gunnersbury Pk. W5 88 CM77
Gunning St. SE18 95 ES77
Gunpowder Sq. EC4 6 E8
Gunpowder Sq. EC4 77 DN72
Gunstor Rd. N16 64 DS63
Gunter Gro. SW10 90 DC79
Gunter Gro., Edg. 46 CR53
Gunterstone Rd. W14 89 CY77
Gunthorpe St. E1 78 DT71
Gunton Rd. E5 64 DV61
Gunton Rd. SW17 104 DG93
Gunwhale Clo. SE16 79 DX74
Gurdon Rd. SE7 94 EG78
Gurnard Clo., West Dr. 70 BK73
Trout Rd.
Gurnell Gro. W13 73 CF70
Gurney Clo. E15 66 EE64
Gurney Rd.
Gurney Clo. E17 51 DX53
Gurney Clo., Bark. 81 EP65
Gurney Cres., Croy. 119 DM102
Gurney Dr. N2 62 DC56
Gurney Rd. E15 66 EE64
Gurney Rd., Cars. 118 DG104
Gurney Rd., Nthlt. 71 BV69
Guthrie St. SW3 8 B10
Gutter La. EC2 7 J8
Gutter La. EC2 78 DQ72
Gutteridge La., Rom. 41 FC44
Guy Barnett Clo. SE3 94 EG83
Casterbridge Rd.
Guy Rd., Wall. 119 DK104
Guy St. SE1 11 L4
Guy St. SE1 92 DR75
Guyatt Gdns., Mitch. 118 DG96
Ormerod Gdns.
Guyscliff Rd. SE13 107 EC85
Guysfield Clo., Rain. 83 FG67
Guysfield Dr., Rain. 83 FG67
Gwalior Rd. SW15 89 CX83
Felsham Rd.
Gwendolen Ave. SW15 89 CX84
Gwendolen Clo. SW15 103 CX85
Gwendoline Ave. E13 80 EH67
Gwendwr Rd. W14 89 CY78
Gwent Clo., Wat. 16 BX34
Gwillim Clo., Sid. 110 EU85
Gwydor Rd., Beck. 121 DX98
Gwydyr Rd., Brom. 122 EF97
Gwyn Clo. SW6 90 DC80
Gwynne Ave., Croy. 121 DX101
Gwynne Clo. W4 89 CT79
Gwynne Pk. Ave., Wdf.Grn. 53 EM51
Gwynne Pl. WC1 6 C3
Gwynne Rd. SW11 90 DD82
Gwynne Rd., Cat. 148 DQ121
Coulsdon Rd.
Gyfford Wk., Wal.Cr. 22 DV31
Hawthorne Clo.
Gylcote Clo. SE5 92 DR84
Gyles Pk., Stan. 45 CJ52
Gyllyngdune Gdns., Ilf. 67 ET62
Gypsy La., Kings L. 15 BR33

H

Ha-Ha Rd. SE18 95 EM79
Haarlem Rd. W14 89 CX76
Haberdasher Pl. N1 7 L2
Haberdasher St. N1 7 L2
Haberdasher St. N1 78 DR69
Habgood Rd., Loug. 38 EL41
Haccombe Rd. SW19 104 DC93
Haydons Rd.
Hackbridge Grn., Wall. 118 DG103
Hackbridge Pk. Gdns., Cars. 118 DG103
Hackbridge Rd., Wall. 118 DG103
Hackford Rd. SW9 91 DM81
Hackforth Clo., Barn. 33 CV43
Hackington Cres., Beck. 107 EA93
Hackney Clo., Borwd. 32 CR43
Hackney Gro. E8 78 DV65
Reading La.
Hackney Rd. E2 7 P2
Hackney Rd. E2 78 DT69
Hadden Rd. SE28 95 ES76
Hadden Way, Grnf. 73 CD65
Haddington Rd., Brom. 107 ED91
Haddo St. SE10 93 EC79
Haddon Clo., Borwd. 32 CN40
Haddon Clo., Enf. 36 DU44
Haddon Clo., N.Mal. 117 CT99
Haddon Clo., Wey. 113 BR104
Haddon Gro., Sid. 109 ET87
Haddon Rd., Orp. 124 EW99
Haddon Rd., Sutt. 132 DB105
Haddonfield SE8 93 DX77
Hadfield Clo., Sthl. 72 BZ69
Adrienne Ave.
Hadfield Rd., Stai. 98 BK86
Hadleigh Clo. E1 78 DW70
Mantus Rd.
Hadleigh Clo. SW20 117 CZ96
Hadleigh Dr., Sutt. 132 DA109
Hadleigh Rd. N9 50 DV45
Hadleigh St. E2 78 DW69
Hadleigh Wk. E6 80 EL72
Kirkham Rd.
Hadley Clo. N21 35 DN44
Hadley Clo., Borwd. 32 CM43
Hadley Common, Barn. 34 DA40
Hadley Gdns. W4 88 CR78
Hadley Gdns., Sthl. 86 BZ78
Hadley Grn., Barn. 33 CZ40
Hadley Grn. Rd., Barn. 33 CZ40
Hadley Grn. W., Barn. 33 CY40
Hadley Gro., Barn. 33 CY40
Hadley Highstone, Barn. 33 CZ39
Hadley Pl., Wey. 126 BN108
Hadley Ridge, Barn. 33 CZ41
Hadley Rd. (Hadley Wd.), Barn. 34 DG38
Hadley Rd. (New Barnet), Barn. 34 DB41
Hadley Rd., Belv. 96 EZ77
Hadley Rd., Enf. 35 DL38
Hadley Rd., Mitch. 119 DK98
Hadley St. NW1 77 DH65
Hadley Way N21 35 DN44
Hadley Wd. Ri., Ken. 147 DP115
Hadlow Pl. SE19 106 DU94
Hadlow Rd., Sid. 110 EU91
Hadlow Rd., Well. 96 EW80
Hadrian Clo., Stai. 98 BL88
Hadrian Way
Hadrian Clo., Wall. 133 DL108
De Havilland Rd.
Hadrian Est. E2 78 DU68
Hackney Rd.
Hadrian St. SE10 94 EE78
Hadrian Way, Stai. 98 BK87
Hadrians Ride, Enf. 36 DT43
Hadyn Pk. Rd. W12 89 CU75
Hafer Rd. SW11 90 DF84
Hafton Rd. SE6 108 EE88
Hagden La., Wat. 29 BT43
Haggard Rd., Twick. 101 CG87
Haggerston Rd. E8 78 DT66
Haggerston Rd., Borwd. 32 CL38
Hague St. E2 78 DU69
Derbyshire St.
Haig Rd., Stan. 45 CJ50
Haig Rd., Uxb. 71 BP71
Haig Rd., West. 150 EL117
Haig Rd. E. E13 80 EJ69
Haig Rd. W. E13 80 EJ69
Haigville Gdns., Ilf. 67 EP56
Hailes Clo. SW19 104 DC93
North Rd.
Hailey Rd., Erith 96 FA75
Haileybury Ave., Enf. 36 DT44
Haileybury Rd., Orp. 138 EU105
Hailsham Ave. SW2 105 DM89
Hailsham Clo., Surb. 115 CK101
Hailsham Dr., Har. 59 CD55
Hailsham Rd. SW17 104 DG93
Hailsham Ter. N18 50 DQ50
Haimo Rd. SE9 108 EK85
Hainault Ct. E17 65 ED56
Hainault Gore, Rom. 68 EY57
Hainault Gro., Chig. 53 EQ49
Hainault Ind. Est., Ilf. 54 EW50
Hainault Rd. E11 65 EC60
Hainault Rd., Chig. 53 EP48
Hainault Rd., Rom. 55 FC54
Hainault Rd. (Chadwell Heath), Rom. 68 EZ58
Hainault Rd. (Hainault), Rom. 68 EV55
Hainault St. SE9 109 EP88
Hainault St., Ilf. 67 EQ61
Haines Ct., Wey. 127 BR106
St. George's Lo.
Haines Way, Wat. 15 BU34
Hainford Clo. SE4 93 DX84
Haining Clo. W4 88 CN78
Wellesley Rd.
Hainthorpe Rd. SE27 105 DP90
Hainton Clo. E1 78 DV72
Halberd Ms. E5 64 DV61
Knightland Rd.
Halbutt Gdns., Dag. 68 EZ62
Halbutt St., Dag. 68 EZ63
Halcomb St. N1 78 DS67
Halcot Ave., Bexh. 111 FB85
Halcrow St. E1 78 DV71
Newark St.
Haldan Rd. E4 51 EC51
Haldane Clo. N10 49 DH52
Haldane Pl. SW18 104 DB88
Haldane Rd. E6 80 EK69
Haldane Rd. SE28 82 EX73
Haldane Rd. SW6 89 CZ80
Haldane Rd., Sthl. 72 CC73
Haldon Clo., Chig. 53 ES50
Haldon Rd. SW18 103 CZ85
Hale, The E4 51 ED52
Hale, The N17 64 DU55
Hale Clo. E4 51 EC48
Hale Clo., Edg. 46 CQ50
Hale Clo., Orp. 137 EQ105
Hale Dr. NW7 46 CQ51
Hale End, Rom. 55 FH51
Hale End Clo., Ruis. 57 BU58
Hale End Rd. E4 51 ED51
Hale End Rd. E17 51 ED53
Hale End Rd., Wdf.Grn. 51 ED52
Hale Gdns. N17 64 DU55
Hale Gdns. W3 74 CN74
Hale Gro. Gdns. NW7 46 CR50
Hale La. NW7 46 CR50
Hale La., Edg. 46 CP50
Hale La., Sev. 153 FE117
Hale Path SE27 105 DP91
Hale Rd. E6 80 EL70
Hale Rd. N17 64 DU55
Hale St. E14 79 EB73
Hale Wk. W7 73 CE71
Benham Rd.
Halefield Rd. N17 50 DU53
Hales St. SE8 93 EA80
Deptford High St.
Halesowen Rd., Mord. 118 DB101
Haleswood, Cob. 127 BV114
Halesworth Clo. E5 64 DW61
Theydon Rd.
Halesworth Rd. SE13 93 EB83
Haley Rd. NW4 61 CW58
Half Acre, Brent. 87 CK79
Half Acre Rd. W7 73 CE74
Half Moon Ct. EC1 7 H7
Half Moon Cres. N1 77 DM68
Half Moon La. SE24 106 DQ86
Half Moon La., Epp. 25 ET31
Half Moon Pas. E1 78 DT72
Braham St.
Half Moon St. W1 9 J2
Half Moon St. W1 77 DH74
Halfhide La. (Cheshunt), Wal.Cr. 23 DX27
Halfhides, Wal.Abb. 23 ED33
Halford Rd. E10 65 ED57
Halford Rd. SW6 90 DA79
Halford Rd., Rich. 102 CL85
Halford Rd., Uxb. 56 BN64
Halfway Grn., Walt. 113 BV104
Halfway St., Sid. 109 ER87
Haliburton Rd., Twick. 101 CG85
Haliday Wk. N1 78 DR65
Balls Pond Rd.
Halidon Clo. E9 64 DW64
Urswick Rd.
Halifax Rd., Enf. 36 DQ40
Halifax Rd., Grnf. 72 CB67
Halifax St. SE26 106 DV91
Halifield Dr., Belv. 96 EY76
Haling Down Pas., S.Croy. 134 DQ109
Kingsdown Ave.
Haling Gro., S.Croy. 134 DQ108
Haling Pk., S.Croy. 134 DQ107
Haling Pk. Gdns., S.Croy. 133 DP107
Haling Pk. Rd., S.Croy. 133 DP107
Haling Rd., S.Croy. 134 DR107
Halkin Arc. SW1 8 F6
Halkin Ms. SW1 8 F6
Halkin Pl. SW1 8 F6
Halkin Pl. SW1 90 DG76
Halkin St. SW1 8 G5
Halkin St. SW1 90 DG75
Hall, The SE3 94 EG83
Hall Ave. N18 50 DR51
Weir Hall Ave.
Hall Clo. W5 74 CL71
Hall Clo., Rick. 42 BG46
Hall Ct., Tedd. 101 CF92
Teddington Pk.
Hall Dr. SE26 106 DW92
Hall Dr. W7 73 CE72
Hall Dr., Uxb. 42 BJ53
Hall Fm. Clo., Stan. 45 CH49
Hall Fm. Dr., Twick. 101 CD87
Hall Gdns. E4 51 DZ49
Hall Gate NW8 76 DC69
Hall Rd.
Hall Hill, Sev. 155 FP123
Hall La. E4 51 DY50
Hall La. NW4 47 CU53
Hall La., Hayes 85 BR80
Hall Oak Wk. NW6 75 CZ65
Maygrove Rd.
Hall Pl. W2 76 DD70
Hall Pl. Cres., Bex. 111 FC85
Hall Pl. Dr., Wey. 127 BS106
Hall Rd. E6 81 EM67
Hall Rd. E15 65 ED63
Hall Rd. NW8 76 DC69
Hall Rd., Islw. 101 CD85
Hall Rd., Rom. 68 EW58
Hall Rd. (Gidea Pk.), Rom. 69 FH55
Hall Rd., Wall. 133 DH109
Hall St. EC1 6 G2
Hall St. EC1 77 DP69
Hall St. N12 48 DC50
Hall Vw. SE9 108 EK89
Hall Way, Pur. 133 DP113
Downs Ct. Rd.
Hallam Clo., Chis. 109 EM92
Hallam Clo., Wat. 30 BW40
Hallam Gdns., Pnr. 44 BY52
Hallam Ms. W1 5 J6
Hallam Rd. N15 63 DP56
Hallam Rd. SW13 89 CV83
Hallam St. W1 5 J5
Hallam St. W1 77 DH71
Halland Way, Nthwd. 43 BR51
Halley Gdns. SE13 93 ED84
Halley Rd. E7 80 EJ65
Halley Rd. E12 80 EK65
Halley St. E14 79 DY71
Halleys Wk., Add. 126 BJ108
Hallfield Est. W2 76 DC72
Cleveland Ter.
Halliards, The, Walt. 113 BU100
Felix Rd.
Halliday Sq., Sthl. 73 CD74
Halliford Clo., Shep. 113 BR98
Halliford Rd., Shep. 113 BS99
Halliford Rd., Sun. 113 BT99
Halliford St. N1 78 DQ66
Hallingbury Ct. E17 65 EB55
Halliwell Rd. SW2 105 DM86
Halliwick Rd. N10 48 DG53
Hallmark Trd. Est. NW10 60 CQ63
Great Cen. Way
Hallmead Rd., Sutt. 118 DB104
Hallowell Ave., Croy. 133 DL105
Hallowell Clo., Mitch. 118 DG97
Hallowell Rd., Nthwd. 43 BS52
Hallowes Cres., Wat. 43 BU48
Hayling Rd.
Hallowfield Way, Mitch. 118 DD97
Hallside Rd., Enf. 36 DT38
Hallsville Rd. E16 80 EF72
Hallswelle Rd. NW11 61 CZ57
Hallywell Cres. E6 81 EM71
Halons Rd. SE9 109 EN87
Halpin Pl. SE17 11 L9
Halsbrook Rd. SE3 94 EJ83
Halsbury Clo., Stan. 45 CH49
Halsbury Rd. W12 75 CU74
Halsbury Rd. E., Nthlt. 58 CC63
Halsbury Rd. W., Nthlt. 58 CB64
Halsend, Hayes 71 BV74
Halsey Ms. SW3 8 D8
Halsey Pk., St.Alb. 18 CM27
Halsey Pl., Wat. 29 BV38
Halsey Rd., Wat. 29 BV41
Halsey St. SW3 8 D8
Halsey St. SW3 90 DF77
Halsham Cres., Bark. 81 ET65
Halsmere Rd. SE5 91 DP81
Halstead Clo., Croy. 120 DQ104
Charles St.
Halstead Ct. N1 7 L1
Halstead Gdns. N21 50 DR46
Halstead Hill (Cheshunt), Wal.Cr. 22 DS29
Halstead La., Sev. 138 EZ114
Halstead Rd. E11 66 EG57
Halstead Rd. N21 50 DR46
Halstead Rd., Enf. 36 DS42
Halstead Rd., Erith 97 FE81
Halston Clo. SW11 104 DF86
Halstow Rd. NW10 75 CX69
Halstow Rd. SE10 94 EG78
Halsway, Hayes 71 BU74
Halt Robin La., Belv. 97 FB77
Halt Robin Rd.
Halt Robin Rd., Belv. 96 FA77
Halter Clo., Borwd. 32 CR43
Clydesdale Clo.
Halton Cross St. N1 77 DP67
Halton Rd.
Halton Rd. N1 77 DP66
Ham, The, Brent. 87 CJ80
Ham Clo., Rich. 101 CJ90
Ham Common, Rich. 101 CK90
Ham Fm. Rd., Rich. 101 CK91
Ham Gate Ave., Rich. 102 CL91
Ham Pk. Rd. E7 80 EG66

Ham Pk. Rd. E15 80 EF66
Ham Ridings, Rich. 102 CM92
Ham St., Rich. 101 CH88
Ham Vw., Croy. 121 DY100
Ham Yd. W1 5 M10
Hambalt Rd. SW4 105 DJ85
Hamble Clo., Ruis. 57 BS61
Chichester Ave.
Hamble Ct., Kings.T. 101 CK94
Hamble St. SW6 90 DB83
Hamble Wk., Nthlt. 72 CA68
Brabazon Rd.
Hambledon Clo., Uxb. 71 BP71
Aldenham Dr.
Hambledon Gdns. SE25 120 DT97
Hambledon Hill, Epsom 144 CQ116
Hambledon Pl. SE21 106 DS88
Hambledon Rd. SW18 103 CZ87
Hambledon Rd., Cat. 148 DQ121
Coulsdon Rd.
Hambledon Vale, Epsom 144 CQ116
Hambledown Rd., Sid. 109 ER87
Hambleton Clo., Wor.Pk. 117 CW103
Cotswold Way
Hamblings Clo., Rad. 17 CK33
Hambridge Way SW2 105 DN87
Hambro Ave., Brom. 122 EG102
Hambro Rd. SW16 105 DK93
Hambrook Rd. SE25 120 DV97
Hambrough Rd., Sthl. 72 BY74
Hamburgh Ct., Wal.Cr. 23 DX28
Hamden Cres., Dag. 69 FB62
Hamel Clo., Har. 59 CK55
Hamelin St. E14 79 EC72
St. Leonards Rd.
Hameway E6 81 EN70
Hamfrith Rd. E15 80 EF65
Hamhaugh Island, Shep. 112 BN103
Hamilton Ave. N9 50 DU45
Hamilton Ave., Cob. 127 BU113
Hamilton Ave., Ilf. 67 EP56
Hamilton Ave., Rom. 55 FD54
Hamilton Ave., Surb. 116 CN103
Hamilton Ave., Sutt. 117 CY102
Hamilton Clo. N17 64 DT55
Hamilton Clo. NW8 76 DD69
Hamilton Clo. SE16 93 DY75
Somerford Way
Hamilton Clo., Barn. 34 DE42
Hamilton Clo., Epsom 130 CQ112
Hamilton Clo., Felt. 99 BT92
Hamilton Clo., Pot.B. 19 CU33
Hamilton Clo., Pur. 133 DP112
Hamilton Clo., St.Alb. 16 CA31
Hamilton Clo., Stan. 45 CF47
Hamilton Ct. W5 74 CM73
Hamilton Ct. W9 76 DC69
Maida Vale
Hamilton Cres. N13 49 DN49
Hamilton Cres., Har. 58 BZ62
Hamilton Cres., Houns. 100 CB85
Hamilton Gdns. NW8 76 DC69
Hamilton La. N5 63 DP63
Hamilton Pk.
Hamilton Ms. W1 9 H4
Hamilton Pk. N5 63 DP63
Hamilton Pk. W. N5 63 DP63
Hamilton Pl. W1 8 G3
Hamilton Pl. W1 76 DG74
Hamilton Pl., Sun. 99 BV94
Hamilton Pl., Tad. 145 CZ122
Hamilton Rd. E15 80 EE69
Hamilton Rd. E17 51 DY54
Hamilton Rd. N2 62 DC55
Hamilton Rd. N9 50 DU45
Hamilton Rd. NW10 61 CU64
Hamilton Rd. NW11 61 CX59
Hamilton Rd. SE27 106 DR91
Hamilton Rd. SW19 104 DB94
Hamilton Rd. W4 88 CS75
Hamilton Rd. W5 74 CL73
Hamilton Rd., Barn. 34 DE42
Hamilton Rd., Bexh. 96 EY82
Hamilton Rd., Brent. 87 CK79
Hamilton Rd., Felt. 99 BT91
Hamilton Rd., Har. 59 CE57
Hamilton Rd., Hayes 71 BV73
Hamilton Rd., Ilf. 67 EP63
Hamilton Rd., Kings L. 15 BQ33
Hamilton Rd., Rom. 69 FH57
Hamilton Rd., Sid. 110 EU91
Hamilton Rd., Sthl. 72 BZ74
Hamilton Rd., Th.Hth. 120 DR97
Hamilton Rd., Twick. 101 CE88
Hamilton Rd., Uxb. 70 BK70
Hamilton Rd., Wat. 43 BV48
Hamilton Sq. SE1 11 L4
Hamilton St. SE8 93 EA79
Deptford High St.
Hamilton St., Wat. 30 BW43
Hamilton Ter. NW8 76 DB68
Hamilton Wk., Erith 97 FF80
Frobisher Rd.
Hamilton Way N3 48 DA51
Hamilton Way N13 49 DP49
Hamilton Way, Wall. 133 DK109
Hamlea Clo. SE12 108 EG85
Hamlet, The SE5 92 DR83
Hamlet Clo. SE13 94 EE84
Old Rd.
Hamlet Clo., Rom. 54 FA52
Hamlet Gdns. W6 89 CU77
Hamlet Rd. SE19 106 DT94
Hamlet Rd., Rom. 54 FA52
Hamlet Sq. NW2 61 CY62
Cricklewood Trd. Est.
Hamlet Sq. NW11 61 CY62
The Vale
Hamlet Way SE1 11 L4
Hamlets Way E3 79 DZ70
Hamlin Cres., Pnr. 58 BW57
Hamlin Rd., Sev. 154 FE121
Hamlyn Clo., Edg. 46 CL48
Hamlyn Gdns. SE19 106 DS94
Hamm Ct., Wey. 112 BM104
Hamm Moor La., Add. 126 BL106
Hammelton Grn. SW9 91 DP81
Cromwell Rd.
Hammelton Rd., Brom. 122 EF95
Hammer Par., Wat. 15 BT33
Hammers Gate, St.Alb. 16 CA25
Hammers La. NW7 47 CU50
Hammersmith Bri. SW13 89 CV78
Hammersmith Bri. Rd. W6 89 CW78
Hammersmith Bdy. W6 89 CW77
Hammersmith Flyover W6 89 CW78
Hammersmith Gro. W6 89 CW75
Hammersmith Rd. W6 89 CX77
Hammersmith Rd. W14 89 CX77
Hammersmith Ter. W6 89 CU78
Hammet Clo., Hayes 72 BX71
Willow Tree La.
Hammett St. EC3 7 P10
Hammond Ave., Mitch. 119 DH96
Hammond Clo., Barn. 33 CY43
Hammond Clo., Grnf. 59 CD64
Lilian Board Way
Hammond Clo., Hmptn. 114 CA95
Hammond Clo. (Cheshunt), Wal.Cr. 22 DS26
Hammond Rd., Enf. 36 DV40
Hammond Rd., Sthl. 86 BY76
Hammond St. NW5 77 DJ65
Hammond Way SE28 82 EV73
Oriole Way
Hammonds Clo., Dag. 68 EW62
Hammondstreet Rd. (Cheshunt), Wal.Cr. 21 DP25
Hamond Clo., S.Croy. 133 DP109
Hamonde Clo., Edg. 46 CP47
Hampden Ave., Beck. 121 DY96
Hampden Clo. NW1 5 N1
Hampden Clo., Epp. 26 FA27
Hampden Cres. (Cheshunt), Wal.Cr. 22 DV31
Hampden Gurney St. W1 4 D9
Hampden La. N17 50 DT53
Hampden Pl., St.Alb. 17 CE29
Hampden Rd. N8 63 DN56
Hampden Rd. N10 48 DG52
Hampden Rd. N17 50 DU53
Hampden Rd. N19 63 DK61
Holloway Rd.
Hampden Rd., Beck. 121 DY96
Hampden Rd., Har. 44 CC53
Hampden Rd., Kings.T. 116 CN97
Hampden Rd., Rom. 55 FB52
Hampden Sq. N14 49 DH46
Osidge La.
Hampden Way N14 49 DH47
Hampden Way, Wat. 29 BS36
Hampermill La., Wat. 43 BT47
Hampshire Clo. N18 50 DV50
Hampshire Hog La. W6 89 CV77
King St.
Hampshire Rd. N22 49 DM52
Hampshire St. NW5 77 DK65
Torriano Ave.
Hampson Way SW8 91 DM81
Hampstead Clo. SE28 82 EV74
Hampstead Gdns. NW11 62 DA58
Hampstead Gdns., Rom. 68 EV57
Hampstead Grn. NW3 62 DE64
Hampstead Gro. NW3 62 DC62
Hampstead High St. NW3 62 DC63
Hampstead Hill Gdns. NW3 62 DD63
Hampstead La. N6 62 DD59
Hampstead La. NW3 62 DD60
Hampstead Rd. NW1 5 K1
Hampstead Rd. NW1 77 DJ68
Hampstead Sq. NW3 62 DC62
Hampstead Wk. E3 79 DZ67
Parnell Rd.
Hampstead Way NW11 61 CZ57
Hampton Clo. N11 49 DH50
Balmoral Ave.
Hampton Clo. NW6 76 DA69
Hampton Clo. SW20 103 CW94
Hampton Ct. N1 77 DP65
Upper St.
Hampton Ct. Ave., E.Mol. 115 CD99
Hampton Ct. Cres., E.Mol. 115 CD97
Hampton Ct. Palace, E.Mol. 115 CE97
Hampton Ct. Par., E.Mol. 115 CE98
Creek Rd.
Hampton Ct. Rd., E.Mol. 115 CF97
Hampton Ct. Rd., Hmptn. 114 CC96
Hampton Ct. Rd., Kings.T. 115 CJ96
Hampton Ct. Way, E.Mol. 115 CE100
Hampton Ct. Way, T.Ditt. 115 CE103
Hampton Fm. Ind. Est., Felt. 100 BY90
Hampton Gro., Epsom 131 CT111
Hampton La., Felt. 100 BY91
Hampton Mead, Loug. 39 EP41
Hampton Ri., Har. 60 CL58
Hampton Rd. E4 51 DZ50
Hampton Rd. E7 66 EH64
Hampton Rd. E11 65 ED60
Hampton Rd., Croy. 120 DQ100
Hampton Rd., Hmptn. 101 CD92
Hampton Rd., Ilf. 67 EP63
Hampton Rd., Tedd. 101 CD92
Hampton Rd., Twick. 101 CD90
Hampton Rd., Wor.Pk. 117 CU103
Hampton Rd. E., Felt. 100 BZ90
Hampton Rd. W., Felt. 100 BY89
Hampton St. SE1 10 G9
Hampton St. SE1 92 DQ77
Hampton St. SE17 10 G9
Hampton St. SE17 91 DP77
Hamsey Grn. Gdns., Warl. 148 DV116
Hamsey Way, S.Croy. 148 DV115
Hamshades Clo., Sid. 109 ET90
Hanah Ct. SW19 103 CX94
Hanameel St. E16 80 EH74
Hanbury Clo. (Cheshunt), Wal.Cr. 23 DX30
Hanbury Dr. N21 35 DM43
Hanbury Dr., West. 136 EH113
Hanbury Ms. N1 78 DQ67
Mary St.
Hanbury Rd. N17 50 DV54
Hanbury Rd. W3 88 CP75
Hanbury St. E1 78 DT71
Hanbury Wk., Bex. 111 FE90
Hancock Ct., Borwd. 32 CQ39
Hancock Rd. E3 79 EC69
Hancock Rd. SE19 106 DR93
Hand Ct. WC1 6 C7
Handa Wk. N1 78 DR65
Clephane Rd.
Handcroft Rd., Croy. 119 DP101
Handel Clo., Edg. 46 CM51
Handel Pl. NW10 74 CR65
Mitchellbrook Way
Handel St. WC1 5 P4
Handel St. WC1 77 DL70
Handel Way, Edg. 46 CN52
Handen Rd. SE12 108 EE85
Handforth Rd. SW9 91 DN80
Handforth Rd., Ilf. 67 EP62
Winston Way
Handley Rd. E9 78 DW67
Handowe Clo. NW4 61 CU56
Hands Wk. E16 80 EG72
Butchers Rd.
Handside Clo., Wor.Pk. 117 CX102
Carters Clo.
Handsworth Ave. E4 51 ED51
Handsworth Rd. N17 64 DR55
Handsworth Way, Wat. 43 BU48
Hayling Rd.
Handtrough Way, Bark. 81 EP68
Fresh Wf. Rd.
Hanford Clo. SW18 104 DA88
Hanford Row SW19 103 CW93
Hangar Ruding, Wat. 44 BZ48
Hanger Grn. W5 74 CN70
Hanger Hill, Wey. 127 BP107
Hanger La. W5 74 CL68
Hanger Vale La. W3 74 CM72
Hanger Vale La. W5 74 CM72
Hanger Vw. Way W3 74 CN72
Hangrove Hill, Orp. 137 EP113
Cudham Rd.
Hankey Pl. SE1 11 L5
Hankey Pl. SE1 92 DR75
Hankins La. NW7 46 CS47
Hanley Pl., Beck. 107 EA94
Hanley Rd. N4 63 DL60
Hanmer Wk. N7 63 DM62
Newington Barrow Way
Hannah Clo. NW10 60 CQ63
Hannah Clo., Beck. 121 EC97
Hannah Mary Way SE1 92 DU77
Simms Rd.
Hannah Ms., Wall. 133 DJ108
Hannards Way, Ilf. 54 EV50
Hannay La. N8 63 DK59
Hannay Wk. SW16 105 DK89
Dingley La.
Hannell Rd. SW6 89 CY80
Hannen Rd. SE27 105 DP90
Norwood High St.
Hannibal Rd. E1 78 DW71
Hannibal Rd., Stai. 98 BK87
Hannibal Way, Croy. 133 DM106
Hannington Rd. SW4 91 DH83
Hanover Ave. E16 80 EG74
Silvertown Way
Hanover Ave., Felt. 99 BU88
Hanover Circle, Hayes 71 BQ72
Hanover Clo., Rich. 88 CN80
Hanover Clo., Sutt. 131 CY105
Hanover Ct. W12 75 CU74
Uxbridge Rd.
Hanover Dr., Chis. 109 EQ91
Hanover Gdns. SE11 91 DN79
Hanover Gdns., Ilf. 53 EQ52
Hanover Gate NW1 4 C3
Hanover Gate NW1 76 DE69
Hanover Pk. SE15 92 DU81
Hanover Pl. WC2 6 A9
Hanover Rd. N15 64 DT56
Hanover Rd. NW10 75 CW66
Hanover Rd. SW19 104 DC94
Hanover Sq. W1 5 J9
Hanover Sq. W1 77 DH72
Hanover St. W1 5 J9
Hanover St. W1 77 DH72
Hanover St., Croy. 119 DP104
Abbey Rd.
Hanover Ter. NW1 4 C3
Hanover Ter. NW1 76 DE69
Hanover Ter., Islw. 87 CG81
Hanover Ter. Ms. NW1 4 C3
Hanover Wk., Wey. 113 BS104
Hanover Way, Bexh. 96 EX83
Hanover W. Ind. Est. NW10 74 CR69
Acton La.
Hanover Yd. N1 77 DP68
Noel Rd.
Hans Cres. SW1 8 D6
Hans Cres. SW1 90 DF76
Hans Pl. SW1 8 E6
Hans Pl. SW1 90 DF76
Hans Rd. SW3 8 D6
Hans Rd. SW3 90 DF76
Hans St. SW1 8 E7
Hansard Ms. W14 89 CX75
Holland Rd.
Hansart Way, Enf. 35 DN39
The Ridgeway
Hanselin Clo., Stan. 45 CF50
Chenduit Way
Hansen Dr. N21 35 DM43
Hansha Dr., Edg. 46 CR53
Hansler Gro., E.Mol. 115 CD99
Hansler Rd. SE22 106 DT85
Hansol Rd., Bexh. 110 EY85
Hanson Clo. SW12 105 DH87
Hanson Clo. SW14 88 CQ83
Hanson Clo., Beck. 107 EB93
Hanson Clo., Loug. 39 EQ40
Hanson Dr.
Hanson Clo., West Dr. 84 BM76
Hanson Dr., Loug. 39 EQ40
Hanson Gdns., Sthl. 86 BY75
Hanson Grn., Loug. 39 EQ40
Hanson Dr.
Hanson St. W1 5 K6
Hanson St. W1 77 DJ71
Hanway Pl. W1 5 M8
Hanway Rd. W7 73 CD72
Hanway St. W1 5 M8
Hanway St. W1 77 DK72
Hanworth Rd., Felt. 99 BV88
Hanworth Rd., Hmptn. 100 BZ91
Hanworth Rd., Houns. 100 BY88
Hanworth Rd., Sun. 99 BU94
Hanworth Ter., Houns. 86 CB84
Hanworth Trd. Est., Felt. 100 BY90
Hanyards End (Cuffley), Pot.B. 21 DL28
Hanyards La. (Cuffley), Pot.B. 21 DK28
Hapgood Clo., Grnf. 59 CD64
Harads Pl. E1 78 DU73
Ensign St.
Harben Rd. NW6 76 DC66
Harberson Rd. E15 80 EF67
Harberson Rd. SW12 105 DH88
Harberton Rd. N19 63 DJ60
Harbet Rd. E4 51 DX50
Harbet Rd. N18 51 DX50
Harbet Rd. W2 4 A7
Harbet Rd. W2 76 DD71
Harbex Clo., Bex. 111 FB87
Harbinger Rd. E14 93 EB77
Harbledown Pl., Orp. 124 EW98
Okemore Gdns.
Harbledown Rd. SW6 90 DA81
Harbledown Rd., S.Croy. 134 DU111
Harbord Clo. SE5 92 DR82
De Crespigny Pk.
Harbord St. SW6 89 CX81
Harborne Clo., Wat. 44 BW50
Harborough Ave., Sid. 109 ES87
Harborough Rd. SW16 105 DM91
Harbour Ave. SW10 90 DC81
Harbour Ex. Sq. E14 93 EB75
Harbour Rd. SE5 92 DQ83
Harbourer Clo., Ilf. 54 EV50
Harbourer Rd., Ilf. 54 EV50
Harbourfield Rd., Bans. 146 DB115
Harbridge Ave. SW15 103 CT87
Harbury Rd., Cars. 132 DE109
Harbut Rd. SW11 90 DD84
Harcombe Rd. N16 64 DS62
Harcourt Ave. E12 67 EM63
Harcourt Ave., Edg. 46 CQ48
Harcourt Ave., Sid. 110 EW86
Harcourt Ave., Wall. 133 DH105
Harcourt Clo., Islw. 87 CG83
Harcourt Fld., Wall. 133 DH105
Harcourt Rd. E15 80 EF68
Harcourt Rd. N22 49 DK53
Harcourt Rd. SE4 93 DY84
Harcourt Rd. SW19 104 DA94
Russell Rd.
Harcourt Rd., Bexh. 96 EY84
Harcourt Rd., Th.Hth. 119 DM100
Harcourt Rd., Wall. 133 DH105
Harcourt Rd. (Bushey), Wat. 30 CC43
Harcourt St. W1 4 C7
Harcourt St. W1 76 DE71
Harcourt Ter. SW10 90 DB78
Hardcastle Clo., Croy. 120 DT100
Hardcourts Clo., W.Wick. 121 EB104
Hardel Ri. SW2 105 DP88
Hardel Wk. SW2 105 DN87
Papworth Way
Hardens Manorway SE7 94 EK76
Harders Rd. SE15 92 DV82
Hardess St. SE24 92 DQ83
Herne Hill Rd.
Hardie Clo. NW10 60 CR64
Hardie Rd., Dag. 69 FC62
Harding Clo. SE17 92 DQ79
Hillingdon St.
Harding Clo., Wat. 16 BW33
Harding Ho., Hayes 71 BU72
Harding Rd., Bexh. 96 EZ82
Harding Rd., Epsom 144 CS119
Hardinge Clo., Uxb. 71 BP72
Dawley Ave.
Hardinge La. E1 78 DW72
Hardinge St.
Hardinge Rd. N18 50 DS50
Hardinge Rd. NW10 75 CV67
Hardinge St. E1 78 DW72
Hardings La. SE20 107 DX93
Hardman Rd. SE7 94 EH78
Hardman Rd., Kings.T. 116 CL96
Hardwick Clo., Lthd. 142 CC115
Hardwick Clo., Stan. 45 CJ50
Hardwick Grn. W13 73 CH71
Hardwick St. EC1 6 E3
Hardwick St. EC1 77 DN69
Hardwicke Ave., Houns. 86 CA81
Hardwicke Pl., St.Alb. 17 CK27
Hardwicke Rd. N13 49 DL51
Hardwicke Rd. W4 88 CQ77
Hardwicke Rd., Rich. 101 CJ91
Hardwicke St., Bark. 81 EQ67
Hardwicks Way SW18 104 DA85
Buckhold Rd.
Hardwidge St. SE1 11 M4
Hardy Ave. E16 80 EG74
Silvertown Way
Hardy Ave., Ruis. 57 BV64
Hardy Clo. SE16 93 DX75
Middleton Dr.
Hardy Clo., Barn. 33 CY43
Hardy Clo., Pnr. 58 BX59
Hardy Rd. E4 51 DZ51
Silver Birch Ave.
Hardy Rd. SE3 94 EF79
Hardy Rd. SW19 104 DB94
Hardy Way, Enf. 35 DN39
Hare & Billet Rd. SE3 93 ED81
Hare Ct. EC4 6 D9
Hare Cres., Wat. 15 BU32
Hare Hall La., Rom. 69 FH56
Hare Hill Clo., Wok. 140 BG115
Hare La., Esher 129 CD106
Hare Marsh E2 78 DU70
Cheshire St.
Hare Pl. EC4 6 E9
Hare Row E2 78 DV68
Hare St. SE18 95 EN76
Hare Wk. N1 7 N1
Hare Wk. N1 78 DS68
Harebell Dr. E6 81 EN71
Harebell Hill, Cob. 128 BX114
Harebreaks, The, Wat. 29 BU36
Harecastle Clo., Hayes 72 BY70
Braunston Dr.
Harecourt Rd. N1 78 DQ65
Harecroft, Lthd. 142 CB123
Haredale Rd. SE24 92 DQ84
Haredon Clo. SE23 106 DW87
Harefield, Esher 115 CE104
Harefield Ave., Sutt. 131 CY109
Harefield Clo., Enf. 35 DN39
Harefield Ms. SE4 93 DZ83
Harefield Rd. N8 63 DK57
Harefield Rd. SE4 93 DZ83
Harefield Rd. SW16 105 DM94
Harefield Rd., Rick. 42 BK47
Harefield Rd., Sid. 110 EX89
Harefield Rd., Uxb. 70 BJ66
Harendon, Tad. 145 CW121
Hares Bank, Croy. 135 ED110
Haresfield Rd., Dag. 82 FA65
Harestone Dr., Cat. 148 DT124
Harewood, Rick. 28 BH42
Harewood Ave. NW1 4 C5
Harewood Ave. NW1 76 DE70
Harewood Ave., Nthlt. 72 BY66
Harewood Clo., Nthlt. 72 BZ66
Harewood Dr., Ilf. 53 EM54
Harewood Gdns., S.Croy. 148 DV115
Harewood Hill, Epp. 39 ES35
Harewood Pl. W1 5 J9
Harewood Rd. SW19 104 DE93
Harewood Rd., Islw. 87 CF80
Harewood Rd., S.Croy. 134 DS107
Harewood Rd., Wat. 43 BV47
Harewood Row NW1 4 C6
Harewood Ter., Sthl. 86 BZ77
Harfield Gdns. SE5 92 DS83
Harfield Rd., Sun. 114 BX96
Harford Clo. E4 51 EB45
Harford Dr., Wat. 29 BS38
Harford Rd. E4 51 EB45
Harford St. E1 79 DY70
Harford Wk. N2 62 DD56
Harfst Way, Swan. 125 FC95
Hargood Clo., Har. 60 CL58
Hargood Rd. SE3 94 EJ81
Hargrave Pk. N19 63 DJ61
Hargrave Pl. N7 63 DK64
Brecknock Rd.
Hargrave Rd. N19 63 DJ61
Hargreaves Ave. (Cheshunt), Wal.Cr. 22 DV30
Hargreaves Clo. (Cheshunt), Wal.Cr. 22 DV31
Hargwyne St. SW9 91 DM83
Haringey Pk. N8 63 DL58
Haringey Pas. N4 63 DP57
Warham Rd.
Haringey Pas. N8 63 DP56
Haringey Rd. N8 63 DL56
Harington Ter. N9 50 DR48
Harington Ter. N18 50 DR48
Harkett Clo., Har. 45 CF54
Byron Rd.

Harkett Ct., Har. 45 CF54
Harkness (Cheshunt), Wal.Cr. 22 DV29
Harkness Clo., Epsom 145 CW116
Harland Ave., Croy. 120 DT104
Harland Ave., Sid. 109 ER90
Harland Clo. SW19 118 DB97
Harland Rd. SE12 108 EG88
Harlands Gro., Orp. 137 EP105
Pinecrest Gdns.
Harlech Gdns., Houns. 86 BW79
Harlech Rd. N14 49 DL48
Harlech Rd., Abb.L. 15 BU31
Harlech Twr. W3 88 CQ75
Harlequin Ave., Brent. 87 CG79
Harlequin Clo., Hayes 72 BX71
Cygnet Way
Harlequin Clo., Islw. 101 CE85
Harlequin Rd., Tedd. 101 CH94
Harlescott Rd. SE15 93 DX84
Harlesden Gdns. NW10 75 CT67
Harlesden La. NW10 75 CU67
Harlesden Rd. NW10 75 CU67
Harleston Clo. E5 64 DW61
Theydon Rd.
Harley Clo., Wem. 73 CK65
Harley Ct. E11 66 EG59
Blake Hall Rd.
Harley Cres., Har. 59 CD56
Harley Gdns. SW10 90 DC78
Harley Gdns., Orp. 137 ES105
Harley Gro. E3 79 DZ69
Harley Pl. W1 5 H7
Harley Pl. W1 77 DH71
Harley Rd. NW3 76 DD66
Harley Rd. NW10 74 CS68
Harley Rd., Har. 59 CD56
Harley St. W1 5 H5
Harley St. W1 77 DH71
Harleyford, Brom. 122 EJ95
Harleyford Rd. SE11 91 DM79
Harleyford St. SE11 91 DN79
Harlington Clo., Hayes 85 BQ80
New Rd.
Harlington Rd., Bexh. 96 EY83
Harlington Rd., Houns. 85 BT84
Harlington Rd., Uxb. 70 BN69
Harlington Rd. E., Felt. 99 BV87
Harlington Rd. W., Felt. 99 BV86
Harlow Gdns., Rom. 55 FC51
Harlow Rd. N13 50 DR48
Harlow Rd., Rain. 83 FF67
Harlton Ct., Wal.Abb. 24 EF34
Harlyn Dr., Pnr. 57 BV55
Harman Ave., Wdf.Grn. 52 EF51
Harman Clo. E4 51 ED49
Harman Clo. NW2 61 CY62
Harman Dr. NW2 61 CY62
Harman Dr., Sid. 109 ET86
Harman Pl., Pur. 133 DP111
Harman Rd., Enf. 36 DT43
Harmondsworth La., West Dr. 84 BL79
Harmondsworth Rd., West Dr. 84 BL78
Harmony Clo. NW11 61 CY57
Harmony Clo., Wall. 133 DK109
Harmony Way NW4 61 CW56
Harmood Gro. NW1 77 DH66
Clarence Way
Harmood Pl. NW1 77 DH66
Harmood St.
Harmood St. NW1 77 DH65
Harmsworth St. SE17 91 DP78
Harmsworth Way N20 47 CZ46
Harnage Rd., Brent. 87 CH80
Harness Rd. SE28 96 EU75
Harnetts Clo., Swan. 125 FD100
Harold Ave., Belv. 96 EZ78
Harold Ave., Hayes 85 BT76
Harold Cres., Wal.Abb. 23 EC32
Harold Est. SE1 11 N7
Harold Est. SE1 92 DS76
Harold Gibbons Ct. SE7 94 EJ79
Victoria Way
Harold Pl. SE11 91 DN78
Kennington La.
Harold Rd. E4 51 EC49
Harold Rd. E11 66 EE60
Harold Rd. E13 80 EH67
Harold Rd. N8 63 DM57
Harold Rd. N15 64 DT57
Harold Rd. NW10 74 CR69
Harold Rd. SE19 106 DR94
Harold Rd., Sutt. 132 DD105
Harold Rd., Wdf.Grn. 52 EG53
Haroldstone Rd. E17 65 DX57
Harp All. EC4 6 F8
Harp Island Clo. NW10 60 CR61
Harp La. EC3 11 M1
Harp Rd. W7 73 CE70
Harpenden Rd. E12 66 EJ61
Harpenden Rd. SE27 105 DP89
Harper Clo. N14 35 DJ43
Alexandra Ct.
Harper La., Rad. 17 CG32
Harper Rd. E6 81 EM72
Harper Rd. SE1 11 J6
Harper Rd. SE1 92 DQ76
Harpers Yd. N17 50 DT53
Ruskin Rd.
Harpley Sq. E1 78 DW69
Harpour Rd., Bark. 81 EQ65
Harpsden St. SW11 90 DG81
Harpur Ms. WC1 6 B6
Harpur St. WC1 6 B6
Harpur St. WC1 77 DM71
Harpurs, Tad. 145 CX122
Harraden Rd. SE3 94 EJ81
Harrap St. E14 79 EC73
Harrier Clo., Horn. 83 FH65
Harrier Ms. SE28 95 ER76
Harrier Rd. NW9 46 CS54
Harrier Way E6 81 EM71
Harrier Way, Wal.Abb. 24 EG34
Harriers Clo. W5 74 CL73
Harries Ct., Wal.Abb. 24 EG32
Harries Rd., Hayes 72 BW70
Harriet Clo. E8 78 DU67
Harriet Gdns., Croy. 120 DU103
Harriet St. SW1 8 E5
Harriet Tubman Clo. SW2 105 DM87
Upper Tulse Hill
Harriet Wk. SW1 8 E5
Harriet Wk. SW1 90 DF75
Harriet Way (Bushey), Wat. 45 CD45
Harringay Gdns. N8 63 DP56
Harringay Rd. N15 63 DP57
Harrington Clo. NW10 60 CR62
Harrington Clo., Croy. 119 DL103
Harrington Gdns. SW7 90 DC77
Harrington Hill E5 64 DV60
Harrington Rd. E11 66 EE60
Harrington Rd. SE25 120 DU98
Harrington Rd. SW7 8 A8
Harrington Rd. SW7 90 DD77
Harrington Sq. NW1 5 K1
Harrington Sq. NW1 77 DJ68
Harrington St. NW1 5 K1
Harrington St. NW1 77 DJ69
Harrington Way SE18 94 EK76
Harriott Clo. SE10 94 EF77
Harriotts Clo., Ash. 143 CJ120
Harriotts La.
Harriotts La., Ash. 143 CJ119
Harris Clo., Enf. 35 DP39
Harris Clo., Houns. 86 CA81
Harris La., Rad. 18 CN34
Harris Rd., Bexh. 96 EY81
Harris Rd., Dag. 68 EZ64
Harris Rd., Wat. 29 BU35
Harris St. E17 65 DZ59
Harris St. SE5 92 DR80
Harris Way, Sun. 113 BS95
Harrison Clo., Nthwd. 43 BQ51
Harrison Ct., Shep. 113 BP99
Greeno Cres.
Harrison Dr., Epp. 27 FB26
Harrison Rd., Dag. 83 FB65
Harrison St. WC1 6 A3
Harrison St. WC1 77 DL69
Harrison Wk. (Cheshunt), Wal.Cr. 23 DX30
Harrison Way, Sev. 154 FG122
Harrisons Ri., Croy. 119 DP104
Harrogate Rd., Wat. 44 BW48
Harrold Rd., Dag. 68 EV64
Harrow Ave., Enf. 36 DT44
Harrow Clo., Add. 112 BH103
Harrow Clo., Chess. 129 CK108
Harrow Cres., Rom. 55 FH52
Harrow Dr. N9 50 DT46
Harrow Dr., Horn. 69 FH58
Harrow Flds. Gdns., Har. 59 CE62
Harrow Gdns., Orp. 138 EV105
Harrow Gdns., Warl. 149 DZ116
Harrow Grn. E11 66 EE62
Harrow Rd.
Harrow La. E14 79 EC73
Harrow Manorway SE2 96 EW76
Harrow Pk., Har. 59 CE61
Harrow Pas., Kings.T. 115 CK96
Market Pl.
Harrow Pl. E1 7 N8
Harrow Pl. E1 78 DS72
Harrow Rd. E6 80 EL67
Harrow Rd. E11 66 EE62
Harrow Rd. NW10 75 CV69
Harrow Rd. W2 75 CX69
Harrow Rd. W9 75 CX69
Harrow Rd. W10 75 CX69
Harrow Rd., Bark. 81 ES67
Harrow Rd., Cars. 132 DE106
Harrow Rd., Felt. 98 BN88
Harrow Rd., Ilf. 67 EQ63
Harrow Rd., Sev. 152 EY115
Harrow Rd., Warl. 149 DZ115
Harrow Rd., Wem. 59 CF63
Harrow Rd. (Tokyngton), Wem. 60 CN64
Harrow Vw., Har. 44 CC53
Harrow Vw., Hayes 71 BU72
Harrow Vw., Uxb. 71 BQ69
Harrow Vw. Rd. W5 73 CH70
Harrow Way, Shep. 113 BQ96
Harrow Way, Wat. 44 BY48
Harrow Weald Pk., Har. 45 CD51
Harroway Rd. SW11 90 DD82
Harrowby St. W1 4 C8
Harrowby St. W1 76 DE72
Harrowdene Clo., Wem. 59 CK63
Harrowdene Gdns., Tedd. 101 CG93
Harrowdene Rd., Wem. 59 CK64
Harrowes Meade, Edg. 46 CN48
Harrowgate Rd. E9 79 DY65
Hart Cres., Chig. 53 ET50
Hart Dyke Cres., Swan. 125 FD97
Hart Dyke Rd.
Hart Dyke Rd., Orp. 124 EW102
Hart Dyke Rd., Swan. 125 FD96
Hart Gro. W5 74 CN74
Hart Gro., Sthl. 72 CA71
Hart Rd., W.Byf. 126 BL113
Hart St. EC3 7 N10
Harte Rd., Houns. 86 BZ82
Hartfield Ave., Borwd. 32 CN43
Hartfield Ave., Nthlt. 71 BV68
Hartfield Clo., Borwd. 32 CN43
Hartfield Cres. SW19 103 CZ94
Hartfield Cres., W.Wick. 122 EG104
Hartfield Gro. SE20 120 DW95
Hartfield Rd. SW19 103 CZ93
Hartfield Rd., Chess. 129 CK106
Hartfield Rd., W.Wick. 136 EG105
Hartfield Ter. E3 79 EA68
Hartford Ave., Har. 59 CG55
Hartford Rd., Bex. 110 FA86
Hartford Rd., Epsom 130 CN107
Hartforde Rd., Borwd. 32 CN40
Harthall La., Hem.H. 15 BP28
Hartham Clo. N7 63 DL64
Hartham Clo., Islw. 87 CG81
Hartham Rd. N7 63 DL64
Hartham Rd. N17 50 DT54
Hartham Rd., Islw. 87 CF81
Harting Rd. SE9 108 EL91
Hartington Clo., Har. 59 CE63
Hartington Ct. W4 88 CP80
Hartington Rd. E16 80 EH72
Hartington Rd. E17 65 DY58
Hartington Rd. SW8 91 DL81
Hartington Rd. W4 88 CP80
Hartington Rd. W13 73 CH73
Hartington Rd., Sthl. 86 BY76
Hartington Rd., Twick. 101 CH87
Hartismere Rd. SW6 89 CZ80
Hartlake Rd. E9 79 DX65
Hartland Clo. N21 36 DQ44
Elmscott Gdns.
Hartland Clo., Add. 126 BJ109
Hartland Clo., Edg. 46 CN47
Hartland Dr., Edg. 46 CN47
Hartland Dr., Ruis. 57 BV62
Hartland Rd. E15 80 EF66
Hartland Rd. N11 48 DF50
Hartland Rd. NW1 77 DH66
Hartland Rd. NW6 75 CZ68
Hartland Rd., Add. 126 BG108
Hartland Rd., Epp. 26 EU31
Hartland Rd., Hmptn. 100 CB91
Hartland Rd., Horn. 69 FG61
Hartland Rd., Islw. 87 CG83
Hartland Rd., Mord. 118 DA101
Hartland Rd. (Cheshunt), Wal.Cr. 23 DX30
Hartland Way, Croy. 121 DY103
Hartland Way, Mord. 117 CZ101
Hartlands Clo., Bex. 110 EZ86
Hartley Ave. E6 80 EL67
Hartley Ave. NW7 47 CT50
Hartley Clo. NW7 47 CT50
Hartley Clo., Brom. 123 EM96
Hartley Down, Pur. 147 DM115
Hartley Fm. Est., Pur. 147 DM115
Hartley Hill, Pur. 147 DM115
Hartley Old Rd., Pur. 147 DM115
Hartley Rd. E11 66 EF60
Hartley Rd., Croy. 119 DP101
Hartley Rd., Well. 96 EW80
Hartley St. E2 78 DW69
Hartley Way, Pur. 147 DM115
Hartmann Rd. E16 80 EK74
Hartmoor Ms., Enf. 37 DX37
Ordnance Rd.
Hartnoll St. N7 63 DM64
Eden Gro.
Harton Clo., Brom. 122 EK95
Harton Rd. N9 50 DV47
Harton St. SE8 93 EA81
Harts Clo. (Bushey), Wat. 30 CA39
Harts Gro., Wdf.Grn. 52 EG50
Harts Hill Clo., Uxb. 70 BN65
Harts La. SE14 93 DY80
Harts La., Bark. 81 EP65
Hartsbourne Ave. (Bushey), Wat. 44 CC47
Hartsbourne Clo. (Bushey), Wat. 45 CD47
Hartsbourne Rd. (Bushey), Wat. 45 CD47
Hartscroft, Croy. 135 DY109
Hartshorn All. EC3 7 N9
Hartshorn Gdns. E6 81 EN70
Hartslands Rd., Sev. 155 FJ123
Hartslock Dr. SE2 96 EX75
Hartsmead Rd. SE9 109 EM89
Hartsmoor Ms., Enf. 37 DX37
Hartspring Ind. Est., Wat. 30 CA40
Hartspring La. (Bushey), Wat. 30 CA40
Hartsway, Enf. 36 DW42
Hartswood Grn. (Bushey), Wat. 45 CD47
Hartswood Rd. W12 89 CT75
Hartsworth Clo. E13 80 EF68
Hartville Rd. SE18 95 ES77
Hartwell Dr. E4 51 EC51
Hartwell St. E8 78 DT65
Dalston La.
Harvard Hill W4 88 CP79
Harvard La. W4 88 CP78
Harvard Rd.
Harvard Rd. SE13 107 EC85
Harvard Rd. W4 88 CP78
Harvard Rd., Islw. 87 CE81
Harvard Wk., Horn. 69 FG63
Harvel Clo., Orp. 124 EU97
Harvel Cres. SE2 96 EX78
Harvest Bank Rd., W.Wick. 122 EF104
Harvest Ct., Shep. 112 BN98
Harvest End, Wat. 30 BX36
Harvest La., T.Ditt. 115 CG100
Harvest Rd., Felt. 99 BU91
Harvest Rd. (Bushey), Wat. 30 CB42
Harvest Way, Swan. 125 FD101
Harvester Rd., Epsom 130 CR110
Harvesters Clo., Islw. 101 CD85
Harvey Gdns. E11 66 EF60
Harvey Rd.
Harvey Gdns. SE7 94 EJ78
Harvey Gdns., Loug. 39 EP41
Harvey Ho., Brent. 88 CL78
Green Dragon La.
Harvey Pt. E16 80 EH71
Fife Rd.
Harvey Rd. E11 66 EE60
Harvey Rd. N8 63 DM57
Harvey Rd. SE5 92 DR81
Harvey Rd., Houns. 100 BZ87
Harvey Rd., Ilf. 67 EP64
Harvey Rd., Nthlt. 72 BW66
Harvey Rd., Rick. 28 BN44
Harvey Rd., St.Alb. 17 CJ26
Harvey Rd., Uxb. 70 BN68
Harvey Rd., Walt. 113 BU101
Harvey St. N1 78 DR67
Harveyfields, Wal.Abb. 23 EC34
Harveys La., Rom. 69 FD61
Harvil Rd. (Harefield), Uxb. 56 BJ56
Harvil Rd. (Ickenham), Uxb. 56 BL60
Harvill Rd., Sid. 110 EX92
Harvington Wk. E8 78 DU66
Wilman Gro.
Harvist Est. N7 63 DN63
Harvist Rd. NW6 75 CX68
Harwater Dr., Loug. 39 EM40
Harwell Clo., Ruis. 57 BR60
Harwell Pas. N2 62 DF56
Harwich La. EC2 7 N6
Harwich La. EC2 78 DS71
Harwood Ave., Brom. 122 EH96
Harwood Ave., Mitch. 118 DE97
Harwood Clo. N12 48 DE51
Summerfields Ave.
Harwood Clo., Wem. 59 CK63
Harrowdene Rd.
Harwood Dr., Uxb. 70 BM67
Harwood Rd. SW6 90 DA80
Harwood Ter. SW6 90 DB81
Harwoods Rd., Wat. 29 BU42
Harwoods Yd. N21 49 DN45
Wades Hill
Hascombe Ter. SE5 92 DR82
Haselbury Rd. N9 50 DS48
Haselbury Rd. N18 50 DS49
Haseldine Rd., St.Alb. 17 CK26
Haseley End SE23 106 DW87
Tyson Rd.
Haselrigge Rd. SW4 91 DK84
Haseltine Rd. SE26 107 DZ91
Haselwood Dr., Enf. 35 DP42
Haskard Rd., Dag. 68 EX63
Haskell Ho. NW10 74 CR67
Hasker St. SW3 8 C8
Hasker St. SW3 90 DE77
Haslam Ave., Sutt. 117 CY102
Haslam Clo. N1 77 DN66
Haslam Clo., Uxb. 57 BQ61
Haslemere Ave. NW4 61 CX58
Haslemere Ave. SW18 104 DB89
Haslemere Ave. W7 87 CG76
Haslemere Ave. W13 87 CG76
Haslemere Ave., Barn. 48 DF46
Haslemere Ave., Houns. 86 BW82
Haslemere Ave., Mitch. 118 DD96
Haslemere Clo., Hmptn. 100 BZ92
Haslemere Clo., Wall. 133 DL106
Stafford Rd.
Haslemere Gdns. N3 61 CZ55
Haslemere Heathrow Est., Houns. 85 BV82
Haslemere Rd. N8 63 DK59
Haslemere Rd. N21 49 DP47
Haslemere Rd., Bexh. 96 EZ82
Haslemere Rd., Ilf. 67 ET61
Haslemere Rd., Th.Hth. 119 DP99
Hasler Clo. SE28 82 EV73
Haslett Rd., Shep. 113 BS96
Hasluck Gdns., Barn. 34 DB44
Hassard St. E2 78 DT68
Hackney Rd.
Hassendean Rd. SE3 94 EH79
Hassett Rd. E9 79 DX65
Hassock Wd., Kes. 136 EK105
Hassocks Clo. SE26 106 DV90
Hassocks Rd. SW16 119 DJ95
Hassop Rd. NW2 61 CX63
Hassop Wk. SE9 108 EL91
Hasted Rd. SE7 94 EK78
Hastings Ave., Ilf. 67 EQ56
Hastings Clo. SE15 92 DU80
Hastings Clo., Barn. 34 DC42
Leicester Rd.
Hastings Dr., Surb. 115 CJ100
Hastings Ho. SE18 95 EM77
Cardwell Rd.
Hastings Rd. N11 49 DJ50
Hastings Rd. N17 64 DR55
Hastings Rd. W13 73 CH73
Hastings Rd., Brom. 122 EL102
Hastings Rd., Croy. 120 DT102
Hastings Rd., Rom. 69 FH57
Hastings St. WC1 5 P3
Hastings St. WC1 77 DL69
Hastings Way, Rick. 29 BQ42
Hastings Way (Bushey), Wat. 30 BY42
Hastoe Clo., Hayes 72 BY70
Kingsash Dr.
Hat and Mitre Ct. EC1 6 G5
Hatch, The, Enf. 37 DX39
Hatch Clo., Add. 112 BH104
Hatch Gdns., Tad. 145 CX120
Hatch Gro., Rom. 68 EY56
Hatch La. E4 51 ED49
Hatch La., Bans. 146 DF115
Rectory La.
Hatch La., Couls. 146 DG115
Hatch La., West Dr. 84 BK80
Hatch La., Wok. 141 BP120
Hatch Pl., Kings.T. 102 CM92
Hatch Rd. SW16 119 DL96
Hatch Side, Chig. 53 EN50
Hatcham Pk. Ms. SE14 93 DX81
Hatcham Pk. Rd.
Hatcham Pk. Rd. SE14 93 DX81
Hatcham Rd. SE15 92 DW79
Hatchard Rd. N19 63 DK61
Hatchcroft NW4 61 CV55
Hatchett Rd., Felt. 99 BQ88
Hatchwood Clo., Wdf.Grn. 52 EF49
Sunset Ave.
Hatcliffe Clo. SE3 94 EF83
Hatcliffe St. SE10 94 EF78
Woolwich Rd.
Hatfield Clo. SE14 93 DX80
Reaston St.
Hatfield Clo., Ilf. 67 EP55
Hatfield Clo., Mitch. 118 DD98
Hatfield Clo., Sutt. 132 DB109
Hatfield Clo., W.Byf. 126 BH112
Hatfield Mead, Mord. 118 DA99
Central Rd.
Hatfield Rd. E15 66 EE64
Hatfield Rd. W4 88 CR75
Hatfield Rd. W13 73 CG74
Hatfield Rd., Ash. 144 CM119
Hatfield Rd., Dag. 82 EY65
Hatfield Rd., Pot.B. 20 DC30
Hatfield Rd., Wat. 29 BV39
Hatfields SE1 10 E2
Hatfields SE1 77 DN74
Hatfields, Loug. 39 EP41
Hathaway Clo., Brom. 123 EM102
Hathaway Clo., Ruis. 57 BT63
Stafford Rd.
Hathaway Clo., Stan. 45 CG50
Hathaway Cres. E12 81 EM65
Hathaway Gdns. W13 73 CF71
Hathaway Gdns., Rom. 68 EX57
Hathaway Rd., Croy. 119 DP101
Hatherleigh Clo., Chess. 129 CK106
Hatherleigh Clo., Mord. 118 DA98
Hatherleigh Gdns., Pot.B. 20 DD31
Hatherleigh Rd., Ruis. 57 BU61
Hatherley Cres., Sid. 110 EU89
Hatherley Gdns. E6 80 EK68
Hatherley Gdns. N8 63 DL58
Hatherley Gro. W2 76 DB72
Hatherley Ms. E17 65 EA56
Hatherley Rd. E17 65 DZ56
Hatherley Rd., Rich. 88 CM81
Hatherley Rd., Sid. 110 EU91
Hatherley St. SW1 9 L9
Hathern Gdns. SE9 109 EN91
The Knole
Hatherop Rd., Hmptn. 100 BZ94
Hatherwood, Lthd. 143 CK121
Hathorne Clo. SE15 92 DV82
Hathway St. SE15 92 DW82
Gibbon Rd.
Hathway Ter. SE14 92 DW82
Gibbon Rd.
Hatley Ave., Ilf. 67 EQ56
Hatley Clo. N11 48 DF50
Hatley Rd. N4 63 DM61
Hatteraick St. SE16 92 DW75
Brunel Rd.
Hatters La., Wat. 29 BR44
Hattersfield Clo., Belv. 96 EZ77
Hatton Clo. SE18 95 ER80
Hatton Ct. E5 65 DY63
Gilpin Rd.
Hatton Gdn. EC1 6 E6
Hatton Gdn. EC1 77 DN70
Hatton Gdns., Mitch. 118 DF99
Hatton Grn., Felt. 85 BU84
Hatton Gro., West Dr. 84 BK75
Hatton Ho. E1 78 DU73
Wellclose Sq.
Hatton Pl. EC1 6 E6
Hatton Pl. EC1 77 DN70
Hatton Rd., Croy. 119 DN102
Hatton Rd., Felt. 99 BQ87
Hatton Rd. (Cheshunt), Wal.Cr. 23 DX29
Hatton Row NW8 4 A5
Hatton St. NW8 4 A5
Hatton Wall EC1 6 D6
Hatton Wall EC1 77 DN71
Haunch of Venison Yd. W1 5 H9
Havana Clo., Rom. 69 FE57
Havana Rd. SW19 104 DA89
Havannah St. E14 93 EA75
Havant Rd. E17 65 EC55
Havant Way SE15 92 DT80
Daniel Gdns.
Havelock Pl., Har. 59 CE58
Havelock Rd. N17 50 DU54
Havelock Rd. SW19 104 DC92

Havelock Rd., Belv. 96 EZ77
Havelock Rd., Brom. 122 EJ98
Havelock Rd., Croy. 120 DT103
Havelock Rd., Dart. 111 FH87
Havelock Rd., Har. 59 CE55
Havelock Rd., Kings L. 14 BM28
Havelock Rd., Sthl. 86 BY76
Havelock St. N1 77 DL67
Havelock St., Ilf. 67 EP61
Havelock Ter. SW8 91 DH80
Havelock Wk. SE23 106 DW88
Haven, The SE26 106 DV92
Springfield Rd.
Haven, The, Rich. 88 CN83
Haven Clo. SE9 109 EM90
Haven Clo. SW19 103 CX90
Haven Clo., Hayes 71 BS71
Haven Clo., Sid. 110 EW93
Haven Clo., Swan. 125 FF96
Haven Grn. W5 73 CK72
Haven Grn. Ct. W5 73 CK72
Haven La. W5 74 CL72
Haven Pl. W5 73 CK73
The Bdy.
Haven Rd., Ashf. 99 BP91
Haven St. NW1 77 DH66
Castlehaven Rd.
Haven Ter. W5 73 CK73
The Bdy.
Havenhurst Ri., Enf. 35 DN40
Havensfield, Kings L. 14 BH31
Nunfield
Havenwood, Wem. 60 CP62
Haverfield Gdns., Rich. 88 CN80
Haverfield Rd. E3 79 DY69
Haverford Way, Edg. 46 CM53
Haverhill Rd. E4 51 EC46
Haverhill Rd. SW12 105 DJ88
Havering Dr., Rom. 69 FE56
Havering Gdns., Rom. 68 EW57
Havering Rd., Rom. 69 FD55
Havering St. E1 79 DX72
Devonport St.
Havering Way, Bark. 82 EV69
Havers Ave., Walt. 128 BX106
Haversfield Est., Brent. 88 CL78
Haversham Clo., Twick. 101 CK86
Haversham Pl. N6 62 DF61
Haverstock Hill NW3 76 DF65
Haverstock Rd. NW5 62 DG64
Haverstock St. N1 6 G1
Haverstock St. N1 77 DP68
Haverthwaite Rd., Orp. 123 ER103
Havil St. SE5 92 DS80
Havisham Pl. SE19 105 DP93
Hawarden Gro. SE24 106 DQ87
Hawarden Hill NW2 61 CU62
Hawarden Rd. E17 65 DX56
Hawarden Rd., Cat. 148 DQ121
Hawbridge Rd. E11 65 ED60
Hawes Clo., Nthwd. 43 BT52
Hawes La. E4 37 EC38
Hawes La., W.Wick. 121 EC102
Hawes Rd. N18 50 DV51
Hawes Rd., Brom. 122 EH95
Hawes Rd., Tad. 145 CX120
Hatch Gdns.
Hawes St. N1 77 DP66
Haweswater Dr., Wat. 16 BW33
Haweswater Ho., Islw. 101 CF85
Hawfield Bank, Orp. 124 EX104
Hawfield Gdns., St.Alb. 17 CD26
Hawgood St. E3 79 EA71
Hawk Clo., Wal.Abb. 24 EG34
Hawkdene E4 37 EB44
Hawke Pk. Rd. N22 63 DP55
Hawke Pl. SE16 93 DX75
Middleton Dr.
Hawke Rd. SE19 106 DS93
Hawker Clo., Wall. 133 DL108
Kingsford Ave.
Hawke's Pl., Sev. 154 FG127
Hawkes Rd., Mitch. 118 DE95
Hawkesbury Rd. SW15 103 CV85
Hawkesfield Rd. SE23 107 DY89
Hawkesley Clo., Twick. 101 CG91
Hawkesworth Clo., Nthwd. 43 BS52
Hawkewood Rd., Sun. 113 BU97
Hawkhirst Rd., Ken. 148 DR115
Hawkhurst, Cob. 128 CA114
Hawkhurst Gdns., Chess. 130 CL105
Hawkhurst Gdns., Rom. 55 FD51
Hawkhurst Rd. SW16 119 DK95
Hawkhurst Way, N.Mal. 116 CR99
Hawkhurst Way, W.Wick. 121 EB103
Hawkinge Wk., Orp. 124 EV97
Farrington Ave.
Hawkins Clo. NW7 46 CR50
Hale La.
Hawkins Clo., Borwd. 32 CQ40
Banks Rd.
Hawkins Clo., Har. 59 CD59
Hawkins Rd., Tedd. 101 CH93
Hawkins Way SE6 107 EA91
Hawkley Gdns. SE27 105 DP89
Hawkridge Clo., Rom. 68 EW58
Hawks Hill, Lthd. 143 CF123
Guildford Rd.
Hawks Hill Clo., Lthd. 143 CF123
Hawks Ms. SE10 93 EC80
Luton Pl.
Hawks Rd., Kings.T. 116 CM96
Hawksbrook La., Beck. 121 EB100
Hawkshaw Clo. SW2 105 DL87
Tierney Rd.
Hawkshead Clo., Brom. 108 EE94
Hawkshead La., Hat. 19 CW28
Hawkshead Rd. NW10 75 CT66
Hawkshead Rd. W4 88 CS75
Hawkshead Rd., Pot.B. 19 CZ28
Hawkshill Clo., Esher 128 CA107
Hawkshill Way, Esher 128 BZ107
Hawkslade Rd. SE15 107 DX85
Hawksley Rd. N16 64 DR62
Hawksmead Clo., Enf. 37 DX35
Hawksmoor, Rad. 18 CN33
North Rd.
Hawksmoor Clo. E6 80 EL72
Allhallows Rd.
Hawksmoor Clo. SE18 95 ES78
Hawksmoor Ms. E1 78 DV73
Cable St.
Hawksmoor St. W6 89 CX79
Hawksmouth E4 51 EB45
Hawkstone Rd. SE16 92 DW77
Hawksview, Cob. 128 BZ113
Hawkwell Ct. E4 51 EC48
Colvin Gdns.
Hawkwell Wk. N1 78 DQ67
Basire St.
Hawkwood Cres. E4 37 EB44
Hawkwood La., Chis. 123 EQ95
Hawkwood Mt. E5 64 DV60
Hawlands Dr., Pnr. 58 BY59
Hawley Clo., Hmptn. 100 BZ93
Hawley Cres. NW1 77 DH66
Hawley Ms. NW1 77 DH66
Hawley St.
Hawley Rd. N18 51 DX50
Hawley Rd. NW1 77 DH66
Hawley St. NW1 77 DH66
Hawley Way, Ashf. 98 BN92
Haws La., Stai. 98 BG86
Hawstead La., Orp. 138 EZ106
Hawstead Rd. SE6 107 EB86
Hawsted, Buck.H. 52 EH45
Hawthorn Ave. N13 49 DL50
Hawthorn Ave., Cars. 132 DG108
Hawthorn Ave., Rain. 83 FH70
Hawthorn Ave., Rich. 88 CL82
Kew Rd.
Hawthorn Ave., Th.Hth. 119 DP95
Hawthorn Cen., Har. 59 CF56
Hawthorn Clo., Abb.L. 15 BU32
Magnolia Ave.
Hawthorn Clo., Bans. 131 CY114
Hawthorn Clo., Hmptn. 100 CA92
Hawthorn Clo., Houns. 85 BV80
Hawthorn Clo., Orp. 123 ER100
Hawthorn Clo., Wat. 29 BT38
Hawthorn Cotts., Well. 96 EU83
Hook La.
Hawthorn Ct., Rich. 88 CP81
West Hall Rd.
Hawthorn Cres. SW17 104 DG92
Hawthorn Dr., Har. 58 CA58
Hawthorn Dr., Uxb. 70 BJ65
Hawthorn Dr., W.Wick. 136 EE105
Hawthorn Gdns. W5 87 CK76
Hawthorn Gro. SE20 106 DV94
Hawthorn Gro., Barn. 33 CT44
Hawthorn Gro., Enf. 36 DR38
Hawthorn Hatch, Brent. 87 CH80
Hawthorn La., Sev. 154 FF122
Hawthorn Ms. NW7 47 CY53
Holders Hill Rd.
Hawthorn Pl., Erith 97 FC78
Hawthorn Pl., Hayes 71 BT73
Central Ave.
Hawthorn Rd. N8 63 DK55
Hawthorn Rd. N18 50 DT51
Hawthorn Rd. NW10 75 CU66
Hawthorn Rd., Bexh. 96 EZ84
Hawthorn Rd., Brent. 87 CH80
Hawthorn Rd., Buck.H. 52 EK49
Hawthorn Rd., Sutt. 132 DE106
Hawthorn Rd., Wall. 133 DH108
Hawthorn Wk. W10 75 CY70
Droop St.
Hawthorn Way N9 50 DS47
Hawthorn Way, Add. 126 BJ110
Hawthorn Way, Stai. 98 BK87
Hawthornden Clo. N12 48 DE51
Fallowfields Dr.
Hawthorndene Clo., Brom. 122 EF103
Hawthorndene Rd., Brom. 122 EF103
Hawthorne Ave., Har. 59 CG58
Hawthorne Ave., Mitch. 118 DD96
Hawthorne Ave., Ruis. 57 BV59
Hawthorne Ave. (Cheshunt), Wal.Cr. 22 DV30
Hawthorne Ave., West. 150 EK115
Hawthorne Clo. N1 78 DS65
Hawthorne Clo., Brom. 123 EM97
Hawthorne Clo., Sutt. 118 DB103
Aultone Way
Hawthorne Clo. (Cheshunt), Wal.Cr. 22 DV31
Hawthorne Ct., Walt. 114 BX103
Ambleside Ave.
Hawthorne Cres., S.Croy. 134 DW111
Hawthorne Cres., West Dr. 84 BM75
Hawthorne Fm. Ave., Nthlt. 72 BY67
Hawthorne Gro. NW9 60 CQ59
Hawthorne Ms., Grnf. 72 CC72
Greenford Rd.
Hawthorne Pl., Epsom 130 CS112
Hawthorne Rd. E17 65 EA55
Hawthorne Rd., Brom. 123 EM97
Hawthorne Rd., Rad. 17 CG34
Hawthorne Way, Shep. 113 BR98
Hawthornes Cen., Har. 59 CF56
Hawthorns, Wdf.Grn. 52 EG48
Hawthorns, The, Epsom 131 CT107
Ewell Bypass
Hawthorns, The, Loug. 39 EN42
Hawtrees, Rad. 31 CF35
Hawtrey Ave., Nthlt. 72 BX68
Hawtrey Dr., Ruis. 57 BU59
Hawtrey Rd. NW3 76 DE66
Haxted Rd., Brom. 122 EH95
North Rd.
Hay Clo. E15 80 EE66
Hay Clo., Borwd. 32 CQ40
Hay Currie St. E14 79 EB72
Hay Hill W1 9 J1
Hay Hill W1 77 DH73
Hay La. NW9 60 CQ56
Hay St. E2 78 DU67
Hayburn Way, Horn. 69 FF60
Haycroft Clo., Couls. 147 DP118
Caterham Dr.
Haycroft Gdns. NW10 75 CU67
Haycroft Rd. SW2 105 DL85
Haycroft Rd., Surb. 115 CK104
Hayday Rd. E16 80 EG71
Hayden Ct., Add. 126 BH111
Hayden Way, Rom. 55 FC54
Haydens Clo., Orp. 124 EW100
Haydens Pl. W11 75 CZ72
Portobello Rd.
Haydn Ave., Pur. 133 DN114
Haydns Ms. W3 74 CQ72
Emanuel Ave.
Haydock Ave., Nthlt. 72 CA65
Haydock Grn., Nthlt. 72 CA65
Haydock Ave.
Haydon Clo. NW9 60 CQ56
Haydon Clo., Enf. 36 DS44
Mortimer Dr.
Haydon Dr., Pnr. 57 BV56
Haydon Pk. Rd. SW19 104 DA92
Haydon Rd., Dag. 68 EW61
Haydon Rd., Wat. 30 BY44
Haydon St. EC3 7 P10
Haydon Wk. E1 78 DT73
Mansell St.
Haydon Way SW11 90 DD84
St. John's Hill
Haydons Rd. SW19 104 DB92
Hayes, The, Epsom 144 CR119
Hayes Chase, W.Wick. 121 ED100
Hayes Clo., Brom. 122 EG103
Hayes Ct. SW2 105 DL88
Hayes Cres. NW11 61 CZ57
Hayes Cres., Sutt. 131 CX105
Hayes Dr., Rain. 83 FH66
Hayes End Clo., Hayes 71 BR70
Hayes End Dr., Hayes 71 BR70
Hayes End Rd., Hayes 71 BR70
Hayes Gdn., Brom. 122 EG103
Hayes Hill, Brom. 122 EE102
Hayes Hill Rd., Brom. 122 EF102
Hayes La., Beck. 121 EC97
Hayes La., Brom. 122 EG99
Hayes La., Ken. 147 DP116
Hayes Mead Rd., Brom. 122 EE102
Hayes Pk., Hayes 71 BS70
Hayes Pl. NW1 4 C5
Hayes Rd., Brom. 122 EG98
Hayes Rd., Sthl. 85 BV77
Hayes St., Brom. 122 EH102
Hayes Wk., Brox. 23 DZ25
Landau Way
Hayes Wk., Pot.B. 20 DB33
Hyde Ave.
Hayes Way, Beck. 121 EC98
Hayes Wd. Ave., Brom. 122 EH102
Hayesford Pk. Dr., Brom. 122 EF99
Hayfield Clo. (Bushey), Wat. 30 CB42
Hayfield Pas. E1 78 DW70
Stepney Grn.
Hayfield Rd., Orp. 124 EU99
Hayfield Yd. E1 78 DW70
Mile End Rd.
Haygarth Pl. SW19 103 CX92
Haygreen Clo., Kings.T. 102 CP93
Hayland Clo. NW9 60 CR56
Hayles St. SE11 10 F8
Hayles St. SE11 91 DP77
Haylett Gdns., Kings.T. 115 CK98
Anglesea Rd.
Hayling Ave., Felt. 99 BU90
Hayling Clo. N16 64 DS64
Pellerin Rd.
Hayling Rd., Wat. 43 BT48
Haymaker Clo., Uxb. 70 BM66
Honey Hill
Hayman Cres., Hayes 71 BR68
Hayman St. N1 77 DP66
Cross St.
Haymarket SW1 9 M1
Haymarket SW1 77 DK73
Haymarket Arc. SW1 9 M1
Haymeads Dr., Esher 128 CC107
Haymer Gdns., Wor.Pk. 117 CU104
Haymerle Rd. SE15 92 DU79
Haymill Clo., Grnf. 73 CF69
Hayne Rd., Beck. 121 DZ96
Hayne St. EC1 6 G6
Haynes Clo. N11 48 DG48
Haynes Clo. N17 50 DV52
Haynes Clo. SE3 94 EE83
Haynes Clo., Wok. 140 BH122
Haynes La. SE19 106 DS93
Haynes Rd., Wem. 74 CL66
Haynt Wk. SW20 117 CY97
Hay's La. SE1 11 M3
Hay's Ms. W1 9 H2
Hay's Ms. W1 77 DH74
Hays Wk., Sutt. 131 CX110
Haysleigh Gdns. SE20 120 DU96
Haysoms Clo., Rom. 69 FE56
Haystall Clo., Hayes 71 BS68
Hayter Rd. SW2 105 DL85
Hayton Clo. E8 78 DT65
Buttermere Wk.
Hayward Clo. SW19 104 DB94
Hayward Clo., Bex. 111 FD85
Hayward Clo., Dart. 111 FD85
Hayward Gdns. SW15 103 CW86
Hayward Rd. N20 48 DC47
Hayward's Pl. EC1 6 F5
Haywood Clo., Pnr. 44 BX54
Haywood Ct., Wal.Abb. 24 EF34
Haywood Ri., Orp. 137 ES105
Haywood Rd., Brom. 122 EK98
Hayworth Clo., Enf. 37 DY40
Green St.
Hazel Ave., West Dr. 84 BN76
Hazel Bank, Surb. 116 CQ102
Hazel Clo. N13 50 DR48
Hazel Clo. N19 63 DJ61
Hargrave Pk.
Hazel Clo. SE15 92 DU82
Copeland Rd.
Hazel Clo., Brent. 87 CH80
Hazel Clo., Croy. 121 DX101
Hazel Clo., Horn. 69 FH62
Hazel Clo., Mitch. 119 DK98
Hazel Clo., Twick. 100 CC87
Hazel Clo., Wal.Cr. 22 DS26
The Laurels
Hazel Dr., Erith 97 FG81
Hazel End, Swan. 125 FE99
Hazel Gdns., Edg. 46 CP49
Hazel Gro. SE26 107 DX91
Hazel Gro., Enf. 36 DU44
Dimsdale Dr.
Hazel Gro., Orp. 123 EP103
Hazel Gro., Rom. 68 EY55
Hazel Gro., Stai. 98 BH93
Hazel Gro., Wat. 29 BV35
Cedar Wd. Dr.
Hazel Gro., Wem. 74 CL67
Carlyon Rd.
Hazel Gro. Est. SE26 107 DX91
Hazel La., Rich. 102 CL89
Hazel Mead, Barn. 33 CV43
Hazel Mead, Epsom 131 CU110
Hazel Rd. E15 66 EE64
Wingfield Rd.
Hazel Rd. NW10 75 CV69
Hazel Rd., Erith 97 FG81
Hazel Rd., St.Alb. 16 CB28
Hazel Rd., W.Byf. 126 BG114
Hazel Tree Rd., Wat. 29 BV37
Hazel Wk., Brom. 123 EN100
Hazel Way E4 51 DZ51
Hazel Way SE1 11 P8
Hazel Way, Couls. 146 DF119
Hazel Way, Lthd. 142 CC122
Hazelbank Ct., Cher. 112 BJ102
Hazelbank Rd. SE6 107 ED89
Hazelbank Rd., Cher. 112 BJ101
Hazelbourne Rd. SW12 105 DH86
Hazelbrouck Gdns., Ilf. 53 ER52
Hazelbury Ave., Abb.L. 15 BQ32
Hazelbury Clo. SW19 118 DA96
Hazelbury Grn. N9 50 DS48
Hazelbury La. N9 50 DS48
Hazelcroft, Pnr. 44 CB51
Hazelcroft Clo., Uxb. 70 BM66
Hazeldean Rd. NW10 74 CR66
Hazeldene, Add. 126 BJ106
Hazeldene, Wal.Cr. 23 DY32
Hazeldene Ct., Ken. 148 DR115
Hazeldene Dr., Pnr. 58 BW55
Hazeldene Gdns., Uxb. 71 BQ67
Hazeldene Rd., Ilf. 68 EV61
Hazeldene Rd., Well. 96 EW82
Hazeldon Rd. SE4 107 DY85
Hazeleigh Gdns., Wdf.Grn. 52 EL50
Hazelgreen Clo. N21 49 DP46
Hazelhurst, Beck. 121 ED95
Hazelhurst Rd. SW17 104 DC91
Hazell Cres., Rom. 55 FB53
Hazellville Rd. N19 63 DK59
Hazelmere Clo., Felt. 99 BR86
Hazelmere Clo., Lthd. 143 CH119
Hazelmere Clo., Nthlt. 72 BZ68
Hazelmere Dr., Nthlt. 72 BZ68
Hazelmere Gdns., Horn. 69 FH57
Hazelmere Rd. NW6 75 CZ67
Hazelmere Rd., Nthlt. 72 BZ68
Hazelmere Rd., Orp. 123 EQ98
Hazelmere Wk., Nthlt. 72 BZ68
Hazelmere Way, Brom. 122 EG100
Hazeltree La., Nthlt. 72 BY69
Hazelwood, Loug. 38 EK43
Hazelwood Ave., Mord. 118 DB98
Hazelwood Clo. W5 88 CL75
Hazelwood Clo., Har. 58 CB56
Hazelwood Ct. NW10 60 CS62
Neasden La. N.
Hazelwood Cres. N13 49 DN49
Hazelwood Cft., Surb. 116 CL100
Hazelwood Dr., Pnr. 43 BV54
Hazelwood Gro., S.Croy. 134 DV113
Hazelwood La. N13 49 DN49
Hazelwood La., Abb.L. 15 BR31
Hazelwood La., Couls. 146 DE118
Hazelwood Pk. Clo., Chig. 53 ES50
Hazelwood Rd. E17 65 DY57
Hazelwood Rd., Enf. 36 DT44
Hazelwood Rd., Rick. 29 BQ44
Hazelwood Rd., Sev. 137 ER112
Hazlebury Rd. SW6 90 DB82
Hazledean Rd., Croy. 120 DR103
Hazledene Rd. W4 88 CQ79
Hazlemere Gdns., Wor.Pk. 117 CU102
Hazlewell Rd. SW15 103 CV85
Hazlewood Clo. E5 65 DY62
Mandeville St.
Hazlewood Cres. W10 75 CY70
Hazlitt Ms. W14 89 CY76
Hazlitt Rd.
Hazlitt Rd. W14 89 CY76
Hazon Way, Epsom 130 CQ112
Heacham Ave., Uxb. 57 BQ62
Head St. E1 79 DX72
Headcorn Pl., Th.Hth. 119 DM98
Headcorn Rd.
Headcorn Rd. N17 50 DT52
Headcorn Rd., Brom. 108 EG92
Headcorn Rd., Th.Hth. 119 DM98
Headfort Pl. SW1 8 G5
Headfort Pl. SW1 90 DG75
Headingley Clo., Ilf. 53 ET51
Headingley Clo., Rad. 18 CL32
Headingley Clo. (Cheshunt), Wal.Cr. 22 DT26
Headington Rd. SW18 104 DC89
Headlam Rd. SW4 105 DK86
Headlam St. E1 78 DV70
Headley App., Ilf. 67 EP57
Headley Ave., Wall. 133 DM106
Headley Clo., Epsom 130 CN107
Headley Ct. SE26 106 DW92
Headley Dr., Croy. 135 EB108
Headley Dr., Epsom 145 CV119
Headley Dr., Ilf. 67 EP58
Headley Gro., Tad. 145 CV120
Headley Rd. (Ashtead Pk.), Epsom 144 CP118
Headley Rd. (Tyrrell's Wd.), Epsom 144 CN122
Headley Rd., Lthd. 143 CJ122
Head's Ms. W11 76 DA72
Artesian Rd.
Headstone Dr., Har. 59 CD55
Headstone Gdns., Har. 58 CC56
Headstone La., Har. 44 CB52
Headstone Rd., Har. 59 CE57
Headway, The, Epsom 131 CT109
Headway Clo., Rich. 101 CJ91
Locksmeade Rd.
Heald St. SE14 93 DZ81
Healey Dr., Orp. 137 ET105
Healey Rd., Wat. 29 BT44
Healey St. NW1 77 DH65
Heanor Ct. E5 65 DX62
Pedro St.
Hearn Ri., Nthlt. 72 BX67
Hearn Rd., Rom. 69 FF58
Hearn St. EC2 7 N5
Hearn St. EC2 78 DS70
Hearne Rd. W4 88 CN79
Hearn's Bldgs. SE17 11 L9
Hearn's Ri., Orp. 124 EX98
Hearn's Rd., Orp. 124 EW98
Hearnville Rd. SW12 104 DG88
Heath, The W7 73 CE74
Lower Boston Rd.
Heath, The, Cat. 148 DQ124
Heath, The, Rad. 17 CG33
Heath Ave., Bexh. 96 EX79
Heath Brow NW3 62 DC62
North End Way
Heath Clo. NW11 62 DB59
Heath Clo. W5 74 CM70
Heath Clo., Bans. 132 DB114
Heath Clo., Hayes 85 BR80
Heath Clo., Orp. 124 EW100
Sussex Rd.
Heath Clo., Pot.B. 20 DB30
Heath Clo., Rom. 69 FG55
Heath Clo., Stai. 98 BJ86
Heath Cotts., Pot.B. 20 DB30
Heath Rd.
Heath Ct., Houns. 86 BZ84
Heath Ct., Uxb. 70 BL66
Heath Dr. NW3 62 DB63
Heath Dr. SW20 117 CW98
Heath Dr., Epp. 39 ES36
Heath Dr., Pot.B. 20 DA30
Heath Dr., Rom. 55 FG53
Heath Dr., Sutt. 132 DC109
Heath End Rd., Bex. 111 FE88
Heath Fm. Ct., Wat. 29 BR37
Grove Mill La.
Heath Gdns., Twick. 101 CF88
Heath Gro. SE20 106 DW94
Maple Rd.
Heath Gro., Sun. 99 BT94
Heath Hurst Rd. NW3 62 DE63
Heath La. SE3 93 ED82
Heath La., Dart. 111 FG89
Heath La. Upper, Dart. 111 FH88
Heath Mead SW19 103 CX90
Heath Pk. Ct., Rom. 69 FG57
Heath Pk. Rd.
Heath Pk. Dr., Brom. 122 EL97
Heath Pk. Rd., Rom. 69 FG57
Heath Ridge Grn., Cob. 128 CA113
Heath Ri. SW15 103 CX86
Heath Ri., Brom. 122 EF100
Heath Ri., Wok. 140 BH123
Heath Rd. SW8 91 DH82
Heath Rd., Bex. 111 FC88
Heath Rd., Cat. 148 DR123
Heath Rd., Dart. 111 FF86

Heath Rd., Har. 58 CC59
Heath Rd., Houns. 86 CB84
Heath Rd., Lthd. 128 CC112
Heath Rd., Pot.B. 20 DA30
Heath Rd., Rom. 68 EX59
Heath Rd., Th.Hth. 120 DQ97
Heath Rd., Twick. 101 CF88
Heath Rd., Uxb. 71 BQ70
Heath Rd., Wat. 44 BX45
Heath Rd., Wey. 126 BN105
Heath Side NW3 62 DD63
Heath Side, Orp. 123 EQ102
Heath St. NW3 62 DC62
Heath Vw. N2 62 DC56
Heath Vw. Clo. N2 62 DC56
Heath Vill. SE18 95 ET78
Heath Vill. SW18 104 DC88
Cargill Rd.
Heath Way, Erith 97 FC81
Heatham Pk., Twick. 101 CF87
Heathbourne Rd., Stan. 45 CE47
Heathbourne Rd. (Bushey), Wat. 45 CE46
Heathbridge, Wey. 126 BN108
Heathclose Ave., Dart. 111 FH87
Heathclose Rd., Dart. 111 FG88
Heathcock Ct. WC2 77 DL73
Strand
Heathcote, Tad. 145 CX121
Heathcote Ave., Ilf. 53 EM54
Heathcote Gro. E4 51 EC48
Heathcote Rd., Epsom 130 CR114
Heathcote Rd., Twick. 101 CH86
Heathcote St. WC1 6 B4
Heathcote St. WC1 77 DM70
Heathcote Way, West Dr. 70 BK74
Tavistock Rd.
Heathcroft NW11 62 DB60
Heathcroft W5 74 CM70
Heathcroft Ave., Sun. 99 BT94
Heathdale Ave., Houns. 86 BY83
Heathdene, Tad. 145 CY119
Canons La.
Heathdene Dr., Belv. 97 FB77
Heathdene Rd. SW16 105 DM94
Heathdene Rd., Wall. 132 DG108
Heathedge SE26 106 DV89
Heathend Rd., Bex. 111 FE88
Heather Ave., Rom. 55 FD54
Heather Clo. E6 81 EP72
Heather Clo. SE13 107 ED87
Heather Clo. SW8 91 DH83
Heather Clo., Abb.L. 15 BU32
Magnolia Ave.
Heather Clo., Add. 126 BH110
Heather Clo., Hmptn. 114 BZ95
Heather Clo., Islw. 101 CD85
Harvesters Clo.
Heather Clo., Rom. 55 FD53
Heather Clo., Tad. 145 CY122
Heather Clo., Uxb. 70 BM71
Violet Ave.
Heather Dr., Dart. 111 FG87
Heather Dr., Enf. 35 DP40
Chasewood Ave.
Heather Dr., Rom. 55 FD54
Heather End, Swan. 125 FD98
Heather Gdns. NW11 61 CY58
Heather Gdns., Rom. 55 FD54
Heather Gdns., Sutt. 132 DA107
Heather Glen, Rom. 55 FD54
Heather La., Wat. 29 BT35
Heather La., West Dr. 70 BL72
Heather Pk. Dr., Wem. 74 CN66
Heather Pl., Esher 128 CB105
Park Rd.
Heather Ri. (Bushey), Wat. 30 BZ40
Heather Rd. E4 51 DZ51
Silver Birch Ave.
Heather Rd. NW2 61 CT61
Heather Rd. SE12 108 EG89
Heather Wk. W10 75 CY70
Droop St.
Heather Wk., Edg. 46 CP50
Heather Wk., Twick. 100 CA87
Stephenson Rd.
Heather Wk., Walt. 127 BT110
Octagon Rd.
Heather Way, Pot.B. 19 CZ32
Heather Way, Rom. 55 FD54
Heather Way, S.Croy. 135 DX109
Heather Way, Stan. 45 CF51
Heatherbank SE9 95 EM82
Heatherbank, Chis. 123 EN96
Heatherbank Clo., Dart. 111 FE86
Heatherdale Clo., Kings.T. 102 CP94
Heatherdene Clo. N12 48 DC53
Bow La.
Heatherdene Clo., Mitch. 118 DE98
Heatherfields, Add. 126 BH110
Heatherlands, Sun. 99 BU93
Heatherley Dr., Ilf. 66 EL55
Heathers, The, Stai. 98 BM87
Heatherset Gdns. SW16 105 DM94
Heatherside Rd., Epsom 130 CR108
Heatherside Rd., Sid. 110 EX90
Wren Rd.
Heathervale Caravan Pk., Add. 126 BJ110
Heathervale Rd., Add. 126 BH110
Heatherwood Clo. E12 66 EJ61
Heatherwood Dr., Hayes 71 BR68
Charville La.
Heathfield E4 51 EC48
Heathfield, Chis. 109 EQ93
Heathfield, Cob. 128 CA114
Heathfield Ave. SW18 104 DD87
Heathfield Rd.
Heathfield Ave., S.Croy. 135 DY109
Heathfield Clo. E16 80 EK71
Heathfield Clo., Kes. 136 EJ106
Heathfield Clo., Pot.B. 20 DB30
Heathfield Dr., Mitch. 118 DE95
Heathfield Gdns. NW11 61 CX58
Heathfield Gdns. SW18 104 DD86
Heathfield Rd.
Heathfield Gdns. W4 88 CQ78
Heathfield Gdns., Croy. 134 DR105
Coombe Rd.
Heathfield La., Chis. 109 EP93
Heathfield N., Twick. 101 CF87
Heathfield Pk. NW2 75 CW65
Heathfield Pk. Dr., Rom. 68 EV57
Barley La.
Heathfield Ri., Ruis. 57 BQ59
Heathfield Rd. SW18 104 DC86
Heathfield Rd. W3 88 CP75
Heathfield Rd., Bexh. 96 EZ84
Heathfield Rd., Brom. 108 EF94
Heathfield Rd., Croy. 134 DR105
Heathfield Rd., Kes. 136 EJ106
Heathfield Rd., Sev. 154 FF122
Heathfield Rd., Walt. 128 BY105
Heathfield Rd. (Bushey), Wat. 30 BY42
Heathfield S., Twick. 101 CF87
Heathfield Sq. SW18 104 DD87
Heathfield St. W11 75 CY73
Portland Rd.
Heathfield Ter. SE18 95 ES79
Heathfield Ter. W4 88 CQ78
Heathfield Vale, S.Croy. 135 DX109
Heathfields Ct., Houns. 100 BY85
Frampton Rd.
Heathgate NW11 62 DB58
Heathland Rd. N16 64 DS60
Heathlands, Tad. 145 CX122
Heathlands Clo., Sun. 113 BT96
Heathlands Clo., Twick. 101 CF88
Heathlands Ri., Dart. 111 FH86
Heathlands Way, Houns. 100 BY85
Frampton Rd.
Heathlee Rd. SE3 94 EF84
Heathlee Rd., Dart. 111 FE86
Heathley End, Chis. 109 EQ93
Heathmans Rd. SW6 89 CZ81
Heathrow Clo., West Dr. 84 BH81
Heathrow International Trd. Est., Houns. 85 BV83
Heaths Clo., Enf. 36 DS40
Heathside, Esher 115 CE104
Heathside, Houns. 100 BZ87
Heathside, Wey. 127 BP106
Heathside Ave., Bexh. 96 EY82
Heathside Clo., Esher 115 CE104
Heathside Clo., Nthwd. 43 BR50
Heathside Ct., Tad. 145 CV123
Heathside Pl., Epsom 145 CX118
Heathside Rd., Nthwd. 43 BR49
Heathstan Rd. W12 75 CU72
Heathurst Rd., S.Croy. 134 DS109
Heathview Ave., Dart. 111 FE86
Heathview Ct. SW19 103 CX89
Heathview Cres., Dart. 111 FG87
Heathview Dr. SE2 96 EX79
Heathview Gdns. SW15 103 CW87
Heathview Rd., Th.Hth. 119 DN98
Heathville Rd. N19 63 DL59
Heathwall St. SW11 90 DF83
Heathway SE3 94 EG80
Heathway, Croy. 121 DZ104
Heathway, Dag. 68 EZ62
Heathway, Lthd. 141 BT124
Heathway, Wdf.Grn. 52 EJ49
Heathwood Gdns. SE7 94 EL77
Heathwood Gdns., Swan. 125 FC96
Heathwood Wk., Bex. 111 FE88
Heaton Ave., Rom. 55 FH52
Heaton Clo. E4 51 EC48
Friars Clo.
Heaton Ct., Wal.Cr. 23 DX29
Heaton Gra. Rd., Rom. 55 FF54
Heaton Rd. SE15 92 DU83
Heaton Rd., Mitch. 104 DG94
Heaver Rd. SW11 90 DD83
Wye St.
Heavitree Clo. SE18 95 ER78
Heavitree Rd. SE18 95 ER78
Hebden Ct. E2 78 DT67
Laburnum St.
Hebden Ter. N17 50 DS51
Commercial Rd.
Hebdon Rd. SW17 104 DE90
Heber Rd. NW2 61 CX64
Heber Rd. SE22 106 DT86
Hebron Rd. W6 89 CV76
Hecham Clo. E17 51 DY54
Heckfield Pl. SW6 90 DA80
Fulham Rd.
Heckford St. E1 79 DX73
The Highway
Hector St. SE18 95 ES77
Heddington Gro. N7 63 DM64
Heddon Clo., Islw. 87 CG84
Heddon Ct. Ave., Barn. 34 DF43
Heddon Rd., Barn. 34 DF43
Heddon St. W1 5 K10
Heddon St. W1 77 DJ73
Hedge Hill, Enf. 35 DP39
Hedge La. N13 49 DP48
Hedge Wk. SE6 107 EB92
Lushington Rd.
Hedgeley, Ilf. 67 EM56
Hedgemans Rd., Dag. 82 EX66
Hedgemans Way, Dag. 82 EY65
Hedgerley Gdns., Grnf. 72 CC68
Hedgerow Wk., Wal.Cr. 23 DX30
Hedgers Gro. E9 79 DY65
Hedgeside Rd., Nthwd. 43 BQ50
Hedgewood Gdns., Ilf. 67 EN56
Hedgley St. SE12 108 EF85
Hedingham Clo. N1 78 DQ66
Popham Rd.
Hedingham Rd., Dag. 68 EV64
Hedley Rd., Twick. 100 CA87
Hedley Row N5 64 DR64
Poets Rd.
Hedworth Ave., Wal.Cr. 23 DX33
Heenan Clo., Bark. 81 EQ65
Glenny Rd.
Heene Rd., Enf. 36 DR39
Heidegger Cres. SW13 89 CV79
Trinity Ch. Rd.
Heigham Rd. E6 80 EL66
Heighton Gdns., Croy. 133 DP106
Heights, The SE7 94 EJ78
Heights, The, Beck. 107 EC94
Heights, The, Loug. 39 EM40
Heights, The, Nthlt. 58 BZ64
Heights, The, Wal.Abb. 24 EH25
Heights, The, Wey. 126 BN110
Heights Clo. SW20 103 CV94
Heights Clo., Bans. 145 CY116
Heiron St. SE17 91 DP79
Helby Rd. SW4 105 DK86
Helder Gro. SE12 108 EF87
Helder St., S.Croy. 134 DR107
Heldmann Clo., Houns. 87 CD84
Helen Ave., Felt. 99 BV87
Helen Clo. N2 62 DC55
Thomas More Way
Helen Clo., Dart. 111 FH87
Helen Clo., W.Mol. 114 CB98
Helen St. SE18 95 EP77
Wilmount St.
Helena Clo., Barn. 34 DD38
Helena Clo., Wall. 133 DL108
Kingsford Ave.
Helena Pl. E9 78 DW67
Fremont St.
Helena Rd. E13 80 EF68
Helena Rd. E17 65 EA57
Helena Rd. NW10 61 CV64
Helena Rd. W5 73 CK71
Helena Sq. SE16 79 DY73
Rotherhithe St.
Helens Gate, Wal.Cr. 23 DZ26
Helen's Pl. E2 78 DW69
Roman Rd.
Helenslea Ave. NW11 61 CZ60
Helford Clo., Ruis. 57 BS61
Chichester Ave.
Helgiford Gdns., Sun. 99 BS94
Helix Gdns. SW2 105 DM86
Helix Rd.
Helix Rd. SW2 105 DM86
Hellings St. E1 78 DU74
Wapping High St.
Helme Clo. SW19 103 CZ92
Helmet Row EC1 7 J4
Helmet Row EC1 78 DQ70
Helmsdale Clo., Hayes 72 BY70
Berrydale Rd.
Helmsdale Clo., Rom. 55 FE52
Helmsdale Rd. SW16 119 DK95
Helmsdale Rd., Rom. 55 FE52
Helmsley Pl. E8 78 DV66
Helsinki Sq. SE16 93 DY76
Finland St.
Helston Clo., Pnr. 44 BZ52
Helston Pl., Abb.L. 15 BT32
Shirley Rd.
Helvetia St. SE6 107 DZ89
Hemans St. SW8 91 DK80
Hemberton Rd. SW9 91 DL83
Hemery Rd., Grnf. 59 CD64
Heming Rd., Edg. 46 CP52
Hemingford Clo. N12 48 DD50
Fenstanton Ave.
Hemingford Rd. N1 77 DM67
Hemingford Rd., Sutt. 131 CW105
Hemingford Rd., Wat. 29 BS36
Hemington Ave. N11 48 DF50
Hemlock Clo., Tad. 145 CY124
Warren Lo. Dr.
Hemlock Rd. W12 75 CT73
Hemmen La., Hayes 71 BT72
Hemming Clo., Hmptn. 114 CA95
Chandler Clo.
Hemming St. E1 78 DU70
Hemming Way, Wat. 29 BU35
Hemmings Clo., Sid. 110 EV89
Hemnall St., Epp. 25 ET31
Hemp Wk. SE17 11 L8
Hempshaw Ave., Bans. 146 DF116
Hempstead Clo., Buck.H. 52 EG47
Hempstead Rd. E17 51 ED54
Hempstead Rd., Kings L. 14 BM26
Hempstead Rd., Wat. 29 BR36
Hemsby Rd., Chess. 130 CM107
Hemstal Rd. NW6 76 DA66
Hemsted Rd., Erith 97 FE80
Hemswell Dr. NW9 46 CS53
Hemsworth Ct. N1 78 DS68
Hemsworth St.
Hemsworth St. N1 78 DS68
Hemus Pl. SW3 90 DE78
Chelsea Manor St.
Hen & Chicken Ct. EC4 77 DN72
Fleet St.
Henbit Clo., Tad. 145 CV119
Henbury Way, Wat. 44 BX48
Henchman St. W12 75 CT72
Hendale Ave. NW4 61 CU55
Henderson Clo. NW10 74 CQ65
Henderson Clo., Horn. 69 FH61
St. Leonards Way
Henderson Dr. NW8 76 DD70
Cunningham Pl.
Henderson Pl., Abb.L. 15 BT27
Henderson Rd. E7 80 EJ65
Henderson Rd. N9 50 DV46
Henderson Rd. SW18 104 DE87
Henderson Rd., Croy. 120 DR100
Henderson Rd., Hayes 71 BU69
Henderson Rd., West. 136 EJ112
Hendham Rd. SW17 104 DE89
Hendon Ave. N3 47 CY53
Hendon Gdns., Rom. 55 FC51
Hendon La. N3 61 CY55
Hendon Pk. Row NW11 61 CZ58
Hendon Rd. N9 50 DU47
Hendon Way NW2 61 CX59
Hendon Way NW4 61 CV58
Hendon Way, Stai. 98 BK86
Hendon Wd. La. NW7 47 CT45
Hendre Rd. SE1 11 N9
Hendren Clo., Grnf. 59 CD64
Dimmock Dr.
Hendrick Ave. SW12 104 DF87
Heneage Cres., Croy. 135 EC110
Heneage La. EC3 7 N9
Heneage St. E1 78 DT71
Henfield Clo. N19 63 DJ60
Henfield Clo., Bex. 110 FA86
Henfield Rd. SW19 117 CZ95
Hengelo Gdns., Mitch. 118 DD98
Hengist Rd. SE12 108 EH87
Hengist Rd., Erith 97 FB80
Hengist Way, Brom. 121 ED98
Hengrave Rd. SE23 106 DW87
Hengrove Ct., Bex. 110 EY88
Hurst Rd.
Hengrove Cres., Ashf. 98 BK90
Henley Ave., Sutt. 117 CY104
Henley Clo., Grnf. 72 CC68
Henley Clo., Islw. 87 CF81
Henley Ct. N14 49 DJ45
Henley Dr. SE1 92 DT77
Henley Dr., Kings.T. 103 CT94
Henley Gdns., Pnr. 57 BV55
Henley Gdns., Rom. 68 EY57
Henley Rd. E16 95 EM75
Henley Rd. N18 50 DS49
Henley Rd. NW10 75 CW67
Henley Rd., Ilf. 67 EQ63
Henley St. SW11 90 DG82
Henley Way, Felt. 100 BX92
Henlow Pl., Rich. 101 CK89
Sandpits Rd.
Hennel Clo. SE23 106 DW90
Henniker Gdns. E6 80 EK69
Henniker Ms. SW3 90 DD79
Callow St.
Henniker Pt. E15 66 EE64
Henniker Rd. E15 65 ED64
Henning St. SW11 90 DE81
Henningham Rd. N17 50 DR53
Henrietta Ms. WC1 6 A4
Henrietta Pl. W1 5 H8
Henrietta Pl. W1 77 DH72
Henrietta St. E15 65 EC64
Henrietta St. WC2 6 A10
Henrietta St. WC2 77 DL73
Henriques St. E1 78 DU72
Henry Clo., Enf. 36 DS38
Henry Cooper Way SE9 108 EK90
Henry Darlot Dr. NW7 47 CX50
Henry Dickens Ct. W11 75 CX73
Henry Jackson Rd. SW15 89 CX83
Henry Rd. E6 80 EL68
Henry Rd. N4 64 DQ60
Henry Rd., Barn. 34 DD43
Henry St., Brom. 122 EH95
Henry's Ave., Wdf.Grn. 52 EF50
Henry's Wk., Ilf. 53 ER52
Henryson Rd. SE4 107 EA85
Hensford Gdns. SE26 106 DV91
Wells Pk. Rd.
Henshall St. N1 78 DR65
Henshaw St. SE17 11 K8
Henshaw St. SE17 92 DR77
Henshawe Rd., Dag. 68 EX62
Henshill Pt. E3 79 EB69
Bromley High St.
Henslowe Rd. SE22 106 DU85
Henson Ave. NW2 61 CW64
Henson Clo., Orp. 123 EP103
Henson Path, Har. 59 CK55
Brancker Rd.
Henson Pl., Nthlt. 72 BW67
Henstridge Pl. NW8 76 DE68
Hensworth Rd., Ashf. 98 BK92
Henty Clo. SW11 90 DE80
Henty Wk. SW15 103 CV85
Henville Rd., Brom. 122 EJ95
Henwick Rd. SE9 94 EK83
Henwood Rd. SE16 92 DW76
Gomm Rd.
Henwood Side, Wdf.Grn. 53 EM51
Love La.
Hepburn Gdns., Brom. 122 EE102
Hepburn Ms. SW11 104 DF85
Webbs Rd.
Hepple Clo., Islw. 87 CH82
Hepplestone Clo. SW15 103 CV86
Dover Pk. Dr.
Hepscott Rd. E9 79 EA65
Hepworth Ct., Bark. 68 EU64
Hepworth Gdns., Bark. 68 EU64
Hepworth Rd. SW16 105 DL94
Hepworth Wk. NW3 62 DE64
Haverstock Hill
Hepworth Way, Walt. 113 BT102
Heracles Clo., Wall. 133 DL108
Gull Clo.
Herald Gdns., Wall. 119 DH104
Herald St. E2 78 DV70
Three Colts La.
Herald's Ct. SE11 10 F9
Herald's Pl. SE11 10 E8
Herbal Hill EC1 6 E5
Herbal Hill EC1 77 DN70
Herbert Cres. SW1 8 E6
Herbert Gdns. NW10 75 CV67
Herbert Gdns. W4 88 CP79
Magnolia Rd.
Herbert Gdns., Rom. 68 EX59
Herbert Pl. SE18 95 EP79
Plumstead Common Rd.
Herbert Rd. E12 66 EL63
Herbert Rd. E17 65 DZ59
Herbert Rd. N11 49 DL52
Herbert Rd. N15 64 DT57
Herbert Rd. NW9 61 CU58
Herbert Rd. SE18 95 EN80
Herbert Rd. SW19 103 CZ94
Herbert Rd., Bexh. 96 EY82
Herbert Rd., Brom. 122 EK99
Herbert Rd., Ilf. 67 ES61
Herbert Rd., Kings.T. 116 CM97
Herbert Rd., Sthl. 72 BZ74
Herbert Rd., Swan. 111 FH93
Herbert St. E13 80 EG68
Herbert St. NW5 76 DG65
Herbert Ter. SE18 95 EP79
Herbert Rd.
Herbrand St. WC1 5 P4
Herbrand St. WC1 77 DL70
Hercies Rd., Uxb. 70 BM66
Hercules Pl. N7 63 DL62
Hercules St.
Hercules Rd. SE1 10 C7
Hercules Rd. SE1 91 DM76
Hercules St. N7 63 DL62
Hercules Twr. SE14 93 DY79
Milton Ct. Rd.
Hereford Ave., Barn. 48 DF46
Hereford Clo., Epsom 130 CR113
Hereford Clo., Stai. 112 BH95
Hereford Gdns. SE13 108 EE85
Longhurst Rd.
Hereford Gdns., Ilf. 66 EL59
Hereford Gdns., Pnr. 58 BY57
Hereford Gdns., Twick. 100 CC88
Hereford Ho. NW6 76 DA68
Hereford Ms. W2 76 DA72
Hereford Rd.
Hereford Pl. SE14 93 DZ80
Hereford Retreat SE15 92 DU80
Bird in Bush Rd.
Hereford Rd. E11 66 EH57
Hereford Rd. W2 76 DA72
Hereford Rd. W3 74 CP73
Hereford Rd. W5 87 CJ76
Hereford Rd., Felt. 100 BW88
Hereford Sq. SW7 90 DC77
Hereford St. E2 78 DU70
Hereford Way, Chess. 129 CJ106
Herent Dr., Ilf. 66 EL56
Hereward Ave., Pur. 133 DN111
Hereward Clo., Wal.Abb. 23 EC32
Hereward Gdns. N13 49 DN50
Hereward Grn., Loug. 39 EQ39
Hereward Rd. SW17 104 DE91
Herga Ct., Har. 59 CE62
Herga Ct., Wat. 29 BU40
Herga Rd., Har. 59 CF56
Heriot Ave. E4 51 EA47
Heriot Rd. NW4 61 CW57
Heriot Rd., Cher. 112 BG101
Heriots Clo., Stan. 45 CG49
Heritage Clo., Uxb. 70 BJ70
Heritage Hill, Kes. 136 EJ106
Heritage Vw., Har. 59 CF62
Herkomer Clo. (Bushey), Wat. 30 CB44
Herkomer Rd. (Bushey), Wat. 30 CA43
Herlwyn Ave., Ruis. 57 BS61
Herlwyn Gdns. SW17 104 DF91
Hermes Pt. W9 76 DA70
Harrow Rd.
Hermes St. N1 6 D1
Hermes Wk., Nthlt. 72 CA68
Hotspur Rd.
Hermes Way, Wall. 133 DK108
Hermiston Ave. N8 63 DL57
Hermit Pl. NW6 76 DB67
Belsize Rd.
Hermit Rd. E16 80 EF70
Hermit St. EC1 6 F2
Hermit St. EC1 77 DP69
Hermitage, The SE23 106 DW88
Hermitage, The SW13 89 CT81
Hermitage, The, Felt. 99 BT90
Hermitage, The, Rich. 102 CL85
Hermitage, The, Uxb. 70 BK65
Hermitage Clo. E18 66 EF56
Hermitage Clo., Enf. 35 DP40
Hermitage Clo., Esher 129 CG107
Hermitage Clo., Shep. 112 BN98
Hermitage Ct. E18 66 EG56

Hermitage Ct. NW2 62 DA62
Hermitage La.
Hermitage Ct., Pot.B. 20 DC33
Southgate Rd.
Hermitage Gdns. NW2 62 DA62
Hermitage Gdns. SE19 106 DQ94
Hermitage La. N18 50 DR50
Hermitage La. NW2 62 DA62
Hermitage La. SE25 120 DU100
Hermitage La. SW16 105 DM94
Hermitage La., Croy. 120 DU100
Hermitage Path SW16 119 DL95
Hermitage Rd. N4 63 DP59
Hermitage Rd. N15 63 DP59
Hermitage Rd. SE19 106 DQ94
Hermitage Rd., Ken. 148 DQ116
Hermitage Row E8 64 DU64
Hermitage St. W2 76 DD71
Harrow Rd.
Hermitage Wk. E18 66 EF56
Hermitage Wall E1 78 DU74
Hermitage Way, Stan. 45 CG53
Hermon Gro., Hayes 71 BU74
Hermon Hill E11 66 EG57
Hermon Hill E18 66 EH55
Herndon Rd. SW18 104 DC85
Herne Clo. NW10 60 CR64
North Circular Rd.
Herne Hill SE24 106 DQ85
Herne Hill Rd. SE24 92 DQ83
Herne Ms. N18 50 DU49
Lyndhurst Rd.
Herne Pl. SE24 105 DP85
Herne Rd., Surb. 115 CK103
Herne Rd. (Bushey), Wat. 30 CB44
Heron Clo. E17 51 DZ54
Heron Clo. NW10 74 CS65
Heron Clo., Buck.H. 52 EG46
Heron Clo., Rick. 42 BK47
Heron Clo., Uxb. 70 BK65
Heron Ct., Brom. 122 EJ98
Heron Cres., Sid. 109 ES90
Heron Dale, Add. 126 BK106
Heron Flight Ave., Horn. 83 FH66
Heron Hill, Belv. 96 EZ78
Heron Ms., Ilf. 67 EP61
Balfour Rd.
Heron Pl. SE16 79 DY74
Heron Quay E14 79 EA74
Heron Rd. SE24 92 DQ84
Heron Rd., Croy. 120 DS103
Tunstall Rd.
Heron Rd., Twick. 87 CG84
Heron Sq., Rich. 101 CK85
Bridge St.
Heron Wk., Nthwd. 43 BS49
Herondale, S.Croy. 135 DX109
Herondale Ave. SW18 104 DD88
Heronfield, Pot.B. 20 DC30
Herongate Rd. E12 66 EJ61
Herongate Rd., Swan. 111 FE93
Herongate Rd. (Cheshunt), Wal.Cr. 23 DY27
Heronry, The, Walt. 127 BU107
Herons, The E11 66 EF58
Herons Cft., Wey. 127 BR107
Heron's Pl., Islw. 87 CH83
Herons Ri., Barn. 34 DE42
Heronsforde W13 73 CJ72
Heronsgate, Edg. 46 CN50
Heronslea, Wat. 30 BW36
Heronslea Dr., Stan. 46 CL50
Heronswood, Wal.Abb. 24 EE34
Roundhills
Heronway, Wdf.Grn. 52 EJ49
Herrick Rd. N5 64 DQ62
Herrick St. SW1 9 N9
Herrick St. SW1 91 DK77
Herries St. W10 75 CY68
Herringham Rd. SE7 94 EJ76
Herrings La., Cher. 112 BG100
Herrongate Clo., Enf. 36 DT40
Hersant Clo. NW10 75 CU67
Herschell Rd. SE23 107 DY87
Hersham Bypass, Walt. 127 BV106
Hersham Clo. SW15 103 CU87
Hersham Gdns., Walt. 128 BW105
Hersham Rd., Walt. 113 BU102
Hersham Trd. Est., Walt. 114 BY103
Hertford Ave. SW14 102 CR85
Hertford Clo., Barn. 34 DD41
Hertford Pl. W1 5 K5
Hertford Rd. N1 78 DS67
Hertford Rd. N2 62 DE55
Hertford Rd. N9 50 DU47
Hertford Rd., Bark. 81 EP66
Hertford Rd., Barn. 34 DC41
Hertford Rd., Enf. 36 DW40
Hertford Rd., Ilf. 67 ES58
Hertford Rd., Wal.Cr. 37 DY35
Hertford Sq., Mitch. 119 DL98
Hertford Way
Hertford St. W1 8 G3
Hertford St. W1 76 DG74
Hertford Wk., Belv. 96 FA78
Hoddesdon Rd.
Hertford Way, Mitch. 119 DL98
Hertslet Rd. N7 63 DM62
Hertsmere Rd. E14 79 EA73
Hervey Clo. N3 48 DA53
Hervey Pk. Rd. E17 65 DY56
Hervey Rd. SE3 94 EH81
Hesa Rd., Hayes 71 BU72
Hesiers Hill, Warl. 150 EE117
Hesiers Rd., Warl. 150 EE117
Hesketh Pl. W11 75 CY73
Hesketh Rd. E7 66 EG62
Heslop Rd. SW12 104 DF88
Hesper Ms. SW5 90 DB78
Hesperus Cres. E14 93 EB77
Hessel Rd. W13 87 CG75
Hessel St. E1 78 DV72
Hesselyn Dr., Rain. 83 FH66
Hessle Gro., Epsom 131 CT111
Hester Rd. N18 50 DU50
Hester Rd. SW11 90 DE80
Hester Ter., Rich. 88 CN83
Chilton Rd.
Hestercombe Ave. SW6 89 CY82
Hesterman Way, Croy. 119 DL102
Heston Ave., Houns. 86 BY79
Heston Gra. La., Houns. 86 BZ79
Heston Ind. Cen., Houns. 86 BW79
Heston Ind. Mall, Houns. 86 BZ80
Heston Rd., Houns. 86 CA79
Heston St. SE14 93 EA81
Heswell Grn., Wat. 43 BU48
Fairhaven Cres.
Hetherington Rd. SW4 91 DL84
Hetherington Rd., Shep. 113 BQ96
Hetherington Way, Uxb. 56 BL63
Hetley Gdns. SE19 106 DT94
Fox Hill
Hetley Rd. W12 75 CV74
Heton Gdns. NW4 61 CU56
Hevelius Clo. SE10 94 EF78
Hever Cft. SE9 109 EN91
Hever Gdns., Brom. 123 EN96
Heverham Rd. SE18 95 ES77
Heversham Rd., Bexh. 96 FA82
Hewens Rd., Hayes 71 BQ70
Hewens Rd., Uxb. 71 BQ70
Hewer St. W10 75 CX71
Hewers Way, Tad. 145 CV120
Hewett Clo., Stan. 45 CH49
Hewett Pl., Swan. 125 FD98
Hewett Rd., Dag. 68 EW64
Hewett St. EC2 7 N5
Hewins Clo., Wal.Abb. 24 EE33
Broomstick Hall Rd.
Hewish Rd. N18 50 DS49
Hewison St. E3 79 DZ68
Hewitt Ave. N22 49 DP54
Hewitt Clo., Croy. 121 EA104
Hewitt Rd. N8 63 DN57
Hewitts Rd., Orp. 138 EZ108
Hewlett Rd. E3 79 DY68
Hexagon, The N6 62 DF60
Hexal Rd. SE6 108 EE90
Hexham Gdns., Islw. 87 CG80
Hexham Rd. SE27 106 DQ89
Hexham Rd., Barn. 34 DB42
Hexham Rd., Mord. 118 DB102
Heybourne Rd. N17 50 DV52
Heybridge Ave. SW16 105 DL94
Heybridge Dr., Ilf. 53 ER54
Heybridge Way E10 65 DY59
Heyford Ave. SW8 91 DL80
Heyford Ave. SW20 117 CZ97
Heyford Rd., Mitch. 118 DE96
Heyford Rd., Rad. 31 CF37
Heygate St. SE17 11 H9
Heygate St. SE17 92 DQ77
Heylyn Sq. E3 79 DZ69
Malmesbury Rd.
Heymede, Lthd. 143 CJ123
Heynes Rd., Dag. 68 EW63
Heysham Dr., Wat. 44 BW50
Heysham La. NW3 62 DB62
Heysham Rd. N15 64 DR58
Heythorp St. SW18 103 CZ88
Heythrop Dr., Uxb. 56 BM63
Heywood Ave. NW9 46 CS53
Heyworth Rd. E5 64 DV63
Heyworth Rd. E15 66 EF63
Hibbert Ave., Wat. 30 BX38
Hibbert Rd. E17 65 DZ59
Hibbert Rd., Har. 45 CF54
Hibbert St. SW11 90 DC83
Hibbs Clo., Swan. 125 FD96
Hibernia Gdns., Houns. 86 CA84
Hibernia Rd., Houns. 86 CA84
Hichisson Rd. SE15 106 DW85
Hickin Clo. SE7 94 EK77
Hickin St. E14 93 EC76
Plevna St.
Hickling Rd., Ilf. 67 EP64
Hickman Ave. E4 51 EC51
Hickman Clo. E16 80 EK71
Hickman Rd., Rom. 68 EW59
Hickmore Wk. SW4 91 DJ83
Hickory Clo. N9 50 DU45
Hicks Ave., Grnf. 73 CD68
Hicks Clo. SW11 90 DE83
Hicks St. SE8 93 DY78
Hidcote Gdns. SW20 117 CV97
Hide E6 81 EN72
Downings
Hide Pl. SW1 9 M9
Hide Pl. SW1 91 DK77
Hide Rd., Har. 58 CC56
Hideaway, The, Abb.L. 15 BU31
Hides St. N7 77 DM65
Sheringham Rd.
Higgins Wk., Hmptn. 100 BY93
Abbott Clo.
High Acres, Abb.L. 15 BR32
High Beech, S.Croy. 134 DS108
High Beech Rd., Loug. 38 EL42
High Beeches, Bans. 131 CW114
High Beeches, Orp. 138 EU107
High Beeches, Sid. 110 EY92
High Beeches Clo., Pur. 133 DK110
High Bri. SE10 93 ED78
High Bri. Wf. SE10 93 ED78
High Bri.
High Broom Cres., W.Wick. 121 EB101
High Canons, Borwd. 32 CQ37
High Cedar Dr. SW20 103 CV94
High Clo., Rick. 28 BJ43
High Coombe Pl., Kings.T. 102 CR94
High Cross, Wat. 31 CD37
High Cross Cen. N15 64 DU56
High Cross Rd. N17 64 DU55
High Dr., Cat. 149 EA122
High Dr., Lthd. 129 CD114
High Dr., N.Mal. 116 CQ95
High Elms, Chig. 53 ES49
High Elms, Wdf.Grn. 52 EG50
High Elms Clo., Nthwd. 43 BR51
High Elms La., Wat. 15 BV31
High Elms Rd., Orp. 137 EN111
High Fld., Bans. 146 DE117
High Firs, Rad. 31 CF35
High Firs, Swan. 125 FE98
High Foleys, Esher 129 CH108
High Gables, Loug. 38 EK43
High Garth, Esher 128 CC107
High Gro. SE18 95 ER80
High Gro., Brom. 122 EJ95
High Hill Est. E5 64 DV60
Mount Pleasant La.
High Hill Ferry E5 64 DV60
High Hill Rd., Warl. 149 EC115
High Holborn WC1 5 P8
High Holborn WC1 77 DL72
High La. W7 73 CD71
High La., Cat. 149 DZ119
High La., Warl. 149 DZ118
High Lawns, Har. 59 CE62
High Level Dr. SE26 106 DU91
High Mead, Chig. 53 EQ47
High Mead, Har. 59 CE57
High Mead, W.Wick. 121 ED103
High Meadow Clo., Pnr. 57 BV56
Daymer Gdns.
High Meadow Cres. NW9 60 CR57
High Meadows, Chig. 53 ER50
High Meads Rd. E16 80 EK72
Fulmer Rd.
High Mt. NW4 61 CU58
High Oaks, Enf. 35 DM38
High Pk. Ave., Rich. 88 CN81
High Pk. Rd., Rich. 88 CN81
High Path SW19 118 DB95
High Pine Clo., Wey. 127 BQ106
High Pines, Warl. 148 DW119
High Pt. N6 62 DG59
High Pt. SE9 109 EP90
High Ridge (Cuffley), Pot.B. 21 DL27
High Ridge Clo., Hem.H. 14 BK25
High Ridge Rd., Hem.H. 14 BK25
High Rd. N2 48 DD53
High Rd. N11 49 DH50
High Rd. N12 48 DC49
High Rd. N15 64 DT58
High Rd. N17 64 DT55
High Rd. N20 48 DC47
High Rd. N22 49 DM51
High Rd. (Willesden) NW10 75 CT65
High Rd., Buck.H. 52 EH48
High Rd., Chig. 53 EN50
High Rd., Couls. 146 DE124
High Rd., Epp. 25 ER32
High Rd. (North Weald Bassett), Epp. 27 FB27
High Rd. (Thornwood), Epp. 26 EV28
High Rd. (Harrow Weald), Har. 45 CE52
High Rd., Ilf. 67 EQ61
High Rd. (Goodmayes), Ilf. 68 EU60
High Rd. (Seven Kings), Ilf. 67 ET60
High Rd., Loug. 38 EJ44
High Rd., Pnr. 57 BV57
High Rd. (Chadwell Heath), Rom. 68 EU60
High Rd., Uxb. 70 BJ71
High Rd. (Ickenham), Uxb. 57 BP62
High Rd. (Bushey), Wat. 45 CD46
High Rd. (Leavesden Grn.), Wat. 29 BT35
High Rd., Wem. 60 CL64
High Rd., W.Byf. 126 BK112
High Rd. Leyton E10 65 EB58
High Rd. Leyton E15 65 EC63
High Rd. Leytonstone E11 66 EE63
High Rd. Leytonstone E15 66 EE63
High Rd. Turnford, Brox. 23 DY25
High Rd. Woodford Grn. E18 52 EF53
High Rd. Woodford Grn., Wdf.Grn. 52 EF51
High Silver, Loug. 38 EK42
High St. E11 66 EG57
High St. E13 80 EG68
High St. E15 79 EC68
High St. E17 65 DY57
High St. N8 63 DL56
High St. N14 49 DK47
High St. NW7 47 CV50
High St. (Harlesden) NW10 75 CT68
High St. SE20 106 DW94
High St. (South Norwood) SE25 120 DT98
High St. SW6 89 CY83
High St. W3 74 CP74
High St. W5 73 CK73
High St., Abb.L. 15 BS31
High St. (Bedmond), Abb.L. 15 BT27
High St., Add. 126 BH105
High St., Bans. 146 DA115
High St., Barn. 33 CY41
High St., Beck. 121 EA96
High St. (Elstree), Borwd. 31 CK44
High St., Brent. 88 CL79
High St., Brom. 122 EG96
High St., Cars. 132 DF105
High St., Cat. 148 DS123
High St., Chis. 109 EP93
High St., Cob. 127 BV114
High St., Croy. 120 DQ104
High St., Edg. 46 CN51
High St. (Ponders End), Enf. 36 DW42
High St., Epp. 25 ET31
High St., Epsom 130 CR113
High St. (Ewell), Epsom 131 CT109
High St., Esher 128 CB105
High St. (Claygate), Esher 129 CF107
High St., Felt. 99 BT90
High St., Hmptn. 114 CB95
High St., Har. 59 CE60
High St. (Wealdstone), Har. 45 CE54
High St., Hayes 85 BR79
High St., Houns. 86 CB83
High St. (Cranford), Houns. 85 BU80
High St., Ilf. 67 EQ55
High St., Kings L. 14 BN29
High St., Kings.T. 115 CK97
High St. (Hampton Wick), Kings.T. 115 CJ95
High St., Lthd. 143 CH122
High St. (Oxshott), Lthd. 129 CD113
High St., N.Mal. 116 CS98
High St., Nthwd. 43 BT53
High St., Orp. 124 EU103
High St. (Downe), Orp. 137 EN111
High St. (Farnborough), Orp. 137 EP106
High St. (Green St. Grn.), Orp. 137 ET108
High St. (St. Mary Cray), Orp. 124 EW100
High St., Pnr. 58 BY55
High St., Pot.B. 20 DC33
High St., Pur. 133 DN111
High St., Rick. 42 BK46
High St., Rom. 69 FE57
High St., Ruis. 57 BS59
High St. (London Colney), St.Alb. 17 CJ25
High St., Sev. 155 FJ126
High St. (Chipstead), Sev. 154 FC122
High St. (Otford), Sev. 153 FF116
High St. (Seal), Sev. 155 FL121
High St. (Shoreham), Sev. 139 FF110
High St., Shep. 113 BP101
High St., Sthl. 72 BZ74
High St. (Stanwell), Stai. 98 BK86
High St., Sutt. 132 DB105
High St. (Cheam), Sutt. 131 CY107
High St., Swan. 125 FF97
High St., Tad. 145 CW123
High St., Tedd. 101 CF92
High St., T.Ditt. 115 CG101
High St., Th.Hth. 120 DQ98
High St. (Whitton), Twick. 100 CC87
High St., Uxb. 70 BJ66
High St. (Cowley), Uxb. 70 BJ69
High St. (Harefield), Uxb. 42 BJ53
High St., Wal.Cr. 23 DX33
High St. (Cheshunt), Wal.Cr. 23 DX29
High St., Walt. 113 BU102
High St., Wat. 29 BV41
High St. (Bushey), Wat. 30 BZ44
High St., Wem. 60 CM63
High St., West Dr. 84 BK79
High St. (Yiewsley), West Dr. 70 BK73
High St., W.Mol. 114 CA98
High St., W.Wick. 121 EB102
High St. (Brasted), West. 152 EV124
High St., Wey. 126 BN105
High St. (Ripley), Wok. 140 BH122
High St. Colliers Wd. SW19 104 DD94
High St. Ms. SW19 103 CY92
High St. N. E6 80 EL66
High St. N. E12 66 EL64
High St. S. E6 81 EM68
High St. Wimbledon SW19 103 CX92
High Timber St. EC4 7 H10
High Timber St. EC4 78 DQ73
High Tor Clo., Brom. 108 EH94
Babbacombe Rd.
High Tree Ct. W7 73 CE73
High Trees SW2 105 DN88
High Trees, Barn. 34 DE43
High Trees, Croy. 121 DY102
High Trees Clo., Cat. 148 DT123
High Vw., Pnr. 58 BW55
High Vw., Rick. 28 BG42
High Vw., Sutt. 131 CZ111
High Vw., Wat. 29 BT44
High Vw. Clo. SE19 120 DT96
High Vw. Clo., Loug. 38 EJ43
High Vw. Rd. E18 66 EF55
High Vw. Rd., Sid. 110 EV91
High Worple, Har. 58 BY59
Higham Hill Rd. E17 51 DY53
Higham Pl. E17 65 DY55
Higham Rd. N17 64 DR55
Higham Rd., Wdf.Grn. 52 EG51
Higham Sta. Ave. E4 51 EA51
Higham St. E17 65 DY55
Higham Vw., Epp. 27 FB26
Highams Lo. Business Cen. E17 65 DX55
Highams Pk. Ind. Est. E4 51 EC51
Highbank Way N8 63 DN58
Highbanks Clo., Well. 96 EV80
Highbanks Rd., Pnr. 44 CA51
Highbarns Rd., Hem.H. 14 BN25
Highbarrow Rd., Croy. 120 DU101
Highbridge SE10 93 ED78
Highbridge Rd., Bark. 81 EP67
Highbridge St., Wal.Abb. 23 EB33
Highbrook Rd. SE3 94 EK83
Highbury Ave., Th.Hth. 119 DN96
Highbury Clo., N.Mal. 116 CQ98
Highbury Clo., W.Wick. 121 EB103
Highbury Cor. N5 77 DP65
Highbury Cres. N5 63 DP64
Highbury Est. N5 64 DQ64
Highbury Gdns., Ilf. 67 ES61
Highbury Gra. N5 64 DQ63
Highbury Gro. N5 77 DP65
Highbury Hill N5 63 DN62
Highbury Ms. N7 77 DN65
Holloway Rd.
Highbury New Pk. N5 64 DQ64
Highbury Pk. N5 63 DP63
Highbury Pk. Ms. N5 64 DQ63
Highbury Gra.
Highbury Pl. N5 77 DP65
Highbury Quad. N5 64 DQ62
Highbury Rd. SW19 103 CY92
Highbury Sta. Rd. N1 77 DN65
Highbury Ter. N5 63 DP64
Highbury Ter. Ms. N5 63 DP64
Highclere Clo., Ken. 148 DQ115
Highclere Rd., N.Mal. 116 CR97
Highclere St. SE26 107 DY91
Highcliffe Dr. SW15 103 CT86
Highcliffe Gdns., Ilf. 66 EL57
Highcombe SE7 94 EH79
Highcombe Clo. SE9 108 EK88
Highcroft NW9 60 CS57
Highcroft Ave., Wem. 74 CN67
Highcroft Ct., Lthd. 142 CA123
Highcroft Gdns. NW11 61 CZ58
Highcroft Rd. N19 63 DL59
Highcroft Rd., Hem.H. 14 BG25
Highcross Way SW15 103 CU88
Highdaun Dr. SW16 119 DM98
Highdown, Wor.Pk. 116 CS103
Highdown La., Sutt. 132 DB111
Highdown Rd. SW15 103 CV86
Higher Dr., Bans. 131 CX112
Higher Dr., Pur. 133 DN113
Higher Grn., Epsom 131 CU113
Highfield, Felt. 99 BU88
Highfield, Kings L. 14 BL28
Highfield Ave. NW9 60 CQ57
Highfield Ave. NW11 61 CX59
Highfield Ave., Erith 97 FB79
Highfield Ave., Grnf. 59 CE64
Highfield Ave., Orp. 137 ET106
Highfield Ave., Pnr. 58 BZ57
Highfield Ave., Wem. 60 CL62
Highfield Clo. N22 49 DN53
Highfield Clo. NW9 60 CQ57
Highfield Clo. SE13 107 ED87
Highfield Clo., Lthd. 129 CD111
Highfield Clo., Nthwd. 43 BS53
Highfield Clo., Rom. 55 FC51
Highfield Clo., Surb. 115 CJ102
Highfield Clo., W.Byf. 126 BG113
Highfield Ct. N14 35 DJ44
Highfield Cres., Nthwd. 43 BS53
Highfield Dr., Brom. 122 EE98
Highfield Dr., Epsom 131 CT108
Highfield Dr., Uxb. 56 BL62
Highfield Dr., W.Wick. 121 EB103
Highfield Gdns. NW11 61 CY58
Highfield Grn., Epp. 25 ES31
Highfield Hill SE19 106 DR94
Highfield Link, Rom. 55 FD51
Highfield Pl., Epp. 25 ES31
Highfield Rd. N21 49 DP47
Highfield Rd. NW11 61 CY58
Highfield Rd. W3 74 CP71
Highfield Rd., Bexh. 110 EZ85
Highfield Rd., Brom. 123 EM98
Highfield Rd., Cat. 148 DU122
Highfield Rd., Cher. 112 BG102
Highfield Rd., Chis. 123 ET97
Highfield Rd., Felt. 99 BU88
Highfield Rd., Islw. 87 CF81
Highfield Rd., Nthwd. 43 BS53
Highfield Rd., Pur. 133 DM110
Highfield Rd., Rom. 55 FC52
Highfield Rd., Sun. 113 BT98
Highfield Rd., Surb. 116 CQ101
Highfield Rd., Sutt. 132 DE106
Highfield Rd. (Cheshunt), Wal.Cr. 22 DS26
Highfield Rd., Walt. 113 BU102
Highfield Rd. (Bushey), Wat. 30 BY43
Highfield Rd., W.Byf. 126 BG113

Highfield Rd., West. 150 EJ117
Highfield Rd., Wdf.Grn. 52 EL52
Highfield Twrs., Rom. 55 FD50
Highfield Way, Pot.B. 20 DB32
Highfield Way, Rick. 28 BG44
Highfields, Ash. 143 CK119
Highfields, Lthd. 143 CD124
Highfields (Cuffley), Pot.B. 21 DL28
Highfields, Rad. 31 CF35
Highfields Gro. N6 62 DF60
Highgate Ave. N6 63 DH59
Highgate Clo. N6 62 DG59
Highgate High St. N6 62 DG60
Highgate Hill N6 63 DH60
Highgate Hill N19 63 DH60
Highgate Rd. NW5 63 DH63
Highgate Wk. SE23 106 DW89
Highgate W. Hill N6 62 DG60
Highgrove Clo. N11 48 DG50
Balmoral Ave.
Highgrove Clo., Chis. 122 EL95
Highgrove Ct., Beck. 107 EA94
Park Rd.
Highgrove Ms., Cars. 118 DF104
Highgrove Rd., Dag. 68 EW64
Highgrove Way, Ruis. 57 BU58
Highland Ave. W7 73 CE72
Highland Ave., Dag. 69 FC62
Highland Ave., Loug. 38 EL44
Highland Cotts., Wall. 133 DH105
Highland Ct. E18 52 EH53
Highland Cft., Beck. 107 EB92
Highland Dr. (Bushey), Wat. 44 CC45
Highland Pk., Felt. 99 BT91
Highland Rd. SE19 106 DS93
Highland Rd., Bexh. 110 FA85
Highland Rd., Brom. 122 EF95
Highland Rd., Nthwd. 43 BT54
Highland Rd., Pur. 133 DN114
Highland Rd., Sev. 139 FB110
Highlands, Ash. 143 CJ119
Highlands, Wat. 44 BW46
Highlands, The, Edg. 46 CP54
Highlands, The, Pot.B. 20 DC30
Highlands, The, Rick. 42 BH45
Highlands Ave. N21 35 DM43
Worlds End La.
Highlands Ave. W3 74 CQ73
Highlands Ave., Lthd. 143 CJ122
Highlands Clo. N4 63 DL59
Mount Vw. Rd.
Highlands Clo., Houns. 86 CB81
Highlands Clo., Lthd. 143 CH122
Highlands Gdns., Ilf. 67 EM60
Highlands Heath SW15 103 CW87
Highlands Hill, Swan. 125 FG96
Highlands Pk., Lthd. 143 CK123
Highlands Pk., Sev. 155 FL121
Highlands Rd., Barn. 34 DA43
Highlands Rd., Lthd. 143 CH122
Highlands Rd., Orp. 124 EV101
Highlea Clo. NW9 46 CS53
Highlever Rd. W10 75 CW71
Highmead SE18 95 ET80
Highmead Cres., Wem. 74 CM66
Highmore Rd. SE3 94 EE80
Highpoint, Wey. 126 BN106
Highridge Clo., Epsom 144 CS115
Highshore Rd. SE15 92 DT82
Highstead Cres., Erith 97 FE80
Highstone Ave. E11 66 EG58
Highview, Cat. 148 DS124
Highview Ave., Edg. 46 CQ49
Highview Ave., Wall. 133 DM106
Highview Clo., Pot.B. 20 DC33
Highview Gdns.
Highview Gdns. N3 61 CY56
Highview Gdns. N11 49 DJ50
Highview Gdns., Edg. 46 CQ50
Highview Gdns., Pot.B. 20 DC33
Highview Ho., Rom. 68 EY56
Highview Rd. SE19 106 DR93
Highview Rd. W13 73 CG71
Highway, The E1 78 DU73
Highway, The E14 79 DX73
Highway, The, Orp. 138 EV106
Highway, The, Stan. 45 CF53
Highway, The, Sutt. 132 DC109
Highwold, Couls. 146 DG118
Highwood, Brom. 121 ED97
Highwood Ave. N12 48 DC49
Highwood Ave. (Bushey), Wat. 30 BZ39
Highwood Clo., Ken. 148 DQ117
Highwood Clo., Orp. 123 EQ103
Highwood Dr., Orp. 123 EQ103
Highwood Gdns., Ilf. 67 EM57
Highwood Gro. NW7 46 CR50
Highwood Hall La., Hem.H. 15 BQ25
Highwood Hill NW7 47 CT47
Highwood La., Loug. 39 EN43
Highwood Rd. N19 63 DL62
Highwoods, Lthd. 143 CJ121
Highworth Rd. N11 49 DK51
Hilary Ave., Mitch. 118 DG97
Hilary Clo. SW6 90 DB80
Hilary Clo., Erith 97 FB81
Hilary Rd. W12 75 CT72
Hilbert Rd., Sutt. 117 CX104
Hilborough Way, Orp. 137 ER106
Hilda May Ave., Swan. 125 FD97
Hilda Rd. E6 80 EK66
Hilda Rd. E16 80 EE70
Hilda Ter. SW9 91 DN82
Hilda Vale Clo., Orp. 137 EP105
Hilda Vale Rd., Orp. 137 EN105
Hilden Dr., Erith 97 FH80
Hildenborough Gdns., Brom. 108 EE93
Hildenlea Pl., Brom. 122 EE96
Hilders, The, Ash. 144 CP117
Hildreth St. SW12 105 DH88
Hildyard Rd. SW6 90 DA79
Hiley Rd. NW10 75 CW69
Hilfield La., Wat. 30 CB39
Hilfield La. S. (Bushey), Wat. 31 CF44
Hilgrove Rd. NW6 76 DC66
Hiliary Gdns., Stan. 45 CJ54
Hill, The, Cat. 148 DT124
Hill Barn, S.Croy. 134 DS111
Hill Brow, Brom. 122 EK95
Hill Brow, Dart. 111 FF86
Hill Brow Clo., Bex. 111 FD91
Hill Clo. NW2 61 CV62
Hill Clo. NW11 62 DA58
Hill Clo., Barn. 33 CW43
Hill Clo., Chis. 109 EP92
Hill Clo., Har. 59 CE62
Hill Clo., Pur. 134 DQ112
Hill Clo., Stan. 45 CH49
Hill Ct., Nthlt. 58 CA64
Hill Cres. N20 48 DB47
Hill Cres., Bex. 111 FC88
Hill Cres., Har. 59 CG57
Hill Cres., Surb. 116 CM99
Hill Cres., Wor.Pk. 117 CW103
Hill Crest, Pot.B. 20 DC34
Hill Crest, Sev. 154 FG122
Hill Crest, Sid. 110 EU87
Hill Crest Gdns. N3 61 CY56
Hill Dr. NW9 60 CQ60
Hill Dr. SW16 119 DM97
Hill End, Orp. 123 ET103
The App.
Hill End Rd., Uxb. 42 BJ52
Hill Fm. Ave., Wat. 15 BU33
Hill Fm. Clo., Wat. 15 BU33
Hill Fm. Rd. W10 75 CW71
Hill Gro., Rom. 69 FE55
Hill Ho. Ave., Stan. 45 CF52
Hill Ho. Clo. N21 49 DN45
Hill Ho. Dr., Wey. 126 BN111
Hill Ho. Rd. SW16 105 DM92
Hill La., Ruis. 57 BQ60
Hill La., Tad. 145 CY121
Hill Leys (Cuffley), Pot.B. 21 DL28
Hill Pk. Dr., Lthd. 143 CF119
Hill Path SW16 105 DM92
Valley Rd.
Hill Ri. N9 36 DV44
Hill Ri. NW11 62 DB56
Hill Ri. SE23 106 DV88
London Rd.
Hill Ri., Esher 115 CH103
Hill Ri., Grnf. 72 CC66
Hill Ri., Pot.B. 20 DC34
Hill Ri. (Cuffley), Pot.B. 21 DL28
Hill Ri., Rich. 101 CK85
Hill Ri., Rick. 42 BH45
Hill Ri., Ruis. 57 BQ60
Hill Ri., Walt. 113 BT101
Hill Rd. N10 48 DF53
Hill Rd. NW8 76 DC68
Hill Rd., Cars. 132 DE107
Hill Rd., Epp. 39 ES38
Hill Rd., Har. 59 CG57
Hill Rd., Lthd. 142 CB122
Hill Rd., Mitch. 119 DH95
Hill Rd., Nthwd. 43 BR51
Hill Rd., Pnr. 58 BY58
Hill Rd., Pur. 133 DM112
Hill Rd., Sutt. 132 DB106
Hill Rd., Wem. 59 CH62
Hill St. W1 8 G2
Hill St. W1 76 DG74
Hill St., Rich. 101 CK85
Hill Top NW11 62 DB56
Hill Top, Loug. 39 EN40
Hill Top, Mord. 118 DB100
Hill Top Clo., Loug. 39 EN41
Hill Top Pl., Loug. 39 EN41
Hill Top Vw., Wdf.Grn. 53 EM51
Hill Vw. Clo., Tad. 145 CW121
Shelvers Way
Hill Vw. Cres., Orp. 123 ET102
Hill Vw. Dr., Well. 95 ES82
Hill Vw. Gdns. NW9 60 CR57
Hill Vw. Rd., Esher 129 CG108
Hill Vw. Rd., Orp. 123 ET102
Hill Vw. Rd., Twick. 101 CG86
Hillars Heath Rd., Couls. 147 DL115
Hillary Cres., Walt. 114 BW102
Hillary Ri., Barn. 34 DA42
Hillary Rd., Sthl. 86 CA76
Hillbeck Clo. SE15 92 DW80
Hillbeck Way, Grnf. 73 CD67
Hillborne Clo., Hayes 85 BU78
Hillborough Ave., Sev. 155 FK122
Hillborough Clo. SW19 104 DC94
Hillbrook Gdns., Wey. 126 BN108
Hillbrook Rd. SW17 104 DF90
Hillbrow, N.Mal. 117 CT97
Hillbrow Rd., Brom. 108 EE94
Hillbrow Rd., Esher 128 CC105
Hillbury Ave., Har. 59 CH57
Hillbury Clo., Warl. 148 DW118
Hillbury Gdns., Warl. 148 DW118
Hillbury Rd. SW17 105 DH90
Hillbury Rd., Warl. 148 DU117
Hillbury Rd., Whyt. 148 DU117
Hillcote Ave. SW16 105 DN94
Hillcourt Ave. N12 48 DB51
Hillcourt Est. N16 64 DR60
Hillcourt Rd. SE22 106 DV86
Hillcrest N6 62 DG59
Hillcrest N21 49 DN45
Hillcrest, Wey. 127 BP105
Hillcrest Ave. NW11 61 CY57
Hillcrest Ave., Edg. 46 CP49
Hillcrest Ave., Pnr. 58 BX56
Hillcrest Clo. SE26 106 DU91
Hillcrest Clo., Beck. 121 DZ99
Hillcrest Clo., Epsom 145 CT115
Hillcrest Gdns. NW2 61 CU62
Hillcrest Gdns., Esher 115 CF104
Hillcrest Par., Couls. 133 DH114
Hillcrest Rd. E17 51 ED54
Hillcrest Rd. E18 52 EF54
Hillcrest Rd. W3 74 CN74
Hillcrest Rd. W5 74 CL71
Hillcrest Rd., Brom. 108 EG91
Hillcrest Rd., Dart. 111 FF87
Hillcrest Rd., Horn. 69 FG59
Hillcrest Rd., Loug. 38 EK44
Hillcrest Rd., Ong. 27 FE30
Hillcrest Rd., Orp. 124 EU103
Hillcrest Rd., Pur. 133 DM110
Hillcrest Rd., Rad. 18 CN33
Hillcrest Rd., West. 150 EK116
Hillcrest Rd., Whyt. 148 DT117
Hillcrest Vw., Beck. 121 DZ100
Hillcrest Way, Epp. 26 EU31
Hillcroft, Loug. 39 EN40
Hillcroft Ave., Pnr. 58 BZ58
Hillcroft Ave., Pur. 133 DJ113
Hillcroft Cres. W5 73 CK72
Hillcroft Cres., Ruis. 58 BX62
Hillcroft Cres., Wat. 43 BU46
Hillcroft Cres., Wem. 60 CM63
Hillcroft Rd. E6 81 EP71
Hillcroome Rd., Sutt. 132 DD107
Hillcross Ave., Mord. 117 CX100
Hilldale Rd., Sutt. 131 CZ105
Hilldeane Rd., Pur. 133 DN109
Hilldown Rd. SW16 105 DL94
Hilldown Rd., Brom. 122 EE102
Hilldrop Cres. N7 63 DK64
Hilldrop Est. N7 63 DK64
Hilldrop La. N7 63 DK64
Hilldrop Rd. N7 63 DK64
Hilldrop Rd., Brom. 108 EG93
Hillend SE18 95 EP81
Hillersdon Ave. SW13 89 CU82
Hillersdon Ave., Edg. 46 CM50
Hillery Clo. SE17 11 L9
Hilley Fld. La., Lthd. 142 CC122
Hillfield Ave. N8 63 DL57
Hillfield Ave. NW9 60 CS57
Hillfield Ave., Mord. 118 DE100
Hillfield Ave., Wem. 74 CL66
Hillfield Clo., Har. 58 CC56
Hillfield Ct. NW3 62 DE64
Hillfield Pk. N10 63 DH55
Hillfield Pk. N21 49 DN47
Hillfield Pk. Ms. N10 63 DH56
Hillfield Rd. NW6 61 CZ64
Hillfield Rd., Hmptn. 100 BZ94
Hillfield Rd., Sev. 153 FE120
Hillfoot Ave., Rom. 55 FC53
Hillfoot Rd., Rom. 55 FC53
Hillgate Pl. SW12 105 DH87
Hillgate Pl. W8 76 DA74
Hillgate St. W8 76 DA74
Hillhouse, Wal.Abb. 24 EF33
Hillhurst Gdns., Cat. 148 DS120
Hilliard Rd., Nthwd. 43 BT53
Hilliards Ct. E1 78 DV74
Wapping High St.
Hilliards Rd., Uxb. 70 BK72
Hilliards St. E1 78 DW74
Wapping High St.
Hillier Clo., Barn. 34 DB44
Hillier Gdns., Croy. 133 DN106
Crowley Cres.
Hillier Pl., Chess. 129 CJ107
Hillier Rd. SW11 104 DF86
Hilliers Ave., Uxb. 70 BN69
Harlington Rd.
Hilliers La., Croy. 119 DL104
Hillingdale, West. 150 EH118
Hillingdon Ave., Sev. 155 FJ121
Hillingdon Ave., Stai. 98 BL88
Hillingdon Hill, Uxb. 70 BL69
Hillingdon Ri., Sev. 155 FK122
Hillingdon Rd., Bexh. 97 FC82
Hillingdon Rd., Uxb. 70 BJ67
Hillingdon Rd., Wat. 15 BU34
Hillingdon St. SE5 91 DP79
Hillingdon St. SE17 91 DP79
Hillington Gdns., Wdf.Grn. 52 EK54
Hillman Clo., Uxb. 56 BL64
Hillman Dr. W10 75 CW70
Hillman St. E8 78 DV65
Hillmarton Rd. N7 63 DL64
Hillmead Dr. SW9 91 DP84
Hillmont Rd., Esher 115 CE104
Hillmore Gro. SE26 107 DX92
Hillreach SE18 95 EM78
Hillrise Ave., Wat. 30 BX38
Hillrise Rd. N19 63 DL59
Hillrise Rd., Rom. 55 FC51
Hills La., Nthwd. 43 BS53
Hills Ms. W5 74 CL73
Hills Pl. W1 5 K9
Hills Rd., Buck.H. 52 EH46
Hillsboro Rd. SE22 106 DS85
Hillsborough Grn., Wat. 43 BU48
Ashburnham Dr.
Hillsgrove Clo., Well. 96 EW80
Hillside NW9 60 CR56
Hillside NW10 74 CQ66
Hillside SW19 103 CX93
Hillside, Bans. 145 CY115
Hillside, Barn. 34 DC43
Hillside, Erith 97 FD77
Hillside, Uxb. 56 BJ57
Hillside, The, Orp. 138 EV109
Hillside Ave. N11 48 DF51
Hillside Ave., Borwd. 32 CP42
Hillside Ave., Pur. 133 DP113
Hillside Ave. (Cheshunt), Wal.Cr. 23 DX31
Hillside Ave., Wem. 60 CM63
Hillside Ave., Wdf.Grn. 52 EJ50
Hillside Clo. NW8 76 DB68
Hillside Clo., Abb.L. 15 BS32
Hillside Clo., Bans. 145 CY116
Hillside Clo., Mord. 117 CY98
Hillside Clo., Wdf.Grn. 52 EJ50
Hillside Ct., Swan. 125 FG98
Hillside Cres., Enf. 36 DR38
Hillside Cres., Har. 58 CC60
Hillside Cres., Nthwd. 43 BU53
Hillside Cres. (Cheshunt), Wal.Cr. 23 DX31
Hillside Cres., Wat. 30 BY44
Pinner Rd.
Hillside Dr., Edg. 46 CN51
Hillside Est. N15 64 DT58
Hillside Gdns. E17 65 ED55
Hillside Gdns. N6 62 DG58
Hillside Gdns. SW2 105 DN89
Hillside Gdns., Barn. 33 CY42
Hillside Gdns., Edg. 46 CM49
Hillside Gdns., Har. 60 CL59
Hillside Gdns., Nthwd. 43 BU52
Hillside Gdns., Wall. 133 DJ108
Hillside Gro. N14 49 DK45
Hillside Gro. NW7 47 CU52
Hillside La., Brom. 122 EG103
Hillside Pas. SW2 105 DM89
Hillside Ri., Nthwd. 43 BU52
Hillside Rd. N15 64 DS58
Hillside Rd. SW2 105 DM89
Hillside Rd. W5 74 CL71
Hillside Rd., Ash. 144 CM117
Hillside Rd., Brom. 122 EF97
Hillside Rd., Couls. 147 DL118
Hillside Rd., Croy. 133 DP106
Hillside Rd., Dart. 111 FG86
Hillside Rd., Epsom 131 CV110
Hillside Rd., Nthwd. 43 BU52
Hillside Rd., Pnr. 43 BV53
Hillside Rd., Rad. 31 CH35
Hillside Rd., Sev. 155 FK123
Hillside Rd., Sthl. 72 CA70
Hillside Rd., Surb. 116 CM98
Hillside Rd., Sutt. 131 CZ108
Hillside Rd. (Bushey), Wat. 30 BY43
Hillside Rd., West. 150 EL119
Hillside Rd., Whyt. 148 DU118
Hillsleigh Rd. W8 75 CZ74
Hillsmead Way, S.Croy. 134 DU113
Hillstowe St. E5 64 DW62
Hilltop, Sutt. 117 CZ101
Hilltop Clo., Lthd. 143 CJ123
Hilltop Clo. (Cheshunt), Wal.Cr. 22 DT26
Hilltop Gdns. NW4 47 CV53
Great N. Way
Hilltop Gdns., Orp. 123 ES103
Hilltop Rd. NW6 76 DA66
Hilltop Rd., Kings L. 15 BR27
Hilltop Rd., Whyt. 148 DS117
Hilltop Wk., Cat. 149 DY120
Hilltop Way, Stan. 45 CG48
Hillview SW20 103 CV94
Hillview, Mitch. 119 DL98
Hillview Ave., Har. 60 CL57
Hillview Clo., Pnr. 44 BZ51
Hillview Clo., Pur. 133 DP111
Hillview Cres., Ilf. 67 EM58
Hillview Gdns. NW4 61 CX56
Hillview Gdns., Har. 58 CA55
Hillview Gdns. (Cheshunt), Wal.Cr. 23 DX27
Hillview Rd. NW7 47 CX49
Hillview Rd., Chis. 109 EN92
Hillview Rd., Pnr. 44 BZ52
Hillview Rd., Sutt. 118 DC104
Hillway N6 62 DG60
Hillway NW9 60 CS59
Hillworth Rd. SW2 105 DN87
Hilly Flds. Cres. SE4 93 EA83
Hillyard Rd. W7 73 CE71
Hillyard St. SW9 91 DN81
Hillyfield E17 65 DY55
Hillyfields, Loug. 39 EN40
Hilsea St. E5 64 DW63
Hilton Ave. N12 48 DD50
Hilton Clo., Uxb. 70 BH68
Hilton Way, S.Croy. 148 DV115
Hilversum Cres. SE22 106 DS85
East Dulwich Gro.
Himalayan Way, Wat. 29 BT43
Himley Rd. SW17 104 DE92
Hinchcliffe Clo., Wall. 133 DM108
Roe Way
Hinchley Clo., Esher 115 CF104
Hinchley Dr., Esher 115 CF104
Hinchley Way, Esher 115 CG104
Hinckler Clo., Wall. 133 DL108
Kingsford Ave.
Hinckley Rd. SE15 92 DU84
Hind Clo., Chig. 53 ET50
Hind Ct. EC4 6 E9
Hind Cres., Erith 97 FD79
Hind Gro. E14 79 EA72
Hinde Ms. W1 76 DG72
Marylebone La.
Hinde St. W1 4 G8
Hinde St. W1 76 DG72
Hindes Rd., Har. 59 CD57
Hindhead Clo. N16 64 DS60
Hindhead Clo., Uxb. 71 BP71
Aldenham Dr.
Hindhead Gdns., Nthlt. 72 BY67
Hindhead Grn., Wat. 44 BW50
Hindhead Way, Wall. 133 DL106
Hindmans Rd. SE22 106 DU85
Hindmans Way, Dag. 82 EZ70
Hindmarsh Clo. E1 78 DU73
Cable St.
Hindrey Rd. E5 64 DV64
Hindsley's Pl. SE23 106 DW89
Hinkler Rd., Har. 59 CK55
Hinkley Clo., Uxb. 56 BJ56
Hinksey Path SE2 96 EX75
Hinstock Rd. SE18 95 EQ79
Hinton Ave., Houns. 86 BX84
Hinton Clo. SE9 108 EL88
Hinton Rd. N18 50 DS49
Hinton Rd. SE24 91 DP83
Hinton Rd., Uxb. 70 BJ67
Hinton Rd., Wall. 133 DJ107
Hippodrome Ms. W11 75 CY73
Portland Rd.
Hippodrome Pl. W11 75 CY73
Hiroshima Wk. SE7 94 EH76
Hiscocks Ho. NW10 74 CQ66
Hitcham Rd. E17 65 DZ59
Hitchcock Clo., Shep. 112 BM97
Hitchen Hatch La., Sev. 154 FG124
Hitchin Sq. E3 79 DY68
Hither Grn. La. SE13 107 EC85
Hitherbroom Rd., Hayes 71 BU74
Hitherfield Rd. SW16 105 DM89
Hitherfield Rd., Dag. 68 EY61
Hitherlands SW12 105 DH89
Hithermoor Rd., Stai. 98 BG86
Hitherwell Dr., Har. 45 CD53
Hitherwood Dr. SE19 106 DT91
Hive Clo. (Bushey), Wat. 45 CD47
Hive Rd. (Bushey), Wat. 45 CD47
Hoadly Rd. SW16 105 DK90
Hobart Clo. N20 48 DE47
Hobart Clo., Hayes 72 BX70
Hobart Dr., Hayes 72 BX70
Hobart Gdns., Th.Hth. 120 DR97
Hobart La., Hayes 72 BX70
Hobart Pl. SW1 9 H6
Hobart Pl. SW1 91 DH76
Hobart Pl., Rich. 102 CM86
Chisholm Rd.
Hobart Rd., Dag. 68 EX63
Hobart Rd., Hayes 72 BX70
Hobart Rd., Ilf. 53 EQ54
Hobart Rd., Wor.Pk. 117 CV104
Hobbayne Rd. W7 73 CD72
Hobbes Wk. SW15 103 CV85
Hobbs Clo. (Cheshunt), Wal.Cr. 23 DX29
Hobbs Clo., W.Byf. 126 BH113
Hobbs Cross Rd., Epp. 40 EW35
Hobbs Grn. N2 62 DC55
Hobbs Ms., Ilf. 67 ET61
Ripley Rd.
Hobbs Pl. Est. N1 78 DS67
Pitfield St.
Hobbs Rd. SE27 106 DQ91
Hobday St. E14 79 EB71
Hobill Wk., Surb. 116 CM100
Hoblands End, Chis. 109 ES93
Hobsons Pl. E1 78 DU71
Hanbury St.
Hobury St. SW10 90 DC79
Hockenden La., Swan. 124 FA97
Hocker St. E2 7 P3
Hockett Clo. SE8 93 DY77
Hockley Ave. E6 80 EL68
Hockley Dr., Rom. 55 FH54
Hocroft Ave. NW2 61 CZ62
Hocroft Rd. NW2 61 CZ63
Hocroft Wk. NW2 61 CZ62
Hodder Dr., Grnf. 73 CF68
Hoddesdon Rd., Belv. 96 FA78
Hoddesdon Rd., Brox. 23 DX26
Hodford Rd. NW11 61 CZ60
Hodges Way, Wat. 29 BU44
Hodgkin Clo. SE28 82 EX73
Fleming Way
Hodnet Gro. SE16 93 DX77
Hawkstone Rd.
Hodsoll Ct., Orp. 124 EX99
Hodson Clo., Har. 58 BZ62
Hodson Cres., Orp. 124 EX99
Hoe, The, Wat. 44 BX47
Hoe La., Enf. 36 DU38
Hoe La., Rom. 40 EV41
Hoe St. E17 65 EA57
Hofland Rd. W14 89 CX76
Hog Hill Rd., Rom. 54 EZ52
Hogan Ms. W2 76 DD71
Porteus Rd.
Hogan Way E5 64 DU61
Geldeston Rd.
Hogarth Ave., Ashf. 99 BQ93
Hogarth Clo. E16 80 EK71
Hogarth Clo. W5 74 CL71
Hogarth Ct. EC3 7 N10

Hogarth Ct. SE19 106 DT91
Fountain Dr.
Hogarth Ct. (Bushey), Wat. 44 CB45
Steeplands
Hogarth Cres. SW19 118 DD95
Hogarth Cres., Croy. 120 DQ101
Hogarth Gdns., Houns. 86 CA80
Hogarth Hill NW11 61 CZ56
Hogarth La. W4 88 CS79
Hogarth Pl. SW5 90 DB77
Hogarth Rd.
Hogarth Reach, Loug. 39 EM43
Hogarth Rd. SW5 90 DB77
Hogarth Rd., Dag. 68 EV64
Hogarth Rd., Edg. 46 CN54
Hogarth Roundabout W4 88 CS79
Hogarth Way, Hmptn. 114 CC95
Hogg La., Borwd. 31 CG42
Hogs Orchard, Swan. 125 FH95
School La.
Hogscross La., Couls. 146 DF123
Hogshead Pas. E1 78 DV73
Pennington St.
Hogshill La., Cob. 127 BV114
Hogsmill Way, Epsom 130 CQ106
Hogtrough Hill, West. 151 ET120
Holbeach Gdns., Sid. 109 ES86
Holbeach Ms. SW12 105 DH88
Harberson Rd.
Holbeach Rd. SE6 107 EA87
Holbeck La. (Cheshunt), Wal.Cr. 22 DT26
Holbeck Row SE15 92 DU80
Holbein Gate, Nthwd. 43 BS50
Holbein Ms. SW1 8 F10
Holbein Ms. SW1 90 DG78
Holbein Pl. SW1 8 F9
Holbein Pl. SW1 90 DG77
Holbein Ter., Dag. 68 EV63
Marlborough Rd.
Holberton Gdns. NW10 75 CV69
Holborn EC1 6 D7
Holborn EC1 77 DN71
Holborn Circ. EC1 6 E7
Holborn Pl. WC1 6 B7
Holborn Rd. E13 80 EH70
Holborn Viaduct EC1 6 E7
Holborn Viaduct EC1 77 DN71
Holborn Way, Mitch. 118 DF96
Holbrook Clo. N19 63 DH60
Dartmouth Pk. Hill
Holbrook Clo., Enf. 36 DT39
Holbrook La., Chis. 109 ER94
Holbrook Rd. E15 80 EF68
Holbrook Way, Brom. 123 EM100
Holbrooke Ct. N7 63 DL62
Holbrooke Pl., Rich. 101 CK85
Hill Ri.
Holburne Clo. SE3 94 EJ81
Holburne Gdns. SE3 94 EK81
Holburne Rd. SE3 94 EJ81
Holcombe Hill NW7 47 CU48
Highwood Hill
Holcombe Rd. N17 64 DT55
Holcombe Rd., Ilf. 67 EN59
Holcombe St. W6 89 CV78
Holcote Clo., Belv. 96 EY76
Blakemore Way
Holcroft Rd. E9 78 DW66
Holdbrook, Wal.Cr. 23 EA34
Holdbrook N., Wal.Cr. 23 DZ34
Eleanor Way
Holdbrook S., Wal.Cr. 23 DZ34
Queens Way
Holden Ave. N12 48 DB50
Holden Ave. NW9 60 CQ60
Holden Clo., Dag. 68 EV62
Holden Pt. E15 79 ED65
Waddington Rd.
Holden Rd. N12 48 DB50
Holden St. SW11 90 DG82
Holdenby Rd. SE4 107 DY85
Holdenhurst Ave. N12 48 DB52
Holder Clo. N3 48 DB52
Holderness Way SE27 105 DP92
Holdernesse Clo., Islw. 87 CG81
Blenheim Way
Holdernesse Rd. SW17 104 DF90
Holders Hill Ave. NW4 47 CX54
Holders Hill Circ. NW7 47 CY52
Dollis Rd.
Holders Hill Cres. NW4 47 CX54
Holders Hill Dr. NW4 61 CX55
Holders Hill Gdns. NW4 47 CY54
Holders Hill Rd. NW4 47 CX54
Holders Hill Rd. NW7 47 CY53
Holdgate St. SE7 94 EK76
Westmoor St.
Holecroft, Wal.Abb. 24 EE34
Holford Pl. WC1 6 C2
Holford Rd. NW3 62 DC62
Holford St. WC1 6 D2
Holford St. WC1 77 DN69
Holgate Ave. SW11 90 DD83
Holgate Gdns., Dag. 82 FA65
Holgate Rd., Dag. 68 FA64
Holland Ave. SW20 117 CT95
Holland Ave., Sutt. 132 DA108
Holland Clo., Barn. 48 DD45
Holland Clo., Brom. 122 EF103
Holland Clo., Rom. 69 FC57
Holland Clo., Stan. 45 CH50
Holland Dr. SE23 107 DY90
Holland Gdns. W14 89 CY76
Holland Gdns., Wat. 30 BW35
Holland Gro. SW9 91 DN80
Holland Pk. W8 89 CZ75
Holland Pk. W11 75 CY74
Holland Pk. Ave. W11 75 CY74
Holland Pk. Ave., Ilf. 67 ES58
Holland Pk. Gdns. W14 89 CY75
Holland Pk. Ms. W11 75 CZ74
Holland Pk. Rd. W14 89 CZ76
Holland Pas. N1 78 DQ67
Basire St.
Holland Pl. W8 90 DB75
Kensington Ch. St.
Holland Rd. E6 81 EM67
Holland Rd. E15 80 EE69
Holland Rd. NW10 75 CU67
Holland Rd. SE25 120 DU99
Holland Rd. W14 89 CX75
Holland Rd., Wem. 73 CK65
Holland St. SE1 10 G2
Holland St. SE1 77 DP74
Holland St. W8 90 DA75
Holland Vill. Rd. W14 89 CY75
Holland Wk. N19 63 DK60
Duncombe Rd.
Holland Wk. W8 89 CZ75
Holland Wk., Stan. 45 CG50
Holland Way, Brom. 122 EF103
Hollands, The, Felt. 100 BX91
Hollands, The, Wor.Pk. 117 CT102
Hollar Rd. N16 64 DT62
Stoke Newington High St.
Hollen St. W1 5 L8
Hollen St. W1 77 DK72
Holles Clo., Hmptn. 100 CA93
Holles St. W1 5 J8
Holles St. W1 77 DH72
Holley Rd. W3 88 CS75
Hollickwood Ave. N12 48 DF51
Holliday Sq. SW11 90 DD83
Fowler Clo.
Hollidge Way, Dag. 83 FB65
Hollies, The E11 66 EG57
Hollies, The N20 48 DD46
Hollies, The, Har. 59 CG56
Hollies Ave., Sid. 109 ET89
Hollies Clo. SW16 105 DN93
Hollies Clo., Twick. 101 CF89
Hollies Ct., Add. 126 BJ106
Hollies End NW7 47 CV50
Hollies Rd. W5 87 CJ77
Hollies Way SW12 104 DG87
Bracken Ave.
Hollies Way, Pot.B. 20 DC31
Holligrave Rd., Brom. 122 EG95
Hollingbourne Ave., Bexh. 96 EZ80
Hollingbourne Gdns. W13 73 CH71
Hollingbourne Rd. SE24 106 DQ85
Hollingbourne Twr., Orp. 124 EX102
Hollingsworth Rd., Croy. 134 DV107
Hollington Cres., N.Mal. 117 CT100
Hollington Rd. E6 81 EM69
Hollington Rd. N17 50 DU54
Hollingworth Clo.,W.Mol. 114 BZ98
Hollingworth Rd., Orp. 123 EP101
Hollman Gdns. SW16 105 DP93
Hollow, The, Wdf.Grn. 52 EF49
Hollow Wk., Rich. 88 CL80
Kew Rd.
Holloway La., West Dr. 84 BK79
Holloway Rd. E6 81 EM69
Holloway Rd. E11 66 EE62
Holloway Rd. N7 63 DL62
Holloway Rd. N19 63 DJ61
Holloway St., Houns. 86 CB83
Hollowfield Wk., Nthlt. 72 BY65
Hollows, The, Brent. 88 CM79
Kew Bri. Rd.
Holly Ave., Add. 126 BG110
Holly Ave., Stan. 46 CL54
Holly Ave., Walt. 114 BX102
Holly Bush Hill NW3 62 DC63
Holly Bush La., Hmptn. 100 BZ94
Holly Bush La., Sev. 155 FJ124
Holly Bush Steps NW3 62 DC63
Heath St.
Holly Bush Vale NW3 62 DC63
Heath St.
Holly Clo. NW10 74 CS66
Holly Clo., Buck.H. 52 EK48
Holly Clo., Felt. 100 BY92
Holly Clo., Wall. 133 DH108
Holly Cres., Beck. 121 DZ99
Holly Cres., Wdf.Grn. 51 ED52
Holly Dr. E4 51 EB45
Holly Dr., Brent. 87 CG79
Holly Dr., Pot.B. 20 DB33
Holly Fm. Rd., Sthl. 86 BY78
Holly Gdns., West Dr. 84 BM75
Holly Grn., Wey. 127 BR105
Holly Gro. NW9 60 CQ59
Holly Gro. SE15 92 DT82
Holly Gro., Pnr. 44 BY53
Holly Gro. (Bushey), Wat. 45 CD45
Holly Hedge Ter. SE13 107 ED85
Holly Hill N21 35 DM44
Holly Hill NW3 62 DC63
Holly Hill Dr., Bans. 146 DA116
Holly Hill Rd., Belv. 97 FB78
Holly Hill Rd., Erith 97 FC78
Holly La., Bans. 146 DA116
Holly La. E., Bans. 146 DB116
Holly La. W., Bans. 146 DB117
Holly Lo. Gdns. N6 62 DG60
Holly Ms. SW10 90 DC78
Drayton Gdns.
Holly Mt. NW3 62 DC63
Holly Bush Hill
Holly Pk. N3 61 CZ55
Holly Pk. N4 63 DL59
Holly Pk. Est. N4 63 DM59
Blythwood Rd.
Holly Pk. Gdns. N3 62 DA55
Holly Pk. Rd. N11 48 DG50
Holly Pk. Rd. W7 73 CF74
Holly Rd. E11 66 EF59
Holly Rd. W4 88 CR77
Dolman Rd.
Holly Rd., Enf. 37 DX36
Holly Rd., Hmptn. 100 CC93
Holly Rd., Houns. 86 CB84
Holly Rd., Orp. 138 EU108
Holly Rd., Twick. 101 CG88
Holly St. E8 78 DT65
Holly St. Est. E8 78 DT66
Holly St.
Holly Ter. N20 48 DC47
Holly Tree Ave., Swan. 125 FE96
Holly Tree Rd., Cat. 148 DS122
Elm Gro.
Holly Vw. Clo. NW4 61 CU58
Holly Wk. NW3 62 DC63
Holly Wk., Enf. 36 DQ41
Gentlemans Row
Holly Wk., Rich. 88 CL82
Holly Way, Mitch. 119 DK98
Hollybank Clo., Hmptn. 100 CA92
Hollybank Rd., W.Byf. 126 BG114
Hollyberry La. NW3 62 DC63
Holly Wk.
Hollybrake Clo., Chis. 109 ER94
Hollybush Clo. E11 66 EG57
Hollybush Clo., Har. 45 CE53
Hollybush Clo., Sev. 155 FJ124
Hollybush Clo., Wat. 44 BW45
Hollybush Ct., Sev. 155 FJ124
Hollybush Gdns. E2 78 DV69
Hollybush Hill E11 66 EF59
Hollybush La., Orp. 138 FA107
Hollybush La., Wok. 140 BK119
Hollybush Pl. E2 78 DV69
Bethnal Grn. Rd.
Hollybush Rd., Kings.T. 102 CL92
Hollybush St. E13 80 EH69
Hollybush Wk. SW9 91 DP84
Hollybush Way, Wal.Cr. 22 DU28
Hollycroft Ave. NW3 62 DA62
Hollycroft Ave., Wem. 60 CM61
Hollycroft Clo., West Dr. 84 BN79
Hollycroft Gdns., West Dr. 84 BN79
Hollydale Dr., Brom. 123 EM104
Hollydale Rd. SE15 92 DW81
Hollydene SE15 92 DV81
Hollydown Way E11 65 ED62
Hollyfield Ave. N11 48 DF50
Hollyfield Rd., Surb. 116 CM101
Hollyfields, Brox. 23 DY26
Hollyhedge Rd., Cob. 127 BV114
Hollymead, Cars. 118 DF104
Hollymead Rd., Couls. 146 DG118
Hollymeoak Rd., Couls. 147 DH119
Hollymoor La., Epsom 130 CR110
Hollymount Clo. SE10 93 EC81
Hollytree Clo. SW19 103 CX88
Hollywood Ct., Borwd. 32 CM42
Deacon's Hill Rd.
Hollywood Gdns., Hayes 71 BV72
Hollywood Ms. SW10 90 DC79
Hollywood Rd.
Hollywood Rd. E4 51 DY50
Hollywood Rd. SW10 90 DC79
Hollywood Way, Erith 97 FH81
Hollywood Way, Wdf.Grn. 51 ED52
Hollywoods, Croy. 135 DZ109
Holm Gro., Uxb. 70 BN66
Holm Oak Clo. SW15 103 CZ86
West Hill
Holm Oak Ms. SW4 105 DL85
King's Ave.
Holm Wk. SE3 94 EG82
Blackheath Pk.
Holman Rd. SW11 90 DD82
Holman Rd., Epsom 130 CQ106
Holmbank Dr., Shep. 113 BS98
Holmbridge Gdns., Enf. 37 DX42
Holmbrook Dr. NW4 61 CX57
Holmbury Ct. SW17 104 DF90
Holmbury Ct. SW19 104 DE94
Cavendish Rd.
Holmbury Gdns., Hayes 71 BT74
Church Rd.
Holmbury Gro., Croy. 135 DZ108
Holmbury Pk., Brom. 108 EL94
Holmbury Vw. E5 64 DV60
Holmbush Rd. SW15 103 CY86
Holmcote Gdns. N5 64 DQ64
Holmcroft Way, Brom. 123 EM99
Holmdale Clo., Borwd. 32 CM40
Holmdale Gdns. NW4 61 CX57
Holmdale Rd. NW6 62 DA64
Holmdale Rd., Chis. 109 EQ92
Holmdale Ter. N15 64 DS59
Holmdene Ave. NW7 47 CU51
Holmdene Ave. SE24 106 DQ85
Holmdene Ave., Har. 58 CB55
Holmdene Clo., Beck. 121 EC96
Holme Chase, Wey. 127 BQ107
Holme Clo. (Cheshunt), Wal.Cr. 23 DY31
Holme Lacey Rd. SE12 108 EF86
Holme Lea, Wat. 16 BW34
Kingsway
Holme Pk., Borwd. 32 CM40
Holme Rd. E6 80 EL67
Holme Way, Stan. 45 CF51
Holmead Rd. SW6 90 DB80
Holmebury Clo. (Bushey), Wat. 45 CE47
Holmefield Ct. NW3 76 DE65
Holmes Ave. E17 65 DZ55
Holmes Ave. NW7 47 CY50
Holmes Pl. SW10 90 DC79
Fulham Rd.
Holmes Rd. NW5 77 DH65
Holmes Rd. SW19 104 DC94
Holmes Rd., Twick. 101 CF89
Holmes Ter. SE1 10 D4
Holmes Ter. SE1 91 DN75
Holmesdale, Wal.Cr. 36 DW35
Holmesdale Ave. SW14 88 CP83
Holmesdale Clo. SE25 120 DT97
Holmesdale Rd. N6 63 DH59
Holmesdale Rd. SE25 120 DR99
Holmesdale Rd., Bexh. 96 EX82
Holmesdale Rd., Croy. 120 DR99
Holmesdale Rd., Rich. 88 CM81
Holmesdale Rd., Tedd. 101 CJ94
Holmesley Rd. SE23 107 DY86
Holmewood Gdns. SW2 105 DM87
Holmewood Rd. SE25 120 DS97
Holmewood Rd. SW2 105 DL87
Holmfield Ave. NW4 61 CX57
Holmhurst Rd., Belv. 97 FB78
Holmleigh Rd. N16 64 DS60
Holmleigh Rd. Est. N16 64 DT60
Holmleigh Rd.
Holms St. E2 78 DU68
Audrey St.
Holmsdale Gro., Bexh. 97 FE82
Holmsdale Rd., Sev. 155 FJ123
Holmshaw Clo. SE26 107 DY91
Holmshill La., Borwd. 32 CS36
Holmside Ri., Wat. 43 BV48
Holmside Rd. SW12 104 DG86
Holmsley Clo., N.Mal. 117 CT100
Holmstall Ave., Edg. 60 CQ55
Holmwood Ave., S.Croy. 134 DT113
Holmwood Clo., Add. 126 BG106
Holmwood Clo., Har. 58 CC55
Holmwood Clo., Nthlt. 72 CB65
Holmwood Clo., Sutt. 131 CX109
Holmwood Gdns. N3 48 DA54
Holmwood Gdns., Wall. 133 DH107
Holmwood Gro. NW7 46 CR50
Holmwood Rd., Chess. 129 CK106
Holmwood Rd., Enf. 37 DX36
Holmwood Rd., Ilf. 67 ES61
Holmwood Rd., Sutt. 131 CW110
Holmwood Vill. SE7 94 EG78
Holne Chase N2 62 DC58
Holne Chase, Mord. 117 CZ100
Holness Rd. E15 80 EF65
Holroyd Clo., Esher 129 CF109
Holroyd Rd. SW15 89 CW84
Holroyd Rd., Esher 129 CF109
Holstein Ave., Wey. 126 BN105
Holstein Way, Erith 96 EX76
Holstock Rd., Ilf. 67 EQ61
Holsworth Clo., Har. 58 CC57
Holsworthy Sq. WC1 6 C5
Holsworthy Way, Chess. 129 CJ106
Holt, The, Ilf. 53 EQ51
Holt, The, Wall. 133 DJ105
Holt Clo. N10 62 DG56
Holt Clo. SE28 82 EV73
Holt Clo., Borwd. 32 CM42
Holt Clo., Chig. 53 ET50
Holt Ct. E15 65 EC64
Clays La.
Holt Rd. E16 80 EL74
Holt Rd., Wem. 59 CH62
Holt Way, Chig. 53 ET50
Holton St. E1 79 DX70
Holtsmere Clo., Wat. 30 BW35
Holtwhite Ave., Enf. 36 DQ40
Holtwhites Hill, Enf. 35 DP39
Holtwood Rd., Lthd. 128 CC114
Holwell Pl., Pnr. 58 BY56
Holwood Clo., Walt. 114 BW103
Holwood Pk. Ave., Orp. 137 EM105
Holwood Pl. SW4 91 DK84
Holybourne Ave. SW15 103 CU87
Holyfield Rd., Wal.Abb. 23 EC29
Holyhead Clo. E3 79 EA69
Holyhead Clo. E6 81 EM71
Valiant Way
Holyoak Rd. SE11 10 F8
Holyoake Ct. SE16 93 DZ75
Bryan Rd.
Holyoake Ter., Sev. 154 FG124
Holyoake Wk. N2 62 DC55
Holyoake Wk. W5 73 CJ70
Holyport Rd. SW6 89 CW80
Holyrood Ave., Har. 58 BY63
Holyrood Gdns., Edg. 60 CP55
Holyrood Rd., Barn. 34 DC44
Holyrood St. SE1 11 M3
Holywell Clo. SE3 94 EG79
Holywell Clo., Stai. 98 BL88
Holywell Ind. Est., Wat. 29 BR44
Holywell La. EC2 7 N4
Holywell La. EC2 78 DS70
Holywell Rd., Wat. 29 BU43
Holywell Row EC2 7 M5
Holywell Row EC2 78 DS70
Holywell Way, Stai. 98 BL88
Home Clo., Cars. 118 DF103
Home Clo., Lthd. 143 CD121
Home Clo., Nthlt. 72 BZ69
Home Ct., Felt. 99 BU88
Home Fm. Clo., Epsom 145 CX117
Home Fm. Clo., Esher 128 CB107
Home Fm. Clo., Shep. 113 BS98
Home Fm. Clo., T.Ditt. 115 CF101
Home Fm. Gdns., Walt. 114 BW103
Home Fm. Rd., Rick. 42 BM49
Home Gdns., Dag. 69 FC62
Home Hill, Swan. 111 FF94
Home Lea, Orp. 137 ET106
Home Mead, Stan. 45 CJ53
Home Meadow, Bans. 146 DA116
Holly La.
Home Pk. Mill Link Rd., Kings L. 15 BP31
Home Pk. Rd. SW19 103 CZ91
Home Pk. Wk., Kings.T. 115 CK98
Home Rd. SW11 90 DE82
Homecroft Gdns., Loug. 39 EP42
Homecroft Rd. N22 49 DP53
Homecroft Rd. SE26 106 DW92
Homedean Rd., Sev. 154 FC122
Homefarm Rd. W7 73 CE72
Homefield, Wal.Abb. 24 EG32
Homefield, Walt. 128 BX105
Homefield Ave., Ilf. 67 ES57
Homefield Clo. NW10 74 CQ65
Homefield Clo., Epp. 26 EU30
Homefield Clo., Hayes 72 BX70
Homefield Clo., Lthd. 143 CJ121
Homefield Clo., Orp. 124 EV98
Homefield Clo., Swan. 125 FF97
Homefield Gdns. N2 62 DD55
Homefield Gdns., Mitch. 118 DC96
Homefield Gdns., Tad. 145 CW120
Homefield Ms., Beck. 121 EA95
Homefield Pk., Sutt. 132 DB107
Homefield Ri., Orp. 124 EU102
Homefield Rd. SW19 103 CX93
Homefield Rd. W4 89 CT78
Homefield Rd., Brom. 122 EJ95
Homefield Rd., Couls. 147 DP119
Homefield Rd., Edg. 46 CR51
Homefield Rd., Rad. 31 CF37
Homefield Rd., Sev. 154 FE122
Homefield Rd., Walt. 114 BY101
Homefield Rd., Warl. 148 DW119
Homefield Rd. (Bushey), Wat. 30 CA42
Homefield Rd., Wem. 59 CG63
Homefield St. N1 7 M1
Homeland Dr., Sutt. 132 DB109
Homelands, Lthd. 143 CJ121
Homelands Dr. SE19 106 DS94
Homeleigh Ct., Wal.Cr. 22 DV29
Homeleigh Rd. SE15 107 DX85
Homemead SW12 105 DH89
Homemead Rd., Brom. 123 EM99
Homemead Rd., Croy. 120 DW100
Homer Clo., Bexh. 97 FC81
Homer Dr. E14 93 EA77
Homer Rd. E9 79 DY65
Homer Rd., Croy. 121 DX100
Homer Row W1 4 C7
Homer Row W1 76 DE71
Homer St. W1 4 C7
Homer St. W1 76 DE71
Homersham Rd., Kings.T. 116 CN96
Homerton Gro. E9 65 DX64
Homerton High St. E9 64 DW64
Homerton Rd. E9 65 DY64
Homerton Row E9 64 DW64
Homerton Ter. E9 78 DW65
Morning La.
Homesdale Clo. E11 66 EG57
Homesdale Rd., Brom. 122 EJ98
Homesdale Rd., Cat. 148 DR123
Homesdale Rd., Orp. 123 ES101
Homesfield NW11 62 DA57
Homestall Rd. SE22 106 DW85
Homestead, The N11 49 DH49
Homestead Clo., St.Alb. 16 CC27
Homestead Gdns., Esher 129 CE106
Homestead Paddock N14 35 DH43
Homestead Pk. NW2 61 CT62
Homestead Rd. SW6 89 CZ80
Homestead Rd., Cat. 148 DR123
Homestead Rd., Dag. 68 EZ61
Homestead Rd., Orp. 138 EV108
Homestead Rd., Rick. 42 BK45
Park Rd.
Homestead Rd., Stai. 98 BH93
Homestead Way, Croy. 135 EC111
Homewaters Ave., Sun. 113 BT95
Homewillow Clo. N21 35 DP44
Homewood Ave. (Cuffley), Pot.B. 21 DL27
Homewood Clo., Hmptn. 100 BZ93
Fearnley Cres.
Homewood Cres., Chis. 109 ES93
Homewood La., Pot.B. 21 DJ27
Honduras St. EC1 7 H4
Honey Clo., Dag. 83 FB65
Honey Hill, Uxb. 70 BM66
Honey La. EC2 7 J9
Honey La., Wal.Abb. 24 EE33
Honeybourne Rd. NW6 62 DB64
Honeybourne Way, Orp. 123 ER102
Honeybrook, Wal.Abb. 24 EE33
Honeybrook Rd. SW12 105 DJ87
Honeycroft, Loug. 39 EN42
Honeycroft Hill, Uxb. 70 BL66
Honeyden Rd., Sid. 110 EY93
Honeyman Clo. NW6 75 CX66
Honeypot Clo. NW9 60 CM56
Honeypot La. NW9 60 CL55
Honeypot La., Stan. 60 CL55
Honeysett Rd. N17 50 DT54
Reform Row
Honeysuckle Clo., Sthl. 72 BY73

Honeysuckle Gdns., Croy. 121 DX102
Primrose La.
Honeywell Rd. SW11 104 DE86
Honeywood Clo., Pot.B. 20 DD33
Honeywood Rd. NW10 75 CT68
Honeywood Rd., Islw. 87 CG84
Honeywood Wk., Cars. 132 DF105
Honister Clo., Stan. 45 CH53
Honister Gdns., Stan. 45 CH53
Honister Heights, Pur. 134 DR114
Honister Pl., Stan. 45 CH53
Honiton Rd. NW6 75 CZ68
Honiton Rd., Rom. 69 FD58
Honiton Rd., Well. 95 ET82
Honley Rd. SE6 107 EB87
Honnor Rd., Stai. 98 BK94
Honor Oak Pk. SE23 107 DX86
Honor Oak Ri. SE23 106 DW86
Honor Oak Rd. SE23 106 DW88
Hood Ave. N14 35 DH44
Hood Ave. SW14 102 CQ85
Hood Ave., Orp. 124 EV99
Hood Clo., Croy. 119 DP102
Parson's Mead
Hood Ct. EC4 6 E9
Hood Rd. SW20 103 CT94
Hood Rd., Rain. 83 FE68
Hood Wk., Rom. 55 FB53
Hoodcote Gdns. N21 49 DP45
Hook, The, Barn. 34 DD44
Hook Fm. Rd., Brom. 122 EK99
Hook Gate, Enf. 36 DV36
Hook Grn. La., Dart. 111 FF90
Hook Hill, S.Croy. 134 DS110
Hook La., Pot.B. 20 DF32
Hook La., Rom. 40 EZ44
Hook La., Well. 95 ET84
Hook Ri. N., Surb. 116 CN104
Hook Ri. S., Surb. 116 CN104
Hook Rd., Chess. 129 CK106
Hook Rd., Epsom 130 CQ108
Hook Rd., Surb. 116 CL104
Hook Wk., Edg. 46 CQ51
Hookers Rd. E17 65 DX55
Hookfield, Epsom 130 CQ113
Hooking Grn., Har. 58 CB57
Hooks Clo. SE15 92 DV81
Woods Rd.
Hooks Hall Dr., Dag. 69 FC62
Hooks Way SE22 106 DU88
Dulwich Common
Hookstone Way, Wdf.Grn. 52 EK52
Hookwood Rd., Orp. 138 EW111
Hoop La. NW11 61 CZ59
Hooper Rd. E16 80 EG72
Hooper Sq. E1 78 DU73
Hooper St.
Hooper St. E1 78 DU73
Hooper's Ct. SW3 8 D5
Hoopers Yd., Sev. 155 FJ126
Hop Gdns. WC2 77 DL73
St. Martin's La.
Hope Clo. N1 78 DQ65
Wallace Rd.
Hope Clo. SE12 108 EH90
Hope Clo., Sutt. 132 DC106
Hope Clo., Wdf.Grn. 52 EJ51
West Gro.
Hope Grn., Wat. 15 BU33
Hope Pk., Brom. 108 EF94
Hope St. SW11 90 DD83
Hopedale Rd. SE7 94 EH79
Hopefield Ave. NW6 75 CY68
Hopes Clo., Houns. 86 CA79
Old Cote Dr.
Hopetown St. E1 78 DT71
Brick La.
Hopewell St. SE5 92 DR80
Hopewell Yd. SE5 92 DR80
Hopewell St.
Hopfield Ave., W.Byf. 126 BL112
Hopgarden La., Sev. 154 FG128
Hopgood St. W12 75 CW74
Macfarlane Rd.
Hopkins Clo. N10 48 DG52
Cromwell Rd.
Hopkins Ms. E15 80 EF67
West Rd.
Hopkins St. W1 5 L9
Hopkinsons Pl. NW1 76 DG67
Fitzroy Rd.
Hoppers Rd. N13 49 DN47
Hoppers Rd. N21 49 DN47
Hoppett Rd. E4 52 EE47
Hoppety, The, Tad. 145 CX122
Hopping La. N1 77 DP65
St. Mary's Gro.
Hoppingwood Ave., N.Mal. 116 CS97
Hoppit Rd., Wal.Abb. 23 EB33
Hoppner Rd., Hayes 71 BQ68
Hopton Gdns. SE1 10 G2
Hopton Gdns., N.Mal. 117 CU100
Hopton Rd. SW16 105 DL92
Hopton St. SE1 10 G2
Hopton St. SE1 77 DP74
Hopwood Clo. SW17 104 DC90
Hopwood Rd. SE17 92 DR79
Hopwood Wk. E8 78 DU66
Wilman Gro.
Horace Ave., Rom. 69 FC60
Horace Rd. E7 66 EH63
Horace Rd., Ilf. 67 EQ55
Horace Rd., Kings.T. 116 CM97
Horatio Ct. SE16 78 DW74
Rotherhithe St.
Horatio Pl. E14 93 EC75
Cold Harbour
Horatio Pl. SW19 104 DA94
Kingston Rd.
Horatio St. E2 78 DU68
Horatius Way, Croy. 133 DM106
Horbury Cres. W11 76 DA73
Horbury Ms. W11 75 CZ73
Ladbroke Rd.
Horder Rd. SW6 89 CY81
Hordle Prom. E. SE15 92 DT80
Daniel Gdns.
Hordle Prom. N. SE15 92 DT80
Daniel Gdns.
Hordle Prom. S. SE15 92 DT80
Pentridge St.
Hordle Prom. W. SE15 92 DS80
Diamond St.
Horizon Way SE7 94 EH77
Horley Clo., Bexh. 110 FA85
Horley Rd. SE9 108 EL91
Hormead Rd. W9 75 CZ70
Horn La. SE10 94 EG77
Horn La. W3 74 CQ74
Horn La., Bexh. 97 FC82
Horn La., Wdf.Grn. 52 EG51
Horn Pk. Clo. SE12 108 EH85
Horn Pk. La. SE12 108 EH85
Hornbeam Clo. SE11 10 D8
Hornbeam Clo., Borwd. 32 CN39
Hornbeam Clo., Buck.H. 52 EK48
Hornbeam Rd.
Hornbeam Clo., Epp. 39 ER37
Hornbeam Clo., Nthlt. 58 BZ64
Hornbeam Cres., Brent. 87 CH80
Hornbeam Gro. E4 52 EE48
Hornbeam La. E4 38 EE43
Hornbeam La., Bexh. 97 FC82
Hornbeam Rd., Buck.H. 52 EK48
Hornbeam Rd., Epp. 39 ER37
Hornbeam Rd., Hayes 72 BW71
Hornbeam Ter., Cars. 118 DE102
Hornbeam Twr. E11 65 ED62
Hollydown Way
Hornbeam Wk., Rich. 102 CM89
Hornbeam Wk., Walt. 127 BT109
Octagon Rd.
Hornbeam Way, Brom. 123 EN100
Hornbeam Way, Wal.Cr. 22 DT29
Hornbeams, St.Alb. 16 BZ30
Hornbeams Ave., Enf. 36 DW35
Hornbeams Ri. N11 48 DG51
Hornbill Clo., Uxb. 70 BK72
Hornblower Clo. SE16 93 DY77
Greenland Quay
Hornbuckle Clo., Har. 59 CD61
Hornby Clo. NW3 76 DD66
Horncastle Clo. SE12 108 EG87
Horncastle Rd. SE12 108 EG87
Hornchurch Clo., Kings.T. 101 CK91
Hornchurch Hill, Whyt. 148 DT117
Hornchurch Rd., Horn. 69 FF60
Horndean Clo. SW15 103 CU88
Bessborough Rd.
Horndon Clo., Rom. 55 FC53
Horndon Grn., Rom. 55 FC53
Horndon Rd., Rom. 55 FC53
Horne Rd., Shep. 112 BM98
Horne Way SW15 89 CW82
Horner La., Mitch. 118 DD96
Hornets, The, Wat. 29 BV42
Hornfair Rd. SE7 94 EJ79
Hornford Way, Rom. 69 FE59
Horniman Dr. SE23 106 DV88
Horning Clo. SE9 108 EL91
Horns End, Pnr. 58 BW56
Horns Rd., Ilf. 67 EQ58
Hornsey La. N6 63 DH60
Hornsey La. N19 63 DH60
Hornsey La. Est. N19 63 DK59
Hornsey La.
Hornsey La. Gdns. N6 63 DJ59
Hornsey Pk. Rd. N8 63 DM55
Hornsey Ri. N19 63 DK59
Hornsey Ri. Gdns. N19 63 DK59
Hornsey Rd. N7 63 DM62
Hornsey Rd. N19 63 DL60
Hornsey St. N7 63 DM64
Hornshay St. SE15 92 DW79
Hornton Pl. W8 90 DA75
Hornton St.
Hornton St. W8 90 DA75
Horsa Clo., Wall. 133 DL108
Kingsford Ave.
Horsa Rd. SE12 108 EJ87
Horsa Rd., Erith 97 FB80
Horse and Dolphin Yd. W1 5 N10
Horse Fair, Kings.T. 115 CK96
Wood St.
Horse Guards Ave. SW1 9 P3
Horse Guards Ave. SW1 77 DL74
Horse Guards Rd. SW1 9 N3
Horse Guards Rd. SW1 77 DK74
Horse Leaze E6 81 EN72
Horse Ride SW1 9 M3
Horse Ride, Cars. 132 DF112
Horse Rd. E7 66 EH62
Centre Rd.
Horse Shoe Cres., Nthlt. 72 CA68
Horse Shoe Yd. W1 5 J10
Horse Yd. N1 77 DP67
Essex Rd.
Horsebridges Clo., Dag. 82 EY67
Horsecroft, Bans. 145 CZ117
Lyme Regis Rd.
Horsecroft Clo., Orp. 124 EV102
Horsecroft Rd., Edg. 46 CR52
Horseferry Pl. SE10 93 EC79
Horseferry Rd. E14 79 DX73
Horseferry Rd. SW1 9 M7
Horseferry Rd. SW1 91 DK77
Horsell Ct., Cher. 112 BH101
Stepgates
Horsell Rd. N5 63 DN64
Horsell Rd., Orp. 124 EV95
Horselydown La. SE1 11 P4
Horselydown La. SE1 92 DT75
Horseman Side, Brwd. 55 FH45
Horsemans Ride, St.Alb. 16 CA25
Horsenden Ave., Grnf. 59 CE64
Horsenden Cres., Grnf. 59 CF64
Horsenden La. N., Grnf. 73 CF65
Horsenden La. S., Grnf. 73 CG67
Horseshoe, The, Bans. 145 CZ115
Horseshoe, The, Couls. 133 DK113
Horseshoe Clo. E14 93 EC78
Ferry St.
Horseshoe Clo. NW2 61 CV61
Horseshoe Clo., Wal.Abb. 24 EG34
Horseshoe Grn., Sutt. 118 DB103
Aultone Way
Horseshoe Hill, Wal.Abb. 24 EH33
Horseshoe La. N20 47 CX46
Horseshoe La., Enf. 36 DQ41
Chase Side
Horseshoe La., Wat. 15 BV32
Horseshoe Ridge, Wey. 127 BQ111
Horsfeld Gdns. SE9 108 EL85
Horsfeld Rd. SE9 108 EK85
Horsford Rd. SW2 105 DM85
Horsham Ave. N12 48 DE50
Horsham Rd., Bexh. 110 FA86
Horsham Rd., Felt. 99 BQ86
Horsley Clo., Epsom 130 CR113
Horsley Dr., Croy. 135 EC108
Horsley Dr., Kings.T. 101 CK92
Horsley Rd. E4 51 EC47
Horsley Rd., Brom. 122 EH95
Palace Rd.
Horsley Rd., Cob. 141 BU122
Horsley St. SE17 92 DR79
Horsmonden Clo., Orp. 123 ET101
Horsmonden Rd. SE4 107 DZ85
Hortensia Rd. SW10 90 DC80
Horticultural Pl. W4 88 CR78
Heathfield Ter.
Horton Ave. NW2 61 CY63
Horton Bri. Rd., West Dr. 70 BM74
Horton Clo., West Dr. 70 BM74
Horton Gdns., Epsom 130 CQ111
Horton Hill
Horton Hill, Epsom 130 CQ111
Horton Ind. Pk., West Dr. 70 BM74
Horton La., Epsom 130 CP109
Horton Rd. E8 78 DV65
Horton Rd., Stai. 98 BG85
Horton Rd., West Dr. 70 BL74
Horton St. SE13 93 EB83
Horton Way, Croy. 121 DX99
Hortus Rd. E4 51 EC47
Hortus Rd., Sthl. 86 BZ75
Horvath Clo., Wey. 127 BR105
Horwood Ct., Wat. 30 BX37
Hosack Rd. SW17 104 DF88
Hoser Ave. SE12 108 EG89
Hosier La. EC1 6 F7
Hosier La. EC1 77 DP71
Hoskins Clo. E16 80 EJ72
Hoskins Clo., Hayes 85 BT78
Cranford Dr.
Hoskins St. SE10 93 ED78
Hospital Bri. Rd., Twick. 100 CB87
Hospital La., Islw. 101 CF85
Hospital Rd. E9 65 DX64
Homerton Row
Hospital Rd., Houns. 86 CA83
Hospital Rd., Sev. 155 FJ121
Hotham Clo., Swan. 125 FH95
Hotham Clo., W.Mol. 114 CA97
Garrick Gdns.
Hotham Rd. SW15 89 CW83
Hotham Rd. SW19 104 DC94
Hotham Rd. Ms. SW19 104 DC94
Haydons Rd.
Hotham St. E15 80 EE67
Hothfield Pl. SE16 92 DW76
Lower Rd.
Hotspur Rd., Nthlt. 72 CA68
Hotspur St. SE11 10 D10
Hotspur St. SE11 91 DN78
Houblon Rd., Rich. 102 CL85
Houblons Hill, Epp. 26 EW31
Houghton Clo. E8 78 DT65
Buttermere Wk.
Houghton Clo., Hmptn. 100 BY93
Houghton Rd. N15 64 DT57
West Grn. Rd.
Houghton St. WC2 6 C9
Houlder Cres., Croy. 133 DP107
Houndsden Rd. N21 35 DM44
Houndsditch EC3 7 N8
Houndsditch EC3 78 DS72
Houndsfield Rd. N9 50 DV45
Hounslow Ave., Houns. 100 CB85
Hounslow Gdns., Houns. 100 CB85
Hounslow Rd. (Feltham), Felt. 99 BV88
Hounslow Rd. (Hanworth), Felt. 100 BX91
Hounslow Rd., Twick. 100 CB86
Houseman Way SE5 92 DR80
Hopewell St.
Houston Pl., Esher 115 CE102
Lime Tree Ave.
Houston Rd. SE23 107 DY89
Hove Ave. E17 65 DZ57
Hove Gdns., Sutt. 118 DB102
Hoveden Rd. NW2 61 CY64
Hoveton Rd. SE28 82 EW72
How La., Couls. 146 DF119
How Wd., St.Alb. 16 CB28
Howard Ave., Bex. 110 EW88
Howard Ave., Epsom 131 CU110
Howard Business Pk., Wal.Abb. 23 ED33
Howard Clo.
Howard Clo. N11 48 DG47
Howard Clo. NW2 61 CY63
Howard Clo. W3 74 CP72
Howard Clo., Ash. 144 CM118
Howard Clo., Hmptn. 100 CC93
Howard Clo., Lthd. 143 CJ123
Windmill Dr.
Howard Clo., Loug. 38 EL44
Howard Clo., Sun. 99 BT93
Catherine Dr.
Howard Clo., Wal.Abb. 23 ED33
Howard Clo., Wat. 29 BU37
Howard Clo. (Bushey), Wat. 45 CE45
Howard Dr., Borwd. 32 CR42
Howard Ms. N5 63 DP63
Hamilton Pk.
Howard Pl. SW1 9 K7
Howard Rd. E6 81 EM68
Howard Rd. E11 66 EE62
Howard Rd. E17 65 EA55
Howard Rd. N15 64 DS58
Howard Rd. N16 64 DR63
Howard Rd. NW2 61 CX63
Howard Rd. SE20 120 DW95
Howard Rd. SE25 120 DU99
Howard Rd., Bark. 81 ER67
Howard Rd., Brom. 108 EG94
Howard Rd., Couls. 147 DJ115
Howard Rd., Ilf. 67 EP63
Howard Rd., Islw. 87 CF83
Howard Rd., Lthd. 141 BU122
Howard Rd., N.Mal. 116 CS97
Howard Rd., Sthl. 72 CB72
Howard Rd., Surb. 116 CM100
Howard St., T.Ditt. 115 CH101
Howard Wk. N2 62 DC56
Howard Way, Barn. 33 CX43
Howards Clo., Pnr. 43 BV54
Howards Crest Clo., Beck. 121 EC96
Howards La. SW15 103 CV85
Howards Rd. E13 80 EG69
Howarth Ct. E15 65 EC64
Taylor Ct.
Howarth Rd. SE2 96 EU78
Howberry Clo., Edg. 45 CK51
Howberry Rd., Edg. 45 CK51
Howberry Rd., Stan. 45 CK51
Howberry Rd., Th.Hth. 120 DR95
Howbury La., Erith 97 FG82
Howbury Rd. SE15 92 DW83
Howcroft Cres. N3 48 DA52
Howcroft La., Grnf. 73 CD69
Cowgate Rd.
Howden Clo. SE28 82 EX73
Howden Rd. SE25 120 DT96
Howden St. SE15 92 DU83
Howe Clo., Rad. 18 CL32
Howe Clo., Rom. 54 FA53
Howe Dr., Cat. 148 DR122
York Gate
Howell Clo., Rom. 68 EX57
Howell Hill Clo., Epsom 131 CW111
Howell Hill Gro., Epsom 131 CW110
Howell Wk. SE1 10 G9
Howes Clo. N3 62 DA55
Howgate Rd. SW14 88 CR83
Howick Pl. SW1 9 L7
Howick Pl. SW1 91 DJ76
Howie St. SW11 90 DE80
Howitt Rd. NW3 76 DE65
Howland Est. SE16 92 DW76
Lower Rd.
Howland Ms. E. W1 5 L6
Howland St. W1 5 K6
Howland St. W1 77 DJ71
Howland Way SE16 93 DY75
Howletts La., Ruis. 57 BQ57
Howletts Rd. SE24 106 DQ86
Howley Pl. W2 76 DC71
Howley Rd., Croy. 119 DP104
Hows Clo., Uxb. 70 BJ67
Hows Rd.
Hows Rd., Uxb. 70 BJ67
Hows St. E2 78 DT68
Howsman Rd. SW13 89 CU79
Howson Rd. SE4 93 DY84
Howson Ter., Rich. 102 CL86
Howton Pl. (Bushey), Wat. 45 CD46
Hoxton Mkt. N1 7 M3
Hoxton Sq. N1 7 M3
Hoxton Sq. N1 78 DS69
Hoxton St. N1 78 DS67
Hoy St. E16 80 EF72
Hoylake Cres., Uxb. 56 BN61
Hoylake Gdns., Mitch. 119 DJ97
Hoylake Gdns., Ruis. 57 BV60
Hoylake Gdns., Wat. 44 BX49
Hoylake Rd. W3 74 CS72
Hoyland Clo. SE15 92 DV80
Commercial Way
Hoyle Rd. SW17 104 DE92
Hubbard Dr., Chess. 129 CJ107
Hubbard Rd. SE27 106 DQ91
Hubbard St. E15 80 EE67
Hubbard's Hill, Sev. 155 FH130
Hubbinet Ind. Est., Rom. 69 FC55
Hubert Gro. SW9 91 DL83
Hubert Rd. E6 80 EK69
Hubert Rd., Rain. 83 FF69
Huddart St. E3 79 DZ71
Huddleston Clo. E2 78 DW68
Huddleston Rd. N7 63 DJ62
Huddlestone Rd. E7 66 EF63
Huddlestone Rd. NW2 75 CV65
Hudson Clo., Wat. 29 BT36
Hudson Ct. SW19 104 DB94
Hudson Gdns., Orp. 137 ET107
Superior Dr.
Hudson Pl. SE18 95 EQ78
Hudson Rd., Bexh. 96 EZ82
Hudson Rd., Hayes 85 BR79
Hudsons, Tad. 145 CX121
Hudson's Pl. SW1 9 K8
Huggin Ct. EC4 7 J10
Huggin Hill EC4 7 J10
Huggins Pl. SW2 105 DM88
Roupell Rd.
Hugh Dalton Ave. SW6 89 CZ79
Rylston Rd.
Hugh Gaitskell Clo. SW6 89 CZ79
Rylston Rd.
Hugh Ms. SW1 9 J9
Hugh Pl. SW1 9 M8
Hugh St. SW1 9 J9
Hugh St. SW1 91 DH77
Hughan Rd. E15 65 ED64
Hughenden Ave., Har. 59 CH57
Hughenden Gdns., Nthlt. 72 BW69
Hughenden Rd., Wor.Pk. 117 CU101
Hughendon Ter. E15 65 EC63
Westdown Rd.
Hughes Rd., Ashf. 99 BQ94
Hughes Rd., Hayes 71 BU73
Hughes Wk., Croy. 120 DQ101
St. Saviours Rd.
Hugo Gdns., Rain. 83 FF65
Hugo Rd. N19 63 DJ63
Hugon Rd. SW6 90 DB83
Huguenot Pl. E1 78 DT71
Huguenot Pl. SW18 104 DC85
Huguenot Sq. SE15 92 DV83
Scylla Rd.
Hull Clo. SE16 93 DX75
Hull Clo., Sutt. 132 DB110
Yardbridge Clo.
Hull St. EC1 7 H3
Hullbridge Ms. N1 78 DR67
Sherborne St.
Hulse Ave., Bark. 81 ER65
Hulse Ave., Rom. 55 FB53
Hulse Ter., Ilf. 67 EQ64
Loxford La.
Hulsewood Clo., Dart. 111 FH90
Hulton Clo., Lthd. 143 CJ123
Windmill Dr.
Hulverston Clo., Sutt. 132 DB110
Humber Dr. W10 75 CX70
Humber Rd. NW2 61 CV61
Humber Rd. SE3 94 EF79
Humberstone Rd. E13 80 EJ69
Humberton Clo. E9 65 DY64
Marsh Hill
Humbolt Rd. W6 89 CY79
Hume Ter. E16 80 EJ72
Prince Regent La.
Hume Way, Ruis. 57 BU58
Humes Ave. W7 87 CE76
Humphrey Clo., Ilf. 53 EM53
Humphrey Clo., Lthd. 142 CC122
Humphrey St. SE1 11 P10
Humphrey St. SE1 92 DT78
Humphries Clo., Dag. 68 EZ63
Hundred Acre NW9 47 CT54
Hungerdown E4 51 EC46
Hungerford Bri. SE1 10 B3
Hungerford Bri. SE1 77 DM74
Hungerford Bri. WC2 10 B3
Hungerford Bri. WC2 77 DM74
Hungerford La. WC2 10 A2
Hungerford Rd. N7 77 DK65
Hungerford Sq., Wey. 127 BR105
Rosslyn Pk.
Hungerford St. E1 78 DV72
Commercial Rd.
Hungry Hill, Wok. 140 BK124
Hungry Hill La.
Hungry Hill La., Wok. 140 BK124
Hunsdon Clo., Dag. 82 EY65
Hunsdon Dr., Sev. 155 FH123
Hunsdon Rd. SE14 93 DX80
Hunslett St. E2 78 DW68
Royston St.
Hunston Rd., Mord. 118 DB102
Hunt Rd., Sthl. 86 CA76
Hunt St. W11 75 CX74
Hunt Way SE22 106 DU88
Dulwich Common
Hunter Clo. SE1 11 L7
Hunter Clo. SW12 104 DG88
Balham Pk. Rd.
Hunter Clo., Borwd. 32 CQ43
Hunter Clo., Pot.B. 20 DB33
Hunter Ho., Felt. 99 BU88
Hunter Rd. SW20 117 CW95
Hunter Rd., Ilf. 67 EP64
Hunter Rd., Th.Hth. 120 DR97
Hunter St. WC1 6 A4
Hunter St. WC1 77 DL70
Hunter Wk. E13 80 EG67
Stratford Rd.

Hunter Wk., Borwd. 32 CQ43
Ashley Dr.
Huntercrombe Gdns., Wat. 44 BW50
Hunters, The, Beck. 121 EC95
Hunters Clo., Bex. 111 FE90
Hunters Clo., Epsom 130 CQ113
Marshalls Clo.
Hunters Ct., Rich. 101 CK85
Friars La.
Hunters Gro., Har. 59 CJ56
Hunters Gro., Hayes 71 BU74
Hunters Gro., Orp. 137 EP105
Hunters Gro., Rom. 55 FB50
Hunters Hall Rd., Dag. 68 FA63
Hunters Hill, Ruis. 58 BW62
Hunters La., Wat. 15 BT33
Hunters Meadow SE19 106 DS91
Dulwich Wd. Ave.
Hunters Reach, Wal.Cr. 22 DT29
Hunters Ride, St.Alb. 16 CA31
Hunters Rd., Chess. 116 CL104
Hunters Sq., Dag. 68 FA63
Hunters Wk., Sev. 138 EY114
Hunters Way, Croy. 134 DS105
Brownlow Rd.
Hunters Way, Enf. 35 DN39
Hunting Clo., Esher 128 CA105
Hunting Gate Clo., Enf. 35 DN41
Hunting Gate Dr., Chess. 130 CL108
Hunting Gate Ms., Sutt. 118 DB104
Hunting Gate Ms., Twick. 101 CE88
Colne Rd.
Huntingdon Clo., Mitch. 119 DL98
Huntingdon Gdns. W4 88 CQ80
Huntingdon Gdns., Wor.Pk. 117 CW104
Huntingdon Rd. N2 62 DE55
Huntingdon Rd. N9 50 DW46
Huntingdon St. E16 80 EF72
Huntingdon St. N1 77 DM66
Huntingfield, Croy. 135 DZ108
Huntingfield Rd. SW15 89 CU84
Huntings Rd., Dag. 82 FA65
Huntland Clo., Rain. 83 FH71
Huntley Dr. N3 48 DA51
Huntley St. WC1 5 L5
Huntley St. WC1 77 DJ70
Huntley Way SW20 117 CU96
Huntly Rd. SE25 120 DS98
Hunton Bri. Hill, Kings L. 15 BQ33
Hunton Bri. Ind. Est., Kings L. 15 BQ33
Hunton St. E1 78 DU71
Hunt's Clo. SE3 94 EG82
Hunt's Ct. WC2 9 N1
Hunts La. E15 79 EC68
Hunts Mead, Enf. 37 DX41
Hunts Mead Clo., Chis. 109 EM94
Hunts Slip Rd. SE21 106 DS90
Huntsman Clo., Warl. 148 DW119
Huntsman Rd., Ilf. 54 EU51
Huntsman St. SE17 11 L9
Huntsman St. SE17 92 DS77
Huntsmans Clo., Felt. 99 BV91
Huntsmans Clo., Lthd. 143 CD124
The Grn.
Huntsmoor Rd., Epsom 130 CR106
Huntspill St. SW17 104 DC90
Huntsworth Ms. NW1 4 D5
Hurley Clo., Walt. 113 BV103
Hurley Cres. SE16 93 DX75
Marlow Way
Hurley Rd., Grnf. 72 CB72
Hurlingham Ct. SW6 89 CZ83
Hurlingham Gdns. SW6 89 CZ83
Hurlingham Rd. SW6 89 CZ82
Hurlingham Rd., Bexh. 96 EZ80
Hurlingham Sq. SW6 90 DB83
Peterborough Rd.
Hurlock St. N5 63 DP62
Hurlstone Rd. SE25 120 DR99
Hurn Ct. Rd., Houns. 86 BX82
Renfrew Rd.
Hurnford Clo., S.Croy. 134 DS110
Huron Clo., Orp. 137 ET107
Winnipeg Dr.
Huron Rd. SW17 104 DG89
Hurren Clo. SE3 94 EE83
Hurricane Way, Abb.L. 15 BU32
Abbey Dr.
Hurricane Way, Epp. 26 FA27
Hurry Clo. E15 80 EE66
Hursley Rd., Chig. 53 ET50
Tufter Rd.
Hurst Ave. E4 51 EA49
Hurst Ave. N6 63 DJ58
Hurst Clo. E4 51 EA48
Hurst Clo. NW11 62 DB58
Hurst Clo., Brom. 122 EF102
Hurst Clo., Chess. 130 CN106
Hurst Clo., Nthlt. 72 BZ65
Hurst Dr., Wal.Cr. 23 DX34
Hurst Est. SE2 96 EX78
Hurst Gro., Walt. 113 BT102
Hurst La. SE2 96 EX78
Hurst La., E.Mol. 114 CC98
Hurst La., Epsom 144 CQ124
Hurst Pl., Nthwd. 43 BP53
Hurst Ri., Barn. 34 DA41
Hurst Rd. E17 65 EB55
Hurst Rd. N21 49 DN46
Hurst Rd., Bex. 110 EW88
Hurst Rd., Buck.H. 52 EK46
Hurst Rd., Croy. 134 DR106
Hurst Rd., E.Mol. 114 CA97
Hurst Rd., Epsom 130 CR111
Hurst Rd. (Headley), Epsom 144 CR123
Hurst Rd., Erith 97 FC81
Hurst Rd., Sid. 110 EU89
Hurst Rd., Tad. 145 CU123
Hurst Rd., Walt. 114 BW99
Hurst Rd., W.Mol. 114 CA97
Hurst Springs, Bex. 110 EY88
Hurst St. SE24 105 DP86
Hurst Vw. Rd., S.Croy. 134 DS108
Hurst Way, Sev. 155 FJ127
Hurst Way, S.Croy. 134 DS107
Hurstbourne, Esher 129 CF107
Hurstbourne Gdns., Bark. 81 ES65
Hurstbourne Rd. SE23 107 DY88
Hurstcourt Rd., Sutt. 118 DB102
Hurstdene Ave., Brom. 122 EF102
Hurstdene Ave., Stai. 98 BH93
Hurstdene Gdns. N15 64 DS59
Hurstfield, Brom. 122 EG99
Hurstfield Cres., Hayes 71 BS70
Hurstfield Rd., W.Mol. 114 CA97
Hurstleigh Gdns., Ilf. 53 EM53
Hurstmead Ct., Edg. 46 CP49
Hurstway Wk. W11 75 CX73
Whitchurch Rd.
Hurstwood Ave. E18 66 EH56
Hurstwood Ave., Bex. 110 EY88
Hurstwood Ave., Bexh. 97 FE81
Hurstwood Ave., Erith 97 FE81
Hurstwood Dr., Brom. 123 EM97
Hurstwood Rd. NW11 61 CY56
Hurtwood Rd., Walt. 114 BZ101
Huson Clo. NW3 76 DE66
Hussars Clo., Houns. 86 BY83
Husseywell Cres., Brom. 122 EG102
Hutchings St. E14 93 EA75
Hutchings Wk. NW11 62 DB56
Hutchingsons Rd., Croy. 135 EC111
Hutchins Clo. E15 79 EC66
Gibbins Rd.
Hutchinson Ter., Wem. 59 CK62
Hutton Clo., Grnf. 59 CD64
Mary Peters Dr.
Hutton Clo., Wdf.Grn. 52 EH51
Hutton Gdns., Har. 44 CC52
Hutton Wk.
Hutton Gro. N12 48 DB50
Hutton La., Har. 44 CC52
Hutton Row, Edg. 46 CQ52
Pavilion Way
Hutton St. EC4 6 E9
Hutton Wk., Har. 44 CC52
Huxbear St. SE4 107 DZ85
Huxley Clo., Nthlt. 72 BY67
Huxley Clo., Uxb. 70 BK70
Huxley Dr., Rom. 68 EV59
Huxley Gdns. NW10 74 CM69
Huxley Par. N18 50 DQ50
Huxley Pl. N13 49 DP48
Huxley Rd. E10 65 EC61
Huxley Rd. N18 50 DR49
Huxley Rd., Well. 95 ET83
Huxley Sayze N18 50 DQ50
Huxley St. W10 75 CY69
Hyacinth Clo., Hmptn. 100 CA93
Gresham Rd.
Hyacinth Ct., Pnr. 58 BW55
Tulip Ct.
Hyacinth Dr., Uxb. 70 BL66
Hyacinth Rd. SW15 103 CU88
Hyburn Clo., St.Alb. 16 BZ30
Hycliffe Gdns., Chig. 53 EQ49
Hyde, The NW9 60 CS56
Hyde Ave., Pot.B. 20 DB33
Hyde Clo. E13 80 EG68
Pelly Rd.
Hyde Clo., Ashf. 99 BS93
Hyde Ter.
Hyde Clo., Barn. 33 CZ41
Hyde Ct. N20 48 DD48
Hyde Cres. NW9 60 CS57
Hyde Dr., Orp. 124 EV98
Hyde Est. Rd. NW9 61 CT57
Hyde Ho. NW9 60 CS57
The Hyde
Hyde La. SW11 90 DE81
Battersea Bri. Rd.
Hyde La., Hem.H. 14 BN27
Hyde La., St.Alb. 17 CE28
Hyde La., Wok. 140 BN120
Hyde Pk. SW7 8 B2
Hyde Pk. SW7 76 DE74
Hyde Pk. W1 8 B2
Hyde Pk. W1 76 DE74
Hyde Pk. W2 8 B2
Hyde Pk. W2 76 DE74
Hyde Pk. Ave. N21 50 DQ47
Hyde Pk. Cor. W1 8 G4
Hyde Pk. Cor. W1 90 DG75
Hyde Pk. Cres. W2 4 B9
Hyde Pk. Cres. W2 76 DE72
Hyde Pk. Gdns. N21 50 DQ46
Hyde Pk. Gdns. W2 4 A10
Hyde Pk. Gdns. W2 76 DD73
Hyde Pk. Gdns. Ms. W2 4 A10
Hyde Pk. Gate SW7 90 DC75
Hyde Pk. Gate Ms. SW7 90 DC75
Hyde Pk. Gate
Hyde Pk. Pl. W2 4 C10
Hyde Pk. Sq. W2 4 B9
Hyde Pk. Sq. W2 76 DE72
Hyde Pk. Sq. Ms. W2 4 B9
Hyde Pk. St. W2 4 B9
Hyde Pk. St. W2 76 DE72
Hyde Rd. N1 78 DS67
Hyde Rd., Bexh. 96 EZ82
Hyde Rd., Rich. 102 CM85
Albert Rd.
Hyde Rd., S.Croy. 134 DR113
Hyde Rd., Wat. 29 BU40
Hyde St. SE8 93 EA79
Deptford High St.
Hyde Ter., Ashf. 99 BS93
Hyde Vale SE10 93 ED81
Hyde Wk., Mord. 118 DA101
Glastonbury Rd.
Hyde Way N9 50 DT47
Hyde Way, Hayes 85 BT77
Hydefield Clo. N21 50 DR46
Hydefield Ct. N9 50 DS47
Hyderabad Way E15 80 EE66
Hydes Pl. N1 77 DP66
Compton Ave.
Hydeside Gdns. N9 50 DT47
Hydethorpe Ave. N9 50 DT47
Hydethorpe Rd. SW12 105 DJ88
Hyland Clo., Horn. 69 FH59
Hyland Way, Horn. 69 FH59
Hylands Clo., Epsom 144 CQ115
Hylands Ms., Epsom 144 CQ115
Hylands Rd. E17 51 ED54
Hylands Rd., Epsom 144 CQ115
Hylton St. SE18 95 ET77
Hyndewood SE23 107 DX90
Hyndman St. SE15 92 DV79
Hynton Rd., Dag. 68 EW61
Hyperion Pl., Epsom 130 CR109
Hyrstdene, S.Croy. 133 DP105
Hyson Rd. SE16 92 DV77
Galleywall Rd.
Hythe Ave., Bexh. 96 EY80
Hythe Clo. N18 50 DU49
Hythe Clo., Orp. 124 EW98
Sandway Rd.
Hythe Path, Th.Hth. 120 DR97
Buller Rd.
Hythe Rd. NW10 75 CU70
Hythe Rd., Th.Hth. 120 DR96
Hyver Hill NW7 32 CR44

I

Ian Sq., Enf. 37 DX39
Lansbury Rd.
Ibbetson Path, Loug. 39 EP41
Ibbotson Ave. E16 80 EF72
Ibbott St. E1 78 DW70
Mantus Rd.
Iberian Ave., Wall. 133 DK105
Ibis La. W4 88 CQ81
Ibis Way, Hayes 72 BX72
Cygnet Way
Ibscott Clo., Dag. 83 FC65
Ibsley Gdns. SW15 103 CU88
Ibsley Way, Barn. 34 DE43
Iceland Rd. E3 79 EA67
Ickburgh Est. E5 64 DV62
Ickburgh Rd.
Ickburgh Rd. E5 64 DV62
Ickenham Clo., Ruis. 57 BR61
Ickenham Rd., Ruis. 57 BQ61
Ickenham Rd., Uxb. 57 BQ61
Ickleton Rd. SE9 108 EL91
Icklingham Gate, Cob. 128 BW112
Icklingham Rd.
Icklingham Rd., Cob. 128 BW112
Icknield Dr., Ilf. 67 EP57
Ickworth Pk. Rd. E17 65 DY56
Ida Rd. N15 64 DR57
Ida St. E14 79 EC72
Iden Clo., Brom. 122 EE97
Idlecombe Rd. SW17 104 DG93
Idmiston Rd. E15 66 EF64
Idmiston Rd. SE27 106 DQ90
Idmiston Rd., Wor.Pk. 117 CT101
Idmiston Sq., Wor.Pk. 117 CT102
Idol La. EC3 11 M1
Idonia St. SE8 93 EA80
Iffley Clo., Uxb. 70 BK66
Iffley Rd. W6 89 CV76
Ifield Rd. SW10 90 DB79
Ifor Evans Pl. E1 79 DX70
Mile End Rd.
Ightham Rd., Erith 96 FA80
Ikea Twr. NW10 60 CR64
Ikona Ct., Wey. 127 BQ106
Ilbert St. W10 75 CX69
Ilchester Gdns. W2 76 DB73
Ilchester Pl. W14 89 CZ76
Ilchester Rd., Dag. 68 EV64
Ildersly Gro. SE21 106 DR89
Ilderton Rd. SE15 92 DW80
Ilderton Rd. SE16 92 DV78
Ilex Clo., Sun. 114 BW96
Oakington Dr.
Ilex Ho. N4 63 DM59
Ilex Rd. NW10 75 CT65
Ilex Way SW16 105 DN92
Ilford Hill, Ilf. 67 EN62
Ilford La., Ilf. 67 EP62
Ilfracombe Gdns., Rom. 68 EV59
Ilfracombe Rd., Brom. 108 EF90
Iliffe St. SE17 10 G10
Iliffe St. SE17 91 DP78
Iliffe Yd. SE17 10 G10
Ilkeston Ct. E5 65 DX63
Overbury St.
Ilkley Clo. SE19 106 DR93
Ilkley Rd. E16 80 EJ71
Ilkley Rd., Wat. 44 BX50
Illingworth Clo., Mitch. 118 DD97
Illingworth Way, Enf. 36 DS42
Ilmington Rd., Har. 59 CK58
Ilminster Gdns. SW11 90 DE84
Imber Clo. N14 49 DJ45
Imber Clo., Esher 115 CD102
Ember La.
Imber Ct. Ind. Est., E.Mol. 115 CD100
Imber Gro., Esher 115 CD101
Imber Pk. Rd., Esher 115 CD102
Imber St. N1 78 DR67
Imer Pl., T.Ditt. 115 CF101
Imperial Ave. N16 64 DT62
Victorian Rd.
Imperial Clo., Har. 58 CA58
Imperial College Rd. SW7 90 DD76
Imperial Cres., Wey. 113 BQ104
Churchill Dr.
Imperial Dr., Har. 58 CA59
Imperial Gdns., Mitch. 119 DH97
Imperial Ms. E6 80 EJ68
Central Pk. Rd.
Imperial Rd. N22 49 DL53
Imperial Rd. SW6 90 DB81
Imperial Rd., Felt. 99 BS87
Imperial Sq. SW6 90 DB81
Imperial St. E3 79 EC69
Imperial Way, Chis. 109 EQ90
Imperial Way, Croy. 133 DN107
Imperial Way, Har. 60 CL58
Imperial Way, Wat. 30 BW39
Inca Dr. SE9 109 EP87
Ince Rd., Walt. 127 BS108
Inchmery Rd. SE6 107 EB89
Inchwood, Croy. 135 EB105
Independent Pl. E8 64 DT64
Downs Pk. Rd.
Independents Rd. SE3 94 EF83
Blackheath Village
Inderwick Rd. N8 63 DM57
Indescon Ct. E14 93 EA75
India Pl. WC2 6 B10
India St. EC3 7 P9
India Way W12 75 CV73
Indus Rd. SE7 94 EJ80
Industry Ter. SW9 91 DN83
Canterbury Cres.
Ingal Rd. E13 80 EG70
Ingate Pl. SW8 91 DH81
Ingatestone Rd. E12 66 EJ60
Ingatestone Rd. SE25 120 DV99
Ingatestone Rd., Wdf.Grn. 52 EH52
Ingelow Rd. SW8 91 DH82
Ingels Mead, Epp. 25 ET29
Ingersoll Rd. W12 75 CV74
Ingersoll Rd., Enf. 36 DW38
Ingestre Pl. W1 5 L9
Ingestre Rd. E7 66 EG63
Ingestre Rd. NW5 63 DH63
Ingham Clo., S.Croy. 135 DX109
Ingham Rd. NW6 62 DA63
Ingham Rd., S.Croy. 134 DW109
Ingle Clo., Pnr. 58 BZ55
Inglebert St. EC1 6 D2
Ingleboro Dr., Pur. 134 DQ113
Ingleborough St. SW9 91 DN82
Ingleby Clo., Dag. 83 FB65
Ingleby Dr., Har. 59 CD62
Ingleby Gdns., Chig. 54 EV48
Ingleby Rd. N7 63 DL62
Ingleby Rd., Dag. 83 FB65
Ingleby Rd., Ilf. 67 EP60
Ingleby Way, Chis. 109 EN92
Ingleby Way, Wall. 133 DJ109
Ingledew Rd. SE18 95 ER78
Inglefield, Pot.B. 20 DA30
Inglehurst, Add. 126 BH110
Inglehurst Gdns., Ilf. 67 EM57
Inglemere Rd. SE23 107 DX90
Inglemere Rd., Mitch. 104 DF94
Inglesham Wk. E9 79 DZ65
Beanacre Clo.
Ingleside Clo., Beck. 107 EA94
Ingleside Gro. SE3 94 EF79
Inglethorpe St. SW6 89 CX81
Ingleton Ave., Well. 110 EU85
Ingleton Rd. N18 50 DU51
Ingleton Rd., Cars. 132 DE109
Ingleton St. SW9 91 DN82
Ingleway N12 48 DD51
Inglewood, Croy. 135 DY109
Middlefields
Inglewood Clo. E14 93 EA77
Inglewood Clo., Ilf. 53 ET51
Inglewood Copse, Brom. 122 EL96
Inglewood Rd. NW6 62 DA64
Inglewood Rd., Bexh. 97 FD84
Inglis Barracks NW7 47 CY50
Inglis Rd. W5 74 CM73
Inglis Rd., Croy. 120 DT102
Inglis St. SE5 91 DP81
Ingram Ave. NW11 62 DC59
Ingram Clo. SE11 10 C8
Ingram Clo., Stan. 45 CJ50
Ingram Rd. N2 62 DE56
Ingram Rd., Th.Hth. 120 DQ95
Ingram Way, Grnf. 73 CD67
Ingrams Clo., Walt. 128 BW106
Ingrave Ho., Dag. 82 EV67
Ingrave Rd., Rom. 69 FD56
Ingrave St. SW11 90 DD83
Ingrebourne Rd., Rain. 83 FH70
Ingress St. W4 88 CS78
Devonshire Rd.
Inigo Jones Rd. SE7 94 EL80
Inigo Pl. WC2 5 P10
Inkerman Rd. NW5 77 DH65
Inks Grn. E4 51 EB50
Inman Rd. NW10 74 CS67
Inman Rd. SW18 104 DC87
Inmans Row, Wdf.Grn. 52 EG49
Inner Circle NW1 4 F3
Inner Circle NW1 76 DG69
Inner Pk. Rd. SW19 103 CX88
Inner Ring E., Houns. 85 BP83
Inner Ring W., Houns. 84 BN83
Inner Temple La. EC4 6 D9
Innes Clo. SW20 117 CY96
Innes Gdns. SW15 103 CV86
Innes Yd., Croy. 120 DQ104
High St.
Inniskilling Rd. E13 80 EJ68
Inskip Clo. E10 65 EB61
Inskip Rd., Dag. 68 EX60
Institute Pl. E8 64 DV64
Amhurst Rd.
Institute Rd., Epp. 26 EX29
Instone Clo., Wall. 133 DL108
De Havilland Rd.
Integer Gdns. E11 65 ED59
Forest Rd.
Interchange E. Ind. Est. E5 64 DW60
Theydon Rd.
International Ave., Houns. 86 BW78
International Trd. Est., Sthl. 85 BV76
Inver Clo. E5 64 DW61
Theydon Rd.
Inver Ct. W2 76 DB72
Inverness Ter.
Inveraray Pl. SE18 95 ER79
Old Mill Rd.
Inverclyde Gdns., Rom. 68 EX56
Inveresk Gdns., Wor.Pk. 117 CT104
Inverforth Clo. NW3 62 DC61
North End Way
Inverforth Rd. N11 49 DH50
Inverine Rd. SE7 94 EH78
Invermore Pl. SE18 95 EQ77
Inverness Ave., Enf. 36 DS39
Inverness Dr., Ilf. 53 ES51
Inverness Gdns. W8 76 DB74
Vicarage Gate
Inverness Ms. W2 76 DB73
Inverness Ter.
Inverness Pl. W2 76 DB73
Inverness Rd. N18 50 DV50
Aberdeen Rd.
Inverness Rd., Houns. 86 BZ84
Inverness Rd., Sthl. 86 BY77
Inverness Rd., Wor.Pk. 117 CX102
Inverness St. NW1 77 DH67
Inverness Ter. W2 76 DB72
Inverton Rd. SE15 93 DX84
Invicta Clo., Chis. 109 EN92
Invicta Gro., Nthlt. 72 BZ69
Invicta Plaza SE1 77 DP74
Southwark St.
Invicta Rd. SE3 94 EG80
Inville Rd. SE17 92 DR78
Inwen Ct. SE8 93 DY78
Inwood Ave., Couls. 147 DN120
Inwood Ave., Houns. 86 CC83
Inwood Clo., Croy. 121 DY103
Inwood Ct., Walt. 114 BW103
Inwood Rd., Houns. 86 CB84
Inworth St. SW11 90 DE82
Inworth Wk. N1 78 DQ67
Popham St.
Ion Sq. E2 78 DU68
Hackney Rd.
Iona Clo. SE6 107 EA87
Ipswich Rd. SW17 104 DG93
Ireland Clo. E6 81 EM71
Bradley Stone Rd.
Ireland Pl. N22 49 DL52
Whittington Rd.
Ireland Row E14 79 DZ72
Commercial Rd.
Ireland Yd. EC4 6 G9
Irene Rd. SW6 90 DA81
Irene Rd., Cob. 128 CB114
Irene Rd., Orp. 123 ET101
Ireton Ave., Walt. 113 BS103
Ireton Clo. N10 48 DG52
Cromwell Rd.
Ireton St. E3 79 EA70
Tidworth Rd.
Iris Ave., Bex. 110 EY86
Iris Clo. E6 80 EL71
Iris Clo., Croy. 121 DX102
Iris Clo., Surb. 116 CM101
Iris Ct., Pnr. 58 BW55
Iris Cres., Bexh. 96 EZ79
Iris Rd., Epsom 130 CP106
Iris Way E4 51 DZ51
Irkdale Ave., Enf. 36 DT39
Iron Bri. Clo. NW10 60 CS64
Iron Bri. Clo., Sthl. 72 CC74
Iron Bri. Rd., Uxb. 84 BN75
Iron Bri. Rd., West Dr. 84 BN75
Iron Mill La., Dart. 97 FE84
Iron Mill Pl. SW18 104 DB86
Garratt La.
Iron Mill Pl., Dart. 97 FF84
Iron Mill Rd. SW18 104 DB86
Ironmonger La. EC2 7 K9
Ironmonger Pas. EC1 7 J3
Ironmonger Row EC1 7 J3
Ironmonger Row EC1 78 DQ69
Ironmongers Pl. E14 93 EA77
Spindrift Ave.
Irons Way, Rom. 55 FC52
Ironside Clo. SE16 93 DX75
Kinburn St.

Irvine Ave., Har. 59 CG55
Irvine Clo. N20 48 DE47
Irvine Way, Orp. 123 ET101
Irving Ave., Nthlt. 72 BX67
Irving Gro. SW9 91 DM82
Irving Rd. W14 89 CX76
Irving St. WC2 9 N1
Irving St. WC2 77 DK73
Irving Way NW9 61 CT57
Irving Way, Swan. 125 FD96
Irwin Ave. SE18 95 ES80
Irwin Gdns. NW10 75 CV67
Isabel St. SW9 91 DM81
Isabella Clo. N14 49 DJ45
Isabella Dr., Orp. 137 EQ105
Isabella Rd. E9 64 DW64
Isabella St. SE1 10 F3
Isabella St. SE1 77 DP74
Isabelle Clo., Wal.Cr. 22 DQ29
Doverfield
Isambard Clo., Uxb. 70 BK70
Isambard Ms. E14 93 EC76
Isambard Pl. SE16 78 DW74
Rotherhithe St.
Isbell Gdns., Rom. 55 FE52
Isel Way SE22 106 DS85
East Dulwich Gro.
Isham Rd. SW16 119 DL96
Isis Clo. SW15 89 CW84
Isis Clo., Ruis. 57 BQ58
Isis St. SW18 104 DC89
Isla Rd. SE18 95 EQ79
Island Fm. Ave., W.Mol. 114 BZ99
Island Fm. Rd., W.Mol. 114 BZ99
Island Rd., Mitch. 104 DF94
Island Row E14 79 DY72
Commercial Rd.
Islay Gdns., Houns. 100 BX85
Islay Wk. N1 78 DQ66
Douglas Rd.
Isledon Rd. N7 63 DN62
Islehurst Clo., Chis. 123 EN95
Islington Grn. N1 77 DP67
Islington High St. N1 77 DN68
Islington Pk. Ms. N1 77 DN66
Islington Pk. St.
Islington Pk. St. N1 77 DN66
Islip Gdns., Edg. 46 CR52
Islip Gdns., Nthlt. 72 BY66
Islip Manor Rd., Nthlt. 72 BY66
Islip St. NW5 63 DJ64
Ismailia Rd. E7 80 EH66
Isom Clo. E13 80 EJ70
Belgrave Rd.
Ivanhoe Clo., Uxb. 70 BK71
Ivanhoe Dr., Har. 59 CG55
Ivanhoe Rd. SE5 92 DT83
Ivanhoe Rd., Houns. 86 BX83
Ivatt Pl. W14 89 CZ78
Ivatt Way N17 63 DP55
Ive Fm. Clo. E10 65 EA61
Ive Fm. La. E10 65 EA61
Iveagh Ave. NW10 74 CN68
Iveagh Clo. E9 79 DX67
Iveagh Clo. NW10 74 CN68
Iveagh Clo., Nthwd. 43 BP53
Iveagh Ter. NW10 74 CN68
Iveagh Ave.
Ivedon Rd., Well. 96 EW82
Iveley Rd. SW4 91 DJ82
Iver La., Iver 70 BG72
Iver La., Uxb. 70 BH70
Iver Rd., Iver 70 BG72
Ivere Dr., Barn. 34 DB44
Iverhurst Clo., Bexh. 110 EX85
Iverna Ct. W8 90 DA76
Iverna Gdns. W8 90 DA76
Iverna Gdns., Felt. 99 BR85
Ivers Way, Croy. 135 EB108
Iverson Rd. NW6 75 CZ65
Ives Gdns., Rom. 69 FF56
Sims Clo.
Ives Rd. E16 80 EE71
Ives St. SW3 8 C8
Ives St. SW3 90 DE77
Ivestor Ter. SE23 106 DW87
Ivimey St. E2 78 DU69
Ivinghoe Clo., Enf. 36 DS39
Ivinghoe Clo., Wat. 30 BX35
Ivinghoe Rd., Dag. 68 EV64
Ivinghoe Rd., Rick. 42 BG45
Ivinghoe Rd. (Bushey), Wat. 45 CD45
Ivor Gro. SE9 109 EP88
Ivor Pl. NW1 4 D5
Ivor Pl. NW1 76 DF70
Ivor St. NW1 77 DJ66
Ivory Sq. SW11 90 DC83
Gartons Way
Ivorydown, Brom. 108 EG91
Ivy Chimneys Rd., Epp. 25 ES32
Ivy Clo., Har. 58 BZ63
Ivy Clo., Pnr. 58 BW59
Ivy Clo., Sun. 114 BW96
Ivy Cotts. E14 79 EB73
Grove Vill.
Ivy Ct. SE16 92 DU78
Argyle Way
Ivy Cres. W4 88 CQ77
Ivy Gdns. N8 63 DL58
Ivy Gdns., Mitch. 119 DK97
Ivy Ho. La., Sev. 153 FD118
Ivy La., Houns. 86 BZ84
Ivy La., Sev. 152 EY116
Ivy Lea, Rick. 42 BG46
Springwell Ave.
Ivy Pl., Surb. 116 CM100
Alpha Rd.
Ivy Rd. E16 80 EG72
Pacific Rd.
Ivy Rd. E17 65 EA58
Ivy Rd. N14 49 DJ45
Ivy Rd. NW2 61 CW63
Ivy Rd. SE4 93 DZ84
Ivy Rd. SW17 104 DE92
Tooting High St.
Ivy Rd., Houns. 86 CB84
Ivy Rd., Surb. 116 CN103
Ivy St. N1 78 DS68
Ivy Wk., Dag. 82 EY65
Ivybridge Clo., Twick. 101 CG87
Ivybridge Clo., Uxb. 70 BL69
Ivybridge Est., Islw. 101 CF85
Ivybridge La. WC2 10 A1
Ivychurch Clo. SE20 106 DW94
Ivychurch La. SE17 11 N10
Ivydale Rd. SE15 93 DX83
Ivydale Rd., Cars. 118 DF103
Ivyday Gro. SW16 105 DM90
Ivydene, W.Mol. 114 BZ99
Ivydene Clo., Sutt. 132 DC105
Ivyhouse Rd., Dag. 82 EX65
Ivyhouse Rd., Uxb. 57 BP63
Ivymount Rd. SE27 105 DN90
Ixworth Pl. SW3 8 B10
Ixworth Pl. SW3 90 DE78
Izane Rd., Bexh. 96 EZ84

J

Jacaranda Clo., N.Mal. 116 CS97
Jack Barnett Way N22 49 DM54
Mayes Rd.
Jack Clow Rd. E15 80 EE68
Jack Cornwell St. E12 67 EN63
Jack Dash Way E6 80 EL70
Jack Walker Ct. N5 63 DP63
Jackass La., Kes. 136 EH106
Jackets La., Nthwd. 43 BP53
Jackets La., Uxb. 43 BP53
Jacketts Fld., Abb.L. 15 BT31
Jacklin Grn., Wdf.Grn. 52 EG49
Jackman Ms. NW10 60 CS62
Jackman St. E8 78 DV67
Jacks La., Uxb. 42 BG52
Jackson Clo., Epsom 130 CR114
Jackson Clo., Uxb. 70 BL66
Jackson Rd.
Jackson Rd. N7 63 DM63
Jackson Rd., Bark. 81 ER67
Jackson Rd., Barn. 34 DD44
Jackson Rd., Brom. 122 EL103
Jackson Rd., Uxb. 70 BL66
Jackson St. SE18 95 EN79
Jackson Way, Sthl. 86 CB75
Jacksons Dr., Wal.Cr. 22 DU28
Jacksons La. N6 62 DG59
Jacksons Pl., Croy. 120 DR102
Cross Rd.
Jacksons Way, Croy. 121 EA104
Jacob St. SE1 92 DT75
Jacobs Clo., Dag. 69 FB63
Jacobs Ho. E13 80 EJ69
Jacob's Well Ms. W1 4 G8
Jacqueline Clo., Nthlt. 72 BZ67
Canford Ave.
Jade Clo. E16 80 EK72
Jade Clo. NW2 61 CX59
Marble Dr.
Jade Clo., Dag. 68 EW60
Jaffe Rd., Ilf. 67 ER60
Jaffray Pl. SE27 105 DP91
Chapel Rd.
Jaffray Rd., Brom. 122 EK98
Jaggard Way SW12 104 DF87
Jago Clo. SE18 95 EQ79
Jago Wk. SE5 92 DR80
Lomond Gro.
Jail La. (Biggin Hill), West. 150 EK115
Jamaica Rd. SE1 92 DT75
Jamaica Rd. SE16 92 DU76
Jamaica Rd., Th.Hth. 119 DP100
Jamaica St. E1 78 DW71
James Ave. NW2 61 CW64
James Ave., Dag. 68 EZ60
James Bedford Clo., Pnr. 44 BW54
James Boswell Clo. SW16 105 DN91
Curtis Fld. Rd.
James Clo. E13 80 EG68
Richmond St.
James Clo. NW11 61 CY58
Woodlands
James Clo., Rom. 69 FG57
James Clo. (Bushey), Wat. 30 BY43
Aldenham Rd.
James Collins Clo. W9 75 CZ70
Fermoy Rd.
James Ct. N1 78 DQ66
Morton Rd.
James Dudson Ct. NW10 74 CQ66
James Gdns. N22 49 DP52
James Hammett Ho. E2 78 DT69
Ravenscroft St.
James Joyce Wk. SE24 91 DP84
Shakespeare Rd.
James La. E10 65 ED59
James La. E11 65 ED58
James Martin Clo., Uxb. 56 BG58
James Newman Ct. SE9 109 EN90
Great Harry Dr.
James Pl. N17 50 DT53
Ruskin Rd.
James Rd., Dart. 111 FF87
James Sinclair Pt. E13 80 EJ67
James St. W1 4 G8
James St. W1 76 DG72
James St. WC2 6 A10
James St., Bark. 81 EQ66
James St., Enf. 36 DT43
James St., Epp. 25 ET28
James St., Houns. 87 CD83
James Ter. SW14 88 CR83
Addington Ct.
James Yd. E4 51 ED51
Larkshall Rd.
Jameson Clo. W3 88 CQ75
Acton La.
Jameson St. W8 76 DA74
James's Cotts., Rich. 88 CN80
Kew Rd.
Jamestown Rd. NW1 77 DH67
Jamieson Ho., Houns. 100 BZ86
Jane St. E1 78 DV72
Commercial Rd.
Janet St. E14 93 EA76
Janeway Pl. SE16 92 DV75
Janeway St.
Janeway St. SE16 92 DU75
Janice Ms., Ilf. 67 EP62
Oakfield Rd.
Jansen Wk. SW11 90 DD84
Hope St.
Janson Clo. E15 66 EE64
Janson Rd.
Janson Clo. NW10 60 CS62
Janson Rd. E15 66 EE64
Jansons Rd. N15 64 DS55
Japan Cres. N4 63 DM59
Japan Rd., Rom. 68 EX58
Jardine Rd. E1 79 DX73
Jarrett Clo. SW2 105 DP88
Jarrow Clo., Mord. 118 DB99
Jarrow Rd. N17 64 DV56
Jarrow Rd. SE16 92 DW77
Jarrow Rd., Rom. 68 EW58
Jarrow Way E9 65 DZ64
Jarvis Cleys (Cheshunt), Wal.Cr. 22 DT26
Roundcroft
Jarvis Clo., Barn. 33 CX43
Jarvis Rd. SE22 92 DS84
Melbourne Gro.
Jarvis Rd., S.Croy. 134 DR107
Jasmin Clo., Nthwd. 43 BT53
Jasmin Rd., Epsom 130 CP107
Jasmine Clo., Ilf. 67 EP64
Jasmine Clo., Orp. 123 EP103
Jasmine Clo., Sthl. 72 BY73
Jasmine Gdns., Croy. 121 EA104
Jasmine Gdns., Har. 58 CA61
Jasmine Gro. SE20 120 DV95
Jasmine Ter., West Dr. 84 BN75
Jasmine Way, E.Mol. 115 CE98
Hampton Ct. Way
Jason Clo., Wey. 127 BQ106
Jason Ct. W1 76 DG72
Marylebone La.
Jason Wk. SE9 109 EN91
Jasper Clo., Enf. 36 DW38
Jasper Pas. SE19 106 DT93
Jasper Rd. E16 80 EK72
Jasper Rd. SE19 106 DT93
Jasper Wk. N1 7 K2
Javelin Way, Nthlt. 72 BX69
Jay Gdns., Chis. 109 EM91
Jay Ms. SW7 90 DC75
Jaycroft, Enf. 35 DN39
The Ridgeway
Jays Covert, Couls. 146 DG120
Jebb Ave. SW2 105 DL86
Jebb St. E3 79 EA68
Jedburgh Rd. E13 80 EJ69
Jedburgh St. SW11 90 DG84
Jeddo Rd. W12 89 CT75
Jefferies Ho. NW10 74 CR66
Jefferson Clo. W13 87 CH76
Jefferson Clo., Ilf. 67 EP57
Jefferson Wk. SE18 95 EN79
Kempt St.
Jeffreys Pl. NW1 77 DJ66
Jeffreys St.
Jeffreys Rd. SW4 91 DL82
Jeffreys Rd., Enf. 37 DZ41
Jeffreys St. NW1 77 DJ66
Jeffreys Wk. SW4 91 DL82
Jeffs Clo., Hmptn. 100 CB93
Uxbridge Rd.
Jeffs Rd., Sutt. 131 CZ105
Jeger Ave. E2 78 DT67
Jeken Rd. SE9 94 EJ84
Jelf Rd. SW2 105 DN85
Jellicoe Gdns., Stan. 45 CF51
Jellicoe Rd. E13 80 EG70
Jutland Rd.
Jellicoe Rd. N17 50 DR52
Jellicoe Rd., Wat. 29 BU44
Jengar Clo., Sutt. 132 DB105
Jenkins Ave., St.Alb. 16 BY30
Jenkins La. E6 81 EN68
Jenkins La., Bark. 81 EP68
Jenkins Rd. E13 80 EH70
Jenner Ave. W3 74 CR71
Jenner Ho. SE3 94 EE79
Jenner Pl. SW13 89 CV79
Jenner Rd. N16 64 DT62
Jennett Rd., Croy. 119 DN104
Jennifer Rd., Brom. 108 EF90
Jennings Clo., Add. 126 BJ109
Woodham La.
Jennings Rd. SE22 106 DT86
Jennings Way, Barn. 33 CW41
Jenningtree Rd., Erith 97 FH80
Jenningtree Way, Belv. 97 FC75
Jenny Hammond Clo. E11 66 EF62
Newcomen Rd.
Jenson Way SE19 106 DT94
Jenton Ave., Bexh. 96 EY81
Jephson Rd. E7 80 EJ66
Jephson St. SE5 92 DR81
Grove La.
Jephtha Rd. SW18 104 DA86
Jeppos La., Mitch. 118 DF98
Jerdan Pl. SW6 90 DA80
Fulham Bdy.
Jeremiah St. E14 79 EB72
Jeremys Grn. N18 50 DV49
Jermyn St. SW1 9 L2
Jermyn St. SW1 77 DJ74
Jerningham Ave., Ilf. 53 EP54
Jerningham Rd. SE14 93 DY82
Jerome Cres. NW8 4 B4
Jerome Cres. NW8 76 DE70
Jerome St. E1 7 P5
Jerrard St. N1 7 N1
Jerrard St. SE13 93 EB83
Jersey Ave., Stan. 45 CH54
Jersey Dr., Orp. 123 ER100
Jersey Par., Houns. 86 CB81
Jersey Rd. E11 65 ED60
Jersey Rd. E16 80 EJ72
Prince Regent La.
Jersey Rd. SW17 105 DH93
Jersey Rd. W7 87 CG75
Jersey Rd., Houns. 86 CB81
Jersey Rd., Ilf. 67 EP63
Jersey Rd., Islw. 87 CD80
Jersey Rd., Rain. 83 FG66
Jersey St. E2 78 DV69
Bethnal Grn. Rd.
Jerusalem Pas. EC1 6 F5
Jervis Ave., Enf. 37 DY36
Jervis Ct. W1 5 J9
Jerviston Gdns. SW16 105 DN92
Jesmond Ave., Wem. 74 CM65
Jesmond Clo., Mitch. 118 DG97
Jesmond Rd., Croy. 120 DT101
Jesmond Way, Stan. 46 CL50
Jessam Ave. E5 64 DV60
Jessamine Rd. W7 73 CE74
Jessamine Ter., Swan. 125 FC95
Birchwood Rd.
Jessamy Rd., Wey. 113 BP103
Jesse Rd. E10 65 EC60
Jessel Dr., Loug. 39 EQ39
Jessett Clo., Erith 97 FD77
West St.
Jessica Rd. SW18 104 DC86
Jessie Blythe La. N19 63 DL59
Hillrise Rd.
Jessiman Ter., Shep. 112 BN99
Jessop Ave., Sthl. 86 BZ77
Jessop Rd. SE24 91 DP84
Milkwood Rd.
Jessops Way, Croy. 119 DJ100
Jessup Clo. SE18 95 EQ77
Jetstar Way, Nthlt. 72 BY69
Jevington Way SE12 108 EH88
Jewel Rd. E17 65 EA55
Jewels Hill, West. 136 EG112
Jewry St. EC3 7 P9
Jewry St. EC3 78 DT72
Jew's Row SW18 90 DB84
Jews Wk. SE26 106 DV91
Jeymer Ave. NW2 61 CV64
Jeymer Dr., Grnf. 72 CC67
Jeypore Rd. SW18 104 DC87
Jillian Clo., Hmptn. 100 CA94
Jim Bradley Clo. SE18 95 EN77
John Wilson St.
Joan Cres. SE9 108 EK87
Joan Gdns., Dag. 68 EY61
Joan Rd., Dag. 68 EY60
Joan St. SE1 10 F3
Joan St. SE1 77 DP74
Jocelyn Rd., Rich. 88 CL83
Jocelyn St. SE15 92 DU81
Jockey's Flds. WC1 6 C6
Jockey's Flds. WC1 77 DM71
Jodane St. SE8 93 DZ77
Jodrell Clo., Islw. 87 CG81
Blenheim Way
Jodrell Rd. E3 79 DZ67
Joel St., Nthwd. 57 BU55
Joel St., Pnr. 57 BU55
Johanna St. SE1 10 D5
John Adam St. WC2 10 A1
John Adam St. WC2 77 DL73
John Aird Ct. W2 76 DC71
Howley Pl.
John Ashby Clo. SW2 105 DL86
John Barnes Wk. E15 80 EF65
Hamfrith Rd.
John Bradshaw Rd. N14 49 DK46
High St.
John Burns Dr., Bark. 81 ES66
John Campbell Rd. N16 64 DS64
John Carpenter St. EC4 6 E10
John Carpenter St. EC4 77 DP73
John Cobb Rd., Wey. 126 BN108
John Cornwall VC Ho. E12 67 EN63
John Deed Ind. Est., Mitch. 118 DF100
John Felton Rd. SE16 92 DU75
John Fisher St. E1 78 DU73
John Gooch Dr., Enf. 35 DP39
John Groom's Est., Edg. 46 CQ49
John Horner Ms. N1 78 DQ68
Frome St.
John Islip St. SW1 9 N10
John Islip St. SW1 91 DK78
John Keats Ho. N22 49 DM52
John Maurice Clo. SE17 11 K8
John Maurice Clo. SE17 92 DR77
John McKenna Wk. SE16 92 DU76
Tranton Rd.
John Newton Ct., Well. 96 EV83
Danson La.
John Parker Clo., Dag. 83 FB66
John Parker Sq. SW11 90 DD83
Thomas Baines Rd.
John Penn St. SE13 93 EB81
John Perrin Pl., Har. 60 CL59
John Princes St. W1 5 J8
John Princes St. W1 77 DH72
John Rennie Wk. E1 78 DV74
Wine Clo.
John Roll Way SE16 92 DU76
John Ruskin St. SE5 91 DP80
John Silkin La. SE8 93 DX78
John Smith Ave. SW6 89 CZ80
John Spencer Sq. N1 77 DP65
John St. E15 80 EF67
John St. SE25 120 DU98
John St. WC1 6 C5
John St. WC1 77 DM70
John St., Enf. 36 DT43
John St., Houns. 86 BY82
John Trundle Ct. EC2 78 DQ71
Beech St.
John Walsh Twr. E11 66 EF61
John Williams Clo. SE14 93 DX79
John Wilson St. SE18 95 EN76
John Woolley Clo. SE13 93 ED84
Johnby Clo., Enf. 37 DY37
Manly Dixon Dr.
Johns Ave. NW4 61 CW56
Johns Clo., Ashf. 99 BQ91
Johns La., Mord. 118 DC99
John's Ms. WC1 6 C5
John's Ms. WC1 77 DM70
John's Pl. E1 78 DV72
Damien St.
Johns Rd., West. 150 EK120
John's Ter., Croy. 120 DS102
Johns Wk., Whyt. 148 DU119
Johnson Clo. E8 78 DU67
Johnson Rd., Brom. 122 EK99
Johnson Rd., Croy. 120 DR101
Johnson Rd., Houns. 86 BW80
Johnson St. E1 78 DW73
Cable St.
Johnson St., Sthl. 86 BW76
Johnsons Ave., Sev. 139 FB110
Johnsons Clo., Cars. 118 DE104
Johnson's Ct. EC4 77 DN72
Fleet St.
Johnsons Ct., Sev. 155 FM121
School La.
Johnsons Dr., Hmptn. 114 CC95
Johnson's Pl. SW1 91 DJ78
Johnsons Way NW10 74 CP70
Johnsons Yd., Uxb. 70 BJ66
Redford Way
Johnston Clo. SW9 91 DM81
Hackford Rd.
Johnston Rd., Wdf.Grn. 52 EG50
Johnston Ter. NW2 61 CX62
Campion Ter.
Johnstone Rd. E6 81 EM69
Joiner St. SE1 11 L3
Joiner's Arms Yd. SE5 92 DR81
Denmark Hill
Joinville Pl., Add. 126 BK105
Jollys La., Har. 59 CD60
Lower Rd.
Jollys La., Hayes 72 BX71
Jonathan St. SE11 10 B10
Jonathan St. SE11 91 DM78
Jones Rd. E13 80 EH70
Holborn Rd.
Jones Rd. (Cheshunt), Wal.Cr. 21 DP30
Jones St. W1 9 H1
Jones Wk., Rich. 102 CM86
Pyrland Rd.
Jonquil Gdns., Hmptn. 100 BZ93
Partridge Rd.
Jonson Clo., Hayes 71 BU71
Jonson Clo., Mitch. 119 DH98
Joram Way SE16 92 DV78
Egan Way
Jordan Clo., Dag. 69 FB63
Muggeridge Rd.
Jordan Clo., Har. 58 BZ62
Hamilton Cres.
Jordan Clo., S.Croy. 134 DT111
Jordan Clo., Wat. 29 BT35
Jordan Rd., Grnf. 73 CH67
Jordans Clo., Islw. 87 CE81
Jordans Clo., Stai. 98 BJ87
Jordans Rd., Rick. 42 BG45
Jordans Way, St.Alb. 16 BZ30
Joseph Ave. W3 74 CR72
Joseph Locke Way, Esher 114 CA103
Mill Rd.
Joseph Powell Clo. SW12 105 DH86
Hazelbourne Rd.
Joseph Ray Rd. E11 66 EE61
High Rd. Leytonstone
Joseph St. E3 79 DZ70
Josephine Ave. SW2 105 DM85
Joshua St. E14 79 EC72
St. Leonards Rd.

Joubert St. SW11 90 DF82
Jowett St. SE15 92 DT80
Joyce Ave. N18 50 DT50
Joyce Ct., Wal.Abb. 23 ED34
Joyce Dawson Way SE28 82 EU73
Thamesmere Dr.
Joyce Page Clo. SE7 94 EK79
Lansdowne La.
Joyce Wk. SW2 105 DN86
Joydens Wd. Rd., Bex. 111 FD91
Joydon Dr., Rom. 68 EV58
Joyners Clo., Dag. 68 EZ63
Jubb Powell Ho. N15 64 DS58
Jubilee Ave. E4 51 EC51
Jubilee Ave., Rom. 69 FB57
Jubilee Ave., St.Alb. 17 CK26
Jubilee Ave., Twick. 100 CC87
Jubilee Clo. NW9 60 CR58
Jubilee Clo., Pnr. 44 BW54
Jubilee Clo., Rom. 69 FB57
Jubilee Clo., Stai. 98 BJ87
Jubilee Ct., Stai. 98 BG92
Leacroft
Jubilee Cres. E14 93 EC76
Jubilee Cres. N9 50 DU46
Jubilee Cres., Add. 126 BK106
Jubilee Dr., Ruis. 58 BX63
Jubilee Gdns., Sthl. 72 CA72
Jubilee Pl. SW3 8 C10
Jubilee Pl. SW3 90 DE78
Jubilee Ri., Sev. 155 FM121
Jubilee Rd., Grnf. 73 CH67
Jubilee Rd., Orp. 138 FA107
Jubilee Rd., Sutt. 131 CX108
Jubilee Rd., Wat. 29 BU38
Jubilee St. E1 78 DW72
Jubilee Wk., Wat. 43 BV49
Muirfield Rd.
Jubilee Way SW19 118 DB95
Jubilee Way, Chess. 130 CN105
Jubilee Way, Felt. 99 BT88
Jubilee Way, Sid. 110 EU89
Judd St. WC1 5 P3
Judd St. WC1 77 DL69
Jude St. E16 80 EF72
Judge Heath La., Hayes 71 BQ72
Judge Heath La., Uxb. 71 BQ72
Judge St., Wat. 29 BV38
Judge Wk., Esher 129 CE107
Judges Hill, Pot.B. 20 DE29
Judith Ave., Rom. 55 FB51
Juer St. SW11 90 DE80
Juglans Rd., Orp. 124 EU102
Julia Gdns., Bark. 82 EX68
Julia St. NW5 62 DG63
Oak Village
Julian Ave. W3 74 CP73
Julian Clo., Barn. 34 DB41
Julian Hill, Har. 59 CE61
Julian Hill, Wey. 126 BN108
Julian Pl. E14 93 EB78
Julian Rd., Orp. 138 EU107
Juliana Clo. N2 62 DB55
East End Rd.
Julians Clo., Sev. 154 FG127
Julians Way, Sev. 154 FG127
Julien Rd. W5 87 CJ77
Julien Rd., Couls. 147 DK115
Juliette Rd. E13 80 EF68
Junction App. SE13 93 EC83
Loampit Vale
Junction App. SW11 90 DE83
Junction Ave. W10 75 CW69
Harrow Rd.
Junction Ms. W2 4 B8
Junction Pl. W2 4 A8
Junction Rd. E13 80 EH68
Junction Rd. N9 50 DU46
Junction Rd. N17 64 DU55
Junction Rd. N19 63 DJ63
Junction Rd. W5 87 CK77
Junction Rd., Ashf. 99 BQ92
Junction Rd., Brent. 87 CK77
Junction Rd., Har. 59 CE58
Junction Rd., Rom. 69 FF56
Junction Rd., S.Croy. 134 DR106
Junction Rd. E., Rom. 68 EY59
Kenneth Rd.
Junction Rd. W., Rom. 68 EY59
Junction Wf. N1 7 H1
Junction Wf. N1 78 DQ68
June Clo., Couls. 133 DH114
Juniper Ave., St.Alb. 16 CA31
Juniper Clo., Barn. 33 CX43
Juniper Clo., Brox. 23 DZ25
Juniper Clo., Chess. 130 CM107
Juniper Clo., Rick. 42 BK48
Juniper Clo., Wem. 60 CN64
Juniper Clo., West. 150 EL117
Juniper Cres. NW1 76 DG66
Juniper Gdns. SW16 119 DJ95
Leonard Rd.
Juniper Gdns., Sun. 99 BT93
Juniper Gate, Rick. 42 BK47
Juniper Gro., Wat. 29 BU38
Bay Tree Wk.
Juniper La. E6 80 EL71
Juniper Rd., Ilf. 67 EP63
Juniper St. E1 78 DW73
Juniper Wk., Swan. 125 FD96
Pear Tree Clo.
Juniper Way, Hayes 71 BR73
Juno Way SE14 93 DX79
Jupiter Way N7 77 DM65
Jupp Rd. E15 79 ED66
Jupp Rd. W. E15 79 EC67
Justice Wk. SW3 90 DE79
Lawrence St.
Justin Clo., Brent. 87 CK80
Justin Rd. E4 51 DZ51
Jute La., Enf. 37 DY40
Jutland Clo. N19 63 DL60
Sussex Way
Jutland Gdns., Couls. 147 DL120
Goodenough Way
Jutland Rd. E13 80 EG70
Jutland Rd. SE6 107 EC87
Jutsums Ave., Rom. 69 FB58
Jutsums La., Rom. 69 FB58
Juxon Clo., Har. 44 CB53
Augustine Rd.
Juxon St. SE11 10 C8
Juxon St. SE11 91 DM77

K

Kaduna Clo., Pnr. 57 BV57
Kale Rd., Erith 96 EY75
Kambala Rd. SW11 90 DD83
Kangley Bri. Rd. SE26 107 DZ91
Kaplan Dr. N21 35 DL43
Pennington Dr.
Karen Clo., Rain. 83 FE68
Karen Ct. SE4 93 DZ82
Wickham Rd.
Karen Ct., Brom. 122 EF95
Blyth Rd.
Karen Ter. E11 66 EF61
Montague Rd.
Karoline Gdns., Grnf. 73 CD68
Oldfield La. N.
Kashgar Rd. SE18 95 ET77
Kashmir Clo., Add. 126 BK109
Kashmir Rd. SE7 94 EK80
Kassala Rd. SW11 90 DF81
Katella Trd. Est., Bark. 81 ES69
Kates Clo., Barn. 33 CU43
Katharine St., Croy. 120 DQ104
Katherine Clo., Add. 126 BG107
Katherine Gdns. SE9 94 EK84
Katherine Gdns., Ilf. 53 EQ52
Katherine Rd. E6 80 EK66
Katherine Rd. E7 80 EJ65
Katherine Rd., Twick. 101 CG88
London Rd.
Katherine Sq. W11 75 CY74
Wilsham St.
Kathleen Ave. W3 74 CQ71
Kathleen Ave., Wem. 74 CL66
Kathleen Rd. SW11 90 DF83
Kay Rd. SW9 91 DL82
Kay St. E2 78 DU68
Kay St. E15 79 ED66
Kay St., Well. 96 EV81
Kaye Don Way, Wey. 126 BN111
Kayemoor Rd., Sutt. 132 DE108
Kean St. WC2 6 B9
Kean St. WC2 77 DM72
Kearton Clo., Ken. 148 DQ117
Keatley Grn. E4 51 DZ51
Keats Ave., Rom. 55 FH52
Keats Clo. E11 66 EH57
Nightingale La.
Keats Clo. NW3 62 DE63
Keats Gro.
Keats Clo. SE1 11 P9
Keats Clo. SW19 104 DD93
North Rd.
Keats Clo., Chig. 53 EQ51
Keats Clo., Enf. 37 DX43
Keats Clo., Hayes 71 BU71
Keats Gro. NW3 62 DE63
Keats Ho., Beck. 107 EA93
Keats Pl. EC2 7 K7
Keats Rd., Belv. 97 FC76
Keats Rd., Well. 95 ES81
Keats Way, Croy. 120 DW100
Keats Way, Grnf. 72 CB71
Keats Way, West Dr. 84 BM77
Keble Clo., Nthlt. 58 CC64
Keble Clo., Wor.Pk. 117 CT102
Keble Pl. SW13 89 CV79
Trinity Ch. Rd.
Keble St. SW17 104 DC91
Keble Ter., Abb.L. 15 BT32
Kechill Gdns., Brom. 122 EG101
Kedelston Ct. E5 65 DX63
Redwald Rd.
Kedleston Dr., Orp. 123 ET100
Kedleston Wk. E2 78 DV69
Middleton St.
Keedonwood Rd., Brom. 108 EE92
Keel Clo. SE16 79 DX74
Keel Clo., Bark. 82 EY69
Choats Rd.
Keele Clo., Wat. 30 BW40
Keeley Rd., Croy. 120 DQ103
Keeley St. WC2 6 B9
Keeley St. WC2 77 DM72
Keeling Rd. SE9 108 EK85
Keely Clo., Barn. 34 DE43
Keemor Clo. SE18 95 EN80
Llanover Rd.
Keens Clo. SW16 105 DK92
Keens Rd., Croy. 134 DQ105
Keens Yd. N1 77 DP65
St. Paul's Rd.
Keep, The SE3 94 EG82
Keep, The, Kings.T. 102 CM93
Keep La. N11 48 DG49
Gardeners Clo.
Keepers Ms., Tedd. 101 CJ93
Keesey St. SE17 92 DR79
Keetons Rd. SE16 92 DV76
Keevil Dr. SW19 103 CX87
Keighley Clo. N7 63 DL64
Penn Rd.
Keightley Dr. SE9 109 EQ88
Keilder Clo., Uxb. 70 BN68
Charnwood Rd.
Keildon Rd. SW11 90 DF84
Keir, The SW19 103 CW92
West Side Common
Keir Hardie Est. E5 64 DV60
Springfield
Keir Hardie Ho. W6 89 CW79
Lochaline St.
Keir Hardie Way, Bark. 82 EU66
Keir Hardie Way, Hayes 71 BU69
Keith Connor Clo. SW8 91 DH83
Daley Thompson Way
Keith Gro. W12 89 CU75
Keith Pk. Cres., West. 136 EH113
Keith Pk. Rd., Uxb. 70 BM66
Keith Rd. E17 51 DZ53
Keith Rd., Bark. 81 ER68
Keith Rd., Hayes 85 BS76
Kelbrook Rd. SE3 94 EL82
Kelburn Way, Rain. 83 FG69
Dominion Way
Kelby Path SE9 109 EP90
Kelceda Clo. NW2 61 CU61
Kelf Gro., Hayes 71 BT72
Kelfield Gdns. W10 75 CW72
Kelfield Ms. W10 75 CX72
Kelfield Gdns.
Kell St. SE1 10 G6
Kelland Clo. N8 63 DK57
Palace Rd.
Kelland Rd. E13 80 EG70
Kellaway Rd. SE3 94 EJ82
Keller Cres. E12 66 EK63
Kellerton Rd. SE13 108 EE85
Kellett Rd. SW2 91 DN84
Kelling Gdns., Croy. 119 DP101
Kellino St. SW17 104 DF91
Kellner Rd. SE28 95 ET76
Kelly Clo., Shep. 113 BS96
Kelly Ct., Borwd. 32 CR40
Kelly Rd. NW7 47 CY51
Kelly St. NW1 77 DH65
Kelly Way, Rom. 68 EY57
Kelman Clo. SW4 91 DK82
Kelman Clo., Wal.Cr. 23 DX31
Kelmore Gro. SE22 92 DU84
Kelmscott Clo. E17 51 DZ54
Kelmscott Clo., Wat. 29 BU43
Kelmscott Cres., Wat. 29 BU43
Kelmscott Gdns. W12 89 CU76
Kelmscott Rd. SW11 104 DE85
Kelross Pas. N5 64 DQ63
Kelross Rd.
Kelross Rd. N5 64 DQ63
Kelsall Clo. SE3 94 EH82
Kelsey La., Beck. 121 EA97
Kelsey Pk. Ave., Beck. 121 EB96
Kelsey Pk. Rd., Beck. 121 EA96
Kelsey Rd., Orp. 124 EV96
Kelsey Sq., Beck. 121 EA96
High St.
Kelsey St. E2 78 DU70
Kelsey Way, Beck. 121 EA97
Kelshall, Wat. 30 BY36
Kelshall Ct. N4 64 DQ61
Brownswood Rd.
Kelsie Way, Ilf. 53 ES51
Kelso Pl. W8 90 DB76
Kelso Rd., Cars. 118 DC101
Kelson Ho. E14 93 EC76
Kelston Rd., Ilf. 53 EP54
Kelvedon Ave., Walt. 127 BS108
Kelvedon Clo., Kings.T. 102 CN93
Kelvedon Rd. SW6 89 CZ80
Kelvedon Wk., Rain. 83 FE67
Ongar Way
Kelvedon Way, Wdf.Grn. 53 EM51
Kelvin Ave. N13 49 DM51
Kelvin Ave., Lthd. 143 CF119
Kelvin Ave., Tedd. 101 CE93
Kelvin Clo., Epsom 130 CN107
Kelvin Cres., Har. 45 CE52
Kelvin Dr., Twick. 101 CH86
Kelvin Gdns., Croy. 119 DL101
Kelvin Gdns., Sthl. 72 CA72
Kelvin Gro. SE26 106 DV90
Kelvin Gro., Chess. 116 CL104
Kelvin Ind. Est., Grnf. 72 CB66
Kelvin Par., Orp. 123 ES102
Kelvin Rd. N5 63 DP63
Kelvin Rd., Well. 96 EU83
Kelvinbrook, W.Mol. 114 CB97
Kelvington Clo., Croy. 121 DY101
Kelvington Rd. SE15 107 DX85
Kember St. N1 77 DM66
Carnoustie Dr.
Kemble Clo., Pot.B. 20 DD33
Kemble Clo., Wey. 127 BR105
Kemble Cotts., Add. 112 BG104
Emley Rd.
Kemble Dr., Brom. 122 EL104
Kemble Par., Pot.B. 20 DC32
High St.
Kemble Rd. N17 50 DU53
Kemble Rd. SE23 107 DX88
Kemble Rd., Croy. 119 DN104
Kemble St. WC2 6 B9
Kemble St. WC2 77 DM72
Kembleside Rd., West. 150 EJ118
Kemerton Rd. SE5 92 DQ83
Kemerton Rd., Beck. 121 EB96
Kemerton Rd., Croy. 120 DT101
Kemeys St. E9 65 DY64
Kemnal Rd., Chis. 109 EQ94
Kemp Gdns., Croy. 120 DQ100
St. Saviours Rd.
Kemp Pl. (Bushey), Wat. 30 CA44
Kemp Rd., Dag. 68 EX60
Kempe Rd. NW6 75 CX68
Kempe Rd., Enf. 36 DV36
Kempis Way SE22 106 DS85
East Dulwich Gro.
Kemplay Rd. NW3 62 DD63
Kemprow, Wat. 31 CD36
Kemp's Ct. W1 5 L9
Kemps Dr. E14 79 EA73
Morant St.
Kemps Dr., Nthwd. 43 BT52
Kemps Gdns. SE13 107 EC85
Thornford Rd.
Kempsford Gdns. SW5 90 DA78
Kempsford Rd. SE11 10 F9
Kempsford Rd. SE11 91 DN77
Kempshott Rd. SW16 105 DK94
Kempson Rd. SW6 90 DA81
Kempt St. SE18 95 EN79
Kempthorne Rd. SE8 93 DY77
Kempton Ave., Nthlt. 72 CA65
Kempton Ave., Sun. 113 BV95
Kempton Clo., Erith 97 FC79
Kempton Clo., Uxb. 57 BQ63
Kempton Ct., Sun. 113 BV95
Kempton Rd. E6 81 EM67
Kempton Rd., Hmptn. 114 BZ96
Kempton Wk., Croy. 121 DY100
Kemsing Clo., Bex. 110 EY87
Kemsing Clo., Brom. 122 EF103
Bourne Way
Kemsing Clo., Th.Hth. 120 DQ98
Kemsing Rd. SE10 94 EG78
Kemsley Rd., West. 150 EK119
Ken Way, Wem. 60 CQ61
Kenbury Clo., Uxb. 56 BN62
Kenbury Gdns. SE5 92 DQ82
Kenbury St.
Kenbury St. SE5 92 DQ82
Kenchester Clo. SW8 91 DL80
Kencot Way, Erith 96 EZ75
Kendal Ave. N18 50 DR49
Kendal Ave. W3 74 CN70
Kendal Ave., Bark. 81 ES66
Kendal Ave., Epp. 26 EU30
Kendal Clo. SW9 91 DP80
Kendal Clo., Felt. 99 BT88
Ambleside Dr.
Kendal Clo., Hayes 71 BS68
Kendal Clo., Wdf.Grn. 52 EF47
Kendal Cft., Horn. 69 FG64
Kendal Gdns. N18 50 DR49
Kendal Gdns., Sutt. 118 DC103
Kendal Par. N18 50 DR49
Great Cambridge Rd.
Kendal Pl. SW15 103 CZ85
Upper Richmond Rd.
Kendal Rd. NW10 61 CU63
Kendal St. W2 4 C9
Kendal St. W2 76 DE72
Kendale Rd., Brom. 108 EE92
Kendall Ave., Beck. 121 DY96
Kendall Ave., S.Croy. 134 DR109
Kendall Ave. S., S.Croy. 134 DQ110
Kendall Ct. SW19 104 DD93
Byegrove Rd.
Kendall Pl. W1 4 F7
Kendall Rd., Beck. 121 DY96
Kendall Rd., Islw. 87 CG82
Kendalmere Clo. N10 49 DH53
Kendals Clo., Rad. 31 CE36
Kender St. SE14 92 DW81
Kendoa Rd. SW4 91 DK84
Kendon Clo. E11 66 EH57
The Ave.
Kendor Ave., Epsom 130 CQ111
Kendra Hall Rd., S.Croy. 133 DP108
Kendrey Gdns., Twick. 101 CE86
Kendrick Ms. SW7 90 DD77
Reece Ms.
Kendrick Pl. SW7 90 DD77
Kenelm Clo., Har. 59 CG62
Kenerne Dr., Barn. 33 CY43
Kenford Clo., Wat. 15 BV32
Kenilford Rd. SW12 105 DH87
Kenilworth Ave. E17 51 EA54
Kenilworth Ave. SW19 104 DA92
Kenilworth Ave., Cob. 128 CB114
Kenilworth Ave., Har. 58 BZ63
Kenilworth Clo., Bans. 146 DB116
Kenilworth Clo., Borwd. 32 CQ41
Kenilworth Ct. SW15 89 CX83
Kenilworth Ct., Wat. 29 BU39
Hempstead Rd.
Kenilworth Cres., Enf. 36 DS39
Kenilworth Dr., Borwd. 32 CQ41
Kenilworth Dr., Rick. 29 BP42
Kenilworth Dr., Walt. 114 BX104
Kenilworth Gdns. SE18 95 EP82
Kenilworth Gdns., Hayes 71 BT71
Kenilworth Gdns., Ilf. 67 ET61
Kenilworth Gdns., Loug. 39 EM44
Kenilworth Gdns., Sthl. 72 BZ69
Kenilworth Gdns., Stai. 98 BJ92
Kenilworth Gdns., Wat. 44 BW50
Kenilworth Rd. E3 79 DY68
Kenilworth Rd. NW6 75 CZ67
Kenilworth Rd. SE20 121 DX95
Kenilworth Rd. W5 74 CL74
Kenilworth Rd., Ashf. 98 BK90
Kenilworth Rd., Edg. 46 CQ48
Kenilworth Rd., Epsom 131 CU106
Kenilworth Rd., Orp. 123 EQ100
Kenley Ave. NW9 46 CS53
Kenley Clo., Bex. 110 FA87
Kenley Clo., Cat. 148 DR120
Kenley Clo., Chis. 123 ES97
Kenley Gdns., Th.Hth. 119 DP98
Kenley La., Ken. 134 DQ114
Kenley Rd. SW19 117 CZ96
Kenley Rd., Kings.T. 116 CP96
Kenley Rd., Twick. 101 CG86
Kenley Wk. W11 75 CY73
Princedale Rd.
Kenley Wk., Sutt. 131 CX105
Kenlor Rd. SW17 104 DD92
Kenmare Dr., Mitch. 104 DF94
Kenmare Gdns. N13 50 DQ49
Kenmare Rd., Th.Hth. 119 DN100
Kenmere Gdns., Wem. 74 CN67
Kenmere Rd., Well. 96 EW82
Kenmont Gdns. NW10 75 CV69
Kenmore Ave., Har. 59 CG56
Kenmore Clo., Rich. 88 CN80
Kent Rd.
Kenmore Cres., Hayes 71 BT69
Kenmore Gdns., Edg. 46 CP54
Kenmore Rd., Har. 59 CK55
Kenmore Rd., Ken. 133 DP114
Kenmure Rd. E8 64 DV64
Kenmure Yd. E8 64 DV64
Kenmure Rd.
Kennard Rd. E15 79 ED66
Kennard Rd. N11 48 DF50
Kennard St. E16 81 EM74
Kennard St. SW11 90 DG81
Kennedy Ave., Enf. 36 DW44
Kennedy Clo. E13 80 EG68
Kennedy Clo., Mitch. 118 DG95
Kennedy Clo., Orp. 123 ER102
Kennedy Clo., Pnr. 44 BZ51
Kennedy Clo. (Cheshunt), Wal.Cr. 23 DY28
Kennedy Gdns., Sev. 155 FJ123
Kennedy Path W7 73 CF70
Harp Rd.
Kennedy Rd. W7 73 CE71
Kennedy Rd., Bark. 81 ES67
Kennedy Wk. SE17 92 DR77
Flint St.
Kennel Clo., Lthd. 142 CC124
Kennel Hill SE22 92 DS83
Kennel La., Lthd. 142 CC122
Kennelwood Cres., Croy. 135 ED111
Kennet Clo. SW11 90 DD84
Maysoule Rd.
Kennet Rd. W9 75 CZ70
Kennet Rd., Dart. 97 FG83
Kennet Rd., Islw. 87 CF83
Kennet Sq., Mitch. 118 DE95
Kennet St. E1 78 DU74
Kennet Wf. La. EC4 7 J10
Kenneth Ave., Ilf. 67 EP63
Kenneth Cres. NW2 61 CV64
Kenneth Gdns., Stan. 45 CG51
Kenneth More Rd., Ilf. 67 EP62
Oakfield Rd.
Kenneth Rd., Bans. 146 DD115
Kenneth Rd., Rom. 68 EX59
Kenneth Robbins Ho. N17 50 DV52
Kennett Ct., Swan. 125 FE97
Kennett Dr., Hayes 72 BY71
Kenning St. SE16 92 DW75
Railway Ave.
Kenning Ter. N1 78 DS67
Kenninghall Rd. E5 64 DU62
Kenninghall Rd. N18 50 DW50
Kennings Way SE11 10 F10
Kennings Way SE11 91 DN78
Kennington Grn. SE11 91 DN78
Montford Pl.
Kennington Gro. SE11 91 DM79
Oval Way
Kennington La. SE11 91 DL78
Kennington Oval SE11 91 DM79
Kennington Pk. Est. SE11 91 DN79
Harleyford St.
Kennington Pk. Gdns. SE11 91 DN79
Montford Pl.
Kennington Pk. Pl. SE11 91 DN79
Kennington Pk. Rd. SE11 91 DN79
Kennington Rd. SE1 10 D6
Kennington Rd. SE1 91 DN76
Kennington Rd. SE11 10 D8
Kennington Rd. SE11 91 DN76
Kenny Rd. NW7 47 CY50
Kennylands Rd., Ilf. 54 EU52
Kenrick Pl. W1 4 F7
Kensal Rd. W10 75 CX70
Kensington Ave. E12 80 EL65
Kensington Ave., Th.Hth. 119 DN95
Kensington Ave., Wat. 29 BT42
Kensington Ch. Ct. W8 90 DB75
Kensington Ch. St. W8 76 DA74
Kensington Ch. Wk. W8 90 DB75
Kensington Clo. N11 48 DG51
Kensington Ct. W8 90 DB75
Kensington Ct. Gdns. W8 90 DB76
Kensington Ct. Pl.
Kensington Ct. Ms. W8 90 DB75
Kensington Ct. Pl.
Kensington Ct. Pl. W8 90 DB76
Kensington Dr., Wdf.Grn. 52 EK54
Kensington Gdns. W2 76 DB74
Kensington Gdns., Ilf. 67 EM60

Kensington Gdns., 115 CK97
Kings.T.
Portsmouth Rd.
Kensington Gdns. Sq. W2 76 DB72
Kensington Gate W8 90 DC76
Kensington Gore SW7 90 DC75
Kensington Hall Gdns. 89 CZ78
W14
Beaumont Ave.
Kensington High St. W8 90 DA76
Kensington High St. W14 89 CZ76
Kensington Mall W8 76 DA74
Kensington Palace Gdns. 76 DB74
W8
Kensington Pk. Gdns. W11 75 CZ73
Kensington Pk. Ms. W11 75 CZ72
Kensington Pk. Rd.
Kensington Pk. Rd. W11 75 CZ72
Kensington Pl. W8 76 DA74
Kensington Rd. W8 90 DB75
Kensington Rd., Nthlt. 72 CA69
Kensington Rd., Rom. 69 FC58
Kensington Sq. W8 90 DB75
Kensington Ter., S.Croy. 134 DR108
Sanderstead Rd.
Kent Ave. W13 73 CH71
Kent Ave., Dag. 82 FA70
Kent Ave., Well. 109 ET85
Kent Clo., Borwd. 32 CR38
Kent Clo., Mitch. 119 DL98
Kent Clo., Orp. 137 ES107
Kent Clo., Stai. 98 BK93
Kent Clo., Uxb. 70 BJ65
Kent Dr., Barn. 34 DG42
Kent Dr., Tedd. 101 CE92
Kent Gdns. W13 73 CH71
Kent Gdns., Ruis. 57 BV58
Kent Gate Way, Croy. 135 DZ107
Kent Ho. La., Beck. 107 DY92
Kent Ho. Rd. SE20 107 DX94
Kent Ho. Rd. SE26 107 DY92
Kent Ho. Rd., Beck. 107 DX94
Kent Pas. NW1 **4** **D4**
Kent Rd. N21 50 DR46
Kent Rd. W4 88 CQ76
Kent Rd., Dag. 69 FB64
Kent Rd., E.Mol. 114 CC98
Kent Rd., Kings.T. 115 CK97
Kent Rd., Orp. 124 EV100
Kent Rd., Rich. 88 CN80
Kent Rd., W.Wick. 121 EB102
Kent St. E2 78 DT68
Kent St. E13 80 EH69
Kent Ter. NW1 **4** **C3**
Kent Ter. NW1 76 DE69
Kent Twrs. SE20 106 DV94
Kent Vw. Gdns., Ilf. 67 ES61
Kent Wk. SW9 91 DP84
Moorland Rd.
Kent Way SE15 92 DT81
Sumner Est.
Kent Way, Sutt. 116 CL104
Kent Yd. SW7 **8** **C5**
Kentford Way, Nthlt. 72 BY67
Kentish Bldgs. SE1 **11** **K4**
Kentish La., Hat. 20 DC26
Kentish Rd., Belv. 96 FA77
Kentish Town Rd. NW1 77 DH66
Kentish Town Rd. NW5 77 DH65
Kentish Way, Brom. 122 EG96
Kentmere Rd. SE18 95 ES77
Kenton Ave., Har. 59 CF59
Kenton Ave., Sthl. 72 CA73
Kenton Ave., Sun. 114 BX96
Kenton Ct. W14 89 CZ76
Kensington High St.
Kenton Gdns., Har. 59 CJ57
Kenton La., Har. 45 CF51
Kenton Pk. Ave., Har. 59 CK56
Kenton Pk. Clo., Har. 59 CJ56
Kenton Pk. Cres., Har. 59 CK56
Kenton Pk. Rd., Har. 59 CJ56
Kenton Rd. E9 79 DX65
Kenton Rd., Har. 59 CF59
Kenton St. WC1 **5** **P4**
Kenton St. WC1 77 DL70
Kenton Way, Hayes 71 BS69
Exmouth Rd.
Kents Pas., Hmptn. 114 BZ95
Kentwode Grn. SW13 89 CU80
Kenver Ave. N12 48 DD51
Kenward Rd. SE9 108 EJ85
Kenway, Rom. 55 FC54
Kenway Rd. SW5 90 DB77
Kenwood Ave. N14 35 DK43
Kenwood Ave. SE14 93 DX81
Besson St.
Kenwood Clo. NW3 62 DD60
Kenwood Clo., West Dr. 84 BN79
Kenwood Dr., Beck. 121 EC97
Kenwood Dr., Walt. 127 BV107
Kenwood Gdns. E18 66 EH55
Kenwood Gdns., Ilf. 67 EN56
Kenwood Pk., Wey. 127 BR107
Kenwood Ridge, Ken. 147 DP117
Kenwood Rd. N6 62 DF58
Kenwood Rd. N9 50 DU46
Kenworth Clo., Wal.Cr. 23 DX33
Kenworthy Rd. E9 65 DY64
Kenwyn Dr. NW2 60 CS62
Kenwyn Rd. SW4 91 DK84
Kenwyn Rd. SW20 117 CW95
Kenya Rd. SE7 94 EK80
Kenyngton Dr., Sun. 99 BU92
Kenyngton Pl., Har. 59 CJ57
Kenyon St. SW6 89 CX81

Keogh Rd. E15 80 EE65
Kepler Rd. SW4 91 DL84
Keppel Rd. E6 81 EM66
Keppel Rd., Dag. 68 EY63
Keppel Row SE1 **11** **H3**
Keppel St. WC1 **5** **N6**
Keppel St. WC1 77 DK71
Kerbela St. E2 78 DU70
Cheshire St.
Kerbey St. E14 79 EB72
Kerdistone Clo., Pot.B. 20 DB30
Kerfield Cres. SE5 92 DR81
Grove La.
Kerfield Pl. SE5 92 DR81
Kerri Clo., Barn. 33 CW42
Kerridge Ct. N1 78 DS65
Kingsbury Rd.
Kerrill Ave., Couls. 147 DN119
Kerrison Rd. E15 79 ED67
Kerrison Rd. SW11 90 DE83
Kerrison Rd. W5 73 CK74
Kerrison Vill. W5 73 CK74
Kerrison Pl.
Kerry Ave., Stan. 45 CK49
Kerry Clo. E16 80 EH72
Kerry Clo. N13 49 DM47
Kerry Ct., Stan. 45 CK49
Kerry Path SE14 93 DZ79
Kerry Rd.
Kerry Rd. SE14 93 DZ79
Kersey Dr., S.Croy. 134 DW112
Kersey Gdns. SE9 108 EL91
Kersfield Rd. SW15 103 CX86
Kershaw Clo. SW18 104 DD86
Westover Rd.
Kershaw Rd., Dag. 68 FA62
Kersley Ms. SW11 90 DF82
Kersley Rd. N16 64 DS61
Kersley St. SW11 90 DF82
Kerstin Clo., Hayes 71 BT73
St. Mary's Rd.
Kerswell Clo. N15 64 DS57
Kerwick Clo. N7 77 DM66
Sutterton St.
Keslake Rd. NW6 75 CX68
Kessock Clo. N17 64 DV57
Kesteven Clo., Ilf. 53 ET51
Kestlake Rd., Bex. 110 EW86
East Rochester Way
Keston Ave., Add. 126 BG111
Keston Ave., Couls. 147 DN119
Keston Ave., Kes. 136 EJ106
Keston Clo. N18 50 DR48
Keston Clo., Well. 96 EW80
Keston Gdns., Kes. 136 EJ105
Keston Ms., Wat. 29 BV40
Nascot La.
Keston Pk. Clo., Kes. 123 EM104
Keston Rd. N17 64 DR55
Keston Rd. SE15 92 DU83
Keston Rd., Th.Hth. 119 DM100
Kestrel Ave. E6 80 EL71
Swan App.
Kestrel Ave. SE24 105 DP85
Kestrel Clo. NW9 46 CS54
Kestrel Clo. NW10 60 CR64
Kestrel Clo., Horn. 83 FH66
Kestrel Clo., Ilf. 54 EW49
Kestrel Clo., Wat. 16 BY34
Kestrel Ho. EC1 **7** **H2**
Kestrel La. W13 73 CF70
Kestrel La., Kings.T. 101 CK92
Kestrel Pl. SE14 93 DY79
Milton Ct. Rd.
Kestrel Way, Wal.Abb. 24 EG34
Kestrel Way, Croy. 135 ED109
Keswick Ave. SW15 102 CS92
Keswick Ave. SW19 118 DA96
Keswick Bdy. SW15 103 CY85
Upper Richmond Rd.
Keswick Clo., Sutt. 132 DC105
Keswick Dr., Enf. 36 DW36
Keswick Gdns., Ilf. 66 EL53
Keswick Gdns., Ruis. 57 BR58
Keswick Gdns., Wem. 60 CL63
Keswick Ms. W5 74 CL74
Keswick Rd. SW15 103 CY85
Keswick Rd., Bexh. 96 FA82
Keswick Rd., Lthd. 142 CC124
Keswick Rd., Orp. 123 ET102
Keswick Rd., Twick. 100 CC86
Keswick Rd., W.Wick. 122 EE103
Kett Gdns. SW2 105 DM85
Kettering Rd., Enf. 37 DX37
Beaconsfield Rd.
Kettering St. SW16 105 DJ93
Kettlebaston Rd. E10 65 DZ60
Kettlewell Ct., Swan. 125 FF96
Kevan Ho. SE5 92 DQ80
Wyndham Rd.
Kevelioc Rd. N17 50 DQ53
Kevin Clo., Houns. 86 BW82
Kevington Clo., Orp. 123 ET98
Kevington Dr., Chis. 123 ES98
Kevington Dr., Orp. 124 EU98
Kew Bri., Brent. 88 CM79
Kew Bri., Rich. 88 CM79
Kew Bri. Arches, Rich. 88 CM79
Kew Bri.
Kew Bri. Ct. W4 88 CN78
Kew Bri. Rd., Brent. 88 CM79
Kew Cres., Sutt. 117 CY104
Kew Foot Rd., Rich. 88 CL84
Kew Gdns. Rd., Rich. 88 CM80
Kew Grn., Rich. 88 CM79
Kew Meadow Path, Rich. 88 CP81

Kew Palace, Rich. 88 CL80
Kew Rd., Rich. 88 CL84
Kewferry Dr., Nthwd. 43 BP50
Kewferry Rd., Nthwd. 43 BQ51
Key Clo. E1 78 DV70
Keybridge Ho. SW8 91 DL79
Keyes Rd. NW2 61 CX64
Keymer Clo., West. 150 EJ116
Keymer Rd. SW2 105 DM89
Keynes Clo. N2 62 DF56
Keynsham Ave., Wdf.Grn. 52 EE49
Keynsham Gdns. SE9 108 EL85
Keynsham Rd. SE9 108 EK85
Keynsham Rd., Mord. 118 DB102
Keynsham Wk., Mord. 118 DB102
Hunston Rd.
Keyse Rd. SE1 **11** **P7**
Keysham Ave., Houns. 85 BU81
The Ave.
Keystone Cres. N1 **6** **A1**
Keywood Dr., Sun. 99 BU93
Keyworth Clo. E5 65 DY63
Keyworth St. SE1 **10** **G6**
Keyworth St. SE1 91 DP76
Kezia St. SE8 93 DY78
Trundleys Rd.
Khama Rd. SW17 104 DE91
Khartoum Rd. E13 80 EH69
Khartoum Rd. SW17 104 DD91
Khartoum Rd., Ilf. 67 EP64
Khyber Rd. SW11 90 DE82
Kibworth St. SW8 91 DM80
Kidbrooke Gdns. SE3 94 EG82
Kidbrooke Gro. SE3 94 EG81
Kidbrooke La. SE9 94 EL84
Kidbrooke Pk. Clo. SE3 94 EH81
Kidbrooke Pk. Rd. SE3 94 EH81
Kidbrooke Way SE3 94 EH82
Kidd Pl. SE7 94 EL78
Kidderminster Pl., Croy. 119 DP102
Kidderminster Rd.
Kidderminster Rd., Croy. 119 DP102
Kidderpore Ave. NW3 62 DA63
Kidderpore Gdns. NW3 62 DA63
Kidlington Way NW9 46 CS54
Kidron Way E9 78 DW67
Clermont Rd.
Kielder Clo., Ilf. 53 ET51
Kiffen St. EC2 **7** **L4**
Kilberry Clo., Islw. 87 CD81
Kilburn Bri. NW6 75 CZ66
Kilburn High Rd.
Kilburn Bldgs. NW6 76 DB67
Kilburn High Rd.
Kilburn Gate NW6 76 DB68
Kilburn Priory
Kilburn High Rd. NW6 75 CZ66
Kilburn La. W9 75 CX69
Kilburn La. W10 75 CX69
Kilburn Pk. Rd. NW6 76 DA69
Kilburn Pl. NW6 76 DA67
Kilburn Priory NW6 76 DB67
Kilburn Sq. NW6 76 DA67
Kilburn High Rd.
Kilburn Vale NW6 76 DB67
Belsize Rd.
Kilby Clo., Wat. 30 BX35
Kilcorral Clo., Epsom 131 CU114
Kildare Clo., Ruis. 58 BW60
Kildare Gdns. W2 76 DA72
Kildare Rd. E16 80 EG71
Kildare Ter. W2 76 DA72
Kildare Wk. E14 79 EA72
Farrance St.
Kildonan Clo., Wat. 29 BT39
Kildoran Rd. SW2 105 DL85
Kildowan Rd., Ilf. 68 EU60
Kilgour Rd. SE23 107 DY86
Kilkie St. SW6 90 DC82
Killarney Rd. SW18 104 DC86
Killasser Ct., Tad. 145 CW123
Killearn Rd. SE6 107 ED88
Killester Gdns., Wor.Pk. 131 CV105
Killewarren Way, Orp. 124 EW100
Killick Clo., Sev. 154 FE121
Killick St. N1 77 DM68
Killieser Ave. SW2 105 DL88
Killip Clo. E16 80 EF72
Killowen Ave., Nthlt. 58 CC64
Killowen Rd. E9 79 DX65
Killyon Rd. SW8 91 DJ82
Killyon Ter. SW8 91 DJ82
Killyon Rd.
Kilmaine Rd. SW6 89 CY80
Kilmarnock Gdns., Dag. 68 EW62
Lindsey Rd.
Kilmarnock Rd., Wat. 44 BX49
Kilmarsh Rd. W6 89 CW77
Kilmartin Ave. SW16 119 DM97
Kilmartin Rd., Ilf. 68 EU61
Kilmartin Way, Horn. 69 FH64
Kilmeston Way SE15 92 DT80
Daniel Gdns.
Kilmington Rd. SW13 89 CU79
Kilmiston Ave., Shep. 113 BQ100
Kilmorey Gdns., Twick. 87 CH84
Kilmorey Rd., Twick. 87 CH84
Kilmorie Rd. SE23 107 DY88
Kiln Clo., Hayes 85 BR79
Brickfield La.
Kiln La., Epsom 130 CS111
Kiln La., Wok. 140 BG124
Kiln Ms. SW17 104 DD92
Kiln Pl. NW5 62 DG63
Kiln Rd., Epp. 26 FA27
Kiln Way, Nthwd. 43 BS51
Kilner St. E14 79 EA71

Kilnside, Esher 129 CG108
Kilnwood, Sev. 138 EZ113
Kilpatrick Way, Hayes 72 BY71
Kilravock St. W10 75 CY69
Kilross Rd., Felt. 99 BR88
Kilrue La., Walt. 127 BT105
Kilsby Wk., Dag. 82 EV65
Rugby Rd.
Kilsha Rd., Walt. 113 BV100
Kilsmore La., Wal.Cr. 23 DX28
Kilvinton Dr., Enf. 36 DR38
Kimbell Gdns. SW6 89 CY81
Kimber Rd. SW18 104 DA87
Kimberley Ave. E6 80 EL68
Kimberley Ave. SE15 92 DV82
Kimberley Ave., Ilf. 67 ER59
Kimberley Ave., Rom. 69 FC58
Kimberley Dr., Sid. 110 EX89
Kimberley Gdns. N4 63 DP57
Kimberley Gdns., Enf. 36 DT41
Kimberley Gate, Brom. 108 EF94
Oaklands Rd.
Kimberley Pl., Pur. 133 DN111
Brighton Rd.
Kimberley Ride, Cob. 128 CB113
Littleheath La.
Kimberley Rd. E4 52 EE46
Kimberley Rd. E11 65 ED61
Kimberley Rd. E16 80 EF70
Kimberley Rd. E17 51 DZ53
Kimberley Rd. N17 50 DU54
Kimberley Rd. N18 50 DV51
Kimberley Rd. NW6 75 CY67
Kimberley Rd. SW9 91 DL82
Kimberley Rd., Beck. 121 DX96
Kimberley Rd., Croy. 119 DP100
Kimberley Way E4 52 EE46
Kimble Clo., Wat. 29 BS44
Kimble Cres. (Bushey), 44 CC45
Wat.
Kimble Rd. SW19 104 DD93
Kimbolton Clo. SE12 108 EF86
Kimbolton Grn., Borwd. 32 CQ42
Kimbolton Row SW3 **8** **B9**
Kimmeridge Gdns. SE9 108 EL91
Kimmeridge Rd. SE9 108 EL91
Kimpton Ind. Est., Sutt. 117 CZ103
Kimpton Pl., Wat. 16 BX34
Kimpton Rd. SE5 92 DR81
Kimpton Rd., Sutt. 117 CZ104
Kimptons Clo., Pot.B. 19 CX33
Kimptons Mead, Pot.B. 19 CX32
Kinburn St. SE16 93 DX75
Kincaid Rd. SE15 92 DV80
Kincardine Gdns. W9 75 CZ70
Harrow Rd.
Kinch Gro., Wem. 60 CM59
Kincraig Dr., Sev. 154 FG124
Kinder Clo. SE28 82 EX73
Kinder St. E1 78 DV72
Cannon St. Rd.
Kindersley Way, Abb.L. 15 BQ31
Kinfauns Rd. SW2 105 DN89
Kinfauns Rd., Ilf. 68 EU60
King Alfred Ave. SE6 107 EA91
King & Queen Clo. SE9 108 EL91
Beaconsfield Rd.
King & Queen St. SE17 **11** **J10**
King & Queen St. SE17 92 DQ78
King Arthur Clo. SE15 92 DW80
King Arthur Ct., Wal.Cr. 23 DY31
King Charles Cres., Surb. 116 CM101
King Charles Rd., Rad. 18 CL32
King Charles Rd., Surb. 116 CM99
King Charles St. SW1 **9** **P4**
King Charles St. SW1 91 DK75
King Charles Ter. E1 78 DV73
Sovereign Clo.
King Charles Wk. SW19 103 CY88
Princes Way
King David La. E1 78 DW73
King Edward Dr., Chess. 116 CL104
Kelvin Gro.
King Edward Ms. SW13 89 CU81
King Edward Rd. E10 65 EC60
King Edward Rd. E17 65 DY55
King Edward Rd., Barn. 34 DA42
King Edward Rd., Rad. 18 CM33
King Edward Rd., Rom. 69 FF58
King Edward Rd., Wal.Cr. 23 DY33
King Edward Rd., Wat. 30 BY44
King Edward St. EC1 **7** **H8**
King Edward St. EC1 78 DQ72
King Edward Wk. SE1 **10** **E6**
King Edward Wk. SE1 91 DN76
King Edward's Gdns. W3 74 CN74
King Edwards Gro., 101 CH93
Tedd.
King Edward's Pl. W3 74 CN74
King Edward's Gdns.
King Edwards Rd. E9 78 DV67
King Edwards Rd. N9 50 DV45
King Edwards Rd., Bark. 81 ER67
King Edward's Rd., Enf. 37 DX42
King Edwards Rd., Ruis. 57 BR60
King Gdns., Croy. 133 DP106
King George Ave. E16 80 EK72
King George Ave., Ilf. 67 ER57
King George Ave., Walt. 114 BX102
King George Ave. 30 CB44
(Bushey), Wat.
King George Clo., Rom. 69 FC55
King George Clo., Sun. 99 BT92
King George Rd., 23 EC34
Wal.Abb.
King George VI Ave., 118 DF98
Mitch.

King George VI Ave., 150 EK116
West.
King George Sq., Rich. 102 CM86
King George St. SE10 93 ED80
King Georges Ave., Wat. 29 BS42
King Georges Dr., Add. 126 BG110
King Georges Dr., Sthl. 72 BZ71
King Harolds Way, Bexh. 96 EX80
King Henry Ms., Orp. 137 ET106
Osgood Ave.
King Henry St. N16 64 DS64
King Henry Ter. E1 78 DV73
Sovereign Clo.
King Henry's Dr., Croy. 135 EB109
King Henry's Ms., Enf. 37 EA37
King Henry's Rd. NW3 76 DE66
King Henrys Rd., Kings.T. 116 CP97
King Henry's Wk. N1 78 DS65
King James Ave. 21 DL29
(Cuffley), Pot.B.
King James St. SE1 **10** **G5**
King James St. SE1 91 DP75
King John Ct. EC2 **7** **N4**
King John St. E1 79 DX71
King John's Wk. SE9 108 EK88
King Sq. EC1 **7** **H3**
King Stairs Clo. SE16 92 DV75
Elephant La.
King St. E13 80 EG70
King St. EC2 **7** **J9**
King St. EC2 78 DQ72
King St. N2 62 DD55
King St. N17 50 DT53
King St. SW1 **9** **L3**
King St. SW1 77 DJ74
King St. W3 74 CP74
King St. W6 89 CU77
King St. WC2 **5** **P10**
King St. WC2 77 DL73
King St., Cher. 112 BG102
King St., Rich. 101 CK85
King St., Sthl. 86 BY76
King St., Twick. 101 CG88
King St., Wat. 30 BW42
King William IV Gdns. 106 DW93
SE20
St. John's Rd.
King William La. SE10 94 EE78
Orlop St.
King William St. EC4 **11** **L1**
King William St. EC4 78 DR73
King William Wk. SE10 93 EC79
Kingaby Gdns., Rain. 83 FG66
Kingcup Clo., Croy. 121 DX102
Primrose La.
Kingdon Rd. NW6 76 DA65
Kingfield Rd. W5 73 CK70
Kingfield St. E14 93 EC77
Kingfisher Clo. SE28 82 EW73
Kingfisher Clo., Har. 45 CF52
Kingfisher Clo., Nthwd. 43 BP53
Kingfisher Clo., Orp. 124 EX98
Kingfisher Clo., Walt. 128 BY106
Old Esher Rd.
Kingfisher Ct. SW19 103 CY89
Queensmere Rd.
Kingfisher Dr., Rich. 101 CH91
Kingfisher Gdns., S.Croy. 135 DX111
Kingfisher Lure, Kings L. 15 BP29
Kingfisher Lure, Rick. 28 BH42
Kingfisher Sq. SE8 93 DZ79
Dorking Clo.
Kingfisher St. E6 80 EL71
Kingfisher Way NW10 74 CR65
Kingfisher Way, Beck. 121 DX99
Kingham Clo. SW18 104 DC87
Kingham Clo. W11 89 CY75
Kinghorn St. EC1 **7** **H7**
Kinglake Est. SE17 **11** **N10**
Kinglake St. SE17 92 DS78
Kingly Ct. W1 **5** **L10**
Kingly St. W1 **5** **K10**
Kingly St. W1 77 DJ73
Kings Arbour, Sthl. 86 BY78
Ringway
Kings Arms Ct. E1 78 DU71
Old Montague St.
Kings Arms Yd. EC2 **7** **K8**
Kings Ave. N10 62 DG55
Kings Ave. N21 49 DP46
King's Ave. SW4 105 DL85
King's Ave. SW12 105 DK88
Kings Ave. W5 73 CK72
Kings Ave., Brom. 108 EF93
Kings Ave., Buck.H. 52 EK47
Kings Ave., Cars. 132 DE108
Kings Ave., Grnf. 72 CB72
Kings Ave., Houns. 86 CB81
Kings Ave., N.Mal. 116 CS98
Kings Ave., Rom. 68 EZ58
Kings Ave., Sun. 99 BT92
Kings Ave., Wat. 29 BT42
Kings Ave., W.Byf. 126 BK112
Kings Ave., Wdf.Grn. 52 EH51
Kings Bench St. SE1 **10** **G4**
Kings Bench Wk. EC4 **6** **E9**
Kings Chase, E.Mol. 114 CC97
Kings Clo. E10 65 EB59
Kings Clo. NW4 61 CX56
Kings Clo., Dart. 97 FE84
Kings Clo., Kings L. 14 BH31
Kings Clo., Nthwd. 43 BT51
Kings Clo., Stai. 98 BK94
Kings Clo., T.Ditt. 115 CG100
Kings Clo., Walt. 113 BV100

Kin–Kni This index reads in the sequence: Street Name / Postal District or Post Town / Map Page Number / Grid Reference

King's Clo., Wat. 29 BV42
Lady's Clo.
Kings College Rd. NW3 76 DE66
Kings College Rd., Ruis. 57 BT58
Kings Ct. E13 80 EH67
Kings Ct. W6 89 CU77
King St.
Kings Ct., Tad. 145 CW122
Kings Ct., Wem. 60 CP61
Kings Cres. N4 64 DQ62
Kings Cres. Est. N4 64 DQ61
King's Cross Bri. N1 6 A2
King's Cross Rd. WC1 6 B2
King's Cross Rd. WC1 77 DM69
Kings Dr., Edg. 46 CM49
Kings Dr., Surb. 116 CN101
Kings Dr., Tedd. 101 CD92
Kings Dr., T.Ditt. 115 CH100
Kings Dr., Wem. 60 CP61
Kings Dr., The, Walt. 127 BT109
Kings Fm. Ave., Rich. 88 CN84
Kings Gdns. NW6 76 DA66
West End La.
Kings Gdns., Ilf. 67 ER60
King's Garth Ms. SE23 106 DW89
London Rd.
Kings Grn., Loug. 38 EL41
Kings Gro. SE15 92 DV81
Kings Gro., Rom. 69 FG57
Kings Hall Rd., Beck. 107 DY94
Kings Head Hill E4 51 EB45
Kings Head La., W.Byf. 126 BK111
Kings Head Yd. SE1 11 K3
Kings Highway SE18 95 ES79
Kings Hill, Loug. 38 EL40
Kings Keep, Kings.T. 116 CL98
Beaufort Rd.
Kings La., Kings L. 14 BG31
Kings La., Sutt. 132 DD107
Kings Langley Bypass, Kings L. 14 BJ25
Kings Mead Pk., Esher 129 CE108
Kings Meadow, Kings L. 14 BN28
Kings Ms. SW4 105 DL85
King's Ave.
King's Ms. WC1 6 C5
King's Ms. WC1 77 DM70
Kings Ms., Chig. 53 EQ47
King's Orchard SE9 108 EL86
Kings Paddock, Hmptn. 114 CC95
Kings Par., Cars. 118 DE104
Wrythe La.
King's Pas. E11 66 EE59
Kings Pas., Kings.T. 115 CK96
Kings Pl. SE1 11 H5
Kings Pl. W4 88 CQ77
Chiswick High Rd.
Kings Pl., Buck.H. 52 EK47
King's Reach Twr. SE1 10 E2
Kings Ride Gate, Rich. 88 CN84
Kings Rd. E4 51 ED46
Kings Rd. E6 80 EJ67
Kings Rd. E11 66 EE59
King's Rd. N17 50 DT53
Kings Rd. N18 50 DU50
Kings Rd. N22 49 DM53
Kings Rd. NW10 75 CV66
Kings Rd. SE25 120 DU97
King's Rd. SW1 90 DD79
King's Rd. SW3 90 DD79
King's Rd. SW6 90 DB80
King's Rd. SW10 90 DC80
Kings Rd. SW14 88 CR83
Kings Rd. SW19 104 DA93
Kings Rd. W5 73 CK71
Kings Rd., Add. 126 BH110
Kings Rd., Bark. 81 EQ66
North St.
Kings Rd., Barn. 33 CW41
Kings Rd., Felt. 100 BW88
Kings Rd., Har. 58 BZ61
Kings Rd., Kings.T. 102 CL94
Kings Rd., Mitch. 118 DG97
Kings Rd., Orp. 137 ET105
Kings Rd., Rich. 102 CM86
Kings Rd., Rom. 69 FG57
Kings Rd. (London Colney), St.Alb. 17 CJ26
Kings Rd., Surb. 115 CJ102
Kings Rd., Sutt. 132 DA110
Kings Rd., Tedd. 101 CD92
Kings Rd., Twick. 101 CH86
Kings Rd., Uxb. 70 BK68
Kings Rd., Wal.Cr. 23 DY34
Kings Rd., Walt. 113 BV103
Kings Rd., West Dr. 84 BM75
Kings Rd., West. 150 EH118
King's Scholars' Pas. SW1 9 K7
King's Ter. NW1 77 DJ67
Plender St.
Kings Ter., Islw. 87 CG83
Worple Rd.
Kings Wk., Kings.T. 115 CK95
Kings Wk., S.Croy. 134 DV114
Kings Way, Har. 59 CE56
Kingsand Rd. SE12 108 EG89
Kingsash Dr., Hayes 72 BY70
Kingsbridge Ave. W3 88 CM75
Kingsbridge Cres., Sthl. 72 BZ71
Kingsbridge Rd. W10 75 CW72
Kingsbridge Rd., Bark. 81 ER68
Kingsbridge Rd., Mord. 117 CX101
Kingsbridge Rd., Sthl. 86 BZ77
Kingsbridge Rd., Walt. 113 BV101
Kingsbridge Way, Hayes 71 BS69
Bradenham Rd.
Kingsbrook, Lthd. 143 CG118
Ryebrook Rd.
Kingsbury Circle NW9 60 CN57
Kingsbury Rd. N1 78 DS65
Kingsbury Rd. NW9 60 CN57
Kingsbury Ter. N1 78 DS65
Kingsbury Trd. Est. NW9 60 CR58
Kingsclere Clo. SW15 103 CU87
Kingscliffe Gdns. SW19 103 CZ88
Kingscote Rd. W4 88 CR76
Kingscote Rd., Croy. 120 DV101
Kingscote Rd., N.Mal. 116 CR97
Kingscote St. EC4 6 F10
Kingscourt Rd. SW16 105 DK90
Kingscroft Rd. NW2 75 CZ65
Kingscroft Rd., Bans. 146 DD115
Kingscroft Rd., Lthd. 143 CH120
Kingsdale Gdns. W11 75 CX74
Kingsdale Rd. SE18 95 ET79
Kingsdale Rd. SE20 107 DX94
Kingsdene, Tad. 145 CV121
Kingsdown Ave. W3 74 CS73
Kingsdown Ave. W13 87 CH75
Kingsdown Ave., S.Croy. 133 DP109
Kingsdown Clo. W10 75 CX72
Kingsdown Rd. E11 66 EE62
Kingsdown Rd. N19 63 DL62
Kingsdown Rd., Epsom 131 CU113
Kingsdown Rd., Sutt. 131 CY106
Kingsdown Way, Brom. 122 EG101
Kingsdowne Rd., Surb. 116 CL101
Kingsend, Ruis. 57 BR60
Kingsfield Ave., Har. 58 CB56
Kingsfield Ct., Wat. 44 BX45
Kingsfield Dr., Enf. 37 DX35
Kingsfield Ho. SE9 108 EK90
Kingsfield Rd., Har. 59 CD59
Kingsfield Rd., Wat. 44 BX45
Kingsfield Way, Enf. 37 DX35
Kingsford Ave., Wall. 133 DL108
Kingsford St. NW5 62 DF64
Kingsford Way E6 81 EM71
Kingsgate, Wem. 60 CQ62
Kingsgate Ave. N3 62 DA55
Kingsgate Clo., Bexh. 96 EY81
Kingsgate Clo., Orp. 124 EW97
Main Rd.
Kingsgate Pl. NW6 76 DA66
Kingsgate Rd. NW6 76 DA66
Kingsgate Rd., Kings.T. 116 CL95
Kingsground SE9 108 EL87
Kingshall Ms. SE13 93 EC83
Lewisham Rd.
Kingshill Ave., Har. 59 CH56
Kingshill Ave., Hayes 71 BS69
Kingshill Ave., Nthlt. 71 BU69
Kingshill Ave., Rom. 55 FC51
Kingshill Ave., Wor.Pk. 117 CU101
Kingshill Dr., Har. 45 CH54
Kingshold Rd. E9 78 DW66
Kingsholm Gdns. SE9 94 EK84
Kingshurst Rd. SE12 108 EG87
Kingsland NW8 76 DE67
Broxwood Way
Kingsland, Pot.B. 19 CZ33
Kingsland Grn. E8 78 DS65
Kingsland High St. E8 78 DT65
Kingsland Pas. E8 78 DS65
Kingsland Grn.
Kingsland Rd. E2 7 N2
Kingsland Rd. E2 78 DS69
Kingsland Rd. E8 78 DS67
Kingsland Rd. E13 80 EJ69
Kingslawn Clo. SW15 103 CV85
Howards La.
Kingslea, Lthd. 143 CG120
Kingsleigh Pl., Mitch. 118 DF97
Chatsworth Pl.
Kingsleigh Wk., Brom. 122 EF98
Stamford Dr.
Kingsley Ave. W13 73 CG72
Kingsley Ave., Bans. 146 DA115
Kingsley Ave., Borwd. 32 CM40
Kingsley Ave., Houns. 86 CC82
Kingsley Ave., Sthl. 72 CA73
Kingsley Ave., Sutt. 132 DD105
Kingsley Ave. (Cheshunt), Wal.Cr. 22 DV29
Kingsley Clo. N2 62 DC57
Kingsley Clo., Dag. 69 FB63
Kingsley Ct., Edg. 46 CP47
Kingsley Dr., Wor.Pk. 117 CT103
Badgers Copse
Kingsley Flats SE1 92 DS77
Old Kent Rd.
Kingsley Gdns. E4 51 EA50
Kingsley Ms. E1 78 DV73
Wapping La.
Kingsley Ms. W8 90 DB76
Stanford Rd.
Kingsley Ms., Chis. 109 EP93
Kingsley Pl. N6 62 DG59
Kingsley Rd. E7 80 EG66
Kingsley Rd. E17 51 EC54
Kingsley Rd. N13 49 DN49
Kingsley Rd. NW6 75 CZ67
Kingsley Rd. SW19 104 DB92
Kingsley Rd., Croy. 119 DN102
Kingsley Rd., Har. 58 CC63
Kingsley Rd., Houns. 86 CB81
Kingsley Rd., Ilf. 53 EQ53
Kingsley Rd., Loug. 39 ER41
Kingsley Rd., Orp. 137 ET107
Kingsley Rd., Pnr. 58 BZ56
Kingsley St. SW11 90 DF83
Kingsley Way N2 62 DC57
Kingsley Wd. Dr. SE9 109 EM90
Kingslyn Cres. SE19 120 DS95
Kingsman Par. SE18 95 EM76
Woolwich Ch. St.
Kingsman St. SE18 95 EM76
Kingsmead, Barn. 34 DA42
Kingsmead (Cuffley), Pot.B. 21 DL28
Kingsmead, Rich. 102 CM86
Kingsmead, Wal.Cr. 23 DX28
Kingsmead, West. 150 EK116
Kingsmead Ave. N9 50 DV46
Kingsmead Ave. NW9 60 CR59
Kingsmead Ave., Mitch. 119 DJ97
Kingsmead Ave., Rom. 69 FE58
Kingsmead Ave., Sun. 114 BW96
Kingsmead Ave., Surb. 116 CN103
Kingsmead Ave., Wor.Pk. 117 CV103
Kingsmead Clo., Epsom 130 CR108
Kingsmead Clo., Sid. 110 EU89
Kingsmead Clo., Tedd. 101 CH93
Kingsmead Dr., Nthlt. 72 BZ66
Kingsmead Est. E9 65 DY63
Kingsmead Way
Kingsmead Rd. SW2 105 DN89
Kingsmead Way E9 65 DY63
Kingsmere Clo. SW15 89 CY83
Felsham Rd.
Kingsmere Pk. NW9 60 CP60
Kingsmere Rd. SW19 103 CX89
Kingsmill Gdns., Dag. 68 EZ64
Kingsmill Rd., Dag. 68 EZ64
Kingsmill Ter. NW8 76 DD68
Kingsnympton Pk., Kings.T. 102 CP94
Kingspark Ct. E18 66 EG55
Kingsridge SW19 103 CY89
Kingsthorpe Rd. SE26 107 DX91
Kingston Ave., Felt. 99 BS86
Kingston Ave., Lthd. 143 CH121
Kingston Ave., Sutt. 117 CY104
Kingston Ave., West Dr. 70 BM73
Kingston Bri., Kings.T. 115 CK96
Kingston Bypass SW15 102 CS91
Kingston Bypass SW20 102 CS93
Kingston Bypass, Esher 115 CE103
Kingston Bypass, N.Mal. 117 CU98
Kingston Bypass, Surb. 115 CH104
Kingston Clo., Nthlt. 72 BZ66
Kingston Clo., Rom. 68 EY55
Kingston Clo., Tedd. 101 CH93
Kingston Ct. N4 64 DQ58
Wiltshire Gdns.
Kingston Cres., Ashf. 98 BJ92
Kingston Cres., Beck. 121 DZ95
Kingston Gdns., Croy. 119 DL104
Wandle Rd.
Kingston Hall Rd., Kings.T. 115 CK97
Kingston Hill, Kings.T. 116 CN95
Kingston Hill Ave., Rom. 68 EY55
Kingston Hill Pl., Kings.T. 102 CQ91
Kingston Ho. Gdns., Lthd. 143 CG121
Upper Fairfield Rd.
Kingston La., Tedd. 101 CG92
Kingston La., Uxb. 70 BL69
Kingston La., West Dr. 84 BM75
Kingston Pk. Est., Kings.T. 102 CP93
Kingston Pl., Har. 45 CF52
Richmond Gdns.
Kingston Ri., Add. 126 BG110
Kingston Rd. N9 50 DU47
Kingston Rd. SW15 103 CU89
Kingston Rd. SW19 117 CY96
Kingston Rd. SW20 117 CW96
Kingston Rd., Ashf. 98 BL93
Kingston Rd., Barn. 34 DD43
Kingston Rd., Epsom 130 CS105
Kingston Rd., Ilf. 67 EP63
Kingston Rd., Kings.T. 116 CP97
Kingston Rd., Lthd. 143 CG121
Kingston Rd., N.Mal. 116 CR98
Kingston Rd., Rom. 69 FF56
Kingston Rd., Sthl. 86 BZ75
Kingston Rd., Stai. 98 BH93
Kingston Rd., Surb. 116 CP103
Kingston Rd., Tedd. 101 CH92
Kingston Rd., Wor.Pk. 116 CQ104
Kingston Sq. SE19 106 DR92
Kingston Vale SW15 102 CR91
Kingstown St. NW1 76 DG67
Kingswater Pl. SW11 90 DE80
Battersea Ch. Rd.
Kingsway N12 48 DC51
Kingsway SW14 88 CP83
Kingsway WC2 6 B8
Kingsway WC2 77 DM72
Kingsway, Croy. 133 DM106
Kingsway, Enf. 36 DV43
Kingsway, Hayes 71 BQ71
Kingsway, N.Mal. 117 CW98
Kingsway, Orp. 123 EQ99
Kingsway (Cuffley), Pot.B. 21 DL30
Kingsway, Stai. 98 BK88
Kingsway, Wat. 29 BT35
Kingsway, Wem. 60 CL63
Kingsway, W.Wick. 122 EE104
Kingsway, Wdf.Grn. 52 EJ50
Kingsway, The, Epsom 130 CS111
Kingsway Ave., S.Croy. 134 DW109
Kingsway Business Pk., Hmptn. 114 BZ95
Kingsway Cres., Har. 58 CC56
Kingsway Ind. Est. N18 51 DX51
Kingsway Rd., Sutt. 131 CY107
Kingswear Rd. NW5 63 DH62
Kingswear Rd., Ruis. 57 BU61
Kingswell Ride (Cuffley), Pot.B. 21 DL30
Kingswood Ave. NW6 75 CY67
Kingswood Ave., Belv. 96 EZ77
Kingswood Ave., Brom. 122 EE97
Kingswood Ave., Hmptn. 100 CB93
Kingswood Ave., Houns. 86 BZ81
Kingswood Ave., S.Croy. 148 DV115
Kingswood Ave., Swan. 125 FF98
Kingswood Ave., Th.Hth. 119 DN99
Kingswood Clo. N20 48 DC45
Kingswood Clo. SW8 91 DL80
Kenchester Clo.
Kingswood Clo., Enf. 36 DS43
Kingswood Clo., N.Mal. 117 CT100
Motspur Pk.
Kingswood Clo., Orp. 123 ER101
Kingswood Clo., Surb. 116 CL101
Kingswood Clo., Wey. 127 BP108
Kingswood Dr. SE19 106 DS91
Kingswood Dr., Cars. 118 DF102
Kingswood Dr., Sutt. 132 DB109
Kingswood Est. SE21 106 DS91
Bowen Dr.
Kingswood La., Warl. 148 DW115
Kingswood Pk. N3 47 CZ54
Kingswood Pl. SE13 94 EE84
Kingswood Rd. SE20 106 DW93
Kingswood Rd. SW2 105 DL86
Kingswood Rd. SW19 103 CZ94
Kingswood Rd. W4 88 CQ76
Kingswood Rd., Brom. 121 ED98
Kingswood Rd., Ilf. 68 EU60
Kingswood Rd., Sev. 153 FE120
Kingswood Rd., Tad. 145 CV121
Kingswood Rd., Wat. 15 BV34
Kingswood Rd., Wem. 60 CN62
Kingswood Ter. W4 88 CQ76
Kingswood Rd.
Kingswood Way, S.Croy. 134 DW113
Kingswood Way, Wall. 133 DL106
Kingsworth Clo., Beck. 121 DY99
Shirley Cres.
Kingsworthy Clo., Kings.T. 116 CM97
Kingthorpe Rd. NW10 74 CR66
Kingthorpe Ter. NW10 74 CR65
Kingwell Rd., Barn. 34 DD38
Kingwood Rd. SW6 89 CY80
Kinlet Rd. SE18 95 EQ81
Kinloch Dr. NW9 60 CR59
Kinloch St. N7 63 DM62
Hornsey Rd.
Kinloss Gdns. N3 61 CZ55
Kinloss Rd., Cars. 118 DC101
Kinnaird Ave. W4 88 CQ80
Kinnaird Ave., Brom. 108 EF93
Kinnaird Clo., Brom. 108 EF93
Kinnaird Way, Wdf.Grn. 53 EM51
Kinnear Rd. W12 89 CT75
Kinnerton Pl. N. SW1 8 E5
Kinnerton Pl. S. SW1 8 E5
Kinnerton St. SW1 8 F5
Kinnerton St. SW1 90 DG75
Kinnerton Yd. SW1 8 E5
Kinnoul Rd. W6 89 CY79
Kinross Ave., Wor.Pk. 117 CU103
Kinross Clo., Edg. 46 CP47
Tayside Dr.
Kinross Clo., Har. 60 CL57
Kinross Clo., Sun. 99 BT92
Kinross Dr., Sun. 99 BT92
Kinsale Rd. SE15 92 DU83
Kintore Way SE1 11 P8
Kintyre Clo. SW16 119 DM96
Kinveachy Gdns. SE7 94 EL78
Kinver Rd. SE26 106 DW91
Kipings, Tad. 145 CX122
Heathcote
Kipling Dr. SW19 104 DD93
Kipling Est. SE1 11 L5
Kipling Est. SE1 92 DR75
Kipling Pl., Stan. 45 CF51
Uxbridge Rd.
Kipling Rd., Bexh. 96 EY81
Kipling St. SE1 11 L5
Kipling St. SE1 92 DR75
Kipling Ter. N9 50 DR48
Kipling Twrs., Rom. 55 FH52
Kippington Clo., Sev. 154 FF124
Kippington Dr. SE9 108 EK88
Kippington Rd., Sev. 154 FG124
Kirby Clo., Epsom 131 CT106
Kirby Clo., Ilf. 53 ES51
Kirby Clo., Loug. 52 EL45
Kirby Clo., Nthwd. 43 BT51
Kirby Est. SE16 92 DV76
Kirby Gro. SE1 11 M4
Kirby Gro. SE1 92 DS75
Kirby St. EC1 6 E6
Kirby Way, Walt. 114 BW100
Kirchen Rd. W13 73 CH73
Kirk Ct., Sev. 154 FG123
Kirk La. SE18 95 EQ79
Kirk Ri., Sutt. 118 DB104
Kirk Rd. E17 65 DZ58
Kirkcaldy Grn., Wat. 44 BW48
Trevose Way
Kirkdale SE26 106 DW91
Kirkdale Rd. E11 66 EE60
Kirkfield Clo. W13 73 CH74
Broomfield Rd.
Kirkham Rd. E6 80 EL72
Kirkham St. SE18 95 ES79
Kirkland Ave., Ilf. 53 EN54
Kirkland Clo., Sid. 109 ES86
Kirkland Wk. E8 78 DT65
Laurel St.
Kirkleas Rd., Surb. 116 CL102
Kirklees Rd., Dag. 68 EW64
Kirklees Rd., Th.Hth. 119 DN99
Kirkley Rd. SW19 118 DA95
Kirkly Clo., S.Croy. 134 DS109
Kirkman Pl. W1 5 M7
Kirkmichael Rd. E14 79 EC72
Dee St.
Kirks Pl. E14 79 DZ71
Rhodeswell Rd.
Kirkside Rd. SE3 94 EG79
Kirkstall Ave. N17 64 DR56
Kirkstall Gdns. SW2 105 DK88
Kirkstall Rd. SW2 105 DK88
Kirkstead Ct. E5 65 DY62
Mandeville St.
Kirksted Rd., Mord. 118 DB102
Kirkstone Way, Brom. 108 EE93
Kirkton Rd. N15 64 DS56
Kirkwall Pl. E2 78 DW69
Kirkwood Rd. SE15 92 DV82
Kirn Rd. W13 73 CH73
Kirchen Rd.
Kirrane Clo., N.Mal. 117 CT99
Kirtley Rd. SE26 107 DY91
Kirtling St. SW8 91 DJ80
Kirton Clo. W4 88 CR77
Dolman Rd.
Kirton Gdns. E2 78 DT69
Chambord St.
Kirton Rd. E13 80 EJ68
Kirton Wk., Edg. 46 CQ52
Kirwyn Way SE5 91 DP80
Kitcat Ter. E3 79 EA69
Kitchener Rd. E7 80 EH65
Kitchener Rd. E17 51 EB53
Kitchener Rd. N2 62 DE55
Kitchener Rd. N17 64 DR55
Kitchener Rd., Dag. 83 FB65
Kitchener Rd., Th.Hth. 120 DR97
Kite Yd. SW11 90 DF81
Cambridge Rd.
Kitley Gdns. SE19 120 DT95
Kitson Rd. SE5 92 DR80
Kitson Rd. SW13 89 CU81
Kitswell Way, Rad. 17 CF33
Kitters Grn., Abb.L. 15 BS31
High St.
Kittiwake Clo., S.Croy. 135 DY110
Kittiwake Rd., Nthlt. 72 BX69
Kittiwake Way, Hayes 72 BX71
Kitto Rd. SE14 93 DX82
Kitt's End Rd., Barn. 33 CX36
Kiver Rd. N19 63 DK61
Kiwi Clo., Twick. 101 CH86
Crown Rd.
Klea Ave. SW4 105 DJ86
Knapdale Clo. SE23 106 DV89
Knapmill Rd. SE6 107 EA89
Knapmill Way SE6 107 EB89
Knapp Clo. NW10 74 CS65
Knapp Rd. E3 79 EA70
Knapp Rd., Ashf. 98 BM91
Knapton Ms. SW17 104 DG93
Seely Rd.
Knaresborough Dr. SW18 104 DB88
Knaresborough Pl. SW5 90 DB77
Knatchbull Rd. NW10 74 CR67
Knatchbull Rd. SE5 91 DP82
Knebworth Ave. E17 51 EA53
Knebworth Path, Borwd. 32 CR42
Knebworth Rd. N16 64 DS63
Nevill Rd.
Knee Hill SE2 96 EW77
Knee Hill Cres. SE2 96 EW77
Kneller Gdns., Islw. 101 CD86
Kneller Rd. SE4 93 DY84
Kneller Rd., N.Mal. 116 CS101
Kneller Rd., Twick. 100 CC86
Knighten St. E1 78 DU74
Knightland Rd. E5 64 DV61
Knighton Clo., Rom. 69 FD58
Knighton Clo., S.Croy. 133 DP108
Knighton Clo., Wdf.Grn. 52 EH49
Knighton Dr., Wdf.Grn. 52 EH49
Knighton La., Buck.H. 52 EH47
Knighton Pk. Rd. SE26 107 DX92
Knighton Rd. E7 66 EG62
Knighton Rd., Rom. 69 FC58
Knighton Rd., Sev. 153 FF116
Knighton St. E1 78 DU74
Knighton Way La., Uxb. 70 BH65
Knightrider Ct. EC4 78 DQ73
Godliman St.
Knightrider St. EC4 78 DQ73
Godliman St.
Knights Arc. SW1 8 D5
Knights Ave. W5 88 CL75
Knights Clo. E9 64 DW64
Churchill Wk.
Knights Ct., Kings.T. 116 CL97
Knights Ct., Rom. 68 EY58
Knights Hill SE27 105 DP92
Knights Hill Sq. SE27 105 DP91
Knights Hill
Knights La. N9 50 DU48
Knights Pk., Kings.T. 116 CL97
Knights Ridge, Orp. 138 EV106
Stirling Dr.
Knights Rd. E16 94 EG75
Knights Rd., Stan. 45 CJ49
Knights Wk. SE11 10 F9
Knights Wk., Rom. 40 EV41
Knights Way, Ilf. 53 EQ51
Knightsbridge SW1 8 E4

Knightsbridge SW1 90 DF75
Knightsbridge SW7 8 C5
Knightsbridge SW7 90 DE75
Knightsbridge Cres., Stai. 98 BH93
Knightsbridge Gdns., Rom. 69 FD57
Knightsbridge Grn. SW1 8 D5
Knightsbridge Grn. SW1 90 DF75
Knightswood Clo., Edg. 46 CQ47
Knightwood Cres., N.Mal. 116 CS100
Knipp Hill, Cob. 128 BZ113
Knivet Rd. SW6 90 DA79
Knobs Hill Rd. E15 79 EB67
Knockholt Clo., Sutt. 132 DB110
Knockholt Main Rd., Sev. 152 EY115
Knockholt Rd. SE9 108 EK85
Knockholt Rd., Sev. 138 EZ113
Knole, The SE9 109 EN91
Knole Clo., Croy. 120 DW100
Stockbury Rd.
Knole Gate, Sid. 109 ES90
Woodside Cres.
Knole La., Sev. 155 FJ126
Knole Rd., Dart. 111 FG87
Knole Rd., Sev. 155 FK123
Knole Way, Sev. 155 FJ125
Knoll, The W13 73 CJ71
Knoll, The, Beck. 121 EB95
Knoll, The, Brom. 122 EG102
Knoll, The, Cob. 128 CA113
Knoll, The, Lthd. 143 CJ121
Knoll Ct. SE19 106 DT92
Knoll Cres., Nthwd. 43 BS54
Knoll Dr. N14 48 DG45
Knoll Ri., Orp. 123 ET102
Knoll Rd. SW18 104 DC85
Knoll Rd., Bex. 110 FA87
Knoll Rd., Sid. 110 EV92
Knollmead, Surb. 116 CQ102
Knolls, The, Epsom 145 CW116
Knolls Clo., Wor.Pk. 117 CV104
Knollys Clo. SW16 105 DN90
Knollys Rd. SW16 105 DM90
Knottisford St. E2 78 DW69
Knotts Grn. Ms. E10 65 EB58
Knotts Grn. Rd.
Knotts Grn. Rd. E10 65 EB58
Knotts Pl., Sev. 154 FG124
Knowl Pk., Borwd. 32 CL43
Knowl Way, Borwd. 32 CM43
Knowle, The, Tad. 145 CW121
Knowle Ave., Bexh. 96 EY80
Knowle Clo. SW9 91 DN83
Knowle Grn., Stai. 98 BG92
Knowle Pk., Cob. 142 BY115
Knowle Pk. Ave., Stai. 98 BH93
Knowle Rd., Brom. 122 EL103
Knowle Rd., Twick. 101 CE88
Knowles Clo., West Dr. 70 BL74
Knowles Hill Cres. SE13 107 ED85
Knowles Wk. SW4 91 DJ83
Knowlton Grn., Brom. 122 EF99
Knowsley Ave., Sthl. 72 CB74
Knowsley Rd. SW11 90 DF82
Knox Rd. E7 80 EF65
Knox St. W1 4 D6
Knox St. W1 76 DF71
Knoyle St. SE14 93 DY79
Chubworthy St.
Knutsford Ave., Wat. 30 BX38
Koh-i-noor Ave. 30 CA44
(Bushey), Wat.
Kohat Rd. SW19 104 DB92
Koonowla Clo., West. 150 EK115
Kooringa, Warl. 148 DV119
Korda Clo., Shep. 112 BM97
Kossuth St. SE10 94 EE78
Kotree Way SE1 92 DU77
Beatrice Rd.
Kramer Ms. SW5 90 DA78
Kempsford Gdns.
Kreedman Wk. E8 64 DU64
Kreisel Wk., Rich. 88 CM79
Kuala Gdns. SW16 119 DM95
Kuhn Way E7 66 EG64
Forest La.
Kydbrook Clo., Orp. 123 EQ101
Kylemore Clo. E6 80 EK68
Parr Rd.
Kylemore Rd. NW6 76 DA66
Kymberley Rd., Har. 59 CE58
Kyme Rd., Horn. 69 FF58
Kynance Gdns., Stan. 45 CJ53
Kynance Ms. SW7 90 DC76
Kynance Pl. SW7 90 DC76
Kynaston Ave. N16 64 DT62
Dynevor Rd.
Kynaston Ave., Th.Hth. 120 DQ99
Kynaston Clo., Har. 45 CD52
Kynaston Cres., Th.Hth. 120 DQ99
Kynaston Rd. N16 64 DS62
Kynaston Rd., Brom. 108 EG92
Kynaston Rd., Enf. 36 DR39
Kynaston Rd., Orp. 124 EV101
Kynaston Rd., Th.Hth. 120 DQ99
Kynaston Wd., Har. 45 CD52
Kynock Rd. N18 50 DW49
Kyrle Rd. SW11 104 DF86
Kytes Dr., Wat. 16 BX33
Kytes Est., Wat. 16 BX33
Kyverdale Rd. N16 64 DT59

L

La Tourne Gdns., Orp. 123 EQ104
Laburnham Ave., West Dr. 70 BM73
Laburnum Ave. N9 50 DS47
Laburnum Ave. N17 50 DR52
Laburnum Ave., Horn. 69 FF62
Laburnum Ave., Sutt. 118 DE104
Laburnum Ave., Swan. 125 FC97
Laburnum Clo. E4 51 DZ51
Laburnum Clo. N11 48 DG51
Laburnum Clo. SE15 92 DW80
Clifton Way
Laburnum Clo. 23 DX31
(Cheshunt), Wal.Cr.
Laburnum Ct. E2 78 DT67
Laburnum St.
Laburnum Ct., Stan. 45 CJ49
Laburnum Cres., Sun. 113 BV95
Batavia Rd.
Laburnum Gdns. N21 50 DQ47
Laburnum Gdns., Croy. 121 DX101
Laburnum Gro. N21 50 DQ47
Laburnum Gro. NW9 60 CQ59
Laburnum Gro., Houns. 86 BZ84
Laburnum Gro., N.Mal. 116 CR96
Laburnum Gro., Ruis. 57 BR58
Laburnum Gro., St.Alb. 16 CB25
Laburnum Gro., Sthl. 72 BZ70
Laburnum Ho., Dag. 68 FA61
Althorne Way
Laburnum Rd. SW19 104 DC94
Laburnum Rd., Cher. 112 BG102
Laburnum Rd., Epp. 26 EW29
Laburnum Rd., Epsom 130 CS113
Laburnum Rd., Hayes 85 BT77
Laburnum Rd., Mitch. 118 DG96
Laburnum St. E2 78 DT67
Laburnum Way, Brom. 123 EN101
Laburnum Way, Stai. 98 BM88
Laburnum Way 21 DP28
(Cheshunt), Wal.Cr.
Millcrest Rd.
Lacebark Clo., Sid. 109 ET87
Lacey Ave., Couls. 147 DN120
Lacey Clo. N9 50 DU47
Lacey Dr., Couls. 147 DN120
Lacey Dr., Dag. 68 EV63
Lacey Dr., Edg. 46 CL49
Lacey Dr., Hmptn. 114 BZ95
Lacey Grn., Couls. 147 DN120
Lacey Wk. E3 79 EA68
Lackford Rd., Couls. 146 DF118
Lackington St. EC2 7 L6
Lackington St. EC2 78 DR71
Lackmore Rd., Enf. 36 DW35
Lacock Clo. SW19 104 DC93
Lacon Rd. SE22 92 DU84
Lacy Rd. SW15 89 CX84
Ladas Rd. SE27 106 DQ91
Ladbroke Cres. W11 75 CY72
Ladbroke Gro.
Ladbroke Gdns. W11 75 CZ73
Ladbroke Gro. W10 75 CX70
Ladbroke Gro. W11 75 CY72
Ladbroke Ms. W11 75 CY74
Ladbroke Rd.
Ladbroke Rd. W11 75 CZ74
Ladbroke Rd., Enf. 36 DT44
Ladbroke Rd., Epsom 130 CR114
Ladbroke Sq. W11 75 CZ73
Ladbroke Ter. W11 75 CZ73
Ladbroke Wk. W11 75 CZ74
Ladbrook Clo., Pnr. 58 BZ57
Ladbrook Rd. SE25 120 DR97
Ladbrooke Clo., Pot.B. 20 DA32
Strafford Gate
Ladbrooke Cres., Sid. 110 EX90
Ladbrooke Dr., Pot.B. 20 DA32
Ladderstile Ride, Kings.T. 102 CQ92
Ladderswood Way N11 49 DJ50
Ladds Way, Swan. 125 FD98
Lady Booth Rd., Kings.T. 116 CL96
Lady Hay, Wor.Pk. 117 CT103
Lady Margaret Rd. N19 63 DJ63
Lady Margaret Rd. NW5 63 DJ64
Lady Margaret Rd., Sthl. 72 BZ71
Lady Somerset Rd. NW5 63 DH63
Ladybower Ct. E5 65 DY63
Gilpin Rd.
Ladycroft Gdns., Orp. 137 EQ106
Ladycroft Rd. SE13 93 EB83
Ladycroft Wk., Stan. 45 CK53
Ladycroft Way, Orp. 137 EQ106
Ladyfield Clo., Loug. 39 EP42
Ladyfields, Loug. 39 EP42
Ladygate La., Ruis. 57 BP58
Ladygrove, Croy. 135 DY109
Ladymeadow, Kings L. 14 BK27
Lady's Clo., Wat. 29 BV42
Ladysmith Ave. E6 80 EL68
Ladysmith Ave., Ilf. 67 ER59
Ladysmith Rd. E16 80 EF69
Ladysmith Rd. N17 50 DU54
Ladysmith Rd. N18 50 DV50
Ladysmith Rd. SE9 109 EN86
Ladysmith Rd., Enf. 36 DS41
Ladysmith Rd., Har. 45 CE54
Ladythorpe Clo., Add. 126 BH105
Church Rd.
Ladywell Clo. SE4 93 DZ84
Adelaide Ave.
Ladywell Heights SE4 107 DZ86
Ladywell Rd. SE13 107 EB85
Ladywell St. E15 80 EF67
Plaistow Gro.
Ladywood Ave., Orp. 123 ES99
Ladywood Clo., Rick. 28 BH41
Ladywood Rd., Surb. 116 CN103
Lafone Ave., Felt. 100 BW88
Alfred Rd.
Lafone St. SE1 11 P4
Lafone St. SE1 92 DT75
Lagado Ms. SE16 79 DX74
Lagonda Ave., Ilf. 53 ET51
Lagoon Rd., Orp. 124 EV99
Laing Clo., Ilf. 53 ER51
Laing Dean, Nthlt. 72 BW67
Laings Ave., Mitch. 118 DF96
Lainlock Pl., Houns. 86 CB81
Spring Gro. Rd.
Lainson St. SW18 104 DA87
Laird Ho. SE5 92 DQ80
Redcar St.
Lairdale Clo. SE21 106 DQ88
Lairs Clo. N7 77 DL65
Manger Rd.
Laitwood Rd. SW12 105 DH88
Lake, The (Bushey), Wat. 44 CC46
Lake Ave., Brom. 108 EG93
Lake Clo. SW19 103 CZ92
Lake Rd.
Lake Clo., W.Byf. 126 BK112
Lake Dr. (Bushey), Wat. 44 CC47
Lake Gdns., Dag. 68 FA64
Lake Gdns., Rich. 101 CH89
Lake Gdns., Wall. 119 DH104
Lake Ho. Rd. E11 66 EG62
Lake Ri., Rom. 55 FF54
Lake Rd. SW19 103 CZ92
Lake Rd., Croy. 121 DZ103
Lake Rd., Rom. 68 EX56
Lake Vw., Edg. 46 CM50
Lake Vw., Pot.B. 20 DC33
Lake Vw. Rd., Sev. 154 FG123
Lakedale Rd. SE18 95 ES78
Lakefield Rd. N22 49 DP54
Lakehall Gdns., Th.Hth. 119 DP99
Lakehall Rd., Th.Hth. 119 DP99
Lakehurst Rd., Epsom 130 CS106
Lakeland Clo., Chig. 54 EV49
Lakeland Clo., Har. 45 CD51
Lakenheath N14 35 DJ43
Laker Pl. SW15 103 CY86
Lakers Ri., Bans. 146 DE116
Lakes Rd., Kes. 136 EJ106
Lakeside N3 48 DB54
Lakeside W13 73 CJ72
Edgehill Rd.
Lakeside, Beck. 121 EB97
Lakeside, Enf. 35 DK42
Lakeside, Wall. 119 DH104
Derek Ave.
Lakeside, Wey. 113 BS103
Lakeside Ave. SE28 82 EU74
Lakeside Ave., Ilf. 66 EK56
Lakeside Clo. SE25 120 DU96
Lakeside Clo., Chig. 53 ET49
Lakeside Clo., Ruis. 57 BR56
Lakeside Clo., Sid. 110 EW85
Lakeside Ct. N4 63 DP61
Lakeside Ct., Borwd. 32 CN43
Cavendish Cres.
Lakeside Cres., Barn. 34 DF43
Lakeside Cres., Wey. 113 BQ104
Churchill Dr.
Lakeside Dr., Brom. 122 EL104
Lakeside Dr., Esher 128 CC107
Lakeside Pl., St.Alb. 17 CK27
Lakeside Rd. N13 49 DM49
Lakeside Rd. W14 89 CX76
Lakeside Rd. (Cheshunt), 22 DW28
Wal.Cr.
Lakeside Way, Wem. 60 CN63
Lakeswood Rd., Orp. 123 EP99
Lakeview Ct. SW19 103 CY89
Victoria Dr.
Lakeview Rd. SE27 105 DN92
Lakeview Rd., Well. 96 EV84
Lakis Clo. NW3 62 DC63
Flask Wk.
Laleham Ave. NW7 46 CR48
Laleham Pk., Stai. 112 BJ99
Laleham Reach, Cher. 112 BH96
Laleham Rd. SE6 107 EC87
Laleham Rd., Shep. 112 BL98
Lalor St. SW6 89 CY82
Lamb Clo., Wat. 16 BW34
Lamb La. E8 78 DV66
Lamb St. E1 7 P6
Lamb St. E1 78 DT71
Lamb Wk. SE1 11 M5
Lamb Yd., Wat. 30 BX43
Lambarde Ave. SE9 109 EN91
Lambarde Dr., Sev. 154 FG123
Lambarde Rd., Sev. 154 FG122
Lambardes Clo., Orp. 138 EW110
Lamberhurst Clo., Orp. 124 EX102
Lamberhurst Rd. SE27 105 DN91
Lamberhurst Rd., Dag. 68 EY60
Lambert Ave., Rich. 88 CN83
Lambert Clo., West. 150 EK116
Lambert Ct. (Bushey), 30 BX42
Wat.
Lambert Jones Ms. EC2 78 DQ71
Beech St.
Lambert Rd. E16 80 EH72
Lambert Rd. N12 48 DC50
Lambert Rd. SW2 105 DL85
Lambert Rd., Bans. 132 DA114
Lambert St. N1 77 DN66
Lambert Wk., Wem. 59 CK62
Clarendon Gdns.
Lambert Way N12 48 DC50
Woodhouse Rd.
Lamberts Pl., Croy. 120 DR102
Lamberts Rd., Surb. 116 CL99
Lambeth Bri. SE1 10 A8
Lambeth Bri. SE1 91 DL77
Lambeth Bri. SW1 10 A8
Lambeth Bri. SW1 91 DL77
Lambeth High St. SE1 10 B8
Lambeth High St. SE1 91 DM77
Lambeth Hill EC4 7 H10
Lambeth Hill EC4 78 DQ73
Lambeth Palace Rd. SE1 10 B7
Lambeth Palace Rd. SE1 91 DM76
Lambeth Rd. SE1 10 D7
Lambeth Rd. SE1 91 DM76
Lambeth Rd. SE11 91 DM76
Lambeth Rd., Croy. 119 DN101
Lambeth Wk. SE11 10 C8
Lambeth Wk. SE11 91 DM77
Lamble St. NW5 62 DG64
Lambley Rd., Dag. 82 EV65
Lambolle Pl. NW3 76 DE65
Lambolle Rd. NW3 76 DE65
Lambourn Chase, Rad. 31 CF36
Lambourn Clo. W7 87 CF75
Lambourn Rd. SW4 91 DH83
Lambourne Ave. SW19 103 CZ91
Lambourne Clo., Chig. 54 EV47
Lambourne Rd.
Lambourne Cres., Chig. 54 EV47
Lambourne Dr., Cob. 142 BX115
Lambourne Gdns. E4 51 EA47
Lambourne Gdns., Bark. 81 ET66
Lambourne Rd.
Lambourne Gdns., Enf. 36 DT40
Lambourne Gro., Kings.T. 116 CP96
Kenley Rd.
Lambourne Pl. SE3 94 EH81
Shooter's Hill Rd.
Lambourne Rd. E11 65 ED59
Lambourne Rd., Bark. 81 ES66
Lambourne Rd., Chig. 53 ET49
Lambourne Rd., Ilf. 67 ES61
Lambrook Ter. SW6 89 CY81
Lamb's Bldgs. EC1 7 K5
Lambs Clo. (Cuffley), 21 DM29
Pot.B.
Lambs Conduit Pas. WC1 6 B6
Lamb's Conduit St. WC1 6 B5
Lamb's Conduit St. WC1 77 DM70
Lambs La., Rain. 83 FH71
Lambs Meadow, 52 EK54
Wdf.Grn.
Lambs Ms. N1 77 DP67
Colebrooke Row
Lamb's Pas. EC1 7 K6
Lamb's Pas. EC1 78 DR71
Lambs Ter. N9 50 DR47
Lambs Wk., Enf. 36 DQ40
Lambscroft Ave. SE9 108 EJ90
Lambton Ave., Wal.Cr. 23 DX32
Lambton Pl. W11 75 CZ72
Westbourne Gro.
Lambton Rd. N19 63 DL60
Lambton Rd. SW20 117 CW95
Lamerock Rd., Brom. 108 EF91
Lamerton Rd., Ilf. 53 EP54
Lamerton St. SE8 93 EA79
Lamford Clo. N17 50 DR52
Lamington St. W6 89 CV77
Lamlash St. SE11 10 F8
Lammas Ave., Mitch. 118 DG96
Lammas Grn. SE26 106 DV90
Lammas La., Esher 128 CA106
Lammas Pk. W5 87 CJ75
Lammas Pk. Gdns. W5 73 CJ74
Lammas Pk. Rd. W5 73 CJ74
Lammas Rd. E9 79 DX66
Lammas Rd. E10 65 DY61
Lammas Rd., Rich. 101 CJ91
Lammas Rd., Wat. 30 BW43
Lammermoor Rd. SW12 105 DH87
Lamont Rd. SW10 90 DC79
Lamont Rd. Pas. SW10 90 DD79
Lamont Rd.
Lamorbey Clo., Sid. 109 ET88
Lamorna Clo. E17 51 EC54
Lamorna Clo., Orp. 124 EU101
Lamorna Clo., Rad. 17 CH34
Lamorna Gro., Stan. 45 CK53
Lampard Gro. N16 64 DT60
Lampern Sq. E2 78 DU69
Nelson Gdns.
Lampeter Sq. W6 89 CY79
Humbolt Rd.
Lamplighter Clo. E1 78 DW70
Cleveland Way
Lamplighters Clo., 24 EG34
Wal.Abb.
Lampmead Rd. SE12 108 EF85
Lamport Clo. SE18 95 EM77
Lampton Ave., Houns. 86 CB81
Lampton Ho. Clo. SW19 103 CX91
Lampton Pk. Rd., Houns. 86 CB82
Lampton Rd., Houns. 86 CB82
Lamson Rd., Rain. 83 FF70
Lanacre Ave. NW9 46 CR53
Lanark Clo. W5 73 CJ71
Lanark Pl. W9 76 DC70
Lanark Rd. W9 76 DB68
Lanark Sq. E14 93 EB76
Lanata Wk., Hayes 72 BX70
Ramulis Dr.
Lanbury Rd. SE15 93 DX84
Lancashire Ct. W1 5 J10
Lancaster Ave. E18 66 EH56
Lancaster Ave. SE27 105 DP89
Lancaster Ave. SW19 103 CX92
Lancaster Ave., Bark. 81 ES66
Lancaster Ave., Barn. 34 DC38
Lancaster Ave., Mitch. 119 DL99
Lancaster Clo. N1 78 DS66
Hertford Rd.
Lancaster Clo. N17 50 DU52
Park La.
Lancaster Clo. NW9 47 CT52
Corner Mead
Lancaster Clo., Brom. 122 EF98
Lancaster Clo., Kings.T. 101 CK92
Lancaster Cotts., Rich. 102 CL86
Lancaster Pk.
Lancaster Ct. SE27 105 DP89
Lancaster Ct. SW6 89 CZ80
Lancaster Ct. W2 76 DC73
Lancaster Gate
Lancaster Ct., Bans. 131 CZ114
Lancaster Ct., Walt. 113 BU101
Lancaster Dr. E14 79 EC74
Prestons Rd.
Lancaster Dr. NW3 76 DE65
Lancaster Dr., Horn. 69 FH64
Lancaster Dr., Loug. 38 EL44
Lancaster Gdns. SW19 103 CY92
Lancaster Gdns. W13 87 CH75
Lancaster Gdns., Kings.T. 101 CK92
Lancaster Gate W2 76 DC73
Lancaster Gro. NW3 76 DD65
Lancaster Ms. SW18 104 DB85
East Hill
Lancaster Ms. W2 76 DC73
Lancaster Ms., Rich. 102 CL86
Richmond Hill
Lancaster Pk., Rich. 102 CL85
Lancaster Pl. SW19 103 CX92
Lancaster Rd.
Lancaster Pl. WC2 6 B10
Lancaster Pl. WC2 77 DM73
Lancaster Pl., Houns. 86 BW82
Lancaster Pl., Ilf. 67 EQ64
Staines Rd.
Lancaster Pl., Twick. 101 CG86
Lancaster Rd. E7 80 EG66
Lancaster Rd. E11 66 EE61
Lancaster Rd. E17 51 DX54
Lancaster Rd. N4 63 DM59
Lancaster Rd. N11 49 DK51
Lancaster Rd. N18 50 DT50
Lancaster Rd. NW10 61 CU64
Lancaster Rd. SE25 120 DT96
Lancaster Rd. SW19 103 CX92
Lancaster Rd. W11 75 CY72
Lancaster Rd., Barn. 34 DD43
Lancaster Rd., Enf. 36 DR39
Lancaster Rd., Epp. 26 FA26
Lancaster Rd., Har. 58 CA57
Lancaster Rd., Nthlt. 72 CC65
Lancaster Rd., Sthl. 72 BY73
Lancaster Rd., Uxb. 70 BK65
Lancaster St. SE1 10 G5
Lancaster St. SE1 91 DP75
Lancaster Ter. W2 76 DD73
Lancaster Wk. W2 76 DD74
Lancaster Wk., Hayes 71 BQ72
Lancaster Way, Abb.L. 15 BT31
Lance Rd., Har. 58 CC59
Lancefield St. W10 75 CZ69
Lancell St. N16 64 DS61
Stoke Newington Ch. St.
Lancelot Ave., Wem. 59 CK63
Lancelot Cres., Wem. 59 CK63
Lancelot Gdns., Barn. 48 DG45
Lancelot Pl. SW7 8 D5
Lancelot Pl. SW7 90 DF75
Lancelot Rd., Ilf. 53 ES51
Lancelot Rd., Well. 96 EU84
Lancelot Rd., Wem. 59 CK63
Lancer Sq. W8 90 DB75
Old Ct. Pl.
Lancey Clo. SE7 94 EK77
Cleveley Clo.
Lanchester Rd. N6 62 DF57
Lancing Gdns. N9 50 DT46
Lancing Rd. W13 73 CH73
Drayton Grn. Rd.
Lancing Rd., Croy. 119 DM100
Lancing Rd., Felt. 99 BT89
Lancing Rd., Ilf. 67 ER58
Lancing Rd., Orp. 124 EU103
Lancing St. NW1 5 M3
Lancing Way, Rick. 29 BP43
Lancresse Clo., Uxb. 70 BK65
Lancresse Ct. N1 78 DS67
Landau Way, Brox. 23 DZ25
Landcroft Rd. SE22 106 DT85
Landells Rd. SE22 106 DT86
Landford Clo., Rick. 42 BL47
Landford Rd. SW15 89 CW83
Landgrove Rd. SW19 104 DA92
Landmann Way SE14 93 DX79
Landmead Rd. 23 DY29
(Cheshunt), Wal.Cr.
Landon Pl. SW1 8 D6
Landon Pl. SW1 90 DF76
Landon Wk. E14 79 EB73
Cottage St.
Landon Way, Ashf. 99 BP93
Courtfield Rd.
Landons Clo. E14 79 EC74
Landor Rd. SW9 91 DL83
Landor Wk. W12 89 CU75
Landport Way SE15 92 DT80
Daniel Gdns.
Landra Gdns. N21 35 DP44
Landridge Rd. SW6 89 CZ82
Landrock Rd. N8 63 DL58
Lands End, Borwd. 31 CK44
Landscape Rd., Warl. 148 DV119
Landscape Rd., Wdf.Grn. 52 EH52

Landseer Ave. E12 67 EN64
Landseer Clo. SW19 118 DC95
Brangwyn Cres.
Landseer Clo., Edg. 46 CN54
Landseer Clo., Horn. 69 FH60
Landseer Rd. N19 63 DL62
Landseer Rd., Enf. 36 DU43
Landseer Rd., N.Mal. 116 CR101
Landseer Rd., Sutt. 132 DA107
Landstead Rd. SE18 95 ER80
Landway, The, Orp. 124 EW97
Lane, The NW8 76 DC68
Marlborough Pl.
Lane, The SE3 94 EG83
Lane, The, Cher. 112 BG97
Lane App. NW7 47 CY50
Lane Clo. NW2 61 CV62
Lane Clo., Add. 126 BH106
Lane End, Bexh. 97 FB83
Lane End, Epsom 130 CP114
Lane Gdns. (Bushey), Wat. 45 CE45
Lane Ms. E12 67 EM62
Colchester Ave.
Lanercost Clo. SW2 105 DN89
Lanercost Gdns. N14 49 DL45
Lanercost Rd. SW2 105 DN89
Lanesborough Pl. SW1 8 G4
Laneside, Chis. 109 EP92
Laneside, Edg. 46 CQ50
Laneside Ave., Dag. 68 EZ59
Laneway SW15 103 CV85
Sunnymead Rd.
Lanfranc Rd. E3 79 DY68
Lanfrey Pl. W14 89 CZ78
North End Rd.
Lang Clo., Lthd. 142 CB123
Lang St. E1 78 DW70
Langaller La., Lthd. 142 CB122
Langbourne Ave. N6 62 DG61
Langbourne Way, Esher 129 CG107
Langbrook Rd. SE3 94 EK83
Langcroft Clo., Cars. 118 DF104
Langdale Ave., Mitch. 118 DF97
Langdale Clo. SE17 92 DQ79
Langdale Clo. SW14 88 CP84
Clifford Ave.
Langdale Clo., Dag. 68 EW60
Langdale Clo., Orp. 123 EP104
Grasmere Rd.
Langdale Cres., Bexh. 96 FA80
Langdale Dr., Hayes 71 BS68
Langdale Gdns., Grnf. 73 CH69
Langdale Gdns., Horn. 69 FG64
Langdale Gdns., Wal.Cr. 37 DX35
Langdale Rd. SE10 93 EC80
Langdale Rd., Th.Hth. 119 DN98
Langdale St. E1 78 DV72
Burslem St.
Langdon Ct. NW10 74 CS67
Langdon Cres. E6 81 EN68
Langdon Dr. NW9 60 CQ60
Langdon Pk. Rd. N6 63 DJ59
Langdon Pl. SW14 88 CQ83
Rosemary La.
Langdon Rd. E6 81 EN67
Langdon Rd., Brom. 122 EH97
Langdon Rd., Mord. 118 DC99
Langdon Shaw, Sid. 109 ET92
Langdon Wk., Mord. 118 DC99
Langdon Rd.
Langdon Way SE1 92 DU77
Simms Rd.
Langford Clo. E8 64 DU64
Langford Clo. N15 64 DS58
Langford Clo. NW8 76 DC68
Langford Pl.
Langford Ct. NW8 76 DC68
Langford Pl.
Langford Cres., Barn. 34 DF42
Langford Grn. SE5 92 DS83
Langford Pl. NW8 76 DC68
Langford Pl., Sid. 110 EU90
Langford Rd. SW6 90 DB82
Gilstead Rd.
Langford Rd., Barn. 34 DE42
Langford Rd., Wdf.Grn. 52 EJ51
Langfords, Buck.H. 52 EK47
Langfords Way, Croy. 135 DY111
Langham Clo. N15 63 DP55
Langham Rd.
Langham Dene, Ken. 147 DP115
Langham Dr., Rom. 68 EV58
Langham Gdns. N21 35 DN43
Langham Gdns. W13 73 CH73
Langham Gdns., Edg. 46 CQ52
Langham Gdns., Rich. 101 CJ91
Langham Gdns., Wem. 59 CJ61
Langham Ho. Clo., Rich. 101 CK91
Langham Pl. N15 63 DP55
Langham Pl. W1 5 J7
Langham Pl. W1 77 DH71
Langham Pl. W4 88 CS79
Hogarth Roundabout
Langham Rd. N15 63 DP55
Langham Rd. SW20 117 CW95
Langham Rd., Edg. 46 CQ51
Langham Rd., Tedd. 101 CH92
Langham St. W1 5 J7
Langham St. W1 77 DH71
Langhedge Clo. N18 50 DT51
Langhedge La.
Langhedge La. N18 50 DT51
Langhedge La. Ind. Est. N18 50 DT51
Langholm Clo. SW12 105 DK87
King's Ave.
Langholme (Bushey), Wat. 44 CC46
Langhorne Rd., Dag. 82 FA66
Langland Ct., Nthwd. 43 BQ52
Langland Cres., Stan. 45 CK54
Langland Dr., Pnr. 44 BY52
Langland Gdns. NW3 62 DB64
Langland Gdns., Croy. 121 DZ103
Langlands Ri., Epsom 130 CQ113
Burnet Gro.
Langler Rd. NW10 75 CW68
Langley Ave., Ruis. 57 BV61
Langley Ave., Surb. 115 CK102
Langley Ave., Wor.Pk. 117 CX102
Langley Clo., Epsom 144 CR119
Langley Ct. SE9 109 EN86
Langley Ct. WC2 5 P10
Langley Ct., Beck. 121 EB99
Langley Cres. E11 66 EH59
Langley Cres., Dag. 82 EW66
Langley Cres., Edg. 46 CQ48
Langley Cres., Hayes 85 BT80
Langley Cres., Kings L. 14 BN30
Langley Dr. E11 66 EH59
Langley Dr. W3 88 CP75
Langley Gdns., Brom. 122 EJ98
Langley Gdns., Dag. 82 EX66
Langley Gdns., Orp. 123 EP100
Langley Gro., N.Mal. 116 CS96
Langley Hill, Kings L. 14 BM29
Langley Hill Clo., Kings L. 14 BN29
Langley La. SW8 91 DL79
Langley La., Abb.L. 15 BT31
Langley Lo. La., Kings L. 14 BL31
Langley Meadow, Loug. 39 ER40
Langley Oaks Ave., S.Croy. 134 DU110
Langley Pk. NW7 46 CS51
Langley Pk. Rd., Sutt. 132 DC106
Langley Rd. SW19 117 CZ95
Langley Rd., Abb.L. 15 BS31
Langley Rd., Beck. 121 DY98
Langley Rd., Islw. 87 CF82
Langley Rd., Kings L. 14 BH30
Langley Rd., S.Croy. 135 DX109
Langley Rd., Surb. 116 CL101
Langley Rd., Wat. 29 BT39
Langley Rd., Well. 96 EW79
Langley Row, Barn. 33 CZ39
Langley St. WC2 5 P9
Langley St. WC2 77 DL72
Langley Vale Rd., Epsom 144 CP120
Langley Way, Wat. 29 BS40
Langley Way, W.Wick. 121 ED102
Langleybury La., Kings L. 29 BP37
Langmead Dr. (Bushey), Wat. 45 CD45
Langmead St. SE27 105 DP91
Beadman St.
Langmore Ct., Bexh. 96 EX83
Regency Way
Langport Ct., Walt. 114 BW102
Langridge Ms., Hmptn. 100 BZ93
Oak Ave.
Langroyd Rd. SW17 104 DF89
Langside Ave. SW15 89 CU84
Langside Cres. N14 49 DK48
Langston Hughes Clo. SE24 91 DP84
Shakespeare Rd.
Langston Rd., Loug. 39 EQ43
Langthorn Ct. EC2 7 L8
Langthorne Rd. E11 65 EC62
Langthorne St. SW6 89 CX81
Langton Ave. E6 81 EN69
Langton Ave. N20 48 DC45
Langton Ave., Epsom 131 CT111
Langton Clo. WC1 6 C4
Langton Clo., Add. 112 BH104
Langton Gro., Nthwd. 43 BQ50
Langton Ri. SE23 106 DV87
Langton Rd. NW2 61 CW62
Langton Rd. SW9 91 DP80
Langton Rd., Har. 44 CC52
Langton Rd., W.Mol. 114 CC99
Langton St. SW10 90 DC79
Langton Way SE3 94 EF81
Langton Way, Croy. 120 DS104
Langtry Rd. NW8 76 DB67
Langtry Rd., Nthlt. 72 BX68
Langtry Wk. NW8 76 DC66
Alexandra Pl.
Langwood Chase, Tedd. 101 CJ93
Langwood Gdns., Wat. 29 BU39
Langworth Dr., Hayes 71 BU72
Lanhill Rd. W9 76 DA70
Lanier Rd. SE13 107 EC86
Lanigan Dr., Houns. 100 CB85
Lankaster Gdns. N2 48 DD53
Lankers Dr., Har. 58 BZ58
Lankton Clo., Beck. 121 EC95
Lannock Rd., Hayes 71 BS74
Lannoy Rd. SE9 109 EQ88
Lanrick Rd. E14 79 ED72
Lanridge Rd. SE2 96 EX76
Lansbury Ave. N18 50 DR50
Lansbury Ave., Bark. 82 EU66
Lansbury Ave., Felt. 99 BV86
Lansbury Ave., Rom. 68 EY57
Lansbury Clo. NW10 60 CQ64
Lansbury Dr., Hayes 71 BS68
Lansbury Est. E14 79 EB72
Lansbury Gdns. E14 79 EC72
Lansbury Rd., Enf. 37 DX39
Lansbury Way N18 50 DS50
Lansbury Ave.
Lansdell Rd., Mitch. 118 DG96
Lansdown Clo., Walt. 114 BW102
St. Johns Dr.
Lansdown Rd. E7 80 EJ66
Lansdown Rd., Sid. 110 EV90
Lansdowne Ave., Bexh. 96 EW80
Lansdowne Ave., Orp. 123 EP102
Lansdowne Clo. SW20 103 CX94
Lansdowne Clo., Surb. 116 CP103
Kingston Rd.
Lansdowne Clo., Twick. 101 CF88
Lion Rd.
Lansdowne Clo., Wat. 30 BX35
Lansdowne Ct., Wor.Pk. 117 CU103
Lansdowne Cres. W11 75 CZ73
Lansdowne Dr. E8 78 DU65
Lansdowne Gdns. SW8 91 DL81
Lansdowne Grn. SW8 91 DL81
Hartington Rd.
Lansdowne Gro. NW10 60 CS63
Lansdowne Hill SE27 105 DP90
Lansdowne La. SE7 94 EK78
Lansdowne Ms. SE7 94 EK78
Lansdowne Ms. W11 75 CZ74
Lansdowne Rd.
Lansdowne Pl. SE1 11 L6
Lansdowne Pl. SE19 106 DT94
Lansdowne Ri. W11 75 CY73
Lansdowne Rd. E4 51 EA47
Lansdowne Rd. E11 66 EF61
Lansdowne Rd. E17 65 EA58
Lansdowne Rd. E18 66 EG55
Lansdowne Rd. N3 47 CZ52
Lansdowne Rd. N10 49 DJ54
Lansdowne Rd. N17 50 DU53
Lansdowne Rd. SW20 103 CW94
Lansdowne Rd. W11 75 CY73
Lansdowne Rd., Brom. 108 EG94
Lansdowne Rd., Croy. 120 DQ103
Lansdowne Rd., Epsom 130 CQ108
Lansdowne Rd., Har. 59 CE59
Lansdowne Rd., Houns. 86 CB83
Lansdowne Rd., Ilf. 67 ET60
Lansdowne Rd., Pur. 133 DN112
Lansdowne Rd., Sev. 155 FK122
Lansdowne Rd., Stai. 98 BH94
Lansdowne Rd., Stan. 45 CJ51
Lansdowne Rd., Uxb. 71 BP72
Lansdowne Row W1 9 J2
Lansdowne Ter. WC1 6 A5
Lansdowne Ter. WC1 77 DL70
Lansdowne Wk. W11 75 CZ74
Lansdowne Way SW8 91 DK81
Lansdowne Wd. Clo. SE27 105 DP90
Lansfield Ave. N18 50 DU49
Lant St. SE1 11 H4
Lant St. SE1 92 DQ75
Lantern Clo. SW15 89 CU84
Lantern Clo., Wem. 59 CK64
Lanterns Ct. E14 93 EA75
Lanvanor Rd. SE15 92 DW82
Lapford Clo. W9 75 CZ70
Lapponum Wk., Hayes 72 BX71
Lochan Clo.
Lapse Wd. Wk. SE23 106 DV89
Lapstone Gdns., Har. 59 CJ58
Lapwing Clo., Erith 97 FH80
Lapwing Clo., S.Croy. 135 DY110
Lapwing Ct., Surb. 116 CN104
Chaffinch Clo.
Lapwing Way, Abb.L. 23 DX31
College Rd.
Lapwing Way, Hayes 72 BX72
Lapworth Clo., Orp. 124 EW103
Lara Clo. SE13 107 EC86
Lara Clo., Chess. 130 CL108
Larbert Rd. SW16 105 DJ94
Larby Pl., Epsom 130 CS110
Larch Ave. W3 74 CS74
Larch Ave., St.Alb. 16 BY30
Larch Clo. E13 80 EH70
Larch Clo. N11 48 DG52
Larch Clo. N19 63 DJ61
Bredgar Rd.
Larch Clo. SE8 93 DZ79
Clyde St.
Larch Clo. SW12 105 DH88
Larch Clo., Tad. 146 DC121
Larch Clo., Wal.Cr. 22 DS27
The Firs
Larch Clo., Warl. 149 DY119
Larch Cres., Epsom 130 CP107
Larch Cres., Hayes 72 BW70
Larch Dr. W4 88 CN78
Gunnersbury Ave.
Larch Grn. NW9 46 CS53
Clayton Fld.
Larch Gro., Sid. 109 ET88
Larch Ms. N19 63 DJ61
Bredgar Rd.
Larch Rd. E10 65 EA61
Walnut Rd.
Larch Rd. NW2 61 CW63
Larch Tree Way, Croy. 121 EA104
Larch Wk., Swan. 125 FD96
Larch Way, Brom. 123 EN101
Larchdene, Orp. 123 EN103
Larches, The N13 50 DQ48
Larches, The, Nthwd. 43 BQ51
Larches, The, Uxb. 71 BP68
Larches, The, Wat. 30 BY43
Larches Ave. SW14 88 CR84
Larches Ave., Enf. 36 DW35
Larchwood Ave., Rom. 55 FB51
Larchwood Clo., Bans. 145 CY115
Larchwood Clo., Rom. 55 FC51
Larchwood Rd. SE9 109 EP89
Larcom St. SE17 11 J9
Larcom St. SE17 92 DQ77
Larcombe Clo., Croy. 134 DT105
Larden Rd. W3 74 CS74
Largewood Ave., Surb. 116 CM103
Largo Wk., Erith 97 FE81
Selkirk Dr.
Larissa St. SE17 11 L10
Lark Row E2 78 DW67
Lark Way, Cars. 118 DE101
Larkbere Rd. SE26 107 DY91
Larken Dr. (Bushey), Wat. 44 CC46
Larkfield, Cob. 127 BU113
Larkfield Ave., Har. 59 CH55
Larkfield Clo., Brom. 122 EF103
Larkfield Rd., Rich. 88 CL84
Larkfield Rd., Sev. 154 FC123
Larkfield Rd., Sid. 109 ET90
Larkhall Clo., Walt. 128 BW107
Larkhall Ct., Rom. 55 FC54
Larkhall La. SW4 91 DK82
Larkhall Ri. SW4 91 DJ83
Larkham Clo., Felt. 99 BS90
Larkhill Ter. SE18 95 EN80
Larkin Clo., Couls. 147 DM117
Larks Gro., Bark. 81 ES66
Larksfield Gro., Enf. 36 DV39
Larkshall Cres. E4 51 EC49
Larkshall Rd. E4 51 EC50
Larkspur Clo. E6 80 EL71
Larkspur Clo. N17 50 DR52
Fryatt Rd.
Larkspur Clo. NW9 60 CP57
Old Kenton La.
Larkspur Clo., Orp. 124 EW103
Larkspur Clo., Ruis. 57 BQ59
Glovers Gro.
Larkspur Way, Epsom 130 CP106
Larkswood Clo., Erith 97 FG81
Larkswood Ct. E4 51 ED50
Larkswood Ri., Pnr. 58 BW56
Larkswood Rd. E4 51 EA49
Larkway Clo. NW9 60 CR56
Larmans Rd., Enf. 36 DW36
Larnach Rd. W6 89 CX79
Larne Rd., Ruis. 57 BT59
Larner Rd., Erith 97 FE80
Larpent Ave. SW15 103 CW85
Larsen Dr., Wal.Abb. 23 ED34
Larwood Clo., Grnf. 59 CD64
Las Palmas Est., Shep. 113 BQ101
Lascelles Ave., Har. 59 CD59
Lascelles Clo. E11 65 ED61
Lascotts Rd. N22 49 DM51
Lassa Rd. SE9 108 EL85
Lassell St. SE10 93 ED78
Lasseter Pl. SE3 94 EF79
Vanbrugh Hill
Lasterton St. E8 78 DV65
Wilton Way
Latchett Rd. E18 52 EH53
Latchford Pl., Chig. 54 EV49
Manford Way
Latchingdon Ct. E17 65 DX56
Latchingdon Gdns., Wdf.Grn. 52 EL51
Latchmere Clo., Rich. 102 CL92
Latchmere La., Kings.T. 102 CM93
Latchmere Pas. SW11 90 DE82
Cabul Rd.
Latchmere Rd. SW11 90 DF82
Latchmere Rd., Kings.T. 102 CL94
Latchmere St. SW11 90 DF82
Lateward Rd., Brent. 87 CK79
Latham Clo. E6 80 EL72
Oliver Gdns.
Latham Clo., Twick. 101 CG87
Latham Clo., West. 150 EJ116
Latham Ho. E1 79 DX72
Latham Rd., Bexh. 110 FA85
Latham Rd., Twick. 101 CF87
Lathams Way, Croy. 119 DM102
Lathkill Clo., Enf. 50 DT45
Lathom Rd. E6 80 EL66
Latimer SE17 92 DS78
Beaconsfield Rd.
Latimer Ave. E6 81 EM67
Latimer Clo., Pnr. 44 BW53
Latimer Clo., Wat. 43 BS45
Latimer Clo., Wor.Pk. 131 CV105
Latimer Gdns., Pnr. 44 BW53
Latimer Pl. W10 75 CW72
Latimer Rd. E7 66 EH63
Latimer Rd. N15 64 DS58
Latimer Rd. SW19 104 DB93
Latimer Rd. W10 75 CW71
Latimer Rd., Barn. 34 DB41
Latimer Rd., Croy. 119 DP104
Abbey Rd.
Latimer Rd., Tedd. 101 CF92
Latimer St. E1 79 DX71
Stepney Way
Latona Rd. SE15 92 DU79
Lattimer Pl. W4 89 CT80
Latton Clo., Esher 128 CB105
Latton Clo., Walt. 114 BY101
Latymer Clo., Wey. 127 BQ105
Latymer Ct. W6 89 CX77
Latymer Rd. N9 50 DT47
Latymer Way N9 50 DR47
Laud St. SE11 10 B10
Laud St., Croy. 120 DQ104
Lauder Clo., Nthlt. 72 BX68
Lauderdale Dr., Rich. 101 CK90
Lauderdale Pl. EC2 78 DQ71
Aldersgate St.
Lauderdale Rd. W9 76 DB69
Lauderdale Rd., Kings L. 15 BQ33
Lauderdale Twr. EC2 78 DQ71
Beech St.
Laughton Ct., Borwd. 32 CR40
Banks Rd.
Laughton Rd., Nthlt. 72 BX67
Launcelot Rd., Brom. 108 EG91
Launcelot St. SE1 10 D5
Launceston Gdns., Grnf. 73 CJ67
Launceston Pl. W8 90 DC76
Launceston Rd., Grnf. 73 CJ67
Launch St. E14 93 EC76
Laundress La. N16 64 DU62
Laundry La. N1 78 DQ67
Greenman St.
Laundry La., Wal.Abb. 24 EE25
Laundry Rd. W6 89 CY79
Laura Clo. E11 66 EJ57
Laura Clo., Enf. 36 DS43
Laura Dr., Swan. 111 FG94
Laura Pl. E5 64 DW63
Lauradale Rd. N2 62 DF56
Laurel Ave., Pot.B. 19 CZ32
Laurel Ave., Twick. 101 CF88
Laurel Bank Gdns. SW6 89 CZ82
New Kings Rd.
Laurel Bank Rd., Enf. 36 DQ39
Laurel Bank Vill. W7 73 CE74
Lower Boston Rd.
Laurel Clo. N19 63 DJ61
Hargrave Pk.
Laurel Clo. SW17 104 DE92
Laurel Clo., Ilf. 53 EQ51
Laurel Clo., Sid. 110 EU90
Laurel Cres., Croy. 121 EA104
Laurel Cres., Rom. 69 FE60
Laurel Dr. N21 49 DN45
Laurel Flds., Pot.B. 19 CZ31
Laurel Gdns. E4 51 EB45
Laurel Gdns. NW7 46 CR48
Laurel Gdns. W7 73 CE74
Laurel Gdns., Houns. 86 BY84
Laurel Gro. SE20 106 DV94
Laurel Gro. SE26 107 DX91
Laurel La., West Dr. 84 BL77
Laurel Lo. La., Barn. 33 CW36
Dancers La.
Laurel Pk., Har. 45 CF52
Laurel Rd. SW13 89 CU82
Laurel Rd. SW20 117 CV95
Laurel Rd., Hmptn. 101 CD92
Laurel St. E8 78 DT65
Laurel Vw. N12 48 DB48
Laurel Way E18 66 EF56
Laurel Way N20 48 DA48
Laurels, The, Bans. 145 CZ117
Laurels, The, Cob. 142 BY115
Laurels, The, Wal.Cr. 22 DS27
Laurels, The, Wey. 113 BR104
Laurence Ms. W12 89 CU75
Askew Rd.
Laurence Pountney Hill EC4 7 K10
Laurence Pountney La. EC4 7 K10
Laurie Gro. SE14 93 DY81
Laurie Rd. W7 73 CE71
Laurie Wk., Rom. 69 FE56
Laurier Rd. NW5 63 DH62
Laurier Rd., Croy. 120 DT101
Laurimel Clo., Stan. 45 CH51
September Way
Laurino Pl. (Bushey), Wat. 44 CC47
Lauriston Rd. E9 79 DX67
Lauriston Rd. SW19 103 CX93
Lausanne Rd. N8 63 DN56
Lausanne Rd. SE15 92 DW81
Lauser Rd., Stai. 98 BJ87
Lavell St. N16 64 DR63
Lavender Ave. NW9 60 CQ60
Lavender Ave., Mitch. 118 DE95
Lavender Ave., Wor.Pk. 117 CW104
Lavender Clo. SW3 90 DD79
Danvers St.
Lavender Clo., Brom. 122 EL100
Lavender Clo., Cars. 133 DH105
Lavender Clo., Couls. 147 DJ119
Lavender Clo. (Cheshunt), Wal.Cr. 22 DT27
Lavender Ct., W.Mol. 114 CB97
Molesham Way
Lavender Gdns. SW11 90 DF84
Lavender Gdns., Enf. 35 DP39
Lavender Gdns., Har. 45 CE51
Uxbridge Rd.
Lavender Gro. E8 78 DU66
Lavender Gro., Mitch. 118 DE95
Lavender Hill SW11 90 DF84
Lavender Hill, Enf. 35 DN39
Lavender Hill, Swan. 125 FD97
Lavender Ms., Wall. 133 DL107
Lavender Pk. Rd., W.Byf. 126 BG112
Lavender Pl., Ilf. 67 EP64
Lavender Ri., West Dr. 84 BN75
Lavender Rd. SE16 79 DY74
Lavender Rd. SW11 90 DD83
Lavender Rd., Cars. 132 DG105
Lavender Rd., Croy. 119 DM100
Lavender Rd., Enf. 36 DR39
Lavender Rd., Epsom 130 CP106
Lavender Rd., Sutt. 132 DD105
Lavender Rd., Uxb. 70 BM71
Lavender Sq. E11 65 ED62
Anglian Rd.
Lavender St. E15 80 EE65
Manbey Gro.
Lavender Sweep SW11 90 DF84

Lavender Ter. SW11 90 DE83
Falcon Rd.
Lavender Vale, Wall. 133 DK107
Lavender Wk. SW11 90 DF84
Lavender Wk., Mitch. 118 DG97
Lavender Way, Croy. 121 DX100
Lavengro Rd. SE27 106 DQ89
Lavenham Rd. SW18 103 CZ89
Lavernock Rd., Bexh. 96 FA82
Lavers Rd. N16 64 DS62
Laverstoke Gdns. SW15 103 CT87
Laverton Ms. SW5 90 DB77
Laverton Pl.
Laverton Pl. SW5 90 DB77
Lavidge Rd. SE9 108 EL89
Lavina Gro. N1 77 DM68
Wharfdale Rd.
Lavington Rd. W13 73 CH74
Lavington Rd., Croy. 119 DM104
Lavington St. SE1 10 G3
Lavington St. SE1 77 DP74
Lavinia Ave., Wat. 16 BX34
Lavrock La., Rick. 42 BM45
Law Ho., Bark. 82 EU68
Law St. SE1 11 L6
Law St. SE1 92 DR76
Lawdons Gdns., Croy. 133 DP105
Lawford Clo., Wall. 133 DL109
Lawford Gdns., Ken. 148 DQ116
Lawford Rd. N1 78 DS66
Lawford Rd. NW5 77 DJ65
Lawford Rd. W4 88 CQ80
Lawless St. E14 79 EB73
Lawley Rd. N14 49 DH45
Lawley St. E5 64 DW63
Lawn, The, Sthl. 86 CA78
Lawn Ave., West Dr. 84 BJ75
Lawn Clo. N9 50 DT45
Lawn Clo., Brom. 108 EH93
Lawn Clo., N.Mal. 116 CS96
Lawn Clo., Ruis. 57 BT62
Lawn Clo., Swan. 125 FC96
Lawn Cres., Rich. 88 CN82
Lawn Fm. Gro., Rom. 68 EY56
Lawn Gdns. W7 73 CE74
Lawn Ho. Clo. E14 93 EC75
Lawn La. SW8 91 DL79
Lawn Pk., Sev. 155 FH127
Lawn Pl. SE15 92 DT81
Sumner Est.
Lawn Rd. NW3 62 DF64
Lawn Rd., Beck. 107 DZ94
Lawn Rd., Uxb. 70 BJ66
New Windsor St.
Lawn Ter. SE3 94 EE83
Lawn Vale, Pnr. 44 BY54
Lawnfield NW2 75 CX66
Coverdale Rd.
Lawns, The E4 51 EA50
Lawns, The SE3 94 EE83
Lee Ter.
Lawns, The SE19 120 DR95
Lawns, The, Pnr. 44 CB52
Lawns, The, Sid. 110 EV91
Lawns, The, Sutt. 131 CY108
Lawnside SE3 94 EF84
Lawnsway, Rom. 55 FC52
Lawrance Gdns. (Cheshunt), Wal.Cr. 23 DX28
Lawrence Ave. E12 67 EN63
Lawrence Ave. E17 51 DX53
Lawrence Ave. N13 49 DP49
Lawrence Ave. NW7 46 CS49
Lawrence Ave., N.Mal. 116 CR100
Lawrence Bldgs. N16 64 DT62
Lawrence Campe Clo. N20 48 DD48
Friern Barnet La.
Lawrence Clo. E3 79 EA69
Lawrence Clo. N15 64 DS55
Lawrence Rd.
Lawrence Ct. NW7 46 CS50
Lawrence Cres., Dag. 69 FB62
Lawrence Cres., Edg. 46 CN54
Lawrence Dr., Uxb. 57 BQ63
Lawrence Est., Houns. 86 BW84
Lawrence Gdns. NW7 47 CT48
Lawrence Hill E4 51 EA47
Lawrence La. EC2 7 J9
Lawrence Pl. N1 77 DL67
Outram Pl.
Lawrence Rd. E6 80 EL67
Lawrence Rd. E13 80 EH67
Lawrence Rd. N15 64 DS56
Lawrence Rd. N18 50 DV49
Lawrence Rd. SE25 120 DT98
Lawrence Rd. W5 87 CK77
Lawrence Rd., Erith 97 FB80
Sussex Rd.
Lawrence Rd., Hmptn. 100 BZ94
Lawrence Rd., Hayes 71 BQ68
Lawrence Rd., Houns. 86 BW84
Lawrence Rd., Pnr. 58 BX58
Lawrence Rd., Rich. 101 CJ91
Lawrence Rd., Rom. 69 FH57
Lawrence Rd., W.Wick. 136 EG105
Lawrence St. E16 80 EF71
Lawrence St. NW7 47 CT50
Lawrence St. SW3 90 DE79
Lawrence Way NW10 60 CQ63
Lawrence Weaver Clo., Mord. 118 DB100
Green La.
Lawrie Pk. Ave. SE26 106 DV92
Lawrie Pk. Cres. SE26 106 DV92
Lawrie Pk. Gdns. SE26 106 DV91
Lawrie Pk. Rd. SE26 106 DV93
Lawson Clo. E16 80 EJ71
Lawson Clo. SW19 103 CX90
Lawson Est. SE1 11 K7
Lawson Gdns., Pnr. 57 BV55
Lawson Rd., Enf. 36 DW39
Lawson Rd., Sthl. 72 BZ70
Lawton Rd. E3 79 DY69
Lawton Rd. E10 65 ED60
Lawton Rd., Barn. 34 DD41
Lawton Rd., Loug. 39 EP40
Laxcon Clo. NW10 60 CQ64
Laxey Rd., Orp. 137 ET107
Laxley Clo. SE5 91 DP80
Laxton Pl. NW1 5 J4
Layard Rd. SE16 92 DV77
Layard Rd., Enf. 36 DT39
Layard Rd., Th.Hth. 120 DR96
Layard Sq. SE16 92 DV77
Laycock St. N1 77 DN65
Layer Gdns. W3 74 CN73
Layfield Clo. NW4 61 CV59
Layfield Cres. NW4 61 CV59
Layfield Rd. NW4 61 CV59
Layhams Rd., Kes. 136 EF106
Layhams Rd., W.Wick. 121 ED104
Laymarsh Clo., Belv. 96 EZ76
Laymead Clo., Nthlt. 72 BY65
Laystall St. EC1 6 D5
Laystall St. EC1 77 DN70
Layton Ct., Wey. 127 BP105
Castle Vw. Rd.
Layton Cres., Croy. 133 DN106
Layton Rd. N1 77 DN68
Parkfield St.
Layton Rd., Brent. 87 CK78
Layton Rd., Houns. 86 CB84
Laytons Bldgs. SE1 11 K4
Laytons La., Sun. 113 BT96
Layzell Wk. SE9 108 EK88
Mottingham La.
Lazar Wk. N7 63 DM61
Briset Way
Le Corte Clo., Kings L. 14 BM29
Le May Ave. SE12 108 EH90
Le Personne Rd., Cat. 148 DR122
Lea Bri. Rd. E5 64 DV62
Lea Bri. Rd. E10 65 EA59
Lea Bri. Rd. E17 65 ED57
Lea Bushes, Wat. 30 CA35
Lea Clo. (Bushey), Wat. 30 CB43
Lea Cres., Ruis. 57 BT63
Lea Gdns., Wem. 60 CM63
Lea Hall Rd. E10 65 EA60
Lea Mt., Wal.Cr. 22 DS28
Lea Rd., Beck. 121 EA96
Fairfield Rd.
Lea Rd., Enf. 36 DR39
Lea Rd., Sev. 155 FJ127
Lea Rd., Sthl. 86 BY77
Lea Rd., Wal.Abb. 23 EA34
Lea Rd. Trd. Est., Wal.Abb. 23 EA34
Lea Side Ind. Est., Enf. 37 DZ41
Lea Vale, Dart. 97 FD84
Lea Valley Rd. E4 37 DX43
Lea Valley Rd., Enf. 37 DX43
Lea Valley Viaduct E4 51 DX50
Lea Valley Viaduct N18 51 DX50
Lea Vw. Hos. E5 64 DV60
Springfield
Leabank Clo., Har. 59 CE62
Leabank Sq. E9 79 EA65
Leabank Vw. N15 64 DU58
Leabourne Rd. N16 64 DU58
Leach Gro., Lthd. 143 CJ122
Leacroft, Stai. 98 BG92
Leacroft Ave. SW12 104 DF87
Leacroft Clo., Ken. 148 DQ116
Leacroft Clo., Stai. 98 BH91
Leacroft Clo., West Dr. 70 BL72
Leadale Ave. E4 51 DZ47
Leadale Rd. N15 64 DU58
Leadale Rd. N16 64 DU58
Leadbeaters Clo. N11 48 DF50
Goldsmith Rd.
Leadenhall Mkt. EC3 7 M9
Leadenhall Pl. EC3 7 M9
Leadenhall St. EC3 7 M9
Leadenhall St. EC3 78 DS72
Leader Ave. E12 67 EN64
Leadings, The, Wem. 60 CQ62
Leaf Clo., Nthwd. 43 BR52
Leaf Clo., T.Ditt. 115 CE99
Leaf Gro. SE27 105 DN92
Leafield Clo. SW16 105 DP93
Leafield La., Sid. 110 EZ91
Leafield Rd. SW20 117 CZ97
Leafield Rd., Sutt. 118 DA103
Leaford Cres., Wat. 29 BT37
Leaforis Rd., Wal.Cr. 22 DU28
Leafy Gro., Kes. 136 EJ106
Leafy Oak Rd. SE12 108 EJ91
Leafy Way, Croy. 120 DT103
Leagrave St. E5 64 DW62
Leaholme Way, Ruis. 57 BQ58
Leahurst Rd. SE13 107 ED85
Leake Ct. SE1 10 C4
Leake St. SE1 10 C4
Leake St. SE1 91 DM75
Lealand Rd. N15 64 DT58
Leamington Ave. E17 65 EA57
Leamington Ave., Brom. 108 EJ92
Leamington Ave., Mord. 117 CY98
Leamington Ave., Orp. 137 ES105
Leamington Clo. E12 67 EM64
Leamington Clo., Brom. 108 EJ91
Leamington Clo., Houns. 100 CC85
Leamington Cres., Har. 58 BY62
Leamington Gdns., Ilf. 67 ET61
Leamington Pk. W3 74 CR71
Leamington Pl., Hayes 71 BT70
Leamington Rd., Sthl. 86 BX77
Leamington Rd. Vill. W11 75 CZ71
Leamore St. W6 89 CV77
Leamouth Rd. E6 80 EL72
Leamouth Rd. E14 79 ED72
Leander Ct. SE8 93 EA81
Leander Gdns., Wat. 30 BY37
Leander Rd. SW2 105 DM87
Leander Rd., Nthlt. 72 CA68
Leander Rd., Th.Hth. 119 DM98
Learoyd Gdns. E6 81 EN73
Leas, The, Stai. 98 BG91
Leas, The (Bushey), Wat. 30 BZ39
Leas Clo., Chess. 130 CM108
Leas Dale SE9 109 EN90
Leas Grn., Chis. 109 ET93
Leas La., Warl. 149 DX118
Leas Rd., Warl. 149 DX118
Leaside, Lthd. 142 CA123
Leaside Ave. N10 62 DG55
Leaside Ct., Uxb. 71 BP69
The Larches
Leaside Rd. E5 64 DW60
Leasowes Rd. E10 65 EA60
Leathart Clo., Horn. 83 FH66
Dowding Way
Leather Bottle La., Belv. 96 EZ77
St. Augustine's Rd.
Leather Clo., Mitch. 118 DG96
Leather Gdns. E15 80 EE67
Abbey Rd.
Leather La. EC1 6 D6
Leather La. EC1 77 DN70
Leatherbottle Grn., Erith 96 EZ76
Leatherdale St. E1 78 DW70
Portelet Rd.
Leatherhead Bypass Rd., Lthd. 143 CH120
Leatherhead Clo. N16 64 DS60
Leatherhead Ind. Est., Lthd. 143 CG121
Station Rd.
Leatherhead Rd., Ash. 143 CK121
Leatherhead Rd., Chess. 129 CJ111
Leatherhead Rd. (Great Bookham), Lthd. 143 CK121
Leatherhead Rd. (Oxshott), Lthd. 129 CD114
Leathermarket Ct. SE1 92 DS75
Leathermarket St. SE1 11 M5
Leathermarket St. SE1 92 DS75
Leathersellers Clo., Barn. 33 CY42
The Ave.
Leathsail Rd., Har. 58 CB62
Leathwaite Rd. SW11 90 DF84
Leathwell Rd. SE8 93 EB82
Leaveland Clo., Beck. 121 EA98
Leaver Gdns., Grnf. 73 CD68
Leaves Grn. Cres., Kes. 136 EJ111
Leaves Grn. Rd., Kes. 136 EK111
Leavesden Rd., Stan. 45 CG51
Leavesden Rd., Wat. 29 BV38
Leavesden Rd., Wey. 127 BP106
Leaview, Wal.Abb. 23 EB33
Leaway E10 65 DX60
Leazes Ave., Cat. 147 DN124
Lebanon Ave., Felt. 100 BX92
Lebanon Clo., Wat. 29 BR36
Lebanon Ct., Twick. 101 CH87
Lebanon Dr., Cob. 128 CA113
Lebanon Gdns. SW18 104 DA85
Lebanon Gdns., West. 150 EK117
Lebanon Pk., Twick. 101 CH87
Lebanon Rd. SW18 104 DA85
Lebanon Rd., Croy. 120 DS102
Lebrun Sq. SE3 94 EH83
Lechmere App., Wdf.Grn. 52 EJ54
Lechmere Ave., Chig. 53 EQ49
Lechmere Ave., Wdf.Grn. 52 EK54
Lechmere Rd. NW2 75 CV65
Leckford Rd. SW18 104 DC89
Leckwith Ave., Bexh. 96 EY79
Lecky St. SW7 90 DD78
Leconfield Ave. SW13 89 CT83
Leconfield Rd. N5 64 DR63
Leda Ave., Enf. 37 DX38
Leda Rd. SE18 95 EM76
Ledbury Est. SE15 92 DV80
Ledbury Ms. N. W11 76 DA73
Ledbury Rd.
Ledbury Ms. W. W11 76 DA73
Ledbury Rd.
Ledbury Pl., Croy. 134 DQ105
Ledbury Rd.
Ledbury Rd. W11 75 CZ72
Ledbury Rd., Croy. 134 DQ105
Ledbury St. SE15 92 DU80
Ledgers Rd., Warl. 149 EB119
Ledrington Rd. SE19 106 DU93
Anerley Hill
Ledway Dr., Wem. 60 CM59
Lee Ave., Rom. 68 EY58
Lee Bri. SE13 93 EC83
Lee Ch. St. SE13 94 EE84
Lee Clo. E17 51 DX53
Lee Clo., Barn. 34 DC42
Lee Conservancy Rd. E9 65 DZ64
Lee Grn. SE12 108 EF85
Lee Grn., Orp. 124 EU99
Lee Grn. La., Epsom 144 CP124
Lee Gro., Chig. 53 EN47
Lee High Rd. SE12 94 EF84
Lee High Rd. SE13 93 ED84
Lee Pk. SE3 94 EF84
Lee Pk. Way N9 51 DY48
Lee Pk. Way N18 51 DX50
Lee Rd. NW7 47 CX52
Lee Rd. SE3 94 EF83
Lee Rd. SW19 118 DB95
Lee Rd., Enf. 36 DU44
Lee Rd., Grnf. 73 CJ67
Lee St. E8 78 DT67
Lee Ter. SE3 94 EE83
Lee Ter. SE13 94 EE83
Lee Valley Trd. Est. N18 51 DX50
Lee Vw., Enf. 35 DP39
Leechcroft Ave., Sid. 109 ET85
Leechcroft Ave., Swan. 125 FF97
Leechcroft Rd., Wall. 118 DG104
Leecroft Rd., Barn. 33 CY43
Leeds Clo., Orp. 124 EX103
Leeds Pl. N4 63 DM61
Tollington Pk.
Leeds Rd., Ilf. 67 ER60
Leeds St. N18 50 DU50
Leefe Way, Pot.B. 21 DK28
Leefern Rd. W12 89 CU75
Leegate SE12 108 EF85
Leeke St. WC1 6 B2
Leeke St. WC1 77 DM69
Leeland Rd. W13 73 CG74
Leeland Ter. W13 73 CG74
Leeland Way NW10 61 CT63
Leeming Rd., Borwd. 32 CM39
Leerdam Dr. E14 93 EC76
Lees, The, Croy. 121 DZ103
Lees Ave., Nthwd. 43 BT54
Lees Pl. W1 4 F10
Lees Pl. W1 76 DG73
Lees Rd., Uxb. 71 BP70
Leeside, Barn. 33 CY43
Leeside, Pot.B. 20 DD31
Wayside
Leeside Cres. NW11 61 CY58
Leeside Rd. N17 50 DV51
Leeson Rd. SE24 91 DN84
Leesons Hill, Chis. 123 ES97
Leesons Hill, Orp. 124 EU97
Leesons Way, Orp. 123 ET96
Leeward Gdns. SW19 103 CZ92
Leeway SE8 93 DZ78
Leeway Clo., Pnr. 44 BZ52
Leewood Clo. SE12 108 EF86
Upwood Rd.
Leewood Pl., Swan. 125 FD98
Lefevre Wk. E3 79 DZ67
Old Ford Rd.
Lefroy Rd. W12 89 CT75
Legard Rd. N5 63 DP62
Legatt Rd. SE9 108 EK85
Leggatt Rd. E15 79 EC68
Leggatts Clo., Wat. 29 BT36
Leggatts Ri., Wat. 29 BU35
Leggatts Way, Wat. 29 BT36
Leggatts Wd. Ave., Wat. 29 BV36
Legge St. SE13 107 EC85
Leghorn Rd. NW10 75 CT68
Leghorn Rd. SE18 95 ER78
Legion Clo. N1 77 DN66
Legion Ct., Mord. 118 DA100
Legion Rd., Grnf. 72 CC67
Legion Way N12 48 DE52
Downway
Legon Ave., Rom. 69 FC60
Legrace Ave., Houns. 86 BX82
Leicester Ave., Mitch. 119 DL98
Leicester Clo., Wor.Pk. 131 CW105
Leicester Ct. WC2 5 N10
Leicester Gdns., Ilf. 67 ES59
Leicester Pl. WC2 5 N10
Leicester Rd. E11 66 EH57
Leicester Rd. N2 62 DE55
Leicester Rd. NW10 74 CR66
Leicester Rd., Barn. 34 DB43
Leicester Rd., Croy. 120 DS101
Leicester Sq. WC2 9 N1
Leicester Sq. WC2 77 DK73
Leicester St. WC2 5 N10
Leigh Ave., Ilf. 66 EK56
Leigh Clo., N.Mal. 116 CR98
Leigh Cor., Cob. 128 BW114
Leigh Hill Rd.
Leigh Ct., Borwd. 32 CR40
Banks Rd.
Leigh Ct., Har. 59 CE60
Leigh Ct. Clo., Cob. 128 BW114
Leigh Cres., Croy. 135 EB108
Leigh Gdns. NW10 75 CW68
Leigh Hill Rd., Cob. 128 BW114
Leigh Hunt Dr. N14 49 DK46
Leigh Hunt St. SE1 11 H4
Leigh Orchard Clo. SW16 105 DM90
Leigh Pl. EC1 77 DN71
Baldwin's Gdns.
Leigh Pl., Cob. 128 BW114
Leigh Pl., Well. 96 EU82
Leigh Rd. E6 81 EN65
Leigh Rd. E10 65 EC59
Leigh Rd. N5 63 DP63
Leigh Rd., Cob. 127 BV113
Leigh Rd., Houns. 87 CD84
Leigh Rodd, Wat. 44 BZ48
Leigh St. WC1 5 P4
Leigh St. WC1 77 DL70
Leigh Ter., Orp. 124 EV97
Saxville Rd.
Leigham Ave. SW16 105 DL90
Leigham Ct. Rd. SW16 105 DL89
Leigham Dr., Islw. 87 CE80
Leigham Vale SW2 105 DN89
Leigham Vale SW16 105 DM90
Leighton Ave. E12 67 EN64
Leighton Ave., Pnr. 58 BY55
Leighton Clo., Edg. 46 CN54
Leighton Cres. NW5 63 DJ64
Leighton Gro.
Leighton Gdns. NW10 75 CV68
Leighton Gdns., S.Croy. 134 DV113
Leighton Gro. NW5 63 DJ64
Leighton Pl. NW5 63 DJ64
Leighton Rd. NW5 63 DJ64
Leighton Rd. W13 87 CG75
Leighton Rd., Enf. 36 DT43
Leighton Rd., Har. 45 CD54
Leighton St., Croy. 119 DP102
Leighton Way, Epsom 130 CR114
Leila Parnell Pl. SE7 94 EJ79
Leinster Ave. SW14 88 CQ83
Leinster Gdns. W2 76 DC72
Leinster Ms. W2 76 DC73
Leinster Pl. W2 76 DC72
Leinster Rd. N10 63 DH56
Leinster Rd. NW6 76 DA69
Stafford Rd.
Leinster Sq. W2 76 DA72
Leinster Ter. W2 76 DC73
Leisure La., W.Byf. 126 BH112
Leith Clo. NW9 60 CR60
Leith Hill, Orp. 124 EU95
Leith Hill Grn., Orp. 124 EU95
Leith Hill
Leith Rd. N22 49 DP53
Leith Rd., Epsom 130 CS112
Leith Yd. NW6 76 DA67
Quex Rd.
Leithcote Gdns. SW16 105 DM91
Leithcote Path SW16 105 DM90
Lela Ave., Houns. 86 BW82
Lelitia Clo. E8 78 DU67
Pownall Rd.
Leman St. E1 78 DT72
Lemark Clo., Stan. 45 CJ50
Lemmon Rd. SE10 94 EE79
Lemna Rd. E11 66 EE59
Lemonfield Dr., Wat. 16 BY33
Lemonwell Ct. SE9 109 EQ85
Lemonwell Dr.
Lemonwell Dr. SE9 109 EQ85
Lemsford Clo. N15 64 DU57
Lemsford Ct. N4 64 DQ61
Brownswood Rd.
Lemsford Ct., Borwd. 32 CQ42
Lemuel St. SW18 104 DB86
St. Ann's Hill
Len Freeman Pl. SW6 89 CZ80
John Smith Ave.
Lena Gdns. W6 89 CW76
Lena Kennedy Clo. E4 51 EC51
Lenanton Steps E14 93 EA75
Manilla St.
Lendal Ter. SW4 91 DK83
Lenelby Rd., Surb. 116 CN102
Lenham Rd. SE12 94 EF84
Lenham Rd., Bexh. 96 EZ79
Lenham Rd., Sutt. 132 DB105
Lenham Rd., Th.Hth. 120 DR96
Lennard Ave., W.Wick. 122 EE103
Lennard Clo., W.Wick. 122 EE103
Lennard Rd. SE20 107 DX93
Lennard Rd., Beck. 107 DY94
Lennard Rd., Brom. 123 EM102
Lennard Rd., Croy. 120 DQ102
Lennard Rd., Sev. 153 FE120
Lennon Rd. NW2 75 CW65
Lennox Clo., Rom. 69 FF58
Lennox Gdns. NW10 61 CT63
Lennox Gdns. SW1 8 D7
Lennox Gdns. SW1 90 DF76
Lennox Gdns., Croy. 133 DP105
Lennox Gdns., Ilf. 67 EM60
Lennox Gdns. Ms. SW1 8 D7
Lennox Gdns. Ms. SW1 90 DF76
Lennox Rd. E17 65 DZ58
Lennox Rd. N4 63 DM61
Lenor Clo., Bexh. 96 EY84
Lens Rd. E7 80 EJ66
Lensbury Clo. (Cheshunt), Wal.Cr. 23 DY28
Ashdown Cres.
Lensbury Way SE2 96 EW76
Lenthall Pl. SW7 90 DC77
Gloucester Rd.
Lenthall Rd. E8 78 DT66
Lenthall Rd., Loug. 39 ER42
Lenthorp Rd. SE10 94 EF77
Lentmead Rd., Brom. 108 EF90
Lenton Ri., Rich. 88 CL83
Evelyn Ter.
Lenton St. SE18 95 ER77
Lenville Way SE16 92 DU78
Catlin St.
Leo St. SE15 92 DV80
Leo Yd. EC1 6 G5
Leof Cres. SE6 107 EB92
Leominster Rd., Mord. 118 DC100
Leominster Wk., Mord. 118 DC100
Leonard Ave., Mord. 118 DC99
Leonard Ave., Rom. 69 FD60
Leonard Ave., Sev. 153 FH116
Leonard Rd. E4 51 EA51
Leonard Rd. E7 66 EG63
Leonard Rd. N9 50 DT48
Leonard Rd. SW16 119 DJ95
Leonard Rd., Sthl. 86 BX76
Leonard Robbins Path SE28 82 EV73
Tawney Rd.
Leonard St. E16 80 EL74
Leonard St. EC2 7 L4

Leonard St. EC2 78 DR70
Leontine Clo. SE15 92 DU80
Leopards Ct. EC1 6 D6
Leopold Ave. SW19 103 CZ92
Leopold Ms. E9 78 DW67
Fremont St.
Leopold Rd. E17 65 EA57
Leopold Rd. N2 62 DD55
Leopold Rd. N18 50 DV50
Leopold Rd. NW10 74 CS66
Leopold Rd. SW19 103 CZ91
Leopold Rd. W5 74 CM74
Leopold St. E3 79 DZ71
Leopold Ter. SW19 104 DA92
Dora Rd.
Lepe Clo., Brom. 108 EE91
Winlaton Rd.
Leppoc Rd. SW4 105 DK85
Leret Way, Lthd. 143 CG121
Leroy St. SE1 11 M7
Leroy St. SE1 92 DS77
Lescombe Clo. SE23 107 DY90
Lescombe Rd. SE23 107 DY90
Lesley Clo., Bex. 111 FB87
Lesley Clo., Swan. 125 FD97
Leslie Gdns., Sutt. 132 DA107
Leslie Gro., Croy. 120 DR102
Leslie Gro. Pl., Croy. 120 DR102
Leslie Gro.
Leslie Pk. Rd., Croy. 120 DS102
Leslie Rd. E11 65 EC63
Leslie Rd. E16 80 EH72
Leslie Rd. N2 62 DD55
Leslie Smith Sq. SE18 95 EN79
Nightingale Vale
Lesney Fm. Est., Erith 97 FD80
Lesney Pk., Erith 97 FD79
Lesney Pk. Rd., Erith 97 FD79
Lessar Ave. SW4 105 DH85
Lessing St. SE23 107 DY87
Lessingham Ave. SW17 104 DF91
Lessingham Ave., Ilf. 67 EN55
Lessington Ave., Rom. 69 FC58
Lessness Ave., Bexh. 96 EX80
Lessness Pk., Belv. 96 EZ78
Lessness Rd., Belv. 96 FA78
Stapley Rd.
Lessness Rd., Mord. 118 DC100
Lester Ave. E15 80 EE70
Leston Clo., Rain. 83 FG69
Leswin Pl. N16 64 DT62
Leswin Rd.
Leswin Rd. N16 64 DT62
Letchford Gdns. NW10 75 CU69
Letchford Ms. NW10 75 CU69
Letchford Gdns.
Letchford Ter., Har. 44 CB53
Letchmore Rd., Rad. 31 CG36
Letchworth Ave., Felt. 99 BT87
Letchworth Clo., Brom. 122 EG99
Letchworth Clo., Wat. 44 BX50
Letchworth Dr., Brom. 122 EG99
Letchworth St. SW17 104 DF91
Lethbridge Clo. SE13 93 EC81
Lett Rd. E15 79 ED66
Letter Box La., Sev. 155 FJ129
Letterstone Rd. SW6 89 CZ80
Varna Rd.
Lettice St. SW6 89 CZ81
Lettsom St. SE5 92 DS82
Lettsom Wk. E13 80 EG68
Stratford Rd.
Leucha Rd. E17 65 DY57
Levana Clo. SW19 103 CY88
Levehurst Way SW4 91 DL82
Leven Clo., Wal.Cr. 23 DX33
Leven Clo., Wat. 44 BX50
Leven Dr., Wal.Cr. 23 DX33
Leven Rd. E14 79 EC71
Leven Way, Hayes 71 BS72
Levendale Rd. SE23 107 DY89
Lever St. EC1 6 G3
Lever St. EC1 77 DP69
Leveret Clo., Croy. 135 ED111
Leveret Clo., Wat. 15 BU34
Leverett St. SW3 8 C8
Leverholme Gdns. SE9 109 EN90
Leverson St. SW16 105 DJ93
Leverton Pl. NW5 63 DJ64
Leverton St.
Leverton St. NW5 63 DJ64
Leverton Way, Wal.Abb. 23 EC33
Levett Gdns., Ilf. 67 ET63
Levett Rd., Bark. 81 ES65
Levett Rd., Lthd. 143 CH120
Levine Gdns., Bark. 82 EX68
Levison Way N19 63 DK61
Grovedale Rd.
Lewes Clo., Nthlt. 72 CA65
Lewes Rd. N12 48 DE50
Lewes Rd., Brom. 122 EK96
Lewes Way, Rick. 29 BQ42
Lewesdon Clo. SW19 103 CX88
Leweston Pl. N16 64 DT59
Lewey Ho. E3 79 DZ70
Lewgars Ave. NW9 60 CQ58
Lewin Rd. SW14 88 CR83
Lewin Rd. SW16 105 DK93
Lewin Rd., Bexh. 110 EY85
Lewins Rd., Epsom 130 CP114
Lewis Ave. E17 51 EA53
Lewis Clo. N14 49 DJ45
Orchid Rd.
Lewis Clo., Add. 126 BJ105
Lewis Clo., Uxb. 42 BJ54
Lewis Cres. NW10 60 CQ64
Lewis Gdns. N2 48 DD54
Lewis Gro. SE13 93 EC83
Lewis Rd., Mitch. 118 DD96
Lewis Rd., Rich. 101 CK85
Red Lion St.
Lewis Rd., Sid. 110 EW90
Lewis Rd., Sthl. 86 BY75
Lewis Rd., Sutt. 132 DB105
Lewis Rd., Well. 96 EW83
Lewis St. NW1 77 DH65
Lewis Way, Dag. 83 FB65
Lewisham High St. SE13 107 EB86
Lewisham Hill SE13 93 EC82
Lewisham Pk. SE13 107 EC85
Lewisham Rd. SE13 93 EB81
Lewisham St. SW1 9 N5
Lewisham Way SE4 93 EA82
Lewisham Way SE14 93 DZ81
Lexden Dr., Rom. 68 EV58
Lexden Rd. W3 74 CP74
Lexden Rd., Mitch. 119 DK98
Lexham Gdns. W8 90 DA77
Lexham Gdns. Ms. W8 90 DB76
Lexham Gdns.
Lexham Ho., Bark. 81 ER67
St. Margarets
Lexham Ms. W8 90 DA77
Lexham Wk. W8 90 DB76
Lexham Gdns.
Lexington Clo., Borwd. 32 CM41
Lexington Ct., Pur. 134 DQ110
Lexington St. W1 5 L10
Lexington St. W1 77 DJ73
Lexington Way, Barn. 33 CX42
Lexton Gdns. SW12 105 DK88
Ley St., Ilf. 67 EP61
Leyborne Ave. W13 87 CH75
Leyborne Pk., Rich. 88 CN81
Leybourne Ave., W.Byf. 126 BM113
Leybourne Clo., Brom. 122 EG100
Leybourne Clo., W.Byf. 126 BM113
Leybourne Ave.
Leybourne Rd. E11 66 EF60
Leybourne Rd. NW1 77 DH66
Leybourne Rd. NW9 60 CN57
Leybourne Rd., Uxb. 71 BQ67
Leybourne St. NW1 77 DH66
Hawley St.
Leybridge Ct. SE12 108 EG85
Leyburn Clo. E17 65 EC56
Leyburn Gdns., Croy. 120 DT103
Leyburn Gro. N18 50 DU51
Leyburn Rd. N18 50 DU51
Leycroft Clo., Loug. 39 EN43
Leycroft Gdns., Erith 97 FG81
Leyden St. E1 7 P7
Leydenhatch La., Swan. 125 FC95
Leydon Clo. SE16 79 DX74
Lagado Ms.
Leyes Rd. E16 80 EJ72
Leyfield, Wor.Pk. 116 CS102
Leyhill Clo., Swan. 125 FE99
Leyland Ave., Enf. 37 DY40
Leyland Clo. (Cheshunt), 22 DW28
Wal.Cr.
Leyland Gdns., Wdf.Grn. 52 EJ50
Leyland Rd. SE12 108 EF85
Leylang Rd. SE14 93 DX80
Leys, The N2 62 DC56
Leys, The, Har. 60 CL58
Leys Ave., Dag. 83 FC67
Leys Clo., Dag. 83 FC66
Leys Clo., Har. 59 CD57
Leys Clo., Uxb. 42 BK53
Leys Gdns., Barn. 34 DG43
Leys Rd., Lthd. 129 CD112
Leys Rd. E., Enf. 37 DY39
Leys Rd. W., Enf. 37 DY39
Leysdown Ave., Bexh. 97 FC84
Leysdown Rd. SE9 108 EL89
Leysfield Rd. W12 89 CU76
Leyspring Rd. E11 66 EF60
Leyswood Dr., Ilf. 67 ES57
Leythe Rd. W3 88 CQ75
Leyton Business Cen. E10 65 EA61
Leyton Cross Rd., Dart. 111 FF90
Leyton Gra. E10 65 EB60
Leyton Gra. Est. E10 65 EA60
Leyton Grn. Rd. E10 65 EC58
Leyton Ind. Village E10 65 DX59
Leyton Pk. Rd. E10 65 EC62
Leyton Rd. E15 65 ED64
Leyton Rd. SW19 104 DC94
Leyton Way E11 66 EE59
Leytonstone Rd. E15 80 EE65
Leywick St. E15 80 EE68
Lezayre Rd., Orp. 137 ET107
Liardet St. SE14 93 DY79
Liberia Rd. N5 77 DP65
Liberty, The, Rom. 69 FE57
Liberty Ave. SW19 118 DC95
Liberty Hall Rd., Add. 126 BG106
Liberty La., Add. 126 BG106
Liberty Ms. SW12 105 DH86
Liberty Ri., Add. 126 BG107
Liberty St. SW9 91 DM81
Libra Rd. E3 79 DZ67
Libra Rd. E13 80 EG68
Library Pl. E1 78 DV73
Cable St.
Library St. SE1 10 F5
Library St. SE1 91 DP75
Library Way, Twick. 100 CC87
Nelson Rd.
Lichfield Clo., Barn. 34 DG41
Lichfield Gdns., Rich. 88 CL84
Lichfield Gro. N3 48 DA53
Lichfield Rd. E3 79 DY69
Lichfield Rd. E6 80 EK69
Lichfield Rd. N9 50 DU47
Winchester Rd.
Lichfield Rd. NW2 61 CY63
Lichfield Rd., Dag. 68 EV63
Lichfield Rd., Houns. 86 BW83
Lichfield Rd., Nthwd. 57 BU55
Lichfield Rd., Rich. 88 CM81
Lichfield Rd., Wdf.Grn. 52 EE49
Lichfield Sq., Rich. 88 CL84
Lichfield Gdns.
Lichfield Way, S.Croy. 135 DX110
Lichlade Clo., Orp. 137 ET105
Lidbury Rd. NW7 47 CY51
Lidcote Gdns. SW9 91 DN82
Liddall Way, West Dr. 70 BM74
Liddell Clo., Har. 59 CK55
Liddell Gdns. NW10 75 CW68
Liddell Rd. NW6 76 DA65
Lidding Rd., Har. 59 CK57
Liddington Rd. E15 80 EF67
Liddon Rd. E13 80 EH69
Liddon Rd., Brom. 122 EJ97
Liden Clo. E17 65 DZ60
Hitcham Rd.
Lidfield Rd. N16 64 DR63
Lidgate Rd. SE15 92 DT80
Chandler Way
Lidiard Rd. SW18 104 DC89
Lidlington Pl. NW1 5 L1
Lidlington Pl. NW1 77 DJ68
Lido Sq. N17 50 DR53
Lidyard Rd. N19 63 DJ60
Lieutenant Ellis Way, 22 DU29
Wal.Cr.
Liffler Rd. SE18 95 ES78
Lifford St. SW15 89 CX84
Liffords Pl. SW13 89 CT82
Lightcliffe Rd. N13 49 DN49
Lighter Clo. SE16 93 DY77
Lighterman Ms. E1 79 DX72
Belgrave St.
Lightermans Rd. E14 93 EA75
Lightermans Wk. SW18 90 DA84
Lightfoot Rd. N8 63 DL57
Lightley Clo., Wem. 74 CM66
Stanley Ave.
Ligonier St. E2 7 P4
Lila Pl., Swan. 125 FE98
Lilac Clo. E4 51 DZ51
Lilac Clo. (Cheshunt), 22 DV31
Wal.Cr.
Greenwood Ave.
Lilac Gdns. W5 87 CK76
Lilac Gdns., Croy. 121 EA104
Lilac Gdns., Hayes 71 BS72
Lilac Gdns., Rom. 69 FE60
Lilac Gdns., Swan. 125 FD97
Lilac Pl. SE11 10 B9
Lilac Pl. SE11 91 DM77
Lilac Pl., West Dr. 70 BM73
Cedar Ave.
Lilac St. W12 75 CU73
Lilacs Ave., Enf. 36 DW36
Lilburne Gdns. SE9 108 EL85
Lilburne Rd. SE9 108 EL85
Lilburne Wk. NW10 74 CQ65
Pitfield Way
Lile Cres. W7 73 CE71
Lilestone Est. NW8 76 DD70
Fisherton St.
Lilestone St. NW8 4 B4
Lilestone St. NW8 76 DE70
Lilford Rd. SE5 91 DP82
Lilian Barker Clo. SE12 108 EG85
Lilian Board Way, Grnf. 59 CD64
Lilian Clo. N16 64 DS62
Barbauld Rd.
Lilian Gdns., Wdf.Grn. 52 EH53
Lilian Rd. SW16 119 DJ95
Lillechurch Rd., Dag. 82 EV65
Lilleshall Rd., Mord. 118 DD99
Lilley Clo. E1 78 DU74
Hermitage Wall
Lilley Dr., Tad. 146 DB122
Lilley La. NW7 46 CR50
Lillian Ave. W3 88 CN75
Lillian Rd. SW13 89 CU79
Lillie Rd. SW6 89 CX79
Lillie Rd., West. 150 EK118
Lillie Yd. SW6 90 DA79
Lillieshall Rd. SW4 91 DH83
Lillington Gdns. Est. SW1 9 L9
Lilliots La., Lthd. 143 CG119
Kingston Rd.
Lilliput Ave., Nthlt. 72 BY67
Lilliput Rd., Rom. 69 FD59
Lily Clo. W14 89 CX77
Gliddon Rd.
Lily Gdns., Wem. 73 CJ68
Lily Pl. EC1 6 E6
Lily Pl. EC1 77 DN71
Lily Rd. E17 65 EA58
Lilyville Rd. SW6 89 CZ81
Limbourne Ave., Dag. 68 EZ59
Limburg Rd. SW11 90 DF84
Lime Ave., West Dr. 70 BM73
Lime Clo. E1 78 DU74
Lime Clo., Brom. 122 EL98
Lime Clo., Buck.H. 52 EK48
Lime Clo., Cars. 118 DF103
Lime Clo., Har. 45 CG54
Lime Clo., Pnr. 57 BT55
Lime Clo., Rom. 69 FC56
Lime Clo., Wat. 44 BX45
Lime Ct., Mitch. 118 DD96
Lewis Rd.
Lime Cres., Sun. 114 BW96
Lime Gro. N20 47 CZ46
Lime Gro. W12 89 CW75
Lime Gro., Add. 126 BG105
Lime Gro., Hayes 71 BR73
Lime Gro., Ilf. 53 ET51
Lime Gro., N.Mal. 116 CR97
Lime Gro., Orp. 123 EP103
Lime Gro., Ruis. 57 BV58
Lime Gro., Sid. 109 ET86
Lime Gro., Twick. 101 CF86
Lime Gro., Warl. 149 DY118
Lime Meadow Ave., 134 DU113
S.Croy.
Lime Pit La., Sev. 153 FC117
Lime Rd., Epp. 25 ET31
Lime Rd., Rich. 88 CM84
St. Mary's Gro.
Lime Rd., Swan. 125 FD97
Lime Row, Erith 96 EZ76
Northwood Pl.
Lime St. E17 65 DY56
Lime St. EC3 7 M10
Lime St. EC3 78 DS73
Lime St. Pas. EC3 7 M10
Lime Ter. W7 73 CE73
Manor Ct. Rd.
Lime Tree Ave., Esher 115 CD102
Lime Tree Ave., T.Ditt. 115 CD102
Lime Tree Clo., Lthd. 142 CA124
Lime Tree Gro., Croy. 121 DZ104
Lime Tree Pl., Mitch. 119 DH95
Lime Tree Rd., Houns. 86 CB81
Lime Tree Ter. SE6 107 DZ88
Winterstoke Rd.
Lime Tree Wk., Enf. 36 DQ38
Lime Tree Wk., Rick. 28 BH43
Lime Tree Wk., Sev. 155 FH125
Lime Tree Wk. (Bushey), 45 CE46
Wat.
Lime Tree Wk., W.Wick. 136 EF105
Lime Wk. E15 80 EE67
Church St. N.
Lime Wk., Uxb. 56 BJ64
Limeburner La. EC4 6 F9
Limeburner La. EC4 77 DP72
Limebush Clo., Add. 126 BJ109
Limecroft Clo., Epsom 130 CR108
Limedene Clo., Pnr. 44 BX53
Limeharbour E14 93 EB76
Limehouse Causeway E14 79 DZ73
Limehouse Flds. Est. E14 79 DY71
Limekiln Dr. SE7 94 EH79
Limerick Clo. SW12 105 DJ87
Limerston St. SW10 90 DC79
Limes, The W2 76 DA73
Linden Gdns.
Limes, The, Brom. 122 EL103
Limes Ave. E11 66 EH56
Limes Ave. N12 48 DC49
Limes Ave. NW7 46 CS51
Limes Ave. NW11 61 CY59
Limes Ave. SE20 106 DV94
Limes Ave. SW13 89 CT82
Limes Ave., Cars. 118 DF102
Limes Ave., Chig. 53 EQ50
Limes Ave., Croy. 119 DN104
Limes Ave., The N11 49 DH50
Limes Clo., Ashf. 98 BN92
Limes Fld. Rd. SW14 88 CS83
White Hart La.
Limes Gdns. SW18 104 DA86
Limes Gro. SE13 93 EC84
Limes Pl., Croy. 120 DR101
Limes Rd., Beck. 121 EB96
Limes Rd., Croy. 120 DR100
Limes Rd. (Cheshunt), 23 DX32
Wal.Cr.
Limes Rd., Wey. 126 BN105
Limes Row, Orp. 137 EP106
Orchard Rd.
Limes Wk. SE15 92 DV84
Limes Wk. W5 87 CK75
Chestnut Gro.
Limesdale Gdns., Edg. 46 CQ54
Limesford Rd. SE15 93 DX84
Limestone Wk., Erith 96 EX76
Alsike Rd.
Limetree Clo. SW2 105 DM88
Limetree Ter., Well. 96 EU83
Hook La.
Limetree Wk. SW17 104 DG92
Church La.
Limewood Clo. W13 73 CH72
St. Stephens Rd.
Limewood Ct., Ilf. 67 EM57
Beehive La.
Limewood Rd., Erith 97 FC80
Limpsfield Ave. SW19 103 CX89
Limpsfield Ave., Th.Hth. 119 DM99
Limpsfield Rd., S.Croy. 134 DU112
Limpsfield Rd., Warl. 148 DW116
Linacre Ct. W6 89 CX78
Linacre Rd. NW2 75 CV65
Linberry Wk. SE8 93 DY77
Carteret Way
Linchmere Rd. SE12 108 EF87
Lincoln Ave. N14 49 DJ48
Lincoln Ave. SW19 103 CX90
Lincoln Ave., Rom. 69 FD60
Lincoln Ave., Twick. 100 CB89
Lincoln Clo. SE25 120 DU100
Woodside Grn.
Lincoln Clo., Erith 97 FF82
Lincoln Clo., Grnf. 72 CC67
Lincoln Clo., Har. 58 BZ57
Lincoln Ct. N16 64 DR59
Lincoln Ct., Borwd. 32 CR43
Lincoln Cres., Enf. 36 DS43
Lincoln Dr., Rick. 29 BP44
Lincoln Dr., Wat. 44 BW48
Lincoln Gdns., Ilf. 66 EL59
Lincoln Grn. Rd., Orp. 123 ET99
Lincoln Ms. NW6 75 CZ67
Willesden La.
Lincoln Ms. SE21 106 DR88
Lincoln Rd. E7 80 EK65
Lincoln Rd. E13 80 EH70
Lincoln Rd. E18 52 EG53
Grove Rd.
Lincoln Rd. N2 62 DE55
Lincoln Rd. SE25 120 DV97
Lincoln Rd., Enf. 36 DS42
Lincoln Rd., Erith 97 FF82
Lincoln Rd., Felt. 100 BZ90
Lincoln Rd., Har. 58 BZ57
Lincoln Rd., Mitch. 119 DL99
Lincoln Rd., N.Mal. 116 CQ97
Lincoln Rd., Nthwd. 43 BT54
Lincoln Rd., Sid. 110 EV92
Lincoln Rd., Wem. 73 CK65
Lincoln Rd., Wor.Pk. 117 CV102
Lincoln St. E11 66 EE61
Lincoln St. SW3 8 D9
Lincoln St. SW3 90 DF77
Lincoln Wk., Epsom 130 CR110
Hollymoor La.
Lincoln Way, Enf. 36 DV43
Lincoln Way, Rick. 29 BP44
Lincoln Way, Sun. 113 BS95
Lincolns, The NW7 47 CT48
Lincolns Fld., Epp. 25 ET29
Lincoln's Inn WC2 77 DM72
Chancery La.
Lincoln's Inn Flds. WC2 6 B8
Lincoln's Inn Flds. WC2 77 DM72
Lincombe Rd., Brom. 108 EF90
Lind Rd., Sutt. 132 DC106
Lind St. SE8 93 EA82
Lindal Cres., Enf. 35 DL43
Lindal Rd. SE4 107 DZ85
Lindales, The N17 50 DT51
Brantwood Rd.
Lindbergh Rd., Wall. 133 DL108
Linden Ave. NW10 75 CX68
Linden Ave., Couls. 147 DH116
Linden Ave., Enf. 36 DU39
Linden Ave., Houns. 100 CB85
Linden Ave., Ruis. 57 BU60
Linden Ave., Th.Hth. 119 DP98
Linden Ave., Wem. 60 CM64
Linden Chase Rd., Sev. 155 FH122
Linden Clo. N14 35 DJ44
Linden Clo., Add. 126 BG111
Linden Clo., Orp. 138 EU106
Linden Clo., Ruis. 57 BU60
Linden Clo., Stan. 45 CH50
Linden Clo., Tad. 145 CX120
Linden Clo., T.Ditt. 115 CF101
Linden Clo., Wal.Cr. 22 DV30
Linden Ct. W12 75 CW74
Linden Ct., Lthd. 143 CH121
Linden Cres., Grnf. 73 CF65
Linden Cres., Kings.T. 116 CM96
Linden Cres., Wdf.Grn. 52 EH51
Linden Dr., Cat. 148 DQ124
Linden Gdns. W2 76 DA73
Linden Gdns. W4 88 CS78
Linden Gdns., Enf. 36 DU39
Linden Gdns., Lthd. 143 CJ121
Linden Gro. SE15 92 DV83
Linden Gro. SE26 106 DW93
Linden Gro., N.Mal. 116 CS97
Linden Gro., Tedd. 101 CF92
Waldegrave Rd.
Linden Gro., Walt. 113 BT103
Linden Gro., Warl. 149 DY118
Linden Lawns, Wem. 60 CM63
Linden Lea N2 62 DC57
Linden Lea, Wat. 15 BU33
Linden Leas, W.Wick. 121 ED103
Linden Ms. N1 64 DR64
Mildmay Gro. N.
Linden Ms. W2 76 DA73
Linden Pit Path, Lthd. 143 CH121
Linden Pl., Epsom 130 CS112
East St.
Linden Pl., Mitch. 118 DE98
Linden Rd. E17 65 DZ57
High St.
Linden Rd. N10 63 DH56
Linden Rd. N11 48 DF47
Linden Rd. N15 64 DQ56
Linden Rd., Hmptn. 100 CA94
Linden Rd., Lthd. 143 CH121
Linden Rd., Wey. 127 BQ109
Linden Sq., Sev. 154 FE122
London Rd.
Linden St., Rom. 69 FD56
Linden Wk. N19 63 DJ61
Hargrave Pk.
Linden Way N14 35 DJ44
Linden Way, Pur. 133 DJ110
Linden Way, Shep. 113 BQ99
Lindenfield, Chis. 123 EP96
Lindens, The N12 48 DD50
Lindens, The W4 88 CQ81
Hartington Rd.
Lindens, The, Croy. 135 EC107
Lindens, The, Loug. 39 EM43
Lindeth Clo., Stan. 45 CJ51
Old Ch. La.
Lindfield Gdns. NW3 62 DC64
Lindfield Rd. W5 73 CJ70

Lindfield Rd., Croy. 120 DT100
Lindfield St. E14 79 EA72
Lindisfarne Rd. SW20 103 CU94
Lindisfarne Rd., Dag. 68 EW62
Lindisfarne Way E9 65 DY63
Lindley Est. SE15 92 DU80
Bird in Bush Rd.
Lindley Rd. E10 65 EB61
Lindley Rd., Walt. 114 BX104
Lindley St. E1 78 DW71
Lindo St. SE15 92 DW82
Selden Rd.
Lindore Rd. SW11 90 DF84
Lindores Rd., Cars. 118 DC101
Lindrop St. SW6 90 DC82
Lindsay Clo., Chess. 130 CL108
Lindsay Clo., Epsom 130 CQ113
Lindsay Clo., Stai. 98 BK85
Lindsay Dr., Har. 60 CL58
Lindsay Dr., Shep. 113 BR100
Lindsay Pl., Wal.Cr. 22 DV30
Lindsay Rd., Add. 126 BG110
Lindsay Rd., Hmptn. 100 CB91
Lindsay Rd., Wor.Pk. 117 CV103
Lindsay Sq. SW1 91 DK78
Lindsell St. SE10 93 EC81
Lindsey Clo., Brom. 122 EK97
Lindsey Clo., Mitch. 119 DL98
Lindsey Gdns., Felt. 99 BR87
Lindsey Ms. N1 78 DQ66
Lindsey Rd., Dag. 68 EW63
Lindsey Rd., Uxb. 56 BG62
Lindsey St. EC1 6 G6
Lindsey St. EC1 77 DP71
Lindsey St., Epp. 25 ER28
Lindum Rd., Tedd. 101 CJ94
Lindway SE27 105 DP92
Lindwood Clo. E6 80 EL71
Northumberland Rd.
Linfield Clo. NW4 61 CW55
Linfield Clo., Walt. 127 BV106
Linford Rd. E17 65 EC55
Linford St. SW8 91 DJ81
Ling Rd. E16 80 EG71
Ling Rd., Erith 97 FC79
Lingards Rd. SE13 93 EC84
Lingey Clo., Sid. 109 ET89
Lingfield Ave., Kings.T. 116 CL98
Lingfield Clo., Enf. 36 DS44
Lingfield Clo., Nthwd. 43 BS52
Lingfield Cres. SE9 95 ER84
Lingfield Gdns. N9 50 DV45
Lingfield Gdns., Couls. 147 DP119
Lingfield Rd. SW19 103 CX93
Lingfield Rd., Wor.Pk. 117 CW104
Lingham St. SW9 91 DL82
Lingholm Way, Barn. 33 CX42
Lingmere Clo., Chig. 53 EQ47
Lingmoor Dr., Wat. 16 BW33
Lingrove Gdns., Buck.H. 52 EH47
Beech La.
Lings Coppice SE21 106 DR89
Lingwell Rd. SW17 104 DE90
Lingwood Gdns., Islw. 87 CE80
Lingwood Rd. E5 64 DU59
Linhope St. NW1 4 D4
Linhope St. NW1 76 DF70
Link, The SE9 109 EN90
Sandling Ri.
Link, The W3 74 CP72
Link, The, Enf. 37 DY39
Link, The, Nthlt. 58 BZ64
Eastcote La.
Link, The, Pnr. 58 BW59
Link, The, Wem. 59 CJ60
Nathans Rd.
Link La., Wall. 133 DK107
Link Rd. N11 48 DG49
Link Rd., Add. 126 BL105
Weybridge Rd.
Link Rd., Dag. 83 FB68
Link Rd., Felt. 99 BT87
Link Rd., Wall. 118 DG102
Link Rd. (Bushey), Wat. 30 BX40
Link St. E9 64 DW64
Link Way, Brom. 122 EL101
Link Way, Dag. 68 EW63
Link Way, Pnr. 44 BX53
Link Way, Stai. 98 BH93
Link Way, Uxb. 56 BG58
Linkfield, Brom. 122 EG100
Linkfield, W.Mol. 114 CB97
Linkfield Rd., Islw. 87 CF82
Linklea Clo. NW9 46 CS52
Links, The E17 65 DY56
Links, The (Cheshunt), Wal.Cr. 23 DX26
Links, The, Walt. 113 BU103
Links Ave., Mord. 118 DA98
Links Ave., Rom. 69 FH55
Links Brow, Lthd. 143 CE124
Links Clo., Ash. 143 CJ117
Links Dr. N20 48 DA46
Links Dr., Borwd. 32 CM41
Links Dr., Rad. 17 CF33
Links Gdns. SW16 105 DN94
Links Grn. Way, Cob. 128 CA114
Links Pl., Ash. 143 CK117
Links Rd. NW2 61 CT61
Links Rd. SW17 104 DG93
Links Rd. W3 74 CN72
Links Rd., Ashf. 98 BL92
Links Rd., Ash. 143 CJ118
Links Rd., Epsom 131 CU113
Links Rd., W.Wick. 121 EC102
Links Rd., Wdf.Grn. 52 EG50
Links Side, Enf. 35 DM41
Links Vw. N3 47 CZ52
Links Vw., Dart. 111 FH88
Links Vw. Clo., Stan. 45 CG51
Links Vw. Rd., Croy. 121 EA104
Links Vw. Rd., Hmptn. 100 CC92
Links Way, Beck. 121 EA100
Links Way, Nthwd. 43 BQ52
Links Way, Rick. 29 BQ41
Links Yd. E1 78 DU71
Spelman St.
Linkscroft Ave., Ashf. 99 BP93
Linkside N12 47 CZ51
Linkside, Chig. 53 EQ50
Linkside, N.Mal. 116 CS96
Linkside Clo., Enf. 35 DM41
Linkside Gdns., Enf. 35 DM41
Linksway NW4 47 CX54
Linkway N4 64 DQ59
Linkway SW20 117 CV97
Linkway, Rich. 101 CH90
Linkway, The, Barn. 34 DB44
Linkway, The, Sutt. 132 DC109
Linkwood Wk. NW1 77 DK66
Maiden La.
Linley Cres., Rom. 69 FB55
Linley Rd. N17 50 DS54
Linnell Clo. NW11 62 DB58
Linnell Dr. NW11 62 DB58
Linnell Rd. N18 50 DU50
Fairfield Rd.
Linnell Rd. SE5 92 DS82
Linnet Clo. N9 51 DX46
Linnet Clo. SE28 82 EW73
Linnet Clo., S.Croy. 135 DX110
Linnet Clo. (Bushey), Wat. 44 CC45
Linnet Ms. SW12 104 DG87
Linnet Rd., Abb.L. 15 BU31
College Rd.
Linnett Clo. E4 51 EC49
Linom Rd. SW4 91 DL84
Linscott Rd. E5 64 DW63
Linsdell Rd., Bark. 81 EQ67
Linsey St. SE16 92 DU77
Linslade Clo., Houns. 100 BY85
Frampton Rd.
Linslade Clo., Pnr. 57 BV55
Linslade Rd., Orp. 138 EU107
Linstead Ct. SE9 109 ES86
Linstead St. NW6 76 DA66
Linstead Way SW18 103 CY87
Linster Gro., Borwd. 32 CQ43
Lintaine Clo. W6 89 CY79
Moylan Rd.
Linthorpe Ave., Wem. 73 CJ65
Linthorpe Rd. N16 64 DS59
Linthorpe Rd., Barn. 34 DE41
Linton Ave., Borwd. 32 CM39
Linton Clo., Mitch. 118 DF101
Linton Clo., Well. 96 EV81
Anthony Rd.
Linton Gdns. E6 80 EL72
Linton Glade, Croy. 135 DY109
Linton Gro. SE27 105 DP92
Linton Rd., Bark. 81 EQ66
Linton St. N1 78 DQ67
Lintons, The, Bark. 81 EQ66
Lintons La., Epsom 130 CS112
Lintott Ct., Stai. 98 BK86
Linver Rd. SW6 89 CZ82
Linwood Clo. E6 80 EL71
Northumberland Rd.
Linwood Clo. SE5 92 DT82
Linwood Cres., Enf. 36 DU39
Linwood Way SE15 92 DT80
Daniel Gdns.
Linzee Rd. N8 63 DL56
Lion Ave., Twick. 101 CF88
Lion Rd.
Lion Clo. SE4 107 EA86
Lion Clo., Shep. 112 BL97
Lion Ct., Borwd. 32 CQ39
Lion Gate Gdns., Rich. 88 CM83
Lion Grn. Rd., Couls. 147 DK115
Lion Pk. Ave., Chess. 130 CN105
Lion Rd. E6 81 EM71
Lion Rd. N9 50 DU47
Lion Rd., Bexh. 96 EZ84
Lion Rd., Croy. 120 DQ99
Pawson's Rd.
Lion Rd., Twick. 101 CF88
Lion Way, Brent. 87 CK80
Lion Wf. Rd., Islw. 87 CH83
Lion Yd. SW4 91 DK84
Tremadoc Rd.
Lionel Gdns. SE9 108 EK85
Lionel Ms. W10 75 CY71
Telford Rd.
Lionel Rd. SE9 108 EK85
Lionel Rd., Brent. 88 CL76
Lions Clo. SE9 108 EJ90
Liphook Clo., Horn. 69 FF63
Petworth Way
Liphook Cres. SE23 106 DW87
Liphook Rd., Wat. 44 BX49
Lippitts Hill, Loug. 38 EE39
Lipsham Clo., Bans. 132 DD113
Lipton Clo. SE28 82 EW73
Aisher Rd.
Lipton Rd. E1 79 DX72
Bower St.
Lisbon Ave., Twick. 100 CC89
Lisburne Rd. NW3 62 DF63
Lisford St. SE15 92 DT81
Lisgar Ter. W14 89 CZ77
Liskeard Clo., Chis. 109 EQ93
Liskeard Gdns. SE3 94 EG81
Lisle St. WC2 5 N10
Lisle St. WC2 77 DK73
Lismore Circ. NW5 62 DG64
Wellesley Rd.
Lismore Clo., Islw. 87 CG82
Lismore Rd. N17 64 DR55
Lismore Rd., S.Croy. 134 DS107
Lismore Wk. N1 78 DQ65
Clephane Rd.
Liss Way SE15 92 DT80
Pentridge St.
Lissenden Gdns. NW5 62 DG63
Lissoms Rd., Couls. 146 DG118
Lisson Grn. Est. NW8 4 B3
Lisson Grn. Est. NW8 76 DE69
Lisson Gro. NW1 4 A4
Lisson Gro. NW1 76 DE70
Lisson Gro. NW8 4 A4
Lisson Gro. NW8 76 DD70
Lisson St. NW1 4 B6
Lisson St. NW1 76 DE71
Lister Clo. W3 74 CR71
Lister Clo., Mitch. 118 DE95
Lister Gdns. N18 50 DQ50
Lister Ho. SE3 94 EE79
Lister Rd. E11 66 EE60
Lister St. E13 80 EG69
Sewell St.
Lister Wk. SE28 82 EX73
Haldane Rd.
Liston Rd. N17 50 DU53
Liston Rd. SW4 91 DJ83
Liston Way, Wdf.Grn. 52 EJ52
Listowel Clo. SW9 91 DN80
Mandela St.
Listowel Rd., Dag. 68 FA62
Listria Pk. N16 64 DS61
Litchfield Ave. E15 80 EE65
Litchfield Ave., Mord. 117 CZ101
Litchfield Gdns. NW10 75 CU65
Litchfield Rd., Sutt. 132 DC105
Litchfield St. WC2 5 N10
Litchfield St. WC2 77 DK73
Litchfield Way NW11 62 DB57
Lithos Rd. NW3 76 DC65
Little Acre, Beck. 121 EA97
Little Albany St. NW1 5 J3
Little Argyll St. W1 5 K9
Little Benty, West Dr. 84 BK77
Little Birch Clo., Add. 126 BK109
Little Birches, Sid. 109 ES89
Little Boltons, The SW5 90 DB78
Little Boltons, The SW10 90 DB78
Little Bookham St., Lthd. 142 BZ123
Little Bornes SE21 106 DS91
Little Britain EC1 6 G7
Little Britain EC1 77 DP71
Little Brownings SE23 106 DV89
Little Bury St. N9 50 DR46
Little Bushey La. (Bushey), Wat. 30 CA41
Little Cedars N12 48 DC49
Woodside Ave.
Little Chester St. SW1 9 H6
Little Chester St. SW1 91 DH76
Little College La. EC4 78 DR73
Garlick Hill
Little College St. SW1 9 P6
Little Ct., W.Wick. 122 EE103
Little Dean's Yd. SW1 9 P6
Little Dimocks SW12 105 DH89
Little Dorrit Ct. SE1 11 J4
Little Dorrit Ct. SE1 92 DQ75
Little Dragons, Loug. 38 EK42
Little Ealing La. W5 87 CJ77
Little Edward St. NW1 5 J2
Little Elms, Hayes 85 BR80
Little Essex St. WC2 6 D10
Little Ferry Rd., Twick. 101 CH88
Ferry Rd.
Little Friday Rd. E4 52 EE47
Little Gearies, Ilf. 67 EP56
Little George St. SW1 9 P5
Little Gra., Grnf. 73 CG69
Perivale La.
Little Graylings, Abb.L. 15 BS33
Little Grn., Rich. 87 CK84
Little Grn. La., Rick. 28 BM41
Little Grn. St. NW5 63 DH63
College La.
Little Gregories La., Epp. 39 ER35
Little Gro. (Bushey), Wat. 30 CB42
Little Halliards, Walt. 113 BU100
Felix Rd.
Little Hayes, Kings L. 14 BN29
Little Heath SE7 94 EL78
Little Heath, Rom. 68 EV56
Little Heath Rd., Bexh. 96 EY81
Little How Cft., Abb.L. 15 BQ31
Little Ilford La. E12 67 EM63
Little Julians Hill, Sev. 154 FG128
Little Marlborough St. W1 5 K9
Little Martins (Bushey), Wat. 30 CB43
Little Moreton Clo., W.Byf. 126 BH112
Little Moss La., Pnr. 44 BY54
Little New St. EC4 6 E8
Little Newport St. WC2 5 N10
Little Newport St. WC2 77 DK73
Little Orchard Clo., Abb.L. 15 BR31
Little Orchard Clo., Pnr. 44 BY54
Barrow Pt. La.
Little Oxhey La., Wat. 44 BX50
Little Pk. Dr., Felt. 100 BX89
Little Pk. Gdns., Enf. 36 DQ41
Little Pipers Clo. (Cheshunt), Wal.Cr. 21 DP29
Little Pluckets Way, Buck.H. 52 EJ46
Little Portland St. W1 5 J8
Little Portland St. W1 77 DJ72
Little Potters (Bushey), Wat. 45 CD45
Little Queens Rd., Tedd. 101 CF93
Little Redlands, Brom. 122 EL96
Little Rd., Croy. 120 DS102
Lower Addiscombe Rd.
Little Rd., Hayes 85 BT75
Little Roke Ave., Ken. 133 DP113
Little Roke Rd., Ken. 134 DQ114
Little Russell St. WC1 5 P7
Little Russell St. WC1 77 DL71
Little St. James's St. SW1 9 K3
Little St. James's St. SW1 77 DJ74
Little St. Leonards SW14 88 CQ83
Little Sanctuary SW1 9 N5
Little Smith St. SW1 9 N6
Little Somerset St. E1 7 P9
Little Strand NW9 47 CT54
Little Stream Clo., Nthwd. 43 BS50
Little Thrift, Orp. 123 EQ98
Little Titchfield St. W1 5 K7
Little Trinity La. EC4 7 J10
Little Turnstile WC1 6 B7
Little Wd. Clo., Orp. 124 EU95
Little Woodcote La., Cars. 132 DG112
Little Woodcote La., Pur. 132 DG112
Little Woodcote La., Wall. 132 DG112
Littlebrook Clo., Croy. 121 DX100
Littlebrook Gdns. (Cheshunt), Wal.Cr. 22 DW30
Littlebury Rd. SW4 91 DK83
Littlecombe SE7 94 EH79
Littlecombe Clo. SW15 103 CX86
Littlecote Clo. SW19 103 CX87
Littlecote Pl., Pnr. 44 BZ53
Littlecourt Rd., Sev. 154 FG124
Littlecroft SE9 95 EN83
Littledale SE2 96 EU79
Littlefield Clo. N19 63 DJ63
Tufnell Pk. Rd.
Littlefield Clo., Kings.T. 116 CL96
Fairfield W.
Littlefield Rd., Edg. 46 CQ52
Littlegrove, Barn. 34 DE44
Littleheath La., Cob. 128 BZ114
Littleheath Rd., S.Croy. 134 DV108
Littlejohn Rd. W7 73 CF72
Littlejohn Rd., Orp. 124 EU100
Littlemead, Esher 129 CD105
Littlemede SE9 109 EM90
Littlemoor Rd., Ilf. 67 ER62
Littlemore Rd. SE2 96 EU75
Littlers Clo. SW19 118 DD95
Runnymede
Littlestone Clo., Beck. 107 EA93
Abbey La.
Littleton Ave. E4 52 EF46
Littleton Cres., Har. 59 CF61
Littleton La., Shep. 112 BK101
Littleton Rd., Ashf. 99 BQ94
Littleton Rd., Har. 59 CF61
Littleton St. SW18 104 DC89
Littlewood SE13 107 EC85
Littlewood, Sev. 155 FJ122
Littlewood Clo. W13 87 CH76
Littleworth Ave., Esher 129 CD106
Littleworth Common Rd., Esher 115 CD104
Littleworth La., Esher 129 CD105
Littleworth Pl., Esher 129 CD105
Littleworth Rd., Esher 129 CD106
Livermere Rd. E8 78 DT67
Liverpool Gro. SE17 92 DR78
Liverpool Rd. E10 65 EC58
Liverpool Rd. E16 80 EE71
Liverpool Rd. N1 77 DN66
Liverpool Rd. N7 63 DN64
Liverpool Rd. W5 87 CK75
Liverpool Rd., Kings.T. 102 CN94
Liverpool Rd., Th.Hth. 120 DQ97
Liverpool Rd., Wat. 29 BV43
Liverpool St. EC2 7 M7
Liverpool St. EC2 78 DS71
Livesey Clo., Kings.T. 116 CM97
Livesey Pl. SE15 92 DU79
Peckham Pk. Rd.
Livingston College Twrs. E10 65 EC58
Livingstone Pl. E14 93 EC78
Ferry St.
Livingstone Rd. E15 79 EC67
Livingstone Rd. E17 65 EB58
Livingstone Rd. N13 49 DL51
Livingstone Rd. SW11 90 DD83
Winstanley Rd.
Livingstone Rd., Cat. 148 DR122
Livingstone Rd., Houns. 86 CC84
Livingstone Rd., Sthl. 72 BX73
Livingstone Rd., Th.Hth. 120 DQ96
Livingstone Ter., Rain. 83 FE67
Stanley Rd. N.
Livingstone Wk. SW11 90 DD83
Livonia St. W1 5 L9
Lizard St. EC1 7 J3
Lizard St. EC1 78 DQ69
Lizban St. SE3 94 EH80
Llanelly Rd. NW2 61 CZ61
Llanover Rd. SE18 95 EN79
Llanover Rd., Wem. 59 CK62
Llanthony Rd., Mord. 118 DD100
Llanvanor Rd. NW2 61 CZ61
Llewellyn St. SE16 92 DU75
Chambers St.
Lloyd Ave. SW16 119 DL95
Lloyd Ave., Couls. 132 DG114
Lloyd Baker St. WC1 6 C3
Lloyd Baker St. WC1 77 DM69
Lloyd Ct., Pnr. 58 BX57
Lloyd Pk. Ave., Croy. 134 DT105
Lloyd Rd. E6 81 EM67
Lloyd Rd. E17 65 DX56
Lloyd Rd., Dag. 82 EZ65
Lloyd Rd., Wor.Pk. 117 CW104
Lloyd Sq. WC1 6 D2
Lloyd Sq. WC1 77 DN69
Lloyd St. WC1 6 D2
Lloyd St. WC1 77 DN69
Lloyd's Ave. EC3 7 N9
Lloyd's Ave. EC3 78 DS72
Lloyds Pl. SE3 94 EE82
Lloyd's Row EC1 6 F3
Lloyds Way, Beck. 121 DY99
Loampit Hill SE13 93 EA82
Loampit Vale SE13 93 EB83
Loanda Clo. E8 78 DT67
Clarissa St.
Loates La., Wat. 30 BW41
Loats Rd. SW2 105 DL86
Lobelia Clo. E6 80 EL71
Sorrel Gdns.
Local Board Rd., Wat. 30 BW43
Locarno Rd. W3 74 CQ74
High St.
Locarno Rd., Grnf. 72 CC70
Lochaber Rd. SE13 94 EE84
Lochaline St. W6 89 CW79
Lochan Clo., Hayes 72 BY70
Lochinvar St. SW12 105 DH87
Lochmere Clo., Erith 97 FB79
Lochnagar St. E14 79 EC71
Lock Chase SE3 94 EE83
Lock Clo., Sthl. 86 CC75
Navigator Dr.
Lock Island, Shep. 112 BN103
Lock La., Wok. 140 BH116
Lock Rd., Rich. 101 CJ91
Locke Clo., Rain. 83 FF65
Locke King Clo., Wey. 126 BN108
Locke King Rd., Wey. 126 BN108
Lockesfield Pl. E14 93 EB78
Lockesley Dr., Orp. 123 ET100
Lockesley Sq., Surb. 115 CK100
Locket Rd., Har. 59 CE55
Lockfield Ave., Enf. 37 DY40
Lockgate Clo. E9 65 DZ64
Lee Conservancy Rd.
Lockhart Clo. N7 77 DM65
Lockhart Clo., Enf. 36 DV43
Derby Rd.
Lockhart Rd., Cob. 128 BW113
Lockhart St. E3 79 DZ70
Lockhurst St. E5 65 DX63
Lockie Pl. SE25 120 DU97
Lockier Wk., Wem. 59 CK62
Hutchinson Ter.
Lockington Rd. SW8 91 DH81
Lockmead Rd. N15 64 DU58
Lockmead Rd. SE13 93 EC83
Locks La., Mitch. 118 DF95
Lockside E14 79 DY73
Northey St.
Locksley Est. E14 79 DZ72
Locksley St. E14 79 DZ71
Locksmeade Rd., Rich. 101 CJ91
Lockswood Clo., Barn. 34 DG41
Lockwood Clo. SE26 107 DX91
Lockwood Ind. Pk. N17 64 DV55
Lockwood Sq. SE16 92 DV76
Lockwood Wk., Rom. 69 FE57
Lockwood Way E17 51 DX54
Lockwood Way, Chess. 130 CN106
Lockyer Est. SE1 11 L4
Lockyer St. SE1 11 L5
Loddiges Rd. E9 78 DW66
Loder St. SE15 92 DW80
Lodge Ave. SW14 88 CS83
Lodge Ave., Borwd. 32 CM43
Lodge Ave., Croy. 119 DN104
Lodge Ave., Dag. 82 EU67
Lodge Ave., Har. 60 CL56
Lodge Ave., Rom. 69 FG57
Lodge Clo. N18 50 DQ50
Lodge Clo., Chig. 54 EU48
Lodge Clo., Cob. 142 BZ116
Lodge Clo., Edg. 46 CM51
Lodge Clo., Epsom 131 CW110
Howell Hill Gro.
Lodge Clo., Islw. 87 CH81
Lodge Clo., Lthd. 143 CD122
Lodge Clo., Orp. 124 EV102
Lodge Clo., Uxb. 70 BJ70
Lodge Clo., Wall. 118 DG102
Lodge Cres., Orp. 124 EV102
Lodge Cres., Wal.Cr. 23 DX34
Lodge Dr. N13 49 DN49
Lodge Dr., Rick. 28 BJ42
Lodge End, Rad. 17 CH34
Lodge End, Rick. 29 BR41
Lodge Gdns., Beck. 121 DZ99
Lodge Hill SE2 96 EV80
Lodge Hill, Ilf. 66 EL56
Lodge Hill, Pur. 147 DN115
Lodge Hill, Well. 96 EV80
Lodge La. N12 48 DC50
Lodge La., Bex. 110 EX86
Lodge La., Croy. 135 EA107
Lodge La., Rom. 54 FA52
Lodge La., Wal.Abb. 37 ED35
Lodge Pl., Sutt. 132 DB106
Lodge Rd. NW4 61 CW56

Lodge Rd. NW8 4 A3
Lodge Rd. NW8 76 DD69
Lodge Rd., Brom. 108 EH94
Lodge Rd., Croy. 119 DP100
Lodge Rd., Lthd. 142 CC122
Lodge Rd., Sutt. 132 DB106
Throwley Way
Lodge Rd., Wall. 133 DH106
Lodge Vill., Wdf.Grn. 52 EF52
Lodge Way, Ashf. 98 BL89
Lodge Way, Shep. 113 BQ96
Lodgehill Pk. Clo., Har. 58 CB61
Lodore Gdns. NW9 60 CS57
Lodore Grn., Uxb. 56 BL62
Lodore St. E14 79 EC72
Lofthouse Pl., Chess. 129 CJ107
Loftie St. SE16 92 DU75
Lofting Rd. N1 77 DM66
Loftus Rd. W12 75 CV74
Logan Clo., Enf. 37 DX39
Logan Clo., Houns. 86 BZ83
Logan Ms. W8 90 DA77
Logan Pl. W8 90 DA77
Logan Rd. N9 50 DV47
Logan Rd., Wem. 60 CL61
Loggetts, The SE21 106 DR90
Logs Hill, Brom. 108 EL94
Logs Hill, Chis. 108 EL94
Logs Hill Clo., Chis. 122 EL95
Lois Dr., Shep. 113 BP99
Lolesworth Clo. E1 78 DT71
Commercial St.
Lollard St. SE11 10 C8
Lollard St. SE11 91 DN77
Loman St. SE1 10 G4
Loman St. SE1 91 DP75
Lomas Clo., Croy. 135 EC108
Lomas Ct. E8 78 DT66
Lomas St. E1 78 DU71
Lombard Ave., Enf. 36 DW39
Lombard Ave., Ilf. 67 ES60
Lombard Business Pk. SW19 118 DB96
Lombard Ct. EC3 7 L10
Lombard La. EC4 6 E9
Lombard Rd. N11 49 DH50
Lombard Rd. SW11 90 DD82
Lombard Rd. SW19 118 DB96
Lombard St. EC3 7 L9
Lombard St. EC3 78 DR72
Lombard Wall SE7 94 EH76
Lombardy Pl. W2 76 DB73
Bark Pl.
Lombardy Way, Borwd. 32 CL39
Lomond Clo. N15 64 DS57
Lomond Clo., Wem. 74 CM66
Lomond Gdns., S.Croy. 135 DY108
Lomond Gro. SE5 92 DR80
Lomond Ho. SE5 92 DR81
Lomond Gro.
Loncin Mead Ave., Add. 126 BJ109
Loncroft Rd. SE5 92 DS79
Londesborough Rd. N16 64 DS63
London Bri. EC4 11 L2
London Bri. EC4 78 DR73
London Bri. SE1 11 L2
London Bri. SE1 78 DR74
London Bri. St. SE1 11 L3
London Bri. St. SE1 78 DR74
London Bri. Wk. SE1 11 L2
London City Airport E16 80 EL74
London Colney Bypass, St.Alb. 17 CK25
London Colney Ind. Est., St.Alb. 18 CL27
London Flds. E8 78 DV66
London Flds. E. Side E8 78 DV66
London Flds. W. Side E8 78 DU66
London Ind. Pk. E6 81 EP71
London La. E8 78 DV66
London La., Brom. 108 EF94
London Ms. W2 4 A9
London Rd. E13 80 EG68
London Rd. SE1 10 F6
London Rd. SE1 91 DP76
London Rd. SE23 106 DV88
London Rd. SW16 119 DM95
London Rd. SW17 104 DF94
London Rd., Ashf. 98 BJ90
London Rd., Bark. 81 EP66
London Rd., Borwd. 32 CQ36
London Rd., Brent. 87 CF82
London Rd., Brom. 108 EF94
London Rd., Cat. 148 DR123
London Rd., Croy. 119 DP102
London Rd. (Crayford), Dart. 111 FD85
London Rd., Enf. 36 DR42
London Rd., Epsom 131 CU108
London Rd., Felt. 98 BH90
London Rd., Har. 59 CE61
London Rd., Houns. 86 CC83
London Rd., Islw. 87 CF82
London Rd., Kings.T. 116 CM96
London Rd., Mitch. 118 DE98
London Rd. (Beddington Cor.), Mitch. 118 DG101
London Rd., Mord. 118 DA99
London Rd., Ong. 41 FH36
London Rd., Rad. 18 CM33
London Rd., Rick. 42 BM47
London Rd., Rom. 68 FA58
London Rd. (Abridge), Rom. 40 EU42
London Rd. (Stapleford Tawney), Rom. 41 FC40
London Rd., Sev. 154 FF123
London Rd. (Halstead), Sev. 139 FB112
London Rd. (Longford), Sev. 153 FD119
London Rd., Stai. 98 BH90
London Rd., Stan. 45 CJ50
London Rd., Sutt. 117 CW104
London Rd., Swan. 125 FC95
London Rd., Th.Hth. 119 DN99
London Rd., Twick. 101 CG87
London Rd., Wall. 133 DH105
London Rd. (Bushey), Wat. 30 BY44
London Rd., Wem. 60 CL64
London Stile W4 88 CN78
Wellesley Rd.
London St. EC3 7 N10
London St. W2 76 DD72
London St., Cher. 112 BG101
London Wall EC2 7 J7
London Wall EC2 78 DQ71
London Wall Bldgs. EC2 7 L7
Lonesome Way SW16 119 DH95
Long Acre WC2 5 P10
Long Acre WC2 77 DL73
Long Acre, Orp. 124 EX103
Long Barn Clo., Wat. 15 BU32
Long Copse Clo., Lthd. 142 CB123
Long Ct. WC2 9 N1
Long Deacon Rd. E4 52 EE46
Long Dr. W3 74 CS72
Long Dr., Grnf. 72 CB67
Long Dr., Ruis. 58 BX63
Long Elmes, Har. 44 CB53
Long Elms, Abb.L. 15 BR33
Long Elms Clo., Abb.L. 15 BR33
Long Elms
Long Fallow, St.Alb. 16 CA27
Long Fld. NW9 46 CS52
Long Grn., Chig. 53 ES49
Long Gro. Rd., Epsom 130 CP110
Long Hedges, Houns. 86 CA81
Great W. Rd.
Long Hill, Cat. 149 DX121
Long La. EC1 6 G6
Long La. EC1 77 DP71
Long La. N2 48 DC54
Long La. N3 48 DB52
Long La. SE1 11 K5
Long La. SE1 92 DR75
Long La., Bexh. 96 EX80
Long La., Croy. 120 DV100
Long La., Stai. 98 BM89
Long La., Uxb. 71 BP67
Long Leys E4 51 EB51
Long Lo. Dr., Walt. 114 BW104
Long Mark Rd. E16 80 EK71
Fulmer Rd.
Long Mead NW9 47 CT53
Long Meadow NW5 63 DK64
Torriano Ave.
Long Meadow, Sev. 153 FD119
London Rd.
Long Meadow Clo., W.Wick. 121 EC101
Long Pond Rd. SE3 94 EE81
Long Reach, Wok. 140 BN123
Long Reach Ct., Bark. 81 ER68
Long Reach Rd., Bark. 81 ET70
Long Rd. SW4 91 DH84
Long Shaw, Lthd. 143 CG120
Long St. E2 7 P2
Long St. E2 78 DT69
Long St., Wal.Abb. 24 EL32
Long Wk. SE1 11 N6
Long Wk. SE18 95 EP79
Long Wk. SW13 88 CS82
The Ter.
Long Wk., Epsom 145 CW119
Long Wk., N.Mal. 116 CQ97
Long Wk., Wal.Abb. 23 EA30
Long Wk., W.Byf. 126 BJ114
Long Yd. WC1 6 B5
Long Yd. WC1 77 DM70
Longacre Pl., Cars. 132 DG107
Beddington Gdns.
Longacre Rd. E17 51 ED53
Longbeach Rd. SW11 90 DF83
Longberrys NW2 61 CZ62
Longboat Row, Sthl. 72 BZ72
Longboyds, Cob. 127 BV114
Longbridge Rd., Bark. 81 ER65
Longbridge Rd., Dag. 68 EU63
Longbridge Way SE13 107 EC85
Longbridge Way, Uxb. 70 BH68
Longbury Clo., Orp. 124 EV97
Longbury Dr., Orp. 124 EV97
Longcliffe Path, Wat. 43 BU48
Gosforth La.
Longcroft SE9 109 EM90
Longcroft, Wat. 43 BV45
Longcroft Ave., Bans. 132 DC114
Longcroft Dr., Wal.Cr. 23 DZ34
Longcroft Ri., Loug. 39 EN43
Longcrofte Rd., Edg. 45 CK52
Longcrofts, Wal.Abb. 24 EE34
Roundhills
Longdon Wd., Kes. 122 EL104
Longdown La. N., Epsom 131 CU114
Longdown La. S., Epsom 131 CU114
Longdown Rd. SE6 107 EA91
Longdown Rd., Epsom 131 CU114
Longfellow Rd. E17 65 DZ58
Longfellow Rd., Wor.Pk. 117 CU102
Longfellow Way SE1 92 DT77
Chaucer Dr.
Longfield, Brom. 122 EF95
Longfield, Loug. 38 EJ43
Longfield Ave. E17 65 DY56
Longfield Ave. NW7 47 CU52
Longfield Ave. W5 73 CJ73
Longfield Ave., Enf. 36 DW37
Longfield Ave., Horn. 69 FF59
Longfield Ave., Wall. 118 DG102
Longfield Ave., Wem. 60 CL60
Longfield Cres. SE26 106 DW90
Longfield Cres., Tad. 145 CW120
Longfield Dr. SW14 102 CP85
Longfield Dr., Mitch. 104 DE94
Longfield Est. SE1 92 DT77
Longfield La. (Cheshunt), Wal.Cr. 22 DT27
Longfield Rd. W5 73 CJ72
Longfield St. SW18 104 DA87
Longfield Wk. W5 73 CJ72
Longford Ave., Felt. 99 BS86
Longford Ave., Sthl. 72 CA73
Longford Ave., Stai. 98 BL88
Longford Clo., Hmptn. 100 CA91
Longford Clo., Hayes 72 BX73
Longford Gdns.
Longford Ct. E5 65 DX63
Pedro St.
Longford Ct. NW4 61 CX56
Longford Ct., Epsom 130 CQ105
Longford Gdns., Hayes 72 BX73
Longford Gdns., Sutt. 118 DC104
Longford Rd., Twick. 100 CA88
Longford St. NW1 5 J4
Longford St. NW1 77 DH70
Longford Wk. SW2 105 DN87
Papworth Way
Longford Way, Stai. 98 BL88
Longhayes Ave., Rom. 68 EX56
Longheath Gdns., Croy. 120 DW99
Longhedge Ho. SE26 106 DT91
Longhedge St. SW11 90 DG82
Longhill Rd. SE6 107 ED89
Longhook Gdns., Nthlt. 71 BU68
Longhope Clo. SE15 92 DS79
Longhurst Rd. SE13 107 ED85
Longhurst Rd., Croy. 120 DV100
Longland Ct. SE1 92 DU78
Rolls Rd.
Longland Dr. N20 48 DB48
Longlands Ave., Couls. 132 DG114
Longlands Clo. (Cheshunt), Wal.Cr. 23 DX32
Longlands Ct. W11 75 CZ73
Portobello Rd.
Longlands Ct., Mitch. 118 DG95
Summerhill Way
Longlands Pk. Cres., Sid. 109 ES90
Longlands Rd., Sid. 109 ES90
Longleat Ms., Orp. 124 EW98
High St.
Longleat Rd., Enf. 36 DS43
Longleat Way, Felt. 99 BR87
Longleigh La. SE2 96 EW79
Longleigh La., Bexh. 96 EW79
Longlents Ho. NW10 74 CR67
Shrewsbury Cres.
Longley Ave., Wem. 74 CM67
Longley Rd. SW17 104 DE93
Longley Rd., Croy. 119 DP101
Longley Rd., Har. 58 CC57
Longley St. SE1 92 DU77
Longley Way NW2 61 CW62
Longmead, Chis. 123 EN96
Longmead, Epsom 130 CR110
Longmead Clo., Cat. 148 DS122
Longmead Dr., Sid. 110 EX89
Longmead Rd. SW17 104 DF92
Longmead Rd., Epsom 130 CR111
Longmead Rd., Hayes 71 BT73
Longmead Rd., T.Ditt. 115 CE101
Longmeadow Rd., Sid. 109 ES88
Longmere Gdns., Tad. 145 CW119
Longmoor, Wal.Cr. 23 DY29
Longmoor Pt. SW15 103 CV88
Norley Vale
Longmoore St. SW1 9 K9
Longmoore St. SW1 91 DJ77
Longmore Ave., Barn. 34 DC44
Longmore Rd., Walt. 128 BY105
Longnor Rd. E1 79 DX69
Longport Clo., Ilf. 54 EU51
Longreach Rd., Erith 97 FH80
Longridge La., Sthl. 72 CB72
Longridge Rd. SW5 90 DA77
Longs Clo., Wok. 140 BG116
Longs Ct., Rich. 88 CM84
Crown Ter.
Longshaw Rd. E4 51 ED48
Longshore SE8 93 DZ77
Longspring, Wat. 29 BV38
Longspring Wd., Sev. 154 FF130
Longstaff Cres. SW18 104 DA86
Longstaff Rd. SW18 104 DA86
Longstone Ave. NW10 75 CT66
Longstone Rd. SW17 105 DH92
Longthornton Rd. SW16 119 DJ96
Longton Ave. SE26 106 DU91
Longton Gro. SE26 106 DV91
Longview Way, Rom. 55 FD53
Longville Rd. SE11 10 G8
Longwalk Rd., Uxb. 71 BP74
Longwalk Rd., Uxb. 71 BP74
Longwood Dr. SW15 103 CU86
Longwood Gdns., Ilf. 67 EM56
Longwood Rd., Ken. 148 DR116
Longworth Clo. SE28 82 EX72
Loning, The NW9 60 CS56
Loning, The, Enf. 36 DW38
Lonsdale Ave. E6 80 EK69
Lonsdale Ave., Rom. 69 FC58
Lonsdale Ave., Wem. 60 CL64
Lonsdale Clo. E6 80 EL70
Lonsdale Ave.
Lonsdale Clo. SE9 108 EK90
Lonsdale Clo., Edg. 46 CM50
Orchard Dr.
Lonsdale Clo., Pnr. 44 BY52
Lonsdale Clo., Uxb. 71 BQ71
Dawley Ave.
Lonsdale Cres., Ilf. 67 EP58
Lonsdale Dr., Enf. 35 DK42
Lonsdale Gdns., Th.Hth. 119 DM98
Lonsdale Ms., Rich. 88 CN81
Elizabeth Cotts.
Lonsdale Pl. N1 77 DN66
Barnsbury St.
Lonsdale Rd. E11 66 EF59
Lonsdale Rd. NW6 75 CZ67
Lonsdale Rd. SE25 120 DV98
Lonsdale Rd. SW13 89 CU79
Lonsdale Rd. W4 89 CT77
Lonsdale Rd. W11 75 CZ72
Lonsdale Rd., Bexh. 96 EZ82
Lonsdale Rd., Sthl. 86 BX76
Lonsdale Rd., Wey. 126 BN108
Lonsdale Sq. N1 77 DN67
Loobert Rd. N15 64 DS55
Looe Gdns., Ilf. 67 EP55
Loom La., Rad. 31 CF37
Loom Pl., Rad. 31 CG36
Loop Rd., Chis. 109 EQ93
Loop Rd., Epsom 144 CQ116
Woodcote Side
Loop Rd., Wal.Abb. 23 EB32
Lopen Rd. N18 50 DS49
Loraine Clo., Enf. 36 DW43
Loraine Gdns., Ash. 144 CL117
Loraine Rd. N7 63 DM63
Loraine Rd. W4 88 CP79
Lorane Ct., Wat. 29 BU40
Stratford Rd.
Lord Ave., Ilf. 67 EM56
Lord Chancellor Wk., Kings.T. 116 CQ95
Lord Gdns., Ilf. 66 EL56
Lord Hills Bri. W2 76 DB71
Porchester Rd.
Lord Hills Rd. W2 76 DB71
Lord Holland La. SW9 91 DN81
Myatt's Flds. S.
Lord Knyvett Clo., Stai. 98 BK86
Lord Napier Pl. W6 89 CU78
Upper Mall
Lord N. St. SW1 9 P7
Lord N. St. SW1 91 DL76
Lord Roberts Ms. SW6 90 DB80
Moore Pk. Rd.
Lord Roberts Ter. SE18 95 EN78
Lord St. E16 80 EL74
Lord St., Wat. 30 BW41
Lord Warwick St. SE18 95 EM76
Lordell Pl. SW19 103 CW93
Lorden Wk. E2 78 DU69
Turin St.
Lord's Clo. SE21 106 DQ89
Lords Clo., Felt. 100 BY89
Lords Clo., Rad. 18 CL32
Lord's Vw. NW8 4 A3
Lordsbury Fld., Wall. 133 DJ110
Lordsgrove Clo., Tad. 145 CV120
Whitegate Way
Lordship Gro. N16 64 DR61
Lordship La. N17 50 DQ53
Lordship La. N22 49 DN54
Lordship La. SE22 106 DT86
Lordship La. Est. SE22 106 DU88
Lordship Pk. N16 64 DQ61
Lordship Pk. Ms. N16 64 DQ61
Allerton Rd.
Lordship Pl. SW3 90 DE79
Cheyne Row
Lordship Rd. N16 64 DR60
Lordship Rd., Nthlt. 72 BY66
Lordship Rd. (Cheshunt), Wal.Cr. 22 DV30
Lordship Ter. N16 64 DR61
Lordsmead Rd. N17 50 DS53
Lorenzo St. WC1 6 B1
Lorenzo St. WC1 77 DM69
Loretto Gdns., Har. 60 CL56
Lorian Clo. N12 48 DB49
Loring Rd. N20 48 DE47
Loring Rd., Islw. 87 CF82
Loris Rd. W6 89 CW76
Lorn Ct. SW9 91 DN82
Lorn Rd.
Lorn Rd. SW9 91 DM82
Lorne Ave., Croy. 121 DX101
Lorne Clo. NW8 4 C3
Lorne Gdns. E11 66 EJ56
Lorne Gdns. W11 89 CX75
Lorne Gdns., Croy. 121 DX101
Lorne Rd. E7 66 EH63
Lorne Rd. E17 65 EA57
Lorne Rd. N4 63 DM60
Lorne Rd., Har. 45 CF54
Lorne Rd., Rich. 102 CM85
Albert Rd.
Lorraine Pk., Har. 45 CE52
Lorrimore Rd. SE17 91 DP79
Lorrimore Sq. SE17 91 DP79
Losberne Way SE16 92 DU78
Catlin St.
Loseberry Rd., Esher 129 CD106
Lothair Rd. W5 87 CK75
Lothair Rd. N. N4 63 DP5
Lothair Rd. S. N4 63 DN5
Lothbury EC2 7 K8
Lothbury EC2 78 DR72
Lothian Ave., Hayes 71 BV7
Lothian Clo., Wem. 59 CG6
Lothian Rd. SW9 91 DP8
Lothian Wd., Tad. 145 CV122
Lothrop St. W10 75 CY69
Lots Rd. SW10 90 DC80
Lotus Clo. SE21 106 DQ90
Lotus Rd., West. 151 EM118
Loubet St. SW17 104 DF93
Loudoun Ave., Ilf. 67 EP57
Loudoun Rd. NW8 76 DC66
Loudoun Rd. Ms. NW8 76 DC67
Loudoun Rd.
Loudwater Clo., Sun. 113 BU98
Loudwater Dr., Rick. 28 BJ42
Loudwater Heights, Rick. 28 BH41
Loudwater La., Rick. 28 BK42
Loudwater Ridge, Rick. 28 BJ42
Loudwater Rd., Sun. 113 BU98
Lough Rd. N7 63 DM64
Loughborough Est. SW9 91 DP82
Loughborough Rd.
Loughborough Pk. SW9 91 DP84
Loughborough Rd. SW9 91 DN82
Loughborough St. SE11 91 DM78
Loughton Ct., Wal.Abb. 24 EH33
Stanway Rd.
Loughton La., Epp. 39 ER38
Loughton Way, Buck.H. 52 EK46
Louis Ms. N10 49 DH53
Louisa Gdns. E1 79 DX70
Louisa St.
Louisa Ho. SW15 89 CT84
Arabella Dr.
Louisa St. E1 79 DX70
Louise Aumonier Wk. N19 63 DL59
Hillrise Rd.
Louise Bennett Clo. SE24 91 DP84
Shakespeare Rd.
Louise Gdns., Rain. 83 FE69
Louise Rd. E15 80 EE65
Louisville Rd. SW17 104 DG90
Louvain Way, Wat. 15 BV32
Louvaine Rd. SW11 90 DD84
Lovage App. E6 80 EL71
Lovat Clo. NW2 61 CT62
Lovat La. EC3 11 M1
Lovat Wk., Houns. 86 BY80
Cranford La.
Lovatt Clo., Edg. 46 CP51
Lovatt Dr., Ruis. 57 BT57
Lovatts, Rick. 28 BN42
Love La. EC2 7 J8
Love La. EC2 78 DQ72
Love La. N17 50 DT52
Love La. SE18 95 EP77
Love La. SE25 120 DV97
Love La., Abb.L. 15 BT30
Love La., Bex. 110 EZ86
Love La., Kings L. 14 BL28
Love La., Mitch. 118 DE97
Love La., Mord. 118 DA101
Love La., Pnr. 58 BY55
Love La., Surb. 115 CJ103
Love La., Sutt. 131 CY107
Love La., Wdf.Grn. 53 EM51
Love Wk. SE5 92 DR82
Loveday Rd. W13 73 CH74
Lovegrove St. SE1 92 DU78
Lovegrove Wk. E14 79 EC74
Lovekyn Clo., Kings.T. 116 CM96
Queen Elizabeth Rd.
Lovel Ave., Well. 96 EU82
Lovelace Ave., Brom. 123 EN100
Lovelace Clo., Lthd. 141 BU123
Lovelace Gdns., Bark. 68 EU63
Lovelace Gdns., Surb. 115 CK101
Lovelace Gdns., Walt. 128 BW106
Lovelace Grn. SE9 95 EM83
Lovelace Rd. SE21 106 DQ89
Lovelace Rd., Barn. 48 DE45
Lovelace Rd., Surb. 115 CJ101
Lovelinch Clo. SE15 92 DW79
Lovell Ho. E8 78 DU67
Lovell Pl. SE16 93 DY76
Ropemaker Rd.
Lovell Rd., Enf. 36 DV35
Lovell Rd., Rich. 101 CJ90
Lovell Rd., Sthl. 72 CB72
Lovell Wk., Rain. 83 FG65
Lovelock Clo., Ken. 148 DQ117
Loveridge Ms. NW6 75 CZ65
Loveridge Rd.
Loveridge Rd. NW6 75 CZ65
Lovers Wk. N3 48 DA52
Lovers Wk. NW7 47 CY51
Lovers Wk. SE10 94 EE80
Lover's Wk. W1 8 F2
Lover's Wk. W1 76 DG74
Lovett Dr., Cars. 118 DC101
Lovett Rd., Uxb. 56 BJ55
Lovett Way NW10 60 CQ64
Lovett's Pl. SW18 90 DB84
Old York Rd.
Lovibonds Ave., Orp. 137 EP105
Lovibonds Ave., West Dr. 70 BM72
Low Cross Wd. La. SE21 106 DT90
Low Hall Clo. E4 51 EA45
Low Hall La. E17 65 DY58
Lowbell La., St.Alb. 18 CL27
Lowbrook Rd., Ilf. 67 EP63
Lowdell Clo., West Dr. 70 BL72
Lowden Rd. N9 50 DV46

Lowden Rd. SE24 92 DQ84
Lowden Rd., Sthl. 72 BY73
Lowe, The, Chig. 54 EU49
Lowe Ave. E16 80 EG71
Charford Rd.
Lowe Clo., Chig. 54 EU50
Lowell St. E14 79 DY72
Lowen Rd., Rain. 83 FD68
Lower Aberdeen Wf. E14 79 DZ74
Westferry Rd.
Lower Addiscombe Rd., Croy. 120 DS102
Lower Addison Gdns. W14 89 CY75
Lower Alderton Hall La., Loug. 39 EN43
Lower Barn Rd., Pur. 134 DR113
Lower Bedfords Rd., Rom. 55 FE51
Lower Belgrave St. SW1 9 H7
Lower Belgrave St. SW1 91 DH76
Lower Boston Rd. W7 73 CE74
Lower Broad St., Dag. 82 FA67
Lower Bury La., Epp. 25 ES31
Lower Camden, Chis. 109 EM94
Lower Ch. St., Croy. 119 DP103
Waddon New Rd.
Lower Clapton Rd. E5 64 DW64
Lower Clarendon Wk. W11 75 CY72
Lancaster Rd.
Lower Common S. SW15 89 CV83
Lower Coombe St., Croy. 134 DQ105
Lower Ct. Rd., Epsom 130 CQ111
Lower Cft., Swan. 125 FF98
Lower Downs Rd. SW20 117 CX95
Lower Drayton Pl., Croy. 119 DP103
Drayton Rd.
Lower Dunnymans, Bans. 131 CZ114
Basing Rd.
Lower Fm. Rd., Lthd. 141 BV124
Lower George St., Rich. 101 CK85
George St.
Lower Gravel Rd., Brom. 122 EL102
Lower Grn. Rd., Esher 114 CB103
Lower Grn. W., Mitch. 118 DE97
Lower Grosvenor Pl. SW1 9 H6
Lower Grosvenor Pl. SW1 91 DH76
Lower Gro. Rd., Rich. 102 CM86
Lower Hall La. E4 51 DY50
Lower Ham Rd., Kings.T. 101 CK93
Lower Hampton Rd., Sun. 114 BW97
Lower High St., Wat. 30 BW42
Lower Hill Rd., Epsom 130 CP112
Lower James St. W1 5 L10
Lower John St. W1 5 L10
Lower Kenwood Ave., Enf. 35 DK43
Lower Lea Crossing E14 80 EE73
Lower Maidstone Rd. N11 49 DJ51
Telford Rd.
Lower Mall W6 89 CV78
Lower Mardyke Ave., Rain. 83 FC68
Lower Marsh SE1 10 D5
Lower Marsh SE1 91 DM75
Lower Marsh La., Kings.T. 116 CM98
Lower Meadow, Wal.Cr. 23 DX27
Lower Merton Ri. NW3 76 DE66
Lower Morden La., Mord. 117 CX100
Lower Mortlake Rd., Rich. 88 CL84
Lower Northfield, Bans. 131 CZ114
Lower Paddock Rd., Wat. 30 BY44
Lower Pk. Rd. N11 49 DJ50
Lower Pk. Rd., Belv. 96 FA76
Lower Pk. Rd., Couls. 146 DE118
Lower Pk. Rd., Loug. 38 EK43
Lower Plantation, Rick. 28 BJ41
Lower Queens Rd., Buck.H. 52 EK47
Lower Richmond Rd. SW14 88 CP83
Lower Richmond Rd. SW15 89 CV83
Lower Richmond Rd., Rich. 88 CN83
Lower Rd. SE8 93 DX77
Lower Rd. SE16 92 DW76
Lower Rd., Belv. 97 FB76
Lower Rd., Erith 97 FD77
Lower Rd., Har. 59 CD60
Lower Rd., Hem.H. 14 BN25
Lower Rd., Ken. 133 DP113
Lower Rd., Lthd. 143 CD123
Lower Rd., Loug. 39 EN39
Lower Rd., Orp. 124 EV100
Lower Rd., Sutt. 132 DC105
Lower Rd., Swan. 111 FF94
Lower Robert St. WC2 10 A1
Lower Sawley Wd., Bans. 131 CZ114
Upper Sawley Wd.
Lower Shott (Cheshunt), Wal.Cr. 22 DT26
Lower Sloane St. SW1 8 F9
Lower Sloane St. SW1 90 DG77
Lower Sq., Islw. 87 CH83
Lower Sta. Rd. (Crayford), Dart. 111 FE86
Lower Strand NW9 47 CT54
Lower Sunbury Rd., Hmptn. 114 BZ96
Lower Swaines, Epp. 25 ES30
Lower Sydenham Ind. Est. SE26 107 DZ92
Lower Tail, Wat. 44 BY48
Lower Talbot Wk. W11 75 CY72
Lancaster Rd.
Lower Teddington Rd., Kings.T. 101 CK94
Lower Ter. NW3 62 DC62
Lower Thames St. EC3 11 L1
Lower Thames St. EC3 78 DR73
Lower Tub (Bushey), Wat. 45 CD45
Lower Wd. Rd., Esher 129 CG107
Lowestoft Clo. E5 64 DW61
Theydon Rd.
Lowestoft Rd., Wat. 29 BV39
Loweswater Clo., Wat. 16 BW33
Loweswater Clo., Wem. 59 CK61
Lowfield Rd. NW6 76 DA66
Lowfield Rd. W3 74 CQ72
Lowick Rd., Har. 59 CE56
Lowlands Dr., Stai. 98 BK85
Lowlands Gdns., Rom. 69 FB58
Lowlands Rd., Har. 59 CE58
Lowlands Rd., Pnr. 58 BW58
Lowman Rd. N7 63 DM63
Lowndes Clo. SW1 8 G7
Lowndes Clo. SW1 90 DG76
Lowndes Pl. SW1 8 F7
Lowndes Pl. SW1 90 DG76
Lowndes Sq. SW1 8 E5
Lowndes Sq. SW1 90 DF75
Lowndes St. SW1 8 E6
Lowndes St. SW1 90 DF76
Lowood Ct. SE19 106 DT92
Lowood St. E1 78 DV73
Dellow St.
Lowry Cres., Mitch. 118 DE96
Lowry Rd., Dag. 68 EV64
Lowshoe La., Rom. 54 FA53
Lowson Gro., Wat. 44 BY45
Lowswood Clo., Nthwd. 43 BQ53
Lowth Rd. SE5 92 DQ82
Lowther Clo., Borwd. 32 CM43
Lowther Dr., Enf. 35 DL42
Lowther Gdns. SW7 90 DD75
Prince Consort Rd.
Lowther Hill SE23 107 DY87
Lowther Rd. E17 51 DY54
Lowther Rd. N7 63 DN64
Mackenzie Rd.
Lowther Rd. SW13 89 CT81
Lowther Rd., Kings.T. 116 CM95
Lowther Rd., Stan. 60 CM55
Loxford Ave. E6 80 EK68
Loxford La., Ilf. 67 EQ64
Loxford Rd., Bark. 81 EP65
Loxham Rd. E4 51 EA52
Loxham St. WC1 6 A3
Loxley Clo. SE26 107 DX92
Loxley Rd. SW18 104 DD88
Loxley Rd., Hmptn. 100 BZ91
Loxton Rd. SE23 107 DX88
Loxwood Clo., Felt. 99 BR88
Loxwood Clo., Orp. 124 EX103
Loxwood Rd. N17 64 DS55
Lubbock Rd., Chis. 109 EM94
Lubbock St. SE14 92 DW80
Lucan Dr., Stai. 98 BK94
Lucan Pl. SW3 8 B9
Lucan Pl. SW3 90 DE77
Lucan Rd., Barn. 33 CY41
Lucas Ave. E13 80 EH67
Lucas Ave., Har. 58 CA61
Lucas Ct., Har. 58 CA60
Lucas Ct., Wal.Abb. 24 EF33
Lucas Rd. SE20 106 DW93
Lucas Sq. NW11 62 DA58
Hampstead Way
Lucas St. SE8 93 EA81
Lucerne Clo. N13 49 DL48
Lucerne Ct., Erith 96 EY76
Middle Way
Lucerne Gro. E17 65 ED56
Lucerne Ms. W8 76 DA74
Kensington Mall
Lucerne Rd. N5 63 DP63
Lucerne Rd., Orp. 123 ET102
Lucerne Rd., Th.Hth. 119 DP99
Lucey Rd. SE16 92 DU76
Lucey Way SE16 92 DU76
Linsey St.
Lucie Ave., Ashf. 99 BP93
Lucien Rd. SW17 104 DG91
Lucien Rd. SW19 104 DB89
Lucknow St. SE18 95 ES80
Lucorn Clo. SE12 108 EF86
Lucton Ms., Loug. 39 EP42
Luctons Ave., Buck.H. 52 EJ46
Lucy Cres. W3 74 CQ71
Lucy Gdns., Dag. 68 EY62
Grafton Rd.
Luddesdon Rd., Erith 96 FA79
Ludford Clo. NW9 46 CS54
Ludford Clo., Croy. 133 DP105
Warrington Rd.
Ludgate Bdy. EC4 6 F9
Ludgate Bdy. EC4 77 DP72
Ludgate Circ. EC4 6 F9
Ludgate Hill EC4 6 F9
Ludgate Hill EC4 77 DP72
Ludgate Sq. EC4 6 G9
Ludham Clo. SE28 82 EW72
Rollesby Way
Ludlow Clo., Brom. 122 EG97
Ludlow Clo., Har. 58 BZ63
Ludlow Mead, Wat. 43 BV48
Ludlow Rd. W5 73 CJ70
Ludlow Rd., Felt. 99 BU91
Ludlow St. EC1 7 H4
Ludlow Way N2 62 DC56
Ludlow Way, Rick. 29 BQ42
Ludovick Wk. SW15 88 CS84
Ludwick Ms. SE14 93 DY80
Luffield Rd. SE2 96 EV76
Luffman Rd. SE12 108 EH90
Lugard Rd. SE15 92 DV82
Lugg App. E12 67 EN62
Luke Ho. E1 78 DV72
Luke St. EC2 7 M4
Luke St. EC2 78 DS70
Lukin Cres. E4 51 ED48
Lukin St. E1 78 DW72
Lukintone Clo., Loug. 38 EL44
Lullarook Clo., West. 150 EJ116
Lullingstone Ave., Swan. 125 FF97
Lullingstone Clo., Orp. 110 EV94
Lullingstone Cres.
Lullingstone Cres., Orp. 110 EU94
Lullingstone La. SE13 107 ED86
Lullingstone Rd., Belv. 96 EZ79
Lullington Garth N12 47 CZ50
Lullington Garth, Borwd. 32 CP43
Lullington Garth, Brom. 108 EE94
Lullington Rd. SE20 106 DU94
Lullington Rd., Dag. 82 EY66
Lulot Gdns. N19 63 DH61
Dartmouth Pk. Hill
Lulworth SE17 11 K10
Lulworth Ave., Houns. 86 CB80
Lulworth Ave. (Cheshunt), Wal.Cr. 21 DP29
Lulworth Ave., Wem. 59 CJ59
Lulworth Clo., Har. 58 BZ62
Lulworth Cres., Mitch. 118 DE96
Lulworth Dr., Pnr. 58 BX59
Lulworth Dr., Rom. 55 FB50
Lulworth Gdns., Har. 58 BY61
Lulworth Rd. SE9 108 EL89
Lulworth Rd. SE15 92 DV82
Lulworth Rd., Well. 95 ET82
Lulworth Waye, Hayes 71 BV72
Lumen Rd., Wem. 59 CK61
Lumley Clo., Belv. 96 FA79
Lumley Ct. WC2 10 A1
Lumley Gdns., Sutt. 131 CY106
Lumley Rd., Sutt. 131 CY107
Lumley St. W1 4 G9
Lumley St. W1 76 DG72
Luna Rd., Th.Hth. 120 DQ97
Lunar Clo., West. 150 EK116
Lunar Ho., Croy. 120 DQ102
Lundin Wk., Wat. 44 BX49
Woodhall La.
Lundy Dr., Hayes 85 BS77
Lundy Wk. N1 78 DQ65
Clephane Rd.
Lunghurst Rd., Cat. 149 DZ120
Lunham Rd. SE19 106 DS93
Lupin Clo. SW2 105 DP89
Palace Rd.
Lupin Clo., Croy. 121 DX102
Primrose La.
Lupin Clo., West Dr. 84 BK78
Magnolia St.
Lupin Cres., Ilf. 67 EP62
Ilford La.
Lupton Clo. SE12 108 EH91
Lupton St. NW5 63 DJ63
Lupus St. SW1 91 DH78
Luralda Gdns. E14 93 EC78
Saunders Ness Rd.
Lurgan Ave. W6 89 CX79
Lurline Gdns. SW11 90 DG81
Luscombe Ct., Brom. 122 EE96
Luscombe Way SW8 91 DL80
Lushes Ct., Loug. 39 EP43
Lushes Rd.
Lushes Rd., Loug. 39 EP43
Lushington Dr., Cob. 127 BV114
Lushington Rd. NW10 75 CV68
Lushington Rd. SE6 107 EB92
Lushington Ter. E8 64 DU64
Wayland Ave.
Lusted Hall La., West. 150 EJ120
Lusted Rd., Sev. 153 FE120
Luther Clo., Edg. 46 CQ47
Luther King Clo. E17 65 DY58
Luther Rd., Tedd. 101 CF92
Luton Pl. SE10 93 EC80
Luton Rd. E17 65 DZ55
Luton Rd., Sid. 110 EW90
Luton St. NW8 4 A5
Luton St. NW8 76 DD70
Lutton Ter. NW3 62 DD63
Flask Wk.
Luttrell Ave. SW15 103 CV85
Lutwyche Rd. SE6 107 DZ89
Luxborough La., Chig. 52 EL48
Luxborough St. W1 4 F5
Luxborough St. W1 76 DG71
Luxemburg Gdns. W6 89 CX77
Luxfield Rd. SE9 108 EL88
Luxford St. SE16 93 DX77
Luxmore Gdns. SE4 93 DZ81
Luxmore St.
Luxmore St. SE4 93 DZ81
Luxor St. SE5 92 DQ83
Luxted Rd., Orp. 137 EN112
Lyal Rd. E3 79 DY68
Lyall Ave. SE21 106 DS90
Lyall Ms. SW1 8 F7
Lyall Ms. SW1 90 DG76
Lyall Ms. W. SW1 8 F7
Lyall St. SW1 8 F7
Lyall St. SW1 90 DG76
Lycett Pl. W12 89 CU75
Becklow Rd.
Lych Gate, Wat. 16 BX33
Lych Gate Rd., Orp. 124 EU102
Lych Gate Wk., Hayes 71 BT73
Lyconby Gdns., Croy. 121 DY101
Lydd Clo., Sid. 109 ES90
Lydd Rd., Bexh. 96 EZ80
Lydden Ct. SE9 109 ES86
Lydden Gro. SW18 104 DB87
Lydden Rd. SW18 104 DB87
Lydeard Rd. E6 81 EM66
Lydford Clo. N16 64 DS64
Pellerin Rd.
Lydford Rd. N15 64 DR57
Lydford Rd. NW2 75 CW65
Lydford Rd. W9 75 CZ70
Lydhurst Ave. SW2 105 DM89
Lydia Rd., Erith 97 FF79
Lydney Clo. SE15 92 DS80
Blakes Rd.
Lydney Clo. SW19 103 CY89
Princes Way
Lydon Rd. SW4 91 DJ83
Lydstep Rd., Chis. 109 EN91
Lye, The, Tad. 145 CW122
Lye La., St.Alb. 16 CA28
Lyfield, Lthd. 128 CB114
Lyford Rd. SW18 104 DD87
Lygon Pl. SW1 9 H7
Lyham Clo. SW2 105 DL86
Lyham Rd. SW2 105 DL85
Lyle Clo., Mitch. 118 DG101
Lyle Pk., Sev. 155 FH123
Lymbourne Clo., Sutt. 132 DA110
Lyme Fm. Rd. SE12 94 EG84
Lyme Gro. E9 78 DW66
St. Thomas's Sq.
Lyme Regis Rd., Bans. 145 CZ117
Lyme Rd., Well. 96 EV81
Lyme St. NW1 77 DJ66
Lyme Ter. NW1 77 DJ66
Royal College St.
Lymer Ave. SE19 106 DT92
Lymescote Gdns., Sutt. 118 DA103
Lyminge Clo., Sid. 109 ET91
Lyminge Gdns. SW18 104 DE88
Lymington Ave. N22 49 DN54
Lymington Clo. E6 81 EM71
Valiant Way
Lymington Clo. SW16 119 DK96
Lymington Dr., Ruis. 57 BR61
Lymington Gdns., Epsom 131 CT106
Lymington Rd. NW6 76 DB65
Lymington Rd., Dag. 68 EX60
Lympstone Gdns. SE15 92 DU80
Lyn Ms. E3 79 DZ69
Tredegar Sq.
Lynbridge Gdns. N13 49 DP49
Lynbrook Clo. SE15 92 DS80
Blakes Rd.
Lynbrook Clo., Rain. 83 FD68
Lynceley Gra., Epp. 26 EU29
Lynch, The, Uxb. 70 BJ67
New Windsor St.
Lynch Clo., Uxb. 70 BJ66
New Windsor St.
Lynch Wk. SE8 93 DZ79
Prince St.
Lynchen Clo., Houns. 85 BU81
The Ave.
Lyncott Cres. SW4 91 DH84
Lyncroft Ave., Pnr. 58 BY57
Lyncroft Gdns. NW6 62 DA64
Lyncroft Gdns. W13 87 CJ75
Lyncroft Gdns., Epsom 131 CT109
Lyncroft Gdns., Houns. 100 CC85
Lyndale NW2 61 CZ63
Lyndale Ave. NW2 61 CZ62
Lyndale Clo. SE3 94 EF79
Lyndale Ct., W.Byf. 126 BG113
Parvis Rd.
Lynden Way, Swan. 125 FC97
Lyndhurst Ave. N12 48 DF51
Lyndhurst Ave. NW7 46 CS51
Lyndhurst Ave. SW16 119 DK96
Lyndhurst Ave., Pnr. 43 BV53
Lyndhurst Ave., Sthl. 72 CB74
Lyndhurst Ave., Sun. 113 BU97
Lyndhurst Ave., Surb. 116 CP102
Lyndhurst Ave., Twick. 100 BZ88
Lyndhurst Clo. NW10 60 CR62
Lyndhurst Clo., Bexh. 97 FB83
Lyndhurst Clo., Croy. 120 DT104
Lyndhurst Clo., Orp. 137 EP105
Lyndhurst Dr. E10 65 EC59
Lyndhurst Dr., N.Mal. 116 CS100
Lyndhurst Dr., Sev. 154 FE124
Lyndhurst Gdns. N3 47 CY53
Lyndhurst Gdns. NW3 62 DD64
Lyndhurst Gdns., Bark. 81 ES65
Lyndhurst Gdns., Enf. 36 DS42
Lyndhurst Gdns., Ilf. 67 ER58
Lyndhurst Gdns., Pnr. 43 BV53
Lyndhurst Gro. SE15 92 DS82
Lyndhurst Ri., Chig. 53 EN49
Lyndhurst Rd. E4 51 EC52
Lyndhurst Rd. N18 50 DU49
Lyndhurst Rd. N22 49 DM51
Lyndhurst Rd. NW3 62 DD64
Lyndhurst Rd., Bexh. 97 FB83
Lyndhurst Rd., Couls. 146 DG116
Lyndhurst Rd., Grnf. 72 CB70
Lyndhurst Rd., Th.Hth. 119 DN98
Lyndhurst Sq. SE15 92 DT81
Lyndhurst Ter. NW3 62 DD64
Lyndhurst Way SE15 92 DT81
Lyndhurst Way, Sutt. 132 DA108
Lyndon Ave., Pnr. 44 BY51
Lyndon Ave., Sid. 109 ET85
Lyndon Ave., Wall. 118 DG104
Lyndon Rd., Belv. 96 FA77
Lyne Cres. E17 51 DZ53
Lynegrove Ave., Ashf. 99 BQ92
Lyneham Wk. E5 65 DY64
Ashenden Rd.
Lyneham Wk., Pnr. 57 BT55
Wiltshire La.
Lynett Rd., Dag. 68 EX61
Lynette Ave. SW4 105 DH86
Lynford Clo., Edg. 46 CQ53
Lynford Gdns., Edg. 46 CP48
Lynford Gdns., Ilf. 67 ET61
Lynhurst Cres., Uxb. 71 BQ66
Lynhurst Rd., Uxb. 71 BQ66
Lynmere Rd., Well. 96 EV82
Lynmouth Ave., Enf. 36 DT44
Lynmouth Ave., Mord. 117 CX101
Lynmouth Dr., Ruis. 57 BV61
Lynmouth Gdns., Grnf. 73 CH67
Lynmouth Gdns., Houns. 86 BX81
Lynmouth Ri., Orp. 124 EV98
Lynmouth Rd. E17 65 DY58
Lynmouth Rd. N2 62 DF56
Lynmouth Rd. N16 64 DT60
Lynmouth Rd., Grnf. 73 CH67
Lynn Clo., Ashf. 99 BR92
Goffs Rd.
Lynn Clo., Har. 45 CD54
Lynn Ms. E11 66 EE61
Lynn Rd.
Lynn Rd. E11 66 EE61
Lynn Rd. SW12 105 DH87
Lynn Rd., Ilf. 67 ER59
Lynn St., Enf. 36 DR39
Lynne Clo., Orp. 137 ET107
Lynne Clo., S.Croy. 134 DW111
Lynne Wk., Esher 128 CC106
Lynne Way NW10 74 CS65
Lynne Way, Nthlt. 72 BX68
Lynscott Way, S.Croy. 133 DP109
Lynsted Clo., Bexh. 111 FB85
Lynsted Clo., Brom. 122 EJ96
Lynsted Ct., Beck. 121 DY96
Churchfields Rd.
Lynsted Gdns. SE9 94 EK83
Lynton Ave. N12 48 DD49
Lynton Ave. NW9 61 CT56
Lynton Ave. W13 73 CG72
Lynton Ave., Orp. 124 EV98
Lynton Ave., Rom. 54 FA53
Lynton Clo. NW10 60 CS64
Lynton Clo., Chess. 130 CL105
Lynton Clo., Islw. 87 CF84
Lynton Cres., Ilf. 67 EP58
Lynton Crest, Pot.B. 20 DA32
Strafford Gate
Lynton Est. SE1 92 DU77
Lynton Rd.
Lynton Gdns. N11 49 DK51
Lynton Gdns., Enf. 50 DS45
Lynton Mead N20 48 DA48
Lynton Par., Wal.Cr. 23 DX30
Turners Hill
Lynton Rd. E4 51 EB50
Lynton Rd. N8 63 DK57
Lynton Rd. NW6 75 CZ67
Lynton Rd. SE1 92 DT77
Lynton Rd. W3 74 CN73
Lynton Rd., Croy. 119 DN100
Lynton Rd., Har. 58 BY61
Lynton Rd., N.Mal. 116 CR99
Lynton Wk., Hayes 71 BS69
Exmouth Rd.
Lynwood Ave., Couls. 147 DH115
Lynwood Ave., Epsom 131 CT114
Lynwood Clo. E18 52 EJ53
Gordon Rd.
Lynwood Clo., Har. 58 BY62
Lynwood Clo., Rom. 55 FB51
Lynwood Dr., Nthwd. 43 BS53
Lynwood Dr., Rom. 55 FB51
Lynwood Dr., Wor.Pk. 117 CU103
Lynwood Gdns., Croy. 133 DM105
Lynwood Gdns., Sthl. 72 BZ71
Lynwood Gro. N21 49 DN46
Lynwood Gro., Orp. 123 ES101
Lynwood Heights, Rick. 28 BH43
Lynwood Rd. SW17 104 DF90
Lynwood Rd. W5 74 CL70
Lynwood Rd., Epsom 131 CT114
Lynwood Rd., T.Ditt. 115 CF103
Lyon Business Pk., Bark. 81 ES68
Lyon Meade, Stan. 45 CJ53
Lyon Pk. Ave., Wem. 74 CL65
Lyon Rd. SW19 118 DC95
Lyon Rd., Har. 59 CF58
Lyon Rd., Rom. 69 FF59
Lyon Rd., Walt. 114 BY103
Lyon St. N1 77 DM66
Caledonian Rd.
Lyon Way, Grnf. 73 CE67
Lyons Pl. NW8 76 DD70
Lyons Wk. W14 89 CY77
Lyonsdown Ave., Barn. 34 DC44
Lyonsdown Rd., Barn. 34 DB44
Lyoth Rd., Orp. 123 EQ103
Lyric Dr., Grnf. 72 CB70
Lyric Rd. SW13 89 CT81
Lysander Gdns., Surb. 116 CM100
Ewell Rd.
Lysander Gro. N19 63 DK60
Lysander Rd., Croy. 133 DM107
Lysander Rd., Ruis. 57 BR61
Lysander Way, Abb.L. 15 BU32
Lysander Way, Orp. 123 EQ104
Lysia St. SW6 89 CX80
Lysias Rd. SW12 105 DH86

Lysons Wk. SW15 103 CU85
Swinburne Rd.
Lytchet Rd., Brom. 108 EH94
Lytchet Way, Enf. 36 DW39
Lytchgate Clo., S.Croy. 134 DS108
Lytcott Dr., W.Mol. 114 BZ97
Freeman Dr.
Lytcott Gro. SE22 106 DT85
Lyte St. E2 78 DW68
Bishops Way
Lytham Ave., Wat. 44 BX50
Lytham Gro. W5 74 CM69
Lytham St. SE17 92 DR78
Lyttelton Clo. NW3 76 DE66
Hawtrey Rd.
Lyttelton Rd. E10 65 EB62
Lyttelton Rd. N2 62 DC57
Lyttleton Rd. N8 63 DN55
Lytton Ave. N13 49 DN47
Lytton Ave., Enf. 37 DY38
Lytton Clo. N2 62 DC58
Lytton Clo., Loug. 39 ER41
Lytton Clo., Nthlt. 72 BZ66
Lytton Gdns., Wall. 133 DK105
Lytton Gro. SW15 103 CX85
Lytton Rd. E11 66 EE59
Lytton Rd., Barn. 34 DC42
Lytton Rd., Pnr. 44 BY52
Lytton Rd., Rom. 69 FH57
Lytton Strachey Path SE28 82 EV73
Titmuss Ave.
Lyveden Rd. SE3 94 EH80
Lyveden Rd. SW17 104 DE93
Lywood Clo., Tad. 145 CW122

M

Mabbotts, Tad. 145 CX121
Mabbutt Clo., St.Alb. 16 BY30
Mabel Rd., Swan. 111 FG93
Maberley Cres. SE19 106 DU94
Maberley Rd. SE19 120 DT95
Maberley Rd., Beck. 121 DX97
Mabledon Pl. WC1 5 N3
Mabledon Pl. WC1 77 DK69
Mablethorpe Rd. SW6 89 CY80
Mabley St. E9 65 DY64
Macaret Clo. N20 48 DC45
MacArthur Clo. E7 80 EG65
Macarthur Ter. SE7 94 EK79
Macaulay Ave., Esher 115 CE103
Macaulay Ct. SW4 91 DH83
Macaulay Rd. E6 80 EK68
Macaulay Rd. SW4 91 DH83
Macaulay Rd., Cat. 148 DS122
Macaulay Sq. SW4 91 DH84
Macaulay Way SE28 82 EV73
Booth Clo.
Macauley Ms. SE13 93 EC81
Macbean St. SE18 95 EP76
Macbeth St. W6 89 CV78
Macclesfield Bri. NW1 76 DE68
Macclesfield Rd. EC1 7 H2
Macclesfield Rd. EC1 78 DQ69
Macclesfield Rd. SE25 120 DV99
Macclesfield St. W1 5 N10
Macdonald Ave., Dag. 69 FB62
Macdonald Rd. E7 66 EG63
Macdonald Rd. E17 51 EC54
Macdonald Rd. N11 48 DF50
Macdonald Rd. N19 63 DJ61
Macdonnell Gdns., Wat. 29 BT35
High Rd.
Macduff Rd. SW11 90 DG81
Mace Clo. E1 78 DV74
Kennet St.
Mace La., Sev. 137 ER113
Mace St. E2 79 DX68
MacFarlane La., Islw. 87 CF79
Macfarlane Rd. W12 75 CW74
Macfarren Pl. NW1 4 G5
Macgregor Rd. E16 80 EJ71
Machell Rd. SE15 92 DW83
Macintosh Clo., Wal.Cr. 21 DP25
Hammondstreet Rd.
Mackay Rd. SW4 91 DH83
Mackennal St. NW8 76 DE68
Mackenzie Rd. N7 77 DM65
Mackenzie Rd., Beck. 120 DW96
Mackenzie Wk. E14 79 EA74
South Colonnade
Mackeson Rd. NW3 62 DF63
Mackie Rd. SW2 105 DN87
Mackintosh La. E9 65 DX64
Homerton High St.
Macklin St. WC2 6 A8
Macklin St. WC2 77 DL72
Mackrow Wk. E14 79 EC73
Robin Hood La.
Macks Rd. SE16 92 DU77
Mackworth St. NW1 5 K2
Mackworth St. NW1 77 DJ69
Maclaren Ms. SW15 89 CW84
Clarendon Dr.
Maclean Rd. SE23 107 DY86
Macleod Rd. N21 35 DL43
Macleod St. SE17 92 DQ78
Maclise Rd. W14 89 CY76
Macoma Rd. SE18 95 ER79
Macoma Ter. SE18 95 ER79
Maconochies Rd. E14 93 EB78
Macquarie Way E14 93 EB77
Macready Pl. N7 63 DL63
Warlters Rd.
Macroom Rd. W9 75 CZ69
Mada Rd., Orp. 123 EP103
Madans Wk., Epsom 144 CR115
Maddams St. E3 79 EB70
Maddison Clo., Tedd. 101 CF93
Maddock Way SE17 91 DP79
Cooks Rd.
Maddocks Clo., Sid. 110 EX92
Maddox La., Lthd. 142 BY123
Maddox Pk., Lthd. 142 BY123
Maddox St. W1 5 J10
Maddox St. W1 77 DH73
Madeira Ave., Brom. 108 EE94
Madeira Gro., Wdf.Grn. 52 EJ51
Madeira Rd. E11 65 ED60
Madeira Rd. N13 49 DP49
Madeira Rd. SW16 105 DL92
Madeira Rd., Mitch. 118 DF98
Madeley Rd. W5 74 CL72
Madeline Gro., Ilf. 67 ER64
Madeline Rd. SE20 106 DU94
Madells, Epp. 25 ET31
Madge Gill Way E6 80 EL67
Ron Leighton Way
Madinah Rd. E8 78 DU65
Madison Cres., Bexh. 96 EW80
Madison Gdns., Bexh. 96 EW80
Madison Gdns., Brom. 122 EF97
Madison Way, Sev. 154 FF123
Madras Pl. N7 77 DN65
Madras Rd., Ilf. 67 EP63
Madresfield Ct., Rad. 18 CL32
Russet Dr.
Madrid Rd. SW13 89 CU81
Madrigal La. SE5 91 DP80
Madron St. SE17 11 N10
Madron St. SE17 92 DS78
Maesmaur Rd., West. 150 EK121
Mafeking Ave. E6 80 EL68
Mafeking Ave., Brent. 88 CL79
Mafeking Ave., Ilf. 67 ER59
Mafeking Rd. E16 80 EF70
Mafeking Rd. N17 50 DU54
Mafeking Rd., Enf. 36 DT41
Magazine Pl., Lthd. 143 CH122
Magazine Rd., Cat. 147 DP122
Magdala Ave. N19 63 DH61
Magdala Rd., Islw. 87 CG83
Magdala Rd., S.Croy. 134 DR108
Napier Rd.
Magdalen Clo., W.Byf. 126 BL114
Magdalen Cres., W.Byf. 126 BL114
Magdalen Gro., Orp. 138 EV105
Magdalen Pas. E1 78 DT73
Prescot St.
Magdalen Rd. SW18 104 DC88
Magdalen St. SE1 11 M3
Magdalen St. SE1 78 DS74
Magdalene Clo. SE15 92 DV82
Heaton Rd.
Magdalene Gdns. E6 81 EN70
Magdalene Rd., Shep. 112 BM97
Magee St. SE11 91 DN79
Maggie Blake's Cause SE1 11 P3
Magnaville Rd. (Bushey), Wat. 45 CE45
Magnet Rd., Wem. 59 CK61
Magnin Clo. E8 78 DU67
Wilde Clo.
Magnolia Ave., Abb.L. 15 BU32
Magnolia Clo., Kings.T. 102 CP93
Magnolia Clo., St.Alb. 17 CD27
Magnolia Ct., Har. 60 CM59
Magnolia Ct., Rich. 88 CP81
West Hall Rd.
Magnolia Dr., West. 150 EK116
Magnolia Gdns. E10 65 EB61
Oliver Rd.
Magnolia Pl. SW4 105 DL85
Magnolia Pl. W5 74 CL71
Montpelier Rd.
Magnolia Rd. W4 88 CP79
Magnolia St., West Dr. 84 BK77
Magnolia Way, Epsom 130 CQ106
Magpie All. EC4 6 E9
Magpie Clo. E7 66 EF64
Magpie Clo. NW9 46 CS54
Eagle Dr.
Magpie Clo., Couls. 147 DJ118
Ashbourne Clo.
Magpie Clo., Enf. 36 DU39
Magpie Hall Clo., Brom. 122 EL100
Magpie Hall La., Brom. 122 EL101
Magpie Hall Rd. (Bushey), Wat. 45 CE47
Magpie Pl. SE14 93 DY79
Milton Ct. Rd.
Magri Wk. E1 78 DW71
Ashfield St.
Maguire Dr., Rich. 101 CJ91
Maguire St. SE1 92 DT75
Mahatma Gandhi Ho., Wem. 60 CM64
Mahlon Ave., Ruis. 57 BV64
Mahogany Clo. SE16 79 DY74
Mahon Clo., Enf. 36 DT39
Maida Ave. E4 51 EB45
Maida Ave. W2 76 DC71
Maida Rd., Belv. 96 FA76
Maida Vale W9 76 DB68
Maida Vale Rd., Dart. 111 FG85
Maida Way E4 51 EB45
Maiden Erlegh Ave., Bex. 110 EY88
Maiden La. NW1 77 DK66
Maiden La. SE1 11 J2
Maiden La. WC2 6 A10
Maiden La. WC2 77 DL73
Maiden La., Dart. 97 FG83
Maiden Rd. E15 80 EE66
Maidenshaw Rd., Epsom 130 CR112
Maidenstone Hill SE10 93 EC81
Maids of Honour Row, Rich. 101 CK85
The Grn.
Maidstone Ave., Rom. 55 FC54
Maidstone Bldgs. SE1 11 K3
Maidstone Ho. E14 79 EB72
Carmen St.
Maidstone Rd. N11 49 DJ51
Maidstone Rd., Sev. 154 FE122
Maidstone Rd. (Seal), Sev. 155 FN121
Maidstone Rd., Sid. 110 EX93
Maidstone Rd., Swan. 125 FC95
Maidstone St. E2 78 DU68
Audrey St.
Main Ave., Enf. 36 DT43
Main Ave., Nthwd. 43 BQ48
Main Dr., Wem. 59 CK62
Main Rd., Kes. 136 EJ112
Main Rd., Orp. 124 EW98
Main Rd., Rom. 69 FF56
Main Rd. (Knockholt), Sev. 151 ET119
Main Rd. (Sundridge), Sev. 152 EX124
Main Rd., Sid. 109 ES90
Main Rd., Swan. 111 FF94
Main Rd. (Crockenhill), Swan. 125 FC100
Main Rd., West. 136 EJ114
Main St., Felt. 100 BX92
Mainridge Rd., Chis. 109 EN91
Maisemore St. SE15 92 DU80
Peckham Pk. Rd.
Maisie Webster Clo., Stai. 98 BK87
Lauser Rd.
Maitland Clo. SE10 93 EB80
Maitland Clo., Houns. 86 BZ83
Maitland Clo., W.Byf. 126 BG113
Maitland Pk. Est. NW3 76 DF65
Maitland Pk. Rd. NW3 76 DF65
Maitland Pk. Vill. NW3 76 DF65
Maitland Pl. E5 64 DV63
Clarence Rd.
Maitland Rd. E15 80 EF65
Maitland Rd. SE26 107 DX93
Maize Row E14 79 DZ73
Commercial Rd.
Majendie Rd. SE18 95 ER78
Majestic Way, Mitch. 118 DF96
Major Rd. E15 65 ED64
Major Rd. SE16 92 DU76
Jamaica Rd.
Makepeace Ave. N6 62 DG61
Makepeace Rd. E11 66 EG56
Makepeace Rd., Nthlt. 72 BY67
Makins St. SW3 8 C9
Makins St. SW3 90 DE77
Malabar St. E14 93 EA75
Malam Gdns. E14 79 EB73
Wades Pl.
Malan Clo., West. 150 EL117
Malan Sq., Rain. 83 FH65
Malbrook Rd. SW15 89 CV84
Malcolm Ct., Stan. 45 CJ50
Malcolm Cres. NW4 61 CU58
Malcolm Dr., Surb. 115 CK102
Malcolm Pl. E2 78 DW70
Malcolm Rd. E1 78 DW70
Malcolm Rd. SE20 106 DW94
Malcolm Rd. SE25 120 DU100
Malcolm Rd. SW19 103 CY93
Malcolm Rd., Couls. 147 DK115
Malcolm Rd., Uxb. 56 BM63
Malcolm Way E11 66 EG57
Malcolms Way N14 35 DJ43
Malden Ave. SE25 120 DV97
Malden Ave., Grnf. 59 CE64
Malden Cres. NW1 76 DG65
Malden Grn. Ave., Wor.Pk. 117 CT102
Malden Hill, N.Mal. 117 CT97
Malden Hill Gdns., N.Mal. 117 CT97
Malden Pk., N.Mal. 117 CT100
Malden Pl. NW5 62 DG64
Grafton Ter.
Malden Rd. NW5 62 DF64
Malden Rd., Borwd. 32 CN41
Malden Rd., N.Mal. 116 CS99
Malden Rd., Sutt. 117 CW104
Malden Rd., Wat. 29 BU40
Malden Rd., Wor.Pk. 117 CT101
Malden Way, N.Mal. 116 CR100
Maldon Clo. E15 65 ED64
David St.
Maldon Clo. N1 78 DQ67
Maldon Clo. SE5 92 DS83
Maldon Rd. N9 50 DT48
Maldon Rd. W3 74 CQ73
Maldon Rd., Rom. 69 FC59
Maldon Rd., Wall. 133 DH106
Maldon Wk., Wdf.Grn. 52 EJ51
Malet Pl. WC1 5 M5
Malet Pl. WC1 77 DK70
Malet St. WC1 5 M5
Malet St. WC1 77 DK70
Maley Ave. SE27 105 DP89
Malford Ct. E18 52 EG54
Malford Gro. E18 66 EF56
Malfort Rd. SE5 92 DS83
Malham Rd. SE23 107 DX88
Malins Clo., Barn. 33 CV43
Mall, The E15 79 ED66
Broadway
Mall, The N14 49 DL48
Mall, The SW1 9 L4
Mall, The SW1 91 DJ75
Mall, The SW14 102 CQ85
Mall, The W5 74 CL73
Mall, The, Brom. 122 EG97
High St.
Mall, The, Croy. 120 DQ102
Poplar Wk.
Mall, The, Har. 60 CM58
Mall, The, Horn. 69 FH60
Mall, The, St.Alb. 16 CC27
Mall, The, Surb. 115 CK99
Mall Rd. W6 89 CV78
Mallams Ms. SW9 91 DP83
St. James's Cres.
Mallard Clo. E9 79 DZ65
Mallard Clo. W7 87 CE75
Mallard Clo., Barn. 34 DD44
The Hook
Mallard Clo., Twick. 100 CA87
Stephenson Rd.
Mallard Path SE28 95 ER76
Tom Cribb Rd.
Mallard Pl., Twick. 101 CH90
Mallard Rd., Abb.L. 15 BT31
College Rd.
Mallard Rd., S.Croy. 135 DX110
Mallard Wk. SE28 95 ER76
Goosander Way
Mallard Wk., Beck. 121 DX99
Mallard Wk., Sid. 110 EW93
Cray Rd.
Mallard Way NW9 60 CQ59
Mallard Way, Nthwd. 43 BQ52
Mallard Way, Wall. 133 DJ109
Mallard Way, Wat. 30 BY36
Mallards, The, Stai. 112 BH96
Thames Side
Mallards Reach, Wey. 113 BR103
Mallards Rd., Wdf.Grn. 52 EH52
Mallet Dr., Nthlt. 58 BZ64
Mallet Rd. SE13 107 ED86
Malling Clo., Croy. 120 DW100
Malling Gdns., Mord. 118 DC100
Malling Way, Brom. 122 EF101
Mallinson Rd. SW11 104 DE85
Mallinson Rd., Croy. 119 DK104
Mallion Ct., Wal.Abb. 24 EF33
Mallord St. SW3 90 DD79
Mallory Clo. SE4 93 DY84
Mallory Gdns., Barn. 48 DG45
Mallory St. NW8 4 B5
Mallory St. NW8 76 DE70
Mallow Clo., Croy. 121 DX102
Marigold Way
Mallow Clo., Tad. 145 CV119
Mallow Mead NW7 47 CY52
Mallow St. EC1 7 K4
Mallow Wk., Wal.Cr. 22 DR28
Mallows, The, Uxb. 57 BP62
Malm Clo., Rick. 42 BK47
Malmains Clo., Beck. 121 ED98
Malmains Way, Beck. 121 EC98
Malmesbury Clo., Pnr. 57 BT56
Malmesbury Rd. E3 79 DZ69
Malmesbury Rd. E16 80 EE71
Malmesbury Rd. E18 52 EF53
Malmesbury Rd., Mord. 118 DC101
Malmesbury Ter. E16 80 EF71
Malpas Dr., Pnr. 58 BX57
Malpas Rd. E8 78 DV65
Malpas Rd. SE4 93 DZ82
Malpas Rd., Dag. 82 EX65
Malt La., Rad. 31 CG35
Newlands Ave.
Malt St. SE1 92 DU79
Malta Rd. E10 65 EA60
Malta St. EC1 6 G4
Maltby Clo., Orp. 124 EU102
Vinson Clo.
Maltby Dr., Enf. 36 DV38
Maltby Rd., Chess. 130 CN107
Maltby St. SE1 11 P5
Maltby St. SE1 92 DT76
Malthouse Dr. W4 88 CS79
Malthouse Dr., Felt. 100 BX92
Malthouse Pas. SW13 88 CS82
The Ter.
Malthouse Pl., Rad. 17 CG34
Malthus Path SE28 82 EW74
Owen Clo.
Malting Ho. E14 79 DZ73
Oak La.
Malting Way, Islw. 87 CF83
Maltings, The, Kings L. 15 BQ33
Maltings, The, Orp. 123 ET102
Maltings, The, W.Byf. 126 BM113
Maltings Clo. SW13 88 CS82
Cleveland Gdns.
Maltings Dr., Epp. 26 EU29
Palmers Hill
Maltings La., Epp. 26 EU29
Maltings Ms., Sid. 110 EU90
Station Rd.
Maltings Pl. SW6 90 DB81
Malton Ms. SE18 95 ES79
Malton St.
Malton Ms. W10 75 CY72
Cambridge Gdns.
Malton Rd. W10 75 CY72
St. Marks Rd.
Malton St. SE18 95 ES79
Maltravers St. WC2 6 C10
Malva Clo. SW18 104 DB85
St. Ann's Hill
Malvern Ave. E4 51 ED52
Malvern Ave., Bexh. 96 EY80
Malvern Ave., Har. 58 BY62
Malvern Clo. SE20 120 DU96
Derwent Rd.
Malvern Clo. W10 75 CZ71
Malvern Clo., Mitch. 119 DJ97
Malvern Clo., Surb. 116 CL102
Malvern Clo., Uxb. 56 BN61
Malvern Ct. SE14 92 DW80
Avonley Rd.
Malvern Ct. SW7 8 A8
Malvern Ct. SW7 90 DD77
Malvern Dr., Felt. 100 BX92
Malvern Dr., Ilf. 67 ET63
Malvern Dr., Wdf.Grn. 52 EJ50
Malvern Gdns. NW2 61 CY61
Malvern Gdns. NW6 75 CZ68
Malvern Gdns., Har. 60 CL56
Malvern Gdns., Loug. 39 EM44
Malvern Ms. NW6 76 DA69
Malvern Rd.
Malvern Pl. NW6 75 CZ69
Malvern Rd. E6 80 EL67
Malvern Rd. E8 78 DU66
Malvern Rd. E11 66 EE61
Malvern Rd. N8 63 DM55
Malvern Rd. N17 64 DU55
Malvern Rd. NW6 76 DA69
Malvern Rd., Enf. 37 DY36
Malvern Rd., Hmptn. 100 CA94
Malvern Rd., Hayes 85 BS80
Malvern Rd., Horn. 69 FG58
Malvern Rd., Orp. 138 EV105
Malvern Rd., Surb. 116 CL103
Malvern Rd., Th.Hth. 119 DN98
Malvern Ter. N1 77 DN67
Malvern Ter. N9 50 DT46
Malvern Way W13 73 CH71
Templewood
Malvern Way, Rick. 29 BP43
Malwood Rd. SW12 105 DH86
Malyons, The, Shep. 113 BR100
Gordon Rd.
Malyons Rd. SE13 107 EB86
Malyons Rd., Swan. 111 FF94
Malyons Ter. SE13 107 EB85
Managers St. E14 79 EC74
Prestons Rd.
Manatee Pl., Wall. 119 DK104
Croydon Rd.
Manaton Clo. SE15 92 DV83
Manaton Cres., Sthl. 72 CA72
Manbey Gro. E15 80 EE65
Manbey Pk. Rd. E15 80 EE65
Manbey Rd. E15 80 EE65
Manbey St. E15 80 EE65
Manborough Ave. E6 81 EM69
Manbre Rd. W6 89 CW79
Manchester Dr. W10 75 CY70
Manchester Gro. E14 93 EC78
Manchester Ms. W1 4 F7
Manchester Rd. E14 93 EC78
Manchester Rd. N15 64 DR58
Manchester Rd., Th.Hth. 120 DQ97
Manchester Row, Dart. 111 FE85
Manchester Sq. W1 4 F8
Manchester Sq. W1 76 DG72
Manchester St. W1 4 F7
Manchester St. W1 76 DG71
Manchester Way, Dag. 69 FB63
Manchuria Rd. SW11 104 DG86
Manciple St. SE1 11 L5
Manciple St. SE1 92 DR75
Mandalay Rd. SW4 105 DJ85
Mandarin St. E14 79 EA73
Salter St.
Mandarin Way, Hayes 72 BX72
Mandela Clo. NW10 74 CQ66
Mandela Rd. E16 80 EG72
Mandela St. NW1 77 DJ67
Mandela St. SW9 91 DN80
Mandela Way SE1 11 N8
Mandela Way SE1 92 DS77
Mandeville Clo. SE3 94 EF80
Vanbrugh Pk.
Mandeville Clo. SW20 117 CY95
Mandeville Clo., Wat. 29 BT38
Mandeville Ct. E4 51 DY49
Mandeville Dr., Surb. 115 CK102
Mandeville Pl. W1 4 G8
Mandeville Pl. W1 76 DG72
Mandeville Rd. N14 49 DH47
Mandeville Rd., Enf. 37 DY36
Mandeville Rd., Islw. 87 CG82
Mandeville Rd., Nthlt. 72 BZ66
Mandeville Rd., Pot.B. 20 DC32
Mandeville Rd., Shep. 112 BN99
Mandeville St. E5 65 DY62
Mandrake Rd. SW17 104 DF89
Mandrake Way E15 80 EE66
Elliot Clo.
Mandrell Rd. SW2 105 DL85
Manette St. W1 5 N9
Manette St. W1 77 DK72
Manford Clo., Chig. 54 EU49
Manford Cross, Chig. 54 EU50
Manford Way, Chig. 53 ES49
Manfred Rd. SW15 103 CZ85
Manger Rd. N7 77 DL65
Mangold Way, Erith 96 EY76
Manhattan Ct., Nthlt. 72 BX69
Manhattan Wf. E16 94 EG75
Manilla St. E14 93 EA75
Manister Rd. SE2 96 EU76
Manitoba Ct. SE16 92 DW75
Renforth St.

Manitoba Gdns., Orp. 137 ET107
Superior Dr.
Manley Ct. N16 64 DT62
Stoke Newington High St.
Manley St. NW1 76 DG67
Manly Dixon Dr., Enf. 37 DY37
Mann Clo., Croy. 120 DQ104
Salem Pl.
Mannamead, Epsom 144 CS119
Mannamead Clo., Epsom 144 CS119
Mannamead
Mannin Rd., Rom. 68 EV59
Manning Gdns., Har. 59 CK59
Manning Pl., Rich. 102 CM86
Grove Rd.
Manning Rd. E17 65 DY57
Southcote Rd.
Manning Rd., Dag. 82 FA65
Manning Rd., Orp. 124 EX99
Manningford Clo. EC1 6 F2
Manningtree Clo. SW19 103 CY88
Manningtree Rd., Ruis. 57 BV63
Manningtree St. E1 78 DU72
White Ch. La.
Mannock Dr., Loug. 39 EQ40
Mannock Rd. N22 63 DP55
Manns Clo., Islw. 101 CF85
Manns Rd., Edg. 46 CN51
Manoel Rd., Twick. 100 CC89
Manor Ave. SE4 93 DZ82
Manor Ave., Cat. 148 DS124
Manor Ave., Houns. 86 BX83
Manor Ave., Nthlt. 72 BZ66
Manor Chase, Wey. 127 BP106
Manor Clo. E17 51 DY54
Manor Rd.
Manor Clo. NW7 46 CR50
Manor Dr.
Manor Clo. NW9 60 CP57
Manor Clo. SE28 82 EW73
Manor Clo., Barn. 33 CY42
Manor Clo., Dag. 83 FD65
Manor Clo. (Crayford), Dart. 97 FD84
Manor Clo. (Wilmington), Dart. 111 FG90
Manor Clo., Rom. 69 FG57
Manor Rd.
Manor Clo., Ruis. 57 BT60
Manor Clo., Warl. 149 DY117
Manor Clo., Wor.Pk. 116 CS102
Manor Cotts., Nthwd. 43 BT53
Manor Cotts. App. N2 48 DC54
Manor Ct. E10 65 EB60
Grange Pk. Rd.
Manor Ct. N2 62 DF57
Manor Ct. SW6 90 DB81
Bagley's La.
Manor Ct., Enf. 36 DV36
Manor Rd.
Manor Ct., Rad. 31 CF38
Manor Ct., Twick. 100 CC89
Manor Ct., Wem. 60 CL64
Manor Ct., Wey. 127 BP105
Manor Ct. Rd. W7 73 CE73
Manor Cres., Surb. 116 CN100
Manor Cres., W.Byf. 126 BM113
Manor Dr. N14 49 DH45
Manor Dr. N20 48 DE48
Manor Dr. NW7 46 CR50
Manor Dr., Add. 126 BG110
Manor Dr., Epsom 130 CS107
Manor Dr., Esher 115 CF104
Manor Dr., Felt. 100 BX92
Lebanon Ave.
Manor Dr., St.Alb. 16 CA27
Manor Dr., Sun. 113 BU96
Manor Dr., Surb. 116 CM100
Manor Dr., Wem. 60 CM63
Manor Dr., The, Wor.Pk. 116 CS102
Manor Dr. N., N.Mal. 116 CR100
Manor Dr. N., Wor.Pk. 116 CS102
Manor Est. SE16 92 DV77
Manor Fm. Ave., Shep. 113 BP100
Manor Fm. Clo., Wor.Pk. 116 CS102
Manor Fm. Dr. E4 52 EE48
Manor Fm. Rd., Enf. 36 DV36
Manor Fm. Rd., Th.Hth. 119 DN96
Manor Fm. Rd., Wem. 73 CK67
Manor Flds. SW15 103 CX86
Manor Gdns. N7 63 DL62
Manor Gdns. SW20 117 CZ96
Manor Gdns. W3 88 CN77
Manor Gdns., Hmptn. 100 CB94
Manor Gdns., Rich. 88 CM84
Manor Gdns., Ruis. 58 BW64
Manor Gdns., S.Croy. 134 DT107
Manor Gdns., Sun. 113 BU95
Manor Gate, Nthlt. 72 BY66
Manor Grn. Rd., Epsom 130 CP113
Manor Gro. SE15 92 DW79
Manor Gro., Beck. 121 EB96
Manor Gro., Rich. 88 CN84
Manor Hall Ave. NW4 47 CW54
Manor Hall Dr. NW4 47 CX54
Manor Ho. Ct., Epsom 130 CQ113
Manor Ho. Ct., Shep. 113 BP101
Manor Ho. Dr. NW6 75 CX66
Manor Ho. Dr., Nthwd. 43 BP52
Manor Ho. Gdns., Abb.L. 15 BR31
Manor Ho. Way, Islw. 87 CH83
Manor La. SE12 108 EE86
Manor La. SE13 108 EE85
Manor La., Felt. 99 BU89
High St.
Manor La., Hayes 85 BR79
Manor La., Sun. 113 BU96
Manor La., Sutt. 132 DC106
Manor La. Ter. SE13 94 EE84
Manor Ms. NW6 76 DA68
Cambridge Ave.
Manor Ms. SE4 93 DZ82
Manor Mt. SE23 106 DW88
Manor Par. NW10 75 CT68
Station Rd.
Manor Pk. SE13 107 ED85
Manor Pk., Chis. 123 ER96
Manor Pk., Rich. 88 CM84
Manor Pk. Clo., W.Wick. 121 EB102
Manor Pk. Cres., Edg. 46 CN51
Manor Pk. Dr., Har. 58 CB55
Manor Pk. Gdns., Edg. 46 CN50
Manor Pk. Par. SE13 93 ED84
Lee High Rd.
Manor Pk. Rd. E12 66 EK63
Manor Pk. Rd. N2 62 DC55
Manor Pk. Rd. NW10 75 CT67
Manor Pk. Rd., Chis. 123 EQ95
Manor Pk. Rd., Sutt. 132 DC106
Manor Pk. Rd., W.Wick. 121 EB102
Manor Pl. SE17 11 H10
Manor Pl. SE17 91 DP78
Manor Pl., Chis. 123 ER96
Manor Pl., Felt. 99 BU88
Manor Pl., Mitch. 119 DJ97
Manor Pl., Stai. 98 BH92
Manor Pl., Sutt. 132 DB106
Manor Pl., Walt. 113 BT101
Manor Rd.
Manor Rd. E10 65 EA59
Manor Rd. E15 80 EE68
Manor Rd. E16 80 EE70
Manor Rd. E17 51 DY54
Manor Rd. N16 64 DR61
Manor Rd. N17 50 DU53
Manor Rd. N22 49 DL51
Manor Rd. SE25 120 DU98
Manor Rd. SW20 117 CZ96
Manor Rd. W13 73 CG73
Manor Rd., Ashf. 98 BM92
Manor Rd., Bark. 81 ET65
Manor Rd., Barn. 33 CY43
Manor Rd., Beck. 121 EA96
Manor Rd., Bex. 111 FB88
Manor Rd., Chig. 53 EN51
Manor Rd., Dag. 83 FC65
Manor Rd., Dart. 97 FE84
Manor Rd., E.Mol. 115 CD98
Manor Rd., Enf. 36 DQ40
Manor Rd., Erith 97 FF79
Manor Rd., Har. 59 CG58
Manor Rd., Hayes 71 BU72
Manor Rd., Loug. 38 EH44
Manor Rd. (High Beach), Loug. 38 EH39
Manor Rd., Mitch. 119 DJ98
Manor Rd., Pot.B. 19 CZ31
Manor Rd., Rich. 88 CM83
Manor Rd., Rom. 69 FG57
Manor Rd. (Chadwell Heath), Rom. 68 EX58
Manor Rd. (Lambourne End), Rom. 54 EW47
Manor Rd., Ruis. 57 BR60
Manor Rd. (London Colney), St.Alb. 17 CJ26
Manor Rd., Sev. 152 EX124
Manor Rd., Sid. 110 EU90
Manor Rd., Sutt. 131 CZ108
Manor Rd., Tedd. 101 CG92
Manor Rd., Twick. 100 CC89
Manor Rd., Wall. 133 DH105
Manor Rd., Wal.Abb. 23 ED33
Manor Rd., Walt. 113 BT101
Manor Rd., Wat. 29 BU39
Manor Rd., W.Wick. 121 EB103
Manor Rd., West. 150 EL120
Manor Rd., Wdf.Grn. 53 EM51
Manor Rd. N., Esher 115 CF104
Manor Rd. N., T.Ditt. 115 CG103
Manor Rd. N., Wall. 133 DH105
Manor Rd. S., Esher 129 CE105
Manor Sq., Dag. 68 EW61
Manor Vale, Brent. 87 CJ78
Manor Vw. N3 48 DB54
Manor Wk., Wey. 127 BP106
Manor Way E4 51 ED49
Manor Way NW9 60 CS56
Manor Way SE3 94 EF84
Manor Way, Bans. 146 DF116
Manor Way, Beck. 121 EA96
Manor Way, Bex. 110 FA88
Manor Way, Bexh. 97 FD83
Manor Way, Borwd. 32 CQ40
Manor Way, Brom. 122 EL100
Manor Way, Har. 58 CB56
Manor Way, Lthd. 142 CC115
Manor Way, Mitch. 119 DJ97
Manor Way, Orp. 123 EQ99
Manor Way, Pot.B. 20 DA30
Manor Way, Pur. 133 DL112
Manor Way, Rain. 83 FE72
Manor Way, Rick. 28 BN42
Manor Way, Ruis. 57 BS59
Manor Way, S.Croy. 134 DS107
Manor Way, Sthl. 86 BX77
Manor Way (Cheshunt), Wal.Cr. 23 DY31
Russells Ride
Manor Way, Wor.Pk. 116 CS102
Manor Way, The, Wall. 133 DH105
Manor Waye, Uxb. 70 BK67
Manor Wd. Rd., Pur. 133 DL113
Manorbrook SE3 94 EG84
Manordene Clo., T.Ditt. 115 CG102
Manordene Rd. SE28 82 EW72
Manorfield Clo. N19 63 DJ63
Tufnell Pk. Rd.
Manorfields Clo., Chis. 123 ET97
Manorgate Rd., Kings.T. 116 CN95
Manorhall Gdns. E10 65 EA60
Manorside, Barn. 33 CY42
Manorside Clo. SE2 96 EW77
Manorway, Enf. 50 DS45
Manorway, Wdf.Grn. 52 EJ50
Manpreet Ct. E12 67 EM64
Morris Ave.
Manresa Rd. SW3 90 DE78
Mansard Beeches SW17 104 DG92
Mansard Clo., Horn. 69 FG61
Mansard Clo., Pnr. 58 BX55
Manse Clo., Hayes 85 BR79
Manse Rd. N16 64 DT62
Manse Way, Swan. 125 FG98
Mansel Gro. E17 51 EA53
Mansel Rd. SW19 103 CY93
Mansell Rd. W3 88 CR75
Mansell Rd., Grnf. 72 CB71
Mansell St. E1 78 DT72
Mansell Way, Cat. 148 DR122
Manser Rd., Rain. 83 FE69
Mansergh Clo. SE18 94 EL80
Mansfield Ave. N15 64 DR56
Mansfield Ave., Barn. 34 DF44
Mansfield Ave., Ruis. 57 BV60
Mansfield Clo. N9 36 DU44
Mansfield Clo., Orp. 124 EX101
Mansfield Clo., Wey. 127 BP106
Mansfield Dr., Hayes 71 BS70
Mansfield Hill E4 51 EB46
Mansfield Ms. W1 5 H7
Mansfield Pl. NW3 62 DC63
New End
Mansfield Rd. E11 66 EH58
Mansfield Rd. E17 65 DZ56
Mansfield Rd. NW3 62 DF64
Mansfield Rd. W3 74 CP70
Mansfield Rd., Chess. 129 CJ106
Mansfield Rd., Ilf. 67 EN61
Mansfield Rd., S.Croy. 134 DR107
Mansfield Rd., Swan. 111 FE93
Mansfield St. W1 5 H7
Mansfield St. W1 77 DH71
Mansford St. E2 78 DU68
Manship Rd., Mitch. 104 DG94
Mansion Gdns. NW3 62 DB62
Mansion Ho. EC4 7 K9
Mansion Ho. Pl. EC4 7 K9
Manson Ms. SW7 90 DC77
Manson Pl. SW7 90 DD77
Manstead Gdns., Rain. 83 FH72
Mansted Gdns., Rom. 68 EW59
Manston Ave., Sthl. 86 CA77
Manston Clo. SE20 120 DW95
Garden Rd.
Manston Clo. (Cheshunt), Wal.Cr. 22 DW30
Manston Gro., Kings.T. 101 CK92
Manston Way, Horn. 83 FH65
Manstone Rd. NW2 61 CY64
Manthorp Rd. SE18 95 EQ78
Mantilla Rd. SW17 104 DG91
Mantle Rd. SE4 93 DY83
Mantle Way E15 80 EE66
Romford Rd.
Mantlet Clo. SW16 105 DJ94
Manton Ave. W7 87 CF75
Manton Clo., Hayes 71 BS73
Manton Rd. SE2 96 EU77
Mantua St. SW11 90 DD83
Mantus Clo. E1 78 DW70
Mantus Rd.
Mantus Rd. E1 78 DW70
Manus Way N20 48 DC47
Blakeney Clo.
Manville Gdns. SW17 105 DH89
Manville Rd. SW17 104 DG89
Manwood Rd. SE4 107 DZ85
Manwood St. E16 81 EM74
Manygate La., Shep. 113 BQ101
Manygates SW12 105 DH89
Mape St. E2 78 DV70
Mapesbury Rd. NW2 75 CY66
Mapeshill Pl. NW2 75 CW65
Maple Ave. E4 51 DZ50
Maple Ave. W3 74 CS74
Maple Ave., Har. 58 CB61
Maple Ave., West Dr. 70 BL73
Maple Clo. N16 64 DU58
Maple Clo. SW4 105 DK86
Maple Clo., Buck.H. 52 EK48
Maple Clo., Epp. 39 ER37
Loughton La.
Maple Clo., Hmptn. 100 BZ93
Maple Clo., Hayes 72 BX69
Maple Clo., Horn. 69 FH62
Maple Clo., Ilf. 53 ES50
Maple Clo., Mitch. 119 DH95
Maple Clo., Orp. 123 ER99
Maple Clo., Ruis. 57 BV58
Maple Clo., Swan. 125 FE96
Maple Clo. (Bushey), Wat. 30 BY40
Maple Clo., Whyt. 148 DT117
Maple Ct., N.Mal. 116 CR97
Maple Cres., Sid. 110 EU86
Maple Gdns., Edg. 46 CS52
Maple Gdns., Stai. 98 BL89
Maple Gate, Loug. 39 EN40
Maple Gro. NW9 60 CQ59
Maple Gro. W5 87 CJ76
Maple Gro., Brent. 87 CH80
Maple Gro., Sthl. 72 BZ71
Maple Gro., Wat. 29 BU39
Maple Ind. Est., Felt. 99 BU90
Maple Leaf Clo., Abb.L. 15 BU32
Magnolia Ave.
Maple Leaf Clo., West. 150 EK116
Main Rd.
Maple Leaf Dr., Sid. 109 ET88
Maple Leaf Sq. SE16 93 DX75
St. Elmos Rd.
Maple Ms. NW6 76 DB68
Kilburn Pk. Rd.
Maple Ms. SW16 105 DM92
Maple Pl. W1 5 L5
Maple Pl., Bans. 145 CX115
Maple Pl., West Dr. 70 BM73
Maple Ave.
Maple Rd. E11 66 EE58
Maple Rd. SE20 120 DV95
Maple Rd., Ash. 143 CK119
Maple Rd., Hayes 72 BW69
Maple Rd., Surb. 115 CK100
Maple Rd., Whyt. 148 DT117
Maple Rd., Wok. 140 BG124
Maple Springs, Wal.Abb. 24 EG33
Maple St. W1 5 K6
Maple St. W1 77 DJ71
Maple St., Rom. 69 FC56
Maple Wk. W10 75 CX70
Droop St.
Maple Wk., Sutt. 132 DB110
Maple Way, Couls. 147 DH121
Maple Way, Felt. 99 BU90
Maplecroft Clo. E6 80 EL72
Allhallows Rd.
Mapledale Ave., Croy. 120 DU103
Mapledene, Chis. 109 EQ92
Kemnal Rd.
Mapledene Rd. E8 78 DU66
Maplefield, St.Alb. 16 CB29
Maplehurst, Lthd. 143 CD123
Maplehurst Clo., Kings.T. 116 CL98
Mapleleafe Gdns., Ilf. 67 EP55
Maples, The, Bans. 132 DB114
Maples, The, Wal.Cr. 22 DS28
Burton La.
Maples Pl. E1 78 DV71
Raven Row
Maplestead Rd. SW2 105 DM87
Maplestead Rd., Dag. 82 EV67
Maplethorpe Rd., Th.Hth. 119 DN98
Mapleton Clo., Brom. 122 EG100
Mapleton Cres. SW18 104 DB86
Mapleton Cres., Enf. 36 DW38
Mapleton Rd. E4 51 EC48
Mapleton Rd. SW18 104 DA86
Mapleton Rd., Enf. 36 DV40
Maplin Clo. N21 35 DM44
Maplin Rd. E16 80 EG72
Maplin St. E3 79 DZ69
Mapperley Dr., Wdf.Grn. 52 EE52
Forest Dr.
Maran Way, Erith 96 EX75
Marban Rd. W9 75 CZ69
Marble Arch W1 4 D10
Marble Arch W1 76 DF73
Marble Clo. W3 74 CP74
Marble Dr. NW2 61 CX60
Marble Hill Clo., Twick. 101 CH87
Marble Hill Gdns., Twick. 101 CH87
Marble Quay E1 78 DU74
Marbles Way, Tad. 145 CX119
Marbrook Ct. SE12 108 EJ90
Marcellina Way, Orp. 123 ES104
March Rd., Twick. 101 CG87
March Rd., Wey. 126 BN106
Marchant Rd. E11 65 ED61
Marchant St. SE14 93 DY79
Sanford St.
Marchbank Rd. W14 89 CZ79
Marchmont Gdns., Rich. 102 CM85
Marchmont Rd.
Marchmont Rd., Rich. 102 CM85
Marchmont Rd., Wall. 133 DJ108
Marchmont St. WC1 5 P4
Marchmont St. WC1 77 DL70
Marchside Clo., Houns. 86 BX81
Springwell Rd.
Marchwood Clo. SE5 92 DS80
Marchwood Cres. W5 73 CJ72
Marcia Rd. SE1 11 N9
Marcia Rd. SE1 92 DS77
Marcilly Rd. SW18 104 DD85
Marco Rd. W6 89 CV76
Marcon Pl. E8 64 DV64
Marconi Rd. E10 65 EA60
Marconi Way, Sthl. 72 CB72
Marcourt Lawns W5 74 CL70
Marcus Ct. E15 80 EE67
Marcus Garvey Way SE24 91 DN84
Marcus Rd., Dart. 111 FG87
Marcus St. E15 80 EE67
Marcus St. SW18 104 DB86
Marcus Ter. SW18 104 DB86
Marcuse Rd., Cat. 148 DQ121
Coulsdon Rd.
Mardale Dr. NW9 60 CR57
Mardell Rd., Croy. 121 DX99
Marden Ave., Brom. 122 EF100
Marden Clo., Chig. 54 EV47
Marden Cres., Bex. 111 FC85
Marden Cres., Croy. 119 DM100
Marden Rd. N17 64 DS55
Marden Rd., Croy. 119 DM100
Marden Rd., Rom. 69 FE58
Kingsmead Ave.
Marden Sq. SE16 92 DV76
Marder Rd. W13 87 CG75
Mardon St. E14 79 DY71
Mare St. E8 78 DV67
Marechal Niel Ave., Sid. 109 ER90
Mares Fld., Croy. 120 DS104
Maresfield Gdns. NW3 62 DC64
Marfleet Clo., Cars. 118 DE103
Margaret Ave. E4 37 EB44
Margaret Bondfield Ave., Bark. 82 EU66
Margaret Bldgs. N16 64 DT60
Margaret Rd.
Margaret Clo., Abb.L. 15 BT32
Margaret Clo., Epp. 26 EU29
Margaret Rd.
Margaret Clo., Pot.B. 20 DC33
Margaret Clo., Rom. 69 FH57
Margaret Rd.
Margaret Clo., Stai. 98 BK93
Charles Rd.
Margaret Clo., Wal.Abb. 23 EC33
Margaret Ct. W1 5 K8
Margaret Gardner Dr. SE9 109 EM89
Margaret Ingram Clo. SW6 89 CZ79
Rylston Rd.
Margaret Rd. N16 64 DT60
Margaret Rd., Barn. 34 DD42
Margaret Rd., Bex. 110 EX86
Margaret Rd., Epp. 26 EU29
Margaret Rd., Rom. 69 FH57
Margaret Sq., Uxb. 70 BJ67
Margaret St. W1 5 J8
Margaret St. W1 77 DH72
Margaret Way, Couls. 147 DP118
Margaret Way, Ilf. 66 EL58
Margaretta Ter. SW3 90 DE79
Margaretting Rd. E12 66 EJ60
Margate Rd. SW2 105 DL85
Margeholes, Wat. 44 BY47
Margery Pk. Rd. E7 80 EG65
Margery Rd., Dag. 68 EX62
Margery St. WC1 6 D3
Margery St. WC1 77 DN69
Margherita Pl., Wal.Abb. 24 EG34
Margherita Rd., Wal.Abb. 24 EG34
Margin Dr. SW19 103 CX92
Margravine Gdns. W6 89 CX78
Margravine Rd. W6 89 CX78
Marham Gdns. SW18 104 DE88
Marham Gdns., Mord. 118 DC100
Maria Clo. SE1 92 DU77
Beatrice Rd.
Maria Ter. E1 79 DX70
Maria Theresa Clo., N.Mal. 116 CR99
Marian Clo., Hayes 72 BX70
Marian Ct., Sutt. 132 DB106
Marian Pl. E2 78 DV68
Marian Rd. SW16 119 DJ95
Marian Sq. E2 78 DU68
Pritchard's Rd.
Marian St. E2 78 DV68
Hackney Rd.
Marian Way NW10 75 CT66
Maricas Ave., Har. 45 CD52
Marie Lloyd Gdns. N19 63 DL59
Hornsey Ri. Gdns.
Marie Lloyd Wk. E8 78 DU65
Forest Rd.
Mariette Way, Wall. 133 DL109
Marigold All. SE1 10 F1
Marigold Clo., Sthl. 72 BY73
Lancaster Rd.
Marigold Rd. N17 50 DW52
Marigold St. SE16 92 DV75
Marigold Way E4 51 DZ51
Silver Birch Ave.
Marigold Way, Croy. 121 DX102
Marina App., Hayes 72 BY71
Marina Ave., N.Mal. 117 CV99
Marina Clo., Brom. 122 EG97
Marina Clo., Cher. 112 BH102
Marina Dr., Well. 95 ES82
Marina Gdns., Rom. 69 FB57
Marina Gdns. (Cheshunt), Wal.Cr. 22 DW30
Marina Way, Tedd. 101 CK94
Fairways
Marine Dr. SE18 95 EM77
Marine St. SE16 92 DU76
Enid St.
Marinefield Rd. SW6 90 DB82
Mariner Gdns., Rich. 101 CJ90
Mariner Rd. E12 67 EM63
Dersingham Ave.
Mariners Ms. E14 93 ED77
Mariners Wk., Erith 97 FF79
Frobisher Rd.
Marion Ave., Shep. 113 BP99
Marion Clo., Ilf. 53 ER52
Marion Clo. (Bushey), Wat. 30 BZ39
Marion Cres., Orp. 124 EU99
Marion Gro., Wdf.Grn. 52 EE50
Marion Rd. NW7 47 CU50
Marion Rd., Th.Hth. 120 DQ99
Marischal Rd. SE13 93 ED83
Maritime St. E3 79 DZ70
Marius Pas. SW17 104 DG89
Marius Rd.
Marius Rd. SW17 104 DG89
Marjorams Ave., Loug. 39 EM40
Marjorie Gro. SW11 90 DF84
Marjorie Ms. E1 79 DX72
Arbour Sq.
Mark Ave. E4 37 EB44
Mark Clo., Bexh. 96 EY81

Mark Clo., Sthl. 72 CB74
Longford Ave.
Mark La. EC3 7 N10
Mark La. EC3 78 DS73
Mark Oak La., Lthd. 142 CA122
Mark Rd. N22 49 DP54
Mark St. E15 80 EE66
West Ham La.
Mark St. EC2 7 M4
Mark Way, Swan. 125 FG99
Markab Rd., Nthwd. 43 BT50
Marke Clo., Kes. 136 EL105
Markedge La., Couls. 146 DE124
Markeston Grn., Wat. 44 BX49
Market Ct. W1 5 K8
Market Est. N7 77 DL65
Clock Twr. Pl.
Market Hill SE18 95 EN76
Market La., Edg. 46 CQ53
Market Link, Rom. 69 FE56
Market Meadow, Orp. 124 EW98
Market Ms. W1 9 H3
Market Par. SE15 92 DU82
Rye La.
Market Pl. N2 62 DE55
Market Pl. NW11 62 DC56
Market Pl. SE16 92 DU77
Southwark Pk. Rd.
Market Pl. W1 5 K8
Market Pl. W3 74 CQ74
Market Pl., Bexh. 96 FA84
Market Pl., Brent. 87 CK80
Lion Way
Market Pl., Enf. 36 DR41
The Town
Market Pl., Kings.T. 115 CK96
Market Pl., Rom. 69 FE57
Market Pl. (Abridge), Rom. 40 EV41
Market Rd. N7 77 DL65
Market Rd., Rich. 88 CN83
Market Row SW9 91 DN84
Atlantic Rd.
Market Sq. E14 79 EB72
Chrisp St.
Market Sq. N9 50 DU47
New Rd.
Market Sq., Brom. 122 EG96
Market Sq., Uxb. 70 BJ66
High St.
Market Sq., Wal.Abb. 23 EC33
Leverton Way
Market St. E6 81 EM68
Market St. SE18 95 EN77
Market St., Wat. 29 BV42
Market Way E14 79 EB72
Kerbey St.
Markfield, Croy. 135 DZ110
Markfield Gdns. E4 51 EB45
Markfield Rd. N15 64 DU56
Markham Pl. SW3 8 D10
Markham Pl. SW3 90 DF78
Markham Sq. SW3 8 D10
Markham Sq. SW3 90 DF78
Markham St. SW3 8 C10
Markham St. SW3 90 DE78
Markhole Clo., Hmptn. 100 BZ94
Priory Rd.
Markhouse Ave. E17 65 DY58
Markhouse Rd. E17 65 DZ57
Markmanor Ave. E17 65 DY59
Marks Rd., Rom. 69 FC57
Marks Rd., Warl. 149 DY118
Marksbury Ave., Rich. 88 CN83
Markway, The, Sun. 114 BW96
Markwell Clo. SE26 106 DV91
Longton Gro.
Markwell Clo., W.Wick. 122 EE103
Deer Pk. Way
Markyate Rd., Dag. 68 EV64
Marl Rd. SW18 90 DB84
Marl St. SW18 90 DC84
Marl Rd.
Marlands Rd., Ilf. 66 EL55
Marlborough Ave. E8 78 DU67
Marlborough Ave. N14 49 DJ48
Marlborough Ave., Edg. 46 CP48
Marlborough Ave., Ruis. 57 BQ58
Marlborough Bldgs. SW3 8 C8
Marlborough Bldgs. SW3 90 DE77
Marlborough Clo. N20 48 DF48
Marlborough Gdns.
Marlborough Clo. SE17 11 H9
Marlborough Clo. SW19 104 DE94
Marlborough Clo., Orp. 123 ET101
Aylesham Rd.
Marlborough Clo., Walt. 114 BX104
Arch Rd.
Marlborough Ct. W8 90 DA77
Marlborough Cres. W4 88 CR76
Marlborough Cres., Sev. 154 FE124
Marlborough Dr., Ilf. 66 EL55
Marlborough Dr., Wey. 113 BQ104
Marlborough Gdns. N20 48 DF48
Marlborough Gate Ho. W2 76 DD73
Elms Ms.
Marlborough Gro. SE1 92 DU78
Marlborough Hill NW8 76 DC67
Marlborough Hill, Har. 59 CD56
Marlborough La. SE7 94 EJ79
Marlborough Pk. Ave., Sid. 110 EU88
Marlborough Pl. NW8 76 DC68
Marlborough Rd. E4 51 EA51
Marlborough Rd. E7 80 EJ66
Marlborough Rd. E15 66 EE63
Borthwick Rd.
Marlborough Rd. E18 66 EG55
Marlborough Rd. N9 50 DT46
Marlborough Rd. N19 63 DK61
Marlborough Rd. N22 49 DL52
Marlborough Rd. SW1 9 L3
Marlborough Rd. SW1 77 DJ74
Marlborough Rd. SW19 104 DE93
Marlborough Rd. W4 88 CQ78
Marlborough Rd. W5 87 CK75
Marlborough Rd., Ashf. 98 BK92
Marlborough Rd., Bexh. 96 EX83
Marlborough Rd., Brom. 122 EJ98
Marlborough Rd., Dag. 68 EV63
Marlborough Rd., Felt. 100 BX89
Marlborough Rd., Hmptn. 100 CA93
Marlborough Rd., Islw. 87 CH81
Marlborough Rd., Rich. 102 CL86
Marlborough Rd., Rom. 68 FA56
Marlborough Rd., S.Croy. 134 DQ108
Marlborough Rd., Sthl. 86 BW76
Marlborough Rd., Sutt. 118 DA104
Marlborough Rd., Uxb. 71 BP70
Marlborough Rd., Wat. 29 BV42
Marlborough St. SW3 8 B9
Marlborough St. SW3 90 DE77
Marlborough Yd. N19 63 DK61
Marlborough Rd.
Marld, The, Ash. 144 CM118
Marle Gdns., Wal.Abb. 23 EC32
Marler Rd. SE23 107 DY88
Marlescroft Way, Loug. 39 EP43
Marley Ave., Bexh. 96 EX79
Marley Clo. N15 63 DP56
Stanmore Rd.
Marley Clo., Grnf. 72 CA69
Marley Wk. NW2 61 CW64
Lennon Rd.
Marlin Clo., Sun. 99 BS93
Marlin Sq., Abb.L. 15 BT31
Marlingdene Clo., Hmptn. 100 CA93
Marlings Clo., Chis. 123 ES98
Marlings Clo., Whyt. 148 DS117
Marlings Pk. Ave., Chis. 123 ES98
Marlins, The, Nthwd. 43 BT50
Marlins Clo., Sutt. 132 DC106
Turnpike La.
Marlins Meadow, Wat. 29 BR44
Marloes Clo., Wem. 59 CK63
Marloes Rd. W8 90 DB76
Marlow Clo. SE20 120 DV97
Marlow Ct. NW6 75 CX66
Marlow Ct. NW9 60 CS55
Marlow Cres., Twick. 101 CF86
Marlow Dr., Sutt. 117 CX103
Marlow Gdns., Hayes 85 BR76
Marlow Rd. E6 81 EM69
Marlow Rd. SE20 120 DV97
Marlow Rd., Sthl. 86 BZ76
Marlow Way SE16 93 DX75
Marlowe Clo., Chis. 109 ER93
Marlowe Clo., Ilf. 53 EQ53
Marlowe Gdns. SE9 109 EN86
Marlowe Rd. E17 65 EC56
Marlowe Sq., Mitch. 119 DJ98
Marlowe Way, Croy. 119 DL103
Marlowes, The NW8 76 DD67
Marlowes, The, Dart. 97 FD84
Marlpit Ave., Couls. 147 DL117
Marlpit La., Couls. 147 DK116
Marlton St. SE10 94 EF78
Woolwich Rd.
Marlwood Clo., Sid. 109 ES89
Marlyon Rd., Ilf. 54 EV50
Marmadon Rd. SE18 95 ET77
Marmion App. E4 51 EA49
Marmion Ave. E4 51 DZ49
Marmion Clo. E4 51 DZ49
Marmion Ms. SW11 90 DG83
Taybridge Rd.
Marmion Rd. SW11 90 DG84
Marmont Rd. SE15 92 DU81
Marmora Rd. SE22 106 DW86
Marmot Rd., Houns. 86 BX83
Marne Ave. N11 49 DH49
Marne Ave., Well. 96 EU83
Marne St. W10 75 CY69
Marnell Way, Houns. 86 BX83
Marney Rd. SW11 90 DG84
Marneys Clo., Epsom 144 CN115
Marnfield Cres. SW2 105 DM87
Upper Tulse Hill
Marnham Ave. NW2 61 CY63
Marnham Cres., Grnf. 72 CB69
Marnock Rd. SE4 107 DZ85
Maroon St. E14 79 DY71
Maroons Way SE6 107 EA92
Marquess Rd. N1 78 DR65
Marquis Clo., Wem. 74 CM66
Marquis Rd. N4 63 DM60
Marquis Rd. N22 49 DM51
Marquis Rd. NW1 77 DK65
Marrabon Clo., Sid. 110 EU88
Marrick Clo. SW15 89 CU84
Marrilyne Ave., Enf. 37 DZ38
Marriots Clo. NW9 61 CT58
Marriott Clo., Felt. 99 BR86
Marriott Lo. Clo., Add. 126 BJ105
Marriott Rd. E15 80 EE67
Marriott Rd. N4 63 DM60
Marriott Rd. N10 48 DF53
Marriott Rd., Barn. 33 CX41
Marrowells, Wey. 113 BS104
Marryat Pl. SW19 103 CY91
Marryat Rd. SW19 103 CX92
Marryat Rd., Enf. 36 DV35
Marryat Sq. SW6 89 CY81
Marsala Rd. SE13 93 EB84
Marsden Rd. N9 50 DV47
Marsden Rd. SE15 92 DT83
Marsden St. NW5 76 DG65
Marsden Way, Orp. 123 ES104
Marsh Ave., Epsom 130 CS110
Marsh Ave., Mitch. 118 DF96
Marsh Clo. NW7 47 CT48
Marsh Clo., Wal.Cr. 23 DY33
Marsh Ct. SW19 118 DC95
High Path
Marsh Dr. NW9 61 CT58
Marsh Fm. Rd., Twick. 101 CF88
Marsh Grn. Rd., Dag. 82 FA67
Marsh Hill E9 65 DY64
Marsh La. E10 65 EA61
Marsh La. N17 50 DV53
Marsh La. NW7 46 CR49
Marsh La., Add. 126 BH105
Marsh La., Stan. 45 CJ50
Marsh Rd., Pnr. 58 BY56
Marsh Rd., Wem. 73 CK69
Marsh St. E14 93 EB77
Harbinger Rd.
Marsh Ter., Orp. 124 EX98
Buttermere Rd.
Marsh Wall E14 79 EA74
Marsh Way, Rain. 83 FD72
Marshall Clo. SW18 104 DC86
Allfarthing La.
Marshall Clo., Har. 59 CD59
Bowen Rd.
Marshall Clo., Houns. 100 BZ85
Marshall Clo., S.Croy. 134 DU113
Marshall Dr., Hayes 71 BT71
Marshall Path SE28 82 EV73
Attlee Rd.
Marshall Pl., Add. 126 BJ109
Marshall Rd. N17 50 DR53
Marshall St. W1 5 L9
Marshall St. W1 77 DJ72
Marshalls Clo. N11 49 DH49
Marshalls Clo., Epsom 130 CQ113
Marshalls Dr., Rom. 69 FE55
Marshall's Gro. SE18 94 EL77
Marshalls Pl. SE16 92 DT76
Spa Rd.
Marshalls Rd., Rom. 69 FD56
Marshall's Rd., Sutt. 132 DB105
Marshalsea Rd. SE1 11 J4
Marshalsea Rd. SE1 92 DQ75
Marsham Clo., Chis. 109 EP92
Marsham St. SW1 9 N7
Marsham St. SW1 91 DK76
Marshbrook Clo. SE3 94 EK83
Marshcroft Dr. (Cheshunt), Wal.Cr. 23 DY30
Marshe Clo., Pot.B. 20 DD32
Marshfield St. E14 93 EC76
Marshgate La. E15 79 EB66
Marshgate Path SE28 95 EQ77
Tom Cribb Rd.
Marshgate Sidings E15 79 EB66
Marshgate La.
Marshside Clo. N9 50 DW46
Marsland Clo. SE17 91 DP78
Marston, Epsom 130 CQ110
Marston Ave., Chess. 130 CL107
Marston Ave., Dag. 68 FA61
Marston Clo. NW6 76 DC66
Fairfax Rd.
Marston Clo., Dag. 68 FA62
Marston Ct., Walt. 114 BW102
St. Johns Dr.
Marston Dr., Warl. 149 DY118
Marston Rd., Ilf. 52 EL53
Marston Rd., Tedd. 101 CH92
Kingston Rd.
Marston Way SE19 105 DP94
Marsworth Ave., Pnr. 44 BX53
Marsworth Clo., Hayes 72 BY71
Marsworth Clo., Wat. 29 BS44
Mart St. WC2 6 A10
Martaban Rd. N16 64 DT61
Martel Pl. E8 78 DT65
Dalston La.
Martell Rd. SE21 106 DR90
Martello St. E8 78 DV66
Martello Ter. E8 78 DV66
Marten Rd. E17 51 EA54
Martens Ave., Bexh. 97 FB84
Martens Clo., Bexh. 97 FC84
Martha Ct. E2 78 DV68
Cambridge Heath Rd.
Martha Rd. E4 51 DZ51
Martha Rd. E15 80 EE65
Martha St. E1 78 DV72
Martham Clo. SE28 82 EX73
Marthorne Cres., Har. 45 CD54
Martin Bowes Rd. SE9 95 EM83
Martin Clo. N9 51 DX46
Martin Clo., S.Croy. 135 DX111
Martin Clo., Uxb. 70 BL68
Valley Rd.
Martin Clo., Warl. 148 DV116
Martin Cres., Croy. 119 DN102
Martin Dale Ind. Est., Enf. 36 DV41
Martin Dene, Bexh. 110 EZ85
Martin Dr., Nthlt. 58 BZ64
Martin Dr., Rain. 83 FH70
Martin Gdns., Dag. 68 EW63
Martin Gro., Mord. 118 DA97
Martin La. EC4 7 L10
Martin Ri., Bexh. 110 EZ85
Martin Rd., Dag. 68 EW63
Martin Way SW20 117 CX96
Martin Way, Mord. 118 DA97
Martinbridge Trd. Est., Enf. 36 DU42
Martindale SW14 102 CQ85
Martindale Ave. E16 80 EG73
Martindale Ave., Orp. 138 EU106
Martindale Rd. SW12 105 DH87
Martindale Rd., Houns. 86 BY84
Martineau Clo., Esher 129 CD105
Martineau Est. E1 78 DW73
Martineau Ms. N5 63 DP63
Martineau Rd.
Martineau Rd. N5 63 DP63
Martineau St. E1 78 DW73
Lukin St.
Martingale Clo., Sun. 113 BU98
Martingales Clo., Rich. 101 CK90
Martins Clo., Orp. 124 EX97
Martins Clo., Rad. 31 CE36
Martins Clo., W.Wick. 121 ED103
Martins Dr. (Cheshunt), Wal.Cr. 23 DY28
Martins Mt., Barn. 34 DA42
Martins Rd., Brom. 122 EE96
Martins Shaw, Sev. 154 FC122
Martins Wk. N10 48 DG53
Martins Wk., Borwd. 32 CN42
Siskin Clo.
Martinsfield Clo., Chig. 53 ES49
Martlet Gro., Nthlt. 72 BX69
Javelin Way
Martlett Ct. WC2 6 A9
Martley Dr., Ilf. 67 EP57
Martock Clo., Har. 59 CG56
Marton Clo. SE6 107 EA90
Marton Rd. N16 64 DS61
Martys Yd. NW3 62 DD63
Hampstead High St.
Marvell Ave., Hayes 71 BU71
Marvels Clo. SE12 108 EH89
Marvels La. SE12 108 EH89
Marville Rd. SW6 89 CZ80
Marvin St. E8 78 DV65
Sylvester Rd.
Marwell Clo., Rom. 69 FG58
Marwell Clo., W.Wick. 122 EF103
Deer Pk. Way
Marwood Clo., Kings L. 14 BN29
Marwood Clo., Well. 96 EV83
Marwood Way SE16 92 DV78
Catlin St.
Mary Adelaide Clo. SW15 102 CS91
Mary Ann Gdns. SE8 93 EA79
Mary Clo., Stan. 60 CM56
Mary Datchelor Clo. SE5 92 DR81
Mary Gardener Dr. SE9 109 EM89
Mary Grn. NW8 76 DB67
Mary Hill Clo., Ken. 148 DQ117
Mary Kingsley Ct. N19 63 DL59
Hillrise Rd.
Mary Lawrenson Pl. SE3 94 EG80
Heathway
Mary Macarthur Ho. W6 89 CY79
Field Rd.
Mary Peters Dr., Grnf. 59 CD64
Mary Pl. W11 75 CY73
Mary Rose Clo., Hmptn. 114 CA95
Ashley Rd.
Mary Rose Mall E6 81 EN71
Frobisher Rd.
Mary Rose Way N20 48 DD46
Mary Seacole Clo. E8 78 DT67
Clarissa St.
Mary St. E16 80 EF71
Barking Rd.
Mary St. N1 78 DQ67
Mary Ter. NW1 77 DH67
Arlington Rd.
Maryatt Ave., Har. 58 CB61
Marybank SE18 95 EM77
Maryfield Clo., Bex. 111 FE90
Maryland Pk. E15 66 EE64
Maryland Pt. E15 80 EE65
Leytonstone Rd.
Maryland Rd. E15 65 ED64
Maryland Rd. N22 49 DM51
Maryland Rd., Th.Hth. 119 DP95
Maryland Sq. E15 66 EE64
Maryland St. E15 65 ED64
Maryland Wk. N1 78 DQ67
Popham St.
Maryland Way, Sun. 113 BU96
Marylands Rd. W9 76 DA70
Marylebone Flyover NW1 4 B7
Marylebone Flyover W2 4 A7
Marylebone High St. W1 4 G6
Marylebone High St. W1 76 DG71
Marylebone La. W1 4 G7
Marylebone La. W1 76 DG72
Marylebone Ms. W1 5 H7
Marylebone Ms. W1 77 DH71
Marylebone Pas. W1 5 L8
Marylebone Rd. NW1 4 E6
Marylebone Rd. NW1 76 DE71
Marylebone St. W1 4 G7
Marylebone St. W1 76 DG71
Marylee Way SE11 10 C10
Marylee Way SE11 91 DM77
Maryon Gro. SE7 94 EL77
Maryon Ms. NW3 62 DE63
South End Rd.
Maryon Rd. SE7 94 EL77
Maryon Rd. SE18 94 EL77
Mary's Clo. N17 50 DT53
Kemble Rd.
Mary's Ter., Twick. 101 CG87
Masbro Rd. W14 89 CX76
Mascalls Ct. SE7 94 EJ79
Victoria Way
Mascalls Rd. SE7 94 EJ79
Mascotte Rd. SW15 89 CX84
Mascotts Clo. NW2 61 CV62
Masefield Ave., Borwd. 32 CP43
Masefield Ave., Sthl. 72 CA73
Masefield Ave., Stan. 45 CF50
Masefield Clo., Erith 97 FF81
Masefield Cres. N14 35 DJ43
Masefield Gdns. E6 81 EN70
Masefield La., Hayes 71 BV70
Masefield Rd., Hmptn. 100 BZ91
Wordsworth Rd.
Masefield Vw., Orp. 123 EQ104
Masefield Way, Stai. 98 BM88
Mashie Rd. W3 74 CS72
Mashiters Hill, Rom. 55 FD54
Mashiters Wk., Rom. 69 FE55
Maskall Clo. SW2 105 DN88
Maskani Wk. SW16 105 DJ94
Bates Cres.
Maskell Rd. SW17 104 DC90
Maskelyne Clo. SW11 90 DE81
Mason Bradbear Ct. N1 78 DR65
St. Paul's Rd.
Mason Clo. E16 80 EG73
Mason Clo. SE16 92 DU78
Stevenson Cres.
Mason Clo. SW20 117 CX95
Mason Clo., Bexh. 97 FB83
Mason Clo., Borwd. 32 CR40
Mason Clo., Hmptn. 114 BZ95
Mason Rd., Wdf.Grn. 52 EE49
Mason St. SE17 11 L8
Mason St. SE17 92 DR77
Mason Way, Wal.Abb. 24 EE33
Masons Arms Ms. W1 5 J10
Masons Ave. EC2 7 K8
Masons Ave., Croy. 120 DQ104
Masons Ave., Har. 59 CF56
Masons Ct., Wem. 60 CN61
Mayfields
Masons Grn. La. W3 74 CN70
Dukes Rd.
Masons Hill SE18 95 EP77
Masons Hill, Brom. 122 EG97
Mason's Pl. EC1 7 H2
Mason's Pl. EC1 78 DQ69
Masons Pl., Mitch. 118 DF95
Masons Rd., Enf. 36 DV36
Mason's Yd. SW1 9 L2
Mason's Yd. SW19 103 CX92
High St. Wimbledon
Massey Clo. N11 49 DH50
Grove Rd.
Massie Rd. E8 78 DU65
Graham Rd.
Massinger St. SE17 11 M9
Massingham St. E1 79 DX70
Masson Ave., Ruis. 72 BW65
Mast Ho. Ter. E14 93 EA77
Mast Leisure Pk. SE16 93 DX76
Surrey Quays Rd.
Master Gunner Pl. SE18 94 EL80
Masterman Ho. SE5 92 DR80
Lomond Gro.
Masterman Rd. E6 80 EL69
Masters Dr. SE16 92 DV78
Masters St. E1 79 DX71
Mastmaker Rd. E14 93 EA75
Maswell Pk. Cres., Houns. 100 CC85
Maswell Pk. Rd., Houns. 100 CB85
Matcham Rd. E11 66 EE62
Matchless Dr. SE18 95 EN80
Matfield Clo., Brom. 122 EG99
Matfield Rd., Belv. 96 FA79
Matham Gro. SE22 92 DT84
Matham Rd., E.Mol. 115 CD99
Matheson Rd. W14 89 CZ77
Mathews Pk. Ave. E15 80 EF65
Mathias Clo., Epsom 130 CQ113
Matilda St. N1 77 DM67
Matlock Clo. SE24 92 DQ84
Matlock Clo., Barn. 33 CX44
Matlock Ct. SE5 92 DR84
Denmark Hill Est.
Matlock Cres., Sutt. 131 CY105
Matlock Cres., Wat. 44 BW48
Matlock Gdns., Sutt. 131 CY105
Matlock Pl., Sutt. 131 CY105
Matlock Rd. E10 65 EC58
Matlock Rd., Cat. 148 DS121
Matlock St. E14 79 DY72
Matlock Way, N.Mal. 116 CR95
Matrimony Pl. SW8 91 DJ82
Wandsworth Rd.
Matson Ct., Wdf.Grn. 52 EE52
Bridle Path
Matthew Arnold Clo., Cob. 127 BU114
Matthew Arnold Clo., Stai. 98 BJ93
Elizabeth Ave.
Matthew Clo. W10 75 CX70
Matthew Ct., Mitch. 119 DK99
Matthew Parker St. SW1 9 N5
Matthew Parker St. SW1 91 DK75
Matthews Ave. E6 81 EN68
Matthews Gdns., Croy. 135 ED111
Matthews Rd., Grnf. 59 CD64
Matthews St. SW11 90 DF82
Matthews Yd. WC2 5 P9
Matthias Rd. N16 64 DR64
Mattingley Way SE15 92 DT80
Daniel Gdns.
Mattison Rd. N4 63 DN58
Mattock La. W5 73 CJ74
Mattock La. W13 73 CH74
Maud Cashmore Way SE18 95 EM76
Maud Gdns. E13 80 EF67

Maud Gdns., Bark. 81 ET68
Maud Rd. E10 65 EC62
Maud Rd. E13 80 EF68
Maud St. E16 80 EF71
Maude Cres., Wat. 29 BV37
Maude Rd. E17 65 DY57
Maude Rd. SE5 92 DS81
Maude Rd., Swan. 111 FG93
Maude Ter. E17 65 DY56
Maudlin's Grn. E1 78 DU74
Marble Quay
Maudslay Rd. SE9 95 EM83
Maudsley Ho., Brent. 88 CL78
Green Dragon La.
Mauleverer Rd. SW2 105 DL85
Maundeby Wk. NW10 74 CS65
Neasden La.
Maunder Rd. W7 73 CE74
Maunsel St. SW1 9 M8
Maunsel St. SW1 91 DK77
Maurice Ave. N22 49 DP54
Maurice Ave., Cat. 148 DR122
Maurice Brown Clo. NW7 47 CX50
Maurice St. W12 75 CV72
Maurice Wk. NW11 62 DC56
Maurier Clo., Nthlt. 72 BW67
Mauritius Rd. SE10 94 EE77
Maury Rd. N16 64 DU61
Mavelstone Clo., Brom. 122 EL95
Mavelstone Rd., Brom. 122 EK95
Maverton Rd. E3 79 EA67
Mavis Ave., Epsom 130 CS106
Mavis Clo., Epsom 130 CS106
Mavis Wk. E6 80 EL71
Tollgate Rd.
Mawbey Est. SE1 92 DT78
Mawbey Pl. SE1 92 DT78
Mawbey Rd. SE1 92 DT78
Old Kent Rd.
Mawbey St. SW8 91 DL80
Mawney Clo., Rom. 55 FB54
Mawney Rd., Rom. 55 FB54
Mawson Clo. SW20 117 CY96
Mawson La. W4 89 CT79
Great W. Rd.
Maxey Gdns., Dag. 68 EY63
Maxey Rd. SE18 95 EQ77
Maxey Rd., Dag. 68 EY64
Maxfield Clo. N20 48 DC45
Maxilla Gdns. W10 75 CX72
Cambridge Gdns.
Maxilla Wk. W10 75 CX72
Kingsdown Clo.
Maxim Rd. N21 35 DN44
Maxim Rd., Dart. 111 FE85
Maxim Rd., Erith 97 FE77
Maximfeldt Rd., Erith 97 FE78
Maxted Pk., Har. 59 CE59
Maxted Rd. SE15 92 DT83
Maxwell Clo., Croy. 119 DL101
Maxwell Clo., Rick. 42 BG47
Maxwell Dr., W.Byf. 126 BJ111
Maxwell Gdns., Orp. 123 ET104
Maxwell Ri., Wat. 44 BY45
Maxwell Rd. SW6 90 DB80
Maxwell Rd., Ashf. 99 BQ93
Maxwell Rd., Borwd. 32 CP41
Maxwell Rd., Nthwd. 43 BR52
Maxwell Rd., Well. 96 EU83
Maxwell Rd., West Dr. 84 BM77
Maxwelton Ave. NW7 46 CR50
Maxwelton Clo. NW7 46 CR50
May Ave., Orp. 124 EV99
May Clo., Chess. 130 CM107
May Cotts., Wat. 30 BW43
Watford Fld. Rd.
May Ct. SW19 118 DB95
May Gdns., Wem. 73 CJ69
May Rd. E4 51 EA51
May Rd. E13 80 EG68
May Rd., Twick. 101 CE88
May St. W14 89 CZ78
North End Rd.
May Tree La., Stan. 45 CF52
May Wk. E13 80 EH68
Queens Rd. W.
Maya Rd. N2 62 DC56
Mayall Rd. SE24 105 DP85
Maybank Ave. E18 52 EH54
Maybank Ave., Wem. 59 CF64
Maybank Gdns., Pnr. 57 BU57
Maybank Rd. E18 52 EH53
Maybells Commercial Est., Bark. 82 EX68
Mayberry Pl., Surb. 116 CM101
Maybourne Clo. SE26 106 DV92
Maybrook Meadow Est., Bark. 68 EU64
Maybury Ave. (Cheshunt), Wal.Cr. 22 DV28
Maybury Clo., Loug. 39 EP42
Maybury Clo., Orp. 123 EP99
Maybury Clo., Tad. 145 CY119
Ballards Grn.
Maybury Gdns. NW10 75 CV65
Maybury Ms. N6 63 DJ59
Maybury Rd. E13 80 EJ70
Maybury Rd., Bark. 81 ET68
Maybury St. SW17 104 DE92
Maychurch Clo., Stan. 45 CK52
Maycock Gro., Nthwd. 43 BT51
Maycroft, Pnr. 43 BV54
Maycroft Rd. (Cheshunt), Wal.Cr. 22 DS26
Maycross Ave., Mord. 117 CZ97
Mayday Gdns. SE3 94 EL82
Mayday Rd., Th.Hth. 119 DP100
Maydwell Lo., Borwd. 32 CM40
Mayell Clo., Lthd. 143 CJ123
Mayerne Rd. SE9 108 EK85
Mayes Clo., Swan. 125 FG98
Mayes Clo., Warl. 149 DX118
Mayes Rd. N22 49 DM54
Mayesbrook Rd., Bark. 81 ET67
Mayesbrook Rd., Dag. 68 EV62
Mayesbrook Rd., Ilf. 68 EU62
Mayesford Rd., Rom. 68 EW59
Mayeswood Rd. SE12 108 EJ90
Mayfair Ave., Bexh. 96 EX81
Mayfair Ave., Ilf. 67 EM61
Mayfair Ave., Rom. 68 EX58
Mayfair Ave., Twick. 100 CC87
Mayfair Ave., Wor.Pk. 117 CT102
Mayfair Clo., Beck. 121 EB95
Mayfair Clo., Surb. 116 CL102
Mayfair Gdns. N17 50 DQ51
Mayfair Gdns., Wdf.Grn. 52 EG52
Mayfair Ms. NW1 76 DF66
Regents Pk. Rd.
Mayfair Pl. W1 9 J2
Mayfair Pl. W1 77 DH74
Mayfair Ter. N14 49 DK45
Mayfare, Rick. 29 BR43
Mayfield, Bexh. 96 EZ83
Mayfield, Wal.Abb. 23 ED34
Roundhills
Mayfield Ave. N12 48 DC49
Mayfield Ave. N14 49 DJ47
Mayfield Ave. W4 88 CS77
Mayfield Ave. W13 87 CH76
Mayfield Ave., Add. 126 BH110
Mayfield Ave., Har. 59 CH57
Mayfield Ave., Orp. 123 ET101
Mayfield Ave., Wdf.Grn. 52 EG51
Mayfield Clo. E8 78 DT65
Forest Rd.
Mayfield Clo. SW4 105 DK85
Mayfield Clo., Add. 126 BJ110
Mayfield Clo., Ashf. 99 BP93
Mayfield Clo., T.Ditt. 115 CH102
Mayfield Clo., Uxb. 71 BP69
Mayfield Clo., Walt. 127 BU105
Mayfield Cres. N9 36 DV44
Mayfield Cres., Th.Hth. 119 DM98
Mayfield Dr., Pnr. 58 BZ56
Mayfield Gdns. NW4 61 CX58
Mayfield Gdns. W7 73 CD72
Mayfield Gdns., Walt. 127 BU105
Mayfield Rd. E4 51 EC47
Mayfield Rd. E8 78 DT66
Mayfield Rd. E13 80 EF70
Mayfield Rd. E17 51 DY54
Mayfield Rd. N8 63 DM57
Mayfield Rd. SW19 117 CZ95
Mayfield Rd. W3 74 CP73
Mayfield Rd. W12 88 CS75
Mayfield Rd., Belv. 97 FC77
Mayfield Rd., Brom. 122 EL99
Mayfield Rd., Dag. 68 EW60
Mayfield Rd., Enf. 37 DX40
Mayfield Rd., S.Croy. 134 DR109
Mayfield Rd., Sutt. 132 DD107
Mayfield Rd., Th.Hth. 119 DM98
Mayfield Rd., Walt. 127 BU105
Mayfield Rd., Wey. 126 BM106
Mayfields, Wem. 60 CN61
Mayfields Clo., Wem. 60 CN61
Mayflower Clo. SE16 93 DX77
Greenland Quay
Mayflower Ct. SE16 92 DW75
St. Marychurch St.
Mayflower Rd. SW9 91 DL83
Mayflower Rd., St.Alb. 16 CB27
Mayflower St. SE16 92 DW75
Mayfly Clo., Orp. 124 EX98
Mayfly Clo., Pnr. 58 BW59
Mayfly Gdns., Nthlt. 72 BX69
Ruislip Rd.
Mayford Clo. SW12 104 DF87
Mayford Clo., Beck. 121 DX97
Mayford Rd. SW12 104 DF87
Maygood St. N1 77 DM68
Maygoods Clo., Uxb. 70 BK71
Maygoods Grn., Uxb. 70 BK71
Worcester Rd.
Maygoods La., Uxb. 70 BK71
Maygoods Vw., Uxb. 70 BJ71
Benbow Waye
Maygreen Cres., Horn. 69 FG59
Maygrove Rd. NW6 75 CZ65
Mayhew Clo. E4 51 EA48
Mayhill Rd. SE7 94 EH79
Mayhill Rd., Barn. 33 CY43
Maylands Ave., Horn. 69 FH63
Maylands Dr., Sid. 110 EX90
Maylands Dr., Uxb. 70 BK65
Maylands Rd., Wat. 44 BW49
Maynard Clo. N15 64 DS56
Brunswick Rd.
Maynard Clo. SW6 90 DB80
Cambria St.
Maynard Clo., Erith 97 FF80
Maynard Ct., Wal.Abb. 24 EF34
Maynard Path E17 65 EC57
Maynard Rd.
Maynard Pl., Pot.B. 21 DM29
Maynard Rd. E17 65 EC57
Maynards Quay E1 78 DW73
Garnet St.
Maynooth Gdns., Cars. 118 DF101
Middleton Rd.
Mayo Clo. (Cheshunt), Wal.Cr. 22 DV28
Mayo Rd. NW10 74 CS65
Mayo Rd., Croy. 120 DR99
Mayo Rd., Walt. 113 BT101
Mayola Rd. E5 64 DW63
Mayow Rd. SE23 107 DX90
Mayow Rd. SE26 107 DX91
Mayplace Ave., Dart. 97 FG84
Mayplace Clo., Bexh. 97 FB83
Mayplace La. SE18 95 EP80
Mayplace Rd. E., Bexh. 97 FB83
Mayplace Rd. E., Dart. 97 FE84
Mayplace Rd. W., Bexh. 96 FA84
Maypole Cres., Ilf. 53 ER52
Maypole Dr., Chig. 54 EU48
Maypole Rd., Orp. 138 EZ106
Mayroyd Ave., Surb. 116 CN103
Mays Clo., Wey. 126 BM110
Mays Ct. WC2 9 P1
Mays Hill Rd., Brom. 122 EE96
Mays La. E4 51 ED47
Mays La., Barn. 47 CU45
Mays Rd., Tedd. 101 CD92
Maysoule Rd. SW11 90 DD84
Mayswood Gdns., Dag. 83 FC65
Maythorne Clo., Wat. 29 BS42
Mayton St. N7 63 DM62
Maytree Clo., Edg. 46 CQ48
Maytree Clo., Rain. 83 FE68
Maytree Cres., Wat. 29 BT35
Maytree Gdns. W5 87 CK75
South Ealing Rd.
Maytree Wk. SW2 105 DN89
Kingsmead Rd.
Maytrees, Rad. 31 CG37
Mayville Est. N16 64 DS64
King Henry St.
Mayville Rd. E11 66 EE61
Mayville Rd., Ilf. 67 EP64
Maywater Clo., S.Croy. 134 DR111
Maywood Clo., Beck. 107 EB94
Maze Hill SE3 94 EE80
Maze Hill SE10 94 EE79
Maze Rd., Rich. 88 CN80
Mazenod Ave. NW6 76 DA66
McAdam Dr., Enf. 35 DP40
Rowantree Rd.
McAuley Clo. SE1 10 D6
McAuley Clo. SE1 91 DN76
McAuley Clo. SE9 109 EP85
McCall Clo. SW4 91 DL82
Jeffreys Rd.
McCall Cres. SE7 94 EL78
McCarthy Rd., Felt. 100 BX92
McCoid Way SE1 11 H5
McCrone Ms. NW3 76 DD65
Belsize La.
McCullum Rd. E3 79 DZ67
McDermott Clo. SW11 90 DE83
McDermott Rd. SE15 92 DU83
McDonough Clo., Chess. 130 CL105
McDowall Rd. SE5 92 DQ81
McDowell Clo. E16 80 EF71
McEntee Ave. E17 51 DY53
McEwan Way E15 79 ED67
McGrath Rd. E15 66 EF64
McGredy (Cheshunt), Wal.Cr. 22 DV29
McGregor Rd. W11 75 CZ71
McIntosh Clo., Rom. 69 FE55
McIntosh Clo., Wall. 133 DL108
McIntosh Rd., Rom. 69 FE55
McKay Rd. SW20 103 CV94
McKellar Clo. (Bushey), Wat. 44 CC47
McKerrell Rd. SE15 92 DU81
McLeod Rd. SE2 96 EU77
McLeod's Ms. SW7 90 DB77
McMillan St. SE8 93 EA79
McNeil Rd. SE5 92 DS82
McNicol Dr. NW10 74 CQ68
McRae La., Mitch. 118 DF101
Mead, The N2 48 DC54
Mead, The W13 73 CH71
Mead, The, Ash. 144 CL119
Mead, The, Beck. 121 EC95
Mead, The, Stan. 45 CJ53
Mead, The, Uxb. 56 BN61
Mead, The, Wall. 133 DK107
Mead, The (Cheshunt), Wal.Cr. 22 DW29
Mead, The, Wat. 44 BY48
Mead, The, W.Wick. 121 ED102
Mead Clo., Har. 45 CD53
Mead Clo., Loug. 39 EP40
Mead Clo., Rom. 55 FG54
Mead Clo., Swan. 125 FG99
Mead Clo., Uxb. 56 BG61
Mead Ct. NW9 60 CQ57
Mead Ct., Wal.Abb. 23 EB34
Mead Cres. E4 51 EC49
Mead Cres., Sutt. 132 DE105
Mead End, Ash. 144 CM117
Mead Gro., Rom. 68 EX55
Mead Ho. Rd., Hayes 71 BR70
Mead La., Cher. 112 BJ102
Mead La. Caravan Pk., Cher. 112 BJ102
Mead Path SW17 104 DC91
Mead Pl. E9 78 DW65
Mead Pl., Croy. 119 DP102
Mead Pl., Rick. 42 BH46
Mead Plat NW10 74 CQ65
Mead Rd., Cat. 148 DT123
Mead Rd., Chis. 109 EQ93
Mead Rd., Edg. 46 CN51
Mead Rd., Rad. 18 CN33
Mead Rd., Rich. 101 CJ90
Mead Rd., Uxb. 70 BK65
Mead Rd., Walt. 128 BY105
Mead Row SE1 10 D6
Mead Way, Brom. 122 EE100
Mead Way, Couls. 147 DL118
Mead Way, Croy. 121 DY103
Mead Way (Bushey), Wat. 30 BY40
Meadcroft Rd. SE11 91 DP79
Meade Clo. W4 88 CN79
Meade Ct., Tad. 145 CU124
Meades, The, Wey. 127 BR107
Meadfield, Edg. 46 CP47
Meadfield Grn., Edg. 46 CP47
Meadfoot Rd. SW16 105 DJ94
Meadgate Ave., Wdf.Grn. 52 EL50
Meadhurst Rd., Cher. 112 BH102
Meadlands Dr., Rich. 101 CK89
Meadow, The, Chis. 109 EQ93
Meadow Ave., Croy. 121 DX100
Meadow Bank N21 35 DM44
Meadow Clo. E4 51 EB46
Mount Echo Ave.
Meadow Clo. E9 65 DZ64
Meadow Clo. SE6 107 EA92
Meadow Clo. SW20 117 CW98
Meadow Clo., Barn. 33 CZ44
Meadow Clo., Bexh. 110 EZ85
Meadow Clo., Chis. 109 EP92
Meadow Clo., Enf. 37 DY38
Meadow Clo., Esher 115 CF104
Meadow Clo., Houns. 100 CA86
Meadow Clo., Nthlt. 72 CA68
Meadow Clo., Pur. 133 DK113
Meadow Clo., Rich. 102 CL88
Meadow Clo., Ruis. 57 BT58
Meadow Clo. (Bricket Wd.), St.Alb. 16 CA29
Meadow Clo. (London Colney), St.Alb. 17 CK27
Meadow Clo., Sev. 154 FG123
Meadow Clo., Sutt. 118 DB103
Aultone Way
Meadow Clo., Walt. 128 BZ105
Meadow Ct., Epsom 130 CQ113
Meadow Dr. N10 62 DG55
Meadow Dr. NW4 47 CW54
Meadow Gdns., Edg. 46 CP51
Meadow Garth NW10 74 CQ65
Meadow Hill, N.Mal. 116 CS100
Meadow Hill, Pur. 133 DJ113
Meadow La., Cars. 118 DE103
Meadow La., Lthd. 142 CC121
Meadow Ms. SW8 91 DM79
Meadow Pl. SW8 91 DL80
Meadow Pl. W4 88 CS80
Edensor Rd.
Meadow Ri., Couls. 133 DK113
Meadow Rd. SW8 91 DM80
Meadow Rd. SW19 104 DC94
Meadow Rd., Ashf. 99 BR92
Meadow Rd., Ash. 144 CL117
Meadow Rd., Bark. 81 ET66
Meadow Rd., Borwd. 32 CP40
Meadow Rd., Brom. 122 EE95
Meadow Rd., Dag. 82 EZ65
Meadow Rd., Epp. 25 ET29
Meadow Rd., Esher 129 CE106
Meadow Rd., Felt. 100 BY89
Meadow Rd., Loug. 38 EL43
Meadow Rd., Pnr. 58 BX56
Meadow Rd., Rom. 69 FC60
Meadow Rd., Sthl. 72 BZ73
Meadow Rd., Sutt. 132 DE106
Meadow Rd., Wat. 15 BU34
Meadow Rd. (Bushey), Wat. 30 CB43
Meadow Row SE1 11 H7
Meadow Row SE1 92 DQ76
Meadow Stile, Croy. 120 DQ104
High St.
Meadow Vw., Har. 59 CE60
Meadow Vw., Sid. 110 EV87
Meadow Vw. Rd., Hayes 71 BQ70
Meadow Vw. Rd., Th.Hth. 119 DP99
Meadow Wk. E18 66 EG56
Meadow Wk., Dag. 82 EZ65
Meadow Wk., Epsom 130 CS107
Meadow Wk., Tad. 145 CV124
Meadow Wk., Wall. 119 DH104
Meadow Way NW9 60 CR57
Meadow Way, Abb.L. 15 BT27
Meadow Way, Add. 126 BH105
Meadow Way, Chess. 130 CL106
Meadow Way, Chig. 53 EQ48
Meadow Way, Kings L. 14 BN30
Meadow Way (Great Bookham), Lthd. 142 CB123
Meadow Way, Orp. 123 EN104
Meadow Way, Pot.B. 20 DA34
Meadow Way, Rick. 42 BJ45
Meadow Way, Ruis. 57 BV58
Meadow Way, Tad. 145 CY117
Meadow Way, Wem. 59 CK63
Meadow Way, The, Har. 45 CE53
Meadow Waye, Houns. 86 BY79
Meadowbank NW3 76 DF66
Meadowbank SE3 94 EF83
Meadowbank, Kings L. 14 BN30
Meadowbank, Surb. 116 CM100
Meadowbank, Wat. 44 BW45
Meadowbank Clo. SW6 89 CW80
Meadowbank Clo., Barn. 33 CT43
Meadowbank Gdns., Houns. 85 BU81
Meadowbank Rd. NW9 60 CR59
Meadowbanks, Barn. 33 CU43
Barnet Rd.
Meadowcourt Rd. SE3 94 EF84
Meadowcroft, Brom. 123 EM97
Meadowcroft (Bushey), Wat. 30 CB44
Meadowcroft Rd. N13 49 DN47
Meadowcross, Wal.Abb. 24 EE34
Meadowlands, Cob. 127 BU113
Meadowlands Pk., Add. 112 BL104
Meadowlea Clo., West Dr. 84 BK79
Meadows, The, Orp. 138 EW107
Meadows, The, Sev. 138 EZ113
Meadows, The, Warl. 149 DX117
Meadows Clo. E10 65 EA61
Meadows End, Sun. 113 BU95
Meadows Leigh Clo., Wey. 113 BQ104
Meadowside SE9 94 EJ84
Meadowside, Lthd. 142 CA123
Meadowside, Walt. 114 BW103
Meadowside Rd., Sutt. 131 CY109
Meadowsweet Clo. E16 80 EK71
Monarch Dr.
Meadowview, Orp. 124 EW97
Meadowview Rd. SE6 107 EA91
Meadowview Rd., Bex. 110 EY86
Meadowview Rd., Epsom 130 CS109
Meads, The, Edg. 46 CR51
Meads, The, St.Alb. 16 BZ29
Meads, The, Sutt. 117 CY104
Meads, The, Uxb. 70 BL70
Meads La., Ilf. 67 ES59
Meads Rd. N22 49 DP54
Meads Rd., Enf. 37 DY39
Meadvale Rd. W5 73 CH70
Meadvale Rd., Croy. 120 DT101
Meadway N14 49 DK47
Meadway NW11 62 DB58
Meadway SW20 117 CW98
Meadway, Ashf. 98 BN91
Meadway, Barn. 33 CZ42
Meadway, Beck. 121 EC95
Meadway, Enf. 36 DW37
Meadway, Epsom 130 CQ113
Meadway, Esher 128 CB109
Meadway, Ilf. 67 ES63
Meadway (Oxshott), Lthd. 129 CD114
Meadway, Rom. 55 FG54
Meadway, Ruis. 57 BR58
Meadway, Sev. 138 EZ113
Meadway, Stai. 98 BG94
Meadway, Surb. 116 CQ102
Meadway, Twick. 101 CD88
Meadway, Warl. 148 DW116
Meadway, Wdf.Grn. 52 EJ50
Meadway, The SE3 93 ED82
Heath La.
Meadway, The, Buck.H. 52 EK46
Meadway, The, Loug. 39 EM44
Meadway, The, Orp. 138 EV106
Meadway, The (Cuffley), Pot.B. 21 DM28
Meadway, The, Sev. 154 FF122
Meadway Clo. NW11 62 DB58
Meadway Clo., Barn. 34 DA42
Meadway Clo., Pnr. 44 CB51
Highbanks Rd.
Meadway Ct. NW11 62 DB58
Meadway Dr., Add. 126 BJ108
Meadway Gdns., Ruis. 57 BR58
Meadway Gate NW11 62 DA58
Meaford Way SE20 106 DV94
Meakin Est. SE1 11 M6
Meakin Est. SE1 92 DS76
Meanley Rd. E12 66 EL63
Meard St. W1 5 M9
Meard St. W1 77 DK72
Meare Clo., Tad. 145 CW123
Meath Clo., Orp. 124 EV99
Meath Rd. E15 80 EF68
Meath Rd., Ilf. 67 EQ62
Meath St. SW11 91 DH81
Mechanics Path SE8 93 EA80
Deptford High St.
Mecklenburgh Pl. WC1 6 B4
Mecklenburgh Pl. WC1 77 DM70
Mecklenburgh Sq. WC1 6 B4
Mecklenburgh Sq. WC1 77 DM70
Mecklenburgh St. WC1 6 B4
Mecklenburgh St. WC1 77 DM69
Medburn St. NW1 77 DK68
Medcalf Rd., Enf. 37 DZ37
Medcroft Gdns. SW14 88 CQ84
Mede Fld., Lthd. 143 CD124
Medebourne Clo. SE3 94 EG83
Medesenge Way N13 49 DP51
Medfield St. SW15 103 CU87
Medhurst Clo. E3 79 DY68
Arbery Rd.
Medhurst Rd. E3 79 DY68
Arbery Rd.
Median Rd. E5 64 DW64
Medina Ave., Esher 115 CE104
Medina Gro. N7 63 DN62
Medina Rd.
Medina Rd. N7 63 DN62
Medland Clo., Wall. 118 DG102
Medlar Clo., Nthlt. 72 BY68
Parkfield Ave.
Medlar St. SE5 92 DQ81
Medley Rd. NW6 76 DA65
Medman Clo., Uxb. 70 BJ68
Chiltern Vw. Rd.
Medora Rd. SW2 105 DM87
Medora Rd., Rom. 69 FD56
Medow Mead, Rad. 17 CF33
Medusa Rd. SE6 107 EB86
Medway Bldgs. E3 79 DY68
Medway Rd.

Midfield Way, Orp. 124 EU95
Midford Pl. W1 5 L5
Midgarth Clo., Lthd. 128 CC114
Midholm NW11 62 DB56
Midholm, Wem. 60 CN60
Midholm Clo. NW11 62 DB56
Midholm Rd., Croy. 121 DY103
Midhope St. WC1 6 A3
Midhurst Ave. N10 62 DG55
Midhurst Ave., Croy. 119 DN101
Midhurst Clo., Horn. 69 FG63
Midhurst Gdns., Uxb. 71 BQ66
Midhurst Hill, Bexh. 110 FA86
Midhurst Rd. W13 87 CG75
Midland Pl. E14 93 EC78
Ferry St.
Midland Rd. E10 65 EC59
Midland Rd. NW1 5 N1
Midland Rd. NW1 77 DK68
Midland Ter. NW2 61 CX62
Midland Ter. NW10 74 CS70
Shaftesbury Gdns.
Midleton Rd., N.Mal. 116 CQ96
Midlothian Rd. E3 79 DY71
Midmoor Rd. SW12 105 DJ88
Midmoor Rd. SW19 117 CX95
Midship Clo. SE16 79 DX74
Surrey Water Rd.
Midstrath Rd. NW10 60 CS63
Midsummer Ave., Houns. 86 BZ84
Midway, Sutt. 117 CZ101
Midway, Walt. 113 BV103
Midway Ave., Cher. 112 BG97
Eastern Ave.
Midwinter Clo., Well. 96 EU83
Hook La.
Midwood Clo. NW2 61 CV62
Miena Way, Ash. 143 CK117
Miers Clo. E6 81 EN67
Mighell Ave., Ilf. 66 EK57
Milborne Gro. SW10 90 DC78
Milborne St. E9 78 DW65
Milborough Cres. SE12 108 EE86
Milbourne La., Esher 128 CC107
Milbrook, Esher 128 CC107
Milburn Dr., West Dr. 70 BL73
Milburn Wk., Epsom 144 CS115
Milcote St. SE1 10 F5
Milcote St. SE1 91 DP75
Mildenhall Rd. E5 64 DW63
Mildmay Ave. N1 78 DR65
Mildmay Gro. N. N1 64 DR64
Mildmay Gro. S. N1 64 DR64
Mildmay Pk. N1 64 DR64
Mildmay Pl., Sev. 139 FF111
Mildmay Rd. N1 64 DR64
Mildmay Rd., Ilf. 67 EP62
Winston Way
Mildmay Rd., Rom. 69 FC57
Mildmay St. N1 78 DR65
Mildred Ave., Borwd. 32 CN42
Mildred Ave., Hayes 85 BR77
Mildred Ave., Nthlt. 58 CB64
Mildred Ave., Wat. 29 BT42
Mildred Rd., Erith 97 FE78
Mile Clo., Wal.Abb. 23 EC33
Mile End, The E17 51 DX53
Mile End Pl. E1 79 DX70
Mile End Rd. E1 78 DW71
Mile End Rd. E3 79 DY70
Mile Rd., Wall. 119 DH102
Miles La., Cob. 128 BY113
Miles Pl. NW1 4 B6
Miles Pl., Surb. 116 CM98
Villiers Ave.
Miles Rd. N8 63 DL55
Miles Rd., Epsom 130 CR112
Miles Rd., Mitch. 118 DD97
Miles St. SW8 91 DL79
Miles Way N20 48 DE47
Milespit Hill NW7 47 CV50
Milestone Clo. N9 50 DU47
Chichester Rd.
Milestone Clo., Sutt. 132 DD107
Milestone Clo., Wok. 140 BG122
Milestone Rd. SE19 106 DT93
Milfoil St. W12 75 CU73
Milford Clo. SE2 96 EY79
Milford Gdns., Croy. 121 DX99
Tannery Clo.
Milford Gdns., Edg. 46 CN52
Milford Gdns., Wem. 59 CK63
Milford Gro., Sutt. 132 DC105
Milford La. WC2 6 D10
Milford La. WC2 77 DM73
Milford Ms. SW16 105 DM90
Milford Rd. W13 73 CH74
Milford Rd., Sthl. 72 CA73
Milford Way SE15 92 DT81
Sumner Est.
Milk St. E16 81 EP74
Milk St. EC2 7 J8
Milk St., Brom. 108 EH93
Milk Yd. E1 78 DW73
Milking La., Kes. 136 EK112
Milking La., Orp. 136 EL112
Milkwell Gdns., Wdf.Grn. 52 EH52
Milkwell Yd. SE5 92 DQ81
Milkwood Rd. SE24 105 DP85
Mill Ave., Uxb. 70 BJ68
Mill Brook Rd., Orp. 124 EW98
Mill Clo., Cars. 118 DG103
Mill Clo., Hem.H. 14 BN25
Mill Clo., Lthd. 142 CA124
Mill Clo., West Dr. 84 BK76
Mill Cor., Barn. 33 CZ39
Mill Ct. E10 65 EC62
Mill Fm. Ave., Sun. 99 BS94
Mill Fm. Clo., Pnr. 44 BW54
Mill Fm. Cres., Houns. 100 BY88
Mill Gdns. SE26 106 DV91
Mill Grn., Mitch. 118 DG101
London Rd.
Mill Grn. Rd., Mitch. 118 DF101
Mill Hill SW13 89 CU82
Mill Hill Rd.
Mill Hill Circ. NW7 47 CT50
Watford Way
Mill Hill Gro. W3 74 CP74
Mill Hill Rd.
Mill Hill Rd. SW13 89 CU82
Mill Hill Rd. W3 88 CP75
Mill La. E4 37 EB41
Mill La. NW6 61 CY64
Mill La. SE18 95 EN78
Mill La., Cars. 132 DF105
Mill La., Croy. 119 DM104
Mill La., Epsom 131 CT109
Mill La., Kings L. 14 BN29
Mill La., Lthd. 143 CG122
Mill La. (Toot Hill), Ong. 27 FE29
Mill La. (Downe), Orp. 137 EN110
Mill La., Rick. 29 BQ44
Watford Rd.
Mill La. (Chadwell Heath), Rom. 68 EY58
Mill La. (Navestock), Rom. 41 FH38
Mill La., Sev. 155 FJ121
Mill La. (Shoreham), Sev. 139 FF110
Mill La., Wal.Cr. 23 DY28
Mill La., W.Byf. 126 BM113
Mill La., Wok. 140 BK119
Mill La., Wdf.Grn. 52 EF50
Mill Mead Ind. Cen. N17 50 DV54
Mill Mead Rd. N17 64 DV55
Mill Pl. E14 79 DZ72
East India Dock Rd.
Mill Pl., Chis. 123 EP95
Mill Pl., Dart. 97 FG84
Mill Pl., Kings.T. 116 CM97
Mill Plat, Islw. 87 CG82
Mill Plat Ave., Islw. 87 CG82
Mill Pond Clo., Sev. 155 FK121
Mill Ridge, Edg. 46 CM50
Mill Rd. E16 80 EH74
Mill Rd. SE13 93 EC83
Loampit Vale
Mill Rd. SW19 104 DC94
Mill Rd., Cob. 142 BW115
Mill Rd., Epsom 131 CT112
Mill Rd., Erith 97 FC80
Mill Rd., Esher 114 CA103
Mill Rd., Ilf. 67 EN62
Mill Rd., Sev. 154 FE121
Mill Rd., Tad. 145 CX123
Mill Rd., Twick. 100 CC89
Mill Rd., West Dr. 84 BJ76
Mill Row N1 78 DS67
Mill Shot Clo. SW6 89 CW81
Mill St. SE1 92 DT75
Mill St. W1 5 K10
Mill St. W1 77 DJ73
Mill St., Kings.T. 116 CL97
Mill Trd. Est., The NW10 74 CQ69
Mill Vale, Brom. 122 EF96
Mill Vw. Clo., Epsom 131 CT108
Mill Vw. Gdns., Croy. 121 DX104
Mill Way, Felt. 99 BV85
Mill Way, Lthd. 144 CM124
Mill Way (Bushey), Wat. 30 BY40
Mill Yd. E1 78 DU73
Cable St.
Millais Ave. E12 67 EN64
Millais Gdns., Edg. 46 CN54
Millais Rd. E11 65 EC63
Millais Rd., Enf. 36 DT43
Millais Rd., N.Mal. 116 CS101
Millais Way, Epsom 130 CQ105
Millan Clo., Add. 126 BH110
Milland Ct., Borwd. 32 CR39
Millard Clo. N16 64 DS64
Boleyn Rd.
Millard Ter., Dag. 82 FA65
Church Elm La.
Millbank SW1 9 P6
Millbank SW1 91 DL77
Millbank, Stai. 98 BH92
Millbank Twr. SW1 9 P9
Millbank Twr. SW1 91 DL77
Millbank Way SE12 108 EG85
Millbourne Rd., Felt. 100 BY91
Millbro, Swan. 111 FG94
Millbrook, Wey. 127 BS105
Millbrook Ave., Well. 95 ER84
Millbrook Gdns., Rom. 55 FE54
Millbrook Gdns. (Chadwell Heath), Rom. 68 EZ58
Millbrook Rd. N9 50 DV46
Millbrook Rd. SW9 91 DP83
Millbrook Rd. (Bushey), Wat. 30 BZ39
Millcrest Rd. (Cheshunt), Wal.Cr. 21 DP28
Millender Wk. SE16 92 DW77
Millennium Pl. E2 78 DV68
Millennium Sq. SE1 92 DT75
Tooley St.
Miller Clo., Mitch. 118 DF101
Miller Clo., Pnr. 44 BW54
Miller Rd. SW19 104 DD93
Miller Rd., Croy. 119 DM102
Miller St. NW1 77 DJ68
Miller Wk. SE1 10 E3
Miller Wk. SE1 77 DN74
Miller's Ave. E8 64 DT64
Millers Clo. NW7 47 CU49
Millers Clo., Chig. 54 EV46
Millers Clo., Stai. 98 BH92
Millers Copse, Epsom 144 CR119
Millers Ct. W4 89 CT78
Chiswick Mall
Millers Grn. Clo., Enf. 35 DP41
Miller's La., Chig. 54 EV46
Millers Meadow Clo. SE3 108 EF85
Meadowcourt Rd.
Miller's Ter. E8 64 DT64
Millers Way W6 89 CW75
Millet Rd., Grnf. 72 CB69
Millfield, Sun. 113 BR95
Millfield Ave. E17 51 DY53
Millfield La. N6 62 DF61
Millfield Pl. N6 62 DG61
Millfield Rd., Edg. 46 CQ54
Millfield Rd., Houns. 100 BY88
Millfields Clo., Orp. 124 EV98
Millfields Est. E5 65 DX62
Denton Way
Millfields Rd. E5 64 DW63
Millgrove St. SW11 90 DG81
Millharbour E14 93 EB76
Millhaven Clo., Rom. 68 EV58
Millhedge Clo., Cob. 142 BY116
Millhoo Ct., Wal.Abb. 24 EF34
Millhouse La., Abb.L. 15 BU27
Millhouse Pl. SE27 105 DP91
Millicent Rd. E10 65 DZ60
Milligan St. E14 79 DZ73
Milliners Ct., Loug. 39 EN40
The Cft.
Milling Rd., Edg. 46 CR52
Millington Rd., Hayes 85 BS76
Millman Ms. WC1 6 B5
Millman Ms. WC1 77 DM70
Millman Pl. WC1 6 B5
Millman St. WC1 6 B5
Millman St. WC1 77 DM70
Millmark Gro. SE14 93 DY82
Millmarsh La., Enf. 37 DY40
Millmead, W.Byf. 126 BM112
Millpond Ct., Add. 126 BL106
Millpond Est. SE16 92 DV75
West La.
Mills Clo., Uxb. 70 BN68
Mills Ct. EC2 7 M4
Mills Gro. E14 79 EC71
Dewberry St.
Mills Gro. NW4 61 CX55
Mills Rd., Walt. 128 BW106
Mills Row W4 88 CR77
Bridge St.
Millside, Cars. 118 DF103
Millside Pl., Islw. 87 CH82
Millsmead Way, Loug. 39 EM40
Millson Clo. N20 48 DD47
Millstead Clo., Tad. 145 CV122
Millstream Clo. N13 49 DN50
Millstream Rd. SE1 11 P5
Millstream Rd. SE1 92 DT75
Millthorn Clo., Rick. 28 BM43
Millwall Dock Rd. E14 93 EA76
Millway NW7 46 CS50
Millway Gdns., Nthlt. 72 BZ65
Millwell Cres., Chig. 53 ER50
Millwood Rd., Houns. 100 CC85
Millwood Rd., Orp. 124 EW97
Millwood St. W10 75 CY71
St. Charles Sq.
Milman Clo., Pnr. 58 BX55
Milman Rd. NW6 75 CX68
Milman's St. SW10 90 DD79
Milne Feild, Pnr. 44 CA52
Milne Gdns. SE9 108 EL85
Milne Pk. E., Croy. 135 ED111
Milne Pk. W., Croy. 135 ED111
Milne Way, Uxb. 42 BH53
Milner App., Cat. 148 DU121
Milner Clo., Cat. 148 DU121
Milner Clo., Wat. 15 BV34
Milner Ct. (Bushey), Wat. 30 CB44
Milner Dr., Cob. 128 BZ112
Milner Dr., Twick. 101 CD87
Milner Pl. N1 77 DN67
Milner Pl., Cars. 132 DG105
High St.
Milner Rd. E15 80 EE69
Milner Rd. SW19 118 DB95
Milner Rd., Cat. 148 DU122
Milner Rd., Dag. 68 EW61
Milner Rd., Kings.T. 115 CK97
Milner Rd., Mord. 118 DD99
Milner Rd., Th.Hth. 120 DR97
Milner Sq. N1 77 DP66
Milner St. SW3 8 D8
Milner St. SW3 90 DF77
Milnthorpe Rd. W4 88 CR79
Milo Rd. SE22 106 DT86
Milroy Wk. SE1 10 F2
Milson Rd. W14 89 CX76
Milton Ave. E6 80 EK66
Milton Ave. N6 63 DJ59
Milton Ave. NW9 60 CQ55
Milton Ave. NW10 74 CQ67
Milton Ave., Barn. 33 CZ43
Milton Ave., Croy. 120 DR101
Milton Ave., Horn. 69 FF61
Milton Ave., Sev. 139 FB110
Milton Ave., Sutt. 118 DD104
Milton Clo. N2 62 DC57
Milton Clo. SE1 11 P9
Milton Clo. SE1 92 DT77
Milton Clo., Hayes 71 BU72
Milton Clo., Sutt. 118 DD104
Milton Ct. EC2 7 K6
Milton Ct., Uxb. 57 BP62
Milton Ct., Wal.Abb. 23 EC34
Milton Ct. Rd. SE14 93 DY79
Milton Cres., Ilf. 67 EQ59
Milton Dr., Borwd. 32 CP43
Milton Dr., Shep. 112 BL98
Milton Gdn. Est. N16 64 DS63
Milton Gro.
Milton Gdns., Epsom 130 CS114
Milton Gdns., Stai. 98 BM88
Milton Gro. N11 49 DJ50
Milton Gro. N16 64 DR63
Milton Pk. N6 63 DJ59
Milton Pl. N7 63 DN64
George's Rd.
Milton Rd. E17 65 EA56
Milton Rd. N6 63 DJ59
Milton Rd. N15 63 DP56
Milton Rd. NW7 47 CU50
Milton Rd. NW9 61 CU59
West Hendon Bdy.
Milton Rd. SE24 105 DP86
Milton Rd. SW14 88 CR83
Milton Rd. SW19 104 DC93
Milton Rd. W3 74 CR74
Milton Rd. W7 73 CF73
Milton Rd., Add. 126 BG107
Milton Rd., Belv. 96 FA77
Milton Rd., Cat. 148 DR121
Milton Rd., Croy. 120 DR102
Milton Rd., Hmptn. 100 CA94
Milton Rd., Har. 59 CE56
Milton Rd., Mitch. 104 DG94
Milton Rd., Rom. 69 FG58
Milton Rd., Sev. 154 FE121
Milton Rd., Sutt. 118 DA104
Milton Rd., Uxb. 56 BN63
Milton Rd., Wall. 133 DJ107
Milton Rd., Walt. 114 BX104
Milton Rd., Well. 95 ET81
Milton St. EC2 7 K6
Milton St. EC2 78 DR71
Milton St., Wal.Abb. 23 EC34
Milton St., Wat. 29 BV38
Milton Way, West Dr. 84 BM77
Milverton Dr., Uxb. 57 BQ63
Milverton Gdns., Ilf. 67 ET61
Milverton Rd. NW6 75 CW66
Milverton St. SE11 91 DN78
Milverton Way SE9 109 EN91
Milward St. E1 78 DV71
Stepney Way
Milward Wk. SE18 95 EN79
Spearman St.
Mimms Hall Rd., Pot.B. 19 CX31
Mimms La., Pot.B. 18 CQ33
Mimms La., Rad. 18 CN33
Mimosa Clo., Orp. 124 EW104
Berrylands
Mimosa Rd., Hayes 72 BW71
Mimosa St. SW6 89 CZ81
Mina Rd. SE17 92 DS78
Mina Rd. SW19 118 DA95
Minard Rd. SE6 108 EE87
Minchenden Cres. N14 49 DJ48
Minchin Clo., Lthd. 143 CG122
Mincing La. EC3 7 M10
Mincing La. EC3 78 DS73
Minden Rd. SE20 120 DV95
Minden Rd., Sutt. 117 CZ103
Minehead Rd. SW16 105 DM92
Minehead Rd., Har. 58 CA62
Minera Ms. SW1 8 G8
Minera Ms. SW1 90 DG77
Mineral St. SE18 95 ES77
Minerva Clo. SW9 91 DN80
Minerva Clo., Sid. 109 ES90
Minerva Dr., Wat. 29 BS36
Minerva Rd. E4 51 EB52
Minerva Rd. NW10 74 CQ69
Minerva Rd., Kings.T. 116 CM96
Minerva St. E2 78 DV68
Minet Ave. NW10 74 CS68
Minet Dr., Hayes 71 BU74
Minet Gdns. NW10 74 CS68
Minet Gdns., Hayes 71 BU74
Minet Rd. SW9 91 DP82
Minford Gdns. W14 89 CX75
Ming St. E14 79 EA73
Mingard Wk. N7 63 DM61
Hornsey Rd.
Ministry Way SE9 109 EM89
Miniver Pl. EC4 78 DQ73
Garlick Hill
Mink Ct., Houns. 86 BW82
Minniedale, Surb. 116 CM99
Minnow St. SE17 92 DS77
East St.
Minnow Wk. SE17 11 N9
Minorca Rd., Wey. 126 BN105
Minories EC3 7 P9
Minories EC3 78 DT72
Minshull Pl., Beck. 107 EA94
Minshull St. SW8 91 DK81
Wandsworth Rd.
Minson Rd. E9 79 DX67
Minstead Gdns. SW15 103 CT87
Minstead Way, N.Mal. 116 CS100
Minster Ave., Sutt. 118 DA103
Leafield Rd.
Minster Ct. EC3 78 DR73
Mincing La.
Minster Dr., Croy. 134 DS105
Minster Gdns., W.Mol. 114 BZ99
Molesey Ave.
Minster Pavement EC3 78 DR73
Mincing La.
Minster Rd. NW2 61 CY64
Minster Rd., Brom. 108 EH94
Minster Wk. N8 63 DL56
Lightfoot Rd.
Minsterley Ave., Shep. 113 BS98
Minstrel Gdns., Surb. 116 CM99
Mint Clo., Uxb. 71 BP69
Mint Rd., Bans. 146 DC116
Mint Rd., Wall. 133 DH105
Mint St. SE1 11 H4
Mint Wk., Croy. 120 DQ104
High St.
Mint Wk., Warl. 149 DX117
Mintern Clo. N13 49 DP48
Mintern St. N1 78 DR68
Minterne Ave., Sthl. 86 CA77
Minterne Rd., Har. 60 CM57
Minterne Waye, Hayes 72 BW72
Minton Ms. NW6 76 DB65
Lymington Rd.
Mirabel Rd. SW6 89 CZ80
Miranda Clo. E1 78 DW71
Sidney St.
Miranda Ct. W3 74 CM72
Queens Dr.
Miranda Rd. N19 63 DJ60
Mirfield St. SE7 94 EK76
Miriam Rd. SE18 95 ES78
Mirror Path SE9 108 EJ90
Lambscroft Ave.
Misbourne Rd., Uxb. 70 BN67
Missenden Clo., Felt. 99 BT88
Missenden Gdns., Mord. 118 DC100
Mission Gro. E17 65 DY57
Mission Pl. SE15 92 DU81
Mission Sq., Brent. 88 CL79
Netley Rd.
Mistletoe Clo., Croy. 121 DX102
Marigold Way
Misty's Fld., Walt. 114 BW102
Mitali Pas. E1 78 DU72
Back Ch. La.
Mitcham Gdn. Village, Mitch. 118 DG99
Mitcham Ind. Est., Mitch. 118 DG95
Mitcham La. SW16 105 DH93
Mitcham Pk., Mitch. 118 DE98
Mitcham Rd. E6 80 EL69
Mitcham Rd. SW17 104 DF92
Mitcham Rd., Croy. 119 DL100
Mitcham Rd., Ilf. 67 ET59
Mitchell Clo. SE2 96 EW77
Mitchell Clo., Abb.L. 15 BU32
Mitchell Clo., Belv. 97 FC76
Mitchell Rd. N13 49 DP50
Mitchell Rd., Orp. 137 ET105
Mitchell St. EC1 7 H4
Mitchell St. EC1 78 DQ70
Mitchell Wk. E6 80 EL71
Oliver Gdns.
Mitchell Way NW10 74 CQ65
Mitchell Way, Brom. 122 EG95
Mitchellbrook Way NW10 74 CR65
Mitchison Rd. N1 78 DR65
Mitchley Ave., Pur. 134 DQ113
Mitchley Ave., S.Croy. 134 DS113
Mitchley Gro., S.Croy. 134 DU113
Mitchley Hill, S.Croy. 134 DS113
Mitchley Rd. N17 64 DU55
Mitchley Vw., S.Croy. 134 DU113
Mitford Clo., Chess. 129 CJ107
Merritt Gdns.
Mitford Rd. N19 63 DL61
Mitre, The E14 79 DZ73
Three Colt St.
Mitre Ave. E17 65 DZ55
Greenleaf Rd.
Mitre Clo., Brom. 122 EF96
Beckenham La.
Mitre Clo., Shep. 113 BR100
Gordon Dr.
Mitre Clo., Sutt. 132 DC108
Mitre Ct. EC2 7 J8
Mitre Ct. EC4 6 E9
Mitre Rd. E15 80 EE68
Mitre Rd. SE1 10 E4
Mitre Rd. SE1 91 DN75
Mitre Sq. EC3 7 N9
Mitre St. EC3 7 N9
Mitre St. EC3 78 DS72
Mitre Way W10 75 CV70
Mixbury Gro., Wey. 127 BR107
Mizen Clo., Cob. 128 BX114
Mizen Way, Cob. 142 BW115
Moat, The, N.Mal. 116 CS95
Moat, The, Ong. 27 FF29
Moat Clo., Orp. 137 ET107
Moat Clo., Sev. 154 FB123
Moat Clo. (Bushey), Wat. 30 CB43
Moat Ct., Ash. 144 CL117
Moat Cres. N3 62 DB55
Moat Cft., Well. 96 EW83
Moat Dr. E13 80 EJ68
Boundary Rd.
Moat Dr., Har. 58 CC56
Moat Dr., Ruis. 57 BS59
Moat Fm. Rd., Nthlt. 72 BZ65
Moat La., Erith 97 FG81
Moat Pl. SW9 91 DM83
Moat Pl. W3 74 CP72
Moat Pl., Uxb. 56 BH63
Moatfield Rd. (Bushey), Wat. 30 CB43

Morley Cres. W., Stan. 59 CJ55
Morley Hill, Enf. 36 DR38
Morley Rd. E10 65 EC60
Morley Rd. E15 80 EF68
Morley Rd. SE13 93 EC84
Morley Rd., Bark. 81 ER67
Morley Rd., Chis. 123 EQ95
Morley Rd., Rom. 68 EY57
Morley Rd., S.Croy. 134 DT110
Morley Rd., Sutt. 117 CZ102
Morley Rd., Twick. 101 CK86
Morley St. SE1 10 E6
Morley St. SE1 91 DN76
Morna Rd. SE5 92 DQ82
Morning La. E9 78 DW65
Morning Ri., Rick. 28 BK41
Morningside Rd., Wor.Pk. 117 CV103
Mornington Ave. W14 89 CZ77
Mornington Ave., Brom. 122 EJ97
Mornington Ave., Ilf. 67 EN59
Mornington Clo., West. 150 EK117
Mornington Clo., Wdf.Grn. 52 EG49
Mornington Ct., Bex. 111 FC88
Mornington Cres. NW1 77 DJ68
Mornington Cres., Houns. 85 BV81
Mornington Gro. E3 79 EA69
Mornington Ms. SE5 92 DQ81
Mornington Pl. NW1 77 DH68
Mornington Ter.
Mornington Rd. E4 51 ED45
Mornington Rd. E11 66 EF60
Mornington Rd. SE8 93 DZ80
Mornington Rd., Ashf. 99 BQ92
Mornington Rd., Grnf. 72 CB71
Mornington Rd., Loug. 39 EQ41
Mornington Rd., Rad. 17 CH34
Mornington Rd., Wdf.Grn. 52 EF49
Mornington St. NW1 77 DH68
Mornington Ter. NW1 77 DH68
Mornington Wk., Rich. 101 CJ91
Morocco St. SE1 11 M5
Morocco St. SE1 92 DS75
Morpeth Ave., Borwd. 32 CM38
Morpeth Gro. E9 79 DX67
Morpeth Rd. E9 78 DW67
Morpeth St. E2 79 DX69
Morpeth Ter. SW1 9 K7
Morpeth Ter. SW1 91 DJ76
Morpeth Wk. N17 50 DV52
West Rd.
Morrab Gdns., Ilf. 67 ET62
Morrell Clo., Barn. 34 DC41
Galdana Ave.
Morris Ave. E12 67 EM64
Morris Clo., Croy. 121 DY100
Morris Clo., Orp. 123 ES104
Morris Ct. E4 51 EB48
Flaxen Rd.
Morris Ct., Wal.Abb. 24 EF34
Morris Gdns. SW18 104 DA87
Morris Pl. N4 63 DN61
Morris Rd. E14 79 EB71
Morris Rd. E15 65 ED63
Morris Rd., Dag. 68 EZ61
Morris Rd., Islw. 87 CF83
Morris Rd., Rom. 55 FH52
Morris St. E1 78 DV72
Morris Way, St.Alb. 17 CK26
Morrish Rd. SW2 105 DL87
Morrison Ave. N17 64 DS55
Morrison Rd., Bark. 82 EY68
Morrison Rd., Hayes 71 BV69
Morrison St. SW11 90 DG83
Morriston Clo., Wat. 44 BW50
Morse Clo. E13 80 EG69
Morse Clo., Uxb. 42 BJ54
Morshead Rd. W9 76 DA69
Morson Rd., Enf. 37 DY44
Morston Clo., Tad. 145 CV120
Waterfield
Morston Gdns. SE9 109 EM91
Morten Clo. SW4 105 DK86
Morten Gdns., Uxb. 56 BG59
Morteyne Rd. N17 50 DR53
Mortgramit Sq. SE18 95 EN76
Powis St.
Mortham St. E15 80 EE67
Mortimer Clo. NW2 61 CZ62
Mortimer Clo. SW16 105 DK89
Mortimer Clo. (Bushey), Wat. 30 CB44
Mortimer Cres. NW6 76 DB67
Mortimer Cres., Wor.Pk. 116 CR104
Mortimer Dr., Enf. 36 DS43
Mortimer Est. NW6 76 DB67
Mortimer Gate, Wal.Cr. 23 DZ27
Mortimer Mkt. WC1 5 L5
Mortimer Pl. NW6 76 DB67
Mortimer Rd. E6 81 EM69
Mortimer Rd. N1 78 DS66
Mortimer Rd. NW10 75 CW69
Mortimer Rd. W13 73 CJ72
Mortimer Rd., Erith 97 FD79
Mortimer Rd., Mitch. 118 DF95
Mortimer Rd., Orp. 124 EU102
Mortimer Rd., West. 136 EJ112
Mortimer Sq. W11 75 CX73
St. Anns Rd.
Mortimer St. W1 5 K8
Mortimer St. W1 77 DJ72
Mortimer Ter. NW5 63 DH63
Gordon Ho. Rd.
Mortlake Clo., Croy. 119 DL104
Richmond Rd.
Mortlake Dr., Mitch. 118 DE95
Mortlake High St. SW14 88 CR83
Mortlake Rd. E16 80 EH72
Mortlake Rd., Ilf. 67 EQ63
Mortlake Rd., Rich. 88 CN80
Mortlake Ter., Rich. 88 CN80
Kew Rd.
Mortlock Clo. SE15 92 DV81
Cossall Wk.
Morton, Tad. 145 CX121
Morton Cres. N14 49 DK49
Morton Gdns., Wall. 133 DJ106
Morton Ms. SW5 90 DB77
Earls Ct. Gdns.
Morton Pl. SE1 10 D7
Morton Rd. E15 80 EF66
Morton Rd. N1 78 DQ66
Morton Rd., Mord. 118 DD99
Morton Way N14 49 DJ48
Morval Rd. SW2 105 DN85
Morvale Clo., Belv. 96 EZ77
Morven Clo., Pot.B. 20 DC31
Morven Rd. SW17 104 DF90
Morville St. E3 79 EA68
Morwell St. WC1 5 N7
Moscow Pl. W2 76 DB73
Moscow Rd.
Moscow Rd. W2 76 DB73
Moselle Ave. N22 49 DN54
Moselle Clo. N8 63 DM55
Miles Rd.
Moselle Ho. N17 50 DT52
Moselle Pl. N17 50 DT52
High Rd.
Moselle Rd., West. 150 EL118
Moselle St. N17 50 DT52
Mospey Cres., Epsom 145 CT115
Moss Clo. E1 78 DU71
Old Montague St.
Moss Clo., Pnr. 44 BZ54
Moss Clo., Rick. 42 BK47
Moss Gdns., Felt. 99 BU89
Rose Gdns.
Moss Gdns., S.Croy. 135 DX108
Warren Ave.
Moss Hall Cres. N12 48 DB51
Moss Hall Gro. N12 48 DB51
Moss La., Pnr. 44 BY53
Moss La., Rom. 69 FF58
Wheatsheaf Rd.
Moss Rd., Dag. 82 FA66
Moss Rd., Wat. 15 BV34
Moss Side, St.Alb. 16 BZ30
Mossborough Clo. N12 48 DB51
Mossbury Rd. SW11 90 DE83
Mossdown Clo., Belv. 96 FA77
Mossendew Clo., Uxb. 42 BK53
Mossfield, Cob. 127 BU113
Mossford Ct., Ilf. 67 EP55
Mossford Grn., Ilf. 67 EP55
Mossford La., Ilf. 53 EP54
Mossford St. E3 79 DZ70
Mossington Gdns. SE16 92 DW77
Abbeyfield Rd.
Mosslea Rd. SE20 106 DW93
Mosslea Rd., Brom. 122 EK99
Mosslea Rd., Orp. 123 EQ104
Mosslea Rd., Whyt. 148 DT116
Mossop St. SW3 8 C8
Mossop St. SW3 90 DE77
Mossville Gdns., Mord. 117 CZ97
Moston Clo., Hayes 85 BT78
Fuller Way
Mostyn Ave., Wem. 60 CM64
Mostyn Gdns. NW10 75 CX69
Mostyn Gro. E3 79 EA68
Mostyn Rd. SW9 91 DN81
Mostyn Rd. SW19 117 CZ95
Mostyn Rd., Edg. 46 CR52
Mostyn Rd. (Bushey), Wat. 30 CC43
Mosul Way, Brom. 122 EL100
Mosyer Dr., Orp. 124 EX103
Motcomb St. SW1 8 E6
Motcomb St. SW1 90 DG76
Mothers Sq., The E5 64 DV63
Motley Ave. EC2 78 DS70
Scrutton St.
Motley St. SW8 91 DJ82
St. Rule St.
Motspur Pk., N.Mal. 117 CT100
Mott St. E4 37 ED38
Mott St., Loug. 38 EE39
Mottingham Gdns. SE9 108 EK88
Mottingham La. SE9 108 EJ88
Mottingham La. SE12 108 EJ88
Mottingham Rd. N9 37 DX44
Mottingham Rd. SE9 108 EL89
Mottisfont Rd. SE2 96 EU76
Motts Hill La., Tad. 145 CU123
Mouchotte Clo., West. 136 EH112
Moulins Rd. E9 78 DW66
Moultain Hill, Swan. 125 FG98
Moulton Ave., Houns. 86 BY82
Mound, The SE9 109 EN90
Moundfield Rd. N16 64 DU58
Mount, The N20 48 DC47
Mount, The NW3 62 DC63
Heath St.
Mount, The, Couls. 146 DG115
Mount, The (Ewell), Epsom 131 CT110
Mount, The, Esher 128 CA107
Mount, The, Lthd. 143 CE123
Mount, The, N.Mal. 117 CT97
Mount, The, Pot.B. 20 DB30
Mount, The, Rick. 28 BJ44
Mount, The (Cheshunt), Wal.Cr. 22 DR26
Mount, The, Warl. 148 DU119
Mount, The, Wem. 60 CP61
Mount, The, Wey. 113 BS103
Mount, The, Wor.Pk. 131 CV105
Mount Adon Pk. SE22 106 DU87
Mount Angelus Rd. SW15 103 CT87
Laverstoke Gdns.
Mount Ararat Rd., Rich. 102 CL85
Mount Ash Rd. SE26 106 DV90
Mount Ave. E4 51 EA48
Mount Ave. W5 73 CJ71
Mount Ave., Cat. 148 DQ124
Mount Ave., Sthl. 72 CA72
Mount Clo. W5 73 CJ71
Mount Clo., Barn. 34 DG42
Mount Clo., Brom. 122 EL95
Mount Clo., Cars. 132 DG109
Mount Clo., Ken. 148 DR116
Mount Clo., Lthd. 143 CE123
Mount Clo., Sev. 154 FF123
Mount Cor., Felt. 100 BX89
Mount Ct. SW15 89 CY83
Weimar St.
Mount Ct., W.Wick. 122 EE103
Mount Culver Ave., Sid. 110 EX93
Mount Dr., Bexh. 110 EY85
Mount Dr., Har. 58 BZ57
Mount Dr., St.Alb. 17 CD25
Mount Dr., Wem. 60 CQ61
Mount Echo Ave. E4 51 EB47
Mount Echo Dr. E4 51 EB46
Mount Ephraim La. SW16 105 DK90
Mount Ephraim Rd. SW16 105 DK90
Mount Est., The E5 64 DV61
Mount Pleasant La.
Mount Felix, Walt. 113 BT102
Mount Gdns. SE26 106 DV90
Mount Grace Rd., Pot.B. 20 DA31
Mount Gro., Edg. 46 CQ48
Mount Harry Rd., Sev. 154 FG123
Mount Ms., Hmptn. 114 CB95
Mount Mills EC1 6 G3
Mount Nod Rd. SW16 105 DM90
Mount Pk., Cars. 132 DG109
Mount Pk. Ave., Har. 59 CD61
Mount Pk. Ave., S.Croy. 133 DP109
Mount Pk. Cres. W5 73 CK72
Mount Pk. Rd. W5 73 CK71
Mount Pk. Rd., Har. 59 CD62
Mount Pk. Rd., Pnr. 57 BU57
Mount Pleasant SE27 106 DQ92
Mount Pleasant WC1 6 D5
Mount Pleasant WC1 77 DN70
Mount Pleasant, Barn. 34 DE42
Mount Pleasant, Epsom 131 CT110
Mount Pleasant, Ruis. 58 BW61
Mount Pleasant, Uxb. 42 BG53
Mount Pleasant, Wem. 74 CL67
Mount Pleasant, West. 150 EK117
Mount Pleasant, Wey. 112 BN104
Mount Pleasant Cres. N4 63 DM59
Mount Pleasant Hill E5 64 DV61
Mount Pleasant La. E5 64 DV61
Mount Pleasant La., St.Alb. 16 BY30
Mount Pleasant Pl. SE18 95 ER77
Orchard Rd.
Mount Pleasant Rd. E17 51 DY54
Mount Pleasant Rd. N17 50 DS53
Mount Pleasant Rd. NW10 75 CW66
Mount Pleasant Rd. SE13 107 EC86
Mount Pleasant Rd. W5 73 CJ70
Mount Pleasant Rd., Cat. 148 DU123
Mount Pleasant Rd., Chig. 53 ER49
Mount Pleasant Rd., N.Mal. 116 CQ97
Mount Pleasant Rd., Rom. 55 FD51
Mount Pleasant Vill. N4 63 DM59
Mount Pleasant Wk., Bex. 111 FC85
Mount Rd. NW2 61 CV62
Mount Rd. NW4 61 CU58
Mount Rd. SE19 106 DR93
Mount Rd. SW19 104 DA89
Mount Rd., Barn. 34 DE43
Mount Rd., Bexh. 110 EX85
Mount Rd., Chess. 130 CM106
Mount Rd., Dag. 68 EZ60
Mount Rd., Dart. 111 FF86
Mount Rd., Epp. 26 EW32
Mount Rd., Felt. 100 BY90
Mount Rd., Hayes 85 BT75
Mount Rd., Ilf. 67 EP64
Mount Rd., Mitch. 118 DD96
Mount Rd., N.Mal. 116 CR97
Mount Row W1 9 H1
Mount Row W1 77 DH73
Mount Sq., The NW3 62 DC62
Heath St.
Mount Stewart Ave., Har. 59 CK58
Mount St. W1 8 F1
Mount St. W1 76 DG73
Mount Ter. E1 78 DV71
New Rd.
Mount Vernon NW3 62 DC63
Mount Vw. NW7 46 CR48
Mount Vw. W5 73 CK70
Mount Vw., Enf. 35 DM38
Mount Vw., Rick. 42 BH46
Mount Vw., St.Alb. 18 CL27
Mount Vw. Rd. E4 51 EC45
Mount Vw. Rd. N4 63 DL59
Mount Vw. Rd. NW9 60 CR57
Mount Vill. SE27 105 DP90
Mount Way, Cars. 132 DG109
Mountacre Clo. SE26 106 DT91
Mountague Pl. E14 79 EC73
Mountbatten Clo. SE18 95 ES79
Mountbatten Clo. SE19 106 DS92
Mountbatten Ct. SE16 78 DW74
Rotherhithe St.
Mountbatten Ct., Buck.H. 52 EK47
Mountbatten Gdns., Beck. 121 DY98
Balmoral Ave.
Mountbatten Ms. SW18 104 DC88
Inman Rd.
Mountbel Rd., Stan. 45 CG53
Mountcombe Clo., Surb. 116 CL101
Mountearl Gdns. SW16 105 DM90
Mountfield Clo. SE6 107 ED87
Mountfield Rd. E6 81 EN68
Mountfield Rd. N3 61 CZ55
Mountfield Rd. W5 73 CK72
Mountfield Way, Orp. 124 EW98
Mountford St. E1 78 DU72
Adler St.
Mountfort Cres. N1 77 DN66
Barnsbury Sq.
Mountfort Ter. N1 77 DN66
Barnsbury Sq.
Mountgrove Rd. N5 63 DP62
Mounthurst Rd., Brom. 122 EF101
Mountington Pk. Clo., Har. 59 CK58
Mountjoy Clo. SE2 96 EV75
Mountjoy Ho. EC2 78 DQ71
The Barbican
Mounts Pond Rd. SE3 93 ED82
Mountsfield Clo., Stai. 98 BG85
Mountsfield Ct. SE13 107 ED86
Mountside, Felt. 100 BY90
Mountside, Stan. 45 CF53
Mountview, Nthwd. 43 BT51
Mountview Ct. N8 63 DP56
Green Las.
Mountview Ct., Wat. 30 CB43
Mountview Rd., Esher 129 CH108
Mountview Rd., Orp. 124 EU101
Mountview Rd. (Cheshunt), Wal.Cr. 22 DS26
Mountway, Pot.B. 20 DA30
Mountwood, W.Mol. 114 CA97
Mountwood Clo., S.Croy. 134 DV110
Movers La., Bark. 81 ER67
Mowatt Clo. N19 63 DK60
Mowbray Ave., W.Byf. 126 BL113
Mowbray Rd. NW6 75 CY66
Mowbray Rd. SE19 120 DT95
Mowbray Rd., Barn. 34 DC42
Mowbray Rd., Edg. 46 CN49
Mowbray Rd., Rich. 101 CJ90
Mowbrays Clo., Rom. 55 FC53
Mowbrays Rd., Rom. 55 FC54
Mowbrey Gdns., Loug. 39 EQ39
Mowlem St. E2 78 DV68
Mowlem Trd. Est. N17 50 DW52
Mowll St. SW9 91 DN80
Moxom Ave. (Cheshunt), Wal.Cr. 23 DY30
Windmill La.
Moxon Clo. E13 80 EF68
Whitelegg Rd.
Moxon St. W1 4 F7
Moxon St. W1 76 DG71
Moxon St., Barn. 33 CZ41
Moye Clo. E2 78 DU67
Dove Row
Moyers Rd. E10 65 EC59
Moylan Rd. W6 89 CY79
Moyne Pl. NW10 74 CN68
Moynihan Dr. N21 35 DL43
Moys Clo., Croy. 119 DL100
Moyser Rd. SW16 105 DH92
Mozart St. W10 75 CZ69
Mozart Ter. SW1 8 G9
Muchelney Rd., Mord. 118 DC100
Mud La. W5 73 CK71
Mudlarks Way SE7 94 EH76
Mudlarks Way SE10 94 EF76
Muggeridge Rd., Dag. 69 FB63
Muir Rd. E5 64 DU63
Muir St. E16 81 EM74
Newland St.
Muirdown Ave. SW14 88 CR84
Muirfield W3 74 CS72
Muirfield Clo. SE16 92 DV78
Ryder Dr.
Muirfield Clo., Wat. 44 BW50
Muirfield Cres. E14 93 EB76
Millharbour
Muirfield Grn., Wat. 44 BW49
Muirfield Rd., Wat. 43 BV49
Muirkirk Rd. SE6 107 EC88
Mulberry Ave., Stai. 98 BL88
Mulberry Clo. E4 51 EA47
Mulberry Clo. N8 63 DL57
Mulberry Clo. NW3 62 DD63
Hampstead High St.
Mulberry Clo. NW4 61 CW55
Mulberry Clo. SE7 94 EK79
Mulberry Clo. SE22 106 DU86
Mulberry Clo. SW3 90 DD79
Beaufort St.
Mulberry Clo. SW16 105 DJ91
Mulberry Clo., Barn. 34 DD42
Mulberry Clo., Nthlt. 72 BY68
Parkfield Ave.
Mulberry Clo., Rom. 69 FH56
Mulberry Clo., St.Alb. 16 CB28
Mulberry Clo., Wey. 113 BP104
Mulberry Ct., Bark. 81 ET66
Westrow Dr.
Mulberry Cres., Brent. 87 CH80
Mulberry Cres., West Dr. 84 BN75
Mulberry La., Croy. 120 DT102
Mulberry Ms., Wall. 133 DJ107
Ross Rd.
Mulberry Par., West Dr. 84 BN76
Mulberry Pl. W6 89 CU78
Chiswick Mall
Mulberry Rd. E8 78 DT66
Mulberry St. E1 78 DU72
Adler St.
Mulberry Trees, Shep. 113 BR101
Mulberry Wk. SW3 90 DD79
Mulberry Way E18 52 EH54
Mulberry Way, Belv. 97 FC75
Mulberry Way, Ilf. 67 EQ56
Mulgrave Rd. NW10 61 CT63
Mulgrave Rd. SW6 89 CZ79
Mulgrave Rd. W5 73 CK70
Mulgrave Rd., Croy. 120 DR104
Mulgrave Rd., Har. 59 CG61
Mulgrave Rd., Sutt. 131 CZ108
Mulholland Clo., Mitch. 119 DH96
Mulkern Rd. N19 63 DK60
Mull Wk. N1 78 DQ65
Clephane Rd.
Mullards Clo., Mitch. 118 DF102
Muller Rd. SW4 105 DK86
Mullet Gdns. E2 78 DU68
St. Peter's Clo.
Mullins Path SW14 88 CR83
Mullion Clo., Har. 44 CB53
Mullion Wk., Wat. 44 BX49
Ormskirk Rd.
Mulready St. NW8 4 B5
Multi Way W3 88 CS75
Valetta Rd.
Multon Rd. SW18 104 DD87
Mulvaney Way SE1 11 L5
Mulvaney Way SE1 92 DR75
Mumford Ct. EC2 7 J8
Mumford Rd. SE24 105 DP85
Railton Rd.
Muncaster Clo., Ashf. 98 BN91
Muncaster Rd. SW11 104 DF85
Muncaster Rd., Ashf. 99 BP92
Muncies Ms. SE6 107 EC89
Mund St. W14 89 CZ78
Mundania Rd. SE22 106 DV86
Munday Rd. E16 80 EG72
Mundells, Wal.Cr. 22 DU27
Munden Dr., Wat. 30 BY37
Colne Way
Munden Gro., Wat. 30 BW38
Munden St. W14 89 CY77
Munden Vw., Wat. 30 BX36
Mundesley Clo., Wat. 44 BW49
Mundford Rd. E5 64 DW61
Mundon Gdns., Ilf. 67 ER60
Mundy St. N1 7 N2
Mundy St. N1 78 DS69
Mungo Pk. Clo. (Bushey), Wat. 44 CC47
Mungo Pk. Rd., Rain. 83 FG65
Mungo Pk. Way, Orp. 124 EW100
Munnery Way, Orp. 123 EN103
Munnings Gdns., Islw. 101 CD85
Munro Dr. N11 49 DJ51
Munro Ms. W10 75 CY71
Munro Rd. (Bushey), Wat. 30 CB43
Munro Ter. SW10 90 DD79
Munslow Gdns., Sutt. 132 DC105
Munster Ave., Houns. 86 BY84
Munster Ct., Tedd. 101 CJ93
Munster Gdns. N13 49 DP49
Munster Ms. SW6 89 CY80
Munster Rd.
Munster Rd. SW6 89 CY80
Munster Rd., Tedd. 101 CH93
Munster Sq. NW1 5 J3
Munster Sq. NW1 77 DH69
Munton Rd. SE17 11 J8
Munton Rd. SE17 92 DQ77
Murchison Ave., Bex. 110 EX88
Murchison Rd. E10 65 EC61
Murdoch Clo., Stai. 98 BG92
Murdock Clo. E16 80 EF72
Rogers Rd.
Murdock St. SE15 92 DV79
Murfett Clo. SW19 103 CY89
Muriel Ave., Wat. 30 BW43
Muriel St. N1 77 DM67
Murillo Rd. SE13 93 ED84
Murphy St. SE1 10 D5
Murphy St. SE1 91 DN75
Murray Ave., Brom. 122 EH97
Murray Ave., Houns. 100 CB85
Murray Cres., Pnr. 44 BX53
Murray Gro. N1 7 J1
Murray Gro. N1 78 DQ68
Murray Ms. NW1 77 DK66
Murray Rd. SW19 103 CX93
Murray Rd. W5 87 CK77
Murray Rd., Nthwd. 43 BS53
Murray Rd., Orp. 124 EV97
Murray Rd., Rich. 101 CH89
Murray Sq. E16 80 EG72
Murray St. NW1 77 DK66
Murray Ter. NW3 62 DD63
Flask Wk.
Murray Ter. W5 87 CK77
Murray Rd.
Murrays La., W.Byf. 126 BK114
Murrells Wk., Lthd. 142 CA123
Murreys, The, Ash. 143 CK118
Mursell Est. SW8 91 DM81
Murthering La., Rom. 55 FF45
Murtwell Dr., Chig. 53 EQ51
Musard Rd. W6 89 CY79
Musard Rd. W14 89 CY79

Musbury St. E1 78 DW72
Muscal W6 89 CY79
Muscatel Pl. SE5 92 DS81
Dalwood St.
Muschamp Rd. SE15 92 DT83
Muschamp Rd., Cars. 118 DE103
Muscovy St. EC3 11 N1
Museum La. SW7 8 A7
Museum Pas. E2 78 DV69
Victoria Pk. Sq.
Museum St. WC1 5 P7
Museum St. WC1 77 DL71
Musgrave Clo., Barn. 34 DC39
Musgrave Clo., Wal.Cr. 22 DT27
Allwood Rd.
Musgrave Cres. SW6 90 DA80
Musgrave Rd., Islw. 87 CF81
Musgrove Rd. SE14 93 DX81
Musjid Rd. SW11 90 DD82
Kambala Rd.
Muskalls Clo. (Cheshunt), Wal.Cr. 22 DU27
Musquash Way, Houns. 86 BW82
Muston Rd. E5 64 DV61
Mustow Pl. SW6 89 CZ82
Munster Rd.
Muswell Ave. N10 49 DH53
Muswell Hill N10 63 DH55
Muswell Hill Bdy. N10 63 DH55
Muswell Hill Pl. N10 63 DH56
Muswell Hill Rd. N6 62 DG58
Muswell Hill Rd. N10 62 DG58
Muswell Ms. N10 63 DH55
Muswell Rd.
Muswell Rd. N10 63 DH55
Mutchetts Clo., Wat. 16 BY33
Mutrix Rd. NW6 76 DA67
Mutton La., Pot.B. 19 CW31
Mutton Pl. NW1 77 DH65
Harmood St.
Muybridge Rd., N.Mal. 116 CQ96
Myatt Rd. SW9 91 DP81
Myatt's Flds. N. SW9 91 DN81
Eythorne Rd.
Myatt's Flds. S. SW9 91 DN82
Mycenae Rd. SE3 94 EG80
Myddelton Ave., Enf. 36 DS38
Myddelton Clo., Enf. 36 DT39
Myddelton Gdns. N21 49 DP45
Myddelton Pk. N20 48 DD48
Myddelton Pas. EC1 6 E2
Myddelton Rd. N8 63 DL56
Myddelton Sq. EC1 6 E2
Myddelton Sq. EC1 77 DN69
Myddelton St. EC1 6 E3
Myddelton St. EC1 77 DN69
Myddleton Ms. N22 49 DL52
Myddleton Path (Cheshunt), Wal.Cr. 22 DV31
Hawthorne Clo.
Myddleton Rd. N22 49 DL52
Myddleton Rd., Uxb. 70 BJ67
Myers La. SE14 93 DX79
Myles Ct., Wal.Cr. 22 DQ29
Mylis Clo. SE26 106 DV91
Mylius Clo. SE14 92 DW81
Kender St.
Mylne Clo., Wal.Cr. 22 DW27
Mylne St. EC1 6 D1
Mylne St. EC1 77 DN68
Mymms Dr., Hat. 20 DA26
Mynns Clo., Epsom 130 CP114
Myra St. SE2 96 EU77
Myrdle St. E1 78 DU71
Myrna Clo. SW19 104 DE94
Myron Pl. SE13 93 EC83
Myrtle Ave., Felt. 85 BS84
Myrtle Ave., Ruis. 57 BU59
Myrtle Clo., Barn. 48 DF46
Myrtle Clo., Erith 97 FE81
Myrtle Clo., Uxb. 70 BM71
Violet Ave.
Myrtle Clo., West Dr. 84 BM76
Myrtle Gdns. W7 73 CE74
Myrtle Gro., Enf. 36 DR38
Myrtle Gro., N.Mal. 116 CQ96
Myrtle Rd. E6 80 EL67
Myrtle Rd. E17 65 DY58
Myrtle Rd. N13 50 DQ48
Myrtle Rd. W3 74 CQ74
Myrtle Rd., Croy. 121 EA104
Myrtle Rd., Hmptn. 100 CC93
Myrtle Rd., Houns. 86 CC82
Myrtle Rd., Ilf. 67 EP61
Myrtle Rd., Sutt. 132 DC106
Myrtle Wk. N1 7 M1
Myrtle Wk. N1 78 DS68
Myrtleberry Clo. E8 78 DT65
Beechwood Rd.
Myrtledene Rd. SE2 96 EU78
Myrtleside Clo., Nthwd. 43 BR52
Mysore Rd. SW11 90 DF83
Myton Rd. SE21 106 DR90

N

Nadine St. SE7 94 EJ78
Nafferton Ri., Loug. 38 EK43
Nagasaki Wk. SE7 94 EJ76
Nagle Clo. E17 51 ED54
Nag's Head Ct. EC1 7 J5
Nags Head La., Well. 96 EV83
Nags Head Rd., Enf. 36 DW42
Nairn Grn., Wat. 43 BU48
Nairn Rd., Ruis. 72 BW65
Nairn St. E14 79 EC71
Nairne Gro. SE24 106 DR85
Naish Ct. N1 77 DL67
Nallhead Rd., Felt. 100 BW92
Namton Dr., Th.Hth. 119 DM98
Nan Clark's La. NW7 47 CT47
Nancy Downs, Wat. 44 BW45
Nankin St. E14 79 EA72
Nansen Rd. SW11 90 DG84
Nant Rd. NW2 61 CZ61
Nant St. E2 78 DV69
Cambridge Heath Rd.
Nantes Clo. SW18 90 DC84
Nantes Pas. E1 7 P6
Naoroji St. WC1 6 D3
Nap, The, Kings L. 14 BN29
Napier Ave. E14 93 EA78
Napier Ave. SW6 89 CZ83
Napier Clo. SE8 93 DZ80
Amersham Vale
Napier Clo. W14 89 CZ76
Napier Rd.
Napier Clo., Horn. 69 FH60
St. Leonards Way
Napier Clo., St.Alb. 17 CK25
Napier Clo., West Dr. 84 BM76
Napier Ct. SW6 89 CZ83
Ranelagh Gdns.
Napier Ct. (Cheshunt), Wal.Cr. 22 DV28
Flamstead End Rd.
Napier Dr. (Bushey), Wat. 30 BY42
Napier Gro. N1 78 DQ68
Napier Ho., Rain. 83 FF69
Napier Pl. W14 89 CZ76
Napier Rd. E6 81 EN67
Napier Rd. E11 66 EE63
Napier Rd. E15 80 EE68
Napier Rd. N17 64 DS55
Napier Rd. NW10 75 CV69
Napier Rd. SE25 120 DV98
Napier Rd. W14 89 CY76
Napier Rd., Ashf. 99 BR94
Napier Rd., Belv. 96 EZ77
Napier Rd., Brom. 122 EH98
Napier Rd., Enf. 37 DX43
Napier Rd., Houns. 84 BK81
Napier Rd., Islw. 87 CG84
Napier Rd., S.Croy. 134 DR108
Napier Rd., Wem. 59 CK64
Napier Ter. N1 77 DP65
Napoleon Rd. E5 64 DV62
Napoleon Rd., Twick. 101 CH87
Napsbury Ave., St.Alb. 17 CJ26
Napton Clo., Hayes 72 BY70
Kingsash Dr.
Narbonne Ave. SW4 105 DJ85
Narboro Ct., Rom. 69 FG57
Manor Rd.
Narborough Clo., Uxb. 57 BQ61
Aylsham Dr.
Narborough St. SW6 90 DB82
Narcissus Rd. NW6 62 DA64
Naresby Fold, Stan. 45 CJ51
Narford Rd. E5 64 DU62
Narrow La., Warl. 148 DV119
Narrow St. E14 79 DY73
Narrow Way, Brom. 122 EL100
Nascot Pl., Wat. 29 BV40
Stamford Rd.
Nascot Rd., Wat. 29 BV40
Nascot St. W12 75 CW72
Nascot St., Wat. 29 BV40
Nascot Wd. Rd., Wat. 29 BT37
Naseby Clo. NW6 76 DC66
Fairfax Rd.
Naseby Clo., Islw. 87 CE81
Naseby Ct., Walt. 114 BW103
Clements Rd.
Naseby Rd. SE19 106 DR93
Naseby Rd., Dag. 68 FA62
Naseby Rd., Ilf. 53 EM53
Nash Clo., Borwd. 32 CM42
Nash Grn., Brom. 108 EG93
Nash Grn., Hem.H. 14 BM25
Nash La., Kes. 136 EG108
Nash Pl. E14 79 EB74
South Colonnade
Nash Rd. N9 50 DW47
Nash Rd. SE4 93 DY84
Nash Rd., Rom. 68 EX56
Nash St. NW1 5 J2
Nash's Yd., Uxb. 70 BK66
Bakers Rd.
Nasmyth St. W6 89 CV76
Nassau Path SE28 82 EW74
Disraeli Clo.
Nassau Rd. SW13 89 CT81
Nassau St. W1 5 K7
Nassau St. W1 77 DJ71
Nassington Rd. NW3 62 DE63
Natal Rd. N11 49 DL51
Natal Rd. SW16 105 DK93
Natal Rd., Ilf. 67 EP63
Natal Rd., Th.Hth. 120 DR97
Natalie Clo., Felt. 99 BR87
Natalie Ms., Twick. 101 CD90
Sixth Cross Rd.
Nathan Way SE28 95 ES76
Nathaniel Clo. E1 78 DT71
Thrawl St.
Nathans Rd., Wem. 59 CJ60
Nation Way E4 51 EC46
Naval Row E14 79 EC73
Naval Wk., Brom. 122 EG97
High St.
Navarino Gro. E8 78 DU65
Navarino Rd. E8 78 DU65
Navarre Gdns., Rom. 55 FB50
Navarre Rd. E6 80 EL68
Navarre St. E2 7 P4
Navarre St. E2 78 DT70
Navenby Wk. E3 79 EA70
Rounton Rd.
Navestock Clo. E4 51 EC48
Mapleton Rd.
Navestock Cres., Wdf.Grn. 52 EJ53
Navestock Ho., Bark. 82 EV68
Navigator Dr., Sthl. 86 CC75
Navy St. SW4 91 DK83
Naylor Gro., Enf. 37 DX43
South St.
Naylor Rd. N20 48 DC47
Naylor Rd. SE15 92 DV80
Nazareth Gdns. SE15 92 DV82
Nazeing Wk., Rain. 83 FE67
Ongar Way
Nazrul St. E2 7 P2
Nazrul St. E2 78 DT69
Neagle Clo., Borwd. 32 CQ39
Balcon Way
Neal Ave., Sthl. 72 BZ69
Neal Clo., Nthwd. 43 BU53
Neal Ct., Wal.Abb. 24 EF33
Neal St. WC2 5 P9
Neal St. WC2 77 DL72
Neal St., Wat. 30 BW43
Nealden St. SW9 91 DM83
Neale Clo. N2 62 DC55
Neal's Yd. WC2 5 P9
Near Acre NW9 47 CT53
Neasden Clo. NW10 60 CS64
Neasden La. NW10 60 CS62
Neasden La. N. NW10 60 CR62
Neasden Underpass NW10 60 CR62
Neasham Rd., Dag. 68 EV64
Neate St. SE5 92 DS79
Neath Gdns., Mord. 118 DC100
Neathouse Pl. SW1 9 K8
Neats Acre, Ruis. 57 BR59
Neatscourt Rd. E6 80 EK71
Nebraska St. SE1 11 K5
Neckinger SE16 92 DT76
Neckinger Est. SE16 92 DT76
Neckinger St. SE1 92 DT75
Nectarine Way SE13 93 EB82
Needham Rd. W11 76 DA72
Westbourne Gro.
Needham Ter. NW2 61 CX62
Needleman St. SE16 93 DX75
Neela Clo., Uxb. 57 BP63
Neeld Cres. NW4 61 CV57
Neeld Cres., Wem. 60 CN64
Neil Clo., Ashf. 99 BQ92
Neil Wates Cres. SW2 105 DN88
Nelgarde Rd. SE6 107 EA87
Nell Gwynn Clo., Rad. 18 CL32
Nell Gwynne Ave., Shep. 113 BR100
Nella Rd. W6 89 CX79
Nelldale Rd. SE16 92 DW77
Nellgrove Rd., Uxb. 71 BP70
Nello James Gdns. SE27 106 DR91
Nelson Clo., Croy. 119 DP102
Nelson Clo., Felt. 99 BT88
Nelson Clo., Rom. 55 FB53
Nelson Clo., Uxb. 71 BP69
Nelson Clo., Walt. 113 BV102
Nelson Clo., West. 150 EL117
Nelson Ct. SE16 78 DW74
Brunel Rd.
Nelson Gdns. E2 78 DU69
Nelson Gdns., Houns. 100 CA86
Nelson Gro. Rd. SW19 118 DB95
Nelson La., Uxb. 71 BP69
Nelson Rd.
Nelson Mandela Clo. N10 48 DG54
Nelson Mandela Rd. SE3 94 EJ83
Nelson Pas. EC1 7 J3
Nelson Pas. EC1 78 DQ69
Nelson Pl. N1 6 G1
Nelson Pl. N1 77 DP68
Nelson Pl., Sid. 110 EU91
Nelson Rd. E4 51 EA51
Nelson Rd. E11 66 EG56
Nelson Rd. N8 63 DM57
Nelson Rd. N9 50 DV47
Nelson Rd. N15 64 DS56
Nelson Rd. SE10 93 EC79
Nelson Rd. SW19 104 DB94
Nelson Rd., Ashf. 98 BL92
Nelson Rd., Belv. 96 EZ78
Nelson Rd., Brom. 122 EJ98
Nelson Rd., Cat. 148 DR123
Nelson Rd., Enf. 37 DX44
Nelson Rd., Har. 59 CD60
Nelson Rd., Houns. 100 CA86
Nelson Rd. (Heathrow Airport), Houns. 84 BM81
Nelson Rd., N.Mal. 116 CR99
Nelson Rd., Rain. 83 FF68
Nelson Rd., Sid. 110 EU91
Nelson Rd., Stan. 45 CJ51
Nelson Rd., Twick. 100 CB87
Nelson Rd., Uxb. 71 BP69
Nelson Sq. SE1 10 F4
Nelson Sq. SE1 91 DP75
Nelson St. E1 78 DV72
Nelson St. E6 81 EM68
Nelson St. E16 80 EF73
Huntingdon St.
Nelson Ter. N1 6 G1
Nelson Ter. N1 77 DP68
Nelson Trd. Est. SW19 118 DB95
Nelson Wk. SE16 79 DY74
Rotherhithe St.
Nelson's Row SW4 91 DK84
Nelsons Yd. NW1 77 DJ68
Mornington Cres.
Nemoure Rd. W3 74 CQ73
Nene Gdns., Felt. 100 BZ89
Nene Rd., Houns. 85 BP81
Nepaul Rd. SW11 90 DE82
Afghan Rd.
Nepean St. SW15 103 CU86
Neptune Rd., Har. 59 CD58
Neptune Rd. (Heathrow Airport), Houns. 85 BR81
Neptune St. SE16 92 DW76
Nesbit Rd. SE9 94 EK84
Nesbitt Clo. SE3 94 EE83
Hurren Clo.
Nesbitt Sq. SE19 106 DS94
Coxwell Rd.
Nesbitts All., Barn. 33 CZ41
Bath Pl.
Nesham St. E1 78 DU74
Ness St. SE16 92 DU76
Spa Rd.
Nesta Rd., Wdf.Grn. 52 EE51
Nestles Ave., Hayes 85 BT76
Neston Rd., Wat. 30 BW37
Nestor Ave. N21 35 DP44
Nether Clo. N3 48 DA52
Nether St. N3 48 DA53
Nether St. N12 48 DB51
Netheravon Rd. W7 73 CF74
Netheravon Rd. N. W4 89 CT77
Netheravon Rd. S. W4 89 CT78
Netherbury Rd. W5 87 CK76
Netherby Gdns., Enf. 35 DL42
Netherby Pk., Wey. 127 BR106
Netherby Rd. SE23 106 DW87
Nethercourt Ave. N3 48 DA51
Netherfield Gdns., Bark. 81 ER65
Netherfield Rd. N12 48 DB50
Netherfield Rd. SW17 104 DG90
Netherford Rd. SW4 91 DJ82
Netherhall Gdns. NW3 76 DC65
Netherhall Way NW3 62 DC64
Netherhall Gdns.
Netherlands, The, Couls. 147 DJ119
Netherlands Rd., Barn. 34 DD44
Netherleigh Clo. N6 63 DH60
Nethern Ct. Rd., Cat. 149 EA123
Netherne La., Couls. 147 DJ123
Netherne La., Red. 147 DJ123
Netherpark Dr., Rom. 55 FF54
Netherton Gro. SW10 90 DC79
Netherton Rd. N15 64 DR58
Seven Sisters Rd.
Netherton Rd., Twick. 101 CG85
Netherwood N2 48 DD54
Netherwood Pl. W14 89 CX76
Netherwood Rd.
Netherwood Rd. W14 89 CX76
Netherwood St. NW6 75 CZ66
Netley Clo., Croy. 135 EC108
Netley Clo., Sutt. 131 CX106
Netley Dr., Walt. 114 BZ101
Netley Gdns., Mord. 118 DC101
Netley Rd. E17 65 DZ57
Netley Rd., Brent. 88 CL79
Netley Rd. (Heathrow Airport), Houns. 85 BR81
Netley Rd., Ilf. 67 ER57
Netley Rd., Mord. 118 DC101
Netley St. NW1 5 K3
Nettlecombe Clo., Sutt. 132 DB109
Nettleden Ave., Wem. 74 CN65
Nettlefold Pl. SE27 105 DP90
Nettlestead Clo., Beck. 107 DZ94
Copers Cope Rd.
Nettleton Rd. SE14 93 DX81
Nettleton Rd., Houns. 85 BP81
Nettleton Rd., Uxb. 56 BM63
Nettlewood Rd. SW16 105 DK94
Neuchatel Rd. SE6 107 DZ89
Nevada Clo., N.Mal. 116 CQ98
Georgia Rd.
Nevada St. SE10 93 EC79
Nevern Pl. SW5 90 DA77
Nevern Rd. SW5 90 DA77
Nevern Sq. SW5 90 DA77
Nevil Clo., Nthwd. 43 BR50
Nevill Clo. W3 88 CQ75
Acton La.
Nevill Gro., Wat. 29 BV39
Nevill Rd. N16 64 DS63
Nevill Way, Loug. 52 EL45
Valley Hill
Neville Ave., N.Mal. 116 CR95
Neville Clo. E11 66 EF62
Neville Clo. NW1 5 N1
Neville Clo. NW6 75 CZ68
Neville Clo. SE15 92 DU80
Neville Clo., Bans. 132 DB114
Neville Clo., Esher 128 BZ107
Neville Clo., Houns. 86 CB82
Neville Clo., Pot.B. 19 CZ31
Neville Clo., Sid. 109 ET91
Neville Dr. N2 62 DC58
Neville Gdns., Dag. 68 EX62
Neville Gill Clo. SW18 104 DB86
Neville Pl. N22 49 DM53
Neville Rd. E7 80 EG66
Neville Rd. NW6 75 CZ68
Neville Rd. W5 73 CK70
Neville Rd., Croy. 120 DR101
Neville Rd., Dag. 68 EX61
Neville Rd., Ilf. 53 EQ53
Neville Rd., Kings.T. 116 CN96
Neville Rd., Rich. 101 CJ89
Neville St. SW7 90 DD78
Neville Ter. SW7 90 DD78
Neville Wk., Cars. 118 DE101
Green Wrythe La.
Nevilles Ct. NW2 61 CU62
Nevin Dr. E4 51 EB46
Nevis Clo., Rom. 55 FE51
Nevis Rd. SW17 104 DG89
New Ash Clo. N2 62 DD55
Oakridge Dr.
New Barn La., Sev. 151 EQ116
New Barn La., West. 151 EQ118
New Barn La., Whyt. 148 DS116
New Barn Rd., Swan. 125 FE95
New Barn St. E13 80 EG70
New Barns Ave., Mitch. 119 DK98
New Barns Way, Chig. 53 EP48
New Berry La., Walt. 128 BX106
New Bond St. W1 5 H9
New Bond St. W1 77 DH72
New Brent St. NW4 61 CW57
New Bri. St. EC4 6 F9
New Bri. St. EC4 77 DP72
New Broad St. EC2 7 M7
New Bdy. W5 73 CJ73
New Bdy., Hmptn. 101 CD92
Hampton Rd.
New Burlington Ms. W1 5 K10
New Burlington Pl. W1 5 K10
New Burlington St. W1 5 K10
New Burlington St. W1 77 DJ73
New Butt La. SE8 93 EA80
New Butt La. N. SE8 93 EA80
Reginald Rd.
New Cavendish St. W1 4 G7
New Cavendish St. W1 76 DG71
New Change EC4 7 H9
New Change EC4 78 DQ72
New Chapel Sq., Felt. 99 BV88
New Charles St. EC1 6 G2
New Ch. Rd. SE5 92 DR80
New City Rd. E13 80 EJ69
New Clo. SW19 118 DC97
New Clo., Felt. 100 BY92
New College Ms. N1 77 DN66
Islington Pk. St.
New Compton St. WC2 5 N9
New Compton St. WC2 77 DK72
New Ct. EC4 6 D10
New Ct., Add. 112 BJ104
New Covent Gdn. Mkt. SW8 91 DK80
New Coventry St. W1 9 N1
New Crane Pl. E1 78 DW74
Garnet St.
New Cross Rd. SE14 92 DW80
New End NW3 62 DC63
New End Sq. NW3 62 DD63
New Era Est. N1 78 DS67
Phillipp St.
New Fm. Ave., Brom. 122 EG98
New Fm. Dr., Rom. 40 EW41
New Fm. La., Nthwd. 43 BS53
New Ferry App. SE18 95 EN76
New Fetter La. EC4 6 E8
New Fetter La. EC4 77 DN72
New Ford Rd., Wal.Cr. 23 DZ34
New Forest La., Chig. 53 EN51
New Gdn. Dr., West Dr. 84 BL75
Drayton Gdns.
New Globe Wk. SE1 11 H2
New Globe Wk. SE1 78 DQ74
New Goulston St. E1 7 P8
New Haw Rd., Add. 126 BJ106
New Heston Rd., Houns. 86 BZ80
New Horizon Ct., Brent. 87 CG79
Shield Dr.
New Ho. La., Epp. 27 FC25
New Inn Bdy. EC2 7 N4
New Inn Pas. WC2 6 C9
New Inn St. EC2 7 N4
New Inn Yd. EC2 7 N4
New Inn Yd. EC2 78 DS70
New James Ct. SE15 92 DV83
Nunhead La.
New Kent Rd. SE1 11 H7
New Kent Rd. SE1 92 DQ76
New King St. SE8 93 EA79
New Kings Rd. SW6 89 CZ82
New London St. EC3 7 N10
New Lydenburgh St. SE7 94 EJ76
New Mill Rd., Orp. 124 EW95
New Mt. St. E15 79 ED66
New N. Pl. EC2 7 M5
New N. Rd. N1 78 DQ66
New N. Rd., Ilf. 53 ER52
New N. St. WC1 6 B6
New N. St. WC1 77 DM71
New Oak Rd. N2 48 DC54
New Orleans Wk. N19 63 DK59
New Oxford St. WC1 5 N8
New Oxford St. WC1 77 DK72
New Par., Ashf. 98 BM91
Church Rd.
New Pk. Ave. N13 50 DQ48
New Pk. Clo., Nthlt. 72 BY65
New Pk. Ct. SW2 105 DL87
New Pk. Par. SW2 105 DL86
Doverfield Rd.
New Pk. Rd. SW2 105 DK88
New Pk. Rd., Ashf. 99 BQ92
New Pk. Rd., Uxb. 42 BJ53
New Peachey La., Uxb. 70 BK72
New Pl. Sq. SE16 92 DV76

New Plaistow Rd. E15 80 EE67
New Printing Ho. Sq. WC1 77 DM70
Gray's Inn Rd.
New Priory Ct. NW6 76 DA66
Mazenod Ave.
New Quebec St. W1 4 E9
New Quebec St. W1 76 DF72
New Ride SW7 8 B4
New River Ct. (Cheshunt), Wal.Cr. 22 DV30
Pengelly Clo.
New River Cres. N13 49 DP49
New River Wk. N1 78 DQ65
St. Paul's Rd.
New Rd. E1 78 DV71
New Rd. E4 51 EB49
New Rd. N8 63 DL57
New Rd. N9 50 DU48
New Rd. N17 50 DT53
New Rd. N22 50 DQ53
New Rd. NW7 47 CY52
New Rd. (Barnet Gate) NW7 47 CT45
New Rd. SE2 96 EX77
New Rd., Borwd. 31 CK44
New Rd., Brent. 87 CK78
New Rd., Dag. 82 FA67
New Rd., Epp. 26 FA32
New Rd., Esher 114 CC104
New Rd. (Claygate), Esher 129 CF110
New Rd., Felt. 99 BR86
New Rd. (East Bedfont), Felt. 99 BV88
New Rd. (Hanworth), Felt. 100 BY92
New Rd., Har. 59 CF63
New Rd., Hayes 85 BQ80
New Rd., Houns. 86 CB84
Station Rd.
New Rd., Ilf. 67 ES61
New Rd., Kings.T. 102 CN94
New Rd., Lthd. 129 CF110
New Rd., Mitch. 118 DF102
New Rd., Orp. 124 EU101
New Rd., Pot.B. 19 CU33
New Rd., Rad. 31 CE36
New Rd. (Shenley), Rad. 18 CN34
New Rd., Rain. 83 FC68
New Rd., Rich. 101 CJ91
New Rd., Rick. 28 BN43
New Rd., Rom. 40 EX44
New Rd., Sev. 152 EX124
New Rd., Shep. 112 BN97
New Rd., Swan. 125 FF97
New Rd. (Hextable), Swan. 111 FF94
New Rd., Tad. 145 CW123
New Rd., Uxb. 71 BQ70
New Rd., Wat. 30 BW42
New Rd. (Letchmore Heath), Wat. 31 CE39
New Rd., Well. 96 EV82
New Rd., W.Mol. 114 CA97
New Rd., Wey. 127 BQ106
New Rd. Hill, Kes. 136 EL109
New Rd. Hill, Orp. 136 EL109
New Row WC2 5 P10
New Row WC2 77 DL73
New Spring Gdns. Wk. SE11 91 DL78
Goding St.
New Sq. E6 81 EM72
Porter Rd.
New Sq. WC2 6 C8
New Sq. WC2 77 DM72
New Sq., Felt. 99 BQ88
New Sq. Pas. WC2 77 DM72
New Sq.
New St. EC2 7 N7
New St. EC2 78 DS71
New St., Stai. 98 BG91
New St., Wat. 30 BW42
New St. Hill, Brom. 108 EH92
New St. Sq. EC4 6 E8
New Trinity Rd. N2 62 DD55
New Turnstile WC1 6 B7
New Union Clo. E14 93 EC76
New Union St. EC2 7 K7
New Union St. EC2 78 DR71
New Wanstead E11 66 EF58
New Way Rd. NW9 60 CS56
New Wf. Rd. N1 77 DL68
New Windsor St., Uxb. 70 BJ66
New Years Grn. La., Uxb. 56 BL58
New Years La., Orp. 151 ET115
New Years La., Sev. 151 ET115
New Zealand Ave., Walt. 113 BT102
New Zealand Way W12 75 CV73
India Way
New Zealand Way, Rain. 83 FF69
Newall Rd., Houns. 85 BQ81
Newark Clo., Wok. 140 BG121
Newark Cotts., Wok. 140 BG121
Newark Ct., Walt. 114 BW102
St. Johns Dr.
Newark Cres. NW10 74 CR69
Newark Grn., Borwd. 32 CR41
Newark Knok E6 81 EN72
Newark La., Wok. 140 BG121
Newark Rd., S.Croy. 134 DR107
Newark St. E1 78 DV71
Newark Way NW4 61 CU56
Newberries Ave., Rad. 31 CH35
Newbery Rd., Erith 97 FF80
Newbiggin Path, Wat. 44 BW49
Newbolt Ave., Sutt. 131 CW106
Newbolt Rd., Stan. 45 CF50
Newborough Grn., N.Mal. 116 CR98
Newburgh Rd. W3 74 CQ74
Newburgh St. W1 5 K9
Newburgh St. W1 77 DJ72
Newburn St. SE11 91 DM78
Newbury Ave., Enf. 37 DZ38
Newbury Clo., Nthlt. 72 BZ65
Newbury Gdns., Epsom 131 CT105
Newbury Ho. N22 49 DL53
Newbury Ms. NW5 76 DG65
Malden Rd.
Newbury Rd. E4 51 EC51
Newbury Rd., Brom. 122 EG97
Newbury Rd., Houns. 84 BM81
Newbury Rd., Ilf. 67 ES58
Newbury St. EC1 7 H6
Newbury Way, Nthlt. 72 BZ65
Newby Clo., Enf. 36 DS40
Newby Pl. E14 79 EC73
Newby St. SW8 91 DH83
Newcastle Ave., Ilf. 54 EU51
Newcastle Clo. EC4 6 F8
Newcastle Pl. W2 4 A7
Newcastle Pl. W2 76 DD71
Newcastle Row EC1 6 E5
Newcombe Gdns. SW16 105 DL91
Newcombe Pk. NW7 46 CS50
Newcombe Pk., Wem. 74 CM67
Newcombe Ri., West Dr. 70 BL72
Newcombe St. W8 76 DA74
Kensington Pl.
Newcome Path, Rad. 18 CN34
Newcome Rd.
Newcome Rd., Rad. 18 CN34
Newcomen Rd. E11 66 EF62
Newcomen Rd. SW11 90 DD83
Newcomen St. SE1 11 K4
Newcomen St. SE1 92 DR75
Newcourt, Uxb. 70 BJ71
Newcourt St. NW8 4 B1
Newcourt St. NW8 76 DE68
Newcroft Clo., Uxb. 70 BM71
Newdales Clo. N9 50 DU47
Balham Rd.
Newdene Ave., Nthlt. 72 BX68
Newdigate Grn., Uxb. 42 BK53
Newdigate Rd., Uxb. 42 BJ53
Newdigate Rd. E., Uxb. 42 BK53
Newell St. E14 79 DZ72
Newent Clo. SE15 92 DS80
Newent Clo., Cars. 118 DF102
Newfield Clo., Hmptn. 114 CA95
Percy Rd.
Newfield Ri. NW2 61 CV62
Newgale Gdns., Edg. 46 CM53
Newgate, Croy. 120 DQ102
Newgate Clo., Felt. 100 BY89
Newgate St. E4 52 EF48
Newgate St. EC1 6 G8
Newgate St. EC1 77 DP72
Newgate St. Village, Hert. 21 DL25
Newgatestreet Rd. (Cheshunt), Wal.Cr. 21 DP25
Newhall Ct., Wal.Abb. 24 EF33
Newham Way E6 81 EN70
Newham Way E16 80 EF71
Newhams Clo., Brom. 123 EM97
Newhams Row SE1 11 N5
Newhaven Clo., Hayes 85 BT77
Newhaven Cres., Ashf. 99 BR92
Newhaven Gdns. SE9 94 EK84
Newhaven La. E16 80 EF70
Newhaven Rd. SE25 120 DR99
Newhouse Ave., Rom. 68 EX55
Newhouse Clo., N.Mal. 116 CS101
Newhouse Cres., Wat. 15 BV32
Newhouse Wk., Mord. 118 DC101
Newick Clo., Bex. 111 FB86
Newick Rd. E5 64 DV62
Newing Grn., Brom. 108 EK94
Newington Barrow Way N7 63 DM62
Newington Butts SE1 10 G9
Newington Butts SE1 91 DP77
Newington Butts SE11 10 G9
Newington Butts SE11 91 DP77
Newington Causeway SE1 10 G7
Newington Causeway SE1 91 DP76
Newington Grn. N1 64 DR64
Newington Grn. N16 64 DR64
Newington Grn. Rd. N1 78 DR65
Newington Way N7 63 DM61
Hornsey Rd.
Newland Clo., Pnr. 44 BY51
Newland Ct., Wem. 60 CN61
Forty Ave.
Newland Dr., Enf. 36 DV39
Newland Gdns. W13 87 CG75
Newland Rd. N8 63 DL55
Newland St. E16 80 EL74
Newlands, The, Wall. 133 DJ108
Newlands Ave., Rad. 17 CF34
Newlands Ave., T.Ditt. 115 CE102
Newlands Clo., Edg. 46 CL48
Newlands Clo., Sthl. 86 BY78
Newlands Clo., Walt. 128 BY105
Newlands Clo., Wem. 73 CJ65
Newlands Ct. SE9 109 EN86
Newlands Mobile Home Pk., Abb.L. 15 BT26
Newlands Pk. SE26 107 DX92
Newlands Pl., Barn. 33 CX43
Newlands Quay E1 78 DW73
Newlands Rd. SW16 119 DL96
Newlands Rd., Wdf.Grn. 52 EF47
Newlands Wk., Wat. 16 BX33
Trevellance Way
Newlands Way, Chess. 129 CJ106
Newlands Way, Pot.B. 20 DB30
Newlands Wd., Croy. 135 DZ109
Newling Clo. E6 81 EM72
Porter Rd.
Newlyn Clo., St.Alb. 16 BY30
Newlyn Clo., Uxb. 70 BN71
Newlyn Gdns., Har. 58 BZ59
Newlyn Rd. N17 50 DT53
Newlyn Rd. NW2 61 CW60
Tilling Rd.
Newlyn Rd., Barn. 33 CZ42
Newlyn Rd., Well. 95 ET82
Newman Pas. W1 5 L7
Newman Rd. E13 80 EH69
Newman Rd. E17 65 DX57
Southcote Rd.
Newman Rd., Brom. 122 EG95
Newman Rd., Croy. 119 DM102
Newman Rd., Hayes 71 BV73
Newman St. W1 5 L7
Newman St. W1 77 DJ71
Newman Yd. W1 5 L8
Newmans Clo., Loug. 39 EP41
Newman's Ct. EC3 7 L9
Newmans La., Loug. 39 EN41
Newmans La., Surb. 115 CK100
Newman's Row WC2 6 C7
Newmans Way, Barn. 34 DC39
Newmarket Ave., Nthlt. 58 CB64
Newmarket Grn. SE9 108 EK87
Middle Pk. Ave.
Newminster Rd., Mord. 118 DC100
Newnes Path SW15 89 CV84
Putney Pk. La.
Newnham Ave., Ruis. 58 BW60
Newnham Clo., Loug. 38 EK44
Newnham Clo., Nthlt. 58 CC64
Newnham Clo., Th.Hth. 120 DQ96
Newnham Gdns., Nthlt. 72 CC65
Newnham Ms. N22 49 DM53
Newnham Rd.
Newnham Rd. N22 49 DM53
Newnham Ter. SE1 10 D6
Newnham Way, Har. 60 CL57
Newnhams Clo., Brom. 123 EM97
Newnton Clo. N4 64 DR59
Newpiece, Loug. 39 EP41
Newport Ave. E13 80 EH70
Palmer Rd.
Newport Clo., Enf. 37 DY37
Newport Ct. WC2 5 N10
Newport Mead, Wat. 44 BX49
Kilmarnock Rd.
Newport Pl. WC2 5 N10
Newport Pl. WC2 77 DK73
Newport Rd. E10 65 EC61
Newport Rd. E17 65 DY56
Newport Rd. SW13 89 CU81
Newport Rd., Hayes 71 BR71
Uxbridge Rd.
Newport Rd., Houns. 84 BN81
Newport St. SE11 10 B9
Newport St. SE11 91 DM77
Newports, Swan. 125 FD101
Newquay Cres., Har. 58 BY61
Newquay Gdns., Wat. 43 BV47
Fulford Gro.
Newquay Rd. SE6 107 EB89
Newry Rd., Twick. 101 CG85
Newsam Ave. N15 64 DR57
Newsholme Dr. N21 35 DM43
Worlds End La.
Newstead Ave., Orp. 123 ER104
Newstead Clo. N12 48 DE51
Summerfields Ave.
Newstead Rd. SE12 108 EF87
Newstead Wk., Cars. 118 DC101
Newstead Way SW19 103 CX91
Newteswell Dr., Wal.Abb. 23 ED32
Newton Ave. N10 48 DG53
Newton Ave. W3 88 CQ75
Newton Clo. E17 65 DY58
Newton Cres., Borwd. 32 CQ42
Newton Gro. W4 88 CS77
Newton Rd. E15 65 ED64
Newton Rd. N15 64 DT57
Newton Rd. NW2 61 CW62
Newton Rd. SW19 103 CY94
Newton Rd. W2 76 DB72
Newton Rd., Chig. 54 EV50
Newton Rd., Har. 45 CE54
Newton Rd., Islw. 87 CF82
Newton Rd., Pur. 133 DJ112
Newton Rd., Well. 96 EU83
Newton Rd., Wem. 74 CM66
Newton St. WC2 6 A8
Newton St. WC2 77 DL72
Newton Wk., Edg. 46 CP53
North Rd.
Newton Way N18 50 DQ50
Newton Wd. Rd., Ash. 144 CM116
Newtons Clo., Rain. 83 FF66
Newtons Yd. SW18 104 DB85
Wandsworth High St.
Newtown Rd., Uxb. 70 BH65
Newtown St. SW11 91 DH81
Strasburg Rd.
Niagara Ave. W5 87 CJ77
Niagara Clo. N1 78 DR68
Cropley St.
Niagara Clo. (Cheshunt), Wal.Cr. 23 DX29
Nibthwaite Rd., Har. 59 CE57
Nichol Clo. N14 49 DK46
Nichol La., Brom. 108 EG94
Nicholas Clo., Grnf. 72 CB68
Nicholas Clo., Wat. 29 BV37
Nicholas Ct. E13 80 EH69
Tunmarsh La.
Nicholas Dr., Sev. 155 FH126
Nicholas Gdns. W5 87 CK75
Nicholas La. EC4 7 L10
Nicholas Pas. EC4 78 DR72
Lombard St.
Nicholas Rd. E1 78 DW70
Nicholas Rd., Borwd. 32 CM44
Nicholas Rd., Croy. 133 DL105
Nicholas Rd., Dag. 68 EZ61
Nicholas Way, Nthwd. 43 BQ53
Nicholay Rd. N19 63 DK61
Fairbridge Rd.
Nicholes Rd., Houns. 86 CA84
Nicholl Rd., Epp. 25 ET31
Nicholl St. E2 78 DU67
Nicholls Ave., Uxb. 70 BN70
Nichollsfield Wk. N7 63 DM64
Hillmarton Rd.
Nichols Clo. N4 63 DM60
Osborne Rd.
Nichols Clo., Chess. 129 CJ107
Merritt Gdns.
Nichols Grn. W5 74 CL71
Montpelier Rd.
Nicholson Dr. (Bushey), Wat. 44 CC46
Nicholson Rd., Croy. 120 DT102
Nicholson St. SE1 10 F3
Nicholson St. SE1 77 DP74
Nicholson Way, Sev. 155 FK122
Nickelby Clo. SE28 82 EW72
Nickelby Clo., Uxb. 71 BP72
Dickens Ave.
Nicol Clo., Twick. 101 CH86
Cassilis Rd.
Nicola Clo., Har. 45 CD54
Nicola Clo., S.Croy. 134 DQ107
Nicola Ms., Ilf. 53 EP52
Nicoll Pl. NW4 61 CV58
Nicoll Rd. NW10 74 CS67
Nicoll Way, Borwd. 32 CR43
Nicolson Rd., Orp. 124 EX101
Nicosia Rd. SW18 104 DE87
Niederwald Rd. SE26 107 DY91
Nield Rd., Hayes 85 BT75
Nigel Clo., Nthlt. 72 BY67
Church Rd.
Nigel Ms., Ilf. 67 EP63
Nigel Playfair Ave. W6 89 CV77
King St.
Nigel Rd. E7 66 EJ64
Nigel Rd. SE15 92 DU83
Nigeria Rd. SE7 94 EJ80
Nightingale Ave. E4 52 EE50
Nightingale Ave., Lthd. 141 BR124
Nightingale Clo. E4 52 EE49
Nightingale Clo. W4 88 CQ79
Grove Pk. Ter.
Nightingale Clo., Abb.L. 15 BU31
College Rd.
Nightingale Clo., Cars. 118 DG103
Nightingale Clo., Cob. 128 BX111
Nightingale Clo., Pnr. 58 BW57
Nightingale Clo., Rad. 31 CF36
Nightingale Dr., Epsom 130 CP107
Nightingale Est. E5 64 DU62
Nightingale Gro. SE13 107 ED85
Nightingale La. E11 66 EH57
Nightingale La. N6 62 DE59
Nightingale La. N8 63 DL56
Nightingale La. SW4 105 DH86
Nightingale La. SW12 104 DF87
Nightingale La., Brom. 122 EJ96
Nightingale La., Rich. 102 CL87
Nightingale La., Sev. 154 FB130
Nightingale Ms. E3 79 DY68
Chisenhale Rd.
Nightingale Ms., Kings.T. 115 CK97
South La.
Nightingale Pl. SE18 95 EN79
Nightingale Pl. SW10 90 DC79
Fulham Rd.
Nightingale Pl., Rick. 42 BK45
Nightingale Rd. E5 64 DV62
Nightingale Rd. N9 36 DW44
Nightingale Rd. N22 49 DL53
Nightingale Rd. NW10 75 CT68
Nightingale Rd. W7 73 CF74
Nightingale Rd., Cars. 118 DF104
Nightingale Rd., Esher 128 BZ106
Nightingale Rd., Hmptn. 100 CA92
Nightingale Rd., Orp. 123 EQ100
Nightingale Rd., Rick. 42 BJ45
Nightingale Rd., S.Croy. 135 DX111
Nightingale Rd., Walt. 113 BV101
Nightingale Rd. (Bushey), Wat. 30 CA43
Nightingale Rd., W.Mol. 114 CB99
Nightingale Sq. SW12 104 DG87
Nightingale Vale SE18 95 EN79
Nightingale Wk. SW4 105 DH86
Nightingale Way E6 80 EL71
Nightingale Way, Swan. 125 FE97
Nightingales, Wal.Abb. 24 EE34
Roundhills
Nightingales, The, Stai. 98 BM87
Nile Path SE18 95 EN79
Jackson St.
Nile Rd. E13 80 EJ68
Nile St. N1 7 J2
Nile St. N1 78 DR69
Nile Ter. SE15 92 DT78
Nimbus Rd., Epsom 130 CR110
Nimegen Way SE22 106 DS85
East Dulwich Gro.
Nimmo Dr. (Bushey), Wat. 45 CD45
Nimrod Clo., Nthlt. 72 BX69
Britannia Clo.
Nimrod Pas. N1 78 DS65
Tottenham Rd.
Nimrod Rd. SW16 105 DH93
Nimrod Rd., Houns. 84 BN81
Northern Perimeter Rd.
Nine Acres Clo. E12 66 EL64
Nine Elms Ave., Uxb. 70 BK71
Nine Elms Clo., Felt. 99 BT88
Nine Elms Clo., Uxb. 70 BK72
Nine Elms La. SW8 91 DJ80
Nine Stiles Clo., Uxb. 70 BH65
Nineacres Way, Couls. 147 DL116
Ninefields, Wal.Abb. 24 EF33
Ninehams Clo., Cat. 148 DR120
Ninehams Gdns., Cat. 148 DR120
Ninehams Rd., Cat. 148 DR121
Ninehams Rd., West. 150 EJ121
Nineteenth Rd., Mitch. 119 DL98
Ninhams Wd., Orp. 137 EN105
Ninth Ave., Hayes 71 BU73
Nisbet Ho. E9 65 DX64
Homerton High St.
Nithdale Rd. SE18 95 EP80
Nithsdale Gro., Uxb. 57 BQ62
Tweeddale Gro.
Niton Clo., Barn. 33 CX44
Niton Rd., Rich. 88 CN83
Niton St. SW6 89 CX80
Niven Clo., Borwd. 32 CQ39
Nobel Dr., Hayes 85 BR80
Nobel Rd. N18 50 DW49
Noble St. EC2 7 H8
Noble St. EC2 78 DQ72
Noble St., Walt. 113 BV104
Noel Pk. Rd. N22 49 DN54
Noel Rd. E6 80 EL70
Noel Rd. N1 77 DP68
Noel Rd. W3 74 CN72
Noel Sq., Dag. 68 EW63
Noel St. W1 5 L9
Noel St. W1 77 DJ72
Noel Ter. SE23 106 DW89
Dartmouth Rd.
Noke La., St.Alb. 16 BY26
Noke Side, St.Alb. 16 CA27
Nolan Way E5 64 DU63
Nolton Pl., Edg. 46 CM53
Nonsuch Clo., Ilf. 53 EP51
Nonsuch Ct. Ave., Epsom 131 CV110
Nonsuch Wk., Sutt. 131 CW110
Nora Gdns. NW4 61 CX56
Norbiton Ave., Kings.T. 116 CN95
Norbiton Common Rd., Kings.T. 116 CP97
Norbiton Rd. E14 79 DZ72
Norbreck Gdns. NW10 74 CM69
Lytham Gro.
Norbreck Par. NW10 74 CM69
Lytham Gro.
Norbroke St. W12 75 CT73
Norburn St. W10 75 CY71
Chesterton Rd.
Norbury Ave. SW16 119 DM95
Norbury Ave., Houns. 87 CD84
Norbury Ave., Th.Hth. 119 DN96
Norbury Ave., Wat. 30 BW39
Norbury Clo. SW16 119 DN95
Norbury Ct. Rd. SW16 119 DL97
Norbury Cres. SW16 119 DM95
Norbury Cross SW16 119 DL97
Norbury Gdns., Rom. 68 EX57
Norbury Gro. NW7 46 CS48
Norbury Hill SW16 105 DN94
Norbury Ri. SW16 119 DL97
Norbury Rd. E4 51 EA50
Norbury Rd., Th.Hth. 120 DQ96
Norcombe Gdns., Har. 59 CJ58
Norcott Clo., Hayes 72 BW70
Willow Tree La.
Norcott Rd. N16 64 DU61
Norcroft Gdns. SE22 106 DU87
Norcutt Rd., Twick. 101 CE88
Nordenfeldt Rd., Erith 97 FD78
Norfield Rd., Dart. 111 FC91
Norfolk Ave. N13 49 DP51
Norfolk Ave. N15 64 DT58
Norfolk Ave., S.Croy. 134 DT110
Norfolk Ave., Wat. 30 BW38
Norfolk Clo. N2 62 DE55
Park Rd.
Norfolk Clo. N13 49 DP51
Norfolk Clo., Barn. 34 DG42
Norfolk Clo., Twick. 101 CH86
Cassilis Rd.
Norfolk Cres. W2 4 B8
Norfolk Cres. W2 76 DE72
Norfolk Cres., Sid. 109 ES87
Norfolk Gdns., Bexh. 96 EZ81
Norfolk Gdns., Borwd. 32 CR42
Norfolk Ho. SE3 94 EE79
Norfolk Ho. Rd. SW16 105 DK90
Norfolk Pl. W2 4 A8
Norfolk Pl. W2 76 DD72
Norfolk Pl., Well. 96 EU82
Norfolk Rd. E6 81 EM67
Norfolk Rd. E17 51 DX54
Norfolk Rd. NW8 76 DD67
Norfolk Rd. NW10 74 CS66
Norfolk Rd. SW19 104 DE94
Norfolk Rd., Bark. 81 ES66

Norfolk Rd., Barn. 34 DA41
Norfolk Rd., Dag. 69 FB64
Norfolk Rd., Enf. 36 DV44
Norfolk Rd., Esher 129 CE106
Norfolk Rd., Felt. 100 BW88
Norfolk Rd., Har. 58 CB57
Norfolk Rd., Ilf. 67 ES60
Norfolk Rd., Rick. 42 BL46
Norfolk Rd., Rom. 69 FC58
Norfolk Rd., Th.Hth. 120 DQ97
Norfolk Rd., Uxb. 70 BK65
Norfolk Row SE1 10 B8
Norfolk Row SE1 91 DM76
Norfolk Sq. W2 4 A9
Norfolk Sq. W2 76 DD72
Norfolk Sq. Ms. W2 4 A9
Norfolk St. E7 66 EG64
Norfolk Ter. W6 89 CY78
Field Rd.
Norgrove St. SW12 104 DG88
Norheads La., Warl. 150 EG119
Norheads La., West. 150 EH117
Norhyrst Ave. SE25 120 DT97
Nork Gdns., Bans. 131 CY114
Nork Ri., Bans. 145 CX115
Nork Way, Bans. 131 CY114
Norland Pl. W11 75 CY74
Norland Rd. W11 75 CX74
Norland Sq. W11 75 CY74
Norlands Cres., Chis. 123 EP95
Norlands Gate, Chis. 123 EP95
Norley Vale SW15 103 CU88
Norlington Rd. E10 65 EC60
Norlington Rd. E11 65 ED60
Norman Ave. N22 49 DP53
Norman Ave., Epsom 131 CT112
Norman Ave., Felt. 100 BY89
Norman Ave., S.Croy. 134 DQ110
Norman Ave., Sthl. 72 BY73
Norman Ave., Twick. 101 CH87
Norman Clo., Orp. 123 EQ104
Norman Clo., Rom. 55 FB54
Norman Clo., Wal.Abb. 23 ED33
Norman Ct., Ilf. 67 ER59
Norman Ct., Pot.B. 20 DC30
Norman Cres., Houns. 86 BX80
Norman Cres., Pnr. 44 BW53
Norman Gro. E3 79 DY68
Norman Rd. E6 81 EM70
Norman Rd. E11 65 ED61
Norman Rd. N15 64 DT57
Norman Rd. SE10 93 EB80
Norman Rd. SW19 104 DC94
Norman Rd., Ashf. 99 BR93
Norman Rd., Belv. 97 FB76
Norman Rd., Horn. 69 FG59
Norman Rd., Ilf. 67 EP64
Norman Rd., Sutt. 132 DA106
Norman Rd., Th.Hth. 119 DP99
Norman St. EC1 7 H3
Norman Way N14 49 DL47
Norman Way W3 74 CP71
Normanby Clo. SW15 103 CZ85
Manfred Rd.
Normanby Rd. NW10 61 CT63
Normand Gdns. W14 89 CY79
Greyhound Rd.
Normand Ms. W14 89 CY79
Normand Rd.
Normand Rd. W14 89 CZ79
Normandy Ave., Barn. 33 CZ43
Normandy Dr., Hayes 71 BQ72
Normandy Rd. SW9 91 DN81
Normandy Ter. E16 80 EH72
Normandy Way, Erith 97 FE81
Normanhurst, Ashf. 98 BN92
Normanhurst Ave., Bexh. 96 EX81
Normanhurst Dr., Twick. 101 CH85
St. Margarets Rd.
Normanhurst Rd. SW2 105 DM89
Normanhurst Rd., Orp. 124 EV96
Normanhurst Rd., Walt. 114 BX103
Norman's Bldgs. EC1 78 DQ69
Ironmonger Row
Normans Clo. NW10 74 CR65
Normans Clo., Uxb. 70 BM71
Normans Mead NW10 74 CR65
Normansfield Ave., Tedd. 101 CJ94
Normansfield Clo. (Bushey), Wat. 44 CB45
Normanshire Ave. E4 51 EC49
Normanshire Dr.
Normanshire Dr. E4 51 EA49
Normanton Ave. SW19 104 DA89
Normanton Pk. E4 52 EE48
Normanton Rd., S.Croy. 134 DS106
Normanton St. SE23 107 DX89
Normington Clo. SW16 105 DN92
Norrice Lea N2 62 DD57
Norris St. SW1 9 M1
Norris Way, Dart. 97 FF83
Norroy Rd. SW15 89 CX84
Norrys Clo., Barn. 34 DF42
Norrys Rd., Barn. 34 DF42
Norseman Clo., Ilf. 68 EV60
Norseman Way, Grnf. 72 CB67
Olympic Way
Norstead Pl. SW15 103 CU89
Norsted La., Orp. 138 EU112
North Access Rd. E17 65 DX58
North Acre NW9 46 CS53
North Acre, Bans. 145 CZ116
North Acton Rd. NW10 74 CR68
North App., Nthwd. 43 BQ47
North App., Wat. 29 BT35
North Audley St. W1 4 F9
North Audley St. W1 76 DG73
North Ave. N18 50 DU49
North Ave. W13 73 CH71
North Ave., Cars. 132 DG108
North Ave., Har. 58 CB58
North Ave., Hayes 71 BU73
North Ave., Rad. 18 CL32
North Ave., Rich. 88 CN81
Sandycoombe Rd.
North Ave., Sthl. 72 BZ73
North Ave., Walt. 127 BS109
North Bank NW8 4 B3
North Bank NW8 76 DE69
North Birkbeck Rd. E11 65 ED62
North Branch Ave. W10 75 CW69
Harrow Rd.
North Carriage Dr. W2 4 B10
North Carriage Dr. W2 76 DE73
North Circular Rd. E4 51 DZ52
North Circular Rd. E18 52 EH53
North Circular Rd. N3 61 CZ56
North Circular Rd. N12 48 DD53
North Circular Rd. N13 49 DN50
North Circular Rd. NW2 60 CS62
North Circular Rd. NW10 60 CS63
North Circular Rd. NW11 61 CX58
North Clo., Barn. 33 CW43
North Clo., Bexh. 96 EX84
North Clo., Chig. 54 EU50
North Clo., Dag. 82 FA67
North Clo., Felt. 99 BR86
North Rd.
North Clo., Mord. 117 CY98
North Clo., St.Alb. 16 CB25
North Colonnade E14 79 EA74
North Common, Wey. 127 BP105
North Common Rd. W5 74 CL73
North Common Rd., Uxb. 56 BK64
North Cotts., St.Alb. 17 CG25
North Countess Rd. E17 51 DZ54
North Ct. W1 5 L6
North Ct., Rick. 42 BG46
Hall Clo.
North Cray Rd., Bex. 110 FA89
North Cray Rd., Sid. 110 EY93
North Cres. E16 79 ED70
North Cres. N3 47 CZ54
North Cres. WC1 5 M6
North Cross Rd. SE22 106 DT85
North Cross Rd., Ilf. 67 EQ56
North Dene NW7 46 CR48
North Dene, Houns. 86 CB81
North Down, S.Croy. 134 DS111
North Downs Cres., Croy. 135 EB110
North Downs Rd., Croy. 135 EB109
North Downs Way, Sev. 153 FD118
North Downs Way, West. 151 ER121
North Dr. SW16 105 DJ91
North Dr., Houns. 86 CC82
North Dr., Orp. 137 ES105
North Dr., Ruis. 57 BS59
North End NW3 62 DC61
North End, Buck.H. 52 EJ45
North End, Croy. 120 DQ103
North End Ave. NW3 62 DC61
North End Cres. W14 89 CZ77
North End Ho. W14 89 CY77
North End La., Orp. 137 EN111
North End Par. W14 89 CY77
North End Rd.
North End Rd. NW11 62 DA60
North End Rd. SW6 89 CZ79
North End Rd. W14 89 CY77
North End Rd., Wem. 60 CN62
North End Way NW3 62 DC61
North Eyot Gdns. W6 89 CT78
St. Peter's Sq.
North Feltham Trd. Est., Felt. 99 BV85
North Flockton St. SE16 92 DU75
Chambers St.
North Gdn. E14 79 DZ74
Westferry Circ.
North Gdns. SW19 104 DD94
North Glade, The, Bex. 110 EZ87
Camden Rd.
North Gower St. NW1 5 L3
North Gower St. NW1 77 DJ69
North Grn. NW9 46 CS52
Clayton Fld.
North Gro. N6 62 DG59
North Gro. N15 64 DR57
North Hatton Rd. (Heathrow Airport), Houns. 85 BR81
North Hill N6 62 DF58
North Hill Ave. N6 62 DF58
North Hyde Gdns., Hayes 85 BU77
North Hyde La., Houns. 86 BY79
North Hyde La., Sthl. 86 BX78
North Hyde Rd., Hayes 85 BS76
North La., Tedd. 101 CF93
North Lo. Clo. SW15 103 CX85
Westleigh Ave.
North Mall N9 50 DV47
St. Martins Rd.
North Ms. WC1 6 C5
North Ms. WC1 77 DM70
North Orbital Rd., St.Alb. 16 BY30
North Orbital Rd., Wat. 15 BV34
North Par., Chess. 130 CL106
North Pk. SE9 109 EN86
North Pas. SW18 104 DA85
North Peckham Est. SE15 92 DS80
North Perimeter Rd., Uxb. 70 BL69
Kingston La.
North Pl., Mitch. 104 DF94
North Pl., Tedd. 101 CF93
North Pl., Wal.Abb. 23 EB33
Highbridge St.
North Pole La., Kes. 136 EF107
North Pole Rd. W10 75 CW71
North Ride W2 8 B1
North Ride W2 76 DE74
North Riding, St.Alb. 16 BZ30
North Rd. N6 62 DG59
North Rd. N7 77 DL65
North Rd. N9 50 DV46
North Rd. SE18 95 ES77
North Rd. SW19 104 DC93
North Rd. W5 87 CK76
North Rd., Belv. 97 FB76
North Rd., Brent. 88 CL79
North Rd., Brom. 122 EH95
North Rd., Dart. 111 FF87
North Rd., Edg. 46 CP53
North Rd., Felt. 99 BR86
North Rd., Hayes 71 BR71
North Rd., Ilf. 67 ES61
North Rd., Rich. 88 CN83
North Rd., Rom. 68 EY57
North Rd., Rom. (Havering-atte-Bower) 55 FE48
North Rd., Sthl. 72 CA72
North Rd., Surb. 115 CK100
North Rd., Wal.Cr. 23 DY33
North Rd., Walt. 128 BW106
North Rd., West Dr. 84 BM76
North Rd., W.Wick. 121 EB102
North Row W1 4 E10
North Row W1 76 DF73
North Several SE3 93 ED82
Orchard Dr.
North Sq. N9 50 DV47
St. Martins Rd.
North Sq. NW11 62 DA57
North St. E13 80 EH68
North St. NW4 61 CW57
North St. SW4 91 DJ83
North St., Bark. 81 EP65
North St., Bexh. 96 FA84
North St., Brom. 122 EG95
North St., Cars. 118 DF104
North St., Islw. 87 CG83
North St., Lthd. 143 CG121
North St., Rom. 69 FD55
North St. Pas. E13 80 EH68
North St.
North Tenter St. E1 78 DT72
North Ter. SW3 8 B7
North Verbena Gdns. W6 89 CU78
St. Peter's Sq.
North Vw. SW19 103 CW92
North Vw. W5 73 CJ70
North Vw., Ilf. 54 EU52
North Vw., Pnr. 58 BW59
North Vw. Cres. NW10 61 CT63
North Vw. Cres., Epsom 145 CV117
North Vw. Dr., Wdf.Grn. 52 EK54
North Vw. Rd. N8 63 DK55
North Vw. Rd., Sev. 155 FJ121
Seal Rd.
North Vill. NW1 77 DK65
North Wk. W2 76 DC73
Bayswater Rd.
North Wk., Croy. 135 EB107
North Way N9 51 DX47
North Way N11 49 DJ51
North Way NW9 60 CP55
North Way, Mord. 117 CY97
North Way, Pnr. 58 BW55
North Way, Uxb. 70 BL66
North Weald Ind. Est., Epp. 26 FA26
North Western Ave., Wat. 29 BR35
North Wf. Rd. W2 76 DD71
North Woolwich Rd. E16 80 EG74
North Woolwich Roundabout E16 80 EK74
North Woolwich Rd.
North Worple Way SW14 88 CR83
Northall Rd., Bexh. 97 FC82
Northampton Gro. N1 78 DR65
Northampton Pk.
Northampton Pk. N1 78 DQ65
Northampton Rd. EC1 6 E4
Northampton Rd. EC1 77 DN70
Northampton Rd., Croy. 120 DU103
Northampton Rd., Enf. 37 DY42
Northampton Sq. EC1 6 F3
Northampton Sq. EC1 77 DP69
Northampton St. N1 78 DQ66
Northanger Rd. SW16 105 DL93
Northaw Pk., Pot.B. 20 DF32
Northaw Rd. E. (Cuffley), Pot.B. 21 DK31
Northaw Rd. W., Pot.B. 20 DG30
Northbank Rd. E17 51 EC54
Northborough Rd. SW16 119 DK97
Northbourne, Brom. 122 EG101
Northbourne Rd. SW4 91 DK84
Northbrook Dr., Nthwd. 43 BS53
Northbrook Rd. N22 49 DL52
Northbrook Rd. SE13 107 ED85
Northbrook Rd., Barn. 33 CY44
Northbrook Rd., Croy. 120 DR99
Northbrook Rd., Ilf. 67 EN61
Northburgh St. EC1 6 G5
Northburgh St. EC1 77 DP70
Northchurch SE17 11 L10
Northchurch Rd. N1 78 DR66
Northchurch Rd., Wem. 74 CN65
Northchurch Ter. N1 78 DS66
Northcliffe Clo., Wor.Pk. 116 CS104
Northcliffe Dr. N20 47 CZ46
Northcote, Add. 126 BK105
Northcote Ave. W5 74 CL73
Northcote Ave., Islw. 101 CG85
Northcote Ave., Sthl. 72 BY73
Northcote Ave., Surb. 116 CN101
Northcote Pk., Lthd. 128 CC114
Northcote Rd. E17 65 DY56
Northcote Rd. NW10 74 CS66
Northcote Rd. SW11 104 DE85
Northcote Rd., Croy. 120 DR100
Northcote Rd., N.Mal. 116 CR97
Northcote Rd., Sid. 109 ES91
Northcote Rd., Twick. 101 CG85
Northcott Ave. N22 49 DL53
Northcotts, Abb.L. 15 BR33
Long Elms
Northcourt, Rick. 42 BG46
Springwell Ave.
Northcroft Rd. W13 87 CH75
Northcroft Rd., Epsom 130 CR108
Northcroft Ter. W13 87 CH75
Northcroft Rd.
Northdene, Chig. 53 ER50
Northdene Gdns. N15 64 DT58
Northdown Clo., Ruis. 57 BT62
Northdown Gdns., Ilf. 67 ES57
Northdown Rd., Cat. 149 EA123
Northdown Rd., Horn. 69 FH59
Northdown Rd., Sutt. 132 DA110
Northdown Rd., Well. 96 EV82
Northdown St. N1 77 DL68
Northend Rd., Dart. 97 FF81
Northend Rd., Erith 97 FF81
Northern Ave. N9 50 DS47
Northern Perimeter Rd., Houns. 85 BP81
Northern Perimeter Rd. W., Houns. 84 BK81
Northern Relief Rd., Bark. 81 EP66
Northern Rd. E13 80 EH68
Northern Service Rd., Barn. 33 CY41
Northernhay Wk., Mord. 117 CY98
Northey Ave., Sutt. 131 CX110
Northey St. E14 79 DY73
Northfield, Loug. 38 EK42
Northfield Ave. W5 73 CH74
Northfield Ave. W13 73 CH74
Northfield Ave., Orp. 124 EW100
Northfield Ave., Pnr. 58 BX56
Northfield Clo., Brom. 122 EL95
Northfield Clo., Hayes 85 BT76
Northfield Ct., Stai. 112 BH95
Northfield Cres., Sutt. 131 CY105
Northfield Gdns., Dag. 68 EZ63
Northfield Rd.
Northfield Gdns., Wat. 30 BW37
Northfield Pk., Hayes 85 BS76
Northfield Path, Dag. 68 EZ63
Connor Rd.
Northfield Pl., Wey. 127 BP108
Northfield Rd. E6 81 EM66
Northfield Rd. N16 64 DS59
Northfield Rd. W13 87 CH75
Northfield Rd., Barn. 34 DE41
Northfield Rd., Borwd. 32 CP39
Northfield Rd., Cob. 127 BU113
Northfield Rd., Dag. 68 EZ63
Northfield Rd., Enf. 36 DV43
Northfield Rd., Houns. 86 BX80
Northfield Rd., Stai. 112 BH95
Northfield Rd., Wal.Cr. 23 DY32
Northfields SW18 90 DA84
Northfields, Ash. 144 CL119
Northfields Ind. Est., Wem. 74 CN67
Northfields Rd. W3 74 CP71
Northgate, Nthwd. 43 BQ52
Northgate Dr. NW9 60 CS58
Northgate Path, Borwd. 32 CM38
Northiam N12 48 DA49
Northiam St. E9 78 DV67
Northington St. WC1 6 C5
Northington St. WC1 77 DM70
Northlands, Pot.B. 20 DD31
Northlands Ave., Orp. 137 ES105
Northlands St. SE5 92 DQ82
Northolm, Edg. 46 CR49
Northolme Gdns., Edg. 46 CN53
Northolme Ri., Orp. 123 ES103
Northolme Rd. N5 64 DQ63
Northolt Ave., Ruis. 57 BV64
Northolt Gdns., Grnf. 59 CF64
Northolt Ind. Est., Nthlt. 72 CB66
Northolt Rd., Har. 58 CB63
Northolt Rd., Houns. 84 BK81
Northover, Brom. 108 EF90
Northport St. N1 78 DR67
Northrop Rd., Houns. 85 BS82
Northside Rd., Brom. 122 EG95
Mitchell Way
Northspur Rd., Sutt. 118 DA104
Northstead Rd. SW2 105 DN89
Northumberland All. EC3 7 N9
Northumberland All. EC3 78 DS72
Northumberland Ave. E12 66 EJ60
Northumberland Ave. WC2 9 P2
Northumberland Ave. WC2 77 DL74
Northumberland Ave., Enf. 36 DV39
Northumberland Ave., Islw. 87 CF81
Northumberland Ave., Well. 95 ER84
Northumberland Clo., Erith 97 FC80
Northumberland Clo., Stai. 98 BL86
Northumberland Cres., Felt. 99 BS86
Northumberland Gdns. N9 50 DT48
Northumberland Gdns., Brom. 123 EN98
Northumberland Gdns., Islw. 87 CG80
Northumberland Ave.
Northumberland Gdns., Mitch. 119 DK99
Northumberland Gro. N17 50 DV52
Northumberland Pk. N17 50 DT52
Northumberland Pk., Erith 97 FC80
Northumberland Pl. W2 76 DA72
Northumberland Pl., Rich. 101 CK86
Northumberland Rd. E6 80 EL72
Northumberland Rd. E17 65 EA59
Northumberland Rd., Barn. 34 DC44
Northumberland Rd., Har. 58 BZ57
Northumberland Row, Twick. 101 CE88
Colne Rd.
Northumberland St. WC2 9 P2
Northumberland St. WC2 77 DL74
Northumberland Way, Erith 97 FC81
Northumbria St. E14 79 EA72
Northview, Swan. 125 FE96
Northway NW7 47 CU52
Northway NW11 62 DB57
Northway, Rick. 42 BK45
Northway, Wall. 133 DJ105
Northway Circ. NW7 46 CR49
Northway Cres. NW7 46 CR49
Northway Rd. SE5 92 DQ83
Northway Rd., Croy. 120 DT100
Northweald La., Kings.T. 101 CK92
Northwest Pl. N1 77 DN68
Chapel Mkt.
Northwick Ave., Har. 59 CG58
Northwick Circle, Har. 59 CJ58
Northwick Clo. NW8 76 DD70
Northwick Ter.
Northwick Pk. Rd., Har. 59 CF58
Northwick Rd., Wat. 44 BW49
Northwick Rd., Wem. 73 CK67
Northwick Ter. NW8 76 DD70
Northwick Wk., Har. 59 CF59
Peterborough Rd.
Northwold Dr., Pnr. 58 BW55
Cuckoo Hill
Northwold Est. E5 64 DU61
Northwold Rd. E5 64 DU61
Northwold Rd. N16 64 DT61
Northwood Ave., Horn. 69 FG63
Northwood Ave., Pur. 133 DN112
Northwood Clo., Wal.Cr. 22 DT27
Northwood Gdns. N12 48 DD50
Northwood Gdns., Grnf. 59 CF64
Northwood Gdns., Ilf. 67 EN56
Northwood Hall N6 63 DJ59
Northwood Ho. SE27 106 DR91
Northwood Pl., Erith 96 EZ76
Northwood Rd. N6 63 DH59
Northwood Rd. SE23 107 DZ88
Northwood Rd., Cars. 132 DG107
Northwood Rd., Houns. 84 BK81
Northwood Rd., Th.Hth. 119 DP96
Northwood Rd., Uxb. 42 BJ53
Northwood Way SE19 106 DR93
Roman Ri.
Northwood Way, Nthwd. 43 BU53
Northwood Way, Uxb. 42 BK53
Norton Ave., Surb. 116 CP101
Norton Clo. E4 51 EA50
Norton Clo., Borwd. 32 CN39
Norton Clo., Enf. 36 DV40
Brick La.
Norton Folgate E1 7 N6
Norton Folgate E1 78 DS71
Norton Gdns. SW16 119 DL96
Norton La., Cob. 141 BT119
Norton Rd. E10 65 DZ60
Norton Rd., Dag. 83 FD65
Norton Rd., Uxb. 70 BK69
Norton Rd., Wem. 73 CK65
Norval Rd., Wem. 59 CH61
Norway Gate SE16 93 DY76
Norway Pl. E14 79 DZ72
East India Dock Rd.
Norway St. SE10 93 EB79
Norwich Ho. E14 79 EB72
Cordelia St.
Norwich Ms., Ilf. 68 EU60
Ashgrove Rd.
Norwich Pl., Bexh. 96 FA84
Norwich Rd. E7 66 EG64
Norwich Rd., Dag. 82 FA68
Norwich Rd., Grnf. 72 CB67
Norwich Rd., Nthwd. 57 BT55
Norwich Rd., Th.Hth. 120 DQ97
Norwich St. EC4 6 D8
Norwich St. EC4 77 DN72
Norwich Wk., Edg. 46 CQ52
Norwich Way, Rick. 29 BP41
Norwood Ave., Rom. 69 FD59
Norwood Ave., Wem. 74 CM67
Norwood Clo., Sthl. 86 CA77
Norwood Clo., Twick. 101 CD89
Fourth Cross Rd.

255

Oaks Way, Epsom 145 CV119
Epsom La. N.
Oaks Way, Ken. 134 DQ114
Oaks Way, Surb. 115 CK103
Oaksford Ave. SE26 106 DV90
Oakshade Rd., Brom. 107 ED91
Oakshade Rd., Lthd. 128 CC114
Oakshaw Rd. SW18 104 DB87
Oakside, Uxb. 70 BH65
Oakthorpe Rd. N13 49 DN50
Oaktree Ave. N13 49 DP48
Oaktree Clo., Wal.Cr. 21 DP28
Oaktree Gro., Ilf. 67 ER64
Oakview Clo., Wal.Cr. 22 DV28
Oakview Gdns. N2 62 DD56
Oakview Gro., Croy. 121 DY102
Oakview Rd. SE6 107 EB92
Oakway SW20 117 CW98
Oakway, Brom. 121 ED96
Oakway Clo., Bex. 110 EY86
Oakways SE9 109 EP86
Oakwood, Wall. 133 DH109
Oakwood, Wal.Abb. 37 ED35
Roundhills
Oakwood Ave. N14 49 DK45
Oakwood Ave., Beck. 121 EC96
Oakwood Ave., Borwd. 32 CP42
Oakwood Ave., Brom. 122 EH97
Oakwood Ave., Mitch. 118 DD96
Oakwood Ave., Pur. 133 DP112
Oakwood Ave., Sthl. 72 CA73
Oakwood Clo. N14 35 DJ44
Oakwood Clo., Chis. 109 EM93
Oakwood Clo., Wdf.Grn. 52 EL51
Green Wk.
Oakwood Ct. W14 89 CZ76
Oakwood Cres. N21 35 DL44
Oakwood Cres., Grnf. 73 CG65
Oakwood Dr. SE19 106 DR93
Oakwood Dr., Bexh. 97 FD84
Oakwood Dr., Edg. 46 CQ51
Oakwood Dr., Sev. 155 FH123
Oakwood Gdns., Ilf. 67 ET61
Oakwood Gdns., Orp. 123 EQ103
Oakwood Gdns., Sutt. 118 DA103
Oakwood Hill, Loug. 39 EM44
Oakwood Hill Ind. Est., Loug. 39 EP43
Oakwood La. W14 89 CZ76
Oakwood Pk. Rd. N14 49 DK45
Oakwood Pl., Croy. 119 DN100
Oakwood Rd. NW11 62 DA56
Oakwood Rd. SW20 117 CU95
Oakwood Rd., Croy. 119 DN100
Oakwood Rd., Orp. 123 EQ103
Oakwood Rd., Pnr. 43 BV54
Oakwood Rd., St.Alb. 16 BY29
Oakwood Vw. N14 35 DK43
Oakworth Rd. W10 75 CW71
Oasthouse Way, Orp. 124 EV98
Oat La. EC2 7 J8
Oat La. EC2 78 DQ72
Oates Clo., Brom. 121 ED97
Oates Rd., Rom. 55 FB50
Oatfield Rd., Orp. 123 ET102
Oatfield Rd., Tad. 145 CV121
Oatland Ri. E17 51 DY54
Oatlands Ave., Wey. 127 BQ106
Oatlands Chase, Wey. 113 BS104
Oatlands Clo., Wey. 127 BQ105
Oatlands Dr., Wey. 113 BR104
Oatlands Grn., Wey. 113 BR104
Oatlands Dr.
Oatlands Mere, Wey. 113 BR104
Oatlands Rd., Enf. 36 DW39
Oatlands Rd., Tad. 145 CY119
Oban Clo. E13 80 EJ70
Oban Ho., Bark. 81 ER68
Wheelers Cross
Oban Rd. E13 80 EJ69
Oban Rd. SE25 120 DR98
Oban St. E14 79 ED72
Oberon Clo., Borwd. 32 CQ39
Oberon Way, Shep. 112 BL97
Oberstein Rd. SW11 90 DD84
Oborne Clo. SE24 105 DP85
Observatory Gdns. W8 90 DA75
Observatory Rd. SW14 88 CQ84
Occupation La. SE18 95 EP81
Occupation La. W5 87 CK77
Occupation Rd. SE17 11 H10
Occupation Rd. SE17 92 DQ78
Occupation Rd. W13 87 CH75
Occupation Rd., Wat. 29 BV43
Ocean Est. E1 79 DX70
Ocean St. E1 79 DX71
Ockendon Rd. N1 78 DR65
Ockham Dr., Lthd. 141 BR124
Ockham Dr., Orp. 110 EU94
Ockham La., Cob. 141 BR120
Ockham La., Wok. 140 BN121
Ockham Rd. N., Lthd. 141 BQ123
Ockham Rd. N., Wok. 140 BL120
Ockley Rd. SW16 105 DL91
Ockley Rd., Croy. 119 DM101
Octagon Arc. EC2 7 M7
Octagon Rd., Walt. 127 BS109
Octavia Clo., Mitch. 118 DE99
Octavia Rd., Islw. 87 CF83
Octavia St. SW11 90 DE81
Octavia Way SE28 82 EV73
Booth Clo.
Octavia Way, Stai. 98 BG93
Octavius St. SE8 93 EA80
Odard Rd., W.Mol. 114 CA98
Down St.
Oddesey Rd., Borwd. 32 CP39
Odessa Rd. E7 66 EF63
Odessa Rd. NW10 75 CU68
Odessa St. SE16 93 DZ75
Odger St. SW11 90 DF82
Odhams Wk. WC2 5 P9
Odyssey Business Pk., Ruis. 57 BV64
Offas Mead E9 65 DY63
Lindisfarne Way
Offenbach Ho. E2 79 DX68
Mace St.
Offenham Rd. SE9 109 EM91
Offerton Rd. SW4 91 DJ83
Offham Slope N12 47 CZ50
Offley Rd. SW9 91 DN80
Offord Clo. N17 50 DU52
Offord Rd. N1 77 DM66
Offord St. N1 77 DM66
Ogilby St. SE18 95 EM77
Oglander Rd. SE15 92 DT84
Ogle St. W1 5 K6
Ogle St. W1 77 DJ71
Oglethorpe Rd., Dag. 68 EZ62
Ohio Rd. E13 80 EF70
Oil Mill La. W6 89 CU78
Okeburn Rd. SW17 104 DG92
Okehampton Clo. N12 48 DD50
Okehampton Cres., Well. 96 EV81
Okehampton Rd. NW10 75 CW67
Okemore Gdns., Orp. 124 EW98
Olaf St. W11 75 CX73
Old Acre, Wok. 126 BG114
Old Ave., Wey. 127 BQ108
Old Bailey EC4 6 G9
Old Bailey EC4 77 DP72
Old Barn Clo., Sutt. 131 CY108
Old Barn La., Ken. 148 DT116
Old Barn La., Rick. 28 BM43
Old Barn Rd., Epsom 144 CQ117
Old Barn Way, Bexh. 97 FD83
Old Barrack Yd. SW1 8 F5
Old Barrowfield E15 80 EE67
New Plaistow Rd.
Old Bethnal Grn. Rd. E2 78 DU69
Old Bexley La., Bex. 111 FD89
Old Bexley La., Dart. 111 FF88
Old Bond St. W1 9 K1
Old Bond St. W1 77 DJ73
Old Brewers Yd. WC2 5 P9
Old Brewery Ms. NW3 62 DD63
Hampstead High St.
Old Bri. Clo., Nthlt. 72 CA68
Old Bri. St., Kings.T. 115 CK96
Old Broad St. EC2 7 L9
Old Broad St. EC2 78 DR72
Old Bromley Rd., Brom. 107 ED92
Old Brompton Rd. SW5 90 DB78
Old Brompton Rd. SW7 90 DB78
Old Bldgs. WC2 6 D8
Old Burlington St. W1 5 K10
Old Burlington St. W1 77 DJ73
Old Carriageway, The, Sev. 154 FC122
Old Castle St. E1 7 P8
Old Castle St. E1 78 DT72
Old Cavendish St. W1 5 H8
Old Cavendish St. W1 77 DH72
Old Change Ct. EC4 78 DQ72
Carter La.
Old Chapel Rd., Swan. 125 FC101
Old Charlton Rd., Shep. 113 BQ99
Old Chelsea Ms. SW3 90 DD79
Danvers St.
Old Chestnut Ave., Esher 128 CA107
Old Ch. La. NW9 60 CR61
Old Ch. La., Grnf. 73 CG69
Perivale La.
Old Ch. La., Stan. 45 CH50
Old Ch. Path, Esher 128 CB105
High St.
Old Ch. Rd. E1 79 DX72
Old Ch. Rd. E4 51 EA49
Old Ch. St. SW3 90 DD78
Old Claygate La., Esher 129 CG107
Old Clem Sq. SE18 95 EN79
Kempt St.
Old Common Rd., Cob. 127 BU112
Old Compton St. W1 5 M10
Old Compton St. W1 77 DK73
Old Cote Dr., Houns. 86 CA79
Old Ct., Ash. 144 CL119
Old Ct. Pl. W8 90 DB75
Old Deer Pk. Gdns., Rich. 88 CL83
Old Devonshire Rd. SW12 105 DH87
Old Dock Clo., Rich. 88 CN79
Watcombe Cotts.
Old Dover Rd. SE3 94 EG80
Old Esher Clo., Walt. 128 BX106
Old Esher Rd.
Old Esher Rd., Walt. 128 BX106
Old Farleigh Rd., S.Croy. 134 DW110
Old Farleigh Rd., Warl. 149 DY117
Old Fm. Ave. N14 49 DJ45
Old Fm. Ave., Sid. 109 ER88
Old Fm. Clo., Houns. 86 BZ84
Old Fm. Gdns., Swan. 125 FF97
Old Fm. Pas., Hmptn. 114 CC95
Old Fm. Rd. N2 48 DD53
Old Fm. Rd., Hmptn. 100 BZ93
Old Fm. Rd., West Dr. 84 BK75
Old Fm. Rd. E., Sid. 110 EU89
Old Fm. Rd. W., Sid. 109 ET89
Old Farmhouse Dr., Lthd. 143 CD115
Old Fish St. Hill EC4 7 H10
Old Fleet La. EC4 6 F8
Old Fold Clo., Barn. 33 CZ39
Old Fold La.
Old Fold La., Barn. 33 CZ39
Old Fold Vw., Barn. 33 CW41
Old Ford Rd. E2 78 DW68
Old Ford Rd. E3 79 DX68
Old Forge Clo., Stan. 45 CG49
Old Forge Clo., Wat. 15 BU33
Old Forge Cres., Shep. 113 BP100
Old Forge Ms. W12 89 CV75
Goodwin Rd.
Old Forge Rd., Enf. 36 DT38
Old Forge Way, Sid. 110 EV91
Old Fox Clo., Cat. 147 DP121
Old Fox Footpath, S.Croy. 134 DS108
Essenden Rd.
Old Gannon Clo., Nthwd. 43 BQ50
Old Gdn., The, Sev. 154 FD123
Old Gloucester St. WC1 6 A6
Old Gloucester St. WC1 77 DL71
Old Hall Clo., Pnr. 44 BY53
Old Hall Dr., Pnr. 44 BY53
Old Harrow La., West. 151 EQ119
Old Hatch Manor, Ruis. 57 BT59
Old Hill, Chis. 123 EN95
Old Hill, Orp. 137 ER107
Old Homesdale Rd., Brom. 122 EJ98
Old Hospital Clo. SW12 104 DF88
Old Ho. Clo. SW19 103 CY92
Old Ho. Clo., Epsom 131 CT110
Old Ho. Gdns., Twick. 101 CJ86
Old Ho. La., Kings L. 28 BL35
Old Howlett's La., Ruis. 57 BR58
Bury St.
Old Jamaica Rd. SE16 92 DU76
Old James St. SE15 92 DV83
Old Jewry EC2 7 K9
Old Jewry EC2 78 DR72
Old Kent Rd. SE1 11 M8
Old Kent Rd. SE1 92 DS77
Old Kent Rd. SE15 92 DV79
Old Kenton La. NW9 60 CP57
Old Kingston Rd., Wor.Pk. 116 CQ104
Old La., Cob. 141 BP117
Old La., West. 150 EK121
Old La. Gdns., Cob. 141 BT122
Old Lo. La., Ken. 147 DN116
Old Lo. La., Pur. 133 DM113
Old Lo. Pl., Twick. 101 CH86
St. Margarets Rd.
Old Lo. Way, Stan. 45 CG50
Old London Rd., Epsom 145 CU118
Old London Rd., Sev. 138 EY109
Old London Rd. (Knockholt Pound), Sev. 152 EY115
Old Maidstone Rd., Sid. 110 EZ94
Old Malden La., Wor.Pk. 116 CR104
Old Manor Dr., Islw. 100 CC86
Old Manor Ho. Ms., Shep. 112 BN97
Squires Bri. Rd.
Old Manor Way, Bexh. 97 FD82
Old Manor Way, Chis. 109 EM92
Old Manor Yd. SW5 90 DB77
Earls Ct. Rd.
Old Marylebone Rd. NW1 4 C7
Old Marylebone Rd. NW1 76 DE71
Old Ms., Har. 59 CE57
Hindes Rd.
Old Mill Ct. E18 66 EJ55
Old Mill La. W6 89 CU78
Old Mill La., Uxb. 70 BH71
Old Mill Pl., Rom. 69 FD58
Old Mill Rd. SE18 95 ER79
Old Mill Rd., Kings L. 15 BQ34
Old Mill Rd., Uxb. 56 BG62
Old Mitre Ct. EC4 77 DN72
Fleet St.
Old Montague St. E1 78 DU71
Old Nichol St. E2 7 P4
Old Nichol St. E2 78 DT70
Old N. St. WC1 6 B6
Old Oak Ave., Couls. 146 DE119
Old Oak Common La. NW10 74 CS70
Old Oak Common La. W3 74 CS71
Old Oak La. NW10 75 CT69
Old Oak Rd. W3 75 CT73
Old Oaks, Wal.Abb. 24 EE32
Old Orchard, St.Alb. 16 CC26
Old Orchard, Sun. 114 BW96
Old Orchard, W.Byf. 126 BM112
Old Orchard, The NW3 62 DF63
Nassington Rd.
Old Orchard Clo., Barn. 34 DD38
Old Orchard Clo., Uxb. 70 BN72
Old Otford Rd., Sev. 153 FH117
Old Palace La., Rich. 101 CJ85
Old Palace Rd., Croy. 119 DP104
Old Palace Rd., Wey. 113 BP104
Old Palace Ter., Rich. 101 CK85
King St.
Old Palace Yd. SW1 9 P6
Old Palace Yd. SW1 91 DL76
Old Palace Yd., Rich. 101 CK85
Old Paradise St. SE11 10 B8
Old Paradise St. SE11 91 DM77
Old Pk. Ave. SW12 104 DG86
Old Pk. Ave., Enf. 36 DQ42
Old Pk. Gro., Enf. 36 DQ42
Old Pk. La. W1 8 G3
Old Pk. La. W1 76 DG74
Old Pk. Ms., Houns. 86 BZ80
Old Pk. Ride, Wal.Cr. 21 DP31
Old Pk. Ridings N21 35 DP44
Old Pk. Rd. N13 49 DM49
Old Pk. Rd. SE2 96 EU78
Old Pk. Rd., Enf. 35 DP41
Old Pk. Rd. S., Enf. 35 DP42
Old Pk. Vw., Enf. 35 DN41
Old Parkbury La., St.Alb. 17 CF29
Old Parvis Rd., W.Byf. 126 BJ112
Old Perry St., Chis. 109 ES93
Old Polhill, Sev. 151 ET115
Old Pound Clo., Islw. 87 CG81
Old Pye St. SW1 9 M6
Old Pye St. SW1 91 DK76
Old Quebec St. W1 4 E9
Old Quebec St. W1 76 DF72
Old Queen St. SW1 9 N5
Old Queen St. SW1 91 DK75
Old Rectory Clo., Tad. 145 CU124
Old Rectory Gdns., Edg. 46 CN51
Old Rectory Rd., Ong. 27 FH34
Old Redding, Har. 44 CB50
Old Rd. SE13 94 EE84
Old Rd., Dart. 111 FD85
Old Rd., Enf. 36 DW39
Old Rope Wk., Sun. 113 BV97
The Ave.
Old Royal Free Pl. N1 77 DN67
Liverpool Rd.
Old Royal Free Sq. N1 77 DN67
Old Ruislip Rd., Nthlt. 72 BW68
Old Savill's Cotts., Chig. 53 EQ49
The Chase
Old Sch. Clo. SW19 118 DA96
Old Sch. Clo., Beck. 121 DX96
Old Sch. Ms., Wey. 127 BR105
Old Schools La., Epsom 131 CT109
Old Seacoal La. EC4 6 F9
Old Shire La., Wal.Abb. 38 EG35
Old S. Clo., Pnr. 44 BX53
Old S. Lambeth Rd. SW8 91 DL80
Old Sq. WC2 6 C8
Old Sq. WC2 77 DM72
Old Sta. App., Lthd. 143 CG121
Old Sta. Rd., Hayes 85 BT76
Old Sta. Rd., Loug. 38 EL43
Old Stockley Rd., West Dr. 85 BP75
Old St. E13 80 EH68
Old St. EC1 7 H5
Old St. EC1 78 DQ70
Old Swan Yd., Cars. 132 DF105
Old Town SW4 91 DJ83
Old Town, Croy. 119 DP104
Old Tram Yd. SE18 95 ES77
Lakedale Rd.
Old Tye Ave., West. 150 EL116
Old Wk., The, Sev. 153 FH117
Old Watford Rd., St.Alb. 16 BY30
Old Westhall Clo., Warl. 148 DW119
Old Woolwich Rd. SE10 93 ED78
Old York Rd. SW18 104 DB85
Oldacre Ms. SW12 105 DH87
Balham Gro.
Oldberry Rd., Edg. 46 CR51
Oldborough Rd., Wem. 59 CJ61
Oldbury Clo., Orp. 124 EX98
Oldbury Pl. W1 4 G6
Oldbury Pl. W1 76 DG71
Oldbury Rd., Enf. 36 DU40
Oldchurch Gdns., Rom. 69 FD59
Oldchurch Ri., Rom. 69 FD59
Oldchurch Rd., Rom. 69 FE58
Olden La., Pur. 133 DN112
Oldfield Circ., Nthlt. 72 CC65
The Fairway
Oldfield Clo., Brom. 123 EM98
Oldfield Clo., Grnf. 59 CE64
Oldfield Clo., Stan. 45 CG50
Oldfield Clo. (Cheshunt), Wal.Cr. 23 DY28
Oldfield Dr. (Cheshunt), Wal.Cr. 23 DY28
Oldfield Fm. Gdns., Grnf. 73 CD67
Oldfield Gdns., Ash. 143 CK119
Oldfield Gro. SE16 93 DX77
Oldfield La. N., Grnf. 73 CD68
Oldfield La. S., Grnf. 72 CC69
Oldfield Ms. N6 63 DJ59
Oldfield Rd. N16 64 DS62
Oldfield Rd. NW10 75 CT66
Oldfield Rd. SW19 103 CY93
Oldfield Rd. W3 89 CT75
Valetta Rd.
Oldfield Rd., Bexh. 96 EY82
Oldfield Rd., Brom. 122 EL98
Oldfield Rd., Hmptn. 114 BZ95
Oldfield Rd., St.Alb. 17 CK25
Oldfields Rd., Sutt. 117 CZ104
Oldham Ter. W3 74 CQ74
Oldhill St. N16 64 DU60
Oldridge Rd. SW12 104 DG87
Olds App., Wat. 43 BP46
Olds Clo., Wat. 43 BP46
Oldstead Rd., Brom. 107 ED91
Oleander Clo., Orp. 137 ER106
O'Leary Sq. E1 78 DW71
Oley Pl. E1 79 DX71
Redman's Rd.
Olinda Rd. N16 64 DT58
Oliphant St. W10 75 CX69
Olive Rd. E13 80 EJ69
Olive Rd. NW2 61 CW63
Olive Rd. SW19 104 DC94
Norman Rd.
Olive Rd. W5 87 CK76
Olive St., Rom. 69 FD57
Oliver Ave. SE25 120 DT97
Oliver Clo. W4 88 CP79
Oliver Clo., Add. 126 BG105
Oliver Clo., St.Alb. 17 CD27
Oliver Gdns. E6 80 EL72
Oliver Goldsmith Est. SE15 92 DU81
Goldsmith Rd.
Oliver Gro. SE25 120 DT98
Oliver Rd. E10 65 EB61
Oliver Rd. E17 65 EC57
Oliver Rd., N.Mal. 116 CQ96
Oliver Rd., Rain. 83 FF67
Oliver Rd., Sutt. 132 DD105
Oliver Rd., Swan. 125 FD97
Olivers Yd. EC1 7 L4
Olivette St. SW15 89 CX83
Felsham Rd.
Olivia Gdns., Uxb. 42 BJ53
Ollards Gro., Loug. 38 EK42
Ollerton Grn. E3 79 DZ67
Ollerton Rd. N11 49 DK50
Olley Clo., Wall. 133 DL107
Ollgar Clo. W12 75 CT74
Olliffe St. E14 93 EC76
Olmar St. SE1 92 DU79
Olney Rd. SE17 91 DP79
Olron Cres., Bexh. 110 EX85
Olven Rd. SE18 95 EQ79
Olveston Wk., Cars. 118 DD100
Olwen Ms., Pnr. 44 BX54
Olyffe Ave., Well. 96 EU81
Olyffe Dr., Beck. 121 EC95
Olympia Ms. W2 76 DB73
Queensway
Olympia Way W14 89 CY76
Olympic Way, Grnf. 72 CB67
Olympic Way, Wem. 60 CN62
Olympus Sq. E5 64 DU63
Nolan Way
Oman Ave. NW2 61 CV63
O'Meara St. SE1 11 J3
O'Meara St. SE1 78 DQ74
Omega Clo. E14 93 EB76
Tiller Rd.
Omega Pl. N1 6 A1
Omega St. SE14 93 EA81
Ommaney Rd. SE14 93 DX81
Omnibus Way E17 51 EA54
On The Hill, Wat. 44 BY47
Ondine Rd. SE15 92 DT84
One Tree Clo. SE23 106 DW86
Onega Gate SE16 93 DY76
O'Neill Path SE18 95 EN79
Kempt St.
Ongar Clo., Rom. 68 EW57
Ongar Pl., Add. 126 BG107
Ongar Rd. SW6 90 DA79
Ongar Rd., Add. 126 BG106
Ongar Rd., Rom. 40 EV41
Ongar Way, Rain. 83 FE67
Onra Rd. E17 65 EA59
Onslow Ave., Rich. 102 CL85
Onslow Ave., Sutt. 131 CZ110
Onslow Clo. E4 51 ED47
Onslow Clo., T.Ditt. 115 CE102
Onslow Cres., Chis. 123 EP95
Onslow Dr., Sid. 110 EX90
Onslow Gdns. E18 66 EH55
Onslow Gdns. N10 63 DH57
Onslow Gdns. N21 35 DN43
Onslow Gdns. SW7 90 DD78
Onslow Gdns., S.Croy. 134 DU112
Onslow Gdns., T.Ditt. 115 CE102
Onslow Gdns., Wall. 133 DJ107
Onslow Ms., Cher. 112 BG100
Onslow Ms. E. SW7 90 DD77
Cranley Pl.
Onslow Ms. W. SW7 90 DD77
Cranley Pl.
Onslow Rd., Croy. 119 DN102
Onslow Rd., N.Mal. 117 CU98
Onslow Rd., Rich. 102 CL85
Onslow Rd., Walt. 127 BT105
Onslow Sq. SW7 8 A9
Onslow Sq. SW7 90 DD77
Onslow St. EC1 6 E5
Onslow Way, T.Ditt. 115 CE102
Ontario St. SE1 10 G7
Ontario Way E14 79 EA73
Opal Clo. E16 80 EK72
Opal Ms. NW6 75 CZ67
Priory Pk. Rd.
Opal Ms., Ilf. 67 EP61
Ley St.
Opal St. SE11 10 F10
Opal St. SE11 91 DP77
Openshaw Rd. SE2 96 EV77
Openview SW18 104 DC88
Ophelia Gdns. NW2 61 CY62
The Vale
Ophir Ter. SE15 92 DU81
Opossum Way, Houns. 86 BW82
Oppenheim Rd. SE13 93 EC82
Oppidans Ms. NW3 76 DF66
Meadowbank
Oppidans Rd. NW3 76 DF66
Orange Ct. E1 78 DU74
Hermitage Wall
Orange Ct. La., Orp. 137 EM109
Orange Gro. E11 66 EE62
Orange Hill Rd., Edg. 46 CQ52
Orange Pl. SE16 92 DW76
Lower Rd.
Orange St. WC2 9 N1
Orange St. WC2 77 DK73
Orange Tree Hill, Rom. (Havering-atte-Bower) 55 FD50
Orange Yd. W1 5 N9
Orangery, The, Rich. 101 CJ89
Orangery La. SE9 109 EM85

Owen Rd., Hayes 71 BV69
Owen St. EC1 6 E1
Owen Wk. SE20 106 DU94
Sycamore Gro.
Owen Waters Ho., Ilf. 53 EN53
Owen Way NW10 60 CQ64
Owenite St. SE2 96 EV77
Owen's Ct. EC1 6 F2
Owen's Row EC1 6 F2
Owens Way SE23 107 DY87
Owens Way, Rick. 28 BN43
Owgan Clo. SE5 92 DR80
Benhill Rd.
Owl Clo., S.Croy. 135 DX110
Ownstead Gdns., S.Croy. 134 DT111
Ownsted Hill, Croy. 135 EC110
Ox La., Epsom 131 CU109
Church St.
Oxberry Ave. SW6 89 CY82
Oxdowne Clo., Cob. 128 CB114
Oxenden Wd. Rd., Orp. 138 EW108
Oxendon St. SW1 9 M1
Oxendon St. SW1 77 DK73
Oxenford St. SE15 92 DT83
Oxenholme NW1 5 L1
Oxenholme NW1 77 DJ68
Oxenpark Ave., Wem. 60 CL60
Oxestalls Rd. SE8 93 DY78
Oxford Ave. SW20 117 CY96
Oxford Ave., Hayes 85 BT80
Oxford Ave., Houns. 86 CA78
Oxford Circ. Ave. W1 5 K9
Oxford Clo. N9 50 DV47
Oxford Clo., Ashf. 99 BQ94
Oxford Clo., Mitch. 119 DJ97
Oxford Clo., Nthwd. 43 BQ49
Oxford Clo. (Cheshunt), Wal.Cr. 22 DW29
Oxford Ct. EC4 7 K10
Oxford Ct. W3 74 CN72
Queens Dr.
Oxford Ct., Felt. 100 BX91
Oxford Way
Oxford Cres., N.Mal. 116 CR100
Oxford Dr., Ruis. 58 BW61
Oxford Gdns. N20 48 DD46
Oxford Gdns. N21 50 DQ45
Oxford Gdns. W4 88 CN78
Oxford Gdns. W10 75 CX72
Oxford Gdns., Uxb. 56 BG62
Oxford Rd.
Oxford Gate W6 89 CX77
Oxford Ms., Bex. 110 FA87
Bexley High St.
Oxford Pl. NW10 60 CR62
Neasden La. N.
Oxford Rd. E15 79 ED65
Oxford Rd. N4 63 DN60
Oxford Rd. N9 50 DV47
Oxford Rd. NW6 76 DA68
Oxford Rd. SE19 106 DR93
Oxford Rd. SW15 89 CY84
Oxford Rd. W5 73 CK73
Oxford Rd., Cars. 132 DE107
Oxford Rd., Enf. 36 DV43
Oxford Rd., Har. 58 CC58
Oxford Rd. (Wealdstone), Har. 59 CF55
Oxford Rd., Ilf. 67 EQ64
Oxford Rd., Sid. 110 EV92
Oxford Rd., Tedd. 101 CD92
Oxford Rd., Uxb. 70 BJ65
Oxford Rd., Wall. 133 DJ106
Oxford Rd., Wdf.Grn. 52 EK50
Oxford Rd. N. W4 88 CP78
Oxford Rd. S. W4 88 CN78
Oxford Sq. W2 4 C9
Oxford Sq. W2 76 DE72
Oxford St. W1 4 F9
Oxford St. W1 76 DG72
Oxford St., Wat. 29 BV43
Oxford Wk., Sthl. 72 BZ74
Oxford Way, Felt. 100 BX91
Oxgate Gdns. NW2 61 CV62
Oxgate La. NW2 61 CV61
Oxhawth Cres., Brom. 123 EN99
Oxhey Ave., Wat. 44 BX45
Oxhey Dr., Nthwd. 43 BV49
Oxhey Dr., Wat. 44 BW48
Oxhey Dr. S., Nthwd. 43 BV50
Oxhey La., Har. 44 CA50
Oxhey La., Pnr. 44 CA50
Oxhey La., Wat. 44 BY46
Oxhey Ridge Clo., Nthwd. 43 BU50
Oxhey Rd., Wat. 30 BW44
Oxleas E6 81 EP72
Oxleas Clo., Well. 95 ER82
Oxleay Ct., Har. 58 CA60
Oxleay Rd., Har. 58 CA60
Oxleigh Clo., N.Mal. 116 CS99
Oxley Clo. SE1 92 DT78
Oxleys Rd. NW2 61 CV62
Oxleys Rd., Wal.Abb. 24 EG33
Oxlip Clo., Croy. 121 DX102
Marigold Way
Oxlow La., Dag. 68 EZ63
Oxonian St. SE22 92 DT84
Oxshott Ri., Cob. 128 BX113
Oxshott Rd., Lthd. 143 CE116
Oxshott Way, Cob. 142 BY115
Oxted Clo., Mitch. 118 DD97
Oxtoby Way SW16 119 DK95
Oyster Catchers Clo. E16 80 EH72
Freemasons Rd.
Oyster La., W.Byf. 126 BK110
Oyster Row E1 78 DW72
Lukin St.
Ozolins Way E16 80 EG72

P

Pablo Neruda Clo. SE24 91 DP84
Shakespeare Rd.
Pace Pl. E1 78 DV72
Bigland St.
Paceheath Clo., Rom. 55 FD51
Pachesham Dr., Lthd. 143 CF116
Oxshott Rd.
Pachesham Pk., Lthd. 143 CF117
Pacific Clo., Felt. 99 BT88
Pacific Rd. E16 80 EG72
Packet Boat La., Uxb. 70 BH72
Packham Clo., Orp. 124 EW104
Berrylands
Packhorse La., Borwd. 32 CS37
Buckettsland La.
Packhorse La., Pot.B. 18 CR32
Packhorse Rd., Sev. 154 FC123
Packington Rd. W3 88 CQ76
Packington Sq. N1 78 DQ67
Packington St. N1 77 DP67
Packmores Rd. SE9 109 ER85
Padbury SE17 92 DS78
Bagshot St.
Padbury Clo., Felt. 99 BR88
Padbury Ct. E2 78 DT69
Padcroft Rd., West Dr. 70 BK74
Paddenswick Rd. W6 89 CU76
Paddington Clo., Hayes 72 BX70
Paddington Grn. W2 4 A6
Paddington Grn. W2 76 DD71
Paddington St. W1 4 F6
Paddington St. W1 76 DG71
Paddock, The, Uxb. 57 BP63
Paddock Clo. SE3 94 EG83
Paddock Clo. SE26 107 DX91
Paddock Clo., Nthlt. 72 CA68
Paddock Clo., Orp. 137 EP105
State Fm. Ave.
Paddock Clo., Wor.Pk. 116 CS102
Paddock Gdns. SE19 106 DS93
Westow St.
Paddock Rd. NW2 61 CU62
Paddock Rd., Bexh. 96 EY84
Paddock Rd., Ruis. 58 BX62
Paddock Wk., Warl. 148 DV119
Paddock Way, Chis. 109 ER94
Paddocks, The, Add. 126 BH110
Paddocks, The, Barn. 34 DF41
Paddocks, The, Rom. 41 FF44
Paddocks, The, Sev. 155 FK124
Paddocks, The, Wem. 60 CP61
Paddocks, The, Wey. 113 BS104
Paddocks Clo., Ash. 144 CL118
Paddocks Clo., Cob. 128 BW114
Paddocks Clo., Har. 58 CB63
Paddocks Clo., Orp. 124 EX103
Paddocks Way, Ash. 144 CL118
Paddocks Way, Cher. 112 BH102
Padfield Rd. SE5 92 DQ83
Padnall Rd., Rom. 68 EX55
Padstow Rd., Enf. 35 DP40
Padstow Wk., Felt. 99 BT88
Padua Rd. SE20 120 DW95
Pagden St. SW8 91 DH81
Page Clo., Dag. 68 EY64
Page Clo., Hmptn. 100 BY93
Page Clo., Har. 60 CM58
Page Cres., Croy. 133 DN106
Page Cres., Erith 97 FF80
Page Grn. Rd. N15 64 DU57
Page Grn. Ter. N15 64 DT57
Page Heath La., Brom. 122 EK97
Page Heath Vill., Brom. 122 EK97
Page Meadow NW7 47 CU52
Page Rd., Felt. 99 BR86
Page St. NW7 47 CU51
Page St. SW1 9 N8
Page St. SW1 91 DK77
Pageant Ave. NW9 46 CR53
Pageant Wk., Croy. 120 DS104
Pageantmaster Ct. EC4 6 F9
Pagehurst Rd., Croy. 120 DV101
Pages Hill N10 48 DG54
Pages La. N10 48 DG54
Pages La., Uxb. 70 BJ65
Pages Wk. SE1 11 M8
Pages Wk. SE1 92 DS77
Pages Yd. W4 88 CS79
Church St.
Paget Ave., Sutt. 118 DD104
Paget Clo., Hmptn. 101 CD91
Paget Gdns., Chis. 123 EP95
Paget La., Islw. 87 CD83
Paget Pl., Kings.T. 102 CQ93
Paget Pl., T.Ditt. 115 CG102
Brooklands Rd.
Paget Ri. SE18 95 EN79
Paget Rd. N16 64 DR60
Paget Rd., Ilf. 67 EP63
Paget Rd., Uxb. 71 BQ70
Paget St. EC1 6 F2
Paget Ter. SE18 95 EN79
Pagitts Gro., Barn. 34 DB39
Pagnell St. SE14 93 DZ80
Pagoda Ave., Rich. 88 CM83
Pagoda Gdns. SE3 93 ED82
Paignton Rd. N15 64 DS58
Paignton Rd., Ruis. 57 BU62
Paines Clo., Pnr. 44 BY54
Paines La., Pnr. 44 BY53
Pains Clo., Mitch. 119 DH96
Painsthorpe Rd. N16 64 DS62
Oldfield Rd.
Painters La., Enf. 37 DY35
Painters Rd., Ilf. 67 ET55
Paisley Rd. N22 49 DP53
Paisley Rd., Cars. 118 DD102
Pakeman St. N7 63 DM62
Pakenham Clo. SW12 104 DG88
Balham Pk. Rd.
Pakenham St. WC1 6 C3
Pakenham St. WC1 77 DM69
Pakes Way, Epp. 39 ES37
Palace Ave. W8 76 DB74
Palace Clo., Kings L. 14 BM30
Palace Ct. NW3 62 DB64
Palace Ct. W2 76 DB73
Palace Ct., Brom. 122 EH95
Palace Gro.
Palace Ct., Har. 60 CL58
Palace Ct. Gdns. N10 63 DJ55
Palace Dr., Wey. 113 BP104
Palace Gdns., Buck.H. 52 EK46
Palace Gdns., Enf. 36 DR42
Sydney Rd.
Palace Gdns. Ms. W8 76 DA74
Palace Gdns. Ter. W8 76 DA74
Palace Gate W8 90 DC75
Palace Gates Rd. N22 49 DK54
Palace Grn. W8 90 DB75
Palace Grn., Croy. 135 DZ108
Palace Gro. SE19 106 DT94
Palace Gro., Brom. 122 EH95
Palace Ms. E17 65 DZ56
Palace Ms. SW1 8 G9
Palace Ms. SW6 89 CZ80
Hartismere Rd.
Palace Pl. SW1 9 K6
Palace Rd. N8 63 DK57
Palace Rd. N11 49 DK52
Palace Rd. SE19 106 DT94
Palace Rd. SW2 105 DM88
Palace Rd., Brom. 122 EH95
Palace Rd., E.Mol. 115 CD97
Palace Rd., Kings.T. 115 CK98
Palace Rd., Ruis. 58 BY63
Palace Rd., West. 151 EN121
Chestnut Ave.
Palace Rd. Est. SW2 105 DM88
Palace Sq. SE19 106 DT94
Palace St. SW1 9 K6
Palace St. SW1 91 DJ76
Palace Vw. SE12 108 EG89
Palace Vw., Brom. 122 EH97
Palace Vw., Croy. 135 DZ105
Palace Vw. Rd. E4 51 EB50
Palace Way, Wey. 113 BP104
Palace Dr.
Palamos Rd. E10 65 EA60
Palatine Ave. N16 64 DT63
Stoke Newington Rd.
Palatine Rd. N16 64 DS63
Palermo Rd. NW10 75 CU68
Palestine Gro. SW19 118 DD95
Palewell Clo., Orp. 124 EV96
Palewell Common Dr. SW14 102 CR85
Palewell Pk. SW14 102 CR85
Paley Gdns., Loug. 39 EP41
Palfrey Pl. SW8 91 DM80
Palgrave Ave., Sthl. 72 CA73
Palgrave Rd. W12 89 CT76
Palissy St. E2 7 P3
Pall Mall SW1 9 L3
Pall Mall SW1 77 DJ74
Pall Mall E. SW1 9 N2
Pall Mall E. SW1 77 DK74
Pall Mall Pl. SW1 9 L3
Pallant Way, Orp. 123 EN104
Pallet Way SE18 94 EL81
Palliser Dr., Rain. 83 FG71
Palliser Rd. W14 89 CY78
Palm Ave., Sid. 110 EX93
Palm Clo. E10 65 EB62
Palm Gro. W5 88 CL76
Palm Rd., Rom. 69 FC57
Palmar Cres., Bexh. 96 FA83
Palmar Rd., Bexh. 96 FA82
Palmarsh Clo., Orp. 124 EX98
Wotton Grn.
Palmeira Rd., Bexh. 96 EX83
Palmer Ave., Sutt. 131 CW105
Palmer Ave. (Bushey), Wat. 30 CB43
Palmer Clo., Houns. 86 CA81
Palmer Clo., W.Wick. 121 ED104
Palmer Cres., Kings.T. 116 CL97
Palmer Gdns., Barn. 33 CX43
Palmer Pl. N7 63 DN64
Palmer Rd. E13 80 EH70
Palmer Rd., Dag. 68 EX60
Palmer St. SW1 9 M6
Palmer St. SW1 91 DK76
Palmers Gro., W.Mol. 114 CA98
Palmers Hill, Epp. 26 EU29
Palmers La., Enf. 36 DW39
Palmers Moor La., Iver 70 BG70
Palmers Orchard, Sev. 139 FF111
Palmers Pas. SW14 88 CQ83
Palmers Rd.
Palmers Rd. E2 79 DX68
Palmers Rd. N11 49 DJ50
Palmers Rd. SW14 88 CQ83
Palmers Rd. SW16 119 DM96
Palmers Rd., Borwd. 32 CP39
Palmers Way (Cheshunt), Wal.Cr. 23 DY29
Palmersfield Rd., Bans. 132 DA114
Palmerston Cres. N13 49 DM50
Palmerston Cres. SE18 95 EQ79
Palmerston Gro. SW19 104 DA94
Palmerston Rd. E7 66 EH64
Palmerston Rd. E17 65 DZ55
Palmerston Rd. N22 49 DM52
Palmerston Rd. NW6 75 CZ66
Palmerston Rd. SW14 88 CQ84
Palmerston Rd. SW19 104 DA94
Palmerston Rd. W3 88 CQ76
Palmerston Rd., Buck.H. 52 EH47
Palmerston Rd., Cars. 132 DF105
Palmerston Rd., Croy. 120 DR99
Palmerston Rd., Har. 59 CE55
Palmerston Rd., Orp. 137 EQ105
Palmerston Rd., Sutt. 132 DC105
Vernon Rd.
Palmerston Rd., Twick. 101 CE86
Palmerston Way SW8 91 DH80
Bradmead
Pamela Gdns., Pnr. 57 BV57
Pamela Wk. E8 78 DU67
Marlborough Ave.
Pampisford Rd., Pur. 133 DN111
Pampisford Rd., S.Croy. 134 DQ107
Pams Way, Epsom 130 CR106
Pancras La. EC4 7 J9
Pancras Rd. NW1 5 P1
Pancras Rd. NW1 77 DK68
Pancroft, Rom. 40 EV41
Pandora Rd. NW6 76 DA65
Panfield Ms., Ilf. 67 EN58
Cranbrook Rd.
Panfield Rd. SE2 96 EU76
Pangbourne Ave. W10 75 CW71
Pangbourne Dr., Stan. 45 CK50
Pankhurst Clo. SE14 93 DX80
Briant St.
Pankhurst Clo., Islw. 87 CF83
Pankhurst Rd., Walt. 114 BW101
Panmuir Rd. SW20 117 CV95
Panmure Clo. N5 63 DP63
Panmure Rd. SE26 106 DV90
Pannard Pl., Sthl. 72 CB73
Pansy Gdns. W12 75 CU73
Panters, Swan. 111 FF94
Pantile Rd., Wey. 127 BR105
Pantile Wk., Uxb. 70 BJ66
High St.
Pantiles, The NW11 61 CZ57
Willifield Way
Pantiles, The, Bexh. 96 EZ80
Pantiles, The, Brom. 122 EL97
Pantiles, The (Bushey), Wat. 45 CD45
Pantiles Clo. N13 49 DP50
Princes Ave.
Panton St. SW1 9 M1
Panyer All. EC4 7 H8
Papermill Clo., Cars. 132 DG105
Papillons Wk. SE3 94 EG83
Papworth Gdns. N7 63 DM64
Liverpool Rd.
Papworth Way SW2 105 DN87
Parade, The SW11 90 DF80
Parade, The, Dart. 111 FF85
Crayford Way
Parade, The, Epsom 130 CR113
Parade, The, Esher 129 CE107
Parade, The, Sun. 99 BT94
Parade, The, Wat. 29 BV41
Parade, The (Carpenders Pk.), Wat. 44 BY48
Parade Ms. SE27 105 DP89
Norwood Rd.
Paradise Clo. (Cheshunt), Wal.Cr. 22 DV28
Paradise Pas. N7 77 DN65
Sheringham Rd.
Paradise Pl. SE18 94 EL77
Woodhill
Paradise Rd. SW4 91 DL82
Paradise Rd., Rich. 102 CL85
Paradise Rd., Wal.Abb. 23 EC34
Paradise Row E2 78 DV69
Bethnal Grn. Rd.
Paradise St. SE16 92 DV75
Paradise Wk. SW3 90 DF79
Paragon, The SE3 94 EF82
Paragon Clo. E16 80 EG72
Paragon Gro., Surb. 116 CM100
Paragon Ms. SE1 11 L8
Paragon Pl. SE3 94 EF82
Paragon Pl., Surb. 116 CM100
Berrylands Rd.
Paragon Rd. E9 78 DW65
Parbury Ri., Chess. 130 CL107
Parbury Rd. SE23 107 DY86
Parchmore Rd., Th.Hth. 119 DP96
Parchmore Way, Th.Hth. 119 DP96
Pardon St. EC1 6 G4
Pardoner St. SE1 11 L6
Pardoner St. SE1 92 DR76
Parfett St. E1 78 DU71
Parfitt Clo. NW3 62 DC61
North End
Parfour Dr., Ken. 148 DQ116
Parfrey St. W6 89 CW79
Parham Dr., Ilf. 67 EP58
Parham Way N10 49 DJ54
Paris Gdns. SE1 10 F2
Paris Gdns. SE1 77 DP74
Parish Clo., Horn. 69 FH61
St. Leonards Way
Parish Gate Dr., Sid. 109 ES86
Parish La. SE20 107 DX93
Parish Ms. SE20 107 DX94
Parish Wf. Pl. SE18 94 EL77
Woodhill
Park, The N6 62 DG58
Park, The NW11 62 DB60
Park, The SE19 106 DS94
Park, The SE23 106 DV88
Park Hill
Park, The W5 73 CK74
Park, The, Cars. 132 DF106
Park, The, Lthd. 142 CA123
Park, The, Sid. 110 EU91
Park App., Well. 96 EV84
Park Ave. E6 81 EN67
Park Ave. E15 80 EE65
Park Ave. N3 48 DB53
Park Ave. N13 49 DN48
Park Ave. N18 50 DU49
Park Ave. N22 49 DL54
Park Ave. NW2 75 CV65
Park Ave. NW10 74 CM68
Park Ave. NW11 62 DB60
Park Ave. SW14 88 CR84
Park Ave., Bark. 81 EQ65
Park Ave., Barn. 34 DC43
Park Ave., Brom. 108 EF94
Park Ave., Cars. 132 DG107
Park Ave., Cat. 148 DS124
Park Ave., Chis. 123 ES97
Park Ave., Enf. 36 DR43
Park Ave., Houns. 100 CB86
Park Ave., Ilf. 67 EN60
Park Ave., Mitch. 105 DH94
Park Ave., Orp. 124 EU103
Park Ave. (Farnborough), Orp. 123 EM104
Park Ave., Pot.B. 20 DC34
Park Ave., Rad. 17 CH34
Park Ave., Rick. 28 BG43
Park Ave., Ruis. 57 BR58
Park Ave., Sthl. 86 BZ75
Park Ave., Wat. 29 BU41
Park Ave. (Bushey), Wat. 30 BX41
Park Ave., W.Wick. 121 EC103
Park Ave., Wdf.Grn. 52 EH50
Park Ave. E., Epsom 131 CU107
Park Ave. Ms., Mitch. 105 DH94
Park Ave.
Park Ave. N. N8 63 DK55
Park Ave. N. NW10 61 CV64
Park Ave. Rd. N17 50 DV52
Park Ave. S. N8 63 DK56
Park Ave. W., Epsom 131 CU107
Park Boul., Rom. 55 FF53
Park Chase, Wem. 60 CM63
Park Clo. E9 78 DW67
Skipworth Rd.
Park Clo. NW2 61 CV62
Park Clo. NW10 74 CM69
Park Clo. SW1 8 D5
Park Clo. W4 88 CR78
Park Clo. W14 89 CZ76
Park Clo., Add. 126 BH110
Park Clo., Cars. 132 DF107
Park Clo., Epp. 26 FA27
Park Clo., Esher 128 BZ107
Park Clo., Hmptn. 114 CC95
Park Clo., Har. 45 CE53
Park Clo., Hat. 19 CZ26
Park Clo., Houns. 100 CC85
Park Clo., Kings.T. 116 CN95
Park Clo., Lthd. 143 CD124
Park Clo., Rick. 43 BP49
Park Clo., Walt. 113 BT103
Park Clo. (Bushey), Wat. 30 BX41
Park Ct. SE26 106 DV93
Park Ct., Kings.T. 115 CJ95
Park Ct., N.Mal. 116 CR98
Park Ct., Wem. 60 CL64
Park Ct., W.Byf. 126 BG113
Park Cres. N3 48 DB52
Park Cres. W1 5 H5
Park Cres. W1 77 DH70
Park Cres., Borwd. 32 CM41
Park Cres., Enf. 36 DR42
Park Cres., Erith 97 FC79
Park Cres., Har. 45 CE53
Park Cres., Horn. 69 FG59
Park Cres., Twick. 101 CD88
Park Cres. Ms. E. W1 5 J5
Park Cres. Ms. W. W1 5 H5
Park Cres. Rd., Erith 97 FD79
Park Cft., Edg. 46 CQ53
Park Dale N11 49 DK51
Bounds Grn. Rd.
Park Dr. N21 36 DQ44
Park Dr. NW11 62 DB60
Park Dr. SE7 94 EL79
Park Dr. SW14 88 CR84
Park Dr. W3 88 CN76
Park Dr., Dag. 69 FC62
Park Dr., Har. 58 CA59
Park Dr. (Harrow Weald), Har. 45 CE51
Park Dr., Pot.B. 20 DA31
Park Dr., Rom. 69 FD56
Park Dr., Wey. 127 BP106
Park Dr. Clo. SE7 94 EL78
Park End NW3 62 DE63
South Hill Pk.
Park End, Brom. 122 EF95
Park End Rd., Rom. 69 FE56
Park Fm. Clo. N2 62 DC55
Park Fm. Clo., Pnr. 57 BV57
Field End Rd.

Park Fm. Rd., Brom. 122 EK95
Park Fm. Rd., Kings.T. 102 CL94
Park Gdn. Pl. W2 4 A9
Park Gdns. NW9 60 CP55
Park Gdns., Erith 97 FD77
Valley Rd.
Park Gdns., Kings.T. 102 CM92
Park Gate N2 62 DD55
Park Gate N21 49 DM45
Park Gate W5 73 CK71
Mount Ave.
Park Gra. Gdns., Sev. 155 FJ127
Solefields Rd.
Park Grn., Lthd. 142 CA124
Park Gro. E15 80 EG67
Park Gro. N11 49 DK52
Park Gro., Bexh. 97 FC84
Park Gro., Brom. 122 EH95
Park Gro., Edg. 46 CM50
Park Gro. Rd. E11 66 EE61
Park Hall Rd. N2 62 DE56
Park Hall Rd. SE21 106 DR90
Park Hill SE23 106 DV89
Park Hill SW4 105 DK85
Park Hill W5 73 CK71
Park Hill, Brom. 122 EL98
Park Hill, Cars. 132 DE107
Park Hill, Loug. 38 EK43
Park Hill, Rich. 102 CM86
Park Hill Clo., Cars. 132 DE106
Park Hill Ct. SW17 104 DF90
Beeches Rd.
Park Hill Ri., Croy. 120 DS103
Park Hill Rd., Brom. 122 EE96
Park Hill Rd., Croy. 120 DS103
Park Hill Rd., Sid. 109 ES90
Park Hill Rd., Wall. 133 DH107
Park Ho. N21 49 DM45
Park Ho. Gdns., Twick. 101 CJ86
Park Ind. Est., St.Alb. 17 CE27
Park La. E15 79 ED67
High St.
Park La. N9 50 DS48
Park La. N17 50 DT52
Park La. N18 50 DS49
Sheldon Rd.
Park La. W1 4 E10
Park La. W1 76 DF73
Park La., Ash. 144 CM118
Park La., Bans. 146 DD118
Park La., Cars. 132 DG105
Park La., Couls. 147 DK121
Park La., Croy. 120 DR104
Park La., Har. 58 CB62
Park La., Hayes 71 BS71
Park La., Horn. 69 FF58
Park La. (Elm Pk.), Horn. 83 FH65
Park La., Houns. 85 BU80
Park La., Rich. 87 CK84
Park La. (Chadwell Heath), Rom. 68 EX58
Park La., Sev. 155 FJ124
Park La. (Seal), Sev. 155 FN121
Park La., Stan. 45 CG48
Park La., Sutt. 131 CY107
Park La., Tedd. 101 CF93
Park La., Uxb. 42 BG53
Park La., Wall. 132 DG105
Park La., Wal.Cr. 22 DW33
Park La. (Cheshunt), Wal.Cr. 22 DU26
Park La., Wem. 60 CL64
Park La. Clo. N17 50 DU52
Park La. Paradise (Cheshunt), Wal.Cr. 22 DU25
Park Lawn Rd., Wey. 127 BQ105
Park Lawns, Wem. 60 CM63
Park Ley Rd., Cat. 149 DX120
Park Mead, Har. 58 CB62
Park Mead, Sid. 110 EV85
Park Ms. SE24 106 DQ86
Croxted Rd.
Park Ms., Chis. 109 EP93
Park Ms., E.Mol. 114 CC98
Park Ms., Hmptn. 100 CC92
Park Rd.
Park Nook Gdns., Enf. 36 DR37
Park Par. NW10 75 CT68
Park Pl. E14 79 EA74
Park Pl. SW1 9 K3
Park Pl. SW1 77 DJ74
Park Pl. W3 88 CN77
Park Pl. W5 73 CK74
Park Pl., Hmptn. 100 CC93
Park Pl., St.Alb. 17 CD27
Park Pl., Sev. 154 FD123
Park Pl., Wem. 60 CM63
Park Pl. Vill. W2 76 DC71
Park Ridings N8 63 DN55
Park Ri. SE23 107 DY88
Park Ri., Har. 45 CE53
Park Ri., Lthd. 143 CH121
Park Ri. Clo., Lthd. 143 CH121
Park Ri. Rd. SE23 107 DY88
Park Rd. E6 80 EJ67
Park Rd. E10 65 EA60
Park Rd. E12 66 EH60
Park Rd. E15 80 EG67
Park Rd. E17 65 DZ57
Park Rd. N2 62 DD55
Park Rd. N8 63 DJ56
Park Rd. N11 49 DK52
Park Rd. N14 49 DK45
Park Rd. N15 63 DP56
Park Rd. N18 50 DT49
Park Rd. NW1 4 D4
Park Rd. NW1 76 DF70
Park Rd. NW4 61 CU59
Park Rd. NW8 4 B2
Park Rd. NW8 76 DE69
Park Rd. NW9 60 CR59
Park Rd. NW10 74 CS67
Park Rd. SE25 120 DS98
Park Rd. SW19 104 DD94
Park Rd. W4 88 CQ80
Park Rd. W7 73 CF73
Park Rd., Ashf. 99 BP92
Park Rd., Ash. 144 CL118
Park Rd., Bans. 146 DB115
Park Rd., Barn. 33 CZ42
Park Rd. (New Barnet), Barn. 34 DD42
Park Rd., Beck. 107 DZ94
Park Rd., Brom. 122 EH95
Park Rd., Cat. 148 DS123
Park Rd., Chis. 109 EP93
Park Rd., E.Mol. 114 CC98
Park Rd., Enf. 37 DY36
Park Rd., Esher 128 CB105
Park Rd., Felt. 100 BX91
Park Rd., Hmptn. 100 CB91
Park Rd., Hayes 71 BS71
Park Rd., Houns. 100 CB85
Park Rd., Ilf. 67 ER62
Park Rd., Islw. 87 CH81
Park Rd., Ken. 147 DP115
Park Rd., Kings.T. 102 CM92
Park Rd. (Hampton Wick), Kings.T. 115 CJ95
Park Rd., N.Mal. 116 CR98
Park Rd., Orp. 124 EW99
Park Rd., Pot.B. 20 DG30
Park Rd., Rad. 31 CG35
Park Rd., Rich. 102 CM86
Park Rd., Rick. 42 BK45
Park Rd., Shep. 112 BN102
Park Rd., Stai. 98 BH86
Park Rd., Sun. 99 BV94
Park Rd., Surb. 116 CM100
Park Rd., Sutt. 131 CY107
Park Rd., Swan. 125 FF98
Park Rd., Tedd. 101 CF94
Park Rd., Twick. 101 CJ86
Park Rd., Uxb. 70 BL66
Park Rd., Wall. 133 DH106
Park Rd. (Hackbridge), Wall. 119 DH103
Park Rd., Wal.Cr. 23 DX33
Park Rd., Warl. 136 EE114
Park Rd., Wat. 29 BV39
Park Rd. (Bushey), Wat. 30 CA44
Park Rd., Wem. 74 CL65
Park Rd. E. W3 88 CP75
Park Rd. E., Uxb. 70 BK68
Hillingdon Rd.
Park Rd. N. W3 88 CP75
Park Rd. N. W4 88 CR78
Park Rd. W., Kings.T. 115 CJ95
Park Row SE10 93 ED79
Park Royal Rd. NW10 74 CQ70
Park Royal Rd. W3 74 CQ70
Park Side, Add. 126 BH111
Park Side, Sutt. 131 CY107
Park Sq., Esher 128 CB105
Park Rd.
Park Sq. E. NW1 5 H4
Park Sq. E. NW1 77 DH70
Park Sq. Ms. NW1 5 H5
Park Sq. Ms. NW1 77 DH70
Park Sq. W. NW1 5 H4
Park Sq. W. NW1 77 DH70
Park St. SE1 11 H2
Park St. SE1 78 DQ74
Park St. W1 4 F10
Park St. W1 76 DG73
Park St., Croy. 120 DQ103
Park St., St.Alb. 17 CD26
Park St., Tedd. 101 CE93
Park St. La., St.Alb. 16 CB30
Park Ter. (Sundridge), Sev. 152 EX124
Main Rd.
Park Ter., Wor.Pk. 117 CU102
Park Vw. N21 49 DM45
Park Vw. W3 74 CQ71
Park Vw., N.Mal. 117 CT97
Park Vw., Pnr. 44 BZ53
Park Vw., Pot.B. 20 DC33
Park Vw., Wem. 60 CP64
Park Vw. Ct., Ilf. 67 ES58
Brancaster Rd.
Park Vw. Cres. N11 49 DH49
Park Vw. Est. E2 79 DX68
Sewardstone Rd.
Park Vw. Gdns. NW4 61 CX58
Park Vw. Gdns., Bark. 81 ES68
River Rd.
Park Vw. Gdns., Ilf. 67 EM56
Woodford Ave.
Park Vw. Rd. N3 48 DB53
Park Vw. Rd. N17 64 DU55
Park Vw. Rd. NW10 61 CT63
Park Vw. Rd. W5 74 CL71
Park Vw. Rd., Cat. 149 DY122
Park Vw. Rd., Pnr. 43 BV52
Park Vw. Rd., Sthl. 72 CA74
Park Vw. Rd., Uxb. 70 BM72
Park Vw. Rd., Well. 96 EV83
Park Village E. NW1 77 DH68
Park Village W. NW1 77 DH68
Park Vill., Rom. 68 EX58
Park Vista SE10 93 ED79
Park Wk. N6 62 DG59
North Rd.
Park Wk. SW10 90 DC79
Park Wk., Ash. 144 CM119
Rectory La.
Park Way N20 48 DF49
Park Way NW11 61 CY57
Park Way, Bex. 111 FE90
Park Way, Edg. 46 CP53
Park Way, Enf. 35 DN40
Park Way, Felt. 99 BV87
Park Way, Ilf. 67 ET62
Park Way, Lthd. 142 CA123
Park Way, Rick. 42 BJ46
Park Way, Ruis. 57 BU60
Park Way, W.Mol. 114 CB97
Park W. W2 4 A9
Park W. Pl. W2 4 C8
Parkcroft Rd. SE12 108 EF87
Parkdale Cres., Wor.Pk. 116 CR104
Parkdale Rd. SE18 95 ES78
Parke Rd. SW13 89 CU81
Parke Rd., Sun. 113 BU98
Parker Clo. E16 80 EL74
Parker Ms. WC2 6 A8
Parker Rd., Croy. 134 DQ105
Parker St. E16 80 EL74
Parker St. WC2 6 A8
Parker St. WC2 77 DL72
Parker St., Wat. 29 BV39
Parkers Clo., Ash. 144 CL119
Parkers Hill, Ash. 144 CL119
Parkers La., Ash. 144 CL119
Parkers Row SE1 92 DT75
Jamaica Rd.
Parkes Rd., Chig. 53 ES50
Parkfield, Sev. 155 FM123
Parkfield Ave. SW14 88 CS84
Parkfield Ave., Felt. 99 BU90
Parkfield Ave., Har. 44 CC54
Parkfield Ave., Nthlt. 72 BX68
Parkfield Ave., Uxb. 71 BP69
Parkfield Clo., Edg. 46 CP51
Parkfield Clo., Nthlt. 72 BY68
Parkfield Cres., Felt. 99 BU90
Parkfield Cres., Har. 44 CC54
Parkfield Cres., Ruis. 58 BY62
Parkfield Dr., Nthlt. 72 BX68
Parkfield Gdns., Har. 58 CB55
Parkfield Rd. NW10 75 CU66
Parkfield Rd. SE14 93 DZ81
Parkfield Rd., Felt. 99 BU90
Parkfield Rd., Har. 58 CC62
Parkfield Rd., Nthlt. 72 BY68
Parkfield Rd., Uxb. 57 BP61
Parkfield St. N1 77 DN68
Parkfield Way, Brom. 123 EM100
Parkfields SW15 89 CW84
Parkfields, Croy. 121 DZ102
Parkfields, Lthd. 129 CD111
Parkfields Ave. NW9 60 CR60
Parkfields Ave. SW20 117 CV96
Parkfields Clo., Cars. 132 DG105
Devonshire Rd.
Parkfields Rd., Kings.T. 102 CM92
Parkgate SE3 94 EF83
Parkgate Ave., Barn. 34 DC39
Parkgate Clo., Kings.T. 102 CP93
Warboys App.
Parkgate Cres., Barn. 34 DC39
Parkgate Gdns. SW14 102 CR85
Parkgate Rd. SW11 90 DE80
Parkgate Rd., Orp. 139 FB105
Parkgate Rd., Wall. 132 DG106
Parkgate Rd., Wat. 30 BW37
Parkham Ct., Brom. 122 EE96
Parkham St. SW11 90 DD81
Parkhill Rd. E4 51 EC46
Parkhill Rd. NW3 62 DF64
Parkhill Rd., Bex. 110 EZ87
Parkhill Rd., Epsom 131 CT111
Parkhill Wk. NW3 62 DF64
Parkholme Rd. E8 78 DU65
Parkhouse St. SE5 92 DR80
Parkhurst, Epsom 130 CQ110
Parkhurst Gdns., Bex. 110 FA87
Parkhurst Rd. E12 67 EN63
Parkhurst Rd. E17 65 DY56
Parkhurst Rd. N7 63 DL63
Parkhurst Rd. N11 48 DG49
Parkhurst Rd. N17 50 DU54
Parkhurst Rd. N22 49 DM51
Parkhurst Rd., Bex. 110 FA87
Parkhurst Rd., Sutt. 132 DD105
Parkland Ave., Rom. 69 FE55
Parkland Clo., Chig. 53 EQ48
Parkland Clo., Sev. 155 FJ129
Parkland Gdns. SW19 103 CX88
Parkland Gro., Ashf. 98 BN91
Parkland Rd. N22 49 DM54
Parkland Rd., Ashf. 98 BN91
Parkland Rd., Wdf.Grn. 52 EG52
Parkland Wk. N4 63 DN59
Parkland Wk. N6 63 DJ59
Parkland Wk. N10 63 DH56
Parklands N6 63 DH59
Parklands, Add. 126 BJ106
Parklands, Chig. 53 EQ48
Parklands, Epp. 26 EX29
Parklands, Lthd. 142 CA123
Parklands, Surb. 116 CM99
Parklands, Wal.Abb. 23 EC33
Parklands Clo. SW14 102 CQ85
Parklands Clo., Barn. 34 DD38
Parklands Ct., Houns. 86 BX82
Parklands Dr. N3 61 CY55
Parklands Rd. SW16 105 DH92
Parklands Way, Wor.Pk. 116 CS103
Parklawn Ave., Epsom 130 CP113
Parklea Clo. NW9 46 CS53
Parkleigh Rd. SW19 118 DB96
Parkleys, Rich. 101 CK91
Parkmead SW15 103 CV86
Parkmead, Loug. 39 EN43
Parkmead Gdns. NW7 47 CT51
Parkmore Clo., Wdf.Grn. 52 EG49
Parkshot, Rich. 88 CL84
Parkside N3 48 DB53
Parkside NW2 61 CU62
Parkside NW7 47 CU51
Parkside SE3 94 EF80
Parkside SW19 103 CX91
Parkside, Buck.H. 52 EH47
Parkside, Hmptn. 101 CD92
Parkside, Pot.B. 20 DC32
High St.
Parkside, Sev. 138 EZ113
Parkside, Sid. 110 EV89
Parkside, Wal.Cr. 23 DY34
Parkside, Wat. 30 BW44
Parkside Ave. SW19 103 CX92
Parkside Ave., Bexh. 97 FD82
Parkside Ave., Brom. 122 EL98
Parkside Ave., Rom. 69 FD55
Parkside Clo. SE20 106 DW94
Parkside Ct., Wey. 126 BN105
Parkside Cres. N7 63 DN62
Parkside Cres., Surb. 116 CQ100
Parkside Cross, Bexh. 97 FE82
Parkside Dr., Edg. 46 CN48
Parkside Dr., Wat. 29 BS40
Parkside Est. E9 78 DW67
Rutland Rd.
Parkside Gdns. SW19 103 CX91
Parkside Gdns., Barn. 48 DF46
Parkside Gdns., Couls. 147 DH117
Parkside Ho., Dag. 69 FC62
Parkside Rd. SW11 90 DG81
Parkside Rd., Belv. 97 FB77
Parkside Rd., Houns. 100 CB85
Parkside Rd., Nthwd. 43 BT50
Parkside Ter. N18 50 DR49
Great Cambridge Rd.
Parkside Way, Har. 58 CB56
Parkstead Rd. SW15 103 CU85
Parkstone Ave. N18 50 DT50
Parkstone Rd. E17 65 EC55
Parkstone Rd. SE15 92 DU82
Rye La.
Parkthorne Clo., Har. 58 CB58
Parkthorne Dr., Har. 58 CA58
Parkthorne Rd. SW12 105 DK87
Parkview Ct. SW18 104 DA86
Broomhill Rd.
Parkview Dr., Mitch. 118 DD96
Parkview Rd. SE9 109 EP88
Parkview Rd., Croy. 120 DU102
Parkville Rd. SW6 89 CZ80
Parkway N14 49 DL47
Parkway NW1 77 DH67
Parkway SW20 117 CX98
Parkway, Croy. 135 EB109
Parkway, Erith 96 EY76
Parkway, Rain. 83 FG70
Upminster Rd. S.
Parkway, Rom. 55 FF54
Parkway, Uxb. 70 BN66
Parkway, Wey. 127 BR105
Parkway, Wdf.Grn. 52 EJ50
Parkway, The, Hayes 72 BW72
Parkway, The (Cranford), Houns. 85 BU79
Parkway Ms., Mitch. 105 DH94
Park Ave.
Parkway Trd. Est., Houns. 86 BW79
Parkwood N20 48 DF48
Parkwood, Beck. 121 EA95
Parkwood Ave., Esher 114 CC102
Parkwood Clo., Bans. 145 CX115
Parkwood Gro., Sun. 113 BU97
Parkwood Ms. N6 63 DH58
Parkwood Rd. SW19 103 CZ92
Parkwood Rd., Bans. 145 CX115
Parkwood Rd., Bex. 110 EZ87
Parkwood Rd., Islw. 87 CF81
Parkwood Rd., West. 150 EL121
Parkwood Vw., Bans. 145 CW116
Parliament Ct. E1 78 DS71
Sandy's Row
Parliament Hill NW3 62 DE63
Parliament Ms. SW14 88 CQ82
Thames Bank
Parliament Sq. SW1 9 P5
Parliament Sq. SW1 91 DL75
Parliament St. SW1 9 P5
Parliament St. SW1 91 DL75
Parma Cres. SW11 90 DF84
Parmiter St. E2 78 DV68
Parnell Clo., Abb.L. 15 BT30
Parnell Clo., Edg. 46 CP49
Parnell Rd. E3 79 DZ67
Parnham St. E14 79 DY72
Blount St.
Parolles Rd. N19 63 DJ60
Paroma Rd., Belv. 96 FA76
Parr Ave., Epsom 131 CV109
Parr Clo. N9 50 DV49
Parr Clo. N18 50 DV49
Parr Clo., Lthd. 143 CF120
Parr Ct., Felt. 100 BW91
Parr Rd. E6 80 EK67
Parr Rd., Stan. 45 CK53
Parr St. N1 78 DR68
Parrotts Clo., Rick. 28 BN42
Parrs Clo., S.Croy. 134 DR109
Florence Rd.
Parrs Pl., Hmptn. 100 CA94
Parry Ave. E6 81 EM72
Parry Clo., Epsom 131 CU107
Parry Dr., Wey. 126 BN110
Parry Pl. SE18 95 EP77
Parry Rd. SE25 120 DS97
Parry Rd. W10 75 CY69
Parry St. SW8 91 DL79
Parsifal Rd. NW6 62 DA64
Parsley Gdns., Croy. 121 DX102
Primrose La.
Parsloes Ave., Dag. 68 EX63
Parson St. NW4 61 CW56
Parsonage Clo., Abb.L. 15 BS30
Parsonage Clo., Hayes 71 BT72
Parsonage Clo., Warl. 149 DY116
Parsonage Gdns., Enf. 36 DQ40
Parsonage La., Enf. 36 DR40
Parsonage La., Sid. 110 EZ91
Parsonage Manorway, Belv. 96 FA79
Parsonage Rd., Rick. 42 BK45
Parsonage St. E14 93 EC77
Parsons Cres., Edg. 46 CN48
Parsons Grn. SW6 90 DA82
Parsons Grn. La. SW6 90 DA81
Parsons Gro., Edg. 46 CN48
Parsons Hill SE18 95 EN76
Powis St.
Parson's Ho. W2 76 DD70
Edgware Rd.
Parsons La., Dart. 111 FG90
Parson's Mead, Croy. 119 DP102
Parsons Mead, E.Mol. 114 CC97
Parsons Pightle, Couls. 147 DN120
Coulsdon Rd.
Parsons Rd. E13 80 EJ68
Old St.
Parsonsfield Clo., Bans. 145 CX115
Parsonsfield Rd., Bans. 145 CX115
Parthenia Rd. SW6 90 DA81
Parthia Clo., Tad. 145 CV119
Partingdale La. NW7 47 CX50
Partington Clo. N19 63 DK60
Partridge Clo. E16 80 EK71
Fulmer Rd.
Partridge Clo., Barn. 33 CW44
Partridge Clo. (Bushey), Wat. 44 CB46
Partridge Ct. EC1 77 DP70
Percival St.
Partridge Dr., Orp. 123 EQ104
Partridge Grn. SE9 109 EN90
Partridge Knoll, Pur. 133 DP112
Partridge Mead, Bans. 145 CW116
Partridge Rd., Hmptn. 100 BZ93
Partridge Rd., Sid. 109 ES90
Partridge Sq. E6 80 EL71
Nightingale Way
Partridge Way N22 49 DL53
Parvills Rd., Wal.Abb. 23 ED32
Parvin St. SW8 91 DK81
Parvis Rd., W.Byf. 126 BG113
Pasadena Clo., Hayes 85 BU75
Pascal St. SW8 91 DK80
Pascoe Rd. SE13 107 ED85
Pasfield, Wal.Abb. 23 ED33
Pasley Clo. SE17 92 DQ78
Penrose St.
Pasquier Rd. E17 65 DY55
Passey Pl. SE9 109 EM86
Passfield Dr. E14 79 EB71
Uamvar St.
Passfield Path SE28 82 EV73
Booth Clo.
Passing All. EC1 6 F5
Passmore Gdns. N11 49 DK51
Passmore St. SW1 8 F9
Passmore St. SW1 90 DG78
Pasteur Clo. NW9 46 CS54
Pasteur Gdns. N18 49 DP50
Paston Clo. E5 65 DX62
Caldecott Way
Paston Cres. SE12 108 EH87
Pastor St. SE11 10 G8
Pastor St. SE11 91 DP77
Pasture Clo. (Bushey), Wat. 44 CC45
Pasture Clo., Wem. 59 CH62
Pasture Rd. SE6 108 EE88
Pasture Rd., Dag. 68 EZ63
Pasture Rd., Wem. 59 CH61
Pastures, The N20 47 CZ46
Pastures, The, Wat. 44 BW45
Pastures Mead, Uxb. 70 BN65
Patch, The, Sev. 154 FE122
Patcham Ct., Sutt. 132 DC109
Patcham Ter. SW8 91 DH81
Pater St. W8 90 DA76
Paternoster Clo., Wal.Abb. 24 EF32
Paternoster Hill, Wal.Abb. 24 EF32
Paternoster Row EC4 7 H9
Paternoster Sq. EC4 6 G8
Paterson Rd., Ashf. 98 BK92
Pates Manor Dr., Felt. 99 BR87
Path, The SW19 118 DB95
Pathfield Rd. SW16 105 DK93
Pathway, The, Rad. 31 CF36
Pathway, The, Wat. 44 BX46
Anthony Clo.
Patience Rd. SW11 90 DE82
Patio Clo. SW4 105 DK86
Patmore Est. SW8 91 DJ81
Patmore La., Walt. 127 BT107
Patmore Rd., Wal.Abb. 24 EE34
Patmore St. SW8 91 DJ81

Pat–Pen This index reads in the sequence: Street Name / Postal District or Post Town / Map Page Number / Grid Reference

Patmore Way, Rom. 55 FB50
Patmos Rd. SW9 91 DP80
Paton Clo. E3 79 EA69
Paton St. EC1 7 H3
Patricia Ct., Chis. 123 ER95
Manor Pk. Rd.
Patricia Ct., Well. 96 EV80
Patricia Gdns., Sutt. 132 DA111
The Cres.
Patrick Connolly Gdns. E3 79 EB69
Talwin St.
Patrick Pas. SW11 90 DE82
Patrick Rd. E13 80 EJ69
Patrington Clo., Uxb. 70 BJ69
Boulmer Rd.
Patriot Sq. E2 78 DV68
Patrol Pl. SE6 107 EB86
Patshull Pl. NW5 77 DJ65
Patshull Rd.
Patshull Rd. NW5 77 DJ65
Patten All., Rich. 101 CK85
The Hermitage
Patten Rd. SW18 104 DE87
Pattenden Rd. SE6 107 DZ88
Patterdale Clo., Brom. 108 EF93
Patterdale Rd. SE15 92 DW80
Patterson Ct. SE19 106 DT94
Patterson Rd. SE19 106 DT93
Pattinson Pt. E16 80 EG71
Fife Rd.
Pattison Rd. NW2 62 DA62
Pattison Wk. SE18 95 EQ78
Sandbach Pl.
Paul Clo. E15 80 EE66
Paul St.
Paul Gdns., Croy. 120 DT103
Paul Robeson Clo. E6 81 EN69
Eastbourne Rd.
Paul St. E15 80 EE67
Paul St. EC2 7 L5
Paul St. EC2 78 DR70
Paulet Rd. SE5 91 DP82
Paulhan Rd., Har. 59 CJ56
Paulin Dr. N21 49 DN45
Pauline Cres., Twick. 100 CC88
Paulinus Clo., Orp. 124 EW96
Pauls Grn., Wal.Cr. 23 DY33
Eleanor Rd.
Paul's Pl., Ash. 144 CP119
Pauls Wk. EC4 78 DQ73
Upper Thames St.
Paultons Sq. SW3 90 DD79
Paultons St. SW3 90 DD79
Pauntley St. N19 63 DJ60
Paved Ct., Rich. 101 CK85
King St.
Paveley Dr. SW11 90 DE80
Paveley St. NW8 4 C3
Paveley St. NW8 76 DE70
Pavement, The SW4 91 DJ84
Pavement, The W5 88 CL76
Popes La.
Pavement Ms., Rom. 68 EX59
Clarissa Rd.
Pavement Sq., Croy. 120 DU102
Pavet Clo., Dag. 83 FB65
Pavilion Gdns., Stai. 98 BH94
Pavilion Ms. N3 48 DA54
Windermere Ave.
Pavilion Rd. SW1 8 E5
Pavilion Rd. SW1 90 DF76
Pavilion Rd., Ilf. 67 EM59
Pavilion St. SW1 8 E7
Pavilion Ter., E.Mol. 115 CF98
Pavilion Ter., Ilf. 67 ES57
Southdown Cres.
Pavilion Way, Edg. 46 CP52
Pavilion Way, Ruis. 58 BW61
Pavilions, The, Epp. 27 FC25
Pawleyne Clo. SE20 106 DW94
Pawsey Clo. E13 80 EG67
Plashet Rd.
Pawson's Rd., Croy. 120 DQ100
Paxford Rd., Wem. 59 CH61
Paxton Clo., Rich. 88 CM82
Paxton Clo., Walt. 114 BW101
Shaw Dr.
Paxton Pl. SE27 106 DS91
Paxton Rd. N17 50 DT52
Paxton Rd. SE23 107 DY90
Paxton Rd. W4 88 CS79
Paxton Rd., Brom. 108 EG94
Paxton Ter. SW1 91 DH79
Payne Rd. E3 79 EB68
Payne St. SE8 93 DZ79
Paynell Ct. SE3 94 EE83
Lawn Ter.
Paynes Wk. W6 89 CY79
Ancill Clo.
Paynesfield Ave. SW14 88 CR83
Paynesfield Rd. (Bushey), Wat. 45 CF45
Paynesfield Rd., West. 150 EJ121
Peabody Ave. SW1 91 DH78
Sutherland St.
Peabody Clo. SE10 93 EB81
Devonshire Dr.
Peabody Dws. WC1 5 P4
Peabody Est. EC1 7 J5
Peabody Est. N17 50 DS53
Peabody Est. SE1 10 E3
Peabody Est. SE24 106 DQ87
Peabody Est. SW3 90 DE79
Margaretta Ter.
Peabody Est. W6 89 CW78
Peabody Est. W10 75 CW70
Peabody Hill SE21 105 DP88
Peabody Hill Est. SE21 105 DP88
Peabody Sq. N1 77 DP67
Essex Rd.
Peabody Sq. SE1 10 F5
Peabody Sq. SE1 91 DP75
Peabody Trust SE1 11 H3
Peabody Yd. N1 78 DQ67
Greenman St.
Peace Clo. N14 35 DH43
Peace Clo. SE25 120 DS98
Peace Clo., Wal.Cr. 22 DU29
Goffs La.
Peace Gro., Wem. 60 CP61
Peace St. SE18 95 EP79
Nightingale Vale
Peach Rd. W10 75 CX69
Peach Tree Ave., West Dr. 70 BM72
Pear Tree Ave.
Peaches Clo., Sutt. 131 CY108
Peachey Clo., Uxb. 70 BK72
Peachey La., Uxb. 70 BK71
Peachum Rd. SE3 94 EF79
Peacock Ave., Felt. 99 BR88
Peacock Gdns., S.Croy. 135 DY110
Peacock St. SE17 10 G9
Peacock Wk. E16 80 EH72
Sophia Rd.
Peacock Wk., Abb.L. 15 BU31
College Rd.
Peacock Yd. SE17 10 G9
Peak, The SE26 106 DW90
Peak Hill SE26 106 DW91
Peak Hill Ave. SE26 106 DW91
Peak Hill Gdns. SE26 106 DW91
Peakes La. (Cheshunt), Wal.Cr. 22 DT27
Peakes Way (Cheshunt), Wal.Cr. 22 DT27
Peaketon Ave., Ilf. 66 EK56
Peaks Hill, Pur. 133 DK110
Peaks Hill Ri., Pur. 133 DL110
Peal Gdns. W13 73 CG70
Ruislip Rd. E.
Peall Rd., Croy. 119 DM100
Pear Clo. NW9 60 CR56
Pear Clo. SE14 93 DY80
Southerngate Way
Pear Pl. SE1 10 D4
Pear Rd. E11 65 ED62
Pear Tree Ave., West Dr. 70 BM72
Pear Tree Clo. E2 78 DT67
Pear Tree Clo., Add. 126 BG106
Pear Tree Rd.
Pear Tree Clo., Swan. 125 FD96
Pear Tree Ct. EC1 6 E5
Pear Tree Ct. EC1 77 DN70
Pear Tree Rd., Add. 126 BG106
Pear Tree Rd., Ashf. 99 BQ92
Pear Tree Wk. (Cheshunt), Wal.Cr. 22 DR26
Pearce Clo., Mitch. 118 DG96
Pearce Rd., W.Mol. 114 CB97
Pearcefield Ave. SE23 106 DW88
Pearcroft Rd. E11 65 ED61
Peardon St. SW8 91 DH82
Peareswood Gdns., Stan. 45 CK53
Peareswood Rd., Erith 97 FF81
Pearfield Rd. SE23 107 DY90
Pearl Clo. E6 81 EN72
Pearl Clo. NW2 61 CX59
Marble Dr.
Pearl Rd. E17 65 EA55
Pearl St. E1 78 DV74
Penang St.
Pearmain Clo., Shep. 113 BP99
Laleham Rd.
Pearman St. SE1 10 E6
Pearman St. SE1 91 DN76
Pears Rd., Houns. 86 CC83
Pearscroft Ct. SW6 90 DB81
Pearscroft Rd. SW6 90 DB81
Pearson St. E2 78 DT68
Pearsons Ave. SE14 93 EA81
Tanners Hill
Peartree Ave. SW17 104 DC90
Peartree Clo., Erith 97 FD81
Peartree Clo., Mitch. 118 DE96
Peartree Clo., S.Croy. 134 DV114
Peartree Gdns., Dag. 68 EV63
Peartree Gdns., Rom. 55 FB54
Peartree La. E1 78 DW73
Glamis Rd.
Peartree Rd., Enf. 36 DS41
Peartree St. EC1 6 G4
Peartree St. EC1 77 DP70
Peary Pl. E2 78 DW69
Kirkwall Pl.
Pease Clo., Horn. 83 FH66
Dowding Way
Peatfield Clo., Sid. 109 ES90
Woodside Rd.
Peatmore Ave., Wok. 140 BG116
Peatmore Clo., Wok. 140 BG116
Pebworth Rd., Har. 59 CG61
Peckarmans Wd. SE26 106 DT90
Peckett Sq. N5 64 DQ63
Highbury Gra.
Peckford Pl. SW9 91 DN82
Peckham Gro. SE15 92 DS80
Peckham High St. SE15 92 DU81
Peckham Hill St. SE15 92 DU80
Peckham Pk. Rd. SE15 92 DU80
Peckham Rd. SE5 92 DS81
Peckham Rd. SE15 92 DT81
Peckham Rye SE15 92 DU83
Peckham Rye SE22 92 DU84
Peckwater St. NW5 63 DJ64
Pedham Pl. Est., Swan. 125 FG99
Pedlars Wk. N7 77 DL65
Pedley Rd., Dag. 68 EW60
Pedley St. E1 78 DU70
Pedro St. E5 65 DX62
Pedworth Gdns. SE16 92 DW77
Rotherhithe New Rd.
Peek Cres. SW19 103 CX92
Peel Clo. E4 51 EB47
Peel Clo. N9 50 DU48
Plevna Rd.
Peel Dr. NW9 61 CT55
Peel Dr., Ilf. 66 EL55
Peel Gro. E2 78 DW68
Peel Pas. W8 76 DA74
Peel St.
Peel Pl., Ilf. 52 EL54
Peel Prec. NW6 76 DA68
Peel Rd. E18 52 EF53
Peel Rd. NW6 75 CZ69
Peel Rd., Har. 59 CF55
Peel Rd., Orp. 137 EQ106
Peel Rd., Wem. 59 CK62
Peel St. W8 76 DA74
Peel Way, Uxb. 70 BL70
Peerless Dr., Uxb. 56 BJ56
Peerless St. EC1 7 K3
Peerless St. EC1 78 DR69
Pegamoid Rd. N18 50 DW48
Pegasus Ct., Abb.L. 15 BT32
Furtherfield
Pegasus Pl. SE11 91 DN79
Clayton St.
Pegg Rd., Houns. 86 BX80
Peggotty Way, Uxb. 71 BP72
Dickens Ave.
Pegley Gdns. SE12 108 EG89
Pegmire La., Wat. 30 CC39
Pegwell St. SE18 95 ES80
Pekin Clo. E14 79 EA72
Pekin St.
Pekin St. E14 79 EA72
Peldon Ct., Rich. 88 CM84
Peldon Wk. N1 77 DP67
Britannia Row
Pelham Ave., Bark. 81 ET67
Pelham Clo. SE5 92 DS83
Pelham Cres. SW7 8 B9
Pelham Cres. SW7 90 DE77
Pelham Pl. SW7 8 B8
Pelham Pl. SW7 90 DE77
Pelham Rd. E18 66 EH55
Pelham Rd. N15 64 DT56
Pelham Rd. N22 49 DN54
Pelham Rd. SW19 104 DA94
Pelham Rd., Beck. 120 DW96
Pelham Rd., Bexh. 96 FA83
Pelham Rd., Ilf. 67 ER61
Pelham St. SW7 8 A8
Pelham St. SW7 90 DD77
Pelhams, The, Wat. 30 BX35
Pelhams Clo., Esher 128 CA105
Pelhams Wk., Esher 114 CA104
Pelican Est. SE15 92 DT81
Pelican Pas. E1 78 DW70
Cambridge Heath Rd.
Pelican Wk. SW9 91 DP84
Loughborough Pk.
Pelier St. SE17 92 DQ79
Langdale Clo.
Pelinore Rd. SE6 108 EE89
Pellant Rd. SW6 89 CY80
Pellatt Gro. N22 49 DN53
Pellatt Rd. SE22 106 DT85
Pellatt Rd., Wem. 59 CK61
Pellerin Rd. N16 64 DS64
Pelling St. E14 79 EA72
Pellipar Clo. N13 49 DN48
Pellipar Gdns. SE18 95 EM78
Pelly Rd. E13 80 EG67
Pelter St. E2 7 P2
Pelter St. E2 78 DT69
Pelton Ave., Sutt. 132 DB110
Pelton Rd. SE10 94 EE78
Pembar Ave. E17 65 DY55
Pember Rd. NW10 75 CX69
Pemberton Gdns. N19 63 DJ62
Pemberton Gdns., Rom. 68 EY57
Pemberton Gdns., Swan. 125 FE97
Pemberton Ho. SE26 106 DU91
High Level Dr.
Pemberton Pl. E8 78 DV66
Mare St.
Pemberton Pl., Esher 114 CC104
Carrick Gate
Pemberton Rd. N4 63 DN57
Pemberton Rd., E.Mol. 114 CC98
Pemberton Row EC4 6 E8
Pemberton Ter. N19 63 DJ62
Pembridge Ave., Twick. 100 BZ88
Pembridge Cres. W11 76 DA73
Pembridge Gdns. W2 76 DA73
Pembridge Ms. W11 76 DA73
Pembridge Pl. W2 76 DA73
Pembridge Rd. W11 76 DA73
Pembridge Sq. W2 76 DA73
Pembridge Vill. W2 76 DA73
Pembridge Vill. W11 76 DA73
Pembroke Ave., Enf. 36 DV38
Pembroke Ave., Har. 59 CG55
Pembroke Ave., Surb. 116 CP99
Pembroke Ave., Walt. 128 BX105
Pembroke Clo. SW1 8 G5
Pembroke Clo. SW1 90 DG75
Pembroke Clo., Bans. 146 DB117
Pembroke Clo., Erith 97 FD77
Pembroke Dr. (Cheshunt), Wal.Cr. 21 DP29
Pembroke Gdns. W8 89 CZ77
Pembroke Gdns., Dag. 69 FB62
Pembroke Gdns. Clo. W8 89 CZ76
Pembroke Ms. E3 79 DY69
Morgan St.
Pembroke Ms. N10 48 DG53
Pembroke Rd.
Pembroke Ms. W8 90 DA76
Earls Wk.
Pembroke Ms., Sev. 155 FH125
Pembroke Rd.
Pembroke Pl. W8 90 DA76
Pembroke Pl., Edg. 46 CN52
Pembroke Rd. E6 81 EM71
Pembroke Rd. E17 65 EB57
Pembroke Rd. N8 63 DL56
Pembroke Rd. N10 48 DG53
Pembroke Rd. N13 50 DQ48
Pembroke Rd. N15 64 DT57
Pembroke Rd. SE25 120 DS98
Pembroke Rd. W8 90 DA77
Pembroke Rd., Brom. 122 EJ96
Pembroke Rd., Erith 97 FC78
Pembroke Rd., Grnf. 72 CB69
Pembroke Rd., Ilf. 67 ET60
Pembroke Rd., Mitch. 118 DG96
Pembroke Rd., Nthwd. 43 BQ48
Pembroke Rd., Ruis. 57 BS60
Pembroke Rd., Sev. 155 FH125
Pembroke Rd., Wem. 59 CK62
Pembroke Sq. W8 90 DA76
Pembroke St. N1 77 DL66
Pembroke Studios W8 89 CZ76
Pembroke Vill. W8 90 DA77
Pembroke Vill., Rich. 87 CK84
Pembroke Wk. W8 90 DA77
Pembroke Way, Hayes 85 BQ76
Pembury Ave., Wor.Pk. 117 CU102
Pembury Clo., Brom. 122 EF101
Pembury Clo., Couls. 132 DG114
Pembury Ct., Hayes 85 BR79
Pembury Cres., Sid. 110 EY90
Pembury Pl. E5 64 DV64
Pembury Rd. E5 64 DV64
Pembury Rd. N17 50 DT53
Pembury Rd. SE25 120 DU98
Pembury Rd., Bexh. 96 EY80
Pemdevon Rd., Croy. 119 DN101
Pemell Clo. E1 78 DW70
Colebert Ave.
Pemerich Clo., Hayes 85 BT78
Pempath Pl., Wem. 59 CK61
Penally Pl. N1 78 DR67
Shepperton Rd.
Penang St. E1 78 DV74
Penarth St. SE15 92 DW79
Penates, Esher 129 CD105
Penberth Rd. SE6 107 EC88
Penbury Rd., Sthl. 86 BZ77
Pencombe Ms. W11 75 CZ73
Denbigh Rd.
Pencraig Way SE15 92 DV79
Penda Rd., Erith 97 FB80
Pendarves Rd. SW20 117 CW95
Penda's Mead E9 65 DY63
Lindisfarne Way
Pendell Ave., Hayes 85 BT80
Pendennis Clo., W.Byf. 126 BG114
Pendennis Rd. N17 64 DR55
Pendennis Rd. SW16 105 DL91
Pendennis Rd., Orp. 124 EW103
Pendennis Rd., Sev. 155 FH123
Penderel Rd., Houns. 100 CA85
Penderry Ri. SE6 107 ED89
Penderyn Way N7 63 DK63
Pendle Rd. SW16 105 DH93
Pendlestone Rd. E17 65 EB57
Pendragon Rd., Brom. 108 EF90
Pendragon Wk. NW9 60 CS58
Pendrell Rd. SE4 93 DY82
Pendrell St. SE18 95 ER79
Pendula Dr., Hayes 72 BX70
Pendulum Ms. E8 64 DT64
Birkbeck Rd.
Penerley Rd. SE6 107 EB88
Penerley Rd., Rain. 83 FH71
Penfold Clo., Croy. 119 DN104
Epsom Rd.
Penfold La., Bex. 110 EX88
Carisbrooke Ave.
Penfold Pl. NW1 4 B6
Penfold Pl. NW1 76 DE71
Penfold Rd. N9 51 DX46
Penfold St. NW1 4 A5
Penfold St. NW1 76 DD70
Penfold St. NW8 4 A5
Penfold St. NW8 76 DD70
Penford Gdns. SE9 94 EK83
Penford St. SE5 91 DP82
Pengarth Rd., Bex. 110 EX85
Penge Ho. SW11 90 DD83
Wye St.
Penge La. SE20 106 DW94
Penge Rd. E13 80 EJ67
Penge Rd. SE20 120 DU97
Penge Rd. SE25 120 DU97
Pengelly Clo. (Cheshunt), Wal.Cr. 22 DV30
Penhall Rd. SE7 94 EK77
Penhill Rd., Bex. 110 EW86
Penhurst Rd., Ilf. 53 EP52
Penifather La., Grnf. 73 CD69
Peninsular Clo., Felt. 99 BR86
Penistone Rd. SW16 105 DL94
Penketh Dr., Har. 59 CD62
Penman Clo., St.Alb. 16 CA27
Penmon Rd. SE2 96 EU76
Penn Clo., Grnf. 72 CB68
Penn Clo., Har. 59 CJ56
Penn Clo., Uxb. 70 BK70
Penn Gdns., Chis. 123 EP96
Penn Gdns., Rom. 54 FA52
Penn La., Bex. 110 EX86
Penn Pl., Rick. 42 BK45
Northway
Penn Rd. N7 63 DL64
Penn Rd., St.Alb. 16 CC27
Penn Rd., Wat. 29 BV39
Penn St. N1 78 DR67
Pennack Rd. SE15 92 DT79
Pennant Ms. W8 90 DB77
Pennant Ter. E17 51 DZ54
Pennard Rd. W12 89 CW75
Pennards, The, Sun. 114 BW96
Penne Clo., Rad. 17 CF34
Penner Clo. SW19 103 CY89
Victoria Dr.
Pennethorne Clo. E9 78 DW67
Victoria Pk. Rd.
Pennethorne Rd. SE15 92 DV80
Pennine Dr. NW2 61 CX61
Pennine La. NW2 61 CY61
Pennine Dr.
Pennine Way, Bexh. 97 FE81
Pennine Way, Hayes 85 BR80
Pennington Clo. SE27 106 DR91
Hamilton Rd.
Pennington Clo., Rom. 54 FA51
Pennington Dr. N21 35 DL43
Pennington Dr., Wey. 113 BS104
Pennington St. E1 78 DU73
Pennington Way SE12 108 EJ89
Penniston Clo. N17 50 DQ54
Penny Clo., Rain. 83 FH69
Penny La., Shep. 113 BS101
Penny Ms. SW12 105 DH87
Caistor Rd.
Penny Rd. NW10 74 CP69
Pennycroft, Croy. 135 DY109
Pennyfield, Cob. 127 BU113
Pennyfields E14 79 EA73
Pennymoor Wk. W9 75 CZ69
Ashmore Rd.
Pennyroyal Ave. E6 81 EN72
Penpoll Rd. E8 78 DV65
Penpool La., Well. 96 EV83
Penrhyn Ave. E17 51 DZ53
Penrhyn Cres. E17 51 EA53
Penrhyn Cres. SW14 88 CQ84
Penrhyn Gro. E17 51 EA53
Penrhyn Rd., Kings.T. 116 CL98
Penrith Clo. SW15 103 CY85
Penrith Clo., Beck. 121 EB95
Albemarle Rd.
Penrith Clo., Uxb. 70 BK66
Chippendale Waye
Penrith Cres., Rain. 69 FG64
Penrith Pl. SE27 105 DP89
Harpenden Rd.
Penrith Rd. N15 64 DR57
Penrith Rd., Ilf. 53 ET51
Penrith Rd., N.Mal. 116 CR98
Penrith Rd., Th.Hth. 120 DQ96
Penrith St. SW16 105 DJ93
Penrose Ave., Wat. 44 BX47
Penrose Gro. SE17 92 DQ78
Penrose Ho. SE17 92 DQ78
Penrose St.
Penrose Rd., Lthd. 142 CC122
Penrose St. SE17 92 DQ78
Penry St. SE1 11 N9
Penryn St. NW1 77 DK68
Pensbury Pl. SW8 91 DJ82
Pensbury St. SW8 91 DJ82
Penscroft Gdns., Borwd. 32 CR42
Pensford Ave., Rich. 88 CN82
Penshurst Ave., Sid. 110 EU86
Penshurst Gdns., Edg. 46 CP50
Penshurst Grn., Brom. 122 EF99
Penshurst Rd. E9 79 DX66
Penshurst Rd. N17 50 DT52
Penshurst Rd., Bexh. 96 EZ81
Penshurst Rd., Pot.B. 20 DD31
Penshurst Rd., Th.Hth. 119 DP99
Penshurst Wk., Brom. 122 EF99
Hayesford Pk. Dr.
Penshurst Way, Orp. 124 EW98
Star La.
Penshurst Way, Sutt. 132 DA108
Pensons La., Ong. 27 FG28
Penstemon Clo. N3 48 DA51
Penstock Footpath N22 63 DL55
Pentavia Retail Pk. NW7 47 CT52
Bunns La.
Pentelowe Gdns., Felt. 99 BU86
Pentire Rd. E17 51 ED53
Pentland Ave., Edg. 46 CP47
Pentland Ave., Shep. 112 BN99
Pentland Clo. NW11 61 CY61
Pentland Gdns. SW18 104 DC86
St. Ann's Hill
Pentland Pl., Nthlt. 72 BY67
Pentland Rd. (Bushey), Wat. 30 CC44
Pentland St. SW18 104 DC86
Pentland Way, Uxb. 57 BQ62
Pentlands Clo., Mitch. 119 DH97
Pentlow St. SW15 89 CW83
Pentlow Way, Buck.H. 52 EL45
Pentney Rd. E4 51 ED46
Pentney Rd. SW12 105 DJ88

Pentney Rd. SW19 117 CY95
Midmoor Rd.
Penton Dr. (Cheshunt), Wal.Cr. 23 DX29
Penton Gro. N1 6 D1
Penton Hall Dr., Stai. 112 BG95
Penton Hook Rd., Stai. 98 BG94
Penton Pk. Est., Cher. 112 BH97
Penton Pl. SE17 10 G10
Penton Pl. SE17 91 DP78
Penton Ri. WC1 6 C2
Penton Ri. WC1 77 DM69
Penton St. N1 6 D1
Penton St. N1 77 DN68
Pentonville Rd. N1 6 B1
Pentonville Rd. N1 77 DM68
Pentrich Ave., Enf. 36 DU38
Pentridge St. SE15 92 DT80
Pentyre Ave. N18 50 DR50
Penwerris Ave., Islw. 86 CC80
Penwith Rd. SW18 104 DA89
Penwortham Rd. SW16 105 DH93
Penwortham Rd., S.Croy. 134 DQ110
Penylan Pl., Edg. 46 CN52
Penywern Rd. SW5 90 DA78
Penzance Clo., Uxb. 42 BK53
Penzance Pl. W11 75 CY74
Penzance St. W11 75 CY74
Peony Ct., Wdf.Grn. 52 EE52
Bridle Path
Peony Gdns. W12 75 CU73
Peplins Clo., Hat. 19 CY26
Peplins Way, Hat. 19 CY25
Peploe Rd. NW6 75 CX68
Peplow Clo., West Dr. 70 BK74
Tavistock Rd.
Pepper All., Loug. 38 EF40
Pepper Clo. E6 81 EM71
Pepper St. E14 93 EB76
Pepper St. SE1 11 H4
Peppermead Sq. SE13 107 EA85
Peppermint Clo., Croy. 119 DL101
Peppermint Pl. E11 66 EE62
Birch Gro.
Peppie Clo. N16 64 DS61
Bouverie Rd.
Pepys Clo., Ash. 144 CN117
Pepys Clo., Uxb. 57 BP63
Pepys Cres. E16 80 EG74
Silvertown Way
Pepys Cres., Barn. 33 CW43
Pepys Ri., Orp. 123 ET102
Pepys Rd. SE14 93 DX81
Pepys Rd. SW20 117 CW96
Pepys St. EC3 7 N10
Pepys St. EC3 78 DS73
Perceval Ave. NW3 62 DE64
Perch St. E8 64 DT63
Percheron Clo., Islw. 87 CG83
Percheron Rd., Borwd. 32 CR44
Percival Ct. N17 50 DT52
High Rd.
Percival Ct., Nthlt. 58 CA64
Percival Gdns., Rom. 68 EW58
Percival Rd. SW14 88 CQ84
Percival Rd., Enf. 36 DT42
Percival Rd., Felt. 99 BT89
Percival Rd., Orp. 123 EP103
Percival St. EC1 6 F4
Percival St. EC1 77 DP70
Percival Way, Epsom 130 CQ105
Percy Ave., Ashf. 98 BN92
Percy Bryant Rd., Sun. 99 BS94
Percy Bush Rd., West Dr. 84 BM76
Percy Circ. WC1 6 C2
Percy Circ. WC1 77 DM69
Percy Gdns., Enf. 37 DX43
Percy Gdns., Hayes 71 BS69
Percy Gdns., Islw. 87 CG83
Percy Gdns., Wor.Pk. 116 CS102
Percy Ms. W1 5 M7
Percy Pas. W1 5 L7
Percy Rd. E11 66 EE59
Percy Rd. E16 80 EE71
Percy Rd. N12 48 DC50
Percy Rd. N21 50 DQ45
Percy Rd. NW6 76 DA69
Stafford Rd.
Percy Rd. SE20 121 DX95
Percy Rd. SE25 120 DU99
Percy Rd. W12 89 CU75
Percy Rd., Bexh. 96 EY82
Percy Rd., Hmptn. 100 CA94
Percy Rd., Ilf. 68 EU59
Percy Rd., Islw. 87 CG84
Percy Rd., Mitch. 118 DG101
Percy Rd., Rom. 69 FB55
Percy Rd., Twick. 100 CB88
Percy Rd., Wat. 29 BV42
Percy St. W1 5 M7
Percy St. W1 77 DK71
Percy Way, Twick. 100 CC88
Percy Yd. WC1 6 C2
Peregrin Rd., Wal.Abb. 24 EG34
Peregrine Clo. NW10 60 CR64
Peregrine Clo., Wat. 16 BY34
Peregrine Ct. SW16 105 DM91
Leithcote Gdns.
Peregrine Ct., Well. 95 ET81
Peregrine Gdns., Croy. 121 DY103
Peregrine Ho. EC1 6 G2
Peregrine Ho. EC1 77 DP69
Peregrine Rd., Ilf. 54 EV50
Peregrine Rd., Sun. 113 BT96
Peregrine Wk., Horn. 83 FH65
Heron Flight Ave.
Peregrine Way SW19 103 CW94
Perham Rd. W14 89 CY78
Perham Way, St.Alb. 17 CK26
Peridot St. E6 80 EL71
Perifield SE21 106 DQ88
Perimeade Rd., Grnf. 73 CJ68
Periton Rd. SE9 94 EK84
Perivale Gdns. W13 73 CH70
Bellevue Rd.
Perivale Gdns., Wat. 15 BV34
Perivale Gra., Grnf. 73 CG69
Perivale Ind. Pk., Grnf. 73 CG67
Perivale La., Grnf. 73 CG69
Perivale New Business Cen., Grnf. 73 CH68
Perkins Clo., Wem. 59 CH64
Perkins Ct., Ashf. 98 BM92
Perkin's Rents SW1 9 M6
Perkin's Rents SW1 91 DK76
Perkins Rd., Ilf. 67 ER57
Perkins Sq. SE1 11 J2
Perks Clo. SE3 94 EE83
Hurren Clo.
Perpins Rd. SE9 109 ER86
Perram Clo., Brox. 23 DY26
Perran Rd. SW2 105 DP89
Christchurch Rd.
Perran Wk., Brent. 88 CL78
Burford Rd.
Perren St. NW5 77 DH65
Ryland Rd.
Perrers Rd. W6 89 CV77
Perrin Clo., Ashf. 98 BM92
Fordbridge Rd.
Perrin Rd., Wem. 59 CG63
Perrins Ct. NW3 62 DC63
Hampstead High St.
Perrins La. NW3 62 DC63
Perrin's Wk. NW3 62 DC63
Perriors Clo. (Cheshunt), Wal.Cr. 22 DU27
Perrott St. SE18 95 EQ77
Perry Ave. W3 74 CR72
Perry Clo., Rain. 83 FD68
Lowen Rd.
Perry Clo., Uxb. 71 BQ72
Harlington Rd.
Perry Ct. N15 64 DS58
Albert Rd.
Perry Gdns. N9 50 DS48
Deansway
Perry Garth, Nthlt. 72 BW67
Perry Hall Clo., Orp. 124 EU101
Perry Hall Rd., Orp. 123 ET100
Perry Hill SE6 107 DZ90
Perry How, Wor.Pk. 117 CT102
Perry Mead, Enf. 35 DP40
Perry Mead (Bushey), Wat. 44 CB45
Perry Oaks Dr. (Heathrow Airport), Houns. 84 BH82
Perry Oaks Dr., West Dr. 84 BH82
Perry Ri. SE23 107 DY90
Perry Rd., Dag. 82 EZ70
Perry St., Chis. 109 ER93
Perry St., Dart. 97 FE84
Perry St. Gdns., Chis. 109 ES93
Old Perry St.
Perry Vale SE23 106 DW89
Perryfield Way NW9 61 CT58
Perryfield Way, Rich. 101 CH89
Perryman Ho., Bark. 81 EQ67
Perrymans Fm. Rd., Ilf. 67 ER58
Perrymead St. SW6 90 DA81
Perryn Rd. SE16 92 DV76
Drummond Rd.
Perryn Rd. W3 74 CR74
Perrys La., Sev. 138 EV113
Perrys Pl. W1 5 M8
Perrysfield Rd. (Cheshunt), Wal.Cr. 23 DY26
Persant Rd. SE6 108 EE90
Perseverance Pl. SW9 91 DN80
Perseverance Pl., Rich. 88 CL83
Shaftesbury Rd.
Persfield Clo., Epsom 131 CT110
Pershore Clo., Ilf. 67 EP57
Pershore Gro., Cars. 118 DD100
Pert Clo. N10 49 DH51
Perth Ave. NW9 60 CR59
Perth Ave., Hayes 72 BW70
Perth Clo. SW20 117 CU96
Perth Rd. E10 65 DY60
Perth Rd. E13 80 EH68
Perth Rd. N4 63 DN60
Perth Rd. N22 49 DP53
Perth Rd., Bark. 81 ER67
Perth Rd., Beck. 121 EC96
Perth Rd., Ilf. 67 EN58
Perth Ter., Ilf. 67 EQ59
Perwell Ave., Har. 58 BZ60
Perwell Ct., Har. 58 BZ60
Peter Ave. NW10 75 CV66
Peter St. W1 5 M10
Peter St. W1 77 DK73
Peterboat Clo. SE10 94 EE77
Tunnel Ave.
Peterborough Gdns., Ilf. 66 EL59
Peterborough Ms. SW6 90 DA82
Peterborough Rd. E10 65 EC57
Peterborough Rd. SW6 90 DA82
Peterborough Rd., Cars. 118 DE100
Peterborough Rd., Har. 59 CE60
Peterborough Vill. SW6 90 DB81
Peterchurch Ho. SE15 92 DV79
Commercial Way
Petergate SW11 90 DC84
Peters Ave., St.Alb. 17 CJ26
Peters Clo., Dag. 68 EX60
Peters Clo., Stan. 45 CK51
Peters Clo., Well. 95 ES82
Peters Hill EC4 7 H9
Peter's La. EC1 6 F6
Peters Path SE26 106 DV91
Petersfield Ave., Stai. 98 BJ92
Petersfield Clo. N18 50 DQ50
Petersfield Cres., Couls. 147 DL115
Petersfield Ri. SW15 103 CV88
Petersfield Rd. W3 88 CQ75
Petersfield Rd., Stai. 98 BJ92
Petersham Ave., W.Byf. 126 BL112
Petersham Clo., Rich. 101 CK89
Petersham Clo., Sutt. 131 CZ106
Petersham Clo., W.Byf. 126 BL112
Petersham Dr., Orp. 123 ET96
Petersham Gdns., Orp. 123 ET96
Petersham La. SW7 90 DC76
Petersham Ms. SW7 90 DC76
Petersham Pl. SW7 90 DC76
Petersham Rd., Rich. 101 CK86
Petersham Ter., Croy. 119 DL104
Richmond Grn.
Peterstone Rd. SE2 96 EV76
Peterstow Clo. SW19 103 CY89
Peterwood Way, Croy. 119 DM103
Petherton Rd. N5 64 DQ64
Petley Rd. W6 89 CW79
Peto Pl. NW1 5 J4
Peto Pl. NW1 77 DH70
Peto St. N. E16 80 EF73
Victoria Dock Rd.
Petrie Clo. NW2 75 CY65
Pett Clo., Horn. 69 FH61
St. Leonards Way
Pett St. SE18 94 EL77
Petten Clo., Orp. 124 EX102
Petten Gro., Orp. 124 EW102
Petters Rd., Ash. 144 CM116
Petticoat Sq. E1 7 P8
Pettits Boul., Rom. 55 FE53
Pettits Clo., Rom. 55 FE54
Pettits La., Rom. 55 FE54
Pettits La. N., Rom. 55 FD53
Pettits Pl., Dag. 68 FA64
Pettits Rd., Dag. 68 FA64
Pettiward Clo. SW15 89 CW84
Pettley Gdns., Rom. 69 FD57
Pettman Cres. SE28 95 ER76
Petts Hill, Nthlt. 58 CB64
Petts La., Shep. 112 BN98
Petts Wd. Rd., Orp. 123 EQ99
Pettsgrove Ave., Wem. 59 CJ64
Petty France SW1 9 L6
Petty France SW1 91 DJ76
Petworth Clo., Couls. 147 DJ119
Petworth Clo., Nthlt. 72 BZ66
Petworth Gdns. SW20 117 CV97
Hidcote Gdns.
Petworth Gdns., Uxb. 71 BQ67
Petworth Rd. N12 48 DE50
Petworth Rd., Bexh. 110 FA85
Petworth St. SW11 90 DE81
Petworth Way, Horn. 69 FF63
Petyt Pl. SW3 90 DE79
Old Ch. St.
Petyward SW3 8 C9
Petyward SW3 90 DE77
Pevel Ho., Dag. 68 FA61
Pevensey Ave. N11 49 DK50
Pevensey Ave., Enf. 36 DR40
Pevensey Clo., Islw. 86 CC80
Pevensey Rd. E7 66 EF63
Pevensey Rd. SW17 104 DD91
Pevensey Rd., Felt. 100 BY88
Peverel E6 81 EN72
Downings
Peveret Clo. N11 49 DH50
Woodland Rd.
Peveril Dr., Tedd. 101 CD92
Pewsey Clo. E4 51 EA50
Peyton Pl. SE10 93 EC80
Pharaoh Clo., Mitch. 118 DF101
Pharaoh's Island, Shep. 112 BM103
Pheasant Clo. E16 80 EG72
Maplin Rd.
Pheasant Clo., Pur. 133 DP113
Pheasants Way, Rick. 42 BH45
Phelp St. SE17 92 DR79
Phelps Way, Hayes 85 BT77
Phene St. SW3 90 DE79
Phil Brown Pl. SW8 91 DH82
Heath Rd.
Philan Way, Rom. 55 FD51
Philbeach Gdns. SW5 90 DA78
Philchurch Pl. E1 78 DU72
Ellen St.
Philip Ave., Rom. 69 FD60
Philip Ave., Swan. 125 FD98
Philip Clo., Rom. 69 FD60
Philip Ave.
Philip Gdns., Croy. 121 DZ103
Philip La. N15 64 DR56
Philip Rd. SE15 92 DU83
Peckham Rye
Philip Rd., Rain. 83 FE69
Philip Rd., Stai. 98 BK93
Philip St. E13 80 EG70
Philip Wk. SE15 92 DV83
Philipot Path SE9 109 EM86
Court Yd.
Philippa Gdns. SE9 108 EK85
Philips Clo., Cars. 118 DG102
Phillimore Gdns. NW10 75 CW67
Phillimore Gdns. W8 90 DA75
Phillimore Gdns. Clo. W8 90 DA76
Phillimore Gdns.
Phillimore Pl. W8 90 DA75
Phillimore Pl., Rad. 31 CE36
Phillimore Wk. W8 90 DA76
Phillipers, Wat. 30 BX36
Phillipp St. N1 78 DS67
Phillips Clo., Dart. 111 FH86
Philpot La. EC3 7 M10
Philpot Path, Ilf. 67 EQ62
Sunnyside Rd.
Philpot Sq. SW6 90 DB83
Peterborough Rd.
Philpot St. E1 78 DV72
Philpots Clo., West Dr. 70 BK73
Phineas Pett Rd. SE9 94 EL83
Phipp St. EC2 7 M4
Phipp St. EC2 78 DS70
Phipps Bri. Rd. SW19 118 DC96
Phipps Bri. Rd., Mitch. 118 DC96
Phipps Hatch La., Enf. 36 DQ38
Phipp's Ms. SW1 9 H7
Phoebeth Rd. SE4 107 EA85
Phoenix Clo. E8 78 DT67
Stean St.
Phoenix Clo., Nthwd. 43 BT49
Phoenix Clo., W.Wick. 121 ED103
Phoenix Dr., Kes. 122 EK104
Phoenix Pk., Brent. 87 CK78
Phoenix Pl. WC1 6 C4
Phoenix Pl. WC1 77 DM70
Phoenix Rd. NW1 77 DK69
Phoenix Rd. SE20 106 DW93
Phoenix St. WC2 5 N9
Phoenix Way, Houns. 86 BW79
Phoenix Wf. SE10 94 EF75
Phyllis Ave., N.Mal. 117 CV99
Physic Pl. SW3 90 DF79
Royal Hospital Rd.
Piazza, The WC2 77 DL73
Covent Gdn.
Picardy Manorway, Belv. 97 FB76
Picardy Rd., Belv. 96 FA78
Picardy St., Belv. 96 FA76
Piccadilly W1 9 J3
Piccadilly W1 77 DH74
Piccadilly Arc. SW1 9 K2
Piccadilly Circ. W1 9 M1
Piccadilly Circ. W1 77 DJ73
Piccadilly Pl. W1 9 L1
Pick Hill, Wal.Abb. 24 EF32
Pickard St. EC1 6 G2
Pickering Ave. E6 81 EN68
Pickering Gdns., Croy. 120 DT100
Pickering Ms. W2 76 DB72
Bishops Bri. Rd.
Pickering Pl. SW1 9 L3
Pickering St. N1 77 DP67
Essex Rd.
Pickets Clo. (Bushey), Wat. 45 CD46
Pickets St. SW12 105 DH87
Pickett Cft., Stan. 45 CK53
Picketts Lock La. N9 50 DW47
Pickford Clo., Bexh. 96 EY82
Pickford La., Bexh. 96 EY82
Pickford Rd., Bexh. 96 EY84
Pickford Wf. N1 7 H1
Pickford Wf. N1 78 DQ68
Pickhurst Grn., Brom. 122 EF101
Pickhurst La., Brom. 122 EF101
Pickhurst La., W.Wick. 122 EE99
Pickhurst Mead, Brom. 122 EF101
Pickhurst Pk., Brom. 122 EE99
Pickhurst Ri., W.Wick. 121 EC101
Pickle Herring St. SE1 78 DS74
Tooley St.
Pickmoss La., Sev. 153 FH116
Pickwick Clo., Houns. 100 BY85
Dorney Way
Pickwick Ct. SE9 108 EL88
West Pk.
Pickwick Ms. N18 50 DS50
Pickwick Pl., Har. 59 CE59
Pickwick Rd. SE21 106 DR87
Pickwick St. SE1 11 H5
Pickwick Way, Chis. 109 EQ93
Pickworth Clo. SW8 91 DL80
Kenchester Clo.
Picquets Way, Bans. 145 CZ117
Picton Pl. W1 4 G9
Picton St. SE5 92 DR80
Piedmont Rd. SE18 95 ER78
Pield Heath Ave., Uxb. 70 BN70
Pield Heath Rd., Uxb. 70 BL70
Pier Head E1 78 DV74
Wapping High St.
Pier Par. E16 95 EN75
Pier Rd.
Pier Rd. E16 95 EN75
Pier Rd., Erith 97 FE79
Pier Rd., Felt. 99 BV85
Pier St. E14 93 EC77
Pier Ter. SW18 90 DC84
Jew's Row
Pier Way SE28 95 ER76
Piercing Hill, Epp. 39 ER35
Piermont Grn. SE22 106 DV85
Piermont Pl., Brom. 122 EL96
Piermont Rd. SE22 106 DV85
Pierrepoint Arc. N1 77 DP68
Islington High St.
Pierrepoint Rd. W3 74 CP73
Pierrepoint Row N1 77 DP68
Islington High St.
Pigeon La., Hmptn. 100 CA91
Pigott St. E14 79 EA72
Pike Clo., Brom. 108 EH92
Pike Rd. NW7 46 CR49
Ellesmere Ave.
Pike Way, Epp. 26 FA27
Pikes End, Pnr. 57 BV56
Pikes Hill, Epsom 130 CS113
Pikestone Clo., Hayes 72 BY70
Berrydale Rd.
Pilgrim Clo., Mord. 118 DB101
Pilgrim Clo., St.Alb. 16 CC27
Pilgrim Hill SE27 106 DQ91
Pilgrim Hill, Orp. 124 EX96
Pilgrim St. EC4 6 F9
Pilgrim St. EC4 77 DP72
Pilgrimage St. SE1 11 K5
Pilgrimage St. SE1 92 DR75
Pilgrims Clo. N13 49 DM49
Pilgrims Clo., Nthlt. 58 CC64
Pilgrims Clo., Wat. 16 BX33
Kytes Dr.
Pilgrims Ct. SE3 94 EG81
Pilgrim's La. NW3 62 DD63
Pilgrims La., West. 150 EL123
Pilgrims Pl. NW3 62 DD63
Hampstead High St.
Pilgrims Ri., Barn. 34 DE43
Pilgrims Way E6 80 EL67
High St. N.
Pilgrims Way N19 63 DK60
Pilgrims Way (Sundridge), Sev. 152 EV121
Pilgrims Way, S.Croy. 134 DT107
Bench Fld.
Pilgrim's Way, Wem. 60 CP60
Pilgrims Way, West. 151 EM123
Pilgrims Way W., Sev. 153 FD116
Pilkington Rd. SE15 92 DV82
Pilkington Rd., Orp. 123 EQ103
Pilot Ind. Est. NW10 74 CR70
Pilsdon Clo. SW19 103 CX88
Inner Pk. Rd.
Piltdown Rd., Wat. 44 BX49
Pimento Ct. W5 87 CK76
Olive Rd.
Pimlico Rd. SW1 8 F10
Pimlico Rd. SW1 90 DG78
Pimlico Wk. N1 7 M2
Pinchbeck Rd., Orp. 137 ET107
Pinchin St. E1 78 DU73
Pincott Pl. SE4 93 DX83
Billingford Clo.
Pincott Rd. SW19 104 DC94
Pincott Rd., Bexh. 110 FA85
Pindar St. EC2 7 M6
Pindar St. EC2 78 DS71
Pindock Ms. W9 76 DB70
Warwick Ave.
Pine Ave. E15 65 ED64
Pine Ave., W.Wick. 121 EB102
Pine Clo. E10 65 EB61
Walnut Rd.
Pine Clo. N14 49 DJ45
Pine Clo. N19 63 DJ61
Hargrave Pk.
Pine Clo. SE20 106 DW94
Graveney Gro.
Pine Clo., Add. 126 BH111
Pine Clo., Ken. 148 DR117
Pine Clo., Stan. 45 CH49
Pine Clo., Swan. 125 FF98
Pine Clo. (Cheshunt), Wal.Cr. 23 DX28
Pine Coombe, Croy. 135 DX105
Pine Cres., Cars. 132 DD111
Pine Gdns., Ruis. 57 BV60
Pine Gdns., Surb. 116 CN100
Pine Glade, Orp. 137 EM105
Pine Gro. N4 63 DL61
Pine Gro. N20 47 CZ46
Pine Gro. SW19 103 CZ92
Pine Gro., Hat. 20 DB25
Pine Gro., St.Alb. 16 BZ30
Pine Gro. (Bushey), Wat. 30 BZ40
Pine Gro., Wey. 127 BP106
Pine Gro. Ms., Wey. 127 BQ106
Pine Hill, Epsom 144 CR115
Pine Pl., Bans. 131 CX114
Pine Pl., Hayes 71 BT70
Pine Ridge, Cars. 132 DG109
Pine Rd. N11 48 DG47
Pine Rd. NW2 61 CW63
Pine St. EC1 6 D4
Pine St. EC1 77 DN70
Pine Tree Clo., Houns. 85 BV81
Pine Trees Dr., Uxb. 56 BL63
Pine Vw. Manor, Epp. 26 EU30
Pine Wk., Bans. 146 DF117
Pine Wk., Cars. 132 DD110
Pine Wk., Cat. 148 DS122
Pine Wk., Cob. 128 BX114
Pine Wk., Surb. 116 CN100
Pine Wk. E., Cars. 132 DD111
Pine Wk. W., Cars. 132 DD111
Pine Wd., Sun. 113 BU95
Pineapple Ct. SW1 9 K6
Pinecrest Gdns., Orp. 137 EP105
Pinecroft Cres., Barn. 33 CY42
Hillside Gdns.
Pinedene SE15 92 DV81
Meeting Ho. La.
Pinefield Clo. E14 79 EA73
Pinehurst, Sev. 155 FL121
Pinehurst Clo., Abb.L. 15 BS32
Pinehurst Clo., Tad. 146 DA122
Pinehurst Wk., Orp. 123 ES102
Andover Rd.

Pinelands Clo. SE3 94 EF80
St. John's Pk.
Pinemartin Clo. NW2 61 CW62
Pineneedle La., Sev. 155 FH123
Pines, The N14 35 DJ43
Pines, The, Borwd. 32 CM40
Anthony Rd.
Pines, The, Pur. 134 DQ113
Pines, The, Sun. 113 BU97
Pines, The, Wdf.Grn. 52 EG48
Pines Ave., Enf. 36 DV36
Pines Clo., Nthwd. 43 BS51
Pines Rd., Brom. 122 EL96
Pinewood Ave., Add. 126 BJ109
Pinewood Ave., Pnr. 44 CB51
Pinewood Ave., Rain. 83 FH70
Pinewood Ave., Sev. 155 FK121
Pinewood Ave., Sid. 109 ES88
Pinewood Ave., Uxb. 70 BM72
Pinewood Clo., Borwd. 32 CR39
Pinewood Clo., Croy. 121 DY104
Pinewood Clo., Nthwd. 43 BV50
Oxhey Dr. S.
Pinewood Clo., Orp. 123 ER102
Pinewood Clo., Pnr. 44 CB51
Pinewood Clo., Wat. 29 BU39
Pinewood Dr., Orp. 137 ES106
Pinewood Dr., Pot.B. 19 CZ31
Pinewood Dr., Stai. 98 BG92
Cotswold Clo.
Pinewood Gro. W5 73 CJ72
Pinewood Gro., Add. 126 BH110
Pinewood Pk., Add. 126 BH111
Pinewood Rd. SE2 96 EX79
Pinewood Rd., Brom. 122 EG98
Pinewood Rd., Felt. 99 BV90
Pinewood Rd., Rom. 55 FD49
(Havering-atte-Bower)
Pinfold Rd. SW16 105 DL91
Pinfold Rd. (Bushey), Wat. 30 BZ40
Pinglestone Clo., West Dr. 84 BL80
Pinkcoat Clo., Felt. 99 BV90
Tanglewood Way
Pinkerton Pl. SW16 105 DK91
Riggindale Rd.
Pinkham Way N11 48 DG52
Pinks Hill, Swan. 125 FE99
Pinkwell Ave., Hayes 85 BR77
Pinkwell La., Hayes 85 BQ77
Pinley Gdns., Dag. 82 EV67
Stamford Rd.
Pinn Clo., Uxb. 70 BK72
High Rd.
Pinn Way, Ruis. 57 BR59
Pinnacle Hill, Bexh. 97 FB84
Pinnacle Hill N., Bexh. 97 FB83
Pinnacles, Wal.Abb. 24 EE34
Pinnell Pl. SE9 94 EK84
Pinnell Rd. SE9 94 EK84
Pinner Ct., Pnr. 58 CA56
Pinner Grn., Pnr. 44 BW54
Pinner Gro., Pnr. 58 BY56
Pinner Hill, Pnr. 43 BV52
Pinner Hill Rd., Pnr. 44 BW53
Pinner Pk., Pnr. 44 BZ53
Pinner Pk. Ave., Har. 58 CB55
Pinner Pk. Gdns., Har. 44 CC54
Pinner Rd., Har. 58 CB57
Pinner Rd., Nthwd. 43 BT53
Pinner Rd., Pnr. 58 BZ56
Pinner Rd., Wat. 30 BX44
Pinner Vw., Har. 58 CC56
Pintail Clo. E6 80 EL71
Swan App.
Pintail Rd., Wdf.Grn. 52 EH52
Pintail Way, Hayes 72 BX71
Pinto Clo., Borwd. 32 CR44
Percheron Rd.
Pinto Way SE3 94 EH84
Pioneer Pl., Croy. 135 EA109
Featherbed La.
Pioneer St. SE15 92 DU81
Pioneer Way W12 75 CV72
Du Cane Rd.
Pioneer Way, Swan. 125 FE97
Pioneer Way, Wat. 29 BT44
Piper Clo. N7 63 DM64
Piper Rd., Kings.T. 116 CN97
Pipers Clo., Cob. 142 BX115
Piper's Gdns., Croy. 121 DY101
Pipers Grn. NW9 60 CQ57
Pipers Grn. La., Edg. 46 CL48
Pipewell Rd., Cars. 118 DE100
Pippin Clo. NW2 61 CV62
Pippin Clo., Croy. 121 DZ102
Pippins Clo., West Dr. 84 BK76
Pippins Ct., Ashf. 99 BP93
Piquet Rd. SE20 120 DW96
Pirbright Cres., Croy. 135 EC107
Pirbright Rd. SW18 103 CZ88
Pirie Clo. SE5 92 DR83
Denmark Hill
Pirie St. E16 80 EH74
Pitcairn Clo., Rom. 68 FA56
Pitcairn Rd., Mitch. 104 DF94
Pitchfont La., Oxt. 150 EF124
Pitchford St. E15 79 ED66
Pitfield Cres. SE28 82 EU74
Pitfield Est. N1 7 M2
Pitfield St. N1 7 M3
Pitfield St. N1 78 DS69
Pitfield Way NW10 74 CQ65
Pitfield Way, Enf. 36 DW39
Pitfold Clo. SE12 108 EG86
Pitfold Rd. SE12 108 EG86
Pitlake, Croy. 119 DP103
Pitman St. SE5 92 DQ80
Pitsea Pl. E1 79 DX72
Pitsea St.
Pitsea St. E1 79 DX72
Pitshanger La. W5 73 CH70
Pitshanger Pk. W13 73 CG70
Pitson Clo., Add. 126 BK105
Pitt Cres. SW19 104 DB91
Pitt Pl., Epsom 130 CS114
Pitt Rd., Croy. 120 DQ99
Pitt Rd., Epsom 130 CS114
Pitt Rd., Orp. 137 EQ105
Pitt Rd., Th.Hth. 120 DQ99
Pitt St. SE15 92 DT80
Pitt St. W8 90 DA75
Pittman Gdns., Ilf. 67 EQ64
Pitt's Head Ms. W1 8 G3
Pitt's Head Ms. W1 76 DG74
Pittsmead Ave., Brom. 122 EG101
Pittville Gdns. SE25 120 DU97
Pitwood Grn., Tad. 145 CW120
Pixfield Ct., Brom. 122 EF96
Beckenham La.
Pixley St. E14 79 DZ72
Pixton Way, Croy. 135 DY109
Place Fm. Ave., Orp. 123 ER102
Placehouse La., Couls. 147 DM119
Plain, The, Epp. 26 EV29
Plaistow Gro. E15 80 EF67
Plaistow Gro., Brom. 108 EH94
Plaistow La., Brom. 108 EG94
Plaistow Pk. Rd. E13 80 EH68
Plaistow Rd. E13 80 EF67
Plaistow Rd. E15 80 EF67
Plaitford Clo., Rick. 42 BL47
Plane St. SE26 106 DV90
Plane Tree Cres., Felt. 99 BV90
Plane Tree Wk. SE19 106 DS93
Central Hill
Planes, The, Cher. 112 BJ101
Plantaganet Pl., Wal.Abb. 23 EB33
Plantagenet Clo., Wor.Pk. 130 CR105
Plantagenet Gdns., Rom. 68 EX59
Broomfield Rd.
Plantagenet Pl., Rom. 68 EX59
Broomfield Rd.
Plantagenet Rd., Barn. 34 DC42
Plantain Gdns. E11 65 ED62
Hollydown Way
Plantain Pl. SE1 11 K4
Plantation, The SE3 94 EG82
Plantation Dr., Orp. 124 EX102
Plantation La., Warl. 149 DX119
Plantation Rd., Erith 97 FG81
Plantation Rd., Swan. 111 FG94
Plantation Wf. SW11 90 DC83
Plasel Ct. E13 80 EG67
Plashet Rd.
Plashet Gro. E6 80 EJ67
Plashet Rd. E13 80 EG67
Plassy Rd. SE6 107 EB87
Platina St. EC2 7 L4
Plato Rd. SW2 91 DL84
Platt, The SW15 89 CX83
Platt St. NW1 77 DK68
Platts Ave., Wat. 29 BV41
Platt's Eyot, Hmptn. 114 CA96
Platt's La. NW3 62 DA63
Platts Rd., Enf. 36 DW39
Plawsfield Rd., Beck. 121 DX95
Plaxtol Clo., Brom. 122 EJ95
Plaxtol Rd., Erith 96 FA79
Playfair St. W6 89 CW78
Winslow Rd.
Playfield Ave., Rom. 55 FC53
Playfield Cres. SE22 106 DT85
Playfield Rd., Edg. 46 CQ54
Playford Rd. N4 63 DM61
Playgreen Way SE6 107 EA90
Playground Clo., Beck. 121 DX96
Churchfields Rd.
Playhouse Yd. EC4 6 F9
Plaza W., Houns. 86 CB81
Pleasance, The SW15 89 CV84
Pleasance Rd. SW15 103 CV85
Pleasance Rd., Orp. 124 EV96
Pleasant Gro., Croy. 121 DZ104
Pleasant Pl. N1 77 DP66
Pleasant Pl., Walt. 128 BW107
Pleasant Rd., Kings.T. 116 CQ97
Pleasant Row NW1 77 DH67
Camden High St.
Pleasant Vw., Erith 97 FE78
Pleasant Vw. Pl., Orp. 137 EP106
High St.
Pleasant Way, Wem. 73 CJ68
Pleasure Pit Rd., Ash. 144 CP118
Plender St. NW1 77 DJ67
Plender St. Est. NW1 77 DJ67
Plender St.
Pleshey Rd. N7 63 DK63
Plesman Way, Wall. 133 DL109
Plevna Cres. N15 64 DS58
Plevna Rd. N9 50 DU48
Plevna Rd., Hmptn. 114 CB95
Plevna St. E14 93 EC76
Pleydell Ave. SE19 106 DT94
Pleydell Ave. W6 89 CT77
Pleydell Ct. EC4 77 DN72
Fleet St.
Pleydell Est. EC1 78 DQ69
Radnor St.
Pleydell St. EC4 6 E9
Plimsoll Clo. E14 79 EB72
Grundy St.
Plimsoll Rd. N4 63 DN62
Plough Ct. EC3 7 L10
Plough Fm. Clo., Ruis. 57 BR58
Plough Hill (Cuffley), Pot.B. 21 DL28
Plough Ind. Est., Lthd. 143 CG120
Kingston Rd.
Plough La. SE22 106 DT86
Plough La. SW17 104 DC91
Plough La. SW19 104 DB92
Plough La., Cob. 141 BU117
Plough La., Pur. 133 DM109
Plough La., Tedd. 101 CG92
High St.
Plough La., Uxb. 42 BJ51
Plough La., Wall. 133 DL105
Plough La. Clo., Wall. 133 DL106
Plough Ms. SW11 90 DD84
Plough Ter.
Plough Pl. EC4 6 E8
Plough Rd. SW11 90 DD83
Plough Rd., Epsom 130 CR109
Plough St. E1 78 DT72
Leman St.
Plough Ter. SW11 90 DD84
Plough Way SE16 93 DX77
Plough Yd. EC2 7 N5
Plough Yd. EC2 78 DS70
Ploughmans Clo. NW1 77 DK67
Crofters Way
Ploughmans End, Islw. 101 CD85
Plover Way SE16 93 DY76
Plover Way, Hayes 72 BX72
Plowden Bldgs. EC4 77 DN72
Middle Temple La.
Plowman Clo. N18 50 DR50
Plowman Way, Dag. 68 EW60
Plum Garth, Brent. 87 CK77
Plum La. SE18 95 EP80
Plumbers Row E1 78 DU71
Plumbridge St. SE10 93 EC81
Blackheath Hill
Plummer La., Mitch. 118 DF96
Plummer Rd. SW4 105 DK87
Plummers Cft., Sev. 154 FE121
Plumpton Clo., Nthlt. 72 CA65
Plumpton Way, Cars. 118 DE104
Plumstead Common Rd. SE18 95 EP79
Plumstead High St. SE18 95 ER77
Plumstead Rd. SE18 95 EP77
Plumtree Clo., Dag. 83 FC65
Plumtree Clo., Wall. 133 DK108
Plumtree Ct. EC4 6 F8
Plumtree Mead, Loug. 39 EN41
Plymouth Dr., Sev. 155 FJ124
Plymouth Ho., Rain. 83 FF69
Plymouth Pk., Sev. 155 FJ124
Plymouth Rd. E16 80 EG71
Plymouth Rd., Brom. 122 EH95
Plymouth Wf. E14 93 ED77
Plympton Ave. NW6 75 CZ66
Plympton Clo., Belv. 96 EY76
Halifield Dr.
Plympton Pl. NW8 4 B5
Plympton Rd. NW6 75 CZ66
Plympton St. NW8 4 B5
Plympton St. NW8 76 DE70
Plymstock Rd., Well. 96 EW80
Pocklington Clo. NW9 46 CS54
Pocock Ave., West Dr. 84 BM76
Brickfields Way
Pocock St. SE1 10 F4
Pocock St. SE1 91 DP75
Podmore Rd. SW18 90 DC84
Poets Gate, Wal.Cr. 22 DQ28
St. James Rd.
Poets Rd. N5 64 DR64
Poets Way, Har. 59 CE56
Blawith Rd.
Point, The, Ruis. 57 BU63
Bedford Rd.
Point Clo. SE10 93 EC81
Point Hill
Point Hill SE10 93 EC80
Point of Thomas Path E1 78 DW73
Glamis Rd.
Point Pl., Wem. 74 CP66
Point Pleasant SW18 90 DA84
Pointalls Clo. N3 48 DC54
Pointer Clo. SE28 82 EX72
Pointers, The, Ash. 144 CL120
Pointers Clo. E14 93 EB78
Pointers Rd., Cob. 141 BQ116
Poland St. W1 5 L8
Poland St. W1 77 DJ72
Pole Cat All., Brom. 122 EF103
Pole Hill Rd. E4 51 EC45
Pole Hill Rd., Hayes 71 BQ69
Pole Hill Rd., Uxb. 71 BP70
Polebrook Rd. SE3 94 EJ83
Polecroft La. SE6 107 DZ89
Polehamptons, The, Hmptn. 100 CC94
High St.
Polesden Gdns. SW20 117 CV96
Polesteeple Hill, West. 150 EK117
Polesworth Ho. W2 76 DA71
Polesworth Rd., Dag. 82 EX66
Polhill, Sev. 139 FC114
Police Sta. La. (Bushey), Wat. 44 CB45
Sparrows Herne
Police Sta. Rd., Walt. 128 BW107
Pollard Clo. E16 80 EG73
Pollard Clo. N7 63 DM63
Pollard Clo., Chig. 54 EU50
Pollard Rd. N20 48 DE47
Pollard Rd., Mord. 118 DD99
Pollard Row E2 78 DU69
Pollard St. E2 78 DU69
Pollard Wk., Sid. 110 EW93
Evry Rd.
Pollards Clo., Loug. 38 EJ43
Pollards Clo. (Cheshunt), Wal.Cr. 22 DQ29
Pollards Cres. SW16 119 DL97
Pollards Hill E. SW16 119 DM97
Pollards Hill N. SW16 119 DL97
Pollards Hill S. SW16 119 DL97
Pollards Hill W. SW16 119 DL97
Pollards Wd. Rd. SW16 119 DL96
Pollen St. W1 5 K9
Pollitt Dr. NW8 4 A4
Polperro Clo., Orp. 123 ET100
Cotswold Ri.
Polsted Rd. SE6 107 DZ87
Polthorne Est. SE18 95 EQ77
Polthorne Gro.
Polthorne Gro. SE18 95 EQ77
Polworth Rd. SW16 105 DL92
Polygon, The SW4 91 DJ84
Old Town
Polygon Rd. NW1 5 M1
Polygon Rd. NW1 77 DK68
Polytechnic St. SE18 95 EN77
Pomell Way E1 78 DT72
Commercial St.
Pomeroy Cres., Wat. 29 BV36
Pomeroy St. SE14 92 DW81
Pomfret Rd. SE5 91 DP83
Flaxman Rd.
Pomoja La. N19 63 DK61
Pond Clo. SE3 94 EF82
Pond Clo., Ash. 144 CL117
Pond Clo., Uxb. 42 BJ54
Pond Clo., Walt. 127 BT107
Pond Cottage La., W.Wick. 121 EA102
Pond Cotts. SE21 106 DS88
Pond Fld. End, Loug. 52 EJ45
Pond Grn., Ruis. 57 BS61
Pond Hill Gdns., Sutt. 131 CY107
Pond Mead SE21 106 DR86
Pond Path, Chis. 109 EP93
Heathfield La.
Pond Piece, Lthd. 128 CB113
Pond Pl. SW3 8 B9
Pond Pl. SW3 90 DE77
Pond Rd. E15 80 EE68
Pond Rd. SE3 94 EF82
Pond Rd., Hem.H. 14 BN25
Pond Sq. N6 62 DG60
South Gro.
Pond St. NW3 62 DE64
Pond Way, Tedd. 101 CJ93
Holmesdale Rd.
Ponder St. N7 77 DM66
Ponders End Ind. Est., Enf. 37 DZ42
Pondfield Rd., Brom. 122 EE102
Pondfield Rd., Dag. 69 FB64
Pondfield Rd., Ken. 147 DP117
Pondfield Rd., Orp. 123 EP104
Ponds, The, Wey. 127 BS107
Ellesmere Rd.
Pondside Clo., Hayes 85 BR80
Providence La.
Pondwood Ri., Orp. 123 ES101
Ponler St. E1 78 DV72
Ponsard Rd. NW10 75 CV69
Ponsford St. E9 64 DW64
Ponsonby Pl. SW1 9 N10
Ponsonby Pl. SW1 91 DK78
Ponsonby Rd. SW15 103 CV87
Ponsonby Ter. SW1 9 N10
Ponsonby Ter. SW1 91 DK78
Pont St. SW1 8 D7
Pont St. SW1 90 DF76
Pont St. Ms. SW1 8 D7
Pont St. Ms. SW1 90 DF76
Pontefract Rd., Brom. 108 EF92
Pontoise Clo., Sev. 154 FF122
Ponton Rd. SW8 91 DK79
Pontypool Pl. SE1 10 F4
Pony Chase, Cob. 128 BZ113
Pool Clo., Beck. 107 EA92
Pool Clo., W.Mol. 114 BZ99
Pool Ct. SE6 107 EA89
Pool End Clo., Shep. 112 BN99
Pool Gro., Croy. 135 DY112
Pool Rd., Har. 59 CD59
Pool Rd., W.Mol. 114 BZ99
Poole Clo., Ruis. 57 BS61
Chichester Ave.
Poole Ct. Rd., Houns. 86 BY82
Vicarage Fm. Rd.
Poole Rd. E9 79 DX65
Poole Rd., Epsom 130 CR107
Poole St. N1 78 DR67
Poole Way, Hayes 71 BR69
Pooles Bldgs. EC1 6 D5
Pooles La. SW10 90 DC80
Lots Rd.
Pooles La., Dag. 82 EY68
Pooles Pk. N4 63 DN61
Seven Sisters Rd.
Poolmans St. SE16 93 DX75
Poolsford Rd. NW9 60 CS56
Poonah St. E1 78 DW72
Hardinge St.
Pope Clo. SW19 104 DD93
Shelley Way
Pope Clo., Felt. 99 BT88
Pope Rd., Brom. 122 EK99
Pope St. SE1 11 N5
Pope St. SE1 92 DS75
Popes Ave., Twick. 101 CE89
Popes Dr. N3 48 DA53
Popes Gro., Croy. 121 DZ104
Popes Gro., Twick. 101 CE89
Pope's Head All. EC3 78 DR72
Cornhill
Popes La. W5 87 CK76
Popes La., Wat. 29 BV37
Popes Rd. SW9 91 DN83
Popes Rd., Abb.L. 15 BS31
Popham Clo., Felt. 100 BZ90
Popham Gdns., Rich. 88 CN83
Lower Richmond Rd.
Popham Rd. N1 78 DQ67
Popham St. N1 78 DQ67
Poplar Ave., Lthd. 143 CH122
Poplar Ave., Mitch. 118 DF95
Poplar Ave., Orp. 123 EP103
Poplar Ave., Sthl. 86 CB76
Poplar Ave., West Dr. 70 BM73
Poplar Bath St. E14 79 EB73
Lawless St.
Poplar Business Pk. E14 79 EC73
Poplar High St.
Poplar Clo. E9 65 DZ64
Lee Conservancy Rd.
Poplar Clo., Pnr. 44 BX53
Poplar Ct. SW19 104 DA92
Poplar Cres., Epsom 130 CQ107
Poplar Dr., Bans. 131 CY114
Poplar Fm. Clo., Epsom 130 CQ107
Poplar Gdns., N.Mal. 116 CR96
Poplar Gro. N11 48 DG51
Poplar Gro. W6 89 CW75
Poplar Gro., N.Mal. 116 CR97
Poplar Gro., Wem. 60 CQ62
Poplar High St. E14 79 EB73
Poplar Mt., Belv. 97 FB77
Poplar Pl. SE28 82 EW73
Poplar Pl. W2 76 DB73
Poplar Pl., Hayes 71 BU73
Central Ave.
Poplar Rd. SE24 92 DQ84
Poplar Rd. SW19 118 DA96
Poplar Rd., Ashf. 99 BQ93
Poplar Rd., Lthd. 143 CH122
Poplar Rd., Sutt. 117 CZ102
Poplar Rd., Uxb. 56 BJ64
Poplar Rd. S. SW19 118 DA97
Poplar Row, Epp. 39 ES37
Poplar Shaw, Wal.Abb. 24 EF33
Poplar St., Rom. 69 FC56
Poplar Vw., Wem. 59 CK61
Magnet Rd.
Poplar Wk. SE24 92 DQ84
Poplar Wk., Cat. 148 DS123
Poplar Wk., Croy. 120 DQ103
Poplar Way, Felt. 99 BU90
Poplar Way, Ilf. 67 EQ56
Poplars, The N14 35 DH43
Poplars, The, Rom. 40 EV41
Hoe La.
Poplars, The, Wal.Cr. 22 DS27
The Laurels
Poplars Ave. NW10 75 CW65
Poplars Clo., Ruis. 57 BS60
Poplars Clo., Wat. 15 BV32
Poplars Rd. E17 65 EB58
Poppins Ct. EC4 6 F9
Poppleton Rd. E11 66 EE58
Poppy Clo., Wall. 118 DG102
Poppy La., Croy. 120 DW101
Poppy Wk., Wal.Cr. 22 DR28
Porch Way N20 48 DF48
Porchester Gdns. W2 76 DB73
Porchester Gdns. Ms. W2 76 DB72
Porchester Gdns.
Porchester Mead, Beck. 107 EA93
Porchester Ms. W2 76 DB72
Porchester Sq.
Porchester Pl. W2 4 C9
Porchester Pl. W2 76 DE72
Porchester Rd. W2 76 DB71
Porchester Rd., Kings.T. 116 CP96
Porchester Sq. W2 76 DB72
Porchester Ter. W2 76 DC73
Porchester Ter. N. W2 76 DB72
Porchfield Clo., Sutt. 132 DB110
Porcupine Clo. SE9 108 EL89
Porden Rd. SW2 91 DM84
Porlock Ave., Har. 58 CC60
Porlock Rd. W10 75 CX70
Ladbroke Gro.
Porlock Rd., Enf. 50 DT45
Porlock St. SE1 11 L4
Porlock St. SE1 92 DR75
Porrington Clo., Chis. 123 EN95
Port Cres. E13 80 EH70
Jenkins Rd.
Port Hill, Orp. 138 EV112
Portal Clo. SE27 105 DN90
Portal Clo., Ruis. 57 BU63
Portal Clo., Uxb. 70 BL66
Portbury Clo. SE15 92 DU81
Clayton Rd.
Portchester Clo. SE5 92 DR84
Portcullis Lo. Rd., Enf. 36 DR41
Portelet Rd. E1 79 DX69
Porten Rd. W14 89 CY76
Porter Rd. E6 81 EM72
Porter Sq. N19 63 DL60
Hornsey Rd.
Porter St. SE1 11 J2
Porter St. W1 4 E6
Porters Ave., Dag. 82 EV65
Porters Pk. Dr., Rad. 17 CK33

Porters Wk. E1 78 DV73
Pennington St.
Porters Way, West Dr. 84 BM76
Portersfield Rd., Enf. 36 DS42
Porteus Rd. W2 76 DC71
Portgate Clo. W9 75 CZ70
Porthcawe Rd. SE26 107 DY91
Porthkerry Ave., Well. 96 EU84
Portia Way E3 79 DZ70
Portinscale Rd. SW15 103 CY85
Portland Ave. N16 64 DT59
Portland Ave., N.Mal. 117 CT101
Portland Ave., Sid. 110 EU86
Portland Clo., Rom. 68 EY57
Portland Cres. SE9 108 EL89
Portland Cres., Felt. 99 BR91
Portland Cres., Grnf. 72 CB70
Portland Cres., Stan. 45 CK54
Portland Dr., Enf. 36 DS38
Clay Hill
Portland Dr. (Cheshunt), Wal.Cr. 22 DU31
Portland Gdns. N4 63 DP58
Portland Gdns., Rom. 68 EX57
Portland Gro. SW8 91 DM81
Portland Heights, Nthwd. 43 BT49
Portland Ms. W1 5 L9
Portland Pl. W1 5 H5
Portland Pl. W1 77 DH71
Portland Pl., Epsom 130 CS112
Portland Ri. N4 63 DP60
Portland Ri. Est. N4 63 DP60
Portland Rd. N15 64 DT56
Portland Rd. SE9 108 EL89
Portland Rd. SE25 120 DU98
Portland Rd. W11 75 CY73
Portland Rd., Ashf. 98 BL90
Portland Rd., Brom. 108 EJ91
Portland Rd., Hayes 71 BS69
Portland Rd., Kings.T. 116 CL97
Portland Rd., Mitch. 118 DE96
Portland Rd., Sthl. 86 BZ76
Portland Sq. E1 78 DV74
Watts St.
Portland St. SE17 11 K10
Portland St. SE17 92 DR78
Portland Ter., Rich. 87 CK84
Portland Wk. SE17 92 DR79
Portland St.
Portley La., Cat. 148 DS121
Portley Wd. Rd., Whyt. 148 DT121
Portman Ave. SW14 88 CR83
Portman Clo. W1 4 E8
Portman Clo. W1 76 DF72
Portman Clo., Bex. 111 FE88
Portman Clo., Bexh. 96 EX83
Queen Anne's Gate
Portman Dr., Wdf.Grn. 52 EK54
Portman Gdns. NW9 46 CR54
Portman Gdns., Uxb. 70 BN66
Portman Gate NW1 4 C5
Portman Ms. S. W1 4 F9
Portman Ms. S. W1 76 DG72
Portman Pl. E2 78 DW69
Portman Rd., Kings.T. 116 CM96
Portman Sq. W1 4 F8
Portman Sq. W1 76 DG72
Portman St. W1 4 F9
Portman St. W1 76 DG72
Portmeadow Wk. SE2 96 EX75
Portmeers Clo. E17 65 DZ58
Lennox Rd.
Portmore Gdns., Rom. 54 FA50
Portmore Pk. Rd., Wey. 126 BN105
Portmore Quays, Wey. 126 BM105
Bridge Rd.
Portmore Way, Wey. 112 BN104
Portnall Rd. W9 75 CZ68
Portnalls Clo., Couls. 147 DH116
Portnalls Ri., Couls. 147 DH116
Portnalls Rd., Couls. 147 DH118
Portnoi Clo., Rom. 55 FD54
Portobello Ct. W11 75 CZ73
Westbourne Gro.
Portobello Ms. W11 76 DA73
Portobello Rd.
Portobello Rd. W10 75 CY71
Portobello Rd. W11 75 CZ72
Porton Ct., Surb. 115 CJ100
Portpool La. EC1 6 D6
Portpool La. EC1 77 DN71
Portree Clo. N22 49 DM52
Nightingale Rd.
Portree St. E14 79 ED72
Portsdown, Edg. 46 CN50
Rectory La.
Portsdown Ave. NW11 61 CZ58
Portsdown Ms. NW11 61 CZ58
Portsea Ms. W2 4 C9
Portsea Pl. W2 4 C9
Portslade Rd. SW8 91 DJ82
Portsmouth Ave., T.Ditt. 115 CG101
Portsmouth Rd. SW15 103 CV87
Portsmouth Rd., Cob. 141 BQ115
Portsmouth Rd., Esher 128 BZ108
Portsmouth Rd., Kings.T. 115 CK98
Portsmouth Rd., Surb. 115 CJ100
Portsmouth Rd., T.Ditt. 115 CE103
Portsmouth Rd., Wok. 140 BM119
Portsmouth St. WC2 6 B9
Portsoken St. E1 7 P10
Portsoken St. E1 78 DT73
Portswood Pl. SW15 103 CT87
Danebury Ave.
Portugal Gdns., Twick. 100 CC89
Fulwell Pk. Ave.
Portugal St. WC2 6 B9
Portugal St. WC2 77 DM72
Portway E15 80 EF67
Portway, Epsom 131 CU110
Portway Cres., Epsom 131 CU109
Portway Gdns. SE18 94 EK80
Shooter's Hill Rd.
Post La., Twick. 101 CD88
Post Office App. E7 66 EH64
Post Office Ct. EC3 7 L9
Post Office Way SW8 91 DK80
Postern Grn., Enf. 35 DN40
Postmill Clo., Croy. 121 DX104
Postway Ms., Ilf. 67 EP62
Clements Rd.
Potier St. SE1 11 L7
Potier St. SE1 92 DR76
Pott St. E2 78 DV69
Potter Clo., Mitch. 119 DH96
Potter St., Nthwd. 43 BU53
Potter St., Pnr. 43 BV53
Potter St. Hill, Pnr. 43 BV51
Potterne Clo. SW19 103 CX87
Castlecombe Dr.
Potters Clo., Croy. 121 DY102
Potters Clo., Loug. 38 EL40
Potters Flds. SE1 78 DS74
Tooley St.
Potters Gro., N.Mal. 116 CQ98
Potters Heights Clo., Pnr. 43 BV52
Potters La. SW16 105 DK93
Potters La., Barn. 34 DA42
Potters La., Borwd. 32 CQ39
Potters Rd. SW6 90 DC82
Potters Rd., Barn. 34 DB42
Pottery La. W11 75 CY73
Portland Rd.
Pottery Rd., Bex. 111 FC89
Pottery Rd., Brent. 88 CL79
Pottery St. SE16 92 DV75
Poulett Gdns., Twick. 101 CF88
Poulett Rd. E6 81 EM68
Poulner Way SE15 92 DT80
Daniel Gdns.
Poulters Wd., Kes. 136 EK106
Poultney Clo., Rad. 18 CM32
Poulton Ave., Sutt. 118 DD104
Poulton Clo. E8 64 DV64
Spurstowe Ter.
Poultry EC2 7 K9
Poultry EC2 78 DR72
Pound Clo., Orp. 123 ER103
Pound Clo., Surb. 115 CJ102
Pound Ct., Ash. 144 CM118
Pound Ct. Dr., Orp. 123 ER103
Pound Cres., Lthd. 143 CD121
Pound Fld., Wat. 29 BT35
Ashfields
Pound La. NW10 75 CU65
Pound La., Epsom 130 CQ112
Pound La., Rad. 18 CM33
Pound La., Sev. 152 EX115
Pound La. (Knockholt Pound), Sev. 155 FJ124
Pound Pk. Rd. SE7 94 EK77
Pound Pl. SE9 109 EN86
Pound Rd., Bans. 145 CZ117
Pound Rd., Cher. 112 BH101
Pound St., Cars. 132 DF106
Pound Way, Chis. 109 EQ94
Royal Par.
Poundfield Rd., Loug. 39 EN43
Pounsley Rd., Sev. 154 FE121
Pountney Rd. SW11 90 DG83
Poverest Rd., Orp. 123 ET99
Powder Mill La., Twick. 100 BZ87
Powdermill La., Wal.Abb. 23 EB33
Powdermill Ms., Wal.Abb. 23 EB33
Powdermill La.
Powdermill Way, Wal.Abb. 23 EB32
Powell Clo., Chess. 129 CK106
Coppard Gdns.
Powell Clo., Edg. 46 CM51
Powell Clo., Wall. 133 DK108
Hermes Way
Powell Gdns., Dag. 68 FA63
Powell Rd. E5 64 DV62
Powell Rd., Buck.H. 52 EJ45
Powell's Wk. W4 88 CS79
Power Rd. W4 88 CN77
Powers Ct., Twick. 101 CK87
Powerscroft Rd. E5 64 DW63
Powerscroft Rd., Sid. 110 EW93
Powis Ct., Pot.B. 20 DC34
Powis Gdns. NW11 61 CZ59
Powis Gdns. W11 75 CZ72
Powis Ms. W11 75 CZ72
Westbourne Pk. Rd.
Powis Pl. WC1 6 A5
Powis Pl. WC1 77 DL70
Powis Rd. E3 79 EB69
Powis Sq. W11 75 CZ72
Powis St. SE18 95 EN76
Powis Ter. W11 75 CZ72
Powle Ter., Ilf. 67 EQ64
Loxford La.
Powlett Pl. NW1 77 DH65
Harmood St.
Pownall Gdns., Houns. 86 CB84
Pownall Rd. E8 78 DU67
Pownall Rd., Houns. 86 CB84
Pownsett Ter., Ilf. 67 EQ64
Powster Rd., Brom. 108 EH92
Powys Clo., Bexh. 96 EX79
Powys La. N13 49 DL49
Powys La. N14 49 DL49
Poynders Ct. SW4 105 DJ86
Poynders Rd.
Poynders Gdns. SW4 105 DJ87
Poynders Rd. SW4 105 DJ86
Poynings Clo., Orp. 124 EW103
Poynings Rd. N19 63 DJ62
Poynings Way N12 48 DA50
Poyntell Cres., Chis. 123 ER95
Poynter Rd., Enf. 36 DU43
Poynton Rd. N17 50 DU54
Poyntz Rd. SW11 90 DF82
Poyser St. E2 78 DV68
Praed Ms. W2 4 A8
Praed St. W2 4 A8
Praed St. W2 76 DD72
Pragel St. E13 80 EH68
Pragnell Rd. SE12 108 EH89
Prague Pl. SW2 105 DL85
Prah Rd. N4 63 DN61
Prairie Clo., Add. 112 BH104
Prairie Rd., Add. 112 BH104
Prairie St. SW8 90 DG82
Pratt Ms. NW1 77 DJ67
Pratt St.
Pratt St. NW1 77 DJ67
Pratt Wk. SE11 10 C8
Pratt Wk. SE11 91 DM77
Pratts La., Walt. 128 BX105
Molesey Rd.
Pratts Pas., Kings.T. 116 CL96
Eden St.
Prayle Gro. NW2 61 CX60
Prebend Gdns. W4 89 CT77
Prebend Gdns. W6 89 CT77
Prebend St. N1 78 DQ67
Precinct, The, W.Mol. 114 CB97
Victoria Ave.
Precinct Rd., Hayes 71 BU73
Precincts, The, Mord. 118 DB100
Green La.
Premier Cor. W9 75 CZ68
Kilburn La.
Premier Pl. SW15 89 CY84
Putney High St.
Premiere Pl. E14 79 EA73
Garford St.
Prendergast Rd. SE3 94 EE83
Prentis Rd. SW16 105 DK91
Prentiss Ct. SE7 94 EK77
Presburg Rd., N.Mal. 116 CS99
Presburg St. E5 65 DX62
Glyn Rd.
Prescelly Pl., Edg. 46 CM53
Prescot St. E1 78 DT73
Prescott Ave., Orp. 123 EP100
Prescott Clo. SW16 105 DL94
Prescott Clo., Horn. 69 FH60
St. Leonards Way
Prescott Grn., Loug. 39 EQ41
Prescott Ho. SE17 91 DP79
Hillingdon St.
Prescott Pl. SW4 91 DK83
Prescott Rd. (Cheshunt), Wal.Cr. 23 DY27
Presentation Ms. SW2 105 DM88
Palace Rd.
President Dr. E1 78 DV74
Waterman Way
President St. EC1 7 H2
Press Rd. NW10 60 CR62
Press Rd., Uxb. 70 BK65
Prestage Way E14 79 EC73
Prestbury Cres., Bans. 146 DF116
Prestbury Rd. E7 80 EJ66
Prestbury Sq. SE9 109 EM91
Prested Rd. SW11 90 DE84
St. John's Hill
Preston Ave. E4 51 ED51
Preston Clo. SE1 11 M8
Preston Clo., Ash. 143 CJ116
Preston Clo., Twick. 101 CE90
Preston Ct., Walt. 114 BW102
St. Johns Dr.
Preston Dr. E11 66 EJ57
Preston Dr., Bexh. 96 EX81
Preston Dr., Epsom 130 CS107
Preston Gdns. NW10 74 CS65
Church Rd.
Preston Gdns., Enf. 37 DY37
Preston Gdns., Ilf. 66 EL58
Preston Gro., Ash. 143 CJ117
Preston Hill, Har. 60 CL59
Preston La., Tad. 145 CV121
Preston Pl. NW2 75 CU65
Preston Pl., Rich. 102 CL85
Preston Rd. E11 66 EE58
Preston Rd. SE19 105 DP93
Preston Rd. SW20 103 CT94
Preston Rd., Har. 60 CL59
Preston Rd., Shep. 112 BN99
Preston Rd., Wem. 60 CL61
Preston Waye, Har. 60 CL60
Prestons Rd. E14 93 EC75
Prestons Rd., Brom. 122 EG104
Prestwick Clo., Sthl. 86 BY78
Ringway
Prestwick Rd., Wat. 44 BW46
Prestwood Ave., Har. 59 CH56
Prestwood Clo. SE18 96 EU80
Prestwood Clo., Har. 59 CH56
Prestwood Dr., Rom. 55 FC50
Prestwood Gdns., Croy. 120 DQ101
Prestwood St. N1 7 J1
Pretoria Ave. E17 65 DY56
Pretoria Clo. N17 50 DT52
Pretoria Rd.
Pretoria Cres. E4 51 EC46
Pretoria Rd. E4 51 EC46
Pretoria Rd. E11 65 ED60
Pretoria Rd. E16 80 EF70
Pretoria Rd. N17 50 DT52
Pretoria Rd. SW16 105 DH93
Pretoria Rd., Ilf. 67 EP64
Pretoria Rd., Rom. 69 FC56
Pretoria Rd., Wat. 29 BU42
Pretoria Rd. N. N18 50 DT51
Prevost Rd. N11 48 DG47
Price Clo. NW7 47 CY51
Price Clo. SW17 104 DF90
Price Rd., Croy. 133 DP105
Price Way, Hmptn. 100 BY93
Victors Dr.
Price's Yd. N1 77 DM67
Pricklers Hill, Barn. 34 DB44
Prickley Wd., Brom. 122 EF102
Priddy's Yd., Croy. 120 DQ103
Crown Hill
Prideaux Pl. W3 74 CR73
Friars Pl. La.
Prideaux Pl. WC1 6 C2
Prideaux Pl. WC1 77 DM69
Prideaux Rd. SW9 91 DL83
Pridham Rd., Th.Hth. 120 DR98
Priest Ct. EC2 7 H8
Priest Pk. Ave., Har. 58 CA61
Priestfield Rd. SE23 107 DY90
Priestlands Pk. Rd., Sid. 109 ET90
Priestley Clo. N16 64 DT59
Ravensdale Rd.
Priestley Gdns., Rom. 68 EV58
Priestley Rd., Mitch. 118 DG96
Priestley Way E17 65 DX55
Priestley Way NW2 61 CU60
Priests Ave., Rom. 55 FD54
Priests Bri. SW14 88 CS83
Priests Bri. SW15 88 CS83
Prima Rd. SW9 91 DN80
Primrose Ave., Enf. 36 DR39
Primrose Ave., Rom. 68 EU59
Primrose Clo. SE6 107 EC92
Primrose Clo., Har. 58 BZ62
Primrose Clo., Wall. 119 DH101
Primrose Gdns. NW3 76 DE65
Primrose Gdns., Ruis. 58 BW64
Primrose Gdns. (Bushey), Wat. 44 CB45
Primrose Hill EC4 6 E9
Primrose Hill, Kings L. 15 BP28
Primrose Hill Ct. NW3 76 DF66
Primrose Hill Rd. NW3 76 DF66
Primrose Hill Studios NW1 76 DG67
Fitzroy Rd.
Primrose La., Croy. 120 DW102
Primrose Ms. NW1 76 DF66
Sharpleshall St.
Primrose Ms. SE3 94 EH80
Primrose Path (Cheshunt), Wal.Cr. 22 DU31
Primrose Rd. E10 65 EB60
Primrose Rd. E18 52 EH54
Primrose Rd., Walt. 128 BW106
Primrose St. EC2 7 M6
Primrose St. EC2 78 DS71
Primrose Wk., Epsom 131 CT108
Primrose Way, Wem. 73 CK68
Primula St. W12 75 CU72
Prince Albert Rd. NW1 4 C1
Prince Albert Rd. NW1 76 DF68
Prince Albert Rd. NW8 4 C1
Prince Albert Rd. NW8 76 DE69
Prince Arthur Ms. NW3 62 DC63
Perrins La.
Prince Arthur Rd. NW3 62 DC64
Prince Charles Dr. NW4 61 CW59
Prince Charles Rd. SE3 94 EF82
Prince Charles Way, Wall. 119 DH104
Prince Consort Dr., Chis. 123 ER95
Prince Consort Rd. SW7 90 DC76
Prince Edward Rd. E9 79 DZ65
Prince George Ave. N14 35 DJ42
Prince George Duke of Kent Ct., Chis. 109 ER94
Holbrook La.
Prince George Rd. N16 64 DS63
Prince George's Ave. SW20 117 CW96
Prince George's Rd. SW19 118 DD95
Prince Henry Rd. SE7 94 EK80
Prince Imperial Rd. SE18 95 EM81
Prince Imperial Rd., Chis. 109 EP94
Prince John Rd. SE9 108 EL85
Prince of Orange La. SE10 93 EC80
Greenwich High Rd.
Prince of Wales Clo. NW4 61 CV56
Church Ter.
Prince of Wales Dr. SW8 91 DH80
Prince of Wales Dr. SW11 90 DE81
Prince of Wales Footpath, Enf. 37 DX37
St. Stephens Rd.
Prince of Wales Gate SW7 8 B4
Prince of Wales Gate SW7 90 DE75
Prince of Wales Pas. NW1 5 K3
Prince of Wales Rd. E16 80 EJ72
Prince of Wales Rd. NW5 76 DG65
Prince of Wales Rd. SE3 94 EF81
Prince of Wales Rd., Sutt. 118 DD103
Prince of Wales Ter. W4 88 CS78
Prince of Wales Ter. W8 90 DB75
Kensington Rd.
Prince Regent Ct. SE16 79 DY74
Rotherhithe St.
Prince Regent La. E13 80 EH69
Prince Regent La. E16 80 EJ71
Prince Regent Rd., Houns. 86 CC83
Prince Rd. SE25 120 DS99
Prince Rupert Rd. SE9 95 EM84
Prince St. SE8 93 DZ79
Prince St., Wat. 30 BW41
Princedale Rd. W11 75 CY74
Princelet St. E1 78 DT71
Prince's Arc. SW1 9 L2
Princes Ave. N3 48 DA53
Princes Ave. N10 63 DH55
Princes Ave. N13 49 DN50
Princes Ave. N22 49 DK53
Princes Ave. NW9 60 CN56
Princes Ave. W3 88 CN76
Princes Ave., Cars. 132 DF108
Princes Ave., Enf. 37 DY36
Princes Ave., Grnf. 72 CB72
Princes Ave., Orp. 123 ES99
Princes Ave., S.Croy. 148 DV115
Princes Ave., Surb. 116 CN102
Princes Ave., Wat. 29 BT43
Princes Ave., Wdf.Grn. 52 EH49
Princes Clo. N4 63 DP60
Princes Clo. NW9 60 CN56
Princes Clo. SW4 91 DJ83
Old Town
Princes Clo., Edg. 46 CN50
Princes Clo., Epp. 27 FC25
Princes Clo., Sid. 110 EX90
Princes Clo., S.Croy. 148 DV115
Princes Clo., Tedd. 101 CD91
Princes Ct. E1 78 DV73
Princes Ct., Wem. 60 CL64
Princes Dr., Har. 59 CE55
Prince's Dr., Lthd. 129 CE112
Princes Gdns. SW7 8 A6
Princes Gdns. SW7 90 DD76
Princes Gdns. W3 74 CN71
Princes Gdns. W5 73 CJ70
Princes Gate SW7 8 A5
Princes Gate SW7 90 DE75
Princes Gate Ct. SW7 8 A5
Princes Gate Ms. SW7 8 A6
Princes Gate Ms. SW7 90 DD76
Princes La. N10 63 DH55
Princes Ms. W2 76 DA73
Hereford Rd.
Princes Par., Pot.B. 20 DC32
High St.
Princes Pk., Rain. 83 FG66
Princes Pk. Ave. NW11 61 CY58
Princes Pk. Ave., Hayes 71 BR73
Princes Pk. Circle, Hayes 71 BR73
Princes Pk. Clo., Hayes 71 BR73
Princes Pk. La., Hayes 71 BR73
Princes Pk. Par., Hayes 71 BR73
Princes Pk. La.
Princes Pl. SW1 9 L2
Princes Pl. W11 75 CY74
Princes Plain, Brom. 122 EL101
Princes Ri. SE13 93 EC82
Princes Riverside Rd. SE16 79 DX74
Princes Rd. N18 50 DW49
Princes Rd. SE20 107 DX93
Princes Rd. SW14 88 CR83
Princes Rd. SW19 104 DA93
Princes Rd. W13 73 CH74
Broomfield Rd.
Princes Rd., Ashf. 98 BM92
Princes Rd., Buck.H. 52 EJ47
Princes Rd., Dart. 111 FG86
Princes Rd., Felt. 99 BT89
Princes Rd., Ilf. 67 ER56
Princes Rd., Kings.T. 116 CN95
Princes Rd., Rich. 102 CM85
Princes Rd. (Kew), Rich. 88 CM81
Princes Rd., Rom. 69 FG57
Princes Rd., Swan. 111 FG93
Princes Rd., Tedd. 101 CD91
Princes Rd., Wey. 127 BP106
Princes Sq. W2 76 DB73
Princes St. EC2 7 K9
Princes St. EC2 78 DR72
Princes St. N17 50 DS51
Queen St.
Princes St. W1 5 J9
Princes St. W1 77 DH72
Princes St., Bexh. 96 EZ84
Princes St., Rich. 102 CL85
Sheen Rd.
Princes St., Sutt. 132 DD105
Princes Ter. E13 80 EH67
Princes Way SW19 103 CX87
Princes Way, Buck.H. 52 EJ47
Princes Way, Croy. 133 DM106
Princes Way, Ruis. 58 BY63
Princes Way, W.Wick. 136 EF105
Princes Yd. W11 75 CY74
Princedale Rd.
Princesfield Rd., Wal.Abb. 24 EH33
Princess Ave., Wem. 60 CL61
Princess Ct. SE16 93 DZ76
Princess Cres. N4 63 DP61
Princess La., Ruis. 57 BS60
Princess Mary's Rd., Add. 126 BJ105
Princess May Rd. N16 64 DS63
Princess Ms. NW3 76 DD65
Belsize Cres.

Princess Par., Orp. 123 EN104
Crofton Rd.
Princess Rd. NW1 76 DG67
Princess Rd. NW6 76 DA68
Princess Rd., Croy. 120 DQ100
Princess St. SE1 10 G7
Princess St. SE1 91 DP76
Princesses Wk., Rich. 88 CL80
Kew Rd.
Princethorpe Ho. W2 76 DB71
Princethorpe Rd. SE26 107 DX91
Princeton Ct. SW15 89 CX83
Felsham Rd.
Princeton St. WC1 6 B7
Princeton St. WC1 77 DM71
Pringle Gdns. SW16 105 DJ91
Print Village SE15 92 DT82
Chadwick Rd.
Printer St. EC4 77 DN72
New Fetter La.
Printers Inn Ct. EC4 77 DN72
Cursitor St.
Printing Ho. Yd. E2 7 N3
Printinghouse La., Hayes 85 BS75
Priolo Rd. SE7 94 EJ78
Prior Ave., Sutt. 132 DE108
Prior Bolton St. N1 77 DP65
Prior Rd., Ilf. 67 EN62
Prior St. SE10 93 EC80
Prioress Rd. SE27 105 DP90
Prioress St. SE1 11 L7
Prioress St. SE1 92 DR76
Priors, The, Ash. 143 CK119
Priors Cft. E17 51 DY54
Priors Fld., Nthlt. 72 BY65
Arnold Rd.
Priors Gdns., Ruis. 58 BW64
Priors Mead, Enf. 36 DS39
Priorsford Ave., Orp. 124 EU98
Priory, The SE3 94 EF84
Priory Ave. E4 51 DZ48
Priory Ave. E17 65 EA57
Priory Ave. N8 63 DK56
Priory Ave. W4 88 CS77
Priory Ave., Orp. 123 ER100
Priory Ave., Sutt. 131 CX105
Priory Ave., Uxb. 56 BJ56
Priory Ave., Wem. 59 CF63
Priory Clo. E4 51 DZ48
Priory Clo. E18 52 EG53
Priory Clo. N3 47 CZ53
Church Cres.
Priory Clo. N14 35 DH43
Priory Clo. N20 47 CZ45
Priory Clo. SW19 118 DB95
High Path
Priory Clo., Beck. 121 DY97
Priory Clo., Chis. 123 EM95
Priory Clo., Hmptn. 114 BZ95
Priory Gdns.
Priory Clo., Hayes 71 BV73
Priory Clo., Ruis. 57 BT60
Priory Clo., Stan. 45 CF48
Priory Clo., Sun. 99 BU94
Priory Clo. (Denham), Uxb. 56 BG62
Priory Clo. (Harefield), Uxb. 56 BH56
Priory Clo., Walt. 113 BU104
Priory Clo. (Sudbury), Wem. 59 CF63
Priory Ct. E17 51 DZ54
Priory Ct. EC4 77 DP72
Pilgrim St.
Priory Ct. SW8 91 DK81
Priory Ct. (Bushey), Wat. 44 CC46
Sparrows Herne
Priory Ct. Est. E17 51 DZ54
Priory Cres. SE19 106 DQ94
Priory Cres., Sutt. 131 CX105
Priory Cres., Wem. 59 CG62
Priory Dr. SE2 96 EX78
Priory Dr., Stan. 45 CF48
Priory Fld. Dr., Edg. 46 CP49
Priory Gdns. N6 63 DH58
Priory Gdns. SE25 120 DT98
Priory Gdns. SW13 89 CT83
Priory Gdns. W4 88 CS77
Priory Gdns. W5 74 CL69
Hanger La.
Priory Gdns., Ashf. 99 BR92
Priory Gdns., Hmptn. 100 BZ94
Priory Gdns., Uxb. 56 BJ56
Priory Gdns., Wem. 59 CG63
Priory Gate, Wal.Cr. 23 DZ27
Priory Grn., Stai. 98 BH92
Priory Grn. Est. N1 77 DM68
Priory Gro. SW8 91 DL81
Priory Hill, Wem. 59 CG63
Priory La. SW15 102 CS86
Priory La., Rich. 88 CN80
Forest Rd.
Priory La., W.Mol. 114 CA98
Priory Ms. SW8 91 DL81
Priory Ms., Stai. 98 BH92
Chestnut Manor Clo.
Priory Pk. SE3 94 EF83
Priory Pk. Rd. NW6 75 CZ67
Priory Pk. Rd., Wem. 59 CG63
Priory Pl., Walt. 113 BU104
Priory Rd. E6 80 EK67
Priory Rd. N8 63 DJ56
Priory Rd. NW6 76 DB67
Priory Rd. SW19 104 DD94
Priory Rd. W4 88 CR76
Priory Rd., Bark. 81 ER66
Priory Rd., Chess. 116 CL104
Priory Rd., Croy. 119 DN101
Priory Rd., Hmptn. 100 BZ94
Priory Rd., Houns. 100 CC85
Priory Rd., Loug. 38 EL42
Priory Rd., Rich. 88 CN80
Priory Rd., Sutt. 131 CX105
Priory St. E3 79 EB69
St. Leonards St.
Priory Ter. NW6 76 DB67
Priory Ter., Sun. 99 BU94
Priory Clo.
Priory Vw. (Bushey), Wat. 45 CE45
Priory Wk. SW10 90 DC78
Priory Way, Har. 58 CB56
Priory Way, Sthl. 86 BX76
Western Rd.
Priory Way, West Dr. 84 BL79
Pritchard's Rd. E2 78 DU68
Priter Rd. SE16 92 DU76
Priter Way SE16 92 DU76
Dockley Rd.
Private Rd., Enf. 36 DR43
Probert Rd. SW2 105 DN85
Probyn Rd. SW2 105 DP89
Procter St. WC1 6 B7
Procter St. WC1 77 DM71
Proctor Clo., Mitch. 118 DG95
Proctors Clo., Felt. 99 BU88
Profumo Rd., Walt. 128 BX106
Progress Business Pk., The, Croy. 119 DM103
Progress Way N22 49 DN53
Progress Way, Croy. 119 DM103
Progress Way, Enf. 36 DU43
Promenade, The W4 88 CS81
Promenade App. Rd. W4 88 CS80
Promenade de Verdun, Pur. 133 DK111
Prospect Business Pk., Loug. 39 ER42
Langston Rd.
Prospect Clo. SE26 106 DV91
Prospect Clo., Belv. 96 FA77
Prospect Clo., Houns. 86 BZ81
Prospect Clo., Ruis. 58 BX59
Prospect Cotts. SW18 90 DA84
Point Pleasant
Prospect Cres., Twick. 100 CC86
Prospect Hill E17 65 EB56
Prospect Pl. E1 78 DW74
Prospect Pl. N2 62 DD56
Prospect Pl. N17 50 DS53
Church Rd.
Prospect Pl. NW2 61 CZ62
Ridge Rd.
Prospect Pl. NW3 62 DC63
Holly Wk.
Prospect Pl., Brom. 122 EH97
Prospect Pl., Epsom 130 CS113
Clayton Rd.
Prospect Pl., Rom. 55 FC54
Prospect Ring N2 62 DD55
Prospect Rd. NW2 61 CZ62
Prospect Rd., Barn. 34 DA43
Prospect Rd., Sev. 155 FJ123
Prospect Rd., Surb. 115 CJ100
Prospect Rd. (Cheshunt), Wal.Cr. 22 DW29
Prospect Rd., Wdf.Grn. 52 EJ51
Prospect St. SE16 92 DV75
Jamaica Rd.
Prospect Vale SE18 94 EL77
Prospero Rd. N19 63 DJ60
Prossers, Tad. 145 CX121
Croffets
Prothero Gdns. NW4 61 CV57
Prothero Ho. NW10 74 CR66
Prothero Rd. SW6 89 CY80
Prout Gro. NW10 60 CS63
Prout Rd. E5 64 DV62
Provence St. N1 78 DQ68
St. Peters St.
Providence Ct. W1 4 G10
Providence Ct. W1 76 DG73
Providence La., Hayes 85 BR80
Providence Pl. N1 77 DP67
Upper St.
Providence Pl., Epsom 130 CS112
Providence Pl., Rom. 54 EZ54
Providence Pl., Wok. 126 BG114
Providence Rd., West Dr. 70 BL74
Providence Row N1 6 B1
Providence Sq. SE1 92 DT75
Mill St.
Providence St. N1 78 DQ68
St. Peters St.
Providence Yd. E2 78 DU69
Ezra St.
Provident Ind. Est., Hayes 85 BU75
Provost Est. N1 7 K2
Provost Est. N1 78 DR68
Provost Rd. NW3 76 DF66
Provost St. N1 7 K1
Provost St. N1 78 DR68
Prowse Ave. (Bushey), Wat. 44 CC47
Prowse Pl. NW1 77 DH66
Bonny St.
Pruden Clo. N14 49 DJ47
Prudent Pas. EC2 7 K8
Prusom St. E1 78 DV74
Pryor Clo., Abb.L. 15 BT32
Pryors, The NW3 62 DD62
Puck La., Wal.Abb. 23 ED29
Pudding La. EC3 11 L1
Pudding La. EC3 78 DR73
Pudding La., Chig. 39 ES44
Pudding La., Sev. 155 FN121
Church St.
Pudding Mill La. E15 79 EB67
Puddle Dock EC4 6 G10
Puddledock La., Dart. 111 FE92
Puffin Clo., Beck. 121 DX99
Pulborough Rd. SW18 103 CZ87
Pulborough Way, Houns. 86 BW84
Pulford Rd. N15 64 DR58
Pulham Ave. N2 62 DC56
Puller Rd., Barn. 33 CY40
Pulleyns Ave. E6 80 EL69
Pullman Ct. SW2 105 DL88
Pullman Gdns. SW15 103 CW86
Pullman Pl. SE9 108 EL85
Pulross Rd. SW9 91 DM83
Pulteney Clo. E3 79 DZ67
Pulteney Rd. E18 66 EH55
Pulteney Ter. N1 77 DM67
Pulton Pl. SW6 90 DA80
Puma Ct. E1 7 P6
Pump All., Brent. 87 CK80
Pump Clo., Nthlt. 72 CA68
Union Rd.
Pump Ct. EC4 6 D9
Pump Hill, Loug. 39 EM40
Pump La. SE14 92 DW80
Pump La., Hayes 85 BT75
Pump La., Orp. 139 FB106
Pump Pail N., Croy. 120 DQ104
Old Town
Pump Pail S., Croy. 120 DQ104
Southbridge Rd.
Pumping Sta. Rd. W4 88 CS80
Pundersons Gdns. E2 78 DV69
Punjab La., Sthl. 72 BZ74
Herbert Rd.
Purbeck Ave., N.Mal. 117 CT100
Purbeck Dr. NW2 61 CX61
Purbeck Rd., Horn. 69 FG59
Purberry Gro., Epsom 131 CT110
Purbrock Ave., Wat. 29 BV36
Purbrook Est. SE1 11 N5
Purbrook St. SE1 11 N6
Purcell Clo., Borwd. 31 CK39
Purcell Clo., Ken. 134 DR114
Purcell Cres. SW6 89 CX80
Purcell Ms. NW10 74 CS66
Suffolk Rd.
Purcell Rd., Grnf. 72 CB71
Purcell St. N1 78 DS68
Purcells Ave., Edg. 46 CN50
Purcells Clo., Ash. 144 CM118
Albert Rd.
Purchese St. NW1 77 DK68
Purdy St. E3 79 EB70
Purelake Ms. SE13 93 ED83
Purland Clo., Dag. 68 EZ60
Purland Rd. SE28 95 ET75
Purleigh Ave., Wdf.Grn. 52 EL51
Purley Ave. NW2 61 CY61
Purley Bury Ave., Pur. 134 DQ111
Purley Bury Clo., Pur. 134 DQ111
Purley Clo., Ilf. 53 EN54
Purley Downs Rd., Pur. 134 DQ110
Purley Downs Rd., S.Croy. 134 DQ110
Purley Hill, Pur. 133 DP112
Purley Knoll, Pur. 133 DM111
Purley Oaks Rd., S.Croy. 134 DR109
Purley Pk. Rd., Pur. 133 DP110
Purley Pl. N1 77 DP66
Islington Pk. St.
Purley Ri., Pur. 133 DM112
Purley Rd. N9 50 DR48
Purley Rd., Pur. 133 DN111
Purley Rd., S.Croy. 134 DR108
Purley Vale, Pur. 133 DP113
Purley Way, Croy. 119 DM101
Purley Way, Pur. 133 DN111
Purlieu Way, Epp. 39 ES35
Purlings Rd. (Bushey), Wat. 30 CB43
Purneys Rd. SE9 94 EK84
Purrett Rd. SE18 95 ET78
Purser's Cross Rd. SW6 89 CZ81
Pursewardens Clo. W13 73 CJ74
Pursley Gdns., Borwd. 32 CN38
Pursley Rd. NW7 47 CV52
Purves Rd. NW10 75 CV68
Puteaux Ho. E2 79 DX68
Mace St.
Putney Bri. SW6 89 CY83
Putney Bri. SW15 89 CY83
Putney Bri. App. SW6 89 CY83
Putney Bri. Rd. SW15 89 CY84
Putney Bri. Rd. SW18 104 DA85
Putney Common SW15 89 CW83
Putney Heath SW15 103 CV87
Putney Heath La. SW15 103 CX86
Putney High St. SW15 89 CX84
Putney Hill SW15 103 CX86
Putney Pk. Ave. SW15 89 CU84
Putney Pk. La. SW15 89 CV84
Putney Rd., Enf. 37 DX36
Puttenham Clo., Wat. 44 BX47
Pycroft Way N9 50 DU48
Pye Clo., Cat. 148 DQ121
Coulsdon Rd.
Pyecombe Cor. N12 47 CZ49
Pyghtle, The, Uxb. 56 BG59
Savay La.
Pylbrook Rd., Sutt. 118 DA104
Pylon Way, Croy. 119 DL102
Pym Clo., Barn. 34 DD43
Pym Orchard, West. 152 EW124
Pymers Mead SE21 106 DQ88
Pymmes Clo. N13 49 DM50
Pymmes Clo. N17 50 DV53
Pymmes Gdns. N. N9 50 DT48
Pymmes Gdns. S. N9 50 DT48
Pymmes Grn. Rd. N11 49 DH49
Pymmes Rd. N13 49 DL51
Pymms Brook Dr., Barn. 34 DE42
Pynchester Clo., Uxb. 56 BN61
Pyne Rd., Surb. 116 CN102
Pyne Ter. SW19 103 CX88
Windlesham Gro.
Pynest Grn. La., Wal.Abb. 38 EG38
Pynham Clo. SE2 96 EV76
Pynnacles Clo., Stan. 45 CH50
Pyrcroft La., Wey. 127 BP106
Pyrford Lock, Wok. 140 BJ116
Pyrford Rd., W.Byf. 126 BG113
Pyrford Rd., Wok. 140 BH116
Pyrland Rd. N5 64 DR64
Pyrland Rd., Rich. 102 CM86
Pyrles Grn., Loug. 39 EP39
Pyrles La., Loug. 39 EP40
Pyrmont Gro. SE27 105 DP90
Pyrmont Rd. W4 88 CN79
Pyrmont Rd., Ilf. 67 EQ61
High Rd.
Pytchley Cres. SE19 106 DQ93
Pytchley Rd. SE22 92 DS83

Q

Quadrangle, The W2 76 DE72
Norfolk Cres.
Quadrant, The SE24 106 DQ85
Herne Hill
Quadrant, The SW20 117 CY95
Quadrant, The, Bexh. 96 EX80
Quadrant, The, Rich. 88 CL84
Quadrant, The, Sutt. 132 DC107
Quadrant Arc. W1 9 L1
Quadrant Arc., Rom. 69 FE57
Quadrant Gro. NW5 62 DF64
Quadrant Rd., Rich. 87 CK84
Quadrant Rd., Th.Hth. 119 DP98
Quaggy Wk. SE3 94 EG84
Quail Gdns., S.Croy. 135 DY110
Quainton St. NW10 60 CR62
Quaker Clo., Sev. 155 FK123
Quaker La., Sthl. 86 CA76
Quaker La., Wal.Abb. 23 EC34
Quaker St. E1 7 P5
Quaker St. E1 78 DT70
Quakers Course NW9 47 CT53
Quakers Hall La., Sev. 155 FJ122
Quakers La., Islw. 87 CG81
Quakers La., Pot.B. 20 DB30
Quakers Wk. N21 36 DR44
Quality Ct. WC2 6 D8
Quantock Clo., Hayes 85 BR80
Quantock Dr., Wor.Pk. 117 CW103
Cotswold Way
Quantock Gdns. NW2 61 CX61
Quantock Rd., Bexh. 97 FE82
Cumbrian Ave.
Quarles Clo., Rom. 54 FA52
Quarley Way SE15 92 DT80
Daniel Gdns.
Quarr Rd., Cars. 118 DD100
Quarrendon St. SW6 90 DA82
Quarry Cotts., Sev. 154 FG123
Quarry Hill, Sev. 155 FK123
Quarry Pk. Rd., Sutt. 131 CZ107
Quarry Ri., Sutt. 131 CZ107
Quarry Rd. SW18 104 DC86
Quarter Mile La. E10 65 EB63
Quarterdeck, The E14 93 EA75
Quay W., Tedd. 101 CH92
Quebec Ms. W1 4 E9
Quebec Rd., Hayes 72 BW73
Quebec Rd., Ilf. 67 EP59
Quebec Way SE16 93 DX75
Queen Adelaide Rd. SE20 106 DW93
Queen Alexandra's Ct. SW19 103 CZ92
Queen Anne Ave. N15 64 DT57
Suffield Rd.
Queen Anne Ave., Brom. 122 EF97
Queen Anne Clo., Esher 129 CE108
Queen Anne Ms. W1 5 J7
Queen Anne Rd. E9 79 DX65
Queen Anne St. W1 5 H8
Queen Anne St. W1 77 DH71
Queen Anne Ter. E1 78 DV73
Sovereign Clo.
Queen Anne's Clo., Twick. 101 CD90
Queen Anne's Gdns. W4 88 CS76
Queen Annes Gdns. W5 88 CL75
Queen Annes Gdns., Enf. 36 DS44
Queen Annes Gdns., Lthd. 143 CH121
Upper Fairfield Rd.
Queen Anne's Gdns., Mitch. 118 DF97
Queen Anne's Gate SW1 9 M5
Queen Anne's Gate SW1 91 DK75
Queen Anne's Gate, Bexh. 96 EX83
Queen Anne's Gro. W4 88 CS76
Queen Annes Gro. W5 88 CL75
Queen Annes Gro., Enf. 50 DR45
Queen Annes Pl., Enf. 36 DS44
Queen Annes Ter., Lthd. 143 CH121
Upper Fairfield Rd.
Queen Anne's Wk. WC1 6 A5
Queen Caroline Est. W6 89 CW78
Queen Caroline St. W6 89 CW78
Queen Elizabeth Gdns., Mord. 118 DA98
Queen Elizabeth Rd. E17 65 DY55
Queen Elizabeth Rd., Kings.T. 116 CM96
Queen Elizabeth St. SE1 11 P4
Queen Elizabeth St. SE1 92 DT75
Queen Elizabeth Wk. SW13 89 CU81
Queen Elizabeth Wk., Wall. 133 DK105
Queen Elizabeths Clo. N16 64 DR61
Queen Elizabeths Dr. N14 49 DK46
Queen Elizabeth's Dr., Croy. 135 ED110
Queen Elizabeth's Gdns., Croy. 135 ED110
Queen Elizabeth's Dr.
Queen Elizabeths Wk. N16 64 DR61
Queen Margaret's Gro. N1 64 DS64
Queen Mary Ave., Mord. 117 CX99
Queen Mary Clo., Rom. 69 FF58
Queen Mary Clo., Surb. 116 CN104
Queen Mary Rd. SE19 105 DP93
Queen Mary Rd., Shep. 113 BQ96
Queen Mary's Ave., Cars. 132 DF108
Queen Marys Ave., Wat. 29 BS42
Queen of Denmark Ct. SE16 93 DZ76
Queen Sq. WC1 6 A6
Queen Sq. WC1 77 DL70
Queen Sq. Pl. WC1 6 A5
Queen St. EC4 7 J10
Queen St. EC4 78 DQ73
Queen St. N17 50 DS51
Queen St. W1 9 H2
Queen St. W1 77 DH74
Queen St., Bexh. 96 EZ83
Queen St., Cher. 112 BG102
Queen St., Croy. 120 DQ104
Church Rd.
Queen St., Erith 97 FE79
Queen St., Kings L. 14 BG31
Queen St., Rom. 69 FD58
Queen St. Pl. EC4 11 J1
Queen Victoria Ave., Wem. 73 CK66
Queen Victoria St. EC4 6 G10
Queen Victoria St. EC4 77 DP73
Queen Victoria Ter. E1 78 DV73
Sovereign Clo.
Queenborough Gdns., Chis. 109 ER93
Queenborough Gdns., Ilf. 67 EN56
Queenhill Rd., S.Croy. 134 DV110
Queenhithe EC4 7 J10
Queenhithe EC4 78 DQ73
Queens Acre, Sutt. 131 CX108
Queens All., Epp. 25 ET31
Hemnall St.
Queens Ave. N3 48 DC52
Queens Ave. N10 62 DG55
Queens Ave. N20 48 DD47
Queen's Ave. N21 49 DP46
Queens Ave., Felt. 100 BW91
Queens Ave., Grnf. 72 CB72
Queens Ave., Stan. 59 CH55
Queens Ave., Wat. 29 BT42
Queens Ave., W.Byf. 126 BK112
Queens Ave., Wdf.Grn. 52 EH50
Queen's Circ. SW8 91 DH80
Queenstown Rd.
Queens Circ. SW11 91 DH80
Queenstown Rd.
Queens Clo., Edg. 46 CN50
Queens Clo., Tad. 145 CU124
Queens Clo., Wall. 133 DH106
Queens Rd.
Queens Club Gdns. W14 89 CY79
Queens Ct. SE23 106 DW89
Queens Ct., Rich. 102 CM86
Queens Ct., Wey. 127 BR106
Queens Ct. Ride, Cob. 127 BU113
Queens Cres. NW5 76 DG65
Queens Cres., Rich. 102 CM85
Queens Dr. E10 65 EA59
Queens Dr. N4 63 DP61
Queens Dr. W3 74 CM72
Queens Dr. W5 74 CM72
Queens Dr., Abb.L. 15 BT32
Queens Dr., Lthd. 128 CC111
Queens Dr., Surb. 116 CN101
Queens Dr., T.Ditt. 115 CG101
Queens Dr., Wal.Cr. 23 EA34
Queen's Elm Sq. SW3 90 DD78
Old Ch. St.
Queens Gdns. NW4 61 CW57
Queens Gdns. W2 76 DC72
Queens Gdns. W5 73 CJ71
Queen's Gdns., Houns. 86 BY81
Queens Gdns., Rain. 83 FD68
Queen's Gate SW7 90 DC76
Queen's Gate Gdns. SW7 90 DC76
Queens Gate Gdns. SW15 89 CV84
Upper Richmond Rd.
Queen's Gate Ms. SW7 90 DC76
Queen's Gate Pl. SW7 90 DC76

Queen's Gate Pl. Ms. SW7 90 DC76
Queen's Gate Ter. SW7 90 DC76
Queen's Gro. NW8 76 DD67
Queen's Gro. Ms. NW8 76 DD67
Queen's Gro.
Queens Gro. Rd. E4 51 ED46
Queen's Head St. N1 77 DP67
Queens Head Yd. SE1 11 K3
Queens Ho., Tedd. 101 CF93
Queens La. N10 63 DH55
Queens La., Ashf. 98 BM91
Clarendon Rd.
Queens Mkt. E13 80 EJ67
Green St.
Queens Ms. W2 76 DB73
Salem Rd.
Queens Par. N11 48 DF50
Colney Hatch La.
Queens Par. W5 74 CM72
Queens Pk. Ct. W10 75 CX69
Queens Pk. Gdns., Felt. 99 BU90
Vernon Rd.
Queens Pk. Rd., Cat. 148 DS123
Queens Pas., Chis. 109 EP93
High St.
Queens Pl., Mord. 118 DA98
Queens Pl., Wat. 30 BW41
Queen's Prom., Kings.T. 115 CK97
Portsmouth Rd.
Queens Reach, E.Mol. 115 CE98
Queens Ride SW13 89 CU83
Queens Ride SW15 89 CW83
Queen's Ride, Rich. 102 CP88
Queens Ri., Rich. 102 CM86
Queens Rd. E11 65 ED59
Queens Rd. E13 80 EH67
Queen's Rd. E17 65 DZ58
Queens Rd. N3 48 DC53
Queens Rd. N9 50 DV48
Queen's Rd. N11 49 DL52
Queens Rd. NW4 61 CW57
Queens Rd. SE14 92 DV81
Queens Rd. SE15 92 DV81
Queens Rd. SW14 88 CR83
Queens Rd. SW19 103 CZ93
Queens Rd. W5 74 CL72
Queens Rd., Bark. 81 EQ65
Queens Rd., Barn. 33 CX41
Queens Rd., Beck. 121 DY96
Queens Rd., Brom. 122 EG96
Queens Rd., Buck.H. 52 EH47
Queens Rd., Chis. 109 EP93
Queen's Rd., Croy. 119 DP100
Queens Rd., Enf. 36 DS42
Queens Rd., Epp. 27 FB26
Queen's Rd., Erith 97 FE79
Queens Rd., Felt. 99 BV88
Queens Rd., Hmptn. 100 CB91
Queens Rd., Hayes 71 BS72
Queen's Rd., Houns. 86 CB83
Queens Rd., Ilf. 81 EQ65
Queens Rd., Kings.T. 102 CN94
Queens Rd., Loug. 38 EL41
Queens Rd., Mitch. 118 DD96
Queens Rd., Mord. 118 DA98
Queens Rd., N.Mal. 117 CT98
Queens Rd., Rich. 102 CM86
Queens Rd., Sthl. 86 BX75
Queens Rd., Sutt. 132 DA110
Queen's Rd., Tedd. 101 CE93
Queens Rd., T.Ditt. 115 CF99
Queens Rd., Twick. 101 CF87
Queens Rd., Uxb. 70 BJ69
Queens Rd., Wall. 133 DH106
Queens Rd., Wal.Cr. 23 DY34
Queens Rd., Walt. 127 BS106
Queens Rd., Wat. 30 BW42
Queen's Rd., Well. 96 EV82
Queens Rd., West Dr. 84 BM75
Queens Rd., Wey. 127 BP105
Queens Rd. W. E13 80 EG68
Queen's Row SE17 92 DR79
Queens Ter. E13 80 EH67
Queen's Ter. NW8 76 DD67
Queens Ter., Islw. 87 CG84
Queens Ter. Cotts. W7 87 CE75
Boston Rd.
Queens Wk. E4 51 ED46
The Grn. Wk.
Queens Wk. NW9 60 CQ61
Queen's Wk. SW1 9 K3
Queens Wk. SW1 77 DJ74
Queens Wk. W5 73 CJ70
Queens Wk., Ashf. 98 BK91
Queens Wk., Har. 59 CE56
Queens Wk., Ruis. 58 BX62
Queen's Wk., The SE1 78 DR74
London Bri.
Queens Way NW4 61 CW57
Queens Way, Felt. 100 BW91
Queens Way, Rad. 18 CL32
Queens Way, Wal.Cr. 23 DZ34
Queens Well Ave. N20 48 DE49
Queen's Wd. Rd. N10 63 DH58
Queens Yd. WC1 5 L5
Queensberry Ms. W. SW7 90 DD77
Queen's Gate
Queensberry Pl. SW7 90 DD77
Queensberry Way SW7 90 DD77
Harrington Rd.
Queensborough Ms. W2 76 DC73
Porchester Ter.
Queensborough Pas. W2 76 DC73
Porchester Ter.
Queensborough S. Bldgs. W2 76 DC73
Porchester Ter.
Queensborough Studios W2 76 DC73
Porchester Ter.
Queensborough Ter. W2 76 DB73
Queensbridge Pk., Islw. 101 CE85
Queensbridge Rd. E2 78 DT67
Queensbridge Rd. E8 78 DT66
Queensbury Circle Par., Har. 60 CL55
Streatfield Rd.
Queensbury Circle Par., Stan. 60 CL55
Streatfield Rd.
Queensbury Pl., Rich. 101 CK85
Friars La.
Queensbury Rd. NW9 60 CR59
Queensbury Rd., Wem. 74 CM68
Queensbury Sta. Par., Edg. 60 CM55
Queensbury St. N1 78 DQ66
Queenscourt, Wem. 60 CL63
Queenscroft Rd. SE9 108 EK86
Queensdale Cres. W11 75 CX74
Queensdale Pl. W11 75 CY74
Queensdale Rd. W11 75 CX74
Queensdale Wk. W11 75 CY74
Queensdown Rd. E5 64 DV63
Queensferry Wk. N17 64 DV56
Jarrow Rd.
Queensgate, Cob. 128 BX112
Queensgate Gdns., Chis. 123 ER95
Queensgate Pl. NW6 76 DA66
Queensland Ave. N18 50 DQ51
Queensland Ave. SW19 118 DB95
Queensland Pl. N7 63 DN63
Queensland Rd.
Queensland Rd. N7 63 DN63
Queensmead NW8 76 DD67
Queensmead, Lthd. 128 CC111
Queensmead Ave., Epsom 131 CV110
Queensmead Rd., Brom. 122 EF96
Queensmere Clo. SW19 103 CX89
Queensmere Rd. SW19 103 CX89
Queensmill Rd. SW6 89 CX80
Queensthorpe Rd. SE26 107 DX91
Queenstown Gdns., Rain. 83 FF69
Queenstown Ms. SW8 91 DH82
Queenstown Rd.
Queenstown Rd. SW8 91 DH79
Queensville Rd. SW12 105 DK87
Queensway W2 76 DB72
Queensway, Croy. 133 DM107
Queensway, Enf. 36 DV42
Queensway, Orp. 123 EQ99
Queensway, Sun. 113 BV96
Queensway, W.Wick. 122 EE104
Queensway N., Walt. 128 BW105
Robinsway
Queensway S., Walt. 128 BW106
Trenchard Clo.
Queenswood Ave. E17 51 EC53
Queenswood Ave., Hmptn. 100 CB93
Queenswood Ave., Houns. 86 BZ82
Queenswood Ave., Th.Hth. 119 DN99
Queenswood Ave., Wall. 133 DK105
Queenswood Cres., Wat. 15 BU33
Queenswood Gdns. E11 66 EH60
Queenswood Pk. N3 47 CY54
Queenswood Rd. SE23 107 DX90
Queenswood Rd., Sid. 109 ET85
Quemerford Rd. N7 63 DM64
Quendon Dr., Wal.Abb. 23 ED33
Quennell Clo., Ash. 144 CL119
Parkers La.
Quentin Pl. SE13 94 EE83
Quentin Rd. SE13 94 EE83
Quernmore Clo., Brom. 108 EG93
Quernmore Rd. N4 63 DN58
Quernmore Rd., Brom. 108 EG93
Querrin St. SW6 90 DC82
Quex Ms. NW6 76 DA67
Quex Rd.
Quex Rd. NW6 76 DA67
Quick Pl. N1 77 DP67
Quick Rd. W4 88 CS78
Quick St. N1 6 G1
Quick St. N1 77 DP68
Quick St. Ms. N1 6 F1
Quickmoor La., Kings L. 14 BH33
Quicks Rd. SW19 104 DB94
Quickswood NW3 76 DE66
King Henry's Rd.
Quickwood Clo., Rick. 28 BG44
Quiet Clo., Add. 126 BG105
Quiet Nook, Brom. 122 EK104
Croydon Rd.
Quill La. SW15 89 CX84
Quill St. N4 63 DN62
Quill St. W5 74 CL69
Quillot, The, Walt. 127 BT106
Quilp St. SE1 11 H4
Quilter Gdns., Orp. 124 EW102
Tintagel Rd.
Quilter Rd., Orp. 124 EW102
Quilter St. E2 78 DU69
Quilter St. SE18 95 ET78
Quinta Dr., Barn. 33 CV43
Quintin Ave. SW20 117 CZ95
Quintin Clo., Pnr. 57 BV57
Eastcote High Rd.
Quinton Clo., Beck. 121 EC97
Quinton Clo., Houns. 85 BV80
Quinton Clo., Wall. 133 DH105
Quinton Rd., T.Ditt. 115 CG102
Quinton St. SW18 104 DC89
Quixley St. E14 79 ED73
Quorn Rd. SE22 92 DS84

R

Rabbit La., Walt. 127 BU108
Rabbit Row W8 76 DA74
Kensington Mall
Rabbits Rd. E12 66 EL63
Rabournmead Dr., Nthlt. 58 BY64
Raby Rd., N.Mal. 116 CR98
Raby St. E14 79 DY72
Salmon La.
Raccoon Way, Houns. 86 BW82
Rachel Pt. E5 64 DU63
Muir Rd.
Rackham Ms. SW16 105 DJ93
Westcote Rd.
Racton Rd. SW6 90 DA79
Radbourne Ave. W5 87 CJ77
Radbourne Clo. E5 65 DX63
Overbury St.
Radbourne Cres. E17 51 ED54
Radbourne Rd. SW12 105 DJ87
Radcliffe Ave. NW10 75 CU68
Radcliffe Ave., Enf. 36 DQ39
Radcliffe Gdns., Cars. 132 DE108
Radcliffe Ms., Hmptn. 100 CC92
Taylor Clo.
Radcliffe Path SW8 91 DJ82
St. Rule St.
Radcliffe Rd. N21 49 DP46
Radcliffe Rd., Croy. 120 DT103
Radcliffe Rd., Har. 45 CG54
Radcliffe Sq. SW15 103 CX86
Radcliffe Way, Nthlt. 72 BX69
Radcot Pt. SE23 107 DX90
Radcot St. SE11 91 DN78
Methley St.
Raddington Rd. W10 75 CY71
Radfield Way, Sid. 109 ER87
Radford Rd. SE13 107 EC85
Radford Way, Bark. 81 ET69
Radipole Rd. SW6 89 CZ81
Radland Rd. E16 80 EF72
Radlet Ave. SE26 106 DV90
Radlett Clo. E7 80 EF65
Radlett La., Rad. 31 CK35
Radlett Pk. Rd., Rad. 17 CG34
Radlett Pl. NW8 76 DE67
Radlett Rd., St.Alb. 17 CE28
Radlett Rd., Wat. 30 BW41
Radlett Rd. (Aldenham), Wat. 30 CB39
Radley Ave., Ilf. 67 ET63
Radley Clo., Felt. 99 BT88
Radley Ct. SE16 93 DX75
Thame Rd.
Radley Gdns., Har. 60 CL56
Radley Ms. W8 90 DA76
Radley Rd. N17 50 DS54
Radley's La. E18 52 EG54
Radleys Mead, Dag. 83 FB65
Radlix Rd. E10 65 EA60
Radnor Ave., Har. 59 CE57
Radnor Ave., Well. 110 EV85
Radnor Clo., Chis. 109 ES93
Homewood Cres.
Radnor Clo., Mitch. 119 DL98
Radnor Cres. SE18 96 EU80
Radnor Cres., Ilf. 67 EM57
Radnor Gdns., Enf. 36 DS39
Radnor Gdns., Twick. 101 CF89
Radnor Gro., Uxb. 70 BN68
Charnwood Rd.
Radnor Ms. W2 4 A9
Radnor Pl. W2 4 B9
Radnor Pl. W2 76 DE72
Radnor Rd. NW6 75 CY67
Radnor Rd. SE15 92 DU80
Radnor Rd., Har. 59 CD57
Radnor Rd., Twick. 101 CF88
Radnor Rd., Wey. 112 BN104
Radnor St. EC1 7 J3
Radnor St. EC1 78 DQ69
Radnor Ter. W14 89 CZ77
Radnor Wk. E14 93 EA77
Copeland Dr.
Radnor Wk. SW3 90 DE78
Radnor Wk., Croy. 121 DY100
Radnor Way NW10 74 CP70
Radolphs, Tad. 145 CX122
Heathcote
Radstock Ave., Har. 59 CG55
Radstock St. SW11 90 DE80
Radwell Path, Borwd. 32 CL39
Cromwell Rd.
Raebarn Gdns., Barn. 33 CV43
Raeburn Ave., Dart. 111 FH85
Raeburn Ave., Surb. 116 CP102
Raeburn Clo. NW11 62 DC58
Raeburn Clo., Kings.T. 101 CK94
Raeburn Rd., Edg. 46 CN54
Raeburn Rd., Hayes 71 BR68
Raeburn Rd., Sid. 109 ES86
Raeburn St. SW2 91 DL84
Rafford Way, Brom. 122 EH96
Raft Rd. SW18 90 DA84
North Pas.
Rag Hill Clo., West. 150 EL121
Rag Hill Rd., West. 150 EK121
Raggleswood, Chis. 123 EN95
Raglan Ave., Wal.Cr. 23 DX34
Raglan Clo., Houns. 100 BY85
Vickers Way
Raglan Ct. SE12 108 EG85
Raglan Ct., S.Croy. 133 DP106
Raglan Ct., Wem. 60 CM63
Raglan Gdns., Wat. 43 BV46
Raglan Rd. E17 65 EC57
Raglan Rd. SE18 95 EQ78
Raglan Rd., Belv. 96 EZ78
Raglan Rd., Brom. 122 EJ98
Raglan Rd., Enf. 50 DS45
Raglan St. NW5 77 DH65
Raglan Ter., Har. 58 CB63
Raglan Way, Nthlt. 72 CC65
Ragley Clo. W3 88 CQ75
Church Rd.
Rags La. (Cheshunt), Wal.Cr. 22 DS28
Rahn Rd., Epp. 26 EU31
Raider Clo., Rom. 54 FA53
Railey Ms. NW5 63 DJ64
Railpit La., Warl. 150 EE115
Railshead Rd., Islw. 87 CH84
Railton Rd. SE24 91 DN84
Railway App. N4 63 DN58
Wightman Rd.
Railway App. SE1 11 L3
Railway App. SE1 78 DR74
Railway App., Har. 59 CF56
Railway App., Twick. 101 CG87
Railway App., Wall. 133 DH107
Railway Ave. SE16 92 DW75
Railway Cotts., Wat. 29 BV39
Railway Ms. E3 79 EA69
Wellington Way
Railway Ms. W10 75 CY72
Ladbroke Gro.
Railway Pas., Tedd. 101 CG93
Victoria Rd.
Railway Pl. SW19 103 CZ93
Hartfield Rd.
Railway Pl., Belv. 96 FA76
Railway Ri. SE22 92 DS84
Grove Vale
Railway Rd., Tedd. 101 CF91
Railway Rd., Wal.Cr. 23 DY33
Railway Side SW13 88 CS83
Railway St. N1 6 A1
Railway St. N1 77 DL68
Railway St., Rom. 68 EW60
Railway Ter. SE13 107 EB85
Ladywell Rd.
Railway Ter., Felt. 99 BU88
Railway Ter., Hem.H. 14 BN27
Rainborough Clo. NW10 74 CQ65
Rainbow Ave. E14 93 EB78
Rainbow Ct., Wat. 30 BW44
Oxhey Rd.
Rainbow Ind. Est., West Dr. 70 BK73
Rainbow Quay SE16 93 DY76
Rope St.
Rainbow St. SE5 92 DS80
Raine St. E1 78 DV74
Rainer Clo. (Cheshunt), Wal.Cr. 23 DX29
Rainham Clo. SE9 109 ER86
Rainham Clo. SW11 104 DE86
Rainham Rd. NW10 75 CW69
Rainham Rd., Rain. 83 FG69
Rainham Rd. N., Dag. 68 FA61
Rainham Rd. S., Dag. 69 FB63
Rainhill Way E3 79 EA69
Rainsborough Ave. SE8 93 DY77
Rainsford Clo., Stan. 45 CJ50
Rainsford Rd. NW10 74 CP68
Rainsford St. W2 4 B8
Rainsford Way, Horn. 69 FG60
Rainton Rd. SE7 94 EG78
Rainville Rd. W6 89 CW79
Raisins Hill, Pnr. 58 BW55
Raith Ave. N14 49 DK48
Raleana Rd. E14 79 EC74
Raleigh Ave., Hayes 71 BV71
Raleigh Ave., Wall. 133 DK105
Raleigh Clo. NW4 61 CW57
Raleigh Clo., Erith 97 FF79
Raleigh Clo., Pnr. 58 BX59
Raleigh Clo., Ruis. 57 BT61
Raleigh Ct. SE16 79 DX74
Rotherhithe St.
Raleigh Ct., Stai. 98 BG91
Raleigh Ct., Wall. 133 DH107
Raleigh Dr. N20 48 DE48
Raleigh Dr., Esher 129 CD106
Raleigh Dr., Surb. 116 CQ102
Raleigh Gdns. SW2 105 DM86
Brixton Hill
Raleigh Gdns., Mitch. 118 DF97
Raleigh Ms. N1 77 DP67
Queen's Head St.
Raleigh Ms., Orp. 137 ET106
Osgood Ave.
Raleigh Rd. N8 63 DN56
Raleigh Rd. SE20 107 DX94
Raleigh Rd., Enf. 36 DR42
Raleigh Rd., Felt. 99 BT90
Raleigh Rd., Rich. 88 CM83
Raleigh Rd., Sthl. 86 BY78
Raleigh St. N1 77 DP67
Raleigh Way N14 49 DK46
Raleigh Way, Felt. 100 BW91
Ralliwood Rd., Ash. 144 CN119
Ralph Ct. W2 76 DB72
Queensway
Ralph Perring Ct., Beck. 121 EA98
Ralston St. SW3 90 DF78
Tedworth Sq.
Ralston Way, Wat. 44 BX47
Ram Pas., Kings.T. 115 CK96
High St.
Ram Pl. E9 78 DW65
Chatham Pl.
Ram St. SW18 104 DB85
Rama Clo. SW16 105 DL94
Rama Ct., Har. 59 CE61
Ramac Ind. Est. SE7 94 EG77
Ramac Way SE7 94 EH78
Rambler Clo. SW16 105 DJ91
Rame Clo. SW17 104 DG92
Ramilles Clo. SW2 105 DL86
Ramillies Pl. W1 5 K9
Ramillies Pl. W1 77 DJ72
Ramillies Rd. NW7 46 CS47
Ramillies Rd. W4 88 CR77
Ramillies Rd., Sid. 110 EV86
Ramillies St. W1 5 K9
Ramney Dr., Enf. 37 DY36
Ramornie Clo., Walt. 128 BZ106
Rampart St. E1 78 DV72
Commercial Rd.
Rampayne St. SW1 9 M10
Rampayne St. SW1 91 DK78
Rampton Clo. E4 51 EA48
Rams Gro., Rom. 68 EY56
Ramsay Pl., Har. 59 CE60
Ramsay Rd. E7 66 EE63
Ramsay Rd. W3 88 CQ76
Ramscroft Clo. N9 50 DS45
Ramsdale Rd. SW17 104 DG92
Ramsden Clo., Orp. 124 EW102
Ramsden Dr., Rom. 54 FA52
Ramsden Rd. N11 48 DF50
Ramsden Rd. SW12 104 DG86
Ramsden Rd., Erith 97 FD80
Ramsden Rd., Orp. 124 EV101
Ramsey Clo. NW9 61 CT58
West Hendon Bdy.
Ramsey Clo., Grnf. 59 CD64
Ramsey Clo., Hat. 20 DD27
Ramsey Ho., Wem. 74 CL65
Ramsey Ms. SW3 90 DE79
King's Rd.
Ramsey Rd., Th.Hth. 119 DM100
Ramsey St. E2 78 DU70
Ramsey Wk. N1 78 DR65
Clephane Rd.
Ramsey Way N14 49 DJ45
Ramsgate St. E8 78 DT65
Dalston La.
Ramsgill App., Ilf. 67 ET56
Ramsgill Dr., Ilf. 67 ET57
Ramulis Dr., Hayes 72 BX70
Ramus Wd. Ave., Orp. 137 ES106
Rancliffe Gdns. SE9 94 EL84
Rancliffe Rd. E6 80 EL68
Randall Ave. NW2 60 CS61
Randall Clo. SW11 90 DE81
Randall Clo., Erith 97 FC79
Randall Pl. SE10 93 EC80
Randall Rd. SE11 10 B9
Randall Rd. SE11 91 DM78
Randall Row SE11 10 B9
Randalls Cres., Lthd. 143 CG120
Randalls Pk. Ave., Lthd. 143 CG120
Randalls Pk. Dr., Lthd. 143 CG121
Randalls Rd.
Randalls Rd., Lthd. 143 CE119
Randalls Way, Lthd. 143 CG121
Randell's Rd. N1 77 DL67
Randle Rd., Rich. 101 CJ91
Randles La., Sev. 152 EX115
Randlesdown Rd. SE6 107 EA91
Randolph App. E16 80 EJ72
Baxter Rd.
Randolph Ave. W9 76 DB68
Randolph Clo., Bexh. 97 FC83
Randolph Clo., Cob. 142 CA115
Randolph Clo., Kings.T. 102 CQ92
Randolph Cres. W9 76 DC70
Randolph Gdns. NW6 76 DB68
Randolph Gro., Rom. 68 EW57
Donald Dr.
Randolph Ho., Croy. 120 DQ102
Randolph Ms. W9 76 DC70
Randolph Rd. E17 65 EB57
Randolph Rd. W9 76 DC70
Randolph Rd., Epsom 131 CT114
Randolph Rd., Sthl. 86 BZ75
Randolph St. NW1 77 DJ66
Randon Clo., Har. 44 CB54
Ranelagh Ave. SW6 89 CZ83
Ranelagh Ave. SW13 89 CU82
Ranelagh Bri. W2 76 DB71
Gloucester Ter.
Ranelagh Clo., Edg. 46 CN49
Ranelagh Dr., Edg. 46 CN49
Ranelagh Dr., Twick. 87 CH84
Ranelagh Gdns. E11 66 EJ57
Ranelagh Gdns. SW6 89 CZ83
Ranelagh Gdns. W4 88 CQ80
Grove Pk. Gdns.
Ranelagh Gdns. W6 89 CT76
Ranelagh Gdns., Ilf. 67 EM60
Ranelagh Gro. SW1 8 G10
Ranelagh Gro. SW1 90 DG78
Ranelagh Ms. W5 87 CK75
Ranelagh Rd.
Ranelagh Pl., N.Mal. 116 CS99
Rodney Rd.
Ranelagh Rd. E6 81 EN67
Ranelagh Rd. E11 66 EE63
Ranelagh Rd. E15 80 EE67
Ranelagh Rd. N17 64 DS55
Ranelagh Rd. N22 49 DM53

This index reads in the sequence: Street Name / Postal District or Post Town / Map Page Number / Grid Reference

Reede Gdns., Dag. 69 FB64
Reede Rd.
Reede Rd., Dag. 82 FA65
Reede Way, Dag. 83 FB65
Reedham Clo. N17 64 DV56
Reedham Clo., St.Alb. 16 CA29
Reedham Dr., Pur. 133 DM113
Reedham Pk. Ave., Pur. 147 DN116
Reedham St. SE15 92 DU82
Reedholm Vill. N16 64 DR63
Winston Rd.
Reeds Cres., Wat. 30 BW40
Reeds Pl. NW1 77 DJ66
Royal College St.
Reeds Rest La., Tad. 145 CZ119
Reeds Wk., Wat. 30 BW40
Orphanage Rd.
Reedsfield Clo., Ashf. 99 BP91
The Yews
Reedsfield Rd., Ashf. 99 BP91
Reedworth St. SE11 10 E9
Reedworth St. SE11 91 DN77
Reenglass Rd., Stan. 45 CK49
Rees Gdns., Croy. 120 DT100
Rees St. N1 78 DQ67
Reesland Clo. E12 81 EN65
Reets Fm. Clo. NW9 60 CS58
Reeves Ave. NW9 60 CR59
Reeves Cor., Croy. 119 DP103
Roman Way
Reeves Cres., Swan. 125 FD97
Reeves Ms. W1 8 F1
Reeves Ms. W1 76 DG73
Reeves Rd. E3 79 EB70
Reeves Rd. SE18 95 EP79
Reform Row N17 50 DT54
Reform St. SW11 90 DF82
Regal Clo. E1 78 DU71
Old Montague St.
Regal Clo. W5 73 CK71
Regal Ct. N18 50 DT50
College Clo.
Regal Cres., Wall. 119 DH104
Regal Dr. N11 49 DH50
Regal La. NW1 76 DG67
Regents Pk. Rd.
Regal Row SE15 92 DW81
Queens Rd.
Regal Way, Har. 60 CL58
Regal Way, Wat. 30 BW38
Regan Way N1 7 M1
Regan Way N1 78 DS68
Regarder Rd., Chig. 54 EU50
Regarth Ave., Rom. 69 FE58
Regency Clo. W5 74 CL72
Regency Clo., Chig. 53 EQ50
Regency Clo., Hmptn. 100 BZ92
Regency Cres. NW4 47 CX54
Regency Dr., Ruis. 57 BS60
Regency Gdns., Walt. 114 BW102
Regency Lo., Buck.H. 52 EK47
Regency Ms. NW10 75 CU65
High Rd.
Regency Ms., Beck. 121 EC95
Regency Ms., Islw. 101 CE85
Queensbridge Pk.
Regency Pl. SW1 9 N8
Regency St. SW1 9 N8
Regency St. SW1 91 DK77
Regency Ter. SW7 90 DD78
Fulham Rd.
Regency Wk., Croy. 121 DY100
Regency Wk., Rich. 102 CL86
Friars Stile Rd.
Regency Way, Bexh. 96 EX83
Regent Ave., Uxb. 71 BP66
Regent Clo. N12 48 DC50
Nether St.
Regent Clo., Add. 126 BK109
Regent Clo., Har. 60 CL58
Regent Clo., Houns. 85 BV81
Regent Gdns., Ilf. 68 EU58
Regent Pk. Ind. Est., Lthd. 143 CG118
Regent Pl. SW19 104 DB92
Haydons Rd.
Regent Pl. W1 5 L10
Regent Pl., Croy. 120 DT102
Grant Rd.
Regent Rd. SE24 105 DP86
Regent Rd., Epp. 25 ET30
Regent Rd., Surb. 116 CM99
Regent Sq. E3 79 EB69
Regent Sq. WC1 6 A3
Regent Sq. WC1 77 DL69
Regent Sq., Belv. 97 FB77
Regent St. NW10 75 CX69
Wellington Rd.
Regent St. SW1 9 M1
Regent St. SW1 77 DK73
Regent St. W1 5 J8
Regent St. W1 77 DH72
Regent St. W4 88 CN78
Regent St., Wat. 29 BV38
Regents Ave. N13 49 DN50
Regents Bri. Gdns. SW8 91 DL80
Regents Clo., Hayes 71 BS71
Grange Par.
Regents Clo., Rad. 17 CG34
Regents Clo., S.Croy. 134 DS107
Regents Clo., Whyt. 148 DS118
Regents Dr., Kes. 136 EK106
Regents Ms. NW8 76 DC68
Langford Pl.
Regent's Pk. NW1 4 D1
Regent's Pk. NW1 76 DF68
Regent's Pk. Est. NW1 5 K3
Regents Pk. Rd. N3 61 CZ56
Regents Pk. Rd. NW1 76 DF67
Regents Pk. Ter. NW1 77 DH67
Oval Rd.
Regent's Pl. NW1 77 DJ70
Hampstead Rd.
Regent's Pl. SE3 94 EG82
Regents Row E8 78 DU67
Regina Clo., Barn. 33 CX41
Regina Rd. N4 63 DM60
Regina Rd. SE25 120 DU97
Regina Rd. W13 73 CG74
Regina Rd., Sthl. 86 BY77
Regina Ter. W13 73 CH74
Reginald Rd. E7 80 EG65
Reginald Rd. SE8 93 EA80
Reginald Rd., Nthwd. 43 BT53
Reginald Sq. SE8 93 EA80
Regis Rd. NW5 63 DH64
Regnart Bldgs. NW1 5 L4
Reid Ave., Cat. 148 DR121
Reid Clo., Pnr. 57 BU56
Reidhaven Rd. SE18 95 ES77
Reigate Ave., Sutt. 118 DA103
Reigate Rd., Brom. 108 EF90
Reigate Rd., Epsom 131 CU110
Reigate Rd., Ilf. 67 ET61
Reigate Rd., Lthd. 143 CJ122
Reigate Rd., Tad. 145 CY119
Reigate Way, Wall. 133 DL106
Reighton Rd. E5 64 DU62
Relay Rd. W12 75 CW74
Relf Rd. SE15 92 DU83
Relko Ct., Epsom 130 CR111
Relko Gdns., Sutt. 132 DD106
Relton Ms. SW7 8 C6
Rembrandt Clo. E14 93 ED76
Rembrandt Clo. SW1 8 F9
Rembrandt Rd. SE13 94 EE84
Rembrandt Rd., Edg. 46 CN54
Rembrandt Way, Walt. 113 BV103
Remington Rd. E6 80 EL72
Remington Rd. N15 64 DR58
Remington St. N1 6 G1
Remington St. N1 77 DP68
Remnant St. WC2 6 B8
Rempstone Ms. N1 78 DR68
Mintern St.
Remus Rd. E3 79 EA66
Monier Rd.
Rendle Clo., Croy. 120 DT99
Rendlesham Ave., Rad. 31 CF37
Rendlesham Rd. E5 64 DU63
Rendlesham Rd., Enf. 35 DP39
Renforth St. SE16 92 DW75
Renfree Way, Shep. 112 BM101
Renfrew Clo. E6 81 EN73
Renfrew Rd. SE11 10 F8
Renfrew Rd. SE11 91 DP77
Renfrew Rd., Houns. 86 BX82
Renfrew Rd., Kings.T. 102 CP94
Renmans, The, Ash. 144 CM116
Renmuir St. SW17 104 DF93
Rennell St. SE13 93 EC83
Lewisham High St.
Rennels Way, Islw. 87 CE82
St. John's Rd.
Renness Rd. E17 65 DY55
Rennets Clo. SE9 109 ES85
Rennets Wd. Rd. SE9 109 ER85
Rennie Clo., Ashf. 98 BK90
Rennie Est. SE16 92 DV77
Rennie St. SE1 10 F2
Rennie St. SE1 77 DP74
Rennison Clo., Wal.Cr. 22 DT27
Allwood Rd.
Renown Clo., Croy. 119 DP102
Renown Clo., Rom. 54 FA53
Rensburg Rd. E17 65 DX57
Renshaw Clo., Belv. 96 EZ79
Grove Rd.
Renters Ave. NW4 61 CW58
Renton Dr., Orp. 124 EX101
Renwick Ind. Est., Bark. 82 EV67
Renwick Rd., Bark. 82 EV70
Repens Way, Hayes 72 BX70
Stipularis Dr.
Rephidim St. SE1 11 L7
Replingham Rd. SW18 103 CZ88
Reporton Rd. SW6 89 CY81
Repository Rd. SE18 95 EM79
Repton Ave., Hayes 85 BR77
Repton Ave., Rom. 69 FG55
Repton Ave., Wem. 59 CJ63
Repton Clo., Cars. 132 DE106
Repton Ct., Beck. 121 EB95
Repton Dr., Rom. 69 FG56
Repton Gdns., Rom. 69 FG55
Repton Gro., Ilf. 53 EM53
Repton Rd., Har. 60 CM56
Repton Rd., Orp. 124 EU104
Repton St. E14 79 DY72
Repton Way, Rick. 28 BN43
Repulse Clo., Rom. 55 FB53
Reservoir Rd. N14 35 DJ43
Reservoir Rd. SE4 93 DY82
Reservoir Rd., Ruis. 57 BQ57
Resolution Wk. SE18 95 EM76
Venus Rd.
Restell Clo. SE3 94 EE79
Reston Clo., Borwd. 32 CN38
Reston Path, Borwd. 32 CN38
Reston Clo.
Reston Pl. SW7 90 DC75
Hyde Pk. Gate
Restons Cres. SE9 109 ER86
Restormel Clo., Houns. 100 CA85
Retcar Clo. N19 63 DH61
Dartmouth Pk. Hill
Retcar Pl. N19 63 DH61
Dartmouth Pk. Hill
Retford Clo., Borwd. 32 CN38
The Campions
Retingham Way E4 51 EB47
Retreat, The NW9 60 CR57
Retreat, The SW14 88 CS83
South Worple Way
Retreat, The, Abb.L. 15 BQ31
Abbots Rd.
Retreat, The, Add. 126 BK106
Retreat, The, Har. 58 CA59
Retreat, The, Orp. 138 EV107
Retreat, The, Surb. 116 CM100
Retreat, The, Th.Hth. 120 DR98
Retreat, The, Wor.Pk. 117 CV103
Retreat Clo., Har. 59 CJ57
Retreat Pl. E9 78 DW65
Retreat Rd., Rich. 101 CK85
Retreat Way, Chig. 54 EV48
Reunion Row E1 78 DV73
Pennington St.
Reveley Sq. SE16 93 DY75
Howland Way
Revell Clo., Lthd. 142 CB122
Revell Dr., Lthd. 142 CB122
Revell Ri. SE18 95 ET79
Revell Rd., Kings.T. 116 CP96
Revell Rd., Sutt. 131 CZ107
Revelon Rd. SE4 93 DY83
Revelstoke Rd. SW18 103 CZ89
Reventlow Rd. SE9 109 EQ88
Reverdy Rd. SE1 92 DU77
Reverend Clo., Har. 58 CB62
Revesby Rd., Cars. 118 DD100
Review Rd. NW2 61 CT61
Review Rd., Dag. 83 FB67
Rewell St. SW6 90 DC80
Rewley Rd., Cars. 118 DD100
Rex Ave., Ashf. 98 BN93
Rex Clo., Rom. 55 FB52
Rex Pl. W1 8 G1
Reydon Ave. E11 66 EJ58
Reynard Clo. SE4 93 DY83
Foxwell St.
Reynard Clo., Brom. 123 EM97
Reynard Dr. SE19 106 DT94
Reynard Pl. SE14 93 DY79
Milton Ct. Rd.
Reynards Way, St.Alb. 16 BZ30
Reynardson Rd. N17 50 DQ52
Reynolds Ave. E12 67 EN64
Reynolds Ave., Chess. 130 CL108
Reynolds Ave., Rom. 68 EW59
Reynolds Clo. NW11 62 DB59
Reynolds Clo. SW19 118 DD95
Reynolds Clo., Cars. 118 DF102
Reynolds Ct. E11 66 EF62
Cobbold Rd.
Reynolds Dr., Edg. 60 CM55
Reynolds Pl. SE3 94 EH80
Reynolds Pl., Rich. 102 CM86
Cambrian Rd.
Reynolds Rd. SE15 106 DW85
Reynolds Rd. W4 88 CQ76
Reynolds Rd., Hayes 72 BW70
Reynolds Rd., N.Mal. 116 CR101
Reynolds Way, Croy. 134 DS105
Rheidol Ms. N1 78 DQ68
Rheidol Ter.
Rheidol Ter. N1 78 DQ67
Rheingold Way, Wall. 133 DL109
Rheola Clo. N17 50 DT53
Rhoda St. E2 78 DT70
Brick La.
Rhodes Ave. N22 49 DJ53
Rhodes Moorhouse Ct., Mord. 118 DA100
Rhodes St. N7 63 DM64
Mackenzie Rd.
Rhodes Way, Wat. 30 BX40
Rhodesia Rd. E11 65 ED61
Rhodesia Rd. SW9 91 DL82
Rhodeswell Rd. E14 79 DY71
Rhodrons Ave., Chess. 130 CL106
Rhondda Gro. E3 79 DY69
Rhyl Rd., Grnf. 73 CF68
Rhyl St. NW5 76 DG65
Rhys Ave. N11 49 DK52
Rialto Rd., Mitch. 118 DG96
Ribble Clo., Wdf.Grn. 52 EJ51
Prospect Rd.
Ribbledale, St.Alb. 18 CM27
Ribblesdale Ave., Nthlt. 72 CB65
Ribblesdale Rd. N8 63 DM56
Ribblesdale Rd. SW16 105 DH93
Ribbon Dance Ms. SE5 92 DR81
Camberwell Gro.
Ribchester Ave., Grnf. 73 CF69
Ribston Clo., Brom. 123 EM102
Ribston Clo., Rad. 17 CK33
Wayside
Ricardo Path SE28 82 EW74
Byron Clo.
Ricardo St. E14 79 EB72
Ricards Rd. SW19 103 CZ92
Rich La. SW5 90 DB78
Warwick Rd.
Rich St. E14 79 DZ73
Richard Clo. SE18 94 EL77
Richard Foster Clo. E17 65 DZ59
Richard St. E1 78 DV72
Commercial Rd.
Richards Ave., Rom. 69 FC57
Richards Clo., Har. 59 CG57
Richards Clo., Hayes 85 BR79
Richards Clo., Uxb. 70 BN67
Richards Clo. (Bushey), Wat. 45 CD45
Richards Pl. E17 65 EA55
Richards Pl. SW3 8 C8
Richards Rd., Cob. 128 CB114
Richardson Clo. E8 78 DT67
Clarissa St.
Richardson Clo., St.Alb. 18 CL27
Richardson Rd. E15 80 EE68
Richardson's Ms. W1 5 K5
Richbell Clo., Ash. 143 CK118
Richbell Pl. WC1 6 B6
Richborne Ter. SW8 91 DM80
Richborough Clo., Orp. 124 EX98
Richborough Rd. NW2 61 CY63
Riches Rd., Ilf. 67 EQ61
Richfield Rd. (Bushey), Wat. 44 CC45
Richford Rd. E15 80 EF67
Richford St. W6 89 CW75
Richland Ave., Couls. 132 DG114
Richlands Ave., Epsom 131 CU105
Richmer Rd., Erith 97 FG80
Richmond Ave. E4 51 ED50
Richmond Ave. N1 77 DM67
Richmond Ave. NW10 75 CW65
Richmond Ave. SW20 117 CY95
Richmond Ave., Felt. 99 BS86
Richmond Ave., Uxb. 71 BP65
Richmond Bri., Rich. 101 CK85
Richmond Bri., Twick. 101 CK86
Richmond Bldgs. W1 5 M9
Richmond Clo. E17 65 DZ58
Richmond Clo., Borwd. 32 CQ43
Ripon Way
Richmond Clo., Epsom 130 CS114
Richmond Clo., Lthd. 142 CC124
Richmond Clo. (Cheshunt), Wal.Cr. 22 DW29
Richmond Clo., West. 150 EH119
Richmond Ct., Pot.B. 20 DC31
Richmond Cres. E4 51 ED50
Richmond Cres. N1 77 DM67
Richmond Cres. N9 50 DU46
Richmond Dr., Shep. 113 BQ100
Richmond Dr., Wat. 29 BS40
Richmond Gdns. NW4 61 CU57
Richmond Gdns., Har. 45 CF52
Richmond Grn., Croy. 119 DL104
Richmond Gro. N1 77 DP66
Richmond Gro., Surb. 116 CM100
Ewell Rd.
Richmond Hill, Rich. 102 CL86
Richmond Hill Ct., Rich. 102 CL86
Richmond Ms. W1 5 M9
Richmond Ms., Tedd. 101 CF93
Broad St.
Richmond Pk., Kings.T. 102 CN88
Richmond Pk., Rich. 102 CN88
Richmond Pk. Rd. SW14 102 CQ85
Richmond Pk. Rd., Kings.T. 116 CL95
Richmond Pl. SE18 95 EQ77
Richmond Retail Pk., Rich. 88 CP81
Richmond Rd. E4 51 ED46
Richmond Rd. E7 66 EH64
Richmond Rd. E8 78 DT66
Richmond Rd. E11 65 ED61
Richmond Rd. N2 48 DC54
Richmond Rd. N11 49 DL51
Richmond Rd. N15 64 DS58
Richmond Rd. SW20 117 CV95
Richmond Rd. W5 88 CL75
Richmond Rd., Barn. 34 DB43
Richmond Rd., Couls. 147 DH115
Richmond Rd., Croy. 119 DL104
Richmond Rd., Ilf. 67 EQ62
Richmond Rd., Islw. 87 CG83
Richmond Rd., Kings.T. 101 CK92
Richmond Rd., Pot.B. 20 DC31
Richmond Rd., Rom. 69 FF58
Richmond Rd., Th.Hth. 119 DP97
Richmond Rd., Twick. 101 CG88
Richmond St. E13 80 EG68
Richmond Ter. SW1 9 P4
Richmond Ter. SW1 91 DL75
Richmond Ter. Ms. SW1 91 DL75
Parliament St.
Richmond Way E11 66 EG61
Richmond Way W12 89 CX75
Richmond Way W14 89 CX75
Richmond Way, Lthd. 142 CB124
Richmond Way, Rick. 29 BQ42
Richmount Gdns. SE3 94 EG83
Rick Roberts Way E15 79 EC67
Rickard Clo. NW4 61 CU56
Rickard Clo. SW2 105 DN88
Rickard Clo., West Dr. 84 BK76
Rickards Clo., Surb. 116 CL102
Rickett St. SW6 90 DA79
Ricketts Hill Rd., West. 150 EK121
Rickman Cres., Add. 112 BH104
Rickman Hill, Couls. 147 DH117
Rickman Hill Rd., Couls. 147 DH118
Rickman St. E1 78 DW69
Mantus Rd.
Rickmansworth Rd., Nthwd. 43 BP50
Rickmansworth Rd., Pnr. 43 BV54
Rickmansworth Rd., Uxb. 42 BJ53
Rickmansworth Rd., Wat. 29 BS42
Rickthorne Rd. N19 63 DL61
Landseer Rd.
Rickyard Path SE9 94 EL84
Ridding La., Grnf. 59 CF64
Riddlesdown Ave., Pur. 134 DQ111
Riddlesdown Rd., Pur. 134 DQ110
Riddons Rd. SE12 108 EJ90
Ride, The, Brent. 87 CH78
Ride, The, Enf. 36 DW41
Rideout St. SE18 95 EM77
Rider Clo., Sid. 109 ES86
Ridgdale St. E3 79 EA68
Ridge, The, Bex. 110 EZ87
Ridge, The, Couls. 133 DL114
Ridge, The, Epsom 144 CQ118
Ridge, The, Lthd. 143 CD124
Ridge, The, Orp. 123 ER103
Ridge, The, Pur. 133 DJ110
Ridge, The, Surb. 116 CN99
Ridge, The, Twick. 101 CD87
Ridge Ave. N21 50 DQ45
Ridge Ave., Dart. 111 FF86
Ridge Clo. NW4 47 CX54
Ridge Clo. NW9 60 CR56
Ridge Crest, Enf. 35 DM39
Ridge Hill NW11 61 CY60
Ridge La., Wat. 29 BS38
Ridge Langley, S.Croy. 134 DU109
Ridge Pk., Pur. 133 DK110
Ridge Rd. N8 63 DM58
Ridge Rd. N21 50 DQ46
Ridge Rd. NW2 61 CZ62
Ridge Rd., Mitch. 105 DH94
Ridge Rd., Sutt. 117 CY102
Ridge St., Wat. 29 BV38
Ridge Way SE19 106 DS93
Central Hill
Ridge Way, Dart. 111 FF86
Ridge Way, Felt. 100 BY90
Ridge Way, Rick. 42 BH45
Ridge Way, The, S.Croy. 134 DS109
Ridgebrook Rd. SE3 94 EJ83
Ridgecroft Clo., Bex. 111 FC88
Ridgefield, Wat. 29 BS37
Ridgehurst Ave., Wat. 15 BT34
Ridgelands, Lthd. 143 CD124
Ridgemont Gdns., Edg. 46 CQ49
Ridgemount, Wey. 113 BS103
Ridgemount Ave., Couls. 147 DH117
Ridgemount Ave., Croy. 121 DX103
Ridgemount Clo. SE20 106 DV94
Anerley Pk.
Ridgemount Gdns., Enf. 35 DP41
Ridgeview, St.Alb. 18 CM28
Ridgeview Clo., Barn. 33 CX44
Ridgeview Rd. N20 48 DB48
Ridgeway, Brom. 122 EG103
Ridgeway, Epsom 130 CQ112
Ridgeway, Wdf.Grn. 52 EJ49
Ridgeway, The E4 51 EB47
Ridgeway, The N3 48 DB52
Ridgeway, The N11 48 DF49
Ridgeway, The N14 49 DL47
Ridgeway, The NW7 47 CU48
Ridgeway, The NW9 60 CS56
Ridgeway, The NW11 61 CZ60
Ridgeway, The W3 88 CN76
Ridgeway, The, Croy. 119 DM104
Ridgeway, The, Enf. 35 DN39
Ridgeway, The, Har. 58 BZ57
Ridgeway, The (Kenton), Har. 59 CJ58
Ridgeway, The, Lthd. 128 CC114
Ridgeway, The (Oxshott), Lthd. 143 CD123
Ridgeway, The, Pot.B. 20 DD34
Ridgeway, The (Cuffley), Pot.B. 20 DE28
Ridgeway, The, Rad. 31 CF37
Ridgeway, The (Gidea Pk.), Rom. 69 FG56
Ridgeway, The, Ruis. 57 BU59
Ridgeway, The, Stan. 45 CJ51
Ridgeway, The, Sutt. 132 DD107
Ridgeway, The, Wat. 29 BS37
Ridgeway Ave., Barn. 34 DF44
Ridgeway Clo., Lthd. 128 CC114
Ridgeway Cres., Orp. 123 ES104
Ridgeway Cres. Gdns., Orp. 123 ES103
Ridgeway Dr., Brom. 108 EH92
Ridgeway E., Sid. 109 ET85
Ridgeway Gdns. N6 63 DJ59
Ridgeway Gdns., Ilf. 66 EL57
Ridgeway Rd. SW9 91 DP83
Ridgeway Rd., Islw. 87 CE80
Ridgeway Rd. N., Islw. 87 CE79
Ridgeway Wk., Nthlt. 72 BY65
Fortunes Mead
Ridgeway W., Sid. 109 ES85
Ridgewell Clo. N1 78 DQ67
Basire St.
Ridgewell Clo. SE26 107 DZ91
Ridgewell Clo., Dag. 83 FB67
Ridgmount Gdns. WC1 5 M6
Ridgmount Pl. WC1 5 M6
Ridgmount Rd. SW18 104 DB85
Ridgmount St. WC1 5 M6
Ridgway SW19 103 CW94
Ridgway, Wok. 140 BG115
Ridgway Gdns. SW19 103 CX94
Ridgway Pl. SW19 103 CY93
Ridgwell Rd. E16 80 EJ71
Riding, The NW11 61 CZ59
Golders Grn. Rd.
Riding Hill, S.Croy. 134 DU113
Riding Ho. St. W1 5 J7
Riding Ho. St. W1 77 DJ71
Ridings, The W5 74 CM70
Ridings, The, Ash. 143 CK117

This index reads in the sequence: Street Name / Postal District or Post Town / Map Page Number / Grid Reference **Rod–Ros**

Rodney Ct. W9 76 DC70
Maida Vale
Rodney Gdns., Pnr. 57 BV57
Rodney Gdns., W.Wick. 136 EG105
Rodney Grn., Walt. 114 BW103
Rodney Pl. E17 51 DY54
Rodney Pl. SE17 11 J8
Rodney Pl. SE17 92 DQ77
Rodney Pl. SW19 118 DC95
Rodney Rd. E11 66 EH56
Rodney Rd. SE17 11 J8
Rodney Rd. SE17 92 DQ77
Rodney Rd., Mitch. 118 DE96
Rodney Rd., N.Mal. 116 CS99
Rodney Rd., Twick. 100 CA87
Rodney Rd., Walt. 114 BW103
Rodney St. N1 77 DM68
Rodney Way, Rom. 54 FA53
Rodona Rd., Wey. 127 BR111
Rodway Rd. SW15 103 CU87
Rodway Rd., Brom. 122 EH95
Rodwell Clo., Ruis. 58 BW60
Rodwell Ct., Add. 126 BJ105
Garfield Rd.
Rodwell Pl., Edg. 46 CN51
Whitchurch La.
Rodwell Rd. SE22 106 DT86
Roe End NW9 60 CQ56
Roe Grn. NW9 60 CQ57
Roe La. NW9 60 CP56
Roe Way, Wall. 133 DL108
Roebourne Way E16 95 EN75
Roebuck Clo., Ash. 144 CL120
Roebuck Clo., Felt. 99 BV91
Roebuck La. N17 50 DT51
High Rd.
Roebuck La., Buck.H. 52 EJ45
Roebuck Rd., Chess. 130 CN106
Roebuck Rd., Ilf. 54 EV50
Roedean Ave., Enf. 36 DW39
Roedean Clo., Enf. 36 DW39
Roedean Clo., Orp. 138 EV105
Roedean Cres. SW15 102 CS86
Roehampton Clo. SW15 89 CU84
Roehampton Dr., Chis. 109 EQ93
Roehampton Gate SW15 102 CS86
Roehampton High St. SW15 103 CU87
Roehampton La. SW15 89 CU84
Roehampton Vale SW15 103 CT90
Rofant Rd., Nthwd. 43 BS51
Roffes La., Cat. 148 DR124
Roffey Clo., Pur. 147 DP116
Roffey St. E14 93 EC75
Rogate Ho. E5 64 DU62
Muir Rd.
Roger St. WC1 6 C5
Roger St. WC1 77 DM70
Rogers Clo., Cat. 148 DV122
Tillingdown Hill
Rogers Clo., Couls. 147 DP118
Rogers Ct., Swan. 125 FG98
Rogers Gdns., Dag. 68 FA64
Rogers La., Warl. 149 DZ118
Rogers Rd. E16 80 EF72
Rogers Rd. SW17 104 DD91
Rogers Rd., Dag. 68 FA64
Rogers Ruff, Nthwd. 43 BQ53
Rogers Wk. N12 48 DB48
Brook Meadow
Rojack Rd. SE23 107 DX88
Roke Clo., Ken. 134 DQ114
Roke Lo. Rd., Ken. 133 DP113
Roke Rd., Ken. 148 DQ115
Rokeby Gdns., Wdf.Grn. 52 EG53
Rokeby Pl. SW20 103 CV94
Rokeby Rd. SE4 93 DZ82
Rokeby St. E15 79 ED67
Roker Pk. Ave., Uxb. 56 BL63
Rokesby Clo., Well. 95 ER82
Rokesby Pl., Wem. 59 CK64
Rokesly Ave. N8 63 DL57
Roland Gdns. SW7 90 DC78
Roland Gdns., Felt. 100 BZ90
Roland Ms. E1 79 DX71
Stepney Grn.
Roland Rd. E17 65 ED56
Roland Way SE17 92 DR78
Roland Way SW7 90 DC78
Roland Gdns.
Roland Way, Wor.Pk. 117 CT103
Roles Gro., Rom. 68 EX56
Rolfe Clo., Barn. 34 DE42
Rolinsden Way, Kes. 136 EK105
Roll Gdns., Ilf. 67 EN57
Rollesby Rd., Chess. 130 CN107
Rollesby Way SE28 82 EW73
Rolleston Ave., Orp. 123 EP100
Rolleston Clo., Orp. 123 EP101
Rolleston Rd., S.Croy. 134 DR108
Rollins St. SE15 92 DW79
Rollit Cres., Houns. 100 CA85
Rollit St. N7 63 DM64
Hornsey Rd.
Rollo Rd., Swan. 111 FF94
Rolls Bldgs. EC4 6 D8
Rolls Pk. Ave. E4 51 EA51
Rolls Pk. Rd. E4 51 EB50
Rolls Pas. EC4 6 D8
Rolls Rd. SE1 92 DT78
Rollscourt Ave. SE24 106 DQ85
Rolt St. SE8 93 DY79
Rolvenden Gdns., Brom. 108 EK94
Rolvenden Pl. N17 50 DU53
Manor Rd.
Rom Cres., Rom. 69 FF59
Rom Valley Way, Rom. 69 FE58
Roma Read Clo. SW15 103 CV87
Bessborough Rd.
Roma Rd. E17 65 DY55
Roman Clo. W3 88 CP75
Avenue Gdns.
Roman Clo., Felt. 100 BW85
Roman Clo., Rain. 83 FD68
Roman Clo., Uxb. 42 BG53
Roman Gdns., Kings L. 15 BP30
Roman Ri. SE19 106 DR93
Roman Rd. E2 78 DW69
Roman Rd. E3 79 DY68
Roman Rd. E6 80 EK70
Roman Rd. N10 49 DH52
Roman Rd. NW2 61 CW62
Roman Rd. SW2 105 DM87
Upper Tulse Hill
Roman Rd. W4 89 CT77
Roman Rd., Ilf. 81 EP65
Roman Sq. SE28 82 EU74
Roman Way N7 77 DM65
Roman Way SE15 92 DW80
Clifton Way
Roman Way, Croy. 119 DP103
Roman Way, Dart. 111 FE85
Roman Way, Enf. 36 DT43
Roman Way Ind. Est. N1 77 DM66
Offord St.
Romanhurst Ave., Brom. 122 EE98
Romanhurst Gdns., Brom. 122 EE98
Romans Way, Wok. 140 BG115
Romany Gdns. E17 51 DY53
McEntee Ave.
Romany Gdns., Sutt. 118 DA101
Romany Ri., Orp. 123 EQ102
Romberg Rd. SW17 104 DG90
Romborough Gdns. SE13 107 EC85
Romborough Way SE13 107 EC85
Romeland, Borwd. 31 CK44
Romeland, Wal.Abb. 23 EC33
Romero Clo. SW9 91 DM83
Stockwell Rd.
Romero Sq. SE3 94 EJ84
Romeyn Rd. SW16 105 DM90
Romford Rd. E7 66 EH64
Romford Rd. E12 66 EL63
Romford Rd. E15 80 EE65
Romford Rd., Chig. 54 EU48
Romford Rd., Rom. 54 EY52
Romford St. E1 78 DU71
Romilly Dr., Wat. 44 BY49
Romilly Rd. N4 63 DP61
Romilly St. W1 5 M10
Romilly St. W1 77 DK73
Rommany Rd. SE27 106 DR91
Romney Clo. N17 50 DV53
Romney Clo. NW11 62 DC60
Romney Clo. SE14 92 DW80
Kender St.
Romney Clo., Ashf. 99 BQ92
Romney Clo., Chess. 130 CL105
Romney Clo., Har. 58 CA59
Romney Dr., Brom. 108 EK94
Romney Dr., Har. 58 CA59
Romney Gdns., Bexh. 96 EZ81
Romney Ms. W1 4 F6
Romney Par., Hayes 71 BR68
Romney Rd.
Romney Rd. SE10 93 EC79
Romney Rd., Hayes 71 BR68
Romney Rd., N.Mal. 116 CR100
Romney Row NW2 61 CX61
Brent Ter.
Romney St. SW1 9 P7
Romney St. SW1 91 DL76
Romola Rd. SE24 105 DP88
Romsey Clo., Orp. 137 EP105
Romsey Gdns., Dag. 82 EX67
Romsey Rd. W13 73 CG73
Romsey Rd., Dag. 82 EX67
Ron Leighton Way E6 80 EL67
Rona Rd. NW3 62 DG63
Rona Wk. N1 78 DR65
Clephane Rd.
Ronald Ave. E15 80 EE69
Ronald Clo., Beck. 121 DZ98
Ronald St. E1 78 DW72
Devonport St.
Ronalds Rd. N5 63 DN64
Ronalds Rd., Brom. 122 EG95
Ronaldstone Rd., Sid. 109 ES86
Ronart St., Har. 59 CF55
Stuart Rd.
Rondu Rd. NW2 61 CY64
Ronelean Rd., Surb. 116 CM104
Roneo Cor., Horn. 69 FF60
Hornchurch Rd.
Roneo Link, Horn. 69 FF60
Ronfearn Ave., Orp. 124 EX99
Ronneby Clo., Wey. 113 BS104
Ronson Way, Lthd. 143 CG121
Randalls Rd.
Ronver Rd. SE12 108 EG88
Baring Rd.
Rood La. EC3 7 M10
Rood La. EC3 78 DS73
Rook Clo., Horn. 83 FG66
Rook La., Cat. 147 DM124
Rook Wk. E6 80 EL72
Allhallows Rd.
Rookdean, Sev. 154 FC122
Rooke Way SE10 94 EF78
Rookeries Clo., Felt. 99 BV90
Rookery Clo. NW9 61 CT57
Rookery Clo., Lthd. 143 CE124
Rookery Cres., Dag. 83 FB66
Rookery Dr., Chis. 123 EN95
Rookery Gdns., Orp. 124 EW99
Rookery Hill, Ash. 144 CN118
Rookery La., Brom. 122 EK100
Rookery Rd. SW4 91 DJ84
Rookery Rd., Orp. 137 EM110
Rookery Rd., Stai. 98 BH92
Rookery Way NW9 61 CT57
Rookesley Rd., Orp. 124 EX101
Rookfield Ave. N10 63 DJ56
Rookfield Clo. N10 63 DJ56
Cranmore Way
Rookley Clo., Sutt. 132 DB110
Rooks Hill, Rick. 28 BK42
Rooksmead Rd., Sun. 113 BT96
Rookstone Rd. SW17 104 DF92
Rookwood Ave., Loug. 39 EQ41
Rookwood Ave., N.Mal. 117 CU98
Rookwood Ave., Wall. 133 DK105
Rookwood Gdns. E4 52 EF46
Whitehall Rd.
Rookwood Gdns., Loug. 39 EQ41
Rookwood Ho., Bark. 81 ER68
St. Marys
Rookwood Rd. N16 64 DT59
Roosevelt Way, Dag. 83 FD65
Rootes Dr. W10 75 CX70
Rope St. SE16 93 DY76
Rope Wk., Sun. 114 BW97
Rope Wk. Gdns. E1 78 DU72
Commercial Rd.
Rope Yd. Rails SE18 95 EP76
Ropemaker Rd. SE16 93 DY75
Ropemaker St. EC2 7 K6
Ropemaker St. EC2 78 DR71
Ropemakers Flds. E14 79 DZ73
Narrow St.
Roper La. SE1 11 N5
Roper St. SE9 109 EM86
Roper Way, Mitch. 118 DG96
Ropers Ave. E4 51 EB50
Ropers Wk. SW2 105 DN87
Brockwell Pk. Gdns.
Ropery St. E3 79 DZ70
Ropley St. E2 78 DU68
Rosa Alba Ms. N5 64 DQ63
Kelross Rd.
Rosa Ave., Ashf. 98 BN91
Rosaline Rd. SW6 89 CY80
Rosamond St. SE26 106 DV90
Rosamund Clo., S.Croy. 134 DR105
Rosary Clo., Houns. 86 BY82
Rosary Ct., Pot.B. 20 DB30
Rosary Gdns. SW7 90 DC77
Rosary Gdns., Ashf. 99 BP91
Rosaville Rd. SW6 89 CZ80
Roscoe St. EC1 7 J5
Roscoff Clo., Edg. 46 CQ53
Rose All. SE1 11 J2
Rose All. SE1 78 DQ74
Rose & Crown Ct. EC2 7 H8
Rose & Crown Yd. SW1 9 L2
Rose Ave. E18 52 EH54
Rose Ave., Mitch. 118 DF95
Rose Ave., Mord. 118 DC99
Rose Bates Dr. NW9 60 CN56
Rose Bushes, Epsom 145 CV116
Rose Ct. E1 78 DS71
Sandy's Row
Rose Ct. SE26 106 DV89
Rose Ct., Pnr. 58 BW55
Nursery Rd.
Rose Ct., Wal.Cr. 22 DU27
Rose Dale, Orp. 123 EP103
Rose End, Wor.Pk. 117 CX102
Rose Gdn. Clo., Edg. 46 CL51
Rose Gdns. W5 87 CK76
Rose Gdns., Felt. 99 BU89
Rose Gdns., Sthl. 72 CA70
Rose Gdns., Stai. 98 BK87
Diamedes Ave.
Rose Gdns., Wat. 29 BU43
Rose Glen NW9 60 CR56
Rose Glen, Rom. 69 FE60
Rose Hill, Sutt. 118 DB104
Rose La., Rom. 68 EX55
Rose La., Wok. 140 BJ121
Rose Lawn (Bushey), Wat. 44 CC46
Rose St. WC2 5 P10
Rose Wk., Pur. 133 DK111
Rose Wk., Surb. 116 CP99
Rose Wk., W.Wick. 121 EC103
Rose Wk., The, Rad. 31 CH37
Rose Way SE12 108 EG85
Roseacre Clo. W13 73 CH71
Middlefielde
Roseacre Clo., Shep. 112 BN99
Roseacre Rd., Well. 96 EV83
Roseary Clo., West Dr. 84 BK77
Rosebank SE20 106 DV94
Rosebank, Epsom 130 CQ114
Rosebank, Wal.Abb. 24 EE33
Rosebank Ave., Wem. 59 CF63
Rosebank Clo. N12 48 DE50
Rosebank Clo., Tedd. 101 CG93
Rosebank Gdns. E3 79 DZ68
Rosebank Gro. E17 65 DZ55
Rosebank Rd. E17 65 EB58
Rosebank Rd. W7 87 CE75
Rosebank Vill. E17 65 EA56
Rosebank Wk. NW1 77 DK66
Maiden La.
Rosebank Wk. SE18 94 EL77
Woodhill
Rosebank Way W3 74 CR72
Roseberry Ct., Wat. 29 BU39
Grandfield Ave.
Roseberry Gdns. N4 63 DP58
Roseberry Gdns., Orp. 123 ES104
Roseberry Pl. E8 78 DT65
Roseberry St. SE16 92 DV77
Rosebery Ave. E12 80 EL65
Rosebery Ave. EC1 6 D4
Rosebery Ave. EC1 77 DN70
Rosebery Ave. N17 50 DU54
Rosebery Ave., Epsom 130 CS114
Rosebery Ave., Har. 58 BY63
Rosebery Ave., N.Mal. 117 CT96
Rosebery Ave., Sid. 109 ES87
Rosebery Ave., Th.Hth. 120 DQ96
Rosebery Clo., Mord. 117 CX100
Rosebery Ct. EC1 77 DN70
Rosebery Ave.
Rosebery Gdns. N8 63 DL57
Rosebery Gdns. W13 73 CG72
Rosebery Gdns., Sutt. 132 DB105
Rosebery Ms. N10 49 DJ54
Rosebery Ms. SW2 105 DL86
Rosebery Rd.
Rosebery Rd. N9 50 DU48
Rosebery Rd. N10 49 DJ54
Rosebery Rd. SW2 105 DL86
Rosebery Rd., Epsom 144 CR119
Rosebery Rd., Houns. 100 CC85
Rosebery Rd., Kings.T. 116 CP96
Rosebery Rd., Sutt. 131 CZ107
Rosebery Rd. (Bushey), Wat. 44 CB45
Rosebery Sq. EC1 6 D5
Rosebery Sq., Kings.T. 116 CP96
Rosebine Ave., Twick. 101 CD87
Rosebriar Clo., Wok. 140 BG116
Rosebriar Wk., Wat. 29 BT36
Rosebriars, Cat. 148 DS120
Salmons La. W.
Rosebriars, Esher 128 CC106
Rosebury Rd. SW6 90 DB82
Rosebury Vale, Ruis. 57 BU61
Rosecourt Rd., Croy. 119 DM100
Rosecroft Ave. NW3 62 DA62
Rosecroft Clo., Orp. 124 EW100
Rosecroft Clo., West. 151 EM118
Lotus Rd.
Rosecroft Dr., Wat. 29 BS36
Rosecroft Gdns. NW2 61 CU62
Rosecroft Gdns., Twick. 101 CD88
Rosecroft Rd., Sthl. 72 CA70
Rosecroft Wk., Pnr. 58 BX57
Rosecroft Wk., Wem. 59 CK64
Rosedale, Ash. 143 CJ118
Rosedale, Cat. 148 DS123
Rosedale Ave., Hayes 71 BR71
Rosedale Ave. (Cheshunt), Wal.Cr. 22 DT29
Rosedale Clo. SE2 96 EV76
Finchale Rd.
Rosedale Clo. W7 87 CF75
Boston Rd.
Rosedale Clo., St.Alb. 16 BY30
Rosedale Clo., Stan. 45 CH51
Rosedale Ct. N5 63 DP63
Panmure Clo.
Rosedale Gdns., Dag. 82 EV66
Rosedale Rd. E7 66 EJ64
Rosedale Rd., Dag. 82 EV66
Rosedale Rd., Epsom 131 CU106
Rosedale Rd., Rich. 88 CL84
Rosedale Rd., Rom. 55 FC54
Rosedale Ter. W6 89 CV76
Dalling Rd.
Rosedale Way (Cheshunt), Wal.Cr. 22 DU27
Rosedene NW6 75 CX67
Rosedene Ave. SW16 105 DM90
Rosedene Ave., Croy. 119 DL101
Rosedene Ave., Grnf. 72 CA69
Rosedene Ave., Mord. 118 DA99
Rosedene Ct., Ruis. 57 BS60
Rosedene Gdns., Ilf. 67 EN56
Rosedene Ter. E10 65 EB61
Rosedew Rd. W6 89 CX79
Rosefield, Sev. 154 FG124
Rosefield Clo., Cars. 132 DE106
Alma Rd.
Rosefield Gdns. E14 79 EA73
Rosefield Rd., Stai. 98 BG91
Roseford Ct. W12 89 CX75
Shepherds Bush Grn.
Rosehart Ms. W11 76 DA72
Westbourne Gro.
Rosehatch Ave., Rom. 68 EX55
Roseheath Rd., Houns. 100 BZ85
Rosehill, Esher 129 CG107
Rosehill, Hmptn. 114 CA95
Rosehill Ave., Sutt. 118 DC102
Rosehill Fm. Meadow, Bans. 146 DB115
The Tracery
Rosehill Gdns., Abb.L. 15 BQ32
Rosehill Gdns., Grnf. 59 CF64
Rosehill Gdns., Sutt. 118 DB103
Rosehill Pk. W., Sutt. 118 DB102
Rosehill Rd. SW18 104 DC86
Rosehill Rd., West. 150 EJ117
Roseland Clo. N17 50 DR52
Cavell Rd.
Roseleigh Ave. N5 63 DP63
Roseleigh Clo., Twick. 101 CK86
Rosemary Ave. N3 48 DB54
Rosemary Ave. N9 50 DV46
Rosemary Ave., Enf. 36 DR39
Rosemary Ave., Houns. 86 BX82
Rosemary Ave., Rom. 69 FF55
Rosemary Ave., W.Mol. 114 CA97
Rosemary Clo., Croy. 119 DL101
Rosemary Clo., Uxb. 70 BN71
Rosemary Dr. E14 79 ED72
Rosemary Dr., Ilf. 66 EK57
Rosemary Gdns. SW14 88 CQ83
Rosemary La.
Rosemary Gdns., Chess. 130 CL105
Rosemary Gdns., Dag. 68 EZ60
Rosemary La. SW14 88 CQ83
Rosemary Pl. N1 78 DR67
Shepperton Rd.
Rosemary Rd. SE15 92 DT80
Rosemary Rd. SW17 104 DC90
Rosemary Rd., Well. 95 ET81
Rosemary St. N1 78 DR67
Shepperton Rd.
Rosemead NW9 61 CT59
Rosemead, Cher. 112 BH101
Rosemead, Pot.B. 20 DC30
Rosemead Ave., Felt. 99 BT89
Rosemead Ave., Mitch. 119 DJ96
Rosemead Ave., Wem. 60 CL64
Rosemont Ave. N12 48 DC51
Rosemont Rd. NW3 76 DC65
Rosemont Rd. W3 74 CP73
Rosemont Rd., Kings.T. 116 CQ97
Rosemont Rd., N.Mal. 116 CQ97
Rosemont Rd., Rich. 102 CL86
Rosemont Rd., Wem. 74 CL67
Rosemoor St. SW3 8 D9
Rosemoor St. SW3 90 DF77
Rosemount Ave., W.Byf. 126 BG113
Rosemount Clo., Wdf.Grn. 53 EM51
Chapelmount Rd.
Rosemount Dr., Brom. 123 EM98
Rosemount Rd. W13 73 CG72
Rosenau Cres. SW11 90 DE81
Rosenau Rd. SW11 90 DE81
Rosendale Rd. SE21 106 DQ87
Rosendale Rd. SE24 106 DQ87
Roseneath Ave. N21 49 DP46
Roseneath Clo., Orp. 138 EW108
Roseneath Rd. SW11 104 DG86
Roseneath Wk., Enf. 36 DR42
Rosens Wk., Edg. 46 CP48
Rosenthal Rd. SE6 107 EB86
Rosenthorpe Rd. SE15 107 DX85
Roserton St. E14 93 EC75
Rosery, The, Croy. 121 DX100
Roses, The, Wdf.Grn. 52 EF52
Rosethorn Clo. SW12 105 DK87
Rosetta Clo. SW8 91 DL80
Kenchester Clo.
Rosetti Ter., Dag. 68 EV63
Marlborough Rd.
Roseveare Rd. SE12 108 EJ91
Roseville Ave., Houns. 100 CA85
Roseville Rd., Hayes 85 BU78
Rosevine Rd. SW20 117 CW95
Roseway SE21 106 DR86
Rosewell Clo. SE20 106 DV94
Rosewood, Dart. 111 FF91
Rosewood, Esher 115 CG103
Rosewood, Sutt. 132 DC110
Rosewood Ave., Grnf. 59 CG64
Rosewood Ave., Horn. 69 FG64
Rosewood Clo., Sid. 110 EW90
Rosewood Ct., Brom. 122 EJ95
Rosewood Ct., Rom. 68 EW57
Tendring Way
Rosewood Dr., Enf. 35 DN35
Rosewood Dr., Shep. 112 BM99
Rosewood Gdns. SE13 93 EC82
Lewisham Rd.
Rosewood Gro., Sutt. 118 DC103
Rosewood Sq. W12 75 CU72
Primula St.
Rosewood Ter. SE20 106 DW94
Laurel Gro.
Rosher Clo. E15 79 ED66
Rosina St. E9 65 DX64
Roskell Rd. SW15 89 CX83
Roslin Rd. W3 88 CP76
Roslin Way, Brom. 108 EG92
Roslyn Clo., Mitch. 118 DD96
Roslyn Gdns., Rom. 55 FE54
Roslyn Rd. N15 64 DR57
Rosmead Rd. W11 75 CY73
Rosoman Pl. EC1 6 E4
Rosoman St. EC1 6 E3
Rosoman St. EC1 77 DN69
Ross Ave. NW7 47 CY50
Ross Ave., Dag. 68 EZ61
Ross Clo., Har. 44 CC52
Ross Clo., Hayes 85 BR76
Ross Ct. SW15 103 CX87
Ross Cres., Wat. 29 BU35
Ross Par., Wall. 133 DH107
Ross Rd. SE25 120 DR97
Ross Rd., Cob. 128 BW113
Ross Rd., Dart. 111 FG86
Ross Rd., Twick. 100 CB88
Ross Rd., Wall. 133 DJ106
Ross Way SE9 94 EL83
Ross Way, Nthwd. 43 BT49
Rossall Clo., Horn. 69 FG58
Rossall Cres. NW10 74 CM69
Rossdale, Sutt. 132 DE106
Rossdale Dr. N9 36 DW44
Rossdale Dr. NW9 60 CQ60
Rossdale Rd. SW15 89 CW84
Rosse Ms. SE3 94 EH81
Rossendale St. E5 64 DV61
Rossendale Way NW1 77 DJ67

Rossetti Gdns., Couls. 147 DM118
Rossetti Rd. SE16 92 DV78
Rossignol Gdns., Cars. 118 DG103
Rossindel Rd., Houns. 100 CA85
Rossington Ave., Borwd. 32 CL38
Rossington St. E5 64 DU61
Rossiter Flds., Barn. 33 CY44
Rossiter Rd. SW12 105 DH88
Rossland Clo., Bexh. 111 FB85
Rosslyn Ave. E4 52 EF47
Rosslyn Ave. SW13 88 CS83
Rosslyn Ave., Barn. 34 DE44
Rosslyn Ave., Dag. 68 EZ59
Rosslyn Ave., Felt. 99 BU86
Rosslyn Clo., Hayes 71 BR71
Morgans La.
Rosslyn Clo., Sun. 99 BS93
Cadbury Rd.
Rosslyn Clo., W.Wick. 122 EF104
Rosslyn Cres., Har. 59 CF56
Rosslyn Cres., Wem. 60 CL63
Rosslyn Hill NW3 62 DD63
Rosslyn Ms. NW3 62 DD63
Rosslyn Hill
Rosslyn Pk., Wey. 127 BR105
Rosslyn Pk. Ms. NW3 62 DD64
Lyndhurst Rd.
Rosslyn Rd. E17 65 EC56
Rosslyn Rd., Bark. 81 ER66
Rosslyn Rd., Twick. 101 CJ86
Rosslyn Rd., Wat. 29 BV41
Rossmore Rd. NW1 4 C5
Rossmore Rd. NW1 76 DE70
Rossway Dr. (Bushey), Wat. 30 CC43
Rosswood Gdns., Wall. 133 DH107
Rostella Rd. SW17 104 DD91
Rostrevor Ave. N15 64 DT58
Rostrevor Gdns., Hayes 71 BS74
Rostrevor Gdns., Sthl. 86 BY78
Rostrevor Ms. SW6 89 CZ81
Rostrevor Rd.
Rostrevor Rd. SW6 89 CZ81
Rostrevor Rd. SW19 104 DA92
Roswell Clo. (Cheshunt), Wal.Cr. 23 DY30
Rotary St. SE1 10 F6
Roth Wk. N7 63 DM62
Durham Rd.
Rothbury Ave., Rain. 83 FH71
Rothbury Gdns., Islw. 87 CG80
Rothbury Rd. E9 79 DZ66
Rothbury Wk. N17 50 DU52
Northumberland Gro.
Rother Clo., Wat. 16 BW34
Rotherfield Rd., Cars. 132 DG105
Rotherfield Rd., Enf. 37 DX37
Rotherfield St. N1 78 DQ66
Rotherham Wk. SE1 10 F3
Rotherhill Ave. SW16 105 DK93
Rotherhithe New Rd. SE16 92 DV78
Rotherhithe Old Rd. SE16 93 DX77
Rotherhithe St. SE16 92 DW75
Rotherhithe Tunnel E1 79 DX74
Rotherhithe Tunnel App. E14 79 DY73
Rotherhithe Tunnel App. SE16 92 DW75
Rothermere Rd., Croy. 133 DM106
Rotherwick Hill W5 74 CM70
Rotherwick Rd. NW11 62 DA59
Rotherwood Clo. SW20 117 CY95
Rotherwood Rd. SW15 89 CX83
Rothery St. N1 77 DP67
Gaskin St.
Rothery Ter. SW9 91 DP80
Foxley Rd.
Rothesay Ave. SW20 117 CY96
Rothesay Ave., Grnf. 73 CD65
Rothesay Ave., Rich. 88 CP84
Rothesay Rd. SE25 120 DR98
Rothsay Rd. E7 80 EJ66
Rothsay St. SE1 11 M6
Rothsay St. SE1 92 DS76
Rothsay Wk. E14 93 EA77
Charnwood Gdns.
Rothschild Rd. W4 88 CQ76
Rothschild St. SE27 105 DP91
Rothwell Gdns., Dag. 82 EW66
Rothwell Rd., Dag. 82 EW67
Rothwell St. NW1 76 DF67
Rotten Row SW1 8 C4
Rotten Row SW7 8 C4
Rotten Row SW7 90 DE75
Rotterdam Dr. E14 93 EC76
Rouel Rd. SE16 92 DU76
Rougemont Ave., Mord. 118 DA100
Roughs, The, Nthwd. 43 BS48
Roughtallys, Epp. 26 EZ27
Roughwood Clo., Wat. 29 BS38
Round Gro., Croy. 121 DX101
Round Hill SE26 106 DW90
Round Oak Rd., Wey. 126 BM105
Roundacre SW19 103 CX89
Inner Pk. Rd.
Roundaway Rd., Ilf. 53 EM53
Roundcroft (Cheshunt), Wal.Cr. 22 DT26
Roundel Clo. SE4 93 DZ84
Adelaide Ave.
Roundhay Clo. SE23 107 DX89
Roundhedge Way, Enf. 35 DM38
Roundhill Dr., Enf. 35 DM42
Roundhill Way, Cob. 128 CB112
Roundhills, Wal.Abb. 23 ED34
Roundmead Ave., Loug. 39 EN40
Roundmead Clo., Loug. 39 EN41
Roundmoor Dr. (Cheshunt), Wal.Cr. 23 DX29
Roundtable Rd., Brom. 108 EF90
Roundtree Rd., Wem. 59 CH64
Roundway, West. 150 EK116
Norheads La.
Roundway, The N17 50 DQ53
Roundway, The, Esher 129 CF107
Roundway, The, Wat. 29 BT44
Roundways, The, Ruis. 57 BT62
Roundwood, Chis. 123 EP96
Roundwood, Kings L. 14 BL27
Roundwood Ave., Uxb. 71 BQ74
Roundwood Clo., Ruis. 57 BR59
Roundwood Rd. NW10 75 CT65
Roundwood Vw., Bans. 145 CX115
Roundwood Way, Bans. 145 CX115
Rounton Rd. E3 79 EA70
Rounton Rd., Wal.Abb. 24 EE33
Roupell Rd. SW2 105 DM88
Roupell St. SE1 10 E3
Roupell St. SE1 77 DN74
Rous Rd., Buck.H. 52 EL46
Rousden St. NW1 77 DJ66
Rouse Gdns. SE21 106 DS91
Rousebarn La., Rick. 28 BM38
Routemaster Clo. E13 80 EH69
Routh Ct., Felt. 99 BS88
Loxwood Clo.
Routh Rd. SW18 104 DE87
Routh St. E6 81 EM71
Routledge Clo. N19 63 DK60
Rover Ave., Ilf. 53 ET51
Rowallan Rd. SW6 89 CY80
Rowan Ave. E4 51 DZ51
Rowan Clo. SW16 119 DJ95
Rowan Clo. W5 88 CL75
Rowan Clo., N.Mal. 116 CS96
Rowan Clo. (Bricket Wd.), St.Alb. 16 CA31
Rowan Clo., Stan. 45 CF51
Woodlands Dr.
Rowan Clo., Wem. 59 CG62
Rowan Ct., Borwd. 32 CL39
Theobald St.
Rowan Cres. SW16 119 DJ95
Rowan Dr. NW9 61 CU55
Rowan Gdns., Croy. 120 DT104
Radcliffe Rd.
Rowan Grn., Couls. 147 DH121
Rowan Grn., Wey. 127 BR105
Rowan Gro., Couls. 147 DH121
Rowan Ind. Est., Croy. 120 DS101
Rowan Pl., Hayes 71 BT73
West Ave.
Rowan Rd. SW16 119 DJ96
Rowan Rd. W6 89 CX77
Rowan Rd., Bexh. 96 EY83
Rowan Rd., Brent. 87 CH80
Rowan Rd., Swan. 125 FD97
Rowan Rd., West Dr. 84 BK77
Rowan Ter. W6 89 CX77
Bute Gdns.
Rowan Wk. N2 62 DC57
Rowan Wk. N19 63 DJ61
Bredgar Rd.
Rowan Wk. W10 75 CY70
Droop St.
Rowan Wk., Brom. 123 EM104
Rowan Way, Rom. 68 EW55
Rowans, The N13 49 DP48
Rowans, The, Sun. 99 BT92
Rowans Way, Loug. 39 EM42
Rowantree Clo. N21 50 DR46
Rowantree Rd. N21 50 DR46
Rowantree Rd., Enf. 35 DP40
Rowanwood Ave., Sid. 110 EU88
Rowben Clo. N20 48 DB46
Rowberry Clo. SW6 89 CW80
Rowcross St. SE1 92 DT78
Rowdell Rd., Nthlt. 72 CA67
Rowden Pk. Gdns. E4 51 EA51
Rowden Rd.
Rowden Rd. E4 51 EA51
Rowden Rd., Beck. 121 DY95
Rowden Rd., Epsom 130 CP105
Rowditch La. SW11 90 DG82
Rowdon Ave. NW10 75 CV66
Rowdown Cres., Croy. 135 ED109
Rowdowns Rd., Dag. 82 EZ67
Rowe Gdns., Bark. 81 ET68
Rowe La. E9 64 DW64
Rowe Wk., Har. 58 CA62
Rowena Cres. SW11 90 DE82
Rowfant Rd. SW17 104 DG88
Rowhill Rd. E5 64 DV63
Rowhill Rd., Dart. 111 FF93
Rowhill Rd., Swan. 111 FF93
Rowhurst Ave., Add. 126 BH107
Rowhurst Ave., Lthd. 143 CF117
Rowington Clo. W2 76 DB71
Rowland Ave., Har. 59 CJ55
Rowland Ct. E16 80 EF70
Rowland Cres., Chig. 53 ES49
Rowland Gro. SE26 106 DV90
Dallas Rd.
Rowland Hill Ave. N17 50 DQ52
Rowland Hill St. NW3 62 DE64
Rowland Wk., Rom. (Havering-atte-Bower) 55 FE48
Rowland Way SW19 118 DB95
Hayward Clo.
Rowland Way, Ashf. 99 BQ94
Rowlands Ave., Pnr. 44 CA50
Rowlands Clo. N6 62 DG58
North Hill
Rowlands Clo. NW7 47 CU52
Rowlands Clo. (Cheshunt), Wal.Cr. 23 DX30
Rowlands Flds. (Cheshunt), Wal.Cr. 23 DX29
Rowlands Rd., Dag. 68 EZ61
Rowley Ave., Sid. 110 EV87
Rowley Clo., Wat. 30 BY44
Lower Paddock Rd.
Rowley Clo., Wem. 74 CM66
Rowley Clo., Wok. 140 BG116
Rowley Ct., Cat. 148 DR122
Fairbourne La.
Rowley Gdns. N4 64 DQ59
Rowley Gdns. (Cheshunt), Wal.Cr. 23 DX28
Warwick Dr.
Rowley Grn. Rd., Barn. 33 CT43
Rowley Ind. Est. W3 88 CP76
Rowley La., Barn. 32 CS42
Rowley La., Borwd. 32 CR39
Rowley Mead, Epp. 26 EW25
Rowley Rd. N15 64 DQ57
Rowley Way NW8 76 DB67
Rowlheys Pl., West Dr. 84 BL76
Rowlls Rd., Kings.T. 116 CM97
Rowney Gdns., Dag. 82 EW65
Rowney Rd., Dag. 82 EV65
Rowntree Clifford Clo. E13 80 EH69
Liddon Rd.
Rowntree Path SE28 82 EV73
Booth Clo.
Rowntree Rd., Twick. 101 CE88
Rowse Clo. E15 79 EC67
Rowsley Ave. NW4 61 CW55
Rowstock Gdns. N7 63 DK64
Rowton Rd. SE18 95 EQ80
Rowzill Rd., Swan. 111 FF93
Roxborough Ave., Har. 59 CE59
Roxborough Ave., Islw. 87 CF80
Roxborough Pk., Har. 59 CE59
Roxborough Rd., Har. 59 CD57
Roxbourne Clo., Nthlt. 72 BX65
Roxburgh Rd. SE27 105 DP92
Roxburn Way, Ruis. 57 BT62
Roxby Pl. SW6 90 DA79
Roxeth Ct., Ashf. 98 BN92
Roxeth Grn. Ave., Har. 58 CB62
Roxeth Gro., Har. 58 CB63
Roxeth Hill, Har. 59 CD61
Roxford Clo., Shep. 113 BS99
Roxley Rd. SE13 107 EB86
Roxton Gdns., Croy. 135 EA106
Roxwell Rd. W12 89 CU75
Roxwell Rd., Bark. 82 EU68
Roxwell Trd. Pk. E10 65 DY59
Roxwell Way, Wdf.Grn. 52 EJ52
Roxy Ave., Rom. 68 EW59
Roy Gdns., Ilf. 67 ES56
Roy Gro., Hmptn. 100 CB93
Roy Rd., Nthwd. 43 BT52
Roy Sq. E14 79 DY73
Narrow St.
Royal Albert Dock E16 80 EL73
Royal Albert Roundabout E16 94 EK75
Royal Albert Way
Royal Albert Way E16 80 EJ73
Royal Arc. W1 9 K1
Royal Ave. SW3 8 D10
Royal Ave. SW3 90 DF78
Royal Ave., Wal.Cr. 23 DY33
Royal Ave., Wor.Pk. 116 CS103
Royal Circ. SE27 105 DN90
Royal Clo. N16 64 DS60
Manor Rd.
Royal Clo., Ilf. 68 EU59
Royal Clo., Uxb. 70 BM72
Royal Clo., Wor.Pk. 116 CS103
Royal College St. NW1 77 DJ66
Royal Ct. EC3 78 DR72
Cornhill
Royal Ct. SE16 93 DZ76
Finland St.
Royal Cres. W11 75 CX74
Royal Cres., Ruis. 58 BY63
Royal Cres. Ms. W11 75 CX74
Queensdale Rd.
Royal Docks Rd. E6 81 EP72
Royal Docks Rd., Bark. 81 EP72
Royal Dr., Epsom 145 CV118
Royal Ex. EC3 7 L9
Royal Ex. EC3 78 DR72
Royal Ex. Ave. EC3 7 L9
Royal Ex. Bldgs. EC3 7 L9
Royal Ex. Steps EC3 78 DR72
Cornhill
Royal Hill SE10 93 EC80
Royal Hospital Rd. SW3 90 DF79
Royal La., Uxb. 70 BM71
Royal La., West Dr. 70 BM72
Royal London Est., The N17 50 DU51
Royal London Ind. Est. NW10 74 CR68
North Acton Rd.
Royal Mint Ct. EC3 78 DT73
Royal Mint Pl. E1 78 DT73
Blue Anchor Yd.
Royal Mint St. E1 78 DT73
Royal Mt. Ct., Twick. 101 CE90
Royal Naval Pl. SE14 93 DZ80
Royal Oak Ct. N1 78 DS69
Pitfield St.
Royal Oak Pl. SE22 106 DV86
Royal Oak Rd. E8 78 DV65
Royal Oak Rd., Bexh. 110 EZ85
Royal Opera Arc. SW1 9 M2
Royal Orchard Clo. SW18 103 CY87
Royal Par. SE3 94 EF82
Royal Par. SW6 89 CY80
Dawes Rd.
Royal Par. W5 74 CL69
Western Ave.
Royal Par., Chis. 109 EQ94
Royal Par. Ms. SE3 94 EF82
Royal Par.
Royal Par. Ms., Chis. 109 EQ94
Royal Pl. SE10 93 EC80
Royal Rd. E16 80 EJ72
Royal Rd. SE17 91 DP79
Royal Rd., Sid. 110 EX90
Royal Rd., Tedd. 101 CD92
Royal Route, Wem. 60 CN63
Royal St. SE1 10 C6
Royal St. SE1 91 DM76
Royal Victor Pl. E3 79 DX68
Royal Victoria Dock E16 80 EG73
Royal Wk., Wall. 119 DH104
Prince Charles Way
Royal Windsor Ct., Surb. 116 CN102
Royalty Ms. W1 5 M9
Roycraft Ave., Bark. 81 ET68
Roycraft Clo., Bark. 81 ET68
Roycroft Clo. E18 52 EH53
Roycroft Clo. SW2 105 DN88
Roydene Rd. SE18 95 ES79
Roydon Clo. SW11 91 DH81
Reform St.
Roydon Clo., Loug. 52 EL45
Roydon Ct., Walt. 127 BU105
Roydon St. SW11 91 DH81
Southolm St.
Royle Clo., Rom. 69 FH57
Royle Cres. W13 73 CG70
Royston Ave. E4 51 EA50
Royston Ave., Sutt. 118 DD104
Royston Ave., Wall. 133 DK105
Royston Ave., W.Byf. 126 BL112
Royston Clo., Houns. 85 BV81
Royston Clo., Walt. 113 BU102
Royston Ct. SE24 106 DQ86
Burbage Rd.
Royston Ct., Rich. 88 CM81
Lichfield Rd.
Royston Ct., Surb. 116 CN104
Hook Ri. N.
Royston Gdns., Ilf. 66 EK58
Royston Gro., Pnr. 44 CA51
Royston Par., Ilf. 66 EK58
Royston Pk. Rd., Pnr. 44 BZ51
Royston Rd. SE20 121 DX95
Royston Rd., Dart. 111 FF86
Royston Rd., Rich. 102 CL85
Royston Rd., W.Byf. 126 BL112
Royston St. E2 78 DW68
Roystons, The, Surb. 116 CP99
Rozel Ct. N1 78 DS67
Rozel Rd. SW4 91 DJ83
Rubastic Rd., Sthl. 86 BW76
Rubens Rd., Nthlt. 72 BW68
Rubens St. SE6 107 DZ89
Ruberoid Rd., Enf. 37 DZ41
Ruby Ms. E17 65 EA55
Ruby Rd.
Ruby Rd. E17 65 EA55
Ruby St. SE15 92 DV79
Ruby Triangle SE15 92 DV79
Sandgate St.
Ruckholt Clo. E10 65 EB62
Ruckholt Rd. E10 65 EB63
Rucklers La., Kings L. 14 BG28
Rucklidge Ave. NW10 75 CT68
Rudall Cres. NW3 62 DD63
Willoughby Rd.
Ruddington Clo. E5 65 DY63
Ruddstreet Clo. SE18 95 EP77
Ruddy Way NW7 47 CU51
Flower La.
Ruden Way, Epsom 145 CV116
Rudland Rd., Bexh. 97 FB83
Rudloe Rd. SW12 105 DJ87
Rudolf Pl. SW8 91 DL79
Miles St.
Rudolph Ct. SE22 106 DU87
Rudolph Rd. E13 80 EF68
Rudolph Rd. NW6 76 DA68
Rudolph Rd. (Bushey), Wat. 30 CA44
Rudyard Gro. NW7 46 CQ51
Rue de St. Lawrence, Wal.Abb. 23 EC34
Quaker La.
Ruffetts, The, S.Croy. 134 DV108
Ruffetts Clo., S.Croy. 134 DV108
Ruffetts Way, Tad. 145 CY118
Rufford Clo., Har. 59 CG58
Rufford St. N1 77 DL67
Rufford Twr. W3 74 CP74
Rufus Clo., Ruis. 58 BY62
Rufus St. N1 7 M3
Rugby Ave. N9 50 DT46
Rugby Ave., Grnf. 73 CD65
Rugby Ave., Wem. 59 CH64
Rugby Clo., Har. 59 CE56
Rugby Gdns., Dag. 82 EW65
Rugby La., Sutt. 131 CX109
Nonsuch Wk.
Rugby Rd. NW9 60 CN56
Rugby Rd. W4 88 CS75
Rugby Rd., Dag. 82 EV65
Rugby Rd., Islw. 101 CE85
Rugby Rd., Twick. 101 CE85
Rugby St. WC1 6 B5
Rugby St. WC1 77 DM70
Rugby Wk., Sutt. 131 CX109
Nonsuch Wk.
Rugby Way, Rick. 29 BP43
Rugg St. E14 79 EA73
Rugged La., Wal.Abb. 24 EK33
Ruggles-Brise Rd., Ashf. 98 BK92
Ruislip Clo., Grnf. 72 CB70
Ruislip Rd., Grnf. 72 CA69
Ruislip Rd., Nthlt. 72 BX69
Ruislip Rd., Sthl. 72 CA69
Ruislip Rd. E. W7 73 CD70
Ruislip Rd. E. W13 73 CF70
Ruislip Rd. E., Grnf. 73 CD70
Ruislip St. SW17 104 DF91
Rum Clo. E1 78 DW73
Rumbold Rd. SW6 90 DB80
Rumsey Clo., Hmptn. 100 BZ93
Rumsey Ms. N4 63 DP62
Monsell Rd.
Rumsey Rd. SW9 91 DM83
Rumsley, Wal.Cr. 22 DU27
Runbury Circle NW9 60 CR61
Runciman Clo., Orp. 138 EW110
Runcorn Clo. N17 64 DV56
Runcorn Pl. W11 75 CY73
Rundell Cres. NW4 61 CV57
Runes Clo., Mitch. 118 DD98
Runnel Fld., Har. 59 CE62
Running Horse Yd., Brent. 88 CL79
Pottery Rd.
Runnymede SW19 118 DC95
Runnymede Clo., Twick. 100 CB87
Runnymede Ct., Croy. 120 DT103
Runnymede Cres. SW16 119 DK95
Runnymede Gdns., Grnf. 73 CD68
Runnymede Gdns., Twick. 100 CB87
Runnymede Rd., Twick. 100 CB86
Runway, The, Ruis. 57 BV64
Rupack St. SE16 92 DW75
St. Marychurch St.
Rupert Ave., Wem. 60 CL64
Rupert Ct. W1 5 M10
Rupert Gdns. SW9 91 DP82
Rupert Rd. N19 63 DK62
Holloway Rd.
Rupert Rd. NW6 75 CZ68
Rupert Rd. W4 88 CS76
Rupert St. W1 5 M10
Rupert St. W1 77 DK73
Rural Clo., Horn. 69 FH60
Rural Way SW16 105 DH94
Ruscoe Rd. E16 80 EF72
Ruscombe Dr., St.Alb. 16 CB26
Ruscombe Way, Felt. 99 BT87
Rush, The SW19 117 CZ95
Kingston Rd.
Rush Grn. Gdns., Rom. 69 FC60
Rush Grn. Rd., Rom. 69 FC60
Rush Gro. St. SE18 95 EM77
Rush Hill Ms. SW11 90 DG83
Rush Hill Rd.
Rush Hill Rd. SW11 90 DG83
Rusham Rd. SW12 104 DF86
Rushbrook Cres. E17 51 DZ53
Rushbrook Rd. SE9 109 EQ89
Rushcroft Rd. E4 51 EA52
Rushcroft Rd. SW2 91 DN84
Rushden Clo. SE19 106 DR94
Rushden Gdns. NW7 47 CW51
Rushden Gdns., Ilf. 53 EN54
Rushdene SE2 96 EW76
Rushdene Ave., Barn. 48 DE45
Rushdene Clo., Nthlt. 72 BW68
Rushdene Cres., Nthlt. 72 BW68
Rushdene Rd., Pnr. 58 BX58
Rushdene Wk., West. 150 EK117
Rushdon Clo., Rom. 69 FG57
Rushen Wk., Cars. 118 DD102
Paisley Rd.
Rushes Mead, Uxb. 70 BJ67
Frays Waye
Rushet Rd., Orp. 124 EU96
Rushett Clo., T.Ditt. 115 CH102
Rushett La., Chess. 129 CJ111
Rushett La., Epsom 129 CJ111
Rushett Rd., T.Ditt. 115 CH101
Rushey Clo., N.Mal. 116 CR98
Rushey Grn. SE6 107 EB87
Rushey Hill, Enf. 35 DM42
Rushey Mead SE4 107 EA85
Rushfield, Pot.B. 19 CX32
Rushford Rd. SE4 107 DZ86
Rushgrove Ave. NW9 60 CS57
Rushleigh Ave. (Cheshunt), Wal.Cr. 23 DX31
Rushley Clo., Kes. 136 EK105
Rushmead E2 78 DV69
Florida St.
Rushmead, Rich. 101 CH90
Rushmead Clo., Croy. 134 DT105
Rushmere Ct., Wor.Pk. 117 CU103
The Ave.
Rushmere Pl. SW19 103 CX92
Rushmoor Clo., Pnr. 57 BV56
Rushmoor Clo., Rick. 42 BK47
Rushmore Clo., Brom. 122 EL97
Rushmore Cres. E5 65 DX63
Rushmore Rd.
Rushmore Hill, Orp. 138 EW109
Rushmore Hill, Sev. 138 EX112
Rushmore Rd. E5 64 DW63
Rusholme Ave., Dag. 68 FA62
Rusholme Gro. SE19 106 DS92
Rusholme Rd. SW15 103 CX86
Rushout Ave., Har. 59 CH58

Rushton Ave., Wat. 29 BU35
Rushton St. N1 78 DR68
Rushworth Ave. NW4 61 CU55
Rushworth Gdns.
Rushworth Gdns. NW4 61 CU55
Rushworth St. SE1 10 G4
Rushworth St. SE1 91 DP75
Rushy Meadow La., Cars. 118 DE103
Ruskin Ave. E12 80 EL65
Ruskin Ave., Felt. 99 BT86
Ruskin Ave., Rich. 88 CN80
Ruskin Ave., Wal.Abb. 24 EE34
Ruskin Ave., Well. 96 EU82
Ruskin Clo. NW11 62 DB58
Ruskin Clo. (Cheshunt), Wal.Cr. 22 DS26
Ruskin Dr., Orp. 123 ES104
Ruskin Dr., Well. 96 EU83
Ruskin Dr., Wor.Pk. 117 CV103
Ruskin Gdns. W5 73 CK70
Ruskin Gdns., Har. 60 CM56
Ruskin Gdns., Rom. 55 FH52
Ruskin Gro., Well. 96 EU82
Ruskin Pk. Ho. SE5 92 DR83
Ruskin Rd. N17 50 DT53
Ruskin Rd., Belv. 96 FA77
Ruskin Rd., Cars. 132 DF106
Ruskin Rd., Croy. 119 DP103
Ruskin Rd., Islw. 87 CF83
Ruskin Rd., Sthl. 72 BY73
Ruskin Wk. N9 50 DU47
Durham Rd.
Ruskin Wk. SE24 106 DQ85
Ruskin Wk., Brom. 122 EL100
Ruskin Way SW19 118 DD95
Rusland Ave., Orp. 123 ER104
Rusland Pk. Rd., Har. 59 CE56
Rusper Clo. NW2 61 CW62
Rusper Clo., Stan. 45 CJ49
Rusper Rd. N22 49 DP54
Rusper Rd., Dag. 82 EW65
Russell Ave. N22 49 DN54
Russell Clo. NW10 74 CQ66
Russell Clo. SE7 94 EJ80
Russell Clo. W4 89 CT79
Russell Clo., Beck. 121 EB97
Russell Clo., Bexh. 96 FA84
Russell Clo., Dart. 97 FG83
Russell Clo., Nthwd. 43 BQ50
Russell Clo., Ruis. 58 BW61
Russell Ct. SW1 9 L3
Russell Ct., Lthd. 143 CH122
Russell Ct., St.Alb. 16 CA30
Russell Cres., Wat. 29 BT35
High Rd.
Russell Dr., Stai. 98 BK86
Russell Gdns. N20 48 DE47
Russell Gdns. NW11 61 CY58
Russell Gdns. W14 89 CY76
Russell Gdns., Rich. 101 CJ89
Russell Gdns., West Dr. 84 BN78
Russell Gdns. Ms. W14 89 CY75
Russell Grn. Clo., Pur. 133 DN110
Russell Gro. NW7 46 CS50
Russell Gro. SW9 91 DN81
Russell Hill, Pur. 133 DM110
Russell Hill Pl., Pur. 133 DN111
Purley Way
Russell Hill Rd., Pur. 133 DN110
Russell Kerr Clo. W4 88 CQ80
Burlington La.
Russell La. N20 48 DE47
Russell La., Wat. 29 BR36
Russell Mead, Har. 45 CF52
Russell Pl. NW3 62 DE64
Aspern Gro.
Russell Pl. SE16 93 DY76
Onega Gate
Russell Rd. E4 51 DZ49
Russell Rd. E10 65 EB58
Russell Rd. E16 80 EG72
Russell Rd. E17 65 DZ55
Russell Rd. N8 63 DK58
Russell Rd. N13 49 DM51
Russell Rd. N15 64 DS57
Russell Rd. N20 48 DE47
Russell Rd. NW9 61 CT58
Russell Rd. SW19 104 DA94
Russell Rd. W14 89 CY76
Russell Rd., Buck.H. 52 EH46
Russell Rd., Enf. 36 DT38
Russell Rd., Mitch. 118 DE97
Russell Rd., Nthlt. 58 CC64
Russell Rd., Nthwd. 43 BQ48
Russell Rd., Shep. 113 BP101
Russell Rd., Twick. 101 CF86
Russell Rd., Walt. 113 BU100
Russell Sq. WC1 5 P5
Russell Sq. WC1 77 DL70
Russell St. WC2 6 A10
Russell St. WC2 77 DL73
Russell Wk., Rich. 102 CM86
Park Hill
Russell Way, Sutt. 132 DA106
Russell Way, Wat. 43 BV45
Russells, Tad. 145 CX122
Russell's Footpath SW16 105 DL92
Russells Ride (Cheshunt), Wal.Cr. 23 DY30
Russet Clo., Uxb. 71 BQ70
Uxbridge Rd.
Russet Clo., Walt. 114 BX104
Russet Cres. N7 63 DM64
Stock Orchard Cres.
Russet Dr., Croy. 121 DY102
Russet Dr., Rad. 18 CL32
Russets Clo. E4 51 ED49
Larkshall Rd.
Russett Clo., Orp. 138 EV106
Russett Clo., Wal.Cr. 22 DS26
Russett Way SE13 93 EB82
Conington Rd.
Russett Way, Swan. 125 FD96
Russia Ct. EC2 7 J9
Russia Dock Rd. SE16 79 DY74
Russia La. E2 78 DW68
Russia Row EC2 7 J9
Russia Wk. SE16 93 DX75
Archangel St.
Russington Rd., Shep. 113 BR100
Rust Sq. SE5 92 DR80
Rusthall Ave. W4 88 CR77
Rusthall Clo., Croy. 120 DW100
Rustic Ave. SW16 105 DH94
Rustic Pl., Wem. 59 CK63
Rustic Wk. E16 80 EH72
Lambert Rd.
Rustington Wk., Mord. 117 CZ101
Ruston Ave., Surb. 116 CP101
Ruston Gdns. N14 34 DG44
Farm La.
Ruston Ms. W11 75 CY72
St. Marks Rd.
Ruston St. E3 79 DZ67
Rutford Rd. SW16 105 DL92
Ruth Clo., Stan. 60 CM56
Ruthen Clo., Epsom 130 CP114
Rutherford Clo., Borwd. 32 CQ40
Rutherford Clo., Sutt. 132 DD107
Rutherford St. SW1 9 M8
Rutherford St. SW1 91 DK77
Rutherford Twr., Sthl. 72 CB72
Rutherford Way (Bushey), Wat. 45 CD46
Rutherford Way, Wem. 60 CN62
Rutherglen Rd. SE2 96 EU79
Rutherwick Ri., Couls. 147 DL117
Rutherwyke Clo., Epsom 131 CU107
Ruthin Clo. NW9 60 CS58
Ruthin Rd. SE3 94 EG79
Ruthven Ave., Wal.Cr. 23 DX33
Ruthven St. E9 79 DX67
Lauriston Rd.
Rutland Ave., Sid. 110 EU87
Rutland Clo. SW14 88 CP83
Rutland Clo. SW19 104 DE94
Rutland Rd.
Rutland Clo., Ash. 144 CL117
Rutland Clo., Bex. 110 EX88
Rutland Clo., Chess. 130 CM107
Rutland Clo., Epsom 130 CR110
Rutland Ct., Enf. 36 DV43
Rutland Dr., Mord. 117 CZ100
Rutland Dr., Rich. 101 CK88
Rutland Gdns. N4 63 DP58
Rutland Gdns. SW7 8 C5
Rutland Gdns. SW7 90 DE75
Rutland Gdns. W13 73 CG71
Rutland Gdns., Croy. 134 DS105
Rutland Gdns., Dag. 68 EW64
Rutland Gdns. Ms. SW7 8 C5
Rutland Gate SW7 8 C5
Rutland Gate SW7 90 DE75
Rutland Gate, Belv. 97 FB78
Rutland Gate, Brom. 122 EF98
Rutland Gate Ms. SW7 8 B5
Rutland Gro. W6 89 CV78
Rutland Ms. NW8 76 DB67
Boundary Rd.
Rutland Ms. E. SW7 8 B6
Rutland Ms. S. SW7 8 B6
Rutland Pk. NW2 75 CW65
Rutland Pk. SE6 107 DZ89
Rutland Pl. EC1 6 G6
Rutland Pl. (Bushey), Wat. 45 CD46
The Rutts
Rutland Rd. E7 80 EK66
Rutland Rd. E9 78 DW67
Rutland Rd. E11 66 EH57
Rutland Rd. E17 65 EA58
Rutland Rd. SW19 104 DE94
Rutland Rd., Har. 58 CC58
Rutland Rd., Hayes 85 BR77
Rutland Rd., Ilf. 67 EP63
Rutland Rd., Sthl. 72 CA70
Rutland Rd., Twick. 101 CD89
Rutland St. SW7 8 C6
Rutland St. SW7 90 DE76
Rutland Wk. SE6 107 DZ89
Rutland Way, Orp. 124 EW100
Rutley Clo. SE17 91 DP79
Royal Rd.
Rutlish Rd. SW19 118 DA95
Rutson Rd., W.Byf. 126 BM114
Rutter Gdns., Mitch. 118 DD98
Rutters Clo., West Dr. 84 BN75
Rutts, The (Bushey), Wat. 45 CD46
Rutts Ter. SE14 93 DX81
Ruvigny Gdns. SW15 89 CX83
Ruxley Clo., Epsom 130 CP106
Ruxley Clo., Sid. 110 EY93
Ruxley Cor. Ind. Est., Sid. 110 EX93
Ruxley Cres., Esher 129 CH107
Ruxley La., Epsom 130 CP107
Ruxley Ms., Epsom 130 CP106
Ruxley Ridge, Esher 129 CG108
Ruxton Clo., Swan. 125 FE97
Ryall Clo., St.Alb. 16 BY29
Ryalls Ct. N20 48 DF48
Ryan Clo. SE3 94 EJ84
Ryan Clo., Ruis. 57 BV60
Ryan Dr., Brent. 87 CG79
Ryan Way, Wat. 30 BW39
Ryarsh Cres., Orp. 137 ES105
Rycott Path SE22 106 DU87
Lordship La.
Rycroft La., Sev. 154 FE130
Rycroft Way N17 64 DT55
Ryculff Sq. SE3 94 EF82
Rydal Clo. NW4 47 CX53
Rydal Clo., Pur. 134 DR113
Rydal Ct., Wat. 15 BV32
Grasmere Clo.
Rydal Cres., Grnf. 73 CH69
Rydal Dr., Bexh. 96 EZ82
Rydal Dr., W.Wick. 122 EE103
Rydal Gdns. NW9 60 CS57
Rydal Gdns. SW15 102 CS92
Rydal Gdns., Houns. 100 CB86
Rydal Gdns., Wem. 59 CJ60
Rydal Rd. SW16 105 DK91
Rydal Way, Enf. 36 DW44
Rydal Way, Ruis. 58 BW63
Ryde, The, Stai. 112 BH95
Ryde Clo., Wok. 140 BJ121
Ryde Pl., Twick. 101 CJ86
Ryde Vale Rd. SW12 105 DH89
Rydens Ave., Walt. 113 BV103
Rydens Clo., Walt. 114 BW103
Rydens Gro., Walt. 128 BX105
Rydens Pk., Walt. 114 BX103
Rydens Rd.
Rydens Rd., Walt. 113 BV104
Ryder Clo., Brom. 108 EH92
Ryder Clo. (Bushey), Wat. 30 CB44
Ryder Ct. SW1 9 L2
Ryder Dr. SE16 92 DV78
Ryder Gdns., Rain. 83 FF65
Ryder Ms. E9 64 DW64
Homerton High St.
Ryder St. SW1 9 L2
Ryder St. SW1 77 DJ74
Ryder Yd. SW1 9 L2
Ryders Ter. NW8 76 DC68
Blenheim Ter.
Rydon St. N1 78 DQ67
St. Paul St.
Rydons Clo. SE9 94 EL83
Rydon's La., Couls. 148 DQ120
Rydons Pk., Walt. 113 BT102
Rydon's Wd. Clo., Couls. 148 DQ120
Rydston Clo. N7 77 DM66
Sutterton St.
Rye, The N14 49 DJ45
Rye Clo., Bex. 111 FB86
Rye Cres., Orp. 124 EW102
Rye Fld., Orp. 124 EX103
Rye Hill Est. SE15 92 DW84
Rye Hill Pk. SE15 92 DW84
Rye La. SE15 92 DU82
Rye La., Sev. 153 FE120
Rye Pas. SE15 92 DU83
Rye Rd. SE15 93 DX84
Rye Wk. SW15 103 CX85
Chartfield Ave.
Rye Way, Edg. 46 CM51
Canons Dr.
Ryebridge Clo., Lthd. 143 CG118
Ryebrook Rd., Lthd. 143 CG118
Ryecotes Mead SE21 106 DS88
Ryecroft Ave., Ilf. 53 EP54
Ryecroft Ave., Twick. 100 CB87
Ryecroft Cres., Barn. 33 CV43
Ryecroft Rd. SE13 107 EC85
Ryecroft Rd. SW16 105 DN93
Ryecroft Rd., Orp. 123 ER100
Ryecroft Rd., Sev. 153 FG116
Ryecroft St. SW6 90 DB81
Ryedale SE22 106 DV86
Ryefield Ave., Uxb. 71 BP66
Ryefield Path SW15 103 CU88
Ryefield Rd. SE19 106 DQ93
Ryeland Clo., West Dr. 70 BL72
Ryelands Clo., Cat. 148 DS121
Ryelands Ct., Lthd. 143 CG118
Ryelands Cres. SE12 108 EJ86
Ryelands Pl., Wey. 113 BS104
Ryfold Rd. SW19 104 DA90
Ryhope Rd. N11 49 DH49
Ryland Clo., Felt. 99 BT91
Ryland Ho., Croy. 120 DQ104
Ryland Rd. NW5 77 DH65
Rylandes Rd. NW2 61 CU62
Rylandes Rd., S.Croy. 134 DV109
Rylett Cres. W12 89 CT75
Rylett Rd. W12 89 CT76
Rylston Rd. N13 50 DR48
Rylston Rd. SW6 89 CZ79
Rymer Rd., Croy. 120 DS101
Rymer St. SE24 105 DP86
Rymill St. E16 81 EN74
Rysbrack St. SW3 8 D6
Rysbrack St. SW3 90 DF76
Rythe Ct., T.Ditt. 115 CG101
Rythe Rd., Esher 129 CD106

S

Sabah Ct., Ashf. 98 BN91
Sabbarton St. E16 80 EF72
Victoria Dock Rd.
Sabella Ct. E3 79 DZ68
Mostyn Gro.
Sabine Rd. SW11 90 DF83
Sable Clo., Houns. 86 BW83
Sable St. N1 77 DP66
Canonbury Rd.
Sach Rd. E5 64 DV61
Sackville Ave., Brom. 122 EG102
Sackville Clo., Har. 59 CD62
Sackville Clo., Sev. 155 FH122
Sackville Est. SW16 105 DL90
Sackville Gdns., Ilf. 67 EM60
Sackville Rd., Sutt. 132 DA108
Sackville St. W1 9 L1
Sackville St. W1 77 DJ73
Sackville Way SE22 106 DU88
Dulwich Common
Saddle Yd. W1 77 DH74
Hay's Ms.
Saddlebrook Pk., Sun. 99 BS94
Saddlers Clo., Borwd. 32 CR44
Farriers Way
Saddlers Clo., Pnr. 44 CA51
Saddlers Ms., Wem. 59 CF63
The Boltons
Saddlers Way, Epsom 144 CR119
Saddlescombe Way N12 48 DA50
Sadler Clo., Mitch. 118 DF96
Sadlers Ride, W.Mol. 114 CB97
Saffron Ave. E14 79 ED73
Saffron Clo. NW11 61 CZ57
Saffron Clo., Croy. 119 DL100
Saffron Ct., Felt. 99 BQ87
Staines Rd.
Saffron Hill EC1 6 E6
Saffron Hill EC1 77 DN70
Saffron Rd., Rom. 55 FC54
Saffron St. EC1 6 E6
Saffron Way, Surb. 115 CK102
Sage Clo. E6 81 EM71
Bradley Stone Rd.
Sage St. E1 78 DW73
Cable St.
Sage Way WC1 6 B3
Saigasso Clo. E16 80 EK72
Royal Rd.
Sail St. SE11 10 C8
Sail St. SE11 91 DM77
Sainfoin Rd. SW17 104 DG89
Sainsbury Rd. SE19 106 DS92
St. Agatha's Dr., Kings.T. 102 CM93
St. Agathas Gro., Cars. 118 DF102
St. Agnes Clo. E9 78 DW67
Gore Rd.
St. Agnes Pl. SE11 91 DP79
St. Agnes Well EC1 78 DR70
Old St.
St. Aidans Ct., Bark. 82 EV69
Choats Rd.
St. Aidan's Rd. SE22 106 DV86
St. Aidans Rd. W13 87 CH75
St. Albans Ave. E6 81 EM69
St. Alban's Ave. W4 88 CR76
St. Albans Ave., Felt. 100 BX92
St. Albans Ave., Wey. 112 BN104
St. Albans Clo. NW11 62 DA60
St. Albans Cres. N22 49 DN53
St. Alban's Cres., Wdf.Grn. 52 EG52
St. Alban's Gdns., Tedd. 101 CG92
St. Albans Gro. W8 90 DB76
St. Alban's Gro., Cars. 118 DE101
St. Albans La. NW11 62 DA60
West Heath Dr.
St. Albans La., Abb.L. 15 BT26
St. Albans Ms. W2 4 A6
St. Alban's Pl. N1 77 DP67
St. Albans Rd. NW5 62 DG62
St. Albans Rd. NW10 74 CS67
St. Albans Rd., Barn. 33 CW35
St. Albans Rd., Epp. 26 EX29
St. Albans Rd., Ilf. 67 ET60
St. Alban's Rd., Kings.T. 102 CL93
St. Albans Rd. (Dancers Hill), Pot.B. 33 CV35
St. Albans Rd. (South Mimms), Pot.B. 18 CS30
St. Albans Rd., Rad. 18 CN28
St. Albans Rd. (London Colney), St.Alb. 18 CN28
St. Alban's Rd., Sutt. 131 CZ105
St. Albans Rd., Wat. 29 BV40
St. Alban's Rd., Wdf.Grn. 52 EG52
St. Albans St. SW1 9 M1
St. Albans Ter. W6 89 CY79
Margravine Rd.
St. Albans Twr. E4 51 DZ51
St. Alfege Pas. SE10 93 EC79
St. Alfege Rd. SE7 94 EK79
St. Alphage Gdns. EC2 7 J7
St. Alphage Highwalk EC2 78 DR71
London Wall
St. Alphage Wk., Edg. 46 CQ54
St. Alphege Rd. N9 50 DW45
St. Alphonsus Rd. SW4 91 DK84
St. Amunds Clo. SE6 107 EA91
St. Andrew St. EC4 6 E7
St. Andrew St. EC4 77 DN71
St. Andrews Ave., Horn. 69 FF64
St. Andrews Ave., Wem. 59 CG63
St. Andrew's Clo. N12 48 DC49
Woodside Ave.
St. Andrews Clo. NW2 61 CV62
St. Andrews Clo. SE16 92 DV78
Ryder Dr.
St. Andrew's Clo., Islw. 87 CD81
St. Andrews Clo., Ruis. 58 BX61
St. Andrew's Clo., Shep. 113 BR98
St. Andrews Clo., Stan. 45 CJ54
St. Andrew's Ct. SW18 104 DC89
Waynflete St.
St. Andrews Ct., Wat. 29 BV39
St. Andrews Dr., Orp. 124 EV100
St. Andrews Dr., Stan. 45 CJ53
St. Andrews Gdns., Cob. 128 BW113
St. Andrew's Gro. N16 64 DR60
St. Andrew's Hill EC4 6 G10
St. Andrew's Hill EC4 77 DP73
St. Andrew's Ms. N16 64 DS60
St. Andrews Ms. SE3 94 EG80
Mycenae Rd.
St. Andrews Pl. NW1 5 J4
St. Andrews Rd. E11 66 EE58
St. Andrews Rd. E13 80 EH69
St. Andrews Rd. E17 51 DX54
St. Andrews Rd. N9 50 DW45
St. Andrews Rd. NW9 60 CR60
St. Andrews Rd. NW10 75 CV65
St. Andrews Rd. NW11 61 CZ58
St. Andrews Rd. W3 74 CS72
St. Andrews Rd. W7 87 CE75
Church Rd.
St. Andrews Rd. W14 89 CY79
St. Andrews Rd., Cars. 118 DE104
St. Andrews Rd., Couls. 147 DH116
St. Andrews Rd., Croy. 134 DQ105
Lower Coombe St.
St. Andrews Rd., Enf. 36 DR41
St. Andrews Rd., Ilf. 67 EM59
St. Andrews Rd., Rom. 69 FD58
St. Andrews Rd., Sid. 110 EX90
St. Andrew's Rd., Surb. 115 CK100
St. Andrews Rd., Uxb. 70 BL67
St. Andrews Rd., Wat. 44 BX48
Bridlington Rd.
St. Andrews Sq. W11 75 CY72
St. Marks Rd.
St. Andrew's Sq., Surb. 115 CK100
St. Andrews Twr., Sthl. 72 CC73
St. Andrews Wk., Cob. 141 BV115
St. Andrews Way E3 79 EB70
St. Anna Rd., Barn. 33 CX43
Sampson Ave.
St. Annes Ave., Stai. 98 BK87
St. Anne's Clo. N6 62 DG62
Highgate W. Hill
St. Annes Clo. (Cheshunt), Wal.Cr. 22 DU28
St. Anne's Clo., Wat. 44 BW49
St. Anne's Ct. W1 5 M9
St. Annes Gdns. NW10 74 CM69
St. Anne's Ho. N16 64 DS60
St. Annes Pas. E14 79 DZ72
Newell St.
St. Annes Rd. E11 65 ED61
St. Annes Rd., St.Alb. 17 CK27
St. Anne's Rd., Uxb. 56 BJ55
St. Anne's Rd., Wem. 59 CK64
St. Anne's Row E14 79 DZ72
St. Anne's St. E14 79 DZ72
Commercial Rd.
St. Ann's, Bark. 81 EQ67
St. Ann's Cres. SW18 104 DB86
St. Ann's Gdns. NW5 76 DG65
Queens Cres.
St. Ann's Hill SW18 104 DB85
St. Ann's La. SW1 9 N6
St. Ann's Pk. Rd. SW18 104 DC86
St. Ann's Pas. SW13 88 CS83
Cross St.
St. Anns Rd. N9 50 DT47
St. Ann's Rd. N15 63 DP57
St. Ann's Rd. SW13 89 CT82
St. Anns Rd. W11 75 CX73
St. Ann's Rd., Bark. 81 EQ67
Axe St.
St. Ann's Rd., Har. 59 CE58
St. Ann's St. SW1 9 N6
St. Ann's St. SW1 91 DK76
St. Ann's Ter. NW8 76 DD68
St. Anns Vill. W11 75 CX74
St. Anns Way, S.Croy. 133 DP107
St. Anselm's Pl. W1 5 H9
St. Anselms Rd., Hayes 85 BT75
St. Anthonys Ave., Wdf.Grn. 52 EJ51
St. Anthonys Clo. E1 78 DU74
St. Anthonys Clo. SW17 104 DE89
College Gdns.
St. Anthony's Way, Felt. 85 BT84
St. Antony's Rd. E7 80 EH66
St. Arvans Clo., Croy. 120 DS104
St. Asaph Rd. SE4 93 DX83
St. Aubyn's Ave. SW19 103 CZ92
St. Aubyns Ave., Houns. 100 CA85
St. Aubyns Clo., Orp. 123 ET104
St. Aubyns Gdns., Orp. 123 ET103
St. Aubyn's Rd. SE19 106 DT93
St. Audrey Ave., Bexh. 96 FA82
St. Augustine's Ave. W5 74 CL68
St. Augustines Ave., Brom. 122 EL99
St. Augustine's Ave., S.Croy. 134 DQ107
St. Augustines Ave., Wem. 60 CL62
St. Augustine's Path N5 63 DP64
St. Augustines Rd. NW1 77 DK66
St. Augustine's Rd., Belv. 96 EZ77
St. Austell Clo., Edg. 46 CM54
St. Austell Rd. SE13 93 EC82
St. Awdry's Rd., Bark. 81 ER66
St. Awdry's Wk., Bark. 81 EQ66
Station Par.
St. Barnabas Clo., Beck. 121 EC96
St. Barnabas Ct., Har. 44 CC53
St. Barnabas Rd. E17 65 EA58
St. Barnabas Rd., Mitch. 104 DG94
St. Barnabas Rd., Sutt. 132 DD106
St. Barnabas Rd., Wdf.Grn. 52 EH53

St. Barnabas St. SW1 8 G10
St. Barnabas St. SW1 90 DG78
St. Barnabas Ter. E9 65 DX64
St. Barnabas Vill. SW8 91 DL81
St. Bartholomews Clo. SE26 106 DV91
St. Bartholomew's Rd. E6 81 EM68
St. Bejamins Dr., Orp. 138 EW109
St. Benedict's Clo. SW17 104 DG92
Church La.
St. Benet's Clo. SW17 104 DE89
College Gdns.
St. Benet's Gro., Cars. 118 DC101
St. Benet's Pl. EC3 7 L10
St. Bernards, Croy. 120 DS104
St. Bernard's Clo. SE27 106 DR91
St. Gothard Rd.
St. Bernard's Rd. E6 80 EK67
St. Blaise Ave., Brom. 122 EH96
St. Botolph Row EC3 7 P9
St. Botolph St. EC3 7 P8
St. Botolph St. EC3 78 DT72
St. Botolph's Ave., Sev. 154 FG124
St. Botolph's Rd., Sev. 154 FG124
St. Bride St. EC4 6 F8
St. Bride St. EC4 77 DP72
St. Bride's Ave. EC4 77 DP72
New Bri. St.
St. Brides Ave., Edg. 46 CM53
St. Brides Clo., Erith 96 EX75
St. Katherines Rd.
St. Bride's Pas. EC4 6 F9
St. Catherines Clo. SW17 104 DE89
College Gdns.
St. Catherines Dr. SE14 93 DX82
Kitto Rd.
St. Catherines Fm. Ct., Ruis. 57 BQ58
St. Catherine's Ms. SW3 8 D8
St. Catherines Rd. E4 51 EA47
St. Catherines Rd., Ruis. 57 BR57
St. Chads Clo., Surb. 115 CJ101
St. Chad's Gdns., Rom. 68 EY59
St. Chad's Pl. WC1 6 A2
St. Chad's Pl. WC1 77 DL69
St. Chad's Rd., Rom. 68 EY58
St. Chad's St. WC1 6 A2
St. Chad's St. WC1 77 DL69
St. Charles Ct., Wey. 126 BN106
St. Charles Pl. W10 75 CY71
Chesterton Rd.
St. Charles Pl., Wey. 126 BN106
St. Charles Sq. W10 75 CY71
St. Christopher Rd., Uxb. 70 BK71
St. Christopher's Clo., Islw. 87 CE81
St. Christopher's Dr., Hayes 71 BV73
St. Christophers Gdns., Th.Hth. 119 DN97
St. Christophers Ms., Wall. 133 DJ106
St. Christopher's Pl. W1 4 G8
St. Clair Dr., Wor.Pk. 117 CV104
St. Clair Rd. E13 80 EH68
St. Claire Clo., Ilf. 53 EM54
St. Clair's Rd., Croy. 120 DT103
St. Clare St. EC3 7 P9
St. Clement Clo., Uxb. 70 BK72
St. Clements Ct. EC4 78 DR73
Clements La.
St. Clements Ct. N7 77 DN65
Arundel Sq.
St. Clements Heights SE26 106 DU90
St. Clement's La. WC2 6 C9
St. Clements St. N1 77 DN65
St. Clements St. N7 77 DN65
St. Cloud Rd. SE27 106 DQ91
St. Crispins Clo. NW3 62 DE63
St. Crispins Clo., Sthl. 72 BZ72
St. Cross St. EC1 6 E6
St. Cross St. EC1 77 DN71
St. Cuthberts Gdns., Pnr. 44 BZ52
Westfield Pk.
St. Cuthberts Rd. N13 49 DN51
St. Cuthberts Rd. NW2 75 CZ65
St. Cyprian's St. SW17 104 DF91
St. David Clo., Uxb. 70 BK71
St. Davids, Couls. 147 DM117
St. Davids Clo., Wem. 60 CQ62
St. David's Clo., W.Wick. 121 EB101
St. David's Ct. E17 65 EC55
St. Davids Dr., Edg. 46 CM53
St. Davids Pl. NW4 61 CV59
St. Davids Rd., Swan. 111 FF93
St. Denis Rd. SE27 106 DR91
St. Dionis Rd. SW6 89 CZ82
St. Donatts Rd. SE14 93 DZ81
St. Dunstan's All. EC3 11 M1
St. Dunstans Ave. W3 74 CR73
St. Dunstans Clo., Hayes 85 BT77
St. Dunstan's Ct. EC4 77 DN72
Fleet St.
St. Dunstans Gdns. W3 74 CR73
St. Dunstans Ave.
St. Dunstan's Hill EC3 11 M1
St. Dunstan's Hill EC3 78 DS73
St. Dunstan's Hill, Sutt. 131 CY106
St. Dunstan's La. EC3 11 M1
St. Dunstan's La., Beck. 121 EC100
St. Dunstan's Rd. E7 80 EJ65
St. Dunstans Rd. SE25 120 DT98
St. Dunstans Rd. W6 89 CX78
St. Dunstans Rd. W7 87 CE75
St. Dunstan's Rd., Felt. 99 BT90
St. Dunstans Rd., Houns. 85 BV82
St. Edith Clo., Epsom 144 CN116
Dorking Rd.
St. Edmunds Ave., Ruis. 57 BR58
St. Edmunds Clo. NW8 76 DF67
St. Edmunds Ter.
St. Edmunds Clo. SW17 104 DE89
College Gdns.
St. Edmunds Clo., Erith 96 EX75
St. Katherines Rd.
St. Edmunds Dr., Stan. 45 CG53
St. Edmund's La., Twick. 100 CB87
St. Edmunds Rd. N9 50 DU45
St. Edmunds Rd., Ilf. 67 EM58
St. Edmunds Ter. NW8 76 DE68
St. Edwards Clo. NW11 62 DA58
St. Edwards Clo., Croy. 135 ED111
St. Edwards Way, Rom. 69 FD57
St. Egberts Way E4 51 EC46
St. Elizabeth Dr., Epsom 144 CN116
Dorking Rd.
St. Elmo Rd. W12 75 CT74
St. Elmos Rd. SE16 93 DX75
St. Erkenwald Ms., Bark. 81 ER67
St. Erkenwald Rd.
St. Erkenwald Rd., Bark. 81 ER67
St. Ermin's Hill SW1 9 M6
St. Ervans Rd. W10 75 CZ71
St. Fabian Twr. E4 51 DZ51
St. Faiths Clo., Enf. 36 DQ39
St. Faith's Rd. SE21 105 DP88
St. Fidelis Rd., Erith 97 FD77
St. Fillans Rd. SE6 107 EC88
St. Francis Clo., Orp. 123 ES100
St. Francis Clo., Pot.B. 20 DC33
St. Francis Clo., Wat. 43 BV46
St. Francis Rd. SE22 92 DS84
St. Francis Rd., Erith 97 FD77
West St.
St. Francis Twr. E4 51 DZ51
St. Gabriel's Clo. E11 66 EH60
St. Gabriels Rd. NW2 61 CX64
St. George St. W1 5 J10
St. George St. W1 77 DH73
St. Georges Ave. E7 80 EH66
St. Georges Ave. N7 63 DK63
St. Georges Ave. NW9 60 CQ56
St. George's Ave. W5 87 CK75
St. Georges Ave., Sthl. 72 BZ73
St. George's Ave., Wey. 127 BP107
St. Georges Circ. SE1 10 F6
St. Georges Circ. SE1 91 DP76
St. Georges Clo. NW11 61 CZ58
St. George's Clo. SW8 91 DJ81
Patmore Est.
St. Georges Clo., Wem. 59 CG62
St. George's Clo., Wey. 127 BQ106
St. Georges Ct. E6 81 EM70
St. Georges Ct. EC4 6 F8
St. Georges Ct. SW7 90 DC76
Gloucester Rd.
St. George's Dr. SW1 9 J9
St. George's Dr. SW1 91 DH77
St. Georges Dr., Uxb. 56 BM62
St. Georges Dr., Wat. 44 BY48
St. Georges Flds. W2 4 C9
St. Georges Flds. W2 76 DE72
St. Georges Gdns., Epsom 131 CT114
Lynwood Rd.
St. George's Gdns., Surb. 116 CP103
Hamilton Ave.
St. Georges Gro. SW17 104 DD90
St. Georges Gro. Est. SW17 104 DD90
St. Georges Ind. Est. N17 49 DP52
St. Georges La. EC3 7 L10
St. George's Lo., Wey. 127 BR106
St. Georges Ms. NW1 76 DF66
Regents Pk. Rd.
St. Georges Pl., Twick. 101 CG88
Church St.
St. Georges Rd. E7 80 EH65
St. Georges Rd. E10 65 EC62
St. Georges Rd. N9 50 DU48
St. Georges Rd. N13 49 DM48
St. Georges Rd. NW11 61 CZ58
St. Georges Rd. SE1 10 E6
St. Georges Rd. SE1 91 DN76
St. George's Rd. SW19 103 CZ94
St. Georges Rd. W4 88 CR75
St. Georges Rd. W7 73 CF74
St. Georges Rd., Add. 126 BJ105
St. George's Rd., Beck. 121 EB95
St. Georges Rd., Brom. 123 EM96
St. Georges Rd., Dag. 68 EY64
St. Georges Rd., Enf. 36 DT38
St. George's Rd., Felt. 100 BX91
St. Georges Rd., Ilf. 67 EM59
St. George's Rd., Kings.T. 102 CN94
St. George's Rd., Mitch. 119 DH97
St. Georges Rd., Orp. 123 ER100
St. Georges Rd., Rich. 88 CM83
St. George's Rd., Sev. 155 FH122
St. George's Rd., Sid. 110 EX93
St. Georges Rd., Swan. 125 FF98
St. Georges Rd., Twick. 101 CH85
St. Georges Rd., Wall. 133 DH106
St. Georges Rd., Wat. 29 BV38
St. George's Rd., Wey. 127 BR107
St. Georges Rd. W., Brom. 122 EL95
St. Georges Sq. E7 80 EH66
St. Georges Sq. E14 79 DY73
St. Georges Sq. SE8 93 DZ77
St. George's Sq. SW1 91 DK78
St. George's Sq., N.Mal. 116 CS97
High St.
St. George's Sq. Ms. SW1 91 DK78
St. Georges Ter. NW1 76 DF66
Regents Pk. Rd.
St. Georges Wk., Croy. 120 DQ104
St. Georges Way SE15 92 DS79
St. Gerards Clo. SW4 105 DJ85
St. German's Pl. SE3 94 EG81
St. Germans Rd. SE23 107 DY88
St. Giles Ave., Dag. 83 FB66
St. Giles Ave., Pot.B. 19 CV32
St. Giles Ave., Uxb. 57 BQ63
St. Giles Clo., Dag. 83 FB66
St. Giles Ave.
St. Giles Clo., Orp. 137 ER106
St. Giles High St. WC2 5 N8
St. Giles High St. WC2 77 DK72
St. Giles Pas. WC2 5 N9
St. Giles Rd. SE5 92 DS80
St. Gilles Ho. E2 79 DX68
Mace St.
St. Gothard Rd. SE27 106 DR91
St. Gregory Clo., Ruis. 58 BW63
St. Helena Rd. SE16 93 DX77
St. Helena St. WC1 6 D3
St. Helens Clo., Uxb. 70 BK71
St. Helens Ct., Epp. 26 EU30
Hemnall St.
St. Helens Ct., Rain. 83 FG70
St. Helens Cres. SW16 119 DM95
St. Helens Rd.
St. Helens Gdns. W10 75 CX71
St. Helens Pl. EC3 7 M8
St. Helens Rd. SW16 119 DM95
St. Helen's Rd. W13 73 CH74
Dane Rd.
St. Helens Rd., Erith 96 EX75
St. Helens Rd., Ilf. 67 EM58
St. Helier Ave., Mord. 118 DC101
St. Heliers Ave., Houns. 100 CA85
St. Heliers Rd. E10 65 EC58
St. Hildas Ave., Ashf. 98 BL92
St. Hildas Clo. NW6 75 CX67
St. Hildas Clo. SW17 104 DE89
St. Hilda's Rd. SW13 89 CV79
St. Hughe's Clo. SW17 104 DE89
College Gdns.
St. Hughs Rd. SE20 120 DV95
Ridsdale Rd.
St. Ivians Dr., Rom. 69 FG55
St. James Ave. E2 78 DW68
St. James Ave. N20 48 DE48
St. James Ave. W13 73 CG74
St. James Ave., Epsom 131 CT111
St. James Ave., Sutt. 132 DA106
St. James Clo. N20 48 DE48
St. James Clo. SE18 95 EQ78
Congleton Gro.
St. James Clo., Barn. 34 DD42
St. James Clo., Epsom 130 CS114
St. James Clo., N.Mal. 117 CT99
St. James Clo., Ruis. 58 BW61
St. James Gdns. W11 75 CY74
St. James Gdns., Wem. 73 CK66
St. James Gate NW1 77 DK66
St. Paul's Cres.
St. James Gro. SW11 90 DF82
Reform St.
St. James Ms. E14 93 EC76
St. James Ms., Wey. 127 BP105
St. James Rd. E15 66 EF64
St. James Rd. N9 50 DV47
Queens Rd.
St. James Rd., Cars. 118 DE104
St. James Rd., Kings.T. 115 CK96
St. James Rd., Mitch. 104 DG94
St. James Rd., Pur. 133 DP113
St. James Rd., Sev. 155 FH122
St. James Rd., Surb. 115 CK100
St. James Rd., Sutt. 132 DA106
St. James Rd. (Cheshunt), Wal.Cr. 22 DQ28
St. James Rd., Wat. 29 BV43
St. James St. W6 89 CW78
St. James Wk. EC1 6 F4
St. James Wk. SE15 92 DT80
Commercial Way
St. James Way, Sid. 110 EY92
St. James's SE14 93 DY81
St. James's Ave., Beck. 121 DY97
St. James's Ave., Hmptn. 100 CC92
St. James's Clo. SW17 104 DF89
St. James's Dr.
St. James's Cotts., Rich. 101 CK85
Paradise Rd.
St. James's Ct. SW1 9 L6
St. James's Ct. SW1 91 DJ76
St. James's Cres. SW9 91 DN83
St. James's Dr. SW12 104 DF88
St. James's Dr. SW17 104 DF88
St. James's La. N10 63 DH56
St. James's Mkt. SW1 9 M1
St. James's Ms. E17 65 DY57
St. James's St.
St. James's Palace SW1 9 L3
St. James's Palace SW1 77 DJ74
St. James's Pk. SW1 9 M6
St. James's Pk. SW1 91 DJ75
St. James's Pk., Croy. 120 DQ101
St. James's Pas. EC3 7 N9
St. James's Pl. SW1 9 K3
St. James's Pl. SW1 77 DJ74
St. James's Rd. SE1 92 DU78
St. James's Rd. SE16 92 DU76
St. James's Rd., Croy. 119 DP101
St. James's Rd., Hmptn. 100 CB92
St. James's Row EC1 6 F4
St. James's Sq. SW1 9 L2
St. James's Sq. SW1 77 DK74
St. James's St. E17 65 DY57
St. James's St. SW1 9 K2
St. James's St. SW1 77 DJ74
St. James's Ter. NW8 76 DF68
Prince Albert Rd.
St. James's Ter. Ms. NW8 76 DF67
St. Jeromes Gro., Hayes 71 BQ72
St. Joans Rd. N9 50 DT46
St. John Fisher Rd., Erith 96 EX76
St. John St. EC1 6 F2
St. John St. EC1 77 DN68
St. Johns Ave. N11 48 DF50
St. John's Ave. NW10 75 CT67
St. John's Ave. SW15 103 CX85
St. Johns Ave., Epsom 131 CT112
St. Johns Ave., Lthd. 143 CH121
St. John's Ch. Rd. E9 64 DW64
St. Johns Clo. N14 35 DJ44
Chase Rd.
St. John's Clo. SW6 90 DA80
Dawes Rd.
St. Johns Clo., Lthd. 143 CJ120
St. John's Clo., Pot.B. 20 DC33
St. Johns Clo., Rain. 83 FG66
St. John's Clo., Uxb. 70 BH67
St. John's Clo., Wem. 60 CL64
St. John's Cotts. SE20 106 DW94
Maple Rd.
St. Johns Cotts., Rich. 88 CL84
Kew Foot Rd.
St. Johns Ct., Buck.H. 52 EH46
St. John's Ct., Islw. 87 CF82
St. Johns Ct., Nthwd. 43 BS53
Murray Rd.
St. John's Cres. SW9 91 DN83
St. Johns Dr. SW18 104 DB88
St. Johns Dr., Walt. 114 BW102
St. John's Est. N1 7 L1
St. John's Est. N1 78 DR68
St. John's Est. SE1 11 P5
St. John's Gdns. W11 75 CY73
St. Johns Gro. N19 63 DJ61
St. Johns Gro. SW13 89 CT82
Terrace Gdns.
St. Johns Gro., Rich. 88 CL84
Kew Foot Rd.
St. John's Hill SW11 90 DD84
St. Johns Hill, Couls. 147 DN117
Canon's Hill
St. Johns Hill, Pur. 147 DN116
St. John's Hill, Sev. 155 FJ123
St. John's Hill Gro. SW11 90 DD84
St. John's La. EC1 6 F5
St. John's La. EC1 77 DP70
St. John's Ms. W11 76 DA72
Ledbury Rd.
St. Johns Par., Sid. 110 EU91
Church Rd.
St. John's Pk. SE3 94 EF80
St. Johns Pas. SE23 106 DW88
Davids Rd.
St. John's Pas. SW19 103 CY93
Ridgway Pl.
St. John's Path EC1 6 F5
St. Johns Pathway SE23 106 DW88
Devonshire Rd.
St. John's Pl. EC1 6 F5
St. John's Rd. E4 51 EB48
St. John's Rd. E6 80 EL67
Ron Leighton Way
St. Johns Rd. E16 80 EG72
St. John's Rd. E17 51 EB54
St. Johns Rd. N15 64 DS58
St. Johns Rd. NW11 61 CZ58
St. John's Rd. SE20 106 DW94
St. John's Rd. SW11 90 DE84
St. John's Rd. SW19 103 CY93
St. John's Rd., Bark. 81 ES67
St. John's Rd., Cars. 118 DE104
St. John's Rd., Croy. 119 DP104
Sylverdale Rd.
St. Johns Rd., E.Mol. 115 CD98
St. John's Rd., Epp. 25 ET30
St. Johns Rd., Erith 97 FD78
St. John's Rd., Felt. 100 BY91
St. Johns Rd., Har. 59 CF58
St. Johns Rd., Ilf. 67 ER59
St. John's Rd., Islw. 87 CE82
St. Johns Rd., Kings.T. 115 CJ96
St. Johns Rd., Lthd. 143 CJ121
St. Johns Rd., Loug. 39 EM40
St. John's Rd., N.Mal. 116 CQ97
St. Johns Rd., Orp. 123 ER100
St. John's Rd., Rich. 88 CL84
St. John's Rd., Rom. 55 FC50
St. John's Rd., Sev. 155 FH121
St. John's Rd., Sid. 110 EV91
St. Johns Rd., Sthl. 86 BY76
St. Johns Rd., Sutt. 118 DA103
St. Johns Rd., Uxb. 70 BH67
St. Johns Rd., Wat. 29 BV40
St. John's Rd., Well. 96 EV83
St. John's Rd., Wem. 60 CL64
St. John's Sq. EC1 6 F5
St. Johns Ter. E7 80 EH65
St. Johns Ter. SE18 95 EQ79
St. Johns Ter. SW15 102 CR91
Kingston Vale
St. Johns Ter. W10 75 CX70
Harrow Rd.
St. Johns Ter., Enf. 36 DR37
St. Johns Vale SE8 93 EA82
St. Johns Vill. N19 63 DK61
St. John's Vill. W8 90 DB76
St. Mary's Pl.
St. Johns Way N19 63 DJ61
St. John's Wd. Ct. NW8 4 A3
St. John's Wd. High St. NW8 4 A1
St. John's Wd. High St. NW8 76 DD68
St. John's Wd. Pk. NW8 76 DD67
St. John's Wd. Rd. NW8 76 DD70
St. John's Wd. Ter. NW8 76 DD68
St. Josephs Clo. W10 75 CY71
Bevington Rd.
St. Joseph's Clo., Orp. 137 ET105
St. Joseph's Ct. SE7 94 EH79
St. Josephs Dr., Sthl. 72 BY74
St. Joseph's Gro. NW4 61 CV56
St. Josephs Rd. N9 50 DV45
St. Joseph's Rd., Wal.Cr. 23 DY33
St. Joseph's Vale SE3 93 ED83
St. Jude St. N16 64 DS64
St. Jude's Rd. E2 78 DV68
St. Julians, Sev. 155 FL130
St. Julian's Clo. SW16 105 DN91
St. Julian's Fm. Rd. SE27 105 DN91
St. Julian's Rd. NW6 75 CZ66
St. Justin Clo., Orp. 124 EX97
St. Katharines Prec. NW1 77 DH68
Outer Circle
St. Katharine's Way E1 78 DU74
St. Katherines Rd., Erith 96 EX75
St. Katherine's Row EC3 7 N10
St. Keverne Rd. SE9 108 EL91
St. Kilda Rd. W13 73 CG74
St. Kilda Rd., Orp. 123 ET102
St. Kilda's Rd. N16 64 DR60
St. Kildas Rd., Har. 59 CE58
St. Kitts Ter. SE19 106 DS92
St. Laurence Clo. NW6 75 CX67
St. Laurence Clo., Orp. 124 EX97
Edmunds Ave.
St. Lawrence Clo., Abb.L. 15 BS30
St. Lawrence Clo., Edg. 46 CM52
St. Lawrence Clo., Uxb. 70 BJ71
St. Lawrence Dr., Pnr. 57 BV57
St. Lawrence St. E14 79 EC74
St. Lawrence Ter. W10 75 CY71
St. Lawrence Way SW9 91 DN82
St. Lawrence Way, Cat. 148 DQ121
Coulsdon Rd.
St. Lawrence Way, St.Alb. 16 BZ30
St. Leonards Ave. E4 51 ED51
St. Leonards Ave., Har. 59 CJ57
St. Leonards Clo. (Bushey), Wat. 30 BY42
St. Leonard's Clo., Well. 96 EU83
Hook La.
St. Leonards Ct. N1 7 L2
St. Leonard's Gdns., Houns. 86 BY81
St. Leonards Gdns., Ilf. 67 EQ64
St. Leonards Ri., Orp. 137 ES105
St. Leonards Rd. E14 79 EB71
St. Leonards Rd. NW10 74 CR70
St. Leonard's Rd. SW14 88 CP83
St. Leonards Rd. W13 73 CJ72
St. Leonards Rd., Croy. 119 DP104
St. Leonards Rd., Epsom 145 CW119
St. Leonards Rd., Esher 129 CF107
St. Leonard's Rd., Surb. 115 CK99
St. Leonards Rd., T.Ditt. 115 CG100
St. Leonards Rd., Wal.Abb. 24 EE25
St. Leonards Sq. NW5 76 DG65
St. Leonard's Sq., Surb. 115 CK99
St. Leonard's Rd.
St. Leonards St. E3 79 EB69
St. Leonard's Ter. SW3 90 DF78
St. Leonards Wk. SW16 105 DM94
St. Leonards Way, Horn. 69 FH61
St. Loo Ave. SW3 90 DE79
St. Louis Rd. SE27 106 DQ91
St. Loy's Rd. N17 50 DS54
St. Luke Clo., Uxb. 70 BK72
St. Luke's Ave. SW4 91 DK84
St. Lukes Ave., Enf. 36 DR38
St. Luke's Ave., Ilf. 67 EP64
St. Lukes Clo. EC1 78 DQ70
Old St.
St. Luke's Clo. SE25 120 DV100
St. Lukes Clo., Swan. 125 FD96
St. Luke's Est. EC1 7 K3
St. Luke's Est. EC1 78 DR69
St. Lukes Ms. W11 75 CZ72
Basing St.
St. Lukes Pas., Kings.T. 116 CM95
St. Lukes Rd. W11 75 CZ71
St. Lukes Rd., Uxb. 70 BL66
St. Lukes Rd., Whyt. 148 DT118
Whyteleafe Hill
St. Lukes Sq. E16 80 EF72
St. Luke's St. SW3 8 B10
St. Luke's St. SW3 90 DE78
St. Luke's Yd. W9 75 CZ69
St. Malo Ave. N9 50 DW48
St. Margaret Dr., Epsom 144 CN116
Dorking Rd.
St. Margarets, Bark. 81 EQ67
St. Margarets Ave. N15 63 DP56
St. Margarets Ave. N20 48 DC46
St. Margarets Ave., Ashf. 99 BP92
St. Margarets Ave., Har. 58 CC62
St. Margarets Ave., Sid. 109 ER90
St. Margaret's Ave., Sutt. 117 CY104
St. Margarets Ave., Uxb. 70 BN70
St. Margarets Clo., Orp. 138 EV105
St. Margaret's Ct. SE1 11 K3
St. Margarets Cres. SW15 103 CV85

St. Margaret's Dr., Twick. 101 CH85
St. Margaret's Gro. E11 66 EF62
St. Margaret's Gro. SE18 95 EQ79
St. Margaret's Gro., Twick. 101 CG86
St. Margarets La. W8 90 DB76
St. Margarets Pas. SE13 94 EE83
Church Ter.
St. Margarets Rd. E12 66 EJ61
St. Margarets Rd. N17 64 DS55
St. Margaret's Rd. NW10 75 CW69
St. Margarets Rd. SE4 93 DZ84
St. Margarets Rd. W7 87 CE75
St. Margarets Rd., Couls. 147 DH121
St. Margarets Rd., Edg. 46 CP50
St. Margarets Rd., Islw. 87 CH84
St. Margarets Rd., Ruis. 57 BR58
St. Margarets Rd., Twick. 101 CH86
St. Margarets Sq. SE4 93 DZ84
Adelaide Ave.
St. Margaret's St. SW1 9 P5
St. Margaret's St. SW1 91 DL75
St. Margaret's Ter. SE18 95 EQ78
St. Mark St. E1 78 DT72
St. Marks Clo. SE10 93 EC80
Ashburnham Pl.
St. Marks Clo. W11 75 CY72
Lancaster Rd.
St. Mark's Clo., Barn. 34 DB41
St. Marks Cres. NW1 76 DG67
St. Marks Gate E9 79 DZ66
Cadogan Ter.
St. Mark's Gro. SW10 90 DB79
St. Mark's Hill, Surb. 116 CL100
St. Mark's Pl. SW19 103 CZ93
Wimbledon Hill Rd.
St. Marks Pl. W11 75 CY72
St. Marks Ri. E8 64 DT64
St. Marks Rd. SE25 120 DU98
Coventry Rd.
St. Mark's Rd. W5 74 CL74
The Common
St. Marks Rd. W7 87 CE75
St. Marks Rd. W10 75 CX71
St. Marks Rd. W11 75 CY72
St. Marks Rd., Brom. 122 EH97
St. Marks Rd., Enf. 36 DT43
St. Marks Rd., Epsom 145 CW118
St. Marks Rd., Mitch. 118 DF96
St. Mark's Rd., Tedd. 101 CH94
St. Marks Sq. NW1 76 DG67
Regents Pk. Rd.
St. Martin Clo., Uxb. 70 BK72
St. Martins App., Ruis. 57 BS59
St. Martins Ave. E6 80 EK68
St. Martins Ave., Epsom 130 CS114
St. Martin's Clo. NW1 77 DJ67
St. Martins Clo., Enf. 36 DV39
St. Martins Clo., Epsom 130 CS113
Church Rd.
St. Martins Clo., Erith 96 EX75
St. Helens Rd.
St. Martin's Clo., Wat. 44 BW49
Muirfield Rd.
St. Martin's Clo., West Dr. 84 BK76
St. Martin's Rd.
St. Martin's Ct. WC2 5 P10
St. Martin's Ct., Ashf. 98 BJ92
St. Martins Dr., Walt. 114 BW104
St. Martins Est. SW2 105 DN88
St. Martin's La. WC2 5 P10
St. Martin's La. WC2 77 DL73
St. Martins Meadow, West. 152 EW123
St. Martin's Pl. WC2 9 P1
St. Martin's Pl. WC2 77 DL73
St. Martins Rd. N9 50 DV47
St. Martin's Rd. SW9 91 DM82
St. Martin's Rd., West Dr. 84 BJ76
St. Martin's St. WC2 9 N1
St. Martins Way SW17 104 DC90
St. Martin's-le-Grand EC1 7 H8
St. Martin's-le-Grand EC1 78 DQ72
St. Mary Abbots Pl. W8 89 CZ76
St. Mary Abbots Ter. W14 89 CZ76
St. Mary at Hill EC3 11 M1
St. Mary at Hill EC3 78 DS73
St. Mary Ave., Wall. 118 DG104
St. Mary Axe EC3 7 M9
St. Mary Axe EC3 78 DS72
St. Mary Rd. E17 65 EA56
St. Mary St. SE18 95 EN77
St. Marychurch St. SE16 92 DW75
St. Marys, Bark. 81 ER67
St. Marys App. E12 67 EM64
St. Marys Ave. E11 66 EH58
St. Mary's Ave. N3 47 CY54
St. Mary's Ave., Brom. 122 EE97
St. Mary's Ave., Nthwd. 43 BS50
St. Mary's Ave., Sthl. 86 CA77
St. Mary's Ave., Stai. 98 BK87
St. Mary's Ave., Tedd. 101 CF93
St. Marys Clo. N17 50 DU53
Kemble Rd.
St. Marys Clo., Chess. 130 CM108
St. Marys Clo., Epsom 131 CU108
St. Mary's Clo., Lthd. 143 CD123
St. Marys Clo., Orp. 124 EV96
St. Mary's Clo., Stai. 98 BK87
St. Mary's Clo., Sun. 113 BU98
Green Way
St. Mary's Clo., Uxb. 56 BH55
St. Marys Clo., Wat. 29 BV42
St. Marys Ct. E6 81 EM70
St. Mary's Ct. SE7 94 EK80
St. Mary's Ct. W5 87 CK75
St. Mary's Rd.
St. Mary's Cres. NW4 61 CV55
St. Mary's Cres., Hayes 71 BT73
St. Marys Cres., Islw. 87 CD80
St. Marys Cres., Stai. 98 BK87
St. Marys Dr., Felt. 99 BQ87
St. Mary's Dr., Sev. 154 FE123
St. Mary's Gdns. SE11 10 E8
St. Mary's Gdns. SE11 91 DN77
St. Mary's Gate W8 90 DB76
St. Marys Grn. N2 62 DC55
Thomas More Way
St. Marys Grn., West. 150 EJ118
St. Mary's Gro. N1 77 DP65
St. Mary's Gro. SW13 89 CV83
St. Mary's Gro. W4 88 CP79
St. Mary's Gro., Rich. 88 CM84
St. Marys Gro., West. 150 EJ118
St. Marys Mans. W2 76 DD71
St. Mary's Ms. NW6 76 DB66
Priory Rd.
St. Mary's Ms., Rich. 101 CJ90
Back La.
St. Marys Mt., Cat. 148 DT124
St. Marys Path N1 77 DP67
St. Mary's Pl. SE9 109 EN86
Eltham High St.
St. Mary's Pl. W5 87 CK75
St. Mary's Rd.
St. Mary's Pl. W8 90 DB76
St. Marys Rd. E10 65 EC62
St. Marys Rd. E13 80 EH68
St. Marys Rd. N8 63 DL56
High St.
St. Marys Rd. N9 50 DV46
St. Mary's Rd. NW10 74 CS67
St. Marys Rd. NW11 61 CY59
St. Mary's Rd. SE15 92 DW81
St. Marys Rd. SE25 120 DS97
St. Mary's Rd. (Wimbledon) SW19 103 CY92
St. Mary's Rd. W5 87 CK75
St. Mary's Rd., Barn. 48 DF45
St. Marys Rd., Bex. 111 FC88
St. Marys Rd., E.Mol. 115 CD99
St. Mary's Rd., Hayes 71 BT73
St. Marys Rd., Ilf. 67 EQ61
St. Marys Rd., Lthd. 143 CH122
St. Marys Rd., S.Croy. 134 DR110
St. Marys Rd., Surb. 115 CK100
St. Marys Rd. (Long Ditton), Surb. 115 CJ101
St. Marys Rd., Swan. 125 FD98
St. Mary's Rd. (Harefield), Uxb. 56 BH56
St. Mary's Rd. (Cheshunt), Wal.Cr. 22 DW29
St. Marys Rd., Wat. 29 BV42
St. Marys Rd., Wey. 127 BR105
St. Mary's Rd., Wor.Pk. 116 CS103
St. Marys Sq. W2 76 DD71
St. Mary's Sq. W5 87 CK75
St. Mary's Rd.
St. Marys Ter. W2 76 DD71
St. Marys Vw., Har. 59 CJ57
St. Mary's Wk. SE11 10 E8
St. Mary's Wk. SE11 91 DN77
St. Mary's Wk., Hayes 71 BT73
St. Mary's Rd.
St. Mary's Way, Chig. 53 EN50
St. Matthew Clo., Uxb. 70 BK72
St. Matthew St. SW1 9 M7
St. Matthew's Ave., Surb. 116 CL102
St. Matthews Clo., Rain. 83 FG66
St. Matthews Clo., Wat. 30 BX44
St. Matthew's Dr., Brom. 123 EM97
St. Matthew's Rd. SW2 91 DM84
St. Matthews Rd. W5 74 CL74
The Common
St. Matthew's Row E2 78 DU69
St. Matthias Clo. NW9 61 CT57
St. Maur Rd. SW6 89 CZ81
St. Merryn Clo. SE18 95 ER80
St. Michael's All. EC3 7 L9
St. Michaels Ave. N9 50 DW45
St. Michael's Ave., Wem. 74 CN65
St. Michaels Clo. E16 80 EK71
Fulmer Rd.
St. Michael's Clo. N3 47 CZ54
St. Michaels Clo. N12 48 DE50
St. Michaels Clo., Brom. 122 EL97
St. Michaels Clo., Erith 96 EX75
St. Helens Rd.
St. Michaels Clo., Walt. 114 BW103
St. Michaels Clo., Wor.Pk. 117 CT103
St. Michaels Cres., Pnr. 58 BY58
St. Michaels Dr., Wat. 15 BV33
St. Michaels Gdns. W10 75 CY71
St. Lawrence Ter.
St. Michaels Rd. NW2 61 CW63
St. Michael's Rd. SW9 91 DM82
St. Michael's Rd., Ashf. 98 BN92
St. Michaels Rd., Cat. 148 DR122
St. Michaels Rd., Croy. 120 DQ102
St. Michaels Rd., Wall. 133 DJ107
St. Michaels Rd., Well. 96 EV83
St. Michaels St. W2 4 A8
St. Michaels St. W2 76 DD72
St. Michaels Ter. N22 49 DL54
St. Michaels Way, Pot.B. 20 DB30
St. Mildred's Ct. EC2 7 K9
St. Mildreds Rd. SE12 108 EF87
St. Monica's Rd., Tad. 145 CZ121
St. Neots Clo., Borwd. 32 CN38
St. Nicholas Ave., Horn. 69 FG62
St. Nicholas Clo., Borwd. 31 CK44
St. Nicholas Clo., Uxb. 70 BK72
St. Nicholas Dr., Sev. 155 FJ126
St. Nicholas Dr., Shep. 112 BN101
St. Nicholas Glebe SW17 104 DG92
St. Nicholas Hill, Lthd. 143 CH122
St. Nicholas Rd. SE18 95 ET78
St. Nicholas Rd., Sutt. 132 DB106
St. Nicholas Rd., T.Ditt. 115 CF100
St. Nicholas St. SE8 93 DZ81
Lucas St.
St. Nicholas Way, Sutt. 132 DB105
St. Nicolas La., Chis. 122 EL95
St. Ninian's Ct. N20 48 DF48
St. Norbert Grn. SE4 93 DY84
St. Norbert Rd. SE4 107 DX85
St. Normans Way, Epsom 131 CU110
St. Olaf's Rd. SW6 89 CY80
St. Olaves Ct. EC2 7 K9
St. Olave's Est. SE1 11 N4
St. Olaves Gdns. SE11 10 D8
St. Olaves Rd. E6 81 EN67
St. Olave's Wk. SW16 119 DJ96
St. Olav's Sq. SE16 92 DW75
Albion St.
St. Oswald's Pl. SE11 91 DM78
St. Oswald's Rd. SW16 119 DP95
St. Oswulf St. SW1 9 N9
St. Pancras Way NW1 77 DJ66
St. Patrick's Ct., Wdf.Grn. 52 EE52
St. Paul Clo., Uxb. 70 BK71
St. Paul St. N1 78 DQ67
St. Paul's All. EC4 77 DP72
St. Paul's Chyd.
St. Paul's Ave. NW2 75 CW65
St. Paul's Ave. SE16 79 DX74
St. Pauls Ave., Har. 60 CM57
St. Paul's Chyd. EC4 6 G9
St. Paul's Chyd. EC4 77 DP72
St. Paul's Clo. SE7 94 EK78
St. Paul's Clo. W5 88 CM75
St. Pauls Clo., Add. 126 BG106
St. Pauls Clo., Ashf. 99 BQ92
St. Paul's Clo., Cars. 118 DE102
St. Pauls Clo., Chess. 129 CK105
St. Pauls Clo., Hayes 85 BR78
St. Paul's Clo., Houns. 86 BY82
St. Paul's Ct. W14 89 CX77
Colet Gdns.
St. Pauls Ctyd. SE8 93 EA80
Deptford High St.
St. Pauls Cray Rd., Chis. 123 ER95
St. Paul's Cres. NW1 77 DK66
St. Pauls Dr. E15 65 ED64
St. Paul's Ms. NW1 77 DK66
St. Paul's Cres.
St. Paul's Pl. N1 78 DR65
St. Pauls Ri. N13 49 DP51
St. Paul's Rd. N1 77 DP65
St. Paul's Rd. N17 50 DU52
St. Paul's Rd., Bark. 81 EQ67
St. Paul's Rd., Brent. 87 CK79
St. Paul's Rd., Erith 97 FC80
St. Paul's Rd., Rich. 88 CM83
St. Paul's Rd., Th.Hth. 120 DQ97
St. Paul's Shrubbery N1 78 DR65
St. Pauls Sq., Brom. 122 EG96
St. Paul's Ter. SE17 91 DP79
Westcott Rd.
St. Pauls Twr. E10 65 EC59
St. Pauls Wk., Kings.T. 102 CN94
Alexandra Rd.
St. Paul's Way E3 79 DZ71
St. Paul's Way E14 79 DZ71
St. Paul's Way N3 48 DB52
St. Pauls Way, Wal.Abb. 23 ED33
Rochford Ave.
St. Pauls Way, Wat. 30 BW40
St. Pauls Wd. Hill, Orp. 123 ES96
St. Peter's All. EC3 7 L9
St. Peter's Ave. E2 78 DU68
St. Peter's Clo.
St. Peter's Ave. E17 66 EE56
St. Peters Ave. N18 50 DU49
St. Peter's Clo. E2 78 DU68
St. Peters Clo. SW17 104 DE89
College Gdns.
St. Peters Clo., Barn. 33 CV43
St. Peters Clo., Chis. 109 ER94
St. Peters Clo., Ilf. 67 ES56
St. Peters Clo., Rick. 42 BH46
St. Peters Clo., Ruis. 58 BX61
St. Peters Clo. (Bushey), Wat. 45 CD46
St. Peter's Ct. NW4 61 CW57
St. Peters Ct. SE3 94 EF84
Eltham Rd.
St. Peters Ct. SE4 93 DZ82
Wickham Rd.
St. Peters Ct., W.Mol. 114 CA98
St. Peter's Gdns. SE27 105 DN90
St. Peters Gro. W6 89 CU77
St. Peters La., Orp. 124 EU96
St. Peter's Pl. W9 76 DB70
Shirland Rd.
St. Peters Rd. N9 50 DV46
St. Peter's Rd. W6 89 CU78
St. Peter's Rd., Croy. 134 DR105
St. Peters Rd., Kings.T. 116 CN96
St. Peters Rd., Sthl. 72 CA71
St. Peters Rd., Twick. 101 CH85
St. Peters Rd., Uxb. 70 BK71
St. Peter's Rd., W.Mol. 114 CA98
St. Peter's Sq. E2 78 DU68
St. Peter's Clo.
St. Peter's Sq. W6 89 CU78
St. Peters St. N1 77 DP67
St. Peter's St., S.Croy. 134 DR106
St. Peters Ter. SW6 89 CZ80
St. Peter's Vill. W6 89 CU77
St. Peter's Way N1 78 DS66
St. Peters Way W5 73 CK71
St. Peters Way, Hayes 85 BR78
St. Petersburgh Ms. W2 76 DB73
St. Petersburgh Pl. W2 76 DB73
St. Philip Sq. SW8 91 DH82
St. Philip St. SW8 91 DH82
St. Philip's Ave., Wor.Pk. 117 CV103
St. Philip's Rd. E8 78 DU65
St. Philips Rd., Surb. 115 CK100
St. Philip's Way N1 78 DQ67
Linton St.
St. Pinnock Ave., Stai. 112 BG95
St. Quentin Rd., Well. 95 ET83
St. Quintin Ave. W10 75 CW71
St. Quintin Gdns. W10 75 CW71
St. Quintin Rd. E13 80 EH68
St. Raphael's Way NW10 60 CQ64
St. Regis Clo. N10 49 DH54
St. Ronan's Clo., Barn. 34 DD38
St. Ronans Cres., Wdf.Grn. 52 EG52
St. Rule St. SW8 91 DJ82
St. Saviour's Est. SE1 11 P6
St. Saviour's Est. SE1 92 DT76
St. Saviour's Rd. SW2 105 DM85
St. Saviours Rd., Croy. 119 DP100
St. Silas Pl. NW5 76 DG65
St. Silas St. Est. NW5 76 DG65
St. Simon's Ave. SW15 103 CW85
St. Stephens Ave. E17 65 EC57
St. Stephens Ave. W12 89 CV75
St. Stephens Ave. W13 73 CH72
St. Stephen's Ave., Ash. 144 CL116
St. Stephens Clo. E17 65 EB57
St. Stephens Clo. NW8 76 DE67
St. Stephens Clo., Sthl. 72 CA71
St. Stephens Cres. W2 76 DA72
Talbot Rd.
St. Stephens Cres., Th.Hth. 119 DN97
St. Stephens Gdn. Est. W2 76 DA72
Shrewsbury Rd.
St. Stephens Gdns. SW15 103 CZ85
Manfred Rd.
St. Stephens Gdns. W2 76 DA72
St. Stephens Gdns., Twick. 101 CJ86
St. Stephens Gro. SE13 93 EC83
St. Stephens Ms. W2 76 DA71
Chepstow Rd.
St. Stephen's Par. E7 80 EJ66
Green St.
St. Stephen's Pas., Twick. 101 CJ86
Richmond Rd.
St. Stephen's Rd. E3 79 DY67
St. Stephens Rd. E6 80 EJ66
St. Stephen's Rd. E17 65 EB57
Grove Rd.
St. Stephens Rd. W13 73 CH72
St. Stephen's Rd., Barn. 33 CX43
St. Stephen's Rd., Enf. 37 DX37
St. Stephens Rd., Houns. 100 CA86
St. Stephens Rd., West Dr. 70 BK74
St. Stephens Row EC4 7 K10
St. Stephens Ter. SW8 91 DM80
St. Stephen's Wk. SW7 90 DC77
Southwell Gdns.
St. Swithin's La. EC4 7 K10
St. Swithin's La. EC4 78 DR73
St. Swithun's Rd. SE13 107 ED85
St. Theresa Clo., Epsom 144 CN116
Dorking Rd.
St. Theresa's Rd., Felt. 85 BT84
St. Thomas' Clo., Surb. 116 CM102
St. Thomas Ct., Bex. 110 FA87
St. Thomas Dr., Orp. 123 EQ102
St. Thomas' Dr., Pnr. 44 BY53
St. Thomas Gdns., Ilf. 81 EQ65
St. Thomas Pl. NW1 77 DK66
Maiden La.
St. Thomas Rd. E16 80 EG72
St. Thomas Rd. N14 49 DK45
St. Thomas Rd., Belv. 97 FC75
St. Thomas St. SE1 11 L3
St. Thomas St. SE1 78 DR74
St. Thomas's Clo., Wal.Abb. 24 EH33
St. Thomas's Gdns. NW5 76 DG65
Queens Cres.
St. Thomas's Pl. E9 78 DW66
St. Thomas's Rd. N4 63 DN61
St. Thomas's Rd. NW10 74 CS67
St. Thomas's Rd. W4 88 CQ79
St. Thomas's Sq. E9 78 DW66
St. Thomas's Way SW6 89 CZ80
St. Timothy's Ms., Brom. 122 EH95
Wharton Rd.
St. Ursula Gro., Pnr. 58 BX57
St. Ursula Rd., Sthl. 72 CA72
St. Vincent Clo. SE27 105 DP92
St. Vincent Rd., Twick. 100 CC86
St. Vincent Rd., Walt. 113 BV104
St. Vincent St. W1 4 G7
St. Vincents Way, Pot.B. 20 DC33
St. Wilfrids Clo., Barn. 34 DD43
East Barnet Rd.
St. Wilfrids Rd., Barn. 34 DD43
East Barnet Rd.
St. Winefride's Ave. E12 67 EM64
St. Winifreds, Ken. 148 DQ115
St. Winifreds Clo., Chig. 53 EQ50
St. Winifreds Rd., Tedd. 101 CH93
St. Winifred's Rd., West. 151 EM118
Saints Clo. SE27 105 DP91
Wolfington Rd.
Saints Dr. E7 66 EK64
Saints La., Rick. 42 BN45
Salamanca Pl. SE1 10 B9
Salamanca St. SE1 10 B9
Salamanca St. SE1 91 DM77
Salamander Clo., Kings.T. 101 CJ92
Salamons Way, Rain. 83 FE72
Salcombe Dr., Mord. 117 CX102
Salcombe Dr., Rom. 68 EZ58
Salcombe Gdns. NW7 47 CW51
Salcombe Pk., Loug. 38 EK43
High Rd.
Salcombe Rd. E17 65 DZ59
Salcombe Rd. N16 64 DS64
Salcombe Rd., Ashf. 98 BL91
Salcombe Way, Hayes 71 BS69
Portland Rd.
Salcombe Way, Ruis. 57 BU61
Salcot Cres., Croy. 135 EC110
Salcott Rd. SW11 104 DE85
Salcott Rd., Croy. 119 DL104
Sale Pl. W2 4 B7
Sale Pl. W2 76 DE72
Sale St. E2 78 DU70
Salehurst Clo., Har. 60 CL57
Salehurst Rd. SE4 107 DZ86
Salem Pl., Croy. 120 DQ104
Salem Rd. W2 76 DB73
Salford Rd. SW2 105 DK88
Salhouse Clo. SE28 82 EW72
Rollesby Way
Salisbury Ave. N3 61 CZ55
Salisbury Ave., Bark. 81 ER66
Salisbury Ave., Sutt. 131 CZ107
Salisbury Ave., Swan. 125 FG98
Salisbury Clo. SE17 11 K8
Salisbury Clo., Pot.B. 20 DC32
Salisbury Clo., Wor.Pk. 117 CT104
Salisbury Ct. EC4 6 E9
Salisbury Ct. EC4 77 DP72
Salisbury Cres. (Cheshunt), Wal.Cr. 23 DX32
Salisbury Gdns. SW19 103 CY94
Salisbury Gdns., Buck.H. 52 EK47
Salisbury Hall Gdns. E4 51 EA51
Salisbury Ho. E14 79 EB72
Hobday St.
Salisbury Ms. SW6 89 CZ80
Dawes Rd.
Salisbury Pl. SW9 91 DP80
Salisbury Pl. W1 4 D6
Salisbury Pl. W1 76 DF71
Salisbury Pl., W.Byf. 126 BJ111
Salisbury Rd. E4 51 EA48
Salisbury Rd. E7 80 EG65
Salisbury Rd. E10 65 EC61
Salisbury Rd. E12 66 EK64
Salisbury Rd. E17 65 EC57
Salisbury Rd. N4 63 DP57
Salisbury Rd. N9 50 DU48
Salisbury Rd. N22 49 DP53
Salisbury Rd. SE25 120 DU100
Salisbury Rd. SW19 103 CY94
Salisbury Rd. W13 87 CG75
Salisbury Rd., Bans. 132 DB114
Salisbury Rd., Barn. 33 CY41
Salisbury Rd., Bex. 110 FA88
Salisbury Rd., Brom. 122 EL99
Salisbury Rd., Cars. 132 DF107
Salisbury Rd., Dag. 83 FB65
Salisbury Rd., Enf. 37 DZ37
Salisbury Rd., Felt. 100 BW88
Salisbury Rd., Har. 59 CD57
Salisbury Rd., Houns. 86 BW83
Salisbury Rd. (Heathrow Airport), Houns. 99 BQ85
Salisbury Rd., Ilf. 67 ES61
Salisbury Rd., N.Mal. 116 CR97
Salisbury Rd., Pnr. 57 BU56
Salisbury Rd., Rich. 88 CL84
Salisbury Rd., Rom. 69 FH57
Salisbury Rd., Sthl. 86 BY77
Salisbury Rd., Uxb. 70 BK70
Salisbury Rd., Wat. 29 BV38
Salisbury Rd., Wor.Pk. 130 CR105
Salisbury Sq. EC4 6 E9
Salisbury St. NW8 4 B5
Salisbury St. NW8 76 DE70
Salisbury St. W3 88 CQ75
Salisbury Ter. SE15 92 DW83
Salisbury Wk. N19 63 DJ61
Salix Clo., Sun. 99 BV94
Oak Gro.
Salliesfield, Twick. 101 CD86
Salmen Rd. E13 80 EF68
Salmon La. E14 79 DY72
Salmon Rd., Belv. 96 FA78
Salmon St. E14 79 DZ72
Salmon La.
Salmon St. NW9 60 CP60
Salmond Clo., Stan. 45 CG51
Robb Rd.
Salmons La., Cat. 148 DS120
Salmons La., Whyt. 148 DS120
Salmons La. W., Cat. 148 DS120
Salmons Rd. N9 50 DU46
Salmons Rd., Chess. 129 CK107
Salomons Rd. E13 80 EJ71
Chalk Rd.
Salop Rd. E17 65 DX58
Salt Box Hill, West. 136 EH113
Saltash Clo., Sutt. 131 CZ105
Saltash Rd., Ilf. 53 ER52
Saltash Rd., Well. 96 EW81

Scotland Grn. Rd., Enf. 37 DX43
Scotland Grn. Rd. N., Enf. 37 DX42
Scotland Pl. SW1 9 P3
Scotland Rd., Buck.H. 52 EJ46
Scots Hill, Rick. 28 BM44
Scots Hill Clo., Rick. 28 BM44
Scots Hill
Scotscraig, Rad. 31 CF35
Scotsdale Clo., Orp. 123 ES98
Scotsdale Clo., Sutt. 131 CY108
Scotsdale Rd. SE12 108 EH85
Scotshall La., Warl. 135 EB114
Scotsmill La., Rick. 28 BM44
Scotswood St. EC1 6 E4
Scotswood Wk. N17 50 DU52
Scott Clo. SW16 119 DM95
Scott Clo., Epsom 130 CQ106
Scott Clo., West Dr. 84 BM77
Scott Ct. W3 88 CQ75
Petersfield Rd.
Scott Cres., Erith 97 FF81
Cloudesley Rd.
Scott Cres., Har. 58 CB60
Scott Ellis Gdns. NW8 76 DD69
Scott Fm. Clo., T.Ditt. 115 CH102
Scott Gdns., Houns. 86 BX80
Scott Ho. N18 50 DU50
Scott Lidgett Cres. SE16 92 DU75
Scott Russell Pl. E14 93 EB78
Westferry Rd.
Scott St. E1 78 DV70
Scottes La., Dag. 68 EX60
Valence Ave.
Scotts Ave., Brom. 121 ED96
Scotts Ave., Sun. 99 BS94
Scotts Clo., Stai. 98 BK88
Scotts Dr., Hmptn. 100 CB94
Scotts Fm. Rd., Epsom 130 CQ107
Scotts La., Brom. 121 ED98
Scotts Rd. E10 65 EC60
Scotts Rd. W12 89 CV75
Scotts Rd., Brom. 108 EG94
Scotts Rd., Sthl. 86 BW76
Scotts Way, Sev. 154 FE122
Scotts Way, Sun. 99 BS93
Scott's Yd. EC4 7 K10
Scottswood Clo. (Bushey), Wat. 30 BY40
Scottswood Rd.
Scottswood Rd. (Bushey), Wat. 30 BY40
Scottwell Dr. NW9 61 CT57
Scoulding Rd. E16 80 EG72
Scouler St. E14 79 ED73
Quixley St.
Scout App. NW10 60 CS63
Scout La. SW4 91 DJ83
Old Town
Scout Way NW7 46 CR49
Scovell Cres. SE1 11 H5
Scovell Rd. SE1 11 H5
Scrattons Ter., Bark. 82 EX67
Scriven St. E8 78 DT67
Scrooby St. SE6 107 EB86
Scrubbits Pk. Rd., Rad. 31 CG35
Scrubbits Sq., Rad. 31 CG36
The Dell
Scrubs La. NW10 75 CU69
Scrubs La. W10 75 CU69
Scrutton Clo. SW12 105 DK87
Scrutton St. EC2 7 M5
Scrutton St. EC2 78 DS70
Scudamore La. NW9 60 CQ56
Scutari Rd. SE22 106 DW85
Scylla Cres., Houns. 99 BP87
Scylla Rd. SE15 92 DV83
Scylla Rd., Houns. 99 BP86
Seabright St. E2 78 DV69
Bethnal Grn. Rd.
Seabrook Dr., W.Wick. 122 EE103
Seabrook Gdns., Rom. 68 FA59
Seabrook Rd., Dag. 68 EX62
Seabrook Rd., Kings L. 15 BR27
Seaburn Clo., Rain. 83 FE68
Seacole Clo. W3 74 CR71
Seacourt Rd. SE2 96 EX75
Seacroft Gdns., Wat. 44 BX48
Seafield Rd. N11 49 DJ49
Seaford Clo., Ruis. 57 BR61
Seaford Rd. E17 65 EB55
Seaford Rd. N15 64 DR56
Seaford Rd. W13 73 CH74
Seaford Rd., Enf. 36 DS42
Seaford Rd., Houns. 98 BK85
Seaford St. WC1 6 A3
Seaford St. WC1 77 DM69
Seaforth Ave., N.Mal. 117 CV99
Seaforth Clo., Rom. 55 FE52
Seaforth Cres. N5 64 DQ64
Seaforth Dr., Wal.Cr. 23 DX34
Seaforth Gdns. N21 49 DM45
Seaforth Gdns., Epsom 131 CT105
Seaforth Gdns., Wdf.Grn. 52 EJ50
Seaforth Pl. SW1 9 L6
Seager Pl. E3 79 DZ71
Burdett Rd.
Seagrave Rd. SW6 90 DA79
Seagry Rd. E11 66 EG58
Seal Dr., Sev. 155 FM121
Seal Hollow Rd., Sev. 155 FJ124
Seal Rd., Sev. 155 FJ121
Seal St. E8 64 DT63
Sealand Rd., Houns. 98 BN86
Sealand Wk., Nthlt. 72 BY69
Wayfarer Rd.
Seaman Clo., St.Alb. 17 CD25
Searches La., Abb.L. 16 BW27
Searchwood Rd., Warl. 148 DV118
Searle Pl. N4 63 DM60
Evershot Rd.
Searles Clo. SW11 90 DE80
Searles Rd. SE1 11 L8
Searles Rd. SE1 92 DR77
Sears St. SE5 92 DR80
Seasprite Clo., Nthlt. 72 BX69
Seaton Ave., Ilf. 67 ES64
Seaton Clo. E13 80 EH70
New Barn St.
Seaton Clo. SE11 10 F10
Seaton Clo. SW15 103 CV88
Seaton Clo., Twick. 101 CD86
Seaton Dr., Ashf. 98 BL89
Seaton Gdns., Ruis. 57 BU62
Seaton Pl. NW1 5 K4
Seaton Pt. E5 64 DU63
Nolan Way
Seaton Rd., Dart. 111 FG87
Seaton Rd., Hayes 85 BR77
Seaton Rd., Mitch. 118 DE96
Seaton Rd., St.Alb. 17 CK26
Seaton Rd., Twick. 100 CC86
Seaton Rd., Well. 96 EW80
Seaton Rd., Wem. 74 CL68
Seaton St. N18 50 DU50
Sebastian St. EC1 6 G3
Sebastian St. EC1 77 DP69
Sebastopol Rd. N9 50 DU49
Sebbon St. N1 77 DP66
Sebert Rd. E7 66 EH64
Sebright Pas. E2 78 DU68
Hackney Rd.
Sebright Rd., Barn. 33 CX40
Secker Cres., Har. 44 CC53
Secker St. SE1 10 D3
Second Ave. E12 66 EL63
Second Ave. E13 80 EG69
Second Ave. E17 65 EA57
Second Ave. N18 50 DW49
Second Ave. NW4 61 CX56
Second Ave. SW14 88 CS83
Second Ave. W3 75 CT74
Second Ave. W10 75 CY70
Second Ave., Dag. 83 FB67
Second Ave., Enf. 36 DT43
Second Ave., Hayes 71 BT74
Second Ave., Rom. 68 EW57
Second Ave., Walt. 113 BV100
Second Ave., Wat. 30 BX35
Second Ave., Wem. 59 CK61
Second Clo., W.Mol. 114 CC98
Second Cross Rd., Twick. 101 CD89
Second Way, Wem. 60 CP63
Sedan Way SE17 11 M10
Sedcombe Clo., Sid. 110 EV91
Knoll Rd.
Sedcote Rd., Enf. 36 DW43
Sedding St. SW1 8 F8
Sedding St. SW1 90 DG77
Seddon Ho. EC2 78 DQ71
The Barbican
Seddon Rd., Mord. 118 DD99
Seddon St. WC1 6 C3
Sedge Rd. N17 50 DW52
Sedgebrook Rd. SE3 94 EK82
Sedgecombe Ave., Har. 59 CJ57
Sedgeford Rd. W12 75 CT74
Sedgehill Rd. SE6 107 EA91
Sedgemere Ave. N2 62 DC55
Sedgemere Rd. SE2 96 EW76
Sedgemoor Dr., Dag. 68 FA63
Sedgeway SE6 108 EF88
Sedgewick Ave., Uxb. 71 BP66
Sedgewood Clo., Brom. 122 EF101
Sedgmoor Pl. SE5 92 DS80
Sedgwick Rd. E10 65 EC61
Sedgwick St. E9 65 DX64
Sedleigh Rd. SW18 103 CZ86
Sedlescombe Rd. SW6 89 CZ79
Sedley Gro., Uxb. 56 BJ56
Sedley Pl. W1 5 H9
Sedley Ri., Loug. 39 EM40
Sedum Clo. NW9 60 CP57
Old Kenton La.
Seeley Dr. SE21 106 DS91
Seelig Ave. NW9 61 CU59
Seely Rd. SW17 104 DG93
Seething La. EC3 7 N10
Seething La. EC3 78 DS73
Seething Wells La., Surb. 115 CJ100
Sefton Ave. NW7 46 CR50
Sefton Ave., Har. 45 CD53
Sefton Clo., Orp. 123 ET98
Sefton Rd., Croy. 120 DU102
Sefton Rd., Epsom 130 CR110
Sefton Rd., Orp. 123 ET98
Sefton St. SW15 89 CW83
Sefton Way, Uxb. 70 BJ72
Segal Clo. SE23 107 DY87
Segrave Clo., Wey. 126 BN108
Sekforde St. EC1 6 F5
Sekforde St. EC1 77 DP70
Sekhon Ter., Felt. 100 CA90
Selah Dr., Swan. 125 FC95
Selan Gdns., Hayes 71 BV71
Selbie Ave. NW10 61 CT64
Selborne Ave. E12 67 EN63
Walton Rd.
Selborne Ave. E17 65 DZ56
Selborne Ave., Bex. 110 EY88
Selborne Gdns. NW4 61 CU56
Selborne Gdns., Grnf. 73 CG68
Selborne Rd. E17 65 DZ57
Selborne Rd. N14 49 DL48
Selborne Rd. N22 49 DM53
Selborne Rd. SE5 92 DR82
Denmark Hill
Selborne Rd., Croy. 120 DS104
Selborne Rd., Ilf. 67 EN61
Selborne Rd., N.Mal. 116 CS96
Selborne Rd., Sid. 110 EV91
Selborne Wk. E17 65 DY57
High St.
Selbourne Ave., Add. 126 BH110
Selbourne Ave., Surb. 116 CM103
Selbourne Clo., Add. 126 BH110
Selby Chase, Ruis. 57 BV61
Selby Clo. E6 80 EL71
Linton Gdns.
Selby Clo., Chess. 130 CL108
Selby Clo., Chis. 109 EN93
Selby Gdns., Sthl. 72 CA70
Selby Grn., Cars. 118 DE101
Selby Rd. E11 66 EE62
Selby Rd. E13 80 EH71
Selby Rd. N17 50 DS51
Selby Rd. SE20 120 DU96
Selby Rd. W5 73 CH70
Selby Rd., Ashf. 99 BQ93
Selby Rd., Cars. 118 DE101
Selby St. E1 78 DU70
Selcroft Rd., Pur. 133 DP112
Selden Rd. SE15 92 DW82
Selden Wk. N7 63 DM61
Durham Rd.
Selhurst Clo. SW19 103 CX88
Selhurst New Rd. SE25 120 DS100
Selhurst Pl. SE25 120 DS100
Selhurst Rd. N9 50 DR48
Selhurst Rd. SE25 120 DS99
Selinas La., Dag. 68 EY59
Selkirk Dr., Erith 97 FE81
Selkirk Rd. SW17 104 DE91
Selkirk Rd., Twick. 100 CC89
Sellers Clo., Borwd. 32 CQ39
Sellers Hall Clo. N3 48 DA52
Sellincourt Rd. SW17 104 DE92
Sellindge Clo., Beck. 107 DZ94
Sellon Ms. SE11 10 C9
Sellons Ave. NW10 75 CT67
Sellwood Dr., Barn. 33 CX43
Selsdon Ave., S.Croy. 134 DR107
Selsdon Rd.
Selsdon Clo., Rom. 55 FC53
Selsdon Clo., Surb. 116 CL99
Selsdon Cres., S.Croy. 134 DW110
Selsdon Pk. Rd., S.Croy. 135 DX109
Selsdon Rd. E11 66 EG59
Selsdon Rd. E13 80 EJ67
Selsdon Rd. NW2 61 CT61
Selsdon Rd. SE27 105 DP90
Selsdon Rd., Add. 126 BG111
Selsdon Rd., S.Croy. 134 DR106
Selsdon Rd. Ind. Est., S.Croy. 134 DR107
Selsdon Rd.
Selsdon Way E14 93 EB76
Selsea Pl. N16 64 DS64
Crossway
Selsey Cres., Well. 96 EX81
Selsey St. E14 79 EA71
Selvage La. NW7 46 CR50
Selway Clo., Pnr. 57 BV55
Selwood Clo., Stai. 98 BJ86
Selwood Gdns., Stai. 98 BJ86
Selwood Pl. SW7 90 DD78
Selwood Rd., Chess. 129 CK105
Selwood Rd., Croy. 120 DV103
Selwood Rd., Sutt. 117 CZ102
Selwood Ter. SW7 90 DD78
Neville Ter.
Selworthy Clo. E11 66 EG57
Selworthy Rd. SE6 107 DZ90
Selwyn Ave. E4 51 EC51
Selwyn Ave., Ilf. 67 ET58
Selwyn Ave., Rich. 88 CL83
Selwyn Clo., Houns. 86 BY84
Selwyn Ct. SE3 94 EF83
Selwyn Ct., Edg. 46 CP52
Camrose Ave.
Selwyn Cres., Well. 96 EV83
Selwyn Pl., Orp. 124 EV97
Saxville Rd.
Selwyn Rd. E3 79 DZ68
Selwyn Rd. E13 80 EH67
Selwyn Rd. NW10 74 CR66
Selwyn Rd., N.Mal. 116 CR99
Semley Gate E9 79 DZ65
Eastway
Semley Pl. SW1 8 G9
Semley Pl. SW1 90 DG77
Semley Rd. SW16 119 DL96
Senate St. SE15 92 DW82
Senator Wk. SE28 95 ER76
Broadwater Rd.
Seneca Rd., Th.Hth. 120 DQ98
Senga Rd., Wall. 118 DG102
Senhouse Rd., Sutt. 117 CX104
Senior St. W2 76 DB71
Senlac Rd. SE12 108 EH88
Sennen Rd., Enf. 50 DT45
Sennen Wk. SE9 108 EL90
Nunnington Clo.
Senrab St. E1 79 DX72
Sentinel Clo., Nthlt. 72 BY70
Sentinel Sq. NW4 61 CW56
Sentis Ct., Nthwd. 43 BS51
Carew Rd.
September Way, Stan. 45 CH51
Sequoia Clo. (Bushey), Wat. 45 CD46
Giant Tree Hill
Sequoia Gdns., Orp. 123 ET101
Sequoia Pk., Pnr. 44 CB51
Serbin Clo. E10 65 EC59
Sergeants Grn. La., Wal.Abb. 24 EJ33
Sergehill La., Abb.L. 15 BT27
Serjeants Inn EC4 6 E9
Serle St. WC2 6 C8
Serle St. WC2 77 DM72
Sermon Dr., Swan. 125 FC97
Sermon La. EC4 78 DQ72
Carter La.
Serpentine Ct., Sev. 155 FK122
Serpentine Rd. W2 8 D3
Serpentine Rd. W2 76 DF74
Serpentine Rd., Sev. 155 FJ123
Service Rd., The, Pot.B. 20 DA32
Serviden Dr., Brom. 122 EK95
Setchell Rd. SE1 11 P8
Setchell Way SE1 11 P8
Seth St. SE16 92 DW75
Swan Rd.
Seton Gdns., Dag. 82 EW66
Settle Pt. E13 80 EG68
London Rd.
Settle Rd. E13 80 EG68
London Rd.
Settles St. E1 78 DU71
Settrington Rd. SW6 90 DB82
Seven Acres, Cars. 118 DE103
Seven Acres, Nthwd. 43 BU51
Seven Acres, Swan. 125 FD100
Seven Clo., Cars. 118 DE103
Seven Hills Clo., Walt. 127 BS109
Seven Hills Rd., Cob. 127 BS110
Seven Hills Rd., Walt. 127 BS110
Seven Hills Rd. S., Cob. 127 BS113
Seven Kings Rd., Ilf. 67 ET60
Seven Sisters Rd. N4 64 DQ59
Seven Sisters Rd. N7 63 DM62
Seven Sisters Rd. N15 64 DR58
Seven Stars Cor. W12 89 CU76
Goldhawk Rd.
Sevenoaks Business Cen., Sev. 155 FH121
Sevenoaks Bypass, Sev. 154 FC123
Sevenoaks Clo., Bexh. 97 FB84
Sevenoaks Clo., Sutt. 132 DA110
Sevenoaks Ct., Nthwd. 43 BQ52
Sevenoaks Ho. SE25 120 DU97
Sevenoaks Rd. SE4 107 DY86
Sevenoaks Rd., Orp. 137 ET105
Sevenoaks Rd. (Green St. Grn.), Orp. 137 ET108
Sevenoaks Rd. (Otford), Sev. 153 FH116
Sevenoaks Way, Orp. 124 EW98
Sevenoaks Way, Sid. 110 EW94
Seventh Ave. E12 67 EM63
Seventh Ave., Hayes 71 BT74
Severn Ave., Rom. 69 FH55
Severn Dr., Enf. 36 DU38
Severn Dr., Esher 115 CG103
Severn Dr., Walt. 114 BX103
Severn Way NW10 61 CT64
Severn Way, Wat. 16 BW34
Severnake Clo. E14 93 EA77
Severns Fld., Epp. 26 EU29
Severnvale, St.Alb. 18 CM27
Thamesdale
Severus Rd. SW11 90 DE84
Seville Ms. N1 78 DS66
Seville St. SW1 8 E5
Seville St. SW1 90 DF75
Sevington Rd. NW4 61 CV58
Sevington St. W9 76 DB70
Seward Rd. W7 87 CG75
Seward Rd., Beck. 121 DX96
Seward St. EC1 6 G3
Seward St. EC1 77 DP70
Sewardstone Gdns. E4 37 EB43
Sewardstone Rd. E2 78 DW68
Sewardstone Rd. E4 51 EB45
Sewardstone Rd., Wal.Abb. 37 ED38
Sewardstone St., Wal.Abb. 23 EC34
Sewdley St. E5 65 DX63
Sewell Rd. SE2 96 EU75
Sewell St. E13 80 EG69
Sextant Ave. E14 93 ED77
Sexton Clo., Rain. 83 FF67
Blake Clo.
Seymer Rd., Rom. 69 FD55
Seymour Ave. N17 50 DU54
Seymour Ave., Cat. 148 DQ122
Fairbourne La.
Seymour Ave., Epsom 131 CV109
Seymour Ave., Mord. 117 CX101
Seymour Clo., E.Mol. 114 CC99
Seymour Clo., Loug. 38 EL44
Seymour Clo., Pnr. 44 BZ53
Seymour Ct. E4 52 EF47
Seymour Dr., Brom. 123 EM102
Seymour Gdns. SE4 93 DY83
Seymour Gdns., Felt. 100 BW91
Seymour Gdns., Ilf. 67 EM60
Seymour Gdns., Ruis. 58 BX60
Seymour Gdns., Surb. 116 CM99
Seymour Gdns., Twick. 101 CH87
Seymour Ms. W1 4 F8
Seymour Ms. W1 76 DG72
Seymour Pl. SE25 120 DV98
Seymour Pl. W1 4 C6
Seymour Pl. W1 76 DE71
Seymour Rd. E4 51 EB46
Seymour Rd. E6 80 EK68
Seymour Rd. E10 65 DZ60
Seymour Rd. N3 48 DB52
Seymour Rd. N8 63 DP57
Seymour Rd. N9 50 DV47
Seymour Rd. SW18 103 CZ87
Seymour Rd. SW19 103 CX90
Seymour Rd. W4 88 CQ77
Seymour Rd., Cars. 132 DG106
Seymour Rd., E.Mol. 114 CC99
Seymour Rd., Hmptn. 100 CC92
Seymour Rd., Kings.T. 115 CK95
Seymour Rd., Mitch. 118 DG101
Seymour Rd., W.Mol. 114 CC99
Seymour St. W1 4 D9
Seymour St. W1 76 DF72
Seymour St. W2 4 D9
Seymour St. W2 76 DF72
Seymour Ter. SE20 120 DV95
Seymour Vill. SE20 120 DV95
Seymour Wk. SW10 90 DC79
Seymour Way, Sun. 99 BS94
Seymours, The, Loug. 39 EN39
Seyssel St. E14 93 EC77
Shaa Rd. W3 74 CR73
Shacklands Rd., Sev. 139 FB111
Shacklegate La., Tedd. 101 CE91
Shackleton Clo. SE23 106 DV89
Shackleton Rd., Sthl. 72 BZ73
Shackleton Way, Abb.L. 15 BU32
Lysander Way
Shacklewell Grn. E8 64 DT63
Shacklewell La.
Shacklewell La. E8 64 DT64
Shacklewell Rd. N16 64 DT63
Shacklewell Row E8 64 DT63
Shacklewell St. E2 78 DT69
Shad Thames SE1 11 P3
Shad Thames SE1 92 DT75
Shadbolt Clo., Wor.Pk. 117 CT103
Shadwell Dr., Nthlt. 72 BZ69
Shadwell Gdns. E1 78 DW72
Martha St.
Shadwell Pierhead E1 78 DW73
Glamis Rd.
Shadwell Pl. E1 78 DW73
Sutton St.
Shady Bush Clo. (Bushey), Wat. 44 CC45
Richfield Rd.
Shady La., Wat. 29 BV40
Shaef Way, Tedd. 101 CG94
Shafter Rd., Dag. 83 FC65
Shaftesbury, Loug. 38 EK41
Shaftesbury Ave. W1 5 M10
Shaftesbury Ave. W1 77 DK73
Shaftesbury Ave. WC2 9 M1
Shaftesbury Ave. WC2 77 DK73
Shaftesbury Ave., Barn. 34 DC41
Shaftesbury Ave., Enf. 37 DX40
Shaftesbury Ave., Felt. 99 BU86
Shaftesbury Ave., Har. 58 CB60
Shaftesbury Ave. (Kenton), Har. 59 CK57
Shaftesbury Ave., Sthl. 86 CA77
Shaftesbury Circle, Har. 58 CC60
Shaftesbury Ave.
Shaftesbury Ct. N1 78 DR68
Shaftesbury St.
Shaftesbury Cres., Stai. 98 BK94
Shaftesbury Gdns. NW10 74 CS70
Shaftesbury Ms. SW4 105 DJ85
Clapham Common S. Side
Shaftesbury Ms. W8 90 DA76
Stratford Rd.
Shaftesbury Pt. E13 80 EH68
High St.
Shaftesbury Rd. E4 51 ED46
Shaftesbury Rd. E7 80 EJ66
Shaftesbury Rd. E10 65 EA60
Shaftesbury Rd. E17 65 EB58
Shaftesbury Rd. N18 50 DS51
Shaftesbury Rd. N19 63 DL60
Shaftesbury Rd., Beck. 121 DZ96
Shaftesbury Rd., Cars. 118 DD101
Shaftesbury Rd., Epp. 25 ET29
Shaftesbury Rd., Rich. 88 CL83
Shaftesbury Rd., Rom. 69 FF58
Shaftesbury Rd., Wat. 30 BW41
Shaftesbury St. N1 7 J1
Shaftesbury St. N1 78 DQ68
Shaftesbury Way, Twick. 101 CD90
Shaftesbury Waye, Hayes 72 BW71
Shaftesburys, The, Bark. 81 EQ68
Shafto Ms. SW1 8 D7
Shafton Rd. E9 79 DX67
Shaftsbury Rd., Beck. 121 DZ96
Shaftsbury Way, Kings L. 15 BQ28
Shakespeare Ave. N11 49 DJ50
Shakespeare Ave. NW10 74 CR67
Shakespeare Ave., Felt. 99 BU86
Shakespeare Ave., Hayes 71 BU72
Shakespeare Cres. E12 81 EM65
Shakespeare Cres. NW10 74 CR67
Shakespeare Dr., Har. 60 CM58
Shakespeare Gdns. N2 62 DF56
Shakespeare Ho. N14 49 DK47
High St.
Shakespeare Rd. E17 51 DX54
Shakespeare Rd. N3 48 DA53
Popes Dr.
Shakespeare Rd. NW7 47 CT49
Shakespeare Rd. SE24 105 DP85
Shakespeare Rd. W3 74 CQ74
Shakespeare Rd. W7 73 CF73
Shakespeare Rd., Add. 126 BK105
Shakespeare Rd., Bexh. 96 EY81
Shakespeare Rd., Rom. 69 FF58

Shakespeare Sq., Ilf. 53 EQ51
Shakespeare St., Wat. 29 BV38
Shakespeare Twr. EC2 78 DQ71
Beech St.
Shakespeare Way, Felt. 100 BW91
Shakspeare Ms. N16 64 DS63
Shakspeare Wk.
Shakspeare Wk. N16 64 DS63
Shalcomb St. SW10 90 DC79
Shalcross Dr. (Cheshunt), Wal.Cr. 23 DZ30
Shaldon Dr., Mord. 117 CY99
Shaldon Dr., Ruis. 58 BW62
Shaldon Rd., Edg. 46 CM54
Shaldon Way, Walt. 114 BW104
Shalfleet Dr. W10 75 CX73
Shalford Clo., Orp. 137 EQ105
Shalimar Gdns. W3 74 CQ73
Shalimar Rd. W3 74 CQ73
Hereford Rd.
Shallons Rd. SE9 109 EP91
Shalston Vill., Surb. 116 CM100
Shalstone Rd. SW14 88 CP83
Shamrock Clo., Lthd. 143 CD121
Shamrock Rd., Croy. 119 DM100
Shamrock St. SW4 91 DK83
Shamrock Way N14 49 DH46
Shand St. SE1 11 N4
Shand St. SE1 92 DS75
Shandon Rd. SW4 105 DJ86
Shandy St. E1 79 DX71
Shanklin Clo., Wal.Cr. 22 DT29
Hornbeam Way
Shanklin Gdns., Wat. 44 BW49
Shanklin Rd. N8 63 DK57
Shanklin Rd. N15 64 DU56
Shanklin Way SE15 92 DT80
Pentridge St.
Shannon Clo. NW2 61 CX62
Shannon Clo., Sthl. 86 BX78
Shannon Gro. SW9 91 DM84
Shannon Pl. NW8 76 DE68
Allitsen Rd.
Shannon Way, Beck. 107 EB93
Shap Cres., Cars. 118 DF102
Shapland Way N13 49 DM50
Shardcroft Ave. SE24 105 DP85
Shardeloes Rd. SE14 93 DZ82
Sharland Clo., Th.Hth. 119 DN100
Sharman Ct., Sid. 110 EU91
Sharnbrooke Clo., Well. 96 EW83
Sharon Clo., Epsom 130 CQ113
Sharon Clo., Lthd. 142 CA124
Sharon Clo., Surb. 115 CJ102
Sharon Gdns. E9 78 DW67
Sharon Rd. W4 88 CR78
Sharon Rd., Enf. 37 DY40
Sharpe Clo. W7 73 CF71
Templeman Rd.
Sharpleshall St. NW1 76 DF66
Sharpness Clo., Hayes 72 BY71
Sharps La., Ruis. 57 BR60
Sharratt St. SE15 92 DW79
Sharsted St. SE17 91 DP78
Shavers Pl. SW1 9 M1
Shaw Ave., Bark. 82 EY68
Shaw Clo. SE28 82 EV74
Shaw Clo., Epsom 131 CT111
Shaw Clo., Horn. 69 FH60
Shaw Clo., S.Croy. 134 DT112
Shaw Clo. (Cheshunt), Wal.Cr. 22 DW28
Shaw Clo. (Bushey), Wat. 45 CE47
Shaw Cres., S.Croy. 134 DT112
Shaw Dr., Walt. 114 BW101
Shaw Gdns., Bark. 82 EY68
Shaw Rd. SE22 92 DS84
Shaw Rd., Brom. 108 EF90
Shaw Rd., Enf. 37 DX39
Shaw Rd., West. 150 EJ120
Shaw Sq. E17 51 DY53
Shaw Way, Wall. 133 DL108
Shawbrooke Rd. SE9 108 EJ85
Shawbury Rd. SE22 106 DT85
Shawfield Ct., West Dr. 84 BL76
Shawfield Pk., Brom. 122 EK96
Shawfield St. SW3 90 DE78
Shawford Ct. SW15 103 CU87
Shawford Rd., Epsom 130 CR107
Shawley Cres., Epsom 145 CW118
Shawley Way, Epsom 145 CV118
Shaws Cotts. SE23 107 DY90
Shaxton Cres., Croy. 135 EC109
Shearing Dr., Cars. 118 DC101
Stavordale Rd.
Shearling Way N7 77 DL65
Shearman Rd. SE3 94 EF84
Shearsmith Ho. E1 78 DU73
Cable St.
Shearwater Way, Hayes 72 BX72
Shearwood Cres., Dart. 97 FF83
Sheath's La., Lthd. 128 CB113
Sheaveshill Ave. NW9 60 CS56
Sheen Common Dr., Rich. 88 CN84
Sheen Ct., Rich. 88 CN84
Sheen Rd.
Sheen Ct. Rd., Rich. 88 CN84
Sheen Gate Gdns. SW14 88 CQ84
Sheen Gro. N1 77 DN67
Richmond Ave.
Sheen La. SW14 102 CQ85
Sheen Pk., Rich. 88 CL84
Sheen Rd., Orp. 123 ET98
Sheen Rd., Rich. 102 CL85
Sheen Way, Wall. 133 DM106
Sheen Wd. SW14 102 CQ85
Sheendale Rd., Rich. 88 CM84
Sheenewood SE26 106 DV92
Sheep La. E8 78 DV67
Sheep Wk., Epsom 144 CR122
Sheep Wk., Shep. 112 BM101
Sheep Wk. Ms. SW19 103 CY93
Sheepbarn La., Warl. 136 EF112
Sheepcot Dr., Wat. 16 BW34
Sheepcot La., Wat. 15 BU33
Sheepcote Clo., Houns. 85 BU80
Sheepcote Gdns., Uxb. 56 BG58
Sheepcote La. SW11 90 DF82
Sheepcote La., Orp. 124 EZ100
Sheepcote La., Swan. 124 FA98
Sheepcote Rd., Har. 59 CF58
Sheepcotes Rd., Rom. 68 EX56
Sheephouse Way, N.Mal. 116 CR102
Sheerwater Rd. E16 80 EK71
Sheffield Sq. E3 79 DZ69
Malmesbury Rd.
Sheffield St. WC2 6 B9
Sheffield Ter. W8 76 DA74
Shefton Ri., Nthwd. 43 BU52
Sheila Clo., Rom. 55 FB52
Sheila Rd., Rom. 55 FB52
Shelbourne Clo., Pnr. 58 BZ55
Shelbourne Rd. N17 50 DV54
Shelburne Rd. N7 63 DM63
Shelbury Clo., Sid. 110 EU90
Shelbury Rd. SE22 106 DV85
Sheldon Ave. N6 62 DE59
Sheldon Ave., Ilf. 53 EP54
Sheldon Clo. SE12 108 EH85
Sheldon Clo. SE20 120 DV95
Sheldon Clo. (Cheshunt), Wal.Cr. 22 DS26
Sheldon Rd. N18 50 DS49
Sheldon Rd. NW2 61 CX63
Sheldon Rd., Bexh. 96 EZ81
Sheldon Rd., Dag. 82 EY66
Sheldon St., Croy. 120 DQ104
Wandle Rd.
Sheldrake Clo. E16 81 EM74
Newland St.
Sheldrake Pl. W8 90 DA75
Sheldrick Clo. SW19 118 DD96
Shelduck Clo. E15 66 EF64
Sheldwich Ter., Brom. 122 EL100
Shelford Pl. N16 64 DR62
Stoke Newington Ch. St.
Shelford Ri. SE19 106 DT94
Shelford Rd., Barn. 33 CW44
Shelgate Rd. SW11 104 DE85
Shell Clo., Brom. 122 EL100
Shell Rd. SE13 93 EB83
Shellduck Clo. NW9 46 CS54
Swan Dr.
Shelley Ave. E12 80 EL65
Shelley Ave., Grnf. 73 CD69
Shelley Ave., Horn. 69 FF61
Shelley Clo., Bans. 145 CX115
Shelley Clo., Couls. 147 DM117
Shelley Clo., Edg. 46 CN49
Shelley Clo., Grnf. 73 CD69
Shelley Clo., Hayes 71 BU71
Shelley Clo., Nthwd. 43 BT50
Shelley Clo., Orp. 123 ES104
Shelley Cres., Houns. 86 BX81
Shelley Cres., Sthl. 72 BZ72
Shelley Dr., Well. 95 ES81
Shelley Gdns., Wem. 59 CJ61
Shelley Gro., Loug. 39 EM42
Shelley La., Uxb. 42 BG53
Shelley Way SW19 104 DD93
Shelleys La., Sev. 151 ET116
Shellfield Clo., Stai. 98 BG85
Shellgrove Est. N16 64 DS64
Shellness Rd. E5 64 DV64
Shellwood Rd. SW11 90 DF82
Shelmerdine Clo. E3 79 EA71
Shelson Ave., Felt. 99 BT90
Shelton Ave., Warl. 148 DW117
Shelton Clo., Warl. 148 DW117
Shelton Rd. SW19 118 DA95
Shelton St. WC2 5 P9
Shelton St. WC2 77 DL72
Shelvers Grn., Tad. 145 CW121
Shelvers Hill, Tad. 145 CW121
Ashurst Rd.
Shelvers Spur, Tad. 145 CW121
Shelvers Way, Tad. 145 CW121
Shenden Clo., Sev. 155 FJ128
Shenden Way, Sev. 155 FJ128
Shenfield Clo., Couls. 147 DJ119
Woodfield Clo.
Shenfield Ho. SE18 94 EK80
Shooter's Hill Rd.
Shenfield Rd., Wdf.Grn. 52 EH52
Shenfield St. N1 7 N1
Shenfield St. N1 78 DS68
Shenley Ave., Ruis. 57 BT61
Shenley Hill, Rad. 31 CG35
Shenley La., St.Alb. 17 CG25
Shenley Rd. SE5 92 DS81
Shenley Rd., Borwd. 32 CN42
Shenley Rd., Houns. 86 BY81
Shenley Rd., Rad. 17 CH34
Shenleybury, Rad. 17 CK30
Shenleybury Cotts., Rad. 18 CL31
Shenstone Clo., Dart. 97 FD84
Shepcot Ho. N14 35 DJ44
Shepherd Clo., Abb.L. 15 BT31
Jacketts Fld.
Shepherd Mkt. W1 9 H3
Shepherd St. W1 9 H3
Shepherdess Pl. N1 7 J2
Shepherdess Wk. N1 7 J1
Shepherdess Wk. N1 78 DQ68
Shepherds Bush Grn. W12 89 CW75
Shepherds Bush Mkt. W12 89 CW75
Uxbridge Rd.
Shepherds Bush Pl. W12 89 CX75
Shepherds Bush Rd. W6 89 CW77
Shepherds Clo. N6 63 DH58
Shepherds Clo., Lthd. 143 CK124
Shepherds Clo., Orp. 123 ET104
Stapleton Rd.
Shepherds Clo., Rom. 68 EX57
Shepherds Clo., Shep. 113 BP100
Shepherds Clo. (Cowley), Uxb. 70 BJ70
High St.
Shepherds Ct. W12 89 CX75
Shepherds Bush Grn.
Shepherds Grn., Chis. 109 ER94
Shepherds Hill N6 63 DH58
Shepherds La. E9 79 DX65
Shepherds La., Dart. 111 FG88
Shepherds Path, Nthlt. 72 BY65
Fortunes Mead
Shepherds Pl. W1 4 F10
Shepherds Rd., Wat. 29 BT41
Shepherds Wk. NW2 61 CU61
Shepherds Wk. NW3 62 DD63
Shepherds' Wk., Epsom 144 CP121
Shepherds Wk. (Bushey), Wat. 45 CD47
Shepherds Way, Hat. 20 DB27
Shepherds Way, Rick. 42 BH45
Shepherds Way, S.Croy. 135 DX108
Shepiston La., Hayes 85 BR78
Shepiston La., West Dr. 85 BP77
Shepley Clo., Cars. 118 DG104
Shepley Ms., Enf. 37 EA37
Sheppard Clo., Enf. 36 DV38
Sheppard Clo., Kings.T. 116 CL98
Beaufort Rd.
Sheppard Dr. SE16 92 DV78
Sheppard St. E16 80 EF70
Shepperton Business Pk., Shep. 113 BQ99
Shepperton Clo., Borwd. 32 CR39
Shepperton Ct. Dr., Shep. 113 BP99
Shepperton Rd. N1 78 DQ67
Shepperton Rd., Orp. 123 ER100
Shepperton Rd., Shep. 112 BL98
Shepperton Rd., Stai. 112 BJ97
Sheppey Clo., Erith 97 FH80
Sheppey Gdns., Dag. 82 EW66
Sheppey Rd.
Sheppey Rd., Dag. 82 EV66
Sheppey Wk. N1 78 DQ66
Clephane Rd.
Sheppeys La., Abb.L. 15 BS28
Sherard Rd. SE9 108 EL85
Sheraton Business Cen., Grnf. 73 CH68
Sheraton Clo., Borwd. 32 CM43
Sheraton Dr., Epsom 130 CQ113
Sheraton Ms., Wat. 29 BS42
Sheraton St. W1 5 M9
Sherborne Ave., Enf. 36 DW40
Sherborne Ave., Sthl. 86 CA77
Sherborne Clo., Epsom 145 CW117
Sherborne Clo., Hayes 72 BW72
Sherborne Cres., Cars. 118 DE101
Sherborne Gdns. NW9 60 CN55
Sherborne Gdns. W13 73 CH71
Sherborne Gdns., Rom. 54 FA50
Sherborne La. EC4 7 K10
Sherborne Rd., Chess. 130 CL106
Sherborne Rd., Felt. 99 BR87
Sherborne Rd., Orp. 123 ET98
Sherborne Rd., Sutt. 118 DA103
Sherborne St. N1 78 DR67
Sherborne Wk., Lthd. 143 CJ121
Windfield
Sherborne Way, Rick. 29 BP42
Sherboro Rd. N15 64 DT58
Ermine Rd.
Sherbourne Cotts., Wat. 30 BW43
Watford Fld. Rd.
Sherbourne Gdns., Shep. 113 BS101
Windmill Grn.
Sherbrook Gdns. N21 49 DP45
Sherbrooke Clo., Bexh. 96 FA84
Sherbrooke Rd. SW6 89 CY80
Shere Ave., Sutt. 131 CW110
Shere Clo., Chess. 129 CK106
Shere Rd., Ilf. 67 EN57
Sheredan Rd. E4 51 ED50
Sherfield Ave., Rick. 42 BK48
Sherfield Gdns. SW15 103 CT86
Sheridan Clo., Swan. 125 FF97
Willow Ave.
Sheridan Clo., Uxb. 71 BQ70
Alpha Rd.
Sheridan Ct., Houns. 100 BZ85
Vickers Way
Sheridan Cres., Chis. 123 EP96
Sheridan Gdns., Har. 59 CK58
Sheridan Ms. E11 66 EG58
Woodbine Pl.
Sheridan Pl. SW13 89 CT82
Brookwood Ave.
Sheridan Pl., Hmptn. 114 CB95
Sheridan Rd. E7 66 EF62
Sheridan Rd. E12 66 EL64
Sheridan Rd. SW19 117 CZ95
Sheridan Rd., Belv. 96 FA77
Sheridan Rd., Bexh. 96 EY83
Sheridan Rd., Rich. 101 CJ90
Sheridan Rd., Wat. 44 BX45
Sheridan St. E1 78 DV72
Watney St.
Sheridan Ter., Nthlt. 58 CB64
Whitton Ave. W.
Sheridan Wk. NW11 62 DA58
Sheridan Wk., Cars. 132 DF106
Carshalton Pk. Rd.
Sheridan Way, Beck. 121 DZ95
Turners Meadow Way
Sheriff Way, Wat. 15 BU33
Sheringham Ave. E12 67 EM63
Sheringham Ave. N14 35 DK43
Sheringham Ave., Felt. 99 BU90
Sheringham Ave., Rom. 69 FC58
Sheringham Ave., Twick. 100 BZ88
Sheringham Dr., Bark. 67 ET64
Sheringham Rd. N7 77 DM65
Sheringham Rd. SE20 120 DW97
Sheringham Twr., Sthl. 72 CB73
Sherington Ave., Pnr. 44 CA52
Sherington Rd. SE7 94 EH79
Sherland Rd., Twick. 101 CF87
Sherlies Ave., Orp. 123 ES103
Sherlock Ms. W1 4 F6
Sherman Rd., Brom. 122 EG95
Shermanbury Pl., Erith 97 FF80
Betsham Rd.
Shernbroke Rd., Wal.Abb. 24 EF34
Shernhall St. E17 65 EC55
Sherrard Rd. E7 80 EJ65
Sherrard Rd. E12 80 EK65
Sherrards Way, Barn. 34 DA43
Sherrick Grn. Rd. NW10 61 CV64
Sherriff Rd. NW6 76 DA65
Sherrin Rd. E10 65 EA63
Sherringham Ave. N17 50 DU54
Sherrock Gdns. NW4 61 CU56
Sherwin Rd. SE14 93 DX81
Sherwood Ave. E18 66 EH55
Sherwood Ave. SW16 105 DJ94
Sherwood Ave., Grnf. 73 CE65
Sherwood Ave., Hayes 71 BV70
Sherwood Ave., Pot.B. 19 CY32
Sherwood Ave., Ruis. 57 BS58
Sherwood Clo. SW13 89 CV83
Lower Common S.
Sherwood Clo. W13 73 CH74
Sherwood Clo., Bex. 110 EW86
Sherwood Clo., Lthd. 142 CC122
Sherwood Gdns. E14 93 EA77
Sherwood Gdns. SE16 92 DU78
Sherwood Gdns., Bark. 81 ER66
Sherwood Pk. Ave., Sid. 110 EU87
Sherwood Pk. Rd., Mitch. 119 DJ98
Sherwood Pk. Rd., Sutt. 132 DA106
Sherwood Rd. NW4 61 CW55
Sherwood Rd. SW19 103 CZ94
Sherwood Rd., Couls. 147 DJ116
Sherwood Rd., Croy. 120 DV101
Sherwood Rd., Hmptn. 100 CC92
Sherwood Rd., Har. 58 CC61
Sherwood Rd., Ilf. 67 ER56
Sherwood Rd., Well. 95 ES82
Sherwood St. N20 48 DD48
Sherwood St. W1 5 L10
Sherwood Ter. N20 48 DD48
Green Rd.
Sherwood Way, W.Wick. 121 EB103
Sherwoods Rd., Wat. 44 BY45
Shetland Clo., Borwd. 32 CR44
Percheron Rd.
Shetland Rd. E3 79 DZ68
Shewens Rd., Wey. 127 BR105
Shield Dr., Brent. 87 CG79
Shield Rd., Ashf. 99 BQ91
Shieldhall St. SE2 96 EW77
Shifford Path SE23 107 DX90
Shillibeer Pl. W1 4 C7
Shillibeer Wk., Chig. 53 ET48
Shillingford St. N1 77 DP66
Cross St.
Shillitoe Ave., Pot.B. 19 CX32
Shillitoe Rd. N13 49 DP50
Shinfield St. W12 75 CW72
Shingle Ct., Wal.Abb. 24 EG33
Shinglewell Rd., Erith 96 FA79
Shinners Clo. SE25 120 DU99
Stanger Rd.
Ship All. W4 88 CN79
Thames Rd.
Ship and Mermaid Row SE1 11 L4
Ship Hill, West. 150 EJ121
Ship La. SW14 88 CQ83
Ship St. SE8 93 EA81
Ship Tavern Pas. EC3 7 M10
Ship Yd. E14 93 EB78
Napier Ave.
Ship Yd., Wey. 127 BP105
High St.
Shipfield Clo., West. 150 EJ121
Shipka Rd. SW12 105 DH88
Shipman Rd. E16 80 EH72
Shipman Rd. SE23 107 DX89
Shipton Clo., Dag. 68 EX62
Shipton St. E2 78 DT68
Shipwright Rd. SE16 93 DY75
Shirburn Clo. SE23 106 DW87
Tyson Rd.
Shirbutt St. E14 79 EB73
Shire Clo., Brox. 23 DZ26
Groom Rd.
Shire Ct., Epsom 131 CT108
Shire Ct., Erith 96 EX76
St. John Fisher Rd.
Shire Horse Way, Islw. 87 CF83
Shire La., Kes. 136 EL109
Shire La., Orp. 136 EL109
Shire Pl. SW18 104 DC87
Whitehead Clo.
Shirebrook Rd. SE3 94 EK83
Shirehall Clo. NW4 61 CX58
Shirehall Gdns. NW4 61 CX58
Shirehall La. NW4 61 CX58
Shirehall Pk. NW4 61 CX58
Shiremeade, Borwd. 32 CM43
Shires, The, Rich. 102 CL91
Shires Clo., Ash. 143 CK119
Shires Ho., W.Byf. 126 BL113
Eden Gro. Rd.
Shirland Ms. W9 75 CZ69
Shirland Rd. W9 75 CZ69
Shirley Ave., Bex. 110 EX87
Shirley Ave., Couls. 147 DP119
Shirley Ave., Croy. 120 DW102
Shirley Ave., Sutt. 132 DD105
Shirley Ave. (Cheam), Sutt. 131 CZ109
Shirley Ch. Rd., Croy. 120 DW104
Shirley Clo. E17 65 EB57
Addison Rd.
Shirley Clo., Houns. 100 CC85
Shirley Clo. (Cheshunt), Wal.Cr. 22 DW29
Shirley Ct., Croy. 121 DX104
Shirley Cres., Beck. 121 DY98
Shirley Dr., Houns. 100 CC85
Shirley Gdns. W7 73 CF74
Shirley Gdns., Bark. 81 ES65
Shirley Gro. N9 50 DW45
Shirley Gro. SW11 90 DG83
Shirley Heights, Wall. 133 DJ109
Shirley Hills Rd., Croy. 135 DX106
Shirley Ho. Dr. SE7 94 EJ80
Shirley Oaks Rd., Croy. 121 DX102
Shirley Pk. Rd., Croy. 120 DV102
Shirley Rd. E15 80 EE66
Shirley Rd. W4 88 CR75
Shirley Rd., Abb.L. 15 BT32
Shirley Rd., Croy. 120 DV101
Shirley Rd., Enf. 36 DQ41
Shirley Rd., Sid. 109 ES90
Shirley Rd., Wall. 133 DJ109
Shirley St. E16 80 EF72
Shirley Way, Croy. 121 DY104
Shirlock Rd. NW3 62 DF63
Shobden Rd. N17 50 DR53
Shobroke Clo. NW2 61 CW62
Shoe La. EC4 6 E8
Shoe La. EC4 77 DN72
Shoebury Rd. E6 81 EM66
Sholden Gdns., Orp. 124 EW99
Sholto Rd., Houns. 98 BM85
Shonks Mill Rd., Rom. 41 FG37
Shoot Up Hill NW2 61 CY64
Shooters Ave., Har. 59 CJ56
Shooter's Hill SE18 95 EN81
Shooter's Hill, Well. 95 EQ82
Shooter's Hill Rd. SE3 94 EF81
Shooter's Hill Rd. SE10 93 ED81
Shooter's Hill Rd. SE18 94 EK81
Shooters Rd., Enf. 35 DP39
Shord Hill, Ken. 148 DR116
Shore Clo., Felt. 99 BU87
Shore Clo., Hmptn. 100 BY92
Stewart Clo.
Shore Gro., Felt. 100 CA89
Shore Pl. E9 78 DW66
Shore Rd. E9 78 DW66
Shorediche Clo., Uxb. 56 BM62
Shoreditch High St. E1 7 N5
Shoreditch High St. E1 78 DS70
Shoreham Clo. SW18 104 DB85
Ram St.
Shoreham Clo., Bex. 110 EX88
Stansted Cres.
Shoreham Clo., Croy. 120 DW99
Shoreham La., Orp. 138 FA107
Shoreham La., Sev. 154 FF122
Shoreham La. (Halstead), Sev. 138 EZ112
Shoreham Pl., Sev. 139 FG112
Shoreham Rd., Orp. 124 EV95
Shoreham Rd., Sev. 139 FH112
Shoreham Rd. E., Houns. 98 BL85
Shoreham Rd. W., Houns. 98 BL85
Shoreham Way, Brom. 122 EG100
Shorncliffe Rd. SE1 11 P10
Shorncliffe Rd. SE1 92 DT78
Shorndean St. SE6 107 EC88
Shorne Clo., Orp. 124 EX98
Shorne Clo., Sid. 110 EV86
Shornefield Clo., Brom. 123 EN97
Shornells Way SE2 96 EW78
Willrose Cres.
Shorrolds Rd. SW6 89 CZ80
Short Gate N12 47 CZ49
Short Hedges, Houns. 86 CA81
Lampton Ave.
Short Hill, Har. 59 CE60
High St.
Short La., St.Alb. 16 BZ29
Short La., Stai. 98 BM87
Short Path SE18 95 EP79
Westdale Rd.
Short Rd. E11 66 EE61
Short Rd. E15 79 ED67
Short Rd. W4 88 CS79
Short Rd., Houns. 98 BL86
Short St. NW4 61 CW56
New Brent St.
Short St. SE1 10 E4

Short Wall E15 79 ED69
Bisson Rd.
Short Way N12 48 DE51
Short Way SE9 94 EL83
Short Way, Twick. 100 CC87
Shortcroft Rd., Epsom 131 CT108
Shortcrofts Rd., Dag. 82 EZ65
Shorter St. E1 78 DT73
Shortlands W6 89 CX77
Shortlands, Hayes 85 BR79
Shortlands Clo. N18 50 DR48
Shortlands Clo., Belv. 96 EZ76
Shortlands Gdns., Brom. 122 EE96
Shortlands Gro., Brom. 121 ED97
Shortlands Rd. E10 65 EB59
Shortlands Rd., Brom. 121 ED97
Shortlands Rd., Kings.T. 102 CM94
Shortmead Dr. (Cheshunt), Wal.Cr. 23 DY31
Shorts Cft. NW9 60 CP56
Shorts Gdns. WC2 5 P9
Shorts Gdns. WC2 77 DL72
Shorts Rd., Cars. 132 DE105
Shortwood Ave., Stai. 98 BH90
Shortwood Common, Stai. 98 BH91
Shotfield, Wall. 133 DH107
Shott Clo., Sutt. 132 DC106
Turnpike La.
Shottendane Rd. SW6 90 DA81
Shottery Clo. SE9 108 EL90
Shottfield Ave. SW14 88 CS84
Shoulder of Mutton All. E14 79 DY73
Narrow St.
Shouldham St. W1 4 C7
Shouldham St. W1 76 DE71
Showers Way, Hayes 71 BU74
Shrapnel Clo. SE18 94 EL80
Shrapnel Rd. SE9 95 EM83
Shrewsbury Ave. SW14 88 CQ84
Shrewsbury Ave., Har. 60 CL56
Shrewsbury Clo., Surb. 116 CL103
Shrewsbury Ct. EC1 78 DQ70
Whitecross St.
Shrewsbury Cres. NW10 74 CR67
Shrewsbury La. SE18 95 EP81
Shrewsbury Ms. W2 76 DA71
Chepstow Rd.
Shrewsbury Rd. E7 66 EK64
Shrewsbury Rd. N11 49 DJ51
Shrewsbury Rd. W2 76 DA72
Shrewsbury Rd., Beck. 121 DY97
Shrewsbury Rd., Cars. 118 DE100
Shrewsbury St. W10 75 CW70
Shrewsbury Wk., Islw. 87 CG83
South St.
Shrewton Rd. SW17 104 DF94
Shroffold Rd., Brom. 108 EE91
Shropshire Clo., Mitch. 119 DL98
Shropshire Pl. WC1 5 L5
Shropshire Rd. N22 49 DM52
Shroton St. NW1 4 B6
Shroton St. NW1 76 DE71
Shrubberies, The E18 52 EG54
Shrubberies, The, Chig. 53 EQ50
Shrubbery Clo. N1 78 DQ67
St. Paul St.
Shrubbery Gdns. N21 49 DP45
Shrubbery Rd. N9 50 DU48
Shrubbery Rd. SW16 105 DL91
Shrubbery Rd., Sthl. 72 BZ74
Shrubland Gro., Wor.Pk. 117 CW104
Shrubland Rd. E8 78 DT67
Shrubland Rd. E10 65 EA59
Shrubland Rd. E17 65 EA57
Shrubland Rd., Bans. 145 CZ116
Shrublands, Hat. 20 DB26
Shrublands, The, Pot.B. 19 CY33
Shrublands Ave., Croy. 135 EA105
Shrublands Clo. N20 48 DD46
Shrublands Clo. SE26 106 DW90
Shrublands Clo., Chig. 53 EQ51
Shrubs Rd., Rick. 42 BM51
Shrubsall Clo. SE9 108 EL88
Shuna Wk. N1 78 DR65
St. Paul's Rd.
Shurland Ave., Barn. 34 DD44
Shurland Gdns. SE15 92 DT80
Rosemary Rd.
Shurlock Ave., Swan. 125 FD96
Shurlock Dr., Orp. 137 EQ105
Shuters Sq. W14 89 CZ78
Sun Rd.
Shuttle Clo., Sid. 109 ET87
Shuttle Rd., Dart. 97 FG83
Shuttle St. E1 78 DU70
Buxton St.
Shuttlemead, Bex. 110 EZ87
Shuttleworth Rd. SW11 90 DD82
Sibella Rd. SW4 91 DK82
Sibley Clo., Bexh. 110 EY85
Sibley Gro. E12 80 EL66
Sibthorpe Rd. SE12 108 EH86
Sibton Rd., Cars. 118 DE101
Sicilian Ave. WC1 6 A7
Sicklefield Clo. (Cheshunt), Wal.Cr. 22 DT26
Sidbury St. SW6 89 CY81
Sidcup Bypass, Chis. 109 ES91
Sidcup Bypass, Orp. 110 EV93
Sidcup Bypass, Sid. 109 ES91
Sidcup High St., Sid. 110 EU91
Sidcup Hill, Sid. 110 EV91
Sidcup Hill Gdns., Sid. 110 EW92
Sidcup Hill
Sidcup Pl., Sid. 110 EU92
Sidcup Rd. SE9 108 EJ86
Sidcup Rd. SE12 108 EH85
Sidcup Technology Cen., Sid. 110 EX92
Siddons La. NW1 4 E5
Siddons Rd. N17 50 DU53
Siddons Rd. SE23 107 DY89
Siddons Rd., Croy. 119 DN104
Side Rd. E17 65 DZ57
Sidewood Rd. SE9 109 ER88
Sidford Pl. SE1 10 C7
Sidings, The E11 65 EC60
Sidings, The, Loug. 38 EL44
Sidings, The, Stai. 98 BH91
Leacroft
Sidings Ms. N7 63 DN62
Sidmouth Ave., Islw. 87 CE82
Sidmouth Clo., Wat. 43 BV47
Sidmouth Dr., Ruis. 57 BU62
Sidmouth Par. NW2 75 CW66
Sidmouth Rd.
Sidmouth Rd. E10 65 EC62
Sidmouth Rd. NW2 75 CW66
Sidmouth Rd. SE15 92 DT81
Sidmouth Rd., Orp. 124 EV99
Sidmouth Rd., Well. 96 EW80
Sidmouth St. WC1 6 A3
Sidmouth St. WC1 77 DM69
Sidney Ave. N13 49 DM50
Sidney Elson Way E6 81 EN68
Edwin Ave.
Sidney Est. E1 78 DW72
Sidney Gdns., Brent. 87 CJ79
Sidney Gro. EC1 6 F1
Sidney Rd. E7 66 EG62
Sidney Rd. N22 49 DM52
Sidney Rd. SE25 120 DU99
Sidney Rd. SW9 91 DM82
Sidney Rd., Beck. 121 DY96
Sidney Rd., Epp. 39 ER36
Sidney Rd., Har. 58 CC55
Sidney Rd., Stai. 98 BG91
Sidney Rd., Twick. 101 CG86
Sidney Rd., Walt. 113 BU101
Sidney Sq. E1 78 DW71
Sidney St. E1 78 DW71
Sidworth St. E8 78 DV66
Siebert Rd. SE3 94 EG79
Siemens Rd. SE18 94 EK76
Sigdon Rd. E8 64 DU64
Sigers, The, Pnr. 57 BV58
Signmakers Yd. NW1 77 DH67
Delancey St.
Silbury Ave., Mitch. 118 DE95
Silbury St. N1 7 K2
Silchester Rd. W10 75 CX72
Silecroft Rd., Bexh. 96 FA81
Silesia Bldgs. E8 78 DV66
London La.
Silex St. SE1 10 G5
Silex St. SE1 91 DP75
Silk Clo. SE12 108 EG85
Silk Mill Rd., Wat. 43 BV45
Silk Mills Clo., Sev. 155 FJ121
Silk Mills Path SE13 93 EC82
Silk St. EC2 7 J6
Silk St. EC2 78 DQ71
Silkfield Rd. NW9 60 CS57
Silkin Ho., Wat. 44 BW48
Silkmills Sq. E9 79 DZ65
Silkstream Rd., Edg. 46 CQ53
Silsoe Rd. N22 49 DM54
Silver Birch Ave. E4 51 DZ51
Silver Birch Ave., Epp. 26 EY27
Silver Birch Clo. N11 48 DG51
Silver Birch Clo. SE28 82 EU74
Silver Birch Clo., Dart. 111 FE91
Silver Birch Gdns. E6 81 EM70
Silver Birch Ms., Ilf. 53 EQ51
Fencepiece Rd.
Silver Clo. SE14 93 DY80
Southerngate Way
Silver Clo., Har. 45 CD52
Silver Clo., Tad. 145 CY124
Silver Cres. W4 88 CP77
Silver Dell, Wat. 29 BT35
Silver Jubilee Way, Houns. 85 BV82
Silver La., Pur. 133 DK112
Silver La., W.Wick. 121 ED103
Silver Pl. W1 5 L10
Silver Rd. SE13 93 EB83
Elmira St.
Silver Rd. W12 75 CX73
Silver Spring Clo., Erith 97 FB79
Silver St. N18 50 DR49
Silver St., Enf. 36 DR41
Silver St., Rom. 40 EV41
Silver St., Wal.Abb. 23 EC33
Leverton Way
Silver St. (Cheshunt), Wal.Cr. 21 DP30
Silver Tree Clo., Walt. 127 BU105
Silver Trees, St.Alb. 16 BZ30
West Riding
Silver Wk. SE16 79 DZ74
Silver Way, Rom. 69 FB55
Silverbirch Clo., Uxb. 56 BL63
Silverbirch Wk. NW3 76 DG65
Queens Cres.
Silvercliffe Gdns., Barn. 34 DE42
Silverdale SE26 106 DW91
Silverdale, Enf. 35 DL42
Silverdale Ave., Ilf. 67 ES57
Silverdale Ave., Lthd. 128 CC114
Silverdale Ave., Walt. 113 BT104
Silverdale Clo. W7 73 CE74
Cherington Rd.
Silverdale Clo., Nthlt. 58 BZ64
Silverdale Clo., Sutt. 131 CZ105
Silverdale Ct., Stai. 98 BH92
Silverdale Dr. SE9 108 EL89
Silverdale Dr., Horn. 69 FH64
Silverdale Dr., Sun. 113 BV96
Silverdale Gdns., Hayes 85 BU75
Silverdale Rd. E4 51 ED51
Silverdale Rd., Bexh. 97 FB82
Silverdale Rd., Hayes 85 BT75
Silverdale Rd. (Petts Wd.), Orp. 123 EQ98
Silverdale Rd. (St. Paul's Cray), Orp. 124 EU97
Silverdale Rd. (Bushey), Wat. 30 BY43
Silverhall St., Islw. 87 CG83
Silverholme Clo., Har. 60 CL59
Silverland St. E16 81 EM74
Silverleigh Rd., Th.Hth. 119 DM98
Silvermere Ave., Rom. 55 FB51
Silvermere Rd. SE6 107 EB86
Silverst Clo., Nthlt. 72 CB65
Silverstead La., West. 151 ER121
Silverston Way, Stan. 45 CJ51
Silverthorn Gdns. E4 51 EA47
Silverthorne Rd. SW8 91 DH82
Silverton Rd. W6 89 CX79
Silvertown Way E16 80 EE72
Silvertree La., Grnf. 73 CD69
Cowgate Rd.
Silverwood Clo., Beck. 107 EA94
Silverwood Clo., Croy. 135 EA109
Silverwood Clo., Nthwd. 43 BQ53
Silvester Rd. SE22 106 DT85
Silvester St. SE1 11 K5
Silwood Est. SE16 92 DW77
Millender Wk.
Silwood St. SE16 92 DW77
Simla Clo. SE14 93 DY79
Chubworthy St.
Simla Ho. SE1 11 L5
Simmil Rd., Esher 129 CE106
Simmons Clo. N20 48 DE46
Simmons Clo., Chess. 129 CJ107
Merritt Gdns.
Simmons La. E4 51 ED47
Simmons Rd. SE18 95 EP78
Simmons Way N20 48 DE47
Simms Clo., Cars. 118 DE103
Simms Rd. SE1 92 DU77
Simnel Rd. SE12 108 EH87
Simon Clo. W11 75 CZ73
Portobello Rd.
Simonds Rd. E10 65 EA61
Simone Clo., Brom. 122 EK95
Simone Dr., Ken. 148 DQ116
Simons Wk. E15 65 ED64
Waddington St.
Simplemarsh Ct., Add. 126 BH105
Simplemarsh Rd.
Simplemarsh Rd., Add. 126 BG105
Simpson Clo. N21 35 DL43
Simpson Dr. W3 74 CR72
Simpson Rd., Houns. 100 BZ86
Simpson Rd., Rain. 83 FF65
Simpson Rd., Rich. 101 CJ91
Simpson St. SW11 90 DE82
Simpsons Rd. E14 79 EB73
Simpsons Rd., Brom. 122 EG97
Sims Clo., Rom. 69 FF56
Sims Wk. SE3 94 EF84
Lee Rd.
Sinclair Ct., Beck. 107 EA94
Sinclair Dr., Sutt. 132 DB109
Sinclair Gdns. W14 89 CX75
Sinclair Gro. NW11 61 CX58
Sinclair Rd. E4 51 DY50
Sinclair Rd. W14 89 CX75
Sinclare Clo., Enf. 36 DT39
Sinderby Clo., Borwd. 32 CL39
Singapore Rd. W13 73 CG74
Singer St. EC2 7 L3
Single St., West. 151 EP115
Singles Cross La., Sev. 138 EW114
Singleton Clo. SW17 104 DF94
Singleton Clo., Croy. 120 DQ101
St. Saviours Rd.
Singleton Clo., Horn. 69 FF63
Carfax Rd.
Singleton Rd., Dag. 68 EZ64
Singleton Scarp N12 48 DA50
Singret Pl. (Cowley), Uxb. 70 BJ70
High St.
Sinnott Rd. E17 51 DX53
Sion Rd., Twick. 101 CH87
Sipson Clo., West Dr. 84 BN79
Sipson La., Hayes 85 BQ79
Sipson La., West Dr. 84 BN79
Sipson Rd., West Dr. 84 BN78
Sipson Way, West Dr. 84 BN81
Sir Alexander Clo. W3 75 CT74
Sir Alexander Rd. W3 75 CT74
Sir Cyril Black Way SW19 104 DA94
Sir Thomas More Est. SW3 90 DD79
Beaufort St.
Sirdar Rd. N22 63 DP55
Sirdar Rd. W11 75 CX73
Sirdar Rd., Mitch. 104 DG93
Grenfell Rd.
Sirinham Pt. SW8 91 DM79
Sirus Rd., Nthwd. 43 BU50
Sise La. EC4 7 K9
Siskin Clo., Borwd. 32 CN42
Siskin Clo., Wat. 30 BY42
Sisley Rd., Bark. 81 ES67
Sispara Gdns. SW18 103 CZ86
Sissinghurst Rd., Croy. 120 DU101
Sister Mabel's Way SE15 92 DU80
Radnor Rd.
Sisters Ave. SW11 90 DF83
Sistova Rd. SW12 105 DH88
Sisulu Pl. SW9 91 DN83
Sittingbourne Ave., Enf. 36 DR44
Sitwell Gro., Stan. 45 CF50
Sivill Ho. E2 78 DT69
Siviter Way, Dag. 83 FB66
Siward Rd. N17 50 DR53
Siward Rd. SW17 104 DC90
Siward Rd., Brom. 122 EH97
Six Acres Est. N4 63 DN61
Six Bells La., Sev. 155 FJ126
Sixth Ave. E12 67 EM63
Sixth Ave. W10 75 CY69
Sixth Ave., Hayes 71 BT74
Sixth Ave., Wat. 30 BX35
Sixth Cross Rd., Twick. 100 CC90
Skardu Rd. NW2 61 CY64
Skarnings Ct., Wal.Abb. 24 EG33
Skeena Hill SW18 103 CY87
Skeet Hill La., Orp. 124 EX102
Skeffington Rd. E6 81 EM67
Skelbrook St. SW18 104 DB89
Skelgill Rd. SW15 89 CZ84
Skelley Rd. E15 80 EF66
Skelton Clo. E8 78 DT65
Buttermere Wk.
Skelton Rd. E7 80 EG65
Skeltons La. E10 65 EB59
Skelwith Rd. W6 89 CW79
Skenfrith Ho. SE15 92 DV79
Commercial Way
Skerne Rd., Kings.T. 115 CK95
Sketchley Gdns. SE16 93 DX78
Sketty Rd., Enf. 36 DS41
Skibbs La., Orp. 138 EY106
Skid Hill La., Warl. 136 EF113
Skidmore Way, Rick. 42 BL46
Skiers St. E15 80 EE67
Skiffington Clo. SW2 105 DN88
Skillet Hill, Wal.Abb. 38 EH35
Skinner Ct. E2 78 DV68
Parmiter St.
Skinner Pl. SW1 8 F9
Skinner St. EC1 6 E3
Skinner St. EC1 77 DN69
Skinners La. EC4 7 J10
Skinners La., Ash. 143 CK118
Skinners La., Houns. 86 CB81
Skinner's Row SE10 93 EB81
Blackheath Rd.
Skip La., Uxb. 56 BL60
Skipsey Ave. E6 81 EM69
Skipton Dr., Hayes 85 BQ76
Skipworth Rd. E9 78 DW67
Skomer Wk. N1 78 DQ65
Clephane Rd.
Sky Peals Rd., Wdf.Grn. 51 ED52
Skyport Dr., West Dr. 84 BK80
Slade, The SE18 95 ES79
Slade Ct., Rad. 31 CG35
Slade End, Epp. 39 ES36
Slade Gdns., Erith 97 FF81
Slade Grn. Rd., Erith 97 FG80
Slade Ho., Houns. 100 BZ86
Slade Twr. E10 65 EA61
Slade Wk. SE17 91 DP79
Heiron St.
Sladebrook Rd. SE3 94 EK83
Sladedale Rd. SE18 95 ES78
Slades Clo., Enf. 35 DN41
Slades Dr., Chis. 109 EQ90
Slades Gdns., Enf. 35 DN40
Slades Hill, Enf. 35 DN41
Slades Ri., Enf. 35 DN41
Slagrove Pl. SE13 107 EB85
Ladywell Rd.
Slaidburn St. SW10 90 DC79
Slaithwaite Rd. SE13 93 EC84
Slaney Pl. N7 63 DN64
Hornsey Rd.
Slaney Rd., Rom. 69 FE57
Slater Clo. SE18 95 EN78
Woolwich New Rd.
Slattery Rd., Felt. 100 BW88
Sleaford Grn., Wat. 44 BX48
Sleaford St. SW8 91 DJ80
Sledmore Ct., Felt. 99 BS88
Kilross Rd.
Slievemore Clo. SW4 91 DK83
Voltaire Rd.
Slines New Rd., Cat. 149 DX120
Slines Oak Rd., Cat. 149 EA123
Slines Oak Rd., Warl. 149 EA119
Slingsby Pl. WC2 5 P10
Slippers Pl. SE16 92 DV76
Sloane Ave. SW3 8 C9
Sloane Ave. SW3 90 DE77
Sloane Ct. E. SW3 8 F10
Sloane Ct. W. SW3 8 F10
Sloane Ct. W. SW3 90 DG78
Sloane Gdns. SW1 8 F9
Sloane Gdns. SW1 90 DG77
Sloane Gdns., Orp. 123 EQ104
Partridge Dr.
Sloane Sq. SW1 8 E9
Sloane Sq. SW1 90 DF77
Sloane St. SW1 8 E6
Sloane St. SW1 90 DF75
Sloane Ter. SW1 8 E8
Sloane Ter. SW1 90 DF77
Sloane Wk., Croy. 121 DZ100
Slocum Clo. SE28 82 EW73
Woodpecker Rd.
Slough La. NW9 60 CQ57
Sly St. E1 78 DV72
Cannon St. Rd.
Smallberry Ave., Islw. 87 CF82
Smallbrook Ms. W2 76 DD72
Craven Rd.
Smalley Clo. N16 64 DT62
Smalley Rd. Est. N16 64 DT62
Smalley Clo.
Smallholdings Rd., Epsom 131 CW114
Smallwood Rd. SW17 104 DD91
Smardale Rd. SW18 104 DC85
Alma Rd.
Smarden Clo., Belv. 96 FA78
Essenden Rd.
Smarden Gro. SE9 109 EM91
Smart Clo., Rom. 55 FH53
Smart St. E2 79 DX69
Smarts Grn. (Cheshunt), Wal.Cr. 22 DT26
Smarts La., Loug. 38 EK42
Smarts Pl. N18 50 DU50
Fore St.
Smart's Pl. WC2 6 A8
Smeaton Clo., Chess. 129 CK107
Merritt Gdns.
Smeaton Clo., Wal.Abb. 24 EE32
Smeaton Rd. SW18 104 DA87
Smeaton Rd., Wdf.Grn. 53 EM50
Smeaton St. E1 78 DV74
Smedley St. SW4 91 DK82
Smedley St. SW8 91 DK82
Smeed Rd. E3 79 EA66
Smiles Pl. SE13 93 EC82
Smith Clo. SE16 79 DX74
Smith Sq. SW1 9 P7
Smith Sq. SW1 91 DL76
Smith St. SW3 8 D10
Smith St. SW3 90 DF78
Smith St., Surb. 116 CM100
Smith St., Wat. 30 BW42
Smith Ter. SW3 90 DF78
Smitham Bottom La., Pur. 133 DJ111
Smitham Downs Rd., Pur. 133 DK113
Smithfield St. EC1 6 F7
Smithies Ct. E15 65 EC64
Clays La.
Smithies Rd. SE2 96 EV77
Smith's Ct. W1 5 L10
Smiths Fm. Est., Nthlt. 72 CA68
Smiths La. (Cheshunt), Wal.Cr. 22 DR26
Smiths Yd. SW18 104 DC89
Summerley St.
Smith's Yd., Croy. 120 DQ104
St. Georges Wk.
Smithson Rd. N17 50 DR53
Smithwood Clo. SW19 103 CY88
Smithy St. E1 78 DW71
Smock Wk., Croy. 120 DQ100
Smokehouse Yd. EC1 6 G6
Smokehouse Yd. EC1 77 DP71
Smug Oak Business Pk., St.Alb. 16 CB30
Smug Oak La., St.Alb. 16 CB30
Smugglers Way SW18 90 DB84
Smyrks Rd. SE17 92 DS78
Smyrna Rd. NW6 76 DA66
Smythe St. E14 79 EB73
Snag La., Sev. 137 ER112
Snakes La., Barn. 35 DJ41
Snakes La. E., Wdf.Grn. 52 EJ51
Snakes La. W., Wdf.Grn. 52 EG51
Snaresbrook Dr., Stan. 45 CK49
Snaresbrook Rd. E11 66 EE56
Snarsgate St. W10 75 CW71
Sneath Ave. NW11 61 CZ59
Snellings Rd., Walt. 128 BW106
Snells Pk. N18 50 DT51
Sneyd Rd. NW2 61 CW63
Snipe Clo., Erith 97 FH80
Snodland Clo., Orp. 137 EN110
Mill La.
Snow Hill EC1 6 F7
Snow Hill EC1 77 DP71
Snow Hill Ct. EC1 6 G8
Snowbury Rd. SW6 90 DB82
Snowden Ave., Uxb. 71 BP68
Snowden St. EC2 7 M5
Snowden St. EC2 78 DS70
Snowdon Cres., Hayes 85 BQ76
Snowdon Dr. NW9 60 CS58
Snowdown Clo. SE20 121 DX95
Snowdrop Clo., Hmptn. 100 CA93
Gresham Rd.
Snowman Ho. NW6 76 DB66
Snowsfields SE1 11 L4
Snowsfields SE1 92 DR75
Snowshill Rd. E12 66 EL64
Snowy Fielder Waye, Islw. 87 CH82
Soames St. SE15 92 DT83
Soames Wk., N.Mal. 116 CS95
Socket La., Brom. 122 EH100
Soham Rd., Enf. 37 DZ37
Soho Sq. W1 5 M8
Soho Sq. W1 77 DK72
Soho St. W1 5 M8
Sojourner Truth Clo. E8 78 DV65
Richmond Rd.

Solander Gdns. E1 78 DV73
Dellow St.
Sole Fm. Clo., Lthd. 142 BZ124
Solebay St. E1 79 DY70
Solefields Rd., Sev. 155 FH128
Solent Ri. E13 80 EG69
Solent Rd. NW6 62 DA64
Solent Rd., Houns. 98 BM86
Soleoak Dr., Sev. 155 FH127
Solesbridge La., Rick. 28 BH40
Soley Ms. WC1 6 D2
Solna Ave. SW15 103 CW85
Solna Rd. N21 50 DR46
Solomon Ave. N9 50 DU49
Solomons Hill, Rick. 42 BK45
Northway
Solomon's Pas. SE15 92 DV84
Solom's Ct. Rd., Bans. 146 DD117
Solon New Rd. SW4 91 DL84
Solon New Rd. Est. SW4 91 DL84
Solon New Rd.
Solon Rd. SW2 91 DL84
Solway Clo. E8 78 DT65
Buttermere Wk.
Solway Clo., Houns. 86 BY83
Solway Rd. N22 49 DP53
Solway Rd. SE22 92 DU84
Somaford Gro., Barn. 34 DD44
Somali Rd. NW2 61 CZ64
Somerby Rd., Bark. 81 ER66
Somercoates Clo., Barn. 34 DE41
Somerden Rd., Orp. 124 EX101
Somerfield Clo., Tad. 145 CY119
Somerfield Rd. N4 63 DP61
Somerford Clo., Pnr. 57 BU56
Somerford Gro. N16 64 DT63
Somerford Gro. N17 50 DU52
Somerford Gro. Est. N16 64 DT63
Somerford Gro.
Somerford St. E1 78 DV70
Somerford Way SE16 93 DY75
Somerhill Ave., Sid. 110 EV87
Somerhill Rd., Well. 96 EV82
Somerleyton Pas. SW9 91 DP84
Somerleyton Rd. SW9 91 DN84
Somers Clo. NW1 77 DK68
Platt St.
Somers Cres. W2 4 B9
Somers Cres. W2 76 DE72
Somers Ms. W2 4 B9
Somers Pl. SW2 105 DM87
Somers Rd. E17 65 DZ56
Somers Rd. SW2 105 DM86
Somers Way (Bushey), Wat. 44 CC45
Somersby Gdns., Ilf. 67 EM57
Somerset Ave. SW20 117 CV96
Somerset Ave., Chess. 129 CK105
Somerset Ave., Well. 109 ET85
Somerset Clo. N17 50 DR54
Somerset Clo., Epsom 130 CR109
Somerset Clo., N.Mal. 116 CS100
Somerset Clo., Walt. 127 BV106
Queens Rd.
Somerset Clo., Wdf.Grn. 52 EG53
Somerset Est. SW11 90 DD81
Somerset Gdns. N6 62 DG59
Somerset Gdns. SE13 93 EB82
Somerset Gdns. SW16 119 DM97
Somerset Gdns., Tedd. 101 CE92
Somerset Rd. E17 65 EA57
Somerset Rd. N17 64 DT55
Somerset Rd. N18 50 DT50
Somerset Rd. NW4 61 CW56
Somerset Rd. SW19 103 CX90
Somerset Rd. W4 88 CR76
Somerset Rd. W13 73 CH74
Somerset Rd., Barn. 34 DB43
Somerset Rd., Brent. 87 CK79
Somerset Rd., Dart. 111 FH86
Somerset Rd., Enf. 37 EA38
Somerset Rd., Har. 58 CC58
Somerset Rd., Kings.T. 116 CM96
Somerset Rd., Orp. 124 EU101
Somerset Rd., Sthl. 72 BZ72
Somerset Rd., Tedd. 101 CE92
Somerset Sq. W14 89 CY75
Somerset Waye, Houns. 86 BY80
Somersham Rd., Bexh. 96 EY82
Somerton Ave., Rich. 88 CP83
Somerton Clo., Pur. 147 DN115
Somerton Rd. NW2 61 CX62
Somerton Rd. SE15 92 DV84
Somertrees Ave. SE12 108 EH89
Somervell Rd., Har. 58 BZ64
Somerville Ave. SW13 89 CV79
Trinity Ch. Rd.
Somerville Rd. SE20 107 DX94
Somerville Rd., Cob. 128 CA114
Somerville Rd., Rom. 68 EW58
Sonderburg Rd. N7 63 DM61
Sondes St. SE17 92 DR79
Sonia Clo., Wat. 44 BW45
Sonia Ct., Har. 59 CF58
Sonia Gdns. N12 48 DC49
Woodside Ave.
Sonia Gdns. NW10 61 CT63
Sonia Gdns., Houns. 86 CA80
Sonnet Wk., West. 150 EH118
Kings Rd.
Sonning Gdns., Hmptn. 100 BY93
Sonning Rd. SE25 120 DU100
Soper Clo. E4 51 DZ50
Soper Dr., Cat. 148 DQ121
Coulsdon Rd.
Sopers Rd. (Cuffley), Pot.B. 21 DM29
Sophia Clo. N7 77 DM65
Mackenzie Rd.
Sophia Rd. E10 65 EB60
Sophia Rd. E16 80 EH72
Sophia Sq. SE16 79 DY73
Rotherhithe St.
Sopwith Ave., Chess. 130 CL106
Sopwith Clo., Kings.T. 102 CM92
Sopwith Clo., West. 150 EK116
Sopwith Dr., W.Byf. 126 BL112
Sopwith Dr., Wey. 126 BL111
Sopwith Rd., Houns. 86 BW80
Sopwith Way SW8 91 DH80
Sopwith Way, Kings.T. 116 CL95
Sorbie Clo., Wey. 127 BR107
Sorrel Bank, Croy. 135 DY110
Sorrel Clo. SE28 82 EU74
Sorrel Gdns. E6 80 EL71
Sorrel La. E14 79 ED72
Sorrel Wk., Rom. 69 FF55
Sorrell Clo. SE14 93 DY80
Southerngate Way
Sorrento Rd., Sutt. 118 DA104
Sotheby Rd. N5 64 DQ62
Sotheran Clo. E8 78 DU67
Sotheron Rd. SW6 90 DB80
Sotheron Rd., Wat. 30 BW41
Soudan Rd. SW11 90 DF81
Souldern Rd. W14 89 CX76
Souldern St., Wat. 29 BV43
Sounds Lo., Swan. 125 FC100
South Access Rd. E17 65 DY59
South Acre NW9 47 CT54
South Africa Rd. W12 75 CV74
South App., Nthwd. 43 BR48
South Audley St. W1 8 G1
South Audley St. W1 76 DG73
South Ave. E4 51 EB45
South Ave., Cars. 132 DG108
South Ave., Rich. 88 CN82
Sandycoombe Rd.
South Ave., Sthl. 72 BZ73
South Ave., Walt. 127 BS110
South Ave. Gdns., Sthl. 72 BZ73
South Bank, Chis. 109 EQ90
South Bank, Surb. 116 CL100
South Bank Ter., Surb. 116 CL100
South Birkbeck Rd. E11 65 ED62
South Black Lion La. W6 89 CU78
South Bolton Gdns. SW5 90 DB78
South Border, The, Pur. 133 DK111
South Carriage Dr. SW1 90 DE75
South Carriage Dr. SW7 8 B4
South Carriage Dr. SW7 90 DE75
South Clo. N6 63 DH58
South Clo., Barn. 33 CZ41
South Clo., Bexh. 96 EX84
South Clo., Dag. 82 FA67
South Clo., Mord. 118 DB100
Green La.
South Clo., Pnr. 58 BZ59
South Clo., St.Alb. 16 CB25
South Clo., Twick. 100 CA90
South Clo., West Dr. 84 BM76
South Colonnade E14 79 EA74
South Common Rd., Uxb. 70 BL65
South Countess Rd. E17 65 DZ55
South Cres. E16 79 ED70
South Cres. WC1 5 M7
South Cres. WC1 77 DK71
South Cross Rd., Ilf. 67 EQ57
South Croxted Rd. SE21 106 DR90
South Dene NW7 46 CR48
South Dr., Bans. 132 DE113
South Dr., Couls. 147 DK115
South Dr., Orp. 137 ES106
South Dr. (Cuffley), Pot.B. 21 DL30
South Dr., Ruis. 57 BS60
South Dr., Sutt. 131 CY110
South Ealing Rd. W5 87 CK75
South Eastern Ave. N9 50 DT48
South Eaton Pl. SW1 8 G8
South Eaton Pl. SW1 90 DG77
South Eden Pk. Rd., Beck. 121 EB100
South Edwardes Sq. W8 89 CZ76
South End W8 90 DB76
St. Albans Gro.
South End, Croy. 134 DQ105
South End Clo. NW3 62 DE63
South End Rd. NW3 62 DE63
South End Rd., Horn. 83 FH65
South End Rd., Rain. 83 FG68
South End Row W8 90 DB76
South Esk Rd. E7 80 EJ65
South Gdns. SW19 104 DD94
South Gate Ave., Felt. 99 BR91
South Gipsy Rd., Well. 96 EX83
South Glade, The, Bex. 110 EZ88
Camden Rd.
South Grn. NW9 46 CS53
Clayton Fld.
South Gro. E17 65 DZ57
South Gro. N6 62 DG60
South Gro. N15 64 DR57
South Gro. Ho. N6 62 DG60
Highgate W. Hill
South Hall Dr., Rain. 83 FH71
South Hill, Chis. 109 EM93
South Hill Ave., Har. 58 CC62
South Hill Gro., Har. 59 CE63
South Hill Pk. NW3 62 DE63
South Hill Pk. Gdns. NW3 62 DE63
South Hill Rd., Brom. 122 EE97
South Huxley N18 50 DR50
South Island Pl. SW9 91 DM80
South Kensington Sta. Arc. SW7 90 DD77
Pelham St.
South Lambeth Pl. SW8 91 DL79
South Lambeth Rd. SW8 91 DL79
South La., Kings.T. 115 CK97
South La., N.Mal. 116 CR98
South La. W., N.Mal. 116 CR98
South Lo. Ave., Mitch. 119 DL98
South Lo. Cres., Enf. 35 DK42
South Lo. Dr. N14 35 DK42
South Mall N9 50 DU48
Plevna Rd.
South Mead NW9 47 CT53
South Mead, Epsom 130 CS108
South Meadows, Wem. 60 CM64
South Molton La. W1 5 H9
South Molton La. W1 77 DH72
South Molton Rd. E16 80 EG72
South Molton St. W1 5 H9
South Molton St. W1 77 DH72
South Norwood Hill SE25 120 DS95
South Oak Rd. SW16 105 DM91
South Par. SW3 8 A10
South Par. SW3 90 DD78
South Par. W4 88 CR77
South Par., Wal.Abb. 23 EC33
Sun St.
South Pk. SW6 90 DA82
South Pk., Sev. 155 FH125
South Pk. Cres. SE6 108 EF88
South Pk. Cres., Ilf. 67 ER62
South Pk. Dr., Bark. 67 ES62
South Pk. Dr., Ilf. 67 ES61
South Pk. Gro., N.Mal. 116 CQ98
South Pk. Hill Rd., S.Croy. 134 DR106
South Pk. Ms. SW6 90 DB83
South Pk. Rd. SW19 104 DA93
South Pk. Rd., Ilf. 67 ER62
South Pk. Ter., Ilf. 67 ES62
South Pk. Way, Ruis. 72 BW65
South Penge Pk. Est. SE20 120 DV96
South Perimeter Rd., Uxb. 70 BL69
Kingston La.
South Pl. EC2 7 L7
South Pl. EC2 78 DR71
South Pl., Enf. 36 DW43
South Pl., Surb. 116 CM101
South Pl. Ms. EC2 7 L7
South Ridge, Wey. 127 BP110
South Riding, St.Alb. 16 CA30
South Ri., Cars. 132 DE109
South Ri. Way SE18 95 ER78
South Rd. N9 50 DU46
South Rd. SE23 107 DX89
South Rd. SW19 104 DC93
South Rd. W5 87 CK77
South Rd., Edg. 46 CP53
South Rd., Erith 97 FF80
South Rd., Felt. 100 BX92
South Rd., Hmptn. 100 BY93
South Rd. (Chadwell Heath), Rom. 68 EY58
South Rd. (Little Heath), Rom. 68 EW57
South Rd., Sthl. 86 BZ75
South Rd., Twick. 101 CD90
South Rd., West Dr. 84 BN76
South Rd., Wey. 127 BQ106
South Rd. (St. George's Hill), Wey. 126 BN110
South Row SE3 94 EF82
South Sea St. SE16 93 DZ76
South Side W6 89 CT76
South Sq. NW11 62 DB58
South Sq. WC1 6 D7
South St. W1 8 G2
South St. W1 76 DG74
South St., Brom. 122 EG96
South St., Enf. 36 DW43
South St., Epsom 130 CR113
South St., Islw. 87 CG83
South St., Rain. 83 FC68
South St., Rom. 69 FE57
South Tenter St. E1 78 DT73
South Ter. SW7 8 B8
South Ter. SW7 90 DE77
South Ter., Surb. 116 CL100
South Vale SE19 106 DS93
South Vale, Har. 59 CE63
South Vw., Brom. 122 EH96
South Vw. Dr. E18 66 EH55
South Vw. Rd. N8 63 DK55
South Vw. Rd., Ash. 143 CK119
South Vw. Rd., Loug. 39 EM44
South Vw. Rd., Pnr. 43 BV51
South Vill. NW1 77 DK65
South Wk., Hayes 71 BR71
Middleton Rd.
South Wk., W.Wick. 122 EE104
South Way N9 50 DW47
South Way N11 49 DJ51
Ringway
South Way, Abb.L. 15 BR33
South Way, Brom. 122 EG101
South Way, Cars. 132 DD110
South Way, Croy. 121 DY104
South Way, Har. 58 CA56
South Way, Wem. 60 CN64
South Weald Dr., Wal.Abb. 23 ED33
South W. India Dock Entrance E14 93 EC75
South Western Rd., Twick. 101 CG86
South Wf. Rd. W2 76 DD72
South Woodford to Barking Relief Rd. E11 66 EJ55
South Woodford to Barking Relief Rd. E12 67 EN63
South Woodford to Barking Relief Rd. E18 66 EJ55
South Woodford to Barking Relief Rd., Bark. 67 EN63
South Woodford to Barking Relief Rd., Ilf. 66 EJ55
South Worple Ave. SW14 88 CS83
South Worple Way
South Worple Way SW14 88 CR83
Southacre Way, Pnr. 44 BW53
Southall La., Houns. 85 BV79
Southall La., Sthl. 85 BV79
Southall Pl. SE1 11 K5
Southall Pl. SE1 92 DR75
Southam St. W10 75 CY70
Southampton Bldgs. WC2 6 D7
Southampton Gdns., Mitch. 119 DL99
Southampton Pl. WC1 6 A7
Southampton Pl. WC1 77 DL71
Southampton Rd. NW5 62 DF64
Southampton Rd., Houns. 98 BL86
Southampton Row WC1 6 A6
Southampton Row WC1 77 DL71
Southampton St. WC2 6 A10
Southampton St. WC2 77 DL73
Southampton Way SE5 92 DR80
Southbank, T.Ditt. 115 CH101
Southborough Clo., Surb. 115 CK102
Southborough La., Brom. 122 EL99
Southborough Rd. E9 79 DX66
Southborough Rd., Brom. 122 EL97
Southborough Rd., Surb. 116 CL102
Southbourne, Brom. 122 EG101
Southbourne Ave. NW9 46 CQ54
Southbourne Clo., Pnr. 58 BY59
Southbourne Cres. NW4 61 CY56
Southbourne Gdns. SE12 108 EH85
Southbourne Gdns., Ilf. 67 EQ64
Southbourne Gdns., Ruis. 57 BV60
Southbridge Pl., Croy. 134 DQ105
Southbridge Rd., Croy. 134 DQ105
Southbridge Way, Sthl. 86 BY75
Southbrook Dr. (Cheshunt), Wal.Cr. 23 DX28
Southbrook Ms. SE12 108 EF86
Southbrook Rd. SE12 108 EF86
Southbrook Rd. SW16 119 DL95
Southbury Ave., Enf. 36 DU43
Southbury Rd., Enf. 36 DR41
Southchurch Rd. E6 81 EM68
Southcombe St. W14 89 CY77
Southcote Ave., Felt. 99 BT89
Southcote Ave., Surb. 116 CP101
Southcote Ri., Ruis. 57 BR59
Southcote Rd. E17 65 DX57
Southcote Rd. N19 63 DJ63
Southcote Rd. SE25 120 DV99
Southcote Rd., S.Croy. 134 DS110
Southcroft Ave., Well. 95 ES83
Southcroft Ave., W.Wick. 121 EC103
Southcroft Rd. SW16 105 DH93
Southcroft Rd. SW17 104 DG93
Southcroft Rd., Orp. 123 ES104
Southdale, Chig. 53 ER51
Southdean Gdns. SW19 103 CZ89
Southdene, Sev. 138 EZ113
Southdown Ave. W7 87 CG76
Southdown Cres., Har. 58 CC60
Southdown Cres., Ilf. 67 ES57
Southdown Dr. SW20 103 CX94
Crescent Rd.
Southdown Rd. SW20 117 CX95
Southdown Rd., Cars. 132 DG109
Southdown Rd., Cat. 149 DZ122
Southdown Rd., Horn. 69 FH59
Southdown Rd., Walt. 128 BY105
Southend Clo. SE9 109 EP86
Southend Cres. SE9 109 EP86
Southend La. SE6 107 EA91
Southend La. SE26 107 DZ91
Southend La., Wal.Abb. 24 EH34
Southend Rd. E4 51 DZ51
Southend Rd. E6 81 EM66
Southend Rd. E17 51 ED53
Southend Rd. E18 52 EF54
Southend Rd., Beck. 107 EA94
Southend Rd., Wdf.Grn. 52 EJ54
Southerland Clo., Wey. 127 BQ105
Southern Ave. SE25 120 DT97
Southern Ave., Felt. 99 BU88
Southern Dr., Loug. 39 EM44
Southern Gro. E3 79 DZ69
Southern Perimeter Rd., Houns. 98 BJ85
Southern Pl., Swan. 125 FD98
Southern Rd. E13 80 EH68
Southern Rd. N2 62 DF56
Southern Row W10 75 CY70
Southern St. N1 77 DM68
Southern Way, Rom. 68 FA58
Southerngate Way SE14 93 DY80
Southernhay, Loug. 38 EK42
Southerns La., Couls. 146 DD124
Southerton Rd. W6 89 CW76
Southey Rd. N15 64 DS57
Southey Rd. SW9 91 DN81
Southey Rd. SW19 104 DA94
Southey St. SE20 107 DX94
Southfield, Barn. 33 CX44
Southfield Ave., Wat. 30 BW38
Southfield Clo., Uxb. 70 BN69
Southfield Cotts. W7 87 CF75
Oaklands Rd.
Southfield Gdns., Twick. 101 CF91
Southfield Pk., Har. 58 CB56
Southfield Pl., Wey. 127 BP108
Southfield Rd. N17 50 DS54
Southfield Rd. W4 88 CR75
Southfield Rd., Chis. 123 ET97
Southfield Rd., Enf. 36 DV44
Southfield Rd., Wal.Cr. 23 DY32
Southfields NW4 61 CV55
Southfields, E.Mol. 115 CE100
Southfields, Swan. 111 FE94
Southfields Ave., Ashf. 99 BP93
Southfields Ct. SW19 103 CY88
Southfields Pas. SW18 104 DA86
Southfields Rd.
Southfields Rd. SW18 104 DA86
Southfields Rd., Cat. 149 EB124
Southfleet Rd., Orp. 123 ES104
Southgate Ave., Felt. 99 BR91
Southgate Circ. N14 49 DK46
The Bourne
Southgate Gro. N1 78 DR66
Southgate Rd. N1 78 DR67
Southgate Rd., Barn. 34 DD35
Southgate Rd., Pot.B. 20 DC33
Southholme Clo. SE19 120 DT95
Southill La., Pnr. 57 BV56
Southill Rd., Chis. 108 EL93
Southill St. E14 79 EB72
Chrisp St.
Southland Rd. SE18 95 ET80
Southland Way, Houns. 101 CD85
Southlands Ave., Orp. 137 ER105
Southlands Clo., Couls. 147 DM117
Southlands Gro., Brom. 122 EL97
Southlands Rd., Brom. 122 EJ99
Southly Clo., Sutt. 118 DA104
Southmead Cres. (Cheshunt), Wal.Cr. 23 DY30
Southmead Rd. SW19 103 CY88
Southmont Rd., Esher 115 CE103
Southmoor Way E9 79 DZ65
Southold Ri. SE9 109 EM90
Southolm St. SW11 91 DH81
Southover N12 48 DA48
Southover, Brom. 108 EG92
Southport Rd. SE18 95 ER77
Southridge Pl. SW20 103 CX94
Southsea Ave., Wat. 29 BU42
Southsea Rd., Kings.T. 116 CL98
Southside Common SW19 103 CW93
Southspring, Sid. 109 ER87
Southvale Rd. SE3 94 EE82
Southview Ave. NW10 61 CT64
Southview Clo. SW17 104 DG92
Southview Clo., Bex. 110 EZ86
Southview Clo., Swan. 125 FG98
Southview Clo. (Cheshunt), Wal.Cr. 22 DS26
Southview Cres., Ilf. 67 EP58
Southview Gdns., Wall. 133 DJ108
Southview Rd., Brom. 107 ED91
Southview Rd., Cat. 149 EB124
Southview Rd., Warl. 148 DV119
Southviews, S.Croy. 135 DX109
Southville SW8 91 DK81
Southville Clo., Epsom 130 CR109
Southville Clo., Felt. 99 BS88
Southville Cres., Felt. 99 BS88
Southville Rd., Felt. 99 BS88
Southville Rd., T.Ditt. 115 CG101
Southwark Bri. EC4 11 J1
Southwark Bri. EC4 78 DQ74
Southwark Bri. SE1 11 J1
Southwark Bri. SE1 78 DQ74
Southwark Bri. Rd. SE1 11 H5
Southwark Bri. Rd. SE1 91 DP76
Southwark Gro. SE1 11 H3
Southwark Pk. Est. SE16 92 DV77
Southwark Pk. Rd. SE16 92 DT77
Southwark Pl., Brom. 123 EM97
St. Georges Rd.
Southwark St. SE1 10 G2
Southwark St. SE1 77 DP74
Southwater Clo. E14 79 DZ72
Southwater Clo., Beck. 107 EB94
Southway N20 48 DA47
Southway NW7 47 CU52
Southway NW11 62 DB57
Southway SW20 117 CW98
Southway, Wall. 133 DJ105
Southwell Ave., Nthlt. 72 CA65
Southwell Gdns. SW7 90 DC77
Southwell Gro. Rd. E11 66 EE61
Southwell Rd. SE5 92 DQ83
Southwell Rd., Croy. 119 DN100
Southwell Rd., Har. 59 CK58
Southwest Rd. E11 65 ED60
Southwick Ms. W2 4 A8
Southwick Pl. W2 4 B9
Southwick Pl. W2 76 DE72
Southwick St. W2 4 B8
Southwick St. W2 76 DE72
Southwold Dr., Bark. 68 EU64
Southwold Rd. E5 64 DV61
Southwold Rd., Bex. 111 FB86
Southwold Rd., Wat. 30 BW38
Southwood Ave. N6 63 DH59
Southwood Ave., Couls. 147 DJ115
Southwood Ave., Kings.T. 116 CQ95

Southwood Clo., Brom. 123 EM98
Southwood Clo., Wor.Pk. 117 CX102
Carters Clo.
Southwood Dr., Surb. 116 CQ101
Southwood Gdns., Esher 115 CG104
Southwood Gdns., Ilf. 67 EP56
Southwood La. N6 62 DG59
Southwood Lawn Rd. N6 62 DG59
Southwood Rd. SE9 109 EP89
Southwood Rd. SE28 82 EV74
Southwood Smith St. N1 77 DN67
Barford St.
Soval Ct., Nthwd. 43 BR52
Maxwell Rd.
Sovereign Clo. E1 78 DV73
Sovereign Clo. W5 73 CJ71
Sovereign Clo., Ruis. 57 BS60
Sovereign Ct., Brom. 123 EM99
Sovereign Ct., W.Mol. 114 BZ98
Sovereign Cres. SE16 79 DY74
Rotherhithe St.
Sovereign Gro., Wem. 59 CK62
Sovereign Ms. E2 78 DT68
Pearson St.
Sovereign Pk. NW10 74 CP70
Sovereign Pl., Kings L. 14 BN29
Sovereign Rd., Bark. 82 EW69
Sowerby Clo. SE9 108 EL85
Sowrey Ave., Rain. 83 FF65
Spa Clo. SE25 120 DS95
Spa Dr., Epsom 130 CN114
Spa Grn. Est. EC1 6 E2
Spa Hill SE19 120 DR95
Spa Rd. SE16 11 P7
Spa Rd. SE16 92 DT76
Space Waye, Felt. 99 BU85
Spafield St. EC1 6 D4
Spalding Rd. NW4 61 CW58
Spalding Rd. SW17 105 DH92
Spanby Rd. E3 79 EA70
Spaniards Clo. NW11 62 DD60
Spaniards End NW3 62 DC60
Spaniards Rd. NW3 62 DC62
Spanish Pl. W1 4 G8
Spanish Pl. W1 76 DG72
Spanish Rd. SW18 104 DC85
Spareleaze Hill, Loug. 38 EL43
Sparkbridge Rd., Har. 59 CE56
Sparks Clo. W3 74 CR72
Joseph Ave.
Sparks Clo., Dag. 68 EX61
Sparks Clo., Hmptn. 100 BY93
Victors Dr.
Sparrow Clo., Hmptn. 100 BY93
Sparrow Dr., Orp. 123 EQ102
Sparrow Fm. Dr., Felt. 100 BW86
Sparrow Fm. Rd., Epsom 131 CU105
Sparrow Grn., Dag. 69 FB62
Sparrows Herne (Bushey), Wat. 44 CB45
Sparrows La. SE9 109 EQ87
Sparrows Way (Bushey), Wat. 44 CC46
Sparrows Herne
Sparsholt Rd. N19 63 DM60
Sparsholt Rd., Bark. 81 ES67
Sparta St. SE10 93 EC81
Spear Ms. SW5 90 DA77
Spearman St. SE18 95 EN79
Spearpoint Gdns., Ilf. 67 ET56
Spears Rd. N19 63 DL60
Speart La., Houns. 86 BY80
Spedan Clo. NW3 62 DB62
Speed Ho. EC2 78 DR71
Silk St.
Speedbird Way, West Dr. 84 BH80
Tarmac Way
Speedwell St. SE8 93 EA80
Comet St.
Speedy Pl. WC1 5 P3
Speer Rd., T.Ditt. 115 CF101
Speke Ho. SE5 92 DQ80
Speke Rd., Th.Hth. 120 DR96
Spekehill SE9 109 EM90
Speldhurst Clo., Brom. 122 EG99
Speldhurst Rd. E9 79 DX66
Speldhurst Rd. W4 88 CR76
Spellbrook Wk. N1 78 DQ67
Basire St.
Spelman St. E1 78 DU71
Spelthorne Gro., Sun. 99 BT94
Spelthorne La., Ashf. 113 BQ95
Spence Ave., W.Byf. 126 BL114
Spence Clo. SE16 93 DZ75
Vaughan St.
Spencer Ave. N13 49 DM51
Spencer Ave., Hayes 71 BU71
Spencer Ave. (Cheshunt), Wal.Cr. 22 DS26
Spencer Clo. N3 48 DA54
Spencer Clo. NW10 74 CM69
Spencer Clo., Epsom 144 CS119
Spencer Clo., Orp. 123 ES103
Spencer Clo., Uxb. 70 BJ69
Spencer Clo., Wdf.Grn. 52 EJ50
Spencer Ct. NW8 76 DC68
Marlborough Pl.
Spencer Dr. N2 62 DC58
Spencer Gdns. SE9 109 EM85
Spencer Gdns. SW14 102 CQ85
Spencer Hill SW19 103 CY93
Spencer Hill Rd. SW19 103 CY94
Spencer Ms. W6 89 CY79
Greyhound Rd.
Spencer Pk. SW18 104 DD85
Spencer Pas. E2 78 DV68
Pritchard's Rd.
Spencer Pl. N1 77 DP66
Canonbury La.
Spencer Pl., Croy. 120 DR101
Gloucester Rd.
Spencer Ri. NW5 63 DH63
Spencer Rd. E6 80 EK67
Spencer Rd. E17 51 EC54
Spencer Rd. N8 63 DM57
Spencer Rd. N11 49 DH49
Spencer Rd. N17 50 DU53
Spencer Rd. SW18 90 DD84
Spencer Rd. SW20 117 CV95
Spencer Rd. W3 74 CQ74
Spencer Rd. W4 88 CQ80
Spencer Rd., Brom. 108 EF94
Spencer Rd., Cat. 148 DR121
Spencer Rd., Cob. 141 BV115
Spencer Rd., E.Mol. 115 CD98
Spencer Rd., Har. 45 CE54
Spencer Rd., Ilf. 67 ET60
Spencer Rd., Islw. 86 CC81
Spencer Rd., Mitch. 118 DG97
Spencer Rd. (Beddington), Mitch. 118 DG101
Spencer Rd., Rain. 83 FD69
Spencer Rd., S.Croy. 134 DS106
Spencer Rd., Twick. 101 CE90
Spencer Rd., Wem. 59 CJ61
Spencer St. EC1 6 F3
Spencer St. EC1 77 DP69
Spencer St., Sthl. 86 BX75
Spencer Wk. NW3 62 DC63
Hampstead High St.
Spencer Wk. SW15 89 CX84
Spencer Wk., Rick. 28 BJ43
Spenser Ave., Wey. 126 BN109
Spenser Gro. N16 64 DS63
Spenser Rd. SE24 105 DN85
Spenser St. SW1 9 L6
Spenser St. SW1 91 DJ76
Spensley Wk. N16 64 DR62
Clissold Rd.
Speranza St. SE18 95 ET78
Sperling Rd. N17 50 DS54
Spert St. E14 79 DY73
Spey St. E14 79 EC71
Spey Way, Rom. 55 FE52
Speyside N14 35 DJ44
Spezia Rd. NW10 75 CU68
Spicer Clo. SW9 91 DP82
Spicer Clo., Walt. 114 BW100
Spicers Fld., Lthd. 129 CD113
Spicersfield (Cheshunt), Wal.Cr. 22 DU27
Spice's Yd., Croy. 134 DQ105
Spiers Clo., N.Mal. 117 CT100
Spigurnell Rd. N17 50 DR53
Spikes Bri. Rd., Sthl. 72 BY72
Spilsby Clo. NW9 46 CS54
Kenley Ave.
Spindlewood Gdns., Croy. 134 DS105
Spindlewoods, Tad. 145 CV122
Spindrift Ave. E14 93 EA77
Spinel Clo. SE18 95 ET78
Spinnells Rd., Har. 58 BZ60
Spinney, The N21 49 DN45
Spinney, The SW16 105 DJ90
Spinney, The, Barn. 34 DB40
Spinney, The, Epsom 145 CV118
Spinney, The, Lthd. 128 CC112
Spinney, The (Great Bookham), Lthd. 142 CB124
Spinney, The, Pot.B. 20 DD31
Spinney, The, Pur. 133 DP111
Spinney, The, Sid. 110 EY91
Spinney, The, Stan. 46 CL49
Spinney, The, Sun. 113 BU95
Spinney, The, Sutt. 131 CW105
Spinney, The, Swan. 125 FE96
Spinney, The, Wat. 29 BU39
Spinney, The, Wem. 59 CG62
Spinney Clo., Cob. 128 CA111
Spinney Clo., N.Mal. 116 CS99
Spinney Clo., Rain. 83 FE68
Spinney Clo., West Dr. 70 BL73
Yew Ave.
Spinney Dr., Felt. 99 BQ87
Spinney Gdns. SE19 106 DT92
Spinney Gdns., Dag. 68 EY64
Spinney Oak, Brom. 122 EL96
Spinney Way, Sev. 137 ER111
Spinneycroft, Lthd. 143 CD115
Spinneys, The, Brom. 123 EM96
Spirit Quay E1 78 DU74
Smeaton St.
Spital Sq. E1 7 N6
Spital Sq. E1 78 DS71
Spital St. E1 78 DU71
Spital Yd. E1 7 N6
Spitalfields Mkt. E1 7 P6
Spitalfields Mkt. E1 78 DT71
Spitfire Est., Houns. 86 BW78
Spitfire Way, Houns. 86 BW78
Splendour Wk. SE16 92 DW78
Verney Rd.
Spode Wk. NW6 76 DB65
Lymington Rd.
Spondon Rd. N15 64 DU56
Spoonbill Way, Hayes 72 BX71
Spooner Wk., Wall. 133 DK106
Spooners Dr., St.Alb. 16 CC27
Sportsbank St. SE6 107 EC87
Spottons Gro. N17 50 DQ53
Gospatrick Rd.
Spout Hill, Croy. 135 EA106
Spout La., Stai. 98 BG85
Spout La. N., Stai. 84 BH84
Spratt Hall Rd. E11 66 EG58
Spray La., Twick. 101 CE86
Kneller Rd.
Spray St. SE18 95 EP77
Spreighton Rd., W.Mol. 114 CB98
Spriggs Oak, Epp. 26 EU29
Palmers Hill
Sprimont Pl. SW3 8 D10
Sprimont Pl. SW3 90 DF77
Spring Bri. Ms. W5 73 CK73
Spring Bri. Rd.
Spring Bri. Rd. W5 73 CK73
Spring Clo., Barn. 33 CX43
Spring Clo., Borwd. 32 CN39
Spring Clo., Dag. 68 EX60
Spring Clo., Uxb. 42 BK53
Spring Clo. La., Sutt. 131 CY107
Spring Cotts., Surb. 115 CK99
St. Leonard's Rd.
Spring Ct., Sid. 110 EU90
Station Rd.
Spring Ct. Rd., Enf. 35 DN38
Spring Cfts. (Bushey), Wat. 30 CA43
Spring Dr., Pnr. 57 BU58
Eastcote Rd.
Spring Gdns. N5 64 DQ64
Grosvenor Ave.
Spring Gdns. SW1 9 N2
Spring Gdns., Horn. 69 FH63
Spring Gdns., Orp. 138 EV107
Spring Gdns., Rom. 69 FC57
Spring Gdns., Wall. 133 DJ106
Spring Gdns., Wat. 30 BW35
Spring Gdns., W.Mol. 114 CC99
Spring Gdns., West. 150 EJ118
Spring Gdns., Wdf.Grn. 52 EJ52
Spring Gdns. Ind. Est., Rom. 69 FC57
Spring Gro. SE19 106 DT94
Alma Pl.
Spring Gro. W4 88 CN78
Spring Gro., Hmptn. 114 CB95
Plevna Rd.
Spring Gro., Lthd. 142 CB123
Spring Gro., Loug. 38 EK44
Spring Gro., Mitch. 118 DG95
Spring Gro. Cres., Houns. 86 CC81
Spring Gro. Rd., Houns. 86 CB81
Spring Gro. Rd., Islw. 87 CD81
Spring Gro. Rd., Rich. 102 CM85
Spring Hill E5 64 DU59
Spring Hill SE26 106 DW91
Spring Lake, Stan. 45 CH49
Spring La. E5 64 DV59
Spring La. N10 62 DG55
Spring La. SE25 120 DV100
Spring Ms. W1 4 E6
Spring Ms., Epsom 131 CT109
Old Schools La.
Spring Pk. Ave., Croy. 121 DX103
Spring Pk. Dr. N4 64 DQ60
Spring Pk. Rd., Croy. 121 DX103
Spring Pas. SW15 89 CX83
Embankment
Spring Path NW3 62 DD64
Spring Pl. NW5 63 DH64
Spring Rd., Felt. 99 BT90
Spring Shaw Rd., Orp. 124 EU95
Spring St. W2 76 DD72
Spring St., Epsom 131 CT109
Spring Ter., Rich. 102 CL85
Spring Vale, Bexh. 97 FB84
Spring Vale Clo., Swan. 111 FF94
Spring Vill. Rd., Edg. 46 CN52
Spring Wk. E1 78 DU71
Old Montague St.
Springall St. SE15 92 DV80
Springbank N21 35 DM44
Springbank Rd. SE13 107 ED86
Springbank Wk. NW1 77 DK66
St. Paul's Cres.
Springbourne Ct., Beck. 121 EC95
Springclose La., Sutt. 131 CY107
Springcroft Ave. N2 62 DF56
Springdale Ms. N16 64 DR63
Springdale Rd.
Springdale Rd. N16 64 DR63
Springfield E5 64 DV60
Springfield, Epp. 25 ET32
Springfield (Bushey), Wat. 45 CD46
Springfield Ave. N10 63 DJ55
Springfield Ave. SW20 117 CZ97
Springfield Ave., Hmptn. 100 CB93
Springfield Ave., Swan. 125 FF98
Springfield Clo. N12 48 DB50
Springfield Clo., Pot.B. 20 DD31
Springfield Clo., Rick. 29 BP43
Springfield Clo., Stan. 45 CG48
Springfield Dr., Ilf. 67 EQ58
Springfield Dr., Lthd. 143 CE119
Springfield Gdns. E5 64 DV60
Springfield Gdns. NW9 60 CR57
Springfield Gdns., Brom. 123 EM98
Springfield Gdns., Ruis. 57 BV60
Springfield Gdns., W.Wick. 121 EB103
Springfield Gdns., Wdf.Grn. 52 EJ52
Springfield Gro. SE7 94 EJ79
Springfield Gro., Sun. 113 BT95
Springfield La. NW6 76 DB67
Springfield La., Wey. 127 BP105
Springfield Meadows, Wey. 127 BP105
Springfield Mt. NW9 60 CR57
Springfield Pl., N.Mal. 116 CQ98
Springfield Ri. SE26 106 DV90
Springfield Rd. E4 52 EE46
Springfield Rd. E6 81 EM66
Springfield Rd. E15 80 EE69
Springfield Rd. E17 65 DZ58
Springfield Rd. N11 49 DH50
Springfield Rd. N15 64 DU56
Springfield Rd. NW8 76 DC67
Springfield Rd. SE26 106 DV92
Springfield Rd. SW19 103 CZ92
Springfield Rd. W7 73 CE74
Springfield Rd., Ashf. 98 BM92
Springfield Rd., Bexh. 97 FB83
Springfield Rd., Brom. 123 EM98
Springfield Rd., Epsom 131 CW110
Springfield Rd., Har. 59 CE58
Springfield Rd., Hayes 72 BW74
Springfield Rd., Kings.T. 116 CL97
Springfield Rd., Tedd. 101 CG92
Springfield Rd., Th.Hth. 120 DQ95
Springfield Rd., Twick. 100 CA88
Springfield Rd., Wall. 132 DG106
Springfield Rd. (Cheshunt), Wal.Cr. 23 DY32
Springfield Rd., Wat. 15 BV33
Haines Way
Springfield Rd., Well. 96 EV83
Springfield Wk. NW6 76 DB67
Springfield Wk., Orp. 123 ER102
Place Fm. Ave.
Springfields, Wal.Abb. 24 EE34
Springfields Clo., Cher. 112 BH102
Springhead Rd., Erith 97 FF79
Springhill Clo. SE5 92 DR83
Springholm Clo., West. 150 EJ118
Springhurst Clo., Croy. 135 DZ105
Springpark Dr., Beck. 121 EC97
Springpond Rd., Dag. 68 EY64
Springrice Rd. SE13 107 ED86
Springs, The, Brox. 23 DY25
Springshaw Clo., Sev. 154 FD123
Springvale Ave., Brent. 88 CL78
Springvale Est. W14 89 CY76
Blythe Rd.
Springvale Ter. W14 89 CX76
Springvale Way, Orp. 124 EW97
Springwater Clo. SE18 95 EN81
Springwell Ave. NW10 75 CT67
Springwell Ave., Rick. 42 BG47
Springwell Clo. SW16 105 DN91
Etherstone Rd.
Springwell Ct., Houns. 86 BX82
Springwell La., Rick. 42 BG47
Springwell La., Uxb. 42 BH50
Springwell Rd. SW16 105 DN91
Springwell Rd., Houns. 86 BX82
Springwood (Cheshunt), Wal.Cr. 22 DU26
Springwood Clo., Uxb. 42 BK53
Springwood Cres., Edg. 46 CP47
Springwood Way, Rom. 69 FG57
Sprowston Ms. E7 80 EG65
Sprowston Rd. E7 66 EG64
Spruce Ct. W5 88 CL76
Elderberry Rd.
Spruce Hills Rd. E17 51 EC54
Spruce Pk., Brom. 122 EF98
Cumberland Rd.
Spruce Rd., West. 150 EK116
Spruce Way, St.Alb. 16 CB27
Sprucedale Clo., Swan. 125 FE96
Sprucedale Gdns., Croy. 135 DX105
Sprucedale Gdns., Wall. 133 DK109
Sprules Rd. SE4 93 DY82
Spur, The (Cheshunt), Wal.Cr. 23 DX28
Welsummer Way
Spur Clo., Abb.L. 15 BR33
Spur Clo., Rom. 40 EV41
Spur Dr., Tad. 146 DB121
Spur Rd. N15 64 DR56
Philip La.
Spur Rd. SE1 91 DM75
Lower Marsh
Spur Rd. SW1 9 K5
Spur Rd. SW1 91 DJ75
Spur Rd., Bark. 81 EQ69
Spur Rd., Edg. 46 CL49
Spur Rd., Felt. 99 BV85
Spur Rd., Islw. 87 CH80
Spur Rd., Orp. 124 EU103
Spur Rd. Est., Edg. 46 CM49
Spurfield, W.Mol. 114 CB97
Spurgeon Ave. SE19 120 DR95
Spurgeon Rd. SE19 120 DR95
Spurgeon St. SE1 11 K7
Spurgeon St. SE1 92 DR76
Spurling Rd. SE22 92 DT84
Spurling Rd., Dag. 82 EZ65
Spurrell Ave., Bex. 111 FD91
Spurstowe Rd. E8 78 DV65
Marcon Pl.
Spurstowe Ter. E8 64 DV64
Square, The W6 89 CW78
Square, The, Cars. 132 DG106
Square, The, Hayes 71 BR74
Square, The, Ilf. 67 EN59
Square, The, Rich. 101 CK85
Square, The, Sev. 154 FE122
Amherst Hill
Square, The, Swan. 125 FD97
Square, The, Wat. 29 BV37
The Harebreaks
Square, The, West Dr. 84 BH81
Square, The, West. 150 EJ120
Square, The, Wey. 127 BQ106
Square, The, Wok. 140 BL116
Square, The, Wdf.Grn. 52 EG50
Square Rigger Row SW11 90 DC83
York Pl.
Squarey St. SW17 104 DC90
Squires Bri. Rd., Shep. 112 BM98
Squires Ct. SW19 104 DA91
Squires Ct., Cher. 112 BH102
Springfields Clo.
Squires Fld., Swan. 125 FF95
Squires La. N3 48 DB54
Squires Mt. NW3 62 DD62
East Heath Rd.
Squires Rd., Shep. 112 BM98
Squires Wk., Ashf. 99 BR94
Napier Rd.
Squires Way, Dart. 111 FD91
Squires Wd. Dr., Chis. 109 EM94
Squirrel Clo., Houns. 86 BW83
Squirrel Wd., W.Byf. 126 BH112
Dartnell Ave.
Squirrels, The SE13 93 ED83
Belmont Hill
Squirrels, The, Pnr. 58 BZ55
Squirrels, The (Bushey), Wat. 31 CD44
Squirrels Clo. N12 48 DC49
Woodside Ave.
Squirrels Clo., Uxb. 70 BN66
Squirrels Grn., Lthd. 142 CA123
Squirrels Grn., Wor.Pk. 117 CU103
The Ave.
Squirrels Heath Ave., Rom. 69 FH55
Squirrels La., Buck.H. 52 EK48
Squirrels Ms. W13 73 CG73
Squirrels Trd. Est., The, Hayes 85 BT76
Squirrels Way, Epsom 144 CR115
Squirries St. E2 78 DU69
Stable Clo., Nthlt. 72 CA68
Stable Wk. N2 48 DD53
Old Fm. Rd.
Stable Way W10 75 CW72
Latimer Rd.
Stable Yd. SW1 9 K4
Stable Yd. SW9 91 DM82
Broomgrove Rd.
Stable Yd. SW15 89 CW83
Danemere St.
Stable Yd. Rd. SW1 9 L4
Stable Yd. Rd. SW1 91 DJ75
Stables, The, Buck.H. 52 EJ45
Stables, The, Cob. 128 BZ114
Stables, The, Swan. 125 FH95
Stables End, Orp. 123 EQ104
Stables Ms. SE27 106 DQ92
Stables Way SE11 10 D10
Stables Way SE11 91 DN78
Stacey Ave. N18 50 DW49
Stacey Clo. E10 65 ED57
Halford Rd.
Stacey St. N7 63 DN62
Stacey St. WC2 5 N9
Stacey St. WC2 77 DK72
Stackhouse St. SW3 8 D6
Stacy Path SE5 92 DS80
Harris St.
Stadium Rd. NW2 61 CW59
Stadium Rd. SE18 95 EM80
Stadium St. SW10 90 DC80
Stadium Way, Dart. 111 FE86
Stadium Way, Wem. 60 CM63
Staff St. EC1 7 L3
Staffa Rd. E10 65 DX60
Stafford Clo. E17 65 DZ58
Stafford Clo. N14 35 DJ43
Stafford Clo. NW6 76 DA69
Stafford Clo., Cat. 148 DT123
Stafford Clo., Sutt. 131 CY107
Stafford Clo. (Cheshunt), Wal.Cr. 22 DV29
Stafford Ct. W8 90 DA76
Kensington High St.
Stafford Cross Ind. Est., Croy. 133 DM106
Stafford Gdns., Croy. 133 DM106
Stafford Pl. SW1 9 K6
Stafford Pl. SW1 91 DJ76
Stafford Pl., Rich. 102 CM87
Stafford Rd. E3 79 DZ68
Stafford Rd. E7 80 EJ66
Stafford Rd. NW6 76 DA69
Stafford Rd., Cat. 148 DT122
Stafford Rd., Croy. 133 DN105
Stafford Rd., Har. 44 CC52
Stafford Rd., N.Mal. 116 CQ97
Stafford Rd., Ruis. 57 BT63
Stafford Rd., Sid. 109 ES91
Stafford Rd., Wall. 133 DH107
Stafford Sq., Wey. 127 BR105
Rosslyn Pk.
Stafford St. W1 9 K2
Stafford St. W1 77 DJ74
Stafford Ter. W8 90 DA75
Stafford Way, Sev. 155 FJ127
Staffordshire St. SE15 92 DU81
Stag Clo., Edg. 46 CP54
Stag La. NW9 60 CQ55
Stag La. SW15 103 CT89
Stag La., Buck.H. 52 EH47
Stag La., Edg. 46 CP54
Stag Leys, Ash. 144 CL120
Stag Leys Clo., Bans. 146 DE115
Stag Pl. SW1 9 K6
Stag Pl. SW1 91 DJ76

This index reads in the sequence: Street Name / Postal District or Post Town / Map Page Number / Grid Reference

Stag Ride SW19	103	CT90
Stagbury Ave., Couls.	146	DE118
Stagbury Clo., Couls.	146	DE119
Stagg Hill, Barn.	34	DE36
Stagg Hill, Pot.B.	34	DD35
Staggart Grn., Chig.	54	EU51
Stags Way, Islw.	87	CF79
Stainash Cres., Stai.	98	BH92
Stainash Par., Stai.	98	BH92
Stainbank Rd., Mitch.	119	DH97
Stainby Clo., West Dr.	84	BL76
Stainby Rd. N15	64	DT56
Stainer Rd., Borwd.	31	CK39
Stainer St. SE1	**11**	**L3**
Stainer St. SE1	78	DR74
Staines Ave., Sutt.	117	CX103
Staines Bypass, Ashf.	98	BK92
Staines Hill, Barn.	34	DE36
Staines Rd., Felt.	99	BS87
Staines Rd., Houns.	100	BW85
Staines Rd., Ilf.	67	EQ63
Staines Rd., Stai.	98	BG94
Staines Rd., Twick.	100	CA90
Staines Rd. E., Sun.	99	BU94
Staines Rd. W., Ashf.	99	BP93
Staines Rd. W., Sun.	99	BP94
Staines Wk., Sid.	110	EW93
Evry Rd.		
Stainford Clo., Ashf.	99	BR92
Stainforth Rd. E17	65	EA56
Stainforth Rd., Ilf.	67	ER59
Staining La. EC2	**7**	**J8**
Staining La. EC2	78	DQ72
Royston St.		
Stainmore Clo., Chis.	123	ER95
Stains Clo. (Cheshunt),	23	DY28
Wal.Cr.		
Stainsbury St. E2	78	DW68
Royston St.		
Stainsby Pl. E14	79	EA72
Stainsby Rd. E14	79	EA72
Stainton Rd. SE6	107	ED86
Stainton Rd., Enf.	36	DW39
Stairfoot La., Sev.	154	FC122
Staithes Way, Tad.	145	CV120
Stalbridge St. NW1	**4**	**C6**
Stalham St. SE16	92	DV76
Stalisfield Pl., Orp.	137	EN110
Mill La.		
Stambourne Way SE19	106	DS94
Stambourne Way,	121	EC104
W.Wick.		
Stamford Brook Ave. W6	89	CT76
Stamford Brook Rd. W6	89	CT76
Stamford Clo. N15	64	DU56
Stamford Clo., Har.	45	CE52
Stamford Clo., Pot.B.	20	DD32
Stamford Clo., Sthl.	72	CA73
Stamford Cotts. SW10	90	DB80
Billing St.		
Stamford Ct. W6	89	CT77
Goldhawk Rd.		
Stamford Dr., Brom.	122	EF98
Stamford Gdns., Dag.	82	EW66
Stamford Grn. Rd.,	130	CP113
Epsom		
Stamford Gro. E. N16	64	DU60
Oldhill St.		
Stamford Gro. W. N16	64	DU60
Oldhill St.		
Stamford Hill N16	64	DT61
Stamford Hill Est. N16	64	DT60
Stamford Rd. E6	80	EL67
Stamford Rd. N1	78	DS66
Stamford Rd. N15	64	DU56
Stamford Rd., Dag.	82	EV67
Stamford Rd., Walt.	114	BX104
Kenilworth Dr.		
Stamford Rd., Wat.	29	BV40
Stamford St. SE1	**10**	**D3**
Stamford St. SE1	77	DN74
Stamp Pl. E2	**7**	**P2**
Stamp Pl. E2	78	DT69
Stanard Clo. N16	64	DS59
Stanborough Ave.,	32	CN37
Borwd.		
Stanborough Clo., Borwd.	32	CN38
Stanborough Clo., Hmptn.	100	BZ93
Stanborough Pk., Wat.	29	BV35
Stanborough Pas. E8	78	DT65
Abbot St.		
Stanborough Rd., Houns.	87	CD83
Stanbridge Pl. N21	49	DP47
Stanbridge Rd. SW15	89	CW83
Stanbrook Rd. SE2	96	EV75
Stanbury Ave., Wat.	29	BS37
Stanbury Rd. SE15	92	DV81
Stancroft NW9	60	CS57
Standale Gro., Ruis.	57	BQ57
Standard Ind. Est. E16	95	EM75
Standard Pl. EC2	**7**	**N3**
Standard Rd. NW10	74	CQ70
Standard Rd., Belv.	96	FA78
Standard Rd., Bexh.	96	EY84
Standard Rd., Enf.	37	DY37
Standard Rd., Houns.	86	BY83
Standard Rd., Orp.	137	EN110
Standen Rd. SW18	103	CZ87
Standfield, Abb.L.	15	BS31
Standfield Gdns., Dag.	82	FA65
Standfield Rd.		
Standfield Rd., Dag.	68	FA64
Standish Rd. W6	89	CU77
Standlake Pt. SE23	107	DX90
Stane Clo. SW19	118	DB95
Hayward Clo.		
... St., Lthd.	144	CM124
...e Rd.		
...y SE18	94	EL80

Stane Way, Epsom	131	CU110
Stanfield Rd. E3	79	DY68
Stanford Clo., Hmptn.	100	BZ93
Stanford Clo., Rom.	69	FB58
Stanford Clo., Ruis.	57	BQ58
Stanford Clo., Wdf.Grn.	52	EL50
Stanford Ct., Wal.Abb.	24	EG33
Stanford Ho., Bark.	82	EV68
Stanford Pl. SE17	**11**	**M9**
Stanford Rd. N11	48	DF50
Stanford Rd. SW16	119	DK96
Stanford Rd. W8	90	DB76
Stanford St. SW1	**9**	**M9**
Stanford Way SW16	119	DK96
Stangate Cres., Borwd.	32	CR43
Stangate Gdns., Stan.	45	CH49
Stanger Rd. SE25	120	DU98
Stanham Pl., Dart.	97	FG84
Crayford Way		
Stanhope Ave. N3	61	CZ55
Stanhope Ave., Brom.	122	EF102
Stanhope Ave., Har.	45	CD53
Stanhope Clo. SE16	93	DX75
Middleton Dr.		
Stanhope Gdns. N4	63	DP58
Stanhope Gdns. N6	63	DH58
Stanhope Gdns. NW7	47	CT50
Stanhope Gdns. SW7	90	DC77
Stanhope Gdns., Dag.	68	EZ62
Stanhope Rd.		
Stanhope Gdns., Ilf.	67	EM60
Arlington Rd.		
Stanhope Gate W1	**8**	**G2**
Stanhope Gate W1	76	DG74
Stanhope Gro., Beck.	121	DZ99
Stanhope Heath, Stai.	98	BJ86
Stanhope Ms. E. SW7	90	DC77
Stanhope Ms. S. SW7	90	DC77
Gloucester Rd.		
Stanhope Ms. W. SW7	90	DC77
Stanhope Par. NW1	**5**	**K2**
Stanhope Pk. Rd., Grnf.	72	CC70
Stanhope Pl. W2	**4**	**D9**
Stanhope Pl. W2	76	DF72
Stanhope Rd. E17	65	EB57
Stanhope Rd. N6	63	DJ58
Stanhope Rd. N12	48	DC50
Stanhope Rd., Barn.	33	CW43
Stanhope Rd., Bexh.	96	EY82
Stanhope Rd., Cars.	132	DG108
Stanhope Rd., Croy.	120	DS104
Stanhope Rd., Dag.	68	EZ61
Stanhope Rd., Grnf.	72	CC71
Stanhope Rd., Rain.	83	FG68
Stanhope Rd., Sid.	110	EU91
Stanhope Rd., Wal.Cr.	23	DY33
Stanhope Row W1	**9**	**H3**
Stanhope St. NW1	**5**	**K2**
Stanhope St. NW1	77	DJ69
Stanhope Ter. W2	**4**	**A10**
Stanhope Ter. W2	76	DD73
Stanhope Way, Sev.	154	FD122
Stanhope Way, Stai.	98	BJ86
Stanier Clo. W14	89	CZ78
Aisgill Ave.		
Staniland Dr., Wey.	126	BM111
Stanlake Ms. W12	75	CW74
Stanlake Rd. W12	75	CW74
Stanlake Vill. W12	75	CW74
Stanley Ave., Bark.	81	ET68
Stanley Ave., Beck.	121	EC96
Stanley Ave., Dag.	68	EZ60
Stanley Ave., Grnf.	72	CC67
Stanley Ave., N.Mal.	117	CU99
Stanley Ave., Rom.	69	FG56
Stanley Ave., St.Alb.	16	CA25
Stanley Ave., Wem.	74	CL66
Stanley Clo. SW8	91	DM79
Stanley Clo., Couls.	147	DM117
Stanley Clo., Rom.	69	FG56
Stanley Clo., Uxb.	70	BK67
Stanley Clo., Wem.	74	CL66
Stanley Cres. W11	75	CZ73
Stanley Gdns. NW2	61	CW64
Stanley Gdns. W3	88	CS75
Stanley Gdns. W11	75	CZ73
Stanley Gdns., Borwd.	32	CL39
Stanley Gdns., Mitch.	104	DG93
Ashbourne Rd.		
Stanley Gdns., S.Croy.	134	DU112
Stanley Gdns., Wall.	133	DJ107
Stanley Gdns., Walt.	128	BW107
Stanley Gdns. Ms. W11	75	CZ73
Stanley Cres.		
Stanley Gdns. Rd., Tedd.	101	CE92
Stanley Gro. SW8	90	DG82
Stanley Gro., Croy.	119	DN100
Stanley Pk. Dr., Wem.	74	CM67
Stanley Pk. Rd., Cars.	132	DE108
Stanley Pk. Rd., Wall.	133	DH107
Stanley Pas. NW1	**5**	**P1**
Stanley Rd. E4	51	ED46
Stanley Rd. E10	65	EB58
Stanley Rd. E12	66	EL64
Stanley Rd. E15	79	ED67
Stanley Rd. E18	52	EF53
Stanley Rd. N2	62	DD55
Stanley Rd. N9	50	DT46
Stanley Rd. N10	49	DH52
Stanley Rd. N11	49	DK51
Stanley Rd. N15	63	DP56
Stanley Rd. NW9	61	CU59
West Hendon Bdy.		
Stanley Rd. SW14	88	CP84
Stanley Rd. SW19	104	DA94
Stanley Rd. W3	88	CQ76
Stanley Rd., Ashf.	98	BL92
Stanley Rd., Brom.	122	EH98

Stanley Rd., Cars.	132	DG108
Stanley Rd., Croy.	119	DN101
Stanley Rd., Enf.	36	DS41
Stanley Rd., Har.	58	CC61
Stanley Rd., Houns.	86	CC84
Stanley Rd., Ilf.	67	ER61
Stanley Rd., Mitch.	104	DG94
Stanley Rd., Mord.	118	DA98
Stanley Rd., Nthwd.	43	BU53
Stanley Rd., Orp.	124	EU102
Stanley Rd., Sid.	110	EU90
Stanley Rd., Sthl.	72	BY73
Stanley Rd., Sutt.	132	DB107
Stanley Rd., Tedd.	101	CE91
Stanley Rd., Twick.	101	CD90
Stanley Rd., Wat.	30	BW41
Stanley Rd., Wem.	74	CM65
Stanley Rd. N., Rain.	83	FE67
Stanley Rd. S., Rain.	83	FF68
Stanley Sq., Cars.	132	DF109
Stanley St. SE8	93	DZ80
Stanley Ter. N19	63	DL61
Stanley Way, Orp.	124	EV99
Stanleycroft Clo., Islw.	87	CE81
Stanmer St. SW11	90	DE81
Stanmore Gdns., Rich.	88	CM83
Stanmore Gdns., Sutt.	118	DC104
Stanmore Hill, Stan.	45	CG48
Stanmore Pk., Stan.	45	CH51
Stanmore Pl. NW1	77	DH67
Arlington Rd.		
Stanmore Rd. E11	66	EF60
Stanmore Rd. N15	63	DP56
Stanmore Rd., Belv.	97	FC77
Stanmore Rd., Rich.	88	CM83
Stanmore Rd., Wat.	29	BV39
Stanmore St. N1	77	DM67
Caledonian Rd.		
Stanmore Ter., Beck.	121	EA96
Stanmore Way, Loug.	39	EN39
Stanmount Rd., St.Alb.	16	CA25
Stannard Ms. E8	78	DU65
Stannard Rd.		
Stannard Rd. E8	78	DU65
Stannary Pl. SE11	91	DN78
Stannary St.		
Stannary St. SE11	91	DN79
Stannet Way, Wall.	133	DJ105
Stannington Path, Borwd.	32	CN39
Warenford Way		
Stansfeld Rd. E6	80	EK71
Stansfield Rd. SW9	91	DM83
Stansfield Rd., Houns.	85	BV82
Stansgate Rd., Dag.	68	FA61
Stanstead Clo., Brom.	122	EF99
Stanstead Gro. SE6	107	DZ88
Catford Hill		
Stanstead Manor, Sutt.	132	DA107
Stanstead Rd. E11	66	EH57
Stanstead Rd. SE6	107	DZ88
Catford Hill		
Stanstead Rd. SE23	107	DX88
Stanstead Rd., Houns.	98	BM86
Stansted Clo., Horn.	83	FH65
Stansted Cres., Bex.	110	EX88
Stanswood Gdns. SE5	92	DS80
Sedgmoor Pl.		
Stanthorpe Clo. SW16	105	DL92
Stanthorpe Rd. SW16	105	DL92
Stanton Ave., Tedd.	101	CE92
Stanton Clo., Epsom	130	CP106
Stanton Clo., Orp.	124	EW101
Stanton Clo., Wor.Pk.	117	CX102
Stanton Rd. SE26	107	DZ91
Stanton Way		
Stanton Rd. SW13	89	CT82
Stanton Rd. SW20	117	CX95
Stanton Rd., Croy.	120	DQ101
Stanton Sq. SE26	107	DZ91
Stanton Way		
Stanton St. SE15	92	DU81
Stanton Way SE26	107	DZ91
Stanway Clo., Chig.	53	ES50
Stanway Ct. N1	78	DS68
Hoxton St.		
Stanway Gdns. W3	74	CN74
Stanway Gdns., Edg.	46	CQ51
Stanway Rd., Wal.Abb.	24	EG33
Stanway St. N1	78	DS68
Stanwell Clo., Stai.	98	BK86
Stanwell Gdns., Stai.	98	BK86
Stanwell Moor Rd., Stai.	98	BH90
Stanwell Moor Rd.,	84	BH81
West Dr.		
Stanwell New Rd., Stai.	98	BH90
Stanwell Rd., Ashf.	98	BL89
Stanwell Rd., Felt.	99	BQ87
Stanwick Rd. W14	89	CZ77
Stanworth St. SE1	**11**	**P5**
Stanworth St. SE1	92	DT75
Stanwyck Dr., Chig.	53	EQ50
Stanwyck Gdns., Rom.	55	FH50
Stapenhill Rd., Wem.	59	CH62
Staple Clo., Bex.	111	FD90
Staple Inn Bldgs. WC1	**6**	**D7**
Staple St. SE1	**11**	**L5**
Staple St. SE1	92	DR75
Staplefield Clo. SW2	105	DL88
Staplefield Clo., Pnr.	44	BY52
Stapleford Ave., Ilf.	67	ES57
Stapleford Clo. E4	51	EC48
Stapleford Clo. SW19	103	CY87
Stapleford Clo.,	116	CN97
Kings.T.		
Stapleford Ct., Sev.	154	FF123
Stapleford Gdns., Rom.	54	FA51
Stapleford Rd., Rom.	41	FB43

Stapleford Rd., Wem.	73	CK66
Stapleford Tawney, Ong.	27	FC32
Stapleford Tawney,	41	FC35
Rom.		
Stapleford Way, Bark.	82	EV69
Staplehurst Rd. SE13	108	EE85
Staplehurst Rd., Cars.	132	DE108
Staples Clo. SE16	79	DY74
Staples Cor. NW2	61	CV60
Staples Cor. Business	61	CU60
Pk. NW2		
Staples Rd., Loug.	38	EK41
Stapleton Clo., Pot.B.	20	DE31
Stapleton Cres., Rain.	83	FG65
Stapleton Gdns., Croy.	133	DN106
Stapleton Hall Rd. N4	63	DM60
Stapleton Rd. SW17	104	DG90
Stapleton Rd., Bexh.	96	EZ80
Stapleton Rd., Borwd.	32	CN38
Stapleton Rd., Orp.	123	ET104
Stapley Rd., Belv.	96	FA78
Stapylton Rd., Barn.	33	CY41
Star & Garter Hill, Rich.	102	CL88
Star Hill, Dart.	111	FE85
Star Hill Rd., Sev.	152	EZ115
Star La. E16	80	EE70
Star La., Couls.	146	DG122
Star La., Epp.	26	EU30
Star La., Orp.	124	EW98
Star Path, Nthlt.	72	CA68
Brabazon Rd.		
Star Pl. E1	78	DT73
Thomas More St.		
Star Rd. W14	89	CZ79
Star Rd., Islw.	87	CD82
Star Rd., Uxb.	71	BP70
Star St. E16	80	EF71
Star St. W2	**4**	**A8**
Star St. W2	76	DE72
Star Yd. WC2	**6**	**D8**
Starboard Way E14	93	EA76
Starch Ho. La., Ilf.	53	ER54
Starcross St. NW1	77	DJ69
Starcross St. NW1	**5**	**L3**
Starfield Rd. W12	89	CU75
Starkleigh Way SE16	92	DV78
Egan Way		
Starling Clo., Buck.H.	52	EG46
Starling Clo., Pnr.	58	BW55
Starling La. (Cuffley),	21	DM28
Pot.B.		
Starling Ms. SE28	95	ER75
Whinchat Rd.		
Starling Wk., Hmptn.	100	BY93
Oak Ave.		
Starlings, The, Lthd.	128	CC113
Starmans Clo., Dag.	82	EY67
Starrock La., Couls.	146	DF120
Starrock Rd., Couls.	147	DH119
Starts Clo., Orp.	123	EN104
Starts Hill Ave., Orp.	137	EP105
Starts Hill Rd., Orp.	123	EN104
Starveall Clo., West Dr.	84	BM76
Starwood Clo., W.Byf.	126	BJ111
State Fm. Ave., Orp.	137	EP105
Staten Gdns., Twick.	101	CF88
Lion Rd.		
Statham Ms. N16	64	DQ63
Green Las.		
Statham Gro. N18	50	DS50
Station App. E7	66	EH63
Station App.	66	EG57
(Snaresbrook) E11		
High St.		
Station App. N11	49	DH50
Friern Barnet Rd.		
Station App.	48	DB49
(Woodside Pk.) N12		
Holden Rd.		
Station App.	64	DT61
(Stoke Newington) N16		
Stamford Hill		
Station App. NW10	75	CT69
Station Rd.		
Station App. SE1	**10**	**C5**
Station App. SE3	94	EH83
Kidbrooke Pk. Rd.		
Station App.	109	EM88
(Mottingham) SE9		
Station App.	107	DZ92
(Lower Sydenham) SE26		
Worsley Bri. Rd.		
Station App. (Sydenham)	106	DW91
SE26		
Sydenham Rd.		
Station App. SW6	89	CY83
Station App. SW16	105	DK92
Station App. W7	73	CE74
Station App., Ashf.	98	BM91
Station App., Bex.	110	FA87
Bexley High St.		
Station App., Bexh.	96	EY82
Avenue Rd.		
Station App.	97	FC82
(Barnehurst), Bexh.		
Station App., Brom.	122	EG102
Station App., Buck.H.	52	EK49
Cherry Tree Ri.		
Station App., Chis.	123	EN95
Station App.	108	EL93
(Elmstead Wds.), Chis.		
Station App., Couls.	147	DK115
Station App. (Chipstead),	146	DF118
Couls.		
Station App. (Crayford),	111	FF86
Dart.		

Station App.	39	ES36
(Theydon Bois), Epp.		
Coppice Row		
Station App., Epsom	130	CR113
Station App. (Ewell E.),	131	CV109
Epsom		
Station App. (Ewell W.),	131	CT109
Epsom		
Chessington Rd.		
Station App.	131	CT106
(Stoneleigh), Epsom		
Station App.	115	CF104
(Hinchley Wd.), Esher		
Station App., Grnf.	73	CD86
Station App., Hmptn.	114	CA95
Milton Rd.		
Station App., Har.	59	CE59
Station App., Hayes	85	BT75
Station App., Kings.T.	116	CN96
Station App., Lthd.	143	CG121
Station App. (Oxshott),	128	CC113
Lthd.		
Station App., Loug.	38	EL43
Station App. (Debden),	39	EQ42
Loug.		
Station App., Nthwd.	43	BS52
Station App., Orp.	123	ET103
Station App. (Chelsfield),	138	EV106
Orp.		
Station App.	124	EV99
(St. Mary Cray), Orp.		
Station App., Pnr.	58	BY56
Station App. (Hatch End),	44	CA52
Pnr.		
Uxbridge Rd.		
Station App., Pot.B.	19	CZ32
Wyllyotts Pl.		
Station App., Pur.	133	DN111
Whytecliffe Rd. S.		
Station App., Rad.	31	CG35
Shenley Hill		
Station App., Rich.	88	CN81
Station App., Ruis.	57	BV64
Station App., Shep.	113	BQ99
Station App., Sid.	110	EU89
Station App., S.Croy.	134	DR109
Sanderstead Rd.		
Station App., Stai.	98	BG91
Station App., Sun.	113	BU95
Station App. (Belmont),	132	DB110
Sutt.		
Brighton Rd.		
Station App. (Cheam),	131	CY108
Sutt.		
Station App., Swan.	125	FE98
Station App., Wal.Cr.	23	DY34
Station App. (Cheshunt),	23	DZ30
Wal.Cr.		
Station App., Wat.	29	BT41
Cassiobury Pk. Ave.		
Station App.,	44	BX48
(Carpenders Pk.), Wat.		
Prestwick Rd.		
Station App., Well.	96	EU82
Station App., Wem.	73	CH65
Station App., W.Byf.	126	BG112
Station App., West Dr.	70	BL74
High St.		
Station App., Wey.	126	BN107
Station App., Whyt.	148	DU118
Station App. Rd. W4	88	CQ80
Station App. Rd., Couls.	147	DK115
Station App. Rd., Tad.	145	CW122
Station Ave. SW9	91	DP83
Coldharbour La.		
Station Ave., Cat.	148	DU124
Station Ave., Epsom	130	CS109
Station Ave., N.Mal.	116	CS97
Station Ave., Rich.	88	CN81
Station Ave., Walt.	127	BT105
Station Clo. N3	48	DA53
Station Clo., Hmptn.	114	CB95
Station Clo., Hat.	19	CY26
Station Rd.		
Station Clo., Pot.B.	19	CZ31
Station Cres. N15	64	DR56
Station Cres. SE3	94	EG78
Station Cres., Ashf.	98	BK90
Station Cres., Wem.	73	CH65
Station Est., Beck.	121	DX98
Elmers End Rd.		
Station Est. Rd., Felt.	99	BV88
Station Footpath, Kings L.	15	BP30
Station Gdns. W4	88	CQ80
Station Gro., Wem.	74	CL65
Station Hill, Brom.	122	EG103
Station Ho. Ms. N9	50	DU49
Fore St.		
Station Par. E11	66	EG57
Station Par. N14	49	DK46
High St.		
Station Par. NW2	75	CW65
Station Par. SW12	104	DG88
Balham High Rd.		
Station Par. W3	74	CN72
Station Par., Bark.	81	EQ66
Station Par., Horn.	69	FH63
Rosewood Ave.		
Station Par., Rich.	88	CN81
Station Ave.		
Station Par., Sev.	154	FG124
London Rd.		
Station Par., Uxb.	56	BG59
Station Pas. E18	52	EH54
Maybank Rd.		
Station Pas. SE15	92	DW79
Asylum Rd.		

Station Path E8 78 DV65
Amhurst Rd.
Station Pl. N4 63 DN61
Seven Sisters Rd.
Station Ri. SE27 105 DP89
Norwood Rd.
Station Rd. (Chingford) E4 51 ED46
Station Rd. E7 66 EG63
Station Rd. E10 65 EC62
Station Rd. E12 66 EK63
Station Rd. E17 65 DY58
Station Rd. N3 48 DA53
Station Rd. N11 49 DH50
Station Rd. N17 64 DU55
Hale Rd.
Station Rd. N19 63 DJ62
Station Rd. N21 49 DP46
Station Rd. N22 49 DL54
Station Rd. NW4 61 CU58
Station Rd. NW7 46 CS50
Station Rd. NW10 75 CT68
Station Rd. SE20 106 DW93
Station Rd. 120 DT98
(Norwood Junct.) SE25
Station Rd. SW13 89 CT82
Station Rd. SW19 118 DC95
Station Rd. W5 74 CM72
Station Rd. (Hanwell) W7 73 CE74
Station Rd., Add. 126 BJ105
Station Rd., Ashf. 98 BM91
Station App.
Station Rd., Barn. 34 DB43
Station Rd., Belv. 96 FA76
Station Rd., Bexh. 96 EY83
Station Rd., Borwd. 32 CN42
Station Rd., Brom. 122 EG95
Station Rd. (Shortlands), 122 EE96
Brom.
Station Rd., Cars. 132 DF105
Station Rd., Cat. 149 DY122
Station Rd., Chess. 130 CL106
Station Rd., Chig. 53 EP48
Station Rd., Cob. 142 BY117
Station Rd. 120 DR103
(East Croydon), Croy.
Station Rd. 120 DQ102
(West Croydon), Croy.
Station Rd. (Crayford), 111 FF86
Dart.
Station Rd., Edg. 46 CN51
Station Rd., Epp. 25 ET30
Station Rd., Epp. 27 FB27
(North Weald Bassett)
Station Rd., Esher 115 CD103
Station Rd. (Claygate), 129 CD106
Esher
Station Rd., Hmptn. 114 CA95
Station Rd., Har. 59 CF56
Station Rd. (North 58 CB57
Harrow), Har.
Station Rd., Hat. 19 CX25
Station Rd., Hayes 85 BS77
Station Rd., Houns. 86 CB84
Station Rd., Ilf. 67 EP62
Station Rd. (Barkingside), 67 ER55
Ilf.
Station Rd., Ken. 134 DQ114
Station Rd., Kings L. 15 BP29
Station Rd., Kings.T. 116 CN95
Station Rd. 115 CK95
(Hampton Wick), Kings.T.
Station Rd., Lthd. 143 CG121
Station Rd., Loug. 38 EL42
Station Rd. 117 CV99
(Motspur Pk.), N.Mal.
Station Rd., Orp. 123 ET103
Station Rd. 124 EW98
(St. Mary Cray), Orp.
Station Rd. (Cuffley), 21 DL29
Pot.B.
Station Rd., Rad. 31 CG35
Station Rd., Rick. 42 BK45
Station Rd. (Chadwell 68 EX60
Heath), Rom.
Station Rd. (Gidea Pk.), 69 FH56
Rom.
Station Rd. (Bricket Wd.), 16 CA31
St.Alb.
Station Rd. (Dunton 153 FE120
Grn.), Sev.
Station Rd. (Halstead), 138 EZ110
Sev.
Station Rd. (Otford), Sev. 153 FH116
Station Rd. (Shoreham), 139 FG111
Sev.
Station Rd., Shep. 113 BQ99
Station Rd., Sid. 110 EU91
Station Rd., Sun. 99 BU94
Station Rd. (Belmont), 132 DA110
Sutt.
Station Rd., Swan. 125 FE98
Station Rd., Tedd. 101 CF92
Station Rd., T.Ditt. 115 CF101
Station Rd., Twick. 101 CF88
Station Rd., Uxb. 70 BJ70
Station Rd., Wal.Cr. 23 EA34
Station Rd., Wat. 29 BV40
Station Rd., W.Byf. 126 BG112
Station Rd., West Dr. 70 BK74
Station Rd., W.Wick. 121 EC103
Station Rd., West. 152 EV123
Station Rd., Whyt. 148 DT118
Station Rd., N. Belv. 97 FB76
Station Sq. (Petts Wd.), 123 EQ99
Orp.
Station Sq. 124 EV98
(St. Mary Cray), Orp.
Station St. E15 79 ED66
Station St. E16 81 EP74
Station Ter. NW10 75 CX68
Station Ter. SE5 92 DQ81
Station Vw., Grnf. 73 CD67
Station Way SE15 92 DU82
Rye La.
Station Way 52 EJ49
(Roding Valley), Buck.H.
Station Way (Epsom), 130 CR113
Epsom
High St.
Station Way (Claygate), 129 CE107
Esher
Station Way (Cheam), 131 CY107
Sutt.
Station Yd., Twick. 101 CG87
Stationers Hall Ct. EC4 77 DP72
Ludgate Hill
Staunton Rd., Kings.T. 102 CL93
Staunton St. SE8 93 DZ79
Stave Yd. Rd. SE16 79 DY74
Staveley Clo. E9 64 DW64
Churchill Wk.
Staveley Clo. N7 63 DL63
Penn Rd.
Staveley Clo. SE15 92 DV81
Asylum Rd.
Staveley Gdns. W4 88 CR81
Staveley Rd. W4 88 CQ79
Staveley Rd., Ashf. 99 BR93
Staverton Rd. NW2 75 CW66
Stavordale Rd. N5 63 DP63
Stavordale Rd., Cars. 118 DC102
Stayner's Rd. E1 79 DX70
Stayton Rd., Sutt. 118 DA104
Stead St. SE17 11 K9
Stead St. SE17 92 DR77
Steadfast Rd., Kings.T. 115 CK95
Steam Fm. La., Felt. 85 BT84
Stean St. E8 78 DT67
Stebbing Way, Bark. 82 EU68
Stebondale St. E14 93 EC78
Stedham Pl. WC1 5 P8
Stedman Clo., Bex. 111 FE90
Stedman Clo., Uxb. 56 BN62
Steed Clo., Horn. 69 FH61
St. Leonards Way
Steedman St. SE17 11 H9
Steeds Rd. N10 48 DF53
Steeds Way, Loug. 38 EL41
Steele Rd. E11 66 EE63
Steele Rd. N17 64 DS55
Steele Rd. NW10 74 CQ68
Steele Rd. W4 88 CQ76
Steele Rd., Islw. 87 CG84
Steele Wk., Erith 97 FB80
Sussex Rd.
Steeles Ms. N. NW3 76 DF65
Steeles Rd.
Steeles Ms. S. NW3 76 DF65
Steeles Rd.
Steeles Rd. NW3 76 DF65
Steel's La. E1 78 DW72
Devonport St.
Steels La., Lthd. 128 CB114
Steelyard Pas. EC4 78 DR73
Upper Thames St.
Steen Way SE22 106 DS85
East Dulwich Gro.
Steep Clo., Orp. 137 ET107
Steep Hill SW16 105 DK90
Steep Hill, Croy. 134 DS105
Steeplands (Bushey), 44 CB45
Wat.
Steeple Clo. SW6 89 CY82
Steeple Clo. SW19 103 CY92
Steeple Ct. E1 78 DV70
Coventry Rd.
Steeple Gdns., Add. 126 BH106
Weatherall Clo.
Steeple Heights Dr., 150 EK117
West.
Steeple Wk. N1 78 DQ67
Basire St.
Steeplestone Clo. N18 50 DQ50
Steerforth St. SW18 104 DC89
Steers Mead, Mitch. 118 DF95
Steers Way SE16 93 DY75
Stella Rd. SW17 104 DF93
Stellar Ho. N17 50 DU51
Stelling Rd., Erith 97 FD80
Stellman Clo. E5 64 DU62
Stembridge Rd. SE20 120 DV96
Stents La., Cob. 142 BZ120
Stents La., Lthd. 142 BZ120
Cobham Rd.
Stepgates, Cher. 112 BH101
Stepgates Clo., Cher. 112 BH101
Stephan Clo. E8 78 DU67
Stephen Ave., Rain. 83 FG65
Stephen Clo., Orp. 123 ES104
Stephen Ms. W1 5 M7
Stephen Rd., Bexh. 97 FC83
Stephen St. W1 5 M7
Stephen St. W1 77 DK71
Stephendale Rd. SW6 90 DB83
Stephen's Rd. E15 80 EE67
Stephenson Rd. E17 65 DY57
Stephenson Rd. W7 73 CF72
Stephenson Rd., Twick. 100 CA87
Stephenson St. E16 80 EE70
Stephenson St. NW10 74 CS69
Stephenson Way NW1 5 L4
Stephenson Way NW1 77 DJ70
Stephenson Way, Wat. 30 BX41
Stepney Causeway E1 79 DX72
Stepney Grn. E1 78 DW71
Stepney High St. E1 79 DX71
Stepney Way E1 78 DV71
Sterling Ave., Edg. 46 CM49
Sterling Ave., Wal.Cr. 23 DX34
Sterling Gdns. SE14 93 DY79
Sterling Ind. Est., Dag. 69 FB63
Sterling Pl. W5 88 CL77
Sterling Rd., Enf. 36 DR39
Sterling St. SW7 8 C5
Sterling Way N18 50 DR49
Stern Clo., Bark. 82 EY69
Choats Rd.
Sterndale Rd. W14 89 CX76
Sterne St. W12 89 CX75
Sternhall La. SE15 92 DU83
Sternhold Ave. SW2 105 DK89
Sterry Cres., Dag. 68 FA64
Alibon Rd.
Sterry Dr., Epsom 130 CS105
Sterry Dr., T.Ditt. 115 CE100
Sterry Gdns., Dag. 82 FA65
Sterry Rd., Bark. 81 ET67
Sterry Rd., Dag. 68 FA63
Sterry St. SE1 11 K5
Sterry St. SE1 92 DR75
Steucers La. SE23 107 DY88
Steve Biko La. SE6 107 EA91
Steve Biko Rd. N7 63 DN62
Steve Biko Way, Houns. 86 CA83
Stevedale Rd., Well. 96 EW82
Stevedore St. E1 78 DV74
Waterman Way
Stevenage Cres., Borwd. 32 CL39
Stevenage Rd. E6 81 EN65
Stevenage Rd. SW6 89 CX80
Stevens Ave. E9 78 DW65
Stevens Clo., Beck. 107 EA93
Stevens Clo., Bex. 111 FD91
Stevens Clo., Epsom 130 CS113
Upper High St.
Stevens Clo., Hmptn. 100 BY93
Stevens Clo., Pnr. 58 BW57
Bridle Rd.
Stevens Grn. (Bushey), 44 CC46
Wat.
Stevens La., Esher 129 CG108
Stevens Rd., Dag. 68 EV62
Stevens St. SE1 11 N6
Stevens Way, Chig. 53 ES49
Stevenson Clo., Erith 97 FH80
Stevenson Cres. SE16 92 DU78
Steventon Rd. W12 75 CT73
Stew La. EC4 7 H10
Steward Clo. (Cheshunt), 23 DY30
Wal.Cr.
Steward St. E1 7 N6
Steward St. E1 78 DS71
Stewards Clo., Epp. 26 EU32
Stewards Grn. La., Epp. 26 EV32
Stewards Grn. Rd., Epp. 26 EU33
Stewards Wk., Rom. 69 FE57
Stewart, Tad. 145 CX121
Stewart Ave., Shep. 112 BN98
Stewart Clo. NW9 60 CQ58
Stewart Clo., Abb.L. 15 BT31
Stewart Clo., Chis. 109 EP92
Stewart Clo., Hmptn. 100 BY93
Stewart Rainbird Ho. E12 67 EN64
Stewart Rd. E15 65 EC63
Stewart St. E14 93 EC75
Stewart's Gro. SW3 8 B10
Stewart's Gro. SW3 90 DE78
Stewart's Rd. SW8 91 DJ80
Stewartsby Clo. N18 50 DQ50
Steyne Rd. W3 74 CP74
Steyning Clo., Ken. 147 DP116
Steyning Gro. SE9 109 EM91
Steyning Way, Houns. 86 BW84
Steynings Way N12 48 DA50
Steynton Ave., Bex. 110 EX89
Stickland Rd., Belv. 96 FA77
Picardy Rd.
Stickleton Clo., Grnf. 72 CB69
Stile Hall Gdns. W4 88 CN78
Stile Hall Par. W4 88 CN78
Chiswick High Rd.
Stile Path, Sun. 113 BU97
Stilecroft Gdns., Wem. 59 CH62
Stiles Clo., Brom. 123 EM100
Stiles Clo., Erith 97 FB78
Riverdale Rd.
Stillingfleet Rd. SW13 89 CU79
Stillington St. SW1 9 L8
Stillington St. SW1 91 DJ77
Stillness Rd. SE23 107 DY86
Stilton Cres. NW10 74 CQ66
Stilton Path, Borwd. 32 CN38
Brampton Ter.
Stipularis Dr., Hayes 72 BX70
Stirling Clo. SW16 119 DJ95
Stirling Clo., Bans. 145 CZ117
Stirling Clo., Rain. 83 FH69
Stirling Clo., Uxb. 70 BJ69
Ferndale Cres.
Stirling Dr., Orp. 138 EV106
Stirling Gro., Houns. 86 CC82
Stirling Rd. E13 80 EH68
Stirling Rd. E17 65 DY55
Stirling Rd. N17 50 DU53
Stirling Rd. N22 49 DP53
Stirling Rd. SW9 91 DL82
Stirling Rd. W3 88 CP76
Stirling Rd., Har. 59 CF55
Stirling Rd., Hayes 71 BV73
Stirling Rd., Houns. 98 BM86
Stirling Rd., Twick. 100 CA87
Stirling Rd. Path E17 65 DY55
Stirling Wk., N.Mal. 116 CQ99
Green La.
Stirling Wk., Surb. 116 CP100
Stirling Way, Abb.L. 15 BU32
Stirling Way, Borwd. 32 CR44
Stirling Way, Croy. 119 DL101
Stites Hill Rd., Couls. 147 DP120
Stiven Cres., Har. 58 BZ62
Stoats Nest Rd., Couls. 133 DL114
Stoats Nest Village, 147 DL115
Couls.
Stock Fm. Rd., Rick. 42 BK48
Stock Hill, West. 150 EK116
Stock Orchard Cres. N7 63 DM64
Stock Orchard St. N7 63 DM64
Stock St. E13 80 EG68
Stockbury Rd., Croy. 120 DW100
Stockdale Rd., Dag. 68 EZ61
Stockdove Way, Grnf. 73 CF69
Stockfield Rd. SW16 105 DM90
Stockfield Rd., Esher 129 CE106
Stockham's Clo., S.Croy. 134 DR111
Stockholm Rd. SE16 92 DW78
Stockholm Way E1 78 DU74
Thomas More St.
Stockhurst Clo. SW15 89 CW82
Stockingswater La., Enf. 37 DY41
Stockland Rd., Rom. 69 FD58
Stockley Clo., West Dr. 85 BP75
Stockley Fm. Rd., 85 BP76
West Dr.
Stockley Rd.
Stockley Pk. Business 71 BP74
Pk., Uxb.
Stockley Rd., Uxb. 70 BN72
Stockley Rd., West Dr. 85 BP76
Stockport Rd. SW16 119 DK95
Stocks Pl. E14 79 DZ73
Grenade St.
Stocksfield Rd. E17 65 EC55
Stockton Gdns. N17 50 DQ52
Stockton Rd.
Stockton Gdns. NW7 46 CS48
Stockton Rd. N17 50 DQ52
Stockton Rd. N18 50 DU51
Stockwell Ave. SW9 91 DM83
Stockwell Clo., Brom. 122 EH96
Stockwell Clo. 22 DU27
(Cheshunt), Wal.Cr.
Stockwell Gdns. SW9 91 DM81
Stockwell Gdns. Est. SW9 91 DL82
Stockwell Grn. SW9 91 DM82
Stockwell La. SW9 91 DM82
Stockwell La. (Cheshunt), 22 DV28
Wal.Cr.
Stockwell Ms. SW9 91 DM82
Stockwell Rd.
Stockwell Pk. Cres. SW9 91 DM82
Stockwell Pk. Est. SW9 91 DM82
Stockwell Pk. Rd. SW9 91 DM81
Stockwell Pk. Wk. SW9 91 DM83
Stockwell Rd. SW9 91 DM82
Stockwell St. SE10 93 EC79
Stockwell Ter. SW9 91 DM81
Stodart Rd. SE20 120 DW95
Stofield Gdns. SE9 108 EK90
Aldersgrove Ave.
Stoford Clo. SW19 103 CY87
Stoke Ave., Ilf. 54 EU51
Stoke Clo., Cob. 142 BZ116
Stoke Newington Ch. St. 64 DR62
N16
Stoke Newington 64 DT62
Common N16
Stoke Newington High 64 DT62
St. N16
Stoke Newington Rd. N16 64 DT64
Stoke Pl. NW10 75 CT69
Stoke Rd., Cob. 142 BW115
Stoke Rd., Kings.T. 102 CQ94
Stoke Rd., Walt. 114 BW104
Stokenchurch St. SW6 90 DB81
Stokes Ridings, Tad. 145 CX123
Stokes Rd. E6 80 EL70
Stokes Rd., Croy. 121 DX100
Stokesby Rd., Chess. 130 CM107
Stokesheath Rd., Lthd. 128 CC111
Stokesley St. W12 75 CT72
Stoll Clo. NW2 61 CW62
Stompond La., Walt. 113 BU103
Stoms Path SE6 107 EA92
Sedgehill Rd.
Stonard Rd. N13 49 DN48
Stonard Rd., Dag. 68 EV64
Stonards Hill, Epp. 26 EU29
Stonards Hill, Loug. 39 EM44
Stondon Pk. SE23 107 DY86
Stondon Wk. E6 80 EK68
Arragon Rd.
Stone Bldgs. WC2 6 C7
Stone Bldgs. WC2 77 DM72
Stone Clo. SW4 91 DJ82
Larkhall Ri.
Stone Clo., Dag. 68 EZ61
Stone Clo., West Dr. 70 BM74
Stone Cres., Felt. 99 BT87
Stone Hall Gdns. W8 90 DB76
St. Mary's Gate
Stone Hall Pl. W8 90 DB76
St. Mary's Gate
Stone Hall Rd. N21 49 DM45
Stone Ho. Ct. EC3 7 N8
Stone Pk. Ave., Beck. 121 EA98
Stone Pl., Wor.Pk. 117 CU103
Stone Rd., Brom. 122 EF99
Stone St., Croy. 133 DN106
Stonebanks, Walt. 113 BU101
Stonebridge Common E8 78 DT66
Mayfield Rd.
Stonebridge Pk. NW10 74 CR66
Stonebridge Rd. N15 64 DT57
Stonebridge Way, Wem. 74 CP65
Stonechat Sq. E6 80 EL71
Peridot St.
Stonecot Clo., Sutt. 117 CY102
Stonecot Hill, Sutt. 117 CY102
Stonecroft Clo., Barn. 33 CV42
Stonecroft Rd., Erith 97 FC80
Stonecroft Way, Croy. 119 DL101
Stonecutter Ct. EC4 77 DP72
Stonecutter St.
Stonecutter St. EC4 6 F8
Stonecutter St. EC4 77 DP72
Stonefield Clo., Bexh. 96 FA83
Stonefield Clo., Ruis. 58 BY64
Stonefield St. N1 77 DN67
Stonefield Way SE7 94 EK80
Greenbay Rd.
Stonefield Way, Ruis. 58 BY63
Stonegate Clo., Orp. 124 EW97
Main Rd.
Stonegrove, Edg. 46 CL49
Stonegrove Est., Edg. 46 CL49
Stonegrove Gdns., Edg. 46 CL50
Stonehall Ave., Ilf. 66 EL58
Stoneham Rd. N11 49 DJ50
Stonehill Clo. SW14 102 CR85
Stonehill Grn. Rd., Dart. 111 FC94
Birchwood Rd.
Stonehill Rd. SW14 102 CQ85
Stonehill Rd. W4 88 CN78
Wellesley Rd.
Stonehill Wds. Caravan 111 FB93
Pk., Sid.
Stonehills Ct. SE21 106 DS90
Stonehorse Rd., Enf. 36 DW43
Stonehouse La., Sev. 138 EX109
Stonehouse Rd., Sev. 138 EW110
Stoneings La., Sev. 151 ET118
Stoneleigh Ave., Enf. 36 DV38
Stoneleigh Ave., Wor.Pk. 117 CU104
Stoneleigh Clo., Wal.Cr. 23 DX33
Stoneleigh Cres., Epsom 131 CT106
Stoneleigh Pk., Wey. 127 BQ106
Stoneleigh Pk. Ave., 121 DX100
Croy.
Stoneleigh Pk. Rd., 131 CT107
Epsom
Stoneleigh Pl. W11 75 CX73
Stoneleigh Rd. N17 64 DT55
Stoneleigh Rd., Cars. 118 DE101
Stoneleigh Rd., Ilf. 66 EL55
Stoneleigh St. W11 75 CX73
Stoneleigh Ter. N19 63 DH61
Dartmouth Pk. Hill
Stonells Rd. SW11 104 DF85
Chatham Rd.
Stonenest St. N4 63 DM60
Stones All., Wat. 29 BV42
Exchange Rd.
Stones Cross Rd., Swan. 125 FC99
Stones End St. SE1 11 H5
Stones End St. SE1 92 DQ75
Stones Rd., Epsom 130 CS112
Stonewall E6 81 EN71
Stonewood Rd., Erith 97 FE78
Stoney All. SE18 95 EN82
Stoney La. E1 7 P8
Stoney La. SE19 106 DT93
Church Rd.
Stoney St. SE1 11 K2
Stoney St. SE1 78 DR74
Stoneyard La. E14 79 EB73
Poplar High St.
Stoneycroft Clo. SE12 108 EF87
Stoneycroft Rd., Wdf.Grn. 52 EL51
Stoneydeep, Tedd. 101 CG91
Twickenham Rd.
Stoneydown E17 65 DY56
Stoneydown Ave. E17 65 DY56
Stoneyfield Rd., Couls. 147 DM117
Stoneyfields Gdns., Edg. 46 CQ49
Stoneyfields La., Edg. 46 CQ50
Stonhouse St. SW4 91 DK83
Stonny Cft., Ash. 144 CM117
Stonor Rd. W14 89 CZ77
Stony Path, Loug. 39 EM39
Stonycroft Clo., Enf. 37 DY40
Brimsdown Ave.
Stonyshotts, Wal.Abb. 24 EE34
Stoop Ct., W.Byf. 126 BH112
Stopford Rd. E13 80 EG67
Stopford Rd. SE17 91 DP78
Store Rd. E16 95 EN75
Store St. E15 65 ED64
Store St. WC1 5 M7
Store St. WC1 77 DK71
Storers Quay E14 93 ED77
Storey Rd. E17 65 DZ56
Storey Rd. N6 62 DF58
Storey St. E16 81 EN74
Storey's Gate SW1 9 N5
Storey's Gate SW1 91 DK75
Stories Ms. SE5 92 DS82
Stories Rd. SE5 92 DS83
Stork Rd. E7 80 EF65
Storks Rd. SE16 92 DU76
Storksmead Rd., Edg. 46 CS52
Stormont Rd. N6 62 DF59
Stormont Rd. SW11 90 DG83
Stormont Way, Chess. 129 CJ106
Stormount Dr., Hayes 85 BQ75
Storrington Rd., Croy. 120 DT102

Story St. N1 77 DM66
Carnoustie Dr.
Stothard Pl. EC2 78 DS71
Bishopsgate
Stothard St. E1 78 DW70
Colebert Ave.
Stoughton Ave., Sutt. 131 CX106
Stoughton Clo. SE11 10 C9
Stoughton Clo. SW15 103 CU88
Bessborough Rd.
Stour Ave., Sthl. 86 CA76
Stour Clo., Kes. 136 EJ105
Stour Rd. E3 79 EA66
Stour Rd., Dag. 68 FA61
Stour Rd., Dart. 97 FG83
Stourcliffe St. W1 4 D9
Stourcliffe St. W1 76 DF72
Stourhead Clo. SW19 103 CX87
Castlecombe Dr.
Stourhead Gdns. SW20 117 CU97
Stourton Ave., Felt. 100 BZ91
Stow Cres. E17 51 DY52
Stowage SE8 93 EA79
Stowe Cres., Ruis. 57 BP58
Stowe Gdns. N9 50 DT46
Latymer Rd.
Stowe Pl. N15 64 DS55
Stowe Rd. W12 89 CV75
Stowe Rd., Orp. 138 EV105
Stowell Ave., Croy. 135 ED109
Stowting Rd., Orp. 137 ES105
Stox Mead, Har. 45 CD53
Stracey Rd. E7 66 EG63
Stracey Rd. NW10 74 CR67
Strachan Pl. SW19 103 CW93
Woodhayes Rd.
Stradbroke Dr., Chig. 53 EN51
Stradbroke Gro., Buck.H. 52 EK46
Stradbroke Gro., Ilf. 66 EL55
Stradbroke Pk., Chig. 53 EP51
Stradbroke Rd. N5 64 DQ63
Stradella Rd. SE24 106 DQ86
Strafford Ave., Ilf. 53 EN54
Strafford Clo., Pot.B. 20 DA32
Strafford Gate
Strafford Gate, Pot.B. 20 DA32
Strafford Rd. W3 88 CQ75
Strafford Rd., Barn. 33 CY41
Strafford Rd., Houns. 86 BZ83
Strafford Rd., Twick. 101 CG87
Strafford St. E14 93 EA75
Strahan Rd. E3 79 DY69
Straight, The, Sthl. 86 BX75
Straight Rd., Rom. 55 FH50
Straightsmouth SE10 93 EC80
Strait Rd. E6 80 EL73
Straker's Rd. SE15 92 DV84
Strand WC2 9 P1
Strand WC2 77 DL73
Strand Clo., Epsom 144 CR119
Strand La. WC2 6 C10
Strand on the Grn. W4 88 CN79
Strand Pl. N18 50 DS49
Silver St.
Strand Sch. App. W4 88 CN79
Thames Rd.
Strandfield Clo. SE18 95 ES78
Strangeways, Wat. 29 BS36
Strangways Ter. W14 89 CZ76
Melbury Rd.
Stranraer Rd., Houns. 98 BL86
Stranraer Way N1 77 DL66
Strasburg Rd. SW11 91 DH81
Stratfield Pk. Clo. N21 49 DP45
Stratfield Rd., Borwd. 32 CM41
Stratford Ave. W8 90 DA76
Stratford Rd.
Stratford Ave., Uxb. 70 BM68
Stratford Cen., The E15 79 ED66
Broadway
Stratford Clo., Bark. 82 EU66
Stratford Clo., Dag. 83 FC66
Stratford Ct., N.Mal. 116 CR98
Kingston Rd.
Stratford Gro. SW15 89 CX84
Stratford Ho. Ave., Brom. 122 EL97
Stratford Mkt. E15 79 ED67
Bridge Rd.
Stratford Pl. W1 5 H9
Stratford Pl. W1 77 DH72
Stratford Rd. E13 80 EF67
Stratford Rd. W3 88 CQ75
Bollo Bri. Rd.
Stratford Rd. W8 90 DA76
Stratford Rd., Hayes 71 BV70
Stratford Rd., Houns. 99 BP86
Stratford Rd., Sthl. 86 BY77
Stratford Rd., Th.Hth. 119 DN98
Stratford Rd., Wat. 29 BU40
Stratford Vill. NW1 77 DJ66
Stratford Way, St.Alb. 16 BZ29
Stratford Way, Wat. 29 BT40
Strath Ter. SW11 90 DE84
Strathan Clo. SW18 103 CY86
Strathaven Rd. SE12 108 EH86
Strathblaine Rd. SW11 104 DD85
Strathbrook Rd. SW16 105 DM94
Strathcona Rd., Wem. 59 CK61
Strathdale SW16 105 DM92
Strathdon Dr. SW17 104 DD90
Strathearn Ave., Hayes 85 BT80
Strathearn Ave., Twick. 100 CB88
Strathearn Pl. W2 4 B10
Strathearn Pl. W2 76 DE73
Strathearn Rd. SW19 104 DA92
Strathearn Rd., Sutt. 132 DA106
Stratheden Par. SE3 94 EG80
Stratheden Rd.
Stratheden Rd. SE3 94 EG81
Strathfield Gdns., Bark. 81 ER65
Strathleven Rd. SW2 91 DL84
Strathmore Clo., Cat. 148 DS121
Strathmore Gdns. N3 48 DB53
Strathmore Gdns. W8 76 DA74
Palace Gdns. Ter.
Strathmore Gdns., Edg. 46 CP54
Strathmore Gdns., Horn. 69 FF60
Strathmore Rd. SW19 104 DA90
Strathmore Rd., Croy. 120 DQ101
Strathmore Rd., Tedd. 101 CE91
Strathnairn St. SE1 92 DU77
Strathray Gdns. NW3 76 DE65
Strathville Rd. SW18 104 DA89
Strathyre Ave. SW16 119 DN97
Stratton Ave., Enf. 36 DR37
Stratton Ave., Wall. 133 DK109
Stratton Clo. SW19 118 DA96
Stratton Clo., Bexh. 96 EY83
Stratton Clo., Edg. 46 CM51
Stratton Clo., Houns. 86 BZ81
Stratton Clo., Walt. 114 BW102
St. Johns Dr.
Stratton Dr., Bark. 67 ET64
Stratton Gdns., Sthl. 72 BZ72
Stratton Rd. SW19 118 DA96
Stratton Rd., Bexh. 96 EY83
Stratton Rd., Sun. 113 BT96
Stratton St. W1 9 J2
Stratton St. W1 77 DH74
Strattondale St. E14 93 EC76
Strauss Rd. W4 88 CR75
Straw Clo., Cat. 148 DQ121
Coulsdon Rd.
Strawberry Flds., Swan. 125 FE95
Strawberry Hill, Twick. 101 CF90
Strawberry Hill Clo., Twick. 101 CF91
Strawberry Hill Rd., Twick. 101 CF90
Strawberry La., Cars. 118 DF104
Strawberry Vale N2 48 DD53
Strawberry Vale, Twick. 101 CF90
Strayfield Rd., Enf. 35 DP37
Streakes Fld. Rd. NW2 61 CU61
Stream Clo., W.Byf. 126 BK112
Stream La., Edg. 46 CP50
Stream Way, Belv. 96 EZ79
Streamdale SE2 96 EU79
Streamside Clo. N9 50 DT46
Streamside Clo., Brom. 122 EG98
Streatfield Ave. E6 81 EM67
Streatfield Rd., Har. 60 CL55
Streatham Clo. SW16 105 DL90
Streatham Common N. SW16 105 DL92
Streatham Common S. SW16 105 DL93
Streatham Ct. SW16 105 DL90
Streatham High Rd. SW16 105 DL92
Streatham Hill SW2 105 DL89
Streatham Pl. SW2 105 DL87
Streatham Rd. SW16 118 DG95
Streatham Rd., Mitch. 118 DG95
Streatham St. WC1 5 P8
Streatham Vale SW16 119 DJ95
Streathbourne Rd. SW17 104 DG89
Streatley Pl. NW3 62 DC63
New End Sq.
Streatley Rd. NW6 75 CZ66
Street, The, Ash. 144 CM118
Street, The, Kings L. 14 BG31
Street, The, Lthd. 143 CD121
Streeters La., Wall. 119 DK104
Streetfield Ms. SE3 94 EG83
Streimer Rd. E15 79 EC68
Strelley Way W3 74 CS73
Stretton Rd., Croy. 120 DS101
Stretton Rd., Rich. 101 CJ89
Stretton Way, Borwd. 32 CL38
Strickland Rd., Belv. 96 FA77
Strickland Row SW18 104 DD87
Strickland St. SE8 93 EA81
Strickland Way, Orp. 137 ET105
Stride Rd. E13 80 EF68
Stripling Way, Wat. 29 BU44
Strode Clo. N10 48 DG52
Pembroke Rd.
Strode Rd. E7 66 EG63
Strode Rd. N17 50 DS54
Strode Rd. NW10 75 CU65
Strode Rd. SW6 89 CY80
Strodes Cres., Stai. 98 BJ92
Strone Rd. E7 80 EJ65
Strone Rd. E12 80 EK65
Strone Way, Hayes 72 BY70
Strongbow Cres. SE9 109 EM85
Strongbow Rd. SE9 109 EM85
Strongbridge Clo., Har. 58 CA60
Stronsa Rd. W12 89 CT75
Strood Ave., Rom. 69 FD60
Stroud Cres. SW15 103 CU90
Stroud Fld., Nthlt. 72 BY65
Stroud Gate, Har. 58 CB63
Stroud Grn. Gdns., Croy. 120 DW101
Stroud Grn. Rd. N4 63 DM60
Stroud Grn. Way, Croy. 120 DV101
Stroud Rd. SE25 120 DU100
Stroud Rd. SW19 104 DA90
Stroud Way, Ashf. 99 BP93
Courtfield Rd.
Stroudes Clo., Wor.Pk. 116 CS101
Stroudley Wk. E3 79 EB69
Stroudwater Pk., Wey. 127 BP107
Strouts Pl. E2 7 P2
Strutton Grd. SW1 9 M6
Strutton Grd. SW1 91 DK76
Strype St. E1 7 P7
Stuart Ave. NW9 61 CU59
Stuart Ave. W5 74 CM74
Stuart Ave., Brom. 122 EG102
Stuart Ave., Har. 58 BZ62
Stuart Ave., Walt. 113 BV102
Stuart Clo., Swan. 111 FF94
Stuart Clo., Uxb. 70 BN65
Stuart Ct. (Elstree), Borwd. 31 CK44
High St.
Stuart Cres. N22 49 DM53
Stuart Cres., Croy. 135 DZ105
Stuart Cres., Hayes 71 BQ72
Stuart Evans Clo., Well. 96 EW83
Stuart Gro., Tedd. 101 CE92
Stuart Mantle Way, Erith 97 FD80
Stuart Pl., Mitch. 118 DF95
Stuart Rd. NW6 76 DA69
Stuart Rd. SE15 92 DW84
Stuart Rd. SW19 104 DA90
Stuart Rd. W3 74 CQ74
Stuart Rd., Bark. 81 ET66
Stuart Rd., Barn. 48 DE45
Stuart Rd., Har. 59 CF55
Stuart Rd., Rich. 101 CH89
Stuart Rd., Th.Hth. 120 DQ98
Stuart Rd., Warl. 148 DV120
Stuart Rd., Well. 96 EV81
Stuart Twr. W9 76 DC69
Stuart Way, Stai. 98 BH93
Stuart Way (Cheshunt), Wal.Cr. 22 DV31
Stubbings Hall La., Wal.Abb. 23 EB28
Stubbs Dr. SE16 92 DV78
Stubbs Hill, Sev. 138 EW113
Stubbs Ms., Dag. 68 EV63
Marlborough Rd.
Stubbs Pt. E13 80 EG70
Stubbs Way SW19 118 DD95
Brangwyn Cres.
Stucley Pl. NW1 77 DH66
Hawley Cres.
Stucley Rd., Houns. 86 CC80
Stud Grn., Wat. 15 BV32
Studd St. N1 77 DP67
Studdridge St. SW6 90 DA82
Studholme Ct. NW3 62 DA63
Studholme St. SE15 92 DV80
Studio Ct., Borwd. 32 CQ40
Studio Pl. SW1 8 E5
Studio Way, Borwd. 32 CQ40
Studios, The (Bushey), Wat. 30 CA44
Studios Rd., Shep. 112 BM97
Studland SE17 11 K10
Studland Clo., Sid. 109 ET90
Studland Rd. SE26 107 DX92
Studland Rd. W7 73 CD72
Studland Rd., Kings.T. 102 CL93
Studland Rd., W.Byf. 126 BM113
Studland St. W6 89 CV77
Studley Ave. E4 51 ED52
Studley Clo. E5 65 DY64
Studley Ct., Sid. 110 EV92
Studley Dr., Ilf. 66 EK58
Studley Est. SW4 91 DL81
Studley Gra. Rd. W7 87 CE75
Studley Rd. E7 80 EH65
Studley Rd. SW4 91 DL81
Studley Rd., Dag. 82 EX66
Stukeley Rd. E7 80 EH66
Stukeley St. WC2 6 A8
Stukeley St. WC2 77 DL72
Stumps Hill La., Beck. 107 EA93
Stumps La., Whyt. 148 DS117
Sturdy Rd. SE15 92 DV82
Sturge Ave. E17 51 EB53
Sturge St. SE1 11 H4
Sturgeon Rd. SE17 91 DP78
Sturges Fld., Chis. 109 ER93
Sturgess Ave. NW4 61 CU59
Sturlas Way, Wal.Cr. 23 DX33
Sturmer Way N7 63 DM64
Stock Orchard Cres.
Sturminster Clo., Hayes 72 BW72
Sturrock Clo. N15 64 DR56
Sturry St. E14 79 EB72
Sturt St. N1 7 J1
Sturt St. N1 78 DQ68
Stutfield St. E1 78 DU72
Styles Gdns. SW9 91 DP83
Styles Way, Beck. 121 EC98
Succombs Hill, Warl. 148 DV120
Succombs Hill, Whyt. 148 DV120
Succombs Pl., Warl. 148 DV120
Sudbourne Rd. SW2 105 DL85
Sudbrook Gdns., Rich. 102 CL90
Sudbrook La., Rich. 102 CL88
Sudbrooke Rd. SW12 104 DF86
Sudbury E6 81 EN72
Newark Knok
Sudbury Ave., Wem. 59 CJ64
Sudbury Ct. E5 65 DY63
Sudbury Ct. Dr., Har. 59 CF62
Sudbury Ct. Rd., Har. 59 CF62
Sudbury Cres., Brom. 108 EG93
Sudbury Cres., Wem. 59 CH64
Sudbury Cft., Wem. 59 CF63
Sudbury Gdns., Croy. 134 DS105
Langton Way
Sudbury Heights Ave., Grnf. 59 CF64
Sudbury Hill, Har. 59 CE61
Sudbury Hill Clo., Wem. 59 CF63
Sudbury Rd., Bark. 67 ET64
Sudeley St. N1 6 G1
Sudeley St. N1 77 DP68
Sudicamps Ct., Wal.Abb. 24 EG33
Sudlow Rd. SW18 104 DA85
Sudrey St. SE1 11 H5
Suez Ave., Grnf. 73 CF68
Suez Rd., Enf. 37 DY42
Suffield Clo., S.Croy. 135 DX112
Suffield Rd. E4 51 EB48
Suffield Rd. N15 64 DT57
Suffield Rd. SE20 120 DW96
Suffolk Clo., Borwd. 32 CR43
Clydesdale Clo.
Suffolk Clo., St.Alb. 17 CJ25
Suffolk Ct. E10 65 EA59
Suffolk Ct., Ilf. 67 ES58
Suffolk La. EC4 7 K10
Suffolk Pk. Rd. E17 65 DY56
Suffolk Pl. SW1 9 N2
Suffolk Rd. E13 80 EG69
Suffolk Rd. N15 64 DR58
Suffolk Rd. NW10 74 CS66
Suffolk Rd. SE25 120 DT98
Suffolk Rd. SW13 89 CT80
Suffolk Rd., Bark. 81 ER66
Suffolk Rd., Dag. 69 FC64
Suffolk Rd., Enf. 36 DV43
Suffolk Rd., Har. 58 BZ58
Suffolk Rd., Ilf. 67 ES58
Suffolk Rd., Pot.B. 19 CY32
Suffolk Rd., Sid. 110 EW93
Suffolk Rd., Wor.Pk. 117 CT103
Suffolk St. E7 66 EG64
Suffolk St. SW1 9 N1
Suffolk Way, Sev. 155 FJ125
Sugar Bakers Ct. EC3 7 N9
Sugar Ho. La. E15 79 EC68
Sugar Loaf Wk. E2 78 DW69
Victoria Pk. Sq.
Sugar Quay Wk. EC3 78 DS73
Lower Thames St.
Sugden Rd. SW11 90 DG83
Sugden Rd., T.Ditt. 115 CH102
Sugden Way, Bark. 81 ET68
Sulgrave Gdns. W6 89 CW75
Sulgrave Rd.
Sulgrave Rd. W6 89 CW76
Sulina Rd. SW2 105 DL87
Sulivan Ct. SW6 90 DA82
Sulivan Rd. SW6 90 DA83
Sullivan Ave. E16 80 EK71
Sullivan Clo. SW11 90 DE83
Sullivan Clo., Dart. 111 FH86
Sullivan Clo., W.Mol. 114 CA97
Victoria Ave.
Sullivan Cres., Uxb. 42 BK54
Sullivan Rd. SE11 10 E8
Sullivan Rd. SE11 91 DN77
Sullivan Way, Borwd. 31 CJ44
Sullivans Reach, Walt. 113 BT101
Sultan Rd. E11 66 EH56
Sultan St. SE5 92 DQ80
Sultan St., Beck. 121 DX96
Sumatra Rd. NW6 62 DA64
Sumburgh Rd. SW12 104 DG86
Summer Ave., E.Mol. 115 CE99
Summer Clo., Lthd. 143 CD124
Summer Gdns., E.Mol. 115 CE99
Summer Gro., Borwd. 31 CK44
Summer Hill, Borwd. 32 CN43
Summer Hill, Chis. 123 EN96
Summer Hill Vill., Chis. 123 EN95
Summer Ho. Rd. N16 64 DS61
Stoke Newington Ch. St.
Summer Rd., E.Mol. 115 CE99
Summer Rd., T.Ditt. 115 CF99
Summer St. EC1 6 D5
Summer Trees, Sun. 113 BV95
The Ave.
Summercourt Rd. E1 78 DW72
Summerdene Clo. SW16 105 DJ94
Bates Cres.
Summerfield, Ash. 143 CK119
Summerfield Ave. NW6 75 CY68
Summerfield Clo., St.Alb. 17 CJ26
Summerfield La., Surb. 115 CK103
Summerfield Rd. W5 73 CH70
Summerfield Rd., Loug. 38 EK44
Summerfield Rd., Wat. 29 BU35
Summerfield St. SE12 108 EF87
Summerfields Ave. N12 48 DE51
Summerhays, Cob. 128 BX113
Summerhill Clo., Orp. 123 ES104
Summerhill Gro., Enf. 36 DS44
Summerhill Rd. N15 64 DR56
Summerhill Way, Mitch. 118 DG95
Summerhouse Ave., Houns. 86 BY81
Summerhouse Dr., Bex. 111 FD91
Summerhouse Dr., Dart. 111 FD92
Summerhouse La., Uxb. 42 BG52
Summerhouse La., Wat. 30 CC40
Summerhouse La., West Dr. 84 BK79
Summerhouse La. Ind. Est., Uxb. 42 BG51
Summerhouse Way, Abb.L. 15 BT30
Summerland Gdns. N10 63 DH55
Summerlands Ave. W3 74 CQ73
Summerlay Clo., Tad. 145 CY120
Summerlee Ave. N2 62 DF56
Summerlee Gdns. N2 62 DF56
Summerley St. SW18 104 DB89
Summers Clo., Sutt. 132 DA108
Overton Rd.
Summers Clo., Wem. 60 CP60
Summers Clo., Wey. 126 BN111
Summers La. N12 48 DD52
Summers Row N12 48 DE51
Summersby Rd. N6 63 DH58
Summerstown SW17 104 DC90
Summerswood Clo., Ken. 148 DR116
Longwood Rd.
Summerswood La., Borwd. 32 CS35
Summerton Way SE28 82 EX73
Summerville Gdns., Sutt. 131 CZ107
Summerwood Rd., Islw. 101 CF85
Summit, The, Loug. 39 EM39
Summit Ave. NW9 60 CR57
Summit Clo. N14 49 DJ47
Summit Clo. NW9 60 CR56
Summit Clo., Edg. 46 CN52
Summit Ct. NW2 61 CY64
Summit Dr., Wdf.Grn. 52 EK54
Summit Est. N16 64 DU59
Summit Pl., Wey. 126 BN108
Caenshill Rd.
Summit Rd. E17 65 EB56
Summit Rd., Nthlt. 72 CA66
Summit Rd., Pot.B. 19 CY30
Summit Way N14 49 DH47
Summit Way SE19 106 DS94
Sumner Ave. SE15 92 DT81
Sumner Rd.
Sumner Clo., Orp. 137 EQ105
Sumner Est. SE15 92 DT80
Sumner Gdns., Croy. 119 DN102
Sumner Pl. SW7 8 A9
Sumner Pl. SW7 90 DD77
Sumner Pl., Add. 126 BG106
Sumner Pl. Ms. SW7 8 A9
Sumner Rd. SE15 92 DT80
Sumner Rd., Croy. 119 DN102
Sumner Rd., Har. 58 CC59
Sumner Rd. S., Croy. 119 DN102
Sumner St. SE1 10 G2
Sumner St. SE1 77 DP74
Sumpter Clo. NW3 76 DC65
Sun Ct. EC3 7 L9
Sun Ct., Erith 97 FF82
Sun La. SE3 94 EH80
Sun Pas. SE16 92 DU76
Frean St.
Sun Rd. W14 89 CZ78
Sun St. EC2 7 L6
Sun St. EC2 78 DR71
Sun St., Wal.Abb. 23 EC33
Sun St. Pas. EC2 7 M7
Sun Wk. E1 78 DU74
Mews St.
Sunbeam Cres. W10 75 CW70
Sunbeam Rd. NW10 74 CR70
Sunbury Ave. NW7 46 CR50
Sunbury Ave. SW14 88 CR84
Sunbury Ct., Sun. 114 BX96
Sunbury Ct. Island, Sun. 114 BX96
Sunbury Ct. Ms., Sun. 114 BX96
Lower Hampton Rd.
Sunbury Ct. Rd., Sun. 114 BW96
Sunbury Cres., Felt. 99 BT91
Ryland Clo.
Sunbury Gdns. NW7 46 CR50
Sunbury La. SW11 90 DD81
Sunbury La., Walt. 113 BU100
Sunbury Rd., Felt. 99 BT90
Sunbury Rd., Sutt. 117 CX104
Sunbury St. SE18 95 EM76
Sunbury Way, Felt. 100 BW92
Suncroft Pl. SE26 106 DW90
Sundale Ave., S.Croy. 134 DW110
Sunderland Ct. SE22 106 DU87
Sunderland Mt. SE23 107 DX89
Sunderland Rd.
Sunderland Rd. SE23 107 DX88
Sunderland Rd. W5 87 CK76
Sunderland Ter. W2 76 DB72
Sunderland Way E12 66 EK61
Sundew Ave. W12 75 CU73
Sundial Ave. SE25 120 DT97
Sundorne Rd. SE7 94 EH78
Sundown Ave., S.Croy. 134 DT111
Sundown Rd., Ashf. 99 BQ92
Sundra Wk. E1 79 DX70
Beaumont Gro.
Sundridge Ave., Brom. 122 EK96
Sundridge Ave., Chis. 108 EL94
Sundridge Ave., Well. 95 ER82
Sundridge Ho., Brom. 108 EH92
Burnt Ash La.
Sundridge La., Sev. 152 EV117
Sundridge Pl., Croy. 120 DU102
Inglis Rd.
Sundridge Rd., Croy. 120 DT101
Sundridge Rd., Sev. 152 FA120
Sunfields Pl. SE3 94 EH80
Sunkist Way, Wall. 133 DL109
Sunland Ave., Bexh. 96 EY84
Sunleigh Rd., Wem. 74 CL67
Sunley Gdns., Grnf. 73 CG67
Sunmead Clo., Lthd. 143 CF122
Sunmead Rd., Sun. 113 BU97
Sunna Gdns., Sun. 113 BV96
Sunningdale N14 49 DK50
Wilmer Way
Sunningdale Ave. W3 74 CS73

Sunningdale Ave., Bark. 81 ER67
Sunningdale Ave., Felt. 100 BY89
Sunningdale Ave., Rain. 83 FH70
Sunningdale Ave., Ruis. 58 BW60
Sunningdale Clo. E6 81 EM69
Ascot Rd.
Sunningdale Clo. SE16 92 DV78
Ryder Dr.
Sunningdale Clo. SE28 82 EX72
Summerton Way
Sunningdale Clo., Stan. 45 CG52
Sunningdale Clo., Surb. 116 CL103
Culsac Rd.
Sunningdale Gdns. NW9 60 CQ57
Sunningdale Gdns. W8 90 DA76
Lexham Ms.
Sunningdale Rd., Brom. 122 EL98
Sunningdale Rd., Rain. 83 FG66
Sunningdale Rd., Sutt. 131 CZ105
Sunningfields Cres. NW4 47 CV54
Sunningfields Rd. NW4 61 CV55
Sunninghill Rd. SE13 93 EB82
Sunningvale Ave., West. 150 EJ115
Sunningvale Clo., West. 150 EK116
Sunny Bank SE25 120 DU97
Sunny Bank, Warl. 149 DY117
Sunny Cres. NW10 74 CQ66
Sunny Gdns. Par. NW4 47 CW54
Great N. Way
Sunny Gdns. Rd. NW4 47 CV54
Sunny Hill NW4 61 CV55
Sunny Nook Gdns., S.Croy. 134 DR107
Selsdon Rd.
Sunny Ri., Cat. 148 DR124
Sunny Rd., The, Enf. 37 DX39
Sunny Side, Walt. 114 BW99
Sunny Vw. NW9 60 CR57
Sunny Way N12 48 DE52
Sunnybank, Epsom 144 CQ116
Sunnybank Rd., Pot.B. 20 DA33
Sunnycroft Rd. SE25 120 DU97
Sunnycroft Rd., Houns. 86 CB82
Sunnycroft Rd., Sthl. 72 CA71
Sunnydale, Orp. 123 EN103
Sunnydale Gdns. NW7 46 CR51
Sunnydale Rd. SE12 108 EH85
Sunnydell, St.Alb. 16 CB26
Sunnydene Ave. E4 51 ED50
Sunnydene Ave., Ruis. 57 BU60
Sunnydene Gdns., Wem. 73 CJ65
Sunnydene Rd., Pur. 133 DP113
Sunnydene St. SE26 107 DY91
Sunnyfield NW7 47 CT49
Sunnyfield Rd., Chis. 124 EU97
Sunnyhill Clo. E5 65 DY63
Sunnyhill Rd. SW16 105 DL91
Sunnyhurst Clo., Sutt. 118 DA104
Sunnymead Ave., Mitch. 119 DJ97
Sunnymead Rd. NW9 60 CR59
Sunnymead Rd. SW15 103 CV85
Sunnymede, Chig. 54 EV47
Sunnymede Ave., Cars. 132 DD111
Sunnymede Ave., Epsom 130 CS109
Sunnymede Dr., Ilf. 67 EP57
Sunnyside NW2 61 CZ62
Sunnyside SW19 103 CY93
Sunnyside Dr. E4 51 EC45
Sunnyside Pas. SW19 103 CY93
Sunnyside Pl. SW19 103 CY93
Sunnyside
Sunnyside Rd. E10 65 EA60
Sunnyside Rd. N19 63 DK59
Sunnyside Rd. W5 73 CK74
Sunnyside Rd., Epp. 25 ET32
Sunnyside Rd., Ilf. 67 EQ62
Sunnyside Rd., Tedd. 101 CD91
Sunnyside Rd. E. N9 50 DU48
Sunnyside Rd. N. N9 50 DT48
Sunnyside Rd. S. N9 50 DT48
Sunray Ave. SE24 92 DR84
Sunray Ave., Brom. 122 EL100
Sunray Ave., Surb. 116 CP103
Sunray Ave., West Dr. 84 BK75
Sunrise Clo., Felt. 100 BZ90
Exeter Rd.
Sunset Ave. E4 51 EB46
Sunset Ave., Wdf.Grn. 52 EF49
Sunset Clo., Erith 97 FH80
Sunset Dr., Rom. (Havering-atte-Bower) 55 FH50
Sunset Gdns. SE25 120 DT96
Sunset Rd. SE5 92 DQ84
Sunset Rd. SE28 82 EU74
Sunset Vw., Barn. 33 CY40
Sunshine Way, Mitch. 118 DF96
Sunwell Clo. SE15 92 DV81
Cossall Wk.
Superior Dr., Orp. 137 ET107
Surbiton Ct., Surb. 115 CJ100
Surbiton Cres., Kings.T. 116 CL99
Surbiton Hall Clo., Kings.T. 116 CL98
Surbiton Hill Pk., Surb. 116 CM99
Surbiton Hill Rd., Surb. 116 CL98
Surbiton Par., Surb. 116 CL100
St. Mark's Hill
Surbiton Rd., Kings.T. 115 CK98
Surlingham Clo. SE28 82 EX73
Surma Clo. E1 78 DU70
Surr St. N7 63 DL64
Surrendale Pl. W9 76 DA70
Surrey Canal Rd. SE14 93 DX79
Surrey Canal Rd. SE15 92 DW79
Surrey Cres. W4 88 CN78
Surrey Gdns. N4 64 DQ58
Surrey Gdns., Lthd. 141 BU122
Surrey Gro. SE17 92 DS78
Surrey Sq.
Surrey Gro., Sutt. 118 DD104
Surrey La. SW11 90 DE81
Surrey La. Est. SW11 90 DE81
Surrey Lo. SE1 10 D7
Surrey Ms. SE27 106 DS91
Hamilton Rd.
Surrey Mt. SE23 106 DV88
Surrey Quays Rd. SE16 92 DW76
Surrey Rd. SE15 107 DX85
Surrey Rd., Bark. 81 ES66
Surrey Rd., Dag. 69 FB64
Surrey Rd., Har. 58 CC57
Surrey Rd., W.Wick. 121 EB102
Surrey Row SE1 10 F4
Surrey Row SE1 91 DP75
Surrey Sq. SE17 11 M10
Surrey Sq. SE17 92 DS78
Surrey St. E13 80 EH69
Surrey St. WC2 6 C10
Surrey St. WC2 77 DM73
Surrey St., Croy. 120 DQ103
Surrey Ter. SE17 11 N10
Surrey Ter. SE17 92 DS77
Surrey Water Rd. SE16 79 DX74
Surridge Gdns. SE19 106 DR93
Hancock Rd.
Susan Clo., Rom. 69 FC55
Susan Rd. SE3 94 EH82
Susan Wd., Chis. 123 EN95
Susannah St. E14 79 EB72
Sussex Ave., Islw. 87 CE83
Sussex Clo. N19 63 DL61
Cornwallis Rd.
Sussex Clo., Ilf. 67 EM58
Sussex Clo., N.Mal. 116 CS98
Sussex Clo., Twick. 101 CH86
Westmorland Clo.
Sussex Cres., Nthlt. 72 CA65
Sussex Gdns. N4 64 DQ57
Sussex Gdns. N6 62 DF57
Great N. Rd.
Sussex Gdns. W2 76 DD72
Sussex Gdns., Chess. 129 CK107
Sussex Ms. E. W2 4 A9
Sussex Ms. W. W2 4 A10
Sussex Pl. NW1 4 D3
Sussex Pl. NW1 76 DF70
Sussex Pl. W2 4 A9
Sussex Pl. W2 76 DD72
Sussex Pl. W6 89 CW78
Sussex Pl., Erith 97 FB80
Sussex Pl., N.Mal. 116 CS98
Sussex Ring N12 48 DA50
Sussex Rd. E6 81 EN67
Sussex Rd., Cars. 132 DF107
Sussex Rd., Erith 97 FB80
Sussex Rd., Har. 58 CC57
Sussex Rd., Mitch. 119 DL99
Lincoln Rd.
Sussex Rd., N.Mal. 116 CS98
Sussex Rd., Orp. 124 EW100
Sussex Rd., Sid. 110 EV92
Sussex Rd., S.Croy. 134 DR107
Sussex Rd., Sthl. 86 BX76
Sussex Rd., Uxb. 57 BQ63
Sussex Rd., Wat. 29 BU37
Sussex Rd., W.Wick. 121 EB102
Sussex Sq. W2 4 A10
Sussex Sq. W2 76 DD73
Sussex St. E13 80 EH69
Sussex St. SW1 91 DH78
Sussex Wk. SW9 91 DP84
Sussex Way N7 63 DL61
Sussex Way N19 63 DL60
Sussex Way, Barn. 35 DH43
Sutcliffe Clo. NW11 62 DB57
Sutcliffe Clo. (Bushey), Wat. 30 CC42
Sutcliffe Ho., Hayes 71 BU72
Sutcliffe Rd. SE18 95 ES79
Sutcliffe Rd., Well. 96 EW82
Sutherland Ave. W9 76 DA70
Sutherland Ave. W13 73 CH72
Sutherland Ave., Hayes 85 BU77
Sutherland Ave., Orp. 123 ET100
Sutherland Ave. (Cuffley), Pot.B. 21 DK28
Sutherland Ave., Sun. 113 BT96
Sutherland Ave., Well. 95 ES84
Sutherland Ave., West. 150 EK117
Sutherland Clo., Barn. 33 CY42
Sutherland Ct. NW9 60 CP56
Sutherland Dr. SW19 118 DD95
Willow Vw.
Sutherland Gdns. SW14 88 CS83
Sutherland Gdns., Sun. 113 BT96
Sutherland Ave.
Sutherland Gdns., Wor.Pk. 117 CV101
Sutherland Gro. SW18 103 CY86
Sutherland Gro., Tedd. 101 CE92
Sutherland Pl. W2 76 DA72
Sutherland Pt. E5 64 DV63
Tiger Way
Sutherland Rd. E17 51 DX54
Sutherland Rd. N9 50 DU46
Sutherland Rd. N17 50 DU52
Sutherland Rd. W4 88 CS79
Sutherland Rd. W13 73 CG72
Sutherland Rd., Belv. 96 FA76
Sutherland Rd., Croy. 119 DN101
Sutherland Rd., Enf. 37 DX43
Sutherland Rd., Sthl. 72 BZ72
Sutherland Rd. Path E17 65 DX55
Sutherland Row SW1 9 J10
Sutherland Row SW1 91 DH78
Sutherland Sq. SE17 92 DQ78
Sutherland St. SW1 9 H10
Sutherland St. SW1 91 DH78
Sutherland Wk. SE17 92 DQ78
Sutherland Way (Cuffley), Pot.B. 21 DK28
Sutlej Rd. SE7 94 EJ80
Sutterton St. N7 77 DM65
Sutton Clo., Beck. 121 EB95
Albemarle Rd.
Sutton Clo., Loug. 52 EL45
Sutton Clo., Pnr. 57 BU57
Sutton Common Rd., Sutt. 117 CZ101
Sutton Ct. W4 88 CQ79
Sutton Ct. Rd. E13 80 EJ69
Sutton Ct. Rd. W4 88 CQ80
Sutton Ct. Rd., Sutt. 132 DC107
Sutton Ct. Rd., Uxb. 71 BP67
Sutton Cres., Barn. 33 CX43
Sutton Dene, Houns. 86 CB81
Sutton Est. SW3 8 C10
Sutton Est. SW3 90 DE78
Sutton Est. W10 75 CW71
Sutton Est., The N1 77 DP66
Sutton Gdns., Bark. 81 ES67
Sutton Rd.
Sutton Gdns., Croy. 120 DT99
Sutton Grn., Bark. 81 ES67
Sutton Rd.
Sutton Gro., Sutt. 132 DD105
Sutton Hall Rd., Houns. 86 CA80
Sutton La., Bans. 146 DB115
Sutton La., Houns. 86 BZ83
Sutton La., Sutt. 132 DB111
Sutton La. N. W4 88 CQ78
Sutton La. S. W4 88 CQ79
Sutton Pk. Rd., Sutt. 132 DB107
Sutton Path, Borwd. 32 CN40
Stratfield Rd.
Sutton Pl. E9 64 DW64
Sutton Rd. E13 80 EF70
Sutton Rd. E17 51 DX53
Sutton Rd. N10 48 DG53
Sutton Rd., Bark. 81 ES68
Sutton Rd., Houns. 86 CA81
Sutton Rd., Wat. 30 BW41
Sutton Row W1 5 N8
Sutton Row W1 77 DK72
Sutton Sq. E9 64 DW64
Urswick Rd.
Sutton Sq., Houns. 86 BZ81
Sutton St. E1 78 DW73
Sutton Way W10 75 CW71
Sutton Way, Houns. 86 BZ81
Sutton's Way EC1 7 J5
Swaby Rd. SW18 104 DC88
Swaffham Way N22 49 DP52
White Hart La.
Swaffield Rd. SW18 104 DB87
Swaffield Rd., Sev. 155 FJ122
Swain Clo. SW16 105 DH93
Swain Rd., Th.Hth. 120 DQ99
Swains Clo., West Dr. 84 BL75
Swains La. N6 62 DG60
Swains Rd. SW17 104 DF94
Swainson Rd. W3 89 CT75
Swaisland Dr., Dart. 111 FF85
Swaisland Rd., Dart. 111 FH85
Swakeleys Dr., Uxb. 56 BM63
Swakeleys Rd., Uxb. 56 BL63
Swale Rd., Dart. 97 FG83
Swallands Rd. SE6 107 EA90
Swallow Clo. SE14 93 DX81
Swallow Clo., Erith 97 FE81
Swallow Clo., Rick. 42 BJ45
Swallow Clo. (Bushey), Wat. 44 CC46
Swallow Dr. NW10 74 CR65
Kingfisher Way
Swallow Dr., Nthlt. 72 CA68
Swallow Pas. W1 5 J9
Swallow Pl. W1 5 J9
Swallow St. E6 80 EL71
Swallow St. W1 9 L1
Swallow Wk., Horn. 83 FH65
Heron Flight Ave.
Swallowdale, S.Croy. 135 DX109
Swallowfield Rd. SE7 94 EH78
Swallowfield Way, Hayes 85 BR75
Swallows Oak, Abb.L. 15 BT31
Swallowtail Clo., Orp. 124 EX98
Swan & Pike Rd., Enf. 37 EA38
Swan App. E6 80 EL71
Swan Clo. E17 51 DY53
Swan Clo., Croy. 120 DS101
Swan Clo., Felt. 100 BY91
Swan Clo., Orp. 124 EU97
Swan Clo., Rick. 42 BK45
Parsonage Rd.
Swan Ct. SW3 90 DE78
Flood St.
Swan Dr. NW9 46 CS54
Swan La. EC4 11 K1
Swan La. N20 48 DC48
Swan La., Dart. 111 FF87
Swan La., Loug. 52 EJ45
Swan Mead SE1 11 M7
Swan Mead SE1 92 DS76
Swan Pas. E1 78 DT73
Cartwright St.
Swan Pl. SW13 89 CT82
Swan Rd. SE16 92 DW75
Swan Rd. SE18 94 EK76
Swan Rd., Felt. 100 BY92
Swan Rd., Sthl. 72 CB72
Swan Rd., West Dr. 84 BK75
Swan St. SE1 11 J6
Swan St. SE1 92 DQ76
Swan St., Islw. 87 CH83
Swan Wk. SW3 90 DF79
Swan Wk., Rom. 69 FE57
Swan Wk., Shep. 113 BS101
Swan Way, Enf. 37 DX40
Swan Yd. N1 77 DP65
Highbury Sta. Rd.
Swanage Rd. E4 51 EC52
Swanage Rd. SW18 104 DC86
Swanage Waye, Hayes 72 BW72
Swanbridge Rd., Bexh. 96 FA81
Swandon Way SW18 90 DB84
Swanfield Rd., Wal.Cr. 23 DY33
Swanfield St. E2 7 P3
Swanfield St. E2 78 DT69
Swanland Rd., Hat. 19 CV25
Swanland Rd., Pot.B. 19 CV33
Swanley Bar La., Pot.B. 20 DB28
Swanley Bypass, Sid. 125 FC96
Swanley Bypass, Swan. 125 FC96
Swanley Cres., Pot.B. 20 DB29
Swanley La., Swan. 125 FF97
Swanley Rd., Well. 96 EW81
Swanley Village Rd., Swan. 125 FH95
Swanscombe Rd. W4 88 CS78
Swanscombe Rd. W11 75 CX74
Swansea Rd., Enf. 36 DW42
Swanshope, Loug. 39 EP40
Swansland Gdns. E17 51 DY53
McEntee Ave.
Swanston Path, Wat. 44 BW48
Swanton Gdns. SW19 103 CX88
Swanton Rd., Erith 97 FB80
Swanwick Clo. SW15 103 CT87
Sward Rd., Orp. 124 EU100
Swaton Rd. E3 79 EA70
Swaylands Rd., Belv. 96 FA79
Swaythling Clo. N18 50 DV49
Sweden Gate SE16 93 DY76
Swedenborg Gdns. E1 78 DU73
Sweeney Cres. SE1 92 DT75
Sweeps Ditch Clo., Stai. 98 BG94
Sweeps La., Orp. 124 EX99
Sweet Briar Grn. N9 50 DT48
Sweet Briar Gro. N9 50 DT48
Sweet Briar La., Epsom 130 CR114
Madans Wk.
Sweet Briar Wk. N18 50 DT49
Sweetcroft La., Uxb. 70 BM66
Sweetmans Ave., Pnr. 58 BX55
Sweets Way N20 48 DD47
Swete St. E13 80 EG68
Swetenham Wk. SE18 95 EQ78
Sandbach Pl.
Sweyn Pl. SE3 94 EG82
Swievelands Rd., West. 150 EH119
Swift Clo. E17 51 DY53
Swift Clo., Har. 58 CB61
Swift Clo., Hayes 71 BT72
Church Rd.
Swift Rd., Felt. 100 BX91
Swift Rd., Sthl. 86 BZ76
Swift St. SW6 89 CZ81
Swiftsden Way, Brom. 108 EE93
Swinbrook Rd. W10 75 CY71
Swinburne Ct. SE5 92 DR84
Basingdon Way
Swinburne Cres., Croy. 120 DW100
Swinburne Rd. SW15 89 CU84
Swinderby Rd., Wem. 74 CL65
Swindon Clo., Ilf. 67 ES61
Salisbury Rd.
Swindon Rd., Houns. 99 BQ86
Southern Perimeter Rd.
Swindon St. W12 75 CV74
Swinfield Clo., Felt. 100 BY91
Swinford Gdns. SW9 91 DP83
Swingate La. SE18 95 ES80
Swinnerton St. E9 65 DY64
Swinton Clo., Wem. 60 CP60
Swinton Pl. WC1 6 B2
Swinton Pl. WC1 77 DM69
Swinton St. WC1 6 B2
Swinton St. WC1 77 DM69
Swires Shaw, Kes. 136 EK105
Swiss Ave., Wat. 29 BS42
Swiss Clo., Wat. 29 BS41
Swiss Ter. NW6 76 DD66
Swithland Gdns. SE9 109 EN91
Swyncombe Ave. W5 87 CH77
Swynford Gdns. NW4 61 CU56
Handowe Clo.
Sybil Ms. N4 63 DP58
Lothair Rd. N.
Sybil Phoenix Clo. SE8 93 DX78
Sybil Thorndike Ho. N1 78 DQ65
Clephane Rd.
Sybourn St. E17 65 DZ59
Sycamore App., Rick. 29 BQ43
Sycamore Ave. W5 87 CK76
Sycamore Ave., Hayes 71 BS73
Sycamore Ave., Sid. 109 ET86
Sycamore Clo. E16 80 EE70
Clarence Rd.
Sycamore Clo. N9 50 DU49
Pycroft Way
Sycamore Clo. SE9 108 EL89
Sycamore Clo. W3 74 CS74
Bromyard Ave.
Sycamore Clo., Barn. 34 DD44
Sycamore Clo., Cars. 132 DF105
Sycamore Clo., Felt. 99 BU90
Sycamore Clo., Lthd. 143 CE123
Sycamore Clo., Nthlt. 72 BY67
Sycamore Clo., Wal.Cr. 22 DS27
Sycamore Clo., Wat. 29 BV35
Sycamore Clo. (Bushey), Wat. 30 BY40
Sycamore Clo., West Dr. 70 BM73
Whitethorn Ave.
Sycamore Dr., St.Alb. 17 CD27
Sycamore Dr., Swan. 125 FE97
Sycamore Gdns. W6 89 CV75
Sycamore Gdns., Mitch. 118 DD96
Sycamore Gro. NW9 60 CQ59
Sycamore Gro. SE6 107 EC86
Sycamore Gro. SE20 106 DU94
Sycamore Gro., N.Mal. 116 CR97
Sycamore Hill N11 48 DG51
Sycamore Ms. SW4 91 DJ83
Sycamore Ri., Bans. 131 CX114
Sycamore Rd. SW19 103 CW93
Sycamore Rd., Rick. 29 BQ43
Sycamore St. EC1 7 H5
Sycamore Wk. W10 75 CY70
Fifth Ave.
Sycamore Wk., Ilf. 67 EQ56
Civic Way
Sycamore Way, Tedd. 101 CJ93
Sycamore Way, Th.Hth. 119 DN99
Grove Rd.
Sycamores, The, Rad. 17 CH34
Sydenham Ave. SE26 106 DV92
Sydenham Clo., Rom. 69 FF56
Sydenham Cotts. SE12 108 EJ89
Sydenham Hill SE23 106 DV88
Sydenham Hill SE26 106 DT91
Sydenham Hill Est. SE26 106 DU90
Sydenham Pk. SE26 106 DW90
Sydenham Pk. Rd. SE26 106 DW90
Sydenham Ri. SE23 106 DV89
Sydenham Rd. SE26 107 DX92
Sydenham Rd., Croy. 120 DQ102
Sydmons Ct. SE23 106 DW87
Sydner Ms. N16 64 DT63
Sydner Rd.
Sydner Rd. N16 64 DT63
Sydney Ave., Pur. 133 DM112
Sydney Clo. SW3 8 A9
Sydney Clo. SW3 90 DD77
Sydney Cres., Ashf. 99 BP93
Sydney Gro. NW4 61 CW57
Sydney Ms. SW3 8 A9
Sydney Pl. SW7 8 A9
Sydney Pl. SW7 90 DD77
Sydney Rd. E11 66 EH58
Mansfield Rd.
Sydney Rd. N8 63 DN56
Sydney Rd. N10 48 DG53
Sydney Rd. SE2 96 EW76
Sydney Rd. SW20 117 CX96
Sydney Rd. W13 73 CG74
Sydney Rd., Bexh. 96 EX84
Sydney Rd., Enf. 36 DR41
Sydney Rd., Felt. 99 BU88
Sydney Rd., Ilf. 53 EQ54
Sydney Rd., Rich. 88 CL84
Sydney Rd., Sid. 109 ES91
Sydney Rd., Sutt. 132 DA105
Sydney Rd., Tedd. 101 CF92
Sydney Rd., Wat. 29 BS43
Sydney Rd., Wdf.Grn. 52 EG49
Sydney St. SW3 8 B10
Sydney St. SW3 90 DE78
Sykes Dr., Stai. 98 BH92
Sylvan Ave. N3 48 DA54
Sylvan Ave. N22 49 DM52
Sylvan Ave. NW7 47 CT51
Sylvan Ave., Rom. 68 EZ58
Sylvan Clo., S.Croy. 134 DV110
Sylvan Est. SE19 120 DT95
Sylvan Gdns., Surb. 115 CK101
Sylvan Gro. NW2 61 CX63
Sylvan Gro. SE15 92 DV79
Sylvan Hill SE19 120 DS95
Sylvan Rd. E7 80 EG65
Sylvan Rd. E11 66 EG57
Sylvan Rd. E17 65 EA57
Sylvan Rd. SE19 120 DT95
Sylvan Rd., Ilf. 67 EQ61
Hainault St.
Sylvan Wk., Brom. 123 EM97
Sylvan Way, Chig. 54 EV48
Sylvan Way, Dag. 68 EV62
Sylvan Way, W.Wick. 136 EE105
Sylvana Clo., Uxb. 70 BM67
Sylverdale Rd., Croy. 119 DP104
Sylverdale Rd., Pur. 133 DP113
Sylvester Ave., Chis. 109 EM93
Sylvester Gdns., Ilf. 54 EV50
Sylvester Path E8 78 DV65
Sylvester Rd.
Sylvester Rd. E8 78 DV65
Sylvester Rd. E17 65 DZ59
Sylvester Rd. N2 48 DC54
Sylvester Rd., Wem. 59 CJ64
Sylvestres, Sev. 153 FD119
London Rd.
Sylvestrus Clo., Kings.T. 116 CN95
Sylvia Ave., Pnr. 44 BY51
Sylvia Gdns., Wem. 74 CP66
Symes Ms. NW1 77 DJ68
Camden High St.
Symons St. SW3 8 E9
Symons St. SW3 90 DF77
Syon Gate Way, Brent. 87 CG80
Syon La., Islw. 87 CF79
Syon Pk. Gdns., Islw. 87 CF80

Syon Vista, Rich. 87 CK81
Kew Rd.

T

Tabard Gdn. Est. SE1 11 L5
Tabard Gdn. Est. SE1 92 DR75
Tabard St. SE1 11 K5
Tabard St. SE1 92 DR75
Tabarin Way, Epsom 145 CW116
Tabernacle Ave. E13 80 EG70
Barking Rd.
Tabernacle St. EC2 7 L5
Tabernacle St. EC2 78 DR70
Tableer Ave. SW4 105 DJ85
Tabley Rd. N7 63 DL63
Tabor Gdns., Sutt. 131 CZ107
Tabor Gro. SW19 103 CY94
Tabor Rd. W6 89 CV76
Tachbrook Est. SW1 91 DK78
Tachbrook Ms. SW1 9 K8
Tachbrook Rd., Felt. 99 BT87
Tachbrook Rd., Sthl. 86 BX77
Tachbrook Rd., Uxb. 70 BJ68
Tachbrook St. SW1 9 L9
Tachbrook St. SW1 91 DJ77
Tack Ms. SE4 93 EA83
Tadema Rd. SW10 90 DC80
Tadmor Clo., Sun. 113 BT98
Tadmor St. W12 75 CX74
Tadorne Rd., Tad. 145 CW121
Tadworth Ave., N.Mal. 117 CT99
Tadworth Clo., Tad. 145 CX122
Tadworth Par., Horn. 69 FH63
Maylands Ave.
Tadworth Rd. NW2 61 CU61
Tadworth St., Tad. 145 CW123
Taeping St. E14 93 EB77
Taffy's How, Mitch. 118 DE97
Taft Way E3 79 EB69
St. Leonards St.
Tagg's Island, Hmptn. 115 CD96
Tailworth St. E1 78 DU71
Chicksand St.
Tait Rd., Croy. 120 DS101
Takeley Clo., Rom. 55 FD54
Takeley Clo., Wal.Abb. 23 ED33
Talacre Rd. NW5 76 DG65
Talbot Ave. N2 62 DD55
Talbot Ave., Wat. 44 BY45
Talbot Clo. N15 64 DT56
Talbot Ct. EC3 7 L10
Talbot Cres. NW4 61 CU57
Talbot Gdns., Ilf. 68 EU61
Talbot Ho. E14 79 EB72
Giraud St.
Talbot Pl. SE3 94 EE82
Talbot Rd. E6 81 EN68
Talbot Rd. E7 66 EG63
Talbot Rd. N6 62 DG58
Talbot Rd. N15 64 DT56
Talbot Rd. N22 49 DJ54
Talbot Rd. SE22 92 DS84
Talbot Rd. W2 76 DA72
Talbot Rd. W11 75 CZ72
Talbot Rd. W13 73 CG73
Talbot Rd., Ashf. 98 BK92
Talbot Rd., Brom. 122 EH98
Masons Hill
Talbot Rd., Cars. 132 DG106
Talbot Rd., Dag. 82 EZ65
Talbot Rd., Har. 45 CF54
Talbot Rd., Islw. 87 CG84
Talbot Rd., Rick. 42 BL46
Talbot Rd., Sthl. 86 BY77
Talbot Rd., Th.Hth. 120 DR98
Talbot Rd., Twick. 101 CE88
Talbot Rd., Wem. 59 CK64
Talbot Sq. W2 4 A9
Talbot Sq. W2 76 DD72
Talbot Wk. NW10 74 CS65
Garnet Rd.
Talbot Wk. W11 75 CY72
Lancaster Rd.
Talbot Yd. SE1 11 K3
Taleworth Clo., Ash. 143 CK120
Taleworth Pk., Ash. 143 CK120
Taleworth Rd., Ash. 143 CK119
Talfourd Pl. SE15 92 DT81
Talfourd Rd. SE15 92 DT81
Talgarth Rd. W6 89 CX78
Talgarth Rd. W14 89 CX78
Talgarth Wk. NW9 60 CS57
Talisman Clo., Ilf. 68 EV60
Talisman Sq. SE26 106 DU91
Talisman Way, Epsom 145 CW116
Talisman Way, Wem. 60 CM62
Forty Ave.
Tall Elms Clo., Brom. 122 EF99
Tall Trees SW16 119 DM97
Tallack Clo., Har. 45 CE52
College Hill Rd.
Tallack Rd. E10 65 DZ60
Tallis Clo. E16 80 EH72
Tallis Gro. SE7 94 EH79
Tallis St. EC4 6 E10
Tallis St. EC4 77 DN73
Tallis Vw. NW10 74 CR65
Mitchellbrook Way
Tallis Way, Borwd. 31 CK39
Tally Ho Cor. N12 48 DC50
Talma Gdns., Twick. 101 CE86
Talma Rd. SW2 91 DN84
Talmage Clo. SE23 106 DW87
Tyson Rd.
Talman Gro., Stan. 45 CK51
Talwin St. E3 79 EB69
Tamar Sq., Wdf.Grn. 52 EH51
Tamar St. SE7 94 EL76
Tamar Way N17 64 DT55
Tamarind Yd. E1 78 DU74
Asher Way
Tamarisk Sq. W12 75 CT73
Tamesis Gdns., Wor.Pk. 116 CS103
Tamian Est., Houns. 86 BW84
Tamian Way, Houns. 86 BW84
Tamworth Ave., Wdf.Grn. 52 EE51
Tamworth Gdns., Pnr. 43 BV54
Tamworth La., Mitch. 118 DG96
Tamworth Pk., Mitch. 119 DH98
Tamworth Pl., Croy. 120 DQ103
Tamworth Rd., Croy. 119 DP103
Tamworth St. SW6 90 DA79
Tancred Rd. N4 63 DP58
Tandridge Ct., Cat. 148 DU122
Tandridge Dr., Orp. 123 ER102
Tandridge Gdns., S.Croy. 134 DT113
Tandridge Pl., Orp. 123 ER101
Tandridge Dr.
Tandridge Rd., Warl. 149 DX119
Tanfield Ave. NW2 61 CT63
Tanfield Clo., Wal.Cr. 22 DV27
Spicersfield
Tanfield Rd., Croy. 134 DQ105
Tangier Rd., Rich. 88 CP84
Tangier Way, Tad. 145 CY117
Tangier Wd., Tad. 145 CY118
Tangle Tree Clo. N3 62 DB55
Tanglebury Clo., Brom. 122 EL98
Tangles Clo., Uxb. 70 BN69
Tanglewood Clo., Croy. 120 DW104
Tanglewood Clo., Stan. 45 CE47
Tanglewood Way, Felt. 99 BV90
Tangley Gro. SW15 103 CT87
Tangley Pk. Rd., Hmptn. 100 BZ92
Tanglyn Ave., Shep. 112 BN99
Tangmere Cres., Horn. 83 FH65
Tangmere Gdns., Nthlt. 72 BW68
Tangmere Gro., Kings.T. 101 CK92
Tangmere Way NW9 46 CS54
Tanhurst Wk. SE2 96 EX76
Alsike Rd.
Tankerton Rd., Surb. 116 CM103
Tankerton St. WC1 6 A3
Tankerville Rd. SW16 105 DK94
Tankridge Rd. NW2 61 CV61
Tanner St. SE1 11 N5
Tanner St. SE1 92 DS75
Tanner St., Bark. 81 EQ65
Tanners Clo., Walt. 113 BV100
Tanners Dean, Lthd. 143 CJ122
Tanners End La. N18 50 DS49
Tanners Hill SE8 93 DZ81
Tanners Hill, Abb.L. 15 BT31
Tanners La., Ilf. 67 EQ55
Tanners Wd. Clo., Abb.L. 15 BS32
Tanners Wd. La.
Tanners Wd. La., Abb.L. 15 BS32
Tannery Clo., Beck. 121 DX99
Tannery Clo., Dag. 69 FB62
Tannington Ter. N5 63 DN62
Tannsfeld Rd. SE26 107 DX92
Tansley Clo. N7 63 DK64
Hilldrop Rd.
Tanswell Est. SE1 10 E5
Tanswell St. SE1 10 D5
Tansy Clo. E6 81 EN72
Tant Ave. E16 80 EF72
Tantallon Rd. SW12 104 DG88
Tantony Gro., Rom. 68 EX55
Tanworth Clo., Nthwd. 43 BQ51
Tanyard La., Bex. 110 FA87
Bexley High St.
Tanza Rd. NW3 62 DF63
Tapestry Clo., Sutt. 132 DB108
Taplow NW3 76 DD66
Taplow SE17 92 DR78
Taplow Rd. N13 50 DQ49
Taplow St. N1 7 J1
Taplow St. N1 78 DQ68
Tapp St. E1 78 DV70
Tappesfield Rd. SE15 92 DW83
Tapster St., Barn. 33 CZ41
Tarbert Rd. SE22 106 DS85
Tarbert Wk. E1 78 DW73
Juniper St.
Target Clo., Felt. 99 BS86
Tariff Cres. SE8 93 DZ77
Enterprize Way
Tariff Rd. N17 50 DU51
Tarleton Gdns. SE23 106 DV88
Tarling Clo., Sid. 110 EV90
Tarling Rd. E16 80 EF72
Tarling Rd. N2 48 DC54
Tarling St. E1 78 DV72
Tarling St. Est. E1 78 DW72
Tarmac Way, West Dr. 84 BH80
Tarn St. SE1 11 H7
Tarnbank, Enf. 35 DL43
Tarnwood Pk. SE9 109 EM87
Tarpan Way, Brox. 23 DZ26
Tarquin Ho. SE26 106 DU91
Tarragon Clo. SE14 93 DY80
Tarragon Gdns. SE14 93 DY80
Southerngate Way
Tarragon Gro. SE26 107 DX93
Tarrant Pl. W1 4 D7
Tarrington Clo. SW16 105 DK90
Tarry La. SE8 93 DY77
Tartar Rd., Cob. 128 BW113
Tarver Rd. SE17 91 DP78
Tarves Way SE10 93 EB80
Tash Pl. N11 49 DH50
Woodland Rd.
Tasker Clo., Hayes 85 BQ80
Tasker Ho., Bark. 81 ER68
Dovehouse Mead
Tasker Rd. NW3 62 DF64
Tasman Rd. SW9 91 DL83
Tasman Wk. E16 80 EK72
Royal Rd.
Tasmania Ter. N18 50 DQ51
Tasso Rd. W6 89 CY79
Tatam Rd. NW10 74 CR66
Tate & Lyle Jetty E16 94 EL75
Tate Clo., Lthd. 143 CJ123
Windmill Dr.
Tate Rd. E16 81 EM74
Newland St.
Tate Rd., Sutt. 132 DA106
Tatnell Rd. SE23 107 DY86
Tatsfield App. Rd., West. 150 EH123
Tatsfield La., West. 150 EL121
Tattenham Cor. Rd., Epsom 144 CS117
Tattenham Cres., Epsom 145 CU118
Tattenham Gro., Epsom 145 CV118
Tattenham Way, Tad. 145 CX118
Tattersall Clo. SE9 108 EL85
Tatton Cres. N16 64 DT59
Clapton Common
Tatum St. SE17 11 L9
Tatum St. SE17 92 DR77
Tauber Clo., Borwd. 32 CM42
Taunton Ave. SW20 117 CV96
Taunton Ave., Cat. 148 DT123
Taunton Ave., Houns. 86 CC82
Taunton Clo., Bexh. 97 FD82
Taunton Clo., Ilf. 53 ET51
Taunton Clo., Sutt. 118 DA102
Taunton Ct. N17 50 DS52
Taunton Dr. N2 48 DC54
Taunton Dr., Enf. 35 DN41
Taunton La., Couls. 147 DN119
Taunton Ms. NW1 4 D5
Taunton Pl. NW1 4 D4
Taunton Pl. NW1 76 DF70
Taunton Rd. SE12 108 EE85
Taunton Rd., Grnf. 72 CB67
Taunton Way, Stan. 46 CL54
Tavern Clo., Cars. 118 DE101
Tavern La. SW9 91 DN82
Taverner Sq. N5 64 DQ63
Highbury Gra.
Taverners Clo. W11 75 CY74
Addison Ave.
Taverners Way E4 52 EE46
Douglas Rd.
Tavistock Ave. E17 65 DX55
Tavistock Ave., Grnf. 73 CG68
Tavistock Clo. N16 64 DS64
Crossway
Tavistock Clo., Pot.B. 20 DD31
Tavistock Clo., Stai. 98 BK94
Tavistock Cres. W11 75 CZ71
Tavistock Cres., Mitch. 119 DL98
Tavistock Gdns., Ilf. 67 ES63
Tavistock Gate, Croy. 120 DR102
Tavistock Gro., Croy. 120 DR101
Tavistock Ms. E18 66 EG56
Avon Way
Tavistock Ms. W11 75 CZ72
Lancaster Rd.
Tavistock Pl. E18 66 EG55
Avon Way
Tavistock Pl. N14 49 DH45
Chase Side
Tavistock Pl. WC1 5 P4
Tavistock Pl. WC1 77 DL70
Tavistock Rd. E7 66 EF63
Tavistock Rd. E15 80 EF65
Tavistock Rd. E18 66 EG55
Tavistock Rd. N4 64 DR58
Tavistock Rd. NW10 75 CT68
Tavistock Rd. W11 75 CZ72
Tavistock Rd., Brom. 122 EF98
Tavistock Rd., Cars. 118 DD102
Tavistock Rd., Croy. 120 DR102
Tavistock Rd., Edg. 46 CN53
Tavistock Rd., Uxb. 57 BQ64
Tavistock Rd., Wat. 30 BX39
Tavistock Rd., Well. 96 EW81
Tavistock Rd., West Dr. 70 BK74
Tavistock Sq. WC1 5 N4
Tavistock Sq. WC1 77 DK70
Tavistock St. WC2 6 A10
Tavistock St. WC2 77 DL73
Tavistock Ter. N19 63 DK62
Tavistock Wk., Cars. 118 DD102
Tavistock Rd.
Taviton St. WC1 5 M4
Taviton St. WC1 77 DK70
Tavy Bri. SE2 96 EW76
Tavy Clo. SE11 10 E10
Tawney Common, Epp. 26 FA32
Tawney Rd. SE28 82 EV73
Tawny Clo. W13 73 CH74
Tawny Clo., Felt. 99 BU90
Chervil Clo.
Tawny Way SE16 93 DX77
Tay Way, Rom. 55 FF53
Tayben Ave., Twick. 101 CE86
Taybridge Rd. SW11 90 DG83
Tayburn Clo. E14 79 EC72
Tayfield Clo., Uxb. 57 BQ62
Tayles Hill, Epsom 131 CT110
Taylor Ave., Rich. 88 CP82
Taylor Clo. N17 50 DU52
Taylor Clo., Hmptn. 100 CC92
Taylor Clo., Orp. 137 ET105
Taylor Clo., Rom. 54 FA52
Taylor Ct. E15 65 EC64
Taylor Rd., Ash. 143 CK117
Taylor Rd., Mitch. 104 DE94
Taylor Rd., Wall. 133 DH106
Taylors Bldgs. SE18 95 EP77
Spray St.
Taylors Clo., Sid. 109 ET91
Taylors Grn. W3 74 CS72
Long Dr.
Taylors La. NW10 74 CS66
Taylors La. SE26 106 DV91
Taylors La., Barn. 33 CZ39
Taymount Ri. SE23 106 DW89
Tayport Clo. N1 77 DL66
Tayside Dr., Edg. 46 CP48
Taywood Rd., Nthlt. 72 BZ69
Invicta Gro.
Teak Clo. SE16 79 DY74
Teal Ave., Orp. 124 EX98
Teal Clo. E16 80 EK71
Fulmer Rd.
Teal Clo., S.Croy. 135 DX111
Teal Dr., Nthwd. 43 BQ52
Teale St. E2 78 DU68
Tealing Dr., Epsom 130 CR105
Teardrop Ind. Est., Swan. 125 FH99
Teasel Clo., Croy. 121 DX102
Teasel Way E15 80 EE69
Teazle Wd. Hill, Lthd. 143 CE117
Oaklawn Rd.
Teazlewood Pk., Lthd. 143 CG117
Tebworth Rd. N17 50 DT52
Teck Clo., Islw. 87 CG82
Tedder Clo., Chess. 129 CJ107
Tedder Clo., Ruis. 57 BV64
West End Rd.
Tedder Clo., Uxb. 70 BM66
Tedder Rd., S.Croy. 134 DW108
Teddington Clo., Epsom 130 CR110
Teddington Lock, Tedd. 101 CG91
Teddington Pk., Tedd. 101 CF92
Teddington Pk. Rd., Tedd. 101 CF91
Tedworth Gdns. SW3 90 DF78
Tedworth Sq.
Tedworth Sq. SW3 90 DF78
Tee, The W3 74 CS72
Tees Ave., Grnf. 73 CE68
Teesdale Ave., Islw. 87 CG81
Teesdale Clo. E2 78 DU68
Teesdale Gdns. SE25 120 DS96
Grange Hill
Teesdale Gdns., Islw. 87 CG81
Teesdale Rd. E11 66 EF58
Teesdale St. E2 78 DV68
Teesdale Yd. E2 78 DV68
Teesdale St.
Teeswater Ct., Erith 96 EX76
Middle Way
Teevan Clo., Croy. 120 DU101
Teevan Rd., Croy. 120 DU102
Teignmouth Clo. SW4 91 DK84
Teignmouth Clo., Edg. 46 CM54
Teignmouth Gdns., Grnf. 73 CF68
Teignmouth Rd. NW2 61 CX64
Teignmouth Rd., Well. 96 EW82
Telcote Way, Ruis. 58 BW59
Woodlands Ave.
Telegraph Hill NW3 62 DB62
Telegraph La., Esher 129 CF107
Telegraph Ms., Ilf. 68 EU60
Telegraph Rd. SW15 103 CV87
Telegraph St. EC2 7 K8
Telegraph Track, Wall. 133 DH110
Telemann Sq. SE3 94 EH83
Telephone Pl. SW6 89 CZ79
Lillie Rd.
Telfer Clo. W3 88 CQ75
Church Rd.
Telferscot Rd. SW12 105 DK88
Telford Ave. SW2 105 DK88
Telford Clo. E17 65 DY59
Telford Clo. SE19 106 DT93
St. Aubyn's Rd.
Telford Clo. W3 88 CQ75
Church Rd.
Telford Clo., Wat. 30 BX35
Telford Dr., Walt. 114 BW101
Telford Rd. N11 49 DJ51
Telford Rd. NW9 61 CU58
West Hendon Bdy.
Telford Rd. SE9 109 ER89
Telford Rd. W10 75 CY71
Telford Rd., St.Alb. 17 CJ27
Telford Rd., Sthl. 72 CB73
Telford Rd., Twick. 100 CA87
Telford Ter. SW1 91 DJ79
Telford Way W3 74 CS71
Telford Way, Hayes 72 BY71
Telfords Yd. E1 78 DU73
The Highway
Telham Rd. E6 81 EN68
Tell Gro. SE22 92 DT84
Tellisford, Esher 128 CB105
Tellson Ave. SE18 94 EK81
Telscombe Clo., Orp. 123 ES103
Telston La., Sev. 153 FF117
Temeraire St. SE16 92 DW75
Albion St.
Temperley Rd. SW12 104 DG87
Tempest Ave., Pot.B. 20 DD32
Tempest Way, Rain. 83 FG65
Templar Dr. SE28 82 EX72
Templar Ho. NW2 75 CZ65
Shoot Up Hill
Templar Pl., Hmptn. 100 CA94
Templar St. SE5 91 DP82
Templars Ave. NW11 61 CZ58
Templars Cres. N3 48 DA54
Templars Dr., Har. 45 CD51
Temple EC4 6 D10
Temple EC4 77 DN73
Temple Ave. EC4 6 E10
Temple Ave. EC4 77 DN73
Temple Ave. N20 48 DD45
Temple Ave., Croy. 121 DZ103
Temple Ave., Dag. 68 FA60
Temple Clo. E11 66 EE59
Wadley Rd.
Temple Clo. N3 47 CZ54
Cyprus Rd.
Temple Clo. SE28 95 EQ76
Temple Clo. (Cheshunt), Wal.Cr. 22 DU31
Temple Clo., Wat. 29 BT40
Temple Ct., Pot.B. 19 CY31
Mimms Hall Rd.
Temple Fortune Hill NW11 62 DA57
Temple Fortune La. NW11 61 CZ57
Temple Gdns. N21 49 DP47
Barrowell Grn.
Temple Gdns. NW11 61 CZ58
Temple Gdns., Dag. 68 EX62
Temple Gdns., Rick. 43 BP49
Temple Gro. NW11 62 DA58
Temple Gro., Enf. 35 DP41
Temple La. EC4 6 E9
Temple Mead Clo., Stan. 45 CH51
Temple Mill La. E15 65 EA63
Temple Pk., Uxb. 70 BN69
Temple Pl. WC2 6 C10
Temple Pl. WC2 77 DM73
Temple Rd. E6 80 EL67
Temple Rd. N8 63 DM56
Temple Rd. NW2 61 CW63
Temple Rd. W4 88 CQ76
Temple Rd. W5 87 CK76
Temple Rd., Croy. 134 DR105
Temple Rd., Epsom 130 CR111
Temple Rd., Houns. 86 CB84
Temple Rd., Rich. 88 CM82
Temple Rd., West. 150 EK117
Temple Sheen SW14 88 CP84
Temple Sheen Rd. SW14 88 CP84
Temple St. E2 78 DV68
Temple Way, Sutt. 118 DD104
Temple W. Ms. SE11 10 F7
Temple W. Ms. SE11 91 DP76
Templecombe Rd. E9 78 DW67
Templecombe Way, Mord. 117 CY99
Templecroft, Ashf. 99 BR93
Templedene Ave., Stai. 98 BH94
Templefield Clo., Add. 126 BH107
Templehof Ave. NW2 61 CW59
Templeman Clo., Pur. 147 DP116
Croftleigh Ave.
Templeman Rd. W7 73 CF71
Templemead Clo. W3 74 CS72
Templemere, Wey. 113 BR104
Templepan La., Rick. 28 BL37
Templeton Ave. E4 51 EA49
Templeton Clo. N16 64 DS64
Truman's Rd.
Templeton Clo. SE19 120 DR95
Templeton Pl. SW5 90 DA77
Templeton Rd. N15 64 DR58
Templewood W13 73 CH71
Templewood Ave. NW3 62 DB62
Templewood Gdns. NW3 62 DB62
Tempsford Ave., Borwd. 32 CR42
Tempsford Clo., Enf. 36 DQ41
Gladbeck Way
Temsford Clo., Har. 44 CC54
Ten Acres, Lthd. 143 CD124
Ten Acres Clo., Lthd. 143 CD124
Tenbury Clo. E7 66 EK64
Romford Rd.
Tenbury Ct. SW2 105 DK88
Tenby Ave., Har. 45 CH54
Tenby Clo. N15 64 DT56
Hanover Rd.
Tenby Clo., Rom. 68 EY58
Tenby Gdns., Nthlt. 72 CA65
Tenby Rd. E17 65 DY57
Tenby Rd., Edg. 46 CM53
Tenby Rd., Enf. 36 DW41
Tenby Rd., Rom. 68 EY58
Tenby Rd., Well. 96 EX81
Tench St. E1 78 DV74
Tenda Rd. SE16 92 DV77
Roseberry St.
Tendring Way, Rom. 68 EW57
Tenham Ave. SW2 105 DK89
Tenison Ct. W1 5 K10
Tenison Way SE1 10 C3
Tenison Way SE1 77 DM74
Tennand Clo. (Cheshunt), Wal.Cr. 22 DT26
Tenniel Clo. W2 76 DC72
Porchester Gdns.
Tennis Ct. La., E.Mol. 115 CF97
Hampton Ct. Way
Tennis St. SE1 11 K4
Tennis St. SE1 92 DR75
Tennison Ave., Borwd. 32 CP43
Tennison Clo., Couls. 147 DP120
Tennison Rd. SE25 120 DT98
Tenniswood Rd., Enf. 36 DS39
Tennyson Ave. E11 66 EG59
Tennyson Ave. E12 80 EL66
Tennyson Ave. NW9 60 CQ55
Tennyson Ave., N.Mal. 117 CV99

Tennyson Ave., Twick. 101 CF88
Tennyson Ave., Wal.Abb. 24 EE34
Tennyson Clo., Enf. 37 DX43
Tennyson Clo., Felt. 99 BT86
Tennyson Clo., Well. 95 ET81
Tennyson Rd. E10 65 EB60
Tennyson Rd. E15 80 EE66
Tennyson Rd. E17 65 DZ58
Tennyson Rd. NW6 75 CZ67
Tennyson Rd. NW7 47 CU50
Tennyson Rd. SE20 107 DX94
Tennyson Rd. SW19 104 DC93
Tennyson Rd. W7 73 CF73
Tennyson Rd., Add. 126 BL105
Tennyson Rd., Ashf. 98 BL92
Tennyson Rd., Houns. 86 CC82
Tennyson Rd., St.Alb. 16 CA26
Tennyson Rd., Well. 95 ET81
Tennyson St. SW8 91 DH82
Tennyson Way, Horn. 69 FG61
Tensing Rd., Sthl. 86 CA76
Tent Peg La., Orp. 123 EQ99
Tent St. E1 78 DV70
Tentelow La., Sthl. 86 CA78
Tenter Grd. E1 7 P7
Tenter Pas. E1 78 DT72
Mansell St.
Tenterden Clo. NW4 61 CX55
Tenterden Clo. SE9 109 EM91
Tenterden Dr. NW4 61 CX55
Tenterden Gdns. NW4 61 CX55
Tenterden Gdns., Croy. 120 DU101
Tenterden Gro. NW4 61 CX55
Tenterden Rd. N17 50 DT52
Tenterden Rd., Croy. 120 DU101
Tenterden Rd., Dag. 68 EZ61
Tenterden St. W1 5 J9
Tenterden St. W1 77 DH72
Terborch Way SE22 106 DS85
East Dulwich Gro.
Tercel Path, Chig. 54 EV49
Teresa Gdns., Wal.Cr. 22 DW34
Teresa Ms. E17 65 EA56
Teresa Wk. N10 63 DH57
Connaught Gdns.
Terling Clo. E11 66 EF62
Terling Rd., Dag. 68 FA61
Terling Wk. N1 78 DQ67
Britannia Row
Terminus Pl. SW1 9 J7
Terminus Pl. SW1 91 DH76
Terrace, The E4 52 EE48
Chingdale Rd.
Terrace, The N3 47 CZ54
Hendon La.
Terrace, The NW6 76 DA67
Terrace, The SW13 88 CS82
Terrace, The, Add. 126 BL106
Terrace, The, Har. 59 CH60
Terrace, The, Sev. 154 FD122
Terrace, The, Wdf.Grn. 52 EG51
Broadmead Rd.
Terrace Gdns. SW13 89 CT82
Terrace Gdns., Wat. 29 BV40
St. Albans Rd.
Terrace La., Rich. 102 CL86
Terrace Rd. E9 78 DW66
Terrace Rd. E13 80 EG67
Terrace Rd., Walt. 113 BU101
Terrace Wk., Dag. 68 EY64
Terrapin Rd. SW17 105 DH90
Terretts Pl. N1 77 DP66
Upper St.
Terrick Rd. N22 49 DL53
Terrick St. W12 75 CV72
Terrilands, Pnr. 58 BZ55
Terront Rd. N15 64 DQ57
Tessa Sanderson Pl. SW8 91 DH83
Heath Rd.
Tessa Sanderson Way, Grnf. 59 CD64
Lilian Board Way
Testerton Wk. W11 75 CX73
Whitchurch Rd.
Tetbury Pl. N1 77 DP67
Upper St.
Tetcott Rd. SW10 90 DC80
Tetherdown N10 62 DG55
Tetterby Way SE16 92 DU78
Catlin St.
Tetty Way, Brom. 122 EG96
Teversham La. SW8 91 DL81
Teviot Clo., Well. 96 EV81
Teviot St. E14 79 EC71
Tewkesbury Ave. SE23 106 DV87
Tewkesbury Ave., Pnr. 58 BY57
Tewkesbury Clo. N15 64 DR58
Tewkesbury Rd.
Tewkesbury Clo., Loug. 38 EL44
Tewkesbury Clo., W.Byf. 126 BK111
Tewkesbury Gdns. NW9 60 CP55
Tewkesbury Rd. N15 64 DR58
Tewkesbury Rd. W13 73 CG73
Tewkesbury Rd., Cars. 118 DD102
Tewkesbury Ter. N11 49 DJ51
Tewson Rd. SE18 95 ES77
Teynham Ave., Enf. 36 DR44
Teynham Grn., Brom. 122 EG99
Teynton Ter. N17 50 DQ53
Thackeray Ave. N17 50 DU54
Thackeray Clo. SW19 103 CX94
Thackeray Clo., Har. 58 CA60
Thackeray Clo., Islw. 87 CG82
Thackeray Clo., Uxb. 71 BP72
Dickens Ave.
Thackeray Dr., Ilf. 68 EU59
Thackeray Dr., Rom. 68 EU59
Thackeray Rd. E6 80 EK68
Thackeray Rd. SW8 91 DH82
Thackeray St. W8 90 DB75
Thackrah Clo. N2 48 DC54
Thakeham Clo. SE26 106 DV92
Thalia Clo. SE10 93 ED79
Feathers Pl.
Thame Rd. SE16 93 DX75
Thames Ave. SW10 90 DC81
Thames Ave., Cher. 112 BG97
Thames Ave., Dag. 82 FA70
Thames Ave., Grnf. 73 CF68
Thames Bank SW14 88 CQ82
Thames Circle E14 93 EA77
Westferry Rd.
Thames Clo., Cher. 112 BH101
Thames Clo., Hmptn. 114 CB96
Thames Clo., Rain. 83 FH72
Thames Ct., W.Mol. 114 CB96
Thames Dr., Ruis. 57 BQ58
Thames Mead, Walt. 113 BU101
Thames Meadow, Shep. 113 BR102
Thames Meadow, W.Mol. 114 CA96
Thames Pl. SW15 89 CX83
Thames Rd. E16 80 EK74
Thames Rd. W4 88 CN79
Thames Rd., Bark. 81 ES69
Thames Rd., Dart. 97 FF82
Thames Rd. Ind. Est. E16 80 EK74
Thames Side, Cher. 112 BJ99
Thames Side, Kings.T. 115 CK95
Thames Side, Stai. 112 BH96
Thames Side, Tedd. 101 CK94
Thames St. SE10 93 EB79
Thames St., Hmptn. 114 CB95
Thames St., Kings.T. 115 CK96
Thames St., Sun. 113 BU98
Thames St., Walt. 113 BT101
Thames St., Wey. 113 BP103
Thames Village W4 88 CQ81
Thames Wf. E16 80 EF74
Thamesbank Pl. SE28 82 EW72
Thamesdale, St.Alb. 18 CM27
Thamesfield Ct., Shep. 113 BQ101
Thamesgate Clo., Rich. 101 CH91
Locksmeade Rd.
Thameshill Ave., Rom. 55 FC54
Thameside, Tedd. 101 CJ94
Thameside Ind. Est. E16 94 EL75
Thameside Wk. SE28 82 EV72
Thamesmead, Walt. 113 BU101
Thamesmead Spine Rd., Belv. 97 FC75
Thamesmere Dr. SE28 82 EU73
Thamesvale Clo., Houns. 86 CA82
Thane Vill. N7 63 DM62
Thane Wks. N7 63 DM62
Thane Vill.
Thanescroft Gdns., Croy. 120 DS104
Thanet Dr., Kes. 122 EK104
Phoenix Dr.
Thanet Pl., Croy. 134 DQ105
Thanet Rd., Bex. 110 FA87
Thanet Rd., Erith 97 FE80
Thanet St. WC1 5 P3
Thanet St. WC1 77 DL69
Thanington Ct. SE9 109 ES86
Thant Clo. E10 65 EB62
Tharp Rd., Wall. 133 DK106
Thatcham Gdns. N20 48 DC45
Thatcher Clo., West Dr. 84 BL75
Classon Clo.
Thatchers Clo., Loug. 39 EQ40
Thatchers Way, Islw. 101 CD85
Thatches Gro., Rom. 68 EY56
Thavies Inn EC1 6 E8
Thaxted Pl. SW20 103 CX94
Thaxted Rd. SE9 109 EQ89
Thaxted Rd., Buck.H. 52 EK45
Thaxted Wk., Rain. 83 FF67
Ongar Way
Thaxted Way, Wal.Abb. 23 ED33
Thaxton Rd. W14 89 CZ79
Thayer St. W1 4 G7
Thayer St. W1 76 DG71
Thayers Fm. Rd., Beck. 121 DY95
Thaynesfield, Pot.B. 20 DD31
The Floats, Sev. 153 FD119
London Rd.
Theatre St. SW11 90 DF83
Theberton St. N1 77 DN67
Theed St. SE1 10 E3
Theed St. SE1 77 DN74
Thelma Gdns. SE3 94 EK81
Thelma Gdns., Felt. 100 BY90
Thelma Gro., Tedd. 101 CG93
Theobald Cres., Har. 44 CB53
Theobald Rd. E17 65 DZ59
Theobald Rd., Croy. 119 DP103
Theobald St. SE1 11 K7
Theobald St., Borwd. 32 CL39
Theobald St., Rad. 31 CH36
Theobalds Ave. N12 48 DC49
Theobalds Clo. (Cuffley), Pot.B. 21 DM30
Theobalds Ct. N4 64 DQ61
Queens Dr.
Theobalds La. (Cheshunt), Wal.Cr. 22 DW32
Theobalds Pk. Rd., Enf. 35 DP35
Theobald's Rd. WC1 6 B6
Theobald's Rd. WC1 77 DM71
Theobalds Rd. (Cuffley), Pot.B. 21 DL30
Theodore Rd. SE13 107 ED86
Therapia La., Croy. 119 DK101
Therapia Rd. SE22 106 DW86
Theresa Rd. W6 89 CU77
Theresas Wk., S.Croy. 134 DR110
Sanderstead Rd.
Therfield Ct. N4 64 DQ61
Brownswood Rd.
Thermopylae Gate E14 93 EB77
Theseus Wk. N1 6 G1
Thesiger Rd. SE20 107 DX94
Thessaly Rd. SW8 91 DJ80
Thetford Clo. N13 49 DP51
Thetford Gdns., Dag. 82 EX66
Thetford Rd., Ashf. 98 BL91
Thetford Rd., Dag. 82 EX66
Thetford Rd., N.Mal. 116 CR100
Thetis Ter., Rich. 88 CN79
Kew Grn.
Theydon Bower, Epp. 26 EU31
Theydon Ct., Wal.Abb. 24 EG33
Theydon Gdns., Rain. 83 FE66
Theydon Gate, Epp. 39 ES37
Coppice Row
Theydon Gro., Epp. 26 EU30
Theydon Gro., Wdf.Grn. 52 EJ51
Theydon Pk. Rd., Epp. 39 ES39
Theydon Pl., Epp. 25 ET31
Theydon Rd. E5 64 DW61
Theydon Rd., Epp. 25 ER34
Theydon St. E17 65 DZ59
Thicket, The, West Dr. 70 BL72
Thicket Cres., Sutt. 132 DC105
Thicket Gro. SE20 106 DU94
Anerley Rd.
Thicket Gro., Dag. 82 EW65
Thicket Rd. SE20 106 DU94
Thicket Rd., Sutt. 132 DC105
Thicketts, Sev. 155 FJ123
Thickthorne La., Stai. 98 BJ94
Berryscroft Rd.
Third Ave. E12 66 EL63
Third Ave. E13 80 EG69
Third Ave. E17 65 EA57
Third Ave. W3 75 CT74
Third Ave. W10 75 CY69
Third Ave., Dag. 83 FB67
Third Ave., Enf. 36 DT43
Third Ave., Hayes 71 BT74
Third Ave., Rom. 68 EW58
Third Ave., Wat. 30 BX35
Third Ave., Wem. 59 CK61
Third Clo., W.Mol. 114 CB98
Third Cross Rd., Twick. 101 CD89
Third Way, Wem. 60 CP63
Thirleby Rd. SW1 9 L7
Thirleby Rd. SW1 91 DJ76
Thirleby Rd., Edg. 46 CR53
Thirlmere Ave., Grnf. 73 CJ69
Thirlmere Gdns., Nthwd. 43 BP50
Thirlmere Gdns., Wem. 59 CJ60
Thirlmere Ho., Islw. 101 CF85
Thirlmere Ri., Brom. 108 EF93
Thirlmere Rd. N10 49 DH53
Thirlmere Rd. SW16 105 DK91
Thirlmere Rd., Bexh. 97 FC82
Thirsk Clo., Nthlt. 72 CA65
Thirsk Rd. SE25 120 DR98
Thirsk Rd. SW11 90 DG83
Thirsk Rd., Borwd. 32 CN37
Thirsk Rd., Mitch. 104 DG94
Thistle Gro. SW10 90 DC78
Thistle Mead, Loug. 39 EN41
Thistle Wd. Cres., Croy. 135 ED112
Thistlebrook SE2 96 EW76
Thistlecroft Gdns., Stan. 45 CK53
Thistlecroft Rd., Walt. 128 BW105
Thistledene, T.Ditt. 115 CE100
Thistledene Ave., Har. 58 BY62
Thistledene Ave., Rom. 55 FB50
Thistlemead, Chis. 123 EP96
Thistlewaite Rd. E5 64 DV62
Thistlewood Clo. N7 63 DM61
Thistleworth Clo., Islw. 87 CD80
Thistley Clo. N12 48 DE51
Summerfields Ave.
Thomas Ave., Cat. 148 DQ121
Thomas Baines Rd. SW11 90 DD83
Thomas Darby Ct. W11 75 CY72
Thomas Dean Rd. SE26 107 DZ91
Kangley Bri. Rd.
Thomas Dinwiddy Rd. SE12 108 EJ89
Thomas Doyle St. SE1 10 G6
Thomas Doyle St. SE1 91 DP76
Thomas Hardy Ho. N22 49 DM52
Thomas La. SE6 107 EA87
Thomas More Ho. EC2 78 DQ71
The Barbican
Thomas More St. E1 78 DU73
Thomas More Way N2 62 DC55
Thomas Pl. W8 90 DB76
St. Mary's Pl.
Thomas Rd. E14 79 DZ72
Thomas Rochford Way, Wal.Cr. 23 DY26
Thomas Sims Ct., Horn. 69 FH64
Thomas St. SE18 95 EP77
Thomas Wall Clo., Sutt. 132 DB106
Clarence Rd.
Thomas à Beckett Clo., Wem. 59 CF63
Thompson Ave., Rich. 88 CN83
Thompson Clo., Ilf. 67 EQ61
High Rd.
Thompson Rd. SE22 106 DT86
Thompson Rd., Dag. 68 EZ62
Thompson Rd., Uxb. 70 BL66
Thompson Way, Rick. 42 BG45
Thompson's Ave. SE5 92 DQ80
Thompsons Clo., Wal.Cr. 22 DT29
Thompson's La., Loug. 38 EF38
Thomson Cres., Croy. 119 DN102
Thomson Rd., Har. 59 CE55
Thorburn Sq. SE1 92 DU77
Thorburn Way SW19 118 DD95
Willow Vw.
Thoresby St. N1 7 J2
Thoresby St. N1 78 DQ69
Thorkhill Gdns., T.Ditt. 115 CG102
Thorkhill Rd., T.Ditt. 115 CG102
Thorley Clo., W.Byf. 126 BG114
Thorley Gdns., Wok. 126 BG114
Thorn Ave. (Bushey), Wat. 44 CC46
Thorn Clo., Brom. 123 EN100
Thorn Clo., Nthlt. 72 BZ69
Thorn Ho., Beck. 121 DY95
Thorn Ter. SE15 92 DW83
Nunhead Gro.
Thornaby Gdns. N18 50 DU51
Thornbank Clo., Stai. 98 BG85
Thornbury Ave., Islw. 87 CD80
Thornbury Clo. N16 64 DS64
Truman's Rd.
Thornbury Gdns., Borwd. 32 CQ41
Thornbury Rd. SW2 105 DL86
Thornbury Rd., Islw. 87 CD80
Thornbury Sq. N6 63 DJ60
Thornby Rd. E5 64 DW62
Thorncliffe Rd. SW2 105 DL86
Thorncliffe Rd., Sthl. 86 BZ78
Thorncombe Rd. SE22 106 DS85
Thorncroft, Horn. 69 FH58
Thorncroft Clo., Couls. 147 DN120
Waddington Ave.
Thorncroft Dr., Lthd. 143 CH123
Thorncroft Rd., Sutt. 132 DB105
Thorncroft St. SW8 91 DL80
Thorndean St. SW18 104 DC89
Thorndene Ave. N11 48 DG46
Thorndike Ave., Nthlt. 72 BX67
Thorndike Clo. SW10 90 DC80
Thorndike St. SW1 9 M9
Thorndike St. SW1 91 DK77
Thorndon Clo., Orp. 123 ET96
Thorndon Gdns., Epsom 130 CS106
Thorndon Rd., Orp. 123 ET96
Thorndyke Ct., Pnr. 44 BZ52
Westfield Pk.
Thorne Clo. E11 66 EE63
Thorne Clo. E16 80 EF72
Thorne Clo., Ashf. 99 BQ94
Thorne Clo., Erith 97 FC79
Thorne Pas. SW13 88 CS82
Thorne Rd. SW8 91 DL80
Thorne St. E16 80 EF72
Thorne St. SW13 88 CS83
Thorneloe Gdns., Croy. 133 DN106
Thornes Clo., Beck. 121 EC97
Thornet Wd. Rd., Brom. 123 EN97
Thorney Cres. SW11 90 DD80
Thorney Hedge Rd. W4 88 CP77
Thorney Mill Rd., Iver 84 BG76
Thorney Mill Rd., West Dr. 84 BG76
Thorney St. SW1 9 P8
Thorney St. SW1 91 DL77
Thorneycroft Clo., Walt. 114 BW100
Thornfield Ave. NW7 47 CY53
Thornfield Rd. W12 89 CV75
Thornfield Rd., Bans. 146 DA117
Thornford Rd. SE13 107 EC85
Thorngate Rd. W9 76 DA70
Thorngrove Rd. E13 80 EH67
Thornham Gro. E15 65 ED64
Thornham St. SE10 93 EB79
Thornhaugh Ms. WC1 5 N5
Thornhaugh St. WC1 5 N6
Thornhaugh St. WC1 77 DK71
Thornhill, Epp. 27 FC26
Thornhill Ave. SE18 95 ES80
Thornhill Ave., Surb. 116 CL103
Thornhill Bri. Wf. N1 77 DM67
Caledonian Rd.
Thornhill Cres. N1 77 DM66
Thornhill Gdns. E10 65 EB61
Thornhill Gdns., Bark. 81 ES66
Thornhill Gro. N1 77 DM66
Lofting Rd.
Thornhill Ho. N1 77 DN66
Thornhill Rd.
Thornhill Rd. E10 65 EB61
Thornhill Rd. N1 77 DN66
Thornhill Rd., Croy. 120 DQ101
Thornhill Rd., Nthwd. 43 BQ49
Thornhill Rd., Surb. 116 CL103
Thornhill Rd., Uxb. 56 BM63
Thornhill Sq. N1 77 DM66
Thornhill Way, Shep. 112 BN99
Thornlaw Rd. SE27 105 DN91
Thornley Clo. N17 50 DU52
Thornley Dr., Har. 58 CB61
Thornley Pl. SE10 94 EE78
Caradoc St.
Thorns Meadow, West. 152 EW123
Thornsbeach Rd. SE6 107 EC88
Thornsett Pl. SE20 120 DV96
Thornsett Rd. SE20 120 DV96
Thornsett Rd. SW18 104 DB88
Thornside, Edg. 46 CN51
High St.
Thornton Ave. SW2 105 DK88
Thornton Ave. W4 88 CS77
Thornton Ave., Croy. 119 DM100
Thornton Ave., West Dr. 84 BM76
Thornton Clo., West Dr. 84 BM76
Thornton Ct. SW20 117 CX99
Thornton Cres., Couls. 147 DN119
Thornton Dene, Beck. 121 EA96
Thornton Gdns. SW12 105 DK88
Thornton Gro., Pnr. 44 CA51
Thornton Hill SW19 103 CY94
Thornton Pl. W1 4 D6
Thornton Pl. W1 76 DF71
Thornton Rd. E11 65 ED61
Thornton Rd. N18 50 DW48
Thornton Rd. SW12 105 DK87
Thornton Rd. SW14 88 CR83
Thornton Rd. SW19 103 CX93
Thornton Rd., Barn. 33 CY41
Thornton Rd., Belv. 97 FB77
Thornton Rd., Brom. 108 EG92
Thornton Rd., Cars. 118 DD102
Thornton Rd., Croy. 119 DM101
Thornton Rd., Ilf. 67 EP63
Thornton Rd., Pot.B. 20 DC30
Thornton Rd., Th.Hth. 119 DN99
Thornton Rd. E. SW19 103 CX93
Thornton Rd.
Thornton Row, Th.Hth. 119 DN99
London Rd.
Thornton St. SW9 91 DN82
Thornton Way NW11 62 DB57
Thorntons Fm. Ave., Rom. 69 FC60
Thorntree Rd. SE7 94 EK78
Thornville Gro., Mitch. 118 DC96
Thornville St. SE8 93 EA81
Thornwood Clo. E18 52 EH54
Thornwood Rd. SE13 108 EE85
Thornwood Rd., Epp. 26 EV29
Thorogood Gdns. E15 66 EE64
Thorogood Way, Rain. 83 FE67
Thorold Clo., S.Croy. 135 DX110
Thorold Rd. N22 49 DL52
Thorold Rd., Ilf. 67 EP61
Thorparch Rd. SW8 91 DK81
Thorpe Clo. W10 75 CY72
Cambridge Gdns.
Thorpe Clo., Croy. 135 EC111
Thorpe Clo., Orp. 123 ES103
Thorpe Cres. E17 51 DZ54
Thorpe Cres., Wat. 44 BW45
Thorpe Hall Rd. E17 51 EC53
Thorpe Rd. E6 81 EM67
Thorpe Rd. E7 66 EF63
Thorpe Rd. E17 51 EC54
Thorpe Rd. N15 64 DS58
Thorpe Rd., Bark. 81 ER66
Thorpe Rd., Kings.T. 102 CL94
Thorpebank Rd. W12 75 CU74
Thorpedale Gdns., Ilf. 67 EN56
Thorpedale Rd. N4 63 DL61
Thorpewood Ave. SE26 106 DV89
Thorpland Ave., Uxb. 57 BQ62
Thorsden Way SE19 106 DS91
Oaks Ave.
Thorton Rd. Retail Pk., Croy. 119 DM100
Peall Rd.
Thorverton Rd. NW2 61 CY62
Thoydon Rd. E3 79 DY68
Thrale Rd. SW16 105 DJ91
Thrale St. SE1 11 J3
Thrale St. SE1 78 DQ74
Thrasher Clo. E8 78 DT67
Stean St.
Thrawl St. E1 78 DT71
Threadneedle St. EC2 7 L9
Threadneedle St. EC2 78 DR72
Three Barrels Wk. EC4 74 CQ73
Queen St.
Three Colt St. E14 79 DZ72
Three Colts Cor. E2 78 DU70
Weaver St.
Three Colts La. E2 78 DV70
Three Cors., Bexh. 97 FB82
Three Cups Yd. WC1 6 C7
Three Forests Way, Chig. 54 EW48
Three Kings Rd., Mitch. 118 DG97
Three Kings Yd. W1 5 H10
Three Kings Yd. W1 77 DH73
Three Mill La. E3 79 EC69
Three Oak La. SE1 11 P4
Three Oaks Clo., Uxb. 56 BM62
Threshers Pl. W11 75 CY73
Thriffwood SE26 106 DW90
Thrift Fm. La., Borwd. 32 CQ40
Thrift La., Sev. 151 ER116
Cudham La. S.
Thrifts Mead, Epp. 39 ES37
Thrigby Rd., Chess. 130 CM107
Throckmorten Rd. E16 80 EH72
Throgmorton Ave. EC2 7 L8
Throgmorton Ave. EC2 78 DR72
Throgmorton St. EC2 7 L8
Throgmorton St. EC2 78 DR72
Throwley Clo. SE2 96 EW76
Throwley Rd., Sutt. 132 DB106
Throwley Way, Sutt. 132 DB105
Thrums, The, Wat. 29 BV37
Thrupp Clo., Mitch. 119 DH96
Thrupps Ave., Walt. 128 BX106
Thrupps La., Walt. 128 BX106
Thrush Grn., Har. 58 CA56
Thrush Grn., Rick. 42 BJ45
Thrush La. (Cuffley), Pot.B. 21 DL28
Thrush St. SE17 11 H10
Thruxton Way SE15 92 DT80
Daniel Gdns.
Thunderer Rd., Dag. 82 EY70

Thurbarn Rd. SE6 107 EB92
Thurland Rd. SE16 92 DU76
Thurlby Clo., Har. 59 CG58
Gayton Rd.
Thurlby Clo., Wdf.Grn. 53 EM50
Thurlby Rd. SE27 105 DN91
Thurlby Rd., Wem. 73 CK65
Thurleigh Ave. SW12 104 DG86
Thurleigh Rd. SW12 104 DF87
Thurleston Ave., Mord. 117 CY99
Thurlestone Ave. N12 48 DF51
Thurlestone Ave., Ilf. 67 ET63
Thurlestone Clo., Shep. 113 BQ100
Thurlestone Rd. SE27 105 DN90
Thurloe Clo. SW7 8 B8
Thurloe Clo. SW7 90 DE77
Thurloe Gdns., Rom. 69 FF58
Thurloe Pl. SW7 8 A8
Thurloe Pl. SW7 90 DD77
Thurloe Pl. Ms. SW7 8 A8
Thurloe Sq. SW7 8 B8
Thurloe Sq. SW7 90 DE77
Thurloe St. SW7 8 A8
Thurloe St. SW7 90 DD77
Thurlow Clo. E4 51 EB51
Higham Sta. Ave.
Thurlow Gdns., Ilf. 53 ER51
Thurlow Gdns., Wem. 59 CK64
Thurlow Hill SE21 106 DQ88
Thurlow Pk. Rd. SE21 105 DP88
Thurlow Rd. NW3 62 DD64
Thurlow Rd. W7 87 CG75
Thurlow St. SE17 11 L10
Thurlow St. SE17 92 DR78
Thurlow Ter. NW5 62 DG64
Thurlston Rd., Ruis. 57 BU62
Thurnby Ct., Twick. 101 CE90
Thurnham Way, Tad. 145 CW120
Thursland Rd., Sid. 110 EY92
Thursley Cres., Croy. 135 EC108
Thursley Gdns. SW19 103 CX89
Thursley Rd. SE9 109 EM90
Thurso St. SW17 104 DD91
Thurstan Rd. SW20 103 CV94
Thurston Rd. SE13 93 EB82
Thurston Rd., Sthl. 72 BZ72
Thurtle Rd. E2 78 DT67
Thwaite Clo., Erith 97 FC79
Thyer Clo., Orp. 137 EQ105
Isabella Dr.
Thyra Gro. N12 48 DB51
Tibbatts Rd. E3 79 EB70
Tibbenham Wk. E13 80 EF68
Whitelegg Rd.
Tibberton Sq. N1 78 DQ66
Popham Rd.
Tibbets Clo. SW19 103 CX88
Tibbets Cor. SW19 103 CX87
Tibbet's Ride SW15 103 CX87
Tibbles Clo., Wat. 30 BY35
Tibbs Hill Rd., Abb.L. 15 BT30
Tiber Gdns. N1 77 DM67
Treaty St.
Ticehurst Clo., Orp. 110 EU94
Grovelands Rd.
Ticehurst Rd. SE23 107 DY89
Tichmarsh, Epsom 130 CQ110
Tickford Clo. SE2 96 EW75
Ampleforth Rd.
Tidal Basin Rd. E16 80 EF73
Tidenham Gdns., Croy. 120 DS104
Tideswell Rd. SW15 89 CW84
Tideswell Rd., Croy. 121 EA104
Tideway Clo., Rich. 101 CH91
Locksmeade Rd.
Tidey St. E3 79 EA71
Tidford Rd., Well. 95 ET82
Tidworth Rd. E3 79 EA70
Tidy's La., Epp. 26 EV29
Tiepigs La., Brom. 122 EF102
Tiepigs La., W.Wick. 122 EE103
Tierney Rd. SW2 105 DL87
Tiger La., Brom. 122 EH98
Tiger Way E5 64 DV63
Tilbrook Rd. SE3 94 EJ83
Tilbury Clo. SE15 92 DT80
Willowbrook Rd.
Tilbury Clo., Orp. 124 EV96
Tilbury Rd. E6 81 EM68
Tilbury Rd. E10 65 EC59
Tildesley Rd. SW15 103 CW86
Tile Fm. Rd., Orp. 123 ER104
Tile Kiln La. N6 63 DJ60
Winchester Rd.
Tile Kiln La. N13 50 DQ50
Tile Kiln La., Bex. 111 FC89
Tile Kiln La., Uxb. 57 BP59
Tile Yd. E14 79 DZ72
Commercial Rd.
Tilehouse Clo., Borwd. 32 CM41
Tilehurst Rd. SW18 104 DD88
Tilehurst Rd., Sutt. 131 CY106
Tilekiln Clo., Wal.Cr. 22 DT29
Tileyard Rd. N7 77 DL66
Tilford Ave., Croy. 135 EC108
Tilford Gdns. SW19 103 CX88
Tilia Rd. E5 64 DV63
Clarence Rd.
Tilia Wk. SW9 91 DP84
Moorland Rd.
Tiller Rd. E14 93 EA76
Tillett Clo. NW10 74 CQ65
Tillett Sq. SE16 93 DY75
Howland Way
Tillett Way E2 78 DU69
Gosset St.
Tilley La., Epsom 144 CQ123
Tilling Rd. NW2 61 CW60
Tilling Way, Wem. 59 CK63
Tillingbourne Gdns. N3 61 CZ55
Tillingbourne Grn., Orp. 123 ET98
Tillingbourne Way N3 61 CZ55
Tillingbourne Gdns.
Tillingdown Hill, Cat. 148 DU122
Tillingham Ct., Wal.Abb. 24 EG33
Tillingham Way N12 48 DA49
Tillman St. E1 78 DV72
Bigland St.
Tilloch St. N1 77 DM66
Carnoustie Dr.
Tillotson Rd. N9 50 DT47
Tillotson Rd., Har. 44 CB52
Tillotson Rd., Ilf. 67 EN59
Tilney Ct. EC1 7 J4
Tilney Dr., Buck.H. 52 EG47
Tilney Gdns. N1 78 DR65
Mitchison Rd.
Tilney Rd., Dag. 82 EZ65
Tilney Rd., Sthl. 86 BW77
Tilney St. W1 8 G2
Tilney St. W1 76 DG74
Tilson Gdns. SW2 105 DL87
Tilson Ho. SW2 105 DL87
Tilson Gdns.
Tilson Rd. N17 50 DU53
Tilt Clo., Cob. 142 BY116
Tilt Meadow, Cob. 142 BY116
Tilt Rd., Cob. 142 BW115
Tilt Yd. App. SE9 109 EM86
Tilton St. SW6 89 CY79
Tiltwood, The W3 74 CQ73
Acacia Rd.
Timber Clo., Chis. 123 EN96
Timber Hill Rd., Cat. 148 DU124
Timber La., Cat. 148 DU124
Timber Hill Rd.
Timber Mill Way SW4 91 DK83
Timber Pond Rd. SE16 79 DX74
Timber Ridge, Rick. 28 BJ42
Timber Slip Dr., Wall. 133 DK109
Timber St. EC1 7 H4
Timbercroft, Epsom 130 CS105
Timbercroft La. SE18 95 ES79
Timberdene NW4 47 CX54
Timberdene Ave., Ilf. 53 EQ53
Timberhill, Ash. 144 CL119
Ottways La.
Timberland Rd. E1 78 DV72
Timberling Gdns., S.Croy. 134 DR109
Sanderstead Rd.
Timbertop Rd., West. 150 EJ118
Timberwharf Rd. N16 64 DU58
Time Sq. E8 64 DT64
Times Sq., Sutt. 132 DB106
High St.
Timothy Clo. SW4 105 DJ85
Elms Rd.
Timothy Clo., Bexh. 110 EY85
Timothy Rd. E3 79 DZ71
Timsbury Wk. SW15 103 CU88
Tindal St. SW9 91 DP81
Tindale Clo., S.Croy. 134 DR111
Tinderbox All. SW14 88 CR83
Tine Rd., Chig. 53 ES50
Tinniswood Clo. N5 63 DN64
Drayton Pk.
Tinsley Rd. E1 78 DW71
Tintagel Clo., Epsom 131 CT114
Tintagel Cres. SE22 92 DT84
Tintagel Dr., Stan. 45 CK49
Tintagel Gdns. SE22 92 DT84
Oxonian St.
Tintagel Rd., Orp. 124 EW103
Tintern Ave. NW9 60 CP55
Tintern Clo. SW15 103 CY85
Tintern Clo. SW19 104 DC94
Tintern Gdns. N14 49 DL45
Tintern Path NW9 60 CS58
Ruthin Clo.
Tintern Rd. N22 50 DQ53
Tintern Rd., Cars. 118 DD102
Tintern St. SW4 91 DL84
Tintern Way, Har. 58 CB60
Tinto Rd. E16 80 EG70
Tinwell Ms., Borwd. 32 CQ43
Cranes Way
Tinworth St. SE11 10 A10
Tinworth St. SE11 91 DL78
Tippendell La., St.Alb. 16 CA25
Tippetts Clo., Enf. 36 DQ39
Tipthorpe Rd. SW11 90 DG83
Tipton Cotts., Add. 126 BG105
Oliver Clo.
Tipton Dr., Croy. 134 DS105
Tiptree Clo. E4 51 EC48
Tiptree Cres., Ilf. 67 EN55
Tiptree Dr., Enf. 36 DR42
Tiptree Est., Ilf. 67 EN55
Tiptree Rd., Ruis. 57 BV63
Tirlemont Rd., S.Croy. 134 DQ108
Tirrell Rd., Croy. 120 DQ100
Tisbury Ct. W1 5 M10
Tisbury Rd. SW16 119 DL96
Tisdall Pl. SE17 11 L9
Tisdall Pl. SE17 92 DR77
Titchborne Row W2 4 C9
Titchfield Rd. NW8 76 DF67
Titchfield Rd., Cars. 118 DD102
Titchfield Rd., Enf. 37 DY37
Titchfield Wk., Cars. 118 DD101
Titchfield Rd.
Titchwell Rd. SW18 104 DD87
Tite St. SW3 90 DF79
Tithe Barn Clo., Kings.T. 116 CM95
Tithe Barn Ct., Abb.L. 15 BT29
Tithe Barn Way, Nthlt. 71 BV68
Tithe Clo. NW7 47 CU53
Tithe Fm. Ave., Har. 58 CA62
Tithe Fm. Clo., Har. 58 CA62
Tithe Meadow, Wat. 29 BR44
Tithe Wk. NW7 47 CU53
Tithepit Shaw La., Warl. 148 DV117
Titian Ave. (Bushey), Wat. 45 CE45
Titley Clo. E4 51 EA50
Titmus Clo., Uxb. 71 BQ72
Titmuss Ave. SE28 82 EV73
Titmuss St. W12 89 CV75
Titsey Hill, Oxt. 150 EF123
Tiverton Ave., Ilf. 67 EN55
Tiverton Dr. SE9 109 EQ88
Tiverton Rd. N15 64 DR58
Tiverton Rd. N18 50 DS50
Tiverton Rd. NW10 75 CX67
Tiverton Rd., Edg. 46 CM54
Tiverton Rd., Houns. 86 CC82
Tiverton Rd., Pot.B. 20 DD31
Tiverton Rd., Ruis. 57 BU62
Tiverton Rd., Th.Hth. 119 DN99
Willett Rd.
Tiverton Rd., Wem. 74 CL68
Tiverton St. SE1 11 H7
Tiverton St. SE1 92 DQ76
Tiverton Way, Chess. 129 CJ106
Tivoli Ct. SE16 93 DZ75
Tivoli Gdns. SE18 94 EL77
Tivoli Rd. N8 63 DK57
Tivoli Rd. SE27 106 DQ92
Tivoli Rd., Houns. 86 BY84
Toad La., Houns. 86 BZ84
Tobacco Quay E1 78 DV73
Wapping La.
Tobago St. E14 93 EA75
Manilla St.
Tobin Clo. NW3 76 DE66
Toby La. E1 79 DY70
Toby Way, Surb. 116 CP103
Todds Wk. N7 63 DM61
Andover Rd.
Token Yd. SW15 89 CY84
Montserrat Rd.
Tokenhouse Yd. EC2 7 K8
Tokyngton Ave., Wem. 74 CN65
Toland Sq. SW15 103 CU85
Tolcarne Dr., Pnr. 43 BU54
Toley Ave., Wem. 60 CL59
Tollbridge Clo. W10 75 CY70
Kensal Rd.
Tollers La., Couls. 147 DM119
Tollesbury Gdns., Ilf. 67 ER55
Tollet St. E1 79 DX70
Tollgate Dr. SE21 106 DS89
Tollgate Gdns. NW6 76 DB68
Tollgate Rd. E6 80 EK71
Tollgate Rd. E16 80 EJ71
Tollgate Rd., Wal.Cr. 37 DX35
Tollhouse La., Wall. 133 DJ109
Tollhouse Way N19 63 DJ61
Tollington Pk. N4 63 DM61
Tollington Pl. N4 63 DM61
Tollington Rd. N7 63 DM63
Tollington Way N7 63 DL62
Tolmers Ave. (Cuffley), Pot.B. 21 DL28
Tolmers Gdns. (Cuffley), Pot.B. 21 DM29
Tolmers Ms., Hert. 21 DL25
Tolmers Pk., Hert. 21 DL25
Tolmers Rd. (Cuffley), Pot.B. 21 DK27
Tolmers Sq. NW1 5 L4
Tolpits Clo., Wat. 29 BT43
Tolpits La., Wat. 43 BQ46
Tolpuddle Ave. E13 80 EJ67
Rochester Ave.
Tolpuddle St. N1 77 DN68
Tolsford Rd. E5 64 DV64
Tolson Rd., Islw. 87 CG83
Tolverne Rd. SW20 117 CW95
Tolworth Clo., Surb. 116 CP102
Tolworth Gdns., Rom. 68 EX57
Tolworth Pk. Rd., Surb. 116 CM103
Tolworth Ri. N., Surb. 116 CQ101
Elmbridge Ave.
Tolworth Ri. S., Surb. 116 CQ102
Warren Dr. S.
Tolworth Rd., Surb. 116 CL103
Tom Coombs Clo. SE9 94 EL84
Well Hall Rd.
Tom Cribb Rd. SE28 95 EQ76
Tom Gros. Clo. E15 65 ED64
Maryland St.
Tom Hood Clo. E15 65 ED64
Maryland St.
Tom Mann Clo., Bark. 81 ES67
Tom Nolan Clo. E15 80 EE68
Tom Smith Clo. SE10 94 EE79
Maze Hill
Tom Thumbs Arch E3 79 EA68
Malmesbury Rd.
Tomahawk Gdns., Nthlt. 72 BX69
Javelin Way
Tomkins Clo., Borwd. 32 CL39
Tallis Way
Tomlin Clo., Epsom 130 CR111
Tomlins Gro. E3 79 EA69
Tomlins Orchard, Bark. 81 EQ67
Tomlins Ter. E14 79 DZ71
Rhodeswell Rd.
Tomlins Wk. N7 63 DM61
Briset Way
Tomlinson Clo. E2 78 DT69
Tomlinson Clo. W4 88 CP78
Oxford Rd. N.
Tompion St. EC1 6 F3
Toms Hill, Kings L. 14 BJ33
Bucks Hill
Toms La., Abb.L. 15 BS27
Toms La., Kings L. 15 BP29
Tomswood Ct., Ilf. 53 EQ53
Tomswood Hill, Ilf. 53 EP52
Tomswood Rd., Chig. 53 EN51
Tonbridge Clo., Bans. 132 DF114
Tonbridge Cres., Har. 60 CL56
Tonbridge Ho. SE25 120 DU97
Tonbridge Rd., Sev. 155 FJ126
Tonbridge Rd., W.Mol. 114 BY98
Tonbridge St. WC1 5 P2
Tonbridge St. WC1 77 DL69
Tonbridge Wk. WC1 5 P2
Tonfield Rd., Sutt. 117 CZ102
Tonge Clo., Beck. 121 EA99
Tonsley Hill SW18 104 DB85
Tonsley Pl. SW18 104 DB85
Tonsley Rd. SW18 104 DB85
Tonsley St. SW18 104 DB85
Tonstall Rd., Epsom 130 CR110
Tonstall Rd., Mitch. 118 DG96
Tony Cannell Ms. E3 79 DZ69
Maplin St.
Tooke Clo., Pnr. 44 BY53
Took's Ct. EC4 6 D8
Tooley St. SE1 11 L2
Tooley St. SE1 78 DS74
Toorack Rd., Har. 45 CD54
Toot Hill Rd., Ong. 27 FF30
Tooting Bec Gdns. SW16 105 DK91
Tooting Bec Rd. SW16 105 DH91
Tooting Bec Rd. SW17 104 DG90
Tooting Gro. SW17 104 DE92
Tooting High St. SW17 104 DE93
Tootswood Rd., Brom. 122 EE99
Tooveys Mill Clo., Kings L. 14 BN28
Top Dartford Rd., Swan. 111 FF94
Top Ho. Ri. E4 51 EC45
Parkhill Rd.
Top Pk., Beck. 122 EE99
Topaz Wk. NW2 61 CX59
Marble Dr.
Topcliffe Dr., Orp. 137 ER106
Topham Sq. N17 50 DQ53
Topham St. EC1 6 D4
Topiary, The, Ash. 144 CL121
Topiary Sq., Rich. 88 CM83
Topley St. SE9 94 EK84
Topp Wk. NW2 61 CW61
Topping La., Uxb. 70 BK69
Cleveland Rd.
Topsfield Clo. N8 63 DK57
Wolseley Rd.
Topsfield Par. N8 63 DL57
Tottenham La.
Topsfield Rd. N8 63 DL57
Topsham Rd. SW17 104 DF90
Tor Gdns. W8 90 DA75
Tor La., Wey. 127 BQ111
Tor Rd., Well. 96 EW81
Torbay Rd. NW6 75 CZ66
Torbay Rd., Har. 58 BY61
Torbay St. NW1 77 DH66
Hawley Rd.
Torbitt Way, Ilf. 67 ET57
Torbridge Clo., Edg. 46 CL52
Torbrook Clo., Bex. 110 EY86
Torcross Dr. SE23 106 DW89
Torcross Rd., Ruis. 57 BV62
Torland Dr., Lthd. 129 CD114
Tormead Clo., Sutt. 132 DA107
Tormount Rd. SE18 95 ES79
Toronto Ave. E12 67 EM63
Toronto Rd. E11 65 ED63
Toronto Rd., Ilf. 67 EP60
Torquay Gdns., Ilf. 66 EK56
Torquay St. W2 76 DB71
Harrow Rd.
Torr Rd. SE20 107 DX94
Torrance Clo., Horn. 69 FH60
Torre Wk., Cars. 118 DE102
Torrens Rd. E15 80 EF65
Torrens Rd. SW2 105 DM85
Torrens Sq. E15 80 EF65
Torrens St. EC1 6 E1
Torrens St. EC1 77 DN68
Torriano Ave. NW5 63 DK64
Torriano Cotts. NW5 63 DJ64
Torriano Ave.
Torriano Ms. NW5 63 DK64
Torriano Ave.
Torridge Gdns. SE15 92 DW84
Torridge Rd., Th.Hth. 119 DP99
Torridon Rd. SE6 107 ED87
Torridon Rd. SE13 108 EE87
Torrington Ave. N12 48 DD50
Torrington Clo. N12 48 DD49
Torrington Clo., Esher 129 CE107
Torrington Dr., Har. 58 CB63
Torrington Dr., Loug. 39 EQ42
Torrington Dr., Pot.B. 20 DD32
Torrington Gdns. N11 49 DJ51
Torrington Gdns., Grnf. 73 CJ67
Torrington Gdns., Loug. 39 EQ42
Torrington Gro. N12 48 DE50
Torrington Pk. N12 48 DC50
Torrington Pl. E1 78 DU74
Torrington Pl. WC1 5 L6
Torrington Pl. WC1 77 DK71
Torrington Rd. E18 66 EG55
Torrington Rd., Dag. 68 EZ60
Torrington Rd., Esher 129 CE107
Torrington Rd., Grnf. 73 CJ67
Torrington Rd., Ruis. 57 BT62
Torrington Sq. WC1 5 N5
Torrington Sq. WC1 77 DK70
Torrington Sq., Croy. 120 DR101
Tavistock Gro.
Torrington Way, Mord. 118 DA101
Torver Rd., Har. 59 CE56
Torver Way, Orp. 123 ER103
Torwood La., Whyt. 148 DT120
Torwood Rd. SW15 103 CU85
Torworth Rd., Borwd. 32 CM38
Tothill St. SW1 9 M5
Tothill St. SW1 91 DK75
Totnes Rd., Well. 96 EV80
Totnes Wk. N2 62 DD56
Tottan Ter. E1 79 DX72
Belgrave St.
Tottenhall Rd. N13 49 DN51
Tottenham Ct. Rd. W1 5 L5
Tottenham Ct. Rd. W1 77 DJ70
Tottenham Grn. E. N15 64 DT56
Tottenham La. N8 63 DL57
Tottenham Ms. W1 5 L6
Tottenham Rd. N1 78 DS65
Tottenham St. W1 5 L7
Tottenham St. W1 77 DJ71
Totterdown St. SW17 104 DF91
Totteridge Common N20 47 CU47
Totteridge Grn. N20 48 DA47
Totteridge La. N20 48 DA47
Totteridge Rd., Enf. 37 DX37
Totteridge Village N20 47 CY46
Totternhoe Clo., Har. 59 CJ57
Totton Rd., Th.Hth. 119 DN97
Toulmin St. SE1 11 H5
Toulmin St. SE1 92 DQ75
Toulon St. SE5 92 DQ80
Tournay Rd. SW6 89 CZ80
Toussaint Wk. SE16 92 DU76
John Roll Way
Tovey Clo., St.Alb. 17 CK26
Tovil Clo. SE20 120 DV96
Towcester Rd. E3 79 EB70
Tower Bri. E1 11 P3
Tower Bri. E1 78 DT74
Tower Bri. SE1 11 P3
Tower Bri. SE1 78 DT74
Tower Bri. App. E1 11 P2
Tower Bri. App. E1 78 DT74
Tower Bri. Piazza SE1 78 DT74
Horselydown La.
Tower Bri. Rd. SE1 11 M7
Tower Bri. Rd. SE1 92 DS76
Tower Clo. NW3 62 DD64
Lyndhurst Rd.
Tower Clo. SE20 106 DV94
Tower Clo., Ilf. 53 EP51
Tower Clo., Orp. 123 ET103
Tower Ct. WC2 5 P9
Tower Gdns. Rd. N17 50 DQ53
Tower Gro., Wey. 113 BS103
Tower Hamlets Rd. E7 66 EF63
Tower Hamlets Rd. E17 65 EA55
Tower Hill EC3 11 N1
Tower Hill EC3 78 DS73
Tower Hill Ter. EC3 78 DS73
Byward St.
Tower La., Wem. 59 CK62
Main Dr.
Tower Ms. E17 65 EA56
Tower Pier EC3 11 N2
Tower Pier EC3 78 DS73
Tower Pl. EC3 11 N1
Tower Pt., Enf. 36 DR42
Tower Ri., Rich. 88 CL83
Jocelyn Rd.
Tower Rd. NW10 75 CU66
Tower Rd., Belv. 97 FC77
Tower Rd., Bexh. 96 FA84
Tower Rd., Epp. 25 ES30
Tower Rd., Orp. 123 ET103
Tower Rd., Tad. 145 CW123
Tower Rd., Twick. 101 CF90
Tower Royal EC4 7 J10
Tower St. WC2 5 N9
Tower St. WC2 77 DK72
Tower Ter. N22 49 DM54
Mayes Rd.
Tower Vw., Croy. 121 DX101
Towers, The, Ken. 148 DQ115
Towers Ave., Uxb. 71 BQ69
Towers Pl., Rich. 102 CL85
Eton St.
Towers Rd., Pnr. 44 BY52
Towers Rd., Sthl. 72 CA70
Towers Wk., Wey. 127 BP107
Towfield Rd., Felt. 100 BZ89
Towing Path Wk. N1 77 DK67
York Way
Town, The, Enf. 36 DR41
Town Ct. Path N4 64 DQ60
Town End, Cat. 148 DS122
Town End Clo., Cat. 148 DS122
Town Fld. Way, Islw. 87 CG82
Town Hall App. N16 64 DS63
Milton Gro.
Town Hall App. Rd. N15 64 DT56
Town Hall Ave. W4 88 CR78
Town Hall Rd. SW11 90 DF83
Town La., Stai. 98 BK86
Town Meadow, Brent. 87 CK80
Town Quay, Bark. 81 EP67
Town Rd. N9 50 DV47

Town Sq., Erith 97 FE79
Pier Rd.
Town Tree Rd., Ashf. 98 BN92
Towncourt Cres., Orp. 123 EQ99
Towncourt La., Orp. 123 ER100
Towney Mead, Nthlt. 72 BZ68
Townfield, Rick. 42 BJ45
Townfield Rd., Hayes 71 BT74
Townfield Sq., Hayes 71 BT73
Towngate, Cob. 142 BY115
Townholm Cres. W7 87 CF76
Townley Ct. E15 80 EF65
Townley Rd. SE22 106 DS85
Townley Rd., Bexh. 110 EZ86
Townley St. SE17 11 K10
Townmead Rd. SW6 90 DB83
Townmead Rd., Rich. 88 CP82
Townmead Rd., Wal.Abb. 23 EC34
Townsend Ave. N14 49 DK49
Townsend Ind. Est. NW10 74 CQ68
Townsend La. NW9 60 CR59
Townsend Rd. N15 64 DT57
Townsend Rd., Ashf. 98 BL92
Townsend Rd., Sthl. 72 BY74
Townsend St. SE17 11 M8
Townsend St. SE17 92 DR77
Townsend Way, Nthwd. 43 BT52
Townsend Yd. N6 62 DG60
Townshend Clo., Sid. 110 EV93
Townshend Est. NW8 76 DE68
Townshend Rd. NW8 76 DE67
Townshend Rd., Chis. 109 EP92
Townshend Rd., Rich. 88 CM84
Townshend Ter., Rich. 88 CM84
Townslow La., Wok. 140 BK116
Townson Ave., Nthlt. 71 BU69
Townson Way, Nthlt. 71 BU68
Townson Ave.
Towpath, Shep. 112 BM102
Dockett Eddy La.
Towpath Way, Croy. 120 DT100
Towton Rd. SE27 106 DQ89
Toynbec Clo., Chis. 109 EP91
Beechwood Ri.
Toynbee Rd. SW20 117 CY95
Toynbee St. E1 7 P7
Toynbee St. E1 78 DT71
Toyne Way N6 62 DF58
Gaskell Rd.
Tracery, The, Bans. 146 DB115
Tracey Ave. NW2 61 CW64
Tracy Ct., Stan. 45 CJ52
Trade Clo. N13 49 DN49
Trader Rd. E6 81 EP72
Tradescant Rd. SW8 91 DL80
Trading Est. Rd. NW10 74 CQ70
Trafalgar Ave. N17 50 DS51
Trafalgar Ave. SE15 92 DT78
Trafalgar Ave., Wor.Pk. 117 CX102
Trafalgar Business Cen., Bark. 81 ET70
Trafalgar Clo. SE16 93 DY77
Greenland Quay
Trafalgar Ct., Cob. 127 BU113
Trafalgar Dr., Walt. 113 BU104
Trafalgar Gdns. E1 79 DX71
Trafalgar Gdns. W8 90 DB76
South End Row
Trafalgar Gro. SE10 93 ED79
Trafalgar Pl. E11 66 EG56
Trafalgar Pl. N18 50 DU50
Trafalgar Rd. SE10 93 ED79
Trafalgar Rd. SW19 104 DB94
Trafalgar Rd., Rain. 83 FF68
Trafalgar Rd., Twick. 101 CD89
Trafalgar Sq. SW1 9 N2
Trafalgar Sq. SW1 77 DK74
Trafalgar Sq. WC2 9 N2
Trafalgar Sq. WC2 77 DK74
Trafalgar St. SE17 11 K10
Trafalgar St. SE17 92 DR78
Trafalgar Ter., Har. 59 CE60
Nelson Rd.
Trafalgar Way E14 79 EC74
Trafalgar Way, Croy. 119 DM103
Trafford Clo. E15 65 EB64
Trafford Clo., Ilf. 53 ET51
Trafford Clo., Rad. 18 CL32
Trafford Rd., Th.Hth. 119 DM99
Tramway Ave. E15 80 EE66
Tramway Ave. N9 50 DV45
Tramway Path, Mitch. 118 DE98
London Rd.
Tranby Pl. E9 65 DX64
Homerton High St.
Tranley Ms. NW3 62 DE63
Fleet Rd.
Tranmere Rd. N9 50 DT45
Tranmere Rd. SW18 104 DC88
Tranmere Rd., Twick. 100 CB87
Tranquil Pas. SE3 94 EF82
Tranquil Vale
Tranquil Ri., Erith 97 FE78
West St.
Tranquil Vale SE3 94 EE82
Transay Wk. N1 78 DR65
Marquess Rd.
Transept St. NW1 4 C7
Transept St. NW1 76 DE71
Transmere Clo., Orp. 123 EQ100
Transmere Rd., Orp. 123 EQ100
Transom Clo. SE16 93 DY77
Plough Way
Transom Sq. E14 93 EB77
Transport Ave., Brent. 87 CG78
Tranton Rd. SE16 92 DU76
Traps Hill, Loug. 39 EM41
Traps La., N.Mal. 116 CS95
Travellers Way, Houns. 86 BW82
Travers Clo. E17 51 DX53
Travers Rd. N7 63 DN62
Treacy Clo. (Bushey), Wat. 44 CC47
Treadgold St. W11 75 CX73
Treadway St. E2 78 DV68
Treadwell Rd., Epsom 144 CS116
Treaty Rd., Houns. 86 CB83
Hanworth Rd.
Treaty St. N1 77 DM67
Trebeck St. W1 9 H2
Trebovir Rd. SW5 90 DA78
Treby St. E3 79 DZ70
Trecastle Way N7 63 DK63
Carleton Rd.
Tredegar Ms. E3 79 DZ69
Tredegar Ter.
Tredegar Rd. E3 79 DZ68
Tredegar Rd. N11 49 DK52
Tredegar Rd., Dart. 111 FG89
Tredegar Sq. E3 79 DZ69
Tredegar Ter. E3 79 DZ69
Trederwen Rd. E8 78 DU67
Tredown Rd. SE26 106 DW92
Tredwell Clo., Brom. 122 EL98
Tredwell Rd. SE27 105 DP91
Tree Clo., Rich. 101 CK88
Tree Rd. E16 80 EJ72
Treebourne Rd., West. 150 EJ117
Treen Ave. SW13 88 CS83
Treeside Clo., West Dr. 84 BK77
Treetops, Whyt. 148 DU118
Treetops Clo. SE2 96 EY78
Treetops Clo., Nthwd. 43 BR50
Treeview Clo. SE19 120 DS95
Treewall Gdns., Brom. 108 EH91
Trefgarne Rd., Dag. 68 FA61
Trefil Wk. N7 63 DL63
Trefoil Rd. SW18 104 DC85
Trefusis Wk., Wat. 29 BS39
Tregaron Ave. N8 63 DL58
Tregaron Gdns., N.Mal. 116 CS98
Avenue Rd.
Tregarthen Pl., Lthd. 143 CJ121
Tregarvon Rd. SW11 90 DG84
Tregenna Ave., Har. 58 BZ63
Tregenna Clo. N14 35 DJ43
Tregenna Ct., Har. 58 CA63
Trego Rd. E9 79 EA66
Tregothnan Rd. SW9 91 DL83
Tregunter Rd. SW10 90 DC79
Trehearn Rd., Ilf. 53 ER52
Trehern Rd. SW14 88 CR83
Treherne Ct. SW9 91 DN81
Eythorne Rd.
Treherne Ct. SW17 104 DG91
Trehurst St. E5 65 DY64
Trelawn Rd. E10 65 EC62
Trelawn Rd. SW2 105 DN85
Trelawney Clo. E17 65 EB56
Orford Rd.
Trelawney Est. E9 78 DW65
Trelawney Gro., Wey. 126 BN107
Trelawney Rd., Ilf. 53 ER52
Trellick Twr. W10 75 CZ70
Trellis Sq. E3 79 DZ69
Malmesbury Rd.
Treloar Gdns. SE19 106 DR93
Hancock Rd.
Tremadoc Rd. SW4 91 DK84
Tremaine Clo. SE4 93 EA82
Tremaine Rd. SE20 120 DV96
Trematon Pl., Tedd. 101 CJ94
Tremlett Gro. N19 63 DJ62
Tremlett Ms. N19 63 DJ62
Tremlett Gro.
Trenance Gdns., Ilf. 68 EU62
Trench Yd. Ct., Mord. 118 DB100
Green La.
Trenchard Ave., Ruis. 57 BV63
Trenchard Clo., Stan. 45 CG51
Trenchard Clo., Walt. 128 BW106
Trenchard Ct., Mord. 118 DB100
Trenchard St. SE10 93 ED78
Trenchold St. SW8 91 DL79
Trenham Dr., Warl. 148 DW116
Trenholme Clo. SE20 106 DV94
Trenholme Ct., Cat. 148 DU122
Trenholme Rd. SE20 106 DV94
Trenholme Ter. SE20 106 DV94
Trenmar Gdns. NW10 75 CV69
Trent Ave. W5 87 CJ76
Trent Clo., Rad. 18 CL32
Trent Gdns. N14 35 DH44
Trent Rd. SW2 105 DM85
Trent Rd., Buck.H. 52 EH46
Trent Way, Hayes 71 BS69
Trent Way, Wor.Pk. 117 CW104
Trentbridge Clo., Ilf. 53 ET51
Trentham Dr., Orp. 124 EU98
Trentham St. SW18 104 DA88
Trentwood Side, Enf. 35 DM41
Treport St. SW18 104 DB87
Tresco Clo., Brom. 108 EE93
Tresco Gdns., Ilf. 68 EU61
Tresco Rd. SE15 92 DV84
Trescoe Gdns., Har. 58 BY59
Trescoe Gdns., Rom. 55 FC50
Tresham Cres. NW8 4 B4
Tresham Cres. NW8 76 DE70
Tresham Rd., Bark. 81 ET66
Tresham Wk. E9 64 DW64
Churchill Wk.
Tresilian Ave. N21 35 DM43
Tressell Clo. N1 77 DP66
Sebbon St.
Tressillian Cres. SE4 93 EA83
Tressillian Rd. SE4 93 DZ84
Trestis Clo., Hayes 72 BY71
Jollys La.
Treswell Rd., Dag. 82 EY67
Tretawn Gdns. NW7 46 CS49
Tretawn Pk. NW7 46 CS49
Trevanion Rd. W14 89 CY77
Treve Ave., Har. 58 CC59
Trevellance Way, Wat. 16 BW33
Trevelyan Ave. E12 67 EM63
Trevelyan Cres., Har. 59 CK59
Trevelyan Gdns. NW10 75 CW67
Trevelyan Rd. E15 66 EF63
Trevelyan Rd. SW17 104 DE92
Treveris St. SE1 10 G3
Treverton St. W10 75 CY70
Treves Clo. N21 35 DM43
Worlds End La.
Treville St. SW15 103 CV87
Treviso Rd. SE23 107 DX89
Farren Rd.
Trevithick Clo., Felt. 99 BT88
Trevithick St. SE8 93 EA79
Trevone Gdns., Pnr. 58 BY58
Trevor Clo., Barn. 34 DD44
Trevor Clo., Brom. 122 EF101
Trevor Clo., Har. 45 CF52
Kenton La.
Trevor Clo., Islw. 101 CF85
Trevor Clo., Nthlt. 72 BW68
Trevor Cres., Ruis. 57 BT63
Trevor Gdns., Edg. 46 CR53
Trevor Gdns., Nthlt. 72 BW68
Trevor Gdns., Ruis. 57 BU63
Bedford Rd.
Trevor Pl. SW7 8 C5
Trevor Pl. SW7 90 DE75
Trevor Rd. SW19 103 CY94
Trevor Rd., Edg. 46 CR53
Trevor Rd., Hayes 85 BS75
Trevor Rd., Wdf.Grn. 52 EG52
Trevor Sq. SW7 8 D5
Trevor Sq. SW7 90 DE76
Trevor St. SW7 8 C5
Trevor St. SW7 90 DE75
Trevose Rd. E17 51 ED53
Trevose Way, Wat. 44 BW48
Trewenna Dr., Chess. 129 CK106
Trewenna Dr., Pot.B. 20 DD32
Trewince Rd. SW20 117 CW95
Trewint St. SW18 104 DC89
Trewsbury Rd. SE26 107 DX92
Triandra Way, Hayes 72 BX71
Triangle, The EC1 77 DP70
Goswell Rd.
Triangle, The N13 49 DN49
Lodge Dr.
Triangle, The, Bark. 81 EQ65
Tanner St.
Triangle, The, Hmptn. 114 CC95
High St.
Triangle, The, Kings.T. 116 CQ96
Kenley Rd.
Triangle Ct. E16 80 EK71
Tollgate Rd.
Triangle Pas., Barn. 34 DC42
Station Rd.
Triangle Pl. SW4 91 DK84
Triangle Rd. E8 78 DV67
Trident Gdns., Nthlt. 72 BX69
Jetstar Way
Trident Rd., Wat. 15 BT34
Trident St. SE16 93 DX77
Trident Wk. SE16 93 DX77
Greenland Quay
Trident Way, Sthl. 85 BV76
Trig La. EC4 7 H10
Trigo Ct., Epsom 130 CR111
Blakeney Clo.
Trigon Rd. SW8 91 DM80
Trilby Rd. SE23 107 DX89
Trim St. SE14 93 DZ79
Trimmer Wk., Brent. 88 CL79
Netley Rd.
Trinder Gdns. N19 63 DL60
Trinder Rd.
Trinder Rd. N19 63 DL60
Trinder Rd., Barn. 33 CW43
Tring Ave. W5 74 CM74
Tring Ave., Sthl. 72 BZ72
Tring Ave., Wem. 74 CN65
Tring Clo., Ilf. 67 ER57
Trinidad Gdns., Dag. 83 FD66
Trinidad St. E14 79 DZ73
Trinity Ave. N2 62 DD55
Trinity Ave., Enf. 36 DT44
Trinity Ch. Pas. SW13 89 CV79
Trinity Ch. Rd. SW13 89 CV79
Trinity Ch. Sq. SE1 11 J6
Trinity Ch. Sq. SE1 92 DQ76
Trinity Clo. E8 78 DT65
Trinity Clo. E11 66 EE61
Trinity Clo. NW3 62 DD63
Hampstead High St.
Trinity Clo. SE13 93 ED84
Wisteria Rd.
Trinity Clo., Brom. 122 EL102
Trinity Clo., Houns. 86 BY84
Trinity Clo., Nthwd. 43 BS51
Trinity Clo., S.Croy. 134 DS109
Trinity Clo., Stai. 98 BJ86
Trinity Cotts., Rich. 88 CM83
Trinity Rd.
Trinity Ct. N1 78 DS66
Downham Rd.
Trinity Ct. SE7 94 EK77
Charlton La.
Trinity Cres. SW17 104 DF89
Trinity Gdns. SW9 91 DM84
Trinity Gro. SE10 93 EC81
Trinity Hall Clo., Wat. 30 BW40
Trinity La., Wal.Cr. 23 DY32
Trinity Ms. SE20 120 DV95
Trinity Ms. W10 75 CX72
Cambridge Gdns.
Trinity Path SE26 106 DW90
Sydenham Pk.
Trinity Pl., Bexh. 96 EZ84
Trinity Ri. SW2 105 DN88
Trinity Rd. N2 62 DD55
Trinity Rd. N22 49 DL52
Whittington Rd.
Trinity Rd. SW17 104 DF89
Trinity Rd. SW18 104 DD85
Trinity Rd. SW19 104 DA93
Trinity Rd., Ilf. 67 EQ55
Trinity Rd., Rich. 88 CM83
Trinity Rd., Sthl. 72 BY74
Trinity Sq. EC3 11 N1
Trinity Sq. EC3 78 DS73
Trinity St. E16 80 EG71
Vincent St.
Trinity St. SE1 11 J5
Trinity St. SE1 92 DQ75
Trinity St., Enf. 36 DQ40
Trinity Wk. NW3 76 DC65
Trinity Way E4 51 DZ51
Trinity Way W3 74 CS73
Trio Pl. SE1 11 J5
Tristan Sq. SE3 94 EE83
Tristram Clo. E17 65 ED55
Tristram Rd., Brom. 108 EF91
Triton Sq. NW1 5 K4
Triton Sq. NW1 77 DJ70
Tritton Ave., Croy. 133 DL105
Tritton Rd. SE21 106 DR90
Trittons, Tad. 145 CW121
Triumph Clo., Hayes 85 BQ81
Triumph Ho., Bark. 82 EU69
Triumph Rd. E6 81 EM72
Trojan Ct. NW6 75 CY66
Willesden La.
Trojan Way, Croy. 119 DM104
Troon St. E1 79 DY72
White Horse Rd.
Trosley Rd., Belv. 96 FA79
Trossachs Rd. SE22 106 DS85
Trothy Rd. SE1 92 DU77
Monnow Rd.
Trott Rd. N10 48 DF52
Trott St. SW11 90 DD81
Trotters Bottom, Barn. 33 CU37
Trotwood, Chig. 53 ER51
Troughton Rd. SE7 94 EH78
Trout La., West Dr. 70 BH73
Trout Ri., Rick. 28 BH41
Trout Rd., West Dr. 70 BK74
Troutbeck Rd. SE14 93 DY81
Troutstream Way, Rick. 28 BH42
Trouville Rd. SW4 105 DJ86
Trowbridge Est. E9 79 DZ65
Osborne Rd.
Trowbridge Rd. E9 79 DZ65
Trowley Ri., Abb.L. 15 BS31
Trowlock Ave., Tedd. 101 CJ93
Trowlock Island, Tedd. 101 CJ92
Trowlock Way, Tedd. 101 CK93
Troy Clo., Tad. 145 CV120
Troy Ct. SE18 95 EP77
Troy Rd. SE19 106 DR93
Troy Town SE15 92 DU83
Truesdale Dr., Uxb. 56 BJ56
Truesdale Rd. E6 81 EM72
Trulock Ct. N17 50 DU52
Trulock Rd. N17 50 DU52
Truman Clo., Edg. 46 CP52
Pavilion Way
Truman's Rd. N16 64 DS64
Trump St. EC2 7 J9
Trumper Way, Uxb. 70 BJ67
Trumpers Way W7 87 CE75
Trumpington Rd. E7 66 EF63
Trundle St. SE1 11 H4
Trundlers Way (Bushey), Wat. 45 CE46
Trundleys Rd. SE8 93 DX78
Trundleys Ter. SE8 93 DX77
Trunks All., Swan. 125 FB96
Truro Gdns., Ilf. 66 EL59
Truro Rd. E17 65 DZ56
Truro Rd. N22 49 DL52
Truro St. NW5 76 DG65
Truro Way, Hayes 71 BS69
Portland Rd.
Truslove Rd. SE27 105 DN92
Trussley Rd. W6 89 CW76
Trust Rd., Wal.Cr. 23 DY34
Trust Wk. SE21 105 DP88
Peabody Hill
Trustons Gdns., Horn. 69 FG59
Tryfan Clo., Ilf. 66 EK57
Tryon St. SW3 8 D10
Tryon St. SW3 90 DF78
Trystings Clo., Esher 129 CG107
Tuam Rd. SE18 95 ER79
Tubbenden Clo., Orp. 123 ES103
Tubbenden Dr., Orp. 137 ER105
Tubbenden La., Orp. 137 ER105
Tubbenden La. S., Orp. 137 ER106
Tubbs Rd. NW10 75 CT68
Tubs Hill Par., Sev. 154 FG124
Tuck Rd., Rain. 83 FG65
Tucker St., Wat. 30 BW43
Tudor Ave., Hmptn. 100 CA93
Tudor Ave., Rom. 69 FG55
Tudor Ave. (Cheshunt), Wal.Cr. 22 DU31
Tudor Ave., Wat. 30 BX38
Tudor Ave., Wor.Pk. 117 CV104
Tudor Clo. N6 63 DJ59
Tudor Clo. NW3 62 DE64
Tudor Clo. NW7 47 CU51
Tudor Clo. NW9 60 CQ61
Tudor Clo. SW2 105 DM86
Elm Pk.
Tudor Clo., Ashf. 98 BL91
Tudor Clo., Bans. 145 CY115
Tudor Clo., Chess. 130 CL106
Tudor Clo., Chig. 53 EN49
Tudor Clo., Chis. 123 EM95
Tudor Clo., Cob. 128 BZ113
Tudor Clo., Couls. 147 DN118
Tudor Clo., Dart. 111 FH86
Tudor Clo., Lthd. 142 CA124
Tudor Clo., Pnr. 57 BU57
Tudor Clo., S.Croy. 148 DV115
Tudor Clo., Sutt. 131 CY107
Tudor Clo., Wall. 133 DJ108
Tudor Clo. (Cheshunt), Wal.Cr. 22 DV31
Tudor Clo., Wdf.Grn. 52 EH50
Tudor Ct. E17 65 DZ59
Tudor Ct., Borwd. 32 CL40
Tudor Ct., Felt. 100 BW91
Tudor Ct., Swan. 125 FC101
Tudor Ct. N., Wem. 60 CN64
Tudor Ct. S., Wem. 60 CN64
Tudor Cres., Enf. 36 DQ39
Tudor Cres., Ilf. 53 EP51
Tudor Dr., Kings.T. 101 CK92
Tudor Dr., Mord. 117 CX100
Tudor Dr., Rom. 69 FG56
Tudor Dr., Walt. 114 BX102
Tudor Dr., Wat. 30 BX38
Tudor Est. NW10 74 CP69
Tudor Gdns. NW9 60 CQ61
Tudor Gdns. SW13 88 CS83
Treen Ave.
Tudor Gdns. W3 74 CN71
Tudor Gdns., Rom. 69 FG56
Tudor Gdns., Twick. 101 CF88
Tudor Gdns., W.Wick. 121 EC104
Tudor Gro. E9 78 DW66
Tudor Gro. N20 48 DE48
Church Cres.
Tudor Manor Gdns., Wat. 16 BX32
Tudor Par., Rick. 42 BG45
Berry La.
Tudor Pl. W1 5 M8
Tudor Pl., Mitch. 104 DE94
Tudor Rd. E4 51 EB51
Tudor Rd. E6 80 EJ67
Tudor Rd. E9 78 DV67
Tudor Rd. N9 50 DV45
Tudor Rd. SE19 106 DT94
Tudor Rd. SE25 120 DV99
Tudor Rd., Ashf. 99 BR93
Tudor Rd., Bark. 81 ET67
Tudor Rd., Barn. 34 DA41
Tudor Rd., Beck. 121 EB97
Tudor Rd., Hmptn. 100 CA94
Tudor Rd., Har. 45 CD54
Tudor Rd., Hayes 71 BR72
Tudor Rd., Houns. 87 CD84
Tudor Rd., Kings.T. 102 CN94
Tudor Rd., Pnr. 44 BW54
Tudor Rd., Sthl. 72 BY73
Tudor Sq., Hayes 71 BR71
Tudor St. EC4 6 E10
Tudor St. EC4 77 DN73
Tudor Wk., Bex. 110 EY86
Tudor Wk., Lthd. 143 CF120
Tudor Wk., Wat. 30 BX37
Tudor Wk., Wey. 113 BP104
West Palace Gdns.
Tudor Way N14 49 DK46
Tudor Way W3 88 CN75
Tudor Way, Orp. 123 ER100
Tudor Way, Rick. 42 BG46
Tudor Way, Uxb. 70 BN65
Tudor Way, Wal.Abb. 23 ED33
Tudor Well Clo., Stan. 45 CH50
Tudway Rd. SE3 94 EH83
Tufnell Pk. Rd. N7 63 DK63
Tufnell Pk. Rd. N19 63 DJ63
Tufter Rd., Chig. 53 ET50
Tufton Gdns., W.Mol. 114 CB96
Tufton Rd. E4 51 EA49
Tufton St. SW1 9 P7
Tufton St. SW1 91 DK76
Tugboat St. SE28 95 ES75
Tugela Rd., Croy. 120 DR100
Tugela St. SE6 107 DZ89
Tugmutton Clo., Orp. 137 EP105
Acorn Way
Tuilerie St. E2 78 DU68
Hackney Rd.
Tulip Clo. E6 81 EM71
Bradley Stone Rd.
Tulip Clo., Croy. 121 DX102
Tulip Clo., Hmptn. 100 BZ93
Partridge Rd.
Tulip Clo., Sthl. 86 CC75
Chevy Rd.
Tulip Ct., Pnr. 58 BW55
Tulip Dr., Ilf. 67 EP64
Tulip Gdns., Ilf. 81 EP65

Tull St., Mitch. 118 DF101
Tulse Clo., Beck. 121 EC97
Tulse Hill SW2 105 DN86
Tulse Hill Est. SW2 105 DN86
Tulsemere Rd. SE27 106 DQ89
Tulyar Clo., Tad. 145 CV120
Tumblewood Rd., Bans. 145 CY116
Tumbling Bay, Walt. 113 BU100
Tummons Gdns. SE25 120 DS96
Tun Yd. SW8 91 DH82
Peardon St.
Tuncombe Rd. N18 50 DS49
Tunis Rd. W12 75 CV74
Tunley Grn. E14 79 DZ71
Burdett Rd.
Tunley Rd. NW10 74 CS67
Tunley Rd. SW17 104 DG88
Tunmarsh La. E13 80 EH69
Tunnan Leys E6 81 EN72
Tunnel Ave. SE10 93 ED75
Tunnel Gdns. N11 49 DJ52
Tunnel Rd. SE16 92 DW75
St. Marychurch St.
Tunnel Wd. Clo., Wat. 29 BT37
Tunnel Wd. Rd., Wat. 29 BT37
Tunstall Ave., Ilf. 54 EU51
Tunstall Clo., Orp. 137 ES105
Tunstall Rd. SW9 91 DM84
Tunstall Rd., Croy. 120 DS102
Tunstall Wk., Brent. 88 CL79
Ealing Rd.
Tunstock Way, Belv. 96 EY76
Tunworth Clo. NW9 60 CQ58
Tunworth Cres. SW15 103 CT86
Tupelo Rd. E10 65 EB61
Turenne Clo. SW18 90 DC84
Turin Rd. N9 50 DW45
Turin St. E2 78 DU69
Turkey Oak Clo. SE19 120 DS95
Turkey St., Enf. 36 DU36
Turks Clo., Uxb. 70 BN69
Harlington Rd.
Turk's Head Yd. EC1 6 F6
Turks Row SW3 8 E10
Turks Row SW3 90 DF78
Turle Rd. N4 63 DM60
Turle Rd. SW16 119 DL96
Turlewray Clo. N4 63 DM60
Turley Clo. E15 80 EE67
Turnagain La. EC4 6 F8
Turnagain La., Dart. 111 FG90
Turnage Rd., Dag. 68 EY60
Turnberry Clo. SE16 92 DV78
Ryder Dr.
Turnberry Ct., Wat. 44 BW48
Turnberry Dr., St.Alb. 16 BY30
Turnberry Quay E14 93 EB76
Pepper St.
Turnberry Way, Orp. 123 ER102
Turnbury Clo. SE28 82 EX72
Summerton Way
Turnchapel Ms. SW4 91 DH83
Cedars Rd.
Turner Ave. N15 64 DS56
Turner Ave., Mitch. 118 DF95
Turner Ave., Twick. 100 CC90
Turner Clo. NW11 62 DB58
Turner Clo., Hayes 71 BQ68
Charville La.
Turner Dr. NW11 62 DB58
Turner Rd. E17 65 EC55
Turner Rd., Edg. 46 CL54
Turner Rd., N.Mal. 116 CR101
Turner Rd. (Bushey), Wat. 30 CC42
Turner Rd., West. 136 EJ112
Turner St. E1 78 DV71
Turner St. E16 80 EF72
Turners Clo., Stai. 98 BH92
Turners Gdns., Sev. 155 FJ128
Turners Hill (Cheshunt), Wal.Cr. 23 DX30
Turners La., Walt. 127 BV107
Turners Meadow Way, Beck. 121 DZ95
Turners Rd. E3 79 DZ71
Turners Way, Croy. 119 DN103
Turners Wd. NW11 62 DC60
Turneville Rd. W14 89 CZ79
Turney Rd. SE21 106 DQ87
Turnham Grn. Ter. W4 88 CS77
Turnham Grn. Ter. Ms. W4 88 CS77
Turnham Grn. Ter.
Turnham Rd. SE4 107 DY85
Turnmill St. EC1 6 E5
Turnmill St. EC1 77 DN70
Turnpike Clo. SE8 93 DZ80
Amersham Vale
Turnpike Dr., Orp. 138 EW109
Turnpike Ho. EC1 6 G3
Turnpike La. N8 63 DM56
Turnpike La., Sutt. 132 DC106
Turnpike La., Uxb. 70 BL69
Turnpike Link, Croy. 120 DS103
Turnpike Way, Islw. 87 CG81
Turnpin La. SE10 93 EC79
Turnstone Clo. E13 80 EG69
Turnstone Clo. NW9 46 CS54
Kestrel Clo.
Turnstone Clo., S.Croy. 135 DY110
Turnstone Clo., Uxb. 57 BP64
Turnstones, The, Wat. 30 BY36
Turpentine La. SW1 91 DH78
Sutherland St.
Turpin Ave., Rom. 54 FA51
Turpin La., Erith 97 FG80
Turpin Rd., Felt. 99 BT86
Staines Rd.
Turpin Way N19 63 DK61
Elthorne Rd.
Turpin Way, Wall. 133 DH108
Turpington Clo., Brom. 122 EL100
Turpington La., Brom. 122 EL101
Turpins La., Wdf.Grn. 53 EM50
Turquand St. SE17 11 J9
Turret Gro. SW4 91 DJ83
Turton Rd., Wem. 60 CL64
Turville St. E2 78 DT70
Old Nichol St.
Tuscan Rd. SE18 95 ER78
Tuskar St. SE10 94 EE78
Tustin Est. SE15 92 DW79
Tuttlebee La., Buck.H. 52 EG47
Tuxford Clo., Borwd. 32 CL38
Twankhams All., Epp. 26 EU30
Hemnall St.
Tweed Glen, Rom. 55 FD52
Tweed Grn., Rom. 55 FD52
Tweed Way, Rom. 55 FD52
Tweedale Ct. E15 65 EC64
Tweeddale Gro., Uxb. 57 BQ62
Tweeddale Rd., Cars. 118 DD102
Tweedmouth Rd. E13 80 EH68
Tweedy Rd., Brom. 122 EG95
Tweezer's All. WC2 6 D10
Twelve Acre Clo., Lthd. 142 BZ124
Twelvetrees Cres. E3 79 EC70
Twentyman Clo., Wdf.Grn. 52 EG50
Twickenham Bri., Rich. 101 CJ85
Twickenham Bri., Twick. 101 CJ85
Twickenham Clo., Croy. 119 DM104
Twickenham Gdns., Grnf. 59 CG64
Twickenham Gdns., Har. 45 CE52
Twickenham Rd. E11 65 ED61
Twickenham Rd., Felt. 100 BZ90
Twickenham Rd., Islw. 101 CG85
Twickenham Rd., Rich. 101 CJ85
Twickenham Rd., Tedd. 101 CG91
Twickenham Trd. Est., Twick. 101 CF86
Twig Folly Clo. E2 79 DX68
Roman Rd.
Twigg Clo., Erith 97 FE80
Twilley St. SW18 104 DB87
Twine Clo., Bark. 82 EV69
Thames Rd.
Twine Ct. E1 78 DW73
Twineham Grn. N12 48 DA49
Tillingham Way
Twining Ave., Twick. 100 CC90
Twinn Rd. NW7 47 CY51
Twinoaks, Cob. 128 CA113
Twisden Rd. NW5 63 DH63
Twitton La., Sev. 153 FD115
Twitton Meadows, Sev. 153 FE116
Twybridge Way NW10 74 CQ66
Twyford Abbey Rd. NW10 74 CM69
Twyford Ave. N2 62 DF55
Twyford Ave. W3 74 CN73
Twyford Cres. W3 74 CN74
Twyford Pl. WC2 6 B8
Twyford Rd., Cars. 118 DD102
Twyford Rd., Har. 58 CB60
Twyford Rd., Ilf. 67 EQ64
Twyford St. N1 77 DM67
Tyas Rd. E16 80 EF70
Tybenham Rd. SW19 117 CZ97
Tyberry Rd., Enf. 36 DV41
Tyburn La., Har. 59 CE59
Tyburn Way W1 4 E10
Tycehurst Hill, Loug. 39 EM42
Tydcombe Rd., Warl. 148 DW119
Tye La., Orp. 137 EQ106
Tyers Est. SE1 11 M4
Tyers Est. SE1 92 DS75
Tyers Gate SE1 11 M5
Tyers St. SE11 91 DM78
Tyers Ter. SE11 91 DM78
Tyeshurst Clo. SE2 96 EY78
Tyfield Clo. (Cheshunt), Wal.Cr. 22 DW30
Tykeswater La., Borwd. 31 CJ40
Tylecroft Rd. SW16 119 DL96
Tylehurst Gdns., Ilf. 67 EQ64
Tyler Clo. E2 78 DT68
Tyler Gdns., Add. 126 BJ105
Tyler St. SE10 94 EE78
Tylers Clo., Kings L. 14 BL28
Tylers Clo., Loug. 52 EL45
Tyler's Ct. W1 5 M9
Tylers Gate, Har. 60 CL58
Tylers Grn. Rd., Swan. 125 FC100
Tylers Path, Cars. 132 DF105
Rochester Rd.
Tylers Way, Wat. 31 CE43
Tylersfield, Abb.L. 15 BT31
Tylney Ave. SE19 106 DT92
Tylney Rd. E7 66 EJ63
Tylney Rd., Brom. 122 EK96
Tynan Clo., Felt. 99 BU88
Sandycombe Rd.
Tyndale Ct. E14 93 EB78
Tyndale La. N1 77 DP66
Upper St.
Tyndale Ter. N1 77 DP66
Canonbury La.
Tyndall Rd. E10 65 EC61
Tyndall Rd., Well. 95 ET83
Tyne St. E1 78 DT72
Old Castle St.
Tynedale, St.Alb. 18 CM27
Thamesdale
Tyneham Rd. SW11 90 DG82
Tynemouth Clo. E6 81 EP72
Covelees Wall
Tynemouth Dr., Enf. 36 DU38
Tynemouth Rd. N15 64 DT56
Tynemouth Rd. SE18 95 ET78
Tynemouth Rd., Mitch. 104 DG94
Tynemouth St. SW6 90 DC82
Type St. E2 79 DX68
Tyrawley Rd. SW6 90 DB81
Tyrell Clo., Har. 59 CE63
Tyrell Ct., Cars. 132 DF105
Tyrell Sq., Mitch. 118 DE95
Tyrols Rd. SE23 107 DX88
Wastdale Rd.
Tyron Way, Sid. 109 ES91
Tyrone Rd. E6 81 EM68
Tyrrel Way NW9 61 CT59
Tyrrell Ave., Well. 110 EU85
Tyrrell Rd. SE22 92 DU84
Tyrrells Wd. Dr., Lthd. 143 CH123
Tyrwhitt Rd. SE4 93 EA83
Tysea Hill, Rom. 55 FF45
Tysoe Ave., Enf. 37 DZ36
Tysoe St. EC1 6 D3
Tyson Rd. SE23 106 DW87
Tyssen Pas. E8 78 DT65
Tyssen St.
Tyssen Rd. N16 64 DT62
Tyssen St. E8 78 DT65
Tyssen St. N1 7 N1
Tytherton Rd. N19 63 DK62

U

Uamvar St. E14 79 EB71
Uckfield Gro., Mitch. 118 DG95
Uckfield Rd., Enf. 37 DX37
Udall Gdns., Rom. 54 FA51
Udall St. SW1 9 L9
Udney Pk. Rd., Tedd. 101 CG92
Uffington Rd. NW10 75 CU67
Uffington Rd. SE27 105 DN91
Ufford Clo., Har. 44 CB52
Ufford Rd.
Ufford Rd., Har. 44 CB52
Ufford St. SE1 10 E4
Ufford St. SE1 91 DN75
Ufton Gro. N1 78 DR66
Ufton Rd. N1 78 DR66
Uhura Sq. N16 64 DS62
Ujima Ct. SW16 105 DL91
Sunnyhill Rd.
Ullathorne Rd. SW16 105 DJ91
Ulleswater Rd. N14 49 DL49
Ullin St. E14 79 EC71
St. Leonards Rd.
Ullswater Business Pk., The, Couls. 147 DL116
Ullswater Clo. SW15 102 CR91
Ullswater Clo., Brom. 108 EE94
Ullswater Clo., Hayes 71 BS68
Ullswater Ct., Har. 58 CA59
Oakington Ave.
Ullswater Cres. SW15 102 CR91
Ullswater Cres., Couls. 147 DL116
Ullswater Rd. SE27 105 DP89
Ullswater Rd. SW13 89 CU80
Ullswater Way, Horn. 69 FG64
Ulstan Clo., Cat. 149 EA123
Ulster Gdns. N13 50 DQ49
Ulster Pl. NW1 5 H5
Ulster Ter. NW1 5 H4
Ulundi Rd. SE3 94 EE79
Ulva Rd. SW15 103 CX85
Ravenna Rd.
Ulverscroft Rd. SE22 106 DT85
Ulverston Rd. E17 51 ED54
Ulverstone Rd. SE27 105 DP89
Ulwin Ave., W.Byf. 126 BL113
Ulysses Rd. NW6 61 CZ64
Umberston St. E1 78 DV72
Hessel St.
Umbria St. SW15 103 CU86
Umfreville Rd. N4 63 DP58
Undercliff Rd. SE13 93 EA83
Underhill, Barn. 34 DA43
Underhill Pas. NW1 77 DH67
Camden High St.
Underhill Rd. SE22 106 DU85
Underhill St. NW1 77 DH67
Camden High St.
Underne Ave. N14 49 DH47
Underriver Ho. Rd., Sev. 155 FP130
Undershaft EC3 7 M9
Undershaft EC3 78 DS72
Undershaw Rd., Brom. 108 EF90
Underwood, Croy. 135 EC106
Underwood, The SE9 109 EM89
Underwood Rd. E1 78 DU70
Underwood Rd. E4 51 EB50
Underwood Rd., Wdf.Grn. 52 EJ52
Underwood Row N1 7 J2
Underwood Row N1 78 DQ69
Underwood St. N1 7 J2
Underwood St. N1 78 DQ69
Undine Rd. E14 93 EB77
Undine St. SW17 104 DF92
Uneeda Dr., Grnf. 73 CD67
Union Cotts. E15 80 EE66
Welfare Rd.
Union Ct. EC2 7 M8
Union Ct., Rich. 102 CL85
Eton St.
Union Dr. E1 79 DY70
Solebay St.
Union Gro. SW8 91 DK82
Union Rd. N11 49 DK51
Union Rd. SW4 91 DK82
Union Rd. SW8 91 DK82
Union Rd., Brom. 122 EK99
Union Rd., Croy. 120 DQ101
Union Rd., Nthlt. 72 CA68
Union Rd., Wem. 74 CL65
Union Sq. N1 78 DQ67
Union St. E15 79 EC67
Union St. SE1 10 G3
Union St. SE1 78 DQ74
Union St., Barn. 33 CY42
Union St., Kings.T. 115 CK96
Union Wk. E2 7 N2
Unity Clo. NW10 75 CU65
Unity Clo. SE19 106 DQ92
Unity Clo., Croy. 135 EB109
Castle Hill Ave.
Unity Rd., Enf. 36 DW37
Unity Way SE18 94 EK76
Unity Wf. SE1 92 DT75
Mill St.
University Clo. NW7 47 CT52
University Clo., Wat. 30 CA42
University Gdns., Bex. 110 EZ87
University Pl., Erith 97 FB80
Belmont Rd.
University Rd. SW19 104 DD93
University St. WC1 5 L5
University St. WC1 77 DJ70
Unwin Ave., Felt. 99 BR85
Unwin Clo. SE15 92 DU79
Unwin Rd. SW7 90 DD76
Imperial College Rd.
Unwin Rd., Islw. 87 CE83
Upbrook Ms. W2 76 DC72
Chilworth St.
Upcerne Rd. SW10 90 DC80
Upchurch Clo. SE20 106 DV94
Upcroft Ave., Edg. 46 CQ50
Updale Clo., Pot.B. 19 CY33
Updale Rd., Sid. 109 ET91
Upfield, Croy. 120 DV103
Upfield Rd. W7 73 CF70
Upgrove Manor Way SW2 105 DN87
Trinity Ri.
Uphall Rd., Ilf. 67 EP64
Upham Pk. Rd. W4 88 CS77
Uphill Dr. NW7 46 CS50
Uphill Dr. NW9 60 CQ57
Uphill Gro. NW7 46 CS49
Uphill Rd. NW7 46 CS49
Upland Dr., Hat. 20 DB25
Upland Ms. SE22 106 DU85
Upland Rd.
Upland Rd. E13 80 EF70
Sutton Rd.
Upland Rd. SE22 106 DU85
Upland Rd., Bexh. 96 EZ83
Upland Rd., Cat. 149 EA120
Upland Rd., Epp. 25 ER25
Upland Rd., S.Croy. 134 DR106
Upland Rd., Sutt. 132 DD107
Upland Way, Epsom 145 CW118
Uplands, Ash. 143 CK120
Uplands, Beck. 121 EA96
Uplands, Rick. 28 BM44
Uplands, The, Loug. 39 EM41
Uplands, The, Ruis. 57 BU60
Uplands, The, St.Alb. 16 BY30
Uplands Ave. E17 51 DX54
Blackhorse La.
Uplands Business Pk. E17 65 DX55
Uplands Clo. SW14 102 CP85
Monroe Dr.
Uplands Clo., Sev. 154 FF123
Uplands Dr., Lthd. 129 CD113
Uplands End, Wdf.Grn. 52 EL52
Uplands Pk. Rd., Enf. 35 DN41
Uplands Rd. N8 63 DM57
Uplands Rd., Barn. 48 DG46
Uplands Rd., Ken. 148 DQ116
Uplands Rd., Orp. 124 EV102
Uplands Rd., Rom. 68 EX55
Uplands Rd., Wdf.Grn. 52 EL52
Uplands Way N21 35 DN43
Uplands Way, Sev. 154 FF123
Upminster Rd. S., Rain. 83 FG70
Upney La., Bark. 81 ES65
Upnor Way SE17 11 N10
Uppark Dr., Ilf. 67 EQ58
Upper Abbey Rd., Belv. 96 EZ77
Upper Addison Gdns. W14 89 CY75
Upper Bardsey Wk. N1 78 DQ65
Clephane Rd.
Upper Belgrave St. SW1 8 G6
Upper Belgrave St. SW1 90 DG76
Upper Berkeley St. W1 4 D9
Upper Berkeley St. W1 76 DF72
Upper Beulah Hill SE19 120 DS95
Upper Brighton Rd., Surb. 115 CK100
Upper Brockley Rd. SE4 93 DZ82
Upper Brook St. W1 8 F1
Upper Brook St. W1 76 DG73
Upper Butts, Brent. 87 CJ79
Upper Caldy Wk. N1 78 DQ65
Clephane Rd.
Upper Camelford Wk. W11 75 CY72
Lancaster Rd.
Upper Cavendish Ave. N3 62 DA55
Upper Cheyne Row SW3 90 DE79
Upper Clapton Rd. E5 64 DV60
Upper Clarendon Wk. W11 75 CY72
Lancaster Rd.
Upper Ct. Rd., Cat. 149 EA123
Upper Ct. Rd., Epsom 130 CQ111
Upper Dengie Wk. N1 78 DQ67
Popham Rd.
Upper Dr., West. 150 EJ118
Upper Dunnymans, Bans. 131 CZ114
Basing Rd.
Upper Elmers End Rd., Beck. 121 DY98
Upper Fairfield Rd., Lthd. 143 CH121
Upper Fm. Rd., W.Mol. 114 BZ98
Upper Fosters NW4 61 CW57
New Brent St.
Upper Grn. E., Mitch. 118 DF96
Upper Grn. W., Mitch. 118 DF97
London Rd.
Upper Grenfell Wk. W11 75 CX73
Whitchurch Rd.
Upper Grosvenor St. W1 8 F1
Upper Grosvenor St. W1 76 DG73
Upper Grotto Rd., Twick. 101 CF89
Upper Grd. SE1 10 D2
Upper Grd. SE1 77 DN74
Upper Gro. SE25 120 DS98
Upper Gro. Rd., Belv. 96 EZ79
Upper Gulland Wk. N1 78 DQ65
Clephane Rd.
Upper Halliford Bypass, Shep. 113 BS99
Upper Halliford Grn., Shep. 113 BS98
Holmbank Dr.
Upper Halliford Rd., Shep. 113 BS98
Upper Ham Rd., Rich. 101 CK91
Upper Handa Wk. N1 78 DR65
Clephane Rd.
Upper Harley St. NW1 4 G5
Upper Harley St. NW1 76 DG70
Upper Hawkwell Wk. N1 78 DQ67
Popham Rd.
Upper High St., Epsom 130 CS113
Upper Highway, Abb.L. 15 BR33
Upper Highway, Kings L. 15 BQ32
Upper Hill Ri., Rick. 28 BH44
Upper Hitch, Wat. 44 BY46
Upper Holly Hill Rd., Belv. 97 FB78
Upper James St. W1 5 L10
Upper John St. W1 5 L10
Upper Lismore Wk. N1 78 DQ65
Clephane Rd.
Upper Mall W6 89 CU78
Upper Marsh SE1 10 C6
Upper Marsh SE1 91 DM75
Upper Montagu St. W1 4 D6
Upper Montagu St. W1 76 DF71
Upper Mulgrave Rd., Sutt. 131 CY108
Upper N. St. E14 79 EA71
Upper Paddock Rd., Wat. 30 BY44
Upper Palace Rd., E.Mol. 114 CC97
Upper Pk., Loug. 38 EK42
Upper Pk. Rd. N11 49 DH50
Upper Pk. Rd. NW3 76 DF65
Upper Pk. Rd., Belv. 97 FB77
Upper Pk. Rd., Brom. 122 EH95
Upper Pk. Rd., Kings.T. 102 CN93
Upper Phillimore Gdns. W8 90 DA75
Upper Pines, Bans. 146 DF117
Upper Rainham Rd., Horn. 69 FF60
Upper Ramsey Wk. N1 78 DR65
Clephane Rd.
Upper Rawreth Wk. N1 78 DQ67
Popham Rd.
Upper Richmond Rd. SW15 89 CY84
Upper Richmond Rd. W. SW14 88 CR84
Upper Richmond Rd. W., Rich. 88 CN84
Upper Rd. E13 80 EG69
Upper Rd., Wall. 133 DK106
Upper St. Martin's La. WC2 5 P10
Upper St. Martin's La. WC2 77 DL73
Upper Sawley Wd., Bans. 131 CZ114
Upper Selsdon Rd., S.Croy. 134 DS108
Upper Sheppey Wk. N1 78 DQ66
Clephane Rd.
Upper Sheridan Rd., Belv. 96 FA77
Coleman Rd.
Upper Shirley Rd., Croy. 120 DW103
Upper Shott (Cheshunt), Wal.Cr. 22 DT26
Upper Sq., Islw. 87 CG83
North St.
Upper Sta. Rd., Rad. 31 CG35
Upper St. N1 77 DN68
Upper Sunbury Rd., Hmptn. 114 BY95
Upper Sutton La., Houns. 86 CA80
Upper Swaines, Epp. 25 ET30
Upper Tachbrook St. SW1 9 L8
Upper Tachbrook St. SW1 91 DJ77
Upper Tail, Wat. 44 BY48
Upper Talbot Wk. W11 75 CY72
Lancaster Rd.
Upper Teddington Rd., Kings.T. 101 CJ94

Waldo Rd. NW10 75 CU69
Waldo Rd., Brom. 122 EK97
Waldorf Clo., S.Croy. 133 DP109
Waldram Cres. SE23 106 DW88
Waldram Pk. Rd. SE23 107 DX88
Waldram Pl. SE23 106 DW88
Waldrist Way, Erith 96 EZ75
Waldron Gdns., Brom. 121 ED97
Waldron Ms. SW3 90 DD79
Old Ch. St.
Waldron Rd. SW18 104 DC90
Waldron Rd., Har. 59 CE60
Waldronhyrst, S.Croy. 133 DP105
Waldrons, The, Croy. 133 DP105
Waldrons Path, S.Croy. 134 DQ105
Bramley Hill
Waleran Clo., Stan. 45 CF51
Chenduit Way
Waleran Flats SE1 92 DS77
Old Kent Rd.
Walerand Rd. SE13 93 EC82
Wales Ave., Cars. 132 DE106
Wales Fm. Rd. W3 74 CR71
Waley St. E1 79 DY71
Walfield Ave. N20 48 DB45
Walford Rd. N16 64 DS63
Walford Rd., Uxb. 70 BJ68
Walfrey Gdns., Dag. 82 EY66
Walham Gro. SW6 90 DA80
Walham Ri. SW19 103 CY93
Walham Yd. SW6 90 DA80
Walham Gro.
Walk, The, Pot.B. 20 DA32
Walk, The, Sun. 99 BT94
Walkden Rd., Chis. 109 EN92
Walker Clo. N11 49 DJ49
Walker Clo. SE18 95 EQ77
Walker Clo. W7 73 CE74
Walker Clo., Dart. 97 FF83
Walker Clo., Hmptn. 100 BZ93
Fearnley Cres.
Walkers Ct. E8 78 DU65
Wilton Way
Walkers Ct. W1 5 M10
Walkers Pl. SW15 89 CY83
Felsham Rd.
Walkerscroft Mead SE21 106 DQ88
Walkfield Dr., Epsom 145 CV117
Walkford Way SE15 92 DT80
Daniel Gdns.
Walkley Rd., Dart. 111 FH85
Walks, The N2 62 DD55
Wall End Rd. E6 81 EN66
Wall St. N1 78 DR65
Wallace Clo. SE28 82 EX73
Haldane Rd.
Wallace Clo., Shep. 113 BR98
Wallace Clo., Uxb. 70 BL68
Grays Rd.
Wallace Cres., Cars. 132 DF106
Wallace Flds., Epsom 131 CT112
Wallace Rd. N1 78 DQ65
Wallace Wk., Add. 126 BJ105
Wallace Way N19 63 DK61
Giesbach Rd.
Wallasey Cres., Uxb. 56 BN61
Wallbutton Rd. SE4 93 DY82
Wallcote Ave. NW2 61 CX60
Walled Gdn., The, Tad. 145 CX122
Heathcote
Wallenger Ave., Rom. 69 FH55
Waller Dr., Nthwd. 43 BU54
Waller La., Cat. 148 DT123
Waller Rd. SE14 93 DX81
Wallers Clo., Dag. 82 EY67
Wallers Clo., Wdf.Grn. 53 EM51
Waller's Hoppit, Loug. 38 EL40
Wallflower St. W12 75 CT73
Wallgrave Rd. SW5 90 DB77
Wallhouse Rd., Erith 97 FH80
Wallingford Ave. W10 75 CX71
Wallingford Rd., Uxb. 70 BH68
Wallington Clo., Ruis. 57 BQ58
Wallington Rd., Ilf. 67 ET59
Wallington Sq., Wall. 133 DH107
Woodcote Rd.
Wallis All. SE1 11 J5
Wallis Clo. SW11 90 DD83
Wallis Clo., Dart. 111 FG90
Wallis Clo., Horn. 69 FH60
Wallis Ms. N22 63 DN55
Brampton Pk. Rd.
Wallis Ms., Lthd. 143 CG122
Wallis Rd. E9 79 DZ65
Wallis Rd., Sthl. 72 CB72
Walliss Cotts. SW2 105 DL87
Wallorton Gdns. SW14 88 CR84
Wallside EC2 78 DQ71
Wood St.
Wallwood Rd. E11 65 ED60
Wallwood St. E14 79 DZ71
Walm La. NW2 75 CW65
Walmar Clo., Barn. 34 DD39
Walmer Clo. E4 51 EB47
Walmer Clo., Orp. 137 ER105
Tubbenden La. S.
Walmer Clo., Rom. 55 FB54
Walmer Gdns. W13 87 CG75
Walmer Ho. N9 50 DT46
Walmer Pl. W1 4 D6
Walmer Rd. W10 75 CW72
Latimer Rd.
Walmer Rd. W11 75 CY73
Walmer St. W1 4 D6
Walmer Ter. SE18 95 EQ77
Walmgate Rd., Grnf. 73 CH67
Walmington Fold N12 48 DA51
Walney Wk. N1 78 DQ65
St. Paul's Rd.
Walnut Ave., West Dr. 84 BN76
Walnut Clo. SE8 93 DZ79
Clyde St.
Walnut Clo., Cars. 132 DF106
Walnut Clo., Epsom 145 CT115
Walnut Clo., Hayes 71 BS73
Walnut Clo., Ilf. 67 EQ56
Civic Way
Walnut Clo., St.Alb. 16 CB27
Walnut Ct. W5 88 CL75
Walnut Dr., Tad. 145 CY124
Warren Lo. Dr.
Walnut Flds., Epsom 131 CT109
Walnut Gdns. E15 66 EE63
Burgess Rd.
Walnut Grn. (Bushey), Wat. 30 BZ40
Walnut Gro., Bans. 131 CX114
Walnut Gro., Enf. 36 DR43
Walnut Ms., Sutt. 132 DC108
Walnut Rd. E10 65 EA61
Walnut Tree Ave., Mitch. 118 DE97
Dearn Gdns.
Walnut Tree Clo. SW13 89 CT81
Walnut Tree Clo., Bans. 131 CY112
Walnut Tree Clo., Chis. 123 EQ95
Walnut Tree Clo. (Cheshunt), Wal.Cr. 23 DX31
Walnut Tree Cotts. SW19 103 CY91
Church Rd.
Walnut Tree La., W.Byf. 126 BK112
Walnut Tree Rd. SE10 94 EE78
Walnut Tree Rd., Brent. 88 CL79
Walnut Tree Rd., Dag. 68 EX61
Walnut Tree Rd., Erith 97 FE78
Walnut Tree Rd., Houns. 86 BZ79
Walnut Tree Rd., Shep. 113 BQ96
Walnut Tree Wk. SE11 10 D8
Walnut Tree Wk. SE11 91 DN77
Walnut Way, Buck.H. 52 EK48
Walnut Way, Ruis. 72 BW65
Walnut Way, Swan. 125 FD96
Walnuts, The, Orp. 124 EU102
High St.
Walnuts Rd., Orp. 124 EU102
Walpole Ave., Couls. 146 DF119
Walpole Ave., Rich. 88 CM82
Walpole Clo. W13 87 CJ75
Walpole Clo., Pnr. 44 CA51
Walpole Cres., Tedd. 101 CF92
Walpole Gdns. W4 88 CQ78
Walpole Gdns., Twick. 101 CE89
Walpole Ms. NW8 76 DD67
Queen's Gro.
Walpole Ms. SW19 104 DD93
Walpole Rd.
Walpole Pk. W5 73 CJ74
Walpole Pk., Wey. 126 BN108
Walpole Pl. SE18 95 EP77
Anglesea Rd.
Walpole Pl., Tedd. 101 CF92
Walpole Rd. E6 80 EJ66
Walpole Rd. E17 65 DY56
Walpole Rd. E18 52 EF53
Walpole Rd. N17 64 DQ55
(Downhills Way) N17
Walpole Rd. (Lordship La.) N17 50 DQ54
Walpole Rd. SW19 104 DD93
Walpole Rd., Brom. 122 EK99
Walpole Rd., Croy. 120 DR103
Walpole Rd., Surb. 116 CL101
Walpole Rd., Tedd. 101 CF92
Walpole Rd., Twick. 101 CE89
Walpole St. SW3 8 D10
Walpole St. SW3 90 DF78
Walrond Ave., Wem. 60 CL64
Walsh Cres., Croy. 136 EE112
Walsham Clo. N16 64 DU59
Braydon Rd.
Walsham Clo. SE28 82 EX73
Walsham Rd. SE14 93 DX82
Walsham Rd., Felt. 99 BV87
Walshford Way, Borwd. 32 CN38
Walsingham Gdns., Epsom 130 CS105
Walsingham Pk., Chis. 123 ER96
Walsingham Pl. SW4 90 DF84
Clapham Common W. Side
Walsingham Rd. E5 64 DU62
Walsingham Rd. W13 73 CG74
Walsingham Rd., Croy. 135 EC110
Walsingham Rd., Enf. 36 DR42
Walsingham Rd., Mitch. 118 DF99
Walsingham Rd., Orp. 124 EV95
Walsingham Wk., Belv. 96 FA79
Walsingham Way, St.Alb. 17 CJ27
Walt Whitman Clo. SE24 91 DP84
Shakespeare Rd.
Walter Rodney Clo. E6 81 EM65
Stevenage Rd.
Walter St. E2 79 DX69
Walter St., Kings.T. 116 CL95
Sopwith Way
Walter Ter. E1 79 DX72
Walter Wk., Edg. 46 CQ51
Walters Ho. SE17 91 DP79
Otto St.
Walters Mead, Ash. 144 CL117
Walters Rd. SE25 120 DS98
Walters Rd., Enf. 36 DW43
Walters Way SE23 107 DX86
Walters Yd., Brom. 122 EG96
Walterton Rd. W9 75 CZ70
Waltham Ave. NW9 60 CN58
Waltham Ave., Hayes 85 BQ76
Waltham Clo., Dart. 111 FG86
Waltham Clo., Orp. 124 EX102
Waltham Dr., Edg. 46 CN54
Waltham Gdns., Enf. 36 DW36
Waltham Gate, Wal.Cr. 23 DZ26
Thomas Rochford Way
Waltham Pk. Way E17 51 EA53
Waltham Rd., Cars. 118 DD101
Waltham Rd., Cat. 148 DV122
Waltham Rd., Sthl. 86 BY76
Waltham Rd., Wal.Abb. 24 EE26
Waltham Rd., Wdf.Grn. 52 EL51
Waltham Way E4 51 DZ49
Walthamstow Ave. E4 51 DY50
Walthamstow Business Cen. E17 51 EC54
Waltheof Ave. N17 50 DR53
Waltheof Gdns. N17 50 DR53
Walton Ave., Har. 58 BZ64
Walton Ave., N.Mal. 117 CT98
Walton Ave., Sutt. 117 CY104
Walton Bri., Shep. 113 BS101
Walton Bri. Rd., Shep. 113 BR100
Walton Clo. E5 65 DX62
Orient Way
Walton Clo. NW2 61 CV61
Walton Clo. SW8 91 DL80
Walton Clo., Har. 59 CD56
Walton Cres., Har. 58 BZ63
Walton Dr. NW10 74 CR65
Mitchellbrook Way
Walton Dr., Har. 59 CD56
Walton Gdns. W3 74 CP71
Walton Gdns., Felt. 99 BT91
Walton Gdns., Wal.Abb. 23 EB33
Walton Gdns., Wem. 60 CL61
Walton Grn., Croy. 135 EB109
Walton La., Shep. 113 BR101
Walton La., Wey. 113 BP103
Walton Pk., Walt. 114 BX103
Walton Pk. La., Walt. 114 BX103
Walton Pl. SW3 8 D6
Walton Pl. SW3 90 DF76
Walton Rd. E12 67 EN63
Walton Rd. E13 80 EJ68
Walton Rd. N15 64 DT56
Walton Rd., E.Mol. 114 BY98
Walton Rd. (Epsom Downs), Epsom 145 CT117
Walton Rd. (Headley), Epsom 144 CQ121
Walton Rd., Har. 59 CD56
Walton Rd., Rom. 54 EZ52
Walton Rd., Sid. 110 EW89
Walton Rd., Walt. 114 BW99
Walton Rd. (Bushey), Wat. 30 BX42
Walton Rd., W.Mol. 114 BY98
Walton St. SW3 8 C8
Walton St. SW3 90 DE77
Walton St., Enf. 36 DR39
Walton St., Tad. 145 CU124
Walton Way W3 74 CP71
Walton Way, Mitch. 119 DJ98
Walverns Clo., Wat. 30 BW44
Walworth Pl. SE17 92 DQ78
Walworth Rd. SE1 11 H9
Walworth Rd. SE1 92 DQ77
Walworth Rd. SE17 11 H9
Walworth Rd. SE17 92 DQ77
Walwyn Ave., Brom. 122 EK97
Wanborough Dr. SW15 103 CV88
Wanderer Dr., Bark. 82 EV69
Wandle Bank SW19 104 DD94
Wandle Bank, Croy. 119 DL104
Wandle Ct., Epsom 130 CQ105
Wandle Ct. Gdns., Croy. 119 DL104
Wandle Rd. SW17 104 DE89
Wandle Rd., Croy. 120 DQ104
Wandle Rd. (Waddon), Croy. 119 DL104
Wandle Rd., Mord. 118 DC98
Wandle Rd., Wall. 119 DH103
Wandle Side, Croy. 119 DM104
Wandle Side, Wall. 119 DH104
Wandle Way SW18 104 DB88
Wandle Way, Mitch. 118 DF99
Wandon Rd. SW6 90 DB80
Wandsworth Bri. SW6 90 DB83
Wandsworth Bri. SW18 90 DB83
Wandsworth Bri. Rd. SW6 90 DB81
Wandsworth Business Cen., Grnf. 73 CJ68
Wandsworth Common SW12 104 DF87
St. James's Dr.
Wandsworth Common N. Side SW18 104 DC85
Wandsworth Common W. Side SW18 104 DC85
Wandsworth High St. SW18 104 DA85
Wandsworth Plain SW18 104 DA85
Wandsworth Rd. SW8 91 DH83
Wangey Rd., Rom. 68 EX59
Wanless Rd. SE24 92 DQ83
Wanley Rd. SE5 92 DR84
Wanlip Rd. E13 80 EH70
Wannock Gdns., Ilf. 53 EP52
Wansbeck Rd. E9 79 DZ66
Wansbury Way, Swan. 125 FG99
Wansdown Pl. SW6 90 DB80
Fulham Rd.
Wansey St. SE17 11 J9
Wansey St. SE17 92 DQ77
Wansford Pk., Borwd. 32 CR42
Wansford Rd., Wdf.Grn. 52 EJ53
Wanstead Clo., Brom. 122 EJ96
Wanstead La., Ilf. 66 EL58
Wanstead Pk. E11 66 EJ59
Wanstead Pk. Ave. E12 66 EK61
Wanstead Pk. Rd., Ilf. 66 EL58
Wanstead Pl. E11 66 EG58
Wanstead Rd., Brom. 122 EJ96
Wansunt Rd., Bex. 111 FC88
Wantage Rd. SE12 108 EF85
Wantz La., Rain. 83 FH70
Wantz Rd., Dag. 69 FB63
Waplings, The, Tad. 145 CV124
Deans La.
Wapping Dock St. E1 78 DV74
Cinnamon St.
Wapping High St. E1 78 DU74
Wapping La. E1 78 DV73
Wapping Wall E1 78 DW74
Warbank Clo., Croy. 136 EE110
Warbank Cres., Croy. 136 EE110
Warbank La., Kings.T. 103 CT94
Warbeck Rd. W12 89 CV75
Warberry Rd. N22 49 DM54
Warblers Grn., Cob. 128 BZ114
Warboys App., Kings.T. 102 CP93
Warboys Cres. E4 51 EC50
Warboys Rd., Kings.T. 102 CP93
Warburton Clo., Har. 45 CD51
Warburton Rd. E8 78 DV67
Warburton Rd., Twick. 100 CB88
Warburton St. E8 78 DV67
Warburton Rd.
Warburton Ter. E17 51 EB54
Ward Clo., Erith 97 FD79
Ward Clo., S.Croy. 134 DS106
Ward Clo. (Cheshunt), Wal.Cr. 22 DU27
Spicersfield
Ward La., Warl. 148 DW116
Ward Rd. E15 79 ED67
Ward Rd. N19 63 DJ62
Wardalls Gro. SE14 92 DW80
Wardell Clo. NW7 46 CS52
Wardell Fld. NW9 46 CS53
Warden Ave., Har. 58 BZ60
Warden Ave., Rom. 55 FC50
Warden Rd. NW5 76 DG65
Wardens Fld. Clo., Orp. 137 ES107
Wardens Gro. SE1 11 H3
Wardle St. E9 65 DX64
Wardley St. SW18 104 DB87
Garratt La.
Wardo Ave. SW6 89 CY81
Wardour Ms. W1 5 L9
Wardour St. W1 5 L8
Wardour St. W1 77 DJ72
Wardrobe Pl. EC4 6 G9
Wardrobe Ter. EC4 6 G10
Wards Rd., Ilf. 67 ER59
Wareham Clo., Houns. 86 CB84
Waremead Rd., Ilf. 67 EP57
Warenford Way, Borwd. 32 CN39
Warenne Rd., Lthd. 142 CC122
Warepoint Dr. SE28 95 ER75
Warfield Rd. NW10 75 CX69
Warfield Rd., Felt. 99 BS87
Warfield Rd., Hmptn. 114 CB95
Warfield Yd. NW10 75 CX69
Warfield Rd.
Wargrave Ave. N15 64 DT58
Wargrave Rd., Har. 58 CC62
Warham Rd. N4 63 DN57
Warham Rd., Har. 45 CF54
Warham Rd., Sev. 153 FH116
Warham Rd., S.Croy. 133 DP106
Warham St. SE5 91 DP80
Waring Clo., Orp. 137 ET107
Waring Dr., Orp. 137 ET107
Waring Rd., Sid. 110 EW93
Waring St. SE27 106 DQ91
Warkworth Gdns., Islw. 87 CG80
Warkworth Rd. N17 50 DR52
Warland Rd. SE18 95 ER80
Warley Ave., Dag. 68 EZ59
Warley Ave., Hayes 71 BU72
Warley Clo. E10 65 DZ60
Millicent Rd.
Warley Rd. N9 50 DW47
Warley Rd., Hayes 71 BU72
Warley Rd., Ilf. 53 EN53
Warley Rd., Wdf.Grn. 52 EH52
Warley St. E2 79 DX69
Warlingham Rd., Th.Hth. 119 DP98
Warlock Rd. W9 75 CZ70
Warlters Clo. N7 63 DL63
Warlters Rd.
Warlters Rd. N7 63 DL63
Warltersville Rd. N19 63 DL59
Warmington Clo. E5 65 DX62
Orient Way
Warmington Rd. SE24 106 DQ86
Warmington St. E13 80 EG70
Barking Rd.
Warminster Gdns. SE25 120 DU96
Warminster Rd. SE25 120 DU97
Warminster Sq. SE25 120 DU96
Warminster Rd.
Warminster Way, Mitch. 119 DH95
Warndon St. SE16 92 DW77
Warne Pl., Sid. 110 EV86
Westerham Dr.
Warneford Pl., Wat. 30 BY44
Warneford Rd., Har. 59 CK55
Warneford St. E9 78 DV67
Warner Ave., Sutt. 117 CY103
Warner Clo. E15 66 EE64
Warner Clo. NW9 61 CT59
Warner Clo., Hmptn. 100 BZ92
Tangley Pk. Rd.
Warner Clo., Hayes 85 BR80
Warner Par., Hayes 85 BR80
Warner Pl. E2 78 DU68
Warner Rd. E17 65 DY56
Warner Rd. N8 63 DK56
Warner Rd. SE5 92 DQ81
Warner Rd., Brom. 108 EF94
Warner St. EC1 6 D5
Warner St. EC1 77 DN70
Warner Yd. EC1 6 D5
Warners Clo., Wdf.Grn. 52 EG50
Warners La., Kings.T. 101 CK92
Warners Path, Wdf.Grn. 52 EG50
Warnford Ind. Est., Hayes 85 BS75
Warnford Rd., Orp. 137 ET106
Warnham Ct. Rd., Cars. 132 DF108
Warnham Rd. N12 48 DD50
Warple Ms. W3 88 CS75
Warple Way
Warple Way W3 88 CS75
Warren, The E12 66 EL63
Warren, The, Ash. 144 CL119
Warren, The, Cars. 132 DD109
Warren, The, Hayes 71 BU72
Warren, The, Houns. 86 BZ80
Warren, The, Lthd. 128 CC112
Warren, The, Rad. 17 CG33
Warren, The, Tad. 145 CY123
Warren, The, Wor.Pk. 130 CR105
Warren Ave. E10 65 EC62
Warren Ave., Brom. 108 EE94
Warren Ave., Orp. 137 ET106
Warren Ave., Rich. 88 CP84
Warren Ave., S.Croy. 135 DX108
Warren Ave., Sutt. 131 CZ110
Warren Clo. N9 51 DX45
Warren Clo. SE21 106 DQ87
Lairdale Clo.
Warren Clo., Bexh. 110 FA85
Pincott Rd.
Warren Clo., Esher 128 CB105
Warren Clo., Hayes 71 BV71
Warren Clo., Wem. 59 CK61
Warren Ct., Chig. 53 ER49
Warren Ct., Sev. 155 FJ125
Warren Ct., Wey. 126 BN106
Warren Cres. N9 50 DT45
Warren Cutting, Kings.T. 102 CR94
Warren Dr., Grnf. 72 CB70
Warren Dr., Horn. 69 FG63
Warren Dr., Orp. 138 EV106
Warren Dr., Ruis. 58 BX59
Warren Dr., Tad. 145 CZ122
Warren Dr., The E11 66 EJ59
Warren Dr. N., Surb. 116 CP102
Warren Dr. S., Surb. 116 CQ102
Warren Fld., Epp. 26 EU32
Warren Flds., Stan. 45 CJ49
Valencia Rd.
Warren Footpath, Twick. 101 CJ88
Warren Gdns. E15 65 ED64
Ashton Rd.
Warren Gdns., Orp. 138 EU106
Warren Gro., Borwd. 32 CR42
Warren Hill, Epsom 144 CR116
Warren Hill, Loug. 38 EJ43
Warren Ho. E3 79 EB69
Bromley High St.
Warren La. SE18 95 EP76
Warren La., Lthd. 128 CC111
Warren La., Stan. 45 CF48
Warren La., Wok. 140 BG118
Warren Lo. Dr., Tad. 145 CY124
Warren Mead, Bans. 145 CW115
Warren Ms. W1 5 K5
Warren Pk., Kings.T. 102 CQ93
Warren Pk., Warl. 149 DX118
Warren Pk. Rd., Sutt. 132 DD107
Warren Pl. E1 79 DX72
Pitsea St.
Warren Pond Rd. E4 52 EF46
Warren Ri., N.Mal. 116 CR95
Warren Rd. E4 51 EC47
Warren Rd. E10 65 EC62
Warren Rd. E11 66 EJ58
Warren Rd. NW2 61 CT61
Warren Rd. SW19 104 DE93
Warren Rd., Add. 126 BG110
Warren Rd., Ashf. 99 BS94
Warren Rd., Bans. 131 CW114
Warren Rd., Bexh. 110 FA85
Warren Rd., Brom. 122 EG103
Warren Rd., Croy. 120 DS102
Warren Rd., Ilf. 67 ER57
Warren Rd., Kings.T. 102 CQ93
Warren Rd., Orp. 137 ET106
Warren Rd., Pur. 133 DP112
Warren Rd., Sid. 110 EW90
Warren Rd., Twick. 100 CC86
Warren Rd., Uxb. 56 BL63
Warren Rd. (Bushey), Wat. 44 CC46
Warren St. W1 5 J5
Warren St. W1 77 DJ70
Warren Ter., Rom. 68 EX56
Warren Wk. SE7 94 EJ79
Warren Way NW7 47 CY51
Warren Way, Wey. 127 BQ106
Warren Wd. Clo., Brom. 122 EG103
Hillside La.
Warrender Rd. N19 63 DJ62
Warrender Way, Ruis. 57 BU59
Warreners La., Wey. 127 BR109

Warrenfield Clo. (Cheshunt), Wal.Cr. 22 DU31
Portland Dr.
Warrengate La., Pot.B. 19 CW31
Warrengate Rd., Hat. 19 CV26
Warrens Shawe La., Edg. 46 CP47
Warriner Gdns. SW11 90 DF81
Warrington Cres. W9 76 DC70
Warrington Gdns. W9 76 DC70
Warwick Ave.
Warrington Pl. E14 79 EC74
Yabsley St.
Warrington Rd., Croy. 119 DP104
Warrington Rd., Dag. 68 EX61
Warrington Rd., Har. 59 CE57
Warrington Rd., Rich. 101 CK85
Warrington Sq., Dag. 68 EX61
Warrington St. E13 80 EG70
Doherty Rd.
Warrior Sq. E12 67 EN63
Warsaw Clo., Ruis. 71 BV65
Glebe Ave.
Warsdale Dr. NW9 60 CR57
Mardale Dr.
Warspite Rd. SE18 94 EK76
Warton Rd. E15 79 EC66
Warwall E6 81 EP72
Warwick Ave. W2 76 DC71
Warwick Ave. W9 76 DB70
Warwick Ave., Edg. 46 CP48
Warwick Ave., Har. 58 BZ63
Warwick Ave. (Cuffley), Pot.B. 21 DK27
Warwick Ave., Stai. 98 BJ93
Warwick Clo., Barn. 34 DD43
Warwick Clo., Bex. 110 EZ87
Warwick Clo., Hmptn. 100 CC94
Warwick Clo., Orp. 124 EU104
Warwick Clo. (Cuffley), Pot.B. 21 DK27
Warwick Clo. (Bushey), Wat. 45 CE45
Magnaville Rd.
Warwick Ct. SE15 92 DU82
Warwick Ct. WC1 6 C7
Warwick Ct., Surb. 116 CL103
Hook Rd.
Warwick Cres. W2 76 DC71
Warwick Cres., Hayes 71 BT70
Warwick Dene W5 74 CL74
Warwick Dr. SW15 89 CV83
Warwick Dr. (Cheshunt), Wal.Cr. 23 DX28
Warwick Est. W2 76 DB71
Warwick Gdns. N4 64 DQ57
Warwick Gdns. W14 89 CZ76
Warwick Gdns., Ash. 143 CJ117
Warwick Gdns., Ilf. 67 EP60
Warwick Gdns., T.Ditt. 115 CF99
Warwick Gro. E5 64 DV60
Warwick Gro., Surb. 116 CM101
Warwick Ho. St. SW1 9 N2
Warwick Ho. St. SW1 77 DK74
Warwick La. EC4 6 G9
Warwick La. EC4 77 DP72
Warwick Pas. EC4 77 DP72
Old Bailey
Warwick Pl. W5 87 CK75
Warwick Rd.
Warwick Pl. W9 76 DC71
Warwick Pl., Uxb. 70 BJ66
Warwick Pl. N. SW1 9 K9
Warwick Pl. N. SW1 91 DJ77
Warwick Rd. E4 51 EA50
Warwick Rd. E11 66 EH57
Warwick Rd. E12 66 EL64
Warwick Rd. E15 80 EF65
Warwick Rd. E17 51 DZ53
Warwick Rd. N11 49 DK51
Warwick Rd. N18 50 DS49
Warwick Rd. SE20 120 DV97
Warwick Rd. SW5 89 CZ77
Warwick Rd. W5 87 CK75
Warwick Rd. W14 89 CZ77
Warwick Rd., Ashf. 98 BL92
Warwick Rd., Barn. 34 DB42
Warwick Rd., Borwd. 32 CR41
Warwick Rd., Couls. 133 DJ114
Warwick Rd., Enf. 37 DZ37
Warwick Rd., Houns. 85 BV83
Warwick Rd., Kings.T. 115 CJ95
Warwick Rd., N.Mal. 116 CQ97
Warwick Rd., Sid. 110 EV92
Warwick Rd., Sthl. 86 BZ76
Warwick Rd., Sutt. 132 DC105
Warwick Rd., T.Ditt. 115 CF99
Warwick Rd., Th.Hth. 119 DN97
Warwick Rd., Twick. 101 CE88
Warwick Rd., Well. 96 EW83
Warwick Rd., West Dr. 84 BL75
Warwick Row SW1 9 J6
Warwick Row SW1 91 DH76
Warwick Sq. EC4 6 G8
Warwick Sq. SW1 9 K10
Warwick Sq. SW1 91 DJ78
Warwick Sq. Ms. SW1 9 M9
Warwick St. W1 5 L10
Warwick St. W1 77 DJ73
Warwick Ter. SE18 95 ER79
Warwick Way SW1 9 J10
Warwick Way SW1 91 DH78
Warwick Way, Rick. 29 BQ42
Warwick Yd. EC1 7 J5
Warwickshire Path SE8 93 DZ80
Wash La., Pot.B. 19 CV33
Washington Ave. E12 66 EL63
Washington Clo. E3 79 EB69
St. Leonards St.
Washington Rd. E6 80 EJ66
St. Stephens Rd.
Washington Rd. E18 52 EF54
Washington Rd. SW13 89 CU80
Washington Rd., Kings.T. 116 CN96
Washington Rd., Wor.Pk. 117 CV103
Washneys Rd., Orp. 138 EV113
Washpond La., Warl. 149 EC118
Wastdale Rd. SE23 107 DX88
Wat Tyler Rd. SE3 93 EC82
Wat Tyler Rd. SE10 93 EC82
Watchfield Ct. W4 88 CQ78
Watcombe Cotts., Rich. 88 CN79
Watcombe Pl. SE25 120 DV99
Albert Rd.
Watcombe Rd. SE25 120 DV99
Water Gdns., Stan. 45 CH51
Water La. E15 80 EE65
Water La. EC3 78 DS73
Lower Thames St.
Water La. NW1 77 DH66
Kentish Town Rd.
Water La. SE14 92 DW80
Water La., Cob. 142 BY115
Water La., Ilf. 67 ES62
Water La., Kings L. 15 BP29
Water La., Kings.T. 115 CK95
Water La., Rich. 101 CK85
Water La., Sev. 139 FF112
Water La., Sid. 110 EZ90
Water La., Twick. 101 CG88
The Embk.
Water La., Wat. 30 BW42
Water Lily Clo., Sthl. 86 CC75
Navigator Dr.
Water Rd., Wem. 74 CM67
Water St. WC2 6 C10
Water Twr. Clo., Uxb. 56 BL64
Water Twr. Hill, Croy. 134 DR105
Water Twr. Pl. N1 77 DN67
Liverpool Rd.
Waterbank Rd. SE6 107 EB90
Waterbeach Rd., Dag. 82 EW65
Waterbrook La. NW4 61 CW57
Watercress Pl. N1 78 DS66
Hertford Rd.
Watercroft Rd., Sev. 138 EZ110
Waterdale Rd. SE2 96 EU79
Waterdell Pl., Rick. 42 BG47
Uxbridge Rd.
Waterden Rd. E15 65 EA64
Waterer Gdns., Tad. 145 CX118
Waterer Ri., Wall. 133 DK107
Waterfall Clo. N14 49 DJ48
Waterfall Cotts. SW19 104 DD93
Waterfall Rd. N11 49 DH49
Waterfall Rd. N14 49 DJ48
Waterfall Rd. SW19 104 DD93
Waterfall Ter. SW17 104 DE93
Waterfield, Tad. 145 CV119
Waterfield Clo. SE28 82 EV74
Waterfield Clo., Belv. 96 FA76
Waterfield Dr., Warl. 148 DW119
Waterfield Gdns. SE25 120 DR98
Waterfield Grn., Tad. 145 CV120
Waterfields, Lthd. 143 CH119
Waterfields Way, Wat. 30 BX43
Waterford Rd. SW6 90 DB80
Watergardens, The, Kings.T. 102 CQ93
Watergate EC4 6 F10
Watergate, Wat. 44 BX47
Watergate St. SE8 93 EA79
Watergate Wk. WC2 10 A1
Waterhall Ave. E4 52 EE49
Waterhall Clo. E17 51 DX53
Waterhead Clo., Erith 97 FE80
Waterhouse Clo. E16 80 EK71
Waterhouse Clo. NW3 62 DD64
Lyndhurst Rd.
Waterhouse Clo. W6 89 CX77
Great Ch. La.
Waterhouse La., Ken. 148 DQ119
Hayes La.
Waterhouse La., Tad. 145 CZ121
Waterhouse Sq. EC1 77 DN71
Wateridge Clo. E14 93 EA76
Westferry Rd.
Wateringbury Clo., Orp. 124 EV97
Waterloo Bri. SE1 10 B1
Waterloo Bri. SE1 77 DM74
Waterloo Bri. WC2 10 B1
Waterloo Bri. WC2 77 DM73
Waterloo Clo. E9 64 DW64
Churchill Wk.
Waterloo Clo., Felt. 99 BT88
Waterloo Est. E2 78 DW68
Waterloo Gdns. E2 78 DW68
Waterloo Gdns., Rom. 69 FD58
Waterloo Pas. NW6 75 CZ66
Waterloo Pl. SW1 9 M2
Waterloo Pl. SW1 77 DK74
Waterloo Pl., Rich. 102 CL85
Sheen Rd.
Waterloo Pl. (Kew), Rich. 88 CN79
Waterloo Rd. E6 80 EJ66
Waterloo Rd. E7 66 EF64
Wellington Rd.
Waterloo Rd. E10 65 EA59
Waterloo Rd. NW2 61 CU60
Waterloo Rd. SE1 10 D4
Waterloo Rd. SE1 77 DN74
Waterloo Rd., Epsom 130 CR112
Waterloo Rd., Ilf. 53 EQ54
Waterloo Rd., Rom. 69 FE58
Waterloo Rd., Sutt. 132 DD106
Waterloo Rd., Uxb. 70 BJ67
Waterloo Ter. N1 77 DP66
Waterlow Ct. NW11 62 DB59
Heath Clo.
Waterlow Rd. N19 63 DJ60
Waterman Clo., Wat. 29 BV44
Waterman St. SW15 89 CX83
Waterman Way E1 78 DV74
Waterman's Clo., Kings.T. 102 CL94
Woodside Rd.
Watermans Wk. SE16 79 DY74
Redriff Rd.
Watermans Way, Epp. 26 FA27
Watermead, Felt. 99 BS88
Watermead, Tad. 145 CV121
Watermead La., Cars. 118 DF101
Watermead Rd. SE6 107 EB91
Watermead Way N17 64 DU55
Watermeadow Clo., Erith 97 FH81
Hollywood Way
Watermeadow La. SW6 90 DC82
Watermen's Sq. SE20 106 DW94
Watermill Clo., Rich. 101 CJ90
Watermill La. N18 50 DS50
Watermill Way SW19 118 DC95
Watermill Way, Felt. 100 BZ89
Watermint Clo., Orp. 124 EX98
Wagtail Way
Watermint Quay N16 64 DU58
Waters Dr., Rick. 42 BL46
Waters Gdns., Dag. 68 FA64
Sterry Rd.
Waters Rd. SE6 108 EE90
Waters Rd., Kings.T. 116 CP96
Waters Sq., Kings.T. 116 CP97
Watersedge, Epsom 130 CQ105
Watersfield Way, Edg. 45 CK52
Waterside, Beck. 121 EA95
Rectory Rd.
Waterside, Dart. 111 FE85
Waterside, Kings L. 14 BN29
Waterside, St.Alb. 18 CL27
Waterside, Uxb. 70 BJ71
Waterside Clo. E3 79 DZ67
Parnell Rd.
Waterside Clo. SE16 92 DU75
Bevington St.
Waterside Clo., Bark. 68 EU63
Waterside Clo., Nthlt. 72 BZ69
Waterside Clo., Surb. 116 CL103
Culsac Rd.
Waterside Dr., Walt. 113 BU99
Waterside Pl. NW1 76 DG67
Princess Rd.
Waterside Pt. SW11 90 DE80
Waterside Rd., Sthl. 86 CA76
Waterside Trd. Cen. W7 87 CE76
Waterside Way SW17 104 DC91
Watersmeet Way SE28 82 EW72
Waterson St. E2 7 N2
Waterson St. E2 78 DS69
Watersplash Clo., Kings.T. 116 CL97
Watersplash La., Hayes 85 BU77
North Hyde Rd.
Watersplash La., Houns. 85 BV78
Watersplash Rd., Shep. 112 BN99
Waterview Ho. E14 79 DY71
Carr St.
Waterway Rd., Lthd. 143 CG122
Waterworks La. E5 65 DX61
Waterworks Rd. SW2 105 DM86
Waterworks Yd., Croy. 120 DQ104
Surrey St.
Watery La. SW20 117 CZ96
Watery La., Nthlt. 72 BW68
Watery La., St.Alb. 17 CK28
Watery La., Sid. 110 EV93
Wates Way, Mitch. 118 DF100
Wateville Rd. N17 50 DQ53
Watford Bypass, Borwd. 45 CG45
Watford Clo. SW11 90 DE81
Petworth St.
Watford Fld. Rd., Wat. 30 BW43
Watford Heath, Wat. 44 BX45
Watford Rd. E16 80 EG71
Watford Rd., Borwd. 31 CJ44
Watford Rd., Har. 59 CG59
Watford Rd., Kings L. 14 BN30
Watford Rd., Nthwd. 43 BT52
Watford Rd., Rad. 31 CE35
Watford Rd., Rick. 28 BM44
Watford Rd., St.Alb. 16 CA27
Watford Rd., Wem. 59 CG61
Watford Way NW4 61 CU56
Watford Way NW7 46 CS49
Watkin Rd., Wem. 60 CP62
Watkinson Rd. N7 77 DM65
Watling Ave., Edg. 46 CQ53
Watling Ct. EC4 7 J9
Watling Ct., Borwd. 31 CK44
Watling Fm. Clo., Stan. 45 CJ45
Watling Gdns. NW2 75 CY65
Watling Knoll, Rad. 17 CF33
Watling St. EC4 7 H9
Watling St. EC4 78 DQ72
Watling St., Bexh. 97 FB84
Watling St., Borwd. 31 CH38
Watling St., Rad. 17 CF32
Watling St., St.Alb. 17 CD25
Watling St. Caravan Site (Travellers), St.Alb. 16 CC25
Watlings Clo., Croy. 121 DY100
Watlington Gro. SE26 107 DY92
Watney Mkt. E1 78 DV72
Commercial Rd.
Watney Rd. SW14 88 CQ83
Watney St. E1 78 DV72
Watneys Rd., Mitch. 119 DK99
Watson Ave. E6 81 EN66
Watson Ave., Sutt. 117 CY104
Watson Clo. N16 64 DR64
Matthias Rd.
Watson Clo. SW19 104 DE93
Watson St. E13 80 EH68
Watsons Ms. W1 4 C7
Watsons Rd. N22 49 DM53
Watson's St. SE8 93 EA80
Watsons Yd. NW2 61 CT61
North Circular Rd.
Wattendon Rd., Ken. 147 DP116
Wattisfield Rd. E5 64 DW62
Watts Bri. Rd., Erith 97 FF79
Reddy Rd.
Watts Clo. N15 64 DS57
Seaford Rd.
Watts Clo., Tad. 145 CX122
Watts Gro. E3 79 EB71
Watts La., Chis. 123 EP95
Watts La., Tad. 145 CX122
Watts La., Tedd. 101 CG92
Watts Mead, Tad. 145 CX122
Watts Rd., T.Ditt. 115 CG101
Watts St. E1 78 DV74
Watts Way SW7 8 A6
Wauthier Clo. N13 49 DP50
Wavel Ms. N8 63 DK56
Wavel Ms. NW6 76 DB66
Acol Rd.
Wavel Pl. SE26 106 DT91
Sydenham Hill
Wavell Clo. (Cheshunt), Wal.Cr. 23 DY27
Wavell Dr., Sid. 109 ES86
Wavendon Ave. W4 88 CR78
Waveney Ave. SE15 92 DV84
Waveney Clo. E1 78 DU74
Kennet St.
Waverley Ave. E4 51 DZ49
Waverley Ave. E17 65 ED55
Waverley Ave., Ken. 148 DS116
Waverley Ave., Surb. 116 CP100
Waverley Ave., Sutt. 118 DB103
Waverley Ave., Twick. 100 BZ88
Waverley Ave., Wem. 60 CM64
Waverley Clo. E18 52 EJ54
Waverley Clo., Brom. 122 EK99
Waverley Clo., Hayes 85 BR77
Waverley Cres. SE18 95 ER79
Waverley Gdns. E6 80 EL71
Oliver Gdns.
Waverley Gdns. NW10 74 CM68
Waverley Gdns., Bark. 81 ES68
Waverley Gdns., Ilf. 53 EQ54
Waverley Gdns., Nthwd. 43 BU53
Waverley Gro. N3 61 CX55
Waverley Ind. Pk., Har. 59 CD55
Waverley Pl. N4 63 DP61
Adolphus Rd.
Waverley Pl. NW8 76 DD68
Waverley Pl., Lthd. 143 CH122
Church Rd.
Waverley Rd. E17 65 EC55
Waverley Rd. E18 52 EJ53
Waverley Rd. N8 63 DL58
Waverley Rd. N17 50 DV52
Waverley Rd. SE18 95 EQ78
Waverley Rd. SE25 120 DV98
Waverley Rd., Cob. 128 CB114
Waverley Rd., Enf. 35 DP42
Waverley Rd., Epsom 131 CU107
Waverley Rd., Har. 58 BY60
Waverley Rd., Lthd. 128 CB114
Waverley Rd., Rain. 83 FH69
Waverley Rd., Sthl. 72 CA73
Waverley Rd., Wey. 126 BN106
Waverley Vill. N17 50 DT54
Waverley Wk. W2 76 DA71
Waverley Way, Cars. 132 DE107
Waverton Ho. E3 79 DZ67
Waverton Rd. SW18 104 DC87
Waverton St. W1 9 H2
Waverton St. W1 76 DG74
Wavertree Ct. SW2 105 DM88
Streatham Hill
Wavertree Rd. E18 52 EG54
Wavertree Rd. SW2 105 DL88
Waxlow Cres., Sthl. 72 CA72
Waxlow Rd. NW10 74 CQ68
Waxwell Clo., Pnr. 44 BX54
Waxwell La., Pnr. 44 BX54
Waxwell Ter. SE1 10 C5
Waybourne Gro., Ruis. 57 BQ58
Waye Ave., Houns. 85 BU81
Wayfarer Rd., Nthlt. 72 BX69
Wayfield Link SE9 109 ER86
Wayford St. SW11 90 DE82
Wayland Ave. E8 64 DU64
Waylands, Swan. 125 FF98
Waylands Clo., Sev. 152 EY115
Waylands Mead, Beck. 121 EB95
Wayleave, The SE28 82 EV73
Oriole Way
Waylett Pl. SE27 105 DP90
Waylett Pl., Wem. 59 CK62
Wayman Ct. E8 78 DV65
Wayne Clo., Orp. 123 ET104
Wayneflete Twr. Ave., Esher 114 CA104
Waynflete Ave., Croy. 119 DP104
Waynflete Sq. W10 75 CX72
Waynflete St. SW18 104 DC89
Wayside NW11 61 CY60
Wayside SW14 102 CQ85
Wayside, Croy. 135 EB107
Field Way
Wayside, Kings L. 14 BH30
Wayside, Pot.B. 20 DD33
Wayside, Rad. 17 CK33
Wayside Ave. (Bushey), Wat. 31 CD44
Wayside Clo. N14 35 DJ44
Wayside Clo., Rom. 69 FF55
Wayside Commercial Est., Bark. 82 EU68
Wayside Ct., Twick. 101 CJ86
Wayside Ct., Wem. 60 CN62
Oakington Ave.
Wayside Gdns. SE9 109 EM91
Wayside Gro.
Wayside Gdns., Dag. 68 FA64
Wayside Gro. SE9 109 EM91
Wayside Ms., Ilf. 67 EN57
Gaysham Ave.
Weald, The, Chis. 109 EM93
Weald Clo. SE16 92 DV78
Stevenson Cres.
Weald Clo., Brom. 122 EL103
Weald Hall La., Epp. 26 EW25
Weald La., Har. 45 CD54
Weald Ri., Har. 45 CF52
Weald Rd., Sev. 155 FH129
Weald Rd., Uxb. 70 BN68
Weald Sq. E5 64 DV61
Rossington St.
Weald Way, Hayes 71 BS69
Weald Way, Rom. 69 FB58
Wealdstone Rd., Sutt. 117 CZ103
Wealdwood Gdns., Pnr. 44 CB51
Highbanks Rd.
Weale Rd. E4 51 ED48
Weall Grn., Wat. 15 BV32
Wear Pl. E2 78 DV69
Weardale Gdns., Enf. 36 DR39
Weardale Rd. SE13 93 ED84
Wearside Rd. SE13 107 EB85
Weatherall Clo., Add. 126 BH106
Weatherley Clo. E3 79 DZ71
Weaver Clo. E6 81 EP72
Trader Rd.
Weaver St. E1 78 DU70
Weaver Wk. SE27 106 DQ91
Weavers Clo., Islw. 87 CE84
Weavers La., Sev. 155 FJ121
Weavers Ter. SW6 90 DA79
Micklethwaite Rd.
Weavers Way NW1 77 DK66
Webb Est. E5 64 DU59
Webb Gdns. E13 80 EG70
Kelland Rd.
Webb Pl. NW10 75 CT69
Old Oak La.
Webb Rd. SE3 94 EF79
Webb St. SE1 11 M7
Webb St. SE1 92 DS76
Webber Clo., Borwd. 31 CK44
Rodgers Clo.
Webber Clo., Erith 97 FH80
Webber Row SE1 10 E5
Webber Row SE1 91 DN75
Webber St. SE1 10 F5
Webber St. SE1 91 DN75
Webb's All., Sev. 155 FJ125
Webbs Rd. SW11 90 DF84
Webbs Rd., Hayes 71 BV69
Webbscroft Rd., Dag. 69 FB63
Webster Clo., Lthd. 128 CB114
Webster Clo., Wal.Abb. 24 EG33
Webster Gdns. W5 73 CK74
Webster Rd. E11 65 EC62
Webster Rd. SE16 92 DU76
Wedderburn Rd. NW3 62 DD64
Wedderburn Rd., Bark. 81 ER67
Wedgewood Clo., Epp. 26 EU30
Wedgewood Clo., Nthwd. 43 BQ52
Wedgewood Wk. NW6 62 DB64
Lymington Rd.
Wedgewood Way SE19 106 DQ94
Wedgewoods, West. 150 EJ121
Westmore Rd.
Wedgwood Ms. W1 5 N9
Wedlake St. W10 75 CY70
Kensal Rd.
Wedmore Ave., Ilf. 53 EN53
Wedmore Gdns. N19 63 DK61
Wedmore Ms. N19 63 DK62
Wedmore St.
Wedmore Rd., Grnf. 73 CD69
Wedmore St. N19 63 DK62
Weech Rd. NW6 62 DA63
Weedington Rd. NW5 62 DG64
Weekley Sq. SW11 90 DD83
Thomas Baines Rd.
Weigall Rd. SE12 94 EG84
Weighouse St. W1 4 G9
Weighouse St. W1 76 DG72
Weighton Rd. SE20 120 DV96
Weighton Rd., Har. 45 CD53
Weihurst Gdns., Sutt. 132 DD106
Weimar St. SW15 89 CY83
Weind, The, Epp. 39 ES36
Weir Est. SW12 105 DJ87
Weir Hall Ave. N18 50 DR51
Weir Hall Gdns. N18 50 DR50
Weir Hall Rd. N17 50 DR51
Weir Hall Rd. N18 50 DR50
Weir Rd. SW12 105 DJ87
Weir Rd. SW19 104 DB90
Weir Rd., Bex. 111 FB87
Weir Rd., Cher. 112 BH101

Weir Rd., Walt. 113 BU100
Weirdale Ave. N20 48 DF47
Weir's Pas. NW1 5 N2
Weir's Pas. NW1 77 DK69
Weiss Rd. SW15 89 CX83
Welbeck Ave., Brom. 108 EG91
Welbeck Ave., Hayes 71 BV70
Welbeck Ave., Sid. 110 EU88
Welbeck Clo. N12 48 DD50
Torrington Pk.
Welbeck Clo., Borwd. 32 CN41
Welbeck Clo., Epsom 131 CU108
Welbeck Clo., N.Mal. 117 CT99
Welbeck Rd. E6 80 EK69
Welbeck Rd., Barn. 34 DD44
Welbeck Rd., Cars. 118 DE102
Welbeck Rd., Har. 58 CB60
Welbeck Rd., Sutt. 118 DD103
Welbeck St. W1 4 G7
Welbeck St. W1 76 DG71
Welbeck Wk., Cars. 118 DE102
Welbeck Rd.
Welbeck Way W1 5 H8
Welbeck Way W1 77 DH72
Welby St. SE5 91 DP81
Welch Pl., Pnr. 44 BW53
Welcomes Rd., Ken. 148 DQ116
Welcote Dr., Nthwd. 43 BR51
Weld Pl. N11 49 DH50
Weldon Clo., Ruis. 71 BV65
Weldon Dr., W.Mol. 114 BZ98
Welfare Rd. E15 80 EE66
Welford Clo. E5 65 DX62
Denton Way
Welford Pl. SW19 103 CY91
Welham Rd. SW16 105 DH93
Welham Rd. SW17 104 DG92
Welhouse Rd., Cars. 118 DE102
Well App., Barn. 33 CW43
Well Clo. SW16 105 DM91
Well Clo., Ruis. 58 BY62
Parkfield Cres.
Well Cottage Clo. E11 66 EJ59
Well Ct. EC4 7 J9
Well Ct. SW16 105 DM91
Well End Rd., Borwd. 32 CQ37
Well Fm. Rd., Whyt. 148 DU119
Well Gro. N20 48 DC45
Well Hall Par. SE9 95 EM84
Well Hall Rd.
Well Hall Rd. SE9 94 EL83
Well Hill, Orp. 139 FB107
Well Hill La., Orp. 139 FB108
Well Hill Rd., Sev. 139 FC107
Well La. SW14 102 CQ85
Well Pas. NW3 62 DD62
Well Rd. NW3 62 DD62
Well Rd., Barn. 33 CW43
Well Rd., Pot.B. 20 DB28
Well St. E9 78 DW66
Well St. E15 80 EE65
Well Wk. NW3 62 DD63
Well Way, Epsom 144 CN115
Wellacre Rd., Har. 59 CH58
Wellan Clo., Sid. 110 EV85
Welland Gdns., Grnf. 73 CF68
Welland Ms. E1 78 DU74
Kennet St.
Welland St. SE10 93 EC79
Wellands Clo., Brom. 123 EM96
Wellbrook Rd., Orp. 137 EN105
Wellclose Sq. E1 78 DU73
Wellclose St. E1 78 DU73
The Highway
Welldon Cres., Har. 59 CE58
Weller St. SE1 11 H4
Weller's Ct. N1 5 P1
Wellers Gro. (Cheshunt), Wal.Cr. 22 DU28
Wellesford Clo., Bans. 145 CZ117
Wellesley Ave. W6 89 CV76
Wellesley Ave., Nthwd. 43 BT50
Wellesley Ct. W9 76 DC69
Maida Vale
Wellesley Ct. Rd., Croy. 120 DR103
Wellesley Cres., Pot.B. 19 CY33
Wellesley Cres., Twick. 101 CE89
Wellesley Gro., Croy. 120 DR103
Wellesley Pk. Ms., Enf. 35 DP40
Wellesley Pl. NW1 5 M3
Wellesley Rd. E11 66 EG57
Wellesley Rd. E17 65 EA58
Wellesley Rd. N22 49 DN54
Wellesley Rd. NW5 62 DG64
Wellesley Rd. W4 88 CN78
Wellesley Rd., Croy. 120 DQ102
Wellesley Rd., Har. 59 CE57
Wellesley Rd., Ilf. 67 EP61
Wellesley Rd., Sutt. 132 DC107
Wellesley Rd., Twick. 101 CD90
Wellesley St. E1 79 DX71
Wellesley Ter. N1 7 J2
Wellesley Ter. N1 78 DQ69
Wellfield Ave. N10 63 DH55
Wellfield Gdns., Cars. 132 DE109
Woodmansterne Rd.
Wellfield Rd. SW16 105 DL91
Wellfield Wk. SW16 105 DM92
Wellfields Rd., Loug. 39 EN41
Wellfit St. SE24 91 DP83
Hinton Rd.
Wellgarth, Grnf. 73 CH65
Wellgarth Rd. NW11 62 DB60
Wellhouse La., Barn. 33 CW42
Wellhouse Rd., Beck. 121 DZ98
Welling High St., Well. 96 EU83
Welling Way SE9 95 ER83
Welling Way, Well. 95 ES83
Wellings Ho., Hayes 71 BV74
Wellington Ave. E4 51 EA47
Wellington Ave. N9 50 DV48
Wellington Ave. N15 64 DT58
Wellington Ave., Houns. 100 CA85
Wellington Ave., Pnr. 44 BZ53
Wellington Ave., Sid. 110 EU86
Wellington Ave., Wor.Pk. 117 CW104
Wellington Bldgs. SW1 91 DH78
Ebury Bri. Rd.
Wellington Clo. SE14 93 DX81
Rutts Ter.
Wellington Clo. W11 76 DA72
Ledbury Rd.
Wellington Clo., Dag. 83 FC66
Wellington Clo., Walt. 113 BT102
Hepworth Way
Wellington Ct. NW8 76 DD68
Wellington Rd.
Wellington Ct., Stai. 98 BL87
Wellington Cres., N.Mal. 116 CQ97
Wellington Dr., Dag. 83 FC66
Wellington Dr., Pur. 133 DM110
Wellington Gdns. SE7 94 EJ78
Wellington Gdns., Twick. 101 CD91
Wellington Hill, Loug. 38 EH37
Wellington Ms. SE7 94 EJ79
Wellington Ms. SE22 92 DU84
Peckham Rye
Wellington Pk. Ind. Est. NW2 61 CU60
Wellington Pas. E11 66 EG57
Wellington Rd.
Wellington Pl. N2 62 DE57
Great N. Rd.
Wellington Pl. NW8 4 A2
Wellington Pl. NW8 76 DD69
Wellington Rd. E6 81 EM67
Wellington Rd. E7 66 EF63
Wellington Rd. E10 65 DY60
Wellington Rd. E11 66 EG57
Wellington Rd. E17 65 DY55
Wellington Rd. NW8 76 DD68
Wellington Rd. NW10 75 CX69
Wellington Rd. SW19 104 DA89
Wellington Rd. W5 87 CJ76
Wellington Rd., Ashf. 98 BL92
Wellington Rd., Belv. 96 EZ78
Wellington Rd., Bex. 110 EX85
Wellington Rd., Brom. 122 EJ98
Wellington Rd., Cat. 148 DQ122
Wellington Rd., Croy. 119 DP101
Wellington Rd., Enf. 36 DS42
Wellington Rd., Epp. 26 FA27
Wellington Rd., Felt. 99 BS85
Wellington Rd., Hmptn. 101 CD92
Wellington Rd., Har. 59 CE55
Wellington Rd., Orp. 124 EV100
Wellington Rd., Pnr. 44 BZ52
Wellington Rd. (London Colney), St.Alb. 17 CK26
Wellington Rd., Twick. 101 CD91
Wellington Rd., Uxb. 70 BJ67
Wellington Rd., Wat. 29 BV40
Wellington Rd. N., Houns. 86 BZ83
Wellington Rd. S., Houns. 86 BZ84
Wellington Row E2 78 DT69
Wellington Sq. SW3 8 D10
Wellington Sq. SW3 90 DF78
Wellington St. SE18 95 EN77
Wellington St. WC2 6 A10
Wellington St. WC2 77 DL73
Wellington St., Bark. 81 EQ67
Axe St.
Wellington Ter. E1 78 DV74
Waterman Way
Wellington Ter. N8 63 DN55
Turnpike La.
Wellington Ter., Har. 59 CD60
Wellington Way E3 79 EA69
Wellington Way, Wey. 126 BM110
Wellingtonia Ave., Rom. (Havering-atte-Bower) 55 FE48
Wellmeade Dr., Sev. 155 FH127
Wellmeadow Rd. SE6 108 EE87
Wellmeadow Rd. SE13 108 EE86
Wellmeadow Rd. W7 87 CG77
Wellow Wk., Cars. 118 DD102
Whitland Rd.
Wells, The N14 49 DK45
Wells Clo., Lthd. 142 CB124
Wells Clo., Nthlt. 72 BW69
Yeading La.
Wells Dr. NW9 60 CR60
Wells Gdns., Dag. 69 FB64
Pondfield Rd.
Wells Gdns., Ilf. 66 EL59
Wells Gdns., Rain. 83 FF65
Wells Ho. Rd. NW10 74 CS71
Wells Ms. W1 5 L7
Wells Pk. Rd. SE26 106 DU90
Wells Ri. NW8 76 DF67
Wells Rd. W12 89 CW75
Wells Rd., Brom. 123 EM96
Wells Rd., Epsom 130 CN114
Wells Sq. WC1 6 B3
Wells St. W1 5 K7
Wells St. W1 77 DJ71
Wells Ter. N4 63 DN61
Wells Way SE5 92 DS79
Wells Way SW7 90 DD76
Wells Yd. N7 63 DN64
Holloway Rd.
Wellside Clo., Barn. 33 CW42
Wellside Gdns. SW14 102 CQ85
Well La.
Wellsmoor Gdns., Brom. 123 EN97
Wellsprings Cres., Wem. 60 CP62
Wellstead Ave. N9 50 DW45
Wellstead Rd. E6 81 EN68
Wellstones, Wat. 29 BV41
Wellstones Yd., Wat. 29 BV41
Wellstones
Wellwood Clo., Couls. 133 DL114
The Vale
Wellwood Rd., Ilf. 68 EU60
Welsford St. SE1 92 DU78
Welsh Clo. E13 80 EG69
Welsh Side Wk. NW9 60 CS58
Fryent Gro.
Welshpool Ho. E8 78 DU67
Benjamin Clo.
Welshpool St. E8 78 DV67
Broadway Mkt.
Welsummer Way, Wal.Cr. 23 DX27
Weltje Rd. W6 89 CU77
Welton Rd. SE18 95 ES80
Welwyn Ave., Felt. 99 BT86
Welwyn St. E2 78 DW69
Globe Rd.
Welwyn Way, Hayes 71 BS70
Wembley Commercial Cen., Wem. 59 CK61
Wembley Hill Rd., Wem. 60 CM64
Wembley Pk. Business Cen., Wem. 60 CP62
Wembley Pk. Dr., Wem. 60 CM63
Wembley Pt., Wem. 74 CP66
Wembley Retail Pk., Wem. 60 CP63
Wembley Rd., Hmptn. 100 CA94
Wembley Way, Wem. 74 CP65
Wemborough Rd., Stan. 45 CH53
Wembury Rd. N6 63 DH59
Wemyss Rd. SE3 94 EF82
Wend, The, Couls. 133 DK114
Wend, The, Croy. 135 DY111
Wendela Ct., Har. 59 CE62
Wendell Rd. W12 89 CT76
Wendle Ct. SW8 91 DL79
Wendling Rd., Sutt. 118 DD102
Wendon St. E3 79 DZ67
Wendover SE17 11 M10
Wendover Clo., Hayes 72 BY70
Kingsash Dr.
Wendover Dr., N.Mal. 117 CT100
Wendover Rd. NW10 75 CT68
Wendover Rd. SE9 94 EK83
Wendover Rd., Brom. 122 EH97
Wendover Way, Orp. 124 EU100
Glendower Cres.
Wendover Way (Bushey), Wat. 30 CC44
Wendover Way, Well. 110 EU85
Wendy Clo., Enf. 36 DT44
Wendy Way, Wem. 74 CL67
Wenlack Clo., Uxb. 56 BG62
Lindsey Rd.
Wenlock Ct. N1 7 L1
Wenlock Gdns. NW4 61 CU56
Rickard Clo.
Wenlock Rd. N1 7 H1
Wenlock Rd. N1 78 DQ68
Wenlock Rd., Edg. 46 CP52
Wenlock St. N1 7 J1
Wenlock St. N1 78 DQ68
Wennington Rd. E3 79 DX68
Wennington Rd., Rain. 83 FG70
Wensley Ave., Wdf.Grn. 52 EF52
Wensley Clo. SE9 109 EM86
Wensley Clo., Rom. 54 FA50
Wensley Rd. N18 50 DV51
Wensleydale Ave., Ilf. 52 EL54
Wensleydale Gdns., Hmptn. 100 CB94
Wensleydale Pas., Hmptn. 114 CA95
Wensleydale Rd., Hmptn. 100 CA93
Wensum Way, Rick. 42 BK46
Wentbridge Path, Borwd. 32 CN38
Wentland Clo. SE6 107 ED89
Wentland Rd.
Wentland Rd. SE6 107 ED89
Wentworth Ave. N3 48 DA52
Wentworth Ave., Borwd. 32 CM43
Wentworth Clo. N3 48 DB52
Wentworth Clo. SE28 82 EX72
Summerton Way
Wentworth Clo., Ashf. 99 BP91
Reedsfield Rd.
Wentworth Clo., Brom. 122 EG103
Hillside La.
Wentworth Clo., Mord. 118 DA101
Wentworth Clo., Orp. 137 ES106
Wentworth Clo., Pot.B. 20 DA31
Strafford Gate
Wentworth Clo., Surb. 115 CK103
Wentworth Clo., Wat. 29 BT38
Wentworth Clo., Wok. 140 BH121
Wentworth Cres. SE15 92 DU80
Wentworth Cres., Hayes 85 BR76
Wentworth Dr., Dart. 111 FG86
Wentworth Dr., Pnr. 57 BU57
Wentworth Gdns. N13 49 DP49
Wentworth Hill, Wem. 60 CM60
Wentworth Ms. E3 79 DZ70
Eric St.
Wentworth Pk. N3 48 DA52
Wentworth Pl., Stan. 45 CH51
Greenacres Dr.
Wentworth Rd. E12 66 EK63
Wentworth Rd. NW11 61 CZ58
Wentworth Rd., Barn. 33 CX41
Wentworth Rd., Croy. 119 DN101
Wentworth Rd., Sthl. 86 BW77
Wentworth St. E1 7 P8
Wentworth St. E1 78 DT72
Wentworth Way, Pnr. 58 BX56
Wentworth Way, Rain. 83 FH69
Wentworth Way, S.Croy. 134 DU114
Wenvoe Ave., Bexh. 97 FB82
Wernbrook St. SE18 95 EQ79
Werndee Rd. SE25 120 DU98
Werneth Hall Rd., Ilf. 67 EM55
Werrington St. NW1 5 L1
Werrington St. NW1 77 DJ68
Werter Rd. SW15 89 CY84
Wesley Ave. E16 80 EG74
Silvertown Way
Wesley Ave. NW10 74 CR69
Wesley Ave., Houns. 86 BY82
Wesley Clo. N7 63 DM61
Wesley Clo. SE17 10 G9
Wesley Clo., Har. 58 CC61
Wesley Clo., Orp. 124 EW97
Wesley Clo. (Cheshunt), Wal.Cr. 22 DQ28
Wesley Rd. E10 65 EC59
Wesley Rd. NW10 74 CQ67
Hillside
Wesley Rd. SE17 10 G9
Wesley Rd., Hayes 71 BU73
Wesley Sq. W11 75 CY72
Bartle Rd.
Wesley St. W1 4 G7
Wesleyan Pl. NW5 63 DH63
Gordon Ho. Rd.
Wessels, Tad. 145 CX121
Wessex Ave. SW19 118 DA96
Wessex Clo., Ilf. 67 ES58
Wessex Clo., Kings.T. 116 CP95
Gloucester Rd.
Wessex Dr., Erith 97 FE82
Wessex Dr., Pnr. 44 BY52
Wessex Gdns. NW11 61 CY60
Wessex La., Grnf. 73 CD68
Wessex Rd., Houns. 84 BJ84
Wessex St. E2 78 DW69
Wessex Way NW11 61 CY60
West App., Orp. 123 EQ99
West Arbour St. E1 78 DW72
West Ave. E17 65 EB56
West Ave. N3 48 DA51
West Ave. NW4 61 CX57
West Ave., Hayes 71 BT73
West Ave., Pnr. 58 BZ58
West Ave., St.Alb. 16 CB25
West Ave., Sthl. 72 BZ73
West Ave., Wall. 133 DL106
West Ave., Walt. 127 BS109
West Ave. Rd. E17 65 EA56
West Bank N16 64 DS59
West Bank, Bark. 81 EP67
Highbridge Rd.
West Bank, Enf. 36 DQ40
West Barnes La. SW20 117 CV99
West Barnes La., N.Mal. 117 CV97
West Carriage Dr. W2 8 B1
West Carriage Dr. W2 76 DD73
West Cen. St. WC1 5 P8
West Chantry, Har. 44 CB53
Chantry Rd.
West Clo. N9 50 DT48
West Clo., Ashf. 98 BL91
West Clo., Barn. 33 CV43
West Clo. (Cockfosters), Barn. 34 DG42
West Clo., Grnf. 72 CC68
West Clo., Hmptn. 100 BY93
Oak Ave.
West Clo., Rain. 83 FH70
West Clo., Wem. 60 CM60
West Common Rd., Brom. 122 EG103
West Common Rd., Kes. 122 EH104
West Common Rd., Uxb. 56 BK64
West Cotts. NW6 62 DA64
West Ct. SE18 95 EM80
Prince Imperial Rd.
West Ct., Wem. 59 CJ61
West Cromwell Rd. SW5 89 CZ77
West Cromwell Rd. W14 89 CZ78
West Cross Route W10 75 CX73
West Cross Route W11 75 CX74
West Cross Way, Brent. 87 CH79
West Dene, Sutt. 131 CY107
Park La.
West Dene Way, Wey. 113 BS104
West Drayton Pk. Ave., West Dr. 84 BL76
West Drayton Rd., Uxb. 70 BM72
West Dr. SW16 105 DJ91
West Dr., Cars. 132 DD110
West Dr., Har. 45 CD51
West Dr. (Cheam), Sutt. 131 CX109
West Dr., Tad. 145 CX118
West Dr., Wat. 29 BV36
West Dr. Gdns., Har. 45 CD51
West Eaton Pl. SW1 8 F8
West Eaton Pl. SW1 90 DG77
West Eaton Pl. Ms. SW1 8 F7
West Ella Rd. NW10 74 CS66
West End Ave. E10 65 ED57
West End Ave., Pnr. 58 BX56
West End Ct., Pnr. 58 BX56
West End Gdns., Esher 128 BZ106
West End Gdns., Nthlt. 72 BW68
Edward Clo.
West End La. NW6 62 DA64
West End La., Barn. 33 CX42
West End La., Esher 128 BZ108
West End La., Hayes 85 BQ80
West End La., Pnr. 58 BX55
West End Rd., Nthlt. 72 BW66
West End Rd., Ruis. 57 BU63
West End Rd., Sthl. 72 BY74
West Fm. Ave., Ash. 143 CJ118
West Fm. Clo., Ash. 143 CJ119
West Fm. Dr., Ash. 143 CK119
West Gdn. Pl. W2 4 C9
West Gdns. E1 78 DV73
West Gdns. SW17 104 DE93
West Gdns., Epsom 130 CS110
West Gate W5 74 CL69
West Gorse, Croy. 135 DY112
West Grn. Pl., Grnf. 73 CD67
Uneeda Dr.
West Grn. Rd. N15 63 DP56
West Gro. SE10 93 EC81
West Gro., Walt. 127 BV106
West Gro., Wdf.Grn. 52 EJ51
West Halkin St. SW1 8 F6
West Halkin St. SW1 90 DG76
West Hall Rd., Rich. 88 CP81
West Hallowes SE9 108 EL88
West Ham La. E15 79 ED66
West Ham Pk. E7 80 EF66
West Hampstead Ms. NW6 76 DB65
West Harding St. EC4 6 E8
West Harold, Swan. 125 FD97
West Hatch Manor, Ruis. 57 BT60
West Heath Ave. NW11 62 DA60
West Heath Clo. NW3 62 DA62
West Heath Clo., Dart. 111 FF86
West Heath Rd.
West Heath Dr. NW11 62 DA60
West Heath Gdns. NW3 62 DA61
West Heath La., Sev. 155 FH128
West Heath Rd. NW3 62 DA61
West Heath Rd. SE2 96 EW79
West Heath Rd., Dart. 111 FF86
West Hendon Bdy. NW9 61 CT58
West Hill SW15 103 CX87
West Hill SW18 103 CX87
West Hill, Epsom 130 CP113
West Hill, Har. 59 CE61
West Hill, Orp. 137 EM112
West Hill, S.Croy. 134 DS110
West Hill, Wem. 60 CM60
West Hill Ave., Epsom 130 CP113
West Hill Ct. N6 62 DG62
West Hill Pk. N6 62 DF61
Merton La.
West Hill Rd. SW18 103 CZ86
West Hill Way N20 48 DB46
West Holme, Erith 97 FC81
West Ho. Clo. SW19 103 CY88
West India Ave. E14 79 EA74
West India Dock Rd. E14 79 DZ72
West Kentish Town Est. NW5 76 DG65
Warden Rd.
West La. SE16 92 DV75
West Lo. Ave. W3 74 CN74
West Mall W8 76 DA74
Palace Gdns. Ter.
West Mead, Epsom 130 CS107
West Mead, Ruis. 58 BW63
West Ms. N17 50 DV51
West Ms. SW1 9 K9
West Oak, Beck. 121 ED95
West Palace Gdns., Wey. 113 BP104
West Pk. SE9 108 EL89
West Pk. Ave., Rich. 88 CN81
West Pk. Clo., Houns. 86 BZ79
Heston Gra. La.
West Pk. Clo., Rom. 68 EX57
West Pk. Rd., Epsom 130 CM112
West Pk. Rd., Rich. 88 CN81
West Pk. Rd., Sthl. 72 CC74
West Pier E1 78 DV74
Wapping High St.
West Pl. SW19 103 CW92
West Poultry Ave. EC1 6 F7
West Quarters W12 75 CU72
Du Cane Rd.
West Quay Dr., Hayes 72 BY71
West Ramp, Houns. 84 BN81
West Ridge Gdns., Grnf. 72 CC68
West Riding, St.Alb. 16 BZ30
West Rd. E15 80 EF67
West Rd. N17 50 DV51
West Rd. SW3 90 DF78
West Rd. SW4 105 DK85
West Rd. W5 74 CL71
West Rd., Barn. 48 DG46
West Rd., Chess. 129 CJ111
West Rd., Felt. 99 BR86
West Rd., Kings.T. 116 CQ95
West Rd. (Chadwell Heath), Rom. 68 EX58
West Rd. (Rush Grn.), Rom. 69 FD59
West Rd., West Dr. 84 BM76
West Rd., Wey. 127 BP109
West Row W10 75 CY70
West Sheen Vale, Rich. 88 CM84
West Side, Brox. 23 DY25
High Rd. Turnford
West Side Common SW19 103 CW93
West Smithfield EC1 6 F7
West Smithfield EC1 77 DP71
West Spur Rd., Uxb. 70 BK69
West Sq. SE11 10 F7
West Sq. SE11 91 DP76

West St. E2 78 DV68
West St. E11 66 EE62
West St. E17 65 EB57
Grove Rd.
West St. WC2 5 N9
West St., Bexh. 96 EZ84
West St., Brent. 87 CJ79
West St., Brom. 122 EG95
West St., Cars. 118 DF104
West St., Croy. 134 DQ105
West St., Epsom 130 CQ113
West St. (Ewell), Epsom 130 CS110
West St., Erith 97 FD77
West St., Har. 59 CD60
West St., Sutt. 132 DB106
West St., Wat. 29 BV40
West St. La., Cars. 132 DF105
West Temple Sheen SW14 88 CP84
West Tenter St. E1 78 DT72
West Twrs., Pnr. 58 BX58
West Valley Rd., Hem.H. 14 BJ25
West Vw. NW4 61 CW56
West Vw., Felt. 99 BQ87
West Vw., Loug. 39 EM42
West Vw. Ave., Whyt. 148 DU118
Station Rd.
West Vw. Ct., Borwd. 31 CK44
High St.
West Vw. Gdns., Borwd. 31 CK44
High St.
West Vw. Rd., Swan. 125 FG98
West Vw. Rd. (Crockenhill), Swan. 125 FD100
West Wk. W5 74 CL71
West Wk., Barn. 48 DG45
West Wk., Hayes 71 BU74
West Warwick Pl. SW1 9 K9
West Warwick Pl. SW1 91 DJ77
West Way N18 50 DR49
West Way NW10 60 CR63
West Way, Cars. 132 DD110
West Way, Croy. 121 DY103
West Way, Edg. 46 CP51
West Way, Houns. 86 BZ80
West Way, Pnr. 58 BX56
West Way, Rick. 42 BH46
West Way, Ruis. 57 BT60
West Way, Shep. 113 BR100
West Way, W.Wick. 121 ED100
West Way Gdns., Croy. 121 DX103
West Woodside, Bex. 110 EY87
West World W5 74 CL69
Westacott, Hayes 71 BS71
Westacott Clo. N19 63 DK60
Westacres, Esher 128 BZ108
Westall Rd., Loug. 39 EP41
Westbank Rd., Hmptn. 100 CC93
Westbeech Rd. N22 63 DN55
Westbere Dr., Stan. 45 CK49
Westbere Rd. NW2 61 CY63
Westbourne Ave. W3 74 CR72
Westbourne Ave., Sutt. 117 CY103
Westbourne Bri. W2 76 DC71
Westbourne Clo., Hayes 71 BV70
Westbourne Cres. W2 76 DD73
Westbourne Cres. Ms. W2 76 DD73
Westbourne Cres.
Westbourne Dr. SE23 107 DX89
Westbourne Gdns. W2 76 DB72
Westbourne Gro. W2 76 DA72
Westbourne Gro. W11 75 CZ73
Westbourne Gro. Ms. W11 76 DA72
Westbourne Gro.
Westbourne Gro. Ter. W2 76 DB72
Westbourne Pk. Ms. W2 76 DB72
Westbourne Gdns.
Westbourne Pk. Pas. W2 76 DA71
Westbourne Pk. Rd. W2 76 DA71
Westbourne Pk. Rd. W11 75 CY72
Westbourne Pk. Vill. W2 76 DA71
Westbourne Pl. N9 50 DV48
Eastbournia Ave.
Westbourne Rd. N7 77 DM65
Westbourne Rd. SE26 107 DX93
Westbourne Rd., Bexh. 96 EX80
Westbourne Rd., Croy. 120 DT100
Westbourne Rd., Felt. 99 BT90
Westbourne Rd., Stai. 98 BH94
Westbourne Rd., Uxb. 71 BP70
Westbourne St. W2 76 DD73
Westbourne Ter. SE23 107 DX89
Westbourne Dr.
Westbourne Ter. W2 76 DC72
Westbourne Ter. Ms. W2 76 DC72
Westbourne Ter. Rd. W2 76 DC71
Westbridge Rd. SW11 90 DD81
Westbrook Ave., Hmptn. 100 BZ94
Westbrook Clo., Barn. 34 DD41
Westbrook Cres., Barn. 34 DD41
Westbrook Dr., Orp. 124 EW102
Westbrook Rd. SE3 94 EH81
Westbrook Rd., Houns. 86 BZ80
Westbrook Rd., Th.Hth. 120 DR95
Westbrook Sq., Barn. 34 DD41
Westbrooke Cres., Well. 96 EW83
Westbrooke Rd., Sid. 109 ER89
Westbrooke Rd., Well. 96 EV83
Westbury Ave. N22 63 DP55
Westbury Ave., Esher 129 CF107
Westbury Ave., Sthl. 72 CA70
Westbury Ave., Wem. 74 CL66
Westbury Clo., Ruis. 57 BU59
Westbury Clo., Shep. 113 BP100
Burchetts Way
Westbury Clo., Whyt. 148 DS116
Beverley Rd.
Westbury Gro. N12 48 DA51
Westbury La., Buck.H. 52 EJ47
Westbury Lo. Clo., Pnr. 58 BX55
Westbury Par. SW12 105 DH86
Balham Hill
Westbury Pl., Brent. 87 CK79
Westbury Rd. E7 66 EH64
Westbury Rd. E17 65 DZ56
Westbury Rd. N11 49 DL51
Westbury Rd. N12 48 DA51
Westbury Rd. SE20 121 DX95
Westbury Rd. W5 74 CL72
Westbury Rd., Bark. 81 ER67
Westbury Rd., Beck. 121 DY97
Westbury Rd., Brom. 122 EK95
Westbury Rd., Buck.H. 52 EJ47
Westbury Rd., Croy. 120 DR100
Westbury Rd., Felt. 100 BX88
Westbury Rd., Ilf. 67 EN61
Westbury Rd., N.Mal. 116 CR98
Westbury Rd., Nthwd. 43 BR49
Westbury Rd., Wat. 29 BV43
Westbury Rd., Wem. 74 CL66
Westbury St. SW8 91 DJ82
Westbury Ter. E7 80 EH65
Westcar La., Walt. 127 BV107
Westchester Dr. NW4 61 CX55
Westcombe Ave., Croy. 119 DL100
Westcombe Ct. SE3 94 EF80
Westcombe Pk. Rd.
Westcombe Dr., Barn. 34 DA43
Westcombe Hill SE3 94 EG79
Westcombe Hill SE10 94 EG78
Westcombe Lo. Dr., Hayes 71 BR71
Westcombe Pk. Rd. SE3 94 EE79
Westcoombe Ave. SW20 117 CT95
Westcote Ri., Ruis. 57 BQ59
Westcote Rd. SW16 105 DJ92
Westcott Clo. N15 64 DT58
Ermine Rd.
Westcott Clo., Brom. 122 EL99
Ringmer Way
Westcott Clo., Croy. 135 EB109
Castle Hill Ave.
Westcott Cres. W7 73 CE72
Westcott Rd. SE17 91 DP79
Westcott Way, Sutt. 131 CW110
Westcott Way, Uxb. 70 BJ68
Westcourt, Sun. 113 BV96
Westcroft Clo. NW2 61 CY63
Westcroft Clo., Enf. 36 DW38
Westcroft Gdns., Mord. 117 CZ97
Westcroft Rd., Cars. 132 DG105
Westcroft Rd., Wall. 132 DG105
Westcroft Sq. W6 89 CU77
Westcroft Way NW2 61 CY63
Westdale Pas. SE18 95 EP79
Westdale Rd.
Westdale Rd. SE18 95 EP79
Westdean Ave. SE12 108 EH88
Westdean Clo. SW18 104 DB85
Westdown Rd. E15 65 EC63
Westdown Rd. SE6 107 EA87
Wested La., Swan. 125 FG101
Westel Ho. W5 73 CJ73
Westerdale Rd. SE10 94 EG78
Westerfield Rd. N15 64 DT57
Westergate Rd. SE2 96 EY79
Westerham Ave. N9 50 DR48
Westerham Clo., Add. 126 BJ107
Westerham Clo., Sutt. 132 DA110
Westerham Dr., Sid. 110 EV86
Westerham Hill, West. 151 EN120
Westerham Rd. E10 65 EB58
Westerham Rd., Kes. 136 EK108
Westerham Rd., Sev. 154 FC123
Westerley Cres. SE26 107 DZ92
Westerly Ware, Rich. 88 CN79
Kew Grn.
Western Ave. NW11 61 CX58
Western Ave. W3 74 CN70
Western Ave. W5 74 CM70
Western Ave., Cher. 112 BG97
Western Ave., Dag. 83 FC65
Western Ave., Epp. 25 ET32
Western Ave., Grnf. 73 CE68
Western Ave., Nthlt. 72 BZ67
Western Ave., Ruis. 71 BQ65
Western Ave. (Denham), Uxb. 56 BJ63
Western Ave. (Ickenham), Uxb. 56 BK63
Western Clo., Cher. 112 BG97
Western Ave.
Western Ct. N3 48 DA51
Huntley Dr.
Western Dr., Shep. 113 BR100
Western Gdns. W5 74 CN73
Western Gateway E16 80 EG73
Western Ho. W5 74 CL69
Western La. SW12 104 DG87
Western Ms. W9 75 CZ70
Great Western Rd.
Western Perimeter Rd., Houns. 84 BH83
Western Pl. SE16 92 DW75
Canon Beck Rd.
Western Rd. E13 80 EJ67
Western Rd. E17 65 EC57
Western Rd. N2 62 DF56
Western Rd. N22 49 DM54
Western Rd. NW10 74 CQ70
Western Rd. SW9 91 DN83
Western Rd. SW19 118 DD95
Western Rd. W5 73 CK73
Western Rd., Epp. 25 ES32
Western Rd., Mitch. 118 DE95
Western Rd., Rom. 69 FE57
Western Rd., Sthl. 86 BW77
Western Rd., Sutt. 132 DA106
Western Ter. W6 89 CU78
Chiswick Mall
Western Trd. Est. NW10 74 CP70
Western Vw., Hayes 85 BT75
Station Rd.
Western Way SE28 95 ER76
Western Way, Barn. 34 DA44
Westernville Gdns., Ilf. 67 EQ59
Westferry Circ. E14 79 EA74
Westferry Rd. E14 93 EA75
Westfield, Ash. 144 CM118
Westfield, Loug. 38 EJ43
Westfield, Sev. 155 FJ122
Westfield Ave., S.Croy. 134 DR113
Westfield Ave., Wat. 30 BW37
Westfield Clo. NW9 60 CQ55
Westfield Clo. SW10 90 DC80
Westfield Clo., Enf. 37 DY41
Westfield Clo., Sutt. 131 CZ105
Westfield Clo., Wal.Cr. 23 DY31
Westfield Dr., Har. 59 CK56
Westfield Dr., Lthd. 142 CA122
Westfield Gdns., Har. 59 CK56
Westfield La., Har. 59 CK56
Westfield Par., Add. 126 BK110
Westfield Pk., Pnr. 44 BZ52
Westfield Rd. NW7 46 CR48
Westfield Rd. W13 73 CG74
Westfield Rd., Beck. 121 DZ96
Westfield Rd., Bexh. 97 FC82
Westfield Rd., Croy. 119 DP103
Westfield Rd., Dag. 68 EY63
Westfield Rd., Mitch. 118 DF96
Westfield Rd., Surb. 115 CK99
Westfield Rd., Sutt. 131 CZ105
Westfield Rd., Walt. 114 BY101
Westfield St. SE18 94 EK76
Westfield Wk., Wal.Cr. 23 DZ31
Westfield Clo.
Westfield Way E1 79 DY69
Westfield Way, Ruis. 57 BS62
Westfields SW13 89 CT83
Westfields Ave. SW13 88 CS83
Westfields Rd. W3 74 CP71
Westgate Clo., Epsom 144 CR115
Chalk La.
Westgate Ct., Wal.Cr. 37 DX35
Holmesdale
Westgate Rd. SE25 120 DV98
Westgate Rd., Beck. 121 EB96
Westgate St. E8 78 DV67
Westgate Ter. SW10 90 DB78
Westglade Ct., Har. 59 CK57
Westgrove La. SE10 93 EC81
Westhall Pk., Warl. 148 DW119
Westhall Rd., Warl. 148 DU118
Westhay Gdns. SW14 102 CP85
Westholm NW11 62 DB56
Westholme, Orp. 123 ES101
Westholme Gdns., Ruis. 57 BU60
Westhorne Ave. SE9 108 EK85
Westhorne Ave. SE12 108 EH86
Westhorpe Gdns. NW4 61 CW55
Westhorpe Rd. SW15 89 CW83
Westhurst Dr., Chis. 109 EP92
Westlake Clo. N13 49 DN48
Westlake Clo., Hayes 72 BY70
Lochan Clo.
Westlake Rd., Wem. 59 CK61
Westland Clo., Stai. 98 BL86
Westland Dr., Brom. 122 EF103
Westland Dr., Hat. 19 CY26
Westland Pl. N1 7 K2
Westland Rd., Wat. 29 BV40
Westlands Clo., Hayes 85 BU77
Granville Rd.
Westlands Ct., Epsom 144 CQ115
Westlands Est., Hayes 85 BS76
Westlands Ter. SW12 105 DJ86
Gaskarth Rd.
Westlea Ave., Wat. 30 BY36
Westlea Rd. W7 87 CG76
Westleigh Ave. SW15 103 CV85
Westleigh Ave., Couls. 146 DG116
Westleigh Dr., Brom. 122 EL95
Westleigh Gdns., Edg. 46 CN53
Westlinks, Wem. 73 CK69
Alperton La.
Westmacott Dr., Felt. 99 BT87
Westmead SW15 103 CV87
Westmead Cor., Cars. 132 DE105
Colston Ave.
Westmead Rd., Sutt. 132 DD105
Westmeade Clo. (Cheshunt), Wal.Cr. 22 DV29
Westmede, Chig. 53 EQ51
Westmere Dr. NW7 46 CR48
Westmill Ct. N4 64 DQ61
Brownswood Rd.
Westminster Ave., Th.Hth. 119 DP96
Westminster Bri. SE1 10 A5
Westminster Bri. SE1 91 DM75
Westminster Bri. SW1 10 A5
Westminster Bri. SW1 91 DL75
Westminster Bri. Rd. SE1 10 C5
Westminster Bri. Rd. SE1 91 DM75
Westminster Cathedral Piazza SW1 9 K7
Westminster Clo., Felt. 99 BU88
Westminster Clo., Ilf. 53 ER54
Westminster Clo., Tedd. 101 CG92
Westminster Dr. N13 49 DL50
Westminster Gdns. E4 52 EE46
Westminster Gdns., Bark. 81 ES68
Westminster Gdns., Ilf. 53 EQ54
Westminster Rd. N9 50 DV46
Westminster Rd. W7 73 CE74
Westminster Rd., Sutt. 118 DD103
Westmoat Clo., Beck. 107 EC94
Westmont Rd., Esher 115 CE103
Westmoor Gdns., Enf. 37 DX40
Westmoor Rd., Enf. 37 DX40
Westmoor St. SE7 94 EK76
Westmore Grn., West. 150 EJ121
Westmore Rd., West. 150 EJ121
Westmoreland Ave., Well. 95 ES83
Westmoreland Bldgs. EC1 78 DQ71
Bartholomew Clo.
Westmoreland Dr., Sutt. 132 DB109
Westmoreland Pl. SW1 91 DH78
Westmoreland Pl. W5 73 CK71
Mount Ave.
Westmoreland Rd. NW9 60 CM55
Westmoreland Rd. SE17 92 DR79
Westmoreland Rd. SW13 89 CT81
Westmoreland Rd., Brom. 122 EE99
Westmoreland St. W1 4 G7
Westmoreland St. W1 76 DG71
Westmoreland Ter. SW1 91 DH78
Westmoreland Wk. SE17 92 DR79
Westmoreland Rd.
Westmorland Clo. E12 66 EK61
Westmorland Clo., Epsom 130 CS110
Westmorland Clo., Twick. 101 CH86
Westmorland Rd. E17 65 EA58
Westmorland Rd., Har. 58 CB57
Westmorland Ter. SE20 106 DV94
Hawthorn Gro.
Westmorland Way, Mitch. 119 DK98
Westmount Rd. SE9 95 EM82
Westoe Rd. N9 50 DV47
Weston Ave., Add. 126 BG105
Weston Ave., T.Ditt. 115 CE101
Weston Ave., W.Mol. 114 BY97
Weston Clo., Couls. 147 DM120
Weston Clo., Pot.B. 19 CZ32
Weston Ct. N4 64 DQ62
Queens Dr.
Weston Dr., Stan. 45 CH53
Weston Gdns., Islw. 87 CD81
Weston Grn., Dag. 68 EZ63
Weston Grn., T.Ditt. 115 CE102
Weston Grn. Rd., Esher 115 CD102
Weston Grn. Rd., T.Ditt. 115 CE102
Weston Gro., Brom. 108 EF94
Weston Pk. N8 63 DL58
Weston Pk., Kings.T. 116 CL96
Fairfield W.
Weston Pk., T.Ditt. 115 CE102
Weston Pk. Clo., T.Ditt. 115 CE102
Weston Pk.
Weston Ri. WC1 6 C1
Weston Ri. WC1 77 DM69
Weston Rd. W4 88 CQ76
Weston Rd., Brom. 108 EF94
Weston Rd., Dag. 68 EY63
Weston Rd., Enf. 36 DR39
Weston Rd., Epsom 130 CS111
Weston Rd., T.Ditt. 115 CE102
Weston St. SE1 11 L4
Weston St. SE1 92 DR75
Weston Wk. E8 78 DV66
Mare St.
Westover Clo., Sutt. 132 DB109
Westover Hill NW3 62 DA61
Westover Rd. SW18 104 DC87
Westow Hill SE19 106 DS93
Westow St. SE19 106 DS93
Westpoint Trd. Est. W3 74 CN70
Westpole Ave., Barn. 34 DG42
Westport Rd. E13 80 EH70
Westport St. E1 79 DX72
Westrow SW15 103 CW86
Westrow Dr., Bark. 81 ET65
Westrow Gdns., Ilf. 67 ET61
Westside NW4 47 CV54
Westvale Ms. W3 88 CS75
Westview Clo. NW10 61 CT64
Westview Clo. W7 73 CE72
Westview Clo. W10 75 CW72
Westview Cres. N9 50 DS45
Westview Dr., Wdf.Grn. 52 EK54
Westview Rd., Warl. 148 DV119
Westville Rd. W12 89 CU75
Westville Rd., T.Ditt. 115 CG102
Westward Rd. E4 51 DY50
Westward Way, Har. 60 CL58
Westway NW7 47 CU52
Westway SW20 117 CV97
Westway W2 76 DA71
Westway W9 76 DA71
Westway W10 75 CY72
Westway W12 75 CT73
Westway, Cat. 148 DR122
Westway, Orp. 123 ER99
Westway Clo. SW20 117 CV97
Westways, Epsom 131 CT105
Westwell Clo., Orp. 124 EX102
Westwell Rd. SW16 105 DL93
Westwell Rd. App. SW16 105 DL93
Westwell Rd.
Westwick Gdns. W14 89 CX75
Westwick Gdns., Houns. 85 BV82
Westwick Pl., Wat. 16 BW34
Westwood Ave. SE19 120 DQ95
Westwood Ave., Har. 58 CB6
Westwood Clo., Brom. 122 EK9
Westwood Clo., Esher 114 CC10
Westwood Clo., Pot.B. 20 DA3
Westwood Clo., Ruis. 57 BP5
Westwood Gdns. SW13 89 CT8
Westwood Hill SE26 106 DU9
Westwood La., Sid. 110 EU8
Westwood La., Well. 95 ET8
Westwood Pk. SE23 106 DV8
Westwood Rd. E16 80 EH7
Westwood Rd. SW13 89 CT8
Westwood Rd., Couls. 147 DK11
Westwood Rd., Ilf. 67 ET6
Westwood Way, Sev. 154 FF12
Wetheral Dr., Stan. 45 CJ5
Wetherby Clo., Nthlt. 72 CB6
Wetherby Gdns. SW5 90 DC7
Wetherby Ms. SW5 90 DB7
Bolton Gdns.
Wetherby Pl. SW7 90 DC7
Wetherby Rd., Borwd. 32 CL3
Wetherby Rd., Enf. 36 DQ3
Wetherby Way, Chess. 130 CL10
Wetherden St. E17 65 DZ5
Wetherell Rd. E9 79 DX67
Wetherill Rd. N10 48 DG53
Wettern Clo., S.Croy. 134 DS110
Purley Oaks Rd.
Wexfenne Gdns., Wok. 140 BH116
Wexford Rd. SW12 104 DF87
Wey Ave., Cher. 112 BG97
Wey Clo., W.Byf. 126 BH113
Broadoaks Cres.
Wey Ct., Add. 126 BK109
Wey Ct., Epsom 130 CQ105
Wey Manor Rd., Add. 126 BK109
Wey Meadows, Wey. 126 BL106
Wey Rd., Wey. 112 BM104
Weybank, Wok. 140 BL116
Weybarton, W.Byf. 126 BM113
Weybourne Pl., S.Croy. 134 DR110
Weybourne St. SW18 104 DC89
Weybridge Business Pk., Add. 126 BL105
Weybridge Ct. SE16 92 DU78
Argyle Way
Weybridge Pk., Wey. 126 BN106
Weybridge Pt. SW11 90 DF82
Weybridge Rd., Add. 112 BK104
Weybridge Rd., Th.Hth. 119 DN98
Weybridge Rd., Wey. 112 BK104
Weydown Clo. SW19 103 CY88
Weyhill Rd. E1 78 DU72
Commercial Rd.
Weylands Clo., Walt. 114 BZ102
Weylands Pk., Wey. 127 BS107
Ellesmere Rd.
Weylond Rd., Dag. 68 EY62
Weyman Rd. SE3 94 EJ81
Weymead Clo., Cher. 112 BJ102
Weymede, W.Byf. 126 BM112
Weymouth Ave. NW7 46 CS50
Weymouth Ave. W5 87 CJ76
Weymouth Clo. E6 81 EP72
Covelees Wall
Weymouth Ct., Sutt. 132 DA108
Weymouth Ms. W1 5 H6
Weymouth Ms. W1 77 DH71
Weymouth Rd., Hayes 71 BS69
Weymouth St. W1 4 G7
Weymouth St. W1 76 DG71
Weymouth Ter. E2 78 DT68
Weymouth Wk., Stan. 45 CG51
Weyside Clo., W.Byf. 126 BM112
Weystone Rd., Add. 126 BM105
Weybridge Rd.
Whadcote St. N4 63 DN61
Seven Sisters Rd.
Whalebone Ave., Rom. 68 EZ58
Whalebone Ct. EC2 7 L8
Whalebone Gro., Rom. 68 EZ58
Whalebone La. E15 80 EE66
West Ham La.
Whalebone La. N., Rom. 54 EY54
Whalebone La. S., Dag. 68 EZ59
Whalebone La. S., Rom. 68 EZ58
Whaley Rd., Pot.B. 20 DC33
Wharf La., Rick. 42 BL46
Wharf La., Twick. 101 CG88
Wharf La. (Ripley), Wok. 140 BK119
Mill La.
Wharf Pl. E2 78 DU67
Wharf Rd. E15 79 ED67
Wharf Rd. N1 7 H1
Wharf Rd. N1 78 DQ68
Wharf Rd., Enf. 37 DY44
Wharf Rd. Ind. Est., Enf. 37 DY44
Wharf St. E16 80 EE71
Wharfdale Ct. E5 65 DX63
Rushmore Rd.
Wharfdale Rd. N1 77 DL68
Wharfedale Gdns., Th.Hth. 119 DM98
Wharfedale St. SW10 90 DB78
Coleherne Rd.
Wharfside Rd. E16 80 EE71
Wharncliffe Dr., Sthl. 73 CD74
Wharncliffe Gdns. SE25 120 DS96
Wharncliffe Rd. SE25 120 DS96
Wharton Clo. NW10 74 CS65
Wharton Rd., Brom. 122 EH95
Wharton St. WC1 6 C3
Wharton St. WC1 77 DM69
Whateley Rd. SE20 107 DX94
Whateley Rd. SE22 106 DT85
Whatley Ave. SW20 117 CX97

Whatman Rd. SE23 107 DX87
Whatmore Clo., Stai. 98 BG86
Wheat Knoll, Ken. 148 DQ116
Wheatash Rd., Add. 112 BH103
Wheatcroft (Cheshunt), Wal.Cr. 22 DV28
Wheatfield Way, Kings.T. 116 CL96
Wheatfields E6 81 EP72
Oxleas
Wheatfields, Enf. 37 DY40
Wheathill Rd. SE20 120 DV96
Wheatlands, Houns. 86 CA79
Wheatlands Rd. SW17 104 DG90
Stapleton Rd.
Wheatley Clo. NW4 47 CU54
Wheatley Cres., Hayes 71 BU73
Wheatley Gdns. N9 50 DS47
Wheatley Rd., Islw. 87 CF83
Wheatley St. W1 4 G7
Wheatley Ter. Rd., Erith 97 FF79
Wheatsheaf Clo., Nthlt. 58 BY64
Wheatsheaf Hill (Halstead), Sev. 138 EZ109
Wheatsheaf La. SW6 89 CW80
Wheatsheaf La. SW8 91 DL80
Wheatsheaf Rd., Rom. 69 FF58
Wheatsheaf Ter. SW6 89 CZ80
Bishops Rd.
Wheatstone Clo., Mitch. 118 DE95
Wheatstone Rd. W10 75 CY71
Wheel Fm. Dr., Dag. 69 FC62
Wheeler Gdns. N1 77 DL67
Outram Pl.
Wheelers, Epp. 25 ET29
Wheelers Cross, Bark. 81 ER68
Wheelers Dr., Ruis. 57 BQ58
Wallington Clo.
Wheelers Fm. Gdns., Epp. 27 FB26
Wheelers La., Epsom 130 CP114
Wheelwright Clo. (Bushey), Wat. 30 CB44
Ashfield Ave.
Wheelwright St. N7 77 DM66
Whelan Way, Wall. 119 DK104
Wheler St. E1 7 P5
Wheler St. E1 78 DT70
Whellock Rd. W4 88 CS76
Whenman Ave., Bex. 111 FC89
Whernside Clo. SE28 82 EW73
Whetstone Clo. N20 48 DD47
Oakleigh Rd. N.
Whetstone Pk. WC2 6 B8
Whetstone Rd. SE3 94 EJ82
Whewell Rd. N19 63 DL61
Whichcote St. SE1 10 B3
Whidborne Clo. SE8 93 EA82
Cliff Ter.
Whidborne St. WC1 6 A3
Whidborne St. WC1 77 DL69
Whiffins Orchard, Epp. 26 EX29
Whimbrel Clo. SE28 82 EW73
Whimbrel Way, Hayes 72 BX72
Whinchat Rd. SE28 95 ER76
Whinfell Clo. SW16 105 DK92
Whinyates Rd. SE9 94 EL83
Whippendell Clo., Orp. 124 EV95
Whippendell Hill, Kings L. 14 BJ30
Whippendell Rd., Wat. 29 BS43
Whippendell Way, Orp. 124 EV95
Whipps Cross Rd. E11 65 ED57
Whiskin St. EC1 6 F3
Whiskin St. EC1 77 DP69
Whisper Wd., Rick. 28 BH41
Whisperwood Clo., Har. 45 CE52
Whistler Gdns., Edg. 46 CM54
Whistler Ms., Dag. 68 EV64
Fitzstephen Rd.
Whistler St. N5 63 DP64
Whistler Wk. SW10 90 DD80
World's End Est.
Whistlers Ave. SW11 90 DD80
Whiston Rd. E2 78 DT68
Whit Hern Ct., Wal.Cr. 22 DW30
College Rd.
Whitakers Way, Loug. 39 EM39
Whitbread Clo. N17 50 DU53
Whitbread Rd. SE4 93 DY84
Whitburn Rd. SE13 93 EB84
Whitby Ave. NW10 74 CP69
Whitby Clo., West. 150 EH119
Whitby Gdns. NW9 60 CN55
Whitby Gdns., Sutt. 118 DD103
Whitby Rd. SE18 95 EM77
Whitby Rd., Har. 58 CC62
Whitby Rd., Ruis. 57 BV62
Whitby Rd., Sutt. 118 DD103
Whitby St. E1 7 P4
Whitcher Clo. SE14 93 DY79
Chubworthy St.
Whitcher Pl. NW1 77 DJ66
Rochester Rd.
Whitchurch Ave., Edg. 46 CM52
Whitchurch Clo., Edg. 46 CM51
Whitchurch Gdns., Edg. 46 CM51
Whitchurch La., Edg. 45 CK52
Whitchurch Rd. W11 75 CX73
Whitcomb Ct. WC2 77 DK73
Whitcomb St.
Whitcomb St. WC2 9 N1
Whitcomb St. WC2 77 DK73
White Acre NW9 46 CS54
White Adder Way E14 93 EB77
Spindrift Ave.
White Beam Way, Tad. 145 CU121
White Beams, St.Alb. 16 CB28
White Bear Pl. NW3 62 DD63
New End Sq.
White Butts Rd., Ruis. 58 BX62
White Ch. La. E1 78 DU72
White Ch. Pas. E1 78 DU72
White Ch. La.
White City Clo. W12 75 CW73
White City Est. W12 75 CV73
White City Rd. W12 75 CV73
White Conduit St. N1 77 DN68
Chapel Mkt.
White Craig Clo., Pnr. 44 CA50
White Friars, Sev. 154 FG127
White Gdns., Dag. 82 FA65
Sterry Rd.
White Gate Gdns., Har. 45 CF52
White Hall, Rom. 40 EV41
Market Pl.
White Hart Clo., Sev. 155 FJ128
White Hart Ct. EC2 78 DS72
Bishopsgate
White Hart Ct., Wok. 140 BJ121
White Hart La. N17 50 DQ52
White Hart La. N22 49 DN53
White Hart La. NW10 75 CT65
Church Rd.
White Hart La. SW13 88 CS82
White Hart La., Rom. 54 FA53
White Hart Meadows, Wok. 140 BJ121
White Hart Rd. SE18 95 ES77
White Hart Row, Cher. 112 BG101
Heriot Rd.
White Hart Slip, Brom. 122 EG96
White Hart St. SE11 10 E10
White Hart St. SE11 91 DN78
White Hart Wd., Sev. 155 FJ129
White Hart Yd. SE1 11 K3
White Heart Ave., Uxb. 71 BQ71
White Heron Ms., Tedd. 101 CF93
White Hill, Couls. 146 DC124
White Hill, Rick. 42 BM51
White Hill, S.Croy. 134 DR109
St. Marys Rd.
White Horse Dr., Epsom 130 CQ114
White Horse Hill, Chis. 109 EM91
White Horse La. E1 79 DX70
White Horse La., St.Alb. 17 CK26
White Horse La., Wok. 140 BJ121
White Horse Ms. SE1 10 E6
White Horse Rd. E1 79 DY72
White Horse Rd. E6 81 EM69
White Horse St. W1 9 J3
White Horse St. W1 77 DH74
White Horse Yd. EC2 78 DR72
Coleman St.
White Ho. Dr., Stan. 45 CJ49
White Ho. Rd., Sev. 154 FF130
White Kennet St. E1 7 N8
White Knights Rd., Wey. 127 BQ108
White La., Oxt. 150 EH124
White La., Warl. 150 EH123
White Lion Ct. EC3 7 M9
White Lion Hill EC4 6 G10
White Lion Hill EC4 77 DP73
White Lion St. N1 6 D1
White Lion St. N1 77 DN68
White Lion Yd. W1 5 H10
White Lo. SE19 105 DP94
White Lo. Clo. N2 62 DD58
White Lo. Clo., Sev. 155 FH123
White Lo. Clo., Sutt. 132 DC108
White Lyon Ct. EC2 78 DQ70
Fann St.
White Oak Business Pk., Swan. 125 FE97
London Rd.
White Oak Dr., Beck. 121 EC96
White Orchards N20 47 CZ45
White Orchards, Stan. 45 CG50
White Post La. E9 79 DZ66
White Post St. SE13 93 EA83
White Post St. SE15 92 DW80
White Rd. E15 80 EE66
White Shack La., Rick. 28 BM37
White St., Sthl. 86 BX75
White Swan Ms. W4 88 CS79
Bennett St.
Whiteadder Way E14 93 EB77
Taeping St.
Whitear Wk. E15 79 ED65
Whitebarn La., Dag. 82 FA67
Whitebeam Ave., Brom. 123 EN101
Whitebeam Clo. SW9 91 DM80
Clapham Rd.
Whitebeam Clo., Wal.Cr. 22 DS26
The Laurels
Whitebeam Twr. E17 65 DY55
Whitebridge Ave., Mitch. 118 DD98
Belgrave Wk.
Whitebridge Clo., Felt. 99 BT86
Whitechapel High St. E1 78 DT72
Whitechapel Rd. E1 78 DU71
Whitecote Rd., Sthl. 72 CC72
Whitecroft, Swan. 125 FE96
Whitecroft Clo., Beck. 121 ED98
Whitecroft Way, Beck. 121 EC99
Whitecross Pl. EC2 7 L6
Whitecross St. EC1 7 J4
Whitecross St. EC1 78 DQ70
Whitecross St. EC2 7 J6
Whitecross St. EC2 78 DQ71
Whitefield Ave. NW2 61 CW59
Whitefield Ave., Pur. 147 DN116
Whitefield Clo. SW15 103 CY86
Whitefield Clo., Orp. 124 EW97
Whitefields Rd. (Cheshunt), Wal.Cr. 22 DW28
Whitefoot La., Brom. 107 EC91
Whitefoot Ter., Brom. 108 EE90
Whitefriars Ave., Har. 45 CE54
Whitefriars Dr., Har. 45 CD54
Whitefriars Ave.
Whitefriars St. EC4 6 E9
Whitefriars St. EC4 77 DN72
Whitegate Way, Tad. 145 CV120
Whitegates, Whyt. 148 DU119
Court Bushes Rd.
Whitegates Clo., Rick. 28 BN42
Whitehall SW1 9 P2
Whitehall SW1 77 DL74
Whitehall Clo., Chig. 54 EU47
Whitehall Clo., Uxb. 70 BJ67
Whitehall Ct. SW1 10 A3
Whitehall Ct. SW1 77 DL74
Whitehall Cres., Chess. 129 CK106
Whitehall Gdns. E4 51 ED46
Whitehall Gdns. SW1 9 P3
Whitehall Gdns. W3 74 CN74
Whitehall Gdns. W4 88 CP79
Whitehall La., Buck.H. 52 EG47
Whitehall La., Erith 97 FF82
Whitehall Pk. N19 63 DJ60
Whitehall Pk. Rd. W4 88 CP79
Whitehall Pl. E7 66 EG64
Station Rd.
Whitehall Pl. SW1 9 P3
Whitehall Pl. SW1 77 DL74
Whitehall Pl., Wall. 133 DH105
Bernard Rd.
Whitehall Rd. E4 52 EE47
Whitehall Rd. W7 87 CG75
Whitehall Rd., Brom. 122 EK99
Whitehall Rd., Har. 59 CE59
Whitehall Rd., Th.Hth. 119 DN100
Whitehall Rd., Uxb. 70 BK67
Whitehall Rd., Wdf.Grn. 52 EF47
Whitehall St. N17 50 DT52
Whitehart Rd., Orp. 124 EU101
Whitehaven Clo., Brom. 122 EG98
Whitehaven St. NW8 4 B5
Whitehead Clo. N18 50 DR50
Whitehead Clo. SW18 104 DC87
Whitehead's Gro. SW3 8 C10
Whitehead's Gro. SW3 90 DE78
Whiteheath Ave., Ruis. 57 BQ59
Whitehill La., Wok. 141 BQ123
Whitehill Rd., Dart. 111 FG85
Whitehills Rd., Loug. 39 EN41
Whitehorn Gdns., Croy. 120 DV103
Whitehorse La. SE25 120 DR98
Whitehorse Rd., Croy. 120 DQ101
Whitehorse Rd., Th.Hth. 120 DR98
Whitehouse Ave., Borwd. 32 CP41
Whitehouse La., Abb.L. 15 BV26
Whitehouse La., Enf. 36 DQ39
Brigadier Hill
Whitehouse Way N14 49 DH47
Whiteledges W13 73 CJ72
Whitelegg Rd. E13 80 EF68
Whiteley Rd. SE19 106 DR92
Whiteleys Cotts. W14 89 CZ77
Whiteleys Way, Felt. 100 CA90
Whiteoak Gdns., Sid. 109 ET87
Whiteoaks, Bans. 132 DB113
Whiteoaks La., Grnf. 73 CD68
Whites Ave., Ilf. 67 ES58
Whites Dr., Brom. 122 EF101
Whites Grds. SE1 11 N5
Whites Grds. SE1 92 DS75
Whites Grds. Est. SE1 11 N4
White's Row E1 7 P7
White's Row E1 78 DT71
White's Sq. SW4 91 DK84
Nelson's Row
Whitestile Rd., Brent. 87 CJ78
Whitestone La. NW3 62 DC62
Heath St.
Whitestone Wk. NW3 62 DC62
North End Way
Whitethorn Ave., Couls. 146 DG115
Whitethorn Ave., West Dr. 70 BL73
Whitethorn Gdns., Enf. 36 DR43
Whitethorn Pl., West Dr. 70 BM74
Whitethorn Ave.
Whitethorn St. E3 79 EA70
Whiteways Ct., Stai. 98 BH94
Pavilion Gdns.
Whitewebbs La., Enf. 36 DS35
Whitewebbs Pk., Enf. 36 DQ35
Whitewebbs Rd., Enf. 35 DP35
Whitewebbs Way, Orp. 123 ET95
Whitewood Cotts., West. 150 EJ120
Whitfield Pl. W1 5 K5
Whitfield Rd. E6 80 EJ66
Whitfield Rd. SE3 93 ED81
Whitfield Rd., Bexh. 96 EZ80
Whitfield St. W1 5 K5
Whitfield St. W1 77 DJ70
Whitford Gdns., Mitch. 118 DF97
Whitgift Ave., S.Croy. 133 DP106
Whitgift Shop. Cen., Croy. 120 DQ103
Whitgift St. SE11 10 B8
Whitgift St. SE11 91 DM77
Whitgift St., Croy. 120 DQ104
High St.
Whiting Ave., Bark. 81 EP66
Whitings, Ilf. 67 ER57
Whitings Rd., Barn. 33 CW43
Whitings Way E6 81 EN71
Whitland Rd., Cars. 118 DD102
Whitlars Dr., Kings L. 14 BM28
Whitley Clo., Abb.L. 15 BU32
Whitley Clo., Stai. 98 BL86
Whitley Rd. N17 50 DS54
Whitlock Dr. SW19 103 CY87
Whitman Rd. E3 79 DY70
Whitmead Clo., S.Croy. 134 DS107
Whitmore Clo. N11 49 DH50
Whitmore Est. N1 78 DS68
Nuttall St.
Whitmore Gdns. NW10 75 CW68
Whitmore Rd. N1 78 DS67
Whitmore Rd., Beck. 121 DZ97
Whitmore Rd., Har. 58 CC59
Whitmores Clo., Epsom 144 CQ115
Whitnell Way SW15 103 CW85
Whitney Ave., Ilf. 66 EK56
Whitney Rd. E10 65 EA59
Whitney Wk., Sid. 110 EY93
Whitstable Clo., Beck. 121 DZ95
Whitstable Clo., Ruis. 57 BS61
Chichester Ave.
Whitstable Ho. W10 75 CX72
Silchester Rd.
Whitta Rd. E12 66 EK63
Whittaker Ave., Rich. 101 CK85
Hill St.
Whittaker Rd. E6 80 EK66
Whittaker Rd., Sutt. 117 CZ104
Whittaker St. SW1 8 F9
Whittaker St. SW1 90 DG77
Whittaker Way SE1 92 DU77
Lynton Rd.
Whittell Gdns. SE26 106 DW90
Whittingstall Rd. SW6 89 CZ81
Whittington Ave. EC3 7 M9
Whittington Ave., Hayes 71 BT71
Whittington Ct. N2 62 DF57
Whittington Ms. N12 48 DC49
Fredericks Pl.
Whittington Rd. N22 49 DL52
Whittington Way, Pnr. 58 BY57
Whittle Clo. E17 65 DY58
Whittle Clo., Sthl. 72 CB72
Whittle Rd., Houns. 86 BW80
Whittlebury Clo., Cars. 132 DF108
Whittlesea Clo., Har. 44 CC52
Whittlesea Rd.
Whittlesea Path, Har. 44 CC53
Whittlesea Rd., Har. 44 CC53
Whittlesey St. SE1 10 E3
Whitton Ave. E., Grnf. 59 CE64
Whitton Ave. W., Grnf. 59 CD64
Whitton Ave. W., Nthlt. 58 CB64
Whitton Clo., Grnf. 73 CH65
Whitton Dene, Houns. 100 CB85
Whitton Dene, Islw. 101 CD85
Whitton Dr., Grnf. 73 CG65
Whitton Manor Rd., Islw. 100 CC85
Whitton Rd., Houns. 86 CB84
Whitton Rd., Twick. 101 CE86
Whitton Wk. E3 79 EA69
Whitton Waye, Houns. 100 CA86
Whitwell Rd. E13 80 EG69
Whitwell Rd., Wat. 30 BX35
Whitworth Pl. SE18 95 EP77
Whitworth Rd. SE18 95 EN79
Whitworth Rd. SE25 120 DS97
Whitworth St. SE10 94 EE78
Whorlton Rd. SE15 92 DV83
Whybridge Clo., Rain. 83 FE67
Whymark Ave. N22 63 DN55
Whytebeam Vw., Whyt. 148 DT118
Whytecliffe Rd. N., Pur. 133 DP111
Whytecliffe Rd. S., Pur. 133 DN111
Whytecroft, Houns. 86 BX80
Whyteleafe Hill, Whyt. 148 DS120
Whyteleafe Rd., Cat. 148 DS122
Whyteville Rd. E7 80 EH65
Whichling Clo., Orp. 124 EX102
Wick La. E3 79 DZ66
Wick Rd. E9 79 DX65
Wick Rd., Tedd. 101 CH94
Wick Sq. E9 79 DZ65
Eastway
Wickenden Rd., Sev. 155 FJ122
Wicker St. E1 78 DV72
Burslem St.
Wickers Oake SE19 106 DT91
Wickersley Rd. SW11 90 DG82
Wicket, The, Croy. 135 EA106
Wicket Rd., Grnf. 73 CG69
Wickets, The, Ashf. 98 BL91
Wickets Way, Ilf. 53 ET51
Wickford St. E1 78 DW70
Wickford Way E17 65 DX56
Wickham Ave., Croy. 121 DY103
Wickham Ave., Sutt. 131 CW106
Wickham Chase, W.Wick. 121 ED102
Wickham Clo., Enf. 36 DV41
Wickham Clo., N.Mal. 117 CT99
Wickham Clo., Uxb. 42 BK53
Wickham Ct. Rd., W.Wick. 121 EC103
Wickham Cres., W.Wick. 121 EC103
Wickham Fld., Sev. 153 FF116
Wickham Gdns. SE4 93 DZ83
Wickham Ho. E1 78 DW71
Jamaica St.
Wickham La. SE2 96 EU78
Wickham La., Well. 96 EU78
Wickham Ms. SE4 93 DZ82
Wickham Rd. E4 51 EC52
Wickham Rd. SE4 93 DZ83
Wickham Rd., Beck. 121 EB96
Wickham Rd., Croy. 120 DW103
Wickham Rd., Har. 45 CD54
Wickham St. SE11 10 B10
Wickham St. SE11 91 DM78
Wickham St., Well. 95 ES82
Wickham Way, Beck. 121 EC98
Wickliffe Ave. N3 47 CY54
Wickliffe Gdns., Wem. 60 CP61
Wicklow St. WC1 6 B2
Wicklow St. WC1 77 DM69
Wicks Clo. SE9 108 EK91
Wicksteed Clo., Bex. 111 FD90
Wicksteed Ho., Brent. 88 CM78
Green Dragon La.
Wickwood St. SE5 91 DP82
Widdecombe Ave., Har. 58 BY61
Widdenham Rd. N7 63 DM63
Widdin St. E15 79 ED66
Wide Way, Mitch. 119 DK97
Widecombe Gdns., Ilf. 66 EL56
Widecombe Rd. SE9 108 EL90
Widecombe Way N2 62 DD57
Widegate St. E1 7 N7
Widenham Clo., Pnr. 58 BW57
Bridle Rd.
Widgeon Clo. E16 80 EH72
Maplin Rd.
Widgeon Rd., Erith 97 FH80
Wallhouse Rd.
Widgeon Way, Wat. 30 BY37
Widley Rd. W9 76 DA69
Widmore Lo. Rd., Brom. 122 EK96
Widmore Rd., Brom. 122 EG96
Widmore Rd., Uxb. 71 BP70
Wieland Rd., Nthwd. 43 BU52
Wigan Ho. E5 64 DV60
Warwick Gro.
Wigeon Path SE28 95 ER76
Wigeon Way, Hayes 72 BX72
Wiggenhall Rd., Wat. 29 BV43
Wiggington Ave., Wem. 74 CP65
Wiggins Mead NW9 47 CT52
Wigham Ho., Bark. 81 EQ66
Wightman Rd. N4 63 DN56
Wightman Rd. N8 63 DN56
Wigley Rd., Felt. 100 BX89
Wigmore Pl. W1 5 H8
Wigmore Pl. W1 77 DH72
Wigmore Rd., Cars. 118 DD103
Wigmore St. W1 4 F9
Wigmore St. W1 76 DG72
Wigmore Wk., Cars. 118 DD103
Wigmore Rd.
Wigram Rd. E11 66 EJ58
Wigram Sq. E17 51 ED54
Wigston Clo. N18 50 DS50
Wigston Rd. E13 80 EH70
Wigton Gdns., Stan. 46 CL53
Wigton Pl. SE11 91 DN78
Milverton St.
Wigton Rd. E17 51 DZ53
Wilberforce Rd. N4 63 DP61
Wilberforce Rd. NW9 61 CU58
Wilberforce Way SW19 103 CX93
Wilbraham Pl. SW1 8 E8
Wilbraham Pl. SW1 90 DF77
Wilbury Ave., Sutt. 131 CZ110
Wilbury Way N18 50 DR50
Wilby Ms. W11 75 CZ73
Wilcot Ave., Wat. 44 BY45
Wilcox Clo. SW8 91 DL80
Wilcox Clo., Borwd. 32 CQ39
Wilcox Gdns., Shep. 112 BM97
Wilcox Pl. SW1 9 L7
Wilcox Rd. SW8 91 DL80
Wilcox Rd., Sutt. 132 DB105
Wilcox Rd., Tedd. 101 CD91
Wild Ct. WC2 6 B8
Wild Ct. WC2 77 DM72
Wild Goose Dr. SE14 92 DW81
Wild Hatch NW11 62 DA58
Wild Oaks Clo., Nthwd. 43 BT51
Wild St. WC2 6 A9
Wild St. WC2 77 DL72
Wildacres, W.Byf. 126 BJ111
Wildcroft Gdns., Edg. 45 CK51
Wildcroft Rd. SW15 103 CW87
Wilde Clo. E8 78 DU67
Wilde Pl. N13 49 DP51
Medesenge Way
Wilde Pl. SW18 104 DD87
Heathfield Rd.
Wilde Rd., Erith 97 FB81
Belmont Rd.
Wilder Clo., Ruis. 57 BV60
Wilderness, The, Hmptn. 100 CB91
Park Rd.
Wilderness Rd., Chis. 109 EP94
Wildernesse Ave., Sev. 155 FL122
Wildernesse Mt., Sev. 155 FK122
Wilderton Rd. N16 64 DS59
Wildfell Rd. SE6 107 EB87
Wild's Rents SE1 11 M6
Wild's Rents SE1 92 DS76
Wildwood NW3 62 DC60
Wildwood, Nthwd. 43 BR51
Wildwood Ave., St.Alb. 16 BZ30
Wildwood Clo. SE12 108 EF87
Wildwood Ct., Ken. 148 DR115
Wildwood Gro. NW3 62 DC60
North End Way
Wildwood Ri. NW11 62 DC60
Wildwood Rd. NW11 62 DB58
Wilford Clo., Enf. 36 DR41
Wilford Clo., Nthwd. 43 BR52
Wilfred Ave., Rain. 83 FG71
Wilfred Owen Clo. SW19 104 DC93
Tennyson Rd.
Wilfred St. SW1 9 K6
Wilfred St. SW1 91 DJ76
Wilfrid Gdns. W3 74 CQ71
Wilhelmina Ave., Couls. 147 DJ119
Wilkes Rd., Brent. 88 CL79
Albany Rd.

Windmill La. (Cheshunt), Wal.Cr. 23 DY30
Windmill La. (Bushey), Wat. 45 CD46
Windmill Ms. W4 88 CS77
Chiswick Common Rd.
Windmill Pas. W4 88 CS77
Chiswick Common Rd.
Windmill Ri., Kings.T. 102 CP94
Windmill Rd. N18 50 DR49
Windmill Rd. SW18 104 DD86
Windmill Rd. SW19 103 CW90
Windmill Rd. W4 88 CS77
Windmill Rd. W5 87 CJ77
Windmill Rd., Brent. 87 CK78
Windmill Rd., Croy. 120 DQ101
Windmill Rd., Hmptn. 100 CB92
Windmill Rd., Mitch. 119 DJ99
Windmill Rd., Sev. 155 FH130
Windmill Rd., Sun. 113 BS95
Windmill Rd. W., Sun. 113 BS96
Windmill Row SE11 91 DN78
Windmill St. W1 5 M7
Windmill St. W1 77 DK71
Windmill St. (Bushey), Wat. 45 CE46
Windmill Wk. SE1 10 E3
Windmill Wk. SE1 77 DN74
Windmill Way, Ruis. 57 BT60
Windmore Ave., Pot.B. 19 CW31
Windover Ave. NW9 60 CR56
Windrose Clo. SE16 93 DX75
Windrush Clo. SW11 90 DD84
Maysoule Rd.
Windrush Clo. W4 88 CQ81
Windrush Clo., Uxb. 56 BM63
Windrush La. SE23 107 DX90
Windsock Clo. SE16 93 DZ76
Windsor Ave. E17 51 DY54
Windsor Ave. SW19 118 DC95
Windsor Ave., Edg. 46 CP49
Windsor Ave., N.Mal. 116 CQ99
Windsor Ave., Sutt. 117 CY104
Windsor Ave., Uxb. 71 BP67
Windsor Ave., W.Mol. 114 CA97
Windsor Cen., The SE27 106 DQ91
Advance Rd.
Windsor Clo. N3 47 CY54
Windsor Clo. SE27 106 DQ91
Windsor Clo., Borwd. 32 CN39
Warenford Way
Windsor Clo., Brent. 87 CH79
Windsor Clo., Chis. 109 EP92
Windsor Clo., Har. 58 CA62
Windsor Clo., Nthwd. 43 BU54
Windsor Clo. (Cheshunt), Wal.Cr. 22 DU30
Windsor Ct. N14 49 DJ45
Windsor Ct., Sun. 99 BU93
Windsor Rd.
Windsor Cres., Har. 58 CA62
Windsor Cres., Wem. 60 CP62
Windsor Dr., Ashf. 98 BK91
Windsor Dr., Barn. 34 DF44
Windsor Dr., Dart. 111 FG86
Windsor Dr., Orp. 138 EU107
Windsor Gdns. W9 76 DA71
Windsor Gdns., Croy. 119 DL104
Richmond Rd.
Windsor Gdns., Hayes 85 BR76
Windsor Gro. SE27 106 DQ91
Windsor Pk. Rd., Hayes 85 BT80
Windsor Pl. SW1 9 L7
Windsor Pl., Cher. 112 BG100
Windsor St.
Windsor Rd. E4 51 EB49
Chivers Rd.
Windsor Rd. E7 66 EH64
Windsor Rd. E10 65 EB61
Windsor Rd. E11 66 EG60
Windsor Rd. N3 47 CY54
Windsor Rd. N7 63 DL62
Windsor Rd. N13 49 DN48
Windsor Rd. N17 50 DU54
Windsor Rd. NW2 75 CV65
Windsor Rd. W5 74 CL73
Windsor Rd., Barn. 33 CX44
Windsor Rd., Bexh. 96 EY84
Windsor Rd., Dag. 68 EY62
Windsor Rd., Enf. 37 DX36
Windsor Rd., Har. 45 CD53
Windsor Rd., Houns. 85 BV82
Windsor Rd., Ilf. 67 EP63
Windsor Rd., Kings.T. 102 CL94
Windsor Rd., Rich. 88 CM82
Windsor Rd., Sthl. 86 BZ76
Windsor Rd., Sun. 99 BU93
Windsor Rd., Tedd. 101 CD92
Windsor Rd., Th.Hth. 119 DP96
Windsor Rd., Wat. 30 BW38
Windsor Rd., Wor.Pk. 117 CU103
Windsor St. N1 77 DP67
Windsor St., Cher. 112 BG100
Windsor St., Uxb. 70 BJ66
Windsor Ter. N1 7 J2
Windsor Ter. N1 78 DQ69
Windsor Wk. SE5 92 DR82
Windsor Wk., Walt. 114 BX102
King George Ave.
Windsor Wk., Wey. 127 BP106
Windsor Way W14 89 CX77
Windsor Way, Rick. 42 BG46
Windsor Wf. E9 65 DZ64
Windsor Wd., Wal.Abb. 24 EE33
Monkswood Ave.
Windsors, The, Buck.H. 52 EL47
Windspoint Dr. SE15 92 DV79
Ethnard Rd.
Windus Rd. N16 64 DT60
Windus Wk. N16 64 DT60
Alkham Rd.
Windward Clo., Enf. 37 DX35
Windy Ridge, Brom. 122 EL95
Windycroft Clo., Pur. 133 DK113
Windyridge Clo. SW19 103 CX92
Wine Clo. E1 78 DW73
Wine Office Ct. EC4 6 E9
Winern Glebe, W.Byf. 126 BK113
Winery La., Kings.T. 116 CM97
Winford Ho. E3 79 DZ66
Jodrell Rd.
Winforton St. SE10 93 EC81
Winfrith Rd. SW18 104 DC87
Wingate Cres., Croy. 119 DK100
Wingate Rd. W6 89 CV76
Wingate Rd., Ilf. 67 EP64
Wingate Rd., Sid. 110 EW93
Wingate Trd. Est. N17 50 DT52
Wingfield Clo., Add. 126 BH110
Wingfield Ms. SE15 92 DU83
Wingfield St.
Wingfield Rd. E15 66 EE63
Wingfield Rd. E17 65 EB57
Wingfield Rd., Kings.T. 102 CN93
Wingfield St. SE15 92 DU83
Wingfield Way, Ruis. 71 BV65
Wingford Rd. SW2 105 DL86
Wingmore Rd. SE24 92 DQ83
Wingrave Rd. W6 89 CW79
Wingrove Rd. SE6 108 EE89
Wings Clo., Sutt. 132 DA105
Winifred Gro. SW11 90 DF84
Winifred Rd. SW19 118 DA95
Winifred Rd., Couls. 146 DG116
Winifred Rd., Dag. 68 EY61
Winifred Rd., Dart. 111 FH85
Winifred Rd., Erith 97 FE78
Winifred Rd., Hmptn. 100 CA91
Winifred St. E16 81 EM74
Winifred Ter. E13 80 EG68
Victoria Rd.
Winifred Ter., Enf. 50 DT45
Great Cambridge Rd.
Winkfield Rd. E13 80 EH68
Winkfield Rd. N22 49 DN53
Winkley St. E2 78 DV68
Winkworth Pl., Bans. 131 CZ114
Bolters La.
Winkworth Rd., Bans. 132 DA114
Winlaton Rd., Brom. 107 ED91
Winmill Rd., Dag. 68 EZ62
Winn Common Rd. SE18 95 ES79
Winn Rd. SE12 108 EH88
Winnett St. W1 5 M10
Winnings Wk., Nthlt. 72 BY65
Arnold Rd.
Winnington Clo. N2 62 DD58
Winnington Rd. N2 62 DD60
Winnington Rd., Enf. 36 DW38
Winnipeg Dr., Orp. 137 ET107
Winnock Rd., West Dr. 70 BK74
Winns Ave. E17 65 DY55
Winns Ms. N15 64 DS56
Grove Pk. Rd.
Winns Ter. E17 51 EA54
Winsbeach E17 51 ED54
Winscombe Cres. W5 73 CK70
Winscombe St. N19 63 DH61
Winscombe Way, Stan. 45 CG50
Winsford Rd. SE6 107 DZ90
Winsford Ter. N18 50 DR50
Winsham Gro. SW11 104 DG85
Winslade Rd. SW2 105 DL85
Winslade Way SE6 107 EB87
Rushey Grn.
Winsland Ms. W2 76 DD72
London St.
Winsland St. W2 76 DD72
Winsley St. W1 5 K8
Winsley St. W1 77 DJ72
Winslow SE17 92 DS78
Kinglake St.
Winslow Clo. NW10 60 CS62
Neasden La. N.
Winslow Clo., Pnr. 57 BV58
Winslow Gro. E4 52 EE47
Winslow Rd. W6 89 CW79
Winslow Way, Felt. 100 BX90
Winslow Way, Walt. 114 BW104
Winsor Ter. E6 81 EN71
Winstanley Clo., Cob. 127 BV114
Winstanley Est. SW11 90 DD83
Winstanley Rd. SW11 90 DD83
Winstead Gdns., Dag. 69 FC64
Winston Ave. NW9 60 CS59
Winston Clo., Har. 45 CF51
Winston Clo., Rom. 69 FB56
Winston Ct., Har. 44 CB52
Winston Dr., Cob. 142 BY116
Winston Rd. N16 64 DR63
Winston Wk. W4 88 CR77
Acton La.
Winston Way, Ilf. 67 EP62
Winston Way, Pot.B. 20 DA33
Winstre Rd., Borwd. 32 CN39
Winter Ave. E6 80 EL67
Winter Box Wk., Rich. 88 CM84
Winterborne Ave., Orp. 123 ER104
Winterbourne Gro., Wey. 127 BQ107
Winterbourne Rd. SE6 107 DZ88
Winterbourne Rd., Dag. 68 EW61
Winterbourne Rd., Th.Hth. 119 DN98
Winterbrook Rd. SE24 106 DQ86
Winterdown Gdns., Esher 128 BZ107
Winterdown Rd., Esher 128 BZ107
Winterfold Clo. SW19 103 CY89
Wintergreen Clo. E6 80 EL71
Yarrow Cres.
Winters Rd., T.Ditt. 115 CH101
Winters Way, Wal.Abb. 24 EG33
Wintersells Rd., W.Byf. 126 BK110
Winterstoke Gdns. NW7 47 CU50
Winterstoke Rd. SE6 107 DZ88
Winterton Ho. E1 78 DV72
Winterton Pl. SW10 90 DC79
Park Wk.
Winterwell Rd. SW2 105 DL85
Winthorpe Rd. SW15 89 CY84
Winthrop St. E1 78 DV71
Brady St.
Winthrop Wk., Wem. 60 CL62
Everard Way
Winton App., Rick. 29 BQ43
Winton Ave. N11 49 DJ52
Winton Clo. N9 51 DX45
Winton Cres., Rick. 29 BP43
Winton Dr., Rick. 29 BP44
Winton Dr. (Cheshunt), Wal.Cr. 23 DY29
Winton Gdns., Edg. 46 CM52
Winton Rd., Orp. 137 EP105
Winton Way SW16 105 DN92
Wireless Rd., West. 150 EK115
Wisbeach Rd., Croy. 120 DR99
Wisborough Rd., S.Croy. 134 DT109
Wisdons Clo., Dag. 69 FB60
Wise La. NW7 47 CU50
Wise La., West Dr. 84 BK76
Wise Rd. E15 79 ED67
Wiseman Ct. SE19 106 DT92
Wiseman Rd. E10 65 EA61
Wise's La., Hat. 19 CW27
Wiseton Rd. SW17 104 DE88
Wishart Rd. SE3 94 EK82
Wishford Ct., Ash. 144 CM118
The Marld
Wisley Common, Wok. 140 BM117
Wisley La., Wok. 140 BJ116
Wisley Rd. SW11 104 DG85
Wisley Rd., Orp. 110 EU94
Wisteria Clo. NW7 47 CT51
Wisteria Clo., Ilf. 67 EP64
Wisteria Clo., Orp. 123 EP103
Wisteria Gdns., Swan. 125 FD96
Wisteria Rd. SE13 93 ED84
Witan St. E2 78 DV69
Witches La., Sev. 154 FD123
Witham Clo., Loug. 38 EL44
Witham Rd. SE20 120 DW97
Witham Rd. W13 73 CG74
Witham Rd., Dag. 68 FA64
Witham Rd., Islw. 87 CD81
Witham Rd., Rom. 69 FH57
Withens Clo., Orp. 124 EW98
Witherby Clo., Croy. 134 DS106
Witherfield Way SE16 92 DV78
Egan Way
Witherington Rd. N5 63 DN64
Withers Clo., Chess. 129 CJ107
Coppard Gdns.
Withers Mead NW9 47 CT53
Witherston Way SE9 109 EN89
Witheygate Ave., Stai. 98 BH93
Withies, The, Lthd. 143 CH121
Withy La., Ruis. 57 BQ57
Withy Mead E4 51 ED48
Withy Pl., St.Alb. 16 CC28
Withybed Cor., Tad. 145 CV123
Withycombe Rd. SW19 103 CX87
Witley Cres., Croy. 135 EC107
Witley Gdns., Sthl. 86 BZ77
Witley Rd. N19 63 DJ61
Holloway Rd.
Witney Clo., Pnr. 44 BZ51
Witney Clo., Uxb. 56 BM63
Witney Path SE23 107 DX90
Inglemere Rd.
Wittenham Way E4 51 ED48
Wittering Clo., Kings.T. 101 CK92
Wittersham Rd., Brom. 108 EF92
Wivenhoe Clo. SE15 92 DV83
Wivenhoe Ct., Houns. 86 BZ84
Wivenhoe Rd., Bark. 82 EU68
Wiverton Rd. SE26 106 DW93
Wix Rd., Dag. 82 EX67
Wixs La. SW4 91 DH83
Woburn Ave., Epp. 39 ES37
Woburn Ave., Horn. 69 FG63
Woburn Ave., Pur. 133 DN111
High St.
Woburn Clo. SE28 82 EX72
Summerton Way
Woburn Clo. SW19 104 DC93
Tintern Clo.
Woburn Clo. (Bushey), Wat. 30 CC43
Woburn Hill, Add. 112 BJ103
Woburn Pl. WC1 5 N4
Woburn Pl. WC1 77 DK70
Woburn Rd., Cars. 118 DE102
Woburn Rd., Croy. 120 DQ102
Woburn Sq. WC1 5 N5
Woburn Sq. WC1 77 DK70
Woburn Wk. WC1 5 N3
Woffington Clo., Kings.T. 115 CJ95
Woking Clo. SW15 89 CT84
Wold, The, Cat. 149 EA122
Woldham Pl., Brom. 122 EJ98
Woldham Rd., Brom. 122 EJ98
Woldingham Rd., Cat. 148 DV120
Wolds Dr., Orp. 137 EN105
Wolfe Clo., Brom. 122 EG100
Wolfe Clo., Hayes 71 BV69
Ayles Rd.
Wolfe Cres. SE7 94 EK78
Wolfe Cres. SE16 93 DX75
Wolferton Rd. E12 67 EM63
Wolffe Gdns. E15 80 EF65
Wolffram Clo. SE13 108 EE85
Wolfington Rd. SE27 105 DP91
Wolftencroft Clo. SW11 90 DD83
Wollaston Clo. SE1 11 H8
Wolmer Clo., Edg. 46 CP49
Wolmer Gdns., Edg. 46 CN48
Wolseley Ave. SW19 104 DA89
Wolseley Gdns. W4 88 CP79
Wolseley Rd. E7 80 EH66
Wolseley Rd. N8 63 DK58
Wolseley Rd. N22 49 DM53
Wolseley Rd. W4 88 CQ77
Wolseley Rd., Har. 59 CE55
Wolseley Rd., Mitch. 118 DG101
Wolseley Rd., Rom. 69 FD59
Wolseley St. SE1 92 DU75
Wolsey Ave. E6 81 EN69
Wolsey Ave. E17 65 DZ55
Wolsey Ave., T.Ditt. 115 CF99
Aragon Ave.
Wolsey Ave. (Cheshunt), Wal.Cr. 22 DT29
Wolsey Clo. SW20 103 CV94
Wolsey Clo., Houns. 86 CC84
Wolsey Clo., Kings.T. 116 CP95
Wolsey Clo., Sthl. 86 CC76
Wolsey Clo., Wor.Pk. 131 CU105
Wolsey Cres., Croy. 135 EC109
Wolsey Cres., Mord. 117 CY101
Wolsey Dr., Kings.T. 102 CL92
Wolsey Dr., Walt. 114 BX102
Wolsey Gdns., Ilf. 53 EP51
Wolsey Gro., Edg. 46 CR52
Wolsey Gro., Esher 128 CB105
Wolsey Ms. NW5 77 DJ65
Wolsey Ms., Orp. 137 ET106
Osgood Ave.
Wolsey Pk., Wat. 43 BR45
Wolsey Rd. N1 64 DR64
Wolsey Rd., Ashf. 98 BL91
Wolsey Rd., E.Mol. 115 CD98
Wolsey Rd., Enf. 36 DV40
Wolsey Rd., Esher 128 CB105
Wolsey Rd., Hmptn. 100 CB93
Wolsey Rd., Nthwd. 43 BQ47
Wolsey Rd., Sun. 99 BT94
Wolsey St. E1 78 DW71
Sidney St.
Wolsey Way, Chess. 130 CN106
Wolsley Clo., Dart. 111 FE85
Wolstan Clo., Uxb. 56 BG62
Lindsey Rd.
Wolstonbury N12 48 DA50
Wolvercote Rd. SE2 96 EX75
Wolverley St. E2 78 DV69
Bethnal Grn. Rd.
Wolverton SE17 11 M10
Wolverton Ave., Kings.T. 116 CN95
Wolverton Gdns. W5 74 CM73
Wolverton Gdns. W6 89 CX77
Wolverton Rd., Stan. 45 CH51
Wolverton Way N14 35 DJ43
Wolves La. N13 49 DN51
Wolves La. N22 49 DN52
Womersley Rd. N8 63 DM58
Wonersh Way, Sutt. 131 CX109
Wonford Clo., Kings.T. 116 CS95
Wontford Rd., Pur. 147 DN115
Wontner Clo. N1 78 DQ66
Greenman St.
Wontner Rd. SW17 104 DF89
Wood Clo. E2 78 DU70
Wood Clo. NW9 60 CR59
Wood Clo., Bex. 111 FE90
Wood Clo., Har. 59 CD59
Wood Dr., Chis. 108 EL93
Wood Dr., Sev. 154 FF126
Wood End, Hayes 71 BS72
Wood End, St.Alb. 16 CC28
Wood End Ave., Har. 58 CB63
Wood End Clo., Nthlt. 59 CD64
Wood End Gdns., Nthlt. 58 CC64
Wood End Grn. Rd., Hayes 71 BR71
Wood End La., Nthlt. 72 CB65
Wood End Rd., Har. 59 CD63
Wood End Way, Nthlt. 58 CC64
Wood Grn. Way (Cheshunt), Wal.Cr. 23 DY31
Holme Clo.
Wood La. N6 63 DH58
Wood La. NW9 60 CR59
Wood La. W12 75 CW72
Wood La., Cat. 148 DR124
Wood La., Dag. 68 EW63
Wood La., Horn. 69 FG64
Wood La., Islw. 87 CE79
Wood La., Ruis. 57 BR60
Wood La., Stan. 45 CG48
Wood La., Tad. 145 CZ117
Brighton Rd.
Wood La., Wey. 127 BQ109
Wood La., Wdf.Grn. 52 EF49
Wood Lo. Gdns., Brom. 108 EL94
Wood Lo. La., W.Wick. 121 EC104
Wood Meads, Epp. 26 EU29
Wood Pt. E16 80 EG71
Fife Rd.
Wood Retreat SE18 95 ER80
Clothworkers Rd.
Wood Ride, Barn. 34 DD39
Wood Ride, Orp. 123 ER98
Wood Rd., Shep. 112 BN98
Wood Rd., West. 150 EJ118
Wood St. E16 80 EH73
Ethel Rd.
Wood St. E17 65 EC55
Wood St. EC2 7 J9
Wood St. EC2 78 DQ72
Wood St. W4 88 CS78
Wood St., Barn. 33 CW42
Wood St., Kings.T. 116 CL95
Wood St., Mitch. 118 DG101
Wood Vale N10 63 DJ57
Wood Vale SE23 106 DV88
Wood Vale Est. SE23 106 DW86
Wood Vw. (Cuffley), Pot.B. 21 DL27
Wood Way, Orp. 123 EN103
Wood Wf. SE10 93 EB79
Thames St.
Woodall Clo. E14 79 EB73
Lawless St.
Woodall Rd., Enf. 37 DX44
Woodbank Rd., Brom. 108 EF90
Woodbastwick Rd. SE26 107 DX92
Woodberry Ave. N21 49 DN47
Woodberry Ave., Har. 58 CB56
Woodberry Clo., Sun. 99 BU93
Ashridge Way
Woodberry Cres. N10 63 DH55
Woodberry Down N4 64 DQ59
Woodberry Down, Epp. 26 EU29
Woodberry Down Est. N4 64 DQ59
Woodberry Gdns. N12 48 DC51
Woodberry Gro. N4 64 DQ59
Woodberry Gro. N12 48 DC51
Woodberry Gro., Bex. 111 FD90
Woodberry Way E4 51 EC46
Woodberry Way N12 48 DC51
Woodbine Clo., Twick. 101 CD89
Woodbine Clo., Wal.Abb. 38 EJ35
Woodbine Gro. SE20 106 DV94
Woodbine Gro., Enf. 36 DR38
Woodbine La., Wor.Pk. 117 CV104
Woodbine Pl. E11 66 EG58
Woodbine Rd., Sid. 109 ES88
Woodbine Ter. E9 78 DW65
Morning La.
Woodbines Ave., Kings.T. 115 CK97
Woodborough Rd. SW15 89 CV84
Woodbourne Ave. SW16 105 DK90
Woodbourne Clo. SW16 105 DL90
Woodbourne Ave.
Woodbourne Dr., Esher 129 CF107
Woodbourne Gdns., Wall. 133 DH108
Woodbridge Ave., Lthd. 143 CG118
Woodbridge Clo. N7 63 DM61
Woodbridge Clo. NW2 61 CU62
Woodbridge Ct., Wdf.Grn. 52 EL52
Woodbridge Gro., Lthd. 143 CG118
Woodbridge Rd., Bark. 67 ET64
Woodbridge St. EC1 6 F4
Woodbridge St. EC1 77 DP70
Woodbrook Gdns., Wal.Abb. 24 EE33
Woodbrook Rd. SE2 96 EU79
Woodburn Clo. NW4 61 CX57
Woodburn Clo., Uxb. 71 BP70
Aldenham Dr.
Woodbury Clo. E11 66 EH56
Woodbury Clo., Croy. 120 DT103
Woodbury Clo., West. 151 EM118
Woodbury Dr., Sutt. 132 DC110
Woodbury Hill, Loug. 38 EL41
Woodbury Hollow, Loug. 38 EL40
Woodbury Pk. Rd. W13 73 CH70
Woodbury Rd. E17 65 EB56
Woodbury Rd., West. 151 EM118
Woodbury St. SW17 104 DE92
Woodchester Sq. W2 76 DB71
Woodchurch Clo., Sid. 109 ER90
Woodchurch Dr., Brom. 108 EK94
Woodchurch Rd. NW6 76 DA66
Woodclyffe Dr., Chis. 123 EN96
Woodcock Ct., Har. 60 CL59
Woodcock Dell Ave., Har. 59 CK59
Woodcock Hill, Har. 59 CJ57
Woodcock Hill, Rick. 42 BL50
Woodcock Hill Trd. Est., Rick. 42 BL49
Woodcocks E16 80 EJ71
Woodcombe Cres. SE23 106 DW88
Woodcote Ave. NW7 47 CW51
Woodcote Ave., Horn. 69 FG63
Woodcote Ave., Th.Hth. 119 DP98
Woodcote Ave., Wall. 133 DH109
Woodcote Clo., Enf. 36 DW44
Woodcote Clo., Epsom 130 CR114
Woodcote Clo., Kings.T. 102 CM92
Woodcote Clo. (Cheshunt), Wal.Cr. 22 DW30
Woodcote Dr., Orp. 123 ER102
Woodcote Dr., Pur. 133 DK110
Woodcote End, Epsom 144 CR115
Woodcote Grn., Wall. 133 DJ109
Woodcote Grn. Rd., Epsom 144 CQ116
Woodcote Gro., Couls. 133 DH112
Woodcote Gro. Rd., Couls. 147 DK115
Woodcote Hurst, Epsom 144 CQ116
Woodcote La., Pur. 133 DK111

Woodcote Ms., Wall. 133 DH107
Woodcote Pk. Ave., Pur. 133 DJ112
Woodcote Pk. Rd., Epsom 144 CQ116
Woodcote Pl. SE27 105 DP92
Woodcote Rd. E11 66 EG59
Woodcote Rd., Epsom 130 CR114
Woodcote Rd., Pur. 133 DH107
Woodcote Rd., Wall. 133 DH107
Woodcote Side, Epsom 144 CP115
Woodcote Valley Rd., Pur. 133 DK113
Woodcrest Rd., Pur. 133 DL113
Woodcroft N21 49 DM46
Woodcroft SE9 109 EM90
Woodcroft, Grnf. 73 CG65
Woodcroft Ave. NW7 46 CS52
Woodcroft Ave., Stan. 45 CF53
Woodcroft Cres., Uxb. 71 BP67
Woodcroft Rd., Th.Hth. 119 DP99
Woodedge Clo. E4 52 EF46
Woodend SE19 106 DQ93
Woodend, Esher 114 CC103
Woodend, Sutt. 118 DC103
Woodend, The, Wall. 133 DH109
Woodend Gdns., Enf. 35 DL42
Woodend Pk., Cob. 142 BX115
Woodend Rd. E17 51 EC54
Wooder Gdns. E7 66 EG63
Wooderson Clo. SE25 120 DS98
Woodfall Ave., Barn. 33 CZ43
Woodfall Dr., Dart. 97 FE84
Woodfall Rd. N4 63 DN60
Woodfall St. SW3 90 DF78
Woodfarrs SE5 92 DR84
Woodfield, Ash. 143 CK117
Woodfield Ave. NW9 60 CS56
Woodfield Ave. SW16 105 DK90
Woodfield Ave. W5 73 CJ70
Woodfield Ave., Cars. 132 DG107
Woodfield Ave., Nthwd. 43 BS49
Woodfield Ave., Wem. 59 CJ62
Woodfield Clo. SE19 106 DQ94
Woodfield Clo., Ash. 143 CK117
Woodfield Clo., Couls. 147 DJ119
Woodfield Clo., Enf. 36 DS42
Woodfield Cres. W5 73 CK70
Woodfield Dr., Barn. 48 DG46
Woodfield Dr., Rom. 69 FG56
Woodfield Gdns. W9 75 CZ71
Woodfield Rd.
Woodfield Gdns., N.Mal. 117 CT99
Woodfield Gro. SW16 105 DK90
Woodfield Hill, Couls. 147 DH119
Woodfield La. SW16 105 DK90
Woodfield La., Ash. 144 CL117
Woodfield Pl. W9 75 CZ70
Woodfield Ri. (Bushey), Wat. 45 CD45
Woodfield Rd. W5 73 CJ70
Woodfield Rd. W9 75 CZ71
Woodfield Rd., Ash. 143 CK117
Woodfield Rd., Houns. 85 BV82
Woodfield Rd., Rad. 31 CG36
Woodfield Rd., T.Ditt. 115 CF103
Woodfield Ter., Epp. 26 EW25
High Rd.
Woodfield Ter., Uxb. 42 BH54
Woodfield Way N11 49 DK52
Woodfields, Sev. 154 FD122
Woodfields, The, S.Croy. 134 DT111
Woodford Ave., Ilf. 66 EL55
Woodford Ave., Wdf.Grn. 66 EL55
Woodford Bri. Rd., Ilf. 66 EK55
Woodford Ct. W12 89 CX75
Shepherds Bush Grn.
Woodford Ct., Wal.Abb. 24 EG33
Woodford Cres., Pnr. 43 BV54
Woodford New Rd. E17 66 EE56
Woodford New Rd. E18 66 EE56
Woodford New Rd., Wdf.Grn. 66 EE56
Woodford Pl., Wem. 60 CL60
Woodford Rd. E7 66 EH63
Woodford Rd. E18 66 EG56
Woodford Rd., Wat. 29 BV40
Woodford Trd. Est., Wdf.Grn. 52 EK54
Woodgate, Wat. 15 BV33
Woodgate Ave., Chess. 129 CK106
Woodgate Cres., Nthwd. 43 BU51
Woodgate Dr. SW16 105 DK94
Woodgavil, Bans. 145 CZ116
Woodger Rd. W12 89 CW75
Goldhawk Rd.
Woodgers Gro., Swan. 125 FF96
Woodget Clo. E6 80 EL72
Remington Rd.
Woodgrange Ave. N12 48 DD51
Woodgrange Ave. W5 74 CN74
Woodgrange Ave., Enf. 36 DU44
Woodgrange Ave., Har. 59 CJ57
Woodgrange Clo., Har. 59 CK57
Woodgrange Gdns., Enf. 36 DU44
Woodgrange Rd. E7 66 EH64
Woodgrange Ter., Enf. 36 DU44
Great Cambridge Rd.
Woodgreen Rd., Wal.Abb. 24 EH33
Woodhall Ave. SE21 106 DT90
Woodhall Ave., Pnr. 44 BY54
Woodhall Clo., Uxb. 56 BK64
Woodhall Dr. SE21 106 DT90
Woodhall Dr., Pnr. 44 BX53
Woodhall Gate, Pnr. 44 BX52
Woodhall La., Rad. 32 CL35
Woodhall La., Wat. 44 BX48
Woodhall Rd., Pnr. 44 BX52
Woodham Ct. E18 66 EF56
Woodham La., Add. 126 BG110
Woodham Rd. SE6 107 EC90
Woodhatch Clo. E6 80 EL72
Remington Rd.
Woodhatch Spinney, Couls. 147 DL116
Woodhaven Gdns., Ilf. 67 EQ55
Brandville Gdns.
Woodhayes Rd. SW19 103 CW94
Woodhead Dr., Orp. 123 ES103
Sherlies Ave.
Woodheyes Rd. NW10 60 CR64
Woodhill SE18 94 EL77
Woodhill Cres., Har. 59 CK58
Woodhouse Ave., Grnf. 73 CF68
Woodhouse Clo., Grnf. 73 CF68
Woodhouse Clo., Hayes 85 BS76
Woodhouse Eaves, Nthwd. 43 BU50
Woodhouse Gro. E12 80 EL65
Woodhouse Rd. E11 66 EF62
Woodhouse Rd. N12 48 DC51
Woodhurst Ave., Orp. 123 EQ100
Woodhurst Ave., Wat. 16 BX34
Woodhurst Rd. SE2 96 EU78
Woodhurst Rd. W3 74 CQ73
Woodhyrst Gdns., Ken. 147 DP115
Firs Rd.
Woodington Clo. SE9 109 EN86
Woodison St. E3 79 DY70
Woodknoll Dr., Chis. 123 EM95
Woodland Clo. NW9 60 CQ58
Woodland Clo. SE19 106 DS93
Woodland Hill
Woodland Clo., Epsom 130 CS107
Woodland Clo., Uxb. 57 BP61
Woodland Clo., Wey. 127 BR105
Woodland Gro.
Woodland Clo., Wdf.Grn. 52 EH48
Woodland Cres. SE10 94 EE79
Woodland Dr., Wat. 29 BT39
Woodland Gdns. N10 63 DH57
Woodland Gdns., Islw. 87 CE83
Woodland Gdns., S.Croy. 134 DW111
Woodland Gro. SE10 94 EE78
Woodland Gro., Epp. 26 EU31
Woodland Gro., Wey. 127 BR105
Woodland Hill SE19 106 DS93
Woodland Ri. N10 63 DH56
Woodland Ri., Grnf. 73 CG65
Woodland Ri., Sev. 155 FL123
Woodland Rd. E4 51 EC46
Woodland Rd. N11 49 DH50
Woodland Rd. SE19 106 DT92
Woodland Rd., Loug. 38 EL41
Woodland Rd., Th.Hth. 119 DN98
Woodland St. E8 78 DT65
Dalston La.
Woodland Ter. SE7 94 EL77
Woodland Ter. SE18 94 EL77
Woodland Wk. NW3 62 DE64
Aspern Gro.
Woodland Wk. SE10 94 EE78
Woodland Gro.
Woodland Wk., Brom. 108 EE91
Woodland Way N21 49 DN47
Woodland Way NW7 46 CS51
Woodland Way SE2 96 EX77
Woodland Way, Croy. 121 DY102
Woodland Way, Epp. 39 ER35
Woodland Way, Mitch. 104 DG94
Woodland Way, Mord. 117 CZ98
Woodland Way, Orp. 123 EQ98
Woodland Way, Pur. 133 DN113
Woodland Way, Surb. 116 CP103
Woodland Way, Tad. 145 CY122
Woodland Way (Cheshunt), Wal.Cr. 21 DP28
Woodland Way, W.Wick. 135 EB105
Woodland Way, Wey. 127 BR106
Woodland Way, Wdf.Grn. 52 EH48
Woodlands NW11 61 CY58
Woodlands SW20 117 CW98
Woodlands, Har. 58 CA56
Woodlands, Hat. 20 DB26
Woodlands, Rad. 17 CG34
Woodlands, St.Alb. 16 CC27
Woodlands, The N14 49 DH46
Woodlands, The SE13 107 ED87
Woodlands, The SE19 106 DQ94
Woodlands, The, Esher 114 CC103
Woodlands, The, Islw. 87 CF82
Woodlands, The, Orp. 138 EV107
Woodlands, The, Wall. 133 DH109
Woodlands Ave. E11 66 EG60
Woodlands Ave. N3 48 DC52
Woodlands Ave. W3 74 CP74
Woodlands Ave., N.Mal. 116 CQ95
Woodlands Ave., Rom. 68 EY58
Woodlands Ave., Ruis. 58 BW59
Woodlands Ave., Sid. 109 ES88
Woodlands Ave., Wor.Pk. 117 CT103
Woodlands Clo. NW11 61 CY57
Woodlands Clo., Borwd. 32 CP42
Woodlands Clo., Brom. 123 EM96
Woodlands Clo., Esher 129 CF108
Woodlands Clo., Swan. 125 FF97
Woodlands Dr., Kings L. 15 BQ28
Woodlands Dr., Stan. 45 CF51
Woodlands Dr., Sun. 114 BW96
Woodlands Gro., Couls. 146 DG117
Woodlands Gro., Islw. 87 CE82
Woodlands La., Cob. 142 BY117
Woodlands Par., Ashf. 99 BQ93
Woodlands Pk., Bex. 111 FC91
Woodlands Pk. Rd. N15 63 DP57
Woodlands Pk. Rd. SE10 94 EE79
Woodlands Ri., Swan. 125 FF96
Woodlands Rd. E11 66 EE61
Woodlands Rd. E17 65 EC55
Woodlands Rd. N9 50 DW46
Woodlands Rd. SW13 89 CT83
Woodlands Rd., Bexh. 96 EY83
Woodlands Rd., Brom. 122 EL96
Woodlands Rd., Enf. 36 DR38
Woodlands Rd., Epsom 144 CN115
Woodlands Rd., Har. 59 CF57
Woodlands Rd., Hem.H. 14 BN27
Woodlands Rd., Ilf. 67 EQ62
Woodlands Rd., Islw. 87 CD83
Woodlands Rd., Lthd. 143 CD117
Woodlands Rd., Orp. 138 EU107
Woodlands Rd., Rom. 69 FF55
Woodlands Rd., Sthl. 72 BX74
Woodlands Rd., Surb. 115 CK101
Woodlands Rd. (Bushey), Wat. 30 BY43
Woodlands St. SE13 107 ED87
Woodlands Vw., Sev. 138 FA110
Woodlands Way SW15 103 CZ85
Oakhill Rd.
Woodlands Way, Ash. 144 CN116
Woodlawn Clo. SW15 103 CZ85
Woodlawn Cres., Twick. 100 CB89
Woodlawn Dr., Felt. 100 BX89
Woodlawn Rd. SW6 89 CX80
Woodlea Dr., Brom. 122 EE99
Woodlea Gro., Nthwd. 43 BQ51
Woodlea Rd. N16 64 DS62
Woodleigh Ave. N12 48 DE51
Woodleigh Gdns. SW16 105 DL90
Woodley Clo. SW17 104 DF94
Arnold Rd.
Woodley La., Cars. 118 DE104
Woodley Rd., Orp. 124 EW103
Woodman La. E4 38 EE43
Woodman Path, Ilf. 53 ES51
Woodman Rd., Couls. 147 DJ115
Woodman St. E16 81 EN74
Woodmancote Gdns., W.Byf. 126 BG113
Woodmans Gro. NW10 61 CT64
Woodmans Ms. W12 75 CW71
Wood La.
Woodman's Yd., Wat. 30 BX42
Woodmansterne La., Bans. 146 DB115
Woodmansterne La., Cars. 132 DF112
Woodmansterne La., Wall. 133 DH111
Woodmansterne Rd. SW16 105 DJ94
Woodmansterne Rd., Cars. 132 DF112
Woodmansterne Rd., Couls. 147 DJ115
Woodmansterne St., Bans. 146 DE115
Woodmere SE9 109 EM87
Woodmere Ave., Croy. 120 DW101
Woodmere Ave., Wat. 30 BX38
Woodmere Clo. SW11 90 DG83
Lavender Hill
Woodmere Clo., Croy. 121 DX101
Woodmere Gdns., Croy. 120 DW101
Woodmere Way, Beck. 121 ED99
Woodmount, Swan. 125 FC101
Woodnook Rd. SW16 105 DH92
Woodpecker Clo. N9 36 DV44
Woodpecker Clo., Cob. 128 BY112
Woodpecker Clo., Har. 45 CF53
Woodpecker Clo. (Bushey), Wat. 44 CC46
Woodpecker Mt., Croy. 135 DY109
Woodpecker Rd. SE14 93 DY79
Woodpecker Rd. SE28 82 EW73
Woodplace Clo., Couls. 147 DJ119
Woodplace La., Couls. 147 DJ118
Woodquest Ave. SE24 106 DQ85
Woodredon Fm. La., Wal.Abb. 24 EK33
Woodridden Hill, Wal.Abb. 38 EJ35
Woodridge Clo., Enf. 35 DN39
Woodridge Way, Nthwd. 43 BS51
Woodridings Ave., Pnr. 44 BZ53
Woodridings Clo., Pnr. 44 BZ52
Woodriffe Rd. E11 65 ED59
Woodrise, Pnr. 57 BU57
Woodrow SE18 95 EM77
Woodrow Ave., Hayes 71 BT71
Woodrow Clo., Grnf. 73 CH66
Woodrow Ct. N17 50 DV52
Heybourne Rd.
Woodrush Clo. SE14 93 DY80
Southerngate Way
Woodrush Way, Rom. 68 EX56
Woods, The, Nthwd. 43 BU50
Woods, The, Rad. 17 CH34
Woods, The, Uxb. 57 BP63
Woods Clo. SE19 106 DS93
Woodland Hill
Woods Ms. W1 4 F10
Woods Ms. W1 76 DG73
Woods Pl. SE1 11 N7
Woods Rd. SE15 92 DV81
Woodseer St. E1 78 DT71
Woodsford SE17 92 DR78
Portland St.
Woodsford Sq. W14 89 CY75
Woodshire Rd., Dag. 69 FB62
Woodshots Meadow, Wat. 29 BR43
Woodside NW11 62 DA57
Woodside SW19 103 CZ93
Woodside, Borwd. 32 CM42
Woodside, Buck.H. 52 EJ47
Woodside, Epp. 26 EW26
Woodside, Lthd. 142 CB122
Woodside, Orp. 138 EU106
Woodside (Cheshunt), Wal.Cr. 22 DU31
Woodside, Walt. 113 BU102
Ashley Rd.
Woodside, Wat. 29 BU36
Woodside Ave. N6 62 DF57
Woodside Ave. N10 62 DF57
Woodside Ave. N12 48 DC49
Woodside Ave. SE25 120 DV100
Woodside Ave., Chis. 109 EQ92
Woodside Ave., Esher 115 CE101
Woodside Ave., Walt. 127 BV105
Woodside Ave., Wem. 74 CL67
Woodside Clo., Bexh. 97 FD84
Woodside Clo., Cat. 148 DS124
Woodside Clo., Stan. 45 CH50
Woodside Clo., Surb. 116 CQ102
Woodside Clo., Wem. 74 CL67
Woodside Ct. N12 48 DC49
Woodside Ave.
Woodside Ct. Rd., Croy. 120 DU101
Woodside Cres., Sid. 109 ES90
Woodside Dr., Dart. 111 FE91
Woodside End, Wem. 74 CL67
Woodside Gdns. E4 51 EB50
Woodside Gdns. N17 50 DS54
Woodside Gra. Rd. N12 48 DB49
Woodside Grn. SE25 120 DU100
Woodside Gro. N12 48 DC48
Woodside La. N12 48 DB48
Woodside La., Bex. 110 EX86
Woodside Pk. SE25 120 DU99
Woodside Pk. Ave. E17 65 ED56
Woodside Pk. Rd. N12 48 DB49
Woodside Pl., Wem. 74 CL67
Woodside Rd. E13 80 EJ70
Woodside Rd. N22 49 DM52
Woodside Rd. SE25 120 DV100
Woodside Rd., Abb.L. 15 BV31
Woodside Rd., Bexh. 97 FD84
Woodside Rd., Brom. 122 EL99
Woodside Rd., Cob. 128 CA113
Woodside Rd., Kings.T. 102 CL94
Woodside Rd., N.Mal. 116 CR96
Woodside Rd., Nthwd. 43 BT52
Woodside Rd., Pur. 133 DK113
Woodside Rd., St.Alb. 16 BZ30
Woodside Rd., Sev. 154 FG123
Woodside Rd. (Sundridge), Sev. 152 EX124
Woodside Rd., Sid. 109 ES90
Woodside Rd., Sutt. 118 DC104
Woodside Rd., Wat. 15 BV31
Woodside Rd., Wdf.Grn. 52 EG49
Woodside Way, Croy. 120 DV100
Woodside Way, Mitch. 119 DH95
Woodsome Lo., Wey. 127 BQ107
Woodsome Rd. NW5 62 DG62
Woodspring Rd. SW19 103 CY89
Woodstead Gro., Edg. 46 CL51
Woodstock Ave. NW11 61 CY60
Woodstock Ave. W13 87 CG76
Woodstock Ave., Islw. 101 CG85
Woodstock Ave., Sthl. 72 BZ69
Woodstock Ave., Sutt. 117 CZ101
Woodstock Clo., Bex. 110 EZ87
Woodstock Clo., Stan. 46 CL54
Woodstock Ct. SE12 108 EG86
Woodstock Cres. N9 36 DV44
Woodstock Dr., Uxb. 56 BL63
Woodstock Gdns., Beck. 121 EB95
Woodstock Gdns., Hayes 71 BT71
Woodstock Gdns., Ilf. 68 EU61
Woodstock Gro. W12 89 CX75
Woodstock La., Surb. 115 CJ103
Woodstock La. S., Chess. 129 CJ105
Woodstock La. S., Esher 129 CH106
Woodstock Ms. W1 4 G7
Woodstock Ri., Sutt. 117 CZ101
Woodstock Rd. E7 80 EJ66
Woodstock Rd. E17 51 ED54
Woodstock Rd. N4 63 DN60
Woodstock Rd. NW11 61 CZ59
Woodstock Rd. W4 88 CS76
Woodstock Rd., Cars. 132 DG106
Woodstock Rd., Couls. 147 DH116
Chipstead Valley Rd.
Woodstock Rd., Croy. 120 DR104
Woodstock Rd. (Bushey), Wat. 45 CE45
Woodstock Rd., Wem. 74 CM66
Woodstock St. E16 80 EE72
Victoria Dock Rd.
Woodstock St. W1 5 H9
Woodstock Ter. E14 79 EB73
Woodstock Way, Mitch. 119 DH96
Woodstone Ave., Epsom 131 CU106
Woodsyre SE26 106 DT91
Woodthorpe Rd. SW15 89 CV84
Woodthorpe Rd., Ashf. 98 BK92
Woodtree Clo. NW4 47 CW54
Ashley La.
Woodvale Ave. SE25 120 DT97
Woodvale Wk. SE27 106 DQ92
Elder Rd.
Woodvale Way NW11 61 CX62
The Vale
Woodview, Chess. 129 CJ111
Woodview Ave. E4 51 EC49
Woodview Clo. N4 63 DP59
Woodview Clo. SW15 102 CR91
Woodview Clo., Kings.T. 102 CR9
Woodview Clo., Orp. 123 EQ10
Crofton Rd.
Woodview Clo., S.Croy. 134 DV11
Woodview Rd., Swan. 125 FC9
Woodville SE3 94 EH8
Woodville Clo. SE12 108 EG8
Woodville Clo., Tedd. 101 CG9
Woodville Ct., Wat. 29 BU4
Woodville Gdns. NW11 61 CX5
Hamilton Rd.
Woodville Gdns. W5 74 CL72
Woodville Gdns., Ilf. 67 EP55
Woodville Gdns., Ruis. 57 BQ59
Woodville Gro., Well. 96 EU83
Woodville Pl., Cat. 148 DQ121
Woodville Rd. E11 66 EF60
Woodville Rd. E17 65 DY56
Woodville Rd. E18 52 EH54
Woodville Rd. N16 64 DS64
Woodville Rd. NW6 75 CZ68
Woodville Rd. NW11 61 CX59
Woodville Rd. W5 73 CK72
Woodville Rd., Barn. 34 DB41
Woodville Rd., Lthd. 143 CH120
Woodville Rd., Mord. 118 DA98
Woodville Rd., Rich. 101 CH90
Woodville Rd., Th.Hth. 120 DQ98
Woodville St. SE18 94 EL77
Woodhill
Woodward Ave. NW4 61 CU57
Woodward Clo., Esher 129 CF107
Woodward Gdns., Dag. 82 EW66
Woodward Rd.
Woodward Gdns., Stan. 45 CF52
Woodward Rd., Dag. 82 EV66
Woodwarde Rd. SE22 106 DS86
Woodway Cres., Har. 59 CG58
Woodwaye, Wat. 44 BW45
Woodwell St. SW18 104 DC85
Huguenot Pl.
Woodyard, The, Epp. 26 EX29
Woodyard Clo. NW5 62 DG64
Gillies St.
Woodyard La. SE21 106 DS87
Woodyates Rd. SE12 108 EG86
Wool Rd. SW20 103 CV94
Woolacombe Rd. SE3 94 EJ81
Woolacombe Way, Hayes 85 BS77
Wooler St. SE17 92 DR78
Woolf Clo. SE28 82 EV74
Woolhampton Way, Chig. 54 EV48
Woollard St., Wal.Abb. 23 EC34
Woollaston Rd. N4 63 DP58
Woollett Clo., Dart. 97 FG84
Woolmead Ave. NW9 61 CU59
Woolmer Clo., Borwd. 32 CN38
Woolmer Gdns. N18 50 DU51
Woolmer Rd. N18 50 DU50
Woolmore St. E14 79 EC73
Woolneigh St. SW6 90 DB83
Woolstaplers Way SE16 92 DU77
Yalding Rd.
Woolston Clo. E17 51 DX54
Riverhead Clo.
Woolstone Rd. SE23 107 DY89
Woolwich Ch. St. SE18 94 EL76
Woolwich Common SE18 95 EN79
Woolwich Dockyard Ind. Est. SE18 94 EL76
Woolwich Ferry Pier E16 95 EN75
Woolwich Garrison SE18 95 EN78
Repository Rd.
Woolwich High St. SE18 95 EN76
Woolwich Ind. Est. SE28 95 ES76
Hadden Rd.
Woolwich Manor Way E6 81 EM70
Woolwich Manor Way E16 81 EP73
Woolwich New Rd. SE18 95 EP77
Woolwich Rd. SE2 96 EX79
Woolwich Rd. SE7 94 EH78
Woolwich Rd. SE10 94 EF78
Woolwich Rd., Belv. 96 EZ78
Woolwich Rd., Bexh. 96 FA84
Wooster Gdns. E14 79 ED72
Wooster Pl. SE1 11 L8
Woosters Ms., Har. 58 CC55
Fairfield Dr.
Wootton Clo., Epsom 145 CT116
Wootton Gro. N3 48 DA53
Wootton St. SE1 10 E3
Wootton St. SE1 77 DN74
Worbeck Rd. SE20 120 DV96
Worcester Ave. N17 50 DU52
Worcester Clo., Croy. 121 DZ103
Worcester Clo., Mitch. 118 DG96
Worcester Ct., Walt. 114 BW102
Rodney Rd.
Worcester Cres. NW7 46 CS48
Worcester Cres., Wdf.Grn. 52 EJ49
Worcester Dr., Ashf. 99 BP92
Worcester Gdns. SW11 104 DF85
Grandison Rd.
Worcester Gdns., Grnf. 72 CC65
Worcester Gdns., Ilf. 66 EL59
Worcester Gdns., Wor.Pk. 116 CS103
Worcester Ms. NW6 76 DB65
Lymington Rd.
Worcester Pk. Rd., Wor.Pk. 116 CQ104
Worcester Rd. E12 67 EM63
Worcester Rd. E17 51 DX54
Worcester Rd. SW19 103 CZ92
Worcester Rd., Sutt. 132 DA108
Worcester Rd., Uxb. 70 BJ71
Worcesters Ave., Enf. 36 DU38
Wordsworth Ave. E12 80 EL66

Wordsworth Ave. E18 66 EF55
Wordsworth Ave., Grnf. 73 CD69
Wordsworth Ave., Ken. 148 DR115
Valley Rd.
Wordsworth Dr., Sutt. 131 CW105
Wordsworth Rd. N16 64 DS64
Wordsworth Rd. SE1 11 P9
Wordsworth Rd. SE20 107 DX94
Wordsworth Rd., Add. 126 BK105
Wordsworth Rd., Hmptn. 100 BZ91
Wordsworth Rd., Wall. 133 DJ107
Wordsworth Rd., Well. 95 ES81
Wordsworth Wk. NW11 61 CZ56
Wordsworth Way, West Dr. 84 BL77
Worfield St. SW11 90 DE80
Worgan St. SE11 10 B10
Worgan St. SE11 91 DM78
Worgan St. SE16 93 DX76
Worland Rd. E15 80 EE66
World Trade Cen. E1 78 DT73
World's End, Cob. 127 BU114
World's End Est. SW10 90 DC80
Worlds End La. N21 35 DM43
Worlds End La., Enf. 35 DM42
Worlds End La., Orp. 137 ET107
World's End Pas. SW10 90 DD80
Riley St.
World's End Pl. SW10 90 DC80
King's Rd.
Worlidge St. W6 89 CW78
Worlingham Rd. SE22 92 DT84
Wormholt Rd. W12 75 CU74
Wormingford Ct., Wal.Abb. 24 EG33
Ninefields
Wormley Ct., Wal.Abb. 24 EG33
Winters Way
Wormwood St. EC2 7 M8
Wormwood St. EC2 78 DS72
Wornington Rd. W10 75 CY70
Woronzow Rd. NW8 76 DD67
Worple Ave. SW19 103 CX94
Worple Ave., Islw. 101 CG85
Worple Ave., Stai. 98 BH93
Worple Clo., Har. 58 BZ60
Worple Rd. SW19 103 CY94
Worple Rd. SW20 117 CW96
Worple Rd., Epsom 144 CR115
Worple Rd., Islw. 87 CG84
Worple Rd., Lthd. 143 CH123
Worple Rd., Stai. 98 BH94
Worple Rd. Ms. SW19 103 CZ93
Worple St. SW14 88 CR83
Worple Way, Har. 58 BZ60
Worple Way, Rich. 102 CL85
Worship St. EC2 7 L5
Worship St. EC2 78 DR70
Worships Hill, Sev. 154 FE123
Worslade Rd. SW17 104 DD91
Worsley Bri. Rd. SE26 107 DZ91
Worsley Bri. Rd., Beck. 107 EA92
Worsley Rd. E11 66 EE63
Worsopp Dr. SW4 105 DJ85
Worth Clo., Orp. 137 ES105
Worth Gro. SE17 92 DR78
Merrow St.
Worthfield Clo., Epsom 130 CR108
Worthing Clo. E15 80 EE68
Mitre Rd.
Worthing Rd., Houns. 86 BZ79
Worthington Clo., Mitch. 119 DH98
Worthington Rd., Surb. 116 CM102
Worthy Down Ct. SE18 95 EN80
Prince Imperial Rd.
Wortley Rd. E6 80 EK66
Wortley Rd., Croy. 119 DN101
Worton Gdns., Islw. 87 CD82
Worton Hall Est., Islw. 87 CE84
Worton Pk. Ind. Est., Islw. 87 CF83
Worton Rd., Islw. 87 CD84
Worton Way, Houns. 87 CD82
Worton Way, Islw. 87 CD82
Wotton Grn., Orp. 124 EX98
Wotton Rd. NW2 61 CW62
Wotton Rd. SE8 93 DZ79
Wotton Way, Sutt. 131 CW110
Wouldham Rd. E16 80 EF72
Wrabness Way, Stai. 112 BH95
Wragby Rd. E11 66 EE62
Wrampling Pl. N9 50 DU46
Wrangley Ct., Wal.Abb. 24 EG33
Wrangthorn Wk., Croy. 133 DN105
Epsom Rd.
Wray Ave., Ilf. 67 EN55
Wray Cres. N4 63 DL61
Wray Rd., Sutt. 131 CZ109
Wrayfield Rd., Sutt. 117 CX104
Wrays Way, Hayes 71 BS70
Balmoral Dr.
Wraysbury Clo., Houns. 100 BY85
Dorney Way
Wrekin Rd. SE18 95 EQ80
Wren Ave. NW2 61 CW64
Wren Ave., Sthl. 86 BZ77
Wren Clo. E16 80 EF72
Ibbotson Ave.
Wren Clo. N9 51 DX46
Chaffinch Clo.
Wren Clo., Orp. 124 EX97
Wren Clo., S.Croy. 135 DX109
Wren Cres., Add. 126 BK106
Wren Cres. (Bushey), Wat. 44 CC46
Wren Dr., Wal.Abb. 24 EG34
Wren Dr., West Dr. 84 BK76
Wren Gdns., Dag. 68 EX64
Wren Gdns., Horn. 69 FF60
Wren Landing E14 79 EA74
Cabot Sq.
Wren Path SE28 95 ER76
Wren Rd. SE5 92 DR81
Wren Rd., Dag. 68 EX64
Wren Rd., Sid. 110 EW91
Wren St. WC1 6 C4
Wren St. WC1 77 DM70
Wrens Ave., Ashf. 99 BQ91
Wrens Hill, Lthd. 142 CC115
Wrentham Ave. NW10 75 CX68
Wrenthorpe Rd., Brom. 108 EE91
Wrenwood Way, Pnr. 57 BV56
Wrestlers Ct. EC3 78 DS72
Camomile St.
Wrexham Rd. E3 79 EA68
Wricklemarsh Rd. SE3 94 EJ81
Wrigglesworth St. SE14 93 DX80
Wright Gdns., Shep. 112 BN99
Laleham Rd.
Wright Rd., Houns. 86 BW80
Wrights All. SW19 103 CW93
Wrights Clo. SE13 93 ED84
Wisteria Rd.
Wrights Clo., Dag. 69 FB63
Wrights Grn. SW4 91 DK84
Nelson's Row
Wrights La. W8 90 DB76
Wrights Pl. NW10 74 CQ65
Mitchell Way
Wrights Rd. E3 79 DZ68
Wrights Rd. SE25 120 DS97
Wrights Row, Wall. 133 DH105
Wrights Wk. SW14 88 CR83
North Worple Way
Wrigley Clo. E4 51 ED50
Writtle Wk., Rain. 83 FE67
Wrotham Pk., Barn. 33 CZ36
Wrotham Rd. NW1 77 DJ66
Agar Pl.
Wrotham Rd. W13 73 CH74
Mattock La.
Wrotham Rd., Barn. 33 CY40
Wrotham Rd., Well. 96 EW81
Wroths Path, Loug. 39 EM39
Wrottesley Rd. NW10 75 CU68
Wrottesley Rd. SE18 95 EQ79
Wroughton Rd. SW11 104 DF85
Wroughton Ter. NW4 61 CV56
Wroxall Rd., Dag. 82 EW65
Wroxham Gdns. N11 49 DJ52
Wroxham Gdns., Enf. 35 DN35
Wroxham Gdns., Pot.B. 19 CX31
Wroxham Rd. SE28 82 EX73
Wroxton Rd. SE15 92 DV82
Wrythe Grn., Cars. 118 DF104
Wrythe Grn. Rd., Cars. 118 DF104
Wrythe La., Cars. 118 DC101
Wulfstan St. W12 75 CT71
Wyatt Clo. SE16 93 DZ75
Wyatt Clo., Felt. 100 BX88
Wyatt Clo., Hayes 71 BU71
Wyatt Clo., Wat. 45 CE45
Wyatt Dr. SW13 89 CV79
Wyatt Pk. Rd. SW2 105 DL89
Wyatt Rd. E7 80 EG65
Wyatt Rd. N5 64 DQ62
Wyatt Rd., Dart. 97 FF83
Wyatt Rd., Stai. 98 BG92
Wyatts Clo., Rick. 28 BG41
Wyatts La. E17 65 EC55
Wybert St. NW1 77 DJ70
Stanhope St.
Wyborne Way NW10 74 CQ66
Wyburn Ave., Barn. 33 CZ40
Wych Elm Dr., Brom. 108 EF94
London La.
Wych Elm Pas., Kings.T. 116 CM95
Wych Elms, St.Alb. 16 CB28
Wyche Gro., S.Croy. 134 DR108
Wycherley Clo. SE3 94 EF80
Wycherley Cres., Barn. 34 DB44
Wychwood Ave., Edg. 45 CK51
Wychwood Ave., Th.Hth. 120 DQ97
Wychwood Clo., Edg. 45 CK51
Wychwood Clo., Sun. 99 BU93
Wychwood End N6 63 DJ59
Wychwood Gdns., Ilf. 67 EM56
Wychwood Way SE19 106 DR93
Roman Ri.
Wychwood Way, Nthwd. 43 BT52
Wyclif St. EC1 6 F3
Wycliffe Clo., Well. 95 ET81
Wycliffe Ct., Abb.L. 15 BS32
Wycliffe Rd. SW11 90 DG82
Wycliffe Rd. SW19 104 DB93
Wycombe Gdns. NW11 62 DA61
Wycombe Pl. SW18 104 DC86
Wycombe Rd. N17 50 DU53
Wycombe Rd., Ilf. 67 EM57
Wycombe Rd., Wem. 74 CN67
Wydehurst Rd., Croy. 120 DU101
Wydell Clo., Mord. 117 CX100
Wydeville Manor Rd. SE12 108 EH91
Wye Clo., Ashf. 99 BP91
Wye Clo., Orp. 123 ET101
Wye Clo., Ruis. 57 BQ58
Wye St. SW11 90 DD82
Wyedale, St.Alb. 18 CM27
Wyemead Cres. E4 52 EE47
Wyeth's Ms., Epsom 131 CT113
Wyeths Rd., Epsom 131 CT113
Wyevale Clo., Pnr. 57 BU55
Wyfields, Ilf. 53 EP53
Ravensbourne Gdns.
Wyfold Rd. SW6 89 CY81
Wyhill Wk., Dag. 83 FC65
Wyke Clo., Islw. 87 CF79
Wyke Gdns. W7 87 CF76
Wyke Rd. E3 79 EA66
Wyke Rd. SW20 117 CW96
Wykeham Ave., Dag. 82 EW65
Wykeham Clo., West Dr. 84 BN78
Wykeham Grn., Dag. 82 EW65
Wykeham Hill, Wem. 60 CM60
Wykeham Ri. N20 47 CY46
Wykeham Rd. NW4 61 CW57
Wykeham Rd., Har. 59 CH56
Wylchin Clo., Pnr. 57 BT56
Wyld Way, Wem. 74 CP65
Wyldes Clo. NW11 62 DC60
Wildwood Rd.
Wyldfield Gdns. N9 50 DT47
Wyleu St. SE23 107 DY87
Wylie Rd., Sthl. 86 CA76
Wyllen Clo. E1 78 DW70
Wyllyotts Clo., Pot.B. 19 CZ32
Wyllyotts La., Pot.B. 19 CZ32
Wyllyotts Pl., Pot.B. 19 CZ32
Wylo Dr., Barn. 33 CU44
Wymering Rd. W9 76 DA69
Wymond St. SW15 89 CW83
Wynan Rd. E14 93 EB78
Wynash Gdns., Cars. 132 DE106
Wynaud Ct. N22 49 DM51
Palmerston Rd.
Wyncham Ave., Sid. 109 ES88
Wynchgate N14 49 DK46
Wynchgate N21 49 DL45
Wynchgate, Har. 45 CE52
Wyncote Way, S.Croy. 135 DX109
Wyncroft Clo., Brom. 123 EM97
Wyndale Ave. NW9 60 CN58
Wyndcliff Rd. SE7 94 EH79
Wyndcroft Clo., Enf. 35 DP41
Wyndham Ave., Cob. 127 BU113
Wyndham Clo., Orp. 123 EQ102
Wyndham Clo., Sutt. 132 DA108
Wyndham Cres. N19 63 DJ62
Wyndham Cres., Houns. 100 CA86
Wyndham Est. SE5 92 DQ80
Wyndham Ms. W1 4 D7
Wyndham Pl. W1 4 D7
Wyndham Pl. W1 76 DF71
Wyndham Rd. E6 80 EK66
Wyndham Rd. SE5 92 DQ80
Wyndham Rd. W13 87 CH76
Wyndham Rd., Barn. 48 DF46
Wyndham Rd., Kings.T. 102 CM94
Wyndham St. W1 4 D6
Wyndham St. W1 76 DF71
Wyndham Yd. W1 4 D7
Wyneham Rd. SE24 106 DR85
Wynell Rd. SE23 107 DX90
Wynford Gro., Orp. 124 EV97
Wynford Pl., Belv. 96 FA79
Wynford Rd. N1 77 DM68
Wynford Way SE9 109 EM90
Wynlie Gdns., Pnr. 43 BV54
Wynndale Rd. E18 52 EH53
Wynne Rd. SW9 91 DN82
Wynns Ave., Sid. 110 EU85
Wynnstay Gdns. W8 90 DA76
Wynter St. SW11 90 DC84
Wynton Gdns. SE25 120 DS99
Wynton Gro., Walt. 113 BU104
Wynton Pl. W3 74 CP72
Wynyard Clo., Rick. 28 BG36
Wynyard Ter. SE11 10 C10
Wynyard Ter. SE11 91 DM78
Wynyatt St. EC1 6 F3
Wyre Gro., Edg. 46 CP48
Wyre Gro., Hayes 85 BU77
Wyresdale Cres., Grnf. 73 CF69
Wyteleaf Clo., Ruis. 57 BQ58
Wythburn Pl. W1 4 D9
Wythens Wk. SE9 109 EP86
Wythenshawe Rd., Dag. 68 FA62
Wythes Clo., Brom. 123 EM96
Wythes Rd. E16 80 EL74
Wythfield Rd. SE9 109 EM86
Wyvenhoe Rd., Har. 58 CC62
Wyvern Clo., Orp. 124 EV104
Wyvern Gro., Hayes 85 BP80
Wyvern Rd., Pur. 133 DP110
Wyvern Way, Uxb. 70 BH66
Wyvil Est. SW8 91 DL80
Luscombe Way
Wyvil Rd. SW8 91 DL79
Wyvis St. E14 79 EB71

Y

Yabsley St. E14 79 EC74
Yaffle Rd., Wey. 127 BQ110
Yalding Clo., Orp. 124 EX98
Yalding Rd. SE16 92 DU76
Yale Clo., Houns. 100 BZ85
Bramley Way
Yale Way, Horn. 69 FG63
Yarborough Rd. SW19 118 DD95
Runnymede
Yardbridge Clo., Sutt. 132 DB110
Yardley Clo. E4 37 EB43
Yardley La. E4 37 EB43
Yardley St. WC1 6 D3
Yardley St. WC1 77 DN69
Yarm Clo., Lthd. 143 CJ123
Yarm Ct. Rd., Lthd. 143 CJ123
Yarm Way, Lthd. 143 CJ123
Yarmouth Cres. N17 64 DV57
Yarmouth Pl. W1 9 H3
Yarmouth Rd., Wat. 30 BW38
Yarnfield Sq. SE15 92 DU81
Clayton Rd.
Yarnton Way SE2 96 EX75
Yarnton Way, Erith 96 EX75
Yarrow Cres. E6 80 EL71
Yateley St. SE18 94 EK76
Yates Ct. NW2 75 CX65
Yeading Ave., Har. 58 BY61
Yeading Fork, Hayes 72 BW71
Yeading Gdns., Hayes 71 BV71
Yeading La., Hayes 71 BV72
Yeading La., Nthlt. 72 BW69
Yeames Clo. W13 73 CG72
Yeate St. N1 78 DR66
Yeatman Rd. N6 62 DF58
Yeats Clo. NW10 74 CS65
Yeats Clo. SE13 93 ED82
Eliot Pk.
Yeldham Rd. W6 89 CX78
Yellow Hammer Ct. NW9 46 CS54
Eagle Dr.
Yellowpine Way, Chig. 54 EV49
Yelverton Rd. SW11 90 DD82
Yenston Clo., Mord. 118 DA100
Yeo St. E3 79 EB71
Yeoman Clo. E6 81 EP72
Ferndale St.
Yeoman Clo. SE27 105 DP90
Yeoman Rd., Nthlt. 72 BY66
Yeoman St. SE8 93 DY77
Yeomanry Clo., Epsom 131 CT112
Dirdene Gdns.
Yeomans Acre, Ruis. 57 BU58
Yeomans Meadow, Sev. 154 FG126
Yeoman's Ms., Islw. 101 CE85
Queensbridge Pk.
Yeoman's Row SW3 8 C7
Yeoman's Row SW3 90 DE76
Yeomans Way, Enf. 36 DW40
Yeomans Yd. E1 78 DT73
Chamber St.
Yeomen Way, Ilf. 53 EQ51
Yeovil Clo., Orp. 123 ES103
Yeovilton Pl., Kings.T. 101 CK92
Yerbury Rd. N19 63 DK62
Yester Dr., Chis. 108 EL94
Yester Pk., Chis. 109 EM94
Yester Rd., Chis. 108 EL94
Yew Ave., West Dr. 70 BL73
Yew Clo., Buck.H. 52 EK47
Yew Clo., Wal.Cr. 22 DS27
Yew Gro. NW2 61 CX63
Yew Pl., Wey. 113 BT104
Yew Tree Bottom Rd., Epsom 145 CV116
Yew Tree Clo. N21 49 DN45
Yew Tree Clo., Couls. 146 DF119
Yew Tree Clo., Sev. 154 FD123
Yew Tree Clo., Well. 96 EU81
Yew Tree Clo., Wor.Pk. 116 CS102
Yew Tree Ct., Borwd. 31 CK44
Barnet La.
Yew Tree Gdns., Rom. 69 FD57
Yew Tree Gdns. (Chadwell Heath), Rom. 68 EY57
Yew Tree Rd. W12 75 CT73
Yew Tree Rd., Uxb. 70 BM67
Yew Tree Wk., Houns. 100 BZ85
Yew Tree Wk., Pur. 134 DQ110
Yew Tree Way, Croy. 135 DY110
Yew Trees, Shep. 112 BM98
Laleham Rd.
Yew Wk., Har. 59 CE60
Yewbank Clo., Ken. 148 DR115
Yewdale Clo., Brom. 108 EE93
Yewfield Rd. NW10 75 CT65
Yewlands Clo., Bans. 146 DB115
Yews, The, Ashf. 99 BP91
Yews Ave., Enf. 36 DV36
Yewtree Clo. N22 49 DJ53
Yewtree Clo., Har. 58 CB56
Southfield Pk.
Yewtree End, St.Alb. 16 CB27
Yewtree Gdns., Epsom 144 CP115
Yewtree Rd., Beck. 121 DZ97
Yoakley Rd. N16 64 DS61
Yoke Clo. N7 77 DL65
Ewe Clo.
Yolande Gdns. SE9 108 EL85
Yonge Pk. N4 63 DN62
York Ave. SW14 102 CQ85
York Ave. W7 73 CE74
York Ave., Hayes 71 BQ71
York Ave., Sid. 109 ES89
York Ave., Stan. 45 CH53
York Bri. NW1 4 F4
York Bri. NW1 76 DG70
York Bldgs. WC2 10 A1
York Clo. E6 81 EM72
Boultwood Rd.
York Clo. W7 73 CE74
York Ave.
York Clo., Kings L. 14 BN29
York Clo., Mord. 118 DB98
York Clo., W.Byf. 126 BL112
York Cres., Borwd. 32 CR40
York Cres., Loug. 38 EL41
York Gdns., Walt. 114 BX103
York Gate N14 49 DL45
York Gate NW1 4 F5
York Gate NW1 76 DG70
York Gate, Cat. 148 DR122
York Gro. SE15 92 DW81
York Hill SE27 105 DP90
York Hill, Loug. 38 EL41
York Hill Est. SE27 105 DP90
York Ho., Wem. 60 CM63
York Ho. Pl. W8 90 DB75
York Ms. NW5 63 DH64
Kentish Town Rd.
York Ms., Ilf. 67 EN62
York Rd.
York Par., Brent. 87 CK78
York Pl. SW11 90 DC83
York Pl. WC2 10 A1
York Pl., Dag. 83 FC65
York Pl., Ilf. 67 EN61
York Rd.
York Ri. NW5 63 DH62
York Ri., Orp. 123 ES102
York Rd. E4 51 EA50
York Rd. E7 80 EG65
York Rd. E10 65 EC62
York Rd. E17 65 DX57
York Rd. N11 49 DK51
York Rd. N18 50 DV51
York Rd. N21 50 DR45
York Rd. SE1 10 C4
York Rd. SE1 91 DM75
York Rd. SW11 90 DC84
York Rd. SW18 90 DC84
York Rd. SW19 104 DC93
York Rd. W3 74 CQ72
York Rd. W5 87 CJ76
York Rd., Barn. 34 DC43
York Rd., Brent. 87 CK78
York Rd., Croy. 119 DN101
York Rd., Epp. 26 FA27
York Rd., Houns. 86 CB83
York Rd., Ilf. 67 EN62
York Rd., Kings.T. 102 CM94
York Rd., Nthwd. 43 BU54
York Rd., Rain. 83 FD66
York Rd., Rich. 102 CM85
Albert Rd.
York Rd., S.Croy. 135 DX110
York Rd., Sutt. 132 DA107
York Rd., Tedd. 101 CE91
York Rd., Uxb. 70 BK66
York Rd., Wal.Cr. 23 DY34
York Rd., Wat. 30 BW43
York Rd., W.Byf. 126 BK112
York Rd., West. 150 EH119
York Rd., Wey. 127 BQ105
York Sq. E14 79 DY72
York St. W1 4 D7
York St. W1 76 DF71
York St., Bark. 81 EQ67
Abbey Rd.
York St., Mitch. 118 DG101
York St., Twick. 101 CG88
York Ter., Enf. 36 DQ38
York Ter., Erith 97 FC81
York Ter. E. NW1 4 G5
York Ter. E. NW1 76 DG70
York Ter. W. NW1 4 F5
York Ter. W. NW1 76 DG70
York Way N1 77 DL67
York Way N7 77 DK65
York Way N20 48 DF48
York Way, Borwd. 32 CR40
York Way, Chess. 130 CL108
York Way, Felt. 100 BZ90
York Way, Wat. 30 BX36
York Way Ct. N1 77 DL67
York Way Est. N7 77 DL65
York Way
Yorke Rd., Rick. 28 BN44
Yorkland Ave., Well. 95 ET83
Yorkshire Clo. N16 64 DS62
Yorkshire Gdns. N18 50 DV50
Yorkshire Grey Pl. NW3 62 DC63
Heath St.
Yorkshire Grey Yd. WC1 6 B7
Yorkshire Rd. E14 79 DY72
Yorkshire Rd., Mitch. 119 DL99
Yorkton St. E2 78 DU68
Young Rd. E16 80 EJ72
Young St. W8 90 DB75
Youngmans Clo., Enf. 36 DQ39
Young's Bldgs. EC1 7 J4
Youngs Rd., Ilf. 67 ER57
Yoxley App., Ilf. 67 EQ58
Yoxley Dr., Ilf. 67 EQ58
Yukon Rd. SW12 105 DH87
Yule Clo., St.Alb. 16 BZ30
Yuletide Clo. NW10 74 CS66
Yunus Khan Clo. E17 65 EA57

Z

Zampa Rd. SE16 92 DW78
Zander Ct. E2 78 DU68
St. Peter's Clo.
Zangwill Rd. SE3 94 EK81
Zealand Ave., West Dr. 84 BK80
Zealand Rd. E3 79 DY68
Zelah Rd., Orp. 124 EV101
Zennor Rd. SW12 105 DJ88
Zenoria St. SE22 92 DT84
Zermatt Rd., Th.Hth. 120 DQ98
Zetland St. E14 79 EB71
Zig-Zag Rd., Ken. 148 DQ116
Zion Pl., Th.Hth. 120 DR98
Zion Rd., Th.Hth. 120 DR98
Zion St., Sev. 155 FM121
Church Rd.
Zoar St. SE1 11 H2
Zoffany St. N19 63 DK61

INDEX TO PLACE NAMES

The following is a comprehensive listing of all named places which appear in this atlas. Bold references can be found within the Central London enlarged scale section (pages 4-11). Postal information is in either London postal district or non-London post town form. For an explanation of post town abbreviations please consult page 170.

Place	Page	Grid
Abbey Wood SE2	96	EV76
Abbots Langley, Abb.L.	15	BR31
Abridge, Rom.	40	EV41
Acton W3	74	CN74
Addington, Croy.	135	DZ106
Addiscombe, Croy.	120	DT102
Addlestone, Add.	126	BJ106
Addlestone Moor, Add.	112	BG103
Aldborough Hatch, Ilf.	67	ES55
Aldenham, Wat.	30	CB37
Aldersbrook E12	66	EH61
Alperton, Wem.	74	CL67
Anerley SE20	120	DV96
Aperfield, West.	151	EM117
Arkley, Barn.	33	CU43
Ashford, Ashf.	98	BM92
Ashley Park, Walt.	113	BU104
Ashstead, Ash.	144	CL118
Ashtead Park, Ash.	144	CN118
Avery Hill SE9	109	EQ86
Badgers Mount, Sev.	139	FB110
Balham SW12	104	DF88
Banstead, Bans.	118	DB96
Barbican EC2	**7**	**J7**
Barking, Bark.	81	EP67
Barkingside, Ilf.	67	EP55
Barnehurst, Bexh.	97	FD83
Barnes SW13	89	CU82
Barnes Cray, Dart.	97	FH84
Barnet, Barn.	33	CZ41
Barnet Gate, Barn.	33	CT44
Barnsbury N1	77	DN65
Batchworth, Rick.	42	BM47
Battersea SW11	90	DG82
Bayswater W2	76	DB72
Beacontree, Dag.	68	EX62
Beacontree Heath, Dag.	68	FA60
Beckenham, Beck.	121	EB95
Beckton E6	81	EN71
Beddington, Wall.	119	DK103
Beddington Corner, Mitch.	118	DG101
Bedford Park W4	88	CR76
Bedmond, Abb.L.	15	BS27
Belgravia SW1	**8**	**G8**
Bell Common, Epp.	25	ER32
Bell Green SE6	107	DZ90
Bellingham SE6	107	EA90
Belmont, Har.	45	CG54
Belmont, Sutt.	132	DB111
Belsize Park NW3	76	DE65
Belvedere, Belv.	97	FB77
Benhilton, Sutt.	118	DB103
Bentley Heath, Barn.	33	CZ35
Bermondsey SE1	**11**	**P6**
Berrylands, Surb.	116	CM100
Berry's Green, West.	151	EP116
Bessels Green, Sev.	154	FC124
Bethnal Green E2	78	DU68
Bexley, Bex.	110	FA86
Bexleyheath, Bexh.	110	EZ85
Bickley, Brom.	123	EM97
Biggin Hill, West.	150	EH116
Blackfen, Sid.	109	ET87
Blackheath SE3	94	EE81
Blackheath Park SE3	94	EG84
Bloomsbury WC1	**5**	**P6**
Borehamwood, Borwd.	32	CP41
Borough, The SE1	**11**	**H5**
Botany Bay, Enf.	35	DJ36
Bow E3	79	DZ68
Bower Hill, Epp.	26	EU31
Bowes Park N22	49	DL51
Brasted, West.	152	EW124
Brentford, Brent.	87	CJ79
Bricket Wood, St.Alb.	16	BZ29
Brimsdown, Enf.	37	DY41
Brixton SW2	91	DL84
Broad Green, Croy.	119	DN100
Broadgate EC2	**7**	**L6**
Brockley SE4	107	DY85
Bromley E3	79	EB70
Bromley, Brom.	122	EF96
Bromley Common, Brom.	123	EM101
Bromley Park, Brom.	122	EE95
Brompton SW3	**8**	**B7**
Brondesbury NW2	75	CX65
Brondesbury Park NW6	75	CX66
Brooklands, Wey.	126	BM109
Brookmans Park, Hat.	19	CY26
Brunswick Park N11	48	DF47
Buckhurst Hill, Buck.H.	52	EH45
Bucks Hill, Kings L.	14	BK34
Bulls Cross, Wal.Cr.	36	DT35
Bullsmoor, Enf.	36	DV37
Burgh Heath, Tad.	145	CX119
Burnt Oak, Edg.	46	CQ52
Burwood Park, Walt.	127	BT106
Bury Green, Wal.Cr.	22	DV31
Bush Hill Park, Enf.	36	DS43
Bushey, Wat.	30	CA44
Bushey Heath, Wat.	45	CE46
Bushey Mead SW20	117	CX97
Byfleet, W.Byf.	126	BM113
Camberwell SE5	92	DQ80
Camden Town NW1	77	DJ67
Canning Town E16	80	EG72
Canons Park, Edg.	46	CL52
Carpenders Park, Wat.	44	BZ47
Carshalton, Cars.	132	DE106
Carshalton Beeches, Cars.	132	DD109
Carshalton on the Hill, Cars.	132	DG108
Castelnau SW13	89	CU79
Caterham, Cat.	148	DU123
Caterham-on-the-Hill, Cat.	148	DT122
Catford SE6	107	EB88
Cattlegate, Enf.	21	DL33
Chadwell Heath, Rom.	68	EX58
Chaldon, Cat.	147	DN124
Charlton SE7	94	EJ79
Chase Cross, Rom.	55	FE51
Cheam, Sutt.	131	CX107
Chelsea SW3	90	DD79
Chelsfield, Orp.	138	EW106
Chelsham, Warl.	149	EA117
Chertsey, Cher.	112	BG102
Cheshunt, Wal.Cr.	23	DX31
Chessington, Chess.	130	CL107
Chigwell, Chig.	53	EP48
Chigwell Row, Chig.	54	EU47
Childs Hill NW2	62	DA61
Chingford E4	51	EB46
Chingford Green E4	52	EF46
Chingford Hatch E4	51	ED49
Chipperfield, Kings L.	14	BG31
Chipping Barnet, Barn.	33	CY42
Chipstead, Couls.	146	DG119
Chipstead, Sev.	154	FC122
Chipstead Bottom, Couls.	146	DE121
Chislehurst, Chis.	109	EN94
Chislehurst West, Chis.	109	EN92
Chiswell Green, St.Alb.	16	BZ26
Chiswick W4	88	CR79
Church End N3	47	CZ53
Church End NW10	74	CS65
Clapham SW4	91	DH83
Clapham Park SW4	105	DJ86
Clapton Park E5	65	DY63
Claremont Park, Esher	128	CA108
Clay Hill, Enf.	36	DQ37
Claygate, Esher	129	CE108
Clayhall, Ilf.	53	EM54
Clerkenwell EC1	**6**	**F5**
Cobham, Cob.	141	BV115
Cockfosters, Barn.	34	DE42
Coldblow, Bex.	111	FC89
Collier Row, Rom.	54	FA53
Collier's Wood SW19	104	DD94
Colney Street, St.Alb.	17	CE30
Commonwood, Kings L.	14	BH34
Coombe, Kings.T.	102	CQ94
Coopersale, Epp.	26	EX29
Copse Hill SW20	103	CU94
Copthall Green, Wal.Abb.	24	EK33
Cottenham Park SW20	117	CU95
Coulsdon, Couls.	147	DJ116
Cowley, Uxb.	70	BJ70
Cranbrook, Ilf.	67	EM60
Cranford, Houns.	85	BU80
Crayford, Dart.	111	FD85
Creekmouth, Bark.	81	ET70
Crews Hills, Enf.	35	DP35
Cricklewood NW2	61	CX62
Crockenhill, Swan.	125	FD101
Crouch End N8	63	DJ58
Croxley Green, Rick.	28	BN43
Croydon, Croy.	120	DR103
Cubitt Town E14	93	EC76
Cudham, Sev.	151	ER115
Cuffley, Pot.B.	21	DM28
Custom House E16	80	EK72
Cyprus E6	81	EN73
Dagenham, Dag.	82	FA65
Dalston E8	78	DS66
Dancers Hill, Barn.	33	CW36
Dartmouth Park NW5	63	DH62
Dartnell Park, W.Byf.	126	BJ112
Debden, Loug.	39	ER41
Debden Green, Loug.	39	EQ38
Denham, Uxb.	56	BG62
Deptford SE8	93	DZ78
Derry Downs, Orp.	124	EX100
Dollis Hill NW2	61	CV62

Dormer's Wells, Sthl.	72	CB73
Downe, Orp.	137	EM111
Downham, Brom.	108	EF91
Downside, Cob.	141	BV118
Ducks Island, Barn.	33	CX44
Dulwich SE21	106	DS87
Dunton Green, Sev.	153	FC119
Ealing W5	73	CJ73
Earls Court SW5	89	CZ78
Earlsfield SW18	104	DC88
East Acton W3	74	CS73
East Barnet, Barn.	34	DE44
East Bedfont, Felt.	99	BS88
East Dulwich SE22	106	DU86
East Ewell, Sutt.	131	CX110
East Finchley N2	62	DD56
East Ham E6	80	EL68
East Molesey, E.Mol.	115	CD97
East Sheen SW14	88	CR84
East Wickham, Well.	96	EU80
Eastbury, Nthwd.	43	BS49
Eastcote, Pnr.	58	BW58
Eastcote Village, Pnr.	57	BV57
Eden Park, Beck.	121	EA99
Edgware, Edg.	46	CP50
Edmonton N9	50	DU49
Elm Corner, Wok.	140	BN119
Elm Park, Horn.	69	FH64
Elmers End, Beck.	121	DX97
Elmstead, Chis.	108	EK92
Elstree, Borwd.	31	CK44
Eltham SE9	108	EK86
Enfield, Enf.	36	DT41
Enfield Highway, Enf.	36	DW40
Enfield Lock, Enf.	37	DZ37
Enfield Town, Enf.	36	DR40
Enfield Wash, Enf.	37	DX38
Epping, Epp.	25	ET32
Epsom, Epsom	130	CQ114
Erith, Erith	97	FD79
Esher, Esher	128	CC105
Ewell, Epsom	131	CU110
Fairmile, Cob.	128	BZ112
Falconwood, Well.	95	ER83
Farleigh, Warl.	135	DZ114
Farnborough, Orp.	137	EP106
Feltham, Felt.	99	BU89
Felthamhill, Felt.	99	BT92
Fetcham, Lthd.	143	CD123
Fiddlers Hamlet, Epp.	26	EW32
Finchley N3	48	DB53
Finsbury EC1	**6**	**E2**
Finsbury Park N4	63	DN60
Flamstead End, Wal.Cr.	22	DU28
Foots Cray, Sid.	110	EV93
Forest Gate E7	66	EG64
Forest Hill SE23	107	DX88
Forestdale, Croy.	135	DZ109
Forty Hill, Enf.	36	DS37
Freezy Water, Wal.Cr.	37	DY35
Friday Hill E4	51	ED47
Friern Barnet N11	48	DE49
Frogmore, St.Alb.	17	CE28
Fulham SW6	89	CX81
Fullwell Cross, Ilf.	53	ER53
Furzedown SW17	104	DG92
Gants Hill, Ilf.	67	EN57
Ganwick Corner, Barn.	34	DB35
Garston, Wat.	30	BW35
Gidea Park, Rom.	69	FG55
Goathurst Common, Sev.	154	FB130
Godden Green, Sev.	155	FN125
Goddington, Orp.	124	EW104
Goffs Oak, Wal.Cr.	22	DQ29
Golders Green NW11	62	DA59
Goodmayes, Ilf.	68	EV61
Gospel Oak NW5	62	DG63
Grange Hill, Chig.	53	ER51
Grange Park N21	35	DP43
Green Street, Borwd.	32	CP37
Green Street Green, Orp.	137	ES107
Greenford, Grnf.	72	CB69
Greensted Green, Ong.	27	FH28
Greenwich SE10	93	ED79
Grove Park SE12	108	EG89
Grove Park W4	88	CQ80
Gunnersbury W4	88	CP77
Hackbridge, Wall.	119	DH103
Hackney E8	78	DV65
Hackney Wick E9	65	DZ64
Hadley, Barn.	33	CZ40
Hadley Wood, Barn.	34	DD38
Haggerston E2	78	DT68
Hainault, Ilf.	53	ET52
Hale End E4	51	ED51
Halstead, Sev.	138	EZ113
Ham, Rich.	101	CJ90
Hammersmith W6	89	CW78
Hammond Street, Wal.Cr.	22	DR26
Hampstead NW3	62	DD63
Hampstead Garden Suburb N2	62	DC57
Hampton, Hmptn.	114	CB95
Hampton Hill, Hmptn.	101	CD93
Hampton Wick, Kings.T.	115	CH95
Hamsey Green, Warl.	148	DW116
Hanwell W7	73	CF74
Hanworth, Felt.	100	BX91
Harefield, Uxb.	42	BL53
Harlesden NW10	74	CS68
Harlington, Hayes	85	BQ79
Harmondsworth, West Dr.	84	BK79
Harringay N8	63	DN57
Harrow, Har.	59	CD59
Harrow on the Hill, Har.	59	CE60
Harrow Weald, Har.	45	CE53
Hatch End, Pnr.	44	BY52
Hatton, Felt.	85	BT84
Havering Park, Rom.	54	FA50
Havering-atte-Bower, Rom.	55	FE48
Hayes, Brom.	122	EH101
Hayes, Hayes	71	BS72
Hayes End, Hayes	71	BQ71
Hayes Town, Hayes	85	BS75
Headstone, Har.	58	CC56
Hendon NW4	61	CV56
Herne Hill SE24	106	DQ85
Hersham, Walt.	128	BX107
Heston, Houns.	86	BZ80
Hextable, Swan.	111	FG94
High Barnet, Barn.	33	CX40
High Beach, Loug.	38	EG39
Higham Hill E17	51	DY54
Highams Park E4	51	ED50
Highbury N5	63	DP64
Highgate N6	63	DH59
Highwood Hill NW7	47	CU47
Hill End, Uxb.	42	BJ51
Hillingdon, Uxb.	70	BM69
Hinchley Wood, Esher	115	CF104
Hither Green SE13	108	EE86
Holborn WC2	**6**	**B8**
Holdbrook, Wal.Cr.	23	EA34
Holders Hill NW4	47	CX54
Holloway N7	63	DL63
Holyfield, Wal.Abb.	23	ED28
Holywell, Wat.	29	BS44
Homerton E9	65	DY64
Honor Oak SE23	106	DW86
Honor Oak Park SE4	107	DZ86
Hook Green, Dart.	111	FG91
Hooley, Couls.	146	DG122
Horns Green, Sev.	151	ES117
Hornsey N8	63	DM55
Horton, Epsom	130	CP110
Hounslow, Houns.	86	BZ84
Hounslow West, Houns.	86	BX83
How Wood, St.Alb.	16	CB27
Hoxton N1	**7**	**M1**
Hulberry, Swan.	125	FG103
Hunton Bridge, Kings L.	15	BP33
Hyde, The NW9	61	CT57
Ickenham, Uxb.	57	BQ62
Ilford, Ilf.	67	EQ62
Isleworth, Islw.	87	CF83
Islington N1	77	DN67
Ivy Chimneys, Epp.	25	ES32
Joydens Wood, Bex.	111	FC92
Kenley, Ken.	148	DQ116
Kennington SE11	91	DN79
Kensal Green NW10	75	CW69
Kensal Rise NW6	75	CX68
Kensal Town W10	75	CX70
Kensington W8	75	CZ74
Kentish Town NW5	77	DJ65
Kenton, Har.	59	CH57
Keston, Brom.	136	EH106
Kew, Rich.	88	CN79
Kidbrooke SE3	94	EJ82
Kilburn NW6	75	CZ68
King's Cross N1	77	DK67
Kings Langley, Kings L.	14	BM30
Kingsbury NW9	60	CP58
Kingston upon Thames, Kings.T.	116	CL96
Kingston Vale SW15	102	CS91
Kingswood, Tad.	145	CZ123
Kingswood, Wat.	15	BV34
Kippington, Sev.	154	FG126
Kitt's End, Barn.	33	CY37
Knockholt, Sev.	152	EU116
Knockholt Pound, Sev.	152	EY116
Ladywell SE13	107	EA85
Laleham, Stai.	112	BJ97
Lambeth SE1	**10**	**C6**
Lambourne End, Rom.	40	EX44
Lamorbey, Sid.	109	ET88
Lampton, Houns.	86	CB81
Langley Vale, Epsom	144	CR119
Lea Bridge E5	65	DX62
Leatherhead, Lthd.	143	CF121
Leatherhead Common, Lthd.	143	CF119
Leavesden Green, Wat.	15	BT34
Lee SE12	108	EF86
Lessness Heath, Belv.	97	FB78
Letchmore Heath, Wat.	31	CD38
Lewisham SE13	93	EB83

Leyton E11	65	EB60
Leytonstone E11	65	ED59
Limehouse E14	79	DY73
Lisson Grove NW8	**4**	**A4**
Little Ealing W5	87	CJ77
Little Ilford E12	66	EL64
Little Woodcote, Cars.	132	DG112
Littleton, Shep.	113	BP97
London Colney, St.Alb.	17	CJ27
Long Ditton, Surb.	115	CJ102
Longford, Sev.	153	FD120
Longford, West Dr.	84	BH81
Longlands, Chis.	109	EQ90
Loudwater, Rick.	28	BK41
Loughton, Loug.	39	EM43
Lower Ashstead, Ash.	143	CJ119
Lower Clapton E5	64	DW63
Lower Edmonton N9	50	DT46
Lower Feltham, Felt.	99	BS90
Lower Green, Esher	114	CA103
Lower Holloway N7	63	DM64
Lower Sydenham SE26	107	DX91
Loxford, Ilf.	67	EQ64
Maida Hill W9	75	CZ70
Maida Vale W9	76	DB70
Malden Rushett, Chess.	129	CH111
Manor Park E12	66	EL63
Mark's Gate, Rom.	54	EY54
Martyr's Green, Wok.	141	BR120
Marylebone NW1	**4**	**D8**
Mayfair W1	**9**	**H1**
Maypole, Orp.	138	EZ107
Merry Hill, Wat.	44	CB46
Merton SW19	118	DA95
Merton Park SW19	118	DA96
Mile End E1	79	DY69
Mill Hill NW7	47	CU50
Millwall E14	93	EB76
Mitcham, Mitch.	118	DG97
Moneyhill, Rick.	42	BH46
Monken Hadley, Barn.	33	CZ39
Monks Orchard, Croy.	121	DZ101
Moor Park, Nthwd.	43	BQ49
Morden, Mord.	118	DA97
Morden Park, Mord.	117	CY100
Mortlake SW14	88	CQ83
Motspur Park, N.Mal.	117	CU100
Mottingham SE9	108	EJ89
Mount End, Epp.	26	EZ32
Muswell Hill N10	63	DH55
Nazeing Gate, Wal.Abb.	24	EJ25
Neasden NW2	60	CS62
New Addington, Croy.	135	EC109
New Barnet, Barn.	34	DB42
New Beckenham, Beck.	107	DZ93
New Charlton SE7	94	EJ77
New Cross SE14	93	DY81
New Cross Gate SE14	93	DX81
New Eltham SE9	109	EN89
New Haw, Add.	126	BK108
New Malden, N.Mal.	116	CR97
New Southgate N11	49	DK49
Newbury Park, Ilf.	67	ER57
Newington SE1	**11**	**H8**
Newyears Green, Uxb.	56	BM59
Nine Elms SW8	91	DJ80
Noel Park N22	49	DN54
Norbiton, Kings.T.	116	CP96
Norbury SW16	119	DM95
Nork, Bans.	145	CX115
North Acton W3	74	CR70
North Beckton E6	80	EL70
North Cheam, Sutt.	117	CX104
North Cray, Sid.	110	EZ90
North Finchley N12	48	DD50
North Harrow, Har.	58	CA58
North Hillingdon, Uxb.	71	BQ65
North Hyde, Sthl.	86	BY77
North Kensington W10	75	CW72
North Looe, Epsom	131	CW113
North Sheen, Rich.	88	CN82
North Watford, Wat.	29	BV37
North Weald Bassett, Epp.	27	FB27
North Wembley, Wem.	59	CH61
North Woolwich E16	94	EL75
Northaw, Pot.B.	20	DF30
Northolt, Nthlt.	72	BY66
Northumberland Heath, Erith	97	FC80
Northwood, Nthwd.	43	BR51
Northwood Hills, Nthwd.	43	BT54
Norwood Green, Sthl.	86	CA77
Norwood New Town SE19	106	DQ93
Notting Hill W11	75	CY72
Nunhead SE15	92	DW83
Nuper's Hatch, Rom.	55	FD45
Oakleigh Park N20	48	DD46
Oakwood N14	35	DK44
Oatlands Park, Wey.	127	BR105
Ockham, Wok.	140	BN121
Old Bexley, Bex.	111	FB87
Old Coulsdon, Couls.	147	DN119
Old Ford E3	79	DZ67
Old Malden, Wor.Pk.	116	CR102
Old Oak Common NW10	74	CS71
Orpington, Orp.	123	ET102
Osidge N14	49	DH46
Osterley, Islw.	87	CD80
Otford, Sev.	153	FG116
Oxhey, Wat.	30	BW44
Oxshott, Lthd.	129	CD114
Pachesham Park, Lthd.	143	CG116
Paddington W2	76	DB71
Palmers Green N13	49	DN48
Park Langley, Beck.	121	EC99
Park Royal NW10	74	CN68
Park Street, St.Alb.	17	CD26
Parsons Green SW6	89	CZ81
Patchetts Green, Wat.	30	CC39
Peckham SE15	92	DT80
Penge SE20	106	DW94
Pentonville N1	**6**	**D1**
Perivale, Grnf.	73	CJ67
Petersham, Rich.	102	CL88
Petts Wood, Orp.	123	ER99
Pimlico SW1	**9**	**K10**
Pinner, Pnr.	58	BY56
Pinner Green, Pnr.	44	BW54
Pinnerwood Park, Pnr.	44	BW53
Plaistow E13	80	EF69
Plaistow, Brom.	108	EF93
Plumstead SE18	95	ES78
Ponders End, Enf.	37	DX43
Poplar E14	79	EB73
Potters Bar, Pot.B.	20	DA32
Potters Crouch, St.Alb.	16	BW25
Poverest, Orp.	123	ET99
Pratt's Bottom, Orp.	138	EV110
Preston, Wem.	59	CK60
Primrose Hill NW8	76	DF67
Purley, Pur.	133	DM111
Putney SW15	103	CW85
Putney Heath SW15	103	CW86
Putney Vale SW15	103	CT90
Pyrford Green, Wok.	140	BH117
Pyrford Village, Wok.	140	BG118
Queensbury, Har.	59	CK55
Radlett, Rad.	31	CH35
Rainham, Rain.	83	FG69
Ramsden, Orp.	124	EW102
Rayners Lane, Har.	58	BZ60
Raynes Park SW20	117	CV97
Redbridge, Ilf.	67	EM58
Regent's Park NW1	**5**	**H1**
Richmond, Rich.	102	CL86
Rickmansworth, Rick.	42	BL45
Ridge, Pot.B.	18	CS34
Ripley, Wok.	140	BJ122
Riverhead, Sev.	154	FD122
Roehampton SW15	103	CU85
Romford, Rom.	69	FF57
Rosehill, Sutt.	118	DB102
Rotherhithe SE16	93	DX76
Rowley Green, Barn.	33	CT42
Roxeth, Har.	59	CD61
Ruislip, Ruis.	57	BS59
Ruislip Common, Ruis.	57	BR57
Ruislip Gardens, Ruis.	57	BS63
Ruislip Manor, Ruis.	57	BU61
Rush Green, Rom.	69	FC59
Rydens, Walt.	114	BW103
St. George's Hill, Wey.	127	BQ110
St. Helier, Cars.	118	DD101
St. James's SW1	**9**	**L3**
St. John's SE8	93	EA82
St. John's Wood NW8	76	DC68
St. Luke's EC1	**7**	**J4**
St. Margarets, Twick.	101	CG85
St. Mary Cray, Orp.	124	EV99
St. Pancras WC1	**5**	**P3**
St. Paul's Cray, Orp.	124	EU96
Sanderstead, S.Croy.	134	DT111
Sands End SW6	90	DB81
Sarratt, Rick.	28	BG35
Seal, Sev.	155	FN121
Selhurst SE25	120	DS100
Selsdon, S.Croy.	134	DW110
Seven Kings, Ilf.	67	ES59
Sevenoaks, Sev.	155	FJ125
Sevenoaks Common, Sev.	155	FH129
Sewardstone E4	37	EC39
Sewardstonebury E4	38	EE42
Shacklewell N16	64	DT63
Shadwell E1	78	DW73
Shenley, Rad.	18	CN33
Shepherd's Bush W12	75	CW74
Shepperton, Shep.	113	BP101
Shirley, Croy.	121	DX104
Shooter's Hill SE18	95	EQ81
Shoreditch E1	**7**	**P5**
Shoreham, Sev.	139	FG111
Shortlands, Brom.	122	EE97
Sidcup, Sid.	109	ET91
Silvertown E16	94	EJ75
Single Street, West.	151	EN115
Sipson, West Dr.	84	BN79
Snaresbrook E11	66	EE57
Soho W1	**5**	**M10**

Place	Page	Grid
Somers Town NW1	**5**	**N1**
South Acton W3	88	CP76
South Beddington, Wall.	133	DK107
South Chingford E4	51	DZ50
South Croydon, S.Croy.	134	DQ107
South Hackney E9	78	DW67
South Hampstead NW6	76	DB66
South Harefield, Uxb.	56	BJ56
South Harrow, Har.	58	CB62
South Hornchurch, Rain.	83	FE67
South Kensington SW7	90	DB76
South Lambeth SW8	91	DL81
South Mimms, Pot.B.	19	CT32
South Norwood SE25	120	DT97
South Oxhey, Wat.	44	BW48
South Ruislip, Ruis.	58	BW63
South Street, West.	151	EM119
South Tottenham N15	64	DS57
South Wimbledon SW19	104	DA94
South Woodford E18	52	EF54
Southall, Sthl.	72	BX74
Southborough, Brom.	123	EM100
Southend SE6	107	EC91
Southfields SW18	104	DA88
Southgate N14	49	DJ47
Southwark SE1	**10**	**G3**
Spring Grove, Islw.	87	CE81
Staines, Stai.	98	BG93
Stamford Hill N16	64	DS60
Stanmore, Stan.	45	CG50
Stanwell, Stai.	98	BL87
Stanwell Moor, Stai.	98	BG85
Stapleford Abbotts, Rom.	41	FC43
Stapleford Tawney, Rom.	41	FC37
Stepney E1	78	DW71
Stockwell SW9	91	DK83
Stoke D'Abernon, Cob.	142	BZ116
Stoke Newington N16	64	DS61
Stonebridge NW10	74	CP67
Stoneleigh, Epsom	131	CU106
Strand WC2	**5**	**P10**
Stratford E15	79	EC65
Strawberry Hill, Twick.	101	CE90
Streatham SW16	105	DL91
Streatham Hill SW2	105	DM88
Streatham Park SW16	105	DJ91
Streatham Vale SW16	105	DK94
Stroud Green N4	63	DM58
Sudbury, Wem.	59	CG64
Summerstown SW17	104	DB91
Sunbury, Sun.	113	BV97
Sundridge, Brom.	108	EJ93
Sundridge, Sev.	152	EZ124
Surbiton, Surb.	116	CL101
Sutton, Sutt.	132	DA107
Swanley, Swan.	125	FE98
Swanley Village, Swan.	125	FH95
Sydenham SE26	106	DV92
Tadworth, Tad.	145	CV122
Tatsfield, West.	150	EL120
Tattenham Corner, Epsom	145	CV118
Teddington, Tedd.	101	CG93
Thames Ditton, T.Ditt.	115	CF100
Thamesmead SE28	82	EU74
Thamesmead North SE28	82	EX72
Thamesmead West SE18	95	EQ76
Theydon Bois, Epp.	39	ET37
Theydon Garnon, Epp.	40	EW36
Theydon Mount, Epp.	26	FA34
Thorney, Iver	84	BH76
Thornton Heath, Th.Hth.	119	DP98
Thornwood, Epp.	26	EW25
Tokyngton, Wem.	74	CP65
Tolworth, Surb.	116	CN103
Toot Hill, Ong.	27	FF30
Tooting Graveney SW17	104	DE93
Tottenham N17	50	DS53
Tottenham Hale N17	64	DU55
Totteridge N20	47	CY46
Tufnell Park N7	63	DK63
Tulse Hill SE21	106	DQ88
Turnford, Brox.	23	DZ26
Twickenham, Twick.	101	CG89
Twitton, Sev.	153	FE116
Tyrrell's Wood, Lthd.	144	CM123
Underhill, Barn.	34	DA43
Underriver, Sev.	155	FN130
Upper Clapton E5	64	DV60
Upper Edmonton N18	50	DU50
Upper Elmers End, Beck.	121	DZ99
Upper Halliford, Shep.	113	BS97
Upper Holloway N19	63	DJ62
Upper Norwood SE19	106	DR94
Upper Sydenham SE26	106	DU91
Upper Tooting SW17	104	DE90
Upper Walthamstow E17	65	EC56
Upshire, Wal.Abb.	24	EJ32
Upton E7	80	EH66
Upton Park E6	80	EJ67
Uxbridge, Uxb.	70	BK66
Uxbridge Moor, Iver	70	BG67
Uxbridge Moor, Uxb.	70	BG67
Vauxhall SW8	91	DK79
Waddon, Croy.	119	DN103
Walham Green SW6	90	DB80
Wallington, Wall.	133	DJ106
Waltham Abbey, Wal.Abb.	38	EF35
Waltham Cross, Wal.Cr.	23	DZ33
Walthamstow E17	51	EB54
Walton-on-Thames, Walt.	113	BT103
Walworth SE17	**11**	**H10**
Wandsworth SW18	103	CZ85
Wanstead E11	66	EG59
Wapping E1	78	DU74
Warlingham, Warl.	149	DX118
Water End, Hat.	19	CV26
Watford, Wat.	29	BU41
Watford Heath, Wat.	44	BX46
Wealdstone, Har.	59	CF55
Well End, Borwd.	32	CR38
Well Hill, Orp.	139	FB107
Welling, Well.	96	EU83
Wembley, Wem.	60	CL64
Wembley Park, Wem.	60	CM61
West Acton W3	74	CN72
West Barnes, N.Mal.	117	CV98
West Brompton SW10	90	DA79
West Byfleet, W.Byf.	126	BH113
West Drayton, West Dr.	84	BK76
West Dulwich SE21	106	DR90
West End, Esher	128	BZ107
West Ewell, Epsom	130	CS108
West Green N15	64	DQ56
West Ham E15	80	EF66
West Hampstead NW6	62	DB64
West Harrow, Har.	58	CC59
West Heath SE2	96	EX79
West Hendon NW9	60	CS59
West Kilburn W9	75	CZ69
West Molesey, W.Mol.	114	BZ98
West Norwood SE27	106	DQ90
West Watford, Wat.	29	BU42
West Wickham, W.Wick.	121	EC103
Westbourne Green W2	76	DA71
Westminster SW1	**9**	**K6**
Weston Green, T.Ditt.	115	CF102
Weybridge, Wey.	126	BN105
Whetstone N20	48	DB47
Whitechapel E1	78	DU72
Whiteley Village, Walt.	127	BS110
Whitton, Twick.	100	CB87
Whyteleafe, Cat.	148	DS118
Widmore, Brom.	122	EJ97
Wildernesse, Sev.	155	FL122
Willesden NW10	75	CT65
Willesden Green NW10	75	CV66
Wimbledon SW19	103	CY93
Wimbledon Park SW19	103	CZ90
Winchmore Hill N21	49	DM45
Wisley, Wok.	140	BL116
Woldingham, Cat.	149	EB122
Woldingham Garden Village, Cat.	149	DY121
Wood Green N22	49	DL53
Woodcote, Epsom	144	CQ116
Woodcote, Pur.	133	DK111
Woodford, Wdf.Grn.	52	EH51
Woodford Bridge, Wdf.Grn.	53	EM52
Woodford Green, Wdf.Grn.	52	EG50
Woodford Wells, Wdf.Grn.	52	EH48
Woodlands, Islw.	87	CE82
Woodmansterne, Bans.	146	DE115
Woodside, Croy.	120	DT100
Woodside, Wat.	15	BU33
Woolwich SE18	95	EM78
Worcester Park, Wor.Pk.	117	CT103
World's End, Enf.	35	DN41
Wrythe, The, Cars.	118	DE103
Yeading, Hayes	71	BV69
Yiewsley, West Dr.	70	BL74

The following is a comprehensive listing of the places of interest which appear in this atlas. Bold references can be found within the Central London enlarged scale section (pages 4-11).

AYLESBURY VALE

D A C O R U M

S T.
A L B A N S

WELWYN

HATFIELD

EA

14   15   16   17   18   19   20

CHILTERN

THREE
RIVERS   28   29   30   31   32   33   34

WATFORD

HERTSMERE

W Y C O M B E

42   43   44   45   46   47   48

B A R N E T

HARROW

HA

S O U T H   B U C K S

56   57   58   59   60   61   62

HILLINGDON

BRENT

CAMDEN

70   71   72   73   74   75   76

SLOUGH

E A L I N G

WESTMINSTER

KENSINGTON &
CHELSEA

84   85   86   87   88   89   90

W I N D S O R   &   M A I D E N H E A D

HAMMERSMITH &
FULHAM

HOUNSLOW

WANDSWORTH

WOKINGHAM

98   99   100   101   102   103   104

RICHMOND
UPON THAMES

SPELTHORNE

MERTON

BRACKNELL
FOREST

112   113   114   115   116   117   118

KINGSTON
UPON THAMES

RUNNYMEDE

SUTTON

ELMBRIDGE

126   127   128   129   130   131   132

SURREY HEATH

EPSOM
& EWELL

HART

WOKING

140   141   142   143   144   145   146

RUSHMOOR

REIGATE &

BANSTEAD

G U I L D F O R D

EAST
HANTS

M O L E   V A L L E Y

W A V E R L E Y

CRAWLEY